W. B. Bible

16-5893

4-27-78

The Athenæum Press
GINN AND COMPANY · PRO-
PRIETORS · BOSTON · U.S.A.

ENGLISH PROSE
AND POETRY

(1137-1892)

SELECTED AND ANNOTATED

BY

JOHN MATTHEWS MANLY

PROFESSOR AND HEAD OF THE DEPARTMENT OF ENGLISH
IN THE UNIVERSITY OF CHICAGO

GINN AND COMPANY
BOSTON · NEW YORK · CHICAGO · LONDON
ATLANTA · DALLAS · COLUMBUS · SAN FRANCISCO

CONTENTS

v

CONTENTS

ENGLISH PROSE AND POETRY

EARLY MIDDLE ENGLISH

THE ANGLO–SAXON CHRONICLE (C. 1154)

A MONK OF PETERBOROUGH

FROM THE RECORD FOR 1137

This gære [1] for [2] the king Stephne ofer sæ [3] to Normandi, and ther wes [4] underfangen,[5] for-thi-that [6] hi [7] uuenden [8] that he sculde [9] ben [10] alsuic [11] alse [12] the eom [13] wes, and for [6] he hadde get [14] his tresor; ac [15] he to-deld [16] it and scatered sotlice.[17] Micel [18] hadde Henri king gadered gold and sylver, and na [19] god [20] ne dide me [21] for his saule [22] tharof.[23]

Tha [24] the king Stephne to Englalande com,[25] tha [26] maçod [27] he his gadering [28] æt Oxeneford; and thar he nam [29] the biscop Roger of Sereberi,[30] and Alexander biscop of Lincol and te [31] Canceler Roger his neves,[32] and dide [33] ælle in prisun til hi [7] iafen [34] up here [35] castles. Tha [24] the suikes [36] undergæton [37] that he milde man was and softe and god [20] and na [19] justise [38] ne dide, tha [26] diden hi [7] alle wunder.[39] Hi [7] hadden him [40] manred [41] maked [27] and athes [42] suoren [43] ac [15] hi nan [19] treuthe ne heolden.[44] Alle he [7] wæron [45] forsworen, and here [35] treothes forloren; [46] for ævric [47] rice [48] man his castles makede,[49] and agænes [50] him heolden,[51] and fylden [52] the land ful of castles. Hi suencten [53] suythe [54] the uurecce [55] men of the land mid [56] castel weorces.[57] Tha [24] the castles uuaren [45] maked, tha [58] fylden hi mid deovles and yvele [59] men. Tha [58] namen [60] hi tha [61] men the [62] hi wenden [63] that ani god [64] hefden,[65] bathe [66] be [67] nihtes

This year went King Stephen over the sea to Normandy and was received there, because they thought that he was going to be just such as his uncle was, and because he still had his uncle's treasure; but he dispersed it and scattered it foolishly. Much had Henry the king gathered of gold and silver, and no good did anyone for his soul by means of it.

When King Stephen came to England, then he made his assembly at Oxford; and there he seized the bishop Roger of Salisbury and Alexander, bishop of Lincoln, and the Chancellor Roger, his nephews, and put them all in prison till they gave up their castles. When the traitors perceived that he was a mild man and soft and good, and enforced no justice, then did they all wonders. They had done homage to him and sworn oaths, but they kept no troth. But they were all forsworn and their troths were entirely abandoned; for every powerful man built his castles and held against him, and they filled the land full of castles. They oppressed grievously the wretched men of the land with castle-building.

When the castles were built, then they filled them with devils and evil men. Then they seized the men who they thought had any property, both by night and by day,

[1] year [2] went [3] sea [4] was [5] received [6] because [7] they [8] weened, thought [9] should [10] be [11] just such [12] as [13] uncle [14] yet [15] but [16] dispersed [17] foolishly [18] much [19] no [20] good [21] anyone [22] soul [23] on account of it [24] when [25] came [26] then [27] made [28] assembly [29] seized [30] Salisbury [31] the [32] nephews (*i.e.* the son and nephew of Roger of Salisbury) [33] put [34] gave

[35] their [36] traitors [37] perceived [38] justice, punishment [39] strange things, evils [40] to him [41] homage [42] oaths [43] sworn [44] kept [45] were [46] entirely abandoned [47] every [48] powerful [49] built [50] against [51] held [52] filled [53] oppressed [54] greatly [55] wretched [56] with [57] works [58] then [59] evil [60] seized [61] those [62] who [63] weened, thought [64] property [65] had [66] both [67] by

and be dæies, carlmen [1] and wimmen, and diden [2] heom [3] in prisun efter [4] gold and sylver, and pined [5] heom untellendlice [6] pining,[7] for ne uuæren [8] nævre [9] nan martyrs swa [10] pined alse [11] hi wæron. Me [12] henged [13] up bi the fet [14] and smoked heom mid ful [15] smoke. Me henged bi the thumbes, other [16] bi the hefed,[17] and hengen [18] bryniges [19] on her [20] fet. Me dide [2] cnotted strenges [21] abuton [22] here [20] hæved [17] and uurythen [23] to [24] that it gæde [25] to the hærnes.[26] Hi dyden heom in quarterne [27] thar [28] nadres [29] and snakes and pades [30] wæron inne, and drapen [31] heom swa.[10] . . .

I ne can ne I ne mai [32] tellen alle the wunder [33] ne alle the pines [34] that hi diden wrecce [35] men on [36] this land; and that lastede tha .xix. wintre [37] wile [38] Stephne was king, and ævre [39] it was uuerse [40] and uuerse.

men and women also, and thrust them in prison for gold and silver, and tortured them with unspeakable tortures, for never were any martyrs so tortured as they were. They were hanged up by the feet and smoked with foul smoke. They were hanged by the thumbs, or by the head, and coats of mail were hung on their feet. Knotted strings were put about their heads and twisted till they penetrated to the brains. They put them in dungeons in which were adders and snakes and toads, and killed them thus. . . .

I cannot and I may not tell all the wonders nor all the tortures that they did to wretched men in this land; and that lasted the nineteen years while Stephen was king, and ever it was worse and worse.

From THE POEMA MORALE, OR MORAL ODE (c. 1170)

(Unknown Author)

Ich [41] æm elder then ich [41] wes, a wintre and a
　lore; [42]
Ic [41] wælde [43] more thanne ic dude,[44] mi wit ah [45]
　to ben more.
Wel lange ic [41] habbe [46] child ibeon [47] a weorde
　and ech [48] a dede;
Theh [49] ic beo [50] a wintre eald,[51] to ying [52] I
　eom [50] a rede.[53]
Unnut [54] lyf ic habb ilæd,[55] and yiet,[56] me-
　thincth, ic lede;
Thanne ic me bethenche,[57] wel sore ic me
　adrede.[58]
Mest [59] al thæt ic habbe ydon [60] ys idelnesse
　and chilche; [61]
Wel late ic habbe me bithoht, bute [62] me God
　do milce.[63]
Fele [64] ydele word ic habbe iqueden [65] syth-
　then [66] ic speke cuthe,[67]
And fale [64] yunge [68] dede ido, thet me of-
　thinchet [69] nuthe.[70]　　　　• 10

I am older than I was in winters and in
　lore;
I govern more than e'er I did, my wisdom
　should be more.
Full long time have I been a child in word
　and eke in deed;
Though I be in winters old, too young am I
　in rede.
Useless is the life I lead, and long, methinks,
　have led;
When I remember me of this, full sore am I
　a-dread.
Nearly all that I have done is childish and of
　naught; •
But, save God show me mercy now, too late
　is this my thought.
Many idle speeches have I spoken since
　speech to me was lent;
And many a foolish deed have done, that I
　must now repent.　　　　10

---

[1] men [2] put [3] them [4] after (i.e. to obtain)
[5] tortured [6] unspeakable [7] torture [8] were [9] never
[10] so [11] as [12] one (i.e. they indefinite) [13] hanged
[14] feet [15] foul [16] or [17] head [18] hung [19] corselets
(as weights) [20] their [21] cords [22] about [23] twisted
[24] till [25] went, penetrated [26] brains [27] prison
[28] where [29] adders [30] toads [31] killed [32] may
[33] evils [34] tortures [35] wretched [36] in [37] years

[38] while [39] ever [40] worse [41] I [42] in years and in
knowledge [43] govern [44] did [45] ought [46] have
[47] been [48] also [49] though [50] am [51] old [52] young
[53] counsel [54] useless [55] led [56] still [57] bethink
[58] I am frightened [59] almost [60] done [61] childishness [62] unless [63] mercy [64] many [65] spoken
[66] since [67] could [68] young, silly [69] repents [70] now

Al to lome [1] ic habbe agult [2] a weorche [3] and
    ec [4] a worde;
Al to muchel ic habbe ispend, to litel yleid [5]
    an horde.
Mest [6] al thet me licede [7] ær,[8] nu hit [9] me
    mislicheth; [10]
The [11] mychel [12] folyeth [13] his ywil, him sulfne
    he biswiketh.[14]
Ich mihte habbe bet [15] idon, hadde ic tho [16]
    yselthe; [17]
Nu ic wolde, ac [18] ic ne mei [19] for elde [20] ne
    for unhelthe; [21]
Ylde [20] me is bistolen on, ær ic hit awyste; [22]
Ne mihte ic iseon [23] before me for smeche [24]
    ne for miste.
Ærwe [25] we beoth [26] to done god, and to yfele [27]
    al to thriste; [28]
More æie [29] stent [30] man of manne thanne him
    do of Criste.   20
The [11] wel ne deth [31] the hwile he mei,[32] wel
    oft hit hym scæl ruwen,[33]
Thænne [34] hy [35] mowen sculen [36] and ripen,[37]
    ther [38] hi ær seowen.[39]
Don ec [40] to Gode wet [41] ye muye,[32] the hwile
    ye buth [26] a life;
Ne hopie no man [42] to muchel to childe ne to
    wyfe;
The [11] him selve foryut [43] for wife other for
    childe,
He sceal cume an uvele stede [44] bute [45] hym
    God beo milde.
Sende æch [46] sum god biforen hym, the hwile
    he mei, to heovene;
Betere is an elmesse [47] bifore thenne beon æfter
    seovene.
Ne beo the leovre [48] thene the sulf thi mei [49] ne
    thi maye [50]
Sot [51] is the [11] is othres mannes freond betre
    thene his aye.[52]   30
Ne hopie [53] wif to hire were,[54] ne wer [54] to his
    wife;
Beo [55] for him sulve ævrich [56] man, the hwyle
    he beo [57] alive.
Wis [58] is the [59] him sulfne bithencth [60] the
    hwile he mote [61] libbe,[62]
For sone [63] wulleth [64] him foryite [65] the
    fremde [66] and the sibbe.[67]

All too often have I sinned in deed and eke
    in word;
All too freely have I spent, too little laid in
    hoard.
Almost all I now mislike of things I liked of
    yore;
Who follows over-much his will, betrays him-
    self the more.
Had fortune only favored me, I might have
    done more good;
Now for weakness and for age, I may not,
    though I would.
Old age is stolen me upon, ere that I it wist;
I could not see before me for the smoke and
    for the mist.
Timid we are in doing good, in evil all too
    bold;
More awe of man than awe of Christ doth
    every person hold.   20
Who doth not well, the while he may, shall
    often rue it sore,
When comes the time to mow and reap what
    he has sown before.
Do ye for God the best ye may, the while ye
    are in life;
And let no man hope overmuch in child nor
    yet in wife.
He who doth himself forget for wife or else
    for child
Shall come into an evil place save God to him
    be mild.
Let each some good before him send, the while
    he may, to heaven;
For better is one alms before than afterward
    are seven.
And hold not dearer than thyself thy kins-
    man or thy son;
Foolish to be another's friend rather than thine
    own.   30
And let no wife in husband hope, nor husband
    in his wife;
Be each man for himself alone, the while he
    is in life.
Wise is who bethinks himself the while he
    liveth yet;
For him will stranger — ay, and friend, soon
    enough forget.

[1] all too often [2] sinned [3] deed [4] also [5] laid [6] almost [7] pleased [8] formerly [9] it [10] displeases [11] who
[12] much [13] follows [14] betrays [15] better [16] then
[17] good fortune [18] but [19] may not [20] age [21] weakness [22] before I knew it [23] see [24] smoke [25] timid
[26] are [27] evil [28] bold [29] awe, fear [30] arises to [31] doth
[32] may [33] shall repent [34] when [35] they [36] shall

[37] reap [38] where [39] sowed [40] also [41] what [42] let no
man hope [43] forgets [44] in evil place [45] unless
[46] each [47] one alms [48] dearer [49] kinsman [50] son
[51] foolish [52] own [53] hope not [54] man [55] be [56] every
[57] is [58] wise [59] who [60] bethinks [61] may [62] live
[63] soon [64] will [65] forget [66] stranger [67] kinsman

The [1] wel ne deth [2] the hwile he mei,[3] ne
    sceal he hwenne he wolde.
Manies mannes sare iswinch habbeth oft
    unholde.[4]
Ne scolde nan man don a furst,[5] ne sclawen [6]
    wel to done ;
For mani man bihateth [7] wel, the [1] hit for-
    yiteth sone.
The man the [1] siker [8] wule beon to habbe
    Godes blisse,
Do wel him sulf the hwile he mei, then haveth
    he mid iwisse.[9]   40

Who doth not well, the while he may, he shall
    not when he would ;
Many a man's sore labor oft cometh to no
    good.
In doing good let none postpone or ever
    make delay ;
For many a man doth promise well who yet
    forgets straightway.
The man who would be safe and sure of having
    God's own bliss
If he do well the while he may, he verily shall
    not miss.   40

ORRM (fl. 1200)

From THE ORRMULUM

Nu, [10] broþerr Wallterr, broþerr min
    Affterr þe flæshess kinde ; [11]
& broþerr min i [12] Crisstenndom
    þurrh fulluhht [13] & þurrh trowwþe ; [14]
& broþerr min i [12] Godess hus,
    ðet o[15] þe þride [16] wise,[17]
þurrh þatt witt [18] hafenn [19] tăkenn ba [20]
    An [21] reȝhellboc [22] to follȝhenn,[23]
Unnderr kanunnkess [24] had [25] & lif,
    Swa summ [26] Sannt Awwstin sette ; [27]   10
Icc hafe [28] don swa summ [26] þu badd,[29]
    & forþedd [30] te [31] þin wille,
Icc hafe [28] wennd [32] inntil [33] Ennglissh
    Goddspelless hallȝhe lare,[34]
Affterr þatt little witt [35] tatt [36] me
    Min Drihhtin hafeþþ lenedd [37]
þu þohhtesst [38] tatt [36] itt mihhte wel
    Till [39] mikell frame [40] turrnenn,
ȝiff [41] Ennglissh follk, forr lufe off Crist,
    Itt wollde ȝerne [42] lernenn,   20
& follȝhenn [23] itt, & fillenn [43] itt
    Wiþþ þohht, [44] wiþþ word, wiþþ dede.
& forrþi [45] ȝerrndesst [46] tu þatt icc
    þiss werrc [47] þe sholld wirrkenn ;
& icc itt hafe forþedd [30] te,[31]
    Acc [48] all þurrh Cristess hellpe ;
& unnc birrþ [49] baþe [50] þannkenn Crist
    þatt itt iss brohht till [39] ende.
Icc hafe sammnedd [51] o [52] þiss boc
    þa Goddspelless neh [53] alle   30

Now, brother Walter, brother mine
    After the fleshly nature ;
And brother mine in Christendom
    Through baptism and through fealty ;
And brother mine in God's own house
    In still another manner,
In that we two have taken both
    One book of rules to follow,
Within the life of canonhood,
    Just as St. Austin ordered ;   10
As thou didst bid me, I have done,
    Thy will for thee fulfilling ;
For into English I have turned
    The gospel's holy teaching,
According to the little wit
    With which my Lord endowed me.
Thou thoughtest that it might full well
    Be turned to mickle profit
If English folk, for love of Christ,
    It zealously would study,   20
And follow it, and it fulfil,
    With thought, with word, with action.
And therefore thou didst yearn that I
    This book for thee should render ;
And I for thee have finished it,
    As Christ the Lord did help me ;
And now behooves us both thank Christ
    That it is brought to ending.
I have collected in this book
    Now nearly all the gospels   30

[1] who [2] doth [3] may [4] many a man's sore labor
hath often misfortune [5] no man should postpone
[6] delay [7] promises [8] sure [9] then he hath it certainly
[10] now [11] nature [12] in [13] through baptism [14] faith
[15] on [16] third [17] way, degree [18] we two [19] have [20] both
[21] one [22] rule-book [23] follow [24] canon's [25] order
[26] just as [27] commanded [28] I have [29] badest [30] accomplished [31] thee [32] turned [33] into [34] holy lore
[35] wit, intelligence [36] that [37] my Lord has lent
[38] thoughtest [39] to [40] great benefit [41] if [42] eagerly
[43] fulfil [44] with thought [45] therefore [46] desiredst
[47] work [48] but [49] us two it behooves [50] both [51] collected [52] in [53] nigh, near

þatt sinndenn[1] o the messeboc[2]
Inn all þe ʒer[3] att messe.
& aʒʒ[4] affterr þe Goddspell stannt[5]
þatt tatt[6] te Goddspell meneþþ,[7]
þatt mann birrþ spellenn[8] to þe follc
Off þeʒʒre[9] sawle nede;
& ʒēt tær tekenn mare inoh[10]
þu shallt tæronne[11] findenn
Off þatt tatt[6] Cristess hallʒhe þed[12]
Birrþ[13] trowwenn[14] wel & follʒhenn.[15]   40
Icc hafe sett her o[16] þiss boc
Amang Goddspelless wordess,
All þurrh me sellfenn,[17] maniʒ word
þe rīme[18] swa[19] to fillenn;
Acc þu shallt finndenn þatt min word,
Eʒʒwhær þær[20] itt iss ekedd,[21]
Maʒʒ hellpenn þa[22] þatt redenn itt
To sen & tunnderrstanndenn[23]
All þess te bettre hu þeʒʒm birrþ[24]
þe Goddspell unnderrstanndenn;   50
& forrþi[25] trowwe icc þatt te[26] birrþ
Wel þolenn[27] mine wordess,
Eʒʒwhær þær[20] þu shallt findenn hemm[28]
Amang Godspelless wordess.

That all the year at mass are found
Within the holy massbook.
And aye after the gospel stands
That which the gospel meaneth,
Which must be told unto the folk,
Because the soul doth need it;
And still within it thou shalt find
Enough and more there written
Of what the holy flock of Christ
Must well believe and follow.   40
I have set down here in this book,
Among the words of gospel,
All of myself full many a word,
To fill the measure merely;
But thou shalt find here that my word,
Wherever it is added,
May help the people who shall read
To see and understand too
The better how it them behooves
To understand the gospel;   50
And therefore trow I that thou must
Endure my words with patience,
Wherever thou shalt find them set
Among the words of gospel.

LAYAMON (c. 1205)

From THE BRUT

Arthur for[29] to Cornwale
Mid unimete ferde;[30]   28530
Modred that iherde[31]
And him togeines heolde[32]
Mid unimete[33] folke.
Ther weore monie væie![34]
Uppen there Tambre[35]
Heo[36] tuhten[37] to gadere;
The stude hatte[38] Camelford;
Ever-mare ilast that like weorde![39]
And at Camelforde wes isomned[40]
Sixti thusend
And ma thusend there-to;[41]
Modred wes heore ælder.[42]
Tha[43] thiderward gon[44] ride   28540
Arthur the riche[45]

Arthur went to Cornwall,
The host with him was countless;   28530
Modred heard the tidings
And took his way against him
With host no man could number.
Many there were death-doomed!
By the river Tamar
The troops came together;
The place was christened Camelford;
Forever-more shall last that word!
And at Camelford was assembled
Sixty thousand
And thousands many more too;
Modred was their leader.
Then thitherward went riding   28540
Arthur the royal

[1] are [2] mass-book [3] year [4] always [5] stands [6] that that, that which [7] means [8] that it behooves one to tell [9] of their [10] and besides that, enough more [11] therein [12] holy people [13] behooves [14] believe [15] follow [16] here in [17] by myself [18] rhythm, measure [19] so [20] everywhere where [21] added [22] those [23] to understand [24] all the better for this how it behooves them [25] therefore [26] thee [27] endure, per-mit [28] them [29] went [30] with a numberless army [31] heard [32] and went against him [33] numberless [34] there were many fey (fated to die) [35] upon the Tamar (a river) [36] they [37] came [38] the place was called [39] ever-more shall last that same word (name) [40] was gathered [41] and more thousands besides [42] was their leader [43] then [44] did [45] great

Mid unimete folke,
Væie thah hit weore.[1]
  Uppe there Tambre
Heo tuhte [2] to-somne;[3]
Heven here-marken;[4]
Halden [5] to-gadere;
Luken sweord longe,[6]
Leiden o [7] the helmen;
Fur ut sprengen,[8]   28550
Speren brastlien;[9]
Sceldes gonnen scanen,[10]
Scaftes to-breken.[11]
Ther faht [12] al to-somne [13]
Folc unimete.
Tambre wes on flode [14]
Mid unimete [15] blode.
Mon i than fihte
Non [16] ther ne mihte
I-kenne nenne kempe,[17]
No [18] wha dude [19] wurse, no wha bet,[20]
Swa that withe [21] wes imenged; [22]   28562
For ælc [23] sloh [24] adun riht,
Weore he swein,[25] weore he cniht.[26]
Ther wes Modred of-slawe [27]
And idon of lif-dawe [28]
[29]*   *   *   *   *   *
*   *   *   in than fihte.
Ther weoren of-slawe [27]
Alle tha snelle,[30]
Arthures hired-men,[31]   28570
Heye and lawe,[32]
And tha Bruttes [33] alle
Of Arthures borde,[34]
And alle his fosterlinges [35]
Of feole kineriches,[36]
And Arthur forwunded
Mid wal-spere brade.[37]
Fiftene he hafde
Feondliche wunden; [38]
Mon mihte i thare lasten [39]   28580
Twa gloven ithraste.[40]
  Tha [41] nas ther na mare
I than fehte to lave [42]
Of twa hundred thusend monnen [43]
Tha [44] ther leien [45] to-hauwen [46]
Buten [47] Arthur the king ane [48]
And of his cnihtes tweien.[49]

With army unnumbered,
Doomed though they all were.
  By the river Tamar
The troops came together;
Raised their royal standards;
Rushed there together;
Long swords locked they,
Laying blows on helmets;
Sparks they struck out,   28550
Spears did rattle;
Shields were a-shaking,
Shafts were a-breaking.
There fought all together
Folk beyond counting.
Tamar was a flood·
With measureless blood.
Of men in the fight there
Nobody might there
Distinguish any warrior,
Nor who did better, who did worse,
So was that conflict mingled;   28562
For each struck adown right,
Were he yeoman, or were he knight.
There was Modred stricken,
And life in him did sicken.
*   *   *   *   *   *   *
*   *   *   in that conflict.
There fell in that battle
All of the brave ones,
Arthur's own henchmen,   28570
The high and the lowly,
And all the Britons
Of Arthur's board too,
And all his fosterlings
Of foreign nations many,
And Arthur sorely wounded
With broad blade of war-spear.
Fifteen times was he
Fiendishly wounded;
Even into the smallest   28580
Two gloves might one have thrust.
  Then were there in that battle
Left among the living
Of two hundred thousand soldiers
Who lay there slaughtered
But Arthur the king only
And two of his warriors.

---

[1] fey though they were [2] they came [3] together [4] raised battle-standards [5] rushed [6] locked long swords [7] laid on, struck upon [8] made fire leap out [9] rattled spears [10] shields did shiver [11] shafts broke to pieces [12] fought [13] together [14] a-flood [15] measureless [16] no man in the fight [17] recognize no warrior [18] nor [19] did [20] better [21] conflict [22] confused [23] each [24] struck [25] yeoman [26] knight [27] slain [28] and put from life-days [29] *A line or more is missing here.* [30] the brave [31] retainers [32] high and low [33] the Britons [34] table [35] wards [36] many kingdoms [37] with broad slaughter-spear [38] dreadful wounds [39] in the least [40] thrust [41] then [42] in the fight remaining [43] men [44] who [45] lay [46] hewed to pieces [47] but [48] alone [49] two

Arthur wes for-wunded
Wunder ane swithe.[1]
   Ther to him com a cnave [2]   28590
The [3] wes of his cunne; [4]
He wes Cadores sune,
The Eorles of Cornwaile.
Constantin hehte [5] the cnave;
He wes than [6] kinge deore.
Arthur him lokede on,
Ther he lai on folden,[7]
And thas word [8] seide
Mid sorhfulle heorte:
"Constantin, thu art wilcume!   28600
Thu weore [9] Cadores sone!
Ich the bitache here [10]
Mine kineriche; [11]
And wite [12] mine Bruttes
A to thines lifes; [13]
And hald heom [14] alle tha lawen [15]
Tha habbeoth istonden a mine dawen,[16]
And alle tha lawen gode
Tha bi Utheres dawen stode.
And ich wulle varen [17] to Avalun   28610
To vairest [18] alre [19] maidene,
To Argante there [20] quene,
Alven swithe sceone; [21]
And heo [22] scal mine wunden
Makien alle isunde,[23]
Al hal [24] me makien
Mid haleweiye drenchen.[25]
And seothe [26] ich cumen wulle
To mine kineriche [27]
And wunien [28] mid Brutten   28620
Mid muchelere wunne." [29]
   Æfne than worden [30]
Ther com of se wenden [31]
That wes an sceort bat lithen,[32]
Sceoven mid uthen; [33]
And twa wimmen ther-inne
Wunderliche idihte.[34]
And heo nomen Arthur anan,[35]
And an eovste hine vereden,[36]
And softe hine adun leiden,   28630
And forth gunnen lithen.[37]
   Tha [38] wes hit iwurthen [39]
That Merlin seide whilen,[40]
That weore unimete care [41]

Arthur was wounded
Wondrous severely.
   To him came a child then   28590
Who was of his kindred;
He was Cador's first-born,
Who Earl was of Cornwall.
Constantine his name was;
He was to the king dear.
Arthur looked upon him,
As he lay on the ground there,
And these words spake he
With heart full of sorrow:
"Constantine, welcome art thou!   28600
Thou wert Cador's first-born!
To thee do I commit here
The care of my kingdom;
And guard well my Britons
Ever whilst thou livest;
And keep thou all the customs
That loved were in my life-time,
And all the customs splendid
That Uther's reign attended.
And I will fare to Avalon   28610
To the fairest of all maidens,
Where Queen Argantè tarries,
Most beautiful of fairies;
And she shall every wound
Make both whole and sound,
All whole shall she make me
With health-giving potions.
And come shall I hereafter
Back to my kingdom
And abide with my Britons   28620
With bliss forever."
   E'en as he was speaking
There came from sea speeding
A very small boat gliding
Before the waves a-riding;
And women twain within it
Wondrously attired.
And they raised up Arthur anon,
And aboard rapidly bore him,
And adown softly they set him,   28630
And forth went they sailing.
   Then was fulfilled there
What Merlin said aforetime,
That infinite grieving

[1] wondrously much [2] young man [3] who [4] kin [5] was named [6] to the [7] the ground [8] these words [9] thou wert [10] I commit to thee here [11] kingdom [12] defend [13] ever during thy life [14] keep for them [15] customs, laws [16] that have stood in my days [17] I will go [18] fairest [19] of all [20] the [21] elf very beautiful [22] she [23] well [24] whole [25] with healing draughts [26] afterwards [27] kingdom [28] dwell [29] with great joy [30] even with these words [31] from the sea moving [32] that was a short boat gliding [33] impelled by the waves [34] wondrously attired [35] they took Arthur at once [36] and in haste bore him [37] did glide [38] then [39] fulfilled [40] whilom, formerly [41] that there should be measureless sorrow

Of Arthures forth-fare.[1]
  Bruttes ileveth yete [2]
That he bon on live [3]
And wunnien [4] in Avalun
Mid fairest alre [5] alven;
And lokieth evere Bruttes yete   28640
Whan Arthur cumen lithe.[6]
  Nis naver [7] the mon iboren
Of naver nane burde icoren [8]
The cunne [9] of than sothe [10]
Of Arthur sugen mare.[11]
Bute while [12] wes an witeye [13]
Mærlin ihate,[14]
He bodede [15] mid worde —
His quithes [16] weoren sothe [17] —
That an Arthur sculde yete   28650
Cum Anglen to fulste.[18]

Should be at Arthur's leaving.
  Britons believe ever
That still he is living
And fostered in Avalon
With the fairest of all fairies;
And ever hope the Britons   28640
For Arthur's coming hither.
  Was never the man born
Of mother on lucky morn
Who can of the true tale
Of Arthur tell us further.
But once there was a wizard,
Merlin they called him,
With words he predicted —
His sayings were truthful —
That an Arthur should one day   28650
Come England to succour.

From THE ANCREN RIWLE [19] (c. 1225)

(*Unknown Author*)

NUNS MAY KEEP NO BEAST BUT A CAT

Ye, mine leove [20] süstren,[21] ne schulen [22] habben [23] no best [24] bute kat one.[25] Ancre [26] thet haveth eihte [27] thüncheth [28] bet [29] husewif,[30] ase Marthe was, then ancre; [26] ne none-weis [31] ne mei heo [32] beon [33] Marie mid grithfulnesse [34] of heorte. Vor theonne [35] mot [36] heo thenchen [37] of the kues [38] foddre and of heordemonne [39] huire,[40] oluhnen [41] thene [42] heiward,[43] warien [44] hwon [45] me [46] pünt [47] hire, and yelden,[48] thauh,[49] the hermes.[50] Wat [51] Crist, this is lodlich [52] thing hwon [45] me [46] maketh mone [53] in tune [54] of ancre [55] eihte.[27] Thauh,[49] yif [56] eni mot [36] nede habben [57] ku, loke [58] thet heo [32] none monne ne eilie [59] ne ne hermie; [60] ne thet hire thouht ne beo [61] nout ther-on ivestned.[62] Ancre ne ouh [63] nout to habben [57] no thing thet drawe [64] utward hire heorte.

None cheffare [65] ne drive ye. Ancre thet is cheapild,[66] heo cheapeth [67] hire soule the chepmon [68] of helle.

Ne wite [69] ye nout in oure [70] huse [71] of other

Ye, my dear sisters, shall have no beast but a cat only. A nun that has property seems rather a housewife, as Martha was, than a nun; and in no wise may she be Mary, with peacefulness of heart. For then must she think about the cow's fodder and the herdsmen's wages, flatter the constable, curse when the cow is put in the pound, and pay the damages nevertheless. God knows, it is a hateful thing when complaint is made in the village of a nun's property. However, if anyone must needs have a cow, let her see to it that it disturbs or harms no man; and that her heart be not fastened upon it. A nun ought to have nothing that will draw her heart outward to the world.

Drive ye no bargains. A nun that is a bargainer sells her soul to the merchant of hell.

Keep ye not in your house any of other

---

[1] death [2] believe yet [3] is alive [4] dwells [5] of all
[6] shall come [7] is never [8] of never no (*i.e.* of no)
lady chosen [9] who can [10] the truth [11] say more
[12] once [13] wizard [14] named [15] announced [16] sayings
[17] true [18] come for a help to the English [19] The
Nuns' Rule [20] dear [21] sisters [22] shall [23] have [24] beast
[25] only [26] a nun [27] property [28] seems [29] rather
[30] housewife [31] no-ways [32] she [33] be [34] peacefulness

[35] then [36] must [37] think [38] cow's [39] herdsmen's
[40] hire [41] flatter [42] the [43] heyward, bailiff [44] curse
[45] when [46] one [47] impounds [48] pay [49] nevertheless
[50] damages [51] knows [52] hateful [53] complaint [54] town,
farm [55] a nun's [56] if [57] have [58] look [59] disturb
[60] harm [61] be [62] fastened [63] ought [64] may draw
[65] bargain [66] bargainer [67] sells [68] tradesman
[69] keep, take care of [70] your [71] house

monnes thinges, ne eihte,[1] ne clothes; ne nout ne undervo [2] ye the chirche vestimenz, ne thene [3] caliz,[4] bute-yif [5] strencthe [6] hit makie,[7] other [8] muchel eie; [9] vor of swüche [10] witunge [11] is ikumen [12] muchel üvel [13] ofte-sithen.[14]

men's things, either property or clothes; and do not receive the church vestments or the chalice, unless compulsion or great fear cause you to do so; for such custody has come great evil oftentimes.

FROM KING HORN (C. 1250)

(Unknown Author)

Alle beon he [15] blithe	Joy to none be wanting
That to my song lythe! [16]	Who listens to my chaunting!
A sang ihc schal you singe	A song I shall you sing
Of Murry the kinge. 4	Of Murry the king. 4
King he was bi weste [17]	King he was i' th' west
So longe so hit laste.	While his rule did last.
Godhild het [18] his quen;	Godhild was his queen;
Fairer ne mihte non ben.[19] 8	Fairer might not be seen. 8
He hadde a sone that het [18] Horn;	He had a son whose name was Horn;
Fairer ne mihte non beo born,	Fairer might there none be born,
Ne no rein upon birine,[20]	Nor rain rain on such a one,
Ne sunne upon bischine.[21] 12	Nor upon such shine the sun. 12
Fairer nis non thane he was;	None is fairer than he was;
He was brigt so the glas,	He was bright as the glass,
He was whit so the flur,	As the flower he was white,
Rose-red was his colur.[22] 16	Red as rose his color bright. 16
In none kinge-riche [23]	Within no kingdom great
Nas non his iliche.[24] 20	Could be found his mate. 20
Twelf feren [25] he hadde	Twelve companions had he
That he with him ladde, [26]	That ever with him led he;
Alle riche mannes sones,	Each was a noble's son,
And alle hi were faire gomes [27] 24	And each was a fitting one 24
With him for to pleie.	To share in his playing.
And mest 'he luvede tweie; [28]	Two loved he beyond saying;
That on him het [29] Hathulf child,	The one was called Hathulf child,
And that other Fikenild. 28	And the other Fikenild. 28
Athulf was the beste	Athulf was the best
And Fikenylde the werste.	And Fikenild the worst.
Hit was upon a someres day,	It was upon a summer's day,
Also [30] ihc you telle may, 32	As I to you the story say, 32
Murri the gode king	Murry the noble king
Rod on his pleing [31]	Rode in his pleasuring
Bi the se side,	By the water-side,
Ase he was woned [32] ride.[22] 36	As he was wont to ride. 36
He fond bi the stronde,	He found by the strand there,
Arived on his londe, 40	Arrived in his land there, 40
Schipes fiftene,	Ships fifteen all told

[1] property   [2] receive   [3] the   [4] chalice   [5] unless [6] strength, necessity   [7] make, cause   [8] or   [9] fear [10] such   [11] guarding   [12] come   [13] evil   [14] oft-times [15] they   [16] listen   [17] in the west   [18] was named   [19] fairer

might none be [20] nor any rain rain upon [21] shine [22] *After this line other MSS. insert two other lines.* [23] kingdom   [24] like   [25] companions   [26] led   [27] fellows [28] two   [29] was named   [30] as   [31] in his sport   [32] wont

With Sarazins kene.[1]		Of Saracens full bold.	
He axede what hi sohte [2]		He asked them what they sought	
Other to londe brohte.	44	Or else to land brought.	44
A payn [3] hit of herde [4]		A pagan there beside	
And hym wel sone answerde,		At once to him replied:	
"Thi lond-folk we schulle slon [5]		"All thy people we shall slay	
And alle that Crist leveth [6] upon,	48	And all who hold with Christ this day,	48
And the selve [7] rigt anon;		And thyself without delay;	
Ne schaltu [8] todai henne [9] gon."		Hence shalt thou not go away."	
The kyng ligte of his stede,		The king sprang from his steed then,	
For tho [10] he havede nede,	52	For surely he had need then,	52
And his gode knigtes two;		And with him true knights two —	
Al to fewe he hadde tho.[10]		Of men he had too few.	
Swerd hi [11] gunne [12] gripe		Swords in hand they took	
And to-gadere smite.	56	And together struck.	56
Hy [11] smyten [13] under schelde,		They smote so under shield	
That sume hit yfelde.[14]		That some fell in the field.	
The king hadde al to fewe		The king had all too few	
Togenes so vele schrewe.[15]	60	Against this evil crew.	60
So fele [16] mihten ythe [17]		So many might easily	
Bringe hem thre to dithe.[18]		Put to death these three.	
The pains [19] come to londe		The pagans came to land	
And neme [20] hit in here honde.	64	And seized it in their hand.	64
That folc hi gunne quelle [21]		The people they did kill	
And churchen for to felle.		And churches spoil at will.	
Ther ne moste libbe [22]		There none alive might go,	
The fremde [23] ne the sibbe,[24]	68	Kinsman no more than foe,	68
Bute hi here lawe asoke [25]		But who his faith forsook	
And to here [26] toke.		And that of pagan took.	
Of alle wymmanne		Of all earthly women	
Wurst was Godhild thanne.	72	Saddest was Godhild then.	72
For Murri heo weop [27] sore		For Murry wept she sore	
And for Horn yute [28] more.[29]		And for Horn yet more.	
He [30] wenten ut of halle,	77	She went out of the hall,	77
Fram hire maidenes alle.		Leaving her maidens all.	
Under a roche of stone		Under a rock of stone	
Ther heo [30] livede alone.	80	There lived she all alone.	80
Ther heo [30] servede Gode,		To serve God was she glad,	
Agenes the paynes [31] forbode;[32]		Though the pagans it forbade;	
Ther he [30] servede Criste,		And there she served Christ too,	
That no payn hit ne wiste.[33]	84	And naught the pagans knew.	84
Evere heo bad [34] for Horn Child		Ever she prayed for Horn Child	
That Jesu Crist him beo myld.		That Jesus Christ be to him mild.	
Horn was in paynes honde		Horn was in pagans' hand	
With his feren [35] of the londe.	88	With his fellows of the land.	88
Muchel was his fairhede,[36]		Beauty great had he,	
For Jhesu Crist him makede.		As Christ would have it be.	
Payns him wolde slen [37]		The pagans wished to slay him	
Other al quic flen.[38]	92	Or else alive to flay him.	92

[1] bold [2] they sought [3] pagan [4] heard [5] slay [6] believe [7] thyself [8] thou shalt not [9] hence [10] then [11] they [12] did [13] smote [14] felled [15] against so many wicked [16] many [17] easily [18] death [19] pagans [20] took [21] did kill [22] there might not live [23] foreigner [24] kinsman [25] unless they forsook their faith [26] theirs [27] she wept [28] yet [29] See note on l. 16. [30] she [31] pagans' [32] prohibition [33] knew [34] prayed [35] companions [36] fairness [37] slay [38] flay alive

Gef his fairnesse nere,[1]
The children alle aslawe [2] were.

Thanne spak on Admirald,
Of wordes he was bald,[3]   96
"Horn, thu art wel kene,[4]
And that is wel isene; [5]
Thu art gret and strong,
Fair and evene long.[6]   100
Thu schalt waxe more [7]
Bi fulle seve [8] yere,
Gef thu mote [9] to live [10] go —
And thine feren [11] also.   104
Gef hit so bi-falle,
Ye scholde slen [12] us alle;
Tharvore thu most to stere,[13]
Thu and thine ifere; [11]   108
To schupe schulle ye funde [14]
And sinke to the grunde. [15]
The se you schal adrenche; [16]
Ne schal hit us noht of-thinche,[17]   112
For if thu were alive,
With swerd other with knive
We scholden alle deie,
And thi fader deth abeie." [18]   116

The children hi brohte to stronde,
Wringinde here honde,[19]
Into schupes borde
At the furste worde.   120
Ofte hadde Horn beo wo,[20]
Ac [21] nevere wurs than him was tho.[22]   122
The se bigan to flowe
And Hornchild to rowe.   128
The se that schup so faste drof,
The children dradde ther of;
Hi wenden to-wisse [23]
Of here lif to misse,   132
Al the day and al the niht
Til hit sprang dai liht,
Til Horn say [24] on the stronde
Men gon in the londe.   136
"Feren," [11] quath he, "yinge,
Ihc [25] telle you tithinge.
Ihc here fogeles [26] singe
And that gras him springe.   140
Blithe beo we on lyve,
Ure schup is on ryve." [27]
Of schup hi gunne funde [28]
And setten fout [29] to grunde.[30]   144
Bi the se side

Had he not been so fair,
The children all had perished there.
An admiral then foretold,
In speaking he was bold: 96
"Horn, valour is in thee,
As any man can see;
Thou art now large and strong,
Fair and of body long.   100
Thou shalt grow ever greater
For seven years or better,
If thou alive may go —
And thy comrades also.   104
If so it should befall,
You would surely slay us all;
Therefore thou must to sea,
Thou and thy company;   108
To ship now shall you go,
And sink to the ground below;
The sea shall you swallow,
Nor shall remorse us follow,   112
For if we gave you life,
With sword or else with knife
We all should soon be dead,
And thy sire's death repaid.   116

They brought the boys to the shore,
Wringing their hands full sore.
On shipboard they thrust them,
No longer would they trust them.   120
Oft had Horn suffered woe,
But never worse than he then did know. 122
The sea began a-flowing
And Horn Child a-rowing.   128
The sea so fast the ship did drive,
No hope the boys had to survive.
They thought without a doubt
Their lives would soon go out,   132
All the day and all the night
Till there sprang daylight,
Till Horn saw on the strand
Men walking in the land.   136
"Comrades," said he, "true,
Good news I tell to you.
I hear the birds a-singing
And the grass a-springing.   140
Let us be glad once more,
Our ship has come to shore."
From the ship they went to land
And set foot upon the strand.   144
By the water side

---

[1] if it were not for his beauty [2] slain [3] bold
[4] brave [5] very evident [6] of good height [7] greater
[8] seven [9] mayst [10] alive [11] companions [12] slay
[13] go to ship [14] go [15] bottom [16] drown [17] repent
[18] pay for [19] wringing their hands [20] been sad
[21] but [22] then *See note on* l. 16. [23] they expected
certainly [24] saw [25] I [26] birds [27] shore [28] did go
[29] foot [30] ground

Hi¹ leten that schup ride.
Thanne spak him Child Horn,
In Suddene he was iborn,   148
"Schup, bi the se flode
Daies have thu gode;
Bi the se brinke
No water the na drinke. ²   152
Gef thu cume to Suddenne,
Gret thu wel of myne kenne;   156
Gret thu wel my moder,
Godhild, quen the gode.
And seie the paene ³ kyng,
Jesu Cristes withering,⁴   160
That ihc ⁵ am hol and fer ⁶
On this lond arived her;
And seie that hi ⁷ schal fonde ⁸
The dent of myne honde."   164

*   *   *   *   *

Aylbrus wende ⁹ hire fro;
Horn in halle fond he tho ¹⁰
Bifore the kyng on benche
Wyn for to schenche.¹¹   388
"Horn," quath he, "so hende,¹²
To bure ¹³ nu thu wende ¹⁴   392
After mete stille
With Rymenhild to duelle.¹⁵
Wordes suthe ¹⁶ bolde
In herte thu hem holde.   396
Horn, beo me wel trewe;
Ne schal hit the nevre rewe." ¹⁷
     Horn in herte leide
Al that he him seide.   400
He yeode ¹⁸ in wel rigte
To Rymenhild the brigte.
On knes he him sette,¹⁹
And sweteliche hure grette.²⁰   404
Of his feire sigte
Al the bur gan ligte.
He spac faire speche;
Ne dorte ²¹ him noman teche.   408
"Wel thu sitte and softe,
Rymenhild the brigte,
With thine Maidenes sixe
That the sitteth nixte! ²²   412
Kinges stuard ure ²³
Sende me in to bure.
With the speke ihc scholde;
Seie ²⁴ me what thu woldest.   416
Seie, and ich schal here,
What thi wille were."

They let the ship ride.
Then up spake Child Horn,
In Suddénè he was born: 148
"Ship, by the sea flood
May thou have days good;
By the sea brink
May thee no water sink.   152
To Suddénè if thou come,
Greet well my kin at home;   156
Greet well my mother dear,
Godhild, queen without peer.
And tell the pagan king,
Hateful to Christ in everything,   160
That I am whole and sound
Landed on this ground;
And say that he shall feel
The blow my hand shall deal."   164

*   *   *   *   *

Aylbrus went from her to the hall,
Where Horn did serve before them all
To the king upon the bench
Wine his thirst to quench.   388
"Horn," said he, "my friend,
To bower must thou wend   392
In secret after meat
Rymenhild to greet.
Speeches very bold
In heart thou shalt hold.   396
Horn, to me be true,
And ne'er shalt thou it rue."
     Horn in heart has laid
All he to him said.   400
In he went forthright
To Rymenhild the bright.
He knelt there at her feet,
And sweetly did her greet.   404
Of his lovely sight
The bower grew all bright.
He spoke with courteous speech —
Him needed no man teach: 408
"Sit thou in weal aright,
Rymenhild the bright,
With handmaidens twice three
That ever sit with thee!   412
The steward of our king
A message did me bring:
To bower should I seek
To hear what thou wouldst speak.   416
Speak and tell to me
Thy will, whatso it be."

---

¹ they ² drown ³ pagan ⁴ enemy ⁵ I ⁶ sound ⁷ he   ¹⁸ went ¹⁹ he kneeled ²⁰ greeted ²¹ needed ²² that
⁸ experience ⁹ went ¹⁰ then ¹¹ pour ¹² courteous   sit nearest thee ²³ our ²⁴ tell
¹³ bower ¹⁴ go ¹⁵ remain, be ¹⁶ very ¹⁷ repent

Rymenhild up gan stonde
And tok him by the honde.   420
Heo sette him on pelle, [1]
Of wyn to drinke his fulle. [2]
Heo makede him faire chere
And tok him abute the swere. [3]
Ofte heo him custe, [4]
So wel so hire luste. [5]   426
"Horn," heo sede, "withute strif,   437
Thu schalt have me to thi wif.
Horn, have of me rewthe, [6]
And pligt [7] me thi trewthe."   440
  Horn tho him bithogte
What he speke migte.
"Crist," quath he, "the wisse, [8]
And yive [9] the hevene blisse   444
Of thine husebonde,
Wher he beo in londe!
Ihc am ibore to lowe
Such wimman to knowe.   448
Ihc am icome of thralle,
And fundling bifalle. [10]
Ne feolle [11] hit the of cunde [12]
To spuse [13] beo me bunde. [14]   452
Hit nere no fair wedding
Bitwexe a thral and a king."
  Tho gan Rymenhild mis-lyke,
And sore gan to sike. [15]   456
Armes heo gan buge; [16]
Adun he [17] feol iswoge. [18]
  Horn in herte was ful wo,
And tok hire on his armes two.   460
He gan hire for to kesse,
Wel ofte mid ywisse. [19]
"Lemman," [20] he sede, "dere,
Thin herte nu thu stere. [21]   464
Help me to knigte,
Bi al thine migte,
To my lord the king,
That he me yive dubbing.   468
Thanne is mi thralhod
Iwent [22] in to knigthod,
And i schal wexe more,
And do, lemman, thi lore." [23]   472
  Rymenhild, that swete thing,
Wakede of hire swowning. [24]
"Horn," quath heo, "wel sone
That schal beon idone;   476
Thu schal beo dubbed knigt
Are [25] come seve nigt.
Have her this cuppe,

Rymenhild up did stand
And took him by the hand.   420
On couch she set him fine,
To drink his fill of wine;
She gave him welcome true
And arms about him threw;
Full oft she did him kiss,
Her joy was most in this.   426
"Horn," she said, "without all strife, 437
Thou shalt have me as thy wife.
Horn, have of me ruth
And plight to me thy truth."   440
  Horn in his heart did seek
What words he then might speak.
"May Christ," said he, "now guide thee!
And heaven's bliss betide thee   444
Of thy husband free,
Where'er in land he be!
But I am born too low
Such a woman's love to know.   448
I come of thralls, God wot;
A foundling's was my lot.
Befits thee not by kind
Thyself to me to bind.   452
It were no fit wedding
Betwixt a thrall and a king."
  Rymenhild was grieved thereby
And sore began to sigh.   456
Her arms slipped strengthless down,
And there she fell a-swown.
  Horn such woe could nowise brook
And in his arms the maiden took.   460
And then he did her kiss,
Full oft and oft, i-wis.
"Sweetheart," said he, "dear,
Thy heart now must thou steer.   464
Help me become a knight,
Truly, with all thy might,
To my lord, the king,
That he me grant dubbing.   468
Then shall my thrallhood
Be changèd to knighthood,
And I grow greater still,
And do, sweetheart, thy will."   472
  Rymenhild, that sweetest thing,
Wakened then from her swooning.
"Horn," quoth she, "full soon
That shall all be done;   476
Thou shalt be dubbed a knight
Within this sevennight.
This cup do thou now bear

---

[1] skin, rug [2] fill [3] neck [4] kissed [5] pleased [6] pity
[7] plight [8] direct [9] give [10] chanced [11] it would not
suit [12] nature [13] spouse [14] bound [15] sigh [16] did bow

[17] she [18] a-swoon [19] very often indeed [20] sweetheart [21] direct, control [22] turned [23] teaching
[24] swooning [25] ere

And this ring ther-uppe,[1]   480
To Aylbrus the stuard,
And se he holde foreward.[2]
Seie [3] ich him biseche,
With loveliche speche   484
That he adun falle
Bifore the king in halle
And bidde [4] the king arigte
Dubbe the to knigte.   488
With selver and with golde
Hit wurth [5] him wel iyolde.[6]
Crist him lene spede [7]
Thin erende to bede." [8]   492

*   *   *   *   *   *

And this ring so fair,   480
To Aylbrus bear them both
And bid him keep his oath.
Tell him I him beseech
That he with fairest speech   484
Upon his knees do fall
Before the king in hall
And pray the king aright
Thee to dub as knight.   488
With silver and with gold
Shall his reward be told.
Christ him grant good skill
Well to obtain thy will!''   492

*   *   *   *   *   *

NICHOLAS DE GUILDFORD (?) (fl. 1250)

THE OWL AND THE NIGHTINGALE

Ich [9] was in one sumere dale,[10]
In one swithe digele hale,[11]
I-herede [12] ich holde grete tale [13]
An ule and one nigtingale.
That plait [14] was stif and starc and strong,
Sum wile [15] softe, and lud among; [16]
And aither [17] agen other swal,[18]
And let that vule mod ut al.[19]
And either [17] seide of otheres custe [20]
That alre-worste [21] that hi wuste; [22]   10
And hure and hure [23] of otheres songe
Hi [24] heolde plaiding swithe [25] stronge.
    The nigtingale bi-gon the speche,
In one hurne [26] of one beche;
And sat up one vaire bohe,[27]
Thar were abute [28] blosme i-nohe,[29]
In ore waste [30] thicke hegge,
I-meind mid spire [31] and grene segge.
Heo [32] was the gladur vor [33] the rise,[34]
And song a vele cunne wise.[35]   20
Bet thuhte the drem [36] that he [37] were
Of harpe and pipe, than he [37] nere,[38]
Bet thuhte [39] that he [37] were i-shote
Of harpe and pipe than of throte.
    Tho [40] stod on old stoc thar bi-side,
Thar tho [41] ule song hire tide,[42]
And was mid ivi al bi-growe,
Hit was thare ule earding-stowe.[43]

As I was in a summer dale,
Within a very secret vale,
I heard of talking a great tale
Betwixt an owl and a nightingale.
The strife was stiff and stark and strong;
Sometimes 'twas soft, then loud, their song.
Either against the other swelled,
Let out the rage that in her dwelled.
And each said of the other's ways
The worst she knew to her dispraise;   10
And specially of each other's song
They had a quarrel very strong.
    The nightingale began the speech,
Snug in a corner of a beech;
She sat upon a pretty bough,
There were about her blossoms enow,
All in a lonely, thickset hedge,
Tangled with shoots and green with sedge.
She was the gladder for the sprays,
And sang in many kinds of ways.   20
It rather seemed the sound I heard
Was harp and pipe than song of bird;
For rather seemed the sound to float
From harp and pipe than from bird's throat.
    There stood an old stump there beside,
Wherefrom the owl in her turn cried;
It was with ivy overgrown,
And there the owl dwelled all alone.

---

[1] besides   [2] agreement   [3] say   [4] pray   [5] shall be
[6] paid   [7] grant success   [8] present   [9] I   [10] a summer
dale   [11] a very secret corner   [12] heard   [13] talk   [14] strife
[15] while   [16] at times   [17] each   [18] swelled   [19] the foul
spirit all out   [20] qualities   [21] the very worst   [22] knew
[23] and indeed and indeed   [24] they   [25] very   [26] corner

[27] a fair bough   [28] about   [29] enough   [30] a solitary
[31] mixed with sprouts   [32] she   [33] for   [34] spray   [35] and
sang in many kinds of ways   [36] the sound seemed
rather   [37] it   [38] was not   [39] it seemed rather   [40] then
[41] where the   [42] in her turn   [43] the owl's home

The nihtingale hi [1] i-seh.
And hi [1] bi-heold and over-seh,[2]   30
And thuhte wel vule [3] of thare ule,
For me hi halt [4] lothlich [5] and fule.
"Unwiht," [6] heo sede, "awei thu fleo !
Me is the wers [7] that ich the seo ;
I-wis [8] for thine vule lete [9]
Wel oft ich mine song for-lete ; [10]
Min heorte at-flith,[11] and falt [12] mi tunge,
Wonne [13] thu art to me i-thrunge.[14]
Me luste bet speten [15] thane singe,
Of [16] thine fule gogelinge." [17]   40
    Theos ule abod fort [18] hit was eve,
Heo ne mihte no leng bileve,[19]
Vor hire heorte was so gret,[20]
That wel neh [21] hire fnast at-schet ; [22]
And warp [23] a word thar-after longe :
"Hu thincthe [24] nu bi mine songe ?
Wenst [25] thu that ich ne cunne [26] singe
Theh [27] ich ne cunne [28] of writelinge ? [29]
I-lome [30] thu dest [31] me grame,[32]
And seist me bothe teone [33] and schame ;   50
Gif [34] ich the heolde on min vote,[35]
So hit bi-tide [36] that ich mote ! [37]
And thu were ut of thine rise,[38]
Thu scholdest singe an other wise.

*   *   *   *   *   *

"Yet thu me seist of other thinge,
And telst that ich ne can noht singe,   310
Ac [39] al mi reorde [40] is woning,[41]
And to i-here grislich [42] thing.
That nis noht soth,[43] ich singe efne [44]
Mid fulle dreme [45] and lude stefne.[40]
Thu wenist [25] that ech song beo grislich [46]
That thine pipinge nis i-lich : [47]
Mi stefne [40] is bold and noht un-orne,[48]
Heo [49] is-i lich [50] one grete horne ;
And thin is i-lich [50] one pipe
Of one smale weode un-ripe.[51]   320
Ich singe bet than thu dest ; [52]
Thu chaterest so [53] doth on Irish prest.
Ich singe an eve, a rihte time,
And seoththe,[54] won [13] hit is bed-time,
The thridde sithe [55] at middelnihte,
And so ich mine song adihte [56]
Wone [13] ich i-seo arise veorre [57]

The nightingale her soon espied,
And looked at her with scornful pride.   30
She thought but meanly of the owl,
For men it loathly deem and foul.
"Monster," she said, "away with thee !
The worse for me that thee I see !
Verily for thy ugly look,
I oftentimes my song forsook.
My tongue is mute, my heart takes flight,
When thou appearest in my sight.
I rather wish to spit than sing,
At sound of thy foul sputtering."   40
    The owl abode till eventide,
No longer could she then abide,
So swollen was her heart with wrath
That she could scarcely get her breath ;
And still she made a speech full long :
"How think'st thou now about my song ?
Think'st thou to sing I have no skill
Merely because I cannot trill ?
Oft am I angered by thy blame,
Thou speakest to my hurt and shame ;   50
If I once held thee in my claw,
Would that I might here in this shaw ! —
And thou wert down from off thy spray,
Then should'st thou sing another way !

*   *   *   *   *   *

"And yet thou sayest another thing,
And tellest me I cannot sing,   310
That all my song is mourning drear,
A fearsome sound for men to hear.
That is sooth ; my voice is true,
And full and loud, sonorous too.
Thou thinkest ugly every note
Unlike the thin ones from thy throat.
My voice is bold and not forlorn,
It soundeth like a mighty horn ;
And thine is like a little pipe
Made of a slender reed unripe.   320
Better I sing than thou at least ;
Thou chatterest like an Irish priest.
I sing at eve, a proper time,
And after, when it is bedtime,
And once again at middle-night,
And so ordain my song aright
When I see rising from afar

[1] her [2] despised [3] very foully [4] for everyone
holds her [5] hateful [6] monster [7] I am the worse
[8] truly [9] appearance [10] give up [11] flies away [12] fails
[13] when [14] arrived [15] I feel more like spitting
[16] because of [17] screeching [18] waited till [19] no
longer wait [20] swollen [21] nigh [22] breath choked
[23] threw [24] how does it seem [25] thinkest [26] cannot

[27] though [28] know nothing [29] trilling [30] often
[31] causest [32] anger [33] injury [34] if [35] foot [36] so may
it happen [37] may [38] bough [39] but [40] voice [41] lamentation [42] terrible [43] true [44] precisely [45] sound
[46] ugly [47] that is not like thy piping [48] unpleasing [49] it [50] like [51] green [52] dost [53] as [54] afterwards [55] third time [56] ordain [57] afar

Other [1] dai-rim [2] other [3] dai-sterre.
Ich do god mid mine throte,
And warni men to heore note; [4]   330
Ac [5] thu singest alle longe niht,
From eve fort [6] hit is dai-liht,
And evre lesteth thin o [7] song
So [8] longe so [8] the niht is longe,
And evre croweth thi wrecche crei,[9]
That he ne swiketh [10] niht ne dai.
Mid thine pipinge thu adunest [11]
Thas monnes earen thar [12] thu wunest,[13]
And makest thine song so un-wiht [14]
That me [15] ne telth [16] of the nowiht.[17]   340
Evrich murhthe [18] mai so longe i-leste,
That heo shal liki [19] wel un-wreste; [20]
Vor harpe and pipe and fugeles [21] songe
Misliketh, gif hit is to longe.
Ne beo the song never so murie,
That he ne shal thinche [22] wel un-murie,[23]
Gef he i-lesteth over un-wille.[24]
So thu miht [25] thine song aspille; [26]
Vor hit is soth,[27] Alvred hit seide,
And me [15] hit mai in boke rede,   350
'Evrich thing mai leosen [28] his godhede [29]
Mid unmethe [30] and mid over-dede.'" [31]

* * * * * *

"Ule," heo seide, "wi dostu so?   411
Thu singest a-winter [32] 'wolawo'; [33]
Thu singest so [8] doth hen a [34] snowe:
Al that heo singeth, hit is for wowe; [35]
A-wintere thu singest wrothe [36] and gomere,[37]
And evre thu art dumb a-sumere.
Hit is for thine fule nithe,[38]
That thu ne miht [39] mid us beo blithe,
Vor thu forbernest [40] wel neh [41] for onde,[42]
Wane [43] ure blisse cumeth to londe.   420
Thu farest so [8] doth the ille; [44]
Evrich blisse him is un-wille; [45]
Grucching and luring [46] him beoth rade,[47]
Gif he i-seoth that men beoth glade;
He wolde that he i-seye [48]
Teres in evrich monnes eye;
Ne rohte he [49] theh [50] flockes were
I-meind [51] bi toppes [52] and bi here.[53]
Al-so thu dost on thire [54] side;
Vor wanne [43] snou lith thicke and wide,   430
And alle wihtes [55] habbeth sorhe,[56]

Either day-dawn or else day-star.
I do men good thus with my throat,
And help them with my warning note;   330
But thou art singing all the night,
From eve until it is daylight,
For ever lasts thy only song,
As long as ever the night is long,
And ever crows thy wretched lay,
That ceaseth not, by night or day.
Thy piping is ever in man's ears,
Wherever thou dwellest, thy din he hears;
Thou makest thy song a thing of naught,
No man accounteth thee as aught;   340
For any mirth may last so long
That dislike of it waxeth strong;
For harp or pipe or song of bird
Displeaseth if too long 'tis heard.
Never so merry a song may be
But to disgust shall turn its glee
If it shall last till it annoy;
So mayst thou thy song destroy.
For it is true, as Alfred said,
And in his book it may be read,   350
'Every good its grace may lose
By lack of measure and by abuse.'"

* * * * * *

"Owl," she said, "why dost thou so?   411
Thou singest in winter a song of woe;
Thou singest as doth a hen in snow:
All that she sings it is for woe;
In winter thou singest in wrath and gloom,
In summer thou art ever dumb.
'Tis thy foul malice that hinders thee,
That blithe with us thou may'st not be;
For envy 'tis that in thee burns,
When in the spring our bliss returns.   420
Thou farest as doth the wicked ever,
Whom joy of others pleases never;
For grudging and louring is he mad
Whene'er he sees that men are glad.
Rather would such a one espy
Tears in every person's eye;
Never a whit would that man care
Though flocks were mixed, both head and hair.
So dost thou fare, upon thy side;
For when the snow lies thick and wide,   430
And every creature lives in sorrow,

[1] either [2] dawn [3] or [4] benefit [5] but [6] till [7] lasteth thy one [8] as [9] cry [10] it ceases not [11] dinnest [12] where [13] dwellest [14] horrible [15] one [16] accounts [17] naught [18] every mirth [19] please [20] very badly [21] bird's [22] seem [23] unpleasant [24] if it lasts unto displeasure [25] mayst [26] ruin [27] true [28] lose [29] goodness [30] excess [31] over-doing [32] in winter [33] welaway [34] in [35] woe [36] wrath [37] grief [38] hatred [39] mayst not [40] burnest up [41] nigh [42] envy [43] when [44] wicked man [45] unpleasing [46] louring [47] ready [48] saw [49] he would not care [50] though [51] mixed up [52] heads [53] hair [54] thy [55] creatures [56] sorrow

Thu singest from eve fort amorhe.[1]
Ac [2] ich alle blisse mid me bringe;
Ech wiht [3] is glad for mine thinge,[4]
And blisseth hit [5] wanne [6] ich cume,
And hiheth agen [7] mine kume.[8]
The blostme ginneth springe and sprede
Bothe ine treo and ek on mede;
The lilie mid hire faire wlite [9]
Wolcumeth me, that thu hit wite,[10]   440
Bit [11] me mid hire faire bleo [12]
That ich schulle to hire fleo;
The rose also mide hire rude,[13]
That cumeth ut of the thorne wude,
Bit [11] me that ich shulle singe
Vor hire luve one skentinge." [14]

Then singest thou from eve till morrow.
But I all gladness with me bring,
All men are happy when I sing;
They all rejoice, when I appear,
And hope for me another year.
Blossoms begin to spring and grow,
On tree, in mead, and in hedge-row;
The lily with her fair white hue
Doth welcome me, I would thou knew;   440
With her sweet face she biddeth me
That I to her shall quickly flee;
Likewise the rose with ruddy hood,
That cometh from the thorny wood,
Biddeth me ever that I shall sing
For her dear love in carolling."

* * * * * *   * * * * * *

FROM CURSOR MUNDI (C. 1300)

(*Unknown Author*)

THE FLIGHT INTO EGYPT

An angel thus til [15] him can [16] sai: 210
"Rise up, Joseph, and busk [17] and ga, [18]
Maria and thi child al-sua; [19]
For yow be-hoves nu [20] al thre
In land of Egypt for to fle;
Rise up ar [21] it be dai,
And folus [22] forth the wildrin [23] wai.
Herod, that es the child [24] fa,[25]
Fra nu [26] wil sek him for to sla.[27]
Thare sal [28] yee bide stil wit [29] the barn,[30]
Til that I eft [31] cum yow to warn."   220
    Son [32] was Joseph redi bun; [33]
Wit [34] naghtertale [35] he went o [36] tun,
Wit [34] Maria mild and their meine: [37]
A maiden and thair suanis [38] thre,
That servid tham in thair servis;
With thaim was nan bot war [39] and wis.
    Forth sco rad,[40] that moder mild,
And in hir barm [41] sco ledd [42] hir child,
Til thai come at [43] a cove was [44] depe.
Thar [45] thai tham thoght to rest and slepe;
Thar did [46] thai Mari for to light,[47]   231
Bot son thai sagh [48] an ugli sight.
Als [49] thai loked tham biside,

An angel thus to him did say: 210
"Rise up, Joseph, and busk and go,
Maria and thy child also;
For it behooves you now all three
To the land of Egypt for to flee;
Rise up, then, ere it be day,
And follow forth the desert way.
Herod, that is the infant's foe,
Henceforth will seek to lay him low.
There with the bairn shall ye remain
Till I come back to warn you plain."   220
    Now soon was Joseph ready dight;
He left the town at fall of night,
With Mary mild and their company:
A maiden and their servants three,
That served them well in servants' guise;
With them was none but wary and wise.
    Forth she rode, that mother mild,
And in her bosom bore her child,
Till they came to a cave full deep;
There they had thought to rest and sleep;
There helped they Mary to alight,   231
But soon they saw an ugly sight.
As they were looking them beside,

[1] till morning [2] but [3] creature [4] on my account
[5] rejoices [6] when [7] hopeth for [8] coming [9] face
[10] know [11] bids [12] visage [13] redness [14] pastime [15] to
[16] did [17] get ready [18] go [19] also [20] now [21] ere
[22] follow [23] wilderness [24] child's [25] foe [26] from now
[27] slay [28] shall [29] with [30] child [31] again [32] soon
[33] prepared [34] with [35] night-time [36] from [37] household [38] men-servants [39] none but was wary [40] she
rode [41] bosom [42] carried [43] came to [44] cave that
was [45] there [46] caused [47] alight [48] saw [49] as

Ute o [1] this cove [2] than sagh [3] thai glide
Mani dragons wel [4] sodanli ;
The suanis [5] than bi-gan to cri.
Quen [6] Jesus sagh tham glopnid [7] be,
He lighted of [8] his moder kne
And stod a-pon thaa [9] bestes grim,[10]
And thai tham luted [11] under him.   240
Than com [12] the propheci al cler
To dede [13] that said es in Sauter : [14]
"The dragons, wonand [15] in thair cove,
The Laverd [16] agh [17] yee worthli to lofe." [18]
Jesus he went befor tham than,
Forbed [19] tham harm do ani man.
Maria and Joseph ne-for-thi [20]
For the child war ful dreri ; [21]
Bot Jesus ansuard [22] thaim onan : [23]
"For me drednes haf [24] nu yee nan,[25]   250
Ne haf yee for me na barn-site,[26]
For I am self man al parfite,[27]
And al the bestes that ar wild
For me most [28] be tame and mild."
Leon yode tham als imid ; [29]
And pardes,[30] als [31] the dragons did,
Bifor Maria and Joseph yede,[32]
In right wai tham for to lede.
Quen Maria sagh thaa [9] bestes lute,[33]
First sco [34] was gretli in dute,[35]   260
Til Jesus loked on hir blith
And dridnes [36] bad hir nan to kith.[37]
"Moder," he said, "haf thou na ward [38]
Nother o [39] leon ne o lepard,
For thai com noght us harm to do,
Bot thair servis at [40] serve us to."
Bath [41] ass and ox that wit [42] tham war [43]
And bestes that thair harnais bar
Ute o Jerusalem, thair kyth,[44]
The leons mekli yod [32] tham wit,[42]   270
Wit-uten harm of ox or ass,
Or ani best that wit tham was.
Than was fulfild the propheci,
That said was thoru Jeremi :
"Wolf and wether, leon and ox,
Sal [45] comen samen,[46] and lamb and fox."

Out of this cave then saw they glide
Many dragons full suddenly ;
The servants then began to cry.
When Jesus saw them frightened be,
He lighted from his mother's knee,
And stood upon those beasts so grim,
And low they bowed them under him.   240
Then came the prophecy all clear
As in the Psalter ye may hear :
"Dragons that in their cavern dwell
The praises of the Lord shall tell."
Jesus, he went before them then,
Forbade their harming any men.
Maria and Joseph, none the less,
For the child were in distress ;
But Jesus answered them and said :
"For me have ye no manner dread ;   250
For me as child have ye no fright,
A perfect man am I by right ;
And all the beasts that are so wild,
For me must be both tame and mild."
A lion went them then amid ;
And leopards, as the dragons did,
Before Maria and Joseph lay,
Ready to lead them on their way.
When Mary saw the beasts all lout,
Greatly, at first, she was in doubt,   260
Till Jesus blithely drew anear,
And bade her not at all to fear.
"Mother," said he, "have no regard
For lion or for fierce leopard ;
For they come not us harm to do ;
But us their service to give unto."
Both ass and ox were with them there,
And other beasts that baggage bare
Out of their home, Jerusalem ;
The lions meekly went with them,   270
And did no harm to ox or ass,
Or any beast that with them was.
Then was fulfilled the prophecy
That spoken was by Jeremy :
"Wolf and wether, lion and ox,
Shall come together, and lamb and fox."

[1] out of [2] cave [3] saw [4] very [5] men [6] when [7] terrified [8] off [9] those [10] fierce [11] bowed [12] came [13] to deed, to realization [14] the Psalter [15] dwelling [16] Lord [17] ought [18] praise [19] forbade [20] nevertheless [21] sad [22] answered [23] at once [24] have [25] none

[26] child-sorrow [27] perfect [28] must [29] a lion went with them also [30] leopards [31] as [32] went [33] bow [34] she [35] doubt, fear [36] terror [37] show, feel [38] regard [39] of [40] to [41] both [42] with [43] were [44] country [45] shall [46] together

THOMAS DE HALES (bef. 1300)

A LUVE RON [1]

A mayde Cristes [2] me bit yorne [3]
  That ich hire [4] wurche [5] a luv ron;
For hwan heo [6] myhte best ileorne [7]
  To taken on [8] other soth [9] lefmon [10]
That treowest were of alle berne,[11]
  And best wyte cuthe [12] a freo wymmon.
Ich hire nule [13] nowiht [14] werne,[15]
  Ich hire wule [16] teche as ic con.   8

Mayde, her [17] thu myht [18] biholde
  This worldes luve nys [19] bute o res,[20]
And is byset so fele-volde,[21]
  Vikel,[22] and frakel,[23] and wok,[24] and les.[25]
Theos theines [26] that her weren bolde
  Beoth aglyden [27] so [28] wyndes bles; [29]
Under molde [30] hi liggeth [31] colde
  And faleweth [32] so [28] doth medewe gres.   16

    *   *   *   *   *   *

Nis non [33] so riche, ne non so freo,[34]
  That he ne schal heonne [35] sone away.
Ne may hit never his waraunt beo, —
  Gold ne seolver, vouh [36] ne gray; [37]
Ne beo he no the swift,[38] ne may he fleo,
  Ne weren [39] his lif enne [40] day.
Thus is thes world, as thu mayht [18] seo,
  Al so [41] the schadewe that glyt [42] away.   32

This world fareth hwilynde.[43]
  Hwenne [44] on cumeth, an other goth;
That [45] wes bi-fore nu is bihynde,
  That [45] er [46] was leof [47] nu hit is loth; [48]
For-thi [49] he doth as the blynde
  That in this world his luve doth.[50]
Ye mowen iseo [51] the world aswynde; [52]   39
  That wouh [53] goth forth, abak that soth.[54]

Theo [55] luve that ne may her abyde,
  Thu treowest [56] hire [57] myd muchel wouh,[58]
Al so [59] hwenne hit schal to-glide,[60]
  Hit is fals, and mereuh,[61] and frouh,[62]
And fromward [63] in uychon tide.[64]
  Hwile hit lesteth, is seorewe [65] inouh; [66]

A LOVE LETTER

A maid of Christ doth plead with me
  To write her a letter of love to-day,
From which she can learn most readily
  To take another true love, i'fay,
Who faithfulest of all shall be,
  And best can guard a lady gay.
No wise will I deny her plea,
  But I will teach her as I may.   8

O maiden, here thou mayst behold
  This earthly love is but a race,
And is beset so many fold,
  Fickle and false and weak and base.
Those knights that here were once so bold,
  Like wind have glided from their place;
Under mould they are lying cold,
  And wither as doth the meadow grass.   16

    *   *   *   *   *   *

There's none so rich and none so free
  That hence he shall not soon away.
Nothing may ever his warrant be, —
  Gold, nor silver, nor ermine gay;
Be he ever so swift, he may not flee,
  Nor guard his life a single day.
Thus is this world, as thou mayst see,
  Like as the shadow that glides away.   32

This world fareth like the wind,
  One thing gone, another here;
What was before is now behind,
  What now is loath before was dear;
Therefore he doth as doth the blind,
  Who sets his love on this world's gear.
The world is vanishing, ye shall find;   39
  Evil goes forward, truth to the rear.

The love that may not here abide,
  Thou art wrong to trust it now;
Away from thee that love will glide,
  Capricious and frail and false of vow,
And hasting away at every tide.
  The while it lasts, 'tis sorrow enow;

[1] a love rune (or letter) [2] of Christ's [3] begs me eagerly [4] her [5] make [6] whereby she [7] learn [8] an [9] true [10] lover [11] men [12] could protect [13] will not [14] not at all [15] refuse [16] will [17] here [18] mayst [19] is not [20] a race [21] in so many ways [22] fickle [23] ugly [24] weak [25] false [26] these nobles [27] are passed away [28] as [29] breath [30] the earth [31] they lie [32] wither [33] there is none [34] free, generous [35] hence [36] ermine [37] vair [38] be he never so swift [39] protect [40] a single [41] just as [42] glides [43] swiftly [44] when [45] what [46] formerly [47] dear [48] hated [49] therefore [50] places [51] may see [52] vanish [53] the wrong [54] the true [55] the [56] trustest [57] it [58] very wrongly [59] even so [60] pass away [61] delicate [62] capricious [63] hasting away [64] at every time [65] sorrow [66] enough

An ende,[1] ne werie [2] mon [robe] so syde,[3]
  He schal to-dreosen [4] so lef on bouh.[5]   48

*   *   *   *   *   *

Hwer is Paris and Heleyne,
  That weren so bryht and feyre on bleo ; [6]
Amadas and Dideyne, [7]
  Tristram, Yseude and alle theo ; [8]
Ector, with his scharpe meyne,[9]
  And Cesar, riche of worldes feo? [10]
Heo beoth iglyden [11] ut of the reyne [12]
  So [13] the schef [14] is of the cleo.[15]   72

Hit is of heom [16] al so hit nere ; [17]
  Of heom [16] me haveth [18] wunder itold,
Nere hit reuthe [19] for to here
  Hw hi [20] were with pyne aquold,[21]
And what hi tholeden [22] alyve here.
  Al is heore [23] hot iturnd to cold.
Thus is thes world of false fere ; [24]
  Fol [25] he is the [26] on hire is bold.   80

Theyh [27] he were so riche mon [28]
  As Henry ure [29] kyng,
And al so veyr [30] as Absalon
  That nevede [31] on eorthe non evenyng,[32]
Al were sone his prute [33] agon,
  Hit nere [34] on ende [1] wurth on heryng.[35]
Mayde, if thu wilnest [36] after leofmon,[37]
  Ich teche the enne [38] treowe king.   88

A ! swete, if thu iknowe [39]
  The gode thewes [40] of thisse childe !
He is feyr and bryht on heowe,[41]
  Of glede chere,[42] of mode [43] mylde,
Of lufsum lost,[44] of truste treowe,
  Freo of heorte, of wisdom wilde ; [45]
Ne thurhte the never rewe,[46]
  Myhtestu do the [47] in his hylde.[48]   96

He is ricchest mon of londe ;
  So [13] wide so [13] mon speketh with muth,
Alle heo [49] beoth [50] to his honde
  Est and west, north and suth.
Henri, king of Engelonde,
  Of hym he halt [51] and to hym buhth.[52]
Mayde, to the he send [53] his sonde,[54]
  And wilneth [55] for to beo the cuth.[56]   104

*   *   *   *   *   *

In the end, none wears a robe so wide,
  But he shall fall as leaf from bough.   48

*   *   *   *   *   *

Paris and Helen — where are they,
  That were so bright and fair of face?
Amadas and Ydoine gay,
  Tristram, Yseult, and all that race?
Hector, strong in battle array,
  And Cæsar, great in worldly place?
They all have glided from earth away
  As sheaf from the hill, that leaves no trace. 72

They're now as though they never were here ;
  Of them are many wonders told,
Were it not pity for one to hear
  How they were tortured and died of old,
And what they suffered in life while here.
  All their heat is turned to cold.
Thus all this world doth false appear ;
  Foolish is he who in it is bold.   80

Although he were a man as strong
  As Henry is, our gracious King,
And fair as Absalom the young,
  Whose match no man on earth could bring,
His pride were soon not worth a song,
  In value less than a red herring.
O maid, if thou wilt love full long,
  I will show thee a loyal king.   88

Ah, my sweet, if thou but knew
  The blessed virtues of this Lord !
He is fair and bright of hue,
  Both glad of cheer and mild of word,
Of lovesome grace, of trust most true,
  Free-hearted, rich in wisdom's hoard ;
Never shouldst thou have need to rue,
  If thou but trust thee in his ward.   96

He is the strongest man in land,
  As far as men can speak with mouth,
And all are liegemen in his hand,
  East and west, north and south.
Henry, King of English land,
  Doth hold of him and to him boweth.
O maid, he sends thee his command,
  His will to be thy friend avoweth.   104

*   *   *   *   *   *

[1] at last [2] wear [3] wide [4] fall [5] bough [6] of face
[7] Idoyne [8] those [9] strength [10] wealth [11] they
have slipped away [12] land [13] as [14] sheaf [15] from
the hillside [16] them [17] as if they had not existed
[18] people have [19] were it not pity [20] how they
[21] killed with torture [22] suffered [23] their [24] validity
[25] foolish [26] who [27] though [28] man [29] our [30] beautiful, fair [31] had not [32] equal [33] pride [34] were not [35] a
herring [36] longest [37] a lover [38] I will teach thee a
[39] didst know [40] qualities [41] hue, appearance [42] countenance [43] mood [44] of lovable desire [45] able [46] thou
wouldst never need to repent [47] might'st thou
put thyself [48] grace [49] they [50] are [51] holds [52] bows
[53] sends [54] messenger [55] desires [56] known to thee.

MIDDLE ENGLISH LYRICS

(Unknown Authors)

ALYSOUN (c. 1300)

Bytuene Mersh[1] and Averil,
  When spray biginneth to springe,
The lutel foul[2] hath hire wyl
  On hyre lud[3] to synge.
Ich libbe[4] in love longinge
  For semlokest[5] of alle thinge.
He[6] may me blisse bringe;
Icham[7] in hire baundoun.[8]
  An hendy hap ichabbe yhent,[9]
  Ichot,[10] from hevene it is me sent,   10
  From alle wymmen mi love is lent[11]
And lyht[12] on Alysoun.

On heu[13] hire her is fayr ynoh,
  Hire browe broune, hire eye blake, —
With lossum chere[14] he on me loh![15] —   15
  With middel[16] smal, and wel ymake.[17]
  Bote[18] he me wolle[19] to hire take,
  Forte buen[20] hire owen make,[21]
  Longe to lyuen ichulle[22] forsake,
And feye[23] fallen adoun.   20
  An hendy hap, etc.

Nihtes-when y wende[24] and wake;
  Forthi[25] myn wonges[26] waxeth won.
Levedi,[27] al for thine sake
  Longinge is ylent[28] me on.   25
  In world nis non so wytermon,[29]
  That al hire bounte[30] telle con.[31]
  Hire swyre[32] is whittore then the swon,
And feyrest may[33] in toune.
  An hendi, etc.   30

Icham for wowyng al forwake,[34]
  Wery so water in wore,[35]
Lest eny reve[36] me my make.[21]
  Ychabbe y-yir yore,[37]
  Betere is tholien whyle sore[38]   35
  Then[39] mournen evermore.
  Geynest under gore,[40]
Herkne to my roun![41]
  An hendi, etc.

Betwixt old March and April gay,
  When sprays begin to spring,
The little bird in her own way
  Follows her will to sing.
But I must live in love longing
  For one who is the fairest thing.
'Tis she who may to bliss me bring,
For she my love hath won.
  A blessed fortune is my lot,
  'Tis sent to me from Heaven, I wot,   10
  To other women my love turns not
But lights on Alison.

Fair enough in hue her hair,
  Her brows are brown, and black her eyne.
She smiled on me with lovesome air;   15
  Trim is her waist and neat and fine.
  Unless thou'lt take me to be thine,
  Thy own dear love, O lady mine,
  Of longer living shall I pine,
By death shall be undone.   20
  A blessed fortune is my lot, etc.

Often at night I toss and wake;
  For this my cheeks are pale and wan.
Lady, 'tis all for thy dear sake
  Longing has fallen me upon.   25
  In world is none so wise a man
  That all her goodness tell he can.
  Her neck is whiter than the swan;
My heart she has undone.
  A blessed fortune is my lot, etc.   30

Weary as water in weir I wake,
  And woo thee more and more,
Lest some one rob me of my make.[21]
  For I have heard of yore,
  Better to suffer a while full sore,   35
  Than go a-mourning evermore.
  Gayest under gore,
Hear my orison!
  A blessed fortune is my lot, etc.

---

[1] March [2] little bird [3] in her language [4] I live [5] most beautiful [6] she [7] I am [8] power [9] a pleasant fortune I have got [10] I know [11] departed [12] alighted [13] in color [14] with loving look [15] laughed [16] waist [17] made [18] unless [19] will [20] (for) to be [21] mate [22] I will [23] ready to die [24] at night-time I turn [25] therefore [26] cheeks [27] lady [28] descended

[29] there is no so wise man [30] goodness [31] can [32] neck [33] maid [34] I am for wooing all worn with watching [35] weary as water in weir [36] take away from [37] I have heard long ago [38] it is better to endure hurt for a while [39] than [40] most gracious one alive (in clothing) [41] secret

AE

SPRINGTIME (C. 1300)

Lenten [1] ys come with love to toune,	1	With love is come to town the spring,	1
With blosmen and with briddes roune; [2]		With blossoms and birds' whispering;
That al this blisse bryngeth.		That all this bliss now bringeth.
Dayes-eyes in this [3] dales;		There are daisies in the dales,
Notes suete [4] of nyhtegales;	5	Pipings sweet of nightingales,	5
Uch foul song singeth. [5]		His song each warbler singeth.
The threstercoc him threteth oo; [6]		The throstlecock doth strutting go;
Away is huere [7] wynter woo		Away is all their winter woe
When woderoue [8] springeth.		When up the woodruff springeth.
This [3] foules [9] singeth ferly fele, [10]	10	A thousand birds are singing gay	10
And wlyteth [11] on huere wynter wele, [12]		Of winter's sadness passed away,
That al the wode ryngeth.		Till all the woodland ringeth.

The rose rayleth [13] hire rode, [14]		The rose puts on her ruddy hood,
The leves on the lyhte wode		The leaves within the greening wood
Waxen al with wille. [15]	15	With a will are growing.	15
The mone mandeth [16] hire bleo, [17]		The moon is brightening her face;
The lilie is lossom [18] to seo,		Here is the lily in her grace,
The fenyl and the fille; [19]		With thyme and fennel blowing;
Wowes this wilde drakes, [20]		A-wooing go the wilding drakes,
Miles murgeth huere makes; [21]	20	Beasts are courting now their mates;	20
Ase strem that striketh [22] stille,		The stream is softly flowing;
Mody meneth, so doht mo; [23]		Many a wretch bemoans his lot;
Ichot ycham on of tho, [24]		I am one of them, I wot,
For love that likes ille. [25]		My love for naught bestowing.

The mone mandeth [26] hire lyht,	25	The moon now mendeth fast her light,	25
So doth the semly sonne bryht,		So doth the seemly sun shine bright,
When briddes singeth breme; [27]		When birds are bravely chaunting;
Deawes donketh [28] the dounes; [29]		The dews are falling on the hill;
Deores with huere derne rounes, [30]		For pleas of love in whispers still
Domes forte deme; [31]	30	Sweethearts are not wanting;	30
Wormes woweth under cloude; [32]		The worm is wooing in the clod;
Wymmen waxeth wounder proude,		Women wax now wondrous proud,
So wel hit wol hem seme.		Their joy in life a-vaunting.
Yef [33] me shal wonte [34] wille of on, [35]		If love of one I may not know,
This wunne weole [36] y wole [37] forgon,	35	This blissful boon I will forego,	35
Ant wyht in wode be fleme. [38]		Lonely the wild wood haunting.

[1] spring [2] whisper [3] these [4] sweet [5] each bird sings a song [6] the throstle cock threatens ever [7] their [8] woodruff [9] birds [10] wonderfully many [11] cry [12] weal [13] puts on [14] redness [15] vigorously [16] mends [17] complexion [18] beautiful [19] thyme [20] these wild drakes woo [21] beasts gladden their mates [22] runs [23] the moody man laments, — so do others [24] I know I am one of those [25] pleases ill [26] mends, increases [27] loud [28] dews wet [29] hills [30] lovers with their secret whispers [come] [31] cases [of love] to judge [32] worms woo under clod [33] if [34] lack [35] one [36] boon of joy [37] will [38] and be a banished wight in the forest

UBI SUNT QUI ANTE NOS FUERUNT? (c. 1350)

Were beth [1] they that biforen us weren,
Houndes ladden [2] and havekes beren,[3]
  And hadden feld and wode?
The riche levedies [4] in here [5] bour,
That wereden gold in here [5] tressour,[6]
  With here [5] brighte rode; [7]   6

Eten and drounken, and maden hem glad;
Here lif was al with gamen [8] y-lad,
  Men kneleden hem [9] biforen;
They beren hem wel swithe heye; [10]
And in a twincling of an eye
  Here soules weren forloren.[11]   12

Were is that lawhing [12] and that song,
That trayling and that proude gong,[13]
  Tho havekes [14] and tho houndes?
Al that joye is went away,
That wele [15] is comen to weylaway [16]
  To manye harde stoundes.[17]   18

Here [5] paradis they nomen [18] here,[19]
And nou they lyen in helle y-fere; [20]
  The fyr hit brennes [21] evere:
Long is ay, and long is o,
Long is wy, and long is wo;
  Thennes ne cometh they nevere.   24

Where are they that lived of yore?
Hounds they led and hawks they bore,
  And held both park and chase.
The ladies in their bowers fair,
Who bound with gold their lovely hair,
  And winsome were of face;   6

They ate and drank and made them glad;
Their life was all with pleasure led,
  Men knelt unto their sway;
They bore themselves full haughty and high;
And in the twinkling of an eye
  Their souls were lost for aye.   12

Where is that laughing and that song,
That swaggering step that strode along,
  The hawks and all the hounds?
All that joy is passed away,
That weal is turned to woe for aye,
  To woe that hath no bounds.   18

Their heaven they had ere they did die,
And now together in hell they lie;
  The fire it burneth ever.
Long is ay! and long is oh!
Long is wy! and long is wo!
  Thence escape they never.   24

[1] where are   [2] led   [3] hawks bore   [4] ladies
[5] their   [6] head-dress   [7] complexion   [8] pleasure
[9] them   [10] bore themselves very high   [11] lost

[12] laughing   [13] gait   [14] those hawks   [15] weal   [16] alas
[17] hours   [18] took   [19] here   [20] together   [21] burns

THE AGE OF CHAUCER

WILLIAM LANGLAND? (1332?–1400?)

PIERS THE PLOWMAN

From THE PROLOGUE (A — TEXT)

In a somer sesun, whon softe was the sonne,
I schop[1] me into a shroud,[2] as[3] I a scheep[4] were;
In habite as an hermite unholy of werkes,
Wente I wyde in this world wondres to here;[5]
Bote[6] in a Mayes morwnynge, on Malverne hulles,[7] 5
Me bifel a ferly,[8] of fairie,[9] me-thoughte.
  I was wery, forwandred,[10] and wente me to reste
Undur a brod banke bi a bourne[11] side;
And as I lay and leonede and lokede on the watres,
I slumbrede in a slepynge, hit[12] swyed[13] so murie.[14] 10
  Thenne gon I meeten[15] a mervelous sweven,[16]
That I was in a wildernesse, wuste[17] I never where;
And as I beheold into the est an heigh[18] to the sonne,
I sauh[19] a tour on a toft,[20] tryelyche[21] i-maket;
A deop dale bineothe, a dungun ther-inne, 15
With deop dich and derk and dredful of sighte.
A feir feld full of folk fond[22] I ther bitwene,
Of alle maner of men, the mene and the riche,
Worchinge[23] and wandringe as the world asketh.
  Summe putten hem[24] to the plough, pleiden[25] ful seldene,[26] 20
In settynge and in sowynge swonken[27] ful harde,
And wonnen that[28] theos wasturs[29] with glotonye distruen.[30]

In a summer season when soft was the sunshine,
I got me into a garment that grew on a sheep's back;
In habit like a hermit unholy in living,
I went wide in this world wonders to seek out.
But on a May morning, on Malvern hillside, 5
I met with a marvel, of magic I thought it.
  I was weary, forwandered, and went to refresh me
Under a broad bank by the side of a brooklet.
And as I lay and leaned there and looked on the waters,
I slumbered in a sleeping, the sound was so soothing. 10
  Then came to my mind's eye a marvellous vision,
That I was in a wilderness, where wist I never;
And as I looked into the east and up where the sun was,
I saw a tower on a toft trimly constructed;
A deep dale beneath a dungeon within it, 15
With deep ditch and dark and dreadful to look on.
A fair field full of folk found I between them,
Of all manner of men, the mean and the mighty,
Working and wandering as the world asketh.
  Some put hand to the plow, played very seldom, 20
In setting and sowing sweated they hardly,
And won what these wasters with gluttony devour.

[1] shaped, arrayed [2] garment [3] as if [4] sheep [5] hear [6] but [7] hills [8] strange thing [9] enchantment [10] worn out with wandering [11] burn, brook [12] it [13] whispered, made a low sound [14] merry [15] did I dream [16] dream [17] knew [18] on high [19] saw [20] field, building-site [21] choicely, skilfully [22] found [23] working [24] them [25] played [26] seldom [27] laboured [28] what [29] these wasters [30] destroy

And summe putten hem to pruide,[1] apparaylden hem ther-after,[2]
In cuntenaunce[3] of clothinge comen disgisid.[4]
To preyeres and to penaunce putten hem monye,[5] 25
For love of ur[6] Lord liveden ful streite,
In hope for to have hevene-riche blisse;[7]
As ancres[8] and hermytes that holdeth hem in heore[9] celles,
Coveyte[10] not in cuntre to cairen[11] aboute,
For non likerous lyflode[12] heore licam[13] to plese.
And summe chosen chaffare,[14] to cheeven[15] the bettre, 31
As hit semeth to ure sighte that suche men thryveth.
And summe, murthhes[16] to maken, as munstrals cunne,[17]
And gete gold with here[9] gle, giltles, I trowe;
Bote japers[18] and jangelers,[19] Judas children,
Founden hem fantasyes and fooles hem maaden,
And habbeth wit at heore[9] wille to worchen yif hem luste.[20] 37
That[21] Poul precheth of hem, I dar not preoven[22] heere:
Qui loquitur turpiloquium he is Luciferes hyne.[23]
Bidders[24] and beggers faste aboute eoden,[25]
Til heor bagges and heore balies[26] weren bretful i-crommet;[27] 41
Feyneden hem[28] for heore foode, foughten atte[29] ale;
In glotonye, God wot, gon heo[30] to bedde
And ryseth up with ribaudye[31] this roberdes knaves;[32]
Sleep and sleughthe[33] suweth[34] hem evere.
Pilgrimes and palmers plihten[35] hem togederes 46
For to seche[36] Seint Jame and seintes at Roome;
Wenten forth in heore wey with mony wyse tales,
And hedden[37] leve to lyen al heore lyf aftir.

And some pranked them in pride, appareled them accordingly,
In quaint guise of clothing came they disfigured.
To prayers and to penance put themselves many, 25
All for love of our Lord lived they most strictly,
In hope of having heaven's bliss after;
As nuns and as hermits that in their cells hold them,
Covet not careering about through the country,
With no lustful luxuries their living to pamper. 30
And some took to trade, to thrive by the better,
As to our sight it seemeth that such men prosper.
And some, merriments to make, with minstrels' cunning,
And get gold with their glee, guiltless, methinketh;
But jesters and jugglers, Judas' children,
Forged them wild fantasies as fools pretended, 36
Yet have wit at their will to work, were they willing.
What Paul preacheth of them prove here I dare not:
Qui loquitur turpiloquium he is Lucifer's henchman.
Bidders and beggars fast about bustled,
Till their bags and their bellies were brimful and bulging; 41
Faking for their food, and fighting at the alehouse,
In gluttony, God wot, go they to slumber,
And rise up with ribaldry, these robber rascals;
Sleep and sloth too pursue them forever. 45
Pilgrims and palmers pledged them together
To seek St. James's and saints' shrines at Rome too;
Went they forth on their way with many wise stories,
And had leave to be liars all their lives after.

---

[1] pride [2] accordingly [3] fashion [4] came disguised
[5] many [6] our [7] the joy of the kingdom of heaven
[8] nuns [9] their [10] desire [11] roam [12] luxurious food
[13] body [14] trade [15] thrive [16] amusements [17] know how [18] jesters [19] buffoons [20] to work if they pleased

[21] what [22] prove, declare [23] servant [24] beggars
[25] went [26] bellies [27] brimful crammed [28] shammed
[29] at the [30] go they [31] ribaldry [32] these robber rascals [33] sloth [34] follow [35] plighted [36] seek [37] had

[1] Grete lobres [2] and longe,   that loth weore to swynke,[3]   50
Clotheden hem in copes,   to beo knowen for bretheren ;
And summe schopen hem to [4] hermytes heore ese to have.
I fond there freres,[5]   all the foure ordres, 55
Prechinge the peple   for profyt of heore wombes,[6]
Glosynge [7] the Gospel   as hem good liketh,[8]
For covetyse of copes   construeth hit ille ;
For monye [9] of this maistres mowen [10] clothen hem at lyking,
For moneye [11] and heore marchaundie meeten togedere ;   60
Seththe [12] Charite hath be [13] chapman,[14] and cheef to schriven [15] lordes,
Mony ferlyes han [16] bifalle   in a fewe yeres.
But [17] Holychirche and heo [18] holde bet [19] togedere,
The moste mischeef on molde [20]   is mountyng up faste.
   Ther prechede a pardoner,   as [21] he a prest were,   65
And brought forth a bulle   with bisschopes seles,
And seide that himself mighte asoylen [22] hem alle
Of falsnesse and fastinge   and of vouwes i-broken.[23]
The lewede [24] men levide [25] him wel and likede his speche,
And comen up knelynge   to kissen his bulle ;
He bonchede [26] hem with his brevet and blered [27] heore eiyen,[28]   71
And raughte [29] with his ragemon [30] ringes and broches.
Thus ye giveth oure [31] gold glotonis [32] to helpen ;
And leveth hit to losels [33] that lecherie haunten.[34]
Weore the bisschop i-blesset and worth bothe his eres,[35]   75
His sel shulde not be sent   to deceyve the peple.
Hit is not al bi [36] the bisschop   that the boye precheth,
Bote the parisch prest and the pardoner parte the selver

Great lubbers and long, that loth were to labour,   50
Clothed themselves in copes,   to be counted for "brethren" ;
And some entered as anchorites their ease for to purchase.
   I found there the friars,   all the four orders,
Preaching to the people   for profit of their bellies,   56
Glossing the gospel   as good to them seemed,
For coveting of copes   construe it wrongly ;
For many of these masters   may dress at their fancy,
For money and their merchandise   meet oft together ;   60
Since Charity hath been a chapman,   and chiefly to shrive nobles,
Many freaks have befallen   in a few seasons.
Save Holy-Church and they   hold better together,
The worst mischief in the world   is mounting up swiftly.
   There too preached a pardoner,   as if he a priest were,   65
And brought forth a bull — a bishop had signed it —
And said that himself could   absolve them all fully
Of falseness in fasting   and of vows they had broken.
The unlettered believed him well   and liked what he told them,
And came up kneeling   to kiss his sealed paper ;
He banged them with his brevet   and blinded their vision,
And raked in with his rigmarole   rings and brooches.
Thus ye give up your gold   gluttons to pamper ;
And rain it on rascals   that revel in lewdness.
Were the bishop blessed   and worth both his ears,   75
His seal should not be sent   to deceive thus the people.
But the blame is not all on the bishop   that the boy preaches,
But the parish priest and the pardoner   part the silver

[1] *I have omitted two lines, which probably were not in the earliest version.* [2] lubbers [3] labour [4] shaped them to, became [5] friars [6] bellies [7] interpreting [8] according to their own desire [9] many [10] may [11] money [12] since [13] been [14] trader [15] shrive, confess [16] many wonders have [17] unless [18] they = the friars [19] better [20] earth [21] as if [22] absolve [23] broken vows [24] ignorant [25] believed [26] banged [27] blinded [28] eyes [29] reached, got [30] license [31] your [32] gluttons [33] rascals [34] practice [35] ears [36] it is not all the fault of

That the pore peple of the parisch schulde
have   yif that heo ne weore.[1]
Persones and parisch prestes   playneth[2] to
heore bisschops   80
That heore parisch hath ben pore   seththe[3]
the pestilence tyme,
To have a lycence and leve   at Londun to
dwelle,
To singe ther for simonye,   for selver is
swete.
Ther hovide[4] an hundret   in houves[5] of
selke,
Serjauns hit semide   to serven atte barre; 85
Pleden for pens[6]   and poundes the lawe,
Not for love of ur Lord   unloseth heore lippes
ones.[7]
Thou mightest beter meten[8] the myst   on
Malverne hulles
Then geten a mom[9] of heore mouth   til
moneye weore schewed!
   I saugh ther bisschops bolde   and bachilers
of divyne[10]   ·   90
Bicoome clerkes of acounte   the king for to
serven.
Erchedekenes and denis,[11]   that dignite
haven
To preche the peple   and pore men to
feede,
Beon lopen[12] to Londun,   bi leve of heore
bisschopes,
To ben clerkes of the Kynges Benche,   the
cuntre to schende.[13]
   Barouns and burgeis[14]   and bondages[15]
alse[16]   96
I saugh in that semble,[17]   as ye schul heren
aftur;
Bakers, bochers,   and breusters[18] monye;
Wollene-websteris[19]   and weveris of lynen; 99
Taillours, tanneris,   and tokkeris[20] bothe;
Masons, minours,   and mony other craftes;
Dykers, and delvers,   that don heore dedes
ille,[21]
And driveth forth the longe day   with "*Deu
save Dam Emme!*"[22]
Cookes and heore knaves[23]   cryen "Hote
pies, hote!
"Goode gees and grys![24]   Go we dyne, go
we!"
Taverners to hem tolde   the same tale, 106

That the poor people of the parish   should
have but for these two.
Parsons and parish priests   complain to their
bishops   80
That their parish hath been poor   since the
pestilence season,
To have a license and leave   in London to
linger,
To sing there for simony,   for sweet is silver.
There hovered a hundred   in hoods of silk
stuff;
It seemed they were sergeants   to serve in
the law courts,   85
To plead for pennies   and pounds for ver-
dicts,
Not for love of our Lord   unloose their lips
ever.
Thou couldst better measure the mist   on
Malvern hill sides
Than get a mum of their mouths   till money
were showed them.
   I saw there bishops bold   and bachelors
of divinity   90
Become clerks of account   and king's own
servants.
Archdeacons and deans,   whose duty binds
them
To preach to the people   and poor men to
care for,
Have lighted out to London,   by leave of their
bishops,
To be clerks of the King's Bench,   the country
to injure.
   Barons and burgesses   and bondmen also
I saw in that assembly,   as I shall show
later;   97
Bakers, butchers,   and brewers many;
Woolen-weavers   and weavers of linen;
Tailors, tanners,   and tuckers likewise; 100
Masons, miners,   and many other craftsmen;
Dikers and diggers   that do their deeds
badly,
And drive forth the long day   with "*Dieu
save Dame Emme!*"
Cooks and their cookboys   crying, "Hot
pies! hot!
Good geese and piglets!   Go we dine, go
we!"   105
Tavern-keepers told them   a tale of traffic,

---

[1] if it were not for them [2] complain [3] since [4] lingered [5] hoods [6] pence, money [7] once [8] thou mightst more easily measure [9] syllable [10] divinity [11] deans [12] have run [13] injure [14] burgesses [15] bondmen [16] also [17] assembly [18] brewers [19] woolen-weavers [20] tuckers, finishers of cloth [21] that do their work badly [22] *A popular song of the time.* [23] boys [24] pigs

With wyn of Oseye [1]   and win of Gaskoyne,
Of the Ryn [2] and of the Rochel,   the rost to
defye,[3]
Al this I saugh slepynge,   and seve sithes
more.

With wine of Alsace   and wine of Gascon,
Of the Rhine and the Rochelle,   the roast to
digest well.
All this saw I sleeping,   and seven times
more.

THE FABLE OF BELLING THE CAT

From THE PROLOGUE (B — TEXT)

With that ran there a route [5] of ratones [6]
at ones,[7]
And smale mys [8] with hem,[9] mo then a
thousande,
And comen [10] to a conseille for here [11] com-
une profit;
For a cat of a courte   cam whan hym lyked,
And overlepe hem lyghtlich and laughte [12]
hem at his wille,   150
And pleyde with hem perilouslych and
possed [13] hem aboute.
"For doute [14] of dyverse dredes [15] we dar
noughte wel loke;
And yif [16] we grucche [17] of his gamen,[18]   he wil
greve us alle,
Cracche [19] us, or clawe us   and in his cloches [20]
holde,
That us lotheth the lyf   or [21] he lete us passe.
Myghte we with any witte   his wille with-
stonde,   156
We myghte be lordes aloft   and lyven at
owre ese."
A raton [22] of renon,[23] most renable [24] of
tonge,
Seide for a sovereygne   help to hymselve: [25]—
"I have y-sein [26] segges," [27] quod he, "in the
cité of London
Beren beighes [28] ful brighte abouten here
nekkes,
And some colers of crafty werk; uncoupled
thei wenden [29]   162
Both in wareine [30] and in waste, where hem
leve lyketh; [31]
And otherwhile thei aren elleswhere, as I
here telle.
Were there a belle on here beighe,[32] bi Jesu,
as me thynketh,
Men myghte wite [33] where thei went, and
awei renne ! [34]   166

With that ran there a rabble of rats all
together,
And small mice with them, more than a
thousand,
And came to a counsel for their common
profit;
For a cat of a court came when it pleased him,
And overleaped them lightly and levied on
them freely,   150
And played with them perilously and pushed
them about there.
"For drede of divers deeds we dare not once
look up;
And if his game we grudge him, he will grieve
us also,
Claw us or clinch us and in his clutches
hold us,
Making life to us loathsome ere he let us
scamper.
Might we with any wisdom his wilfulness
hinder,   156
We might be lords aloft and live at our liking."
A rat of high renown, most reasonable of
discourse,
Said for a sovereign help for their sorrow: —
"I have seen swains," said he, "in the city
of London
Wear circlets most splendid about their
necks swinging,
And some collars of crafty work; uncoupled
they ramble   162
Both in warren and in waste land, e'en
where'er it pleases;
And other times are they elsewhere, as I am
advised.
Were a bell borne on the collar, by Jesu, as
me thinketh,
One might wit where they went, and away
scamper !   166

---

[1] Alsatia [2] Rhine [3] digest [4] seven times [5] crowd
[6] rats [7] once [8] mice [9] them [10] came [11] their [12] seized
[13] pushed [14] fear [15] dreads [16] if [17] grudge [18] sport
[19] scratch [20] clutches [21] before [22] rat [23] renown

[24] eloquent [25] themselves [26] seen [27] people (*here*
dogs *are meant*) [28] rings [29] go [30] warren [31] wherever they please [32] collar [33] know [34] run

And right so," quod this raton, "reson me sheweth
To bugge [1] a belle of brasse   or of brighte sylver
And knitten on a colere   for owre comune profit,
And hangen it upon the cattes hals; [2]   than here [3] we mowen [4]
Where [5] he ritt [6] or rest   or renneth [7] to playe.
And yif him list for to laike, [8]   thenne loke we mowen,   172
And peren [9] in his presence   ther-while hym plaie liketh; [10]
And yif him wrattheth, [11]   be y-war   and his weye shonye." [12]
  Alle this route of ratones   to this reson thei assented.   175
Ac tho [13] the belle was y-bought   and on the beighe hanged,
Ther ne was ratoun in alle the route,   for alle the rewme [14] of Fraunce,
That dorst have y-bounden the belle   aboute the cattis nekke,
Ne hangen it aboute the cattes hals,   al Engelond to wynne ;
And helden hem unhardy [15]   and here conseille feble,   180
And leten [16] here laboure lost   and alle here longe studye.
  A mous that moche good   couthe, [17] as me thoughte,
Stroke forth sternly   and stode biforn hem alle,
And to the route of ratones   reherced these wordes :
"Though we culled [18] the catte   yut [19] sholde ther come another   185
To cracchy us and al owre kynde,   though we croupe [20] under benches.
For-thi [21] I conseille alle the comune   to lat the catte worthe, [22]
And be we never so bolde   the belle hym to shewe ;
For I herde my sire seyn, [23]   is sevene yere y-passed,
' There [24] the catte is a kitoun   the courte is ful elyng ' ; [25]   190
That witnisseth Holi-write, who-so wil it rede : *Ve terre ubi puer rex est,* [26] &c.

And right so," said this rat then, "reason doth counsel
To buy a bell of brass   or of bright silver
And clasp on a collar   for our common profit,
And knit it round the cat's neck ;   then may we know clearly
Whether he rides or rests   or runs to disport him.
And if he pleases to play   then may we press forward,   172
And appear in his presence   while playing him pleases ;
And if wrathful he be, then beware   and his way shun well."
  All this rabble of rats   to this reasoning assented.   175
But when the bell had been bought   and bound on the collar,
There was no rat in all the rout   that, for all the realm of France,
Durst have bound that same bell   about the cat's neck there,
Nor have hung it about his head,   to have all England ;
And found themselves fearful,   and of feeble counsel,   180
And allowed their labour lost   and their long study.
  A mouse that much good   marked, as me-thinketh,
Strode forth sternly   and stood out before them,
And to that rabble of rats   rehearsed this wisdom :
"Though we killed the cat,   yet would there come another   185
To catch us and our kin,   though we crept under benches.
Therefore I counsel all the commons   to let the cat flourish,
And be we never so bold   the bell for to show him ;
For I heard my sire say — 'tis seven years since then —
' Where the cat is a kitten   the court will be ailing ' ;   190
That witnesseth Holy-writ,   whoso will read it : *Vae terrae ubi puer rex est,* etc.

[1] buy [2] neck [3] hear [4] may [5] whether [6] rides
[7] runs [8] if he wishes to play [9] appear [10] when he pleases to play [11] he is angry [12] shun [13] but when

[14] realm [15] timid [16] counted [17] knew [18] killed [19] yet
[20] should creep [21] therefore [22] be [23] say [24] where
[25] ailing [26] woe to the land where the king is a boy

For may no renke [1] there rest have for
ratones bi nyghte.
The while he caccheth conynges [2] he coveiteth
nought owre caroyne,[3]
But fet [4] hym al with venesoun,[5] defame
we hym nevere.
For better is a litel losse than a longe sorwe,
The mase [6] amonge us alle though we
mysse [7] a shrewe.[8]   196
For many mannes malt we mys wolde
destruye,
And also ye route [9] of ratones rende mennes
clothes,
Nere [10] that cat of that courte that can yow
overlepe;
For had ye rattes yowre wille, ye couthe [11]
nought reule [12] yowre-selve.   200
I sey for me," quod the mous, "I se so
mykel [13] after,
Shal never the cat ne the kitoun bi my
conseille be greved,
Ne carpyng [14] of this coler that costed [15] me
nevre.
And though it had coste me catel,[16] biknowen[17]
it I nolde,[18]
But suffre as hym-self wolde to do as hym
liketh,   205
Coupled and uncoupled to cacche what thei
mowe.[19]
For-thi uche [20] a wise wighte I warne wite [21]
wel his owne." —
  What this meteles [22] bemeneth,[23] ye men
that be merye,
Devine ye, for I ne dar,[24] bi dere God in
hevene!

For rest there may no man reap for rats in
the night-time.
While that he catcheth conies he coveteth
not our carcases,
But feeds him all with venison, defame we
him never.
For better is a little loss than a long sorrow,
The maze among us all though we miss one
rascal.   196
For many a man's malt we mice would
destroy,
And also ye rabble of rats would rend men's
clothing
But for that cat of that court that can over-
leap you;
For had ye rats your will, ye could not rule
your own selves.   200
I say for me," said that mouse, "I see so
much after,
Shall never the cat nor the kitten by my
counsel be grieved,
Nor chatter of this collar that cost me noth-
ing.
And though it had cost me cash, confess it
I would not,
But suffer him as himself would to do as
doth please him,   205
Coupled and uncoupled to catch all they are
able.
Therefore every wise wight I warn to watch
well his havings." —
  What the mystery means now, ye men
that are merry,
Divine ye, for I dare not, by dear God of
heaven!

SIR JOHN MANDEVILLE? (D. 1371)

THE VOIAGE AND TRAVAILE OF SIR JOHN MAUNDEVILE, KT.

FROM CHAP. IV

And from Ephesim Men gon [25] throghe many
Iles in the See, unto the Cytee of Paterane,
where Seynt Nicholas was born, and so to
Martha, where he was chosen to ben [26] Bis-
schoppe; and there growethe right gode Wyn
and strong; and that Men callen Wyn of
Martha. And from thens [27] gon Men to the
Ile of Crete, that the Emperour yaf [28] som-

And from Ephesus men go through many
isles in the sea unto the city of Pateran, where
St. Nicholas was born, and so to Martha,
where he was chosen to be bishop; and there
groweth right good wine and strong; and
men call it Wine of Martha. And from
thence go men to the isle of Crete, which the
Emperor gave formerly to the Genoese. And

[1] man, person [2] rabbits [3] flesh [4] feeds [5] game
[6] confusion [7] get rid of [8] tyrant [9] crowd [10] were
it not for [11] could [12] rule [13] much [14] talking [15] cost

[16] property [17] confess [18] would not [19] may [20] each
[21] keep [22] dream [23] means [24] dare not [25] go [26] be
[27] thence [28] gave

tyme[1] to Janeweys.[2] And thanne passen Men thorghe the Isles of Colos and of Lango; of the whiche Iles Ypocras was Lord offe. And some Men seyn,[3] that in the Ile of Lango is yit[4] the Doughtre of Ypocras, in forme and lykeness of a gret Dragoun, that is a hundred Fadme[5] of lengthe, as Men seyn: For I have not seen hire. And thei of the Isles callen hire, Lady of the Lond.[6] And sche lyethe in an olde castelle, in a Cave, and schewethe[7] twyes or thryes in the Yeer. And sche dothe none harm to no Man, but-yif[8] Men don hire harm. And sche was thus chaunged and transformed, from a fair Damysele, in-to lyknesse of a Dragoun, be[9] a Goddesse, that was clept[10] Deane.[11] And Men seyn, that sche schalle so endure in that forme of a Dragoun, unto the tyme that a Knyghte come, that is so hardy, that dar come to hire and kiss hire on the Mouthe: And then schalle sche turne ayen[12] to hire owne Kynde,[13] and ben a Woman ayen: But aftre that sche schalle not liven longe. And it is not long siththen,[14] that a Knyghte of the Rodes, that was hardy and doughty in Armes, seyde that he wolde kyssen hire. And whan he was upon his Coursere, and wente to the Castelle, and entred into the Cave, the Dragoun lifte up hire Hed ayenst[15] him. And whan the Knyghte saw hire in that Forme so hidous and so horrible, he fleyghe[16] awey. And the Dragoun bare[17] the Knyghte upon a Roche,[18] mawgre his Hede;[19] and from that Roche, sche caste him in-to the See: and so was lost bothe Hors and Man. And also a yonge[20] Man, that wiste[21] not of the Dragoun, wente out of a Schipp, and wente thorghe the Ile, til that he come to the Castelle, and cam in to the Cave; and wente so longe, til that he fond a Chambre, and there he saughe[22] a Damysele, that kembed[23] hire Hede, and lokede in a Myrour; and sche hadde meche[24] Tresoure abouten hire: and he trowed,[25] that sche hadde ben a comoun Woman, that dwelled there to receyve Men to Folye. And he abode, tille the Damysele saughe the Schadewe of him in the Myrour. And sche turned hire toward him, and asked hym, what he wolde. And he seyde, he wolde ben hire Limman[26] or Paramour. And sche asked him, yif[27] that he were a Knyghte. And he

then men pass through the isles of Colos and Lango; of the which isles Hippocrates was lord. And some men say that in the isle of Lango is yet the daughter of Hippocrates, in form and likeness of a great dragon that is a hundred fathoms in length, as men say; for I have not seen her. And they of the isles call her Lady of the Land. And she lieth in an old castle, in a cave, and appeareth twice or thrice in the year. And she doeth no harm to any man, unless men do harm to her. And she was thus changed and transformed from a fair damsel into likeness of a dragon by a goddess that was called Diana. And men say that she shall so continue in that form of a dragon until the time that a knight shall come who is so hardy that he dares come to her and kiss her on the mouth: and then shall she return to her own nature and be a woman again: but after that she shall not live long. And it is not long since that a knight of the Rhodes that was hardy and doughty in arms said that he would kiss her. And when he was upon his courser, and went to the castle, and entered into the cave, the dragon lifted up her head against him. And when the knight saw her in that form, so hideous and so horrible, he fled away. And the dragon bore the knight upon a rock despite his efforts; and from the rock she cast him into the sea: and so was lost both horse and man. And also a young man, that did not know about the dragon, went out of a ship, and went through the isle till he came to the castle, and came into the cave; and went on till he found a chamber, and there he saw a damsel that was combing her hair and looking in a mirror; and she had much treasure about her: and he supposed that she was a common woman, who dwelt there to receive men to folly. And he waited till the damsel saw his shadow in the mirror. And she turned herself toward him, and asked him what he wished. And he said he would be her lover or paramour. And she asked him if he were a knight. And he said, "Nay." And then she said that he could not be her lover: but she bade him go back to his fellows and make himself a knight, and come again upon the morrow, and she would come out of the cave before him; and then he should come and kiss her on the

---

[1] formerly, once upon a time [2] the Genoese [3] say [4] yet [5] fathom [6] land [7] appears [8] unless [9] by [10] called [11] Diana [12] again, back [13] nature [14] since

[15] against [16] fled [17] bore [18] rock [19] despite his head (= despite all he could do) [20] young [21] knew [22] saw [23] combed [24] much [25] believed, thought [26] lover [27] if

seyde, nay. And than sche seyde, that he myghte not ben hire Lemman:[1] But sche bad him gon ayen[2] unto his Felowes, and make him Knyghte, and come ayen upon the Morwe, and sche scholde come out of the Cave before him; and thanne come and kysse hire on the mowthe, and have no Drede; "for I schalle do the no maner harm, alle be it that thou see me in Lyknesse of a Dragoun. For thoughe thou see me hidouse and horrible to loken onne, I do[3] the to wytene,[4] that it is made be Enchauntement. For withouten doute, I am non other than thou seest now, a Woman; and therfore drede the noughte. And yif thou kysse me, thou schalt haye alle this Tresoure, and be my Lord, and Lord also of alle that Ile." And he departed fro hire and wente to his Felowes to Schippe, and leet[5] make him Knyghte, and cam ayen upon the Morwe, for to kysse this Damysele. And whan he saughe hire comen[6] out of the Cave, in forme of a Dragoun, so hidouse and so horrible, he hadde so grete drede, that he fleyghe[7] ayen to the Schippe; and sche folewed him. And whan sche saughe, that he turned not ayen, sche began to crye, as a thing that hadde meche[8] Sorwe: and thanne sche turned ayen, in-to hire Cave; and anon the Knighte dyede. And siththen[9] hidrewards,[10] myghte no Knighte se hire, but that he dyede anon. But whan a Knyghte comethe, that is so hardy to kisse hire, he schalle not dye; but he schalle turne the Damysele in-to hire righte Forme and kyndely[11] Schapp, and he schal be Lord of alle the Contreyes and Iles aboveseyd.

mouth, and have no dread; "for I shall do thee no manner of harm, albeit that thou see me in likeness of a dragon. For though thou see me hideous and horrible to look upon, I give thee to know that it is caused by enchantment. For without doubt I am none other than thou seest now, a woman; and therefore dread thee naught. And if thou kiss me, thou shalt have all this treasure, and be my lord and lord also of all the isle." And he departed from her and went to his fellows on the ship, and had himself made a knight, and came back upon the morrow to kiss the damsel. And when he saw her come out of the cave, in the form of a dragon, so hideous and so horrible, he had so great dread that he fled back to the ship; and she followed him. And when she saw that he turned not back, she began to cry, as a thing that had great sorrow: and then she turned back into her cave; and at once the knight died. And from then until now no knight has been able to see her but that he died very soon. But when a knight comes that is so bold as to kiss her, he shall not die; but he shall turn the damsel into her right form and natural shape, and he shall be lord of all the countries and isles abovesaid.

From CHAP. XXVII

In the Lond of Prestre John ben many dyverse thinges and many precious Stones, so grete and so large that men maken of hem[12] Vesselle;[13] as Plateres, Dissches, and Cuppes. And many other marveylles ben there; that it were to[14] combrous and to[14] long to putten it in scripture[15] of Bokes.

But of the princypalle Yles and of his Estate and of his Lawe I schalle telle you som partye.[16] This Emperour Prestre John is Cristene; and a gret partie of his Contree also: but yit thei have not alle the Articles of oure Feythe,[17] as wee have. Thei beleven wel in the Fadre, in the Sone, and in the Holy Gost:

In the land of Prester John are many diverse things, and many precious stones so great and so large that men make of them vessels; as platters, dishes and cups. And many other marvels are there; that it were too cumbrous and too long to put it in the writing of books.

But of the principal isles and of his estate and of his law I shall tell you some part. This emperor Prester John is Christian; and a great part of his country also: but yet they have not all the articles of our faith, as we have. They believe well in the Father, in the Son, and in the Holy Ghost: and they are very

[1] lover [2] back [3] cause [4] know [5] let [6] come
[7] fled [8] much [9] since [10] till now [11] natural [12] them

[13] vessels [14] too [15] writing [16] part [17] religion

and thei ben fulle devoute and righte trewe on[1] to another. And thei sette not be[2] no Barettes,[3] ne be Cawteles,[4] ne of no Disceytes.[5] And he hathe undre him 72 Provynces; and in every Provynce is a Kyng. And theise Kynges han[6] Kynges undre hem; and alle ben tributaries to Prestre John. And he hathe in his Lordschipes many grete marveyles. For in his Contree is the See that men clepen[7] the Gravely[8] See, that is alle Gravelle and Sond[9] with-outen ony drope of Watre; and it ebbethe and flowethe in grete Wawes,[10] as other Sees don; and it is never stille ne in pes[11] in no manner[12] cesoun.[13] And no man may passe that See be Navye[14] ne be no maner of craft:[15] and therfore may no man knowe what Lond is beyond that See. And alle-be-it that it have no Watre, yit men fynden[16] there-in and on the Bankes fulle gode Fissche of other maner of kynde and schappe thanne men fynden in ony other See; and thei ben of right goode tast and delycious to mannes mete.

And a 3 journeys long fro that See, ben gret Mountaynes; out of the whiche gothe[17] out a gret Flood,[18] that comethe out of Paradys; and it is fulle of precious Stones, withouten ony drope of Water; and it rennethe[19] thorghe the Desert, on that[20] o[1] syde, so that it makethe the See gravely; and it berethe[17] in-to that See, and there it endethe. And that Flome[18] rénnethe also 3 dayes in the Woke,[21] and bryngethe with him grete Stones and the Roches[22] also therewith, and that gret plentee. And anon as thei ben entred in-to the gravely See, thei ben seyn[23] no more, but lost for evere more. And in tho 3 dayes that that Ryvere rennethe no man dar[24] entren in-to it: but in the other dayes men dar entren wel ynow.[25] Also beyonde that Flome,[18] more upwærd to the Desertes, is a gret Pleyn alle gravelly betwene the Mountaynes; and in that Playn every day at the Sónne risynge begynnen to growe smale Trees; and thei growen til mydday, berynge Frute; but no man dar taken of that Frute, for it is a thing of Fayrye.[26] And aftre mydday thei discrecen[27] and entren ayen[28] in-to the Erthe; so that at the goynge doun of the Sonne thei apperen no more; and so thei don every day: and that is a gret marvaylle.

devout and very true one to another. And they do not practice any tricks, or frauds, or deceits. And he hath under him seventy-two provinces; and in every province is a king. And these kings have kings under them; and all are tributaries to Prester John. And he hath in his lordships many great marvels. For in his country is the sea that men call the Gravelly Sea, that is all gravel and sand, without any drop of water; and it ebbeth and floweth in great waves, as other seas do; and it is never still nor in peace in any season. And no man may pass that sea by ship or by any kind of craft: and therefore may no man know what land is beyond that sea. And albeit that it have no water, yet men find therein and on the banks very good fish of different kinds and shapes from those that men find in any other sea; and they are all very good to eat and delicious for man's food.

And three days' distance from that sea are great mountains; out of which flows a great river, that comes from Paradise; and it is full of precious stones, without any drop of water; and it runs through the desert, on the one side, so that it makes the sea gravelly; and it flows into the sea and ends there. And this river runs three days in the week, and brings with it great stones and rocks also, and that in great abundance. And as soon as they have entered into the Gravelly Sea, they are seen no more but are lost forever. And during the three days that the river runs, no man dares enter into it: but during the other days one may enter well enough. Also beyond that river, further upward towards the deserts, is a great plain of gravel between the mountains; and in that plain, every day at the rising of the sun, there begin to grow small trees; and they grow till midday, bearing fruit; but no man dares take any of that fruit, for it is a thing of faërie. And after midday they decrease and enter again into the earth; so that at the setting of the sun they appear no more; and so they do every day: and that is a great marvel.

---

[1] one [2] set not by (= do not practice) [3] frauds [4] tricks [5] deceits [6] have [7] call [8] gravelly [9] sand [10] waves [11] peace [12] kind of [13] season [14] ship [15] device [16] find [17] goes, flows [18] river [19] runs [20] the [21] week [22] rocks [23] seen [24] dare [25] enough [26] magic [27] decrease [28] again

JOHN WICLIF (D. 1384)

THE GOSPEL OF MATHEW
(FIRST VERSION)
CHAP. V

Jhesus forsothe,[1] seynge [2] cumpanyes, wente up in-to an hill; and when he hadde sete,[3] his disciplis camen nighe to hym. And he, openynge his mouthe, taughte to hem, sayinge, "Blessid be the pore in spirit, for the kingdam in hevenes is heren.[4] Blessid be mylde men, for thei shuln [5] welde [6] the eerthe. Blessid be thei that mournen, for thei shuln [5] be comfortid. Blessid be thei that hungren and thristen rightwisnesse,[7] for thei shuln ben fulfillid. Blessid be mercyful men, for thei shuln gete mercye. Blessid be thei that ben [8] of clene herte, for thei shuln see God. Blessid be pesible men, for thei shuln be clepid [9] the sonys of God. Blessid be thei that suffren persecucioun for rightwisnesse,[7] for the kyngdam of hevenes is herun.[4] Yee shulen [5] be blessid, when men shulen curse you, and shulen pursue you, and shulen say al yvel [10] ayeins [11] you leezing,[12] for me. Joye [13] yee with-yn-forth,[14] and glade yee with-out-forth, for youre meede [15] is plentevouse [16] in hevenes; forsothe so thei han [17] pursued and [18] prophetis that weren before you. Yee ben [8] salt of the erthe; that yif [19] the salt shal vanyshe awey, wherynne shal it be saltid? To no thing it is worth over,[20] no [21] bot [22] that it be sent out, and defoulid of men. Ye ben [8] light of the world; a citee putt on an hill may nat be hid; nether men tendyn [23] a lanterne, and putten it undir a busshel, but on a candilstike, that it yeve [24] light to alle that ben in the hous. So shyyne [25] youre light before men, that thei see youre good werkis, and glorifie youre Fadir that is in hevens. Nyle [26] ye gesse, or deme,[27] that Y came to undo, or distruye, the lawe, or the prophetis; I came not to undo the lawe, but to fulfille. Forsothe [28] I say to you trewthe, til heven and erthe passe, oon [29] i, that is leste [30] lettre, or titil, shal nat passe fro the lawe, til alle thingis be don. Therfore he that undoth, or breketh, oon of these leste [30] maundementis,[31] and techith thus men, shal be clepid [32] the leste in the rewme [33] of hevenes;

THE GOSPEL OF MATHEU
(SECOND VERSION)
CAP. V

And Jhesus, seynge [2] the puple, wente up in-to an hil; and whanne he was set, hise disciplis camen to hym. And he openyde his mouth, and taughte hem, and seide, "Blessed ben pore men in spirit, for the kyngdom of hevenes is herne.[4] Blessid ben mylde men, for thei schulen [5] welde [6] the erthe. Blessid ben thei that mornen, for thei schulen be coumfortid. Blessid ben thei that hungren and thristen rightwisnesse, for thei schulen be fulfillid. Blessid ben merciful men, for thei schulen gete merci. Blessid ben thei that ben of clene herte, for thei schulen se God. Blessid ben pesible men, for thei schulen be clepid [9] Goddis children. Blessid ben thei that suffren persecusioun for rightfulnesse, for the kingdam of hevenes is herne.[4] Ye schulen be blessid, whanne men schulen curse you, and schulen pursue you, and schulen seie al yvel [10] ayens [11] you liynge, for me. Joie [13] ye, and be ye glad, for youre meede [15] is plentevouse [16] in hevenes; for so thei han [17] pursued also profetis that weren bifor you. Ye ben salt of the erthe; that if the salt vanysche awey, whereynne schal it be saltid? To no thing it is worth overe,[20] no [21] but [22] that it be cast out, and be defoulid of men. Ye ben light of the world; a citee set on an hil may not be hid; ne me teendith [23] not a lanterne, and puttith it undur a busschel, but on a candilstike, that it yyve light to alle that ben in the hous. So schyne youre light befor men, that thei se youre goode werkis, and glorifie youre Fadir that is in hevenes. Nil [26] ye deme,[27] that Y cam to undo the lawe, or the profetis; Y cam not to undo the lawe, but to fulfille. Forsothe Y seie to you, til hevene and erthe passe, o [29] lettir or o [29] titel schal not passe fro the lawe, til alle thingis be doon. Therfor he that brekith oon of these leeste [30] maundementis,[31] and techith thus men, schal be clepid [32] the leste in the rewme [33] of hevenes; but he that doith, and techith, schal be clepid greet in the kyngdom of hevenes. And Y seie

---

[1] indeed [2] seeing [3] sat [4] theirs [5] shall [6] rule [7] righteousness [8] are [9] called [10] evil [11] against [12] lying [13] rejoice [14] with-yn-forth = inwardly [15] reward [16] plenteous [17] have [18] also [19] if [20] besides

[21] not [22] but [23] light [24] give [25] *Subj. of command* [26] do not, *literally*, wish not (Lat. *nolite*) [27] think [28] verily [29] one [30] least [31] commandments [32] called [33] kingdom

forsothe, this [1] that doth, and techith, shal be clepid grete in the kyngdame of hevenes. Forsothe Y say to you, no-but-yif [2] youre rightwisnesse shal be more plentevouse than of scribis and Pharisees, yee shulen not entre in-to kyngdam of hevenes. Yee han [3] herde that it is said to olde men, Thou shal nat slea; forsothe he that sleeth, shal be gylty of dome.[4] But I say to you, that evereche [5] that is wrothe to his brother, shal be gylty of dome; forsothe he that shal say to his brother, Racha, that is, a word of scorn, shal be gylty of counseile; [6] sothly he that shal say, Fool, that is, a word of dispisynge, shal be gylti of the fijr [7] of helle. Therfore yif thou offrist thi yift [8] at the auter,[9] and there shalt by-thenke,[10] that thi brother hath sum-what ayeins thee, leeve there thi yift before the auter, and go first for to be recounseilid, or acordid, to thi brother, and thanne thou cum-mynge shalt offre thi yifte. Be thou consent-ynge to thin adversarie soon, the whijle thou art in the way with hym, lest peraventure thin adversarie take [11] thee to the domesman,[12] and the domesman take thee to the mynystre,[13] and thou be sente in-to prisoun. Trewely I say to thee, Thou shalt not go thennes, til thou yelde [14] the last ferthing. Ye han herd, that it was said to olde men, Thou shalt nat do lecherye. Forsothe Y say to you, for-why [15] every man that seeth a womman for to coveite hire, now he hath do lecherie by hire in his herte. That yif thi right eiye sclaundre[16] thee, pulle it out, and cast it fro thee; for it spedith [17] to thee, that oon [18] of thi membris perishe, than al thi body go in-to helle. And yif thi right hond sclaundre thee, kitt [19] it awey, and cast it fro thee; for it spedith to thee, that oon of thi membris perishe, than that al thi body go in-to helle. Forsothe it is said, Who-evere shal leeve his wyf, yeve [20] he to hir a libel, that is, a litil boke, of for-sakyng. Sothely Y say to you, that every man that shal leeve his wyf, outaken [21] cause of fornicacioun, he makith hire do lecherie and he that weddith the forsaken wijf, doth avoutrie.[22] Efte-soonys [23] yee han herd, that it was said to olde men, Thou shalt not for-swere, sothely [24] to the Lord thou shalt yeeld [14] thin oethis.[25] Forsothe Y say to you, to nat

to you, that but your rightfulnesse be more plentevouse than of scribis and of Farisees, ye schulen not entre into the kyngdom of hevenes. Ye han [3] herd that it was seid to elde men, Thou schalt not slee; and he that sleeth, schal be gilti to doom.[4] But Y seie to you, that ech man that is wrooth to his brothir, schal be gilti to doom; and he that seith to his brother, Fy! schal be gilti to the counseil; [6] but he that seith, Fool, schal be gilti to the fier of helle. Therfor if thou offrist thi yifte [8] at the auter,[9] and ther thou bithenkist, that thi brothir hath sum-what ayens thee, leeve there thi yifte bifor the auter, and go first to be recounselid to thi brothir, and thanne thou schalt come, and schalt offre thi yifte. Be thou consentynge to thin adversarie soone, while thou art in the weie with hym, lest peraventure thin adversarie take [11] thee to the domesman,[12] and the domesman take thee to the mynystre,[13] and thou be sent in-to prisoun. Treuli Y seie to thee, thou schalt not go out fro thennus, til thou yelde [14] the last ferthing. Ye han herd that it was seid to elde men, Thou schalt do no letcherie. But Y seie to you, that every man that seeth a womman for to coveite hir, hath now do letcherie bi hir in his herte. That if thi right iye sclaundre [16] thee, pulle hym out, and caste fro thee; for it spedith [17] to thee, that oon [18] of thi membris perische, than that al thi bodi go in-to helle. And if thi right hond sclaundre thee, kitte [19] hym aweye, and caste fro thee; for it spedith to thee that oon [18] of thi membris perische, than that al thi bodi go in-to helle. And it hath be seyd, Who-evere leeveth his wiif, yyve he to hir a libel of forsakyng. But Y seie to you, that every man that leeveth his wiif, outtakun cause of fornycacioun, makith hir to do letcherie, and he that weddith the for-sakun wiif, doith avowtrye. Eftsoone ye han herd, that it was seid to elde men, Thou schalt not forswere, but thou schalt yelde thin othis to the Lord. But Y seie to you, that ye swere not for ony thing; nethir bi hevene, for it is the trone of God; nether bi the erthe, for it is the stole of his feet; nether bi Jerusalem, for it is the citee of a greet kynge; nether thou schalt not swere bi thin heed, for thou maist not make oon heere white ne blacke;

---

[17] profiteth [18] one [19] cut [20] give (*subj. of command*) [21] except [22] adultery [23] again [24] truly [25] oaths

[1] he [2] unless [3] have [4] judgement [5] every one [6] the council [7] fire [8] gift [9] altar [10] remember [11] deliver [12] judge [13] officer [14] pay [15] that [16] slander

swere on al manere; neither by hevene, for
it is the trone of God; nether by the erthe,
for it is the stole of his feet; neither by Jerusalem, for it is the citee of a greet kyng;
neither thou shalt swere by thin heved,[1] for
thou maist not make oon heer whyt or blak;
but be youre word yea, yea; Nay, nay; forsothe that that is more than this, is of yvel.
Yee han herde that it is said, Eiye [2] for eiye,[2]
toth for toth. But Y say to you, to nat ayein-
stonde [3] yvel; but yif any shal smyte thee
in the right cheeke, yeve to hym and [4] the
tother; and to hym that wole stryve with
thee in dome,[5] and take awey thi coote, leeve
thou to hym and [4] thin over-clothe; and who-
evere constrayneth thee a thousand pacis, go
thou with hym other tweyne. Forsothe yif [6]
to hym that axith of thee, and turne thou
nat awey fro hym that wol borwe [7] of thee.
Yee han herd that it is said, Thou shalt love
thin neighbore, and hate thin enmy. But Y
say to you, love yee youre enmyes, do yee wel
to hem [8] that haten [9] you, and preye yee for
men pursuynge, and falsly chalengynge [10] you;
that yee be the sonys of youre Fadir that is in
hevenes, that makith his sune to springe up
upon good and yvel men, and rayneth upon
juste men and unjuste men. For yif ye loven
hem that loven you, what meed [11] shul [12] yee
have? whether and [4] puplicans don nat this
thing? And yif yee greten, or saluten, youre
bretheren oonly, what more over [13] shul yee
don? whether and [4] paynymmys [14] don nat
this thing? Therfore be yee parfit,[15] as and [4]
youre hevenly Fadir is parfit. Take yee hede,
lest ye don your rightwisnesse before men,
that yee be seen of hem, ellis [16] ye shule nat han
meed at youre Fadir that is in hevenes. Therfore when thou dost almesse,[17] nyle [18] thou
synge byfore thee in a trumpe, as ypocritis
don in synagogis and streetis, that thei ben
maad worshipful of men; forsothe Y saye to
you, thei han resceyved her [19] meede. But
thee doynge almesse,[17] knowe nat the left
hond what thi right hond doth, that thi almes
be in hidlis,[20] and thi Fadir that seeth in hidlis,
shal yelde [21] to thee.''

but be youre word, yhe, yhe; Nay, nay; and
that that is more than these, is of yvel. Ye
han herd that it hath be seid, Iye for iye, and
tothe for tothe. But Y seie to you, that ye
ayenstonde [3] not an yvel man; but if ony
smyte thee in the right cheke, schewe to him
also the tothir; and to hym that wole stryve
with thee in doom,[5] and take awey thi coote,
leeve thou to him also thi mantil; and whoever constreyneth thee a thousynde pacis, go
thou with hym othir tweyne. Yyve [6] thou
to hym that axith of thee, and turne not
awey fro hym that wole borewe [7] of thee. Ye
han herd that it was seid, Thou shalt love thi
neighbore, and hate thin enemye. But Y
seie to you, love ye youre enemyes, do ye wel
to hem that hatiden you, and preye ye for
hem [8] that pursuen, and sclaundren you;
that ye be the sones of your Fadir that is in
hevenes, that makith his sunne to rise upon
goode and yvele men, and reyneth on just men
and unjuste. For if ye loven hem [8] that loven
you, what mede [11] schulen ye han? whether
pupplicans doon not this? And if ye greten
youre britheren oonli, what schulen ye do
more? ne doon not hethene men this? Therfore be ye parfit, as youre hevenli Fadir is
parfit.''

*[It will be observed that the Second Version agrees
with the Authorized Version in the division
into chapters, while the First Version contains a few verses usually assigned to Chapter
VI.]*

---

[1] head　[2] eye　[3] resist　[4] also　[5] a lawsuit　[6] give
[7] borrow　[8] them　[9] hate　[10] accusing　[11] reward
[12] shall　[13] besides　[14] heathen　[15] perfect　[16] else
[17] alms　[18] do not　[19] their　[20] secret　[21] pay

SYR GAWAYN AND THE GRENE KNYGHT

(Unknown Author)

FYTTE THE FIRST

XI

Ther wacz[1] lokyng on lenthe,[2] the lude[3] to
  beholde,
For uch[4] mon had mervayle quat[5] hit mene
  myght,
That a hathel[6] and a horse myght such a hwe
  lach.[7]
As growe grene as the gres[8] and grener hit
  semed,
Then[9] grene aumayl[10] on golde lowande[11]
  bryghter.
Al studied that ther stod, and stalked hym
  nerre,[12]
Wyth al the wonder of the worlde, what he
  worch[13] schulde;
For fele sellyez[14] had thay sen, bot such never
  are,[15]
For-thi for fantoum and fayryye[16] the folk
  there hit demed.   240
Ther-fore to answare wacz arghe[17] mony athel
  freke,[18]
And al stouned[19] at his steven,[20] and ston-stil
  seten,
In a swoghe sylence[21] thurgh the sale[22] riche;
As[23] al were slypped upon slepe, so slaked
  hor lotez[24]
      In hyye;[25]
   I deme hit not al for doute,[26]
   Bot sum for cortaysye,
   Let hym that al schulde loute[27]
   Cast[28] unto that wyye.[3]

XI

Long was there looking, that lord to behold,
For each man had marvel what might be the
  meaning
That a horseman and a horse might such a hue
  catch.
As grow-green as the grass and greener yet
  seemed they,
Than green enamel on gold glowing brighter.
All studied that stood there, and stalked to
  him nearer,
With all the wonder in the world what wiles
  he was planning;
For many sights had they seen, but such a
  sight never;
So for phantom and faërie the folk there did
  deem it.
Therefore to answer was fearful many a fine
  fellow,   240
And all were stunned by his speech and stone-
  still sat they,
In a sheer silence through the hall splendid;
As if they had slipped into sleep, so slacked
  they their talking,
      That day;
   Not all for fear, I trow,
   But some in courteous way,
   Let him to whom all bow
   The stranger first assay.

XII

Thenn Arthour bifore the high dece[29] that
  aventure[30] byholdez,[31]   250
And rekenly hym reverenced,[32] for rad[33] was
  he never,
And sayde, "Wyye, welcum iwys[34] to this
  place;
The hede of this ostel[35] Arthour I hat.[36]

XII

Then Arthur before the high dais that incident beholdeth,
And courteously accosted him, for cowed was
  he never,
And said, "Warrior, welcome i-wis to this
  place;
The head of this hostel Arthur I hight.   253

[1] was [2] for a long time [3] man [4] each [5] what
[6] knight [7] catch such a colour [8] grass [9] than
[10] enamel [11] gleaming [12] nearer [13] do [14] many
strange things [15] before [16] therefore as illusion
and magic [17] timid [18] many a noble knight [19] were
amazed [20] voice [21] in a swoon-like silence [22] hall
[23] as if [24] so slackened their noises [25] suddenly
[26] fear [27] but let him to whom all should bow
(= Arthur) [28] speak [29] dais [30] happening [31] observes [32] courteously greeted him [33] afraid [34] indeed [35] house [36] I am called

AE

Light luflych [1] adoun, and lenge,[2] I the
    praye,
And quat-so thy wylle is, we schal wyt [3]
    after.''
''Nay, as help me,'' quoth the hathel, ''He
    that on hyghe syttes,
To wone [4] any quyle [5] in this won,[6] hit wacz
    not myn ernde; [7]
Bot for [8] the los [9] of the lede [10] is lyft up so
    hyghe,
And thy burgh and thy burnes [11] best ar
    holden,
Stifest under stel-gere [12] on stedes to ryde, 260
The wyghtest [13] and the worthyest of the
    worldes kynde,
Preve [14] for to play wyth in other pure laykez ;[15]
And here is kydde [16] cortaysye, as I haf herd
    carp [17] —
And that hacz wayned [18] me hider, iwyis, at
    this tyme.
Ye may be seker [19] bi this braunch that I bere
    here
That I passe as in pes, and no plyght seche.[20]
For, had I founded [21] in fere, in feghtyng wyse,
I have a hauberghe [22] at home and a helme [23]
    bothe,
A schelde, and a scharp spere, schinande
    bryght,
Ande other weppenes to welde,[24] I wene wel
    als.[25]
Bot for [8] I wolde no were,[26] my wedez [27] ar
    softer.
Bot if thou be so bold as alle burnez [11] tellen,
Thou wyl grant me godly [28] the gomen [29] that
    I ask,   273
            Bi ryght.''
        Arthour con onsware [30]
        And sayd, ''Syr cortays knyght,
        If thou crave batayl bare,
        Here faylez thou not to fyght.''

Alight lovesomely down and linger here, so
    please thee,
And whatso thy will is we shall wit later.''
''Nay, so help me,'' quoth the horseman, ''He
    that on high sits,
To dwell any while in this dwelling is not my
    due errand ;
But that the praise of thy people is published
    so widely,
And thy castle and thy comrades choicest
    are counted,
Stiffest under steel-gear on steeds to en-
    counter,   260
The wightest and the worthiest of this world's
    kindred,
Proven to play with in other pleasant contests ;
And here is kept courtesy, as I have heard
    recounted —
'Tis this has drawn me hither, indeed, at this
    season.
You may be certain by this bough that I bear
    with me
That I pass as in peace, and press for no
    quarrel.
For had I faced you in fear or in fighting hu-
    mour,
I have a hauberk at home and a helmet also,
A shield and a sharp spear, shining brightly,
And other weapons to wield, I ween
    well like-wise.
But as I coveted no combat, my clothing is
    softer.
But if thou be as bold as all barons call thee,
Thou wilt grant me graciously the game I shall
    ask thee,   273
            By right.''
        Arthur gave answer there
        And said, ''Sir courteous knight,
        If thou crave battle bare,
        Here fail'st thou not to fight.''

XIII

''Nay, frayst [31] I no fyght, in fayth I the telle ;
Hit arn [32] aboute on this bench bot berdlez
    chylder.
If I were hasped [33] in armes on a heghe [34]
    stede,
Here is no mon me to mach,[35] for myghtez so
    wayke.[36]

XIII

''Nay, to fight am I not fain, in faith as I
    tell thee ;
There are about on this bench but beardless
    children.
If I were clasped in armour on a high charger,
Here is no man to match me, for in might are
    they weaklings.

[1] alight graciously [2] remain [3] know [4] dwell
[5] while [6] place [7] errand [8] because [9] fame [10] people
[11] knights [12] steel-gear, armour [13] stoutest [14] proven
[15] fine sports [16] shown [17] declare [18] has drawn

[19] sure [20] seek no danger [21] come [22] hauberk
[23] helmet [24] wield [25] also [26] war [27] garments
[28] graciously [29] game [30] answered [31] ask [32] there
are [33] clasped [34] high, tall [35] match [36] weak

For-thy[1] I crave in this court a Crystemas gomen,[2]
For hit is Yol and Nwe Yer, and here are yep[3] mony;   284
If any so hardy in this hous holdez hym-selven,
Be so bolde in his blod, brayn[4] in hys hede,
That dar stifly strike a strok for an other,
I schal gif hym of my gyft thys giserne[5] ryche, —
This ax, that is hevé innogh, — to hondele[6] as hym lykes,   289
And I schal bide[7] the fyrst bur,[8] as bare as I sitte.
If any freke[9] be so felle[10] to fonde[11] that[12] I telle,
Lepe[13] lyghtly me to, and lach[14] this weppen—
I quit-clayme hit for ever, kepe hit as his auen[15] —
And I schal stonde hym a strok, stif on this flet,[16]
Ellez thou wyl dight me the dom[17] to dele hym an other;
     Barlay;[18]
  And yet gif hym respite
  A twelmonyth and a day;
  Now hyghe,[19] and let se tite[20]
  Dar any her-inne oght say."   300

Therefore I crave in this court a Christmas gambol,
For it is Yule and New Year, and here are many young braggarts;
If any in this house holds him so hardy,
If he be so bold in his blood, hot-brained of temper
That he dare stiffly strike one stroke for another,
I shall give him of my gift this gisarme splendid —
This axe, that is heavy enough — to handle as he pleases;
And I shall bide the first blow, as bare as I sit here.
If any man be so mad as to make such a trial
Let him leap to me lightly and lay hold of this weapon —   292
I quit-claim it for ever, keep it as his own —
And I shall stand him a stroke, stiff on this floor,
If thou wilt but grant me the grace to give him another,
     In fay;
  Yet respite shall there be
  A twelvemonth and a day;
  Now hasten and let us see
  If any here dare aught say."   300

XIV

If he hem stowned[21] upon fyrst,[22] stiller were thanne
Alle the hered-men[23] in halle, the hygh and the lowe.
The renk[9] on his rounce[24] hym ruched[25] in his sadel
And runischly[26] his rede yyen[27] he reled aboute;
Bende his bresed[28] browez, blycande[29] grene:
Wayved his berde for to wayte[30] quo-so[31] wolde ryse.
When non wolde kepe hym with carp,[32] he coghed ful hyghe[33]
Ande rimed hym ful richley[34] and ryght hym[35] to speke:
"What, is this Arthures hous," quoth the hathel[36] thenne,
"That al the rous rennes of[37] thurgh ryalmes so mony?   310

XIV

If they were astounded at first, now were they stiller,
All the henchmen in hall, the high and the lowly.
The stranger on his steed then settled him in his saddle
And ragingly his red eyes he rolled upon them;
Bent his bushy brows, green and bristling;
Waved his beard as he watched whether any would offer.
When none would come at his challenge, he coughed full loudly
And stretched himself starkly and stayed not in speaking:
"What? is this Arthur's house," quoth then the horseman,
"Whereof all the renown runs through realms unnumbered?   310

[1] therefore [2] game, amusement [3] bold, ready [4] mad [5] pole-axe [6] handle [7] abide, endure [8] blow [9] man [10] fierce [11] try [12] what [13] let him leap [14] seize [15] own [16] floor [17] provided thou wilt give me the right [18] I claim this [19] hasten [20] quickly [21] amazed [22] at first [23] retainers [24] horse [25] settled [26] furiously [27] eyes [28] bristly [29] glittering [30] observe [31] who-so [32] when none would reply [33] coughed aloud [34] and made full preparation [35] got ready [36] knight [37] of which all the fame goes

Where is now your sourquydrye [1] and your conquestes,
Your gryndel-layk,[2] and your greme,[3] and your grete wordes?
Now is the revel and the renoun of the Rounde Table
Over-walt [4] wyth a worde of on wyyes [5] speche;
For al dares [6] for drede, withoute dynt [7] schewed!"
Wyth this he laghes [8] so loude, that the lorde greved;
The blod schot for scham in-to his schyre [9] face

    And lere.[10]
He wex as wroth as wynde;
So did alle that ther were.   320
The kyng, as kene bi kynde,[11]
Then stod that stif mon nere [12]

Where is now your arrogance and all your conquests,
Your fierceness and your fellness and your fine boasting?
Now is the revel and the renown of the Round Table
Overthrown by a word of one man's speech;
For all quail for cowardice, tho' no combat threatens!"
With this he laughed so loud that the lord was grieved;
The blood shot for shame into his fair cheek And face.

    As wrathful then as wind
Grew all men in that place.   320
The king, as bold by kind,
Neared that stout man apace

XV

Ande sayde, "Hathel, by heven thyn askyng is nys,[13]
And as thou foly hacz frayst,[14] fynde the behoves.[15]
I know no gome [16] that is gast [17] of thy grete wordes.
Gif me now thy geserne,[18] upon Godez halve,[19]
And I schal baythen thy bone,[20] that thou boden [14] habbes."
Lyghtly depez he hym to, and laght [21] at his honde;
Then feersly that other freke [16] upon fote lyghtis.
Now hacz Arthure his axe, and the halme [22] grypez,
And sturnely sturez [23] hit aboute, that stryke wyth hit thoght.   331
The stif mon hym bifore stod upon hyght [24] —
Herre [25] then ani in the hous by the hede and more;
Wyth sturne chere [26] ther he stod, he stroked his berde,
And wyth a countenaunce dryye [27] he drow doun his cote,
No more mate [28] ne dismayd for hys mayn dintez [29]

XV

And said, "Horseman, by heaven thy asking is foolish,
And as thou folly hast craved, it behooves that thou find it.
I know no man that is aghast at thy great boasting.
Give me now thy gisarme, in God's name be it,
And I will bestow the boon that thou hast bidden."
Lightly he leaps to him and lays hand on the weapon;
Then fiercely the other man on foot alights there.
Now has Arthur his axe, and by the handle holds it,
And sternly stirs it about, to strike with it thinks he.   331
The stalwart man before him stood at his full height —
Higher than any in the house by a head and more;
With stern look there he stood, stroking his beard,
And with countenance calm he drew down his collar,   335
No more moved nor dismayed for the king's mighty blows

---

[1] haughtiness [2] fierceness [3] grimness [4] overturned [5] one man's [6] all are frightened [7] stroke [8] laughs [9] bright [10] cheek [11] as one bold by nature [12] nearer [13] foolish [14] asked [15] it behooves thee to find

[16] man [17] frightened [18] axe [19] in God's name [20] grant thy boon [21] grasped [22] shaft [23] fiercely moves [24] stood tall [25] taller [26] fierce look [27] dry, without emotion [28] dispirited [29] strong blows

Then any burne [1] upon bench hade broght
    hym to drynk
        Of wyne.
    Gawan, that sate bi the quene,
    To the kyng he can [2] enclyne,   340
    "I be-seche now with sawez sene,[3]
    This melly mot [4] be myne.

XVI

"Wolde ye, worthilych [5] lorde," quoth Gawan
    to the kyng,
"Bid me bowe [6] fro this benche, and stonde by
    yow there,
That I wyth-oute vylanye myght voyde [7] this
    table,
And that my legge [8] lady lyked not ille,
I wolde com to your counseyl, bifore your cort
    ryche; [9]
For me think hit not semly,[10] as hit is soth
    knawen,[11]
Ther [12] such an askyng is hevened [13] so hyghe
    in your sale,[14]
Thagh ye your-self be talenttyf [15] to take hit
    to your-selven,   350
Whil mony so bolde yow aboute upon bench
    sytten,
That under heven, I hope,[16] non hagher [17] er [18]
    of wylle,
Ne better bodyes on bent,[19] ther [12] baret [20] is
    rered.
I am the wakkest,[21] I wot, and of wyt feblest,
And lest lur [22] of my lyf, quo laytes the sothe; [23]
Bot for as much as ye ar myn em,[24] I am
    only to prayse —
No bounté [25] bot your blod I in my bodé
    knowe —
And sythen this note [26] is so nys [27] that noght
    hit yow falles,[28]
And I have frayned [29] hit at yow fyrst, foldez [30]
    hit to me !
And if I carp [31] not comlyly, let alle this cort
    rych [32]
        Bout [33] blame."   361
    Ryche [34] to-geder con roun,[35]
    And sythen thay redden alle same,[36]
    To ryd the kyng wyth croun,[37]
    And gif Gawan the game.

Than if any baron on the bench had brought
    him to drink
        Of wine.
    Gawain, who sat by the queen,
    To the king he did encline,   340
    "Let bounty now be seen,
    And let this game be mine !

XVI

"Would you, most gracious lord," quoth
    Gawain to the king,
"But bid me leave this bench and bide by
    you there,
So that I without rudeness might rise from
    this table,
And that to my liege lady there were lacking
    no courtesy,
I would come to your counsel, before your
    court splendid;
For methinks it is unseemly, as sage men
    weigh things,
When such an asking is honoured so high in
    your hall —
Though you yourself be eager for all under-
    takings —   350
While about you on bench sit so many bold ones,
Than whom under heaven, I think none hard-
    ier are of temper,
Nor better bodies in battle when banners are
    lifted.
I am the weakest, I wot, and of wit feeblest,
And least the loss of my life, if no lie shall be
    spoken;
But forasmuch as you are my uncle I am only
    of merit —
No desert but your blood I in my body
    reckon —
And since this affair is so foolish that you it
    befits not,
And I have sued for it first, let my suit be
    granted !
And if my conduct is not comely, let all this
    court judge me
        To blame."   361
    Nobles 'gan whispering;
    Their verdict was the same,
    To exempt the crownëd king
    And give Gawain the game.

[1] than if any man [2] did [3] courteous words
[4] this encounter may [5] worthy [6] move [7] leave
[8] liege [9] rich (splendid) court [10] fitting [11] is known
for truth [12] where [13] raised [14] hall [15] desirous [16] think
[17] apter, fitter [18] are [19] in field [20] strife [21] weakest
[22] least loss [23] if any one seeks the truth [24] uncle
[25] goodness [26] affair [27] foolish [28] becomes [29] re-
quested [30] grant [31] if I speak [32] judge [33] without
[34] the great ones [35] did whisper [36] and afterwards
they decided unanimously [37] to set aside the
crowned king

XVII

Then comaunded the kyng the knyght for to
 ryse ;
And he ful radly [1] up ros, and ruchched hym
 fayre,[2]
Kneled doun bifore the kyng, and cachez [3]
 that weppen ;
And he luflyly hit hym laft,[4] and lyfte up his
 honde,
And gef hym Goddez blessyng, and gladly
 hym biddes   370
That his hert and his honde schulde hardi be
 bothe.
"Kepe the, cosyn," quoth the kyng, "that
 thou on kyrf sette,[5]
And if thou redez [6] hym ryght, redly I trowe
That thou schal byden the bur [7] that he schal
 bede [8] after."
Gawan gocz [9] to the gome,[10] with giserne [11] in
 honde,
And he baldly hym bydez,[12] he bayst never the
 helder.[13]
Then carppez to Syr Gawan the knyght in the
 grene :
"Refourme we oure forwardes,[14] er we fyrre [15]
 passe.
Fyrst I ethe [16] the, hathel, how that thou
 hattes,[17]
That thou me telle truly, as I tryst [18] may."
"In god fayth," quoth the goode knyght,
 "Gawan I hatte,[19]   381
That bede [8] the this buffet, quat-so bi-fallez
 after,
And at this tyme twelmonyth take at the [20]
 another,
Wyth what weppen so thou wylt, and wyth
 no wy elléz [21]
   On lyve." [22]
  That other onswarez [23] agayn,
  " Sir Gawan, so mot [24] I thryve,
  As I am ferly fayn,[25]
  This dint that thou schal dryve.[26]

XVIII

"Bi Gog," quoth the grene knyght, "Syr
 Gawan, me lykes,[27]   390
That I schal fange at thy fust [28] that [29] I haf
 frayst [30] here ;

XVII

Then kindly the king commanded him to
 rise ;
And he came forward quickly and curtsied
 duly,
Kneels down before the king and catches the
 weapon ;
And he releases it lovingly and lifts up his
 hand
And gives him God's blessing and gladly bids
 him   370
That his heart and his hand should both be
 hardy.
"Take care, cousin," said the king, "that
 thou carve him once,
And if thou touchest him tidily, truly I trow
That thou canst endure any dint that he will
 deal thee."
Gawain goes to the green man, with gisarme
 in hand ;
And he boldly abides him, abashed was he
 never.
Then calls to Sir Gawain the champion in
 green :
"Let us canvass our compact ere we carry
 this further.
First, knight, I must know what thy name is ;
That tell thou me truly that I may trust to it."
"In good faith," quoth the good knight,
 "Gawain men call me,   381
Who shall bid thee this buffet, whate'er be-
 falls after,
And at this time twelve month take from thee
 another,
With what weapon so thou wilt, and from no
 wight else
   Alive."
  That other answers again,
  "Sir Gawain, so may I thrive
  As I am wondrous fain
  'Tis thou this dint shalt drive.'

XVIII

"By God," quoth the Green Knight, "Sir
 Gawain, I like it   390
That I shall have from thy hand what I here
 sought for ;

[1] quickly [2] stooped courteously [3] seizes [4] left,
gave [5] take care, cousin, that thou give one stroke
[6] treatest [7] blow [8] offer [9] goes [10] man [11] axe
[12] awaits [13] he quailed never the more [14] agreements [15] further [16] ask [17] what is thy name [18] believe [19] Gawain is my name [20] from thee [21] no man
else [22] alive [23] answers [24] may [25] wonderfully glad
[26] that thou shalt deliver this blow [27] it pleases
me [28] take from thy fist [29] what [30] asked for

And thou hacz redily rehersed, bi resoun ful
   trwe,
Clanly [1] al the covenaunt that I the kynge
   asked,
Saf that thou schal siker [2] me, segge,[3] by thi
   trawthe,
That thou schal seche [4] me thi-self, where-so
   thou hopes [5]
I may be funde upon folde,[6] and foch [7] the
   such wages
As thou deles me to day, bifore this douthe [8]
   ryche.''
"Where schulde I wale [4] the?" quoth Gauan,
   "Where is thy place?
I wot never where thou wonyes,[9] bi Hym that
   me wroght,
Ne I know not the, kynght, thy cort, ne thi
   name.
Bot teche me truly ther-to, and telle me howe
   thou hattes,[10]   401
And I schal ware [11] alle my wyt to wynne me
   theder,[12]
And that I swere the for sothe, and by my
   seker [13] traweth."
"That is innogh in Nwe Yer, hit nedes no
   more,"
Quoth the gome in the grene to Gawan the
   hende,[14]
"Gif [15] I the telle trwly, quen I the tape [16] have,
And thou me smothely hacz [17] smyten, smartly
   I the teche
Of my hous, and my home, and myn owen
   nome,[18]
Then may thou frayst my fare,[19] and for-
   wardez [20] holde.
And if I spende no speche, thenne spedez
   thou the better,   410
For thou may leng [21] in thy londe, and layt no
   fyrre,[22]
       Bot slokes.[23]
    Ta [24] now thy grymme tole [25] to the,
    And let se how thou cnokez." [26]
    "Gladly, syr, for sothe,"
    Quoth Gawan; his ax he strokes.

XIX

The grene knyght upon grounde graythely
   hym dresses,[27]
A littel lut [28] with the hede, the lere [29] he
   diskoverez,

And thou hast rightly rehearsed, as reason
   was truly,
Clearly all the covenant that of the king I
   asked,
Save that thou must assure me, sir, by thy
   honour,
That thou wilt seek me thyself in what spot
   soever
Thou thinkst to find me, in faith, and fetch
   thee such wages
As thou dealest me to-day before these
   doughty nobles."
"In what climes shall I seek thee? In what
   country is thy dwelling?
Of thy habitation have I ne'er heard, by Him
   that wrought me;
Nor know I thee, knight, thy court, nor thy
   name;   400
But direct me to thy dwelling and disclose
   how men call thee,
And I shall strive with my strength to steer
   my steps thither;
And that I swear thee surely and by my sacred
   honour."
"That is enough at New Year; no more is
   needful,"
Quoth the grim man in green to Gawain the
   courteous;
"If I tell thee truly, when I the tap have taken
And thou hast smoothly smitten me, if
   smartly I teach thee
Of my house and my home and how men call
   me,
Then mayst thou enquire my country and
   hold our covenant.
And if I spend then no speech, thou shalt speed
   the better,   410
For thou mayst stop in this stead and step no
   further,
       But stay.
    Take now thy grim tool duly;
    Let's see thee hack away!"
    "Yea, sir," quoth Gawain, "truly;"
    His axe he strokes in play.

XIX

The Green Knight on the ground goodly prepares him;
Lightly lowers his head and loosens his collar,

[1] entirely [2] promise [3] man [4] seek [5] believest
[6] earth [7] fetch [8] nobility [9] dwellest [10] what is thy
name [11] use [12] to get there [13] sure [14] courteous [15] if
[16] tap, stroke [17] hast [18] name [19] ask my state,
condition [20] the agreements [21] remain [22] seek no
further [23] but cease [24] take [25] instrument [26] knock-
est [27] readily prepares himself [28] bowed [29] cheek

His longe lovelych lokkez he layd over his
   croun,
Let the naked nec to the note [1] schewe.   420
Gauan gripped to his ax, and gederes hit on
   hyght,[2]
The kay [3] fot on the folde [4] he be-fore sette,
Let hit doun lyghtly lyght on the naked,
That the scharp of the schalk [5] schyndered [6]
   the bones
And schrank [7] thrugh the schyire grece,[8] and
   scade [9] hit in twynne,[10]
That the bit of the broun stel bot [11] on the
   grounde.
The fayre hede fro the halce [12] hit [13] to the
   erthe,
That fele [14] hit foyned [15] wyth her fete, there [16]
   hit forth roled.
The blod brayd [17] fro the body, that blykked [18]
   on the grene ;
And nawther [19] faltered ne fel the freke [20]
   never-the-helder,[21]   430
Bot stythly [22] he start forth upon styf schonkes,[23]
And runyschly [24] he raght [25] out, there-as [26]
   renkkez [27] stoden,
Laght [25] to his lufly [28] hed, and lyft hit up sone ;[29]
And sythen bowez [30] to his blonk,[31] the brydel
   he cachchez,
Steppez in to stel-bawe [32] and strydez alofte,
And his hede by the here in his honde haldez ;
And as sadly [33] the segge [34] hym in his sadel
   sette,
As [35] non unhap had hym ayled, thagh [36]
   hedlez nowe,
     In stedde.[37]
     He brayde [38] his blunk [31] aboute,   440
     That ugly bodi that bledde ;
     Moni on of hym had doute,[39]
     Bi that his resounz were redde.[40]

His long lovely locks he lays over backward,
Let the naked neck to the nape glisten.   420
Gawain gripped to his axe and gathered it on
   high,
His left foot on the floor he thrusts before
   him,
Let the axe lightly light on the bare neck,
So that the bright blade all the bones severs
And slices the sinews and slits them asunder,
So that the edge of the axe entered the earth.
The bright head from the body bounded to
   the floor,
And many filliped it with their feet as it
   rolled forward.
The blood gushed from the body and glistened
   on the green ;
But neither faltered nor fell the fearsome
   stranger,   430
But sturdily strode forth on his stiff shanks,
And roughly he reached forth among the
   ranked courtiers,
Laid hold of his lovely head, and lifted it up
   quickly ;
And then strides to his steed, the bridle he
   seizes,
Steps into the stirrup and straddles aloft,
His head by the hair in his hand holding ;
And as steadily the stranger settled him in his
   saddle
As if no harm had happened, though he was
   headless
     I' the stead.
     He turned his steed about,   440
     That ugly body that bled ;
     Many had dread and doubt
     Ere all his words were said.

XX

For the hede in his honde he haldez up even,
To-ward the derrest [41] on the dece [42] he dres-
   sez [43] the face ,
And hit lyfte up the yye-lyddez,[44] and loked
   ful brode,
And meled [45] thus much with his muthe, as ye
   may now here.

XX

For the head in his hand he holds up even,
Toward the most daring on the dais he
   addresses the face ;
And it lifted up its eyelids and looked about
   it,
And held discourse high, as you shall now
   hear.

[1] head [2] high [3] left [4] ground [5] edge [6] sun-
dered [7] cut [8] pure gristle [9] divided [10] two [11] bit,
cut [12] neck [13] fell [14] many [15] thrust [16] where
[17] spouted [18] shone [19] neither [20] man [21] never the
more [22] sturdily [23] shanks [24] roughly [25] reached

[26] where [27] men [28] lovely [29] immediately [30] goes
[31] horse [32] stirrup [33] steadily [34] fellow [35] as if
[36] though [37] in the place [38] turned [39] fear [40] by
the time his remarks were made [41] bravest
[42] dais [43] directs [44] eye-lids [45] spoke

"Loke, Gawan, thou be graythe [1] to go as thou hettez, [2]
And layte [3] as lelly [4] til thou me, lude, [5] fynde,
As thou hacz hette [6] in this halle, herande [7] thise knyghtes. 450
To the grene chapel thou chose, [8] I charge the, to fotte; [9]
Such a dunt [10] as thou hacz dalt [11] disserved thou habbez, [12]
To be yederly yolden [13] on Nw Yeres morn.
The Knyght of the Grene Chapel, men knowen me mony; [14]
For-thi [15] me for to fynde, if thou fraystez, [16] faylez thou never;
Ther-fore com, other [17] recreaunt be calde the be-hoves."
With a runisch route [18] the raynez he tornez,
Halled [19] out at the hal-dor, his hed in his hande,
That the fyr of the flynt flawe [20] from fole hoves. [21]
To quat kyth he be-com, [22] knewe non there,
Never more then thay wyste from quethen [23] he wacz wonnen. [24]   461
            What thenne?
    The kyng and Gawen thare,
    At that Grene thay lage and grenne,
    Yet breved [25] wacz hit ful bare [26]
    A mervayl among tho [27] menne.

"See, Gawain, that thou be sedulous to seek as thou saidest,
And search assiduously till thou, sir, dost find me,
As thou has promised in this presence before these proven knights.
To the Green Chapel do thou go, I charge thee truly.
Such a dint as thou hast dealt deserved hast thou,   452
To be yarely yielded on New Year's morning.
As the Knight of the Green Chapel, I am known to many;
Thou shalt not fail to find me if faithfully thou triest;
Therefore come or coward to be called shall behoove thee."
With reckless roughness the reins he twitches,
Hurls out of the hall-door, his head in his hand,
So that fire from the flint flew from his steed's hoofs.
To what region he rode none could say rightly,   460
Any more than they wist by what way he had come.
            What then?
    The king and Gawain there
    Did laugh at the Knight in Green.
    'Twas counted a marvel rare
    Such as men had never seen.

XXI

Thagh [28] Arther the hende [29] kyng at hert hade wonder,
He let no semblaunt be sene, bot sayde ful hyghe [30]
To the comlych Quene, wyth cortays speche,
"Dere dame, to-day demay [31] yow never; 470
Wel bycommes [32] such craft upon Crist-masse,
Laykyng [33] of enterludez, to laghe and to syng
Among [34] thise kynde [35] caroles of knyghtez and ladyez.
Never-the-lece [36] to my mete [37] I may me wel dres, [38]
For I haf sen a selly, [39] I may not for-sake." [40]

XXI

Though Arthur the high king in his heart had wonder,
He let no semblance be seen, but spoke full gayly
To the comely Queen with courteous phrases,
"Dear Lady, to-day dismay you never.   470
Such crafts are becoming at the Christmas season,
Listening to such interludes and laughing and singing,
While these lords and ladies lead forth their carols.
But now have I license and leave to look on my food,
For strange is the sight that I have seen truly."

[1] ready [2] didst promise [3] seek [4] faithfully [5] man [6] promised [7] hearing [8] go [9] on foot [10] blow [11] hast dealt [12] hast [13] promptly paid [14] many men know me [15] therefore [16] enquirest [17] or [18] sudden noise [19] rushed [20] flew [21] from the horse's hoofs [22] to what land he went [23] whence [24] come [25] accounted [26] entirely [27] those [28] though [29] courteous [30] loud [31] dismay [32] suits [33] playing [34] now and then [35] suitable [36] nevertheless [37] food [38] address [39] marvel [40] deny

He glent [1] upon Syr Gawen, and gaynly [2] he
  sayde,
"Now, syr, heng up thyn ax, that hacz innogh
  hewen."
And hit wacz don [3] abof the dece, on doser [4]
  to henge,
Ther alle men for mervayl myght on hit loke,
And bi trwe tytel ther-of [5] to telle the wonder.
Thenne thay bowed [6] to a borde,[7] thise
  burnes [8] to-geder,   481
The kyng and the gode knyght; and kene [9]
  men hem served
Of alle dayntyez double, as derrest [10] myght
  falle —
Wyth alle maner of mete and mynstralcie
  bothe;
Wyth wele walt thay that day, til worthed an
  ende [11]
      In londe.
    Now thenk wel, Syr Gawan,
    For wothe [12] that thou ne wonde [13]
    This aventure forto frayn [14]
    That thou hacz tan [15] on honde   490

He glanced at Sir Gawain and graciously said
  he,
"Now, sir, hang up thine axe, it has had
  enough hewing."
And it was hung on high behind the dais,
Where all men for a marvel might look
  upon it
And take it as true witness when they told
  of the wonder.   480
Then they turned to the table, these two lords
  together,
The king and the good knight; and gentle
  squires served them
Of all dainties double that were to them
  dearest —
With all manner of meat and minstrelsy also;
With all delights did they deal until that day
  ended
      In land.
    Now think well, Sir Gawain,
    That thou hast taken in hand
    The adventure to maintain,
    Whatever may withstand.   490

PEARL (c. 1350)

(Unknown Author)

I

Perle plesaunte to prynces paye [16]
To clanly clos [17] in golde so clere;
Oute of oryent, I hardyly saye,
Ne proved I never her precios pere,[18]
So rounde, so reken in uche araye,[19]
So smal, so smothe her sydez were;
Queresoever I jugged gemmez gaye,
I sette hyr sengeley in synglere.[20]
  Alas! I leste [21] hyr in on erbere; [22]
  Thurgh gresse to grounde hit fro me
    yot; [23]
  I dewyne, for-dolked of luf-daungere [24]
  Of that pryvy perle withouten spot. 12

I

A radiant pearl for royal array
Clean to enclose in gold so clear;
Out of the Orient, I boldly say,
Found have I never her precious peer,
So pure, so perfect at each assay,
So small, so smooth that blissful sphere;
Wherever I judged of jewels gay,
I set her apart as the prize most dear.
  Alas! in an arbor I lost her here,
  Slipping through grass to earth, I wot;
  I pine, cut off from the loving cheer
  Of my own pearl without a spot. 12

II

Sythen [25] in that spote hit fro me sprange,
Ofte haf I wayted, wyschande [26] that wele,[27]
That wont wacz whyle [28] devoyde [29] my
  wrange

II

There where I lost it, since have I long
Waited and wished for return of the weal
That whilom made me forget my wrong

[1] glanced [2] kindly [3] put [4] tapestry [5] and on the
evidence of it [6] went [7] table [8] knights [9] brave
[10] dearest [11] in joy they spent the day, till it came
to end [12] injury [13] hesitate [14] seek [15] taken [16] delight [17] cleanly to enclose [18] equal [19] fit in every
respect [20] alone in uniqueness [21] lost [22] an arbor [23] departed [24] I pine away, deprived of the
love-dominion [25] since [26] wishing [27] weal [28] was
formerly [29] to remove

And heven[1] my happe and al my hele;[2]
That docz bot thrych my herte thrange,[3]
My breste in bale[4] bot bolne and bele.[5]
Yet thoght me never so swete a sange
As stylle stounde[6] let to me stele;   20
 Forsothe ther fleten[7] to me fele[8] —
 To thenke hir color so clad in clot![9]
 O moul[10] thou marrez a myry juele,[11]
 My privy perle withouten spotte.

*   *   *   *   *   *

V

Bifore that spot my honde I spennd,[12]
For care ful colde that to me caght;[13]   50
A denely dele in my herte denned,[14]
Thagh resoun sette my selven saght.[15]
I playned[16] my perle that ther wacz spenned,[17]
Wyth fyrte skyllez[18] that faste faght;[19]
Thagh kynde of Kryst me comfort kenned,[20]
My wreched wylle in wo ay wraghte.[21]
 I felle upon that floury flaght;[22]
 Suche odour to my hernez[23] schot,
 I slode upon a slepyng-slaghte[24]
 On that precios perle withouten spot.

*   *   *   *   *   *

XIV

More mervayle con my dom adaunt;[25]
I segh[26] by-yonde that myry mere[27]
A crystal clyffe ful relusaunt,[28]
Mony ryal ray con fro hit rere;[29]   160
At the fote thereof ther sete a faunt,[30]
A mayden of menske,[31] ful debonere,
Blysnande whyte wacz hyr bleaunt;[32]
I knew hyr wel, I hade sen hyr ere.[33]
 As glysnande golde that man con
 schere[34]
 So schon that schene anunder schore;[35]
 On lenghe[36] I looked to hyr there;
 The lenger, I knew hyr more and more.[37]

XV

The more I frayste[38] hyr fayre face,
Her figure fyn quen I had fonte,[39]   170
Suche gladande glory con to me glace[40]

And brought me comfort, my spirit to heal,
That now is oppressed with passions strong
Till all my senses whirl and reel.
Yet me-thought was never so sweet a song
As the quiet hour to me let steal;   20
 Many strange fancies did it reveal —
 To think that her fairness earth should
 clot!
 O grave, the rarest of gems thou dost seal,
 My own dear pearl without a spot.

*   *   *   *   *   *

V

Before that spot my hands I spread,
For care full cold that me had caught;   50
In my heart dark sorrow made its bed,
Though reason reconciled my thought.
I prayed for my pearl that thence had sped,
With timid pleas, and fast they fought;
Though the godhead of Christ me comforted,
My wretched will in woe still wrought.
 A bed among the flowers I sought;
 Such fragrance pierced my brain, I wot,
 Me into a sleep of dreams it brought
 Of that precious pearl without a spot.

*   *   *   *   *   *

XIV

More wonder my judgment stole away;
I saw beyond that river fair
A crystal cliff as clear as day,
Its royal rays gleamed through the air;   160
At its foot there sat a child full gay,
A mannerly maiden, debonair,
All argent white was her array;
I knew her well, I had seen her ere.
 As glistening gold, refined and rare,
 So shone she shone upon the shore;
 Long while I looked upon her there;
 The longer, I knew her more and more.

XV

The more I questioned her fair face
And came to know her figure bright,   170
Such joy shed over me its grace

[1] lift up   [2] prosperity   [3] does but oppress my heart grievously   [4] distress   [5] swell and burn   [6] the quiet hour   [7] float   [8] many things   [9] clod   [10] earth [11] jewel   [12] stretched out   [13] that seized upon me [14] a secret sorrow lay in my heart   [15] though reason reconciled all difficulties   [16] lamented   [17] was taken away   [18] timid reasons   [19] fought hard [20] though Christ's nature taught me comfort [21] wrought [22] bed of flowers [23] brains [24] I slided into a dream   [25] a greater wonder daunted my judgment   [26] saw   [27] pleasant water   [28] gleaming [29] many a royal gleam arose from it   [30] child [31] grace [32] gleaming white was her attire   [33] before [34] that one has refined   [35] so shone that beautiful one beneath the cliff   [36] a long time   [37] the longer I looked the more certainly I knew her   [38] questioned   [39] when I had examined   [40] such delight came to me

As lyttel byfore therto wacz wonte;
To calle hyr lyste con me enchace,[1]
Bot baysment [2] gef myn hert a brunt; [3]
I segh hyr in so strange a place,
Such a burre myght make myn herte blunt.[4]
 Thenne verez ho up her fayre frount,[5]
 Hyr vysayge whyt as playn yvore,[6] 178
 That stonge myn hert ful stray
  atount,[7]
 And ever the lenger, the more and
  more.

  * * * * * *

XX

Pyght [8] in perle, that precios pyece
On wyther-half water [9] com doun the schore; [10]
No gladder gome hethen [11] into Grece 231
Then I quen ho on brymme wore.[12]
Ho wacz me nerre [13] then aunte or nece,
My joy forthy wacz [14] much the more.
Ho profered me speche, that special spece,[15]
Enclynande lowe in wommon lore,[16]
 Caghte of her coroun of grete tresore,
 And haylsed me wyth a lote lyghte.[17]
 Wel wacz me that ever I wacz bore,
 To sware [18] that swete in perlez
  pyghte.

XXI

"O Perle," quoth I, "in perlez pyght, 241
Art thou my perle that I haf playned,[19]
Regretted by myn one, on nyghte? [20]
Much longeyng haf I for the layned,[21]
Sythen in-to gresse thou me aglyghte; [22]
Pensyf, payred,[23] I am for-payned,[24]
And thou in a lyf of lykyng lyghte [25]
In paradys erde,[26] of stryf unstrayned.
 What wyrde hacz hyder my juel
  vayned,[27]
 And don me in thys del [28] and gret
  daunger?
 Fro we in twynne wern towen and
  twayned [29]
 I haf ben a joylez jueler." [30] 252

That scarce before I had known delight;
Desire to address her grew apace,
But abashment filled my heart with fright;
Seeing her in so strange a place
Full well my heart astonish might.
 Then lifts she up her forehead white,
 Her visage fairer than e'er before; 178
 Bewildered my heart was at the sight
 And ever the longer, the more and
  more.

  * * * * * *

XX

All decked with pearls that precious piece
Beyond the water came down the shore;
None gladder than I hence unto Greece 231
When she stood on the bank there me before.
She was nearer to me than aunt or niece,
And my joy was therefore much the more.
That special treasure spoke words of peace,
With womanly grace herself she bore,
 Took off the wondrous crown she wore,
 And greeted me with look full bright.
 What happy fortune for me in store —
 To answer that sweet with pearls be-
  dight.

XXI

"O Pearl," quoth I, "with pearls bedight, 241
Art thou my pearl that I still mourn,
Regretted by me alone at night?
With longing for thee am I outworn;
Since in the grass thou wert lost to sight,
Pensive and pining am I forlorn,
And thou, in a life of glad delight,
Strife-free, dost Paradise adorn.
 What Weird hath hither my jewel
  borne,
 Me here in sorrow and stress to find?
 I have been, since we apart were
  torn,
 A joyless jeweler 'mid my kind." 252

---

[1] desire to speak to her seized me [2] timidity [3] attack [4] such a surprise might well astound me [5] then she lifts her fair face [6] ivory [7] that struck me into bewilderment [8] set [9] on the opposite side of the water [10] cliff [11] person from hence [12] than I when she was at the bank [13] she was nearer to me [14] on that account was [15] she spoke to me, that rare one [16] bowing low as women are taught [17] greeted me pleasantly [18] answer [19] lamented [20] alone by night [21] suffered secretly [22] since thou didst slip away from me into the grass [23] weakened [24] worn with grief [25] and thou in a life of delightful pleasure [26] land [27] what fate has brought my jewel hither [28] put me in this grief [29] since we were drawn apart and separated [30] possessor of jewels

XXII

That juel thenne in gemmez gente [1]
Vered up her vyse [2] with yghen [3] graye,
Set on hyr coroun of perle orient,
And soberly after thenne con ho say : [4]
"Syr, ye haf your tale myse-tente, [5]
To say your perle is al awaye,
That is in cofer, so comly clente, [6]
As in this gardyn gracios gaye,   260
  Here-inne to lenge [7] for-ever and play,
  Ther mys nee mornyng [8] com never
   nere ;
  Her were a forser [9] for the, in faye,
  If thou were a gentyl jueler.

XXIII

"Bot, jueler gente, if thou schal lose
Thy joy for a gemme that the wacz lef, [10]
Me thynk the put [11] in a mad porpose,
And busyez the aboute a raysoun bref ; [12]
For that thou lestez [13] wacz bot a rose,
That flowred and fayled as kynde [14] hit gef ;
Now thurgh kynde [14] of the kyste [15] that hyt
  con [16] close,   271
To a perle of prys hit is put in pref ; [17]
  And thou hacz called thy wyrde [18] a thef,
  That oght of noght hacz mad the cler ; [19]
  Thou blamez the bote [20] of thy meschef,
  Thou art no kynde jueler."

 * * * * * *

LXIII

"O maskelez [21] perle, in perlez pure,
That berez," quod I, "the perle of prys,
Quo [22] formed the thy fayre fygure?
That wroght thy wede, [23] he wacz ful wys ;
Thy beaute com never of nature ;
Pymalyon paynted never thy vys ; [24]   750
Ne Arystotel nawther by hys lettrure
Of carped the kynde these propertez. [25]
  Thy colour passez the flour-de-lys,
  Thyn angel-havynge so clene cortez ; [26]
  Breve [27] me, bryght, quat-kyn offys [28]
  Berez the perle so maskellez."

XXII

That jewel in gems so wondrous wrought
Up lifted her face with eyes of grey,
Set on her crown of pearls far-sought,
And soberly after began to say :
"Oh, sir, your mind is all distraught
To say that your pearl hath passed away,
That into so comely a coffer is brought
As in this garden gracious-gay,   260
  Herein to dwell for ever and play,
  Where moan or mourning none shall
   find ;
  Here were a casket for thee, in fay,
  If thou, my jeweller, wert kind.

XXIII

"But, jeweller gentle, if thus is crossed
Thy joy for a gem that was dear to thee,
Methinks thou art by madness tossed,
O'er a trifle to fret so busily ;
It was only a rose that thou hast lost,
Which flowered and faded naturally ;   270
By charm of the chest that it embossed
It was changed to a pearl of price, dost see?
  Thou callest a thief thy destiny,
  That aught of naught has made thee.
  Blind,
  Thou blam'st the bote of thy hurt the remedy ;
  My jeweller, thou art not kind !"

 * * * * * *

LXIII

"O spotless pearl, in pearls so pure,
That the priceless pearl," quoth I, "dost bear,
Who formed for thee thy beauty's lure,
Or wrought thee the weeds that thou dost wear?
Nature was never so cunning, sure ;
Pygmalion to paint thee would never dare ;
Aristotle, for all his literature,   751
Could never recount thy virtues rare ;
  Than the *fleur de lys* thou art more fair,
  In gracious bearing the angels' mate.
  Tell me what troth in heaven there
  Is pledged to the pearl immaculate?"

---

[1] beautiful [2] lifted her face [3] eyes [4] she said
[5] distorted [6] set [7] remain [8] where lack nor mourning
[9] jewel-box [10] was dear to thee [11] I regard thee as
put [12] small affair [13] didst lose [14] nature [15] chest
[16] did [17] put in proof = turned [18] fate [19] that has

clearly made for thee something of nothing
[20] remedy [21] spotless [22] who [23] garment [24] face
[25] described thy beauties of nature [26] courteous
[27] inform [28] what office *or* position

LXIV

"My maskelez Lambe that al may bete," [1]
Quod scho,[2] "my dere destyne,
Me ches [3] to hys make,[4] al-thagh unmete.
Sum tyme semed that assemble,   760
When I wente fro yor worlde wete ; [5]
He calde me to hys bonerte : [6]
'Cum hyder to me, my lemman [7] swete,
For mote ne spot is non in the.'
  He yef [8] me myght and als [9] bewte ;
  In hys blod he wesch my wede [10] on
   dese,[11]
  And coronde clene in vergynte,
  And pyght me in perlez maskellez."

 * * * * * *

LXXXI

"Motelez [12] may, so meke and mylde,"
Then sayde I to that lufly flor,[13]   962
"Bryng me to that bygly bylde,[14]
And let me se thy blysful bor." [15]
That scheue [16] sayde, that [17] God wyl
  schylde,
"Thou may not enter with-inne hys tor,[18]
Bot of the Lombe I have the [19] aquylde [20]
For a syght ther-of thurgh gret favor.
  Ut-wyth [21] to se that clene cloystor,
  Thou may ; bot in-wyth [22] not a fote,
  To strech in the strete thou hacz no
   vygour,   971
  Bot thou wer clene with-outen mote."

 * * * * * *

XCVI

The Lombe delyt non lyste to wene ; [23]
Thagh he were hurt and wounde hade,
In his sembelaunt [24] wacz never sene ;
So wern his glentez [25] gloryous glade.
I loked among his meyny schene,[26]
How thay wyth lyf wern laste and lade,[27]
Then sagh I ther my lyttel quene,
That I wende [28] had standen by me in sclade.[29]
  Lorde ! much of mirthe wacz that ho [30]
   made,
  Among her ferez [31] that wacz so quyt ! [32]
  That syght me gart [33] to think to wade,
  For luf-longyng in gret delyt.   1152

LXIV

"My spotless Lamb, who far and wide
Heals all — my Master dear," quoth she,
"Me all unworthy chose for his bride ;
Oh! long that waiting seemed to me,   760
When I from your damp world did glide!
He called me to his charity :
'Come hither, sweetheart, to my side,
For mote or spot is none in thee.'
  Beauty and strength he gave to me,
  In his blood he washed me, with sin
   bespate,
  He crowned me clean in virginity,
  And decked me with pearls immacu-
   late."

 * * * * * *

LXXXI

"Spotless maid, so mild and meek,"
Then said I to that flower bright,   962
"Me to thy palace bring, and eke
Of thy blissful bower give me sight."
Sweetly — God shield her! — did she speak :
"That tower may enter no earthly wight ;
But of the Lamb did I favour seek
That thou from afar shouldst see its light ;
  From without that cloister see aright
  Thou mayest indeed ; but within,
   step not ;
  To walk in the street thou hast no
   might,
  Unless thou wert clean, without a
   spot."   972

 * * * * * *

XCVI

The Lamb lacked no delight, I ween ;   1141
Hurt though he was, by wounds betrayed,
In his semblance this was no whit seen ;
So did his glorious looks persuade.
I looked among his comrades clean,
How brimming life upon them he laid.
Then saw I there my little queen,
That I thought stood near me in the glade.
  Lord ! much of mirth was that she
   made,
  Among her sisters all so white !
  That vision moved me to think to wade,
  For love-longing in great delight.   1152

---

[1] amend [2] said she [3] chose [4] mate [5] wet [6] goodness [7] sweetheart [8] gave [9] also [10] garment [11] dais [12] spotless [13] flower [14] great building [15] bower [16] beautiful one [17] whom [18] tower [19] for thee [20] obtained [21] from without [22] within [23] wished to doubt [24] appearance [25] looks [26] beautiful company [27] supplied and laden [28] thought [29] valley [30] she [31] companions [32] white [33] caused

XCVII

Delyt me drof in yghe [1] and ere;
My manez [2] mynde to maddyng malte.[3]
Quen I segh [4] my frely,[5] I wolde be there,
By-yonde the water thagh ho [6] were walte.[7]
I thoght that no-thyng myght me dere,[8]
To fech me bur and take me halte; [9]
And to start in the strem schulde non me
    stere,[10]
To swymme the remnaunt, thagh I ther
    swalte; [11]
    Bot of that munt [12] I wacz bi-talt; [13] 1161
    When I schulde start in the strem
    astraye,
    Out of that caste [14] I wacz by-calt; [15]
    Hit wacz not at my pryncez paye.[16]

XCVII

Delight me drove in eye and ear;
My earthly mind was maddened nigh.
When I saw my darling, I would be near,
Beyond the water that she stood by:
"Nothing," methought, "can harm me here,
Deal me a blow and low make lie;
To wade the stream have I no fear,
Or to swim the deeps, though I should
    die."   1160
    But from that purpose withheld was I;
    As unto the stream I started still,
    Clean from that plan I was turned
    awry;
    It was not at my Prince's will.

XCVIII

Hit payed [17] hym not that I so flonc [18]
Over mervelous merez,[19] so mad arayde;
Of raas [20] thagh I were rasch and ronk,[21]
Yet rapely [22] ther-inne I wacz restayed;
For ryght as I sparred un-to the bonc,
That bratthe [23] out of my drem me brayde; [24]
Then wakned I in that erber wlonk,[25]   1171
My hede upon that hylle wacz layde
    Ther as my perle to grounde strayd;
    I raxled [26] and fel in gret affray,[27]
    And sykyng [28] to myself I sayd:
    "Now al be to that pryncez paye." [16]

XCVIII

It pleased him not I should pass quite,
O'er marvellous meres, so mad arrayed;
Though in my rush I had strength and might,
Yet hastily therein I was stayed;
For as I strove to the bank aright,
My haste me of my dream betrayed;   1170
Then waked I in that arbor bright,
My head upon that mound was laid
    Where my own pearl to ground had
    strayed.
    I roused me, with many a fear a-thrill,
    And sighing to myself I said:
    "Now all be at that Prince's will."

JOHN GOWER (1325?–1408)

From CONFESSIO AMANTIS Bk. V

Jason, which sih [4] his fader old,
Upon Medea made him bold
Of art magique, which sche couthe,[29]
And preith hire that his fader [30] youthe
Sche wolde make ayeinward [31] newe.
And sche, that was toward him trewe,   3950
Behihte [32] him that sche wolde it do
Whan that sche time sawh [4] therto.
Bot [33] what sche dede in that matiere
It is a wonder thing to hiere,
Bot yit for the novellerie [34]
I thenke tellen a partie.[35]

Jason, who saw his father old,
Upon Medea made so bold —
Of magic art she knew, in sooth —
And prays her that his father's youth
She would bring back again as new.
And she, that was to him full true,   3950
Promised him that she would it do
When that she saw her time thereto.
But how she wrought this for his cheer
It is a wondrous thing to hear,
Yet for the novelty of it
I think to tell you just a bit.

---

[1] eye [2] man's [3] melted [4] saw [5] gracious one [6] she
[7] kept [8] injure [9] to fetch me an assault and take
me lame [10] prevent [11] perished [12] purpose [13] shaken
[14] intention [15] recalled [16] pleasure [17] pleased

[18] should fling [19] waters [20] onset [21] strong [22] quickly
[23] haste [24] moved [25] fair [26] roused [27] fear [28] sighing
[29] knew [30] father's [31] again [32] promised [33] but
[34] novelty [35] part

Thus it befell upon a nyht
Whan ther was noght bot sterreliht,[1]
Sche was vanyssht riht as hir liste,[2]
That no wyht bot hirself jt wiste,   3960
And that was ate [3] mydnyht tyde.
The world was stille on every side.
With open [4] hed and fot al bare,
Hir her tosprad,[5] sche gan to fare;
Upon hir clothes gert [6] sche was;
Al specheles and [7] on the gras
Sche glod [8] forth as an addre doth —
Non otherwise sche ne goth —
Til sche cam to the freissche flod,
And there a while sche withstod.[9]   3970
Thries sche torned hire aboute,
And thries ek sche gan doun loute [10]
And in the flod sche wette hir her,
And thries on the water ther
Sche gaspeth with a drecchinge [11] onde,[12]
And tho [13] sche tok hir speche on honde.
Ferst sche began to clepe [14] and calle
Upward unto the sterres alle,
To Wynd, to Air, to See, to Lond
Sche preide, and ek hield up hir hond   3980
To Echates [15] and gan to crie,
Which is godesse of sorcerie.
Sche seide, "Helpeth at this nede,
And as ye maden me to spede,[16]
Whan Jason cam the Flees [17] to seche,
So help me nou, I you beseche."
With that sche loketh and was war, [18]
Doun fro the sky ther cam a char,[19]
The which dragouns aboute drowe.
And tho [13] sche gan hir hed doun bowe,
And up sche styh,[20] and faire and wel   3991
Sche drof forth bothe char and whel
Above in thair [21] among the skyes.[22]
The lond of Crete and tho parties [23]
Sche soughte, and faste gan hire hye,[24]
And there upon the hulles [25] hyhe
Of Othrin and Olimpe also,
And ek of othre hulles mo,
Sche fond and gadreth herbes suote.[26]
Sche pulleth up som be the rote,   4000
And manye with a knyf sche scherth,[27]
And alle into hir char sche berth.[28]
Thus whan sche hath the hulles sought,
The flodes [29] ther forgat [30] sche nought,
Eridian and Amphrisos,

Thus it befell upon a night,
When there was nought but starry light,
She stole away right as she list,
So that none but herself it wist,   3960
And that was at the midnight tide,
The world was still on every side.
With head uncovered, feet all bare,
Her hair unbound, she gan to fare;
High up her clothes she girded has;
And, speechless, forth upon the grass
She glided as an adder does —
And in no other wise she goes —
Till she came to the flowing flood,
And there a while full still she stood.   3970
Three times about she turned her now,
And thrice also she low did bow,
And in the flood she wet her hair,
And thrice upon the water there
She with a troubling breath blew fast,
And then unto her speech she passed.
First she began to cry and call
Unto the stars of heaven all;
To Wind, to Air, to Sea, to Land
She prayed there, holding up her hand,   3980
And unto Hecate did she cry,
Who goddess is of sorcery.
She said: "Oh, help me in this need,
And as ye once made me to speed,
When Jason came, the Fleece to seek,
So now your aid I do bespeak."
With that she looked and saw on high
A chariot gliding from the sky,
Which, dragons drawing, downward sped,
And then she bowed adown her head,   3990
And up she rose, drove well and fair
Both car and wheel on through the air,
Above and through the clouds of sky.
The land of Crete and parts near by
She sought, and fast began her hie;
And there upon the mountains high
Of Othrim and Olympus too,
And other mountains eke thereto,
She found and gathers herbs of boot.
She pulleth some up by the root,   4000
And many with a knife she shears,
And all unto her car she bears.
Thus when she hath the mountains sought,
The rivers there forgot she not;
Eridian and Amphrisos,

---

[1] starlight [2] as it pleased her [3] at the [4] uncovered [5] her hair unbound [6] girded [7] *Gower often gives* and *a strange position in the sentence; we should place it before* al. [8] glided [9] stood still

[10] bow [11] troubling [12] breath [13] then [14] cry [15] Hecate [16] succeed [17] fleece [18] aware [19] chariot [20] rose [21] the air [22] clouds [23] those parts [24] hasten [25] hills [26] sweet [27] cuts [28] bears, carries [29] rivers [30] forgot

Peneie and ek Spercheidos.
To hem sche wente and ther sche nom [1]
Bothe of the water and the fom,
The sond and ek the smale stones,
Whiche-as sche ches [2] out for the nones; [3]
And of the Rede See a part   4011
That was behovelich to hire art
Sche tok, and after that aboute
Sche soughte sondri sedes oute
In feldes and in many greves, [4]
And ek a part sche tok of leves;
Bot thing which mihte hire most availe
Sche fond in Crete and in Thessaile.
    In daies and in nyhtes nyne,
With gret travaile and with gret pyne,   4020
Sche was pourveid of every piece,
And torneth homward into Grece.
Before the gates of Eson
Hir char sche let awai to gon,
And tok out ferst that was therinne;
For tho sche thoghte to beginne
Suche thing as semeth impossible,
And made hirselven invisible,
As sche that was with air enclosed
And mihte of noman be desclosed.   4030
Sche tok up turves of the lond
Withoute helpe of mannes hond,
Al heled [5] with the grene gras,
Of which an alter mad ther was
Unto Echates, the goddesse
Of art magique and the maistresse,
And eft [6] an other to Juvente,
As sche which dede hir hole entente. [7]
Tho tok sche fieldwode and verveyne —
Of herbes ben noght betre tueine; [8]   4040
Of which anon withoute let
These alters ben aboute set.
Tuo sondri puttes [9] faste by
Sche made, and with that hastely
A wether which was blak sche slouh, [10]
And out ther-of the blod sche drouh [11]
And dede [12] into the pettes [9] tuo;
Warm melk sche putte also therto
With hony meynd; [13] and in such wise
Sche gan to make hir sacrifice.   4050
And cride and preide forth withal
To Pluto, the god infernal,
And to the queene Proserpine.
And so sche soghte out al the line
Of hem that longen to that craft,
Behinde was no name laft, [14]

Peneie and eke Spercheidos.
To them she went and there took some
Both of the water and the foam,
The sand and eke the little stones,
Whereof she chose out special ones;   4010
And of the Red Sea too a part
That was behooveful for her art
She took, and, after that, about
She sought there sundry seeds then out
In many a wood and many a field;
Their leaves she made the trees to yield;
But that which best her need did meet
She found in Thessaly and Crete.
    Nine days and nights had passed before,
With labour great and pain full sore,   4020
She was purveyed with every piece,
And turneth homeward unto Greece.
At Eson's gates then did she stay,
And let her chariot go away;
But took out first what was therein,
For then her plan was to begin
Such things as seemed impossible,
And made herself invisible,
As she that was with air enclosed
And might to no man be disclosed.   4030
She took up turfs from off the land,
Without the help of human hand,
All covered with the growing grass,
Of which an altar made she has
To Hecate, who was the goddess
Of magic art and the mistress,
And still another to Juvente,
As one fulfilling her intent.
Then took she wormwood and vervain —
Of herbs there be no better twain;   4040
With which anon, without delay,
She set these altars in array.
Two sundry pits quite near thereby
She made, and with that hastily,
A wether which was black she slew,
And out thereof the blood she drew,
And cast in the pits without ado;
And warm milk added she thereto
With honey mixed; and in such wise
Began to make her sacrifice.   4050
And cried and prayed aloud also
To Pluto, god of all below,
And to the queen's self, Proserpine.
And so she sought out all the line
Of those that to that craft belong —
Forgot she none of all the throng —

---

[1] took [2] chose [3] for the purpose [4] groves [5] covered [6] again [7] entire purpose [8] twain, two [9] pits
[10] slew [11] drew [12] put [13] mixed [14] left

AE

And preide hem alle, as sche wel couthe,[1]
To grante Eson his ferste youthe.
  This olde Eson broght forth was tho;[2]
Awei sche bad alle othre go,   4060
Upon peril that mihte falle;
And with that word thei wenten alle,
And leften there hem tuo al-one.
And tho sche gan to gaspe and gone,[3]
And made signes many-on,
And seide hir wordes therupon;
So that with spellinge of hir charmes
Sche took Eson in both hire armes,
And made him forto slepe faste,
And him upon hire herbes caste.   4070
The blake wether tho sche tok,
And hiewh[4] the fleissh, as doth a cok;
On either alter part sche leide,
And with the charmes that sche seide
A fyr doun fro the sky alyhte
And made it forto brenne lyhte.
Bot whan Medea sawh it brenne,
Anon sche gan to sterte and renne[5]
The fyri aulters al aboute.
Ther was no beste which goth oute   4080
More wylde than sche semeth ther:
Aboute hir schuldres hyng[6] hir her,
As thogh sche were oute of hir mynde
And torned in an other kynde.[7]
Tho[2] lay ther certein wode cleft,
Of which the pieces nou and eft[8]
Sche made hem in the pettes wete,
And put hem in the fyri hete,
And tok the brond with al the blase,
And thries sche began to rase   4090
Aboute Eson, ther-as[9] he slepte;
And eft with water, which sche kepte,
Sche made a cercle aboute him thries,
And eft with fyr of sulphre twyes.
Ful many an other thing sche dede,
Which is noght writen in this stede.[10]
Bot tho[2] sche ran so up and doun,
Sche made many a wonder soun,
Somtime lich[11] unto the cock,
Somtime unto the laverock,[12]   4100
Somtime kacleth as a hen,
Somtime spekth as don the men;
And riht so as hir jargoun strangeth,[13]
In sondri wise hir forme changeth,
Sche semeth faie[14] and no womman;
For with the craftes that sche can
Sche was, as who seith, a goddesse.

And prayed them all, as she well could,
To grant Eson his young manhood.
  This old Eson was brought forth, lo !
Away she bade all others go,   4060
On peril of what might befall;
And with that word then went in all,
And left out there alone those two.
Gasping and pacing, with much ado,
She made her signs full many a one,
And said her magic words thereon;
So that with spelling of her charms
She took Eson in both her arms,
And causèd him to sleep full fast,
And on the herbs him sleeping cast.   4070
The wether black then next she took,
And hewed the flesh as doth a cook;
On either altar part she laid,
And with the charms that she hath said
A fire down from the sky did light
And made the flesh to burn full bright.
But when Medea saw it burn,
Anon she leaped and ran in turn
The fiery altars all about.
There was no beast which goeth out   4080
More wild than she herself seemed there;
About her shoulders hung her hair,
As though she were out of her mind
And turned into another kind.
There certain wood lay cleft in twain,
Of which the sticks, now and again,
She made them in the pits full wet,
And in the fiery heat them set;
And took the brand with all the blaze,
And thrice with it, as in a race,   4090
Ran about Eson as he slept,
And then with water which she kept
She made a circle round him thrice,
And then with fire of sulphur twice.
And other things she did, I wot,
Which in this place are written not.
But, running up and down the ground,
She made full many a wondrous sound;
Sometimes like unto the cock,
Sometimes like the laverock,   4100
Sometimes cackleth as a hen,
Sometimes speaketh as do men.
And as she made her jargon strange,
Her form in sundry wise did change,
She seemed no woman but a fay;
For with the crafts she did assay
She was, as one might say, goddéss.

---

[1] could   [2] then   [3] walk   [4] hewed   [5] run   [6] hung   [12] lark   [13] becomes strange   [14] fairy
[7] nature   [8] now and again   [9] where   [10] place   [11] like

And what hir liste, more or lesse,
Sche dede, in bokes as we finde,
That passeth over manneskinde.[1]   4110
Bot who that wole of wondres hiere,
What thing sche wroghte in this matiere,
To make an ende of that sche gan,[2]
Such merveile herde nevere man.

Apointed in the newe mone,
Whan it was time forto done,
Sche sette a caldron on the fyr,
In which was al the hole atir,[3]
Whereon the medicine stod,
Of jus, of water, and of blod,   4120
And let it buile[4] in such a plit,
Til that sche sawh the spume whyt;
And tho sche caste in rynde[5] and rote,
And sed and flour that was for bote,[6]
With many an herbe and many a ston,
Whereof sche hath ther many on.
And ek Cimpheius the serpent
To hire hath alle his scales lent,
Chelidre hire yaf his addres skin,
And sche to builen caste hem in;   4130
A part ek of the horned oule,
The which men hiere on nyhtes houle;
And of a raven, which was told
Of nyne hundred wynter old,
Sche tok the hed with al the bile;[7]
And as the medicine wile,
Sche tok therafter the bouele[8]
Of the seewolf, and for the hele[9]
Of Eson, with a thousand mo
Of thinges that sche hadde tho,   4140
In that caldroun togedre as blyve[10]
Sche putte; and tok thanne of olyve
A drie branche hem with to stere,[11]
The which anon gan floure and bere
And waxe al freissh and grene ayein.
Whan sche this vertu hadde sein,
Sche let the leste drope of alle
Upon the bare flor doun falle;
Anon ther sprong up flour and gras,
Where-as the drope falle was,   4150
And wox anon al medwe[12] grene,
So that it mihte wel be sene.
Medea thanne knew and wiste
Hir medicine is forto triste,[13]
And goth to Eson ther[14] he lay,
And tok a swerd was of assay[15]
With which a wounde upon his side
Sche made, that therout mai slyde

And whatso pleased her, more or less,
She did, as we in books may find,
Deeds that pass skill of human kind.   4110
But whoso will of wonders hear,
What things she wrought by magic clear
To make an end of all her spell,
Of crafts like hers heard no man tell.

Just as the moon had changed to new,
When it was time her task to do,
She laid a cauldron on the fire,
In which was placed the mass entire
Wherein the magic virtues stood
Of juice, of water, and of blood,   4120
And let it boil therein aright
Till she could see the bubbles white;
And then she cast in bark and root,
And seed and flower both to boot,
With many a herb and many a stone,
Whereof she hath there many a one.
And eke Cimpheius, the serpent,
To her hath all his scales now lent,
Chelidre, the adder, gave his skin,
And she to the boiling cast them in;   4130
A part too of the horned owl,
The which men hear at night-time howl;
And of a raven which had told
His full nine hundred winters old,
She took the head with all the bill;
And as the medicine it will,
Of sea wolf she the bowel took,
And for the healing did it cook
Of Eson; — and a thousand more
Of things that she had still in store   4140
Within that cauldron cast full quick.
Of olive then a withered stick
She took, to stir that mixture rare.
And lo, the stick did flower and bear,
And waxed again all fresh and green!
When she this virtue well had seen,
She let the smallest drop of all
Upon the barren earth down fall;
At once there sprang up flower and grass,
Just where the falling drop did pass,   4150
And waxed at once all meadow-green,
So that it clearly might be seen.
Medea then full surely knew
Her medicine was strong and true;
And goes to Eson where he lay,
And took a sword of good assay,
With which a wound within his side
She made, that so thereout may slide

---

[1] that surpasses human nature [2] began [3] equipment [4] boil [5] bark [6] remedy [7] bill [8] intestine [9] healing [10] quickly [11] stir [12] meadow [13] trust [14] where [15] proof

The blod withinne, which was old 4159	The blood within him, which was old
And sek and trouble and fieble and cold.	And sick and troubled and feeble and cold.
And tho sche tok unto his us [1]	And then she took unto his use 4161
Of herbes al the beste jus,	Of all the herbs the potent juice,
And poured it into his wounde;	And poured it all into his wound,
That made his veynes fulle and sounde.	That made his veins all full and sound;
And tho sche made his wounde clos,	And then she made his wound to close;
And tok his hand, and up he ros.	And took his hand, and up he rose.
And tho sche yaf [2] him drinke a drauhte,	A draught to drink she gave him then,
Of which his youthe ayein he cauhte,	From which his youth he caught again,
His hed, his herte and his visage	His head, his heart, and his viságe,
Lich [3] unto twenty wynter age; 4170	Like unto twenty winters' age; 4170
Hise hore heres were away,	His hoary hairs vanished away;
And lich unto the freisshe Maii,	And like unto the lusty May,
Whan passed ben the colde schoures,	When passed are all the chilling showers,
Riht so recovereth he his floures.	Right so recovereth he his flowers.

GEOFFREY CHAUCER (1340?–1400)

TROILUS AND CRISEYDE

FROM BOOK I

And so bifel,[4] whan comen was the tyme
Of Aperil, whan clothed is the mede [5]
With newe grene, of lusty Ver [6] the pryme,
And swote [7] smellen floures whyte and rede,
In sondry wyses shewede, as I rede,
The folk of Troye hir [8] observaunces olde,
Palladiones [9] feste for to holde.   161

And to the temple, in al hir [8] beste wyse,
In general, ther wente many a wight,
To herknen of Palladion the servyse;
And namely,[10] so many a lusty knight,   165
So many a lady fresh and mayden bright,
Ful wel arayed, bothe moste [11] and leste,
Ye,[12] bothe for the seson and the feste.

Among thise othere folk was Criseyda,
In widewes habite blak; but nathelees,   170
Right as our firste lettre is now an A,
In beautee first so stood she, makelees; [13]
Hir goodly looking gladede al the prees.[14]
Nas [15] never seyn thing to ben preysed derre,[16]
Nor under cloude blak so bright a sterre   175

As was Criseyde, as folk seyde everichoon [17]
That hir bihelden in hir blake wede; [18]
And yet she stood ful lowe and stille alloon,
Bihinden othere folk, in litel brede,[19]

And neigh the dore, ay under shames drede,
Simple of atyr, and debonaire of chere,   181
With ful assured loking and manere.

This Troilus, as he was wont to gyde
His yonge knightes, ladde hem up and doun
In thilke [1] large temple on every syde,   185
Biholding ay the ladyes of the toun,
Now here, now there, for no devocioun
Hadde he to noon, to reven [2] him his reste,
But gan to preyse and lakken [3] whom him leste.[4]

And in his walk full fast he gan to wayten [5]
If knight or squyer of his companye   191
Gan for to syke,[6] or lete his eyen bayten [7]
On any woman that he coude aspye;
He wolde smyle, and holden it folye,   194
And seye him thus, "God wot, she slepeth softe
For love of thee, whan thou tornest ful ofte.

"I have herd told, pardieux, of your livinge,
Ye lovers, and your lewede [8] observaunces,
And which [9] a labour folk han [10] in winninge
Of love, and in the keping which [9] dou- taunces; [11]
And whan your preye is lost, wo and pen- aunces;
O verrey foles! nyce [12] and blinde be ye;   202
Ther nis [13] not oon can war [14] by other be."

---

[1] use [2] gave [3] like [4] it happened [5] meadow
[6] spring [7] sweet [8] their [9] of the Palladium [10] especially [11] greatest [12] yea [13] peerless [14] crowd [15] was
not [16] more dearly [17] every one [18] garment [19] space

[1] that same [2] take away [3] blame [4] it pleased
[5] observe [6] sigh [7] feast [8] silly [9] what sort of [10] have
[11] perplexities [12] foolish [13] is not [14] cautious

And with that word he gan cast up the browe,
Ascaunces,[1] "Lo! is this nought wysly
    spoken?"
At which the god of love gan loken rowe [2]
Right for despyt, and shoop [3] for to ben
    wroken; [4]   207
He kidde [5] anoon his bowe nas not broken;
For sodeynly he hit him at the fulle; —
And yet as proud a pekok can he pulle! [6]

O blinde world, O blinde entencioun! [7]   211
How ofte falleth al theffect [8] contraire
Of surquidrye [9] and foul presumpcioun;
For caught is proud, and caught is debonaire.
This Troilus is clomben on the staire,   215
And litel weneth that he moot descenden.
But al-day [10] falleth thing that foles ne
    wenden.[11]

As proude Bayard ginneth for to skippe
Out of the wey, so priketh him his corn,[12]
Til he a lash have of the longe whippe,   220
Than thenketh he, "Though I praunce al
    biforn,
First in the trays, ful fat and newe shorn,
Yet am I but an hors, and horses lawe
I moot endure, and with my feres [13] drawe."

*   *   *   *   *   *

From BOOK II

*   *   *   *   *   *

With this he [14] took his leve, and hoom he
    wente;
And lord, how he was glad and wel bigoon! [15]
Criseyde aroos, no lenger she ne stente,[16]
But straught in-to hir closet wente anoon,
And sette here [17] doun as stille as any stoon,
And every word gan up and doun to winde,
That he hadde seyd, as it com hir to minde;

And wex somdel [18] astonied in hir thought,
Right for the newe cas; but whan that she
Was ful avysed,[19] tho [20] fond she right nought
Of peril, why she oughte afered be.   606
For man may love, of possibilitee,
A womman so his herte may to-breste,[21]
And she nought love ayein, but-if hir leste.[22]

---

[1] as if to say [2] cruel [3] planned [4] avenged [5] made
known [6] pluck [7] purpose [8] result [9] overweening
[10] constantly [11] active [15] happy [16] delayed [17] her [18] some-
[14] i.e. Pandarus [15] happy [16] delayed [17] her [18] somewhat [19] had considered thoroughly [20] then [21] burst
[22] unless it please her

But as she sat allone and thoughte thus,   610
Thascry [1] aroos at skarmish al with-oute,
And men cryde in the strete, "See, Troilus
Hath right now put to flight the Grekes
    route!" [2]
With that gan al hir meynee [3] for to shoute,
"A! go we see, caste up the latis [4] wyde; 615
For thurgh this strete he moot [5] to palays
    ryde;

"For other wey is fro the yate [6] noon
Of Dardanus, ther [7] open is the cheyne." [8]
With that come he and al his folk anoon
An esy pas rydinge, in routes [9] tweyne,   620
Right as his happy day was, sooth to seyne,
For which men say, may nought disturbed be
That shal bityden of necessitee.

This Troilus sat on his baye stede,
Al armed, save his heed, ful richely,   625
And wounded was his hors, and gan to blede,
On whiche he rood a pas, ful softely;
But swych a knightly sighte, trewely,
As was on him, was nought, with-outen faile,
To loke on Mars, that god is of batayle.   630

So lyk a man of armes and a knight
He was to seen, fulfild of heigh prowesse;
For bothe he hadde a body and a might
To doon that thing, as wel as hardinesse;
And eek to seen him in his gere [10] him dresse,
So fresh, so yong, so weldy [11] semed he,   636
It was an heven up-on him for to see.

His helm to-hewen [12] was in twenty places,
That by a tissew heng, his bak bihinde,
His sheld to-dasshed was with swerdes and
    maces,   640
In which men mighte many an arwe finde
That thirled [13] hadde horn and nerf [14] and
    rinde; [15]
And ay the peple cryde, "Here cometh our
    joye,
And, next his brother, holdere up of Troye!"

For which he wex a litel reed for shame,   645
When he the peple up-on him herde cryen,
That to biholde it was a noble game,
How sobreliche he caste doun his yen.
Cryseyda gan al his chere aspyen,

---

[1] the shout [2] crowd [3] household [4] lattice [5] must
[6] gate [7] where [8] chain [9] companies [10] gear, equipment [11] active [12] cut through [13] pierced [14] sinew
[15] hide

And leet [1] so softe it in hir herte sinke,   650
That to hir-self she seyde, "Who yaf [2] me
   drinke?" [3]

For of hir owene thought she wex al reed,
Remembringe hir right thus, "Lo, this is he
Which that myn uncle swereth he moot be
   deed, [4]
But [5] I on him have mercy and pitee;"   655
And with that thought, for pure a-shamed, [6]
   she
Gan in hir heed to pulle, and that as faste,
Whyl he and al the peple for-by paste.

And gan to caste and rolen up and doun
With-inne hir thought his excellent prowesse,
And his estat, and also his renoun,   661
His wit, his shap, and eek his gentillesse;
But most hir favour was for [7] his distresse
Was al for hir, and thoughte it was a routhe [8]
To sleen [9] swich oon, if that he mente trouthe.

Now mighte some envyous jangle thus,   666
"This was a sodeyn love, how mighte it be
That she so lightly lovede Troilus
Right for the firste sighte; ye, pardee?"
Now who-so seyeth so, mote [10] he never
   thee ! [11]   670
For everything, a ginning [12] hath it nede
Er al be wrought, with-outen any drede.

For I sey nought that she so sodeynly
Yaf [2] him her love, but that she gan enclyne
To lyk him first, and I have told yow why;
And after that, his manhood and his pyne 676
Made love with-inne hir herte for to myne,
For which, by proces and by good servyse,
He gat hir love, and in no sodeyn wyse.

  *   *   *   *   *   *   *

From Book V

  *   *   *   *   *   *

The morwe [13] com, and goostly [14] for to speke,
This Diomede is come un-to Criseyde,   1031
And shortly, lest that ye my tale breke,
So wel he for him-selve spak and seyde,
That alle hir sykes [15] sore adoun he leyde.
And fynally, the sothe for to seyne,   1035
He refte [16] hir of the grete [17] of al hir payne.

[1] let [2] gave [3] a potion [4] must die [5] unless [6] for
very shame [7] because [8] pity [9] slay [10] may [11] thrive
[12] beginning [13] morrow [14] spiritually [15] sighs [16] deprived [17] great (most)

And after this the story telleth us,
That she him yaf [1] the faire baye stede,
The which she ones wan of Troilus;
And eek [2] a broche (and that was litel nede)
That Troilus was, she yaf [1] this Diomede.
And eek, the bet [3] from sorwe him to releve,
She made him were [4] a pencel [5] of hir sleve.
                   1043

I finde eek in the stories elles-where,
Whan through the body hurt was Diomede
Of [6] Troilus, tho weep [7] she many a tere,
Whan that she saugh his wyde woundes
   blede;   1047
And that she took to kepen him good hede;
And for to hele him of his sorwes smerte,
Men seyn, I not, [8] that she yaf him hir herte.

But trewely, the story telleth us,   1051
Ther made never womman more wo
Than she, whan that she falsed Troilus.
She seyde, "Allas ! for now is clene a-go [9]
My name of trouthe in love, for ever-mo !
For I have falsed oon the gentileste   1056
That ever was, and oon the worthieste !

"Allas, of me, un-to the worldes ende,
Shal neither been y-writen nor y-songe
No good word, for thise bokes wol me shende. [10]
O, rolled shal I been on many a tonge;   1061
Through-out the world my belle shal be ronge;
And wommen most wol hate me of alle.
Allas, that swich a cas me sholde falle !

"They wol seyn, in as muche as in me is
I have hem [11] don dishonour, weylawey ! 1066
Al be I not the firste that dide amis,
What helpeth that to do [12] my blame awey?
But sin [13] I see there is no bettre way,
And that to late is now for me to rewe, [14] 1070
To Diomede algate [15] I wol be trewe.

"But, Troilus, sin [13] I no better may,
And sin [13] that thus departen ye and I,
Yet preye I God, so yeve [16] yow right good
   day
As for the gentileste, trewely,   1075
That ever I say, [17] to serven feithfully,
And best can ay his lady [18] honour kepe:" —
And with that word she brast [19] anon [20] to
   wepe.

[1] gave [2] also [3] better [4] wear [5] pencil, small flag
[6] by [7] then wept [8] know not [9] gone [10] shame
[11] them [12] put [13] since [14] repent [15] at any rate
[16] give [17] saw [18] lady's [19] burst [20] at once

"And certes, yow ne haten shal I never,
And freendes love, that shal ye han of me,
And my good word, al [1] mighte I liven ever.
And trewely, I wolde sory be   1082
For to seen yow in adversitee.
And giltelees, I woot [2] wel, I yow leve; [3]
But al shal passe; and thus take I my
    leve."   1085

But trewely, how longe it was bitwene,
That she for-sook him for this Diomede,
Ther is non auctor telleth it, I wene. [4]
Take every man now to his bokes hede;
He shal no terme finden, out of drede. [5]   1090
For though that he bigan to wowe hir sone,
Er he hir wan, yet was ther more to done. [6]

THE CANTERBURY TALES

From THE PROLOGUE

Whan that Aprille with hise shoures soote [7]
The droghte of Marche hath perced to the
    roote
And bathed every veyne [8] in swich [9] licour
Of which vertu engendred is the flour;
Whan Zephirus eek with his swete breeth   5
Inspired hath in every holt [10] and heeth
The tendre croppes, [11] and the yonge sonne
Hath in the Ram his halfe cours [12] y-ronne,
And smale foweles [13] maken melodye
That slepen al the nyght with open eye, —
So priketh hem Nature in hir corages, [14] —   11
Thanne longen folk to goon on pilgrimages,
And palmeres for to seken straunge strondes, [15]
To ferne halwes, [16] kowthe [17] in sondry londes;
And specially, from every shires ende   15
Of Engelond, to Caunterbury they wende,
The hooly blisful martir for to seke,
That hem hath holpen whan that they were
    seeke.
Bifil [18] that in that seson on a day,
In Southwerk at the Tabard as I lay,   20
Redy to wenden on my pilgrymage
To Caunterbury with ful devout corage, [19]
At nyght was come into that hostelrye
Wel [20] nyne-and-twenty in a compaignye,
Of sondry folk, by aventure [21] y-falle   25

In felaweshipe, and pilgrimes were they alle,
That toward Caunterbury wolden ryde.
The chambres and the stables weren wyde,
And wel we weren esed atte beste. [1]
And, shortly, whan the sonne was to reste, 30
So hadde I spoken with hem everychon,
That I was of hir felaweshipe anon,
And made forward [2] erly for to ryse,
To take oure wey, ther-as I yow devyse. [3]
    But nathelees, whil I have tyme and space,
Er that I ferther in this tale pace,   36
Me thynketh it accordaunt to resoun
To telle yow al the condicioun [4]
Of ech of hem, so as it semed me,
And whiche [5] they weren and of what degree,
And eek in what array that they were inne;
And at a knyght than wol I first bigynne. 42
    A Knyght ther was and that a worthy man,
That fro the tyme that he first bigan
To riden out, he lovede chivalrie,   45
Trouthe and honour, fredom and curteisie.
Ful worthy was he in his lordes werre,
And thereto [6] hadde he riden, no man ferre, [7]
As wel in Cristendom as in hethenesse,
And ever honoured for his worthynesse.   50
At Alisaundre he was whan it was wonne;
Ful ofte tyme he hadde the bord bigonne [8]
Aboven alle nacions in Pruce. [9]
In Lettow [10] hadde he reysed [11] and in Ruce, [12]
No Cristen man so ofte of his degree. [13]   55
In Gernade [14] at the seege eek hadde he be
Of Algezir, and riden in Belmarye. [15]
At Lyeys [16] was he, and at Satalye, [16]
Whan they were wonne; and in the Grete
    See [17]
At many a noble armee [18] hadde he be.   60
    At mortal batailles hadde he been fiftene,
And foughten for oure feith at Tramyssene [16]
In lystes thries, and ay slayn his foo.
This ilke [19] worthy knyght hadde been also
Somtyme with the lord of Palatye [16]   65
Agayn [20] another hethen in Turkye;
And evermoore he hadde a sovereyn prys. [21]
And though that he were worthy, he was wys,
And of his port [22] as meeke as is a mayde.
He never yet no vileynye [23] ne sayde   70

---

[1] although [2] know [3] abandon [4] think [5] without
doubt [6] do [7] showers sweet [8] vein [9] such [10] forest
[11] twigs [12] *In April the sun's course lies partly in the
zodiacal sign of the Ram and partly in that of the Bull.*
[13] birds [14] in their hearts [15] foreign strands [16] distant shrines [17] known [18] it happened [19] heart [20] full
[21] chance

[1] made comfortable [2] agreement [3] describe
[4] character [5] what sort [6] besides [7] farther [8] begun
the board (sat at the head of the table) [9] Prussia
[10] Lithuania [11] made expeditions [12] Russia [13] rank
[14] Granada [15] *A district in Africa.* [16] *Places in
Asia Minor.* [17] Mediterranean [18] armed expedition
[19] same [20] against [21] high esteem [22] bearing [23] dis-
courtesy

In al his lyf unto no maner wight.
He was a verray, parfit, gentil knyght.
  But for to tellen yow of his array,
His hors were goode, but he was nat gay;
Of fustian [1] he wered a gypon [2]   75
Al bismotered [3] with his habergeon; [4]
For he was late y-come from his viage, [5]
And wente for to doon his pilgrymage.
  With hym ther was his sone, a yong Squier,
A lovyere and a lusty bacheler,   80
With lokkes crulle, [6] as [7] they were leyd in
    presse.
Of twenty yeer of age he was, I gesse.
Of his stature he was of evene lengthe, [8]
And wonderly delyvere [9] and greet of
    strengthe;
And he hadde been somtyme in chyvachye, [10]
In Flaundres, in Artoys and Pycardye,   86
And born hym weel, as of so litel space,
In hope to stonden in his lady [11] grace.
Embrouded was he, as it were a meede [12]
Al ful of fresshe floures whyte and reede;   90
Syngynge he was or floytynge [13] al the day;
He was as fressh as is the monthe of May.
Short was his gowne, with sleves longe and
    wyde;
Wel coude he sitte on hors, and faire ryde;
He coude songes make and wel endite, [14]   95
Juste and eek daunce and weel purtreye and
    write.
So hoote he lovede that by nyghtertale [15]
He sleep namoore than dooth a nyghtyngale.
Curteis he was, lowely and servysable,
And carf [16] biforn his fader at the table.   100
  A Yeman [17] hadde he, [18] and servants namo [19]
At that tyme, for hym liste ride soo;
And he was clad in cote and hood of grene;
A sheef [20] of pocok [21] arwes bright and kene
Under his belt he bar ful thriftily —   105
Wel coude he dresse [22] his takel [23] yemanly;
His arwes drouped noght with fetheres
    lowe [24] —
And in his hand he bar a myghty bowe.
A not-heed [25] hadde he with a broun visage.
Of woodcraft wel koude he al the usage. 110
Upon his arm he bar a gay bracer,
And by his syde a swerd and a bokeler, [26]

And on that oother syde a gay daggere
Harneised wel and sharpe as point of spere;
A Cristofre [1] on his brest of silver sheene;
An horn he bar, the bawdryk [2] was of grene.
A forster was he soothly, as I gesse.   117
  Ther was also a Nonne, a Prioresse,
That of hir smylyng was ful symple and
    coy; [3]
Hire gretteste ooth was but by Seïnt Loy, [4]
And she was cleped [5] madame Eglentyne. 121
Ful weel she songe the service dyvyne,
Entuned in hir nose ful semely;
And Frenssh she spak ful faire and fetisly [6]
After the scole of Stratford-atte-Bowe, [7]   125
For Frenssh of Parys was to hire unknowe.
At mete wel y-taught was she with-alle,
She leet no morsel from hir lippes falle.
Ne wette hir fyngres in hir sauce depe;
Wel coude she carie a morsel and wel kepe
That no drope ne fille upon hire breste.   131
In curteisie was set ful muchel hir leste. [8]
Hire over-lippe wyped she so clene,
That in hir coppe ther was no ferthyng sene
Of grece, whan she dronken hadde hir
    draughte.
Ful semely after hir mete she raughte, [9]   136
And sikerly [10] she was of greet desport, [11]
And ful plesaunt and amyable of port, [12]
And peyned hire [13] to countrefete [14] cheere [15]
Of court, and been estatlich [16] of manere, 140
And to ben holden digne [17] of reverence.
But, for to speken of hire conscience,
She was so charitable and so pitous
She wolde wepe if that she saugh [18] a mous
Caught in a trappe, if it were deed or bledde.
Of smale houndes [19] hadde she, that she fedde
With rosted flessh, or milk and wastel-breed; [20]
But sore wepte she, if oon of hem were deed, [21]
Or if men [22] smoot it with a yerde [23] smerte; [24]
And al was conscience and tendre herte.   150
Ful semyly [25] hir wympul [26] pynched [27] was;
Hire nose tretys, [28] hir eyen greye as glas,
Hir mouth ful smal and ther-to softe and reed;
But sikerly she hadde a fair forheed;
It was almoost a spanne brood I trowe,   155
For, hardily, [29] she was nat undergrowe.

---

[1] an image of his patron saint [2] cord [3] quiet
[4] By St. Eligius, *a very mild oath* [5] named
[6] skilfully [7] *A convent near London.* [8] pleasure
[9] reached [10] certainly [11] good humour [12] bearing
[13] exerted herself [14] imitate [15] fashions [16] dignified
[17] worthy [18] saw [19] little dogs [20] cake bread [21] died
[22] any one [23] stick [24] sharply [25] neatly [26] face-cloth
[27] pinched, plaited [28] well-formed [29] certainly

---

[1] coarse cloth [2] shirt [3] soiled [4] coat of mail
[5] voyage [6] curly [7] as if [8] medium height [9] active
[10] cavalry expeditions [11] lady's [12] meadow [13] whistling [14] compose [15] night-time [16] carved [17] yeoman
[18] *the knight* [19] no more [20] bundle of twenty-four
[21] peacock [22] take care of [23] equipment [24] worn and
clipped short [25] closely cut hair [26] small shield

Ful fetys [1] was hir cloke, as I was war; [2]
Of smal coral aboute hire arm she bar
A peire [3] of bedes gauded [4] al with grene,
And ther-on heng a brooch of gold ful sheene, [5]
On which ther was first write a crowned A,
And after *Amor vincit omnia.*   162
  Another Nonne with hire hadde she,
That was hire chapeleyne; and Preestes thre.
  A Monk ther was, a fair for the maistrie, [6]
An outridere that lovede venerie, [7]   166
A manly man, to been an abbot able.
Ful many a deyntee [8] hors hadde he in stable,
And whan he rood, men myghte his brydel
    heere
Gynglen in a whistlynge wynd as cleere   170
And eek as loude as dooth the chapel-belle
Ther-as this lord was kepere of the celle. [9]
The reule of Seint Maure or of Seint Beneit,
By-cause that it was old and som-del streit [10] —
This ilke monk leet olde thynges pace   175
And heeld after the newe world the space.
He yaf nat of that text a pulled [11] hen
That seith that hunters beth nat hooly men,
Ne that a monk when he is recchelees [12]
Is likned til a fissh that is waterlees;   180
This is to seyn, a monk out of his cloystre.
But thilke text heeld he nat worth an oystre;
And I seyde his opinioun was good;
What sholde he studie and make hym-selven
    wood, [13]
Upon a book in cloystre alwey to poure,   185
Or swynken [14] with his handes and laboure
As Austyn bit? [15]   How shal the world be
    served?
Lat Austyn have his swynk [14] to him reserved.
Therfore he was a pricasour [16] aright;
Grehoundes he hadde, as swift as fowel in flight:
Of prikyng [17] and of huntyng for the hare 191
Was al his lust, [18] for no cost wolde he spare.
I seigh [19] his sleves purfiled [20] at the hond
With grys, [21] and that the fyneste of a lond;
And for to festne his hood under his chyn 195
He hadde of gold y-wroght a curious pyn;
A love-knotte in the gretter ende ther was.
His heed was balled, that shoon as any glas,
And eek his face as it hadde been enoynt.
He was a lord ful fat and in good poynt; [22]

Hise eyen stepe [1] and rollynge in his heed,
That stemed [2] as a forneys of a leed; [3]
His bootes souple, his hors in greet estaat.
Now certeinly he was a fair prelaat.
He was nat pale, as a forpyned [4] goost;   205
A fat swan loved he best of any roost.
His palfrey was as broun as is a berye.
  A Frere ther was, a wantown and a merye,
A lymytour, [5] a ful solempne [6] man.
In alle the ordres foure [7] is noon that can [8]
So muchel of daliaunce and fair langage;   211
He hadde maad ful many a mariage
Of yonge wommen at his owene cost.
Unto his ordre he was a noble post;
Ful wel biloved and famulier was he   215
With frankeleyns [9] over-al in his contree;
And eek with worthy wommen of the toun,
For he hadde power of confessioun,
As seyde hym-self, moore than a curat,
For of his ordre he was licenciat.   220
Ful swetely herde he confessioun,
And plesaunt was his absolucioun.
He was an esy man to yeve penaunce
Ther-as [10] he wiste [11] to have a good pit-
    aunce; [12]
For unto a povre ordre for to yive   225
Is signe that a man is wel y-shryve.
For, if he [13] yaf, he [14] dorste make avaunt
He wiste that a man was repentaunt;
For many a man so harde is of his herte
He may nat wepe al-thogh hym soore smerte.
Therfore instede of wepynge and preyeres
Men moote yeve silver to the povre freres.
His typet was ay farsed [15] full of knyves   233
And pynnes, for to yeven faire wyves.
And certeinly he hadde a murye [16] note;   235
Wel coude he synge and pleyen on a rote; [17]
Of yeddynges [18] he bar outrely the pris.
His nekke whit was as the flour-de-lys;
Ther-to he strong was as a champioun.
He knew the tavernes well in every toun   240
And everich hostiler and tappestere [19]
Bet [20] than a lazar [21] or a beggestere; [22]
For unto swich a worthy man as he
Acorded nat, as by his facultee,
To have with sike lazars aqueyntaunce;   245
It is nat honeste, [23] it may nat avaunce

---

[1] well-made   [2] as I perceived   [3] set   [4] *Every
eleventh bead was a large green one.*   [5] beautiful
[6] an extremely fine one   [7] hunting   [8] fine   [9] *A
cell is a branch monastery.*   [10] strict   [11] plucked
[12] vagabond   [13] crazy   [14] work   [15] bids   [16] hunter
[17] tracking   [18] pleasure   [19] saw   [20] edged   [21] grey fur
[22] *en bon point,* fleshy

[1] large   [2] gleamed   [3] cauldron   [4] tortured to death
[5] licensed to beg in a certain district   [6] imposing
[7] *Dominican, Franciscan, Carmelite and Austin
friars.*   [8] knows   [9] rich farmers   [10] where   [11] knew
[12] pittance, gift   [13] *the man*   [14] *the friar*   [15] stuffed
[16] merry   [17] fiddle   [18] popular songs   [19] bar-maid
[20] better   [21] beggar   [22] female beggar   [23] becoming

For to deelen with no swiche poraille,[1]
But al with riche and selleres of vitaille,
And over-al,[2] ther-as [3] profit sholde arise
Curteis he was and lowely of servyse.   250
Ther nas no man nowher so vertuous ; [4]
He was the beste beggere in his hous,
For thogh a wydwe hadde noght a sho,[5]
So plesaunt was his *In principio*,[6]
Yet wolde he have a ferthyng [7] er he wente :
His purchas [8] was wel bettre than his rente.[9]
And rage he koude, as it were right a whelpe.[10]
In love-dayes [11] ther coude he muchel helpe,
For there he was nat lyk a cloysterer
With a thredbare cope, as is a povre scoler,
But he was lyk a maister, or a pope ;   261
Of double worstede was his semi-cope,[12]
That rounded as a belle, out of the presse.[13]
Somwhat he lipsed for his wantownesse,[14]
To make his Englissh swete upon his tonge ;
And in his harpyng, whan that he hadde songe,   266
Hise eyen twynkled in his heed aryght
As doon the sterres in the frosty nyght.
This worthy lymytour was cleped Huberd.

    A Marchant was ther with a forked berd,
In mottelee,[15] and hye on horse he sat ;   271
Upon his heed a Flaundrish bever hat,
His botes clasped faire and fetisly.[16]
His resons [17] spak he ful solempnely,[18]
Souning [19] alway thencrees [20] of his winning.
He wolde the see were kept for anything [21]
Betwixe Middelburgh and Orewelle.
Wel coude he in eschaunge [22] sheeldes [23] selle.
This worthy man ful well his wit bisette ; [24]
Ther wiste [25] no wight that he was in dette,
So estatly was he of his governaunce   281
With his bargaynes and with his chevisaunce.[26]
For sothe he was a worthy man withalle,
But sooth to seyn,[27] I noot [28] how men him calle.

    A Clerk ther was of Oxenford also   285
That unto logyk hadde longe y-go.
As leene was his hors as is a rake,
And he nas nat right fat, I undertake,

[1] poor folk [2] everywhere [3] where [4] full of good qualities [5] shoe [6] *St. John* i, 1, *used as a greeting.* [7] bit [8] gettings [9] what he paid for his begging privileges *or* his regular income [10] puppy [11] arbitration days [12] short cape [13] *the press in which the semi-cope was kept.* [14] jollity [15] a sober grey [16] neatly [17] remarks, declarations [18] pompously [19] sounding, proclaiming [20] the increase [21] at any cost [22] exchange [23] French coins, *écus* [24] employed [25] knew [26] borrowing [27] say [28] don't know

But looked holwe [1] and ther-to [2] sobrely.
Ful thredbare was his overeste courtepy,[3]   290
For he hadde geten hym yet no benefice,
Ne was so worldly for to have office ;
For hym was levere [4] have at his beddes heed
Twenty bookes clad in blak or reed
Of Aristotle and his philosophie   295
Than robes riche, or fithele,[5] or gay sautrie.[5]
But al be that he was a philosophre,
Yet hadde he but litel gold in cofre ;
But al that he myghte of his freendes hente
On bookes and his lernynge he it spente,   300
And bisily gan for the soules preye
Of hem that gaf hym wher-with to scoleye.[6]
Of studie took he moost cure [7] and moost heede ;
Noght o word spak he moore than was neede,
And that was seyd in forme and reverence,
And short and quyk and ful of hy sentence.[8]
Sownynge in [9] moral vertu was his speche,
And gladly wolde he lerne and gladly teche.

    A Sergeant of the Lawe, war [10] and wys,
That often hadde been at the parvys,[11]   310
Ther was also, ful riche of excellence.
Discreet he was, and of greet reverence —
He semed swich, his wordes weren so wyse.
Justice he was ful often in assyse,[12]
By patente, and by pleyn [13] commissioun ; 315
For his science, and for his heigh renoun,
Of fees and robes hadde he many oon.
So greet a purchasour [14] was nowher noon ;
Al was fee simple to him in effect,
His purchasing mighte nat been infect.[15]   320
Nowher so bisy a man as he ther nas,[16]
And yet he semed bisier than he was.
In termes hadde he caas [17] and domes [18] alle
That from the tyme of king William were falle.
Therto he coude endyte and make a thing,[19]
Ther coude no wight pinche at [20] his wrytyng ;
And every statut coude he pleyn [21] by rote.[22]
He rood but hoomly in a medlee [23] cote
Girt with a ceint [24] of silk, with barres smale ;
Of his array telle I no lenger tale.   330

    A Frankeleyn [25] was in his compaignye ;
Whit was his berd as is the dayesye ;

[1] hollow [2] besides [3] outer short coat [4] he had rather [5] musical instrument [6] go to school [7] care [8] meaning [9] tending to [10] cautious [11] the porch of St. Paul's, where lawyers met clients [12] court of assize [13] full [14] conveyancer [15] invalidated [16] was not [17] cases [18] decisions [19] compose and draw up a document [20] find a defect in [21] fully [22] by heart [23] sober grey [24] girdle [25] rich landowner

Of his complexioun [1] he was sangwyn.
Wel loved he by the morwe [2] a sope [3] in
wyn;
To lyven in delit was evere his wone, [4]   335
For he was Epicurus owne sone,
That heeld opinioun that pleyn delit
Was verraily felicitee parfit.
An housholdere, and that a greet, was he;
Seint Julian [5] he was in his contree;   340
His breed, his ale, was alwey after oon; [6]
A bettre envyned [7] man was no-wher noon.
Withoute bake-mete [8] was nevere his hous,
Of fissh and flessh, and that so plentevous
It snewed [9] in his hous of mete and drynke,
Of alle deyntees that men coude thynke.   346
After the sondry sesons of the yeer,
So chaunged he his mete and his soper.
Ful many a fat partrich hadde he in muwe, [10]
And many a breem [11] and many a luce [11] in
stuwe. [12]   350
Wo was his cook but-if [13] his sauce were
Poynaunt and sharpe, and redy al his geere.
His table dormant [14] in his halle alway
Stood redy covered al the longe day.
At sessiouns ther was he lord and sire;   355
Ful ofte tyme he was knyght of the shire.
An anlaas, [15] and a gipser [16] al of silk
Heeng at his girdel whit as morne milk.
A shirreve hadde he been and a countour; [17]
Was no-wher such a worthy vavasour. [18]   360
   An haberdassher [19] and a carpenter,
A webbe, [20] a dyere, and a tapicer, [21]
And they were clothed alle in o liveree, [22]
Of a solempne and greet fraternitee.
Ful fresh and newe hir gere [23] apyked [24] was;
Hir knyves were y-chaped [25] noght with bras,
But al with silver; wroght ful clene and weel
Hir girdles and hir pouches everydeel.
Wel semed ech of hem a fair burgeys,
To sitten in a yeldhalle [26] on a deys. [27]   370
Everich, for the wisdom that he can, [28]
Was shaply for to been an alderman;
For catel [29] hadde they ynogh and rente, [30]
And eek hir wyves wolde it wel assente;

And elles certein were they to blame.   375
It is ful fair to been y-clept [1] *ma dame*,
And goon to vigilyës [2] al bifore,
And have a mantel roialliche y-bore.
   A Cook they hadde with hem, [3] for the
nones [4]
To boille chiknes with the mary-bones   380
And poudre-marchant tart [5] and galingale. [6]
Wel coude he knowe a draughte of London
ale.
He coude roste, and sethe, [7] and broille, and
frye,
Maken mortreux, [8] and wel bake a pye.
But greet harm was it, as it thoughte me, 385
That on his shine [9] a mormal [10] hadde he.
For blankmanger, [11] that made he with the
beste.
   A Shipman was ther, wonynge [12] fer by
weste;
For aught I woot [13] he was of Dertemouthe.
He rood upon a rouncy [14] as he couthe, [15]   390
In a gowne of faldyng [16] to the knee.
A daggere hangynge on a laas [17] hadde he
Aboute his nekke under his arm adoun.
The hoote somer hadde maad his hewe al
broun.
And certeinly he was a good felawe; [18]   395
Ful many a draughte of wyn hadde he i-
drawe
Fro Burdeuxward, whil that the chapman [19]
sleep.
Of nyce conscience took he no keep. [20]
If that he faught, and hadde the hyer hond,
By water he sente hem hoom to every
lond. [21]   400
But of his craft to rekene wel his tydes,
His stremes [22] and his daungers hym bisides,
His herberwe and his moone, his lodemenage, [23]
Ther nas noon swich from Hulle to Cartage.
Hardy he was, and wys to undertake; [24]   405
With many a tempest hadde his berd been
shake;
He knew wel alle the havenes, as they were,
From Gootlond [25] to the Cape of Fynystere,

---

[1] temperament [2] in the morning [3] sop [4] custom
[5] patron saint of hospitality [6] always of the same
quality [7] provided with wines [8] pasties [9] snowed
[10] coop [11] a kind of fish [12] pond [13] unless [14] a permanent table [15] knife [16] pouch [17] treasurer [18] landholder [19] keeper of a shop for hats or furnishings
[20] weaver [21] upholsterer [22] one uniform [23] apparel
[24] trimmed [25] sheathed [26] guild-hall [27] dais [28] knows
[29] property [30] income

[1] called [2] meetings on the eve of saints' days
[3] them [4] of the right sort, very skilful [5] a tart
flavouring powder [6] a root for flavouring [7] boil
[8] chowders [9] shin [10] sore [11] minced capon with
sugar, cream, and flour [12] dwelling [13] know [14] hackney [15] as well as he could [16] cheap cloth [17] lace,
cord [18] goodfellow = rascal [19] merchant [20] heed
[21] threw them into the sea [22] currents [23] steersman-
ship [24] skilful in his plans [25] Denmark

And every cryke[1] in Britaigne and in
    Spayne.
His barge y-cleped was the Maudelayne. 410
  With us ther was a Doctour of Phisyk,
In al this world ne was ther noon him lyk
To speke of [2] phisik and of surgerye;
For he was grounded in astronomye.
He kepte his pacient a ful greet del   415
In houres, by his magik naturel.
Wel coude he fortunen the ascendent
Of his images for his pacient.[3]
He knew the cause of everich maladye,
Were it of hoot or cold, or moiste, or drye,
And where engendred, and of what humour; [4]
He was a verrey,[5] parfit practisour.
The cause y-knowe, and of his harm the rote,[6]
Anon he yaf the seke man his bote.[7]
Ful redy hadde he his apothecaries,   425
To sende him drogges and his letuaries,[8]
For ech of hem made other for to winne;
Hir frendschipe nas nat newe to biginne.
Wel knew he the olde Esculapius,[9]
And Deiscorides, and eek Rufus;   430
Old Ypocras, Haly, and Galien;
Serapion, Razis, and Avicen;
Averrois, Damascien, and Constantyn;
Bernard, and Gatesden, and Gilbertyn.
Of his diete mesurable was he,   435
For it was of no superfluitee,
But of greet norissing and digestible.
His studie was but litel on the Bible.
In sangwin [10] and in pers [11] he clad was al,
Lyned with taffata [12] and with sendal; [12]   440
And yet he was but esy [13] of dispence; [14]
He kepte that he wan in pestilence.[15]
For gold in phisik is a cordial,[16]
Therfor he lovede gold in special.
  A Good-wif was ther of biside Bathe,   445
But she was som-del deef and that was
    scathe.[17]
Of clooth-makyng she hadde swich an haunt [18]
She passed hem of Ypres and of Gaunt.
In al the parisshe, wif ne was ther noon
That to the offrynge bifore hire sholde goon;

And if ther dide, certeyn so wrooth was she
That she was out of alle charitee.   452
Hir coverchiefs ful fyne weren of ground;
I dorste swere they weyeden ten pound,
That on a Sonday weren upon hir heed.   455
Hir hosen weren of fyn scarlet reed,
Ful streite y-teyd, and shoes ful moyste [1]
    and newe.
Boold was hir face and fair and reed of hewe.
She was a worthy womman al hir lyve;
Housbondes at chirche dore she hadde fyve,
Withouten oother compaignye in youthe, 461
But ther-of nedeth nat to speke as nowthe.[2]
And thries hadde she been at Jerusalem;
She hadde passed many a straunge strem;
At Rome she hadde been and at Boloigne,
In Galice at Seint Jame, and at Cologne;466
She coude [3] muche of wandrynge by the
    weye:
Gat-tothed [4] was she, soothly for to seye.
Upon an amblere esily she sat,
Y-wympled [5] wel, and on her heed an hat 470
As brood as is a bokeler or a targe; [6]
A foot-mantel [7] aboute hir hipes large,
And on hire feet a paire of spores sharpe.
In felaweshipe wel coude she laughe and
    carpe;   474
Of remedies of love she knew per chaunce,[8]
For she coude of that art the olde daunce.[9]
  A good man was ther of religioun,
And was a povre Persoun of a toun;
But riche he was of hooly thoght and werk;
He was also a lerned man, a clerk,   480
That Cristes gospel trewely wolde preche.
Hise parisshens devoutly wolde he teche;
Benygne he was and wonder diligent,
And in adversitee ful pacient;
And swich he was y-preved [10] ofte sithes.[11] 485
Ful looth were hym to cursen [12] for hise tithes,
But rather wolde he yeven, out of doute,
Unto his povre parisshens aboute,
Of his offryng and eek of his substaunce.
He coude in litel thyng have suffisaunce. 490
Wyd was his parisshe, and houses fer asonder,
But he ne lafte [13] nat for reyn ne thonder
In siknesse nor in meschief to visite
The ferreste [14] in his parisshe, muche and
    lite,[15]

---

[1] creek, inlet [2] in regard to, if one is speaking of
[3] *For ll. 415–18, on the use of astrology in treating
patients, see the* Notes. [4] *For the* humours *as
related to diseases, see the* Notes. [5] true [6] root,
cause [7] remedy [8] medicinal syrups [9] *The men
named in ll. 420–34 were famous writers on medicine, ancient and modern.* [10] red [11] blue [12] light silk
[13] moderate [14] expenditure [15] the plague [16] remedy
for heart-disease [17] harm [18] skill

[1] soft [2] at present [3] knew [4] teeth set wide apart,
a sign that one will travel. [5] with a wimple about
her face [6] shield [7] riding-skirt [8] doubtless [9] *This
is a slang phrase.* [10] proved [11] times [12] excommuni-
cate [13] neglected [14] farthest [15] rich and poor

Upon his feet, and in his hand a staf. 495
This noble ensample to his sheepe he gaf,
That firste he wroghte and afterward he
taughte.
Out of the gospel he tho [1] wordes caughte,
And this figure he added eek [2] therto,
That if gold ruste, what shal iren doo? 500
For if a preest be foul, on whom we truste,
No wonder is a lewed [3] man to ruste;
And shame it is, if a prest take keep, [4]
A [filthy] shepherde and a clene sheep.
Wel oghte a preest ensample for to yeve 505
By his clennesse, how that his sheepe sholde
lyve.
He sette nat his benefice to hyre
And leet his sheep encombred in the myre,
And ran to London unto Seïnt Poules
To seken hym a chaunterie for soules, 510
Or with a bretherhed to been withholde; [5]
But dwelte at hoom and kepte wel his folde,
Só that the wolf ne made it nat myscarie;
He was a shepherde, and noght a mercenarie.
And though he hooly were and vertuous, 515
He was to synful man nat despitous, [6]
Ne of his speche daungerous [7] ne digne, [8]
But in his techyng descreet and benygne;
To drawen folk to hevene by fairnesse,
By good ensample, this was his bisynesse.
But it were any persone obstinat, 521
What so he were, of heigh or lowe estat,
Hym wolde he snybben [9] sharply for the
nonys. [10]
A bettre preest I trowe that no-wher noon ys;
He waited after no pompe and reverence, 525
Ne maked him a spiced conscience,
But Cristes loore, and his apostles twelve,
He taughte, but first he folwed it hym-selve.
With him ther was a Plowman, was [11] his
brother,
That hadde y-lad [12] of dong ful many a
fother, [13] 530
A trewe swinkere [14] and a good was he,
Livinge in pees and parfit [15] charitee.
God loved he best with al his hole herte
At alle tymes, thogh him gamed or smerte, [16]
And thanne his neighebour right as him-
selve. 535
He wolde thresshe, and ther-to dyke and
delve,

For Cristes sake, for every povre wight,
Withouten hyre, if it lay in his might.
His tythes payed he ful faire and wel,
Bothe of his propre [1] swink [2] and his catel. [3]
In a tabard [4] he rood upon a mere. 541
Ther was also a Reve [5] and a Millere,
A Somnour [6] and a Pardoner also,
A Maunciple, [7] and my-self; ther were namo.
The Millere was a stout carl for the nones, [8]
Ful byg he was of brawn and eek of bones;
That proved wel, for over-al [9] ther he cam,
At wrastlynge he wolde have alwey the ram. [10]
He was short-shotldred, brood, a thikke
knarre, [11]
Ther nas no dore that he nolde heve of
harre [12]
Or breke it at a rennyng with his heed. 551
His berd, as any sowe or fox, was reed,
And therto brood, as though it were a spade.
Upon the cop [13] right of his nose he hade
A werte, and theron stood a tuft of herys, 555
Reed as the bristles of a sowes erys; [14]
His nosethirles [15] blake were and wyde.
A swerd and a bokeler bar he by his syde.
His mouth as wyde was as a greet forneys;
He was a janglere [16] and a goliardeys, [17] 560
And that was moost of synne and harlotries.
Wel coude he stelen corn and tollen thries,
And yet he hadde a thombe of gold, [18] pardee!
A whit cote and a blew hood wered he;
A baggepipe wel coude he blowe and sowne,
And therwithal he broghte us out of towne.
A gentil Maunciple was ther of a temple, [19]
Of which achatours [20] mighte take exemple
For to be wyse in bying of vitaille. 569
For whether that he payde, or took by taille, [21]
Algate he wayted [22] so in his achat [23]
That he was ay biforn [24] and in good stat.
Now is nat that of God a ful fair grace,
That swich a lewed [25] mannes wit shal pace [26]
The wisdom of an heep of lerned men? 575
Of maistres hadde he mo [27] than thryes ten,
That were of lawe expert and curious;
Of which ther were a doseyn in that hous,
Worthy to been stiwardes of rente and lond
Of any lord that is in Engelond, 580

[1] own [2] labour [3] property [4] short sleeveless jacket
[5] foreman of the laborers on a manor [6] bailiff of
an ecclesiastical court [7] steward of a college or inn
of court [8] for the nones *means* very, extremely
[9] everywhere [10] *the prize* [11] knot [12] heave off its
hinges [13] end [14] ears [15] nostrils [16] loud talker
[17] jester [18] *As all honest millers have.* [19] inn of court
[20] buyers [21] tally, *i.e.* on credit [22] always he watched
[23] purchase [24] ahead [25] ignorant [26] surpass [27] more

[1] those [2] also [3] ignorant [4] heed [5] maintained
[6] pitiless [7] overbearing [8] haughty [9] snub, rebuke
[10] for the nonys *means* very, extremely [11] who was
[12] carried [13] load [14] labourer [15] perfect [16] whether he
was happy or unhappy

To make him live by his propre good,
In honour dettelees, but he were wood,[1]
Or live as scarsly [2] as him list desire;
And able for to helpen al a shire   585
In any cas that mighte falle or happe;
And yit this maunciple sette hir aller cappe.[3]
　The Reeve was a sclendre colerik [4] man.
His berd was shave as ny as ever he can;
His heer was by his eres round y-shorn;
His top was dokked [5] lyk a preest biforn.
Ful longe were his legges, and ful lene,   591
Y-lyk a staf, ther was no calf y-sene.
Wel coude he kepe a gerner [6] and a binne;
Ther was noon auditour coude on him winne.
Wel wiste he, by the droghte, and by the reyn,
The yeldyng of his seed, and of his greyn.   596
His lordes sheep, his neet,[7] his dayerye,
His swyn, his hors, his stoor,[8] and his pultrye,
Was hooly in this reves governing;
And by his covenaunt yaf the rekening [9]   600
Sin [10] that his lord was twenty yeer of age;
Ther coude no man bringe him in arrerage.[11]
Ther nas baillif, ne herde,[12] ne other hyne,[13]
That he ne knew his sleighte and his covyne;[14]
They were adrad of him, as of the deeth.   605
His woning [15] was ful fair up-on an heeth;
With grene treës shadwed was his place;
He coude bettre than his lord purchace.
Ful riche he was astored prively;
His lord wel coude he plesen subtilly,   610
To yeve and lene him of his owne good,
And have a thank, and yet a cote, and hood.[16]
In youthe he lerned hadde a good mister;[17]
He was a wel good wrighte, a carpenter.
This reve sat up-on a ful good stot,[18]   615
That was al pomely [19] grey, and highte Scot.
A long surcote of pers [20] up-on he hade,
And by his syde he bar a rusty blade.
Of Northfolk was this reve of which I telle,
Bisyde a toun men clepen Baldeswelle.   620
Tukked [21] he was, as is a frere, aboute,
And evere he rood the hindreste of our route.
　A Somnour was ther with us in that place,
That hadde a fyr-reed cherubinnes face,
For sawceflem [22] he was, with eyen narwe,

*　*　*　*　*　*　*

With scalled [1] browes blake, and piled [2] berd;
Of his visage children were aferd.
Ther nas quik-silver, litarge,[3] ne brimstoon,
Boras,[4] ceruce,[3] ne oille of tartre noon,   630
Ne oynement that wolde clense and byte,
That him mighte helpen of his whelkes [5] whyte,
Ne of the knobbes sittinge on his chekes.
Wel loved he garleek, oynons, and eek lekes,
And for to drinken strong wyn, reed as blood.
Thanne wolde he speke and crye, as he were wood.[6]
And whan that he wel dronken hadde the wyn,
Than wolde he speke no word but Latyn.
A fewe termes hadde he, two or thre,
That he had lerned out of some decree;   640
No wonder is, he herde it al the day;
And eek ye knowen wel, how that a Jay
Can clepen 'Watte,' [7] as well as can the pope.
But who-so coude in other thing him grope,[8]
Thanne hadde he spent al his philosophye;
Ay "Questio quid iuris" [9] wolde he crye.   646
He was a gentil harlot [10] and a kynde;
A bettre felawe [11] sholde men noght fynde;
He wolde suffre for a quart of wyn
A good felawe to have his [wikked sin]   650
A twelf-month, and excuse him atte fulle;
And prively a finch eek coude he pulle.[12]
And if he fond owher [13] a good felawe,
He wolde techen him to have non awe,
In swich cas, of the erchedeknes curs,[14]   655
But-if [15] a mannes soule were in his purs;[16]
For in his purs he sholde y-punisshed be.
"Purs is the erchedeknes helle," seyde he.
But wel I woot he lyed right in dede;   659
Of cursing oghte ech gulty man him drede [17] —
For curs wol slee, right as assoilling [18] saveth —
And also war him of a significavit.[19]
In daunger [20] hadde he at his owne gyse [21]
The yonge girles [22] of the diocyse,
And knew hir counseil,[23] and was al hir reed.[24]
A gerland hadde he set up-on his heed,   666

[1] crazy [2] economically [3] cheated them all (slang) [4] irascible [5] cut short [6] granary [7] cattle [8] stock of tools, etc. [9] rendered account [10] since [11] find him in arrears [12] herdsman [13] servant [14] whose craft and deceit he did not know [15] dwelling [16] lend his lord's own property to him and receive thanks and gifts [17] trade [18] cob [19] dappled [20] blue [21] his coat was tucked up with a girdle [22] pimpled

[1] scurfy [2] scraggy [3] a lead ointment [4] borax [5] bumps [6] mad [7] call "Walter," as a parrot calls "Poll" [8] test [9] "The question is what is the law" [10] rascal [11] good fellow was slang for a "disreputable person." [12] slang for "rob a greenhorn." [13] anywhere [14] excommunication [15] unless [16] purse [17] be afraid [18] absolving [19] writ for arresting an excommunicated person [20] under his influence [21] way [22] young people of either sex [23] secrets [24] adviser

As greet as it were for an ale-stake;[1]
A bokeler hadde he maad him of a cake.

With him ther rood a gentil Pardoner
Of Rouncivale, his frend and his compeer,670
That streight was comen fro the court of
    Rome.
Ful loude he song, 'Com hider, love, to me.'
This somnour bar to him a stif burdoun,[2]
Was nevere trompe [3] of half so greet a soun.
This pardoner hadde heer as yelow as wex,
But smothe it heng, as doth a strike of flex;[4]
By ounces [5] henge his lokkes that he hadde,
And ther-with he his shuldres overspradde;
But thinne it lay, by colpons [6] oon and oon;
But hood, for jolitee,[7] ne wered he noon, 680
For it was trussed up in his walet.
Him thoughte [8] he rood al of the newe jet;[9]
Dischevele, save his cappe, he rood al bare.
Swiche glaringe eyen hadde he as an hare.
A vernicle [10] hadde he sowed on his cappe. 685
His walet lay biforn him in his lappe,
Bret-ful [11] of pardoun come from Rome al
    hoot.
A voys he hadde as smal as hath a goot.
No berd hadde he, ne nevere sholde have,
As smothe it was as it were late y-shave; 690

* * * * * * *

But of his craft, fro Berwik unto Ware,[12]
Ne was ther swich another pardoner;
For in his male [13] he hadde a pilwe-beer,[14]
Which that, he seyde, was our lady veyl;[15]
He seyde, he hadde a gobet [16] of the seyl [17]
That Sëynt Peter hadde, whan that he wente
Up-on the see, til Iesu Crist him hente;[18]
He hadde a croys [19] of latoun,[20] ful of stones,
And in a glas he hadde pigges bones. 700
But with thise relikes, whan that he fond
A povre person dwelling up-on lond,[21]
Up-on a day he gat him more moneye
Than that the person gat in monthes tweye.
And thus with feyned flaterye and japes,[22] 705
He made the person and the peple his apes.[23]
But trewely to tellen, atte laste,
He was in chirche a noble ecclesiaste.

[1] a pole projecting from the wall of an inn
and usually bearing a garland [2] accompaniment [3] trumpet [4] hank of flax [5] small portions
[6] handfuls [7] for sport [8] it seemed to him [9] new
fashion [10] a duplicate of the handkerchief of St.
Veronica, on which the face of Jesus was imprinted. [11] brimful [12] from one end of England to
the other [13] bag [14] pillow-case [15] Our Lady's veil
[16] bit [17] sail [18] seized [19] cross [20] brass [21] in the country [22] tricks [23] fools

Wel coude he rede a lessoun or a storie,
But alderbest [1] he song an offertorie; 710
For wel he wiste, whan that song was songe,
He moste preche, and wel affyle [2] his tonge,
To winne silver, as he ful wel coude;
Therfore he song so meriely and loude.

Now have I toold you shortly, in a clause,
Thestaat, tharray, the nombre, and eek the
    cause 716
Why that assembled was this compaignye
In Southwerk at this gentil hostelrye,
That highte [3] the Tabard, faste by the Belle.
But now is tyme to you for to telle 720
How that we baren us that ilke nyght,
Whan we were in that hostelrie alyght;
And after wol I telle of our viage [4]
And al the remenaunt of oure pilgrimage.

But first, I pray yow of youre curteisye,
That ye narette it nat [5] my vileynye,[6] 726
Thogh that I pleynly speke in this mateere
To telle yow hir wordes and hir cheere,
Ne thogh I speke hir wordes proprely;[7]
For this ye knowen al-so wel as I, 730
Whoso shal telle a tale after a man,
He moote reherce, as ny as evere he can,
Everich a word, if it be in his charge,
Al [8] speke he never so rudeliche and large,[9]
Or ellis he moot telle his tale untrewe 735
Or feyne thyng, or fynde wordes newe;
He may nat spare, althogh he were his
    brother,
He moot as wel seye o word as another.
Crist spak hymself ful brode in hooly writ,
And wel ye woot no vileynye [10] is it. 740
Eek Plato seith, whoso that can hym rede,
"The wordes moote be cosyn [11] to the dede."

Also I prey yow to foryeve it me
Al [8] have I nat set folk in hir degree
Heere in this tale, as that they sholde stonde;
My wit is short, ye may wel understonde. 746

Greet chiere made oure hoste us everichon,[12]
And to the soper sette he us anon,
And served us with vitaille at the beste;
Strong was the wyn, and wel to drynke us
    leste.[13] 750
A semely man oure Hooste was with-alle
For to han been a marshal in an halle.
A large man he was, with eyen stepe,[14]
A fairer burgeys was ther noon in Chepe;[15]

[1] best of all [2] polish, smooth [3] was called [4] journey [5] do not ascribe it to [6] lack of breeding
[7] accurately [8] although [9] coarsely [10] vulgarity
[11] cousin [12] every one [13] it pleased us [14] big
[15] Cheapside

Boold of his speche, and wys and wel y-taught,
And of manhod hym lakkede right naught.
Eek therto [1] he was right a myrie man,   757
And after soper pleyen he bigan,
And spak of myrthe amonges othere thynges,
Whan that we hadde maad our rekenynges;
And seyde thus: "Now, lordynges, trewely,
Ye been to me right welcome, hertely;   762
For by my trouthe, if that I shal nat lye,
I ne saugh this yeer so myrie a compaignye
At ones in this herberwe [2] as is now;   765
Fayn wolde I doon yow myrthe, wiste I how.[3]
And of a myrthe I am right now bythoght,
To doon yow ese, and it shal coste noght.
    "Ye goon to Canterbury; God yow speede,
The blisful martir quite yow youre meede![4]
And, wel I woot,[5] as ye goon by the weye,
Ye shapen yow to talen [6] and to pleye;   772
For trewely comfort ne myrthe is noon
To ride by the weye doumb as a stoon;
And therfore wol I maken yow disport,   775
As I seyde erst,[7] and doon yow som comfort.
And if you liketh alle, by oon assent,
Now for to stonden at my juggement,
And for to werken as I shal yow seye,
To-morwe, whan ye riden by the weye,   780
Now by my fader soule that is deed,
But [8] ye be myrie, I wol yeve yow myn heed!
Hoold up youre hond withouten moore
    speche."
    Oure conseil was nat longe for to seche;
Us thoughte it was noght worth to make it
    wys,   785
And graunted hym withouten moore avys,[9]
And bad him seye his verdit, as hym leste.[10]
    "Lordynges," [11] quod he, "now herkneth
    for the beste,
But taak it nought, I prey yow, in desdeyn;
This is the poynt, to speken short and pleyn,
That ech of yow, to shorte with your weye,
In this viage shal telle tales tweye   792
To Caunterburyward, — I mean it so, —
And homward he shal tellen othere two,
Of aventures that whilom [12] han bifalle.   795
And which of yow that bereth hym beste of
    alle,
That is to seyn, that telleth in this caas
Tales of best sentence [13] and moost solaas,
Shal have a soper at oure aller cost,[14]
Heere in this place, sittynge by this post, 800

Whan that we come agayn fro Caunterbury.
And, for to make yow the moore mury,[1]
I wol myselven gladly with yow ryde
Right at myn owne cost, and be youre gyde.
And whoso wole my juggement withseye [2] 805
Shal paye al that we spenden by the weye.
And if ye vouche-sauf that it be so,
Tel me anon, withouten wordes mo,
And I wol erly shape me [3] therfore."
    This thyng was graunted, and oure othes
    swore   810
With ful glad herte, and preyden hym also
That he would vouche-sauf for to do so,
And that he wolde been oure governour,
And of our tales juge and reportour,
And sette a soper at a certeyn pris,   815
And we wol reuled been at his devys
In heigh and lowe; and thus by oon assent
We been acorded to his juggement.
And therupon the wyn was fet [4] anon;
We dronken and to reste wente echon   820
Withouten any lenger taryynge.
    Amorwe, whan that day bigan to sprynge,
Up roos oure Hoost and was oure aller cok,[5]
And gadrede us togidre alle in a flok,
And forth we riden, a litel moore than paas,[6]
Unto the Wateryng of Seint Thomas;   826
And there oure Hoost bigan his hors areste,
And seyde, "Lordynges, herkneth, if `yow
    leste!
Ye woot youre forward,[7] and I it yow re-
    corde.
If even-song and morwe-song accorde,   830
Lat se now who shal telle the firste tale.
As evere mote I drynke wyn or ale,
Whoso be rebel to my juggement
Shal paye for all that by the wey is spent!
Now draweth cut, er that we ferrer twynne.[8]
He which that hath the shorteste shal bi-
    gynne.   836
Sire Knyght," quod he, "my mayster and my
    lord,
Now draweth cut, for that is myn accord.
Cometh neer," [9] quod he, "my lady Prioresse,
And ye, sire Clerk, lat be your shamefast-
    nesse,   840
Ne studieth noght; ley hond to, every man."
    Anon to drawen every wight bigan,
And, shortly for to tellen, as it was,
Were it by aventure, or sort,[10] or cas,[11]

---

[1] besides [2] inn [3] if I knew how [4] give you your
reward [5] know [6] tell tales [7] before [8] unless [9] consideration [10] pleased him [11] gentlemen [12] formerly
[3] meaning [14] cost of us all

[1] merry [2] gainsay [3] prepare myself [4] fetched
[5] cock — *waked us all.* [6] a little faster than a
walk [7] agreement [8] farther depart [9] come nearer
[10] fate [11] chance

The sothe is this, the cut fil to the knyght,
Of which ful blithe and glad was every
    wyght :   846
And telle he moste his tale, as was resoun,
By forward [1] and by composicioun,[2]
As ye han herd ; what nedeth wordes mo ?
And whan this goode man saugh that it was
    so,   850
As he that wys was and obedient
To kepe his forward [1] by his free assent,
He seyde, "Syn [3] I shal bigynne the game,
What, welcom be the cut a [4] Goddes name !
Now lat us ryde, and herkneth what I seye."
And with that word, we ryden forth oure
    weye ;
And he bigan with right a myrie cheere   857
His tale anon, and seyde in this manere.

*   *   *   *   *   *   *

A ROUNDEL

FROM THE PARLEMENT OF FOULES

"Now welcom, somer, with thy sonne softe,
That hast this wintres weders [5] over-shake,[6]
And driven awey the longe nightes blake !"

Seynt Valentyn, that art ful hy on-lofte,[7]
Thus singen smale foules [8] for thy sake :   5
    "Now welcom, somer, with thy sonne softe,
    That hast this wintres weders over-shake."

Wel han [9] they cause for to gladen ofte,
Sith [3] ech of hem recovered hath his make ; [10]
Ful blisful may they singen whan they wake :
    "Now welcom, somer, with thy ʾsonne softe,
    That hast this wintres weders over-shake,
    And driven awey the longe nightes blake !"

BALADE DE BON CONSEYL

Fle fro the prees,[11] and dwelle with sothfast-
    nesse,[12]
Suffyce unto thy good, though hit be smal ;
For hord hath hate, and clymbing tikelnesse,[13]
Prees [11] hath envye, and wele blent overal ; [14]
Savour no more than thee bihove shal ;   5
Werk wel thy-self, that other folk canst rede ; [15]
And trouthe shal delivere, hit is no drede.[16]

Tempest [1] thee noght al croked to redresse,
In trust of hir [2] that turneth as a bal ;
Gret reste stant [3] in litel besinesse.   10
And eek be war [4] to sporne [5] ageyn an al ; [6]
Strive noght, as doth the crokke [7] with the
    wal.
Daunte thy-self, that dauntest otheres dede :
And trouthe shal delivere, hit is no drede.

That thee is sent, receyve in buxumnesse,[8] 15
The wrastling for this worlde axeth a fal.
Her nis non hom, her nis but wildernesse :
Forth, pilgrim, forth ! Forth, beste,[9] out of
    thy stal !
Know thy contree ; lok up, thank God of al ;
Hold the hye-wey,[10] and lat thy gost [11] thee
    lede !   20
And trouthe shal delivere, hit is no drede.

ENVOY

Therfore, thou Vache,[12] leve thyn old wrecch-
    ednesse ;
Unto the worlde leve [13] now to be thral ;
Crye Him mercy that [14] of His hy goodnesse
Made thee of noght, and in especial   25
Draw unto Him, and pray in general
For thee, and eek for other, hevenlich mede ; [15]
And trouthe shal delivere, hit is no drede. 28

Explicit Le bon counseill de G. Chaucer

THE COMPLEINT OF CHAUCER TO
HIS EMPTY PURSE

To you, my purse, and to non other wight [16]
Compleyne I, for ye be my lady dere !
I am so sory, now that ye be light ;
For certes, but [17] ye make me hevy chere,[18]
Me were as leef be leyd up-on my bere ; [19]   5
For whiche un-to your mercy thus I crye :
Beth [20] hevy ageyn, or elles mot I dye !

Now voucheth sauf this day, or [21] hit be night,
That I of you the blisful soun may here,
Or see your colour lyk the sonne bright,   10
That of yelownesse hadde never pere.
Ye be my lyf, ye be myn hertes stere,[22]

---

[1] disturb [2] *i.e.* Fortune [3] stands, resides [4] cautious [5] kick [6] awl [7] crock, earthen pot [8] willing
obedience [9] beast [10] highway [11] spirit [12] Sir Philip
la Vache [13] cease [14] thank him who [15] reward
[16] creature [17] unless [18] cheer [19] bier [20] be [21] ere
[22] guide

[1] agreement [2] compact [3] since [4] in [5] storms
[6] overturned [7] above [8] little birds [9] have [10] mate
[11] the crowd [12] truth [13] insecurity [14] prosperity
blinds everywhere [15] advise [16] doubt

AE

Quene of comfort and of good companye,
Beth hevy ageyn, or elles mot I dye !

Now purs, that be to me my lyves light,   15
And saveour, as doun in this worlde here,
Out of this toune help me through your might,
Sin that ye wole nat ben my tresorere ;
For I am shave as nye [1] as any frere.[2]
But yit I pray un-to your curtesye :   20
Beth hevy ageyn, or elles mot I dye !

LENVOY DE CHAUCER

O conquerour of Brutes Albioun !
Which that by lyne and free eleccioun
Ben [3] verray king, this song to you I sende ;
And ye, that mowen [4] al myn harm amende,
Have mynde up-on my supplicacioun !   26

A TREATISE ON THE ASTROLABE [5]

PROLOGUS

Litel Lowis [6] my sone, I have perceived wel
by certeyne evidences thyn abilite to lerne
sciencez touching noumbres and propor-
ciouns ; and as wel considere I thy bisy [7]
preyere [8] in special to lerne the Tretis of the
Astrolabie. Than,[9] for as mechel [10] as a phil-
osofre seith, "he wrappeth him in his frend, that
condescendeth to the rightful preyers of his
frend," therfor have I yeven [11] thee a suffisaunt
Astrolabie as for oure orizonte,[12] compowned [13]
after the latitude of Oxenford ; upon which,
by mediacion [14] of this litel tretis, I purpose to
teche thee a certein nombre of conclusions [15]
apertening [16] to the same instrument. I seye
a certein of conclusions, for three causes.
The furste cause is this : truste wel that alle
the conclusiouns that han [17] ben founde, or
elles [18] possibly mighten be founde in so noble
an instrument as an Astrolabie, ben [3] unknowe perfitly to any mortal man in this
regioun, as I suppose. Another cause is this :
that sothly,[19] in any tretis of the Astrolabie
that I have seyn,[20] there ben [3] some conclusions that wole [21] nat in alle thinges performen
hir [22] bihestes ; [23] and some of hem ben [3] to [24]

harde to thy tendre age of ten yeer to con-
seyve.[1] This tretis, divided in fyve parties [2]
wole [3] I shewe thee under ful lighte [4] rewles [5]
and naked wordes in English ; for Latin ne
canstow [6] yit but smal, my lyte [7] sone. But
natheles,[8] suffyse to thee thise trewe conclusiouns in English, as wel as suffyseth to
thise noble clerkes Grekes thise same conclusiouns in Greek, and to Arabiens in Arabik,
and to Jewes in Ebrew, and to the Latin folk
in Latin ; whiche Latin folk han [9] hem [10] furst
out of othre diverse langages, and writen in
hir [11] owne tonge, that is to sein,[12] in Latin.
And God wot,[13] that in alle thise langages,
and in many mo,[14] han [9] thise conclusiouns
ben [15] suffisantly lerned and taught, and yit
by diverse rewles,[5] right as diverse pathes
leden diverse folk the righte wey to Rome.
Now wol I prey meekly every discret persone
that redeth or hereth this litel tretis, to have
my rewde [16] endyting [17] for excused, and my
superfluite of wordes, for two causes. The
firste cause is, for-that [18] curious [19] endyting [17]
and hard sentence [20] is ful hevy [21] atones [22]
for swich [23] a child to lerne. And the seconde
cause is this, that sothly [24] mesemeth [25] betre
to wryten unto a child twyes [26] a good sentence,
than he forgete it ones.[27] And, Lowis, yif [28]
so be that I shewe thee in my lighte [29] English
as trewe conclusiouns touching this matere,
and naught [30] only as trewe but as many and
as subtil conclusiouns as ben [31] shewed in
Latin in any commune tretis of the Astrolabie,
con me the more thank ; [32] and preye God save
the king, that is lord of this langage, and alle
that him feyth bereth [33] and obeyeth, everech [34]
in his degree, the more [35] and the lasse.[36] But
considere wel, that I ne usurpe nat to have
founde this werk of my labour or of myn
engin.[37] I nam [38] but a lewd [39] compilatour [40]
of the labour of olde Astrologiens, and have hit
translated in myn English only for thy doctrine ; and with this swerd [41] shal I sleen [42]
envye.

---

[1] shaven as close [2] friar [3] are [4] may [5] astronomical instrument ; *consult the dictionary* [6] Lewis
[7] eager [8] prayer, request [9] then [10] much [11] given
[12] horizon [13] composed [14] means [15] problems and
their solutions [16] pertaining [17] have [18] else [19] truly
[20] seen [21] will [22] their [23] promises [24] too

[1] understand [2] parts [3] will [4] easy [5] rules [6] knowest thou [7] little [8] nevertheless [9] have [10] them
[11] their [12] say [13] knows [14] more [15] been [16] rude
[17] composition [18] because [19] elaborate [20] meaning,
sense [21] difficult [22] at once [23] such [24] truly [25] it
seems to me [26] twice [27] once [28] if [29] easy [30] not
[31] are [32] con thank *means* thank, be grateful [33] bear
[34] every one [35] greater [36] less [37] ingenuity [38] am not
[39] ignorant [40] compiler [41] sword [42] slay

JOHN DE TREVISA (1326–1412)

HIGDEN'S POLYCHRONICON

BOOK I. CHAPTER LIX

This apayrynge[1] of the burthe of the tunge is bycause of tweie thinges; oon is for children in scole ayenst the usage and manere of alle othere naciouns beeth compelled for to leve[2] hire[3] owne langage, and for to construe hir[3] lessouns and here[3] thynges in Frensche, and so they haveth[4] seth[5] the Normans come[6] first in-to Engelond. Also gentil-men children beeth i-taught to speke Frensche from the tyme that they beeth i-rokked in here cradel, and kunneth[7] speke and playe with a childes broche;[8] and uplondisshe[9] men wil likne hym-self to gentil-men, and fondeth[10] with greet besynesse for to speke Frensce, for to be i-tolde[11] of. *Trevisa*.[12] This manere was moche i-used to-for[13] [the] Firste Deth[14] and is siththe[15] sumdel[15] i-chaunged; for John Cornwaile, a maister of grammer, chaunged the lore in gramer scole and construccioun of[16] Frensche in-to Englische; and Richard Pencriche lerned the manere[17] techynge of hym and othere men of Pencrich; so that now, the yere of oure Lorde a thowsand thre hundred and foure score and fyve, and of the secounde kyng Richard after the Conquest nyne, in alle the gramere scoles of Engelond, children leveth Frensche and construeth and lerneth an[18] Englische, and haveth[4] therby avauntage in oon side and disavauntage in another side; here[3] avauntage is, that they lerneth her[3] gramer in lasse[19] tyme than children were i-woned[20] to doo; disavauntage is that now children of gramer scole conneth[21] na more Frensche than can[22] hir[3] lift[23] heele, and that is harme for hem[24] and[25] they schulle passe the see and travaille in straunge landes and in many other places. Also gentil-men haveth now moche i-left[26] for to teche here[3] children Frensche.

This deterioration of the birth of the tongue is because of two things: one is because children in school, against the usage and custom of all other nations, are compelled to give up their own language and to construe their lessons and their exercises in French, and so they have since the Normans came first into England. Also gentlemen's children are taught to speak French from the time that they are rocked in their cradles and can talk and play with a baby's brooch; and countrymen wish to be like gentlemen and attempt with great effort to speak French, in order to be highly regarded. *Trevisa:* This custom was much used before the first plague and has since been somewhat changed; for John Cornwaile, master of grammar, changed the teaching in grammar school and the translation of French into English; and Richard Pencriche learned this sort of teaching from him, and other men from Pencriche, so that now, the year of Our Lord 1385 and of the second King Richard after the Conquest nine, in all the grammar schools of England, children give up French and construe and learn in English, and have thereby advantage on one side and disadvantage on another side; their advantage is that they learn their grammar in less time than children were accustomed to do; the disadvantage is that now children in grammar school know no more French than does their left heel; and that is harm for them if they shall pass the sea and travel in strange lands and in many other places. Also gentlemen have now in general ceased to teach their children French.

follows is Trevisa's addition. [13] before [14] the First Plague, 1348–1349 [15] somewhat [16] from [17] kind of [18] in [19] less [20] accustomed [21] know [22] knows [23] left [24] them [25] if [26] ceased

[1] deterioration [2] leave, give up [3] their [4] have [5] since [6] came [7] can [8] brooch (ornament in general) [9] country [10] attempt [11] accounted [12] *What*

THE END OF THE MIDDLE AGES

THOMAS HOCCLEVE
(1370?–1450?)

FROM DE REGIMINE PRINCIPUM

ON CHAUCER

O maister deere and fadir reverent,   1961
  Mi maister Chaucer, flour of eloquence,
Mirour of fructuous entendement,[1]
  O universel fadir in science,
  Allas, that thou thyn excellent prudence
    In thi bed mortel mightist noght by-
     quethe !
  What eiled Deth allas ! why wold he sle
    the?

O Deth, thou didest naght harme singuleer [2]
  In slaughtere of him, but al this land it
    smertith.   1969
But nathelees yit hast thou no power
  His name sle ; his hy vertu astertith [3]
  Unslayn fro the, whiche ay us lyfly hertyth [4]
    With bookes of his ornat endytyng,
    That is to al this land enlumynyng. 1974

    *   *   *   *   *   *   *

My dere maistir (God his soule quyte !) 2077
  And fadir Chaucer fayn wolde han me
    taght,
  But I was dul, and lerned lite or naght.

Allas ! my worthi maister honorable, 2080
  This landes verray tresor and richesse !
Dethe, by thi deth, hath harme irreparable
  Unto us doon ; hir vengeable duresse [5]
  Despoiled hath this land of the swetnesse
    Of rethorik, for unto Tullius
    Was never man so lyk [6] amonges us. 2086

Also who was hier [7] in philosophie 2087
  To Aristotle in our tonge but thow?

[1] fruitful understanding [2] affecting only one
[3] escapes [4] heartens [5] cruel affliction [6] like [7] heir

The steppes of Virgile in poesie
  Thow folwedist eeke, men wot wel ynow.
That combre-world [1] that the, my maistir,
    slow,[2]
  Would I slayne were ! Deth was to
    hastyf,
  To rene [3] on the, and reve [4] the thi lyf.

Deth hath but smal consideracion 2094
  Unto the vertuous, I have espied,
No more, as shewith the probacion,[5]
  Than to a vicious maister losel [6] tried ;
  Among an heep [7] every man is maistried [8]
    With [9] hire, as wel the porre [10] as is the
     riche ;
    Lerede [11] and lewde [12] eeke standen al
     yliche.[13]

She mighte han taryed hir vengeance a while
  Til that some man had egal to the be.[14] 2102
Nay, lat be that ! sche knew wel that this yle
  May never man forth brynge lyk to the,
  And hir office [15] nedes do mot [16] she ;
    God bad hir do so, I truste as for the
     beste ;
    O maister, maister, God thi soule reste !

    *   *   *   *   *   *   *

The firste fyndere of our faire langage 4978
  Hath seyde in caas semblable,[17] and othir
    moo,[18]
So hyly wel, that it is my dotage
  For to expresse or touche any of thoo.[19]
  Alasse ! my fadir fro the worlde is goo,
    My worthi maister Chaucer, hym I mene :
    Be thou advoket [20] for hym, Hevenes
     Quene !

As thou wel knowest, O Blissid Virgyne, 4985
  With lovyng hert and hye devocion
In thyne honour he wroot ful many a lyne ;
  O now thine helpe and thi promocion !

[1] world-cumberer [2] slew [3] run [4] bereave [5] experience [6] rascal [7] in a crowd [8] overcome [9] by
[10] poor [11] learned [12] ignorant [13] alike [14] had been
equal to thee [15] duty [16] must [17] like cases [18] others
also [19] those [20] advocate

To God thi Sone make a mocion
   How he thi servaunt was, Mayden Marie,
And lat his love floure and fructifie! 4991

Al-thogh his lyfe be queynt,[1] the résemblaunce
Of him hath in me so fressh lyflynesse,
That, to putte othir men in rémembraunce
Of his persone, I have heere his lyknesse
Do make,[2] to this ende, in sothfastnesse,
   That thei that have of him lest thought
     and mynde, 4997
By this peynture may ageyn him fynde.

JOHN LYDGATE (1370?–1451?)

FROM THE STORY OF THEBES

HOW FALSLY ETHYOCLES LEYDE A BUSSHEMENT[3] IN THE WAY TO HAVE SLAYN TYDEUS

At a posterne forth they gan to ryde
By a geyn[4] path, that ley oute a-side,
Secrely, that no man hem espie,
Only of[5] tresoun and of felonye.
They haste hem forth al the longe day,
Of cruel malys, forto stoppe his way,
Thorgh a forest, alle of oon assent,
Ful covartly to leyn a busshement
Under an hille, at a streite passage,
To falle on hym at mor avantage,[6] 1110
The same way that Tydeus gan drawe
At thylke[7] mount wher that Spynx was slawe.[8]
He, nothing war in his opynyoun[9]
Of this compassed[10] conspiracioun,
But innocent and lich[11] a gentyl knyght,
Rood ay forth to[12] that it drowe[13] to nyght,
Sool by hym-silf, with-oute companye,
Havyng no man to wisse[14] hym or to gye.[15]
   But at the last, lifting up his hede,
Toward eve, he gan taken hede; 1120
Mid of his waye, right as eny lyne,
Thoght he saugh, ageyn the mone shyne,
Sheldes fresshe and plates borned[16] bright,
The which environ[17] casten a gret lyght;
Ymagynyng in his fantasye
Ther was treson and conspiracye
Wrought by the kyng, his journe[18] forto lette.[19]
And of al that he no-thyng ne sette,[20]

But wel assured in his manly herte,
List[1] nat onys a-syde to dyverte, 1130
But kepte his way, his sheld upon his brest,
And cast his spere manly in the rest,
And the first platly[2] that he mette
Thorgh the body proudely he hym smette,
That he fille ded, chief mayster of hem alle;
And than at onys they upon hym falle
On every part, be[3] compas envyroun.
But Tydeus, thorgh his hegh renoun,
His blody swerde lete about hym glyde,
Sleth and kylleth upon every side 1140
In his ire and his mortal tene;[4]
That mervaile was he myght so sustene
Ageyn hem alle, in every half besette;[5]
But his swerde was so sharpe whette
That his foomen founde ful unsoote.[6]
But he, allas! was mad light a foote,[7]
Be force grounded,[8] in ful gret distresse;
But of knyghthod and of gret prouesse[9]
Up he roos, maugre[10] alle his foon,[11]
And as they cam, he slogh[12] hem oon be oon, 1151
Lik a lyoun rampaunt in his rage,
And on this hille he fond a narow passage,
Which that he took of ful high prudence;
And liche[13] a boor, stondyng at his diffence,
As his foomen proudly hym assaylle,
Upon the pleyn he made her blode to raylle[14]
Al enviroun, that the soyl wex rede,
Now her, now ther, as they fille dede,
That her lay on, and ther lay two or thre, 1160
So mercyles, in his cruelte,
Thilke day he was upon hem founde;
And, attonys[15] his enemyes to confounde,
Wher-as he stood, this myghty champioun,
Be-side he saugh, with water turned doun,
An huge stoon large, rounde, and squar;
And sodeynly, er that thei wer war,
As[16] it hadde leyn ther for the nonys,[17]
Upon his foon he rolled it at onys,
That ten of hem[18] wenten unto wrak,
And the remnaunt amased drogh[19] a-bak;
For on by on they wente to meschaunce.[20]
And fynaly he broght to outraunce[21] 1172
Hem everychoon, Tydeus, as blyve,[22]
That non but on left[23] of ham[18] alyve:
Hym-silf yhurt, and ywounded kene,[24]
Thurgh his harneys bledyng on the grene;

[1] quenched [2] had made [3] ambush [4] convenient [5] purely because of [6] greater advantage [7] the same [8] slain [9] not at all aware in his thought [10] arranged, formed [11] like [12] till [13] drew [14] direct [15] guide [16] burnished [17] around [18] journey [19] hinder [20] he cared nothing for all that

[1] wished [2] absolutely [3] by [4] pain [5] beset on every side [6] unsweet, bitter [7] made to alight on foot [8] brought to ground [9] prowess [10] in spite of [11] foes [12] slew [13] like [14] flow [15] at once [16] as if [17] for the purpose [18] them [19] drew [20] defeat [21] destruction [22] quickly [23] remained [24] sorely

The Theban knyghtes in compas rounde
    aboute
In the vale lay slayne, alle the hoole route,[1]
Which pitously ageyn the mone [2] gape;
For non of hem, shortly,[3] myght eskape, 1180
But dede [4] echon as thei han deserved,
Save oon excepte, the which was reserved
By Tydeus, of intencioun,
To the kyng to make relacioun
How his knyghtes han on her journe
    spedde,[5] —
Everich of hem his lyf left for a wedde,[6] —
And at the metyng how they han hem born;
To tellen al he sured [7] was and sworn
To Tydeus, ful lowly on his kne.

BALLADS

(Authors and Dates Unknown)

ROBIN HOOD AND GUY OF GISBORNE

1. When shawes [8] beene sheene,[9] and
    shradds [10] full fayre,
  And leeves both large and longe,
  It is merry, walking in the fayre fforrest,
    To heare the small birds songe.

2. The woodweele [11] sang, and wold not
    cease,
  Amongst the leaves a lyne; [12]
  And it is by two wight [13] yeomen,
    By deare God, that I meane.

    *   *   *   *   *   *   *

3. "Me thought they did mee beate and
    binde,
  And tooke my bow mee froe;   10
  If I bee Robin a-live in this lande,
    I'le be wrocken [14] on both them towe."

4. "Sweavens [15] are swift, master," quoth
    John,
  "As the wind that blowes ore a hill;
  For if itt be never soe lowde this night,
    To-morrow it may be still."

---

[1] crowd [2] moon [3] to tell it briefly [4] died [5] succeeded, fared [6] pledge [7] assured [8] groves [9] beautiful [10] coppices [11] woodlark [12] of linden [13] stout [14] avenged [15] dreams

5. "Buske [1] yee, bowne [1] yee, my merry
    men all,
  For John shall goe with mee;
  For I'le goe seeke yond wight yeomen
    In greenwood where they bee."   20

6. They cast on their gowne of greene,
    A shooting gone are they,
  Until they came to the merry greenwood,
    Where they had gladdest bee;
  There were they ware of a wight yeoman,
    His body leaned to a tree.

7. A sword and a dagger he wore by his side,
    Had beene many a mans bane,
  And he was cladd in his capull-hyde,[2]
    Topp, and tayle, and mayne.   30

8. "Stand you still, master," quoth Litle
    John,
    "Under this trusty tree,
  And I will goe to yond wight yeoman,
    To know his meaning trulye."

9. "A, John, by me thou setts noe store,
    And that's a ffarley [3] thinge;
  How offt send I my men beffore,
    And tarry my-selfe behinde?

10. "It is noe cunning a knave to ken;
    And a man but heare him speake.   40
  And itt were not for bursting of my bowe,
    John, I wold thy head breake."

11. But often words they breeden bale;
    That parted Robin and John.
  John is gone to Barnesdale,
    The gates [4] he knowes eche one.

12. And when hee came to Barnesdale,
    Great heavinesse there hee hadd;
  He ffound two of his fellowes
    Were slaine both in a slade,[5]   50

13. And Scarlett a-ffoote flyinge was,
    Over stockes and stone,
  For the sheriffe with seven score men
    Fast after him is gone.

14. "Yett one shoote I'le shoote," says Litle
    John,
    "With Crist his might and mayne;
  I'le make yond fellow that flyes soe fast
    To be both glad and ffaine."

---

[1] get ready [2] horse-hide [3] strange [4] ways [5] valley

15. John bent up a good veiwe [1] bow,
    And ffetteled [2] him to shoote;   60
The bow was made of a tender boughe,
    And fell downe to his foote.

16. "Woe worth thee, wicked wood," sayd
    Litle John,
"That ere thou grew on a tree!
For this day thou art my bale,
    My boote [3] when thou shold bee!"

17. This shoote it was but looselye shott,
    The arrowe flew in vaine,
And it mett one of the sheriffes men;
    Good William a Trent was slaine. 70

18. It had beene better for William a Trent
    To hange upon a gallowe
Then for to lye in the greenwoode,
    There slaine with an arrowe.

19. And it is sayd, when men be mett,
    Six can·doe more than three:
And they have tane Litle John,
    And bound him ffast to a tree.

20. "Thou shalt be drawen by dale and
    downe," quoth the sheriffe,
"And hanged hye on a hill:"   80
"But thou may ffayle," quoth Litle John,
    "If itt be Christs owne will."

21. Let us leave talking of Litle John,
    For hee is bound fast to a tree,
And talke of Guy and Robin Hood
    In the green woode where they bee.

22. How these two yeomen together they mett,
    Under the leaves of lyne, [4]
To see what marchandise they made
    Even at that same time. 90

23. "Good morrow, good fellow," quoth Sir
    Guy;
"Good morrow, good ffellow," quoth
    hee;
"Methinkes by this bow thou beares in
    thy hand,
A good archer thou seems to bee."

24. "I am wilfull [5] of my way," quoth Sir
    Guye,
"And of my morning tyde:"

1 yew 2 made ready 3 help 4 linden 5 astray

"I'le lead thee through the wood," quoth
    Robin,
"Good ffellow, I'le be thy guide."

25. "I seeke an outlaw," quoth Sir Guye,
    "Men call him Robin Hood;   100
I had rather meet with him upon a day
    Than forty pound of golde."

26. "If you tow mett, itt wold be seene
    whether were better
Afore yee did part awaye;
Let us some other pastime find,
    Good ffellow, I thee pray.

27. "Let us some other masteryes make,
    And wee will walke in the woods even;
Wee may chance meet with Robin Hoode
    Att some unsett steven." [1] 110

28. They cutt them downe the summer
    shroggs [2]
Which grew both under a bryar,
And sett them three score rood in twinn, [3]
    To shoote the prickes full neare.

29. "Leade on, good ffellow," sayd Sir Guye,
    "Lead on, I doe bidd thee:"
"Nay, by my faith," quoth Robin Hood,
    "The leader thou shalt bee."

30. The first good shoot that Robin ledd,
    Did not shoote an inch the pricke
    ffroe;
Guy was an archer good enoughe, 121
    But he cold neere shoote soe.

31. The second shoote Sir Guy shott,
    He shott within the garlande;
But Robin Hoode shott it better than hee,
    For he clove the good pricke-wande.

32. "Gods blessing on thy heart!" sayes
    Guye,
"Goode ffellow, thy shooting is goode;
For an thy hart be as good as thy hands,
    Thou were better than Robin Hood. 130

33. "Tell me thy name, good ffellow," quoth
    Guy,
"Under the leaves of lyne:"
"Nay, by my faith," quoth good Robin,
    "Till thou have told me thine."

1 hour   2 wands   3 apart

34. "I dwell by dale and downe," quoth
        Guye,
    "And I have done many a curst turne;
    And he that calles me by my right name,
    Calles me Guye of good Gysborne."

35. "My dwelling is in the wood," sayes
        Robin;
    "By thee I set right nought;   140
    My name is Robin Hood of Barnesdale,
    A ffellow thou has long sought."

36. He that had neither beene a kithe nor
        kin
    Might have seene a full fayre sight,
    To see how together these yeomen went,
    With blades both browne and bright;

37. To have seene how these yeomen together
        fought
    Two howers of a summer's day;
    Itt was neither Guy nor Robin Hood
    That ffettled [1] them to flye away.   150

38. Robin was reacheles [2] on a roote,
    And stumbled at that tyde,
    And Guy was quicke and nimble with-all,
    And hitt him ore the left side.

39. "Ah, deere Lady!" sayd Robin Hoode,
    "Thou art both mother and may! [3]
    I thinke it was never mans destinye
    To dye before his day."

40. Robin thought on Our Lady deere,
    And soone leapt up againe,   160
    And thus he came with an awkwarde [4]
        stroke;
    Good Sir Guy hee has slayne.

41. He tooke Sir Guys head by the hayre,
    And sticked itt on his bowes end:
    "Thou hast beene traytor all thy liffe,
    Which thing must have an ende."

42. Robin pulled forth an Irish kniffe,
    And nicked Sir Guy in the fface,
    That hee was never on a woman borne
    Cold tell who Sir Guye was.   170

43. Saies, "Lye there, lye there, good Sir
        Guye,
    And with me be not wrothe;

44. Robin did off his gowne of greene,
    Sir Guye hee did it throwe;
    And hee put on that capull-hyde
    That cladd him topp to toe.

45. "The bowe, the arrowes, and litle horne,
        And [1] with me now I'le beare;   180
    For now I will goe to Barnesdale,
    To see how my men doe ffare."

46. Robin sette Guyes horne to his mouth,
    A lowd blast in it he did blow;
    That beheard the sheriffe of Nottingham,
    As he leaned under a lowe. [2]

47. "Hearken! hearken!" sayd the sheriffe,
    "I heard noe tydings but good;
    For yonder I heare Sir Guyes horne
        blowe,
    For he hath slaine Robin Hoode.   190

48. "For yonder I heare Sir Guyes horne
        blow,
    Itt blowes soe well in tyde,
    For yonder comes that wighty yeoman,
    Cladd in his capull-hyde.

49. "Come hither, thou good Sir Guy,
    Aske of mee what thou wilt have:"
    "I'le none of thy gold," sayes Robin
        Hood,
    "Nor I'le none of itt have.

50. "But now I have slaine the master," he
        sayd,
    "Let me goe strike the knave;   200
    This is all the reward I aske,
    Nor noe other will I have."

51. "Thou art a madman," said the shiriffe,
    "Thou sholdest have had a knights
        ffee;
    Seeing thy asking hath beene soe badd,
    Well granted it shall be."

52. But Litle John heard his master speake,
    Well he knew that was his steven; [3]
    "Now shall I be loset," [4] quoth Litle John,
    "With Christs might in heaven."   210

If thou have had the worse stroakes at my
        hand,
    Thou shalt have the better cloathe."

---

[1] made ready [2] careless [3] maiden [4] back-handed

[1] also   [2] hill   [3] voice   [4] released

53. But Robin hee hyed [1] him towards Litle
John,
   Hee thought hee wold loose him belive; [2]
The sheriffe and all his companye
   Fast after him did drive.

54. "Stand abacke! stand abacke!" sayd
Robin;
   "Why draw you mee soe nere?
Itt was never the use in our countrye
   Ones shrift another shold heere."

55. But Robin pulled forth an Irysh kniffe,
   And losed John hand and ffoote,   220
And gave him Sir Guyes bow in his hand,
   And bade it be his boote. [3]

56. But John tooke Guyes bow in his hand
   (His arrowes were rawstye [4] by the
     roote);
The sherriffe saw Litle John draw a bow
   And ffettle him to shoote.

57. Towards his house in Nottingham
   He ffled full fast away,
And soe did all his companye,
   Not one behind did stay.   230

58. But he cold neither soe fast goe,
   Nor away soe fast runn,
But Litle John, with an arrow broade,
   Did cleave his heart in twinn.

THE BATTLE OF OTTERBURN

1. Yt felle abowght the Lamasse tyde,
   Whan husbondes wynnes [5] ther haye,
The dowghtye Dowglasse bowynd [6] hym
   to ryde,
   In Ynglond to take a praye.

2. The yerlle of Fyffe, wythowghten stryffe,
   He bowynd hym over Sulway;
The grete wolde ever to-gether ryde;
   That raysse [7] they may rewe for aye.

3. Over Hoppertope hyll they cam in,
   And so down by Rodclyffe crage;   10
Upon Grene Lynton they lyghted dowyn,
   Styrande [8] many a stage.

4. And boldely brente [9] Northomberlond,
   And haryed many a towyn;

[1] hastened [2] quickly [3] help [4] clotted [5] dry [6] got
ready [7] raid [8] arousing [9] burned

They dyd owr Ynglyssh men grete
   wrange,
   To battell that were not bowyn.

5. Than spake a berne [1] upon the bent, [2]
   Of comforte that was not colde,
And sayd, "We have brente Northomber-
   lond,
   We have all welth in holde.   20

6. "Now we have haryed all Bamborowe
   schyre,
   All the welth in the world have wee;
I rede we ryde to Newe Castell,
   So styll and stalworthlye."

7. Upon the morowe, [3] when it was day,
   The standerds schone fulle bryght;
To the Newe Castell they toke the waye,
   And thether they cam fulle ryght.

8. Syr Henry Perssy laye at the New Castell,
   I tell yow wythowtten drede; [4]   30
He had byn a march-man all hys dayes,
   And kepte Barwyke upon Twede.

9. To the Newe Castell when they cam,
   The Skottes they cryde on hyght:
"Syr Hary Perssy, and thow byste within,
   Com to the fylde, and fyght.

10. "For we have brente Northomberlonde,
   Thy erytage good and ryght,
And syne [5] my logeyng [6] I have take,   39
   Wyth my brande dubbyd many a
   knyght."

11. Syr Harry Perssy cam to the walles,
   The Skottyssch oste for to se,
And sayd, "And thow hast brente North-
   omberlond,
   Full sore it rewyth me.

12. "Yf thou hast haryed all Bamborowe
   schyre,
   Thow hast done me grete envye; [7]
For the trespasse thow hast me done,
   The tone [8] of us schall dye."

13. "Where schall I byde the?" sayd the
   Dowglas,
   "Or where wylte thow com to me?"   50
"At Otterborne, in the hygh way,
   Ther mast thow well logeed be.

[1] man [2] field [3] morrow [4] doubt [5] since [6] lodging
[7] hostility [8] the one

14. "The roo [1] full rekeles ther sche rinnes,
        To make the game and glee;
    The fawken and the fesaunt both,
        Amonge the holtes on hye.

15. "Ther mast thow have thy welth at wyll,
        Well looged ther mast be;
    Yt schall not be long or I com the tyll,"
        Sayd Syr Harry Perssye.   60

16. "Ther schall I byde the," sayd the
        Dowglas,
        "By the fayth of my bodye."
    "Thether schall I com," sayd Syr Harry
        Perssy
        "My trowth I plyght to the."

17. A pype of wyne he gave them over the
        walles,
        For soth as I yow saye;
    Ther he mayd the Dowglasse drynke,
        And all hys ost that daye.

18. The Dowglas turnyd hym homewarde
        agayne,
        For soth withowghten naye;   70
    He toke his logeyng at Oterborne,
        Upon a Wedynsday.

19. And ther he pyght [2] hys standerd dowyn,
        Hys gettyng more and lesse, [3]
    And syne he warned hys men to goo
        To chose ther geldynges gresse. [4]

20. A Skottysshe knyght hoved [5] upon the
        bent, [6]
        A wache [7] I dare well saye;
    So was he ware on the noble Perssy
        In the dawnyng of the daye.   80

21. He prycked to hys pavyleon dore,
        As faste as he myght ronne;
    "Awaken, Dowglas," cryed the knyght,
        "For Hys love that syttes in trone.

22. "Awaken, Dowglas," cryed the knyght,
        "For thow maste waken wyth wynne; [8]
    Yender have I spyed the prowde Perssye,
        And seven stondardes wyth hym."

23. "Nay by my trowth," the Dowglas sayed,
        "It ys but a fayned taylle;   90

He durst not loke on my brede [1] banner
    For all Ynglonde so haylle.

24. "Was I not yesterdaye at the Newe
        Castell,
    That stondes so fayre on Tyne?
    For all the men the Perssy had,
        He coude not garre [2] me ones to dyne."

25. He stepped owt at his pavelyon dore,
        To loke and it were lesse : [3]
    "Araye yow, lordynges, one and all,
        For here bygynnes no peysse. [4]   100

26. "The yerle of Mentaye, thow arte my
        eme, [5]
    The fowarde [6] I gyve to the :
    The yerlle of Huntlay, cawte and kene, [7]
        He schall be wyth the.

27. "The lorde of Bowghan, in armure
        bryght,
        On the other hand he schall be;
    Lord Jhonstoune and Lorde Maxwell,
        They to schall be with me.

28. "Swynton, fayre fylde upon your pryde !
        To batell make yow bowen   110
    Syr Davy Skotte, Syr Water Stewarde,
        Syr Jhon of Agurstone !"

29. The Perssy cam byfore hys oste,
        Wych was ever a gentyll knyght;
    Upon the Dowglas lowde can [8] he crye,
        "I wyll holde that I have hyght. [9]

30. "For thou haste brente Northomberlonde,
        And done me grete envye;
    For thys trespasse thou hast me done,
        The tone [10] of us schall dye."   120

31. The Dowglas answerde hym agayne,
        Wyth grett wurdes upon hye,
    And sayd, "I have twenty agaynst thy
        one,
        Byholde, and thou maste see."

32. Wyth that the Perssy was grevyd sore,
        For soth as I yow saye;
    He lyghted dowyn upon his foote,
        And schoote [11] hys horsse clene awaye.

[1] roe [2] fixed [3] all he had got [4] grass [5] tarried
[6] field [7] sentinel [8] joy

33. Every man sawe that he dyd soo,
    That ryall[1] was ever in rowght;[2] 130
    Every man schoote hys horsse hym froo,
    And lyght hym rowynde abowght.

34. Thus Syr Hary Perssye toke the fylde,
    For soth as I yow saye;
    Jhesu Cryste in hevyn on hyght
    Dyd helpe hym well that daye.

35. But nyne thowzand, ther was no moo,
    The cronykle wyll not layne;[3]
    Forty thowsande of Skottes and fowre
    That day fowght them agayne. 140

36. But when the batell bygann to joyne,
    In hast ther cam a knyght;
    The letters fayre furth hath he tayne,
    And thus he sayd full ryght:

37. "My lorde your father he gretes yow well,
    Wyth many a noble knyght;
    He desyres yow to byde
    That he may see thys fyght.

38. "The Baron of Grastoke ys com out of
    the west,
    With hym a noble companye; 150
    All they loge at your fathers thys nyght,
    And the batell fayne wolde they see."

39. "For Jhesus love," sayd Syr Harye Perssy,
    "That dyed for yow and me,
    Wende to my lorde my father agayne,
    And saye thow sawe me not with yee.[4]

40. "My trowth ys plyght to yonne Skottysh
    knyght,
    It nedes me not to layne,
    That I schulde byde hym upon thys bent,
    And I have hys trowth agayne. 160

41. "And if that I weynde of[5] thys growende,
    For soth, onfowghten awaye,
    He wolde me call but a kowarde knyght
    In hys londe another daye.

42. "Yet had I lever to be rynde and rente,[6]
    By Mary, that mykkel maye,[7]
    Then ever my manhood schulde be re-
    provyd
    Wyth a Skotte another daye.

43. "Wherefore schote, archars, for my sake,
    And let scharpe arowes flee; 170
    Mynstrells, playe up for your waryson,[1]
    And well quyt it schall bee.

44. "Every man thynke on hys trewe-love,
    And marke hym to the Trenite;
    For to God I make myne avowe
    Thys day wyll I not flee."

45. The blodye harte in the Dowglas armes,
    Hys standerde stood on hye,
    That every man myght full well knowe;
    By syde stode starrës thre. 180

46. The whyte lyon on the Ynglyssh perte,[2]
    For soth as I yow sayne,
    The lucettes[3] and the cressawntes both;
    The Skottes faught them agayne.

47. Upon Sent Androwe lowde can they crye,
    And thrysse they schowte on hyght,[4]
    And syne merked them one owr Yng-
    lysshe men,
    As I have tolde yow ryght.

48. Sent George the bryght, owr Ladyes
    knyght,
    To name they were full fayne; 190
    Owr Ynglyssh men they cryde on hyght,
    And thrysse they schowtte agayne.

49. Wyth that scharpe arowes bygan to flee,
    I tell yow in sertayne;
    Men of armes bygann to joyne,
    Many a dowghty man was ther slayne.

50. The Perssy and the Dowglas mette,
    That ether of other was fayne;
    They swapped[5] together whyll[6] that
    they swette,
    Wyth swordes of fyne collayne:[7] 200

51. Tyll the bloode from ther bassonnettes[8]
    ranne,
    As the roke[9] doth in the rayne;
    "Yelde the to me," sayd the Dowglas,
    "Or elles thow schalt be slayne.

52. "For I see by thy bryght bassonet,
    Thow arte sum man of myght;
    And so I do by thy burnysshed brande;
    Thow arte an yerle, or elles a knyght."

---

[1] royal [2] company [3] conceal [4] eye [5] count
from [6] flayed and drawn [7] powerful maid

[1] reward [2] part [3] pike (fish) [4] aloud [5] smote
[6] till [7] Cologne steel [8] basinets [9] smoke

53. "By my good faythe," sayd the noble
        Perssye,
    "Now haste thou rede [1] full ryght ; 210
    Yet wyll I never yelde me to the,
        Whyll I may stonde and fyght."

54. They swapped together whyll that they
        swette,
    Wyth swordës scharpe and long ;
    Ych on other so faste they beette,
        Tyll ther helmes cam in peyses dowyn.

55. The Perssy was a man of strenghth,
        I tell yow in thys stounde ; [2]
    He smote the Dowglas at the swordes
        length
        That he fell to the growynde.   220

56. The sworde was scharpe, and sore can byte,
        I tell yow in sertayne ;
    To the harte he cowde [3] hym smyte,
        Thus was the Dowglas slayne.

57. The stonderdes stode styll on eke a [4] syde,
        Wyth many a grevous grone ;
    Ther they fowght the day, and all the
        nyght,
        And many a dowghty man was slayne.

58. Ther was no freke [5] that ther wolde flye,
        But styffely in stowre [6] can stond, 230
    Ychone hewyng on other whyll they
        myght drye,[7]
        Wyth many a bayllefull bronde.

59. Ther was slayne upon the Skottës syde,
        For soth and sertenly,
    Syr James a Dowglas ther was slayne,
        That day that he cowde [3] dye.

60. The yerlle of Mentaye he was slayne,
        Grysely [8] groned upon the growynd ;
    Syr Davy Skotte, Syr Water Stewarde,
        Syr Jhon of Agurstoune.   240

61. Syr Charllës Morrey in that place,
        That never a fote wold flee ;
    Syr Hewe Maxwell, a lord he was,
        Wyth the Dowglas dyd he dye.

62. Ther was slayne upon the Skottës syde,
        For soth as I yow saye,

[1] discerned [2] time [3] did [4] every [5] man [6] battle
[7] endure [8] fearfully

Of fowre and forty thowsande Scottes
    Went but eyghtene awaye.

63. Ther was slayne upon the Ynglysshe syde,
        For soth and sertenlye,   250
    A gentell knyght, Syr Jhon Fechewe,
        Yt was the more pety.

64. Syr James Hardbotell ther was slayne,
        For hym ther hartes were sore ;
    The gentyll Lovell ther was slayne,
        That the Perssys standerd bore.

65. Ther was slayne upon the Ynglyssh perte,
        For soth as I yow saye,
    Of nyne thowsand Ynglyssh men
        Fyve hondert cam awaye,   260

66. The other were slayne in the fylde ;
        Cryste kepe ther sowlles from wo !
    Seyng [1] ther was so fewe fryndes
        Agaynst so many a foo.

67. Then on the morne they mayde them
        beerys
    Of byrch and haysell graye ;
    Many a wydowe, wyth wepyng teyres,
        Ther makes they fette [2] awaye.

68. Thys fraye bygan at Otterborne,
        Bytwene the nyght and the day ;   270
    Ther the Dowglas lost hys lyffe,
        And the Perssy was lede awaye.

69. Then was ther a Scottysh prisoner tayne,
        Syr Hewe Mongomery was hys name ;
    For soth as I yow saye,
        He borowed [3] the Perssy home agayne.

70. Now let us all for the Perssy praye
        To Jhesu most of myght,
    To bryng hys sowlle to the blysse of heven,
        For he was a gentyll knyght.   280

SIR PATRICK SPENS

The king sits in Dumferling toune,
    Drinking the blude-reid wine :
"O whar will I get guid sailor,
    To sail this schip of mine ?"

Up and spak an eldern knicht,
    Sat at the kings richt kne :

[1] seeing   [2] fetched   [3] ransomed

"Sir Patrick Spence is the best sailor,
   That sails upon the se."

The king has written a braid letter,
   And signd it wi his hand,   10
And sent it to Sir Patrick Spence,
   Was walking on the sand.

The first line that Sir Patrick red,
   A loud lauch [1] lauched he;
The next line that Sir Patrick red,
   The teir blinded his ee.

"O wha is this has don this deid,
   This ill deid don to me,
To send me out this time o' the yeir,
   To sail upon the se!   20

"Mak hast, mak haste, my mirry men all,
   Our guid schip sails the morne:"
"O say na sae, my master deir,
   For I feir a deadlie storme.

"Late, late yestreen I saw the new moone,
   Wi the auld moone in hir arme,
And I feir, I feir, my deir master,
   That we will cum to harme."

O our Scots nobles wer richt laith [2]
   To weet their cork-heild schoone;   30
Bot lang owre [3] a' the play wer playd,
   Thair hats they swam aboone.[4]

O lang, lang may their ladies sit,
   Wi thair fans into their hand,
Or eir they se Sir Patrick Spence
   Cum sailing to the land.

O lang, lang may the ladies stand,
   Wi thair gold kems [5] in their hair,
Waiting for thair ain deir lords,
   For they'll se thame na mair.   40

Haf owre, haf owre to Aberdour,
   It's fiftie fadom deip,
And thair lies guid Sir Patrick Spence,
   Wi the Scots lords at his feit.

CAPTAIN CAR, OR, EDOM O GORDON

1. It befell at Martynmas,
   When wether waxed colde,
   Captaine Care said to his men,
   "We must go take a holde." [6]

[1] laugh [2] loth [3] ere [4] above [5] combs [6] castle

Syck,[1] sike,[1] and to-towe [2] sike,
   And sike and like to die;
The sikest nighte that ever I abode,
   God Lord have mercy on me!

2. "Haille, master, and wether [3] you will,
   And wether [3] ye like it best."   10
"To the castle of Crecrynbroghe,
   And there we will take our reste."

3. "I knowe wher is a gay castle,
   Is builded of lyme and stone;
Within their is a gay ladie,
   Her lord is riden and gone."

4. The ladie she lend on her castle-walle,
   She loked upp and downe;
There was she ware of an host of men,
   Come riding to the towne.   20

5. "Se yow, my meri men all,
   And se yow what I see?
Yonder I see an host of men,
   I muse who they shold bee."

6. She thought he had ben her wed lord,
   As he comd riding home;
Then was it traitur Captaine Care
   The lord of Ester-towne.

7. They wer no soner at supper sett,
   Then after said the grace,   30
Or Captaine Care and all his men
   Wer lighte aboute the place.

8. "Gyve over thi howsse, thou lady gay,
   And I will make the a bande;
To-nighte thou shall ly within my armes,
   To-morrowe thou shall ere [4] my lande."

9. Then bespacke the eldest sonne,
   That was both whitt and redde:
"O mother dere, geve over your howsse,
   Or elles we shalbe deade."   40

10. "I will not geve over my hous," she saithe,
   "Not for feare of my lyffe;
It shalbe talked throughout the land,
   The slaughter of a wyffe.

11. "Fetch me my pestilett,[5]
   And charge me my gonne,

[1] sick [2] too-too [3] whither [4] possess [5] pistol

That I may shott at this bloddy butcher,
   The lord of Easter-towne."

12. Styfly upon her wall she stode,
    And lett the pellettes flee;   50
But then she myst the blody bucher,
    And she slew other three.

13. "I will not geve over my hous," she
      saithe,
    "Netheir for lord nor lowne;
Nor yet for traitour Captaine Care,
    The lord of Easter-towne.

14. "I desire of Captine Care,
    And all his bloddye band,
That he would save my eldest sonne,
    The eare [1] of all my lande."   60

15. "Lap him in a shete," he sayth,
    "And let him downe to me,
And I shall take him in my armes,
    His waran shall I be."

16. The captayne sayd unto him selfe;
    Wyth sped, before the rest,
He cut his tonge out of his head,
    His hart out of his brest.

17. He lapt them in a handkerchef,
    And knet it of knotes three,   70
And cast them over the castell-wall,
    At that gay ladye.

18. "Fye upon the, Captayne Care,
    And all thy bloddy band!
For thou hast slayne my eldest sonne,
    The ayre of all my land."

19. Then bespake the yongest sonne,
    That sat on the nurses knee,
Sayth, "Mother gay, geve over your
    house;
    For the smoake it smoothers me."   80

20. Out then spake the Lady Margaret,
    As she stood on the stair;
The fire was at her goud [2] garters,
    The lowe [3] was at her hair.

21. "I wold geve my gold," she saith,
    "And so I wolde my ffee,

      [1] heir   [2] gold   [3] flame

For a blaste of the westryn wind,
   To dryve the smoke from thee.

22. "Fy upon the, John Hamleton,
    That ever I paid the hyre!   90
For thou hast broken my castle-wall,
    And kyndled in the ffyre."

23. The lady gate to her close parler,[1]
    The fire fell aboute her head;
She toke up her children two,
    Seth, "Babes, we are all dead."

24. Then bespake the hye steward,
    That is of hye degree;
Saith, "Ladie gay, you are in close,
    Wether ye fighte or flee."   100

25. Lord Hamleton dremd in his dream,
    In Carvall where he laye,
His halle were all of fyre,
    His ladie slayne or daye.[2]

26. "Busk and bowne, my mery men all,
    Even and go ye with me;
For I dremd that my hall was on fyre,
    My lady slayne or day."

27. He buskt him and bownd hym,
    And like a worthi knighte;   110
And when he saw his hall burning,
    His harte was no dele lighte.

28. He sett a trumpett till his mouth,
    He blew as it plesd his grace;
Twenty score of Hamlentons
    Was light aboute the place.

29. "Had I knowne as much yesternighte
    As I do to-daye,
Captain Care and all his men
    Should not have gone so quite.   120

30. "Fye upon the, Captaine Care,
    And all thy blody bande!
Thou haste slayne my lady gay,
    More wurth then all thy lande.

31. "If thou had ought eny ill will," he saith,
    "Thou shoulde have taken my lyffe,
And have saved my children thre,
    All and my lovesome wyffe."

      [1] parlor   [2] ere day

LORD RANDAL

1. "O where hae ye been, Lord Randal, my
    son?
    O where hae ye been, my handsome young
    man?"
    "I hae been to the wild wood; mother,
    make my bed soon,
    For I'm weary wi hunting, and fain wald lie
    down."

2. "Where gat ye your dinner, Lord Randal,
    my son?
    Where gat ye your dinner, my handsome
    young man?"
    "I din'd wi my true-love; mother, make
    my bed soon,
    For I'm weary wi hunting, and fain wald
    lie down."

3. "What gat ye to your dinner, Lord Randal,
    my son?
    What gat ye to your dinner, my handsome
    young man?"   10
    "I gat eels boiled in broo; mother, make
    my bed soon,
    For I'm weary wi hunting, and fain wald lie
    down."

4. "What became of your bloodhounds, Lord
    Randal, my son?
    What became of your bloodhounds, my
    handsome young man?"
    "O they swelld and they died; mother,
    make my bed soon,
    For I'm weary wi hunting, and fain wald
    lie down."

5. "O I fear ye are poison'd, Lord Randal, my
    son!
    O I fear ye are poisond, my handsome
    young man!"
    "O yes! I am poisond; mother, make my
    bed soon,
    For I'm sick at the heart and I fain wald lie
    down."   20

HIND HORN

1. In Scotland there was a babie born,
    Lill lal, etc.
    And his name it was called young Hind
    Horn.
    With a fal lal, etc.

2. He sent a letter to our king
    That he was in love with his daughter
    Jean.

3. The king an angry man was he;
    He sent young Hind Horn to the sea.

4. He's gien to her a silver wand,
    With seven living lavrocks[1] sitting
    thereon.   10

5. She's gien to him a diamond ring,
    With seven bright diamonds set therein.

6. "When this ring grows pale and wan,
    You may know by it my love is gane."

7. One day as he looked his ring upon,
    He saw the diamonds pale and wan.

8. He left the sea and came to land,
    And the first that he met was an old beg-
    gar man.

9. "What news, what news?" said young
    Hind Horn;
    "No news, no news," said the old beggar
    man.   • 20

10. "No news," said the beggar, "no news at a'
    But there is a wedding in the king's ha.

11. "But there is a wedding in the king's ha,
    That has halden these forty days and
    twa."

12. "Will ye lend me your begging coat?
    And I'll lend you my scarlet cloak.

13. "Will you lend me your beggar's rung?[2]
    And I'll gie you my steed to ride upon.

14. "Will you lend me your wig o hair,
    To cover mine, because it is fair?"   30

15. The auld beggar man was bound for the
    mill,
    But young Hind Horn for the king's hall.

16. The auld beggar man was bound for to
    ride,
    But young Hind Horn was bound for the
    bride.

[1] larks   [2] staff

17. When he came to the king's gate,
　　He sought a drink for Hind Horn's sake.

18. The bride came down with a glass of wine,
　　When he drank out the glass, and dropt
　　　in the ring.

19. "O got ye this by sea or land?
　　Or got ye it off a dead man's hand?"　40

20. "I got not it by sea, I got it by land,
　　And I got it, madam, out of your own
　　　hand."

21. "O I'll cast off my gowns of brown,
　　And beg wi you frae town to town.

22. "O I'll cast off my gowns of red,
　　And I'll beg wi you to win my bread."

23. "Ye needna cast off your gowns of
　　brown,
　　For I'll make you lady o many a town.

24. "Ye needna cast off your gowns o red,
　　It's only a sham, the begging o my
　　　bread."　50

ST. STEPHEN AND HEROD

1. Seynt Stevene was a clerk in Kyng
　　Herowdes halle,
　　And servyd him of bred and cloth, as
　　every kyng befalle.

2. Stevyn out of kechone cam, wyth boris[1]
　　hed on honde;
　　He saw a sterre was fayr and brygt over
　　Bedlem stonde.

3. He kyst[2] adoun the boris hed and went
　　in to the halle:
　　"I forsak the, Kyng Herowdes, and thi
　　werkes alle.

4. "I forsak the, Kyng Herowdes, and thi
　　werkes alle;
　　Ther is a chyld in Bedlem born is beter
　　than we alle."

5. "What eylyt[3] the, Stevene? What is the
　　befalle?
　　Lakkyt the eyther mete or drynk in
　　Kyng Herowdes halle?"　10

　　　　[1] boar's　　　[2] cast　　　[3] aileth

6. "Lakit me neyther mete nor drynk in
　　Kyng Herowdes halle;
　　Ther is a chyld in Bedlem born is beter
　　than we alle."

7. "What eylyt the, Stevyn? Art thu
　　wod,[1] or thu gynnyst to brede?[2]
　　Lakkyt the eyther gold or fe,[3] or ony
　　ryche wede?"[4]

8. "Lakyt me neyther gold ne fe, ne non
　　ryche wede;
　　Ther is a chyld in Bedlem born xal helpyn
　　us at our nede."

9. "That is al so soth,[5] Stevyn, al so soth,
　　iwys,[6]
　　As this capoun crowe xal that lyth here
　　in myn dysh."

10. That word was not so sone seyd, that
　　word in that halle,
　　The capoun crew *Cristus natus est!* among
　　the lordes alle.　20

11. "Rysyt[7] up, myn turmentowres,[8] be to[9]
　　and al be on,
　　And ledyt Stevyn out of this toun, and
　　stonyt hym wyth ston!"

12. Tokyn he[10] Stevene, and stonyd hym in
　　the way,
　　And therefore is his evyn on Crystes owyn
　　day.

SIR THOMAS MALORY
(1400?–1470)

LE MORTE DARTHUR
BOOK XXI. From CAPITULUM V

"But I may not stonde, myn hede werches[11]
soo. A, Syr Launcelot," sayd kyng Arthur,
"thys day have I sore myst the. Alas! that
ever I was ayenst[12] the, for now have I my
dethe, wherof Syr Gauwayn me warned in my
dreme." Than Syr Lucan took up the kyng
the one parte, and Syr Bedwere the other parte,
and in the lyftyng the kyng sowned,[13] and Syr

　　[1] crazy　[2] be whimsical　[3] property　[4] garment
[5] true [6] indeed [7] rise [8] executioners [9] by two [10] they
[11] aches [12] against [13] swooned

Lucan fyl in a sowne[1] wyth the lyfte, that the parte of his guttes fyl oute of his bodye. And therwyth the noble knyghtes herte braste.[2] And whan the kyng awake, he behelde Syr Lucan how he laye foomyng at the mowth, and parte of his guttes laye at his feet. "Alas!" sayd the kyng, "thys is to me a ful hevy syght to see thys noble duke so deye for my sake, for he wold have holpen me that had more nede of helpe than I. Alas! he wold not complayne hym, hys herte was so sette to helpe me. Now Jhesu have mercy upon hys soule." Than Syr Bedwere wepte for the deth of his brother. "Leve thys mornyng and wepyng," sayd the kyng, "for al this wyl not avaylle me; for wyte[3] thou wel, and[4] I myght lyve my self, the deth of Syr Lucan wolde greve me ever more, but my tyme hyeth[5] fast," sayd the kyng. "Therfore," sayd Arthur unto Syr Bedwere, "take thou Excalybur, my good swerde, and goo with it to yonder water syde, and whan thou comest there, I charge the[6] throwe my swerde in that water, and come ageyn and telle me what thou there seest." "My lord," sayd Bedwere, "your commaundement shal be doon, and lyghtly brynge you worde ageyn."

So Syr Bedwere departed, and by the waye he behelde that noble swerde, that the pomel and the hafte was al of precyous stones; and thenne he sayd to hym self, "Yf I throwe this ryche swerde in the water, therof shal never come good, but harme and losse." And thenne Syr Bedwere hydde Excalybur under a tree. And so as sone as he myght he came ageyn unto the kyng, and sayd he had ben at the water, and had throwen the swerde in to the water. "What sawe thou there?" sayd the kyng. "Syr," he sayd, "I sawe no thynge but wawes[7] and wyndes." "That is untrewly sayd of the,"[6] sayd the kynge. "Therfore goo thou lyghtelye[8] ageyn, and do my commaundemente; as thou arte to me leef[9] and dere, spare not but throwe it in." Than Syr Bedwere retorned ageyn, and took the swerde in hys hande, and than hym thought synne and shame to throwe awaye that nobyl swerde; and so efte[10] he hydde the swerde, and retorned ageyn and tolde to the kyng that he had ben at the water, and done his commaundemente. "What sawe thou there?" sayd the kyng. "Syr," he sayd, "I

saw no thynge but the waters wappe[1] and wawes wanne."[2] "A, traytour, untrewe," sayd kyng Arthur, "now hast thou betrayed me twyse. Who wold have wente[3] that thou that hast been to me so leef[4] and dere, and thou arte named a noble knyghte, and wold betraye me for the richesse of the swerde? But now goo ageyn lyghtly, for thy longe taryeng putteth me in grete jeopardye of my lyf, for I have taken colde; and but-yf[5] thou do now as I byd the, yf ever I may see the I shal slee[6] the[7] myn owne handes, for thou woldest for my ryche swerde see me dede."[8] Thenne Syr Bedwere departed, and wente to the swerde, and lyghtly took hit up, and wente to the water syde, and there he bounde the gyrdyl aboute the hyltes, and thenne he threwe the swerde as farre in to the water as he myght. And there cam an arme and an hande above the water and mette it, and caught it, and so shoke it thryse and braundysshed; and than vanysshed awaye the hande wyth the swerde in the water. So Syr Bedwere came ageyn to the kyng and tolde hym what he sawe.

"Alas!" sayd the kyng, "helpe me hens,[9] for I drede[10] me I have taryed over longe." Than Syr Bedwere toke the kyng upon his backe, and so wente wyth hym to that water syde, and whan they were at the water syde, evyn fast[11] by the banke hoved[12] a lytyl barge wyth many fayr ladyes in hit, and emonge hem al was a quene, and al they had blacke hoodes, and al they wepte and shryked[13] whan they sawe kyng Arthur. "Now put me in to the barge," sayd the kyng; and so he dyd softelye. And there receyved hym thre quenes wyth grete mornyng, and soo they sette hem doun, and in one of their lappes kyng Arthur layed hys heed, and than that quene sayd, "A, dere broder, why have ye taryed so longe from me? Alas! this wounde on your heed hath caught overmoche colde." And soo than they rowed from the londe, and Syr Bedwere behelde all tho[14] ladyes goo from hym.[15] Than Syr Bedwere cryed, "A, my lord Arthur, what shal become of me, now ye goo from me and leve me here allone emonge myn enemyes?" "Comfort thy self," sayd the kyng, "and doo as wel as thou mayst, for in me is no truste for to truste in. For I wyl

---

[1] swoon [2] burst [3] know [4] if [5] hastens [6] thee [7] waves [8] quickly [9] beloved [10] again

AE

[1] lap, beat [2] grow dark [3] thought [4] beloved [5] unless [6] slay [7] thee [8] dead [9] hence [10] fear [11] close [12] hovered, floated [13] shrieked [14] those [15] *i.e.* Bedwere

in to the vale of Avylyon, to hele me of my grevous wounde. And yf thou here never more of me, praye for my soule." But ever the quenes and ladyes wepte and shryched,[1] that hit was pyte [2] to here. And assone as Syr Bedwere had loste the syght of the baarge, he wepte and waylled, and so took the foreste;[3] and so he wente al that nyght, and in the mornyng he was ware [4] betwyxte two holtes hore [5] of a chapel and an ermytage.[6]

WILLIAM CAXTON (1422?–1491)

PREFACE TO THE BOOKE OF ENEYDOS

And whan I had advysed me in this sayd boke, I delybered [7] and concluded to translate it in to Englysshe, and forthwyth toke a penne and ynke and wrote a leef or tweyne, whyche I oversawe agayn to corecte it; and whan I sawe the fayr and straunge termes therein, I doubted [8] that it sholde not please some gentylmen whiche late blamed me, sayeng that in my translacyons I had over curyous [9] termes, which coude not be understande [10] of comyn peple, and desired me to use olde and homely termes in my translacyons. And fayn wolde I satysfye every man; and, so to doo, toke an olde boke and redde therin; and certaynly the Englysshe was so rude and brood [11] that I coude not wele understande it; and also my lorde abbot of Westmynster ded so shewe to me late certayn evydences [12] wryton in olde Englysshe for to reduce it in to our Englysshe now used, and certaynly it was wreton in suche wyse that it was more lyke to Dutche than Englysshe; I coude not reduce ne brynge it to be understonden. And certaynly our langage now used varyeth ferre [13] from that whiche was used and spoken whan I was borne. For we Englysshe men ben borne under the domynacyon of the mone, whiche is never stedfaste but ever waverynge, wexynge one season and waneth and dyscreaseth [14] another season. And that comyn [15] Englysshe that is spoken in one shyre varyeth from a-nother, in so moche that in my dayes happened that certayn marchauntes were in a ship in Tamyse for to

have sayled over the see into Zelande, and for lacke of wynde, thei taryed atte [1] Forlond, and wente to lande for to refreshe them. And one of theym named Sheffelde, a mercer, cam in to an hows and axed for mete and specyaly he axyed after eggys, and the goode wyf answerde that she could speke no Frenshe. And the marchaunt was angry, for he also coude speke no Frenshe, but wolde have hadde egges; and she understode hym not. And thenne at laste a-nother sayd that he wolde have eyren.[2] Then the good wyf sayd that she understod hym wel. Loo,[3] what sholde a man in thyse dayes now wryte, egges, or eyren? Certaynly it is hard to playse every man, by-cause of dyversite and chaunge of langage; for in these dayes every man that is in ony reputacyon in his countre wyll utter his commynycacyon and maters in suche maners and termes that fewe men shall understonde theym. And som honest and grete clerkes have ben wyth me and desired me to wryte the moste curyous [4] termes that I coude fynde. And thus, betwene playn, rude, and curyous, I stande abasshed. But in my judgemente the comyn termes that be dayly used ben lyghter to be understonde than the olde and auncyent Englysshe. And, foras-moche as this present booke is not for a rude uplondyssh [5] man to laboure therein ne rede it, but onely for a clerke and a noble gentylman that feleth and understondeth in faytes [6] of armes, in love, and in noble chyvalrye, therfor in a meane bytwene bothe I have reduced and translated this sayd booke in our Englysshe, not over rude ne curyous, but in suche termes as shall be understanden, by Goddys grace, accordynge to my copye.

STEPHEN HAWES (d. 1523)

THE PASTIME OF PLEASURE

OF THE GREAT MARIAGE BETWENE GRAUNDE AMOUR AND LABELL PUCELL

FROM CAPIT. XXXIX

Then Perceveraunce in all goodly haste
Unto the stewarde called Liberalitie
Gave warnyng for to make ready fast
Agaynst this tyme of great solemnitie

---

[1] shrieked [2] pity [3] forest [4] he perceived [5] hoary forests [6] hermitage [7] deliberated [8] feared [9] curious, ornate [10] understood [11] broad [12] legal documents [13] far [14] decreases [15] common

[1] at the [2] eggs [3] lo [4] ornate, artificial [5] country [6] deeds

That on the morowe halowed shoulde be.
She warned the cooke called Temperaunce
And after that the ewres,[1] Observaunce,

With Pleasaunce, the panter,[2] and dame
    Curtesy,
The gentle butler, with the ladyes all.
Eche in her office was prepared shortly   10
Agaynst this feast so muche triumphall;
And La Bell Pucell then in speciall
Was up by time in the morowe graye;
Right so was I when I sawe the daye.

And right anone La Bell Pucell me sent,
Agaynst my weddyng, of the saten fyne,
White as the mylke, a goodly garment
Braudred [3] with pearle that clearely dyd
    shine.
And so, the mariage for to determine,
Venus me brought to a royal chapell,   20
Whiche of fine golde was wrought everydell.

And after that the gay and glorious
La Bell Pucell to the chapell was leade
In a white vesture fayre and precious,
With a golden chaplet on her yelowe heade;
And Lex Ecclesie did me to her wedde.
After whiche weddyng then was a great feast;
Nothing we lacked, but had of the best.

What [4] shoulde tary by longe continuance
Of the fest? for of my joy and pleasure   30
Wisdome can judge, without variaunce,
That nougt I lacked, as ye may be sure,
Paiyng the swete due dette of nature.
Thus with my lady, that was fayre and
    cleare,
In joy I lived full ryght, many a yere.

O lusty youth and yong tender hart,
The true companion of my lady bryght!
God let us never from other astart,[5]
But all in joye to live bothe daye and nyght.
Thus after sorowe joye arived aryght;   40
After my payne I had sport and playe;
Full litle thought I that it shoulde decaye,

Tyll that Dame Nature Naturyng [6] had
    made
All thinges to growe unto their fortitude;[7]

[1] eweress, servant in charge of ewers, napkins,
etc. [2] servant in charge of pantry [3] broidered
[4] why [5] start away [6] *Natura naturans*, Nature as
a creative being [7] strength

And Nature Naturyng waxt retrograde,
By strength my youthe so far to exclude,
As was ever her olde consuetude
First to augment and then to abate, —
This is the custome of her hye estate.   49

JOHN SKELTON (1460?–1529)

FROM A DIRGE FOR PHYLLIP SPAROWE

Do mi nus,[1]
Helpe nowe, swete Jesus !
Levavi oculos meos in montes: [2]
Wolde God I had Zenophontes,
Or Socrates the wyse,
To shew me their devyse,   100
Moderatly to take
This sorrow that I make
For Phyllip Sparowes sake !
So fervently I shake,
I fele my body quake;
So urgently I am brought
Into carefull thought.
Like Andromach, Hectors wyfe,
Was wery of her lyfe,
Whan she had lost her joye,   110
Noble Hector of Troye;
In lyke manner also
Encreaseth my dedly wo,
For my sparowe is go.

    It was so pretty a fole,[3]
It wold syt on a stole,
And lerned after my scole
For to kepe his cut,[4]
With, "Phyllyp, kepe your cut !"
It had a velvet cap,   120
And wold syt upon my lap,
And seke after small wormes,
And somtyme white-bred crommes;
And many tymes and ofte
Betwene my brestes softe
It wolde lye and rest;
It was propre and prest.[5]
    Somtyme he wolde gaspe
Whan he sawe a waspe;
A fly or a gnat,   130
He wolde flye at that;
And prytely he wold pant
Whan he saw an ant;

[1] Lord [2] I have lifted up mine eyes to the
mountains. [3] fool [4] to act shy, to keep his distance [5] ready

Lord, how he wolde pry
After the butterfly!
Lorde, how he wolde hop
After the gressop![1]
And whan I sayd, "Phyp! Phyp!"
Than he wold lepe and skyp,
And take me by the lyp.   140
Alas, it wyll me slo,[2]
That Phillyp is gone me fro!

From COLYN CLOUTE

My name is Colyn Cloute.
I purpose to shake oute
All my connyng bagge,   50
Lyke a clerkely hagge;
For though my ryme be ragged,
Tattered and jagged,
Rudely rayne beaten,
Rusty and moughte-eaten,[3]
If ye take well therwith,
It hath in it some pyth.
For, as farre as I can se,
It is wronge with eche degre;
For the temporalte   60
Accuseth the spiritualte;
The spirituall agayne
Dothe grudge and complayne
Upon the temporall men:
Thus eche of other blother[4]
The tone[5] agayng the tother.
Alas, they make me shoder!
For in hoder moder[6]
The Churche is put in faute.[7]
The prelates ben so haut,[8]   70
They say, and loke so hy,
As though they wolde fly
Above the sterry skye.
Laye-men say indede
How they take no hede
Theyr sely shepe to fede,
But plucke away and pull
The fleces of theyr wull;
Unethes[9] they leve a locke
Of wull amonges theyr flocke.   80
And as for theyr connynge,
A glommynge and a mummynge,
And make therof a jape;
They gaspe and they gape,
All to have promocyon,
There is theyr hole devocyon,
With money, if it wyll hap,

To catche the forked cap.
Forsothe they are to lewd
To say so, all beshrewd!   90

THE NUTBROWNE MAIDE
(C. 1500)
(Unknown Author)

"Be it right or wrong, these men among [1]on
  women do complaine,
Affermyng this, how that it is a labour spent
  in vaine
To love them wele, for never a dele they love a
  man agayne;
For lete a man do what he can ther favor to
  attayne,
Yet yf a newe to them pursue, ther furst
  trew lover than[2]
Laboureth for nought, and from her thought
  he is a bannisshed man."

"I say not nay but that all day it is both writ
  and sayde
That woman's fayth is, as who saythe, all
  utterly decayed;
But nevertheless right good witnes in this
  case might be layde
That they love trewe and contynew —
  recorde the Nutbrowne Maide,   10
Whiche from her love, whan, her to prove, he
  cam to make his mone,
Wolde not departe, for in her herte she lovyd
  but hym allone."

"Than betwene us lete us discusse what was
  all the maner
Betwene them too,[3] we wyl also telle all the
  peyne infere[4]
That she was in. Now I begynne, soo that
  ye me answere.
Wherfore alle ye that present be, I pray you
  geve an eare.
I am a knyght, I cum be nyght, as secret as I
  can,
Sayng, 'Alas! thus stondyth the case: I am
  a bannisshed man.'"

"And I your wylle for to fulfylle, in this wyl
  not refuse,
Trusting to shewe in wordis fewe that men
  have an ille use,[5]   20

---

[1] grasshopper [2] slay [3] motheaten [4] complain
[5] the one [6] in secret [7] fault [8] haughty [9] scarcely

[1] continually [2] then [3] two [4] together [5] habit,
custom

To ther owne shame wymen to blame, and
causeles them accuse.
Therfore to you I answere now, alle wymen
to excuse:
'Myn owne hert dere, with you what chiere?
I prey you telle anoon;
For in my mynde of all mankynde I love but
you allon.'''

"It stondeth so, a dede is do wherefore moche
harme shal growe.
My desteny is for to dey a shamful dethe, I
trowe,
Or ellis to flee; the ton [1] must bee, none other
wey I knowe
But to withdrawe as an outlaw and take me to
my bowe.
Wherfore adew, my owne hert trewe, none
other red [2] I can; [3]
For I muste to the grene wode goo, alone, a
bannysshed man." 30

"O Lorde, what is this worldis blisse, that
chaungeth as the mone?
My somers day in lusty May is derked before
the none.
I here you saye 'farwel;' nay, nay, we departe not soo sone.
Why say ye so? wheder wyl ye goo? alas!
what have ye done?
Alle my welfare to sorow and care shulde
chaunge if ye were gon;
For in my mynde of all mankynde I love but
you alone."

"I can beleve it shal you greve, and somwhat
you distrayne;
But aftyrwarde your paynes harde within a
day or tweyne
Shal sone aslake, and ye shal take confort to
you agayne.
Why shuld ye nought? for to take thought,
your labur were in veyne. 40
And thus I do, and pray you, loo! as hertely
as I can;
For I muste too the grene wode goo, alone, a
bannysshed man."

"Now syth that ye have shewed to me the
secret of your mynde,
I shalbe playne to you agayne, lyke as ye shal
me fynde;

Syth it is so that ye wyll goo, I wol not leve [1]
behynde;
Shal ne'er be sayd the Nutbrowne Mayd was
to her love unkind.
Make you redy, for soo am I, all though it
were anoon; [2]
For in my mynde of all mankynde I love but
you alone."

"Yet I you rede to take good hede, what men
wyl thinke and sey;
Of yonge and olde it shalbe tolde that ye be
gone away, 50
Your wanton wylle for to fulfylle, in grene
wood you to play,
And that ye myght from your delyte noo
lenger make delay.
Rather than ye shuld thus for me be called
an ylle woman,
Yet wolde I to the grenewodde goo, alone, a
bannysshed man."

"Though it be songe of olde and yonge that
I shuld be to blame,
Theirs be the charge that speke so large in
hurting of my name;
For I wyl prove that feythful love it is de-
voyd of shame,
In your distresse and hevynesse to parte wyth
you the same;
And sure all thoo [3] that doo not so, trewe
lovers ar they noon;
But in my mynde of all mankynde I love but
you alone." 60

"I councel yow, remembre how it is noo
maydens lawe
Nothing to dought, but to renne out to wod
with an outlawe;
For ye must there in your hands bere a bowe
redy to drawe,
And as a theef thus must ye lyve ever in
drede and awe,
By whiche to yow gret harme myght grow;
yet had I lever than [4]
That I had too the grenewod goo, [5] alone, a
banysshyd man."

"I thinke not nay, but as ye saye, it is noo
maydens lore;
But love may make me for your sake, as ye
have said before,

---

[1] one   [2] plan   [3] know

[1] remain   [2] at once   [3] those   [4] I had rather then
[5] gone

To com on fote, to hunte and shote to get us
    mete and store ;
For soo that I your company may have, I
    aske noo more ;   70
From whiche to parte, it makith myn herte as
    colde as ony ston ;
For in my mynde of all mankynde I love but
    you alone."

"For an outlawe this is the lawe, that men
    hym take and binde,
Wythout pytee hanged to bee, and waver
    wyth the wynde.
Yf I had neede, as God forbede, what rescous [1]
    coude ye finde?
For sothe I trowe, you and your bowe shul
    drawe for fere behynde ;
And noo merveyle, for lytel avayle were in
    your councel than ;
Wherfore I too the woode wyl goo, alone, a
    bannysshd man."

"Ful wel knowe ye that wymen bee ful febyl
    for to fyght ;
Noo womanhed is it indeede to bee bolde as a
    knight ;   80
Yet in suche fere yf that ye were, amonge
    enemys day and nyght,
I wolde wythstonde, with bowe in hande, to
    greve them as I myght,
And you to save, as wymen have from deth
    [ful] many one ;
For in my mynde of all mankynde I love but
    you alone."

"Yet take good hede, for ever I drede that ye
    coude not sustein
The thorney wayes, the depe valeis, the snowe,
    the frost, the reyn,
The colde, the hete ; for, drye or wete, we
    must lodge on the playn,
And, us above, noon other rove [2] but a brake,
    bussh, or twayne ;
Whiche sone shulde greve you, I believe, and
    ye wolde gladly than
That I had too the grenewode goo, alone, a
    banysshed man."   90

"Syth I have here ben partynere with you
    of joy and blysse,
I muste also parte of your woo endure, as
    reason is ;

[1] rescue   [2] roof

Yet am I sure of oo [1] plesure, and shortly it is
    this,
That where ye bee, me semeth, perdè, I coude
    not fare amysse.
Wythout more speche, I you beseche that we
    were soon agone ;
For in my mynde of all mankynde I love but
    you alone."

"Yef ye goo thedyr, ye must consider, whan
    ye have lust to dyne,
Ther shal no mete be fore to gete, nor drinke,
    bere, ale, ne wine,
Ne shetis clene to lye betwene, made of thred
    and twyne,
Noon other house but levys and bowes, to
    kever your hed and myn.   100
Loo ! myn herte swete, this ylle dyet shuld
    make you pale and wan ;
Wherfore I to the wood wyl goo, alone, a ban-
    ysshid man."

"Amonge the wylde dere suche an archier as
    men say that ye bee
Ne may not fayle of good vitayle, where is so
    grete plente ;
And watir cleere of the ryvere shalbe ful
    swete to me,
Wyth whiche in hele [2] I shal right wele endure,
    as ye shal see ;
And, er we goo, a bed or twoo I can provide
    anoon ;
For in my mynde of all mankynde I love but
    you alone."

"Loo ! yet before ye must doo more, yf ye
    wyl goo with me,
As cutte your here up by your ere, your kirtel
    by the knee,   110
Wyth bowe in hande, for to withstonde your
    enmys, yf nede be,
And this same nyght before daylyght to wood-
    ward wyl I flee ;
And if ye wyl all this fulfylle, doo it shortely
    as ye can ;
Ellis wil I to the grenewode goo, alone, a
    banysshyd man."

"I shal, as now, do more for you than longeth
    to womanhede,
To short my here, a bowe to bere to shote in
    time of nede.

[1] one   [2] health

O my swete moder, before all other, for you
    have I most drede;
But now adiew! I must ensue, wher fortune
    doth me leede:
All this make ye; now lete us flee, the day
    cummeth fast upon;
For in my mynde of all mankynde I love but
    you alone."   120

"Nay, nay, not soo, ye shal not goo! and I
    shal tell you why:
Your appetyte is to be lyght of love, I wele
    aspie;
For right as ye have sayd to me, in lykewise
    hardely
Ye wolde answere, whosoever it were, in way
    of company.
It is sayd of olde, 'sone hote, sone colde,' and
    so is a woman;
Wherfore I too the woode wyl goo, alone, a
    banysshid man."

"Yef [1] ye take hede, yet is noo nede, suche
    wordis to say bee [2] me,
For oft ye preyd, and longe assayed, or I you
    lovid, perdee!
And though that I of auncestry a barons
    doughter bee,
Yet have you proved how I you loved, a
    squyer of lowe degree,   130
And ever shal, what so befalle, to dey therfore
    anoon;
For in my mynde of all mankynde I love but
    you alone."

"A barons childe to be begyled, it were a
    curssed dede,
To be felaw with an outlawe, almyghty God
    forbede!
Yet bettyr were the power [3] squyer alone to
    forest yede,[4]
Than ye shal say, another day, that be [2] my
    wyked dede
Ye were betrayed; wherfore, good maide, the
    best red [5] that I can,
Is that I too the grenewode goo, alone, a ban-
    ysshed man."

"Whatsoever befalle, I never shal of this
    thing you upbraid;
But yf ye goo and leve me so, than have ye me
    betraied.   140

[1] if   [2] by   [3] poor   [4] should go   [5] advice

Remembre you wele how that ye dele, for yf
    ye, as ye sayde,
Be so unkynde to leve behynde your love, the
    Notbrowne Maide,
Trust me truly that I shal dey sone after ye
    be gone;
For in my mynde of all mankynde I love but
    you alone."

"Yef that ye went, ye shulde repent, for in
    the forest now
I have purveid me of a maide, whom I love
    more than you, —
Another fayrer than ever ye were, I dare it
    wel avowe;
And of you both, eche shuld be wrothe with
    other, as I trowe.
It were myn ease to lyve in pease; so wyl I yf
    I can;
Wherfore I to the wode wyl goo, alone, a
    banysshid man."   150

"Though in the wood I undirstode ye had a
    paramour,
All this may nought remeve my thought, but
    that I wyl be your;
And she shal fynde me softe and kynde, and
    curteis every our,
Glad to fulfylle all that she wyl commaunde
    me, to my power;
For had ye, loo! an hondred moo, yet wolde I
    be that one;
For in my mynde of all mankynde I love but
    you alone."

"Myn owne dere love, I see the prove that ye
    be kynde and trewe;
Of mayde and wyfe, in all my lyf, the best
    that ever I knewe!
Be mery and glad, be no more sad, the case
    is chaungèd newe;
For it were ruthe that for your trouth you
    shuld have cause to rewe.   160
Be not dismayed, whatsoever I sayd, to you
    whan I began,
I wyl not too the grenewode goo, I am noo
    banysshyd man."

"Theis tidingis be more glad to me than to be
    made a quene,
Yf I were sure they shuld endure; but it is
    often seen,
When men wyl breke promyse, they speke the
    wordis on the splene.[1]

[1] capriciously

Ye shape some wyle, me to begyle, and stele
  fro me, I wene.
Then were the case wurs than it was, and I
  more woo-begone;
For in my mynde of al mankynde I love but
  you alone."

"Ye shal not nede further to drede, I wyl not
  disparage
You, God defende, sith you descende of so
  grete a lynage.   170
Now understonde, to Westmerlande, whiche
  is my herytage,
I wyle you bringe, and wyth a rynge, be wey
  of maryage,
I wyl you take, and lady make, as shortly as
  I can;
Thus have ye wone an erles son, and not a
  bannysshyd man."

Here may ye see that wymen be in love
  meke, kinde, and stable,
Late never man repreve them than, or calle
  them variable,
But rather prey God that we may to them
  be comfortable, —
Whiche somtyme provyth suche as he loveth,
  yf they be charitable.
For sith men wolde that wymen sholde be
  meke to them echeon,
Moche more ought they to God obey, and
  serve but hym alone.   180

EARLY TUDOR LYRICS (c. 1500)

I. RELIGIOUS LYRIC

I

Who shall have my fayr lady?
Who but I? Who but I? Who?
Who shall have my fayr lady?
Who hath more ryght therto?

This lady clere
That I sheu [1] here,
  Man soul yt ys, trust ye;
To Cryst most dere
It hath no pere;
  Therfor thys song syng we.
    Who shall, etc.   7

---

[1] show, declare

"For love swetnes
And joy endles
  I made my lady fre,
Unto my lyknes
I gave her quicnes [1]
  In Paradyse to be.
    Who shall, etc.   14

"O my swet store,
My true love therfore
  Thy place yt ys above;
What man may do more
Than only dy therfore,
  Lady, for thy love?
    Who shall," etc.   21

II. CHRISTMAS CAROLS

I

Thys ender nyght [2]
I saw a syght,
  A star as bright as day;
And ever among
A maydyn song:
  By-by, baby, lullay!

Thys vyrgyn clere
Wythowtyn pere
  Unto hur son gane say:
"My son, my lorde,
My fathere dere,
  Why lyest thow in hay?   12

"Methynk by ryght
Thow, kyng and knyght,
  Shulde lye in ryche aray,
Yet none the lesse
I wyll not cesse [3]
  To syng, By-by, lullay!"   18

Thys babe full bayne [4]
Aunsweryd agayne,
  And thus, me-thought, he sayd:
"I am a kyng
Above all thyng,
  Yn hay yff I be layde;   24

"For ye shall see
That kynges thre
  Shall cum on the twelfe day.
For thys behest
Geffe me thy brest
  And sing, By-by, lullay!"   30

---

[1] life   [2] the other night   [3] cease   [4] readily

"My son, I say
Wythowtyn nay [1]
   Thow art my derling dere;
I shall the kepe
Whyle thow dost slepe
   And make the [2] goode chere;   36

"And all thy wylle
I wyll fulfill,
   Thou wotyst hyt well yn fay.
Yet more then thys, —
I wyll the kys
   And syng, By-by, lullay."   42

"My moder swete,
When I have slepe,
   Then take me up on lofte;
Upon your kne
Thatt ye sett me
   And dandell me full soft;   48

"And in your arme
Lap me ryght warme
   And kepe me nyght and day;
And yff I wepe
And cannott slepe,
   Syng, By, baby, lullay."   54

"My son, my lorde,
My fader dere,
   Syth all ys at thy wyll,
I pray the, son,
Graunte me a bone,
   Yff hyt be ryght and skylle;   60

"That chylde or man,
Whoever can
   Be mery on thys day,
To blys them bryng
And I shall syng:
   By-by, baby, lullay!"   66

"My moder shene,[3]
Of hevyn quene,
   Your askyng shall I spede,
So that the myrth
Dysplease me nott
   Yn wordes nor in dede.   72

"Syng what ye wyll,
So ye fullfyll
   My ten commaundements ay.
Yow for to please
Let them nott sesse [4]
   To syng, Baby, lullay."   78

[1] certainly   [2] thee   [3] beautiful   [4] cease

II

"*Quid petis, o fily?*"
"*Mater dulcissima, ba-ba!*"
"*Quid petis, o fili?*"
"*Michi plausus oscula da-da!*"

   So laughyng in lap layde,
     So pretyly, so pertly,
   So passyngly well a-payd,[1]
     Ful softly and full soberly
   Unto her swet son she said: 5
     "Quid petys," etc.

The moder full manerly and mekly as a
   mayd,
Lokyng on her lytill son so laughyng in lap
   layd,
So pretyly, so partly, so passingly well apayd,
So passyngly wel apayd,   10
     Full softly and full soberly
Unto her son she saide,
Unto her son saide:
     "Quid petis," etc.

I mene this by Mary, our Makers moder of
   myght,
Full lovely lookyng on our Lord, the lanterne of lyght,   16
Thus saying to our Savior; this saw I in my
   syght.

III

Make we mery, bothe more and lasse,
For now ys the tyme of Crystymas!

Let no man cum into this hall,
Grome, page, nor yet marshal,
But that sum sport he bryng withall,
   For now ys the tyme of Crystymas.   4
   Make we mery, etc.

Yffe that he say he can not syng,
Sum oder sport then lett hym bryng,
That yt may please at thys festyng,   8
   For now ys the tyme of Crystymas.
   Make we mery, etc.

Yffe he say he can nowght do,
Then, for my love, aske hym no mo,   12
But to the stokke then lett hym go,
   For now ys the tyme of Crystymas.
   Make we mery, etc.

[1] satisfied

IV   •

What cher ?   Gud cher ! gud cher, gud cher !
Be mery and glad this gud Newyere !

"Lyft up your hartes and be glad
In Crystes byrth," the angell bad;
Say eche to oder, yf any be sad,
        "What cher," etc.   4

Now the kyng of hevyn his byrth hath take,
Joy and myrth we owght to make;
Say eche to oder for hys sake,
        "What cher," etc.   8

I tell you all with hart so fre,
Ryght welcum ye be to me;
Be glad and mery, for charite !
        "What cher," etc.   12

The gudman of this place in fere [1]
You to be mery he prayth you here,
And with gud hert he doth to you say,
        "What cher," etc.   16

III. CONVIVIAL SONGS

I

Fyll the cuppe, Phylyppe,
        And let us drynke a drame !
Ons or twys abowte the howse
        And leave where we began.
I drynke to your swete harte
        Soo mutche as here is in,
Desyeringe yow to followe me
        And doo as I begyn !   8
And yf you will not pledge,
        You shall bere the blame.
I drynke to you with all my harte,
        Yf you will pledge me the same.

II

Make rome,[2] syrs, and let us be mery,
        With "Huffa, galand !"
Synge,[6] "Tyrll on the bery,"
And let the wyde worlde wynde !
        Synge, "Fryska joly,"
        With "Hey, troly loly,"
        For I se well it is but foly
For to have a sad mynd !   8

[1] together   [2] room

IV. LOVE SONGS

I

Lully, lulley, lulley, lulley !
The fawcon hath born my make [1] away !

He bare hym up, he bare hym down,
He bare hym into an orchard brown.
        Lully, lulley, etc.   3

Yn that orchard there was an halle
That was hangid with purpill and pall.
        Lully, lulley, etc.   6

And in that hall there was a bede,
Hit was hangid with gold so rede.
        Lully, lulley, etc.   9

And yn that bed there lythe a knyght,
His wowndis bledyng day and nyght.
        Lully, lulley, etc.   12

By that bedis side kneleth a may,
And she wepeth both night and day.
        Lully, lulley, etc.   15

And by that beddis side there stondith a
        ston,
Corpus Christi wretyn thereon.
        Lully, lulley, etc.   18

II

The lytyll, prety nyghtyngale,
        Among the levys grene,
I wold I were with her all nyght !
        But yet ye wote [2] not whome I mene !

The nyghtyngale sat one a brere
        Among the thornys sherp and keyn
And comfort me wyth mery cher.
        But yet ye wot not whome I mene !

She dyd aper [3] all on [4] hur keynde [5]
        A lady ryght wel be-seyne,   10
Wyth wordys of loff tolde me hur mynde.
        But yet ye wot not whome I mene.

Hyt dyd me goode upon hur to loke,
        Hur corse was closyd all in grene;
Away fro me hur herte she toke,
        But yete ye wot not whome I mene.

"Lady !" I cryed, wyth rufull mone,
        "Have mynd of me, that true hath bene !
For I loved none but you alone."
        But yet ye wot not whome I mene.   20

[1] mate, sweetheart [2] know [3] appear [4] in [5] nature

THE BEGINNING OF THE RENAISSANCE

SIR THOMAS MORE (1478–1535)

A DIALOGUE OF SYR THOMAS MORE, KNYGHTE

FROM THE THIRDE BOKE. THE 16. CHAPTER

The messenger rehearseth some causes which he hath herd laid [1] by some of the clergie wherfore the Scripture should not be suffred in Englishe. And the author sheweth his mind, that it wer convenient to have the Byble in Englishe.

"Syr," quod your frende, "yet for al this, can I see no cause why the cleargie shoulde kepe the Byble out of ley mennes handes, that can [2] no more but theyr mother tong." "I had went," [3] quod I, "that I had proved you playnely that they kepe it not from them. For I have shewed you that they kepe none from them, but such translacion as be either not yet approved for good, or such as be alredi reproved for naught, as Wikliffes was and Tindals. For as for other olde ones, [4] that wer before Wickliffes daies, remain lawful, and be in some folkes handes had and read." "Ye saye well," quod he. "But yet as weomen saye, 'somewhat it was alway that the cat winked whan her eye was oute.' Surelye so is it not for nought that the English Byble is in so few mens handes, whan so many woulde so fayne have it." "That is very trouth," quod I; "for I thinke that though the favourers of a secte of heretikes be so fervent in the setting furth of their secte, that they let [5] not to lay their money together and make a purse among them, for the printyng of an evill made, or evil translated booke: which though it happe to be forboden [6] and burned, yet some be sold ere they be spyed,

[1] alleged [2] know [3] weened, thought [4] *This word is the subject of* remain, *as well as a part of the phrase in which it stands; the construction is curious but common.* [5] hesitate [6] forbidden

and eche of them lese [1] but theyr part: yet I thinke ther will no printer lightly [2] be so hote [3] to put anye Byble in prynte at hys own charge, whereof the losse shoulde lye hole in his owne necke, and than [4] hang upon a doutful tryal, whether the first copy of hys translacion was made before Wickliffes dayes or since. For if it were made synce, it must be approved before the prynting.

"And surelye howe it hathe happed that in all this whyle God hath eyther not suffered, or not provided that any good verteous man hath hadde the mynde in faithful wise to translate it, and therupon ether the clergie or, at the least wise, some one bishop to approve it, thys can I nothing tell. But howesoever it be, I have hearde and heare so muche spoken in the matter, and so muche doute made therin, that peradventure it would let and withdrawe any one bishop from the admitting therof, without the assent of the remenant. And whereas many thinges be laid against it : yet is ther in my mind not one thynge that more putteth good men of the clergie in doubte to suffer it, than thys : that they see sometime much of the worse sort more fervent in the calling for it, than them whom we find farre better. Which maketh them to feare lest such men desyre it for no good, and lest if it wer hadde in every mannes hand, there would great peril arise, and that sedicious people should doe more harme therwith than good and honest folke should take fruite thereby. Whiche feare I promise you nothyng feareth me, but that whosoever woulde of theyr malice or folye take harme of that thing that is of it selfe ordeyned to doe al men good, I would never for the avoyding of their harme, take from other the profit, which they might take, and nothing deserve to lese. [1] For elles [5] if the abuse of a good thing should cause the taking away thereof from other that woulde use it well, Christ should hymself never have been borne, nor brought hys fayth into the

[1] lose [2] easily [3] hot, ready [4] then [5] else

world, nor God should never have made it neither, if he should, for the losse of those that would be damned wretches, have kept away the occasion of reward from them that would with helpe of his grace endevor them to deserve it."

"I am sure," quod your frend, "ye doubte not but that I am full and hole of youre mynde in this matter, that the Byble shoulde be in oure Englishe tong. But yet that the clergie is of the contrary, and would not have it so, that appeareth well, in that they suffer it not to be so. And over [1] that, I heare in everye place almost where I find any learned man of them, their mindes all set theron to kepe the Scripture from us. And they seke out for that parte every rotten reason that they can find, and set them furth solemnely to the shew, though fyve of those reasons bee not woorth a figge. For they begynne as farre as our first father Adam, and shew us that his wyfe and he fell out of paradise with desyre of knowledge and cunning. Nowe if thys woulde serve, it must from the knowledge and studie of Scripture dryve every man, priest and other, lest it drive all out of paradise. Than [2] saye they that God taught his disciples many thynges apart, because the people should not heare it. And therefore they woulde the people should not now be suffered to read all. Yet they say further that it is hard to translate the Scripture out of one tong into an other, and specially they say into ours, which they call a tong vulgare and barbarous. But of all thing specially they say that Scripture is the foode of the soule. And that the comen people be as infantes that must be fedde but with milke and pappe. And if we have anye stronger meate, it must be chammed [3] afore by the nurse, and so putte into the babes mouthe. But me-think though they make us al infantes, they shall fynde many a shrewde brayn among us, that can perceive chalke fro chese well ynough, and if they woulde once take [4] us our meate in our own hand, we be not so evil-tothed [5] but that within a while they shall see us cham it our self as well as they. For let them call us yong babes and [6] they wil, yet, by God, they shal for al that well fynde in some of us that an olde knave is no chylde."

[1] besides [2] then [3] masticated [4] deliver [5] ill-toothed [6] if

WILLIAM TYNDALE (D. 1536)

THE GOSPELL OF S. MATHEW. THE FYFTH CHAPTER

When he sawe the people, he went up into a mountaine, and wen he was sett, hys disciples cam unto him, and he opened his mouth, and taught them sayinge: "Blessed are the poure in sprete: for thers is the kyngdom of heven. Blessed are they that mourne: for they shalbe comforted. Blessed are the meke: for they shall inheret the erthe. Blessed are they which hunger and thurst for rightewesnes: for they shalbe fylled. Blessed are the mercyfull: for they shall obteyne mercy. Blessed are the pure in hert: for they shall se God. Blessed are the maynteyners of peace: for they shalbe called the chyldren of God. Blessed are they which suffre persecucion for rightewesnes sake: for thers is the kyngdom of heven. Blessed are ye when men shall revyle you, and persecute you, and shal falsly saye all manner of evle sayinges agaynst you for my sake. Rejoyce and be gladde, for greate is youre rewarde in heven. For so persecuted they the prophettes which were before youre dayes.

"Ye are the salt of the erthe, but ah! yf the salte be once unsavery, what can be salted there-with? it is thence-forthe good for nothynge, but to be cast out at the dores, and that men treade it under fete. Ye are the light of the worlde. A cite that is sett on an hill cannot be hyd, nether do men light a candle and put it under a busshell, but on a candel-stycke, and it lighteth all those which are in the housse. Se that youre light so schyne before men, that they maye se youre good werkes, and gloryfie youre Father, which is in heven.

"Ye shall not thynke, that y am come to disanull the lawe other [1] the prophettes: no, y am not come to dysanull them, but to fulfyll them. For truely y say unto you, tyll heven and erthe perysshe, one jott, or one tytle of the lawe shall not scape, tyll all be fulfylled.

"Whosoever breaketh one of these leest commaundmentes, and shall teche men so, he shalbe called the leest in the kyngdom of heven. But whosoever shall observe and teache them, that persone shalbe called great in the kyngdom of heven.

[1] or

"For I say unto you, except youre righte-wesnes excede the rightewesnes of the scrybes and pharyses, ye cannot entre into the kyng-dom of heven.

"Ye have herde howe it was sayd unto them of the olde tyme. Thou shalt not kyll. Whosoever shall kyll, shalbe in daunger of judgement. But I say unto you, whosoever ys angre with hys brother, shalbe in daunger of judgement. Whosoever shall say unto his brother, Racha! shalbe in daunger of a counseill. But whosoever shall say unto his brother, Thou fole! shalbe in daunger of hell fyre. Therfore when thou offerest thy gyfte att the altre, and there remembrest that thy brother hath eny thynge agaynst the: leve there thyne offrynge before the altre, and go thy waye fyrst and reconcyle thy silff to thy brother, and then come and offre thy gyfte.

"Agre with thine adversary at once, whyles thou arte in the waye with hym, lest thine adversary delivre the to the judge, and the judge delyvre the to the minister,[1] and then thou be cast into preson. I say unto the verely: thou shalt not come out thence tyll thou have payed the utmoost forthynge.[2]

"Ye have herde howe yt was sayde to them of olde tyme, thou shalt not commytt ad-voutrie.[3] But I say unto you, that whoso-ever eyeth a wyfe, lustynge after her, hathe commytted advoutrie with her alredy in his hert.

"Wherfore yf thy right eye offende the, plucke hym out and caste him from the, Better hit is for the, that one of thy membres perysshe then that thy whole body shuld be caste in to hell. Also yf thy right honde offend the, cutt hym of and caste hym from the. Better hit is that one of thy membres perisshe, then that all thy body shulde be caste in to hell.

"Hit ys sayd, whosoever put[4] awaye his wyfe, let hym geve her a testymonyall of her divorcement. But I say unto you: whoso-ever put[4] awaye hys wyfe (except hit be for fornicacion) causeth her to breake matrimony, And who soever maryeth her that is divorsed, breaketh wedlocke.

"Agayne ye have herde, howe it was said to them of olde tyme, thou shalt not forswere thysilfe, but shalt performe thine othe to God. But I saye unto you swere not at all: nether by heven, for hit ys Goddes seate: nor yet by the erth, For it is hys fote stole: Nether by Jerusalem, for it is the cite of the greate kynge: Nether shalt thou swere by thy heed, because thou canst not make one heer whyte, or blacke: But youre communicacion shalbe, ye, ye: nay, nay. For whatsoever is more then that, commeth of evle.

"Ye have herde howe it is sayd, an eye for an eye: a tothe for a tothe. But I say unto you, that ye withstond[1] not wronge: But yf a man geve the a blowe on thy right cheke, turne to hym the othre. And yf eny man wyll sue the at the lawe, and take thi coote from the, lett hym have thi clooke also. And whosoever wyll compell the to goo a myle, goo wyth him twayne. Geve to him that axeth: and from him that wolde borrowe turne not away.

"Ye have herde howe it is saide: thou shalt love thyne neghbour, and hate thyne enemy. But y saye unto you, love youre enemies. Blesse them that cursse you. Doo good to them that hate you, Praye for them which doo you wronge, and persecute you, that ye maye be the chyldren of youre hevenly Father: for he maketh his sunne to aryse on the evle and on the good, and sendeth his reyne on the juste and on the onjuste. For if ye shall love them, which love you: what rewarde shall ye have? Doo not the publicans even so? And if ye be frendly to youre brethren only: what singuler thynge doo ye? Doo nott the publicans lyke wyse? Ye shall therfore be perfecte, even as youre hevenly Father is perfecte."

SIR THOMAS WYATT (1503–1542)

THE DESERTED LOVER CONSOLETH HIMSELF WITH REMEMBRANCE THAT ALL WOMEN ARE BY NATURE FICKLE

Divers doth use,[2] as I have heard and know,
When that to change their ladies do begin,
To mourn, and wail, and never for to lynn;[3]
Hoping thereby to 'pease their painful woe.
And some there be that when it chanceth so
That women change, and hate where love
  hath been,
They call them false, and think with words
  to win

---

[1] officer [2] farthing [3] adultery [4] puts

[1] resist [2] many are accustomed [3] cease

The hearts of them which otherwhere doth
    grow.[1]
But as for me, though that by chance indeed
Change hath outworn the favour that I had,
I will not wail, lament, nor yet be sad,   11
Nor call her false that falsely did me feed;
But let it pass, and think it is of kind [2]
That often change doth please a woman's
    mind.

THE LOVER COMPLAINETH THE UNKINDNESS OF HIS LOVE

My lute, awake, perform the last
Labour that thou and I shall waste,[3]
And end that I have now begun.
And when this song is sung and past,
My lute, be still, for I have done.

As to be heard where ear is none,
As lead to grave [4] in marble stone,
My song may pierce her heart as soon.
Should we then sigh, or sing, or moan?
No, no, my lute, for I have done.   10

The rocks do not so cruelly
Repulse the waves continually,
As she my suit and affection;
So that I am past remedy,
Whereby my lute and I have done.

Proud of the spoil that thou hast got
Of simple hearts through Lovës shot,
By whom unkind thou hast them won,
Think not he hath his bow forgot,
Although my lute and I have done.   20

Vengeance shall fall on thy disdain
That makest but game on earnest pain.
Think not alone under the sun
Unquit [5] to cause thy lovers plain,[6]
Although my lute and I have done.

May chance thee lie withered and old
In winter nights that are so cold,
Plaining in vain unto the moon;
Thy wishes then dare not be told.
Care then who list, for I have done.   30

And then may chance thee to repent
The time that thou hast lost and spent

----

[1] grow, adhere, to others   [2] of nature, natural
[3] spend   [4] engrave   [5] unpunished   [6] complain

To cause thy lovers sigh and swoon;
Then shalt thou know beauty but lent,
And wish and want, as I have done.

Now cease, my lute, this is the last
Labour that thou and I shall waste,
And ended is that we begun.
Now is this song both sung and past,
My lute, be still, for I have done.   40

A DESCRIPTION OF SUCH A ONE AS HE WOULD LOVE

A face that should content me wondrous well,
Should not be fair, but lovely to behold,
Of lively look, all grief for to repell,
With right good grace, so would I that it
    should
Speak without word, such words as none can
    tell;
The tress also should be of crispéd gold.
With wit and these perchance I might be
    tried,
And knit again with knot that should not
    slide.

OF THE MEAN AND SURE ESTATE

WRITTEN TO JOHN POINS

My mother's maids, when they did sew and
    spin,
They sang sometime a song of the field mouse
That, for because her livelihood was but thin,
Would needs go seek her townish sister's
    house.
She thought herself enduréd too much pain;
The stormy blasts her cave so sore did souse
That when the furrows swimmed with the
    rain,
She must lie cold and wet in sorry plight;
And worse than that, bare meat there did
    remain
To comfort her when she her house had
    dight;   10
Sometime a barly corn; sometime a bean,
For which she laboured hard both day and
    night
In harvest time whilst she might go and glean;
And where store [1] was stroyed [2] with the flood,
Then welaway! for she undone was clean.
Then was she fain to take instead of food
Sleep, if she might, her hunger to beguile.

----

[1] abundance   [2] destroyed

"My sister," quoth she, "hath a living good,
And hence from me she dwelleth not a mile.
In cold and storm she lieth warm and dry 20
In bed of down, the dirt doth not defile
Her tender foot, she laboureth not as I.
Richly she feedeth and at the richman's cost,
And for her meat she needs not crave nor cry.
By sea, by land, of the delicates, the most
Her cater [1] seeks and spareth for no peril,
She feedeth on boiled bacon, meat and roast,
And hath thereof neither charge nor travail;
And when she list, the liquor of the grape
Doth glad her heart till that her belly swell."
  And at this journey she maketh but a
     jape; [2]   36
So forth she goeth, trusting of all this wealth
With her sister her part so for to shape,
That if she might keep herself in health,
To live a lady while her life doth last.
  And to the door now is she come by stealth,
And with her foot anon she scrapeth full fast.
Th' other for fear durst not well scarce appear,
Of every noise so was the wretch aghast.
At last she askèd softly who was there,   40
And in her language as well as she could.
"Peep!" quoth the other sister, "I am here."
"Peace," quoth the town mouse, "why speakest thou so loud?"
And by the hand she took her fair and well.
"Welcome," quoth she, "my sister, by the Rood!"
She feasted her, that joy it was to tell
The fare they had; they drank the wine so clear,
And as to purpose now and then it fell,
She cheerèd her with "Ho, sister, what cheer!"
  Amid this joy befell a sorry chance,   50
That, welaway! the stranger bought full dear
The fare she had, for, as she looks askance,
Under a stool she spied two steaming [3] eyes
In a round head with sharp ears. In France
Was never mouse so fear'd, for, though unwise
Had not i-seen such a beast before,
Yet had nature taught her after her guise [4]
To know her foe and dread him evermore.
The towney mouse fled, she knew whither to go;
Th' other had no shift, but wanders sore   60

¹ caterer ² jest ³ gleaming ⁴ manner, way

Feard of her life. At home she wished her tho,[1]
And to the door, alas! as she did skip,
The Heaven it would, lo! and eke her chance was so,
At the threshold her silly foot did trip;
And ere she might recover it again,
The traitor cat had caught her by the hip,
And made her there against her will remain,
That had forgotten her poor surety and rest
For seeming wealth wherein she thought to reign.
Alas, my Poines, how men do seek the best 70
And find the worst by error as they stray!
And no marvel; when sight is so oppressed,
And blind the guide, anon out of the way
Goeth guide and all in seeking quiet life.
O wretched minds, there is no gold that may
Grant that ye seek; no war; no peace; no strife.
No, no, although thy head were hooped with gold,
Sergeant with mace, halberd, sword nor knife,
Cannot repulse the care that follow should.
Each kind of life hath with him his disease.
Live in delight even as thy lust would,[2]   81
And thou shalt find, when lust doth most thee please,
It irketh straight, and by itself doth fade.
A small thing it is that may thy mind appease.
None of ye all there is that is so mad
To seek grapes upon brambles or briars;
Nor none, I trow, that hath his wit so bad
To set his hay [3] for conies [4] over rivers,
Nor ye set not a drag net for an hare;
And yet the thing that most is your desire 90
Ye do mistake with more travail and care.
Make plain thine heart, that it be not knotted
With hope or dread, and see thy will be bare
From all effects whom vice hath ever spotted.
Thyself content with that is thee assigned,
And use it well that is to thee allotted.
Then seek no more out of thyself to find
The thing that thou hast sought so long before,
For thou shalt feel it sitting in thy mind.
Mad, if ye list to continue your sore,   100
Let present pass and gape on time to come,
And dip yourself in travail more and more.
  Henceforth, my Poines, this shall be all and some,
These wretched fools shall have nought else of me;

¹ then ² desire, wish ³ snare ⁴ rabbits

But to the great God and to his high dome,
None other pain pray I for them to be,
But when the rage doth lead them from the right,
That, looking backward, virtue they may see,
Even as she is so goodly fair and bright,
And whilst they clasp their lusts in arms across,   110
Grant them, good Lord, as Thou mayst of Thy might,
To fret inward for losing such a loss.

HENRY HOWARD, EARL OF SURREY (1517?–1547)

DESCRIPTION OF SPRING, WHEREIN EACH THING RENEWS, SAVE ONLY THE LOVER

The soote [1] season that bud and bloom forth brings
With green hath clad the hill and eke the vale;
The nightingale with feathers new she sings;
The turtle [2] to her make [3] hath told her tale:
Summer is come, for every spray now springs;
The hart hath hung his old head [4] on the pale; [5]
The buck in brake his winter cote he flings;
The fishes flete [6] with new repaired scale;
The adder all her slough away she slings;
The swift swallow pursueth the flies smale; 10
The busy bee her honey now she mings. [7]
Winter is worn, that was the flowers' bale: [8]
And thus I see among these pleasant things
Each care decays, and yet my sorrow springs!

COMPLAINT OF A LOVER REBUKED

Love, that liveth and reigneth in my thought,
That built his seat within my captive breast,
Clad in the arms wherein with me he fought,
Oft in my face he doth his banner rest.
She that me taught to love and suffer pain,
My doubtful hope and eke my hot desire
With shamefast cloak to shadow and refrain,
Her smiling grace converteth straight to ire.
The coward Love then to the heart apace
Taketh his flight, whereas he lurks and plains, [9]   10
His purpose lost, and dare not show his face.

---

[1] sweet   [2] turtle dove   [3] mate   [4] horns   [5] paling
[6] float   [7] mixes   [8] destruction   [9] laments

For my lord's guilt thus faultless bide I pains.
Yet from my lord shall not my foot remove;
Sweet is his death that takes his end by love.

DESCRIPTION AND PRAISE OF HIS LOVE GERALDINE

From Tuscan came my lady's worthy race;
Fair Florence was sometime her ancient seat;
The Western isle whose pleasant shore doth face
Wild Camber's cliffs did give her lively heat;
Fostered she was with milk of Irish breast;
Her sire, an earl; her dame, of princes' blood;
From tender years in Britain she doth rest,
With a king's child, where she tasteth costly food;
Hunsdon did first present her to mine eyes;
Bright is her hue, and Geraldine she hight; [1]
Hampton me taught to wish her first for mine;   11
And Windsor, alas, doth chase me from her sight:
Her beauty of kind, [2] her virtues from above.
Happy is he, that can obtain her love!

THE MEANS TO ATTAIN A HAPPY LIFE

Martial, the things that do attain
The happy life be these, I find:
The riches left, [3] not got with pain;
The fruitful ground; the quiet mind;
The egall [4] friend; no grudge, no strife;
No charge of rule, no governance;
Without disease, the healthful life;
The household of continuance;
The mean [5] diet, no delicate fare;
True wisdom joined with simpleness;   10
The night dischargèd of all care,
Where wine the wit may not oppress;
The faithful wife, without debate;
Such sleeps as may beguile the night:
Contented with thine own estate,
Ne wish for death, ne fear his might.

VIRGIL'S ÆNEID
BOOK II

They whisted [6] all, with fixèd face attent,
When Prince Æneas from the royal seat

---

[1] is named   [2] from nature   [3] inherited   [4] equal
[5] moderate   [6] became silent

Thus 'gan to speak: "O Queen, it is thy will
I should renew a woe cannot be told;
How that the Greeks did spoil and overthrow
The Phrygian wealth and wailful [1] realm of
    Troy.
Those ruthful things that I myself beheld,
And whereof no small part fell to my share;
Which to express, who could refrain from
    tears?
What Myrmidon? or yet what Dolopes? 10
What stern Ulysses' wagèd soldier?
And lo! moist night now from the welkin
    falls,
And stars declining counsel us to rest;
But since so great is thy delight to hear
Of our mishaps and Troyës last decay,
Though to record the same my mind abhors
And plaint eschews, yet thus will I begin: —
The Greekës chieftains, all irked with the war,
Wherein they wasted had so many years,
And oft repulsed by fatal destiny, 20
A huge horse made, high raisèd like a hill,
By the divine science of Minerva, —
Of cloven fir compacted were his ribs, —
For their return a feignèd sacrifice, —
The fame whereof so wandered it at point.[2]
In the dark bulk they closed bodies of men
Chosen by lot, and did enstuff by stealth
The hollow womb with armèd soldiers.
    There stands in sight an isle hight Tenedon,
Rich and of fame while Priam's kingdom stood,
Now but a bay and road unsure for ship. 31
Hither them secretly the Greeks withdrew,
Shrouding themselves under the desert shore;
And, weening we they had been fled and gone,
And with that wind had fet [3] the land of Greece,
Troy discharged her long continued dole.[4]
The gates cast up, we issued out to play,
The Greekish camp desirous to behold,
The places void and the forsaken coasts.
Here Pyrrhus' band, there fierce Achilles
    pight; [5]
Here rode their ships, there did their battles
    join.
Astonied some the scathful [6] gift beheld, 42
Behight [7] by vow unto the chaste Minerve, —
All wondering at the hugeness of the horse.
And first of all Timœtes gan advise
Within the walls to lead and draw the same,
And place it eke amid the palace court, —
Whether of guile, or Troyës fate it would.
Capys, with some of judgment more discreet,

Willed it to drown, or underset with flame, 50
The suspect present of the Greek's deceit,
Or bore and gauge the hollow caves uncouth;
So diverse ran the giddy people's mind.
    Lo! foremost of a route that followed him,
Kindled [1] Laöcoön hasted from the tower,
Crying far off: 'O wretched citizens,
What so great kind of frenzy freteth you?
Deem ye the Greeks, our enemies, to be gone?
Or any Greekish gifts can you suppose
Devoid of guile? Is so Ulysses known? 60
Either the Greeks are in this timber hid,
Or this an engine is to annoy [2] our walls,
To view our towers, and overwhelm our town.
Here lurks some craft. Good Troyans give
    no trust
Unto this horse, for, whatsoever it be,
I dread the Greeks, yea when they offer gifts.'"

* * * * * * *

ROGER ASCHAM (1515–1568)

THE SCHOLEMASTER

FROM THE FIRST BOOKE FOR THE
YOUTH

* * * * * * *

If your scholer do misse sometimes, in
marking rightlie these foresaid six thinges,
chide not hastelie: for that shall, both dull his
witte, and discorage his diligence: but monish
him gentelie: which shall make him, both willing to amende, and glad to go forward in love
and hope of learning. I have now wished,
twise or thrise, this gentle nature, to be in a
Scholemaster: And, that I have done so,
neither by chance, nor without some reason,
I will now declare at large, why, in mine opinion, love is fitter then feare, gentlenes better
than beating, to bring up a childe rightlie in
learninge.
    With the common use of teaching and beat-
ing in common scholes of England, I will not
greatlie contend: which if I did, it were but a
small grammaticall controversie, neither belonging to heresie nor treason,[3] nor greatly
touching God nor the Prince: although in
very deede, in the end, the good or ill bringing
up of children, doth as much serve to the good
or ill service, of. God, our Prince, and our
whole countrie, as any one thing doth beside.

---

[1] lamentable [2] conformably [3] fetched, reached
[4] sorrow [5] camped, *tendebat* [6] harmful [7] promised

AE

---

[1] excited [2] injure [3] *This is a proverbial expression.*

I do gladlie agree with all good Scholemasters in these pointes: to have children
brought to a good perfitnes in learning: to all
honestie in maners: to have all fautes [1] rightlie
amended: to have everie vice severelie corrected: but for the order and waie that lead-
eth rightlie to these pointes, we somewhat
differ. For commonlie, many scholemasters,
some, as I have seen, moe,[2] as I have heard
tell, be of so crooked a nature, as, when they
meete with a hard witted scholer, they rather
breake him than bowe him, rather marre him
then mend him. For whan the scholemaster
is angrie with some other matter, then will he
sonest faul to beate his scholer: and though
he him selfe should be punished for his folie,
yet must he beate some scholer for his pleasure: though there be no cause for him to do
so, nor yet fault in the scholer to deserve so.
These, ye will say, be fond [3] scholemasters,
and fewe they be that be found to be soch.
They be fond in deede, but surelie overmany
soch be found everie where. But this will I
say, that even the wisest of your great beaters,
do as oft punishe nature as they do correcte
faultes. Yea, many times, the better nature
is sorer punished: For, if one, by quicknes of
witte, take his lesson readelie, an other, by
hardnes of witte, taketh it not so speedelie:
the first is alwaies commended, the other is
commonlie punished: whan a wise scholemaster should rather discretelie consider the
right disposition of both their natures, and
not so moch wey [4] what either of them is able
to do now, as what either of them is likelie to
do hereafter. For this I know, not onelie by
reading of bookes in my studie, but also by
experience of life, abrode in the world, that
those which be commonlie the wisest, the best
learned, and best men also, when they be olde,
were never commonlie the quickest of witte,
when they were yonge. The causes why,
amongst other, which be many, that move
me thus to thinke, be these fewe, which I will
recken. Quicke wittes, commonlie, be apte
to take, unapte to keepe: soone hote and
desirous of this and that: as colde and sone
wery of the same againe: more quicke to enter
spedelie, than hable [5] to pearse [6] farre: even
like over sharpe tooles, whose edges be verie
soone turned. Soch wittes delite them selves
in easie and pleasant studies; and never passe
farre forward in hie and hard sciences. And

therefore the quickest wittes commonlie may
prove the best Poetes, but not the wisest
Orators: readie of tonge to speake boldlie,
not deepe of judgement, either for good counsel
or wise writing. Also, for maners and life,
quicke wittes, commonlie, be, in desire, new-
fangle,[1] in purpose unconstant, light to promise any thing, readie to forget every thing:
both benefite and injurie: and thereby neither
fast to frend, nor fearefull to foe: inquisitive
of every trifle, not secret in greatest affaires:
bolde, with any person: busie, in every matter:
sothing [2] soch as be present: nipping any that
is absent: of nature also, alwaies, flattering
their betters, envying their equals, despising
their inferiors: and, by quicknes of witte,
verie quicke and readie, to like none so well as
them selves.

Moreover commonlie, men, very quicke of
witte, be also, verie light of conditions: [3]
and thereby, very readie of disposition, to be
caried over quicklie, by any light cumpanie
to any riot and unthriftines, when they be
yonge: and therfore seldome, either honest
of life, or riche in living, when they be olde.
For, quicke in witte and light in maners, be,
either seldome troubled, or verie sone wery,
in carying a verie hevie purse. Quicke wittes
also be, in most part of all their doinges, over-
quicke, hastie, rashe, headie, and brainsicke.
These two last wordes, Headie, and Brainsicke, be fitte and proper wordes, rising nat-
urallie of the matter, and tearmed aptlie by
the condition, of over moch quickenes of witte.
In yougthe also they be readie scoffers, privie
mockers, and ever over light and mery.
In aige, sone testie, very waspishe, and alwaies
over miserable: and yet fewe of them cum to
any great aige, by reason of their misordered
life when they were yong: but a great deale
fewer of them cum to shewe any great countenance, or beare any great authoritie abrode in
the world, but either live obscurelie, men know
not how, or dye obscurelie, men marke not
whan. They be like trees, that shewe forth
faire blossoms and broad leaves in spring time,
but bring out small and not long lasting fruite
in harvest time: and that, onelie soch as fall
and rotte before they be ripe, and so, never, or
seldome, cum to any good at all. For this ye
shall finde most true by experience, that
amongst a number of quicke wittes in youthe,
fewe be found, in the end, either verie fortu-

---

[1] faults [2] more [3] foolish [4] weigh [5] able [6] pierce   [1] fond of novelty [2] agreeing with [3] character

nate for them selves, or verie profitable to serve the common wealth, but decay and vanish, men know not which way: except a very fewe, to whom peradventure blood and happie parentage may perchance purchace a long standing upon the stage. The which felicitie, because it commeth by others procuring, not by their owne deservinge, and stand by other mens feete, and not by their own, what owtward brag so ever is borne by them, is in deed, of it selfe, and in wise mens eyes, of no great estimation.

* * * * * * *

JOHN FOXE (1516–1587)

ACTS AND MONUMENTS OF THESE LATTER AND PERILLOUS DAYES

From THE BEHAVIOUR OF DR. RIDLEY AND MASTER LATIMER AT THE TIME OF THEIR DEATH

* * * * * * *

Incontinently [1] they were commanded to make them readie, which they with all meeknesse obeyed. Master Ridley tooke his gowne and his tippet, and gave it to his brother-in-lawe Master Shepside, who all his time of imprisonment, although he might not be suffered to come to him, lay there at his owne charges to provide him necessaries, which from time to time he sent him by the sergeant that kept him. Some other of his apparel that was little worth, hee gave away; other the bailiffes took. He gave away besides divers other small things to gentlemen standing by, and divers of them pitifullie weeping, as to Sir Henry Lea he gave a new groat; and to divers of my Lord Williams gentlemen some napkins, some nutmegges, and races [2] of ginger; his diall, and such other things as he had about him, to every one that stood next him. Some plucked the pointes of his hose. Happie was he that might get any ragge of him. Master Latimer gave nothing, but very quickly suffered his keeper to pull off his hose, and his other array, which to look unto was very simple: and being stripped into his shrowd,[3] hee seemed as comly a person to them that were there present as one should lightly see;

and whereas in his clothes hee appeared a withered and crooked sillie olde man, he now stood bolt upright, as comely a father as one might lightly behold.

Then Master Ridley, standing as yet in his trusse,[1] said to his brother: "It were best for me to go in my trusse still." "No," quoth his brother, "it will put you to more paine: and the trusse will do a poore man good." Whereunto Master Ridley said: "Be it, in the name of God;" and so unlaced himselfe. Then being in his shirt, he stood upon the foresaid stone, and held up his hande and said: "O heavenly Father, I give unto thee most heartie thanks, for that thou hast called mee to be a professour of thee, even unto death. I beseech thee, Lord God, take mercie upon this realme of England, and deliver the same from all her enemies."

Then the smith took a chaine of iron, and brought the same about both Dr. Ridleyes and Maister Latimers middles; and as he was knocking in a staple, Dr. Ridley tooke the chaine in his hand, and shaked the same, for it did girde in his belly, and looking aside to the smith, said: "Good fellow, knocke it in hard, for the flesh will have his course." Then his brother did bringe him gunnepowder in a bag, and would have tied the same about his necke. Master Ridley asked what it was. His brother said, "Gunnepowder." "Then," sayd he, "I take it to be sent of God; therefore I will receive it as sent of him. And have you any," sayd he, "for my brother?" meaning Master Latimer. "Yea, sir, that I have," quoth his brother. "Then give it unto him," sayd hee, "betime; [2] least ye come too late." So his brother went, and caried of the same gunnepowder unto Maister Latimer.

In the mean time Dr. Ridley spake unto my Lord Williams, and saide: "My lord, I must be a suter unto your lordshippe in the behalfe of divers poore men, and speciallie in the cause of my poor sister; I have made a supplication to the Queenes Majestie in their behalves. I beseech your lordship for Christs sake, to be a mean to her Grace for them. My brother here hath the supplication, and will resort to your lordshippe to certifie you herof. There is nothing in all the world that troubleth my conscience, I praise God, this only excepted. Whiles I was in the see of London divers poore men tooke leases of me, and agreed with me for

---

[1] immediately [2] roots [3] shirt

[1] a padded jacket [2] early

the same. Now I heare say the bishop that now occupieth the same roome will not allow my grants unto them made, but contrarie unto all lawe and conscience hath taken from them their livings, and will not suffer them to injoy the same. I beseech you, my lord, be a meane for them; you shall do a good deed, and God will reward you."

Then they brought a faggotte, kindled with fire, and laid the same downe at Dr. Ridleys feete. To whome Master Latimer spake in this manner: "Bee of good comfort, Master Ridley, and play the man. Wee shall this day light such a candle, by Gods grace, in England, as I trust shall never bee putte out."

And so the fire being given unto them, when Dr. Ridley saw the fire flaming up towards him, he cried with a wonderful lowd voice: "In manus tuas, Domine, commendo spiritum meum: Domine, recipe spiritum meum." And after, repeated this latter part often in English, "Lord, Lord, receive my spirit;" Master Latimer crying as vehementlie on the other side, "O Father of heaven, receive my soule!" who received the flame as it were imbracing of it. After that he had stroaked his face with his hands, and as it were bathed them a little in the fire, he soone died (as it appeared) with verie little paine or none. And thus much concerning the end of this olde and blessed servant of God, Master Latimer, for whose laborious travailes,[1] fruitfull life, and constant death the whole realme hath cause to give great thanks to almightie God.

But Master Ridley, by reason of the evill making of the fire unto him, because the wooden faggots were laide about the gosse [2] and over-high built, the fire burned first beneath, being kept downe by the wood; which when he felt, hee desired them for Christes sake to let the fire come unto him. Which when his brother-in-law heard, but not well understood, intending to rid him out of his paine (for the which cause hee gave attendance), as one in such sorrow not well advised what hee did, heaped faggots upon him, so that he cleane covered him, which made the fire more vehement beneath, that it burned cleane all his neather parts, before it once touched the upper; and that made him leape up and down under the faggots, and often desire them to let the fire come unto him, saying, "I cannot burne." Which indeed appeared well;

for, after his legges were consumed by reason of his struggling through the paine (whereof hee had no release, but onelie his contentation in God), he showed that side toward us cleane, shirt and all untouched with flame. Yet in all this torment he forgate not to call unto God still, having in his mouth, "Lord have mercy upon me," intermedling [1] this cry, "Let the fire come unto me, I cannot burne." In which paines he laboured till one of the standers by with his bill [2] pulled off the faggots above, and where he saw the fire flame up, he wrested himself unto that side. And when the flame touched the gunpowder, he was seen to stirre no more, but burned on the other side, falling downe at Master Latimers feete. Which some said happened by reason that the chain loosed; other said that he fell over the chain by reason of the poise of his body, and the weakness of the neather lims.

Some said that before he was like to fall from the stake, hee desired them to holde him to it with their billes. However it was, surelie it mooved hundreds to teares, in beholding the horrible sight; for I thinke there was none that had not cleane exiled all humanitie and mercie, which would not have lamented to beholde the furie of the fire so to rage upon their bodies. Signes there were of sorrow on everie side. Some tooke it greevouslie to see their deathes, whose lives they held full deare: some pittied their persons, that thought the soules had no need thereof. His brother mooved many men, seeing his miserable case, seeing (I say) him compelled to such infelicitie, that he thought then to doe him best service when he hastned his end. Some cried out of the lucke, to see his indevor (who most dearelie loved him, and sought his release) turne to his greater vexation and increase of paine. But whoso considered their preferments in time past, the places of honour that they some time occupied in this common wealth, the favour they were in with their princes, and the opinion of learning they had in the university where they studied, could not chuse but sorrow with teares to see so great dignity, honour, and estimation, so necessary members sometime accounted, so many godly vertues, the study of so manie yeres, such excellent learning, to be put into the fire and consumed in one moment. Well! dead they are, and

[1] labors   [2] gorse, furze

[1] intermingling   [2] a kind of weapon consisting of a curved blade fixed at the end of a pole.

the reward of this world they have alreadie.
What reward remaineth for them in heaven,
the day of the Lords glorie, when hee commeth
with his saints, shall shortlie, I trust, declare.

THOMAS SACKVILLE, LORD BUCKHURST (1536–1608)

A MIRROR FOR MAGISTRATES

From THE INDUCTION

Flat down I fell, and with all reverence
Adorèd her, perceiving now that she,
A goddess sent by godly providence,
In earthly shape thus showed herself to me,
To wail and rue this world's uncertainty : 173
And while I honored thus her god-head's
    might
With plaining voice these words to me she
    shright : [1]

"I shall thee guide first to the griesly [2] lake,
And thence unto the blissful place of rest,
Where thou shalt see and hear the plaint they
    make,   178
That whilom here bare swing [3] among the best.
This shalt thou see, but great is the unrest
That thou must bide before thou canst attain
Unto the dreadful place where these remain.

And with these words as I upraisèd stood,
And 'gan to follow her that straightforth
    paced,
Ere I was ware, into a desert wood
We now were come; where, hand in hand em-
    braced,
She led the way, and through the thick so
    traced,
As, but I had been guided by her might,
It was no way for any mortal wight.   189

But lo ! while thus, amid the desert dark,
We passèd on with steps and pace unmeet,
A rumbling roar, confused with howl and bark
Of dogs, shook all the ground under our feet,
And struck the din within our ears so deep,
As half distraught unto the ground I fell,
Besought return, and not to visit hell.   196

But she forth-with uplifting me apace
Removed my dread, and with a steadfast mind

Bade me come on, for here was now the place,
The place where we our travel's end should
    find.   200
Wherewith I arose, and to the place assigned
Astonied I stalk ; when straight we ap-
    proachèd near
The dreadful place, that you will dread to hear.

An hideous hole all vast, withouten shape,
Of endless depth, o'erwhelmed with ragged
    stone,
With ugly mouth and griesly jaws doth gape,
And to our sight confounds itself in one.
Here entered we, and yeding [1] forth, anon
An horrible lothly lake we might discern,
As black as pitch, that clepèd [2] is Averne. 210

A deadly gulf where nought but rubbish grows,
With foul black swelth [3] in thickened lumps
    that lies,
Which up in the air such stinking vapours
    throws,
That over there may fly no fowl but dies,
Choked with the pestilent savours that arise.
Hither we come, whence forth we still did pace,
In dreadful fear amid the dreadful place. 217

And first within the porch and jaws of Hell
Sat deep Remorse of Conscience, all besprent
With tears : and to herself oft would she tell
Her wretchedness, and cursing never stent [4]
To sob and sigh ; but ever thus lament
With thoughtful care, as she that all in vain
Would wear and waste continually in pain. 224

Her eyes unsteadfast, rolling here and there,
Whirled on each place, as place that vengeance
    brought,
So was her mind continually in fear,
Tossed and tormented with the tedious
    thought
Of those detested crimes which she had
    wrought ;
With dreadful cheer and looks thrown to the
    sky,   230
Wishing for death, and yet she could not die.

Next saw we Dread, all trembling how he
    shook,
With foot uncertain proffered here and there ;
Benumbed of speech, and with a ghastly look
Searched every place all pale and dead for
    fear,

---

[1] shrieked   [2] dreadful   [3] bore sway

[1] going   [2] called   [3] scum   [4] cease

His cap borne up with staring [1] of his hair,
Stoynd [2] and amazed at his own shade for
    dread,
And fearing greater dangers than was need. 238

And next within the entry of this lake
Sat fell Revenge, gnashing her teeth for ire,
Devising means how she may vengeance take,
Never in rest till she have her desire;
But frets within so farforth [3] with the fire
Of wreaking flames, that now determines she
To die by Death, or venged by Death to be. 245

When fell Revenge with bloody foul pretence
Had shown herself as next in order set,
With trembling limbs we softly parted thence,
Till in our eyes another sight we met:
When from my heart a sigh forthwith I fet, [4]
Rueing, alas! upon the woeful plight
Of Misery, that next appeared in sight.   252

His face was lean, and somedeal pined away,
And eke his hands consumèd to the bone,
And what his body was I cannot say,
For on his carcass raiment had he none
Save clouts and patches, piecèd one by one.
With staff in hand, and scrip on shoulders cast,
His chief defence against the winter's blast. 259

His food, for most, [5] was wild fruits of the
    trees,
Unless sometime some crumbs fell to his share,
Which in his wallet long, God wot, kept he.
As on the which full daintily would he fare;
His drink the running stream, his cup the bare
Of his palm closed, his bed the hard cold
    ground.
To this poor life was Misery y-bound.   266

Whose wretched state when we had well
    beheld
With tender ruth on him and on his feres [6]
In thoughtful cares, forth then our pace we
    held.
And by and by, another shape appears
Of greedy Care, still brushing up the breres, [7]
His knuckles knobbed, his flesh deep dented in,
With tawèd hands, and hard y-tannèd skin.

The morrow gray no sooner hath begun
To spread his light, even peeping in our eyes,
When he is up and to his work y-run;   276

But let the night's black misty mantles rise,
And with foul dark never so much disguise
The fair bright day, yet ceaseth he no while,
But hath his candles to prolong his toil.   280

By him lay heavy Sleep, the cousin of Death
Flat on the ground, and still as any stone,
A very corpse, save yielding forth a breath.
Small keep [1] took he whom Fortune frownèd
    on
Or whom she lifted up into the throne
Of high renown; but as a living death,
So dead alive, of life he drew the breath.   287

The body's rest, the quiet of the heart,
The travail's ease, the still night's fear was he,
And of our life in earth the better part,
Reaver of sight, and yet in whom we see
Things oft that tide, [2] and oft that never be.
Without respect esteeming equally
King Cresus' pomp, and Irus' poverty.   294

And next in order sad Old Age we found,
His beard all hoar, his eyes hollow and blind,
With drooping cheer still poring on the ground,
As on the place where nature him assigned
To rest, when that the Sisters [3] had untwined
His vital thread, and ended with their knife
The fleeting course of fast declining life.   301

There heard we him with broken and hollow
    plaint
Rue with himself his end approaching fast,
And all for nought his wretched mind torment
With sweet remembrance of his pleasures past,
And fresh delights of lusty youth forwast. [4]
Recounting which, how would he sob and
    shriek,
And to be young again of Jove beseek! [5]   308

But and [6] the cruel fates so fixèd be
That time forepast [7] cannot return again,
This one request of Jove yet prayèd he:
That in such withered plight, and wretched
    pain
As Eld, accompanied with his lothsome train,
Had brought on him, all were it woe and grief,
He might a while yet linger forth his life,   315

And not so soon descend into the pit,
Where Death, when he the mortal corps hath
    slain,

---

[1] standing on end   [2] astounded   [3] excessively
[4] fetched   [5] chiefly   [6] companions   [7] briars

[1] heed   [2] happen   [3] the Fates   [4] wasted away
[5] beseech   [6] if   [7] passed by

With retchless [1] hand in grave doth cover it,
Thereafter never to enjoy again
The gladsome light, but, in the ground y-lain,
In depth of darkness waste and wear to
  nought,
As he had never into the world been brought.

But who had seen him, sobbing how he
  stood   323
Unto himself, and how he would bemoan
His youth forepast, as though it wrought him
  good
To talk of youth, all were his youth foregone,[2]
He would have mused, and marvelled much
  whereon

[1] careless   [2] passed away

This wretched Age should life desire so fain,
And knows full well life doth but length his
  pain.   329

Crookbacked he was, toothshaken, and blear-
  eyed,
Went on three feet, and sometime crept on
  four,
With old lame bones, that rattled by his side,
His scalp all piled [1] and he with elde forlore; [2]
His withered fist still knocking at death's
  door,
Fumbling and drivelling as he draws his
  breath,   335
For brief, the shape and messenger of Death.

[1] bare   [2] worn with age

THE RENAISSANCE

EDMUND SPENSER (1552?–1599)

FROM THE SHEPHEARDS CALENDER

FEBRUARIE

ÆGLOGA SECUNDA

Cuddie   Thenot

CUDDIE. Ah for pittie, wil rancke Winters rage
These bitter blasts never ginne tasswage?
The kene cold blowes through my beaten hyde,
All as I were through the body gryde.[1]
My ragged rontes [2] all shiver and shake,
As doen high Towers in an earthquake:
They wont in the wind wagge their wrigle tailes,
Perke [3] as Peacock; but nowe it avales.[4]
    THE. Lewdly [5] complainest thou, laesie ladde,
Of Winters wracke for making thee sadde.   10
Must not the world wend in his commun course,
From good to badd, and from badde to worse,
From worse unto that is worst of all,
And then returne to his former fall [6]?
Who will not suffer the stormy time,
Where will he live tyll the lusty prime?
Selfe have I worne out thrise threttie yeares,
Some in much ioy, many in many teares,
Yet never complained of cold nor heate,
Of Sommers flame, nor of Winters threat: 20
Ne ever was to Fortune foeman,
But gently tooke, that ungently came;
And ever my flocke was my chiefe care,
Winter or Sommer they mought well fare.
    CUD. No marveile, Thenot, if thou can beare
Cherefully the Winters wrathfull cheare;
For Age and Winter accord full nie,
This chill, that cold, this crooked, that wrye;

And as the lowring Wether lookes downe,
So semest thou like good fryday to frowne, 30
But my flowring youth is foe to frost,
My shippe unwont in stormes to be tost.
    THE. The soveraigne of seas he blames in vaine,
That, once sea-beate, will to sea againe.
So loytring live you little heardgroomes,
Keeping your beasts in the budded broomes:
And when the shining sunne laugheth once,
You deemen, the Spring is come attonce;
Tho gynne [1] you, fond flyes, the cold to scorne,
And crowing in pypes made of greene corne, 40
You thinken to be Lords of the yeare;
But eft,[2] when ye count you freed from feare,
Comes the breme [3] winter with chamfred [4] browes
Full of wrinckles and frostie furrowes:
Drerily shooting his stormy darte,
Which cruddles [5] the blood, and pricks the harte.
Then is your carelesse corage accoied,[6]
Your carefull heards with colde bene annoied.
Then paye you the price of your surquedrie,[7]
With weeping, and wayling, and misery.   50
    CUD. Ah foolish old man, I scorne thy skill,
That wouldest me, my springing youngth to spil:
I deeme thy braine emperished bee
Through rusty elde, that hath rotted thee:
Or sicker [8] thy head veray tottie [9] is,
So on thy corbe [10] shoulder it leanes amisse.
Now thy selfe hast lost both lopp and topp,
Als [11] my budding braunch thou wouldest cropp:
But were thy yeares greene, as now bene myne,
To other delights they would encline.   60
Tho wouldest thou learne to caroll of Love,
And hery [12] with hymnes thy lasses glove.
Tho wouldest thou pype of Phyllis prayse:
But Phyllis is myne for many dayes;
I wonne her with a gyrdle of gelt,[13]

[1] pierced [2] young bullocks [3] pert [4] droops [5] ignorantly [6] condition

[1] then begin [2] again, after [3] bitter [4] wrinkled [5] curdles [6] quieted [7] pride [8] surely [9] unsteady [10] crooked [11] also [12] praise [13] gilt

Embost with buegle about the belt.
Such an one shepheards woulde make full
faine,
Such an one would make thee younge againe.
   THE. Thou art a fon[1] of thy love to boste,
All that is lent to love wyll be lost. 70
   CUD. Seest howe brag[2] yond Bullocke
beares,
So smirke, so smoothe, his prickèd eares?
His hornes bene as broade as Rainebowe bent,
His dewelap as lythe as lasse of Kent,
See howe he venteth[3] into the wynd.
Weenest of love is not his mynd?
Seemeth thy flocke thy counsell can,[4]
So lustlesse[5] bene they, so weake, so wan,
Clothed with cold, and hoary wyth frost,
Thy flocks father his corage hath lost: 80
Thy Ewes, that wont to have blowen[6] bags,
Like wailefull widdowes hangen their crags[7]:
The rather[8] lambes bene starved with cold,
All for their Maister is lustlesse and old.
   THE. Cuddie, I wote thou kenst[9] little
good,
So vainely tadvaunce thy headlesse hood.
For Youngth is a bubble blown up with
breath,
Whose witt is weakenesse, whose wage is
death,
Whose way is wildernesse, whose ynne[10] Pen-
aunce,
And stoope gallant Age the hoste of Gree-
vaunce.
But shall I tel thee a tale of truth, 91
Which I cond[11] of Tityrus in my youth,
Keeping his sheepe on the hils of Kent?
   CUD. To nought more, Thenot, my mind
is bent,
Then to heare novells of his devise:
They bene so well thewed, and so wise,
What ever that good old man bespake.
   THE. Many meete tales of youth did he
make,
And some of love, and some of chevalrie:
But none fitter than this to applie. 100
Now listen a while, and hearken the end.

There grewe an aged Tree on the greene,
A goodly Oake sometime had it bene,
With armes full strong and largely displayd,
But of their leaves they were disarayde:
The bodie bigge, and mightely pight,[12]

Throughly rooted, and of wonderous hight:
Whilome had bene the King of the field,
And mochell mast[1] to the husband did yielde,
And with his nuts larded[2] many swine. 110
But now the gray mosse marred his rine,[3]
His barèd boughes were beaten with stormes,
His toppe was bald, and wasted with wormes,
His honor decayed, his braunches sere.
   Hard by his side grewe a bragging Brere,
Which prowdly thrust into Thelement,
And seemed to threat the Firmament.
Yt was embellisht with blossomes fayre,
And thereto aye wonned[4] to repayre
The shepheards daughters to gather flowres,
To peinct their girlonds with his colowres. 121
And in his small bushes used to shrowde
The sweete Nightingale singing so lowde:
Which made this foolish Brere wexe so bold,
That on a time he cast him[5] to scold
And snebbe[6] the good Oake, for he was old.
   'Why standst there (quoth he), thou brutish
blocke?
'Nor for fruict nor for shadowe serves thy
stocke.
'Seest how fresh my flowers bene spredde,
'Dyed in Lilly white and Cremsin redde, 130
'With Leaves engrained in lusty greene,
'Colours meete to clothe a mayden Queene?
'Thy wast bignes[7] but combers the grownd,
'And dirks[8] the beauty of my blossoms rownd.
'The mouldie mosse, which thee accloieth,[9]
'My Sinamon smell too much annoieth.
'Wherefore soone, I rede[10] thee, hence remove,
'Least thou the price of my displeasure prove.'
So spake this bold brere with great disdaine:
Little him answered the Oake againe, 140
But yielded, with shame and greefe adawed,[11]
That of a weede he was ouerawed.
   Yt chauncèd after vpon a day,
The Hus-bandman selfe to come that way,
Of custome for to survewe[12] his grownd,
And his trees of state in compasse rownd.
Him when the spitefull brere had espyed,
Causlesse complained, and lowdly cryed
Unto his Lord, stirring up sterne strife:
   'O my liege Lord! the God of my life, 150
'Pleaseth you ponder your Suppliants plaint,
'Caused of wrong, and cruell constraint,
'Which I your poore vassall dayly endure:
'And but your goodnes the same recure,[13]

---

[1] fool [2] brisk [3] puffs [4] know [5] without desire
[6] full [7] necks [8] earlier [9] knowest [10] inn [11] learned
[12] firmly set

[1] many acorns [2] fattened [3] rind [4] were accustomed [5] planned [6] reprove [7] vast bignes [8] darkens [9] encumbers [10] advise [11] daunted [12] look over
[13] recover

'Am like for desperate doole [1] to dye,
'Through felonous force of mine enemie.'
　Greatly aghast with this piteous plea,
Him rested the goodman on the lea,
And badde the Brere in his plaint proceede.
With painted words tho [2] gan this proude
　　weede　　　　　　　　　　　　160
(As most usen Ambitious folke)
His colowred crime with crafte to cloke.
　'Ah my soveraigne, Lord of creatures all,
'Thou placer of plants both humble and tall,
'Was not I planted of thine owne hand,
'To be the primrose of all thy land,
'With flowring blossomes, to furnish the prime,
'And scarlet berries in Sommer time?
'Howe falls it then that this faded Oake,
'Whose bodie is sere, whose braunches broke,
'Whose naked Armes stretch unto the fyre,
'Unto such tyrannie doth aspire,　　172
'Hindering with his shade my lovely light,
'And robbing me of the swete sonnes sight?
'So beate his old boughes my tender side,
'That oft the bloud springeth from wounds
　　wyde:
'Untimely my flowres forced to fall,
'That bene the honor of your Coronall.
'And oft he lets his cancker wormes light
'Upon my braunches, to worke me more
　　spight:　　　　　　　　　　　180
'And oft his hoarie locks downe doth cast,
'Where with my fresh flowretts bene defast:
'For this, and many more such outrage,
'Craving your goodlihead [3] to aswage
'Theranckorous rigour of his might,
'Nought aske I, but onely to hold my right:
'Submitting me to your good sufferance,
'And praying to be garded from greevance.'
　To this the Oake cast him to replie
Well as he couth [4]; but his enemie　　190
Had kindled such coles of displeasure,
That the good man noulde [5] stay his leasure,
But home him hasted with furious heate,
Encreasing his wrath with many a threate.
His harmefull Hatchet he hent [6] in hand,
(Alas, that it so ready should stand!)
And to the field alone he speedeth,
(Ay little helpe to harme there needeth!)
Anger nould let him speake to the tree,
Enaunter [7] his rage mought cooled bee;　200
But to the roote bent his sturdy stroke,
And made many wounds in the wast [8] Oake.
The Axes edge did oft turne againe,

[1] grief　[2] then　[3] goodness　[4] could　[5] would not
[6] seized　[7] lest perchance　[8] vast

As halfe unwilling to cutte the graine:
Semed, the sencelesse yron dyd feare,
Or to wrong holy eld did forbeare.
For it had bene an auncient tree,
Sacred with many a mysteree,
And often crost with the priestes crewe,
And often halowed with holy water dewe.　210
But sike [1] fancies weren foolerie,
And broughten this Oake to this miserye.
For nought mought they quitten him from
　　decay:
For fiercely the good man at him did laye.
The blocke oft gronèd under the blow,
And sighed to see his neare overthrow.
In fine, the steele had pierced his pitth:
Tho [2] downe to the earth he fell forthwith:
His wonderous weight made the grounde to
　　quake.
Thearth [3] shronke vnder him, and seemed to
　　shake.　　　　　　　　　　220
There lyeth the Oake, pitied of none.
　Now stands the Brere like a Lord alone,
Puffed up with pryde and vaine pleasaunce.
But all this glee had no continuance;
For eftsones [4] Winter gan to approche,
The blustering Boreas did encroche,
And beate upon the solitarie Brere:
For nowe no succoure was seene him nere. [5]
Now gan he repent his pryde to late;
For naked left and disconsolate,　　230
The byting frost nipt his stalke dead,
The watrie wette weighed downe his head,
And heaped snowe burdned him so sore,
That nowe upright he can stand no more:
And being downe, is trodde in the durt
Of cattell, and brouzed, and sorely hurt.
Such was thend [6] of this Ambitious brere,
For scorning Eld ——
　CUD.　Now I pray thee, shepheard, tel it not
　　forth:
Here is a long tale, and little worth.　　240
So longe have I listened to thy speche,
That graffed to the ground is my breche;
My hartblood is welnigh frorne, [7] I feele,
And my galage [8] growne fast to my heele:
But little ease of thy lewd tale I tasted:
Hye thee home, shepheard, the day is nigh
　　wasted.
　　　　　Thenots Embleme
　　　　Iddio, perchè è vecchio,
　　　　Fa suoi al suo essempio. [9]

[1] such　[2] then　[3] the earth　[4] soon again　[5] near
[6] the end　[7] frozen　[8] shoe　[9] God, because he is
old, makes his own in his image.

THE FAERIE QUEENE

BOOK I. CANTO I

I

A gentle Knight was pricking [2] on the plaine,
  Ycladd in mightie armes and silver shielde,
  Wherein old dints of deepe woundes did re-
    maine,
  The cruell markes of many a bloody fielde;
  Yet armes till that time did he never wield.
  His angry steede did chide his foming bitt,
  As much disdayning to the curbe to yield:
  Full jolly knight he seemd, and faire did sitt,
As one for knightly giusts [3] and fierce en-
  counters fitt.

II

But on his brest a bloodie Crosse he bore, 10
  The deare remembrance of his dying Lord,
  For whose sweete sake that glorious badge
    he wore,
  And dead, as living, ever him ador'd:
  Upon his shield the like was also scor'd,
  For soveraine hope which in his helpe he
    had.
  Right faithfull true he was in deede and
    word;
  But of his cheere [4] did seeme too solemne
    sad;
Yet nothing did he dread, but ever was
  ydrad.[5]

III

Upon a great adventure he was bond,[6]
  That greatest Gloriana to him gave,   20
  (That greatest Glorious Queene of Faery
    lond [7])
  To winne him worshippe, and her grace to
    have,
  Which of all earthly thinges he most did
    crave:
  And ever as he rode his hart did earne [8]
  To prove his puissance in battell brave
  Upon his foe, and his new force to learne,
Upon his foe, a Dragon horrible and stearne.

IV

A lovely Ladie rode him faire beside,
  Upon a lowly Asse more white then snow,
  Yet she much whiter; but the same did
    hide   30
  Under a vele,[1] that wimpled [2] was full low;
  And over all a blacke stole [3] shee did throw:
  As one that inly mournd, so was she sad,
  And heavie sate upon her palfrey slow;
  Seemed in heart some hidden care she had,
And by her, in a line,[4] a milkewhite lambe she
  lad.[5]

V

So pure and innocent, as that same lambe,
  She was in life and every vertuous lore,
  And by descent from Royall lynage came
  Of ancient Kinges and Queenes, that had of
    yore
  Their scepters stretcht from East to
    Westerne shore,   41
  And all the world in their subjection held;
  Till that infernall feend with foule uprore
  Forwasted [6] all their land, and them expeld;
Whom to avenge she had this Knight from far
  compeld.

VI

Behind her farre away a Dwarfe did lag,
  That lasie seemd, in being ever last,
  Or wearièd with bearing of her bag
  Of needments at his backe. Thus as they
    past,
  The day with cloudes was suddeine overcast,
  And angry Jove an hideous storme of raine
  Did poure into his Lemans [7] lap so fast 52
  That everie wight to shroud [8] it did con-
    strain;
And this faire couple eke [9] to shroud them-
  selves were fain.[10]

VII

Enforst to seeke some covert nigh at hand,
  A shadie grove not farr away they spide,
  That promist ayde the tempest to with-
    stand;
  Whose loftie trees, yclad with sommers
    pride,
  Did spred so broad that heavens light did
    hide,

[1] veil [2] folded [3] a long outer garment [4] cord,
or rope [5] led [6] devastated [7] sweetheart's (= earth's)
[8] cover [9] also [10] glad

[1] No greybeard fears God. [2] riding [3] jousts [4] de-
meanor [5] dreaded [6] bound [7] land [8] yearn

Not perceable with power of any starr : 60
And all within were pathes and alleies wide,
With footing worne, and leading inward
   farr.
Faire harbour that them seemes ; so in they
   entred ar.

*   *   *   *   *   *   *

XXIX

At length they chaunst to meet upon the way
An aged Sire, in long blacke weedes yclad,
His feete all bare, his beard all hoarie gray,
And by his belt his booke he hanging had :
Sober he seemde, and very sagely sad,
And to the ground his eyes were lowly bent,
Simple in shew, and voide of malice bad ;
And all the way he prayèd as he went, 260
And often knockt his brest, as one that did re-
   pent.

XXX

He faire the knight saluted, louting [1] low,
   Who faire him quited,[2] as that courteous
     was ;
   And after askèd him, if he did know
   Of straunge adventures, which abroad did
     pas.
"Ah ! my dear sonne," (quoth he) "how
     should, alas ! 266
   Silly old man, that lives in hidden cell,
   Bidding his beades all day for his trespas,
   Tydings of warre and worldly trouble tell ?
With holy father sits [3] not with such thinges to
   mell.[4]

XXXI

"But if of daunger, which hereby doth dwell,
   And homebredd evil ye desire to heare,
   Of a straunge man I can you tidings tell,
   That wasteth all this countrie, farre and
     neare."
   "Of such," (saide he,) "I chiefly doe in-
     quere,
   And shall you well rewarde to shew the
     place
   In which that wicked wight his dayes doth
     weare ;
   For to all knighthood it is foule disgrace, 278
That such a cursèd creature lives so long a
   space."

[1] bowing   [2] answered   [3] suits   [4] meddle

XXXII

"Far hence" (quoth he) "in wastfull wilder-
   nesse
   His dwelling is, by which no living wight
   May ever passe, but thorough [1] great dis-
     tresse."
"Now," (saide the Ladie,) "draweth to-
     ward night,
   And well I wote, that of your later fight
   Ye all forwearied be ; for what so strong,
   But, wanting rest, will also want of might ?
   The Sunne, that measures heaven all day
     long, 287
At night doth baite [2] his steedes the Ocean
   waves emong.

XXXIII

"Then with the Sunne take, Sir, your timely
     rest,
   And with new day new worke at once
     begin :
   Untroubled night, they say, gives counsell
     best."
"Right well, Sir knight, ye have advised
     bin."
   Quoth then that aged man : "the way to
     win
   Is wisely to advise ; now day is spent :
   Therefore with me ye may take up your In
   For this same night." The knight was well
     content ; 296
So with that godly father to his home they
   went.

XXXIV

A litle lowly Hermitage it was,
   Downe in a dale, hard by a forests side,
   Far from resort of people that did pas
   In traveill to and froe : a litle wyde
   There was an holy chappell edifyde,[3]
   Wherein the Hermite dewly wont to say
   His holy thinges each morne and even-tyde ;
   Thereby a christall streame did gently play,
Which from a sacred fountaine wellèd forth
   alway. 306

XXXV

Arrivèd there, the litle house they fill,
   Ne looke for entertainement where none
     was ;

[1] through   [2] feed   [3] built

Rest is their feast, and all thinges at their
    will.
The noblest mind the best contentment has.
With faire discourse the evening so they pas;
For that olde man of pleasing wordes had
    store
And well could file his tongue as smooth as
    glas:
He told of Saintes and Popes, and evermore
He strowd an Ave-Mary after and before. 315

XXXVI

The drouping night thus creepeth on them
    fast,
    And the sad humor loading their eyeliddes,
As messenger of Morpheus,[1] on them cast
    Sweet slombring deaw, the which to sleep
      them biddes.
Unto their lodgings then his guestes he
    riddes:
    Where when all drownd in deadly sleepe he
      findes,
He to his studie goes; and there amiddes
    His magick bookes and artes of sundries
      kindes, 323
He seekes out mighty charmes, to trouble
    sleepy minds.

XXXVII

Then choosing out few words most horrible,
    (Let none them read) thereof did verses
      frame;
    With which, and other spelles like terrible,
He bad awake blacke Plutoes griesly Dame;
    And cursed heven; and spake reprochful
      shame
Of highest God, the Lord of life and light:
    A bold bad man, that dar'd to call by name
Great Gorgon, prince of darknes and dead
    night; 332
At which Cocytus quakes, and Styx is put to
    flight.

XXXVIII

And forth he cald out of deepe darknes dredd
    Legions of Sprights, the which, like litle
      flyes
Fluttring about his ever-damnèd hedd,
    Awaite whereto their service he applyes,
To aide his friendes, or fray[2] his enimies.

1 the god of sleep   2 frighten

Of those he chose out two, the falsest twoo,
    And fittest for to forge true-seeming lyes:
    The one of them he gave a message too, 341
The other by him selfe staide, other worke to
    doo.

XXXIX

He, making speedy way through spersèd[1] ayre,
    And through the world of waters wide and
      deepe,
To Morpheus house doth hastily repaire.
    Amid the bowels of the earth full steepe,
    And low, where dawning day doth never
      peepe,
His dwelling is; there Tethys his wet bed
Doth ever wash, and Cynthia still doth
    steepe
    In silver deaw his ever-drouping hed, 350
Whiles sad Night over him her mantle black
    doth spred.

XL

Whose double gates he findeth lockèd fast,
    The one faire fram'd of burnisht Yvory,
    The other all with silver overcast;
    And wakeful dogges before them farre doe
      lye,
Watching to banish Care their enimy,
Who oft is wont to trouble gentle Sleepe.
By them the Sprite doth passe in quietly,
    And unto Morpheus comes, whom drownèd
      deepe 359
In drowsie fit he findes: of nothing he takes
    keepe.[2]

XLI

And more, to lulle him in his slumber soft,
    A trickling streame from high rock tumbling
      downe,
And ever-drizling raine upon the loft,
    Mixt with a murmuring winde, much like
      the sowne
Of swarming Bees, did cast him in a swowne.
No other noyse, nor peoples troublous cryes,
As still are wont t'annoy the walled towne,
    Might there be heard; but carelesse Quiet
      lyes 368
Wrapt in eternall silence farre from enimyes.

XLII

The Messenger approching to him spake;
    But his waste wordes retournd to him in
      vaine:

1 dispersed   2 heed

So sound he slept that nought mought[1] him
    awake.
Then rudely he him thrust, and pusht with
    paine,
Whereat he gan to stretch; but he againe
Shooke him so hard that forcèd him to
    speake.
As one then in a dreame, whose dryer
    braine
Is tost with troubled sights and fancies
    weake,
He mumbled soft, but would not all his
    silence breake.   378

XLIII

The Sprite then gan more boldly him to wake,
    And threatned unto him the dreaded name
    Of Hecate: whereat he gan to quake,
    And, lifting up his lompish head, with
      blame
Halfe angrie askèd him, for what he came.
"Hether (quoth he) "me Archimago sent,
He that the stubborne Sprites can wisely
    tame,
He bids thee to him send for his intent 386
A fit false dreame, that can delude the sleepers
    sent."

*   *   *   *   *   *   *

CANTO III

I

Nought is there under heav'ns wide hollow-
    nesse,
    That moves more deare compassion of
      mind,
Then beautie brought t'unworthie wretched-
    nesse
Through envies snares, or fortunes freakes
    unkind.
I, whether lately through her brightnes
    blynd,
Or through alleageance and fast fealty,
Which I do owe unto all womankynd,
Feele my hart perst with so great agony, 8
When such I see, that all for pitty I could dy.

II

And now it is empassionèd so deepe,
    For fairest Unaes sake, of whom I sing,

That my frayle eies these lines with teares
    do steepe,
To thinke how she through guyleful han-
    deling,
Though true as touch, though daughter of a
    king,
Though faire as ever living wight was fayre,
Though nor in word nor deede ill meriting,
Is from her knight divorcèd in despayre,
And her dew loves deryv'd to that vile witches
    shayre.   18

III

Yet she, most faithfull Ladie, all this while
    Forsaken, wofull, solitarie mayd,
    Far from all peoples preace,[1] as in exile,
    In wildernesse and wastfull deserts strayd,
    To seeke her knight; who, subtily betrayd
Through that late vision which th' En-
    chaunter wrought,
Had her abandond. She, of nought affrayd,
Through woods and wastnes wide him daily
    sought;   26
Yet wishèd tydinges none of him unto her
    brought.

IV

One day, nigh wearie of the yrksome way,
    From her unhastie beaste she did alight;
    And on the grasse her dainty limbs did lay,
    In secrete shadow, far from all mens sight:
    From her fayre head her fillet she undight,
    And layd her stole aside. Her angels face,
As the great eye of heaven, shynèd bright,
And made a sunshine in the shady place;
Did never mortall eye behold such heavenly
    grace.   36

V

It fortunèd, out of the thickest wood
    A ramping Lyon rushèd suddeinly,
    Hunting full greedy after salvage[2] blood.
    Soone as the royall virgin he did spy,
    With gaping mouth at her ran greedily,
    To have attonce devourd her tender corse;
    But to the pray when as he drew more ny,
His bloody rage aswagèd with remorse,[3] 44
And with the sight amazd, forgat his furious
    forse.

---

[1] might

[1] press, throng   [2] savage   [3] pity

VI

In stead thereof he kist her wearie feet,
    And lickt her lilly hands with fawning tong,
    As he her wronged innocence did weet.[1]
O how can beautie maister the most strong,
And simple truth subdue avenging wrong!
Whose yielded pryde and proud submission,
Still dreading death, when she had markèd
        long,
Her hart gan melt in great compassion; 53
And drizling teares did shed for pure affection.

FROM EPITHALAMION

Ye learnèd sisters, which have oftentimes
Been to me aiding, others to adorn,
Whom ye thought worthy of your graceful
        rimes,
That even the greatest did not greatly scorn
To hear their names sung in your simple lays,
But joyèd in their praise;
And when ye list your own mishaps to mourn,
Which Death, or Love, or Fortune's wreck did
        raise,
Your string could soon to sadder tenor turn,
And teach the woods and waters to lament
Your doleful dreariment: 11
Now lay those sorrowful complaints aside;
And, having all your heads with garlands
        crowned,
Help me mine own love's praises to resound;
Ne let the same of any be envíed;
So Orpheus did for his own bride!
So I unto myself alone will sing;
The woods shall to me answer, and my echo
        ring.

Early, before the world's light-giving lamp
His golden beam upon the hills doth spread,
Having dispersed the night's uncheerful
        damp,   21
Do ye awake, and, with fresh lustihed,[2]
Go to the bower of my belovèd love,
My truest turtle dove;
Bid her awake; for Hymen is awake,
And long since ready forth his mask to move,
With his bright tead[3] that flames with many
        a flake,
And many a bachelor to wait on him,
In their fresh garments trim;
Bid her awake therefore, and soon her dight,
For lo! the wished day is come at last, 31

---

[1] know   [2] lustiness   [3] torch

That shall, for all the pains and sorrows past,
Pay to her usury of long delight:
And, whilst she doth her dight,
Do ye to her of joy and solace sing,
That all the woods may answer, and your
        echo ring.

Bring with you all the nymphs that you can
        hear,
Both of the rivers and the forests green,
And of the sea that neighbours to her near,
All with gay garlands goodly well beseen; 40
And let them also with them bring in hand
Another gay garland,
For my fair love, of lilies and of roses,
Bound truelove-wise with a blue silk riband;
And let them make great store of bridal posies,
And let them eke bring store of other flowers,
To deck the bridal bowers;
And let the ground whereas[1] her foot shall
        tread,
For fear the stones her tender foot should
        wrong,
Be strewed with fragrant flowers all along, 50
And diapered[2] like the discoloured[3] mead;
Which done, do at her chamber door await,
For she will waken straight;
The whiles do ye this song unto her sing,
The woods shall to you answer, and your echo
        ring.

*   *   *   *   *   *   *

Wake now, my love, awake! for it is time;
The rosy morn long since left Tithon's bed, 75
All ready to her silver coach to climb;
And Phœbus[4] 'gins to show his glorious head.
Hark, how the cheerful birds do chant their
        lays
And carol of love's praise.
The merry lark her matins sings aloft;   80
The thrush replies; the mavis descant plays;
The ouzel shrills; the ruddock warbles soft;
So goodly all agree, with sweet concent,[5]
To this day's merriment.
Ah! my dear love, why do ye sleep thus long
When meeter were that ye should now awake,
T' await the coming of your joyous make,[6]
And hearken to the birds' love-learnèd song,
The dewy leaves among!
For they of joy and pleasance to you sing, 90
That all the woods them answer, and their
        echo ring.

---

[1] where   [2] marked   [3] vari-coloured   [4] the sun
[5] harmony   [6] mate

My love is now awake out of her dreams,
And her fair eyes, like stars that dimmèd were
With darksome cloud, now show their goodly
　　　beams
More bright than Hesperus his head doth rear.
Come now, ye damsels, daughters of delight,
Help quickly her to dight :
But first come ye, fair Hours, which were begot,
In Jove's sweet paradise, of Day and Night ;
Which do the seasons of the year allot,　100
And all that ever in this world is fair
Do make and still repair :
And ye three handmaids of the Cyprian queen,
The which do still adorn her beauty's pride,
Help to adorn my beautifulest bride ;
And as ye her array, still throw between
Some graces to be seen,
And, as ye use to Venus, to her sing,
The whiles the woods shall answer, and your
　　　echo ring.

　　*　　*　　*　　*　　*　　*　　*

Lo ! where she comes along with portly pace,
Like Phœbe,[1] from her chamber of the East,
Arising forth to run her mighty race,　150
Clad all in white, that 'seems a virgin best.
So well it her beseems that ye would ween
Some angel she had been.
Her long loose yellow locks like golden wire,
Sprinkled with pearl, and pearling flowers
　　　atween,
Do like a golden mantle her attire ;
And, being crownèd with a garland green,
Seem like some maiden queen.
Her modest eyes, abashèd to behold
So many gazers as on her do stare,　160
Upon the lowly ground affixèd are ;
Ne dare lift up her countenance too bold,
But blush to hear her praises sung so loud,
So far from being proud.
Nathless[2] do ye still loud her praises sing,
That all the woods may answer, and your echo
　　　ring.

　　*　　*　　*　　*　　*　　*　　*

But if ye saw that which no eyes can see,　185
The inward beauty of her lively spright,[3]
Garnished with heavenly gifts of high degree,
Much more then would ye wonder at that
　　　sight,
And stand astonished like to those which read
Medusa's mazeful head.　190
There dwells sweet love, and constant chastity,
Unspotted faith, and comely womanhood,

Regard of honour, and mild modesty ;
There virtue reigns as queen in royal throne,
And giveth laws alone,
The which the base affections do obey,
And yield their services unto her will ;
Ne thought of thing uncomely ever may
Thereto approach, to tempt her mind to ill.
Had ye once seen these her celestial treasures
And unrevealèd pleasures,　201
Then would ye wonder, and her praises sing,
That all the woods should answer, and your
　　　echo ring.

Open the temple gates unto my love,
Open them wide, that she may enter in,
And all the posts adorn as doth behove,
And all the pillars deck with garlands trim,
For to receive this Saint with honour due,
That cometh in to you.
With trembling steps and humble reverence
She cometh in, before th' Almighty's view ;
Of her, ye virgins, learn obedience,　212
When so ye come into those holy places,
To humble your proud faces :
Bring her up to th' high altar, that she may
The sacred ceremonies there partake,
The which do endless matrimony make ;
And let the roaring organs loudly play
The praises of the Lord in lively notes ;
The whiles, with hollow throats,　220
The choristers the joyous anthem sing,
That all the woods may answer, and their echo
　　　ring.

Behold, whiles she before the altar stands,
Hearing the holy priest that to her speaks
And blesseth her with his two happy hands,
How the red roses flush up in her cheeks
And the pure snow with goodly vermeil stain,
Like crimson dyed in grain :
That even th' angels, which continually
About the sacred altar do remain,　230
Forget their service and about her fly,
Oft peeping in her face, that seems more fair,
The more they on it stare.
But her sad [1] eyes, still fast'nèd on the ground,
Are governèd with goodly modesty,
That suffers not one look to glance awry
Which may let in a little thought unsound.
Why blush ye, love, to give to me your hand,
The pledge of all our band ?
Sing, ye sweet angels, Alleluia sing,　240
That all the woods may answer, and your echo
　　　ring.

────────

[1] the moon　　　[2] nevertheless　　　[3] spirit

[1] serious

Now all is done: bring home the bride again;
Bring home the triumph of our victory:
Bring home with you the glory of her gain,
With joyance bring her and with jollity.
Never had man more joyful day than this
Whom heaven would heap with bliss;
Make feast therefore now all this live-long
    day;
This day for ever to me holy is.
Pour out the wine without restraint or stay,
Pour not by cups, but by the bellyful,   251
Pour out to all that will,
And sprinkle all the posts and walls with wine,
That they may sweat and drunken be withal.
Crown ye god Bacchus with a coronal,
And Hymen also crown with wreaths of vine;
And let the Graces dance unto the rest,
For they can do it best:
The whiles the maidens do their carol sing,
To which the woods shall answer, and their
    echo ring.   260

Ring ye the bells, ye young men of the town,
And leave your wonted labours for this day:
This day is holy; do ye write it down,
That ye forever it remember may;
This day the sun is in his chiefest height,
With Barnaby the bright,
From whence declining daily by degrees,
He somewhat loseth of his heat and light,
When once the Crab behind his back he sees.
But for this time it ill ordainèd was,   270
To choose the longest day in all the year,
And shortest night, when longest fitter were:
Yet never day so long, but late would pass.
Ring ye the bells, to make it wear away,
And bonfires make all day;
And dance about them, and about them sing,
That all the woods may answer, and your echo
    ring.

Ah! when will this long weary day have end,
And lend me leave to come unto my love?
How slowly do the hours their numbers spend!
How slowly does sad Time his feathers move!
Haste thee, O fairest planet, to thy home,   282
Within the western foam:
Thy tirèd steeds long since have need of rest.
Long though it be, at last I see it gloom,
And the bright evening-star with golden crest
Appear out of the East.
Fair child of beauty! glorious lamp of love!
That all the hosts of heaven in ranks dost lead,
And guidest lovers through the nightës dread,
How cheerfully thou lookest from above,   291
AE

And seem'st to laugh atween thy twinkling
    light,
As joying in the sight
Of these glad many, which for joy do sing,
That all the woods them answer, and their
    echo ring!

Now cease, ye damsels, your delights forepast;
Enough it is that all the day was yours:
Now day is done, and night is nighing fast,
Now bring the bride into the bridal bowers.
The night is come, now soon her disarray,   300
And in her bed her lay;
Lay her in lilies and in violets,
And silken curtains over her display,
And odoured sheets, and Arras coverlets.
Behold how goodly my fair love does lie,
In proud humility!
Like unto Maia, whenas Jove her took
In Tempe, lying on the flowery grass,
'Twixt sleep and wake, after she weary was
With bathing in the Acidalian brook.   310
Now it is night, ye damsels may be gone,
And leave my love alone,
And leave likewise your former lay to sing:
The woods no more shall answer, nor your echo
    ring.

*   *   *   *   *   *   *

Song! made in lieu of many ornaments,   427
With which my love should duly have been decked,
Which cutting off through hasty accidents,
Ye would not stay your due time to expect,   430
But promised both to recompense;
Be unto her a goodly ornament,
And for short time an endless monument!

AMORETTI

VIII

More than most fair, full of the living fire
Kindled above unto the Maker near;
No eyes, but joys, in which all powers con-
    spire,
That to the world naught else be counted dear;
Through your bright beams doth not the
    blinded guest
Shoot out his darts to base affections wound;
But angels come, to lead frail minds to rest
In chaste desires, on heavenly beauty bound.
You frame my thoughts, and fashion me
    within;
You stop my tongue, and teach my heart to
    speak;   10

You calm the storm that passion did begin,
Strong through your cause, but by your virtue
    weak.
   Dark is the world where your light shinèd
    never;
   Well is he born that may behold you ever.

XXIV

Like as a ship, that through the ocean wide
By conduct of some star doth make her way,
Whenas a storm hath dimmed her trusty
    guide,
Out of her course doth wander far astray;
So I, whose star, that wont with her bright ray
Me to direct, with clouds is overcast,
Do wander now, in darkness and dismay,
Through hidden perils round about me placed;
Yet hope I well that, when this storm is past,
My Helicë, the lodestar of my life,   10
Will shine again, and look on me at last,
With lovely light to clear my cloudy grief:
   Till then I wander careful, comfortless,
   In secret sorrow and sad pensiveness.

PROTHALAMION

Calm was the day, and through the trembling
    air
Sweet breathing Zephyrus did softly play,
A gentle spirit, that lightly did delay
Hot Titan's beams, which then did glister fair;
When I (whom sullen care,
Through discontent of my long fruitless stay
In princes' court, and expectation vain
Of idle hopes, which still do fly away,
Like empty shadows, did afflict my brain)
Walked forth, to ease my pain,   10
Along the shore of silver streaming Thames;
Whose rutty [1] bank, the which his river hems,
Was painted all with variable flowers,
And all the meads adorned with dainty gems,
Fit to deck maidens' bowers,
And crown their paramours,
Against the bridal day, which is not long:
   Sweet Thames! run softly, till I end my
    song.

There, in a meadow, by the river's side,
A flock of nymphs I chancèd to espy,   20
All lovely daughters of the flood thereby,
With goodly greenish locks, all loose untied,

[1] rooty

As each had been a bride:
And each one had a little wicker basket,
Made of fine twigs, entrailèd curiously,
In which they gathered flowers to fill their
    flasket,
And with fine fingers cropt full feateously [1]
The tender stalks on high.
Of every sort which in that meadow grew
They gathered some; the violet, pallid blue,
The little daisy, that at evening closes,   31
The virgin lily, and the primrose true,
With store of vermeil roses,
To deck their bridegroom's posies,
Against the bridal day, which was not long:
   Sweet Thames! run softly, till I end my
    song.

With that, I saw two swans of goodly hue
Come softly swimming down along the Lee; 38
Two fairer birds I yet did never see;
The snow which doth the top of Pindus strew
Did never whiter shew,
Nor Jove himself, when he a swan would be
For love of Leda, whiter did appear;
Yet Leda was, they say, as white as he,
Yet not so white as these, nor nothing near;
So purely white they were,
That even the gentle stream, the which them
    bare,
Seemed foul to them, and bade his billows
    spare
To wet their silken feathers, lest they might
Soil their fair plumes with water not so fair,
And mar their beauties bright,   51
That shone as heaven's light,
Against their bridal day, which was not long:
   Sweet Thames! run softly, till I end my
    song.

Eftsoons the nymphs, which now had flowers
    their fill,
Ran all in haste to see that silver brood,
As they came floating on the crystal flood;
Whom when they saw, they stood amazèd
    still,
Their wondering eyes to fill;   59
Them seemed they never saw a sight so fair
Of fowls so lovely, that they sure did deem
Them heavenly born, or to be that same pair
Which through the sky draw Venus' silver
    team;
For sure they did not seem
To be begot of any earthly seed,

[1] neatly

But rather angels, or of angels' breed;
Yet were they bred of summer's heat, they
    say,
In sweetest season, when each flower and weed
The earth did fresh array;
So fresh they seemed as day,   70
Even as their bridal day, which was not
    long:
    Sweet Thames! run softly, till I end my
        song.

Then forth they all out of their baskets drew
Great store of flowers, the honour of the
    field,
That to the sense did fragrant odours yield,
All which upon those goodly birds they threw,
And all the waves did strew,
That like old Peneus' waters they did seem,
When down along by pleasant Tempe's shore,
Scattered with flowers, through Thessaly they
    stream,   80
That they appear, through lilies' plenteous
    store,
Like a bride's chamber floor.
Two of those nymphs, meanwhile, two gar-
    lands bound
Of freshest flowers which in that mead they
    found,
The which presenting all in trim array,
Their snowy foreheads therewithal they
    crowned,
Whilst one did sing this lay,
Prepared against that day,
Against their bridal day, which was not long:
    Sweet Thames! run softly, till I end my
        song.   90

"Ye gentle birds! the world's fair ornament,
And heaven's glory, whom this happy hour
Doth lead unto your lover's blissful bower,
Joy may you have, and gentle hearts' content
Of your love's couplement;
And let fair Venus, that is queen of love,
With her heart-quelling son upon you smile,
Whose smile, they say, hath virtue to remove
All love's dislike, and friendship's faulty guile
For ever to assoil;   100
Let endless peace your steadfast hearts
    accord,
And blessed plenty wait upon your board;
And let your bed with pleasures chaste
    abound,
That fruitful issue may to you afford,
Which may your foes confound,
And make your joys redound

Upon your bridal day, which is not long:
    Sweet Thames! run softly, till I end my
        song."

So ended she; and all the rest around
To her redoubled that her undersong,   110
Which said their bridal day should not be long:
And gentle Echo from the neighbour ground
Their accents did resound.
So forth those joyous birds did pass along,
Adown the Lee, that to them murmured low,
As he would speak, but that he lacked a
    tongue,
Yet did by signs his glad affection show,
Making his stream run slow.
And all the fowl which in his flood did dwell
'Gan flock about these twain, that did excel
The rest, so far as Cynthia[1] doth shend[2] 121
The lesser stars. So they, enrangèd well,
Did on those two attend,
And their best service lend,
Against their wedding day, which was not long:
    Sweet Thames! run softly, till I end my
        song.

At length they all to merry London came,
To merry London, my most kindly nurse,
That to me gave this life's first native source;
Though from another place I take my name,
An house of ancient fame: 131
There when they came, whereas[3] those bricky
    towers
The which on Thames' broad, agèd back do
    ride,
Where now the studious lawyers have their
    bowers,
There whilom wont the Templar Knights to
    bide,
Till they decayed through pride:
Next whereunto there stands a stately place,
Where oft I gainèd gifts and goodly grace
Of that great lord which therein wont to dwell,
Whose want too well now feels my friendless
    case;   140
But ah! here fits not well
Old woes, but joys, to tell,
Against the bridal day, which is not long:
    Sweet Thames! run softly, till I end my
        song.

Yet therein now doth lodge a noble peer,
Great England's glory, and the world's wide
    wonder,

    [1] the moon   [2] shame   [3] where

Whose dreadful name late through all Spain
    did thunder,
And Hercules' two pillars standing near
Did make to quake and fear:
Fair branch of honour, flower of chivalry! 150
That fillest England with thy triumph's fame,
Joy have thou of thy noble victory,
And endless happiness of thine own name,
That promiseth the same;
That through thy prowess and victorious arms
Thy country may be freed from foreign harms;
And great Elisa's glorious name may ring
Through all the world, filled with thy wide
    alarms,
Which some brave muse may sing
To ages following,   160
Upon the bridal day, which is not long:
  Sweet Thames! run softly, till I end my
    song.

From those high towers this noble lord issuing,
Like radiant Hesper when his golden hair
In th' ocean billows he hath bathèd fair,
Descended to the river's open viewing,
With a great train ensuing.
Above the rest were goodly to be seen
Two gentle knights of lovely face and feature
Beseeming well the bower of any queen, 170
With gifts of wit, and ornaments of nature,
Fit for so goodly stature,
That like the twins of Jove they seemed in
    sight,
Which deck the baldrick of the heavens
    bright;
They two, forth pacing to the river's side,
Received those two fair brides, their love's
    delight;
Which, at th' appointed tide,
Each one did make his bride,   178
Against their bridal day, which is not long:
  Sweet Thames! run softly, till I end my
    song.

From AN HYMN IN HONOUR OF BEAUTY

What time this world's great Workmaster did
    cast
To make all things such as we now behold, 30
It seems that he before his eyes had placed
A goodly pattern, to whose perfect mould
He fashioned them as comely as he could,
That now so fair and seemly they appear
As nought may be amended anywhere.   35

That wondrous pattern, wheresoe'er it be,
Whether in earth laid up in secret store,
Or else in heaven, that no man may it see
With sinful eyes, for fear it to deflore,[1]
Is perfect Beauty, which all men adore;   40
Whose face and feature doth so much excel
All mortal sense, that none the same may tell.

Thereof as every earthly thing partakes
Or more or less, by influence divine,
So it more fair accordingly it makes,   45
And the gross matter of this earthly mine
Which clotheth it, thereafter doth refine,
Doing away the dross which dims the light
Of that fair beam which therein is empight.[2]

For, through infusion of celestial power   50
The duller earth it quickeneth with delight,
And life-full spirits privily doth pour
Through all the parts, that to the looker's sight
They seem to please. That is thy sovereign
    might,
O Cyprian queen! which, flowing from the
    beam
Of thy bright star, thou into them dost stream.

That is the thing which giveth pleasant grace
To all things fair, that kindleth lively fire,
Light of thy lamp; which, shining in the face,
Thence to the soul darts amorous desire,   60
And robs the hearts of those which it admire;
Therewith thou pointest thy son's poisoned
    arrow,
That wounds the life, and wastes the inmost
    marrow.

How vainly then do idle wits invent
That beauty is nought else but mixture made
Of colours fair, and goodly temp'rament[3]   66
Of pure complexions, that shall quickly fade
And pass away, like to a summer's shade;
Or that it is but comely composition   69
Of parts well measured, with meet disposition!

Hath white and red in it such wondrous power,
That it can pierce through th' eyes unto the
    heart,
And therein stir such rage and restless stour,[4]
As nought but death can stint his dolour's
    smart?
Or can proportion of the outward part   75
Move such affection in the inward mind,
That it can rob both sense, and reason blind?

[1] sully   [2] placed   [3] mixture   [4] strife

Why do not then the blossoms of the field,
Which are arrayed with much more orient hue,
And to the sense most dainty odours yield, 80
Work like impression in the looker's view?
Or why do not fair pictures like power shew,
In which ofttimes we nature see of [1] art
Excelled in perfect limning every part? 84

But ah! believe me, there is more than so,
That works such wonders in the minds of men;
I, that have often prov'd, too well it know,
And whoso list the like assays to ken
Shall find by trial, and confess it then,
That Beauty is not, as fond men misdeem, 90
An outward show of things that only seem.

For that same goodly hue of white and red,
With which the cheeks are sprinkled, shall
decay,
And those sweet rosy leaves, so fairly spread
Upon the lips, shall fade and fall away 95
To that they were, even to corrupted clay:
That golden wire, those sparkling stars so
bright
Shall turn to dust, and lose their goodly light.

But that fair lamp, from whose celestial ray
That light proceeds which kindleth lovers' fire,
Shall never be extinguished nor decay; 101
But when the vital spirits do expire,
Unto her native planet shall retire;
For it is heavenly born and cannot die,
Being a parcel of the purest sky. 105

* * * * * * *

So every spirit, as it is most pure, 127
And hath in it the more of heavenly light,
So it the fairer body doth procure
To habit in, and it more fairly dight [2] 130
With cheerful grace and amiable sight;
For of the soul the body form doth take;
For soul is form, and doth the body make.

Therefore, wherever that thou dost behold
A comely corps,[3] with beauty fair endued, 135
Know this for certain, that the same doth hold
A beauteous soul, with fair conditions thewed,[4]
Fit to receive the seed of virtue strewed;
For all·that fair is, is by nature good;
That is a sign to know the gentle blood. 140

Yet oft it falls that many a gentle mind
Dwells in deformèd tabernacle drowned,

Either by chance, against the course of kind,
Or through unaptness in the substance found,
Which it assumèd of some stubborn ground,
That will not yield unto her form's direction,
But is deformed with some foul imperfection.

And oft it falls (ay me, the more to rue!)
That goodly beauty, albe heavenly borne,
Is foul abused, and that celestial hue, 150
Which doth the world with her delight adorn,
Made but the bait of sin, and sinners' scorn,
Whilst every one doth seek and sue to have it,
But every one doth seek but to deprave it.

Yet nathemore [1] is that fair beauty's blame,
But theirs that do abuse it unto ill: 156
Nothing so good, but that through guilty
shame
May be corrupt, and wrested unto will:
Natheless the soul is fair and beauteous still,
However flesh's fault it filthy make; 160
For things immortal no corruption take.

From AN HYMN OF HEAVENLY BEAUTY

The means, therefore, which unto us is lent,
Him to behold, is on his works to look,
Which he hath made in beauty excellent,
And in the same, as in a brazen book, 130
To read enregistered in every nook
His goodness, which his beauty doth declare;
For all that's good is beautiful and fair.

Thence gathering plumes of perfect specula-
tion,
To imp the wings of thy high-flying mind, 135
Mount up aloft, through heavenly contempla-
tion,
From this dark world, whose damps the soul
do blind,
And like the native brood of eagle's kind,
On that bright Sun of Glory fix thine eyes,
Cleared from gross mists of frail infirmities.

Humbled with fear and awful reverence, 141
Before the footstool of his Majesty,
Throw thyself down, with trembling inno-
cence,
Ne dare look up with corruptible eye
On the dread face of that great Deity, 145
For fear lest, if he chance to look on thee,
Thou turn to nought, and quite confounded be.

[1] by [2] adorn [3] body [4] qualities endowed

[1] none the more

But lowly fall before his mercy-seat,
Close covered with the Lamb's integrity
From the just wrath of his avengeful threat 150
That sits upon the righteous throne on high;
His throne is built upon Eternity,
More firm and durable than steel or brass,
Or the hard diamond, which them both doth
    pass.

His sceptre is the rod of Righteousness, 155
With which he bruiseth all his foes to dust
And the great Dragon strongly doth repress
Under the rigour of his judgment just;
His seat is Truth, to which the faithful trust,
From whence proceed her beams so pure and
    bright   160
That all about him sheddeth glorious light.

* * * * * * *

Ah, then, my hungry soul! which long hast
    fed
On idle fancies of thy foolish thought,
And, with false beauty's flattering bait misled,
Hast after vain deceitful shadows sought, 291
Which all are fled, and now have left thee
    nought
But late repentance through thy follies' prief;[1]
Ah! cease to gaze on matter of thy grief:

And look at last up to that Sovereign Light,
From whose pure beams all perfect beauty
    springs,   296
That kindleth love in every godly spright,
Even the love of God; which loathing brings
Of this vile world and these gay-seeming
    things:
With whose sweet pleasures being so possessed,
Thy straying thoughts henceforth forever rest.

SIR PHILIP SIDNEY (1554–1586)

ASTROPHEL AND STELLA

I

Loving in truth, and fain[2] in verse my love to
    show,
That she, dear she, might take some pleasure
    of my pain, —
Pleasure might cause her read, reading might
    make her know,
Knowledge might pity win, and pity grace
    obtain, —

[1] proof   [2] desirous

I sought fit words to paint the blackest face
    of woe;
Studying inventions fine, her wits to enter-
    tain,
Oft turning others' leaves, to see if thence
    would flow
Some fresh and fruitful showers upon my sun-
    burn'd brain.
But words came halting forth, wanting In-
    vention's stay;
Invention, Nature's child, fled step-dame
    Study's blows;   10
And others' feet still seem'd but strangers in
    my way.
Thus, great with child to speak, and helpless
    in my throes,
Biting my truant pen, beating myself for
    spite;.
"Fool," said my Muse to me, "look in thy
    heart, and write."

XV

You that do search for every purling spring
Which from the ribs of old Parnassus flows,
And every flower, not sweet perhaps, which
    grows
Near thereabouts, into your poesie wring;[1]
Ye that do dictionary's method bring
Into your rimes, running in rattling rows;
You that poor Petrarch's long-deceasèd woes
With new-born sighs and denizen'd wit do
    sing;
You take wrong ways; those far-fet[2] helps be
    such
As do bewray a want of inward touch,[3]   10
And sure, at length stol'n goods do come to
    light:
But if, both for your love and skill, your
    name
You seek to nurse at fullest breasts of Fame,
Stella behold, and then begin to endite.

XXXI

With how sad steps, O Moon, thou climb'st
    the skies!
How silently, and with how wan a face!
What, may it be that even in heav'nly place
That busy archer[4] his sharp arrows tries!
Sure, if that long-with-love-acquainted eyes
Can judge of love, thou feel'st a lover's case,
I read it in thy looks; thy languished grace,

[1] force   [2] far-fetched   [3] feeling   [4] Cupid

To me, that feel the like, thy state descries.[1]
Then, ev'n of fellowship, O Moon, tell me,
Is constant love deem'd there but want of
    wit?
Are beauties there as proud as here they be?
Do they above love to be lov'd, and yet   12
Those lovers scorn whom that love doth
    possess?
Do they call virtue there ungratefulness?

XXXIX

Come, Sleep! O Sleep, the certain knot of
    peace,
The baiting-place[2] of wit, the balm of woe,
The poor man's wealth, the prisoner's release,
Th' indifferent judge between the high and
    low,
With shield of proof shield me from out the
    prease[3]
Of those fierce darts Despair at me doth
    throw:
O make in me those civil wars to cease;
I will good tribute pay, if thou do so.
Take thou of me smooth pillows, sweetest bed,
A chamber deaf of noise and blind of light,   10
A rosy garland and a weary head:
And if these things, as being thine in right,
Move not thy heavy grace, thou shalt in me,
Livelier then else-where, Stella's image see.

XLI

Having this day my horse, my hand, my
    lance
Guided so well, that I obtain'd the prize,
Both by the judgment of the English eyes
And of some sent from that sweet enemy
    France;
Horsemen my skill in horsemanship advance,
Town folks my strength; a daintier judge
    applies
His praise to sleight which from good use
    doth rise;
Some lucky wits impute it but to chance;
Others, because of both sides I do take   9
My blood from them who did excell in this,
Think Nature me a man-at-arms did make.
How far they shot awry! the true cause is,
Stella looked on, and from her heav'nly face
Sent forth the beams which made so fair my
    race.

[1] reveals   [2] place of refreshment   [3] throng

THE NIGHTINGALE

The nightingale, as soon as April bringeth
Unto her rested sense a perfect waking,
While late bare earth, proud of new clothing,
    springeth,
Sings out her woes, a thorn her song-book
    making,
And mournfully bewailing,   5
Her throat in tunes expresseth
What grief her breast oppresseth
For Tereus' force on her chaste will prevailing.
O Philomela fair, O take some gladness,
That here is juster cause of painful sadness:
Thine earth now springs, mine fadeth: 11
Thy thorn without, my thorn my heart in-
    vadeth.

HYMN TO APOLLO

Apollo great, whose beams the greater world
    do light,
And in our little world do clear our inward
    sight,
Which ever shine, though hid from earth by
    earthly shade,
Whose lights do ever live, but in our darkness
    fade;
Thou god whose youth was decked with spoil
    of Python's skin   5
(So humble knowledge can throw down the
    snakish sin);
Latona's son, whose birth in pain and travail
    long
Doth teach, to learn the good what travails
    do belong;
In travail of our life (a short but tedious
    space),
While brickle[1] hour-glass runs, guide thou our
    panting pace: 10
Give us foresightful minds; give us minds to
    obey
What foresight tells; our thoughts upon thy
    knowledge stay.
Let so our fruits grow up that Nature be main-
    tained,
But so our hearts keep down, with vice they
    be not stained.
Let this assuréd hold our judgments over-
    take,
That nothing wins the heaven but what doth
    earth forsake.   16

[1] brittle

ARCADIA

BOOK I. CHAP. I

And now they were already come upon the stays,[1] when one of the sailors descried a galley which came with sails and oars directly in the chase of them, and straight perceived it was a well-known pirate, who hunted, not only for goods, but for bodies of men, which he employed either to be his galley-slaves or to sell at the best market. Which when the master understood, he commanded forthwith to set on all the canvas they could and fly homeward, leaving in that sort poor Pyrocles, so near to be rescued. But what did not Musidorus say? what did he not offer, to persuade them to venture the fight? But fear, standing at the gates of their ears, put back all persuasions; so that he had nothing to accompany Pyrocles but his eyes, nor to succour him but his wishes. Therefore praying for him, and casting a long look that way, he saw the galley leave the pursuit of them and turn to take up the spoils of the other wreck; and, lastly, he might well see them lift up the young man; and, "Alas!" said he to himself, "dear Pyrocles, shall that body of thine be enchained? Shall those victorious hands of thine be commanded to base offices? Shall virtue become a slave to those that be slaves to viciousness? Alas, better had it been thou hadst ended nobly thy noble days. What death is so evil as unworthy servitude?" But that opinion soon ceased when he saw the galley setting upon another ship, which held long and strong fight with her; for then he began afresh to fear the life of his friend, and to wish well to the pirates, whom before he hated, lest in their ruin he might perish. But the fishermen made such speed into the haven that they absented his eyes from beholding the issue; where being entered, he could procure neither them nor any other as then[2] to put themselves into the sea; so that, being as full of sorrow for being unable to do anything as void of counsel how to do anything, besides that sickness grew something upon him, the honest shepherds Strephon and Claius (who, being themselves true friends, did the more perfectly judge the justness of his sorrow) advise him that he

should mitigate somewhat of his woe, since he had gotten an amendment in fortune, being come from assured persuasion of his death to have no cause to despair of his life, as one that had lamented the death of his sheep should after know they were but strayed, would receive pleasure, though readily he knew not where to find them.

CHAP. II

"Now, sir," said they, "thus for ourselves it is. We are, in profession, but shepherds, and, in this country of Laconia, little better than strangers, and, therefore, neither in skill nor ability of power greatly to stead you. But what we can present unto you is this: Arcadia, of which country we are, is but a little way hence, and even upon the next confines.

There dwelleth a gentleman, by name Kalander, who vouchsafeth much favour unto us; a man who for his hospitality is so much haunted[1] that no news stir but come to his ears; for his upright dealing so beloved of his neighbours that he hath many ever ready to do him their uttermost service, and, by the great goodwill our Prince bears him, may soon obtain the use of his name and credit, which hath a principal sway, not only in his own Arcadia, but in all these countries of Peloponnesus; and, which is worth all, all these things give him not so much power as his nature gives him will to benefit, so that it seems no music is so sweet to his ear as deserved thanks. To him we will bring you, and there you may recover again your health, without which you cannot be able to make any diligent search for your friend, and, therefore but in that respect, you must labour for it. Besides, we are sure the comfort of courtesy and ease of wise counsel shall not be wanting."

Musidorus (who, besides he was merely[2] unacquainted in the country, had his wits astonished[3] with sorrow) gave easy consent to that from which he saw no reason to disagree; and therefore, defraying[4] the mariners with a ring bestowed upon them, they took their journey together through Laconia, Claius and Strephon by course carrying his chest for him, Musidorus only bearing in his countenance evident marks of a sorrowful mind

---

[1] come upon the stays = go about from one tack to another　[2] as then = at the time

[1] visited　[2] entirely　[3] stricken　[4] paying

supported with a weak body; which they perceiving, and knowing that the violence of sorrow is not, at the first, to be striven withal (being like a mighty beast, sooner tamed with following than overthrown by withstanding) they gave way unto it for that day and the next, never troubling him, either with asking questions or finding fault with his melancholy, but rather fitting to his dolour dolorous discourses of their own and other folk's misfortunes. Which speeches, though they had not a lively entrance to his senses, shut up in sorrow, yet, like one half asleep, he took hold of much of the matters spoken unto him, so as a man may say, ere sorrow was aware, they made his thoughts bear away something else beside his own sorrow, which wrought so in him that at length he grew content to mark their speeches, then to marvel at such wit in shepherds, after to like their company, and lastly to vouchsafe conference; so that the third day after, in the time that the morning did strow roses and violets in the heavenly floor against the coming of the sun, the nightingales, striving one with the other which could in most dainty variety recount their wrong-caused sorrow, made them put off their sleep; and, rising from under a tree, which that night had been their pavilion, they went on their journey, which by and by welcomed Musidorus' eyes, wearied with the wasted soil of Laconia, with delightful prospects. There were hills which garnished their proud heights with stately trees; humble valleys whose base estate seemed comforted with refreshing of silver rivers; meadows enamelled with all sorts of eye-pleasing flowers; thickets which, being lined with most pleasant shade, were witnessed so to by the cheerful disposition of many well-tuned birds; each pasture stored with sheep, feeding with sober security, while the pretty lambs, with bleating oratory, craved the dams' comfort: here a shepherd's boy piping, as though he should never be old; there a young shepherdess knitting, and withal singing, and it seemed that her voice comforted her hands to work, and her hands kept time to her voice's music. As for the houses of the country (for many houses came under their eye) they were all scattered, no two being one by the other, and yet not so far off as that it barred mutual succour: a show, as it were, of an accompanable [1] solitariness, and of a civil [1] wildness. "I pray you," said Musidorus, then first unsealing his long-silent lips, "what countries be these we pass through, which are so diverse in show, the one wanting no store,[2] the other having no store but of want?"

"The country," answered Claius, "where you were cast ashore, and now are passed through, is Laconia, not so poor by the barrenness of the soil (though in itself not passing fertile) as by a civil war, which, being these two years within the bowels of that estate, between the gentlemen and the peasants (by them named helots) hath in this sort, as it were, disfigured the face of nature and made it so unhospitall as now you have found it; the towns neither of the one side nor the other willingly opening their gates to strangers, nor strangers willingly entering, for fear of being mistaken.

"But this country, where now you set your foot, is Arcadia; and even hard by is the house of Kalander, whither we lead you: this country being thus decked with peace and (the child of peace) good husbandry. These houses you see so scattered are of men, as we two are, that live upon the commodity of their sheep, and therefore, in the division of the Arcadian estate, are termed shepherds; a happy people, wanting [3] little, because they desire not much."

"What cause, then," said Musidorus, "made you venture to leave this sweet life and put yourself in yonder unpleasant and dangerous realm?" "Guarded with poverty," answered Strephon, "and guided with love." "But now," said Claius, "since it hath pleased you to ask anything of us, whose baseness is such as the very knowledge is darkness, give us leave to know something of you and of the young man you so much lament, that at least we may be the better instructed to inform Kalander, and he the better know how to proportion his entertainment." Musidorus, according to the agreement between Pyrocles and him to alter their names, answered that he called himself Palladius, and his friend Daïphantus. "But, till I have him again," said he, "I am indeed nothing, and therefore my story is of nothing. His entertainment, since so good a man he is, cannot be so low as I account my estate; and, in sum, the sum of all his courtesy may

---

[1] companionable

[1] civilized   [2] plenty   [3] lacking

be to help me by some means to seek my friend.''

They perceived he was not willing to open himself further, and therefore, without further questioning, brought him to the house; about which they might see (with fit consideration both of the air, the prospect, and the nature of the ground) all such necessary additions to a great house as might well show Kalander knew that provision is the foundation of hospitality, and thrift the fuel of magnificence. The house itself was built of fair and strong stone, not affecting so much any extraordinary kind of fineness as an honourable representing of a firm stateliness; the lights, doors, and stairs rather directed to the use of the guest than to the eye of the artificer, and yet as the one chiefly heeded, so the other not neglected; each place handsome without curiosity, and homely without loathsomeness; not so dainty as not to be trod on, nor yet slubbered up [1] with good-fellowship; [2] all more lasting than beautiful, but that the consideration of the exceeding lastingness made the eye believe it was exceeding beautiful; the servants, not so many in number as cleanly in apparel and serviceable in behaviour, testifying even in their countenances that their master took as well care to be served as of them that did serve. One of them was forthwith ready to welcome the shepherds, as men who, though they were poor, their master greatly favoured; and understanding by them that the young man with them was to be much accounted of, for that they had seen tokens of more than common greatness, howsoever now eclipsed with fortune, he ran to his master, who came presently forth, and pleasantly welcoming the shepherds, but especially applying him to Musidorus, Strephon privately told him all what he knew of him, and particularly that he found this stranger was loth to be known.

"No,'' said Kalander, speaking aloud, "I am no herald to inquire of men's pedigrees; it sufficeth me if I know their virtues; which, if this young man's face be not a false witness, do better apparel his mind than you have done his body.'' While he was speaking, there came a boy, in show like a merchant's prentice, who, taking Strephon by the sleeve, delivered him a letter, written jointly both to him and Claius from Urania; which they no sooner

had read, but that with short leave-taking of Kalander, who quickly guessed and smiled at the matter, and once again, though hastily, recommending the young man unto him, they went away, leaving Musidorus even loth to part with them, for the good conversation he had of them, and obligation he accounted himself tied in unto them; and therefore, they delivering his chest unto him, he opened it, and would have presented them with two very rich jewels, but they absolutely refused them, telling him they were more than enough rewarded in the knowing of him, and without hearkening unto a reply, like men whose hearts disdained all desires but one, gat speedily away, as if the letter had brought wings to make them fly. But by that sight Kalander soon judged that his guest was of no mean calling; [1] and therefore the more respectfully entertaining him, Musidorus found his sickness, which the fight, the sea, and late travel had laid upon him, grow greatly, so that fearing some sudden accident, he delivered the chest to Kalander, which was full of most precious stones, gorgeously and cunningly set in divers manners, desiring him he would keep those trifles, and if he died, he would bestow so much of it as was needful to find out and redeem a young man naming himself Daïphantus, as then in the hands of Laconian pirates.

But Kalander seeing him faint more and more, with careful speed conveyed him to the most commodious lodging in his house; where, being possessed with an extreme burning fever, he continued some while with no great hope of life; but youth at length got the victory of sickness, so that in six weeks the excellency of his returned beauty was a credible ambassador of his health, to the great joy of Kalander, who, as in this time he had by certain friends of his, that dwelt near the sea in Messenia, set forth a ship and a galley to seek and succour Daïphantus, so at home did he omit nothing which he thought might either profit or gratify Palladius.

For, having found in him (besides his bodily gifts, beyond the degree of admiration) by daily discourses, which he delighted himself to have with him, a mind of most excellent composition (a piercing wit, quite void of ostentation, high-erected thoughts seated in a heart of courtesy, an eloquence as sweet in

---

[1] made slovenly   [2] revelry   [1] rank

the uttering as slow to come to the uttering, a behaviour so noble as gave a majesty to adversity, and all in a man whose age could not be above one-and-twenty years), the good old man was even enamoured with a fatherly love towards him, or rather became his servant by the bonds such virtue laid upon him; once, he acknowledged himself so to be, by the badge of diligent attendance.

JOHN LYLY (1554–1606)

FROM EUPHUES AND HIS ENGLAND

"I perceive, Camilla, that be your cloth never so bad, it will take some colour, and your cause never so false, it will bear some show of probability, wherein you manifest the right nature of a woman, who having no way to win, thinketh to overcome with words. This I gather by your answer, that beauty may have fair leaves, and foul fruit, that all that are amiable are not honest, that love proceedeth of the woman's perfection, and the man's follies, that the trial looked for, is to perform whatsoever they promise, that in mind he be virtuous, in body comely, such a husband in my opinion is to be wished for, but not looked for. Take heed, Camilla, that seeking all the wood for a straight stick you choose not at the last a crooked staff, or prescribing a good counsel to others, thou thyself follow the worst: much like to Chius, who selling the best wine to others, drank himself of the lees."

"Truly," quoth Camilla, "my wool was black, and therefore it could take no other colour, and my cause good, and therefore admitteth no cavil: as for the rules I set down of love, they were not coined of me, but learned, and, being so true, believed. If my fortune be so ill that, searching for a wand, I gather a cammock,[1] or, selling wine to other, I drink vinegar myself, I must be content, that of the worst, poor help, patience,[2] which by so much the more is to be borne, by how much the more it is perforce."

As Surius was speaking, the Lady Flavia prevented him, saying, "It is time that you break off your speech, lest we have nothing to speak, for should you wade any farther, you would both waste the night and leave us no time, and take our reasons and leave us no matter; that every one therefore may say somewhat, we command you to cease; that you have both said so well, we give you thanks."

* * * * * * *

The Lady Flavia speaking in his cast,[1] proceeded in this manner:

"Truly, Martius, I had not thought that as yet your colt's tooth stuck in your mouth,[2] or that so old a truant in love, could hitherto remember his lesson. You seem not to infer that it is requisite they should meet, but being in love that it is convenient, lest, falling into a mad mood, they pine in their own peevishness. Why then let it follow, that the drunkard which surfeiteth with wine be always quaffing, because he liketh it, or the epicure which glutteth himself with meat be ever eating, for that it contenteth him, not seeking at any time the means to redress their vices, but to renew them. But it fareth with the lover as it doth with him that poureth in much wine, who is ever more thirsty than he that drinketh moderately, for having once tasted the delights of love, he desireth most the thing that hurteth him most, not laying a plaster to the wound, but a corrosive.

"I am of this mind, that if it be dangerous, to lay flax to the fire, salt to the eyes, sulphur to the nose, that then it cannot be but perilous to let one lover come in presence of the other."

Surius overhearing the lady, and seeing her so earnest, although he were more earnest in his suit to Camilla, cut her off with these words:

"Good Madam, give me leave either to depart, or to speak, for in truth you gall me more with these terms, than you wist,[3] in seeming to inveigh so bitterly against the meeting of lovers, which is the only marrow of love, and though I doubt not but that Martius is sufficiently armed to answer you, yet would I not have those reasons refelled,[4] which I loathe to have repeated. It may be you utter them not of malice you bear to love, but only to move controversy where there is no question:[5] for if thou envy to have lovers meet, why did you grant us; if allow it, why seek you to separate us?"

---

[1] crooked stick [2] = with the only contentment possible at the worst, the poor help patience

[1] style, manner [2] *i.e.* I had not thought that you still retained the wanton tendencies of your youth [3] know [4] refuted [5] difference of opinion

The good lady could not refrain from laughter, when she saw Surius so angry, who in the midst of his own tale, was troubled with hers, whom she thus again answered.

"I cry you mercy,[1] gentleman, I had not thought to have catched you, when I fished for another, but I perceive now that with one bean it is easy to get two pigeons, and with one bait to have divers bites. I see that others may guess where the shoe wrings, besides him that wears it." "Madam," quoth Surius, "you have caught a frog, if I be not deceived, and therefore as good it were not to hurt him, as not to eat him, but if all this while you angled to have a bite at a lover, you should have used no bitter medicines, but pleasant baits."

"I cannot tell," answered Flavia, "whether my bait were bitter or not, but sure I am I have the fish by the gill, that doth me good." Camilla not thinking to be silent, put in her spoke as she thought into the best wheel, saying,

"Lady, your cunning may deceive you in fishing with an angle, therefore to catch him you would have, you were best to use a net." "A net!" quoth Flavia, "I need none, for my fish playeth in a net already." With that Surius began to wince, replying immediately, "So doth many a fish, good lady, that slippeth out, when the fisher thinketh him fast in, and it may be, that either your net is too weak to hold him, or your hand too wet." "A wet hand," quoth Flavia, "will hold a dead herring:" "Aye," quoth Surius, "but eels are no herrings." "But lovers are," said Flavia.

Surius not willing to have the grass mown, whereof he meant to make his hay, began thus to conclude:

"Good Lady, leave off fishing for this time, and though it be Lent, rather break a statute which is but penal, than sew[2] a pond that may be perpetual." "I am content," quoth Flavia, "rather to fast for once, than to want a pleasure forever: yet, Surius, betwixt us two, I will at large prove, that there is nothing in love more venomous than meeting, which filleth the mind with grief and the body with diseases: for having the one, he cannot fail of the other. But now, Philautus and niece Francis, since I am cut off, begin you: but be short, because the time is short, and that I was more short than I would."

---

[1] I beg your pardon   [2] drain, empty

APELLES' SONG

Cupid and my Campaspe played
At cards for kisses; Cupid paid.
He stakes his quiver, bow, and arrows,
His mother's doves and team of sparrows:
Loses them too; then down he throws   5
The coral of his lip, the rose
Growing on's cheek (but none knows how);
With these the crystal of his brow,
And then the dimple of his chin;
All these did my Campaspe win.   10
At last he set her both his eyes;
She won, and Cupid blind did rise.
O Love, has she done this to thee?
What shall, alas! become of me?

SPRING'S WELCOME

What bird so sings, yet so does wail?
O 'tis the ravished nightingale.
"Jug, jug, jug, jug, tereu," she cries,
And still her woes at midnight rise.

Brave prick-song! who is't now we hear?   5
None but the lark so shrill and clear;
Now at heaven's gates she claps her wings,
The morn not waking till she sings.

Hark, hark, with what a pretty throat
Poor robin redbreast tunes his note;   10
Hark how the jolly cuckoos sing,
Cuckoo, to welcome in the spring;
Cuckoo, to welcome in the spring!

FAIRY REVELS

OMNES. Pinch him, pinch him black and
blue;
Saucy mortals must not view
What the queen of stars is doing,
Nor pry into our fairy wooing.
1 FAIRY. Pinch him blue —   5
2 FAIRY. And pinch him black —
3 FAIRY. Let him not lack
Sharp nails to pinch him blue and
red,
Till sleep has rocked his addlehead.
4 FAIRY. For the trespass he hath done,   10
Spots o'er all his flesh shall run.
Kiss Endymion, kiss his eyes,
Then to our midnight heydeguyes.[1]

---

[1] country dances

THOMAS LODGE (1558?–1625)

From ROSALYNDE: EUPHUES' GOLDEN LEGACY

They came no sooner nigh the folds, but they might see where their discontented forester was walking in his melancholy. As soon as Aliena saw him, she smiled, and said to Ganimede: "Wipe your eyes, sweeting, for yonder is your sweetheart this morning, in deep prayers no doubt to Venus, that she may make you as pitiful as he is passionate. Come on, Ganimede, I pray thee let's have a little sport with him." "Content," quoth Ganimede, and with that, to waken him out of his deep *memento*,[1] he[2] began thus:

"Forester, good fortune to thy thoughts, and ease to thy passions! What makes you so early abroad this morn, in contemplation, no doubt, of your Rosalynde? Take heed, forester, step not too far; the ford may be deep, and you slip over the shoes. I tell thee, flies have their spleen, the ants choler, the least hairs shadows, and the smallest loves great desires. 'Tis good, forester, to love, but not to overlove, lest, in loving her that likes not thee, thou fold thyself in an endless labyrinth." Rosader seeing the fair shepherdess and her pretty swain, in whose company he felt the greatest ease of his care, he returned them a salute on this manner:

"Gentle shepherds, all hail, and as healthful be your flocks as you happy in content. Love is restless, and my bed is but the cell of my bane, in that there I find busy thoughts and broken slumbers. Here, although everywhere passionate,[3] yet I brook love with more patience, in that every object feeds mine eye with variety of fancies. When I look on Flora's beauteous tapestry, checkered with the pride of all her treasure, I call to mind the fair face of Rosalynde, whose heavenly hue exceeds the rose and the lily in their highest excellence. The brightness of Phœbus' shine puts me in mind to think of the sparkling flames that flew from her eyes and set my heart first on fire; the sweet harmony of the birds puts me in remembrance of the rare melody of her voice, which like the Syren enchanteth the ears of the hearer. Thus

---

[1] meditation   [2] he = Rosalynde disguised as Ganimede   [3] troubled

in contemplation I salve my sorrows, with applying the perfection of every object to the excellence of her qualities."

"She is much beholding unto you," quoth Aliena, "and so much that I have oft wished with myself that if I should ever prove as amorous as Œnone, I might find as faithful a Paris as yourself."

"How say you by this *Item*, forester?" quoth Ganimede. "The fair shepherdess favours you, who is mistress of so many flocks. Leave off, man, the supposition of Rosalynde's love, whenas, watching at her, you rove beyond the moon; and cast your looks upon my mistress, who no doubt is as fair though not so royal. One bird in the hand is worth two in the wood; better possess the love of Aliena, than catch frivolously at the shadow of Rosalynde."

"I'll tell thee, boy," quoth Rosader; "so is my fancy fixed on my Rosalynde, that were thy mistress as fair as Leda or Danae, whom Jove courted in transformed shapes, mine eyes would not vouch[1] to entertain their beauties; and so hath Love locked me in her perfections, that I had rather only contemplate in her beauties, than absolutely possess the excellence of any other."

"Venus is to blame, forester, if, having so true a servant of you, she reward you not with Rosalynde, if Rosalynde were more fairer than herself. But leaving this prattle, now I'll put you in mind of your promise about those sonnets which you said were at home in your lodge." "I have them about me," quoth Rosader; "let us sit down, and then you shall hear what a poetical fury Love will infuse into a man." With that they sat down upon a green bank shadowed with fig trees, and Rosader, fetching a deep sigh, read them this sonnet:

ROSADER'S SONNET

In sorrow's cell I laid me down to sleep,
But waking woes were jealous of mine eyes.
They made them watch, and bend themselves to weep;
But weeping tears their want could not suffice.
  Yet since for her they wept who guides my heart,
  They, weeping, smile and triumph in their smart.

---

[1] condescend

Of these my tears a fountain fiercely springs,
Where Venus bains [1] herself incensed with
    love;
Where Cupid boweth his fair feathered wings.
But I behold what pains I must approve.
    Care drinks it dry; but when on her I
    think,
    Love makes me weep it full unto the brink.

Meanwhile my sighs yield truce unto my tears,
By them the winds increased and fiercely
    blow;
Yet when I sigh, the flame more plain appears,
And by their force with greater power doth
    glow.
    Amidst these pains all Phœnix-like I thrive,
    Since Love that yields me death may life
    revive.

Rosader, en esperance.[2]

"Now surely, forester," quoth Aliena,
"when thou madest this sonnet, thou wert in
some amorous quandary, neither too fearful,
as despairing of thy mistress' favours, nor too
gleesome, as hoping in thy fortunes." "I
can smile," quoth Ganimede, "at the sonet-
toes, canzones, madrigals, rounds and roundelays, that these pensive patients pour out,
when their eyes are more full of wantonness
than their hearts of passions. Then, as the
fishers put the sweetest bait to the fairest fish,
so these Ovidians,[3] holding *Amo* in their
tongues, when their thoughts come at hap-
hazard, write that they be wrapped in an endless labyrinth of sorrow, when, walking in
the large lease of liberty, they only have their
humours in their inkpot. If they find women
so fond,[4] that they will with such painted
lures come to their lust, then they triumph till
they be full gorged with pleasures; and then
fly they away, like ramage kites, to their own
content, leaving the tame fool, their mistress,
full of fancy, yet without ever a feather. If
they miss (as dealing with some wary wanton,
that wants not such a one as themselves, but
spies their subtilty), they end their amours
with a few feigned sighs; and so their excuse
is, their mistress is cruel, and they smother
passions with patience. Such, gentle forester,
we may deem you to be, that rather pass
away the time here in these woods with writing
amorets, than to be deeply enamoured, as

you say, of your Rosalynde. If you be such
a one, then I pray God, when you think your
fortunes at the highest, and your desires to be
most excellent, then that you may with Ixion
embrace Juno in a cloud, and have nothing
but a marble mistress to release your martyrdom; but if you be true and trusty, eye-
pained and heart-sick, then accursed be
Rosalynde if she prove cruel; for, forester,
(I flatter not) thou art worthy of as fair as
she." Aliena, spying the storm by the wind,
smiled to see how Ganimede flew to the fist
without any call; but Rosader, who took
him flat for a shepherd's swain, made him
this answer:
"Trust me, swain," quoth Rosader, "but
my canzon [1] was written in no such humour;
for mine eye and my heart are relatives, the
one drawing fancy [2] by sight, the other entertaining her by sorrow. If thou sawest my
Rosalynde, with what beauties Nature hath
favoured her, with what perfection the heavens hath graced her, with what qualities the
Gods have endued her, then wouldst thou say,
there is none so fickle that could be fleeting
unto her. If she had been Æneas' Dido, had
Venus and Juno both scolded him from Carthage, yet her excellence, despite of them,
would have detained him at Tyre. If Phyllis
had been as beauteous, or Ariadne as virtuous, or both as honourable and excellent as
she, neither had the philbert tree sorrowed in
the death of despairing Phyllis, nor the stars
have been graced with Ariadne, but Demophoön and Theseus had been trusty to their
paragons. I will tell thee, swain, if with a
deep insight thou couldst pierce into the
secret of my loves, and see what deep impressions of her idea affection hath made in my
heart, then wouldst thou confess I were passing passionate, and no less endued with admirable patience." "Why," quoth Aliena,
"needs there patience in Love?" "Or else
in nothing," quoth Rosader; "for it is a restless sore that hath no ease, a canker that still
frets, a disease that taketh away all hope of
sleep. If, then, so many sorrows, sudden joys,
momentary pleasures, continual fears, daily
griefs, and nightly woes be found in love, then
is not he to be accounted patient, that smoth-
ers all these passions with silence?" "Thou
speakest by experience," quoth Ganimede,
"and therefore we hold all thy words for

----

[1] bathes   [2] in hope   [3] devotees of Ovid's *Art of Love*   [4] foolish   [5] untamed hawks

[1] a kind of song   [2] love

axioms. But is love such a lingering malady?" "It is," quoth he, "either extreme or mean, according to the mind of the party that entertains it; for as the weeds grow longer untouched than the pretty flowers, and the flint lies safe in the quarry, when the emerald is suffering the lapidary's tool, so mean men are freed from Venus' injuries, when kings are environed with a labyrinth of her cares. The whiter the lawn is, the deeper is the mole,[1] the more purer the chrysolite the sooner stained; and such as have their hearts full of honour, have their loves full of the greatest sorrows. But in whomsoever," quoth Rosader, "he fixeth his dart, he never leaveth to assault him, till either he hath won him to folly or fancy; for as the moon never goes without the star Lunisequa,[2] so a lover never goeth without the unrest of his thoughts. For proof you shall hear another fancy of my making." "Now do, gentle forester," quoth Ganimede. And with that he read over this sonetto:

ROSADER'S SECOND SONETTO

Turn I my looks unto the skies,
Love with his arrows wounds mine eyes;
If so I gaze upon the ground,
Love then in every flower is found;
Search I the shade to fly my pain,
He meets me in the shade again;
Wend I to walk in secret grove,
Even there I meet with sacred Love;
If so I bain[3] me in the spring,
Even on the brink I hear him sing; 10
If so I meditate alone,
He will be partner of my moan;
If so I mourn, he weeps with me;
And where I am, there will he be.
Whenas I talk of Rosalynde,
The God from coyness waxeth kind,
And seems in selfsame flames to fry,
Because he loves as well as I.
Sweet Rosalynde, for pity rue,
For-why[4] than Love I am more true; 20
He, if he speed[5] will quickly fly,
But in thy love I live and die.

"How like you this sonnet?" quoth Rosader. "Marry," quoth Ganimede, "for the pen well, for the passion ill; for as I praise the one, I pity the other" . . . .

[1] discolored spot   [2] Moon-follower   [3] bathe
[4] because [5] succeed

ROBERT GREENE (1560?–1592)

SONG

Sweet are the thoughts that savour of content;
  The quiet mind is richer than a crown;
Sweet are the nights in careless slumber spent;
  The poor estate scorns fortune's angry
    frown:
Such sweet content, such minds, such sleep,
  such bliss, 5
Beggars enjoy, when princes oft do miss.

The homely house that harbours quiet rest;
  The cottage that affords no pride nor care;
The mean that 'grees with country music best;
  The sweet consort of mirth and music's fare;
Obscurèd life sets down a type of bliss: 11
A mind content both crown and kingdom is.

PHILOMELA'S ODE

Sitting by a river's side,
Where a silent stream did glide,
Muse I did of many things
That the mind in quiet brings.
I 'gan think how some men deem
Gold their god; and some esteem
Honour is the chief content
That to man in life is lent.
And some others do contend,
Quiet none like to a friend. 10
Others hold there is no wealth
Comparèd to a perfect health.
Some man's mind in quiet stands,
When he is lord of many lands.
But I did sigh, and said all this
Was but a shade of perfect bliss;
And in my thoughts I did approve,
Nought so sweet as is true love.
Love 'twixt lovers passeth these,
When mouth kisseth and heart 'gres, 20
With folded arms and lips meeting,
Each soul another sweetly greeting;
For by the breath the soul fleeteth,
And soul with soul in kissing meeteth.
If love be so sweet a thing,
That such happy bliss doth bring,
Happy is love's sugared thrall,
But unhappy maidens all,
Who esteem your virgin blisses
Sweeter than a wife's sweet kisses. 30
No such quiet to the mind
As true Love with kisses kind;

But if a kiss prove unchaste,
Then is true love quite disgraced.
Though love be sweet, learn this of me.
No sweet love but honesty.

SEPHESTIA'S SONG TO HER CHILD

Weep not, my wanton,[1] smile upon my knee,
When thou art old there's grief enough for
    thee.
    Mother's wag, pretty boy,
    Father's sorrow, father's joy;
    When thy father first did see   5
    Such a boy by him and me,
    He was glad, I was woe,
    Fortune changèd made him so,
    When he left his pretty boy,
    Last his sorrow, first his joy.   10

Weep not, my wanton, smile upon my knee,
When thou art old there's grief enough for
    thee.
    Streaming tears that never stint,
    Like pearl drops from a flint,
    Fell by course from his eyes,   15
    That one another's place supplies;
    Thus he grieved in every part,
    Tears of blood fell from his heart,
    When he left his pretty boy,
    Father's sorrow, father's joy.   20

Weep not, my wanton, smile upon my knee,
When thou art old there's grief enough for
    thee.
    The wanton smiled, father wept,
    Mother cried, baby leapt;
    More he crowed, more he cried,   25
    Nature could not sorrow hide:
    He must go, he must kiss
    Child and mother, baby bless,
    For he left his pretty boy,
    Father's sorrow, father's joy.   30
Weep not, my wanton, smile upon my knee,
When thou art old there's grief enough for
    thee.

THE SHEPHERD'S WIFE'S SONG

Ah, what is love?   It is a pretty thing,
As sweet unto a shepherd as a king;
    And sweeter too:
For kings have cares that wait upon a crown,
And cares can make the sweetest love to
    frown.   5

[1] *a term of endearment* = spoiled darling

    Ah then, ah then,
If country loves such sweet desires do gain,
What lady would not love a shepherd swain?

His flocks are folded, he comes home at night,
As merry as a king in his delight;   10
    And merrier too:
For kings bethink them what the state require,
Where[1] shepherds careless carol by the fire.
    Ah then, ah then,
If country loves such sweet desires do gain, 15
What lady would not love a shepherd swain?

He kisseth first, then sits as blithe to eat
His cream and curds as doth the king his
    meat;
    And blither too:
For kings have often fears when they do sup,
Where[1] shepherds dread no poison in their
    cup.
    Ah then, ah then,   22
If country loves such sweet desires do gain,
What lady would not love a shepherd swain?

To bed he goes, as wanton then, I ween,   25
As is a king in dalliance with a queen;
    More wanton too:
For kings have many griefs affects[2] to move,
Where[1] shepherds have no greater grief than
    love.
    Ah then, ah then,   30
If country loves such sweet desires do gain,
What lady would not love a shepherd swain?

Upon his couch of straw he sleeps as sound,
As doth the king upon his bed of down;
    More sounder too: 35
For cares cause kings full oft their sleep to spill,
Where weary shepherds lie and snort their fill.
    Ah then, ah then,
If country loves such sweet desires do gain,
What lady would not love a shepherd swain?

Thus with his wife he spends the year, as
    blithe   41
As doth the king at every tide or sithe;[3]
    And blither too:
For kings have wars and broils to take in hand
When shepherds laugh and love upon the
    land.   45
    Ah then, ah then,
If country loves such sweet desires do gain,
What lady would not love a shepherd swain?

[1] whereas   [2] emotions   [3] time

FROM A GROAT'S WORTH OF WIT,
BOUGHT WITH A MILLION OF
REPENTANCE

On the other side of the hedge sat one that
heard his sorrow, who getting over, came
towards him, and brake off his passion.
When he approached, he saluted Roberto in
this sort.

"Gentleman," quoth he, "(for so you seem)
I have by chance heard you discourse some
part of your grief; which appeareth to be
more than you will discover, or I can conceit.[1]
But if you vouchsafe [2] such simple comfort
as my ability will yield, assure yourself that
I will endeavour to do the best, that either may
procure your profit, or bring you pleasure:
the rather, for that I suppose you are a
scholar, and pity it is men of learning should
live in lack."

Roberto wondering to hear such good words,
for that this iron age affords few that esteem
of virtue, returned him thankful gratulations,
and (urged by necessity) uttered his present
grief, beseeching his advice how he might be
employed. "Why, easily," quoth he, "and
greatly to your benefit: for men of my profession get by scholars their whole living."
"What is your profession?" said Roberto.
"Truly, sir," said he, "I am a player." "A
player," quoth Roberto, "I took you rather
for a gentleman of great living, for if by outward habit men should be censured,[3] I tell you
you would be taken for a substantial man."
"So am I, where I dwell (quoth the player),
reputed able at my proper cost to build a
windmill.[4] What though the world once went
hard with me, when I was fain to carry my
playing fardel [5] a-footback; *Tempora mutan-
tur*,[6] I know you know the meaning of it better
than I, but I thus construe it; it is otherwise
now; for my very share in playing apparel
will not be sold for two hundred pounds."
"Truly (said Roberto) it is strange, that you
should so prosper in that vain practice, for
that it seems to me your voice is nothing
gracious." "Nay then," said the player,
"I mislike your judgment: why, I am as
famous for Delphrigus, and the King of
Fairies, as ever was any of my time. The
Twelve Labours of Hercules have I terribly
thundered on the stage, and placed three scenes

of the Devil on the Highway to Heaven."
"Have ye so? (said Roberto) then I pray you
pardon me." "Nay, more (quoth the player),
I can serve to make a pretty speech, for I was
a country author; passing at a moral,[1] for
it was I that penned the Moral of Man's Wit,
the Dialogue of Dives, and for seven years
space was absolute interpreter of the puppets.
But now my almanac is out of date.

The people make no estimation,
Of Morals teaching education.

Was not this pretty for a plain rhyme extempore? if ye will, ye shall have more."
"Nay it is enough," said Roberto, "but how
mean you to use me?" "Why, sir, in making
plays," said the other, "for which you shall be
well paid, if you will take the pains."

* * * * * * *

Here (gentlemen) break I off Roberto's
speech; whose life in most parts agreeing with
mine, found one self punishment as I have
done. Hereafter suppose me the said Roberto, and I will go on with that he promised:
Greene will send you now his groatsworth of
wit, that [2] never showed a mitesworth in his
life: and though no man now be by to do me
good, yet, ere I die, I will by my repentance
endeavour to do all men good.

* * * * * * *

And therefore (while life gives leave) will
send warning to my old consorts,[3] which have
lived as loosely as myself, albeit weakness will
scarce suffer me to write, yet to my fellow
scholars about this City, will I direct these
few ensuing lines.

*To those Gentlemen his Quondam acquaintance,
that spend their wits in making Plays,
R. G. wisheth a better exercise, and
wisdom to prevent his extremities.*

If woeful experience may move you (gentlemen) to beware, or unheard-of wretchedness
entreat you to take heed, I doubt not but you
will look back with sorrow on your time past,
and endeavour with repentance to spend that
which is to come. Wonder not (for with thee
will I first begin), thou famous gracer of
tragedians, that Greene, who hath said with
thee like the fool in his heart, "There is no
God," should now give glory unto his great-

---

[1] conceive [2] *supply* to receive [3] judged [4] *pro-
verbially expensive* [5] bundle [6] Times change

AE

[1] morality play [2] who [3] companions

ness: for penetrating is his power, his hand lies heavy upon me, he hath spoken unto me with a voice of thunder, and I have felt he is a God that can punish enemies. Why should thy excellent wit, his gift, be so blinded, that thou shouldst give no glory to the giver? Is it pestilent Machiavellian policy that thou hast studied? O Punish [1] folly! What are his rules but mere confused mockeries, able to extirpate in small time the generation of mankind. For if *Sic volo, sic jubeo*, [2] hold in those that are able to command: and if it be lawful *Fas et nefas* [3] to do anything that is beneficial, only tyrants should possess the earth, and they striving to exceed in tyranny, should each to other be a slaughter man; till the mightiest outliving all, one stroke were left for Death, that in one age man's life should end. The brother [4] of this Diabolical Atheism is dead, and in his life had never the felicity he aimed at: but as he began in craft, lived in fear and ended in despair. *Quam inscrutabilia sunt Dei judicia?* [5] This murderer of many brethren had his conscience seared like Cain: this betrayer of Him that gave his life for him inherited the portion of Judas: this apostata perished as ill as Julian: and wilt thou, my friend, be his disciple? Look unto me, by him persuaded to that liberty, and thou shalt find it an infernal bondage. I know the least of my demerits merit this miserable death, but willful striving against known truth, exceedeth all the terrors of my soul. Defer not (with me) till this last point of extremity; for little knowest thou how in the end thou shalt be visited.

With thee I join young Juvenal, that biting satirist, that lastly with me together writ a comedy. Sweet boy, might I advise thee, be advised, and get not many enemies by bitter words: inveigh against vain men, for thou canst do it, no man better, no man so well: thou hast a liberty to reprove all, and none more; for, one being spoken to, all are offended; none being blamed, no man is injured. Stop shallow water still running, it will rage; tread on a worm and it will turn: then blame not scholars vexed with sharp lines, if they reprove thy too much liberty of reproof.

And thou no less deserving than the other

two, in some things rarer, in nothing inferior; driven (as myself) to extreme shifts, a little have I to say to thee: and were it not an idolatrous oath, I would swear by sweet S. George, thou art unworthy better hap, sith [1] thou dependest on so mean a stay. Base minded men all three of you, if by my misery ye be not warned: for unto none of you, like me, sought those burrs to cleave: those puppets, I mean, that speak from our mouths, those antics garnished in our colours. Is it not strange that I, to whom they all have been beholding: is it not like that you, to whom they all have been beholding, shall, were ye in that case that I am now, be both at once of them forsaken? Yes, trust them not: for there is an upstart Crow, beautified with our feathers, that with his *Tiger's heart wrapped in a Player's hide*, supposes he is as well able to bombast out a blank verse as the best of you: and being an absolute *Johannes fac totum*, is in his own conceit the only Shake-scene in a country. O that I might entreat your rare wits to be employed in more profitable courses: and let those Apes imitate your past excellence, and never more acquaint them with your admired inventions. I know the best husband of you all will never prove an usurer, and the kindest of them all will never prove a kind nurse: yet whilst you may, seek you better masters; for it is pity men of such rare wits, should be subject to the pleasures of such rude grooms.

In this I might insert two more, that both have writ against these buckram gentlemen: but let their own works serve to witness against their own wickedness, if they persevere to maintain any more such peasants. For other new comers, I leave them to the mercy of these painted monsters, who (I doubt not) will drive the best minded to despise them: for the rest, it skills not though they make a jest at them.

But now return I again to you three, knowing my misery is to you no news: and let me heartily entreat you to be warned by my harms. Delight not, as I have done, in irreligious oaths; for from the blasphemer's house a curse shall not depart. Despise drunkenness, which wasteth the wit, and maketh men all equal unto beasts. Fly lust, as the deathsman of the soul, and defile not the temple of the Holy Ghost. Abhor those

---

[1] Punic, treacherous   [2] So I wish, so I command.
[3] whether right or wrong   [4] ? brocher = beginner
[5] How inscrutable are the judgments of God!

[1] since

epicures, whose loose life hath made religion loathsome to your ears; and when they sooth you with terms of mastership, remember Robert Greene, whom they have so often flattered, perishes now for want of comfort. Remember, gentlemen, your lives are like so many lighted tapers, that are with care delivered to all of you to maintain; these with wind-puffed wrath may be extinguished, which drunkenness put out, which negligence let fall: for man's time of itself is not so short, but it is more shortened by sin. The fire of my light is now at the last snuff, and the want of wherewith to sustain it, there is no substance left for life to feed on. Trust not then, I beseech ye, to such weak stays: for they are as changeable in mind, as in many attires. Well, my hand is tired, and I am forced to leave where I would begin; for a whole book cannot contain these wrongs, which I am forced to knit up in some few lines of words.

Desirous that you should live, though
himself be dying,
Robert Greene.

CHRISTOPHER MARLOWE [1]
(1564–1593)

HERO AND LEANDER

FROM THE FIRST SESTIAD

On Hellespont, guilty of true love's blood,
In view and opposite two cities stood,
Sea-borderers, disjoin'd by Neptune's might;
The one Abydos, the other Sestos hight.
At Sestos Hero dwelt; Hero the fair,
Whom young Apollo courted for her hair,
And offer'd as a dower his burning throne,
Where she should sit, for men to gaze upon.
The outside of her garments were of lawn, 9
The lining purple silk, with gilt stars drawn;
Her wide sleeves green, and border'd with a grove,
Where Venus in her naked glory strove
To please the careless and disdainful eyes
Of proud Adonis, that before her lies;
Her kirtle blue, whereon was many a stain,
Made with the blood of wretched lovers slain.
Upon her head she ware a myrtle wreath,
From whence her veil reach'd to the ground beneath;

[1] See also p. 165.

Her veil was artificial flowers and leaves,
Whose workmanship both man and beast deceives.
Many would praise the sweet smell as she past,
When 'twas the odour which her breath forth cast; 22
And there, for honey, bees have sought in vain,
And, beat from thence, have lighted there again.
About her neck hung chains of pebble-stone,
Which, lighten'd by her neck, like diamonds shone.
She ware no gloves; for neither sun nor wind
Would burn or parch her hands, but, to her mind,
Or warm or cool them, for they took delight
To play upon those hands, they were so white.
Buskins of shells, all silver'd, usèd she, 31
And branch'd with blushing coral to the knee;
Where sparrows perch'd of hollow pearl and gold,
Such as the world would wonder to behold:
Those with sweet water oft her handmaid fills,
Which as she went, would chirrup through the bills.
Some say, for her the fairest Cupid pin'd,
And, looking in her face, was strooken blind.
But this is true; so like was one the other,
As he imagin'd Hero was his mother; 40
And oftentimes into her bosom flew,
About her naked neck his bare arms threw,
And laid his childish head upon her breast,
And, with still panting rock, there took his rest.
So lovely-fair was Hero, Venus' nun,
As Nature wept, thinking she was undone,
Because she took more from her than she left,
And of such wondrous beauty her bereft:
Therefore, in sign her treasure suffer'd wrack,
Since Hero's time hath half the world been black.
    Amorous Leander, beautiful and young 51
(Whose tragedy divine Musæus sung),
Dwelt at Abydos; since him dwelt there none
For whom succeeding times make greater moan.
His dangling tresses, that were never shorn,
Had they been cut, and unto Colchos borne,
Would have allur'd the venturous youth of Greece
To hazard more than for the golden fleece.
Fair Cynthia wished his arms might be her Sphere;
Grief makes her pale, because she moves not there.

His body was as straight as Circe's wand; 61
Jove might have sipt out nectar from his hand.
Even as delicious meat is to the taste,
So was his neck in touching, and surpast
The white of Pelops' shoulder : I could tell ye,
How smooth his breast was, and how white
    his belly ;
And whose immortal fingers did imprint
That heavenly path with many a curious dint
That runs along his back ; but my rude pen
Can hardly blazon forth the loves of men, 70
Much less of powerful gods : Let it suffice
That my slack Muse sings of Leander's eyes ;
Those orient cheeks and lips, exceeding his
That leapt into the water for a kiss
Of his own shadow, and, despising many,
Died ere he could enjoy the love of any.
Had wild Hippolytus Leander seen,
Enamour'd of his beauty had he been.
His presence made the rudest peasant melt,
That in the vast uplandish country dwelt ; 80
The barbarous Thracian soldier, mov'd with
    nought,
Was mov'd with him, and for his favour
    sought.
Some swore he was a maid in man's attire,
For in his looks were all that men desire, —
A pleasant-smiling cheek, a speaking eye,
A brow for love to banquet royally ;
And such as knew he was a man, would say,
"Leander, thou art made for amorous play ;
Why art thou not in love, and loved of all?
Though thou be fair, yet be not thine own
    thrall."
    The men of wealthy Sestos every year, 91
For his sake whom their goddess held so dear,
Rose-cheek'd Adonis, kept a solemn feast.
Thither resorted many a wandering guest
To meet their loves ; such as had none at all
Came lovers home from this great festival ;
For every street, like to a firmament,
Glister'd with breathing stars, who, where
    they went,
Frighted the melancholy earth, which deem'd
Eternal heaven to burn, for so it seem'd   100
As if another Phaëton had got
The guidance of the sun's rich chariot.
But, far above the loveliest, Hero shin'd,
And stole away th' enchanted gazer's mind ;
For like sea-nymphs' inveigling harmony,
So was her beauty to the standers by ;
Nor that night-wandering, pale, and watery
    star[1]

(When yawning dragons draw her thirling[1] car
From Latmus' mount up to the gloomy sky,
Where, crown'd with blazing light and maj-
    esty,   110
She proudly sits) more over-rules the flood
Than she the hearts of those that near her
    stood.
Even as, when gaudy nymphs pursue the
    chase,
Wretched Ixion's shaggy-footed race,
Incens'd with savage heat, gallop amain
From steep pine-bearing mountains to the
    plain,
So ran the people forth to gaze upon her,
And all that view'd her were enamour'd
    on her.
And as, in fury of a dreadful fight,
Their fellows being slain or put to flight, 120
Poor soldiers stand with fear of death dead-
    strooken,
So at her presence all surpris'd and tooken,
Await the sentence of her scornful eyes ;
He whom she favours lives ; the other dies.
There might you see one sigh ; another rage ;
And some, their violent passions to assuage,
Compile sharp satires ; but, alas, too late !
For faithful love will never turn to hate.
And many, seeing great princes were denied,
Pin'd as they went, and thinking on her died.
On this feast-day — O cursèd day and hour ! —
Went Hero thorough Sestos, from her tower
To Venus' temple, where unhappily,
As after chanc'd, they did each other spy.
So fair a church as this had Venus none :
The walls were of discolour'd[2] jasper-stone,
Wherein was Proteus carved ; and over-head
A lively vine of green sea-agate spread,
Where by one hand light-headed Bacchus
    hung,
And with the other wine from grapes out-
    wrung.   140
Of crystal shining fair the pavement was ;
The town of Sestos call'd it Venus' glass :

*   *   *   *   *   *   *

And in the midst a silver altar stood :
There Hero, sacrificing turtles' blood,
Vailed[3] to the ground, veiling her eyelids
    close ;
And modestly they opened as she rose. 160
Thence flew Love's arrow with the golden
    head ;
And thus Leander was enamourèd.

----

[1] the moon

[1] piercing the air   [2] vari-colored   [3] bent

Stone-still he stood, and evermore he gaz'd,
Till with the fire that from his countenance
blaz'd
Relenting Hero's gentle heart was strook:
Such force and virtue hath an amorous look.
  It lies not in our power to love or hate,
  For will in us is over-rul'd by fate.
When two are stript, long ere the course begin,
We wish that one should lose, the other win;
And one especially do we affect   171
Of two gold ingots, like in each respect:
The reason no man knows, let it suffice,
What we behold is censur'd[1] by our eyes.
Where both deliberate, the love is slight:
Who ever lov'd, that lov'd not at first sight?

WILLIAM SHAKESPEARE
(1564–1616)

From VENUS AND ADONIS

Thus hoping that Adonis is alive,
Her rash suspect[2] she doth extenuate;[3] 1010
And that his beauty may the better thrive,
With Death she humbly doth insinuate;
  Tells him of trophies, statues, tombs, and
    stories;
  His victories, his triumphs, and his glories.

"O Jove," quoth she, "how much a fool was I
To be of such a weak and silly mind
To wail his death who lives and must not die
Till mutual overthrow of mortal kind!
  For he being dead, with him is beauty slain,
  And, beauty dead, black chaos comes again.

"Fie, fie, fond love, thou art so full of fear 1021
As one with treasure laden, hemm'd with
    thieves;
Trifles, unwitnessèd with eye or ear,
Thy coward heart with false bethinking
    grieves."
  Even at this word she hears a merry horn,
  Whereat she leaps that was but late forlorn.

As falcon to the lure, away she flies;
The grass stoops not, she treads on it so light;
And in her haste unfortunately spies
The foul boar's conquest on her fair delight;
  Which seen, her eyes, as murder'd with the
    view,   1031
  Like stars ashamed of day, themselves with-
    drew;

[1] judged   [2] suspicion   [3] lessen

Or, as the snail, whose tender horns being
    hit,
Shrinks backward in his shelly cave with
    pain,
And there, all smother'd up, in shade doth sit,
Long after fearing to creep forth again;
  So, at his bloody view, her eyes are fled
  Into the deep dark cabins of her head:

Where they resign their office and their light
To the disposing of her troubled brain; 1040
Who bids them still consort with ugly night,
And never wound the heart with looks again;
  Who, like a king perplexèd in his throne,
  By their suggestion gives a deadly groan,

Whereat each tributary subject quakes;
As when the wind, imprison'd in the ground,
Struggling for passage, earth's foundation
    shakes,
Which with cold terror doth men's minds con-
    found.
  This mutiny each part doth so surprise
  That from their dark beds once more leap
    her eyes;   1050

And, being open'd, threw unwilling light
Upon the wide wound that the boar had
    trench'd
In his soft flank; whose wonted lily white
With purple tears, that his wound wept, was
    drench'd.
  No flower was nigh, no grass, herb, leaf, or
    weed,
  But stole his blood and seem'd with him to
    bleed.

This solemn sympathy poor Venus noteth;
Over one shoulder doth she hang her head;
Dumbly she passions, franticly she doteth;
She thinks he could not die, he is not dead:
  Her voice is stopt, her joints forget to bow;
  Her eyes are mad that they have wept till
    now.   1062

Upon his hurt she looks so steadfastly,
That her sight dazzling makes the wound seem
    three;
And then she reprehends her mangling eye,
That makes more gashes where no breach
    should be:
  His face seems twain, each several limb is
    doubled;
  For oft the eye mistakes, the brain being
    troubled.

"My tongue cannot express my grief for one,
And yet," quoth she, "behold two Adons dead !
My sighs are blown away, my salt tears gone,
Mine eyes are turn'd to fire, my heart to lead :
  Heavy heart's lead, melt at mine eyes' red
    fire !
  So shall I die by drops of hot desire.

"Alas, poor world, what treasure hast thou
    lost !
What face remains alive that's worth the
    viewing?
Whose tongue is music now? what canst thou
    boast
Of things long since, or any thing ensuing?
  The flowers are sweet, their colours fresh
    and trim ;   1079
  But true-sweet beauty lived and died with
    him.

"Bonnet nor veil henceforth no creature wear !
Nor sun nor wind will ever strive to kiss you :
Having no fair to lose, you need not fear ;
The sun doth scorn you and the wind doth
    hiss you :
  But when Adonis lived, sun and sharp air
  Lurk'd like two thieves, to rob him of his
    fair : [1]

"And therefore would he put his bonnet on,
Under whose brim the gaudy sun would peep ;
The wind would blow it off and, being gone,
Play with his locks : then would Adonis weep ;
  And straight, in pity of his tender years,
  They both would strive who first should
    dry his tears.   1092

"To see his face the lion walk'd along
Behind some hedge, because he would not
    fear [2] him ;
To recreate himself when he hath sung,
The tiger would be tame and gently hear him ;
  If he had spoke, the wolf would leave his prey
  And never fright the silly lamb that day.

"When he beheld his shadow in the brook,
The fishes spread on it their golden gills ;
When he was by, the birds such pleasure took,
That some would sing, some other in their bills
Would bring him mulberries and ripe-red
    cherries ;   1103
He fed them with his sight, they him with
    berries.

[1] beauty   [2] frighten

"But this foul, grim, and urchin-snouted boar,
Whose downward eye still looketh for a grave,
Ne'er saw the beauteous livery that he wore ;
Witness the entertainment that he gave :
  If he did see his face, why then I know
  He thought to kiss him, and hath kill'd him
    so.

"'Tis true, 'tis true ; thus was Adonis slain :
He ran upon the boar with his sharp spear,
Who did not whet his teeth at him again, 1113
But by a kiss thought to persuade him there ;
  And nuzzling in his flank, the loving swine
  Sheathed unaware the tusk in his soft groin.

"Had I been tooth'd like him, I must confess,
With kissing him I should have kill'd him first ;
But he is dead, and never did he bless 1119
My youth with his ; the more am I accurst."
  With this, she falleth in the place she stood,
  And stains her face with his congealèd blood.

She looks upon his lips, and they are pale ;
She takes him by the hand, and that is cold ;
She whispers in his ears a heavy tale,
As if they heard the woeful words she told ;
  She lifts the coffer-lids that close his eyes,
  Where, lo, two lamps, burnt out, in darkness
    lies ;

Two glasses, where herself herself beheld
A thousand times, and now no more reflect ;
Their virtue lost, wherein they late excell'd,
And every beauty robb'd of his effect : 1132
  "Wonder of time," quoth she, "this is my
    spite,
  That, thou being dead, the day should yet
    be light.

"Since thou art dead, lo, here I prophesy :
Sorrow on love hereafter shall attend :
It shall be waited on with jealousy,
Find sweet beginning, but unsavoury end,
  Ne'er settled equally, but high or low, 1139
  That all love's pleasure shall not match his
    woe.

"It shall be fickle, false, and full of fraud,
Bud and be blasted in a breathing-while ;
The bottom poison, and the top o'erstraw'd [1]
With sweets that shall the truest sight beguile :
  The strongest body shall it make most weak,
  Strike the wise dumb and teach the fool to
    speak.

[1] o'erstrewed

"It shall be sparing and too full of riot;
Teaching decrepit age to tread the measures;
The staring ruffian shall it keep in quiet,
Pluck down the rich, enrich the poor with
　　treasures;　　　　1150
It shall be raging-mad and silly-mild,
Make the young old, the old become a child.

"It shall suspect where is no cause of fear;
It shall not fear where it should most mistrust;
It shall be merciful and too severe,
And most deceiving when it seems most just;
　　Perverse it shall be where it shows most
　　　　toward;
　　Put [1] fear to valour, courage to the coward.

"It shall be cause of war and dire events,
And set dissension 'twixt the son and sire;
Subject and servile to all discontents,　　1161
As dry combustious matter is to fire:
　　Sith in his prime [2] Death doth my love de-
　　　　stroy,
　　They that love best their loves shall not
　　　　enjoy."

SONNETS

XII

When I do count the clock that tells the time,
And see the brave day sunk in hideous night;
When I behold the violet past prime,
And sable curls all silver'd o'er with white;
When lofty trees I see barren of leaves,
Which erst from heat did canopy the herd,
And summer's green all girded up in sheaves
Borne on the bier with white and bristly beard,
Then of thy beauty do I question make,
That thou among the wastes of time must go,
Since sweets and beauties do themselves for-
　　sake　　　　11
And die as fast as they see others grow;
　　And nothing 'gainst Time's scythe can make
　　　　defence
　　Save breed,[3] to brave him when he takes thee
　　　　hence.

XV

When I consider every thing that grows
Holds [4] in perfection but a little moment,
That this huge stage presenteth nought but
　　shows

---

[1] give　　[2] youth　　[3] offspring　　[4] remains

Whereon the stars in secret influence com-
　　ment;
When I perceive that men as plants increase,
Cheerèd and check'd even by the self-same sky,
Vaunt in their youthful sap, at height decrease,
And wear their brave state out of memory;
Then the conceit [1] of this inconstant stay
Sets you most rich in youth before my sight, 10
Where wasteful Time debateth with Decay,
To change your day of youth to sullied night;
　　And all in war with Time for love of you,
　　As he takes from you, I engraft you new.

XVII

Who will believe my verse in time to come,
If it were fill'd with your most high deserts?
Though yet, heaven knows, it is but as a tomb
Which hides your life and shows not half your
　　parts.
If I could write the beauty of your eyes
And in fresh numbers number all your graces,
The age to come would say, "This poet lies;
Such heavenly touches ne'er touch'd earthly
　　faces."
So should my papers yellow'd with their age
Be scorn'd like old men of less truth than
　　tongue,
And your true rights be term'd a poet's rage 11
And stretchèd metre of an antique song:
　　But were some child of yours alive that time,
　　You should live twice; in it and in my
　　　　rhyme.

XXIX

When, in disgrace with fortune and men's eyes,
I all alone beweep my outcast state
And trouble deaf heaven with my bootless cries
And look upon myself and curse my fate,
Wishing me like to one more rich in hope,
Featured like him, like him with friends
　　possess'd,
Desiring this man's art and that man's scope,
With what I most enjoy contented least;
Yet in these thoughts myself almost despising,
Haply I think on thee, and then my state,　　10
Like to the lark at break of day arising
From sullen earth, sings hymns at heaven's
　　gate;
　　For thy sweet love remember'd such wealth
　　　　brings
　　That then I scorn to change my state with
　　　　kings.

---

[1] conception, thought

XXX

When to the sessions of sweet silent thought
I summon up remembrance of things past,
I sigh the lack of many a thing I sought,
And with old woes new wail my dear time's
      waste:
Then can I drown an eye, unused to flow,
For precious friends hid in death's dateless
      night,
And weep afresh love's long since cancell'd
      woe,
And moan the expense of many a vanish'd
      sight:
Then can I grieve at grievances foregone,
And heavily from woe to woe tell o'er   10
The sad account of fore-bemoanèd moan,
Which I new pay as if not paid before.
   But if the while I think on thee, dear friend,
   All losses are restored and sorrows end.

XXXII

If thou survive my well-contented day,
When that churl Death my bones with dust
      shall cover,
And shalt by fortune once more re-survey
These poor rude lines of thy deceasèd lover,
Compare them with the bettering of the time,
And though they be outstripp'd by every pen,
Reserve them for my love, not for their rhyme,
Exceeded by the height of happier men.
O, then vouchsafe me but this loving thought:
"Had my friend's Muse grown with this grow-
      ing age,   10
A dearer birth than this his love had brought,
To march in ranks of better equipage:
   But since he died and poets better prove,
   Theirs for their style I'll read, his for his
      love."

LV

Not marble, nor the gilded monuments
Of princes, shall outlive this powerful rhyme;
But you shall shine more bright in these con-
      tents
Than unswept stone besmear'd with sluttish
      time.
When wasteful war shall statues overturn,
And broils root out the work of masonry,
Nor Mars his[1] sword nor war's quick fire shall
      burn
The living record of your memory.

      [1] Mars's

'Gainst death and all-oblivious[1] enmity
Shall you pace forth; your praise shall still
      find room   10
Even in the eyes of all posterity
That wear this world out to the ending doom.
   So, till the judgement that yourself arise,
   You live in this, and dwell in lover's eyes.

LXIV

When I have seen by Time's fell hand defaced
The rich proud cost of outworn buried age;
When sometime[2] lofty towers I see down-razed
And brass eternal slave to mortal rage;
When I have seen the hungry ocean gain
Advantage on the kingdom of the shore,
And the firm soil win of the watery main,
Increasing store with loss and loss with store;
When I have seen such interchange of state,
Or state itself confounded to decay;   10
Ruin hath taught me thus to ruminate,
That Time will come and take my love away.
   This thought is as a death, which cannot
      choose
   But weep to have that which it fears to lose.

LXV

Since brass, nor stone, nor earth, nor boundless
      sea,
But sad mortality o'er-sways their power,
How with this rage shall beauty hold a plea,
Whose action is no stronger than a flower?
O, how shall summer's honey breath hold out
Against the wreckful siege of battering days,
When rocks impregnable are not so stout,
Nor gates of steel so strong, but Time decays?
O fearful meditation! where, alack,
Shall Time's best jewel from[3] Time's chest lie
      hid?   10
Or what strong hand can hold his swift foot
      back?
Or who his spoil[4] of beauty can forbid?
   O, none, unless this miracle have might,
   That in black ink my love may still shine
      bright.

LXVI

Tired with all these, for restful death I cry, —
As,[5] to behold desert a beggar born,
And needy nothing[6] trimm'd in jollity,
And purest faith unhappily forsworn,

---

[1] blotting out all things   [2] formerly   [3] out of
[4] spoiling   [5] as, for example   [6] i.e., one of no merit

And gilded honour shamefully misplaced,
And maiden virtue rudely strumpeted,
And right perfection wrongfully disgraced,
And strength by limping sway [1] disablèd,
And art made tongue-tied by authority,
And folly doctor-like controlling skill,   10
And simple truth miscall'd simplicity,[2]
And captive good attending captain ill :
    Tired with all these, from these would I be
       gone,
    Save that, to die, I leave my love alone.

LXXI

No longer mourn for me when I am dead
Than you shall hear the surly sullen bell
Give warning to the world that I am fled
From this vile world, with vilest worms to
.   dwell :
Nay, if you read this line, remember not
The hand that writ it ; for I love you so
That I in your sweet thoughts would be forgot
If thinking on me then should make you woe.
O, if, I say, you look upon this verse   9
When I perhaps compounded am with clay,
Do not so much as my poor name rehearse,
But let your love even with my life decay,
    Lest the wise world should look into your
       moan
    And mock you with [3] me after I am gone.

LXXIII

That time of year thou mayst in me behold
When yellow leaves, or none, or few, do hang
Upon those boughs which shake against the
    cold,
Bare ruin'd choirs, where late the sweet birds
    sang.
In me thou see'st the twilight of such day
As after sunset fadeth in the west,
Which by and by black night doth take away,
Death's second self, that seals up all in rest.
In me thou see'st the glowing of such fire
That on the ashes of his [4] youth doth lie,   10
As the death-bed whereon it must expire,
Consumed with that which it was nourish'd
    by.
    This thou perceivest, which makes thy love
       more strong,
    To love that well which thou must leave [5]
       ere long.

[1] power   [2] foolishness   [3] because of   [4] its = the
fire's   [5] give up

XCVII

How like a winter hath my absence been
From thee, the pleasure of the fleeting year !
What freezings have I felt, what dark days
    seen !
What old December's bareness every where !
And yet this time removed was summer's time,
The teeming autumn, big with rich increase,
Bearing the wanton burthen of the prime,
Like widow'd wombs after their lords' decease :
Yet this abundant issue seem'd to me   9
But hope of orphans and unfather'd fruit ;
For summer and his pleasures wait on thee,
And, thou away, the very birds are mute ;
    Or, if they sing, 'tis with so dull a cheer
    That leaves look pale, dreading the winter's
       near.[1]

XCVIII

From you have I been absent in the spring,
When proud-pied April dress'd in all his trim
Hath put a spirit of youth in every thing,
That [2] heavy Saturn laugh'd and leap'd with
    him.
Yet nor the lays of birds nor the sweet smell
Of different flowers in odour and in hue
Could make me any summer's story tell,
Or from their proud lap pluck them where
    they grew ;
Nor did I wonder at the lily's white,
Nor praise the deep vermilion in the rose ;   10
They were but sweet, but figures of delight,
Drawn after you, you pattern of all those.
    Yet seem'd it winter still, and, you away,
    As with your shadow, I with these did play.

XCIX

The forward violet thus did I chide :
Sweet thief, whence didst thou steal thy sweet
    that smells,
If not from my love's breath ?   The purple
    pride
Which on thy soft cheek for complexion dwells
In my love's veins thou hast too grossly dyed.
The lily I condemnèd for thy hand,
And buds of marjoram had stol'n thy hair.
The roses fearfully on thorns did stand,
One blushing shame, another white despair ;
A third, nor red nor white, had stol'n of both
And to his robbery had annex'd thy breath ;   11

[1] nearness   [2] so that

But, for his theft, in pride of all his growth
A vengeful canker eat him up to death.
  More flowers I noted, yet I none could see
  But sweet or colour it had stol'n from thee.

CVI

When in the chronicle of wasted[1] time
I see descriptions of the fairest wights,
And beauty making beautiful old rhyme
In praise of ladies dead and lovely knights,
Then, in the blazon[2] of sweet beauty's best,
Of hand, of foot, of lip, of eye, of brow,
I see their antique pen would have express'd
Even such a beauty as you master now.
So all their praises are but prophecies
Of this our time, all you prefiguring;   10
And, for[3] they look'd but with divining eyes,
They had not skill enough your worth to sing:
  For we, which now behold these present
    days,
  Have eyes to wonder, but lack tongues to
    praise.

CVII

Not mine own fears, nor the prophetic soul
Of the wide world dreaming on things to come,
Can yet the lease of my true love control,
Supposed as forfeit to a cónfined doom.
The mortal moon hath her eclipse endured
And the sad augurs mock their own presage;
Incertainties now crown themselves assured
And peace proclaims olives of endless age.
Now with the drops of this most balmy time 9
My love looks fresh, and Death to me sub-
  scribes,[4]
Since, spite of him, I'll live in this poor rhyme,
While he insults o'er dull and speechless tribes:
  And thou in this shalt find thy monument,
  When tyrants' crests and tombs of brass are
    spent.

CIX

O, never say that I was false of heart,
Though absence seem'd my flame to qualify.[5]
As easy might I from myself depart
As from my soul, which in thy breast doth lie:
That is my home of love: if I have ranged,
Like him that travels I return again,
Just to the time, not with the time exchanged,
So that myself bring water for my stain.

---

[1] past   [2] description   [3] because   [4] submits
[5] diminish

Never believe, though in my nature reign'd
All frailties that besiege all kinds of blood, 10
That it could so preposterously be stain'd,
To leave for nothing all thy sum of good;
  For nothing this wide universe I call,
  Save thou, my rose; in it thou art my all.

CX

Alas, 'tis true I have gone here and there
And made myself a motley[1] to the view,
Gored mine own thoughts, sold cheap what is
  most dear,
Made old offences of affections new;
Most true it is that I have look'd on truth
Askance and strangely; but, by all above,
These blenches[2] gave my heart another youth,
And worse essays proved thee my best of love.
Now all is done, have what shall have no end:
Mine appetite I never more will grind   10
On newer proof, to try an older friend,
A god in love, to whom I am confin'd.[3]
  Then give me welcome, next my heaven the
    best,
  Even to thy pure and most most loving breast.

CXI

O, for my sake do you with Fortune chide,
The guilty goddess of my harmful deeds,
That did not better for my life provide
Than public means which public manners
  breeds.
Thence comes it that my name receives a
  brand,
And almost thence my nature is subdued
To what it works in, like the dyer's hand.
Pity me then and wish I were renew'd;
Whilst, like a willing patient, I will drink
Potions of eisel[4] 'gainst my strong infection;
No bitterness that I will bitter think,   11
Nor double penance, to correct correction.
  Pity me then, dear friend, and I assure ye
  Even that your pity is enough to cure me.

CXVI

Let me not to the marriage of true minds
Admit impediments. Love is not love
Which alters when it alteration finds,
Or bends with the remover to remove:
O, no! it is an ever-fixèd mark

---

[1] fool   [2] failures   [3] bound   [4] a bitter drink used
as a prophylactic

That looks on tempests and is never shaken;
It is the star to every wandering bark,
Whose worth's[1] unknown, although his height
    be taken.
Love's not Time's fool,[2] though rosy lips and
    cheeks
Within his bending sickle's compass come; 10
Love alters not with his brief hours and weeks,
But bears it out even to the edge of doom.
    If this be error and upon me proved,
    I never writ, nor no man ever loved.

CXLVI

Poor soul, the centre of my sinful earth,
[Amidst] these rebel powers that thee array,
Why dost thou pine within and suffer dearth,
Painting thy outward walls so costly gay?
Why so large cost, having so short a lease,
Dost thou upon thy fading mansion spend?
Shall worms, inheritors of this excess,
Eat up thy charge? is this thy body's end?
Then, soul, live thou upon thy servant's loss,
And let that pine to aggravate thy store; 10
Buy terms divine in selling hours of dross;
Within be fed, without be rich no more:
    So shalt thou feed on Death, that feeds on
      men,
    And Death once dead, there's no more dying
      then.

SONGS FROM THE PLAYS

From LOVE'S LABOUR'S LOST

When icicles hang by the wall,
  And Dick the shepherd blows his nail,
And Tom bears logs into the hall,
  And milk comes frozen home in pail,
When blood is nipped and ways be foul,   5
Then nightly sings the staring owl,
Tu-whit, tu-who! a merry note,
While greasy Joan doth keel[3] the pot.

When all aloud the wind doth blow,
  And coughing drowns the parson's saw, 10
And birds sit brooding in the snow,
  And Marian's nose looks red and raw,
When roasted crabs hiss in the bowl,
Then nightly sings the staring owl,
Tu-whit, tu-who! a merry note,
While greasy Joan doth keel the pot.

From A MIDSUMMER NIGHT'S DREAM

Over hill, over dale,
Thorough[1] bush, thorough brier,
Over park, over pale,
Thorough flood, thorough fire,
I do wander everywhere,
Swifter than the moonës sphere;
And I serve the Fairy Queen,
To dew her orbs upon the green.
The cowslips tall her pensioners[2] be;
In their gold coats spots you see: 10
Those be rubies, fairy favours,
In those freckles live their savours.
I must go seek some dewdrops here,
And hang a pearl in every cowslip's ear.

From TWO GENTLEMEN OF VERONA

Who is Silvia? what is she,
  That all our swains commend her?
Holy, fair, and wise is she;
  The heaven such grace did lend her,
That she might admired be.   5

Is she kind as she is fair?
  For beauty lives with kindness.
Love doth to her eyes repair
  To help him of his blindness,
And, being help'd, inhabits there.   10

Then to Silvia let us sing,
  That Silvia is excelling;
She excels each mortal thing
  Upon the dull earth dwelling:
To her let us garlands bring.   15

From THE MERCHANT OF VENICE

Tell me, where is fancy[3] bred,
Or in the heart, or in the head?
How begot, how nourishèd?
    Reply, reply.

It is engendered in the eyes,   5
With gazing fed; and fancy dies
In the cradle where it lies:
Let us all ring fancy's knell;
I'll begin it, — Ding-dong, bell.
    Ding, dong, bell.   10

---

[1] occult influence   [2] dupe   [3] cool, stir

[1] through   [2] body-guard   [3] romantic love

From AS YOU LIKE IT

Under the greenwood tree
Who loves to lie with me,
And turn [1] his merry note
Unto the sweet bird's throat,
Come hither! come hither! come hither!   5
    Here shall he see
    No enemy
But winter and rough weather.

Who doth ambition shun
And loves to live i' the sun,   10
Seeking the food he eats
And pleased with what he gets,
Come hither! come hither! come hither!
    Here shall he see
    No enemy   15
But winter and rough weather.

From AS YOU LIKE IT

Blow, blow, thou winter wind!
Thou art not so unkind
As man's ingratitude;
Thy tooth is not so keen,
Because thou art not seen,   5
    Although thy breath be rude.

Heigh ho! sing, heigh ho! unto the green
    holly:
Most friendship is feigning, most loving mere
    folly:
    Then, heigh ho, the holly!
    This life is most jolly.   10

Freeze, freeze, thou bitter sky!
That dost not bite so nigh
    As benefits forgot;
Though thou the waters warp,
Thy sting is not so sharp   15
    As friend remembered not.

Heigh ho! sing, heigh ho! etc.

From MUCH ADO ABOUT NOTHING

Sigh no more, ladies, sigh no more!
Men were deceivers ever,
One foot in sea and one on shore,
To one thing constant never:

[1] adapt

Then sigh not so, but let them go,
And be you blithe and bonny,
Converting all your sounds of woe
    Into Hey nonny, nonny!   8

Sing no more ditties, sing no moe [1]
Of dumps so dull and heavy!
The fraud of men was ever so,
    Since summer first was leavy:
Then sigh not so, but let them go,
And be you blithe and bonny,
Converting all your sounds of woe
    Into Hey nonny, nonny!   16

From TWELFTH NIGHT

O Mistress mine, where are you roaming?
O, stay and hear; your true love's coming,
    That can sing both high and low:
Trip no further, pretty sweeting,
Journeys end in lovers meeting,
    Every wise man's son doth know.   6

What is love? 'tis not hereafter;
Present mirth hath present laughter;
    What's to come is still unsure:
In delay there lies no plenty;
Then come kiss me, sweet and twenty,[2]
    Youth's a stuff will not endure.   12

From TWELFTH NIGHT

Come away,[3] come away, Death!
    And in sad cypress [4] let me be laid;
Fly away, fly away, breath!
    I am slain by a fair cruel maid.
My shroud of white, stuck all with yew,
    O, prepare it!
My part of death, no one so true
    Did share it.   8

Not a flower, not a flower sweet,
    On my black coffin let there be strown;
Not a friend, not a friend greet
    My poor corpse, where my bones shall be
    thrown:
A thousand thousand sighs to save,
    Lay me, O, where
Sad true lover never find my grave,
    To weep there!   16

[1] more [2] often and often [3] come here [4] a crape used for funerals

From HAMLET

How should I your true love know
  From another one?
By his cockle hat and staff,
  And his sandal shoon.   4

He is dead and gone, lady,
  He is dead and gone;
At his head a grass-green turf,
  At his heels a stone.   8

White his shroud as the mountain snow,
  Larded[1] with sweet flowers,
Which bewept to the grave did go
  With true-love showers.   12

From MEASURE FOR MEASURE

Take, O, take those lips away,
  That so sweetly were forsworn;
And those eyes, the break of day,
  Lights that do mislead the morn: 4
But my kisses bring again,
              Bring again;
Seals of love, but sealed in vain,
              Sealed in vain!   8

From CYMBELINE

Hark, hark! the lark at heaven's gate sings,
  And Phœbus[2] 'gins arise,
His steeds to water at those springs
  On chaliced flowers that lies;   4
And winking Mary-buds begin
  To ope their golden eyes:
With every thing that pretty is,
  My lady sweet, arise!   8
  Arise, arise!

From CYMBELINE

Fear no more the heat o' th' sun,
  Nor the furious winter's rages;
Thou thy worldly task hast done,
  Home art gone, and ta'en thy wages:
Golden lads and girls all must,
As chimney-sweepers, come to dust.   6

Fear no more the frown o' th' great;
  Thou art past the tyrant's stroke;

Care no more to clothe and eat;
  To thee the reed is as the oak:
The Sceptre, Learning, Physic, must
All follow this, and come to dust.   12

Fear no more the lightning-flash,
  Nor th' all-dreaded thunder-stone;[1]
Fear not slander, censure rash;
  Thou hast finished joy and moan:
All lovers young, all lovers must
Consign[2] to thee, and come to dust.   18

No exorciser harm thee!
  Nor no witchcraft charm thee!
Ghost unlaid forbear thee!
  Nothing ill come near thee!
Quiet consummation have;
And renownèd be thy grave!   24

From THE TEMPEST

A SEA DIRGE

Full fathom five thy father lies:
  Of his bones are coral made;
Those are pearls that were his eyes;
  Nothing of him that doth fade
But doth suffer a sea change   5
Into something rich and strange.
Sea-nymphs hourly ring his knell:
              Ding-dong!
Hark! now I hear them, — Ding-dong, bell!

From THE TEMPEST

Where the bee sucks, there suck I;
In a cowslip's bell I lie;
There I couch when owls do cry.
On the bat's back I do fly
After summer merrily.   5
Merrily, merrily, shall I live now
Under the blossom that hangs on the bough.

GEORGE CHAPMAN (1559?-1634)

From THE TWELFTH BOOK OF HOMER'S ODYSSEYS

This said, the golden-throned Aurora rose,
She[3] her way went, and I did mine dispose   220
Up to my ship, weigh'd anchor, and away.
When reverend Circe help'd us to convey

---

[1] covered   [2] the sun

[1] thunder-bolt   [2] surrender   [3] Circe

Our vessel safe, by making well inclined
A seaman's true companion, a forewind,[1]
With which she fill'd our sails; when, fitting all
Our arms close by us, I did sadly fall
To grave relation what concern'd in fate
My friends to know, and told them that the state
Of our affairs' success, which Circe had
Presaged to me alone, must yet be made 230
To one nor only two known, but to all;
That, since their lives and deaths were left to fall
In their elections, they might life elect,
And give what would preserve it fit effect.
　　I first inform'd them, that we were to fly
The heavenly-singing Sirens' harmony,
And flower-adornèd meadow; and that I
Had charge to hear their song, but fetter'd fast
In bands, unfavour'd, to th' erected mast;
From whence, if I should pray, or use command,
To be enlarged, they should with much more band
Contain my strugglings.   This I simply told
To each particular, nor would withhold 243
What most enjoin'd mine own affection's stay,
That theirs the rather might be taught t' obey.
　　In meantime flew our ships, and straight we fetch'd
The Sirens' isle; a spleenless[2] wind so stretch'd
Her wings to waft us, and so urged our keel.
But having reach'd this isle, we could not feel
The least gasp of it, it was stricken dead, 250
And all the sea in prostrate slumber spread:
The Sirens' devil charm'd all.   Up then flew
My friends to work, strook sail, together drew,
And under hatches stow'd them, sat, and plied
Their polish'd oars, and did in curls divide
The white-head waters.   My part then came on:
A mighty waxen cake I set upon,
Chopp'd it in fragments with my sword, and wrought
With strong hand every piece, till all were soft.
The great power of the sun, in such a beam 260
As then flew burning from his diadem,
To liquefaction help'd us.   Orderly
I stopp'd their ears: and they as fair did ply
My feet and hands with cords, and to the mast
With other halsers[3] made me soundly fast.
　　Then took they seat, and forth our passage strook,
The foamy sea beneath their labour shook.

Row'd on, in reach of an erected[1] voice,
The Sirens soon took note, without our noise;
Tuned those sweet accents that made charms so strong, 270
And these learn'd numbers made the Sirens' song:
　　"*Come here, thou worthy of a world of praise,*
That dost so high the Grecian glory raise;
Ulysses! stay thy ship, and that song hear
That none pass'd ever but it bent his ear,
But left him ravish'd and instructed more
By us, than any ever heard before.
For we know all things whatsoever were
In wide Troy labour'd; whatsoever there
The Grecians and the Trojans both sustain'd 280
By those high issues that the Gods ordain'd.
And whatsoever all the earth can show
T' inform a knowledge of desert, we know."
　　This they gave accent in the sweetest strain
That ever open'd an enamour'd vein.[2]
When my constrain'd heart needs would have mine ear
Yet more delighted, force way forth, and hear.
To which end I commanded with all sign
Stern looks could make (for not a joint of mine
Had power to stir) my friends to rise, and give
My limbs free way.   They freely strived to drive
Their ship still on.   When, far from will to loose,
Eurylochus and Perimedes rose 293
To wrap me surer, and oppress'd me more
With many a halser than had use before.
When, rowing on without[3] the reach of sound,
My friends unstopp'd their ears, and me unbound,
And that isle quite we quitted.

SAMUEL DANIEL (1562–1619)

SONNETS TO DELIA

XIX

Restore thy tresses to the golden ore;
　　Yield Cytherea's son[4] those arcs of love:
　　Bequeath the heavens the stars that I adore;
　　And to the orient do thy pearls remove.
Yield thy hands' pride unto the ivory white;
　　To Arabian odours give thy breathing sweet;

---

[1] favorable wind　　[2] gentle　　[3] hawsers

[1] lifted, *i.e.* loud　[2] burst from an enamored heart　[3] beyond　[4] Venus' son, Cupid

Restore thy blush unto Aurora bright;
To Thetis give the honour of thy feet.
Let Venus have thy graces her resigned;
    And thy sweet voice give back unto the
        spheres:
    But yet restore thy fierce and cruel mind
To Hyrcan tigers and to ruthless bears.   12
Yield to the marble thy hard heart again;
So shalt thou cease to plague and I to pain.

LIV

Care-charmer Sleep, son of the sable Night,
    Brother to Death, in silent darkness born:
    Relieve my languish, and restore the light;
    With dark forgetting of my care, return!
And let the day be time enough to mourn
    The shipwreck of my ill-adventured youth:
    Let waking eyes suffice to wail their scorn,
    Without the torment of the night's un-
        truth.
Cease, dreams, the images of day-desires,
    To model forth the passions of the morrow;
    Never let rising sun approve[1] you liars,   11
    To add more grief to aggravate my sorrow.
Still let me sleep, embracing clouds in vain;
And never wake to feel the day's disdain.

LV

Let others sing of knights and paladins
    In agèd accents and untimely words;
    Paint shadows in imaginary lines
    Which well the reach of their high wits
        records:
But I must sing of thee, and those fair eyes
    Authentic[2] shall my verse in time to
        come;
    When yet th' unborn shall say, "Lo where
        she lies
    Whose beauty made him speak that else
        was dumb."
These are the arcs, the trophies I erect,
    That fortify thy name against old age;   10
    And these thy sacred virtues must protect
    Against the dark, and Time's consuming
        rage.
Though the error of my youth in them ap-
    pear,
Suffice they shew I lived and loved thee
    dear.

[1] prove   [2] authenticate

EPISTLE TO THE LADY MARGARET, COUNTESS OF CUMBERLAND

He that of such a height hath built his mind,
And rear'd the dwelling of his thoughts so
        strong,
As neither fear nor hope can shake the frame
Of his resolvèd pow'rs; nor all the wind
Of vanity or malice pierce, to wrong
His settled peace, or to disturb the same:
What a fair seat hath he, from whence he may
The boundless wastes and wilds of man sur-
    vey!

And with how free an eye doth he look down
Upon these lower regions of turmoil!   10
Where all the storms of passions mainly beat
On flesh and blood: where honour, pow'r,
    renown
Are only gay afflictions, golden toil;
Where greatness stands upon as feeble feet
As frailty doth; and only great doth seem
To little minds, who do it so esteem.

He looks upon the mightiest monarchs'
    wars
But only as on stately robberies;
Where evermore the fortune that prevails
Must be the right: the ill-succeeding mars
The fairest and the best-fac'd enterprise.   21
Great Pirate Pompey lesser pirates quails:
Justice, he sees (as if seduced), still
Conspires with pow'r, whose cause must not
    be ill.

He sees the face of Right t' appear as
    manifold
As are the passions of uncertain man;
Who puts it in all colours, all attires,
To serve his ends, and make his courses hold.
He sees, that let deceit work what it can,
Plot and contrive base ways to high desires,
That the all-guiding Providence doth yet   31
All disappoint, and mocks this smoke of wit.

Nor is he mov'd with all the thunder-
    cracks
Of tyrants' threats, or with the surly brow
Of Pow'r, that proudly sits[1] on others' crimes;
Charg'd with more crying sins than those he
    checks.
The storms of sad confusion, that may grow
Up in the present for the coming times,

[1] *as judge*

Appal not him; that hath no side at all,
But himself, and knows the worst can fall. 40

Altho' his heart, so near allied to earth,
Cannot but pity the perplexèd state
Of troublous and distress'd mortality,
That thus make way unto the ugly birth
Of their own sorrows, and do still beget
Affliction upon imbecility:
Yet seeing thus the course of things must run,
He looks thereon not strange, but as foredone.

And whilst distraught ambition compasses,
And is encompass'd; whilst as craft deceives,
And is deceiv'd; whilst man doth ransack
　　man,　　　　　　　　　　　　　　51
And builds on blood, and rises by distress;
And th' inheritance of desolation leaves
To great-expecting hopes: he looks thereon,
As from the shore of peace, with unwet eye,
And bears no venture in impiety.

* 　　* 　　* 　　* 　　* 　　* 　　*

MICHAEL DRAYTON (1563–1631)

IDEA

IV

Bright Star of Beauty! on whose eyelids sit
A thousand nymph-like and enamoured
　　Graces,
The Goddesses of Memory and Wit,
Which there in order take their several places.
　　In whose dear bosom, sweet delicious Love
Lays down his quiver, which he once did bear,
Since he that blessèd paradise did prove;
And leaves his mother's lap, to sport him
　　there.
　　Let others strive to entertain with words!
My soul is of a braver mettle made:　　10
I hold that vile, which vulgar wit affords,
In me's that faith which Time cannot invade!
　　Let what I praise be still made good by
　　　you!
　　Be you most worthy, whilst I am most true!

XX

An evil Spirit (your Beauty) haunts me still,
Wherewith, alas, I have been long possest;
Which ceaseth not to attempt[1] me to each ill,
Nor give me once, but one poor minute's rest.

[1] tempt

In me it speaks, whether I sleep or wake;
And when by means to drive it out I try,
With greater torments then it me doth take,
And tortures me in most extremity.
　　Before my face, it lays down my despairs,
And hastes me on unto a sudden death;　　10
Now tempting me, to drown myself in tears,
And then in sighing to give up my breath.
　　Thus am I still[1] provoked to every evil,
　　By this good-wicked Spirit, sweet Angel-
　　　Devil.

XXXVII

Dear! why should you command me to my
　　rest,
When now the night doth summon all to
　　sleep?
Methinks this time becometh lovers best!
Night was ordained together friends to keep.
　　How happy are all other living things,
Which, through the day, disjoined by several
　　flight,
The quiet evening yet together brings,
And each returns unto his Love at night!
　　O thou that art so courteous else to all,
Why shouldst thou, Night, abuse me only
　　thus?　　　　　　　　　　　　　　10
That every creature to his kind dost call,
And yet 'tis thou dost only sever us!
　　Well could I wish it would be ever day;
　　If, when night comes, you bid me go away!

LXI

Since there's no help, come, let us kiss and
　　part!
Nay, I have done; you get no more of me!
And I am glad, yea, glad, with all my heart,
That thus so cleanly I myself can free.
　　Shake hands for ever! Cancel all our
　　　vows!
And when we meet at any time again,
Be it not seen in either of our brows,
That we one jot of former love retain!
　　Now at the last gasp of Love's latest breath,
When, his pulse failing, Passion speechless
　　lies;　　　　　　　　　　　　　　10
When Faith is kneeling by his bed of death,
And Innocence is closing up his eyes, —
　　Now, if thou wouldst, when all have given
　　　him over,
　　From death to life thou might'st him yet
　　　recover!

[1] constantly

ODE XII

TO THE CAMBRO–BRITANS AND THEIR HARP, HIS BALLAD OF AGINCOURT

Fair stood the wind for France,
When we our sails advance;
Nor now to prove our chance
  Longer will tarry;
But putting to the main,
At Caux, the mouth of Seine,
With all his martial train
  Landed King Harry.

And taking many a fort,
Furnished in warlike sort,   10
Marcheth towards Agincourt
  In happy hour;
Skirmishing, day by day,
With those that stopped his way,
Where the French general lay
  With all his power.

Which, in his height of pride,
King Henry to deride,
His ransom to provide,
  To the King sending;   20
Which he neglects the while,
As from a nation vile,
Yet, with an angry smile,
  Their fall portending.

And turning to his men,
Quoth our brave Henry then:
"Though they to one be ten
  Be not amazèd!
Yet have we well begun:
Battles so bravely won   30
Have ever to the sun
  By Fame been raisèd!

"And for myself," quoth he,
"This my full rest shall be:
England ne'er mourn for me,
  Nor more esteem me!
Victor I will remain,
Or on this earth lie slain;
Never shall She sustain
  Loss to redeem me!   40

"Poitiers and Cressy tell,
When most their pride did swell,
Under our swords they fell.
  No less our skill is,
Than when our Grandsire great,

Claiming the regal seat,
By many a warlike feat
  Lopped the French lilies."

The Duke of York so dread
The eager vanward led;   50
With the main, Henry sped
  Amongst his henchmen:
Exeter had the rear,
A braver man not there!
O Lord, how hot they were
  On the false Frenchmen!

They now to fight are gone;
Armour on armour shone;
Drum now to drum did groan:
  To hear, was wonder;   60
That, with the cries they make,
The very earth did shake;
Trumpet to trumpet spake;
  Thunder to thunder.

Well it thine age became,
O noble Erpingham,
Which didst the signal aim
  To our hid forces!
When, from a meadow by,
Like a storm suddenly,   70
The English archery
  Stuck the French horses.

With Spanish yew so strong;
Arrows a cloth-yard long,
That like to serpents stung,
  Piercing the weather.
None from his fellow starts;
But, playing manly parts,
And like true English hearts,
  Stuck close together.   80

When down their bows they threw,
And forth their bilboes[1] drew,
And on the French they flew:
  Not one was tardy.
Arms were from shoulders sent,[2]
Scalps to the teeth were rent,
Down the French peasants went:
  Our men were hardy.

This while our noble King,
His broad sword brandishing,   90
Down the French host did ding,
  As to o'erwhelm it.

[1] swords   [2] torn

AE

And many a deep wound lent;
His arms with blood besprent,
And many a cruel dent
  Bruisèd his helmet.

Gloucester, that duke so good,
Next of the royal blood,
For famous England stood
  With his brave brother.   100
Clarence, in steel so bright,
Though but a maiden knight,
Yet in that furious fight
  Scarce such another!

Warwick in blood did wade;
Oxford, the foe invade,
And cruel slaughter made,
  Still as they ran up.
Suffolk his axe did ply;
Beaumont and Willoughby   110
Bare them right doughtily;
  Ferrers, and Fanhope.

Upon Saint Crispin's Day
Fought was this noble fray;
Which Fame did not delay
  To England to carry.
O when shall English men
With such acts fill a pen? [1]
Or England breed again
  Such a King Harry?   120

From NYMPHIDIA

THE COURT OF FAIRY

*   *   *   *   *   *

Her chariot ready straight is made
Each thing therein is fitting laid,   130
That she by nothing might be stayed,
  For nought must here be letting;
Four nimble gnats the horses were,
Their harnesses of gossamer,
Fly Cranion her charioteer
  Upon the coach-box getting.

Her chariot of a snail's fine shell,
Which for the colours did excel,
The fair Queen Mab becoming well,
  So lively was the limning;   140
The seat the soft wool of the bee,
The cover, gallantly to see,
The wing of a pied butterflee;
  I trow 'twas simple trimming.

  [1] give a subject for praise

The wheels composed of crickets' bones,
And daintily made for the nonce;
For fear of rattling on the stones
  With thistle-down they shod it;
For all her maidens much did fear
If Oberon had chanc'd to hear   150
That Mab his Queen should have been there,
  He would not have abode it.

She mounts her chariot with a trice,
Nor would she stay, for no advice,
Until her maids that were so nice
  To wait on her were fitted;
But ran herself away alone,
Which when they heard, there was not one
But hasted after to be gone,
  As she had been diswitted.   160

Hop and Mop and Drop so clear
Pip and Trip and Skip that were
To Mab, their sovereign, ever dear,
  Her special maids of honour;
Fib and Tib and Pink and Pin,
Tick and Quick and Jill and Jin,
Tit and Nit and Wap and Win,
  The train that wait upon her.

Upon a grasshopper they got
And, what with amble and with trot,   170
For hedge nor ditch they sparèd not,
  But after her they hie them;
A cobweb over them they throw,
To shield the wind if it should blow;
Themselves they wisely could bestow
  Lest any should espy them.

FRANCIS BACON (1561–1626)

ESSAYS

I. OF TRUTH

What is Truth? said jesting Pilate; [1] and
would not stay for an answer. Certainly
there be that [2] delight in giddiness, and count
it a bondage to fix a belief; affecting free-will
in thinking, as well as in acting. And though
the sects of philosophers of that kind be gone,
yet there remain certain discoursing wits
which are of the same veins, [3] though there be
not so much blood in them as was in those of

  [1] Cf. *John*, xviii: 38   [2] there are those who
  [3] the same ways of thinking

the ancients. But it is not only the difficulty and labour which men take in finding out of truth; nor again that when it is found it imposeth upon men's thoughts; that doth bring lies in favour; but a natural though corrupt love of the lie itself. One of the later school of the Grecians examineth the matter, and is at a stand to think what should be in it, that men should love lies, where neither they make for pleasure, as with poets, nor for advantage, as with the merchant; but for the lie's sake. But I cannot tell: this same truth is a naked and open day-light, that doth not show the masks and mummeries and triumphs of the world, half so stately and daintily as candle-lights. Truth may perhaps come to the price of a pearl, that showeth best by day; but it will not rise to the price of a diamond or carbuncle, that showeth best in varied lights. A mixture of a lie doth ever add pleasure. Doth any man doubt, that if there were taken out of men's minds vain opinions, flattering hopes, false valuations, imaginations as one would, and the like, but it would leave the minds of a number of men poor shrunken things, full of melancholy and indisposition, and unpleasing to themselves? One of the Fathers, in great severity, called poesy *vinum dæmonum*,[1] because it filleth the imagination; and yet it is but with the shadow of a lie. But it is not the lie that passeth through the mind, but the lie that sinketh in and settleth in it, that doth the hurt; such as we spake of before. But howsoever these things are thus in men's depraved judgments and affections, yet truth, which only doth judge itself, teacheth that the inquiry of truth, which is the love-making or wooing of it, the knowledge of truth, which is the presence of it, and the belief of truth, which is the enjoying of it, is the sovereign good of human nature. The first creature of God, in the works of the days, was the light of the sense; the last was the light of reason; and his Sabbath work ever since, is the illumination of his Spirit. First he breathed light upon the face of the matter or chaos; then he breathed light into the face of man; and still he breatheth and inspireth light into the face of his chosen. The poet[2] that beautified the sect[3] that was otherwise inferior to the rest, saith yet excellently well: *It is a pleasure to stand upon the shore, and to see ships tossed upon the sea; a pleasure to stand in the window of a castle, and to see a battle and the adventures thereof below; but no pleasure is comparable to the standing upon the vantage ground of Truth,* (a hill not to be commanded,[1] and where the air is always clear and serene,) *and to see the errors, and wanderings, and mists, and tempests, in the vale below;* so always that this prospect be with pity, and not with swelling or pride. Certainly, it is heaven upon earth, to have a man's mind move in charity, rest in providence, and turn upon the poles of truth.

To pass from theological and philosophical truth, to the truth of civil business; it will be acknowledged even by those that practise it not, that clear and round dealing is the honour of man's nature; and that mixture of falsehood is like allay[2] in coin of gold and silver, which may make the metal work the better, but it embaseth it. For these winding and crooked courses are the goings of the serpent; which goeth basely upon the belly, and not upon the feet. There is no vice that doth so cover a man with shame as to be found false and perfidious. And therefore Montaigne saith prettily, when he inquired the reason, why the word of the lie should be such a disgrace, and such an odious charge? Saith he, *If it be well weighed, to say that a man lieth, is as much to say, as that he is brave towards God and a coward towards men.* For a lie faces God, and shrinks from man. Surely the wickedness of falsehood and breach of faith cannot possibly be so highly expressed, as in that it shall be the last peal to call the judgments of God upon the generations of men; it being foretold, that when Christ cometh, *he shall not find faith upon the earth.*

VIII. OF MARRIAGE AND SINGLE LIFE

He that hath wife and children hath given hostages to fortune; for they are impediments to great enterprises, either of virtue or mischief. Certainly the best works, and of greatest merit for the public, have proceeded from the unmarried or childless men; which both in affection and means have married and endowed the public. Yet it were great reason that those that have children should have greatest care of future times; unto which they

---

[1] devils' wine   [2] Lucretius   [3] Epicureans

[1] looked down on from a higher   [2] alloy

know they must transmit their dearest pledges. Some there are, who though they lead a single life, yet their thoughts do end with themselves, and account future times impertinences.[1] Nay, there are some other that account wife and children but as bills of charges. Nay more, there are some foolish rich covetous men, that take a pride in having no children, because they may be thought so much the richer. For perhaps they have heard some talk, *Such a one is a great rich man*, and another except to it, *Yea, but he hath a great charge of children;* as if it were an abatement to his riches. But the most ordinary cause of a single life is liberty, especially in certain self-pleasing and humorous[2] minds, which are so sensible of every restraint, as they will go near to think their girdles and garters to be bonds and shackles. Unmarried men are best friends, best masters, best servants; but not always best subjects; for they are light to run away; and almost all fugitives are of that condition. A single life doth well with churchmen; for charity will hardly water the ground where it must first fill a pool. It is indifferent for judges and magistrates; for if they be facile and corrupt, you shall have a servant five times worse than a wife. For soldiers, I find the generals commonly in their hortatives[3] put men in mind of their wives and children; and I think the despising of marriage amongst the Turks maketh the vulgar soldier more base. Certainly wife and children are a kind of discipline of humanity; and single men, though they may be many times more charitable, because their means are less exhaust, yet, on the other side, they are more cruel and hardhearted (good to make severe inquisitors), because their tenderness is not so oft called upon. Grave natures, led by custom, and therefore constant, are commonly loving husbands; as was said of Ulysses, *vetulam suam prætulit immortalitati.*[4] Chaste women are often proud and froward, as presuming upon the merit of their chastity. It is one of the best bonds both of chastity and obedience in the wife, if she think her husband wise; which she will never do if she find him jealous. Wives are young men's mistresses; companions for middle age; and old men's nurses.

So as a man may have a quarrel[1] to marry when he will. But yet he was reputed one of the wise men, that made answer to the question, when a man should marry? *A young man not yet, an elder man not at all.* It is often seen that bad husbands have very good wives; whether it be that it raiseth the price of their husband's kindness when it comes; or that the wives take a pride in their patience. But this never fails, if the bad husbands were of their own choosing, against their friends' consent; for then they will be sure to make good their own folly.

XI. OF GREAT PLACE

Men in great place are thrice servants: servants of the sovereign or state; servants of fame; and servants of business. So as they have no freedom; neither in their persons, nor in their actions, nor in their times. It is a strange desire, to seek power and to lose liberty: or to seek power over others and to lose power over a man's self. The rising unto place is laborious; and by pains men come to greater pains; and it is sometimes base; and by indignities men come to dignities. The standing is slippery, and the regress is either a downfall, or at least an eclipse, which is a melancholy thing. *Cum non sis qui fueris, non esse cur velis vivere.*[2] Nay, retire men cannot when they would, neither will they when it were reason; but are impatient of privateness, even in age and sickness, which require the shadow; like old townsmen, that will be still[3] sitting at their street door, though thereby they offer age to scorn. Certainly great persons had need to borrow other men's opinions, to think themselves happy; for if they judge by their own feeling, they cannot find it: but if they think with themselves what other men think of them, and that other men would fain be as they are, then they are happy as it were by report; when perhaps they find the contrary within. For they are the first that find their own griefs, though they be the last that find their own faults. Certainly men in great fortunes are strangers to themselves, and while they are in the puzzle of business they have no time to tend their health either of body or mind. *Illi mors*

---

[1] things which do not concern them [2] notionate [3] exhortations [4] He preferred his old wife to immortality.

[1] reason [2] When you are no longer what you were, there is no reason why you should wish to live. [3] always

gravis incubat, qui notus nimis omnibus, ignotus moritur sibi.[1] In place there is license to do good and evil; whereof the latter is a curse: for in evil the best condition is not to will; the second not to can. But power to do good is the true and lawful end of aspiring. For good thoughts (though God accept them) yet towards men are little better than good dreams, except they be put in act; and that cannot be without power and place, as the vantage and commanding ground. Merit and good works is the end of man's motion; and conscience of the same is the accomplishment of man's rest. For if a man can be partaker of God's theatre, he shall likewise be partaker of God's rest. *Et conversus Deus, ut aspiceret opera quæ fecerunt manus suæ, vidit quod omnia essent bona nimis;*[2] and then the Sabbath. In the discharge of thy place set before thee the best examples; for imitation is a globe[3] of precepts. And after a time set before thee thine own example; and examine thyself strictly whether thou didst not best at first. Neglect not also the examples of those that have carried themselves ill in the same place; not to set off thyself by taxing their memory, but to direct thyself what to avoid. Reform therefore, without bravery or scandal of former times and persons; but yet set it down to thyself as well to create good precedents as to follow them. Reduce things to the first institution, and observe wherein and how they have degenerate;[4] but yet ask counsel of both times; of the ancient time, what is best; and of the latter time, what is fittest. Seek to make thy course regular, that men may know beforehand what they may expect; but be not too positive and peremptory; and express thyself well when thou digressest from thy rule. Preserve the right of thy place; but stir not questions of jurisdiction: and rather assume thy right in silence and *de facto*, than voice it with claims and challenges. Preserve likewise the rights of inferior places; and think it more honour to direct in chief than to be busy in all. Embrace and invite helps and advices touching the execution of thy place; and do not drive away such as bring thee information, as meddlers; but accept of them in good part. The vices of authority are chiefly four; delays, corruption, roughness, and facility. For delays; give easy access; keep times appointed; go through with that which is in hand, and interlace not business but of necessity. For corruption; do not only bind thine own hands or thy servants' hands from taking, but bind the hands of suitors also from offering. For integrity used doth the one; but integrity professed, and with a manifest detestation of bribery, doth the other. And avoid not only the fault, but the suspicion. Whosoever is found variable, and changeth manifestly without manifest cause, giveth suspicion of corruption. Therefore always when thou changest thine opinion or course, profess it plainly, and declare it, together with the reasons that move thee to change; and do not think to steal it. A servant or a favourite, if he be inward,[1] and no other apparent cause of esteem, is commonly thought but a by-way to close corruption. For roughness; it is a needless cause of discontent: severity breedeth fear, but roughness breedeth hate. Even reproofs from authority ought to be grave, and not taunting. As for facility; it is worse than bribery. For bribes come but now and then; but if importunity or idle respects lead a man, he shall never be without. As Salomon saith, *To respect persons is not good; for such a man will transgress for a piece of bread.* It is most true that was anciently spoken, *A place showeth the man.* And it showeth some to the better, and some to the worse. *Omnium consensu capax imperii, nisi imperasset,*[2] saith Tacitus of Galba; but of Vespasian he saith, *Solus imperantium, Vespasianus mutatus in melius:*[3] though the one was meant of sufficiency, the other of manners and affection. It is an assured sign of a worthy and generous spirit, whom honour amends. For honour is, or should be, the place of virtue; and as in nature things move violently to their place and calmly in their place, so virtue in ambition is violent, in authority settled and calm. All rising to great place is by a winding stair; and if there be factions, it is good to side a

---

[1] It is a sad fate for a man to die too well known to everybody else, and still unknown to himself.
[2] And God turned to look upon the works which his hands had made, and saw that all were very good. [3] world [4] degenerated

[1] intimate [2] A man whom everybody would have thought fit for empire if he had not been emperor. [3] He was the only emperor whom the possession of power changed for the better.

man's self whilst he is in the rising, and to balance himself when he is placed. Use the memory of thy predecessor fairly and tenderly; for if thou dost not, it is a debt will sure be paid when thou art gone. If thou have colleagues, respect them, and rather call them when they look not for it, than exclude them when they have reason to look to be called. Be not too sensible or too remembering of thy place in conversation and private answers to suitors; but let it rather be said, *When he sits in place he is another man.*

XVI. OF ATHEISM

I had rather believe all the fables in the Legend, and the Talmud, and the Alcoran, than that this universal frame is without a mind. And therefore God never wrought miracle to convince atheism, because his ordinary works convince it. It is true, that a little philosophy inclineth man's mind to atheism; but depth in philosophy bringeth men's minds about to religion. For while the mind of man looketh upon second causes scattered, it may sometimes rest in them, and go no further; but when it beholdeth the chain of them, confederate and linked together, it must needs fly to Providence and Deity. Nay, even that school which is most accused of atheism doth most demonstrate religion; that is, the school of Leucippus and Democritus and Epicurus. For it is a thousand times more credible, that four mutable elements, and one immutable fifth essence, duly and eternally placed,[1] need no God, than that an army of infinite small portions or seeds unplaced,[2] should have produced this order and beauty without a divine marshal. The Scripture saith, *The fool hath said in his heart, there is no God;* it is not said, *The fool hath thought in his heart;* so as he rather saith it by rote to himself, as that[3] he would have, than that he can throughly believe it, or be persuaded of it. For none deny there is a God, but those for whom it maketh[4] that there were no God. It appeareth in nothing more, that atheism is rather in the lip than in the heart of man, than by this; that atheists will ever be talking of that their opinion, as if they fainted in it within themselves, and would be glad to be

strengthened by the consent of others. Nay more, you shall have atheists strive to get disciples, as it fareth with other sects. And, which is most of all, you shall have of them that will suffer for atheism, and not recant; whereas if they did truly think that there were no such thing as God, why should they trouble themselves? Epicurus is charged that he did but dissemble for his credit's sake, when he affirmed there were blessed natures, but such as enjoyed themselves without having respect to the government of the world. Wherein they say he did temporise; though in secret he thought there was no God. But certainly he is traduced; for his words are noble and divine: *Non Deos vulgi negare profanum; sed vulgi opiniones Diis applicare profanum.*[1] Plato could have said no more. And although he had the confidence to deny the administration, he had not the power to deny the nature. The Indians of the west have names for their particular gods, though they have no name for God: as if the heathens should have had the names Jupiter, Apollo, Mars, etc., but not the word *Deus;* which shows that even those barbarous people have the notion, though they have not the latitude and extent of it. So that against atheists the very savages take part with the very subtlest philosophers. The contemplative atheist is rare: a Diagoras, a Bion, a Lucian perhaps, and some others; and yet they seem to be more than they are; for that all that impugn a received religion or superstition are by the adverse part branded with the name of atheists. But the great atheists indeed are hypocrites; which are ever handling holy things, but without feeling; so as they must needs be cauterised[2] in the end. The causes of atheism are: divisions in religion, if they be many; for any one main division addeth zeal to both sides; but many divisions introduce atheism. Another is, scandal of priests; when it is come to that which St. Bernard saith, *Non est jam dicere, ut populus sic sacerdos; quia nec sic populus ut sacerdos.*[3] A third is, custom of profane scoffing in holy matters; which doth

---

[1] the current theory in Bacon's time   [2] the theory ascribed to the philosophers just mentioned
[3] what   [4] would be advantageous

[1] There is no profanity in refusing to believe in the Gods of the vulgar; the profanity is in believing of the Gods what the vulgar believe of them.
[2] made callous   [3] One cannot now say, the priest is as the people, for the truth is that the people are not so bad as the priest.

by little and little deface the reverence of religion. And lastly, learned times, specially with peace and prosperity; for troubles and adversities do more bow men's minds to religion. They that deny a God destroy man's nobility; for certainly man is of kin to the beasts by his body; and, if he be not of kin to God by his spirit, he is a base and ignoble creature. It destroys likewise magnanimity, and the raising of human nature; for take an example of a dog, and mark what a generosity and courage he will put on when he finds himself maintained by a man; who to him is instead of a God, or *melior natura* ;[1] which courage is manifestly such as that creature, without that confidence of a better nature than his own, could never attain. So man, when he resteth and assureth himself upon divine protection and favour, gathereth a force and faith which human nature in itself could not obtain. Therefore, as atheism is in all respects hateful, so in this, that it depriveth human nature of the means to exalt itself above human frailty. As it is in particular persons, so it is in nations. Never was there such a state for magnanimity as Rome. Of this state hear what Cicero saith: *Quam volumus licet, patres conscripti, nos amemus, tamen nec numero Hispanos, nec robore Gallos, nec calliditate Pœnos, nec artibus Græcos, nec denique hoc ipso hujus gentis et terræ domestico nativoque sensu Italos ipsos et Latinos; sed pietate, ac religione, atque hac una sapientia, quod Deorum immortalium numine omnia regi gubernarique perspeximus, omnes gentes nationesque superavimus.*[2]

XXIII. OF WISDOM FOR A MAN'S SELF

An ant is a wise creature for itself, but it is a shrewd[3] thing in an orchard or garden. And certainly men that are great lovers of

---

[1] a higher being [2] Pride ourselves as we may upon our country, yet are we not in number superior to the Spaniards, nor in strength to the Gauls, nor in cunning to the Carthaginians, nor to the Greeks in arts, nor to the Italians and Latins themselves in the homely and native sense which belongs to this nation and land; it is in piety only and religion, and the wisdom of regarding the providence of the Immortal Gods as that which rules and governs all things, that we have surpassed all nations and peoples. [3] bad

themselves waste the public. Divide with reason between self-love and society; and be so true to thyself, as thou be not false to others; specially to thy king and country. It is a poor centre of a man's actions, *himself*. It is right[1] earth. For that[2] only stands fast upon his own centre; whereas all things that have affinity with the heavens, move upon the center of another, which they benefit. The referring of all to a man's self is more tolerable in a sovereign prince; because themselves are not only themselves, but their good and evil is at the peril of the public fortune. But it is a desperate evil in a servant to a prince, or a citizen in a republic. For whatsoever affairs pass such a man's hands, he crooketh them to his own ends; which must needs be often eccentric to[3] the ends of his master or state. Therefore let princes, or states, choose such servants as have not this mark; except they mean their service should be made but the accessary. That which maketh the effect more pernicious is that all proportion is lost. It were disproportion enough for the servant's good to be preferred before the master's; but yet it is a greater extreme, when a little good of the servant shall carry things against a great good of the master's. And yet that is the case of bad officers, treasurers, ambassadors, generals, and other false and corrupt servants; which set a bias[4] upon their bowl, of their own petty ends and envies, to the overthrow of their master's great and important affairs. And for the most part, the good such servants receive is after the model[5] of their own fortune; but the hurt they sell for that good is after the model of their master's fortune. And certainly it is the nature of extreme self-lovers, as they will set an house on fire, and it were but to roast their eggs; and yet these men many times hold credit with their masters, because their study is but to please them and profit themselves; and for either respect they will abandon the good of their affairs.

Wisdom for a man's self is, in many branches thereof, a depraved thing. It is the wisdom of rats, that will be sure to leave a house somewhat before it fall. It is the wisdom of the fox, that thrusts out the badger,

---

[1] very [2] the earth, according to the Ptolemaic theory [3] not having the same centre as [4] a weight placed in a bowl (ball for bowling) to make it take a curved course [5] size

who digged and made room for him. It is the wisdom of crocodiles, that shed tears when they would devour. But that which is specially to be noted is, that those which (as Cicero says of Pompey) are *sui amantes, sine rivali*,[1] are many times unfortunate. And whereas they have all their time sacrificed to themselves, they become in the end themselves sacrifices to the inconstancy of fortune; whose wings they thought by their self-wisdom to have pinioned.

XXVII. OF FRIENDSHIP

It had been hard for him that spake it to have put more truth and untruth together in few words, than in that speech, *Whosoever is delighted in solitude is either a wild beast or a god*. For it is most true that a natural and secret hatred and aversation towards society in any man, hath somewhat of the savage beast; but it is most untrue that it should have any character at all of the divine nature; except it proceed, not out of a pleasure in solitude, but out of a love and desire to sequester a man's self for a higher conversation: such as is found to have been falsely and feignedly in some of the heathen; as Epimenides the Candian, Numa the Roman, Empedocles the Sicilian, and Apollonius of Tyana; and truly and really in divers of the ancient hermits and holy fathers of the church. But little do men perceive what solitude is, and how far it extendeth. For a crowd is not company; and faces are but a gallery of pictures; and talk but a tinkling cymbal, where there is no love. The Latin adage meeteth with it a little: *Magna civitas, magna solitudo*,[2] because in a great town friends are scattered; so that there is not that fellowship, for the most part, which is in less neighbourhoods. But we may go further, and affirm most truly that it is a mere and miserable solitude to want true friends; without which the world is but a wilderness; and even in this sense also of solitude, whosoever in the frame of his nature and affections is unfit for friendship, he taketh it of the beast, and not from humanity.

A principal fruit of friendship is the ease and discharge of the fulness and swellings of the heart, which passions of all kinds do cause and induce. We know diseases of stoppings and suffocations are the most dangerous in the body; and it is not much otherwise in the mind; you may take sarza to open the liver, steel to open the spleen, flowers of sulphur for the lungs, castoreum for the brain; but no receipt[1] openeth the heart, but a true friend; to whom you may impart griefs, joys, fears, hopes, suspicions, counsels, and whatsoever lieth upon the heart to oppress it, in a kind of civil[2] shrift or confession.

It is a strange thing to observe how high a rate great kings and monarchs do set upon this fruit of friendship whereof we speak: so great, as they purchase it many times at the hazard of their own safety and greatness. For princes, in regard of the distance of their fortune from that of their subjects and servants, cannot gather this fruit, except (to make themselves capable thereof) they raise some persons to be as it were companions and almost equals to themselves, which many times sorteth to[3] inconvenience. The modern languages give unto such persons the name of favourites, or *privadoes*;[4] as if it were matter of grace, or conversation. But the Roman name attaineth the true use and cause thereof, naming them *participes curarum*;[5] for it is that which tieth the knot. And we see plainly that this hath been done, not by weak and passionate princes only, but by the wisest and most politic that ever reigned; who have oftentimes joined to themselves some of their servants; whom both themselves have called friends, and allowed others likewise to call them in the same manner; using the word which is received between private men.

L. Sylla, when he commanded Rome, raised Pompey (after surnamed the Great) to that height, that Pompey vaunted himself for Sylla's over-match. For when he had carried the consulship for a friend of his, against the pursuit[6] of Sylla, and that Sylla did a little resent thereat, and began to speak great, Pompey turned upon him again, and in effect bade him be quiet; *for that more men adored the sun rising than the sun setting*. With Julius Cæsar, Decimus Brutus had obtained that interest, as he set him down in his testament for heir in remainder after his nephew. And this was the man that had power with

---

[1] lovers of themselves, without rival [2] A great town is a great solitude.

[1] recipe [2] non-religious [3] results in [4] intimates [5] sharers of cares [6] candidacy

him to draw him forth to his death. For when Cæsar would have discharged the senate, in regard of some ill presages, and specially a dream of Calpurnia; this man lifted him gently by the arm out of his chair, telling him he hoped he would not dismiss the senate till his wife had dreamt a better dream. And it seemeth his favour was so great, as Antonius, in a letter which is recited *verbatim* in one of Cicero's Philippics, calleth him *venefica*, witch; as if he had enchanted Cæsar. Augustus raised Agrippa (though of mean birth) to that height, as when he consulted with Mæcenas about the marriage of his daughter Julia, Mæcenas took the liberty to tell him, *that he must either marry his daughter to Agrippa, or take away his life: there was no third way, he had made him so great.* With Tiberius Cæsar, Sejanus had ascended to that height, as they two were termed and reckoned as a pair of friends. Tiberius in a letter to him saith, *hæc pro amicitia nostra non occultavi;* [1] and the whole senate dedicated an altar to Friendship, as to a goddess, in respect of the great dearness of friendship between them two. The like or more was between Septimius Severus and Plautianus. For he forced his eldest son to marry the daughter of Plautianus; and would often maintain Plautianus in doing affronts to his son; and did write also in a letter to the senate, by these words: *I love the man so well, as I wish he may over-live me.* Now if these princes had been as a Trajan or a Marcus Aurelius, a man might have thought that this had proceeded of an abundant goodness of nature; but being men so wise, of such strength and severity of mind, and so extreme lovers of themselves, as all these were, it proveth most plainly that they found their own felicity (though as great as ever happened to mortal men) but as an half piece, except they mought [2] have a friend to make it entire; and yet, which is more, they were princes that had wives, sons, nephews; and yet all these could not supply the comfort of friendship.

It is not to be forgotten what Commineus [3] observeth of his first master, Duke Charles the Hardy; namely, that he would communicate his secrets with none; and least of all, those secrets which troubled him most. Whereupon he goeth on and saith that towards his latter time *that closeness did impair and a little perish his understanding.* Surely Commineus mought have made the same judgment also, if it had pleased him, of his second master, Lewis the Eleventh, whose closeness was indeed his tormentor. The parable of Pythagoras [1] is dark, but true; *Cor ne edito: Eat not the heart.* Certainly, if a man would give it a hard phrase, those that want friends to open themselves unto are cannibals of their own hearts. But one thing is most admirable (wherewith I will conclude this first fruit of friendship), which is, that this communicating of a man's self to his friend works two contrary effects; for it redoubleth joys, and cutteth griefs in halfs. For there is no man that imparteth his joys to his friend, but he joyeth the more: and no man that imparteth his griefs to his friend, but he grieveth the less. So that it is in truth of operation upon a man's mind, of like virtue as the alchemists use to attribute to their stone for man's body; that it worketh all contrary effects, but still to the good and benefit of nature. But yet without praying in aid [2] of alchemists, there is a manifest image of this in the ordinary course of nature. For in bodies, union strengtheneth and cherisheth any natural action; and on the other side weakeneth and dulleth any violent impression: and even so is it of minds.

The second fruit of friendship is healthful and sovereign for the understanding, as the first is for the affections. For friendship maketh indeed a fair day in the affections, from storm and tempests; but it maketh daylight in the understanding, out of darkness and confusion of thoughts. Neither is this to be understood only of faithful counsel, which a man receiveth from his friend; but before you come to that, certain it is that whosoever hath his mind fraught with many thoughts, his wits and understanding do clarify and break up, in the communicating and discoursing with another; he tosseth his thoughts more easily; he marshalleth them more orderly; he seeth how they look when they are turned into words: finally, he waxeth wiser than himself; and that more by an hour's discourse than by a day's meditation. It was well said by Themistocles to the king

[1] These things, because of our friendship, I have not concealed from you. [2] might [3] Philippe de Commines, a French statesman

[1] a Greek philosopher [2] calling in as advocates

of Persia, *That speech was like cloth of Arras, opened and put abroad; whereby the imagery doth appear in figure; whereas in thoughts they lie but as in packs.* Neither is this second fruit of friendship, in opening the understanding, restrained only to such friends as are able to give a man counsel; (they indeed are best); but even without that, a man learneth of himself, and bringeth his own thoughts to light, and whetteth his wits as against a stone, which itself cuts not. In a word, a man were better relate himself to a statua [1] or picture, than to suffer his thoughts to pass in smother.

Add now, to make this second fruit of friendship complete, that other point which lieth more open and falleth within vulgar [2] observation; which is faithful counsel from a friend. Heraclitus saith well in one of his enigmas, *Dry light is ever the best.* And certain it is, that the light that a man receiveth by counsel from another, is drier and purer than that which cometh from his own understanding and judgment; which is ever infused and drenched in his affections and customs. So as there is as much difference between the counsel that a friend giveth, and that a man giveth himself, as there is between the counsel of a friend and of a flatterer. For there is no such flatterer as is a man's self; and there is no such remedy against flattery of a man's self, as the liberty of a friend. Counsel is of two sorts: the one concerning manners, the other concerning business. For the first, the best preservative to keep the mind in health is the faithful admonition of a friend. The calling of a man's self to a strict account is a medicine, sometime, too piercing and corrosive. Reading good books of morality is a little flat and dead. Observing our faults in others is sometimes unproper for our case. But the best receipt [3] (best, I say, to work, and best to take) is the admonition of a friend. It is a strange thing to behold what gross errors and extreme absurdities many (especially of the greater sort) do commit, for want of a friend to tell them of them; to the great damage both of their fame and fortune: for, as St. James saith, they are as men *that look sometimes into a glass, and presently forget their own shape and favour.* As for business, a man may think, if he will, that two eyes see no more than one; or that a gamester

seeth always more than a looker-on; or that a man in anger is as wise as he that hath said over the four and twenty letters; or that a musket may be shot off as well upon the arm as upon a rest; and such other fond and high imaginations, to think himself all in all. But when all is done, the help of good counsel is that which setteth business straight. And if any man think that he will take counsel, but it shall be by pieces; asking counsel in one business of one man, and in another business of another man; it is well, (that is to say, better perhaps than if he asked none at all;) but he runneth two dangers: one, that he shall not be faithfully counselled; for it is a rare thing, except it be from a perfect and entire friend, to have counsel given, but such as shall be bowed and crooked to some ends which he hath that giveth it. The other, that he shall have counsel given, hurtful and unsafe, (though with good meaning,) and mixed partly of mischief and partly of remedy; even as if you would call a physician that is thought good for the cure of the disease you complain of, but is unacquainted with your body; and therefore may put you in way for a present cure, but overthroweth your health in some other kind; and so cure the disease and kill the patient. But a friend that is wholly acquainted with a man's estate will beware, by furthering any present business, how he dasheth upon other inconvenience. And therefore rest not upon scattered counsels; they will rather distract and mislead, than settle and direct.

After these two noble fruits of friendship (peace in the affections, and support of the judgment) followeth the last fruit; which is like the pomegranate, full of many kernels; I mean aid and bearing a part in all actions and occasions. Here the best way to represent to life the manifold use of friendship, is to cast and see how many things there are which a man cannot do himself; and then it will appear that it was a sparing speech of the ancients, to say, *that a friend is another himself;* for that a friend is far more than himself. Men have their time, and die many times in desire of some things which they principally take to heart; the bestowing of a child, the finishing of a work, or the like. If a man have a true friend, he may rest almost secure that the care of those things will continue after him. So that a man hath, as it were, two lives in his desires. A man hath a body, and

---

[1] statue   [2] common   [3] prescription

that body is confined to a place; but where friendship is, all offices of life are as it were granted to him and his deputy. For he may exercise them by his friend. How many things are there which a man cannot, with any face or comeliness, say or do himself? A man can scarce allege his own merits with modesty, much less extol them; a man cannot sometimes brook to supplicate or beg; and a number of the like. But all these things are graceful in a friend's mouth, which are blushing in a man's own. So again, a man's person hath many proper relations which he cannot put off. A man cannot speak to his son but as a father; to his wife but as a husband; to his enemy but upon terms: whereas a friend may speak as the case requires, and not as it sorteth[1] with the person. But to enumerate these things were endless; I have given the rule, where a man cannot fitly play his own part; if he have not a friend, he may quit the stage.

XLII. OF YOUTH AND AGE

A man that is young in years may be old in hours, if he have lost no time. But that happeneth rarely. Generally, youth is like the first cogitations, not so wise as the second. For there is a youth in thoughts, as well as in ages. And yet the invention of young men is more lively than that of old; and imaginations stream into their minds better, and as it were more divinely. Natures that have much heat and great and violent desires and perturbations, are not ripe for action till they have passed the meridian of their years; as it was with Julius Cæsar, and Septimius Severus. Of the latter of whom it is said *Juventutem egit erroribus, imo furoribus, plenam*.[2] And yet he was the ablest emperor, almost, of all the list. But reposed natures may do well in youth. As it is seen in Augustus Cæsar, Cosmus Duke of Florence, Gaston de Fois, and others. On the other side, heat and vivacity in age is an excellent composition for business. Young men are fitter to invent than to judge; fitter for execution than for counsel; and fitter for new projects than for settled business. For the experience of age, in things that fall within the compass of it, directeth them; but in new things, abuseth

them. The errors of young men are the ruin of business; but the errors of aged men amount but to this, that more might have been done, or sooner. Young men, in the conduct and manage of actions, embrace more than they can hold; stir more than they can quiet; fly to the end, without consideration of the means and degrees; pursue some few principles which they have chanced upon absurdly; care[1] not to innovate, which draws unknown inconveniences; use extreme remedies at first; and, that which doubleth all errors, will not acknowledge or retract them; like an unready horse, that will neither stop nor turn. Men of age object too much, consult too long, adventure too little, repent too soon, and seldom drive business home to the full period, but content themselves with a mediocrity of success. Certainly it is good to compound employments of both; for that will be good for the present, because the virtues of either age may correct the defects of both; and good for succession, that young men may be learners, while men in age are actors; and, lastly, good for extern accidents, because authority followeth old men, and favour and popularity youth. But for the moral part, perhaps youth will have the pre-eminence, as age hath for the politic. A certain rabbin, upon the text, *Your young men shall see visions, and your old men shall dream dreams*, inferreth that young men are admitted nearer to God than old, because vision is a clearer revelation than a dream. And certainly, the more a man drinketh of the world, the more it intoxicateth: and age doth profit rather in the powers of understanding, than in the virtues of the will and affections. There is some have an over-early ripeness in their years, which fadeth betimes. These are, first, such as have brittle wits, the edge whereof is soon turned; such as was Hermogenes the rhetorician, whose books are exceeding subtle; who afterwards waxed stupid. A second sort is of those that have some natural dispositions which have better grace in youth than in age; such as is a fluent and luxuriant speech; which becomes youth well, but not age: so Tully saith of Hortensius, *Idem manebat, neque idem decebat*.[2] The third is of such as take too high a strain at the first, and are magnanimous more than tract of years can uphold. As

---

[1] agrees [2] He passed a youth full of errors; yea, of madnesses.

[1] hesitate. [2] He continued the same, when the same was not becoming.

was Scipio Africanus, of whom Livy saith in effect, *Ultima primis cedebant.*[1]

MINOR POETRY

MY MIND TO ME A KINGDOM IS

My mind to me a kingdom is,
　Such present joys therein I find
That it excels all other bliss
　That earth affords or grows by kind:
Though much I want which most would have,
Yet still my mind forbids to crave.　6

No princely pomp, no wealthy store,
　No force to win the victory,
No wily wit to salve a sore,
　No shape to feed a loving eye;　10
To none of these I yield as thrall:
For why? My mind doth serve for all.

I see how plenty [surfeits] oft,
　And hasty climbers soon do fall;
I see that those which are aloft　15
　Mishap doth threaten most of all;
They get with toil, they keep with fear:
Such cares my mind could never bear.

Content to live, this is my stay;
　I seek no more than may suffice;　20
I press to bear no haughty sway;
　Look, what I lack my mind supplies:
Lo, thus I triumph like a king,
Content with that my mind doth bring.

Some have too much, yet still do crave;　25
　I little have, and seek no more.
They are but poor, though much they have,
　And I am rich with little store:
They poor, I rich; they beg, I give;
They lack, I leave; they pine, I live.　30

I laugh not at another's loss;
　I grudge not at another's pain;
No worldly waves my mind can toss;
　My state at one doth still remain:
I fear no foe, I fawn no friend;　35
I loathe not life, nor dread my end.

Some weigh their pleasure by their lust,
　Their wisdom by their rage of will;
Their treasure is their only trust;
　A cloakèd craft their store of skill:　40

[1] His last actions were not equal to his first.

But all the pleasure that I find
Is to maintain a quiet mind.

My wealth is health and perfect ease;
　My conscience clear my chief defence;
I neither seek by bribes to please,　45
　Nor by deceit to breed offence:
Thus do I live; thus will I die;
Would all did so as well as I!
　　— Sir Edward Dyer (1550?–1607)

THE SILENT LOVER

I

Passions are liken'd best to floods and
　streams:
　The shallow murmur, but the deep are
　dumb.
So, when affection yields discourse, it seems
　The bottom is but shallow whence they
　come.
They that are rich in words, in words discover
That they are poor in that which makes a
　lover.　6

II

Wrong not, sweet empress of my heart,
　The merit of true passion,
With thinking that he feels no smart,
　That sues for no compassion.

Silence in love bewrays more woe　5
　Than words, though ne'er so witty:
A beggar that is dumb, you know,
　May challenge double pity.

Then wrong not, dearest to my heart,
　My true, though secret passion;　10
He smarteth most that hides his smart,
　And sues for no compassion.
　　— Sir Walter Raleigh (1552?–1618)

THE CONCLUSION

Even such is time, that takes in trust
　Our youth, our joys, our all we have,
And pays us but with earth and dust;
　Who in the dark and silent grave,
When we have wander'd all our ways,　5
Shuts up the story of our days:
But from this earth, this grave, this dust,
My God shall raise me up, I trust.
　　— Sir Walter Raleigh (1552?–1618)

SONG OF PARIS AND ŒNONE

ŒNONE. Fair and fair, and twice so fair,
  As fair as any may be;
  The fairest shepherd on our green,
  A love for any lady.
PARIS. Fair and fair, and twice so fair, 5
  As fair as any may be;
  Thy love is fair for thee alone,
  And for no other lady.
ŒN. My love is fair, my love is gay,
  As fresh as bin the flowers in May,
  And of my love my roundelay, 11
  My merry, merry roundelay,
  Concludes with Cupid's curse, —
  "They that do change old love for
   new,
  Pray gods they change for worse!" 15
AMBO SIMUL. They that do change, etc.
ŒN. Fair and fair, etc.
PAR. Fair and fair, etc.
  Thy love is fair, etc.
ŒN. My love can pipe, my love can sing, 20
  My love can many a pretty thing,
  And of his lovely praises ring
  My merry, merry roundelays,
   Amen to Cupid's curse, —
  "They that do change," etc. 25
PAR. They that do change, etc.
AMBO. Fair and fair, etc.
   — GEORGE PEELE (1558?-1597?)

HARVESTMEN A-SINGING

All ye that lovely lovers be,
Pray you for me:
Lo, here we come a-sowing, a-sowing,
And sow sweet fruits of love;
In your sweet hearts well may it prove! 5

Lo, here we come a-reaping, a-reaping,
To reap our harvest-fruit!
And thus we pass the year so long,
And never be we mute.
   — GEORGE PEELE (1558?-1597?)

FAREWELL TO ARMS

His golden locks time hath to silver turned;
 O time too swift, O swiftness never ceasing!
His youth 'gainst time and age hath ever
 spurned,
 But spurned in vain; youth waneth by
 increasing:

Beauty, strength, youth, are flowers but fading seen; 5
Duty, faith, love, are roots, and ever green.

His helmet now shall make a hive for bees,
 And, lovers' sonnets turned to holy psalms,
A man-at-arms must now serve on his knees,
 And feed on prayers, which are age his[1]
 alms:
But though from court to cottage he depart,
His saint is sure of his unspotted heart. 12

And when he saddest sits in homely cell,
He'll teach his swains this carol for a song, —
"Blessed be the hearts that wish my sovereign
 well, 15
 Cursed be the souls that think her any
 wrong."
Goddess, allow this agèd man his right,
To be your beadsman now that was your
 knight.
   — GEORGE PEELE (1558?-1597?)

THE BURNING BABE

As I in hoary winter's night stood shivering in
 the snow,
Surprised I was with sudden heat which made
 my heart to glow;
And lifting up a fearful eye to view what fire
 was near,
A pretty babe all burning bright did in the
 air appear,
Who scorchèd with exceeding heat such floods
 of tears did shed, 5
As though His floods should quench His
 flames with what[2] His tears were fed;
"Alas!" quoth He, "but newly born, in fiery
 heats I fry,
Yet none approach to warm their hearts or
 feel my fire but I!
My faultless breast the furnace is, the fuel
 wounding thorns;
Love is the fire and sighs the smoke, the
 ashes shame and scorns; 10
The fuel Justice layeth on, and Mercy blows
 the coals;
The metal in this furnace wrought are men's
 defilèd souls;
For which, as now on fire I am, to work them
 to their good,
So will I melt into a bath, to wash them in
 my blood:"

  [1] age's   [2] that with which

With this He vanish'd out of sight, and swiftly
  shrunk away,   15
And straight I called into mind that it was
  Christmas-day.
    — ROBERT SOUTHWELL (1561?–1595)

CHERRY–RIPE

There is a garden in her face
  Where roses and white lilies blow;
A heavenly paradise is that place,
  Wherein all pleasant fruits do flow:
    There cherries grow which none may
      buy   5
    Till "Cherry-ripe" themselves do cry.

Those cherries fairly do enclose
  Of orient pearl a double row,
Which when her lovely laughter shows,   9
  They look like rosebuds fill'd with snow;
    Yet them nor peer nor prince can buy
    Till "Cherry-ripe" themselves do cry.

Her eyes like angels watch them still; [1]
  Her brows like bended bows do stand
Threat'ning with piercing frowns to kill
  All that attempt with eye or hand   16
    Those sacred cherries to come nigh
    Till "Cherry-ripe" themselves do cry.
    — THOMAS CAMPION (d. 1619)

ENGLAND'S HELICON (1600)

PHYLLIDA AND CORYDON

In the merry month of May,
In a morn by break of day,
Forth I walk'd by the wood-side,
When as May was in his pride:
There I spièd all alone,   5
Phyllida and Corydon.
Much ado there was, God wot!
He would love and she would not.
She said, never man was true;
He said, none was false to you.   10
He said, he had loved her long;
She said, love should have no wrong.
Corydon would kiss her then;
She said, maids must kiss no men,
Till they did for good and all;   15
Then she made the shepherd call

      [1] constantly

All the heavens to witness truth:
Never loved a truer youth.
Thus with many a pretty oath,
Yea and nay, and faith and troth,   20
Such as silly [1] shepherds use
When they will not love abuse,
Love which had been long deluded,
Was with kisses sweet concluded;
And Phyllida, with garlands gay,   25
Was made the Lady of the May.
    — N. BRETON (1545?–1626?)

AS IT FELL UPON A DAY

As it fell upon a day,
In the merry month of May,
Sitting in a pleasant shade,
Which a group of myrtles made,
Beasts did leap and birds did sing,   5
Trees did grow and plants did spring,
Everything did banish moan,
Save the nightingale alone;
She, poor bird, as all forlorn,
Lean'd her breast against a thorn,   10
And there sung the dolefull'st ditty,
That to hear it was great pity.
"Fie, fie, fie!" now would she cry;
"Teru, teru!" [2] by-and-by.
That to hear her so complain   15
Scarce I could from tears refrain;
For her griefs so lively shown
Made me think upon mine own.
Ah, thought I, thou mourn'st in vain,
None takes pity on thy pain.   20
Senseless trees, they cannot hear thee;
Ruthless beasts, they will not cheer thee;
King Pandion [3] he is dead,
All thy friends are lapp'd in lead;
All thy fellow birds do sing,   25
Careless of thy sorrowing;
Even so, poor bird, like thee,
None alive will pity me.
    — IGNOTO

PHYLLIDA'S LOVE–CALL TO HER CORYDON, AND HIS REPLYING

PHYL. Corydon, arise my Corydon!
    Titan shineth clear.
COR. Who is it that calleth Corydon?
    Who is it that I hear?

[1] simple and good   [2] Cf. note on Sidney's *The
Nightingale*   [3] the father of Philomela and Progne

PHYL. Phyllida, thy true love, calleth thee, 5
 Arise then, arise then;
  Arise and keep thy flock with me!
COR. Phyllida, my true love, is it she?
 I come then, I come then, 9
  I come and keep my flock with thee.

PHYL. Here are cherries ripe for my Corydon;
 Eat them for my sake.
COR. Here's my oaten pipe, my lovely one,
 Sport for thee to make.
PHYL. Here are threads, my true love, fine as
  silk, 15
 To knit thee, to knit thee,
  A pair of stockings white as milk.
COR. Here are reeds, my true love, fine and
  neat,
 To make thee, to make thee,
  A bonnet to withstand the heat.

PHYL. I will gather flowers, my Corydon, 21
 To set in thy cap.
COR. I will gather pears, my lovely one,
 To put in thy lap.
PHYL. I will buy my true love garters gay,
 For Sundays, for Sundays, 26
  To wear about his legs so tall.
COR. I will buy my true love yellow say,[1]
 For Sundays, for Sundays,
  To wear about her middle small.

PHYL. When my Corydon sits on a hill, 31
 Making melody —
COR. When my lovely one goes to her
  wheel,
 Singing cheerily —
PHYL. Sure methinks my true love doth
  excel 35
 For sweetness, for sweetness,
  Our Pan, that old Arcadian knight.
COR. And methinks my true love bears the
  bell
 For clearness, for clearness, 39
  Beyond the nymphs that be so
   bright.

PHYL. Had my Corydon, my Corydon,
 Been, alack! her swain —
COR. Had my lovely one, my lovely one,
 Been in Ida plain —
PHYL. Cynthia Endymion had refused, 45
 Preferring, preferring,
  My Corydon to play withal.

[1] silk for a girdle or sash

COR. The queen of love had been excused
 Bequeathing, bequeathing,
  My Phyllida the golden ball. 50

PHYL. Yonder comes my mother, Corydon,
 Whither shall I fly?
COR. Under yonder beech, my lovely one,
 While she passeth by.
PHYL. Say to her thy true love was not here;
 Remember, remember, 56
  To-morrow is another day.
COR. Doubt me not, my true love, do not
  fear;
 Farewell then, farewell then,
  Heaven keep our loves alway. 60
       — IGNOTO

THE SHEPHERD'S DESCRIPTION OF LOVE

MELIBŒUS. Shepherd, what's love, I pray
  thee tell?
FAUSTUS. It is that fountain and that well
 Where pleasure and repentance
  dwell;
 It is perhaps that saucing bell[1]
  That tolls all in to heaven or hell:
 And this is Love, as I hear tell. 6
MELI. Yet what is Love, I prithee say?
FAUST. It is a work on holiday,
 It is December match'd with May,
 When lusty bloods in fresh array
  Hear ten months after of the play:
 And this is Love, as I hear say. 12
MELI. Yet what is Love, good shepherd,
  sain[2]?
FAUST. It is a sunshine mix'd with rain,
 It is a tooth-ache, or like[3] pain,
 It is a game, where none doth gain;
  The lass saith no, and would full
   fain:
 And this is Love, as I hear sain. 18
MELI. Yet, shepherd, what is Love, I
  pray?
FAUST. It is a yea, it is a nay,
 A pretty kind of sporting fray,
 It is a thing will soon away,
  Then, nymphs, take vantage while
   ye may:
 And this is Love, as I hear say. 24
MELI. Yet what is Love, good shepherd,
  show?

[1] Sanctus bell   [2] say   [3] similar

Faust. A thing that creeps, it cannot go,
    A prize that passeth to and fro,
    A thing for one, a thing for moe,[1]
      And he that proves shall find it so :
      And, shepherd, this is Love, I
        trow.   30
                — Ignoto

DAMELUS' SONG TO HIS DIAPHENIA

Diaphenia, like the daffadowndilly,
White as the sun, fair as the lily,
    Heigho, how I do love thee !
I do love thee as my lambs
Are belovèd of their dams :
    How blest were I if thou wouldst prove me !

Diaphenia, like the spreading roses,   7
That in thy sweets all sweets encloses,
    Fair sweet, how I do love thee !
I do love thee as each flower
Loves the sun's life-giving power ;
    For dead, thy breath to life might move me.

Diaphenia, like to all things blessèd,   13
When all thy praises are expressèd,
    Dear joy, how I do love thee !
As the birds do love the Spring,
Or the bees their careful king :
    Then in requite, sweet virgin, love me ! 18
                — H. C.

A NYMPH'S DISDAIN OF LOVE

"Hey, down, a down !"[2] did Dian sing,
    Amongst her virgins sitting ;
"Than love there is no vainer thing,
    For maidens most unfitting."
And so think I, with a down, down, derry.[2] 5

When women knew no woe,
    But lived themselves to please,
Men's feigning guiles they did not know,
    The ground of their disease.
Unborn was false suspect,[3]   10
    No thought of jealousy ;
From wanton toys[4] and fond affect,[5]
    The virgin's life was free.
"Hey, down, a down !" did Dian sing, etc.

[1] more   [2] *A meaningless refrain*   [3] suspicion
[4] frivolous trifling   [5] foolish affection

At length men usèd charms,   15
    To which what[1] maids gave ear,
Embracing gladly endless harms,
    Anon enthrallèd were.
Thus women welcomed woe,
    Disguised in name of love,   20
A jealous hell, a painted show :
    So shall they find that prove.
"Hey, down, a down !" did Dian sing,
    Amongst her virgins sitting ;
"Than love there is no vainer thing,   25
    For maidens most unfitting."
And so think I, with a down, down, derry.
                — Ignoto

ROSALIND'S MADRIGAL

Love in my bosom like a bee,
    Doth suck his sweet ;
Now with his wings he plays with me,
    Now with his feet.
Within mine eyes he makes his nest,
His bed amidst my tender breast ;
My kisses are his daily feast,
And yet he robs me of my rest.
    Ah, wanton,[2] will ye ?   9

And if I sleep, then percheth he,
    With pretty slight,
And makes his pillow of my knee,
    The livelong night.
Strike I my lute, he tunes the string ;
He music plays if I but sing ;
He lends me every lovely thing ;
Yet cruel he my heart doth sting.
    Whist, wanton, still ye !   18

Else I with roses every day
    Will ship ye hence,
And bind ye, when ye long to play,
    For your offence.
I'll shut my eyes to keep ye in,
I'll make you fast it for your sin,
I'll count your power not worth a pin.
Alas ! what hereby shall I win
    If he gainsay me ?   27

What if I beat the wanton boy
    With many a rod ?
He will repay me with annoy,
    Because a god.
Then sit thou safely on my knee,

[1] whichever   [2] rascal (*used playfully*)

And let thy bower my bosom be;
Lurk in mine eyes, I like of thee.
O Cupid! so thou pity me,
   Spare not, but play thee.   36

   — THOM. LODGE (1558?–1625)

THE PASSIONATE SHEPHERD TO HIS LOVE

Come live with me and be my love,
And we will all the pleasures prove,
That valleys, groves, hills, and fields,
Woods, or steepy mountains yields.   4

And we will sit upon the rocks,
Seeing the shepherds feed their flocks,
By shallow rivers, to whose falls
Melodious birds sings madrigals.   8

And I will make thee beds of roses,
And a thousand fragrant posies,
A cap of flowers and a kirtle
Embroider'd all with leaves of myrtle: 12

A gown made of the finest wool,
Which from our pretty lambs we pull;
Fair lined slippers for the cold,
With buckles of the purest gold;   16

A belt of straw and ivy buds,
With coral clasps and amber studs;
And if these pleasures may thee move,
Come live with me and be my love.   20

The shepherd swains shall dance and sing
For thy delights each May morning;

If these delights thy mind may move,
Then live with me and be my love.   24

   — CHR. MARLOW (1564–1593)

THE NYMPH'S REPLY TO THE SHEPHERD

If all the world and love were young,
And truth in every shepherd's tongue,
These pretty pleasures might me move,
To live with thee and be thy love.   4

Time drives the flocks from field to fold,
When rivers rage, and rocks grow cold;
And Philomel becometh dumb;
The rest complains of cares to come.   8

The flowers do fade, and wanton fields
To wayward Winter reckoning yields;
A honey tongue, a heart of gall,
Is fancy's spring, but sorrow's fall.   12

Thy gowns, thy shoes, thy beds of roses,
Thy cap, thy kirtle, and thy posies,
Soon break, soon wither, soon forgotten,
In folly ripe, in reason rotten.   16

Thy belt of straw and ivy buds,
Thy coral clasps and amber studs,
All these in me no means can move,
To come to thee and be thy love.   20

But could youth last, and love still breed,
Had joys no date, nor age no need,
Then these delights my mind might move,
To live with thee and be thy love.   24

   — IGNOTO

AE

THE END OF THE RENAISSANCE

THOMAS DEKKER (1570?–1641)

From THE SHOEMAKER'S HOLIDAY

THE SECOND THREE MEN'S SONG

Cold's the wind, and wet's the rain,
　Saint Hugh be our good speed!
Ill is the weather that bringeth no gain,
　Nor helps good hearts in need.　　　　4

Trowl the bowl, the jolly nut-brown bowl,
　And here, kind mate, to thee:
Let's sing a dirge for Saint Hugh's soul,
　And down it merrily.　　　　8

Down a down! hey down a down!
　Hey derry derry, down a down!
Ho, well done; to me let come!
　Ring, compass, gentle joy.　　　　12

Trowl the bowl, the nut-brown bowl,
　And here, kind mate, to thee: etc.

(*Repeat as often as there be men to drink; and
at last when all have drunk, this verse:*)

Cold's the wind, and wet's the rain,
　Saint Hugh be our good speed!　　　　16
Ill is the weather that bringeth no gain,
　Nor helps good hearts in need.

From OLD FORTUNATUS

SONG

Virtue smiles: cry holiday,
Dimples on her cheeks do dwell,
Virtue frowns, cry welladay,
Her love is heaven, her hate is hell,
Since heaven and hell obey her power,　5
Tremble when her eyes do lower.
Since heaven and hell her power obey,
Where she smiles, cry holiday,
Holiday with joy we cry,
And bend, and bend, and merrily　10
Sing hymns to Virtue's deity:
Sing hymns to Virtue's deity.

From PATIENT GRISSILL

CONTENT

Art thou poor, yet hast thou golden slumbers?
　　　O sweet content!
Art thou rich, yet is thy mind perplexed?
　　　O punishment!　　　　4
Dost laugh to see how fools are vexed
To add to golden numbers golden numbers?[1]
　O sweet content, O sweet, O sweet content!

Work apace! apace! apace! apace!
Honest labour bears a lovely face.
Then hey noney, noney; hey noney, noney!

Canst drink the waters of the crispèd spring?
　　　O sweet content!　　　　12
Swim'st thou in wealth, yet sink'st in thine
　own tears?
　　　O punishment!
Then he that patiently want's burden bears　15
No burden bears, but is a king, a king.
　O sweet content, O sweet, O sweet content!

Work apace, apace, etc.

THE GULL'S HORNBOOK

CHAPTER VI

HOW A GALLANT SHOULD BEHAVE HIMSELF IN A PLAY-HOUSE

The theatre is your poets' royal exchange, upon which their muses (that are now turned to merchants) meeting, barter away that light commodity of words for a lighter ware than words, plaudities,[2] and the breath of the great beast;[3] which (like the threatenings of two cowards) vanish all into air. Players and their factors,[4] who put away the stuff, and make the best of it they possibly can (as indeed 'tis their parts so to do), your gallant, your courtier, and your captain, had wont to

[1] trouble themselves to heap up gold　[2] applause
[3] the public　[4] adherents

166

be the soundest paymasters; and I think are still the surest chapmen;[1] and these, by means that their heads are well stocked, deal upon this comical freight by the gross: when your groundling,[2] and gallery-commoner[2] buys his sport by the penny, and, like a haggler,[3] is glad to utter[4] it again by retailing.

Since then the place is so free in entertainment, allowing a stool as well to the farmer's son as to your templer:[5] that your stinkard has the selfsame liberty to be there in his tobacco fumes, which your sweet courtier hath: and that your carman and tinker claim as strong a voice in their suffrage, and sit to give judgment on the play's life and death, as well as the proudest momus[6] among the tribes of critic: it is fit that he, whom the most tailors' bills do make room for, when he comes, should not be basely (like a viol) cased up in a corner.

Whether therefore the gatherers[7] of the public or private playhouse stand to receive the afternoon's rent, let our gallant (having paid it) presently advance himself up to the throne of the stage. I mean not into the lord's room (which is now but the stage's suburbs): no, those boxes, by the iniquity of custom, conspiracy of waiting women and gentlemen ushers, that there sweat together, and the covetousness of sharers,[8] are contemptibly thrust into the rear, and much new satin is there damned, by being smothered to death in darkness. But on the very rushes where the comedy is to dance, yea, and under the state[9] of Cambises himself must our feathered estridge,[10] like a piece of ordnance, be planted, valiantly (because impudently) beating down the mews and hisses of the opposed rascality.

For do but cast up a reckoning, what large comings-in are pursed up by sitting on the stage. First a conspicuous eminence is got; by which means, the best and most essential parts of a gallant (good clothes, a proportionable leg, white hand, the Persian lock, and a tolerable beard) are perfectly revealed.

By sitting on the stage, you have a signed patent to engross the whole commodity of censure; may lawfully presume to be a girder; and stand at the helm to steer the passage of scenes; yet no man shall once offer to hinder

you from obtaining the title of an insolent, overweening coxcomb.

By sitting on the stage, you may (without travelling for it) at the very next door ask whose play it is: and, by that quest of inquiry, the law warrants you to avoid much mistaking: if you know not the author, you may rail against him: and peradventure so behave yourself, that you may enforce the author to know you.

By sitting on the stage, if you be a knight, you may happily[1] get you a mistress: if a mere Fleet-street gentleman, a wife: but assure yourself, by continual residence, you are the first and principal man in election to begin the number of We Three.[2]

By spreading your body on the stage, and by being a justice in examining of plays, you shall put yourself into such true scenical authority, that some poet shall not dare to present his muse rudely upon your eyes, without having first unmasked her, rifled her, and discovered all her bare and most mystical parts before you at a tavern, when you most knightly shall, for his pains, pay for both their suppers.

By sitting on the stage, you may (with small cost) purchase the dear acquaintance of the boys: have a good stool for sixpence:[3] at any time know what particular part any of the infants[4] present: get your match lighted, examine the play-suits' lace,[5] and perhaps win wagers upon laying 'tis copper, etc. And to conclude, whether you be a fool or a justice of peace, a cuckold, or a captain, a lord-mayor's son, or a dawcock,[6] a knave, or an under-sheriff; of what stamp soever you be, current, or counterfeit, the stage, like time, will bring you to most perfect light and lay you open: neither are you to be hunted from thence, though the scarecrows in the yard[7] hoot at you, hiss at you, spit at you, yea, throw dirt even in your teeth: 'tis most gentlemanlike patience to endure all this, and to laugh at the silly animals: but if the rabble, with a full throat, cry, "Away with the fool," you were worse than a madman to tarry by it:. for the gentleman and the fool should never sit on the stage together.

---

[1] buyers [2] occupants of cheap places [3] huckster [4] sell [5] a resident of one of the inns of court [6] a carping critic [7] doorkeepers [8] shareholders in the theatre [9] canopy [10] ostrich

[1] haply, by chance [2] A jest that still survives, — a picture of two fools or asses, with this inscription. [3] the usual price [4] boy players [5] braid, usually of gold or silver [6] simpleton [7] the pit of the theatre, where there were no seats

Marry, let this observation go hand in hand with the rest: or rather, like a country serving-man, some five yards before them. Present not yourself on the stage (especially at a new play) until the quaking prologue hath (by rubbing) got colour into his cheeks, and is ready to give the trumpets[1] their cue, that he's upon point to enter: for then it is time, as though you were one of the properties, or that you dropped out of the hangings, to creep from behind the arras,[2] with your tripos or three-footed stool in one hand, and a teston[3] mounted between a forefinger and a thumb in the other: for if you should bestow your person upon the vulgar, when the belly of the house is but half full, your apparel is quite eaten up, the fashion lost, and the proportion of your body in more danger to be devoured than if it were served up in the counter[4] amongst the poultry: avoid that as you would the bastome.[5] It shall crown you with rich commendation to laugh aloud in the midst of the most serious and saddest scene of the terriblest tragedy: and to let that clapper (your tongue) be tossed so high, that all the house may ring of it: your lords use it; your knights are apes to the lords, and do so too: your in-a-court-man[6] is zany[7] to the knights, and (marry very scurvily) comes likewise limping after it: be thou a beagle to them all, and never lin[8] snuffing, till you have scented them: for by talking and laughing (like a ploughman in a morris[9]) you heap Pelion upon Ossa, glory upon glory: as first, all the eyes in the galleries will leave walking after the players, and only follow you: the simplest dolt in the house snatches up your name, and when he meets you in the streets, or that you fall into his hands in the middle of a watch, his word shall be taken for you: he'll cry "He's such a gallant," and you pass. Secondly, you publish your temperance to the world, in that you seem not to resort thither to taste vain pleasures with a hungry appetite: but only as a gentleman to spend a foolish hour or two, because you can do nothing else: thirdly, you mightily disrelish the audience, and disgrace the author: marry, you take up (though it be at the worst hand) a strong opinion of your own judgment, and enforce the poet

to take pity of your weakness, and, by some dedicated sonnet, to bring you into a better paradise, only to stop your mouth.

If you can (either for love or money), provide yourself a lodging by the water side: for, above the convenience it brings to shun shoulder-clapping,[1] and to ship away your cockatrice[2] betimes in the morning, it adds a kind of state unto you, to be carried from thence to the stairs of your play-house: hate a sculler (remember that) worse than to be acquainted with one o' th' scullery. No, your oars are your only sea-crabs, board them, and take heed you never go twice together with one pair: often shifting is a great credit to gentlemen; and that dividing of your fare will make the poor watersnakes be ready to pull you in pieces to enjoy your custom: no matter whether upon landing, you have money or no: you may swim in twenty of their boats over the river upon ticket:[3] marry, when silver comes in, remember to pay treble their fare, and it will make your flounder-catchers to send more thanks after you, when you do not draw, than when you do; for they know, it will be their own another day.

Before the play begins, fall to cards: you may win or lose (as fencers do in a prize) and beat one another by confederacy, yet share the money when you meet at supper: notwithstanding, to gull the ragamuffins that stand aloof gaping at you, throw the cards (having first torn four or five of them) round about the stage, just upon the third sound,[4] as though you had lost: it skills not[5] if the four knaves lie on their backs, and outface the audience; there's none such fools as dare take exceptions at them, because, ere the play go off, better knaves than they will fall into the company.

Now, sir, if the writer be a fellow that hath either epigrammed you, or hath had a flirt at your mistress, or hath brought either your feather, or your red beard, or your little legs, etc., on the stage, you shall disgrace him worse than by tossing him in a blanket, or giving him the bastinado in a tavern, if, in the middle of his play (be it pastoral or comedy, moral or tragedy), you rise with a screwed and discontented face from your stool to be gone; no matter whether the scenes be good or no:

---

[1] trumpeters (who announced the beginning of the play) [2] cloth hung against the wall of the stage [3] sixpence [4] a prison for debtors [5] cudgel [6] lawyer [7] ape [8] cease [9] a morris dance

[1] by a constable [2] prostitute [3] "on tick" [4] i.e. for the play to begin [5] it doesn't matter

the better they are the worse do you distaste them: and, being on your feet, sneak not away like a coward, but salute all your gentle acquaintance, that are spread either on the rushes, or on stools about you, and draw what troop you can from the stage after you: the mimics[1] are beholden to you, for allowing them elbow room: their poet cries, perhaps, "a pox go with you," but care not for that, there's no music without frets.

Marry, if either the company, or indisposition of the weather bind you to sit it out, my counsel is then that you turn plain ape, take up a rush, and tickle the earnest ears of your fellow gallants, to make other fools fall a-laughing: mew at passionate speeches, blare at merry, find fault with the music, whew at the children's action, whistle at the songs: and above all, curse the sharers, that whereas the same day you had bestowed forty shillings on an embroidered felt and feather (Scotch-fashion) for your mistress in the court, or your punk[2] in the city, within two hours after, you encounter with the very same block[3] on the stage, when the haberdasher swore to you the impression was extant but that morning.

To conclude, hoard up the finest play-scraps you can get, upon which your lean wit may most savoury feed, for want of other stuff, when the Arcadian and Euphuised gentle-women have their tongues sharpened to set upon you: that quality (next to your shuttle-cock) is the only furniture to a courtier that's but a new beginner, and is but in his A B C of compliment. The next places that are filled, after the playhouses be emptied, are (or ought to be) taverns: into a tavern then let us next march, where the brains of one hogshead must be beaten out to make up another.

BEN JONSON (1573?–1637)

SONG TO CELIA

Drink to me only with thine eyes,
    And I will pledge with mine;
Or leave a kiss but in the cup,
    And I'll not look for wine.
The thirst that from the soul doth rise
    Doth ask a drink divine;
But might I of Jove's nectar sup,
    I would not change for thine.

[1] players   [2] prostitute   [3] style of hat

I sent thee late a rosy wreath,
    Not so much honouring thee   10
As giving it a hope, that there
    It could not wither'd be.
But thou thereon didst only breathe,
    And sent'st it back to me;
Since when it grows, and smells, I swear,
    Not of itself, but thee.

THE TRIUMPH OF CHARIS

See the chariot at hand here of Love,
    Wherein my Lady rideth!
Each that draws is a swan or a dove,
    And well the car Love guideth.
As she goes, all hearts do duty
            Unto her beauty;
And enamour'd, do wish, so they might
            But enjoy such a sight,
That they still were to run by her side,
Through swords, through seas, whither she
    would ride.   10

Do but look on her eyes, they do light
    All that Love's world compriseth!
Do but look on her hair, it is bright
    As Love's star when it riseth!
Do but mark, her forehead's smoother
            Than words that soothe her;
And from her arched brows, such a grace
            Sheds itself through the face
As alone there triumphs to the life
All the gain, all the good, of the elements'
    strife.   20

Have you seen but a bright lily grow,
    Before rude hands have touched it?
Have you marked but the fall of the snow,
    Before the soil hath smutched it?
Have you felt the wool of the beaver?
            Or swan's down ever?
Or have smelt o' the bud of the briar?
            Or the nard in the fire?
Or have tasted the bag of the bee?
Oh so white! Oh so soft! Oh so sweet is
    she!   30

TO THE MEMORY OF MY BELOVED, MASTER WILLIAM SHAKESPEARE

To draw no envy, Shakespeare, on thy name
Am I thus ample to thy book and fame;
While I confess thy writings to be such
As neither man, nor muse, can praise too much.

'Tis true, and all men's suffrage.[1] But these ways
Were not the paths I meant unto thy praise;
For silliest ignorance on these may light,
Which, when it sounds at best, but echoes right;
Or blind affection, which doth ne'er advance
The truth, but gropes, and urgeth all by chance;   10
Or crafty malice might pretend this praise,
And think to ruin, where it seemed to raise.
These are, as [2] some infamous bawd or whore
Should praise a matron. What could hurt her more?
But thou art proof against them, and, indeed,
Above the ill fortune of them, or the need.
I therefore will begin. Soul of the age!
The applause, delight, the wonder of our stage!
My Shakespeare, rise! I will not lodge thee by
Chaucer, or Spenser, or bid Beaumont lie   20
A little further, to make thee a room:
Thou art a monument without a tomb,
And art alive still [3] while thy book doth live
And we have wits to read and praise to give.
That I not mix thee so, my brain excuses,
I mean with great, but disproportioned Muses; [4]
For if I thought my judgment were of years,
I should commit thee surely with thy peers,
And tell how far thou didst our Lily outshine,
Or sporting Kyd, or Marlowe's mighty line.   30
And though thou hadst small Latin and less Greek,
From thence to honour thee, I would not seek
For names; but call forth thundering Æschylus,
Euripides, and Sophocles to us;
Pacuvius, Accius, him of Cordova dead, [5]
To life again, to hear thy buskin [6] tread,
And shake a stage; or, when thy socks [7] were on,
Leave thee alone for the comparison
Of all that insolent Greece or haughty Rome
Sent forth, or since did from their ashes come.
Triumph, my Britain, thou hast one to show
To whom all scenes of Europe homage owe.   42
He was not of an age, but for all time!
And all the Muses still were in their prime,
When, like Apollo, he came forth to warm
Our ears, or like a Mercury to charm!
Nature herself was proud of his designs
And joyed to wear the dressing of his lines!
Which were so richly spun, and woven so fit,
As, since, she will vouchsafe no other wit.   50
The merry Greek, tart Aristophanes,
Neat Terence, witty Plautus, now not please;
But antiquated and deserted lie,
As [1] they were not of Nature's family.
Yet must I not give Nature all; thy art,
My gentle Shakespeare, must enjoy a part.
For though the poet's matter nature be,
His art doth give the fashion; and, that he
Who casts [2] to write a living line, must sweat,
(Such as thine are) and strike the second heat
Upon the Muses' anvil; turn the same   61
(And himself with it) that he thinks to frame,
Or, for [3] the laurel, he may gain a scorn;
For a good poet's made, as well as born.
And such wert thou! Look how the father's face
Lives in his issue, even so the race
Of Shakespeare's mind and manners brightly shines
In his well turnèd, and true filèd lines;
In each of which he seems to shake a lance,
As brandished at the eyes of ignorance.   70
Sweet Swan of Avon! what a sight it were
To see thee in our waters yet appear,
And make those flights upon the banks of Thames,
That so did take Eliza, and our James!
But stay, I see thee in the hemisphere
Advanced, and made a constellation there!
Shine forth, thou Star of poets, and with rage
Or influence, chide or cheer the drooping stage,
Which, since thy flight from hence, hath mourned like night,   79
And despairs day, but for thy volume's light.

From A PINDARIC ODE

To the immortal memory and friendship of that noble pair, Sir Lucius Cary and Sir H. Morison.

III

The Strophe, or Turn

It is not growing like a tree
In bulk, doth make men better be;
Or standing long an oak, three hundred year,
To fall a log at last, dry, bald, and sear:

---

[1] vote, opinion   [2] as if   [3] forever   [4] *i.e. poets not equal to thee*   [5] Pacuvius, Accius, and Seneca, the most famous Latin tragedians   [6] the high shoe of tragedy   [7] the low shoe of comedy

[1] as if   [2] attempts   [3] instead of

A lily of a day,
    Is fairer far, in May;   70
Although it fall and die that night,
It was the plant and flower of light.
In small proportions we just beauties see;
And in short measures life may perfect be.

AN EPITAPH ON SALATHIEL PAVY [1]

Weep with me, all you that read
    This little story:
And know, for whom a tear you shed
    Death's self is sorry.
'Twas a child that so did thrive
    In grace and feature,
As heaven and nature seem'd to strive
    Which owned the creature.
Years he numbered scarce thirteen
    When fates turned cruel,   10
Yet three filled zodiacs [2] had he been
    The stage's jewel;
And did act, what now we moan,
    Old men so duly,
As, sooth, the Parcæ [3] thought him one,
    He played so truly.
So, by error, to his fate
    They all consented;
But viewing him since, alas, too late!
    They have repented;   20
And have sought, to give new birth,
    In baths to steep him;
But being so much too good for earth,
    Heaven vows to keep him.

EPITAPH ON ELIZABETH, L. H. [4]

Would'st thou hear what man can say
In a little? Reader, stay.

Underneath this stone doth lie
As much beauty as could die:
Which in life did harbour give
To more virtue than doth live.

If at all she had a fault,
Leave it buried in this vault.
One name was Elizabeth,
The other, let it sleep with death!   10
Fitter, where it died, to tell,
Than that it lived at all.   Farewell!

[1] the most famous child actor of his time
[2] years   [3] the Fates   [4] Lady Herbert

JOHN DONNE (1573–1631)

THE INDIFFERENT

I can love both fair and brown;
  Her whom abundance melts, and her whom
    want betrays;
  Her who loves loneness best, and her who
    masks and plays;
  Her whom the country form'd, and whom the
    town;
  Her who believes, and her who tries;
  Her who still weeps with spongy eyes,
  And her who is dry cork and never cries.
I can love her, and her, and you, and you;
I can love any, so she be not true.   9

Will no other vice content you?
Will it not serve your turn to do as did your
    mothers?
Or have you all old vices spent and now would
    find out others?
Or doth a fear that men are true torment you?
O we are not, be not you so;
Let me — and do you — twenty know;
Rob me, but bind me not, and let me go.
Must I, who came to travel thorough you,   17
Grow your fix'd subject, because you are true?

Venus heard me sigh this song;
And by love's sweetest part, variety, she
    swore,
She heard not this till now; it should be so no
    more.
She went, examined, and return'd ere long,
And said, "Alas! some two or three
Poor heretics in love there be,
Which think to stablish dangerous constancy.
But I have told them, 'Since you will be true,
You shall be true to them who're false to
    you.'"   27

LOVE'S DEITY

I long to talk with some old lover's ghost
  Who died before the god of love was born.
I cannot think that he who then loved most
  Sunk so low as to love one which did scorn.
But since this god produced a destiny,
And that vice-nature,[1] custom, lets it be,
  I must love her that loves not me.   7

[1] Nature's substitute

Sure, they which made him[1] god, meant not so
    much,
  Nor he in his young godhead practiced it.
But when an even flame two hearts did touch,
  His office was indulgently to fit
Actives to passives.   Correspondency
Only his subject was; it cannot be
  Love till I love her who loves me.   14

But every modern god will not extend
  His vast prerogative as far as Jove.
To rage, to lust, to write to, to commend,
  All is the purlieu of the god of love.
O ! were we waken'd by this tyranny
To ungod this child[1] again, it could not be
  I should love her who loves not me.   21

Rebel and atheist too, why murmur I,
  As though I felt the worst that love could
    do?
Love may make me leave loving, or might try
  A deeper plague, to make her love me too;
Which, since she loves before, I'm loth to see.
Falsehood is worse than hate; and that must
  be,
  If she whom I love, should love me.   28

THE FUNERAL

Whoever comes to shroud me, do not harm
    Nor question much
That subtle wreath of hair about mine arm;
  The mystery, the sign you must not touch,
    For 'tis my outward soul,
Viceroy to that which, unto heav'n being gone,
    Will leave this to control
And keep these limbs, her provinces, from dis-
  solution.   8

For if the sinewy thread[2] my brain lets fall
    Through every part
Can tie those parts, and make me one of all;
Those hairs, which upward grew, and strength
    and art
    Have from a better brain,
Can better do't: except she meant that I
    By this should know my pain,
As prisoners then are manacled, when they're
  condemn'd to die.   16

Whate'er she meant by't, bury it with me,
    For since I am

---

[1] the god of love   [2] the spinal cord and nerves

Love's martyr, it might breed idolatry
If into other hands these reliques came.
    As 'twas humility
T'afford to it all that a soul can do,
    So 'tis some bravery
That, since you[1] would have none of me, I
  bury some of you.   24

FORGET

If poisonous minerals, and if that tree
Whose fruit threw death on else immortal us,
If lecherous goats, if serpents envious
Cannot be damn'd, alas ! why should I be?
Why should intent or reason, born in me,
Make sins, else equal, in me more heinous?
And, mercy being easy and glorious
To God, in His stern wrath why threatens He?
  But who am I, that dare dispute with Thee?
O God, O ! of Thine only worthy blood   10
And my tears make a heavenly Lethean flood,
And drown in it my sin's black memory.
That Thou remember them, some claim as
  debt;
I think it mercy if Thou wilt forget.

DEATH

Death, be not proud, though some have callèd
  thee
Mighty and dreadful, for thou art not so;
For those whom thou think'st thou dost over-
  throw
Die not, poor Death; nor yet canst thou kill
  me.
From Rest and Sleep, which but thy picture
  be,
Much pleasure; then from thee much more
  must flow;
And soonest our best men with thee do go —
Rest of their bones and souls' delivery !   8
Thou'rt slave to Fate, Chance, kings, and
  desperate men,
And dost with poison, war, and sickness dwell;
And poppy or charms can make us sleep as
  well
And better than thy stroke.   Why swell'st
  thou then?
One short sleep past, we wake eternally,
And Death shall be no more: Death, thou
  shalt die !

---

[1] *the* she *of ll.* 14, 17

JOHN FLETCHER (1579–1625)

SWEETEST MELANCHOLY

Hence, all you vain delights,
As short as are the nights
  Wherein you spend your folly!
There's nought in this life sweet,
If man were wise to see't,   5
  But only melancholy;
  O sweetest melancholy!

Welcome, folded arms and fixèd eyes,
A sigh that piercing mortifies,
A look that's fastened to the ground,   10
A tongue chained up without a sound!
Fountain heads and pathless groves,
Places which pale passion loves!
Moonlight walks, when all the fowls
Are warmly housed save bats and owls! 15

A midnight bell, a parting groan,
These are the sounds we feed upon.
Then stretch our bones in a still gloomy valley;
Nothing's so dainty sweet as lovely melan-
  choly.

INVOCATION TO SLEEP

Care-charming Sleep, thou easer of all woes,
Brother to Death, sweetly thyself dispose
On this afflicted prince; fall like a cloud
In gentle showers; give nothing that is loud
Or painful to his slumbers; — easy, sweet, 5
And as a purling stream, thou son of Night,
Pass by his troubled senses; sing his pain
Like hollow murmuring wind or silver rain;
Into this prince gently, oh, gently slide,
And kiss him into slumbers like a bride!   10

SONG TO BACCHUS

God Lyæus,[1] ever young,
Ever honoured, ever sung;
Stained with blood of lusty grapes,
In a thousand lusty shapes,
Dance upon the mazer's brim,   5
In the crimson liquor swim;
From thy plenteous hand divine
Let a river run with wine;
God of youth, let this day here
Enter neither care nor fear!   10

[1] the god of relaxation

BEAUTY CLEAR AND FAIR

Beauty clear and fair,
  Where the air
Rather like a perfume dwells;
  Where the violet and the rose
  Their blue veins and blush disclose,
And come to honour nothing else.   6

Where to live near,
  And planted there,
Is to live, and still live new;
  Where to gain a favour is
  More than light, perpetual bliss, —
Make me live by serving you.   12

Dear, again back recall
  To this light
A stranger to himself and all;
  Both the wonder and the story
  Shall be yours, and eke the glory:
I am your servant, and your thrall.   18

WEEP NO MORE

Weep no more, nor sigh, nor groan,
Sorrow calls no time that's gone;
Violets plucked the sweetest rain
Makes not fresh nor grow again;
Trim thy locks, look cheerfully;
Fate's hid ends eyes cannot see;
Joys as wingèd dreams fly fast,
Why should sadness longer last?   8

Grief is but a wound to woe;
Gentlest fair, mourn, mourn no mo.[1]

DIRGE

Lay a garland on my hearse
  Of the dismal yew;
Maidens, willow branches bear;
  Say, I died true.   4

My love was false, but I was firm
  From my hour of birth.
Upon my buried body lie
  Lightly, gentle earth!   8

[1] more

FRANCIS BEAUMONT
(1584-1616)

MASTER FRANCIS BEAUMONT'S LETTER TO BEN JONSON

The sun (which doth the greatest comfort
bring
To absent friends, because the selfsame thing
They know they see, however absent) is
Here our best haymaker ! Forgive me this ;
It is our country's style ! In this warm shine
I lie and dream of your full Mermaid Wine ! 6

*   *   *   *   *   *   *

Methinks the little wit I had is lost   40
Since I saw you ! For wit is like a rest [1]
Held [2] up at tennis, which men do the best
With the best gamesters. What things have
we seen
Done at the Mermaid ! heard words that have
been
So nimble and so full of subtle flame,
As if that every one from whence they came
Had meant to put his whole wit in a jest
And had resolved to live a fool the rest
Of his dull life ! Then, when there hath been
thrown
Wit able enough to justify the town   50
For three days past ! Wit, that might war-
rant be
For the whole city to talk foolishly
Till that were cancelled ! And, when we were
gone,
We left an air behind us, which alone
Was able to make the two next companies
Right witty ! though but downright fools,
more wise !
When I remember this, and see that now
The country gentlemen begin to allow
My wit for dry bobs ; [3] then I needs must cry,
"I see my days of ballading grow nigh !"   60
I can already riddle ; and can sing
Catches, sell bargains ; and I fear shall bring
Myself to speak the hardest words I find
Over as oft as any, with one wind,
That takes no medicines ! But one thought
of thee
Makes me remember all these things to be
The wit of our young men, fellows that show
No part of good, yet utter all they know !
Who, like trees of the guard, have growing
souls.

[1] rally   [2] kept   [3] smart quips or hits

Only strong Destiny, which all controls, 70
I hope hath left a better fate in store
For me, thy friend, than to live ever poor,
Banished unto this home ! Fate, once again,
Bring me to thee, who canst make smooth and
plain
The way of knowledge for me ; and then I,
Who have no good but in thy company,
Protest it will my greatest comfort be
To acknowledge all I have to flow from thee !
Ben, when these scenes are perfect, we'll
taste wine !
I'll drink thy Muse's health ! thou shalt quaff
mine !   80

WILLIAM DRUMMOND
(1585-1649)

SONNET

A passing glance, a lightning 'long the skies,
That, ush'ring thunder, dies straight to our
sight ;
A spark, of contraries which doth arise,
Then drowns in the huge depths of day and
night :
Is this small Small call'd life, held in such price
Of blinded wights, who nothing judge aright.
Of Parthian shaft so swift is not the flight
As life, that wastes itself, and living dies.
O ! what is human greatness, valour, wit ?
What fading beauty, riches, honour, praise ? 10
To what doth serve in golden thrones to sit,
Thrall earth's vast round, triumphal arches
raise ?
All is a dream, learn in this prince's fall,
In whom, save death, nought mortal was at
all.

MADRIGAL I

This life, which seems so fair,
Is like a bubble blown up in the air
By sporting children's breath,
Who chase it everywhere,
And strive who can most motion it bequeath ;
And though it sometime seem of its own might,
Like to an eye of gold, to be fix'd there,   7
And firm to hover in that empty height,
That only is because it is so light.
But in that pomp it doth not long appear ; 10
For even when most admir'd, it in a
thought,
As swell'd from nothing, doth dissolve in
nought.

JOHN FORD (fl. 1639)

SONG

FROM THE BROKEN HEART

Can you paint a thought? or number
Every fancy in a slumber?
Can you count soft minutes roving
From a dial's point by moving?
Can you grasp a sigh? or, lastly,   5
Rob a virgin's honour chastely?
  No, O, no! yet you may
Sooner do both that and this,
This and that, and never miss,
  Than by any praise display   10
Beauty's beauty; such a glory,
As beyond all fate, all story,
  All arms, all arts,
  All loves, all hearts,
Greater than those or they,   15
Do, shall, and must obey.

DIRGE

FROM THE BROKEN HEART

CHOR.   Glories, pleasures, pomps, de-
    lights, and ease,
      Can but please
    The outward senses, when the
    mind
    Is or untroubled or by peace
    refined.
1ST VOICE. Crowns may flourish and decay, 5
    Beauties shine, but fade away.
2ND VOICE. Youth may revel, yet it must
    Lie down in a bed of dust.
3RD VOICE. Earthly honours flow and waste,
    Time alone doth change and
    last.   10
CHOR.   Sorrows mingled with contents
    prepare
      Rest for care;
    Love only reigns in death;
    though art
    Can find no comfort for a broken
    heart.

GEORGE WITHER (1588–1667)

FROM FAIR VIRTUE, THE MISTRESS OF PHILARETE [1]

SONNET IV

Shall I, wasting in despair,
Die, because a woman's fair?
Or make pale my cheeks with care,
'Cause another's rosy are?
Be she fairer than the day,
Or the flowery meads in May!
  If she be not so to me,
  What care I how fair she be?   8

Should my heart be grieved or pined,
'Cause I see a woman kind?
Or a well disposèd nature
Joinèd with a lovely feature?
Be she meeker, kinder than
Turtle dove, or pelican!
  If she be not so to me,
  What care I how kind she be?   16

Shall a woman's virtues move
Me to perish for her love?
Or her well deserving known,
Make me quite forget mine own?
Be she with that goodness blest
Which may gain her, name of best!
  If she be not such to me,
  What care I how good she be?   24

'Cause her fortune seems too high,
Shall I play the fool, and die?
Those that bear a noble mind,
Where they want of riches find,
Think "What, with them, they would do
That, without them, dare to woo!"
  And unless that mind I see,
  What care I though great she be?   32

Great, or good, or kind, or fair,
I will ne'er the more despair!
If she love me (this believe!)
I will die, ere she shall grieve!
If she slight me, when I woo,
I can scorn, and let her go!
  For if she be not for me,
  What care I for whom she be?   40

[1] Philareté *means* lover of virtue

THOMAS HEYWOOD (D. 1650?)

GO, PRETTY BIRDS!

Ye little birds, that sit and sing
  Amidst the shady valleys,
And see how Phillis sweetly walks
  Within her garden alleys,
Go, pretty birds, about her bower!
Sing, pretty birds, she may not lower!
Ah me! methinks, I see her frown!
  Ye pretty wantons, warble!   8

Go, tell her, through your chirping bills,
  As you by me are bidden,
To her is only known my love;
  Which from the world is hidden.
Go, pretty birds, and tell her so!
See that your notes strain not too low!
For still, methinks, I see her frown!
  Ye pretty wantons, warble!   16

Go, tune your voices' harmony,
  And sing, I am her lover!
Strain loud and sweet, that every note
  With sweet content may move her!
And she that hath the sweetest voice,
Tell her, I will not change my choice!
Yet still, methinks, I see her frown!
  Ye pretty wantons, warble!   24

O, fly! Make haste! See, see, she falls
  Into a pretty slumber!
Sing round about her rosy bed,
  That, waking, she may wonder!
Say to her, 'Tis her lover true,
That sendeth love to you! to you!
And when you hear her kind reply,
  Return with pleasant warblings!   32

WILLIAM BROWNE (1591–1643)

BRITANNIA'S PASTORALS

FROM BOOK II, SONG V

Now was the Lord and Lady of the May
Meeting the May-pole at the break of day,
And Cælia, as the fairest on the green,
Not without some maids' envy chosen queen.
Now was the time com'n, when our gentle
  swain

Must in [1] his harvest or lose all again.   146
Now must he pluck the rose lest other
  hands,
Or tempests, blemish what so fairly stands:
And therefore, as they had before decreed,
Our shepherd gets a boat, and with all speed,
In night, that doth on lovers' actions smile,
Arrivèd safe on Mona's fruitful isle.[2]   152
  Between two rocks (immortal, without
    mother,)
That stand as if out-facing one another,
There ran a creek up, intricate and blind, 155
As if the waters hid them from the wind;
Which never wash'd but at a higher tide
The frizzled coats which do the mountains
  hide;
Where never gale was longer known to stay 159
Than from the smooth wave it had swept
  away
The new divorced leaves, that from each
  side
Left the thick boughs to dance out with the
  tide.
At further end the creek a stately wood
Gave a kind shadow to the brackish flood
Made up of trees, not less kenn'd by each
  skiff
Than that sky-scaling Peak of Teneriffe, 166
Upon whose tops the hernshaw [3] bred her
  young,
And hoary moss upon their branches hung;
Whose rugged rinds sufficient were to show,
Without their height, what time they 'gan to
  grow;
And if dry eld by wrinkled skin appears, 171
None could allot them less than Nestor's
  years.
As under their command the thronged creek
Ran lessen'd up. Here did the shepherd seek
Where he his little boat might safely hide, 175
Till it was fraught with what the world beside
Could not outvalue; nor give equal weight
Though in the time when Greece was at her
  height.

EPITAPH

May, be thou never graced with birds that
  sing,
  Nor Flora's pride!
In thee all flowers and roses spring,
  Mine only died.

[1] bring in   [2] the isle of Anglesey   [3] heron

ON THE COUNTESS DOWAGER OF PEMBROKE

Underneath this sable herse
Lies the subject of all verse:
Sidney's sister, Pembroke's mother:
Death, ere thou hast slain another
Fair and learn'd and good as she,
Time shall throw a dart at thee.

ROBERT HERRICK (1591–1674)

CHERRY–RIPE

Cherry-ripe, ripe, ripe, I cry,
Full and fair ones; come and buy;
If so be you ask me where
They do grow? I answer, there,
Where my Julia's lips do smile;   5
There's the land, or cherry-isle,
Whose plantations fully show
All the year where cherries grow.

CORINNA'S GOING A–MAYING

Get up, get up for shame, the blooming morn
Upon her wings presents the god unshorn.[1]
See how Aurora throws her fair
Fresh-quilted colours through the air:
Get up, sweet slug-a-bed, and see
The dew bespangling herb and tree.
Each flower has wept and bow'd toward the
east
Above an hour since: yet you not dress'd;
Nay! not so much as out of bed?
When all the birds have matins said   10
And sung their thankful hymns, 'tis sin,
Nay, profanation, to keep in,
Whereas a thousand virgins on this day
Spring, sooner than the lark, to fetch in May.

Rise and put on your foliage, and be seen
To come forth, like the spring-time, fresh and
green,
And sweet as Flora. Take no care
For jewels for your gown or hair:
Fear not; the leaves will strew
Gems in abundance upon you: 20
Besides, the childhood of the day has kept,
Against you come, some orient pearls unwept;
Come and receive them while the light
Hangs on the dew-locks of the night:

[1] golden-haired Apollo, *i.e.* the sun.

And Titan on the eastern hill
Retires himself, or else stands still
Till you come forth. Wash, dress, be brief in
praying:
Few beads[1] are best when once we go a-Maying.

Come, my Corinna, come; and, coming,
mark   29
How each field turns a street, each street a
park
Made green and trimm'd with trees; see
how
Devotion gives each house a bough
Or branch: each porch, each door ere this
An ark, a tabernacle is,
Made up of white-thorn, neatly interwove;
As if here were those cooler shades of love.
Can such delights be in the street
And open fields and we not see't?
Come, we'll abroad; and let's obey
The proclamation made for May: 40
And sin no more, as we have done, by staying;
But, my Corinna, come, let's go a-Maying.

There's not a budding boy or girl this day
But is got up, and gone to bring in May.
A deal of youth, ere this, is come
Back, and with white-thorn laden home.
Some have despatched their cakes and
cream
Before that we have left[2] to dream:
And some have wept, and woo'd, and plighted
troth,
And chose their priest, ere we can cast off
sloth: 50
Many a green-gown has been given;
Many a kiss, both odd and even:
Many a glance too has been sent
From out the eye, love's firmament;
Many a jest told of the keys betraying
This night, and locks pick'd, yet we're not
a-Maying.

Come, let us go while we are in our prime;
And take the harmless folly of the time.
We shall grow old apace, and die
Before we know our liberty.   60
Our life is short, and our days run
As fast away as does the sun;
And, as a vapour or a drop of rain,
Once lost, can ne'er be found again,
So when or you or I are made
A fable, song, or fleeting shade,

[1] prayers   [2] ceased

All love, all liking, all delight
Lies drowned with us in endless night.
Then while time serves, and we are but decay-
    ing,
Come, my Corinna, come, let's go a-Maying. 70

TO THE VIRGINS, TO MAKE MUCH OF TIME

Gather ye rosebuds while ye may,
  Old Time is still a-flying;
And this same flower that smiles to-day,
  To-morrow will be dying.   4

The glorious lamp of heaven, the sun,
  The higher he's a-getting,
The sooner will his race be run,
  And nearer he's to setting.   8

That age is best which is the first,
  When youth and blood are warmer;
But being spent, the worse and worst
  Times still succeed the former.   12

Then be not coy, but use your time,
  And while ye may, go marry;
For, having lost but once your prime,
  You may forever tarry.   16

UPON JULIA'S CLOTHES

When-as in silks my Julia goes,
Then, then, methinks, how sweetly flows
The liquefaction of her clothes.   3

Next, when I cast mine eyes, and see
That brave vibration, each way free,
O, how that glittering taketh me!   6

TO DAFFODILS

Fair Daffodils, we weep to see
  You haste away so soon;
As yet the early rising sun
  Has not attain'd his noon.
    Stay, stay,   5
  Until the hasting day
    Has run
  But to the even-song;
And, having prayed together, we
  Will go with you along.   10

We have short time to stay, as you,
  We have as short a spring;
As quick a growth to meet decay,
  As you, or anything.
    We die   15
  As your hours do, and dry
    Away,
  Like to the summer's rain;
Or as the pearls of morning's dew,
  Ne'er to be found again.   20

TO KEEP A TRUE LENT

Is this a fast, to keep
    The larder lean,
      And clean,
From fat of veals and sheep?   4

Is it to quit the dish
    Of flesh, yet still
      To fill
The platter high with fish?   8

Is it to fast an hour,
    Or ragg'd to go,
      Or show
A downcast look, and sour?   12

No; 'tis a fast, to dole
    Thy sheaf of wheat
      And meat
Unto the hungry soul.   16

It is to fast from strife,
    From old debate,
      And hate;
To circumcise thy life.   20

To show a heart grief-rent;
    To starve thy sin,
      Not bin; [1]
And that's to keep thy Lent.   24

GEORGE HERBERT (1593-1633)

VIRTUE

Sweet day, so cool, so calm, so bright,
  The bridal of the earth and sky!
The dew shall weep thy fall to-night;
  For thou must die.   4

[1] larder for food

Sweet rose, whose hue, angry and brave,
   Bids the rash gazer wipe his eye.
Thy root is ever in its grave,
   And thou must die.   8

Sweet spring, full of sweet days and roses,
   A box where sweets compacted lie,
My music shows ye have your closes,
   And all must die.   12

Only a sweet and virtuous soul,
   Like seasoned timber, never gives;
But though the whole world turn to coal,
   Then chiefly lives.   16

THE COLLAR

I struck the board, and cried, "No more;
   I will abroad!
What! shall I ever sigh and pine?
My lines and life are free; free as the road,
   Loose as the wind, as large as store.[1]
   Shall I be still in suit?
Have I no harvest but a thorn
To let me blood, and not restore
What I have lost with cordial fruit?
     Sure there was wine   10
Before my sighs did dry it; there was corn
Before my tears did drown it;
   Is the year only lost to me?
   Have I no bays to crown it,
No flowers, no garlands gay? all blasted,
   All wasted?
Not so, my heart; but there is fruit,
   And thou hast hands.
Recover all thy sigh-blown age
On double pleasures; leave thy cold dispute
Of what is fit and not; forsake thy cage, 21
   Thy rope of sands
Which petty thoughts have made; and made
   to thee
Good cable, to enforce and draw,
   And be thy law,
While thou didst wink[2] and wouldst not see.
   Away! take heed;
   I will abroad.
Call in thy death's-head there, tie up thy fears:
   He that forbears   30
   To suit and serve his need
   Deserves his load."
But as I raved, and grew more fierce and wild
   At every word,
Methought I heard one calling, "Child";
   And I replied, "My Lord."

[1] plenty   [2] close the eyes

LOVE

Love bade me welcome; yet my soul drew back,
   Guilty of dust and sin.
But quick-eyed Love, observing me grow slack
   From my first entrance in,
Drew nearer to me, sweetly questioning,
   If I lacked anything.   6

"A guest," I answered, "worthy to be here:"
   Love said, "You shall be he."
"I, the unkind, ungrateful? Ah, my dear,
   I cannot look on Thee!"
Love took my hand and smiling did reply,
   "Who made the eyes but I?"   12

"Truth, Lord; but I have marred them: let my
   shame
   Go where it doth deserve."
"And know you not," says Love, "who bore the
   blame?"
   "My dear, then I will serve."[1]
"You must sit down," says Love, "and taste
   my meat."
So I did sit and eat.   18

IZAAK WALTON (1593–1683)

THE COMPLETE ANGLER

From THE FIRST DAY

A Conference betwixt an Angler, a Falconer, and a Hunter, each commending his Recreation

CHAPTER I. Piscator,[2] Venator,[3] Auceps[4]

Piscator. You are well overtaken, Gentlemen! A good morning to you both! I have stretched my legs up Tottenham Hill to overtake you, hoping your business may occasion you towards Ware, whither I am going this fine fresh May morning.

Venator. Sir, I, for my part, shall almost answer your hopes; for my purpose is to drink my morning's draught at the Thatched House in Hoddesden; and I think not to rest till I come thither, where I have appointed a friend or two to meet me: but for this gentleman that you see with me, I know not how far he intends his journey; he came so lately into

[1] act as servant [2] angler [3] hunter [4] falconer

my company, that I have scarce had time to ask him the question.

Auceps. Sir, I shall by your favour bear you company as far as Theobalds, and there leave you; for then I turn up to a friend's house, who mews[1] a Hawk for me, which I now long to see.

Piscator. Sir, we are all so happy as to have a fine, fresh, cool morning; and I hope we shall each be the happier in the others' company. And, Gentlemen, that I may not lose yours, I shall either abate or amend my pace to enjoy it, knowing that, as the Italians say, "Good company in a journey makes the way to seem the shorter."

Auceps. It may do, Sir, with the help of a good discourse, which, methinks, we may promise from you, that both look and speak so cheerfully: and for my part, I promise you, as an invitation to it, that I will be as free and open hearted as discretion will allow me to be with strangers.

Venator. And, Sir, I promise the like.

Piscator. I am right glad to hear your answers; and, in confidence[2] you speak the truth, I shall put on a boldness to ask you, Sir, whether business or pleasure caused you to be so early up, and walk so fast? for this other gentleman hath declared he is going to see a hawk, that a friend mews for him.

Venator. Sir, mine is a mixture of both, a little business and more pleasure; for I intend this day to do all my business, and then bestow another day or two in hunting the Otter, which a friend, that I go to meet, tells me is much pleasanter than any other chase whatsoever: howsoever, I mean to try it; for to-morrow morning we shall meet a pack of Otter-dogs of noble Mr. Sadler's, upon Amwell Hill, who will be there so early, that they intend to prevent[3] the sunrising.

Piscator. Sir, my fortune has answered my desires, and my purpose is to bestow a day or two in helping to destroy some of those villainous vermin: for I hate them perfectly, because they love fish so well, or rather, because they destroy so much; indeed so much, that, in my judgment all men that keep Otter-dogs ought to have pensions from the King, to encourage them to destroy the very breed of those base Otters, they do so much mischief.

Venator. But what say you to the Foxes of the Nation? would not you as willingly have them destroyed? for doubtless they do as much mischief as Otters do.

Piscator. Oh, Sir, if they do, it is not so much to me and my fraternity, as those base vermin the Otters do.

Auceps. Why, Sir, I pray, of what fraternity are you, that you are so angry with the poor Otters?

Piscator. I am, Sir, a Brother of the Angle, and therefore an enemy to the Otter: for you are to note, that we Anglers all love one another, and therefore do I hate the Otter both for my own, and their sakes who are of my brotherhood.

Venator. And I am a lover of Hounds: I have followed many a pack of dogs many a mile, and heard many merry Huntsmen make sport and scoff at Anglers.

Auceps. And I profess myself a Falconer, and have heard many grave, serious men pity them, it is such a heavy, contemptible, dull recreation.

Piscator. You know, Gentlemen, it is an easy thing to scoff at any art or recreation; a little wit mixed with ill-nature, confidence, and malice will do it; but though they often venture boldly, yet they are often caught, even in their own trap, according to that of Lucian,[1] the father of the family of Scoffers: —

Lucian, well skill'd in scoffing, this hath writ,
Friend, that's your folly, which you think your wit:
This you vent oft, void both of wit and fear,
Meaning another, when yourself you jeer.

If to this you add what Solomon says of Scoffers, that they are an abomination to mankind, let him that thinks fit scoff on, and be a Scoffer still; but I account them enemies to me and all that love Virtue and Angling.

And for you that have heard many grave, serious men pity Anglers; let me tell you, Sir, there be many men that are by others taken to be serious and grave men, whom we contemn and pity. Men that are taken to be grave, because nature hath made them of a sour complexion; money-getting men, men that spend all their time, first in getting, and next, in anxious care to keep it; men that are condemned to be rich, and then always busy or discontented: for these poor rich men, we Anglers pity them perfectly, and stand in no need to borrow their thoughts to

---

[1] keeps in a cage [2] *Supply* that. [3] anticipate

[1] a famous Greek satirist

think ourselves so happy. No, no, Sir, we enjoy a contentedness above the reach of such dispositions, and as the learned and ingenuous Montaigne says, like himself, freely, "When my Cat and I entertain each other with mutual apish tricks, as playing with a garter, who knows but that I make my Cat more sport than she makes me? Shall I conclude her to be simple, that has her time to begin or refuse, to play as freely as I myself have? Nay, who knows but that it is a defect of my not understanding her language, for doubtless Cats talk and reason with one another, that we agree no better: and who knows but that she pities me for being no wiser than to play with her, and laughs and censures my folly, for making sport for her, when we two play together?"

Thus freely speaks Montaigne concerning Cats; and I hope I may take as great a liberty to blame any man, and laugh at him too, let him be never so grave, that hath not heard what Anglers can say in the justification of their Art and Recreation; which I may again tell you, is so full of pleasure, that we need not borrow their thoughts, to think ourselves happy.

THOMAS CAREW (1598?–1639?)

SONG

Ask me no more where Jove bestows,
When June is past, the fading rose,
For in your beauty's orient deep
These flowers, as in their causes, sleep.   4

Ask me no more whither do stray
The golden atoms of the day,
For, in pure love, heaven did prepare
Those powders to enrich your hair.   8

Ask me no more whither doth haste
The nightingale when May is past,
For in your sweet dividing[1] throat
She winters and keeps warm her note.   12

Ask me no more where those stars light
That downwards fall in dead of night,
For in your eyes they sit, and there
Fixèd become as in their sphere.   16

[1] dividing *means* singing in florid style.

AE

Ask me no more if east or west
The Phœnix builds her spicy nest,
For unto you at last she flies,
And in your fragrant bosom dies.   20

SONG

Would you know what's soft? I dare
Not bring you to the down, or air,
Nor to stars to show what's bright,
Nor to snow to teach you white;   4

Nor, if you would music hear,
Call the orbs to take your ear;
Nor, to please your sense, bring forth
Bruisèd nard, or what's more worth;   8

Or on food were your thoughts placed,
Bring you nectar for a taste;
Would you have all these in one,
Name my mistress, and 'tis done!   12

SIR THOMAS BROWNE
(1605–1682)

HYDRIOTAPHIA: URN–BURIAL

CHAPTER V

Now, since these dead bones have already outlasted the living ones of Methuselah, and, in a yard under ground, and thin walls of clay, outworn all the strong and specious[1] buildings above it, and quietly rested under the drums and tramplings of three conquests;[2] what prince can promise such diuturnity unto his relics, or might not gladly say,

"Sic ego componi versus in ossa velim."[3]

Time, which antiquates antiquities, and hath an art to make dust of all things, hath yet spared these minor monuments. In vain we hope to be known by open and visible conservatories,[4] when to be unknown was the means of their continuation, and obscurity their protection.

If they died by violent hands, and were thrust into their urns, these bones become considerable, and some old philosophers would

[1] beautiful [2] the Saxon, the Danish, and the Norman [3] Would that I were turned into bones! [4] repositories

honour them, whose souls they conceived most pure, which were thus snatched from their bodies, and to retain a stronger propension[1] unto them; whereas, they weariedly left a languishing corpse, and with faint desires of reunion. If they fell by long and aged decay, yet wrapped up in the bundle of time, they fall into indistinction, and make but one blot with infants. If we begin to die when we live, and long life be but a prolongation of death, our life is a sad composition; we live with death, and die not in a moment. How many pulses made up the life of Methuselah, were work for Archimedes. Common counters[2] sum up the life of Moses's man.[3] Our days become considerable, like petty sums by minute accumulations, where numerous fractions make up but small round numbers, and our days of a span long make not one little finger.[4]

If the nearness of our last necessity brought a nearer comformity unto it, there were a happiness in hoary hairs, and no calamity in half senses. But the long habit of living indisposeth us for dying; when avarice makes us the sport of death; when even David grew politically[5] cruel; and Solomon could hardly be said to be the wisest of men. But many are too early old, and before the date of age. Adversity stretcheth our days, misery makes Alcmena's nights,[6] and time hath no wings unto it. But the most tedious being is that which can unwish itself, content to be nothing, or never to have been; which was beyond the malecontent of Job, who cursed not the day of his life, but his nativity, content to have so far been as to have a title to future being, although he had lived here but in a hidden state of life, and as it were an abortion.

What song the Sirens sang, or what name Achilles assumed when he hid himself among women, though puzzling questions,[7] are not beyond all conjecture. What time the persons of these ossuaries[8] entered the famous nations of the dead, and slept with princes and counsellors, might admit a wide[9] solution. But who were the proprietaries of these bones, or what bodies these ashes made up, were a question above antiquarianism; not to be resolved by man, nor easily perhaps by spirits, except we consult the provincial guardians or tutelary observators. Had they made as good provision for their names as they have done for their relics, they had not so grossly erred in the art of perpetuation. But to subsist in bones, and be but pyramidally[1] extant, is a fallacy in duration. Vain ashes, which in the oblivion of names, persons, times, and sexes, have found unto themselves a fruitless continuation, and only arise unto late posterity, as emblems of mortal vanities, antidotes against pride, vainglory, and madding vices. Pagan vainglories, which thought the world might last forever, had encouragement for ambition; and finding no Atropos[2] unto the immortality of their names, were never damped with the necessity of oblivion. Even old ambitions had the advantage of ours, in the attempts of their vainglories, who, acting early, and before the probable meridian[3] of time, have by this time found great accomplishment of their designs, whereby the ancient heroes have already outlasted their monuments and mechanical preservations. But in this latter scene of time we cannot expect such mummies unto our memories, when ambition may fear the prophecy of Elias,[4] and Charles the Fifth can never expect to live within two Methuselahs of Hector.[5]

And therefore restless inquietude for the diuturnity of our memories unto present considerations, seems a vanity almost out of date, and superannuated piece of folly. We cannot hope to live so long in our names as some have done in their persons. One face of Janus[6] holds no proportion unto the other. 'Tis too late to be ambitious. The great mutations of the world are acted, or time may be too short for our designs. To extend our memories by monuments, whose death we daily pray for, and whose duration we cannot hope, without injury to our expectations, in the advent of the last day, were a contradiction to our beliefs. We, whose generations are ordained in this setting part of time, are providentially taken off from such imaginations; and being neces-

---

[1] tendency to return [2] disks for counting [3] Psalms xc, 10 [4] *According to the ancient arithmetic of the hand, wherein the little finger of the right hand, contracted, signified a hundred.* [5] with crafty purpose [6] of double length [7] Put by the emperor Tiberius to the grammarians. [8] receptacles for bones [9] vague, general

[1] in a pyramid or other monument [2] the Fate who cuts the thread of life [3] noon, middle [4] *That the world may last only six thousand years.* [5] *Hector's fame having lasted more than twice the life of Methuselah before the birth of Charles* (1500 A.D.). [6] *The two faces of Janus look in opposite directions.*

sitated to eye the remaining particle of futurity, are naturally constituted unto thoughts of the next world, and cannot excusably decline the consideration of that duration, which maketh pyramids pillars of snow, and all that's past a moment.

Circles and right lines limit and close all bodies, and the mortal right-lined circle[1] must conclude and shut up all. There is no antidote against the opium of time, which temporarily considereth all things. Our fathers find their graves in our short memories, and sadly tell us how we may be buried in our survivors. Gravestones tell truth scarce forty years.[2] Generations pass while some trees stand, and old families last not three oaks. To be read by bare inscriptions, like many in Gruter; [3] to hope for eternity by enigmatical epithets, or first letters of our names; to be studied by antiquaries, who we were, and have new names given us, like many of the mummies, are cold consolations unto the students of perpetuity, even by everlasting languages.

To be content that times to come should only know there was such a man, not caring whether they knew more of him, was a frigid ambition in Cardan,[4] disparaging his horoscopal inclination and judgment of himself. Who cares to subsist like Hippocrates's patients, or Achilles's horses in Homer, under naked nominations,[5] without deserts and noble acts, which are the balsam of our memories, the "entelechia"[6] and soul of our subsistences? Yet to be nameless in worthy deeds exceeds an infamous history. The Canaanitish woman lives more happily without a name, than Herodias with one. And who had not rather have been the good thief than Pilate?

But the iniquity[7] of oblivion blindly scattereth her poppy, and deals with the memory of men without distinction to merit of perpetuity. Who can but pity the founder of the pyramids? Erostratus[8] lives that burnt the Temple of Diana; he is almost lost that built

it. Time hath spared the epitaph of Adrian's[1] horse, confounded that of himself. In vain we compute our felicities by the advantage of our good names, since bad have equal durations; and Thersites[2] is like to live as long as Agamemnon.[3] Who knows whether the best of men be known, or whether there be not more remarkable persons forgot than any that stand remembered in the known account of time? Without the favour of the everlasting register, the first man had been as unknown as the last, and Methuselah's long life had been his only chronicle.

Oblivion is not to be hired. The greater part must be content to be as though they had not been, to be found in the register of God, not in the record of man. Twenty-seven names make up the first story,[4] and the recorded names ever since contain not one living century. The number of the dead long exceedeth all that shall live. The night of time far surpasseth the day; and who knows when was the equinox? Every hour adds unto that current arithmetic, which scarce stands one moment. And since death must be the Lucina[5] of life, and even Pagans could doubt whether thus to live were to die; since our longest sun sets at right declensions, and makes but winter arches, and therefore it cannot be long before we lie down in darkness, and have our light in ashes; since the brother of death daily haunts us with dying mementos, and time, that grows old itself, bids us hope no long duration, diuturnity is a dream and folly of expectation.

Darkness and light divide the course of time, and oblivion shares with memory a great part even of our living beings. We slightly remember our felicities, and the smartest strokes of affliction leave but short smart upon us. Sense endureth no extremities, and sorrows destroy us or themselves. To weep into stones are fables. Afflictions induce callosities; miseries are slippery, or fall like snow upon us, which, notwithstanding, is no unhappy stupidity. To be ignorant of evils to come, and forgetful of evils past, is a merciful provision in nature, whereby we digest the mixture of our few and evil days, and our

---

[1] ⊖, the character of death [2] *In old graveyards the old graves were used for new burials*. [3] Gruter's Ancient Inscriptions [4] A famous Italian scholar of the sixteenth century, who said: "I should like it to be known that I lived, I do not care that it should be known what sort of man I was." [5] mere names [6] realizations [7] injustice [8] *The night that Alexander the Great was born, Herostratus burnt the temple of Diana, at Ephesus, to secure immortal fame.*

[1] the emperor Hadrian [2] an impudent coward in the Greek army against Troy, see the *Iliad* or *Troilus and Cressida* [3] leader of the Greeks against Troy [4] *i.e.*, before the flood, see *Gen.*, iv and v [5] goddess of birth

delivered senses not relapsing into cutting remembrances, our sorrows are not kept raw by the edge of repetitions. A great part of antiquity contented their hopes of subsistency with a transmigration of their souls; a good way to continue their memories, while, having the advantage of plural successions, they could not but act something remarkable in such variety of beings, and enjoying the fame of their passed selves, make accumulation of glory unto their last durations. Others, rather than be lost in the uncomfortable night of nothing, were content to recede into the common being, and make one particle of the public soul of all things, which was no more than to return into their unknown and divine original again. Egyptian ingenuity was more unsatisfied, contriving their bodies in sweet consistencies[1] to attend the return of their souls. But all was vanity, feeding the wind and folly. The Egyptian mummies, which Cambyses or time hath spared, avarice now consumeth.[2] Mummy is become merchandise, Mizraim[3] cures wounds, and Pharaoh is sold for balsams.

In vain do individuals hope for immortality, or any patent from oblivion, in preservations below the moon. Men have been deceived even in their flatteries above the sun,[4] and studied conceits to perpetuate their names in heaven. The various cosmography of that part hath already varied the names of contrived constellations. Nimrod[5] is lost in Orion, and Osiris[6] in the Dog-star. While we look for incorruption in the heavens, we find they are but like the earth, durable in their main bodies, alterable in their parts; whereof, beside comets and new stars, perspectives begin to tell tales, and the spots that wander about the sun, with Phaethon's favor, would make clear conviction.

There is nothing strictly immortal but immortality. Whatever hath no beginning, may be confident of no end; which is the peculiar of that necessary essence that cannot destroy itself, and the highest strain of omnipotency to be so powerfully constituted, as not to suffer even from the power of itself. All others have a dependent being, and within the reach of destruction. But the sufficiency of Christian immortality frustrates all earthly glory, and the quality of either state after death makes a folly of posthumous memory. God, who can only destroy our souls, and hath assured our resurrection, either of our bodies or names hath directly promised no duration. Wherein there is so much of chance, that the boldest expectants have found unhappy frustration; and to hold long subsistence seems but a scape in oblivion. But man is a noble animal, splendid in ashes, and pompous in the grave, solemnising nativities and deaths with equal lustre, nor omitting ceremonies of bravery in the infamy of his nature. ... .

EDMUND WALLER (1606–1687)

THE STORY OF PHŒBUS AND DAPHNE, APPLIED

Thyrsis, a youth of the inspired train,
Fair Sacharissa loved, but loved in vain.
Like Phœbus sung the no less amorous boy;
Like Daphne she, as lovely, and as coy!
With numbers[1] he the flying nymph pursues, 5
With numbers such as Phœbus' self might use!
Such is the chase when Love and Fancy leads,
O'er craggy mountains, and through flowery meads;
Invoked to testify the lover's care,
Or form some image of his cruel fair.   10
Urged with his fury, like a wounded deer,
O'er these he fled; and now approaching near,
Had reached the nymph with his harmonious lay,[2]
Whom all his charms could not incline to stay.
Yet what he sung in his immortal strain,   15
Though unsuccessful, was not sung in vain;
All, but the nymph that should redress his wrong,
Attend his passion, and approve his song.
Like Phœbus thus, acquiring unsought praise,
He catched at love, and filled his arm with bays.   20

ON A GIRDLE

That which her slender waist confined,
Shall now my joyful temples bind;
No monarch but would give his crown,
His arms might do what this has done.

---

[1] *Mummies were made by the use of preservative syrups* [2] *Mummies were sold for use as medicines* [3] the ancestor of the Egyptians, according to Hebrew tradition, 1 *Chron.*, i: 8.   [4] in the sky [5] the Chaldaic name for the constellation Orion [6] the Egyptian name for Sirius

[1] verses   [2] song

It was my heaven's extremest sphere,   5
The pale which held that lovely deer.
My joy, my grief, my hope, my love,
Did all within this circle move!

A narrow compass! and yet there
Dwelt all that's good, and all that's fair;   10
Give me but what this ribband bound,
Take all the rest the sun goes round.

GO, LOVELY ROSE!

Go, lovely Rose!
Tell her that wastes her time and me,
That now she knows,
When I resemble her to thee,
How sweet and fair she seems to be.   5

Tell her that's young,
And shuns to have her graces spied,
That hadst thou sprung
In deserts, where no men abide,
Thou must have uncommended died.   10

Small is the worth
Of beauty from the light retired;
Bid her come forth,
Suffer herself to be desired,
And not blush so to be admired.   15

Then die! that she
The common fate of all things rare
May read in thee;
How small a part of time they share
That are so wondrous sweet and fair!   20

THOMAS FULLER (1608–1661)

THE HOLY STATE

BOOK II. CHAPTER XXII

The Life of Sir Francis Drake

Francis Drake was born nigh South Tavistock in Devonshire, and brought up in Kent; God dividing the honour betwixt two counties, that the one might have his birth, and the other his education. His father, being a minister, fled into Kent, for fear of the Six Articles, wherein the sting of Popery still remained in England, though the teeth thereof were knocked out, and the Pope's supremacy abolished. Coming into Kent, he bound his son Francis apprentice to the master of a small bark, which traded into France and Zealand,[1] where he underwent a hard service; and pains with patience in his youth, did knit the joints of his soul, and made them more solid and compacted. His master, dying unmarried, in reward of his industry, bequeathed his bark unto him for a legacy.

For some time he continued his master's profession; but the narrow seas were a prison for so large a spirit, born for greater undertakings. He soon grew weary of his bark; which would scarce go alone, but as it crept along by the shore: wherefore, selling it, he unfortunately ventured most of his estate with Captain John Hawkins into the West Indies, in 1567; whose goods were taken by the Spaniards at St. John de Ulva, and he himself scarce escaped with life: the king of Spain being so tender in those parts, that the least touch doth wound him; and so jealous of the West Indies, his wife, that willingly he would have none look upon her: he therefore used them with the greater severity.

Drake was persuaded by the minister of his ship, that he might lawfully recover in value of the king of Spain, and repair his losses upon him anywhere else. The case was clear in sea-divinity; and few are such infidels, as not to believe doctrines which make for their own profit. Whereupon Drake, though a poor private man, hereafter undertook to revenge himself on so mighty a monarch; who, as not contented that the sun riseth and setteth in his dominions, may seem to desire to make all his own where he shineth. And now let us see how a dwarf, standing on the mount of God's providence, may prove an overmatch for a giant.

After two or three several voyages to gain intelligence in the West Indies, and some prizes taken, at last he effectually set forward from Plymouth with two ships, the one of seventy, the other twenty-five, tons, and seventy-three men and boys in both. He made with all speed and secrecy to Nombre de Dios, as loath to put the town to too much charge (which he knew they would willingly bestow) in providing beforehand for his entertainment; which city was then the granary of the West Indies, wherein the golden harvest brought from Panama was hoarded up till it could be conveyed into Spain. They came

---

[1] Zeeland (in the Netherlands)

hard aboard the shore, and lay quiet all night, intending to attempt the town in the dawning of the day.

But he was forced to alter his resolution, and assault it sooner ; for he heard his men muttering amongst themselves of the strength and greatness of the town : and when men's heads are once fly-blown with buzzes of suspicion, the vermin multiply instantly, and one jealousy[1] begets another. Wherefore, he raised them from their nest before they had hatched their fears ; and, to put away those conceits,[2] he persuaded them it was day-dawning when the moon rose, and instantly set on the town, and won it; being unwalled. In the market-place the Spaniards saluted them with a volley of shot ; Drake returned their greeting with a flight of arrows, the best and ancient English compliment, which drave their enemies away. Here Drake received a dangerous wound, though he valiantly concealed it a long time ; knowing if his heart stooped, his men's would fall, and loath to leave off the action, wherein if so bright an opportunity once setteth, it seldom riseth again. But at length his men forced him to return to his ship, that his wound might be dressed ; and this unhappy accident defeated the whole design. Thus victory sometimes slips through *their* fingers *who* have caught it in their hands.

But his valour would not let him give over the project as long as there was either life or warmth in it ; and therefore, having received intelligence from the Negroes called Symerons,[3] of many mules'-lading of gold and silver, which was to be brought from Panama, he, leaving competent numbers to man his ships, went on land with the rest, and bestowed himself in the woods by the way as they were to pass, and so intercepted and carried away an infinite mass of gold. As for the silver, which was not portable over the mountains, they digged holes in the ground and hid it therein.

There want not those who love to beat down the price of every honourable action, though they themselves never mean to be chapmen. These cry up Drake's *fortune* herein to cry down his *valour ;* as if this his performance were nothing, wherein a golden opportunity ran his head, with his long forelock, into Drake's hands beyond expectation. But, cer-

tainly, his resolution and unconquerable patience deserved much praise, to adventure on such a design, which had in it just no more probability than what was enough to keep it from being impossible. Yet I admire[1] not so much at all the treasure he took, as at the rich and deep mine of God's providence.

Having now full freighted himself with wealth, and burnt at the House of Crosses[2] above two hundred thousand pounds' worth of Spanish merchandise, he returned with honour and safety into England, and, some years after (December 13th, 1577), undertook that his famous voyage about the world, most accurately described by our English authors : and yet a word or two thereof will not be amiss.

Setting forward from Plymouth, he bore up for Cabo-verd,[3] where, near to the island of St. Jago,[4] he took prisoner Nuno de Silva, an experienced Spanish pilot, whose direction he used in the coasts of Brazil and Magellan Straits, and afterwards safely landed him at Guatulco in New Spain.[5] Hence they took their course to the Island of Brava ; and hereabouts they met with those tempestuous winds whose only praise is, that they continue not an hour, in which time they change all the points of the compass. Here they had great plenty of rain, poured (not, as in other places, as it were out of sieves, but) as out of spouts, so that a butt of water falls down in a place ; which, notwithstanding, is but a courteous injury in that hot climate far from land, and where otherwise fresh water cannot be provided. Then cutting the Line,[6] they saw the face of that heaven which earth hideth from us, but therein only three stars of the first greatness, the rest few and small compared to our hemisphere ; as if God, on purpose, had set up the best and biggest candles in that room wherein his civilest guests are entertained.

Sailing the south of Brazil, he afterwards passed the Magellan Straits (August 20th, 1578), and then entered *Mare Pacificum,* came to the southernmost land at the height of 55½ latitudes ; thence directing his course northward, he pillaged many Spanish towns, and took rich prizes of high value in the kingdoms of Chili, Peru, and New Spain. Then,

---

[1] fear [2] ideas [3] Cimarrones, a band of fugitive negroes who gathered on the Isthmus of Panama in the sixteenth century

[1] wonder [2] a Spanish town in Panama [3] Cape Verde [4] Santiago of the Cape Verde Islands [5] Mexico [6] the equator

bending eastwards, he coasted China, and the Moluccas, where, by the king of Terrenate, a true gentleman Pagan, he was most honourably entertained. The king told them, they and he were all of one religion in this respect, — that they believed not in gods made of stocks and stones, as did the Portugals. He furnished them also with all necessaries that they wanted.

On January 9th following (1579), his ship, having a large wind and a smooth sea, ran aground on a dangerous shoal, and struck twice on it; knocking twice at the door of death, which, no doubt, had[1] opened the third time. Here they stuck, from eight o'clock at night till four the next afternoon, having ground too much, and yet too little to land on; and water too much, and yet too little to sail in. Had God (who, as the wise man saith, "holdeth the winds in his fist," Prov. xxx. 4) but opened his little finger, and let out the smallest blast, they had undoubtedly been cast away; but there blew not any wind all the while. Then they, conceiving aright that the best way to lighten the ship was, first, to ease it of the burden of their sins by true repentance, humbled themselves, by fasting, under the hand of God. Afterwards they received the communion, dining on Christ in the sacrament, expecting no other than to sup with him in heaven. Then they cast out of their ship six great pieces of ordnance, threw overboard as much wealth as would break the heart of a miser to think on it, with much sugar, and packs of spices, making a caudle of the sea round about. Then they betook themselves to their prayers, the best lever at such a dead lift indeed; and it pleased God, that the wind, formerly their mortal enemy, became their friend; which, changing from the starboard to the larboard of the ship, and rising by degrees, cleared them off to the sea again, — for which they returned unfeigned thanks to Almighty God.

By the Cape of Good Hope and west of Africa, he returned safe into England, and (November 3rd, 1580) landed at Plymouth, (being almost the first of those that made a thorough light through the world) having, in his whole voyage, though a curious searcher after the time, lost one day through the variation of several climates. He feasted the queen in his ship at Dartford,[1] who knighted him for his service. Yet it grieved him not a little, that some prime courtiers refused the gold he offered them, as gotten by piracy. Some of them would have been loath to have been told, that they had *aurum Tholosanum*[2] in their own purses. Some think, that they did it to show that their envious pride was above their covetousness, who of set purpose did blur the fair copy of his performance, because they would not take pains to write after it.

I pass by his next West-Indian voyage (1585), wherein he took the cities of St. Jago, St. Domingo, Carthagena, and St. Augustine in Florida; as also his service performed in 1588, wherein he, with many others, helped to the waning of that half-moon,[3] which sought to govern all the motion of our sea. I haste to his last voyage.

Queen Elizabeth, in 1595, perceiving that the only way to make the Spaniard a cripple forever, was to cut his sinews of war in the West Indies, furnished Sir Francis Drake, and Sir John Hawkins, with six of her own ships, besides twenty-one ships and barks of their own providing, containing in all two thousand five hundred men and boys, for some service on America. But, alas! this voyage was marred before begun. For, so great preparations being too big for a cover, the king of Spain knew of it, and sent a caraval of adviso[4] to the West Indies; so that they had intelligence three weeks before the fleet set forth of England, either to fortify or remove their treasure; whereas, in other of Drake's voyages, not two of his own men knew whither he went; and managing such a design is like carrying a mine in war, — if it hath any vent, all is spoiled. Besides, Drake and Hawkins, being in joint commission, hindered each other. The latter took himself to be inferior rather in success than skill; and the action was unlike to prosper when neither would follow, and both could not handsomely go abreast. It vexed old Hawkins, that his counsel was not followed, in present sailing to America, but that they spent time in vain in assaulting the Canaries; and the grief that his advice was slighted, say some, was the cause of his death. Others

---

[1] would have

[1] Deptford   [2] Spanish gold, as bribes   [3] *The Armada was drawn up in crescent form.*   [4] ship of notification

impute it to the sorrow he took for the taking of his bark called "the Francis," which five Spanish frigates had intercepted. But when the same heart hath two mortal wounds given it together, it is hard to say which of them killeth.

Drake continued his course for Porto Rico; and, riding within the road, a shot from the Castle entered the steerage of the ship, took away the stool from under him as he sate at supper, wounded Sir Nicholas Clifford, and Brute Brown to death. "Ah, dear Brute!" said Drake, "I could grieve for thee, but now is no time for me to let down my spirits." And, indeed, a soldier's most proper bemoaning a friend's death in war, is in revenging it. And, sure, as if grief had made the English furious, they soon after fired five Spanish ships of two hundred tons apiece, in despite of the Castle.

America is not unfitly resembled to an hourglass, which hath a narrow neck of land (suppose it the hole where the sand passeth) betwixt the parts thereof, — Mexicana and Peruana. Now the English had a design to march by land over this Isthmus, from Porto Rico to Panama, where the Spanish treasure was laid up. Sir Thomas Baskervile, general of the land-forces, undertook the service with seven hundred and fifty armed men. They marched through deep ways, the Spaniards much annoying them with shot out of the woods. One fort in the passage they assaulted in vain, and heard two others were built to stop them, besides Panama itself. They had so much of this breakfast they thought they should surfeit of a dinner and supper of the same. No hope of conquest, except with cloying the jaws of death, and thrusting men on the mouth of the cannon. Wherefore, fearing to find the proverb true, that "gold may be bought too dear," they returned to their ships. Drake afterwards fired Nombre de Dios, and many other petty towns (whose treasure the Spaniards had conveyed away), burning the empty casks, when their precious liquor was run out before, and then prepared for their returning home.

Great was the difference betwixt the Indian cities now, from what they were when Drake first haunted these coasts. At first, the Spaniards here were safe and secure, counting their treasure sufficient to defend itself, the remoteness thereof being the greatest (almost only) resistance, and the fetching of it more than

the fighting for it. Whilst the king of Spain guarded the head and heart of his dominions in Europe, he left his long legs in America open to blows; till, finding them to smart, being beaten black and blue by the English, he learned to arm them at last, fortifying the most important of them to make them impregnable.

Now began Sir Francis's discontent to feed upon him. He conceived, that expectation, a merciless usurer, computing each day since his departure, exacted an interest and return of honour and profit proportionable to his great preparations, and transcending his former achievements. He saw that all the good which he had done in this voyage, consisted in the evil he had done to the Spaniards afar off, whereof he could present but small visible fruits in England. These apprehensions, accompanying, if not causing, the disease of the flux, wrought his sudden death, January 28th, 1595. And sickness did not so much untie his clothes, as sorrow did rend at once the robe of his mortality asunder. He lived by the sea, died on it, and was buried in it. Thus an extempore performance (scarce heard to be begun, before we hear it is ended!) comes off with better applause, or miscarries with less disgrace, than a long-studied and openly-premeditated action. Besides, we see how great spirits, having mounted to the highest pitch of performance, afterwards strain and break their credits in striving to go beyond it. Lastly, God oftentimes leaves the brightest men in an eclipse, to show that they do but borrow their lustre from his reflexion. We will not justify all the actions of any man, though of a tamer profession than a sea-captain, in whom civility is often counted preciseness. For the main, we say that this our captain was a religious man towards God and his houses (generally sparing churches where he came), chaste in his life, just in his dealings, true of his word, and merciful to those that were under him, hating nothing so much as idleness: and therefore, lest his soul should rest in peace, at spare hours he brought fresh water to Plymouth.[1] Careful he was for posterity (though men of his profession have as well an ebb of riot, as a float of fortune) and providently raised a

[1] *He was a member of the parliamentary commission for establishing a system of water-works there.*

worshipful family of his kindred. In a word: should those that speak against him fast till they fetch their bread where he did his, they would have a good stomach[1] to eat it.

JOHN MILTON (1608–1674)

ON THE MORNING OF CHRIST'S NATIVITY

(*Composed 1629*)

This is the month, and this the happy morn,
Wherein the Son of Heaven's eternal King,
Of wedded maid and virgin mother born,
Our great redemption from above did bring;
For so the holy sages once did sing,   5
   That he our deadly forfeit should release,
And with his Father work us a perpetual
   peace.

That glorious form, that light unsufferable,
And that far-beaming blaze of majesty,
Wherewith he wont at Heaven's high council-
   table   10
To sit the midst of Trinal Unity,
He laid aside; and here with us to be,
   Forsook the courts of everlasting day,
And chose with us a darksome house of mortal
   clay.

Say, Heavenly Muse, shall not thy sacred
   vein   15
Afford a present to the Infant God?
Hast thou no verse, no hymn, or solemn strain,
To welcome him to this his new abode,
Now while the heaven, by the sun's team un-
   trod,
   Hath took no print of the approaching light,
And all the spangled host keep watch in
   squadrons bright?   21

See how from far upon the eastern road
The star-led wizards[2] haste with odours sweet!
O run, prevent[3] them with thy humble ode,
And lay it lowly at his blessed feet;   25
Have thou the honour first thy Lord to greet,
   And join thy voice unto the angel quire,
From out his secret altar touched with hal-
   lowed fire.

    [1] appetite   [2] wise men   [3] precede

THE HYMN

It was the winter wild,
While the heaven-born child   30
   All meanly wrapt in the rude manger lies;
Nature, in awe to him,
Had doffed her gaudy trim,
   With her great Master so to sympathize:
It was no season then for her   35
To wanton[1] with the sun, her lusty paramour.[2]

Only with speeches fair
She woos the gentle air
   To hide her guilty front with innocent snow,
And on her naked shame,   40
Pollute[3] with sinful blame,
   The saintly veil of maiden white to throw;
Confounded, that her Maker's eyes
Should look so near upon her foul deformities.

But he, her fears to cease,   45
Sent down the meek-eyed Peace:
   She, crowned with olive green, came softly
    sliding
Down through the turning sphere,
His ready harbinger,
   With turtle[4] wing the amorous clouds
    dividing;   50
And waving wide her myrtle wand,
She strikes a universal peace through sea and
   land.

No war, or battle's sound,
Was heard the world around;
   The idle spear and shield were high up-
    hung;   55
The hookèd[5] chariot stood
Unstained with hostile blood;
   The trumpet spake not to the armèd throng;
And kings sat still with awful eye,
As if they surely knew their sovran Lord was
   by.   60

But peaceful was the night
Wherein the Prince of Light
   His reign of peace upon the earth began:
The winds, with wonder whist,[6]
Smoothly the waters kissed,   65
   Whispering new joys to the mild ocean,
Who now hath quite forgot to rave,
While birds of calm sit brooding on the
   charmèd wave.

    [1] sport   [2] lover   [3] polluted   [4] turtle dove   [5] pro-
vided with scythes at the hubs   [6] silenced

The stars with deep amaze,
Stand fixed in steadfast gaze,   70
    Bending one way their precious influence,
And will not take their flight,
For all the morning light,
    Or Lucifer that often warned them thence;
But in their glimmering orbs did glow,   75
Until their Lord himself bespake and bid
    them go.

And though the shady gloom
Had given day her room,
    The sun himself withheld his wonted speed,
And hid his head for shame,   80
As[1] his inferior flame
    The new-enlightened world no more should
    need:
He saw a greater Sun appear
Than his bright throne or burning axletree
    could bear.

The shepherds on the lawn,   85
Or ere the point of dawn,
    Sat simply chatting in a rustic row;
Full little thought they than,[2]
That the mighty Pan
    Was kindly come to live with them below: 90
Perhaps their loves, or else their sheep,
Was all that did their silly thoughts so busy
    keep.

When such music sweet
Their hearts and ears did greet
    As never was by mortal finger strook,   95
Divinely-warbled voice
Answering the stringèd noise,
    As all their souls in blissful rapture took:
The air, such pleasure loath to lose,
With thousand echoes still prolongs each
    heavenly close.[3]   100

Nature, that heard such sound
Beneath the hollow round
    Of Cynthia's[4] seat the airy region thrilling,
Now was almost won
To think her part was done,   105
    And that her reign had here its last fulfill-
    ing:
She knew such harmony alone
Could hold all heaven and earth in happier
    union.

[1] as if [2] then [3] conclusion of a musical strain
[4] the moon

At last surrounds their sight
A globe of circular light,   110
    That with long beams the shamefaced night
    arrayed;
The helmèd cherubim
And sworded seraphim
    Are seen in glittering ranks with wings dis-
    played,
Harping in loud and solemn quire,   115
With unexpressive[1] notes, to Heaven's new-
    born heir.

Such music (as 'tis said)
Before was never made,
    But when of old the sons of morning sung,[2]
While the Creator great   120
His constellations set,
    And the well-balanced world on hinges hung,
And cast the dark foundations deep,
And bid the weltering waves their oozy
    channel keep.

Ring out, ye crystal spheres!   •   125
Once bless our human ears
    (If ye have power to touch our senses so),
And let your silver chime
Move in melodious time;
    And let the bass of heaven's deep organ
    blow;
And with your ninefold harmony   131
Make up full consort to the angelic symphony.

For if such holy song
Enwrap our fancy long,
    Time will run back and fetch the age of
    gold;
And speckled Vanity   136
Will sicken soon and die,
    And leprous Sin will melt from earthly
    mould;
And Hell itself will pass away,
And leave her dolorous mansions to the peer-
    ing day.   140

Yea, Truth and Justice then
Will down return to men,
    Orbed in a rainbow; and, like glories
    wearing,
Mercy will sit between,
Throned in celestial sheen,   145
    With radiant feet the tissued[3] clouds down
    steering;

[1] inexpressible [2] cf. *Job* xxxviii: 7 [3] rich, as if
woven with threads of silver and gold

And Heaven, as at some festival,
Will open wide the gates of her high Palace
   Hall.

But wisest Fate says no,
This must not yet be so ;   150
   The Babe yet lies in smiling infancy
That on the bitter cross
Must redeem our loss,
So both himself and us to glorify :
Yet first, to those ychained in sleep,   155
   The wakeful trump of doom must thunder
      through the deep,

With such a horrid clang
As on Mount Sinai rang,
   While the red fire and smouldering clouds
      outbrake :
The aged earth, aghast   160
With terror of that blast,
   Shall from the surface to the centre shake,
When at the world's last session,
The dreadful Judge in middle air shall spread
   his throne.

And then at last our bliss   165
Full and perfect is,
   But now begins ; for from this happy day
The old Dragon[1] under ground,
In straiter limits bound,
   Not half so far casts his usurpèd sway ;   170
And wroth to see his kingdom fail,
Swinges the scaly horror of his folded tail.

The oracles are dumb,
No voice or hideous hum
   Runs through the archèd roof in words de-
      ceiving.   175
Apollo from his shrine
Can no more divine,
   With hollow shriek the steep of Delphos[2]
      leaving.
No nightly trance, or breathèd spell,
Inspires the pale-eyed priest from the pro-
   phetic cell.   180

The lonely mountains o'er,
And the resounding shore,
   A voice of weeping heard and loud lament ;
From haunted spring, and dale
Edged with poplar pale,   185
   The parting Genius is with sighing sent ;

[1] Satan [2] *Delphi, where Apollo had a temple, is
perhaps confused with Delos, where he also had one.*

With flower-inwoven tresses torn
The Nymphs in twilight shade of tangled
   thickets mourn.

In consecrated earth,
And on the holy hearth,   190
   The Lars and Lemures[1] moan with midnight
      plaint ;
In urns and altars round,
A drear and dying sound
   Affrights the flamens at their service quaint ;
And the chill marble seems to sweat,   195
While each peculiar power forgoes his wonted
   seat.

Peor and Baälim[2]
Forsake their temples dim,
   With that twice-battered god of Pales-
      tine ;[3]
And moonèd Ashtaroth,[4]   200
Heaven's queen and mother both,
   Now sits not girt with tapers' holy shine ;
The Libyc Hammon[5] shrinks his horn ;
In vain the Tyrian maids their wounded
   Thammuz mourn.[6]

And sullen Moloch, fled,[2]   205
Hath left in shadows dread
   His burning idol all of blackest hue ;
In vain with cymbals' ring
They call the grisly king,
   In dismal dance about the furnace blue ;   210
The brutish gods of Nile as fast,
Isis[7] and Orus[8] and the dog Anubis, haste.

Nor is Osiris[9] seen
In Memphian grove or green,
   Trampling the unshowered[10] grass with low-
      ings loud ;   215
Nor can he be at rest
Within his sacred chest ;[11]
   Naught but profoundest Hell can be his
      shroud ;
In vain, with timbrelled anthems dark,
The sable-stolèd sorcerers bear his worshipped
   ark.   220

[1] ghosts [2] cf. *Par. Lost*, I, 392–482 [3] See 1
Sam. v : 3 and 4 [4] cf. *Par. Lost*, I, 438 ff. [5] an
Egyptian deity represented with large curving
horns [6] cf. *Par. Lost*, I, 446 ff. [7] wife of Osiris
[8] son of Isis [9] *Osiris in the form of Apis, was the
bull god of Memphis.* [10] *It does not rain in Egypt.*
[11] *Isis gathered the scattered limbs of Osiris, who was
cut to pieces by his brother.*

He feels from Juda's land
The dreaded Infant's hand;
  The rays of Bethlehem blind his dusky eyn;
Nor all the gods beside
Longer dare abide,   225
  Not Typhon[1] huge, ending in snaky twine:
Our Babe, to show his Godhead true,
Can in his swaddling bands control the
    damnèd crew.

So when the sun in bed,
Curtained with cloudy red,   230
  Pillows his chin upon an orient wave,
The flocking shadows pale
Troop to the infernal jail,
  Each fettered ghost slips to his several
    grave,
And the yellow-skirted fays   235
Fly after the night-steeds, leaving their
    moon-loved maze.

But see! the Virgin blest
Hath laid her Babe to rest.
  Time is our tedious song should here have
    ending:
Heaven's youngest-teemèd[2] star   240
Hath fixed her polished car,
  Her sleeping Lord with handmaid lamp
    attending;
And all about the courtly stable
Bright-harnessed[3] angels sit in order service-
  able.

L'ALLEGRO

Hence, loathèd Melancholy,
  Of Cerberus and blackest Midnight born
In Stygian cave forlorn,
  'Mongst horrid shapes and shrieks and
    sights unholy!
Find out some uncouth cell,   5
  Where brooding darkness spreads his jeal-
    ous wings,
And the night-raven sings;
  There under ebon shades and low-browed
    rocks,
As ragged as thy locks,
  In dark Cimmerian desert ever dwell.   10
But come, thou Goddess fair and free,
In heaven yclept[4] Euphrosyne,
And by men heart-easing Mirth;
Whom lovely Venus, at a birth,

With two sister Graces more,   15
To ivy-crownèd Bacchus bore;
Or whether (as some sager sing)
The frolic wind that breathes the spring,
Zephyr, with Aurora playing,
As he met her once a-Maying,   20
There on beds of violets blue
And fresh-blown roses washed in dew,
Filled her with thee, a daughter fair,
So buxom, blithe, and debonair.
Haste thee, nymph, and bring with thee   25
Jest, and youthful Jollity,
Quips and cranks and wanton wiles,
Nods and becks and wreathèd smiles,
Such as hang on Hebe's cheek,
And love to live in dimple sleek;   30
Sport that wrinkled Care derides,
And Laughter, holding both his sides.
Come, and trip it as you go,
On the light fantastic toe;
And in thy right hand lead with thee   35
The mountain nymph, sweet Liberty;
And if I give thee honour due,
Mirth, admit me of thy crew,
To live with her, and live with thee,
In unreprovèd pleasures free: 40
To hear the lark begin his flight,
And singing, startle the dull night,
From his watch-tower in the skies,
Till the dappled dawn doth rise;
Then to come in spite of sorrow,   45
And at my window bid good-morrow,
Through the sweet-briar or the vine,
Or the twisted eglantine;
While the cock, with lively din,
Scatters the rear of darkness thin,   50
And to the stack, or the barn-door,
Stoutly struts his dames before:
Oft listening how the hounds and horn
Cheerly rouse the slumbering morn,
From the side of some hoar hill,   55
Through the high wood echoing shrill:
Sometime walking, not unseen,
By hedge-row elms, on hillocks green,
Right against the eastern gate
Where the great sun begins his state,   60
Robed in flames and amber light,
The clouds in thousand liveries dight;
While the ploughman, near at hand,
Whistles o'er the furrowed land,
And the milkmaid singeth blithe,   65
And the mower whets his scythe,
And every shepherd tells his tale[1]

[1] a monster of Greek mythology   [2] newest born,
the star of Bethlehem   [3] in bright armor   [4] called

[1] counts his flock

Under the hawthorn in the dale.
Straight mine eye hath caught new pleasures
Whilst the landskip[1] round it measures: 70
Russet lawns and fallows grey,
Where the nibbling flocks do stray;
Mountains on whose barren breast
The labouring clouds do often rest;
Meadows trim with daisies pied,   75
Shallow brooks and rivers wide;
Towers and battlements it sees
Bosomed high in tufted trees,
Where perhaps some beauty lies,
The cynosure[2] of neighbouring eyes.   80
Hard by, a cottage chimney smokes
From betwixt two aged oaks,
Where Corydon and Thyrsis met
Are at their savoury dinner set
Of herbs and other country messes,   85
Which the neat-handed Phillis dresses;
And then in haste her bower she leaves,
With Thestylis to bind the sheaves;
Or, if the earlier season lead,
To the tanned haycock in the mead.   90
Sometimes, with secure[3] delight,
The upland hamlets will invite,
When the merry bells ring round,
And the jocund rebecks sound
To many a youth and many a maid   95
Dancing in the chequered shade;
And young and old come forth to play
On a sunshine holiday,
Till the livelong daylight fail:
Then to the spicy nut-brown ale,   100
With stories told of many a feat,
How faery Mab the junkets eat.
She[4] was pinched and pulled, she said;
And he,[5] by friar's lantern led,
Tells how the drudging goblin sweat   105
To earn his cream-bowl duly set,
When in one night, ere glimpse of morn,
His shadowy flail hath threshed the corn
That ten day-labourers could not end;
Then lies him down, the lubber fiend,   110
And, stretched out all the chimney's length,
Basks at the fire his hairy strength,
And crop-full out of doors he flings,
Ere the first cock his matin rings.
Thus done the tales, to bed they creep,   115
By whispering winds soon lulled asleep.
Towered cities please us then,
And the busy hum of men,

Where throngs of knights and barons bold,
In weeds[1] of peace high triumphs hold,   120
With store of ladies, whose bright eyes
Rain influence,[2] and judge the prize
Of wit or arms, while both contend
To win her grace whom all commend.
There let Hymen[3] oft appear   125
In saffron robe, with taper clear,
And pomp and feast and revelry,
With mask and antique pageantry;
Such sights as youthful poets dream
On summer eves by haunted stream.   130
Then to the well-trod stage anon,
If Jonson's learnèd sock[4] be on,
Or sweetest Shakespear, Fancy's child,
Warble his native wood-notes wild.
And ever, against eating cares,   135
Lap me in soft Lydian airs,
Married to immortal verse,
Such as the meeting soul may pierce,
In notes with many a winding bout
Of linkèd sweetness long drawn out,   140
With wanton heed and giddy cunning,
The melting voice through mazes running,
Untwisting all the chains that tie
The hidden soul of harmony;
That Orpheus' self may heave his head   145
From golden slumber on a bed
Of heaped Elysian flowers, and hear
Such strains as would have won the ear
Of Pluto to have quite set free
His half-regained Eurydice.   150
These delights if thou canst give,
Mirth, with thee I mean to live.

IL PENSEROSO

Hence, vain deluding Joys,
    The brood of Folly without father bred!
How little you bested,[5]
    Or fill the fixèd mind with all your toys?
Dwell in some idle brain,   5
    And fancies fond[6] with gaudy shapes possess,
As thick and numberless
    As the gay motes that people the sun-beams,
Or likest hovering dreams,
    The fickle pensioners of Morpheus' train.   10
But hail, thou Goddess sage and holy,
Hail, divinest Melancholy!

---

[1] landscape   [2] *Phœnician sailors steered by the
constellation of the Little Bear, Cynosura.*   [3] carefree
[4] one speaker   [5] another

[1] garments   [2] *Originally* influence *meant the power
of the stars over human affairs.*   [3] cf. *Epithalamion*,
ll. 25 ff.   [4] cf. Jonson's lines on Shakespeare, ll. 36–7
[5] aid   [6] foolish

Whose saintly visage is too bright
To hit the sense of human sight,
And therefore to our weaker view   15
O'erlaid with black, staid Wisdom's hue;
Black, but such as in esteem
Prince Memnon's sister[1] might beseem,
Or that starred Ethiop queen[2] that strove
To set her beauty's praise above   20
The sea nymphs, and their powers offended.
Yet thou art higher far descended:
Thee bright-haired Vesta long of yore
To solitary Saturn bore;
His daughter she (in Saturn's reign   25
Such mixture was not held a stain).
Oft in glimmering bowers and glades
He met her, and in secret shades
Of woody Ida's inmost grove,
Whilst yet there was no fear of Jove.   30
Come, pensive Nun, devout and pure,
Sober, steadfast, and demure,
All in a robe of darkest grain,[3]
Flowing with majestic train,
And sable stole of cypress lawn[4]   35
Over thy decent shoulders drawn.
Come, but keep thy wonted state,
With even step, and musing gait,
And looks commercing with the skies,
Thy rapt soul sitting in thine eyes: 40
There, held in holy passion still,
Forget thyself to marble, till
With a sad leaden downward cast
Thou fix them on the earth as fast.
And join with thee calm Peace, and Quiet,   45
Spare Fast, that oft with gods doth diet,
And hears the Muses in a ring
Aye round about Jove's altar sing;
And add to these retired Leisure,
That in trim gardens takes his pleasure;   50
But first, and chiefest, with thee bring
Him that yon[5] soars on golden wing,
Guiding the fiery-wheelèd throne,
The cherub Contemplation;
And the mute Silence hist along,   55
'Less Philomel[6] will deign a song,
In her sweetest, saddest plight,
Smoothing the rugged brow of Night,
While Cynthia checks her dragon yoke[7]
Gently o'er the accustomed oak: 60
Sweet bird,[6] that shunn'st the noise of folly,

[1] Hemera, presumably very beautiful though
black   [2] Cassiopea, who offended the Nereids; and
after her death was placed among the stars   [3] dye
[4] crape   [5] yonder   [6] the nightingale   [7] *The chariot of
the moon, Cynthia, was drawn by dragons.*

Most musical, most melancholy!
Thee, chauntress, oft the woods among,
I woo to hear thy even-song;
And missing thee, I walk unseen   65
On the dry smooth-shaven green,
To behold the wandering moon,
Riding near her highest noon,
Like one that had been led astray
Through the heaven's wide pathless way,   70
And oft, as if her head she bowed,
Stooping through a fleecy cloud.
Oft on a plat of rising ground,
I hear the far-off curfew sound,
Over some wide-watered shore,   75
Swinging slow with sullen roar;
Or if the air will not permit,
Some still removèd place will fit,
Where glowing embers through the room
Teach light to counterfeit a gloom,   80
Far from all resort of mirth,
Save the cricket on the hearth,
Or the bellman's drowsy charm
To bless the doors from nightly harm.
Or let my lamp at midnight hour   85
Be seen in some high lonely tower,
Where I may oft out-watch the Bear,
With thrice-great Hermes; or unsphere
The spirit of Plato, to unfold
What worlds or what vast regions hold   90
The immortal mind that hath forsook
Her mansion in this fleshly nook;
And of those demons that are found
In fire, air, flood, or underground,
Whose power hath a true consent   95
With planet or with element.
Sometime let gorgeous Tragedy
In sceptred pall come sweeping by,
Presenting Thebes', or Pelops' line,
Or the tale of Troy divine,   100
Or what (though rare) of later age
Ennobled hath the buskined[1] stage.
But, O sad Virgin! that thy power
Might raise Musæus from his bower;
Or bid the soul of Orpheus sing   105
Such notes as, warbled to the string,
Drew iron tears down Pluto's cheek,
And made Hell grant what love did seek;
Or call up him that left half-told
The story of Cambuscan bold,   110
Of Camball, and of Algarsife,
And who had Canace to wife,
That owned the virtuous[2] ring and glass,
And of the wondrous horse of brass

[1] tragic   [2] powerful

On which the Tartar king did ride;   115
And if aught else great bards beside
In sage and solemn tunes have sung,
Of turneys, and of trophies hung,
Of forests, and enchantments drear,
Where more is meant than meets the ear.   120
Thus, Night, oft see me in thy pale career,
Till civil-suited[1] Morn appear,
Not tricked and frounced as she was wont
With the Attic boy to hunt,
But kerchieft in a comely cloud,   125
While rocking winds are piping loud,
Or ushered with a shower still,
When the gust hath blown his fill,
Ending on the rustling leaves,
With minute-drops[2] from off the eaves.   130
And when the sun begins to fling
His flaring beams, me, Goddess, bring
To archèd walks of twilight groves,
And shadows brown, that Sylvan[3] loves,
Of pine, or monumental oak,   135
Where the rude axe with heavèd stroke
Was never heard the nymphs to daunt,
Or fright them from their hallowed haunt.
There in close covert by some brook,
Where no profaner eye may look,   140
Hide me from day's garish eye,
While the bee with honeyed thigh,
That at her flowery work doth sing,
And the waters murmuring,
With such consort as they keep,   145
Entice the dewy-feathered Sleep;
And let some strange mysterious dream
Wave at his wings in airy stream
Of lively portraiture displayed,
Softly on my eyelids laid;   150
And as I wake, sweet music breathe
Above, about, or underneath,
Sent by some spirit to mortals good,
Or the unseen Genius of the wood.
But let my due feet never fail   155
To walk the studious cloister's pale,[4]
And love the high embowèd roof,
With antique pillars massy proof,
And storied[5] windows richly dight,
Casting a dim religious light.   160
There let the pealing organ blow,
To the full-voiced quire below,
In service high and anthems clear,
As may with sweetness, through mine ear,
Dissolve me into ecstasies,   165
And bring all Heaven before mine eyes.

---

[1] soberly attired [2] slow drops [3] god of forests
[4] confines, limits [5] with pictures in stained glass

And may at last my weary age
Find out the peaceful hermitage,
The hairy gown, and mossy cell,
Where I may sit and rightly spell[1]   170
Of every star that heaven doth shew,
And every herb that sips the dew,
Till old experience do attain
To something like prophetic strain.
    These pleasures, Melancholy, give,   175
And I with thee will choose to live.

LYCIDAS

*In this Monody the Author bewails a learned
Friend, unfortunately drowned in his passage
from Chester on the Irish Seas, 1637;
and by occasion foretells the ruin
of our corrupted Clergy, then
in their height.*

Yet once more, O ye laurels, and once more,
Ye myrtles brown, with ivy never sere,[2]
I come to pluck your berries harsh and crude,[3]
And with forced fingers rude
Shatter your leaves before the mellowing year.
Bitter constraint and sad occasion dear   6
Compels me to disturb your season due;
For Lycidas is dead, dead ere his prime,
Young Lycidas, and hath not left his peer.
Who would not sing for Lycidas? he knew 10
Himself[4] to sing, and build the lofty rhyme.
He must not float upon his watery bier
Unwept, and welter to the parching wind,
Without the meed of some melodious tear.
    Begin then, Sisters of the sacred well[5]   15
That from beneath the seat of Jove doth
            spring;
Begin, and somewhat loudly sweep the string.
Hence with denial vain and coy excuse;
So may some gentle Muse[6]
With lucky words favour my destined urn,
And as he passes turn,   21
And bid fair peace be to my sable shroud.
    For we were nursed upon the self-same hill,
Fed the same flock, by fountain, shade, and
            rill;
Together both, ere the high lawns appeared 25
Under the opening eyelids of the morn,
We drove a-field, and both together heard
What time the gray-fly winds her sultry horn,
Battening[7] our flocks with the fresh dews of
            night,

---

[1] interpret [2] dry [3] unripe [4] *Supply* how: [5] the
Muses [6] poet [7] feeding

Oft till the star that rose at evening, bright,
Toward heaven's descent had sloped his west-
   ering wheel.   31
Meanwhile the rural ditties were not mute,
Tempered to the oaten flute;
Rough Satyrs danced, and Fauns with cloven
   heel
From the glad sound would not be absent
   long;
And old Damœtas loved to hear our song. 36
   But O the heavy change, now thou art gone,
Now thou art gone, and never must return!
Thee, Shepherd, thee the woods and desert
   caves,
With wild thyme and the gadding vine o'er-
   grown,
And all their echoes, mourn.   41
The willows and the hazel copses green
Shall now no more be seen,
Fanning their joyous leaves to thy soft lays.
As killing as the canker to the rose,   45
Or taint-worm to the weanling herds that
   graze,
Or frost to flowers, that their gay wardrobe
   wear,
When first the white-thorn blows;
Such, Lycidas, thy loss to shepherd's ear.
   Where were ye, Nymphs, when the remorse-
   less deep   50
Closed o'er the head of your loved Lycidas?
For neither were ye playing on the steep
Where your old bards, the famous Druids, lie,
Nor on the shaggy top of Mona[1] high,
Nor yet where Deva[2] spreads her wizard
   stream.
Ay me, I fondly dream!   56
Had ye been there — for what could that have
   done?
What could the Muse[3] herself that Orpheus
   bore,
The Muse herself, for her enchanting son,
Whom universal nature did lament,   60
When by the rout[4] that made the hideous roar
His gory visage down the stream was sent,
Down the swift Hebrus to the Lesbian shore?
   Alas! what boots it with uncessant care
To tend the homely, slighted, shepherd's
   trade,
And strictly meditate the thankless Muse? 66
Were it not better done, as others use,
To sport with Amaryllis in the shade,
Or with the tangles of Neæra's hair?

[1] the isle of Anglesey [2] the river Dee [3] Calliope
[4] mob

Fame is the spur that the clear spirit doth
   raise
(That last infirmity of noble mind)   71
To scorn delights and live laborious days;
But the fair guerdon when we hope to find,
And think to burst out into sudden blaze, 74
Comes the blind Fury[1] with the abhorrèd
   shears,
And slits the thin-spun life. "But not the
   praise,"
Phœbus replied, and touched my trembling
   ears:
"Fame is no plant that grows on mortal soil
Nor in the glistering foil   79
Set off to the world, nor in broad rumour lies;
But lives and spreads aloft by those pure eyes
And perfect witness of all-judging Jove;
As he pronounces lastly on each deed,
Of so much fame in heaven expect thy meed."
   O fountain Arethuse, and thou honoured
   flood,   85
Smooth-sliding Mincius, crowned with vocal
   reeds,
That strain I heard was of a higher mood:
But now my oat[2] proceeds,
And listens to the herald of the sea,
That came in Neptune's plea.   90
He asked the waves, and asked the felon
   winds,
What hard mishap hath doomed this gentle
   swain?
And questioned every gust of rugged wings
That blows from off each beakèd promontory:
They knew not of his story;   95
And sage Hippotades their answer brings,
That not a blast was from his dungeon strayed;
The air was calm, and on the level brine
Sleek Panope with all her sisters played.
It was that fatal and perfidious bark,   100
Built in the eclipse, and rigged with curses
   dark,
That sunk so low that sacred head of thine.
   Next Camus, reverend sire, went footing
   slow,
His mantle hairy, and his bonnet sedge,
Inwrought with figures dim, and on the edge
Like to that sanguine flower inscribed with
   woe.   106
"Ah! who hath reft,"[3] quoth he, "my dearest
   pledge?"
Last came, and last did go,
The pilot of the Galilean lake;[4]

[1] Atropos, the Fate who severs the thread of
life [2] shepherd's pipe [3] taken away [4] St. Peter

Two massy keys he bore of metals twain 110
(The golden opes, the iron shuts amain).
He shook his mitred locks, and stern bespake:
"How well could I have spared for thee, young
    swain,
Enough of such as for their bellies' sake,
Creep and intrude and climb into the fold!
Of other care they little reckoning make 116
Than how to scramble at the shearers' feast,
And shove away the worthy bidden guest.
Blind mouths! that scarce themselves know
    how to hold
A sheep-hook, or have learnt aught else the
    least
That to the faithful herdman's art belongs!
What recks it them? What need they?
    They are sped;¹ 122
And when they list, their lean and flashy songs
Grate on their scrannel² pipes of wretched
    straw;
The hungry sheep look up, and are not fed,
But swoln with wind and the rank mist they
    draw, 126
Rot inwardly, and foul contagion spread;
Besides what the grim wolf with privy paw
Daily devours apace, and nothing said.
But that two-handed engine at the door 130
Stands ready to smite once, and smite no
    more."
  Return, Alpheus; the dread voice is past
That shrunk thy streams; return, Sicilian
    Muse,
And call the vales, and bid them hither cast
Their bells and flowrets of a thousand hues.
Ye valleys low, where the mild whispers use
Of shades and wanton winds and gushing
    brooks, 137
On whose fresh lap the swart³ star sparely
    looks,
Throw hither all your quaint enamelled eyes,
That on the green turf suck the honeyed
    showers, 140
And purple all the ground with vernal flowers.
Bring the rathe primrose that forsaken dies,
The tufted crow-toe, and pale jessamine,
The white pink, and the pansy freaked with
    jet,
The glowing violet, 145
The musk-rose, and the well-attired woodbine,
With cowslips wan that hang the pensive
    head,
And every flower that sad embroidery wears;

Bid amaranthus all his beauty shed,
And daffodillies fill their cups with tears, 150
To strew the laureate hearse where Lycid lies.
For so to interpose a little ease,
Let our frail thoughts dally with false surmise,
Ay me! whilst thee the shores and sounding
    seas
Wash far away, where'er thy bones are hurled;
Whether beyond the stormy Hebrides, 156
Where thou perhaps under the whelming tide
Visit'st the bottom of the monstrous world;¹
Or whether thou, to our moist² vows denied,
Sleep'st by the fable of Bellerus old, 160
Where the great vision of the guarded mount
Looks toward Namancos and Bayona's hold.
Look homeward, Angel, now, and melt with
    ruth;³
And O ye dolphins, waft the hapless youth.
  Weep no more, woeful shepherds, weep no
    more,
For Lycidas, your sorrow,⁴ is not dead, 166
Sunk though he be beneath the watery floor;
So sinks the day-star in the ocean bed,
And yet anon repairs his drooping head,
And tricks his beams, and with new-spangled
    ore
Flames in the forehead of the morning sky:
So Lycidas sunk low, but mounted high, 172
Through the dear might of him that walked
    the waves,
Where, other groves and other streams along,
With nectar pure his oozy locks he laves, 175
And hears the unexpressive⁵ nuptial song,
In the blest kingdoms meek of joy and love.
There entertain him all the saints above,
In solemn troops and sweet societies,
That sing, and singing in their glory move, 180
And wipe the tears for ever from his eyes.
Now, Lycidas, the shepherds weep no more;
Henceforth thou art the Genius of the shore,
In thy large recompense, and shalt be good
To all that wander in that perilous flood. 185
  Thus sang the uncouth swain to the oaks
    and rills,
While the still morn went out with sandals
    gray;
He touched the tender stops of various quills,
With eager thought warbling his Doric lay:
And now the sun had stretched out all the hills,
And now was dropt into the western bay. 191
At last he rose, and twitched his mantle blue:
To-morrow to fresh woods and pastures new.

---

¹ They have what they wish ² thin, slender
³ dark, injurious

¹ world of monsters ² tear-wet ³ pity ⁴ the
object of your sorrow ⁵ inexpressible

AE

ON HIS HAVING ARRIVED AT THE AGE OF TWENTY-THREE

How soon hath Time, the subtle thief of
    youth,
  Stolen on his wing my three and twentieth
    year!
My hasting days fly on with full career,
But my late spring no bud or blossom
    shew'th.
Perhaps my semblance might deceive the
    truth   5
  That I to manhood am arrived so near;
  And inward ripeness doth much less ap-
    pear,
  That some more timely-happy spirits
    endu'th.
Yet be it less or more, or soon or slow,
  It shall be still in strictest measure even 10
To that same lot, however mean or high,
Toward which Time leads me, and the will of
    Heaven;
All is, if I have grace to use it so,
As ever in my great Task-Master's eye.

WHEN THE ASSAULT WAS IN-TENDED TO THE CITY

Captain, or Colonel,[1] or Knight in arms,
  Whose chance on these defenceless doors
    may seize,
  If ever deed of honour did thee please,
  Guard them, and him within protect from
    harms.
He can requite thee; for he knows the
    charms
  That call fame on such gentle acts as
    these,
  And he can spread thy name o'er lands and
    seas,   7
  Whatever clime the sun's bright circle
    warms.
Lift not thy spear against the Muses' bower:
  The great Emathian conqueror [2] bid spare
  The house of Pindarus, when temple and
    tower   11
Went to the ground; and the repeated air
  Of sad Electra's poet[3] had the power
  To save the Athenian walls from ruin
    bare.

[1] *Pronounced trisyllabic*   [2] Alexander the Great
[3] Euripides

TO THE LORD GENERAL CROMWELL

MAY, 1652

*On the Proposals of Certain Ministers at the
Committee for Propagation of the Gospel*

Cromwell, our chief of men, who through a
    cloud
  Not of war only, but detractions rude,
  Guided by faith and matchless fortitude,
  To peace and truth thy glorious way hast
    ploughed,
And on the neck of crownèd Fortune proud 5
  Hast reared God's trophies, and his work
    pursued,
  While Darwen stream,[1] with blood of Scots
    imbrued,
  And Dunbar field,[2] resounds thy praises
    loud,
And Worcester's[3] laureate wreath: yet much
    remains
  To conquer still; peace hath her victories
  No less renowned than war: new foes
    arise,   11
Threatening to bind our souls with secular
    chains.
  Help us to save free conscience from the paw
  Of hireling wolves, whose gospel is their
    maw.[4]

ON THE LATE MASSACRE IN PIEDMONT

Avenge, O Lord, thy slaughtered saints, whose
    bones
  Lie scattered on the Alpine mountains cold;
  Even them who kept thy truth so pure of old
  When all our fathers worshipped stocks
    and stones,
Forget not: in thy book record their groans 5
  Who were thy sheep, and in their ancient
    fold
  Slain by the bloody Piemontese, that rolled
  Mother with infant down the rocks. Their
    moans
The vales redoubled to the hills, and they
  To heaven. Their martyred blood and
    ashes sow   10
  O'er all the Italian fields, where still doth
    sway

[1] near Preston, where Cromwell defeated the
royalist Scots in Aug., 1648 [2] Sept., 1650 [3] Sept.,
1651 [4] Cf. *Lycidas*, ll. 113-131.

The triple tyrant;[1] that from these may grow
A hundredfold, who, having learnt thy way,
Early may fly the Babylonian woe.[2]

ON HIS BLINDNESS

When I consider how my light is spent
  Ere half my days, in this dark world and
    wide,
  And that one talent[3] which is death to hide
Lodged with me useless, though my soul
    more bent
To serve therewith my Maker, and present 5
  My true account, lest he returning chide;
  "Doth God exact day-labour, light denied?"
I fondly ask. But Patience, to prevent
That murmur, soon replies, "God doth not
    need
  Either man's work or his own gifts. Who
    best   10
  Bear his mild yoke, they serve him best.
    His state
Is kingly: thousands at his bidding speed,
  And post o'er land and ocean without rest;
  They also serve who only stand and wait."

TO CYRIACK SKINNER

Cyriack, this three years' day these eyes,
    though clear
  To outward view, of blemish or of spot,
  Bereft of light, their seeing have forgot;
Nor to their idle orbs doth sight appear
Of sun or moon or star throughout the year, 5
  Or man or woman. Yet I argue not
  Against Heaven's hand or will, nor bate a
    jot
Of heart or hope, but still bear up and steer
Right onward. What supports me, dost thou
    ask?
  The conscience,[4] friend, to have lost them
    overplied   10
In liberty's defence, my noble task,
Of which all Europe talks from side to side.
  This thought might lead me through the
    world's vain mask
  Content, though blind, had I no better
    guide.

[1] the Pope (alluding to his triple crown) [2] *The
Puritans interpreted the biblical denunciations
of Babylon as directed prophetically against the
Catholic Church.* [3] his ability to write [4] consciousness

PARADISE LOST

BOOK I

Of Man's first disobedience, and the fruit
Of that forbidden tree, whose mortal [1] taste
Brought death into the world, and all our woe,
With loss of Eden, till one greater Man
Restore us, and regain the blissful seat,   5
Sing, Heavenly Muse, that on the secret top
Of Oreb,[2] or of Sinai,[2] didst inspire
That shepherd who first taught the chosen
    seed
In the beginning how the Heavens and Earth
Rose out of Chaos: or, if Sion hill   10
Delight thee more, and Siloa's brook that
    flowed
Fast by [3] the oracle of God, I thence
Invoke thy aid to my adventurous song,
That with no middle flight intends to soar
Above the Aonian mount,[4] while it pursues 15
Things unattempted yet in prose or rhyme.
And chiefly Thou, O Spirit, that dost prefer
Before all temples the upright heart and pure,
Instruct me, for Thou know'st; Thou from
    the first
Wast present, and, with mighty wings out-
    spread,   20
Dove-like sat'st brooding on the vast Abyss,
And mad'st it pregnant: what in me is dark
Illumine, what is low raise and support;
That to the highth of this great argument [5]
I may assert Eternal Providence,   25
And justify the ways of God to men.
  Say first — for Heaven hides nothing from
    Thy view,
Nor the deep tract of Hell — say first what
    cause
Moved our grand parents, in that happy state,
Favoured of Heaven so highly, to fall off   30
From their Creator, and transgress his will
For one restraint, lords of the world besides.
Who first seduced them to that foul revolt?
  The infernal Serpent; he it was, whose
    guile,   34
Stirred up with envy and revenge, deceived
The mother of mankind, what time [6] his pride
Had cast him out from Heaven, with all his
    host
Of rebel Angels, by whose aid, aspiring

[1] deadly [2] *The Ten Commandments were given on
Horeb or Sinai.* [3] close by [4] Mt. Helicon; here,
figuratively, for Greek poetry [5] subject [6] at the
time when

To set himself in glory above his peers,
He trusted to have equalled the Most High,
If he opposed; and with ambitious aim   41
Against the throne and monarchy of God
Raised impious war in Heaven, and battle
    proud,
With vain attempt. Him the Almighty
    Power
Hurled headlong flaming from the ethereal
    sky,   45
With hideous ruin and combustion, down
To bottomless perdition; there to dwell
In adamantine[1] chains and penal fire,
Who durst defy the Omnipotent to arms.
    Nine times the space that measures day
    and night   50
To mortal men, he with his horrid crew
Lay vanquished, rolling in the fiery gulf,
Confounded, though immortal. But his
    doom
Reserved him to more wrath; for now the
    thought
Both of lost happiness and lasting pain   55
Torments him; round he throws his baleful
    eyes,
That witnessed[2] huge affliction and dismay,
Mixed with obdurate pride and steadfast
    hate.
At once, as far as Angels ken,[3] he views
The dismal situation waste and wild: 60
A dungeon horrible on all sides round
As one great furnace flamed; yet from those
    flames
No light; but rather darkness visible
Served only to discover sights of woe,
Regions of sorrow, doleful shades, where
    peace   65
And rest can never dwell, hope never comes
That comes to all; but torture without end
Still urges, and a fiery deluge, fed
With ever-burning sulphur unconsumed.
Such place Eternal Justice had prepared   70
For those rebellious; here their prison or-
    dained
In utter[4] darkness, and their portion set,
As far removed from God and light of Heaven
As from the centre thrice to the utmost pole.[5]
Oh how unlike the place from whence they
    fell!   75
There the companions of his fall, o'erwhelmed
With floods and whirlwinds of tempestuous
    fire,

---

[1] unbreakable [2] gave evidence of [3] see [4] outer
[5] pole of the universe

He soon discerns; and, weltering by his side,
One next himself in power, and next in crime,
Long after known in Palestine, and named 80
Beëlzebub.   To whom the Arch-Enemy,
And thence in Heaven called Satan, with
    bold words
Breaking the horrid silence, thus began: —
    "If thou beest he — but Oh how fallen!
    how changed
From him, who in the happy realms of light 85
Clothed with transcendent brightness, didst
    outshine
Myriads, though bright! — if he whom mu-
    tual league,
United thoughts and counsels, equal hope
And hazard in the glorious enterprise,
Joined with me once, now misery hath joined
In equal ruin — into what pit thou seest   91
From what highth fallen: so much the
    stronger proved
He with his thunder: and till then who knew
The force of those dire arms? Yet not for
    those,
Nor what the potent Victor in his rage   95
Can else inflict, do I repent, or change,
Though changed in outward lustre, that fixed
    mind,
And high disdain from sense of injured merit,
That with the Mightiest raised me to contend,
And to the fierce contention brought along
Innumerable force of Spirits armed,   101
That durst dislike his reign, and, me preferring,
His utmost power with adverse power opposed
In dubious battle on the plains of Heaven,
And shook his throne. What though the
    field be lost?   105
All is not lost: the unconquerable will,
And study[1] of revenge, immortal hate,
And courage never to submit or yield,
And what is else not to be overcome;   109
That glory never shall his wrath or might
Extort from me. To bow and sue for grace
With suppliant knee, and deify his power
Who, from the terror of this arm, so late
Doubted his empire[2]— that were low indeed;
That were an ignominy and shame beneath
This downfall; since by fate the strength of
    gods   116
And this empyreal[3] substance cannot fail;
Since, through experience of this great event,
In arms not worse, in foresight much ad-
    vanced,

---

[1] continued endeavor [2] authority and power
[3] divine, cf. l. 138

We may with more successful hope resolve
To wage by force or guile eternal war,   121
Irreconcilable to our grand Foe,
Who now triumphs, and in the excess of joy
Sole reigning holds the tyranny of Heaven."
  So spake the apostate Angel, though in pain,   125
Vaunting aloud, but racked with deep despair;
And him thus answered soon his bold compeer : —
  "O Prince ! O Chief of many thronèd powers,
That led the embattled Seraphim to war
Under thy conduct, and, in dreadful deeds
Fearless, endangered Heaven's perpetual King,   131
And put to proof his high supremacy,
Whether upheld by strength, or chance, or fate !
Too well I see and rue the dire event
That with sad overthrow and foul defeat   135
Hath lost us Heaven, and all this mighty host
In horrible destruction laid thus low,
As far as gods and Heavenly essences
Can perish : for the mind and spirit remains
Invincible, and vigor soon returns,   140
Though all our glory extinct, and happy state
Here swallowed up in endless misery.
But what if he our Conqueror (whom I now
Of force,[1] believe almighty, since no less
Than such could have o'erpowered such force as ours)   145
Have left us this our spirit and strength entire,
Strongly to suffer and support our pains,
That we may so suffice his vengeful ire ;
Or do him mightier service, as his thralls
By right of war, whate'er his business be,   150
Here in the heart of Hell to work in fire,
Or do his errands in the gloomy Deep ?
What can it then avail, though yet we feel
Strength undiminished, or eternal being
To undergo eternal punishment ? "   155
  Whereto with speedy words the Arch-Fiend replied : —
"Fallen Cherub, to be weak is miserable,
Doing or suffering : but of this be sure —
To do aught good never will be our task,
But ever to do ill our sole delight,   160
As being the contrary to his high will
Whom we resist. If then his providence
Out of our evil seek to bring forth good,
Our labour must be to pervert that end,
And out of good still to find means of evil ;   165

[1] necessarily

Which ofttimes may succeed so as perhaps
Shall grieve him, if I fail not,[1] and disturb
His inmost counsels from their destined aim.
But see ! the angry Victor hath recalled
His ministers of vengeance and pursuit   170
Back to the gates of Heaven ; the sulphurous hail,
Shot after us in storm, o'erblown hath laid
The fiery surge that from the precipice
Of Heaven received us falling ; and the thunder,
Winged with red lightning and impetuous rage,   175
Perhaps hath spent his [2] shafts, and ceases now
To bellow through the vast and boundless Deep.
Let us not slip the occasion, whether scorn
Or satiate fury yield it from our Foe.
Seest thou yon dreary plain, forlorn and wild,
The seat of desolation, void of light,   181
Save what the glimmering of these livid [3] flames
Casts pale and dreadful ? Thither let us tend [4]
From off the tossing of these fiery waves ;
There rest, if any rest can harbour there ;   185
And, reassembling our afflicted powers,
Consult how we may henceforth most offend [5]
Our Enemy, our own loss how repair,
How overcome this dire calamity,
What reinforcement we may gain from hope,
If not, what resolution from despair."   191
  Thus Satan, talking to his nearest mate,
With head uplift above the wave, and eyes
That sparkling blazed ; his other parts besides,
Prone on the flood, extended long and large,
Lay floating many a rood, in bulk as huge   196
As whom the fables name of monstrous size,
Titanian,[6] or Earth-born, that warred on Jove,
Briareos or Typhon,[7] whom the den
By ancient Tarsus held, or that sea-beast   200
Leviathan,[8] which God of all his works
Created hugest that swim the ocean-stream.
Him, haply slumbering on the Norway foam,
The pilot of some small night-foundered [9] skiff
Deeming some island, oft, as seamen tell,   205
With fixèd anchor in his scaly rind,
Moors by his side under the lee, while night
Invests [10] the sea, and wishèd morn delays.
So stretched out huge in length the Arch-Fiend lay,

[1] if I mistake not   [2] its   [3] blue-black   [4] go   [5] injure
[6] cf. ll. 509 ff.   [7] gigantic monsters of Greek mythology   [8] in *Job* xli : 1 the crocodile, but here the whale   [9] overtaken by night   [10] covers

Chained on the burning lake; nor ever thence
Had risen or heaved his head, but that the
   will   211
And high permission of all-ruling Heaven
Left him at large to his own dark designs,
That with reiterated crimes he might
Heap on himself damnation, while he sought
Evil to others, and enraged might see   216
How all his malice served but to bring forth
Infinite goodness, grace, and mercy, shewn
On Man by him seduced; but on himself
Treble confusion, wrath, and vengeance
   poured.   220
   Forthwith upright he rears from off the pool
His mighty stature; on each hand the flames
Driven backward slope their pointing spires,
   and, rolled
In billows, leave in the midst a horrid vale.
Then with expanded wings he steers his flight
Aloft, incumbent on the dusky air,   226
That felt unusual weight; till on dry land
He lights — if it were land that ever burned
With solid, as the lake with liquid fire,
And such appeared in hue, as when the force
Of subterranean wind transports a hill   231
Torn from Pelorus,[1] or the shattered side
Of thundering Ætna, whose combustible
And fuelled entrails thence conceiving[2] fire,
Sublimed[3] with mineral fury, aid the winds,
And leave a singèd bottom all involved   236
With stench and smoke: such resting found
   the sole
Of unblest feet. Him followed his next mate,
Both glorying to have 'scaped the Stygian
   flood   239
As gods, and by their own recovered strength,
Not by the sufferance of supernal power.
   "Is this the region, this the soil, the clime,"
Said then the lost Archangel, "this the seat
That we must change for Heaven?[4] this
   mournful gloom
For that celestial light? Be it so, since he
Who now is sovran can dispose and bid   246
What shall be right: farthest from him is best,
Whom reason hath equalled, force hath made
   supreme
Above his equals. Farewell, happy fields,
Where joy forever dwells! Hail, horrors!
   hail,   250
Infernal world! and thou, profoundest Hell,
Receive thy new possessor, one who brings

A mind not to be changed by place or time.
The mind is its own place, and in itself
Can make a Heaven of Hell, a Hell of Heaven.
What matter where, if I be still the same,   256
And what I should be, all but less than he
Whom thunder hath made greater? Here at
   least
We shall be free; the Almighty hath not built
Here for his envy,[1] will not drive us hence:
Here we may reign secure, and in my choice
To reign is worth ambition, though in Hell:
Better to reign in Hell, than serve in Heaven.
But wherefore let we then our faithful friends,
The associates and co-partners of our loss,   265
Lie thus astonished[2] on the oblivious[3] pool,
And call them not to share with us their part
In this unhappy mansion,[4] or once more
With rallied arms to try what may be yet
Regained in Heaven, or what more lost in
   Hell?"   270
   So Satan spake; and him Beëlzebub
Thus answered: — "Leader of those armies
   bright
Which but the Omnipotent none could have
   foiled,
If once they hear that voice, their liveliest
   pledge
Of hope in fears and dangers — heard so oft
In worst extremes, and on the perilous edge
Of battle when it raged, in all assaults   277
Their surest signal — they will soon resume
New courage and revive, though now they lie
Grovelling and prostrate on yon lake of fire,
As we erewhile, astounded and amazed: 281
No wonder, fallen such a pernicious highth!"
   He scarce had ceased when the superior
   Fiend
Was moving toward the shore; his ponderous
   shield,
Ethereal temper, massy, large, and round,   285
Behind him cast. The broad circumference
Hung on his shoulders like the moon, whose
   orb
Through optic glass[5] the Tuscan artist[6] views
At evening from the top of Fesole,
Or in Valdarno, to descry new lands,   290
Rivers, or mountains, in her spotty globe.
His spear — to equal which the tallest pine
Hewn on Norwegian hills, to be the mast
Of some great ammiral,[7] were but a wand —
He walked with, to support uneasy steps   295
Over the burning marle, not like those steps

---

[1] the northeast point of Sicily [2] catching [3] gasified [4] *A Latinism, the thing exchanged is put last,* cf. Jonson's *Drink to me only with thine eyes,* l. 8.

[1] hate [2] astounded [3] causing oblivion [4] dwelling [5] telescope [6] Galileo [7] flag-ship

On Heaven's azure; and the torrid clime
Smote on him sore besides, vaulted with fire.
Nathless he so endured, till on the beach
Of that inflamèd sea he stood, and called 300
His legions, angel forms, who lay entranced,
Thick as autumnal leaves that strow the
    brooks
In Vallombrosa, where the Etrurian shades
High over-arched embower; or scattered sedge
Afloat, when with fierce winds Orion[1] armed
Hath vexed the Red-Sea coast, whose waves
    o'erthrew   306
Busiris[2] and his Memphian chivalry,[3]
While with perfidious hatred they pursued
The sojourners of Goshen, who beheld
From the safe shore their floating carcases
And broken chariot-wheels: so thick be-
    strown,   311
Abject and lost, lay these, covering the flood,
Under amazement of their hideous change.
He called so loud that all the hollow deep
Of Hell resounded: — "Princes, Potentates,
Warriors, the Flower of Heaven — once
    yours, now lost,   316
If such astonishment as this can seize
Eternal Spirits! Or have ye chosen this place
After the toil of battle to repose
Your wearied virtue, for the ease you find
To slumber here, as in the vales of Heaven?
Or in this abject posture have ye sworn 322
To adore the Conqueror, who now beholds
Cherub and Seraph rolling in the flood
With scattered arms and ensigns, till anon 325
His swift pursuers from Heaven-gates discern
The advantage, and descending tread us down
Thus drooping, or with linkèd thunderbolts
Transfix us to the bottom of this gulf?
Awake, arise, or be forever fallen!"   330
    They heard, and were abashed, and up they
        sprung
Upon the wing, as when men wont to watch,
On duty sleeping found by whom they dread,
Rouse and bestir themselves ere well awake.
Nor did they not perceive the evil plight 335
In which they were, or the fierce pains not feel;
Yet to their General's voice they soon obeyed
Innumerable. As when the potent rod
Of Amram's son,[4] in Egypt's evil day,
Waved round the coast, up called a pitchy
    cloud   340
Of locusts, warping[5] on the eastern wind,

That o'er the realm of impious Pharaoh hung
Like night, and darkened all the land of Nile:
So numberless were those bad angels seen
Hovering on wing under the cope of Hell, 345
'Twixt upper, nether, and surrounding fires;
Till, as a signal given, the uplifted spear
Of their great Sultan waving to direct
Their course, in even balance down they light
On the firm brimstone, and fill all the plain:
A multitude like which the populous North
Poured never from her frozen loins, to pass
Rhene[1] or the Danaw,[2] when her barbarous
    sons[3]
Came like a deluge on the South, and spread
Beneath[4] Gibraltar to the Libyan sands. 355
Forthwith, from every squadron and each
    band,
The heads and leaders thither haste where,
    stood
Their great Commander; godlike shapes,
    and forms
Excelling human, princely Dignities,   359
And Powers that erst[5] in Heaven sat on
    thrones;
Though of their names in Heavenly records
    now
Be no memorial, blotted out and rased
By their rebellion from the Books of Life.
Nor had they yet among the sons of Eve
Got them new names, till, wandering o'er the
    earth,   365
Through God's high sufferance for the trial of
    man,
By falsities and lies the greatest part
Of mankind they corrupted to forsake
God their Creator, and the invisible
Glory of him that made them, to transform
Oft to the image of a brute, adorned   371
With gay religions[6] full of pomp and gold,
And devils to adore for deities:
Then were they known to men by various
    names,
And various idols through the heathen world.
    Say, Muse, their names then known, who
        first, who last,   376
Roused from the slumber on that fiery couch,
At their great Emperor's call, as next in worth,
Came singly where he stood on the bare strand,
While the promiscuous crowd stood yet aloof.
    The chief were those who, from the pit of
        Hell   381

---

[1] a constellation supposed to cause storms
[2] Pharaoh [3] horsemen [4] Moses [5] moving in irregular flight

[1] Rhine [2] Danube [3] Vandals and other barbarians, who overran the Roman Empire [4] south of
[5] formerly [6] religious rites

Roaming to seek their prey on Earth, durst fix
Their seats, long after, next the seat of God,
Their altars by his altar, gods adored
Among the nations round, and durst abide
Jehovah thundering out of Sion, throned   386
Between the Cherubim; yea, often placed
Within his sanctuary itself their shrines,
Abominations; and with cursèd things
His holy rites and solemn feasts profaned,
And with their darkness durst affront his
    light.   391
First Moloch, horrid king, besmeared with
    blood
Of human sacrifice, and parents' tears,
Though, for the noise of drums and timbrels
    loud,
Their children's cries unheard that passed
. through fire   395
To his grim idol. Him the Ammonite·
Worshipped in Rabba and her watery plain,
In Argob and in Basan, to the stream
Of utmost Arnon. Nor content with such
Audacious neighbourhood, the wisest heart
Of Solomon he led by fraud to build   401
His temple right against the temple of God
On that opprobrious[1] hill, and made his grove
The pleasant valley of Hinnon, Tophet thence
And black Gehenna called, the type of Hell.
Next Chemos, the obscene dread of Moab's
    sons,   406
From Aroar to Nebo and the wild
Of southmost Abarim; in Hesebon
And Horonaim, Seon's realm, beyond
The flowery dale of Sibma clad with vines,
And Elealè to the Asphaltic pool.[2]   411
Peor his other name, when he enticed
Israel in Sittim, on their march from Nile,
To do him wanton rites, which cost them woe.
Yet thence his lustful orgies he enlarged   415
Even to that hill of scandal, by the grove
Of Moloch homicide, lust hard by hate,
Till good Josiah drove them thence to Hell.
With these came they who, from the bordering
    flood
Of old Euphrates to the brook that parts 420
Egypt from Syrian ground, had general names
Of Baälim and Ashtaroth — those male,
These feminine. For Spirits, when they
    please,
Can either sex assume, or both; so soft
And uncompounded is their essence pure, 425
Not tied or manacled with joint or limb,
Nor founded on the brittle strength of bones,

Like cumbrous flesh; but, in what shape they
    choose,
Dilated or condensed, bright or obscure,
Can execute their aery purposes,   430
And works of love or enmity fulfil.
For those the race of Israel oft forsook
Their living Strength, and unfrequented left
His righteous altar, bowing lowly down   434
To bestial gods; for which their heads as low
Bowed down in battle, sunk before the spear
Of despicable foes. With these in troop
Came Astoreth, whom the Phœnicians called
Astarte, Queen of Heaven, with crescent horns;
To whose bright image nightly by the moon
Sidonian virgins paid their vows and songs;
In Sion also not unsung, where stood   442
Her temple on the offensive mountain, built
By that uxorious king[1] whose heart, though
    large,
Beguiled by fair idolatresses, fell   445
To idols foul. Thammuz came next behind,
Whose annual wound in Lebanon allured
The Syrian damsels to lament his fate
In amorous ditties all a summer's day,   449
While smooth Adonis from his native rock
Ran purple to the sea, supposed with blood
Of Thammuz yearly wounded: the love-tale
Infected Sion's daughters with like heat,
Whose wanton passions in the sacred porch
Ezekiel saw,[2] when, by the vision led,   455
His eye surveyed the dark idolatries
Of alienated Judah. Next came one
Who mourned in earnest, when the captive
    ark
Maimed his brute image, head and hands lopt
    off
In his own temple,[3] on the grunsel-edge,[4] 460
Where he fell flat, and shamed his worshippers:
Dagon his name, sea-monster, upward man
And downward fish; yet had his temple high
Reared in Azotus,[5] dreaded through the coast
Of Palestine, in Gath and Ascalon,   465
And Accaron and Gaza's frontier bounds.
Him followed Rimmon, whose delightful seat
Was fair Damascus, on the fertile banks
Of Abbana and Pharphar, lucid streams.
He also against the house of God was bold: 470
A leper[6] once he lost, and gained a king,
Ahaz, his sottish conqueror, whom he drew
God's altar to disparage and displace
For one of Syrian mode, whereon to burn
His odious offerings, and adore the gods   475

---

[1] offensive   [2] the Dead Sea

[1] Solomon   [2] *Ezek.* viii:14   [3] Cf. *Ode on the
Nativity*, l. 199 [4] threshold [5] Ashdod [6] Naaman

Whom he had vanquished. After these ap-
peared
A crew who, under names of old renown,
Osiris, Isis, Orus, and their train,
With monstrous shapes and sorceries abused
Fanatic Egypt and her priests, to seek   480
Their wandering gods disguised in brutish
forms
Rather than human. Nor did Israel 'scape
The infection, when their borrowed gold
composed
The calf in Oreb; and the rebel king
Doubled that sin in Bethel and in Dan,   485
Likening his Maker to the grazèd ox —
Jehovah, who, in one night, when he passed
From Egypt marching, equalled with one
stroke
Both her first-born and all her bleating gods.
Belial came last, than whom a Spirit more
lewd
Fell not from Heaven, or more gross to love
Vice for itself. To him no temple stood 492
Or altar smoked; yet who more oft than he
In temples and at altars, when the priest
Turns atheist, as did Eli's sons, who filled
With lust and violence the house of God? 496
In courts and palaces he also reigns,
And in luxurious cities, where the noise
Of riot ascends above their loftiest towers,
And injury and outrage; and when night 500
Darkens the streets, then wander forth the
sons
Of Belial, flown¹ with insolence and wine.
Witness the streets of Sodom, and that night
In Gibeah, when the hospitable door
Exposed a matron, to avoid worse rape. 505
These were the prime in order and in might;
The rest were long to tell, though far re-
nowned
The Ionian gods — of Javan's² issue held
Gods, yet confessed later than Heaven and
Earth,
Their boasted parents; — Titan, Heaven's
first-born,   510
With his enormous brood, and birthright
seized
By younger Saturn; he from mightier Jove,
His own and Rhea's son, like measure found;
So Jove usurping reigned. These, first in
Crete
And Ida known, thence on the snowy top 515
Of cold Olympus ruled the middle air,

Their highest Heaven; or on the Delphian
cliff,
Or in Dodona, and through all the bounds
Of Doric land; or who with Saturn old
Fled over Adria to the Hesperian fields,¹ 520
And o'er the Celtic roamed the utmost isles.
All these and more came flocking; but with
looks
Downcast and damp, yet such wherein ap-
peared
Obscure some glimpse of joy, to have found
their Chief
Not in despair, to have found themselves not
lost   525
In loss itself; which on his countenance cast
Like doubtful hue. But he, his wonted pride
Soon recollecting,² with high words that bore
Semblance of worth, not substance, gently³
raised
Their fainting courage, and dispelled their
fears: 530
Then straight commands that at the warlike
sound
Of trumpets loud and clarions, be upreared
His mighty standard. That proud honour
claimed
Azazel as his right, a Cherub tall:
Who forthwith from the glittering staff un-
furled   535
The imperial ensign, which, full high advanced,
Shone like a meteor streaming to the wind,
With gems and golden lustre rich emblazed,⁴
Seraphic arms and trophies; all the while
Sonorous metal blowing martial sounds: 540
At which the universal host up-sent
A shout that tore Hell's concave, and beyond
Frighted the reign of Chaos and old Night.
All in a moment through the gloom were seen
Ten thousand banners rise into the air, 545
With orient colours waving; with them rose
A forest huge of spears; and thronging helms
Appeared, and serried shields in thick array
Of depth immeasurable. Anon they move
In perfect phalanx to the Dorian mood⁵ 550
Of flutes and soft recorders — such as raised
To highth of noblest temper heroes old
Arming to battle, and instead of rage
Deliberate valour breathed, firm and unmoved
With dread of death to flight or foul retreat;
Nor wanting power to mitigate and swage,⁶
With solemn touches, troubled thoughts, and
chase   •   557

¹ filled, flushed ² son of Japheth and ancestor
of the Greeks

¹ Italy ² resuming ³ gallantly ⁴ ornamented
⁵ music of the solemn Dorian mode ⁶ assuage

Anguish and doubt and fear and sorrow and
    pain
From mortal or immortal minds. Thus they,
Breathing united force with fixèd thought, 560
Moved on in silence to soft pipes that charmed
Their painful steps o'er the burnt soil; and
    now
Advanced in view they stand, a horrid front
Of dreadful length and dazzling arms, in guise
Of warriors old, with ordered spear and shield,
Awaiting what command their mighty Chief
Had to impose. He through the armèd files
Darts his experienced eye, and soon traverse [1]
The whole battalion views — their order due,
Their visages and stature as of gods; 570
Their number last he sums. And now his
    heart
Distends with pride, and hardening in his
    strength
Glories; for never, since created man,
Met such embodied force as, named with
    these,
Could merit more than that small infantry [2] 575
Warred on by cranes: though all the giant
    brood
Of Phlegra [3] with the heroic race were joined
That fought at Thebes and Ilium, on each side
Mixed with auxiliar gods; and what resounds
In fable or romance of Uther's son, [4] 580
Begirt with British and Armoric knights;
And all who since, baptized or infidel,
Jousted in Aspramont, [5] or Montalban,
Damasco, or Marocco, or Trebisond;
Or whom Biserta sent from Afric shore 585
When Charlemain with all his peerage fell
By Fontarabbia. Thus far these beyond
Compare of mortal prowess, yet observed
Their dread commander. He, above the rest
In shape and gesture proudly eminent, 590
Stood like a tower; his form had yet not lost
All her original brightness, nor appeared
Less than Archangel ruined, and the excess
Of glory obscured: as when the sun new-
    risen
Looks through the horizontal misty air 595
Shorn of his beams, or from behind the moon,
In dim eclipse, disastrous twilight sheds
On half the nations, and with fear of change
Perplexes monarchs. Darkened so, yet shone
Above them all the Archangel; but his face

[1] cross-wise [2] the Pygmies [3] where the gods and
giants fought [4] King Arthur [5] This and the following are places celebrated in the romances of
Charlemagne.

Deep scars of thunder had intrenched, and
    care 601
Sat on his faded cheek, but under brows
Of dauntless courage, and considerate [1] pride
Waiting revenge. Cruel his eye, but cast
Signs of remorse [2] and passion, to behold 605
The fellows of his crime, the followers rather
(Far other once beheld in bliss), condemned
Forever now to have their lot in pain;
Millions of Spirits for his fault amerced [3]
Of Heaven, and from eternal splendors flung
For his revolt; yet faithful how they stood,
Their glory withered: as, when Heaven's fire
Hath scathed [4] the forest oaks or mountain
    pines,
With singèd top their stately growth, though
    bare,
Stands on the blasted heath. He now pre-
    pared 615
To speak; whereat their doubled ranks they
    bend
From wing to wing, and half enclose him
    round
With all his peers: attention held them mute.
Thrice he assayed, and thrice, in spite of scorn,
Tears, such as Angels weep, burst forth: at
    last 620
Words interwove with sighs found out their
    way: —
"O myriads of immortal Spirits! O powers
Matchless, but with the Almighty! — and
    that strife
Was not inglorious, though the event was dire,
As this place testifies, and this dire change, 625
Hateful to utter. But what power of mind,
Foreseeing or presaging, from the depth
Of knowledge past or present, could have
    feared
How such united force of gods, how such
As stood like these, could ever know repulse?
For who can yet believe, though after loss, 631
That all these puissant legions, whose exile
Hath emptied Heaven, shall fail to reascend,
Self-raised, and repossess their native seat?
For me, be witness all the host of Heaven, 635
If counsels different, or dangers shunned
By me, have lost our hopes. But he who
    reigns
Monarch in Heaven, till then as one secure
Sat on his throne, upheld by old repute,
Consent or custom, and his regal state 640
Put forth at full, but still his strength con-
    cealed;

[1] calm [2] pity [3] deprived [4] injured

Which tempted our attempt, and wrought our fall.
Henceforth his might we know, and know our own,
So as not either to provoke, or dread
New war provoked. Our better part remains
To work in close [1] design, by fraud or guile, 646
What force effected not ; that he no less
At length from us may find, who overcomes
By force hath overcome but half his foe.
Space may produce new worlds ; whereof so rife   650
There went a fame in Heaven that he erelong
Intended to create, and therein plant
A generation whom his choice regard
Should favour equal to the Sons of Heaven.
Thither, if but to pry, shall be perhaps   655
Our first eruption : thither or elsewhere ;
For this infernal pit shall never hold
Celestial Spirits in bondage, nor the Abyss
Long under darkness cover. But these thoughts,
Full counsel must mature. Peace is despaired,
For who can think submission ? War, then, war   661
Open or understood,[1] must be resolved."
He spake ; and, to confirm his words, out-flew
Millions of flaming swords, drawn from the thighs
Of mighty Cherubim ; the sudden blaze   665
Far round illumined Hell. Highly they raged
Against the Highest, and fierce with graspèd arms
Clashed on their sounding shields the din of war,
Hurling defiance toward the vault of Heaven.
  There stood a hill not far, whose grisly top   670
Belched fire and rolling smoke ;· the rest entire
Shone with a glossy scurf, undoubted sign
That in his womb[2] was hid metallic ore,
The work of sulphur.   Thither, winged with speed,
A numerous brigade hastened :   as when bands   675
Of pioneers,[3] with spade and pickaxe armed,
Forerun the royal camp, to trench a field,
Or cast a rampart.   Mammon led them on,
Mammon, the least erected [4] Spirit that fell
From Heaven, for even in Heaven his looks and thoughts   680
Were always downward bent, admiring more

The riches of Heaven's pavement, trodden gold,
Than aught divine or holy else enjoyed
In vision beatific.   By him first
Men also, and by his suggestion taught,   685
Ransacked the Centre, and with impious hands
Rifled the bowels of their mother Earth
For treasures better hid.   Soon had his crew
Opened into the hill a spacious wound,
And digged out ribs of gold. Let none admire[1]   690
That riches grow in Hell ; that soil may best
Deserve the precious bane.[2] And here let those
Who boast in mortal things, and wondering tell
Of Babel,[3] and the works of Memphian [4] kings,
Learn how their greatest monuments of fame,
And strength, and art, are easily outdone 696
By Spirits reprobate, and in an hour
What in an age they, with incessant toil
And hands innumerable, scarce perform.
Nigh on the plain, in many cells prepared, 700
That underneath had veins of liquid fire
Sluiced from the lake, a second multitude
With wondrous art founded the massy ore,
Severing each kind, and scummed the bullion dross.
A third as soon had formed within the ground
A various mould, and from the boiling cells 706
By strange conveyance filled each hollow nook :
As in an organ, from one blast of wind,
To many a row of pipes the sound-board breathes.
Anon out of the earth a fabric huge   710
Rose like an exhalation, with the sound
Of dulcet symphonies and voices sweet —
Built like a temple, where pilasters round
Were set, and Doric pillars overlaid
With golden architrave ; nor did there want
Cornice or frieze, with bossy [5] sculptures graven :   716
The roof was fretted gold. Not Babylon,
Nor great Alcairo,[6] such magnificence
Equalled in all their glories, to enshrine
Belus or Serapis [7] their gods, or seat   720
Their kings, when Egypt with Assyria strove
In wealth and luxury. The ascending pile
Stood fixed her stately highth, and straight the doors,

---

[1] secret [2] its interior [3] soldiers who clear the way for an army [4] elevated

[1] wonder [2] destroyer [3] the temple of Balus in Babylon [4] Egyptian [5] projecting from the walls
[6] Memphis in Egypt [7] gods of Babylon and Egypt

Opening their brazen folds, discover, wide
Within, her ample spaces o'er the smooth 725
And level pavement: from the archèd roof,
Pendent by subtle magic, many a row
Of starry lamps and blazing cressets, fed
With naphtha and asphaltus, yielded light
As from a sky. The hasty multitude 730
Admiring entered, and the work some praise,
And some the architect. His hand was known
In Heaven by many a towered structure high,
Where sceptred Angels held their residence,
And sat as Princes, whom the supreme King
Exalted to such power, and gave to rule, 736
Each in his Hierarchy, the Orders[1] bright.
Nor was his name unheard or unadored
In ancient Greece; and in Ausonian[2] land
Men called him Mulciber; and how he fell
From Heaven they fabled, thrown by angry
    Jove 741
Sheer o'er the crystal battlements: from morn
To noon he fell, from noon to dewy eve,
A summer's day; and with the setting sun
Dropt from the zenith, like a falling star, 745
On Lemnos, the Ægæan isle. Thus they relate,
Erring; for he with this rebellious rout[3]
Fell long before; nor aught availed him now
To have built in Heaven high towers; nor
    did he 'scape
By all his engines,[4] but was headlong sent 750
With his industrious crew to build in Hell.
    Meanwhile the wingèd heralds, by com-
    mand
Of sovran power, with awful ceremony
And trumpet's sound, throughout the host
    proclaim
A solemn council forthwith to be held 755
At Pandemonium, the high capital
Of Satan and his peers. Their summons
    called
From every band and squarèd regiment
By place or choice the worthiest; they anon
With hundreds and with thousands trooping
    came 760
Attended. All access was thronged, the gates
And porches wide, but chief the spacious hall
(Though like a covered field, where champions
    bold
Wont ride in armed, and at the Soldan's[5] chair
Defied the best of Paynym chivalry 765
To mortal combat, or career with lance)
Thick swarmed, both on the ground and in
    the air,

Brushed with the hiss of rustling wings. As
    bees
In spring-time, when the Sun with Taurus
    rides,[1] 769
Pour forth their populous youth about the
    hive
In clusters; they among fresh dews and
    flowers
Fly to and fro, or on the smoothèd plank,
The suburb of their straw-built citadel,
New rubbed with balm, expatiate[2] and confer
Their state-affairs. So thick the aery crowd
Swarmed and were straitened;[3] till, the
    signal given, 776
Behold a wonder! they but now who seemed
In bigness to surpass Earth's giant sons,
Now less than smallest dwarfs, in narrow room
Throng numberless, like that pygmean race
Beyond the Indian mount;[4] or faery elves, 781
Whose midnight revels, by a forest-side
Or fountain, some belated peasant sees,
Or dreams he sees, while overhead the Moon
Sits arbitress, and nearer to the Earth 785
Wheels her pale course; they, on their mirth
    and dance
Intent, with jocund music charm his ear;
At once with joy and fear his heart rebounds.
Thus incorporeal Spirits to smallest forms
Reduced their shapes immense, and were at
    large, 790
Though without number still, amidst the hall
Of that infernal court. But far within,
And in their own dimensions like themselves,
The great Seraphic Lords and Cherubim
In close recess[5] and secret conclave sat, 795
A thousand demi-gods on golden seats,
Frequent[6] and full.[7] After short silence then,
And summons read, the great consult began.

OF EDUCATION

TO MASTER SAMUEL HARTLIB

[AN EXTRACT]

(THEIR EXERCISE)

The course of study hitherto briefly described, is what I can guess by reading, likest
to those ancient and famous schools of
Pythagoras, Plato, Isocrates, Aristotle, and

---

[1] *There were nine orders, or classes, of angels.*
[2] Italy [3] company [4] contrivances [5] Sultan's

[1] is in the sign of Taurus, cf. Chaucer, *Prol. of
C. T.*, note on l. 8 [2] move about [3] gathered close
together [4] the Himalaya range [5] secret retirement
[6] numerous [7] complete in number

such others, out of which were bred such a number of renowned philosophers, orators, historians, poets, and princes all over Greece, Italy, and Asia, besides the flourishing studies of Cyrene and Alexandria. But herein it shall exceed them, and supply a defect as great as that which Plato noted in the commonwealth of Sparta; whereas that city trained up their youth most for war, and these in their academies and Lycæum all for the gown, this institution of breeding which I here delineate shall be equally good both for peace and war.

Therefore about an hour and a half ere they eat at noon should be allowed them for exercise, and due rest afterwards; but the time for this may be enlarged at pleasure, according as their rising in the morning shall be early. The exercise which I commend first, is the exact use of their weapon, to guard, and to strike safely with edge or point; this will keep them healthy, nimble, strong, and well in breath, is also the likeliest means to make them grow large and tall, and to inspire them with a gallant and fearless courage, which being tempered with seasonable lectures and precepts to them of true fortitude and patience, will turn into a native and heroic valour, and make them hate the cowardice of doing wrong. They must be also practised in all the locks and grips of wrestling, wherein Englishmen were wont to excel, as need may often be in fight to tug, to grapple, and to close. And this perhaps will be enough, wherein to prove and heat their single strength.

The interim of unsweating themselves regularly, and convenient rest before meat, may both with profit and delight be taken up in recreating and composing their travailed[1] spirits with the solemn and divine harmonies of music heard or learned; either whilst the skilful organist plies his grave and fancied descant[2] in lofty fugues, or the whole symphony with artful and unimaginable touches adorn and grace the well-studied chords of some choice composer; sometimes the lute or soft organ stop waiting on elegant voices, either to religious, martial, or civil ditties; which, if wise men and prophets be not extremely out, have a great power over dispositions and manners, to smooth and make them gentle from rustic harshness and distempered passions. The like also would not

be unexpedient after meat, to assist and cherish nature in her first concoction,[1] and send their minds back to study in good tune and satisfaction.

Where having followed it close under vigilant eyes, till about two hours before supper, they are by a sudden alarum or watchword, to be called out to their military motions, under sky or covert, according to the season, as was the Roman wont; first on foot, then as their age permits, on horseback, to all the art of cavalry; that having in sport, but with much exactness and daily muster, served out the rudiments of their soldiership, in all the skill of embattling,[2] marching, encamping, fortifying, besieging, and battering with all the helps of ancient and modern stratagems, tactics, and warlike maxims, they may as it were out of a long war come forth renowned and perfect commanders in the service of their country. They would not then, if they were trusted with fair and hopeful armies, suffer them for want of just and wise discipline to shed away from about them like sick feathers, though they be never so oft supplied; they would not suffer their empty and unrecruitable[3] colonels of twenty men in a company, to quaff out, or convey into secret hoards, the wages of a delusive[4] list, and a miserable remnant; yet in the meanwhile to be overmastered with a score or two of drunkards, the only soldiery left about them, or else to comply with[5] all rapines and violences. No, certainly, if they knew aught of that knowledge that belongs to good men or good governors, they would not suffer these things.

But to return to our own institute; besides these constant exercises at home, there is another opportunity of gaining experience to be won from pleasure itself abroad; in those vernal seasons of the year when the air is calm and pleasant, it were an injury and sullenness against nature, not to go out and see her riches, and partake in her rejoicing with heaven and earth. I should not therefore be a persuader to them of studying much then, after two or three years that they have well laid their grounds, but to ride out in companies with prudent and staid guides to all the quarters of the land; learning and observing all places of strength, all com-

---

[1] wearied [2] solemn and elaborate variations

[1] process of digestion [2] drawing up in battle array [3] lacking soldiers and incapable of recruiting [4] false [5] allow

modities [1] of building and of soil, for towns and
tillage, harbours and ports for trade. Sometimes taking sea as far as to our navy, to
learn there also what they can in the practical knowledge of sailing and of seafight.
These ways would try all their peculiar gifts
of nature, and if there were any secret excellence among them, would fetch it out, and
give it fair opportunities to advance itself
by, which could not but mightily redound to
the good of this nation, and bring into fashion
again those old admired virtues and excellencies with far more advantage now in this
purity of Christian knowledge.

From AREOPAGITICA

A SPEECH FOR THE LIBERTY OF UN-
LICENSED PRINTING

To the Parliament of England

* * * * * * *

I deny not but that it is of greatest concernment in the church and commonwealth, to
have a vigilant eye how books demean themselves as well as men; and thereafter to confine, imprison, and do sharpest justice on
them as malefactors: for books are not absolutely dead things, but do contain a potency
of life in them to be as active as that soul was
whose progeny they are; nay, they do preserve as in a vial the purest efficacy and
extraction of that living intellect that bred
them. I know they are as lively, and as
vigorously productive, as those fabulous
dragon's teeth; [2] and being sown up and down,
may chance to spring up armed men. And
yet on the other hand, unless wariness be used,
as good almost kill a man as kill a good book;
who kills a man kills a reasonable creature,
God's image; but he who destroys a good
book, kills reason itself, kills the image of
God as it were in the eye. Many a man lives
a burden to the earth; but a good book is the
precious life-blood of a master spirit, im-
balmed and treasured up on purpose to a life
beyond life. 'Tis true, no age can restore a
life, whereof perhaps there is no great loss;
and revolutions of ages do not oft recover the
loss of a rejected truth, for the want of which

whole nations fare the worse. We should be
wary therefore what persecution we raise
against the living labours of public men, how
we spill [1] the seasoned life of man preserved
and stored up in books; since we see a kind
of homicide may be thus committed, sometimes a martyrdom, and if it extend to the
whole impression, a kind of massacre, whereof
the execution ends not in the slaying of an
elemental life, but strikes at that ethereal and
fifth essence, the breath of reason itself, slays
an immortality rather than a life. But lest
I should be condemned of introducing license, while I oppose licensing, I refuse not
the pains to be so much historical as will
serve to show what hath been done by
ancient and famous commonwealths against
this disorder, till the very time that this
project of licensing crept out of the *inquisition*, was catched up by our prelates, and
hath caught some of our presbyters.

* * * * * * *

Good and evil we know in the field of this
world grow up together almost inseparably;
and the knowledge of good is so involved and
interwoven with the knowledge of evil and in
so many cunning resemblances hardly to be
discerned, that those confused seeds, which
were imposed on Psyche [2] as an incessant
labour to cull out and sort asunder, were not
more intermixed. It was from out the rind
of one apple tasted that the knowledge of
good and evil as two twins cleaving together
leaped forth into the world. And perhaps
this is that doom which Adam fell into of
knowing good and evil, that is to say of
knowing good by evil. As therefore the state
of man now is, what wisdom can there be to
choose, what continence to forbear, without
the knowledge of evil? He that can apprehend and consider vice with all her baits and
seeming pleasures, and yet abstain, and yet
distinguish, and yet prefer that which is
truly better, he is the true warfaring Christian. I cannot praise a fugitive and cloistered virtue, unexercised and unbreathed, [3]
that never sallies out and sees her adversary,
but slinks out of the race, where that immortal
garland is to be run for not without dust and
heat. Assuredly we bring not innocence into
the world, we bring impurity much rather:

---

[1] advantages [2] sown by Cadmus, cf. Gayley,
pp. 114–117

[1] destroy [2] in the temple of Venus, cf. Gayley,
p. 156 [3] unpractised

that which purifies us is trial, and trial is by what is contrary. That virtue therefore which is but a youngling in the contemplation of evil, and knows not the utmost that vice promises to her followers, and rejects it, is but a blank virtue, not a pure; her whiteness is but an excremental[1] whiteness; which was the reason why our sage and serious poet Spenser, whom I dare be known to think a better teacher than Scotus or Aquinas,[2] describing true temperance under the person of Guion, brings him in with his palmer through the cave of Mammon and the bower of earthly bliss,[3] that he might see and know, and yet abstain. Since therefore the knowledge and survey of vice is in this world so necessary to the constituting of human virtue, and the scanning of error to the confirmation of truth, how can we more safely and with less danger scout into the regions of sin and falsity than by reading all manner of tractates, and hearing all manner of reason? And this is the benefit which may be had of books promiscuously read.

* * * * * * *

If we think to regulate printing, thereby to rectify manners, we must regulate all recreations and pastimes, all that is delightful to man. No music must be heard, nor song be set or sung, but what is grave and doric. There must be licensing dancers, that no gesture, motion, or deportment be taught our youth but what by their allowance shall be thought honest; for such Plato was provided of. It will ask more than the work of twenty licensers to examine all the lutes, the violins and the guitars in every house; they must not be suffered to prattle as they do, but must be licensed what they may say. And who shall silence all the airs and madrigals that whisper softness in chambers? The windows also, and the balconies must be thought on; there are shrewd[4] books with dangerous frontispieces set to sale; who shall prohibit them? shall twenty licensers? The villages also must have their visitors to inquire what lectures the bagpipe and the rebec reads, even to the ballatry and the gamut of every municipal fiddler, for these are the

countryman's Arcadias and his Montemayors.[1] Next, what more national corruption, for which England hears ill abroad, than household gluttony? who shall be the rectors[2] of our daily rioting? and what shall be done to inhibit the multitudes that frequent those houses where drunkenness is sold and harboured? Our garments also should be referred to the licensing of some more sober work-masters to see them cut into a less wanton garb. Who shall regulate all the mixed conversation of our youth male and female together, as is the fashion of this country? who shall still[3] appoint what shall be discoursed, what presumed, and no further? Lastly, who shall forbid and separate all idle resort, all evil company? These things will be, and must be; but how they shall be least hurtful, how least enticing, herein consists the grave and governing wisdom of a state. To sequester out of the world into Atlantic and Utopian[4] polities, which never can be drawn into use, will not mend our condition; but to ordain wisely as in this world of evil, in the midst whereof God hath placed us unavoidably. Nor is it Plato's licensing of books will do this, which necessarily pulls along with it so many other kinds of licensing, as will make us all both ridiculous and weary, and yet frustrate; but those unwritten, or at least unconstraining laws of virtuous education, religious and civil nurture, which Plato there mentions as the bonds and ligaments of the commonwealth, the pillars and the sustainers of every written statute; these they be which will bear chief sway in such matters as these, when all licensing will be easily eluded. Impunity and remissness, for certain, are the bane of a commonwealth; but here the great art lies to discern in what the law is to bid restraint and punishment, and in what things persuasion only is to work. If every action which is good, or evil in man at ripe years, were to be under pittance[5] and prescription and compulsion, what were virtue but a name, what praise could be then due to well-doing, what gramercy[6] to be sober, just or continent?

* * * * * * *

[1] external [2] Duns Scotus (1265?–1308?) and Thomas Aquinas (1225?–1274), founders of the two chief systems of mediæval philosophy [3] See *Faerie Queene*, II, vii and xii [4] wicked

[1] The Diana Enamorada *of Jorge de Montemayor, published in 1542, was one of the most famous pastoral romances.* [2] controllers [3] constantly [4] *Atlantis and Utopia were imaginary ideal commonwealths described by Plato and Sir Thomas More.* [5] allowance [6] thanks

Lords and Commons of England, consider what nation it is whereof ye are the governors: a nation not slow and dull, but of a quick, ingenious, and piercing spirit, acute to invent, subtle and sinewy to discourse, not beneath the reach of any point the highest that human capacity can soar to. Therefore the studies of learning in her deepest sciences have been so ancient and so eminent among us, that writers of good antiquity and ablest judgment have been persuaded that even the school of Pythagoras and the Persian wisdom[1] took beginning from the old philosophy of this island. And that wise and civil Roman, Julius Agricola, who governed once here for Cæsar, preferred the natural wits of Britain before the laboured studies of the French. Nor is it for nothing that the grave and frugal Transylvanian sends out yearly from as far as the mountainous borders of Russia and beyond the Hercynian wilderness,[2] not their youth, but their staid men, to learn our language and our theologic arts. Yet that which is above all this, the favour and the love of heaven, we have great argument to think in a peculiar manner propitious and propending towards us. Why else was this nation chosen before any other, that out of her as out of Sion should be proclaimed and sounded forth the first tidings and trumpet of reformation to all Europe? And had it not been the obstinate perverseness of our prelates against the divine and admirable spirit of Wiclif, to suppress him as a schismatic and innovator, perhaps neither the Bohemian Huss and Jerome,[3] no, nor the name of Luther or of Calvin had been ever known; the glory of reforming all our neighbours had been completely ours. But now, as our obdurate clergy have with violence demeaned[4] the matter, we are become hitherto the latest and the backwardest scholars, of whom God offered to have made us the teachers.

Now once again by all concurrence of signs and by the general instinct of holy and devout men, as they daily and solemnly express their thoughts, God is decreeing to begin some new and great period in his church, even to the reforming of reformation itself. What does he then but reveal himself to his servants, and as his manner is, first to his Englishmen; I say

as his manner is, first to us, though we mark not the method of his counsels and are unworthy? Behold now this vast city:[1] a city of refuge, the mansion house of liberty, encompassed and surrounded with his protection; the shop of war hath not there more anvils and hammers waking, to fashion out the plates and instruments of armed justice in defence of beleaguered truth, than there be pens and heads there, sitting by their studious lamps, musing, searching, revolving new notions and ideas wherewith to present as with their homage and their fealty the approaching reformation, others as fast reading, trying all things, assenting to the force of reason and convincement. What could a man require more from a nation so pliant and so prone to seek after knowledge? What wants there to such a towardly and pregnant[2] soil but wise and faithful labourers, to make a knowing people, a nation of prophets, of sages, and of worthies? We reckon more than five months yet to harvest; there need not be five weeks; had we but eyes to lift up, the fields are white already.[3]

*   *   *   *   *   *   *

Methinks I see in my mind a noble and puissant nation rousing herself like a strong man after sleep, and shaking her invincible locks. Methinks I see her as an eagle muing[4] her mighty youth, and kindling her undazzled eyes at the full midday beam, purging and unscaling her long abused sight at the fountain itself of heavenly radiance, while the whole noise of timorous and flocking birds, with those also that love the twilight, flutter about, amazed at what she means, and in their envious gabble would prognosticate a year of sects and schisms.

What should ye do then, should ye suppress all this flowery crop of knowledge and new light sprung up and yet springing daily in this city, should ye set an oligarchy of twenty ingrossers[5] over it, to bring a famine upon our minds again, when we shall know nothing but what is measured to us by their bushel? Believe it, Lords and Commons, they who counsel ye to such a suppressing do as good as bid ye suppress yourselves; and I will soon show how. If it be desired to know the immediate

---

[1] the religion of Zoroaster [2] the wooded mountains of central Germany [3] Jerome of Prague, a religious reformer associated with Huss [4] conducted

[1] London [2] productive [3] cf. *St. John* iv: 35 [4] renewing (by moulting) [5] merchants who corner necessaries

cause of all this free writing and free speaking, there cannot be assigned a truer than your own mild and free and humane government; it is the liberty, Lords and Commons, which your own valorous and happy counsels have purchased us, liberty which is the nurse of all great wits;[1] this is that which hath rarefied and enlightened our spirits like the influence of heaven; this is that which hath enfranchised, enlarged and lifted up our apprehensions degrees above themselves. Ye cannot make us now less capable, less knowing, less eagerly pursuing of the truth, unless ye first make yourselves, that made us so, less the lovers, less the founders of our true liberty. We can grow ignorant again, brutish, formal, and slavish, as ye found us; but you then must first become that which ye cannot be, oppressive, arbitrary, and tyrannous, as they were from whom ye have freed us. That our hearts are now more capacious, our thoughts more erected to the search and expectation of greatest and exactest things, is the issue of your own virtue propagated in us; ye cannot suppress that unless ye reinforce an abrogated and merciless law, that fathers may despatch at will their own children. And who shall then stick closest to ye, and excite others? Not he who takes up arms for coat and conduct and his four nobles of Danegelt.[2] Although I dispraise not the defence of just immunities, yet love my peace better, if that were all. Give me the liberty to know, to utter, and to argue freely according to conscience, above all liberties.

What would be best advised, then, if it be found so hurtful and so unequal[3] to suppress opinions for the newness or the unsuitableness to a customary acceptance, will not be my task to say; I only shall repeat what I have learned from one of your own honourable number, a right noble and pious lord, who had he not sacrificed his life and fortunes to the church and commonwealth, we had not now missed and bewailed a worthy and undoubted patron of this argument. Ye know him I am sure; yet I for honour's sake (and may it be eternal to him!) shall name him, the Lord Brook. He writing of episcopacy, and by the way treating of sects and schisms, left ye his vote, or rather now the last words of his dying charge, which I know will ever be of dear

and honoured regard with ye, so full of meekness and breathing charity, that next to His last testament, Who bequeathed love and peace to His disciples, I cannot call to mind where I have read or heard words more mild and peaceful. He there exhorts us to hear with patience and humility those, however they be miscalled, that desire to live purely, in such a use of God's ordinances, as the best guidance of their conscience gives them, and to tolerate them, though in some disconformity to ourselves. The book itself will tell us more at large being published to the world and dedicated to the parliament by him who, both for his life and for his death, deserves that what advice he left be not laid by without perusal.

And now the time in special is by privilege to write and speak what may help to the further discussing of matters in agitation. The temple of Janus with his two controversal[1] faces might now not unsignificantly be set open.[2] And though all the winds of doctrine were let loose to play upon the earth, so Truth be in the field, we do injuriously by licensing and prohibiting to misdoubt her strength. Let her and Falsehood grapple; who ever knew Truth put to the worse in a free and open encounter? Her confuting is the best and surest suppressing. He who hears what praying there is for light and clearer knowledge to be sent down among us, would think of other matters to be constituted beyond the discipline of Geneva, framed and fabricked already to our hands. Yet when the new light which we beg for shines in upon us, there be who envy and oppose, if it come not first in at their casements. What a collusion is this, whenas we are exhorted by the wiseman to use diligence, *to seek for wisdom as for hidden treasures* early and late, that another order shall enjoin us to know nothing but by statute! When a man hath been labouring the hardest labour in the deep mines of knowledge, hath furnished out his findings in all their equipage, drawn forth his reasons as it were a battle[3] ranged, scattered and defeated all objections in his way, calls out his adversary into the plain, offers him the advantage of wind and sun, if he please, only that he may try the matter by dint of argument, for his opponents then to skulk, to

---

[1] intelligences [2] A tax levied for defence against the Danes. [3] unjust

[1] turned opposite ways [2] *His temple at Rome was kept open in time of war.* [3] battalion

lay ambushments, to keep a narrow bridge of licensing where the challenger should pass, though it be valour enough in soldiership, is but weakness and cowardice in the wars of Truth. For who knows not that Truth is strong next to the Almighty? She needs no policies, no stratagems, nor licensings to make her victorious; those are the shifts and the defences that Error uses against her power. Give her but room, and do not bind her when she sleeps, for then she speaks not true, as the old Proteus did, who spake oracles only when he was caught and bound;[1] but then rather she turns herself into all shapes except her own, and perhaps tunes her voice according to the time, as Micaiah did before Ahab,[2] until she be adjured into her own likeness.

SIR JOHN SUCKLING
(1609–1642)

THE CONSTANT LOVER

Out upon it, I have loved
    Three whole days together!
And am like to love three more,
    If it prove fair weather.   4

Time shall moult away his wings
    Ere he shall discover
In the whole wide world again
    Such a constant lover.   8

But the spite on't is, no praise
    Is due at all to me:
Love with me had made no stays,
    Had it any been but she.   12

Had it any been but she,
    And that very face,
There had been at least ere this
    A dozen dozen in her place.   16

WHY SO PALE AND WAN?

Why so pale and wan, fond lover?
    Prithee, why so pale?
Will, when looking well can't move her,
    Looking ill prevail?
Prithee, why so pale?   5

Why so dull and mute, young sinner?
    Prithee, why so mute?
Will, when speaking well can't win her,
    Saying nothing do 't?
Prithee, why so mute?   10

Quit, quit for shame! This will not move;
    This cannot take her.
If of herself she will not love,
    Nothing can make her:
    The devil take her!   15

RICHARD CRASHAW
(1613?–1649)

IN THE HOLY NATIVITY OF OUR LORD GOD
A HYMN SUNG AS BY THE SHEPHERDS
CHORUS

Come, we shepherds, whose blest sight
Hath met Love's noon in Nature's night;
Come, lift we up our loftier song
And wake the sun that lies too long.

To all our world of well-stol'n joy
He slept, and dreamt of no such thing;
    While we found out heaven's fairer eye
And kissed the cradle of our King.
Tell him he rises now, too late
To show us aught worth looking at.   10

Tell him we now can show him more
Than he e'er showed to mortal sight;
    Than he himself e'er saw before;
Which to be seen needs not his light.
Tell him, Tityrus, where th' hast been
Tell him, Thyrsis, what th' hast seen.

TITYRUS. Gloomy night embraced the place
    Where the noble Infant lay.
        The Babe looked up and showed
            His face;
        In spite of darkness, it was day.   20
        It was Thy day, Sweet! and did rise
    Not from the east, but from Thine
        eyes.

CHORUS. It was Thy day, Sweet . . .

THYRSIS. Winter chid aloud; and sent
    The angry North to wage his wars.
        The North forgot his fierce intent;

<hr>

[1] See the story told by Menelaus in the *Odyssey*, Bk. iv [2] cf. 1 *Kings* xxii: 15–16

And left perfumes instead of scars.
   By those sweet eyes' persuasive
     powers,
   Where he meant frost he scattered
     flowers.

CHO.   By those sweet eyes . . .   30

BOTH.   We saw Thee in Thy balmy nest,
   Young Dawn of our Eternal Day !
   We saw Thine eyes break from their
     east
   And chase the trembling shades away.
   We saw Thee, and we blest the
     sight,
   We saw Thee by Thine own sweet
     light.

TIT.   Poor World, said I, what wilt thou
     do
   To entertain this starry Stranger?
   Is this the best thou canst bestow?
   A cold and not too cleanly, manger?
   Contend, the powers of heaven and
     earth,   41
   To fit a bed for this huge birth !

CHO.   Contend the powers . . .

THYR.   Proud world, said I; cease your
     contest
   And let the mighty Babe alone;
   The phœnix builds the phœnix'
     nest,
   Love's architecture is his own;
   The Babe whose birth embraves[1]
     this morn,
   Made His own bed e'er He was
     born.

CHO.   The Babe whose . . .   50

TIT.   I saw the curl'd drops, soft and
     slow,
   Come hovering o'er the place's head;
   Off'ring their whitest sheets of
     snow
   To furnish the fair Infant's bed.
   Forbear, said I; be not too bold;
   Your fleece is white, but 'tis too
     cold.

CHO.   Forbear, said I . . .

---

[1] makes illustrious

THYR.   I saw the obsequious seraphim
   Their rosy fleece[1] of fire bestow,
   For well they now can spare their
     wings   60
   Since Heaven itself lies here below.
   Well done, said I; but are you sure
   Your down so warm, will pass for
     pure?

CHO.   Well done, said I . . .

TIT.   No, no, your King's not yet to seek
   Where to repose His royal head;
   See, see how soon His new-bloomed
     cheek
   'Twixt mother's breasts is gone to
     bed !
   Sweet choice, said we ! no way but so
   Not to lie cold, yet sleep in snow.   70

CHO.   Sweet choice, said we . . .

BOTH.   We saw Thee in Thy balmy nest,
   Bright Dawn of our Eternal Day !
   We saw Thine eyes break from their
     east
   And chase the trembling shades away.
   We saw Thee, and we blest the sight,
   We saw Thee by Thine own sweet
     Light.

CHO.   We saw Thee . . .

FULL CHORUS

Welcome, all wonders in one night !
Eternity shut in a span,   80
   Summer in winter, day in night,
   Heaven in earth, and God in man.
   Great Little One ! Whose all-em-
     bracing birth
   Lifts earth to heaven, stoops heaven
     to earth.

Welcome — though nor to gold nor
     silk,
To more than Cæsar's birthright is;
   Two sister-seas of virgin-milk
   With many a rarely-tempered kiss
   That breathes at once both maid
     and mother,   89
   Warms in the one, cools in the other.

---

[1] not of wool, but of feathers from their wings

Welcome — though not to those
gay flies [1]
Gilded i' th' beams of earthly kings,
Slippery souls in smiling eyes —
But to poor shepherds, homespun
things,
Whose wealth's their flock, whose
wit's to be
Well read in their simplicity.

Yet, when young April's husband
show'rs
Shall bless the fruitful Maia's bed,
We'll bring the first-born of her
flow'rs
To kiss Thy feet and crown Thy head.
To Thee, dread Lamb! Whose love
must keep   101
The Shepherds, more than they the
sheep.

To Thee, meek Majesty! soft King
Of simple graces and sweet loves!
Each of us his lamb will bring,
Each his pair of silver doves!
Till burnt at last in fire of Thy fair
eyes,
Ourselves become our own best sacri-
fice!

JEREMY TAYLOR (1613–1667)

THE RULE AND EXERCISES OF HOLY DYING

CHAP. I. — A GENERAL PREPARATION TOWARDS A HOLY AND BLESSED DEATH, BY WAY OF CONSIDERATION

FROM SECTION II. — [OF THE VANITY AND SHORTNESS OF MAN'S LIFE]: THE CONSIDERATION REDUCED TO PRACTICE

It will be very material to our best and noblest purposes, if we represent this scene of change and sorrow, a little more dressed up in circumstances; for so we shall be more apt to practise those rules the doctrine of which is consequent to this consideration. It is a mighty change, that is made by the death of every person, and it is visible to us, who are alive. Reckon but from the sprightfulness of

_____
[1] *i.e.*, courtiers

youth, and the fair cheeks and full eyes of childhood, from the vigorousness and strong flexure of the joints of five-and-twenty, to the hollowness and dead paleness, to the loathsomeness and horror of a three day's burial, and we shall perceive the distance to be very great and very strange. But so have I seen a rose newly springing from the clefts of its hood, and, at first, it was fair as the morning, and full with the dew of heaven, as a lamb's fleece; but when a ruder breath had forced open its virgin modesty, and dismantled its too youthful and unripe retirements, it began to put on darkness, and to decline to softness and the symptoms of a sickly age; it bowed the head, and broke its stalk, and, at night, having lost some of its leaves and all its beauty, it fell into the portion of weeds and outworn faces. The same is the portion of every man and every woman; the heritage of worms and serpents, rottenness and cold dishonour, and our beauty so changed, that our acquaintance quickly knew us not; and that change mingled with so much horror or else meets so with our fears and weak discoursings, that they who, six hours ago, tended upon us, either with charitable or ambitious services, cannot, without some regret, stay in the room alone, where the body lies stripped of its life and honour. I have read of a fair young German gentleman, who, living, often refused to be pictured, but put off the importunity of his friends' desire, by giving way, that, after a few days' burial, they might send a painter to his vault, and, if they saw cause for it, draw the image of his death unto the life. They did so, and found his face half eaten, and his midriff and backbone full of serpents; and so he stands pictured among his armed ancestors. So does the fairest beauty change, and it will be as bad with you and me; and then, what servants shall we have to wait upon us in the grave? what friends to visit us? what officious people to cleanse away the moist and unwholesome cloud reflected upon our faces from the sides of the weeping vaults, which are the longest weepers for our funeral?

This discourse will be useful, if we consider and practise by the following rules and considerations respectively.

1. All the rich and all the covetous men in the world will perceive, and all the world will perceive for them, that it is but an ill recompense for all their cares, that, by this time, all

that shall be left, will be this, that the neighbours shall say, "He died a rich man;" and yet his wealth will not profit him in the grave, but hugely swell the sad accounts of doomsday. And he that kills the Lord's people with unjust or ambitious wars for an unrewarding interest, shall have this character, that he threw away all the days of his life, that one year might be reckoned with his name, and computed by his reign or consulship; and many men, by great labours and affronts, many indignities and crimes, labour only for a pompous epitaph, and a loud title upon their marble; whilst those, into whose possessions their heirs or kindred are entered, are forgotten, and lie unregarded as their ashes, and without concernment or relation, as the turf upon the face of their grave. A man may read a sermon, the best and most passionate that ever man preached, if he shall but enter into the sepulchres of kings. In the same Escurial,[1] where the Spanish princes live in greatness and power, and decree war or peace, they have wisely placed a cemetery, where their ashes and their glory shall sleep till time shall be no more; and where our kings have been crowned, their ancestors lie interred, and they must walk over their grandsire's head to take his crown. There is an acre sown with royal seed, the copy of the greatest change, from rich to naked, from ceiled roofs to arched coffins, from living like gods to die like men. There is enough to cool the flames of lust, to abate the heights of pride, to appease the itch of covetous desires, to sully and dash out the dissembling colours of a lustful, artificial, and imaginary beauty. There the warlike and the peaceful, the fortunate and the miserable, the beloved and the despised princes mingle their dust, and pay down their symbol of mortality, and tell all the world, that, when we die, our ashes shall be equal to kings', and our accounts easier, and our pains or our crowns shall be less. To my apprehension it is a sad record, which is left by Athenæus[2] concerning Ninus, the great Assyrian monarch, whose life and death are summed up in these words: "Ninus, the Assyrian, had an ocean of gold, and other riches more than the sand in the Caspian Sea; he never saw the stars, and perhaps he never desired it; he never stirred up the holy fire among the Magi, nor touched his god with the sacred rod according to the laws; he never offered sacrifice, nor worshipped the deity, nor administered justice, nor spake to his people, nor numbered them; but he was most valiant to eat and drink, and, having mingled his wines, he threw the rest upon the stones. This man is dead: behold his sepulchre; and now hear where Ninus is. Sometimes I was Ninus, and drew the breath of a living man; but now am nothing but clay. I have nothing, but what I did eat, and what I served to myself in lust, that was and is all my portion. The wealth with which I was esteemed blessed, my enemies, meeting together, shall bear away, as the mad Thyades[1] carry a raw goat. I am gone to hell; and when I went thither, I neither carried gold, nor horse, nor silver chariot. I that wore a mitre,[2] am now a little heap of dust." I know not anything, that can better represent the evil condition of a wicked man, or a changing greatness. From the greatest secular dignity to dust and ashes his nature bears him, and from thence to hell his sins carry him, and there he shall be forever under the dominion of chains and devils, wrath and an intolerable calamity. This is the reward of an unsanctified condition, and a greatness ill gotten or ill administered.

2. Let no man extend his thoughts, or let his hopes wander towards future and far-distant events and accidental contingencies. This day is mine and yours, but ye know not what shall be on the morrow; and every morning creeps out of a dark cloud, leaving behind it an ignorance and silence deep as midnight, and undiscerned as are the phantasms that make a chrisom-child[3] to smile: so that we cannot discern what comes hereafter, unless we had a light from heaven brighter than the vision of an angel, even the spirit of prophecy. Without revelation, we cannot tell, whether we shall eat to-morrow, or whether a squinancy[4] shall choke us: and it is written in the unrevealed folds of Divine predestination, that many, who are this day alive, shall to-morrow be laid upon the cold earth, and the women shall weep over their shroud, and dress them for their funeral.

* * * * * * *

[1] a famous building near Madrid, consisting of a monastery, a church, a palace, and a mausoleum of the Kings of Spain   [2] a gossipy Greek writer of the second century after Christ

[1] worshippers of Bacchus   [2] i.e., crown   [3] newly christened child   [4] quinsy

SIR JOHN DENHAM (1615–1669)

FROM COOPER'S HILL

My eye, descending from the hill, surveys
Where Thames amongst the wanton valleys
    strays;   .   60
Thames, the most loved of all the Ocean's
    sons,
By his old sire to his embraces runs,
Hasting to pay his tribute to the sea,
Like mortal life to meet eternity;
Though with those streams he no resemblance
    hold,
Whose foam is amber, and their gravel gold,
His genuine and less guilty wealth to explore,
Search not his bottom, but survey his shore,
O'er which he kindly spreads his spacious
    wing,
And hatches plenty for th' ensuing spring; 70
Nor then destroys it with too fond a stay,
Like mothers which their infants overlay,
Nor, with a sudden and impetuous wave,
Like profuse kings, resumes the wealth he
    gave;
No unexpected inundations spoil
The mower's hopes, nor mock the plough-
    man's toil,
But godlike his unwearied bounty flows,
First loves to do, then loves the good he
    does;
Nor are his blessings to his banks confined,
But free and common as the sea or wind; 80
When he to boast or to disperse his stores,
Full of the tributes of his grateful shores,
Visits the world, and in his flying towers,[1]
Brings home to us, and makes both Indies
    ours,
Finds wealth where 'tis, bestows it where it
    wants,
Cities in deserts, woods in cities plants;
So that to us no thing, no place is strange,
While his fair bosom is the world's exchange.
O could I flow like thee, and make thy
    stream
My great example, as it is my theme!   90
Though deep, yet clear, though gentle, yet not
    dull,
Strong without rage, without o'erflowing full.

[1] ships

RICHARD LOVELACE (1618–1658)

TO LUCASTA, GOING TO THE WARS

Tell me not, Sweet, I am unkind,
    That from the nunnery
Of thy chaste breast and quiet mind
    To war and arms I fly.   4

True, a new mistress now I chase,
    The first foe in the field;
And with a stronger faith embrace
    A sword, a horse, a shield.   8

Yet this inconstancy is such
    As thou too shalt adore;
I could not love thee, Dear, so much,
    Loved I not Honour more.   12

FROM THE GRASSHOPPER

O Thou that swing'st upon the waving hair
    Of some well-fillèd oaten beard,
Drunk every night with a delicious tear
    Dropt thee from heaven, where thou wert
    rear'd.   4

The joys of earth and air are thine entire,
    That with thy feet and wings dost hop and
    fly;
And when thy poppy works, thou dost retire
    To thy carved acorn-bed to lie.   8

Up with the day, the sun thou welcom'st
    then,
    Sport'st in the gilt plaits of his beams,
And all these merry days mak'st merry, men,
    Thyself, and melancholy streams.   12

TO ALTHEA, FROM PRISON

When Love with unconfinèd wings
    Hovers within my gates,
And my divine Althea brings
    To whisper at the grates;
When I lie tangled in her hair
    And fetter'd to her eye,
The birds that wanton in the air
    Know no such liberty.   8

When flowing cups run swiftly round
    With no allaying Thames,[1]

[1] diluting water

Our careless heads with roses bound,
    Our hearts with loyal flames;
When thirsty grief in wine we steep,
    When healths and draughts go free —.
Fishes that tipple in the deep
    Know no such liberty.   16

When, like committed [1] linnets, I
    With shriller throat shall sing
The sweetness, mercy, majesty,
    And glories of my King;
When I shall voice aloud how good
    He is, how great should be,
Enlargèd winds, that curl the flood,
    Know no such liberty.   24

Stone walls do not a prison make,
    Nor iron bars a cage;
Minds innocent and quiet take
    That for an hermitage;
If I have freedom in my love
    And in my soul am free,
Angels alone, that soar above,
    Enjoy such liberty.   32

ABRAHAM COWLEY (1618–1667)

THE WISH

Well then! I now do plainly see
This busy world and I shall ne'er agree.
The very honey of all earthly joy
Does of all meats the soonest cloy;
    And they, methinks, deserve my pity
    Who for it can endure the stings,
The crowd and buzz and murmurings,
    Of this great hive, the city.   8

Ah, yet, ere I descend to the grave
May I a small house and large garden have;
And a few friends, and many books, both
        true,
Both wise, and both delightful too!
    And since love ne'er will from me flee,
    A Mistress moderately fair,
And good as guardian angels are,
    Only beloved and loving me.   16

O fountains! when in you shall I
Myself eased of unpeaceful thoughts espy?
O fields! O woods! when, when shall I be
    made

[1] caged

The happy tenant of your shade?
    Here's the spring-head of Pleasure's
        flood:
Here's wealthy Nature's treasury,
Where all the riches lie that she
    Has coin'd and stamp'd for good.   24

Pride and ambition here
Only in far-fetch'd metaphors appear;
Here nought but winds can hurtful murmurs
        scatter,
And nought but Echo flatter.
    The gods, when they descended, hither
From heaven did always choose their way:
And therefore we may boldly say
    That 'tis the way too thither.   32

How happy here should I
And one dear She live, and embracing die!
She who is all the world, and can exclude
In deserts solitude.
    I should have then this only fear:
    Lest men, when they my pleasures see,
Should hither throng to live like me,
    And so make a city here.   40

ANDREW MARVELL (1621–1678)

THE GARDEN

How vainly men themselves amaze,
To win the palm, the oak, or bays,
And their incessant labours see
Crowned from some single herb or tree
Whose short and narrow-vergèd shade
Does prudently their toils upbraid,
While all the flowers and trees do close
To weave the garlands of repose!   8

Fair Quiet, have I found thee here,
And Innocence, thy sister dear?
Mistaken long, I sought you then
In busy companies of men.
Your sacred plants, if here below,
Only among the plants will grow;
Society is all but rude
To this delicious solitude.   16

No white nor red was ever seen
So amorous as this lovely green.
Fond lovers, cruel as their flame,
Cut in these trees their mistress' name.
Little, alas! they know or heed,
How far these beauties hers exceed!

Fair trees! wheres'e'er your barks I wound
No name shall but your own be found.   24

When we have run our passion's heat,
Love hither makes his best retreat.
The gods, that mortal beauty chase,
Still in a tree did end their race;
Apollo hunted Daphne so,
Only that she might laurel grow;
And Pan did after Syrinx speed,
Not as a nymph, but for a reed.   32

What wondrous life is this I lead!
Ripe apples drop about my head;
The luscious clusters of the vine
Upon my mouth do crush their wine;
The nectarine, and curious[1] peach,
Into my hands themselves do reach;
Stumbling on melons, as I pass,
Insnared with flowers, I fall on grass.   40

Meanwhile the mind, from pleasure less,
Withdraws into its happiness; —
The mind, that ocean where each kind
Does straight its own resemblance find;
Yet it creates, transcending these,
Far other worlds, and other seas,
Annihilating all that's made
To a green thought in a green shade.   48

Here at the fountain's sliding foot,
Or at some fruit-tree's mossy root,
Casting the body's vest aside,
My soul into the boughs does glide:
There, like a bird, it sits and sings,
Then whets and combs its silver wings,
And, till prepared for longer flight,
Waves in its plumes the various light.   56

Such was that happy garden-state,
While man there walked without a mate.
After a place so pure and sweet,
What other help could yet be meet!
But 'twas beyond a mortal's share
To wander solitary there:
Two paradises 'twere in one,
To live in paradise alone.   64

How well the skilful gardener drew
Of flowers, and herbs, this dial[2] new;
Where, from above, the milder sun
Does through a fragrant zodiac run,
And, as it works, the industrious bee

[1] rare, exotic [2] a bed of various flowers which,
opening at successive hours, indicate the time of
day

Computes its time as well as we!
How could such sweet and wholesome hours
Be reckoned but with herbs and flowers?   72

TO HIS COY MISTRESS

Had we but world enough, and time,
This coyness, Lady, were no crime,
We would sit down and think which way
To walk and pass our long love's day.
Thou by the Indian Ganges' side
Shouldst rubies find; I by the tide
Of Humber would complain. I would
Love you ten years before the Flood,
And you should, if you please, refuse
Till the conversion of the Jews.   10
My vegetable love should grow
Vaster than empires, and more slow;
An hundred years should go to praise
Thine eyes and on thy forehead gaze;
Two hundred to adore each breast,
But thirty thousand to the rest;
An age at least to every part,
And the last age should show your heart.
For, Lady, you deserve this state,
Nor would I love at lower rate.   20
   But at my back I always hear
Time's wingèd chariot hurrying near;
And yonder all before us lie
Deserts of vast eternity.
Thy beauty shall no more be found,
Nor, in thy marble vault, shall sound
My echoing song; then worms shall try
That long preserved virginity,
And your quaint honour turn to dust,
And into ashes all my lust: 30
The grave's a fine and private place,
But none, I think, do there embrace.
   Now therefore, while the youthful hue
Sits on thy skin like morning dew,
And while thy willing soul transpires
At every pore with instant fires,
Now let us sport us while we may,
And now, like amorous birds of prey,
Rather at once our time devour
Than languish in his slow-chapt[1] power.   40
Let us roll all our strength and all
Our sweetness up into one ball,
And tear our pleasures with rough strife
Thorough[2] the iron gates of life:
Thus, though we cannot make our sun
Stand still, yet we will make him run.

[1] *Time is represented as having jaws (chaps)
that move slowly.* [2] through

HENRY VAUGHAN (1622–1695)

THE RETREAT

Happy those early days, when I
Shined in my angel-infancy!
Before I understood this place
Appointed for my second race,
Or taught my soul to fancy ought
But a white, celestial thought;
When yet I had not walked above
A mile or two from my first love,
And looking back — at that short space —
Could see a glimpse of His bright face; 10
When on some gilded cloud or flower
My gazing soul would dwell an hour,
And in those weaker glories spy
Some shadows of eternity;
Before I taught my tongue to wound
My conscience with a sinful sound,
Or had the black art to dispense,
A several sin to every sense,
But felt through all this fleshly dress
Bright shoots of everlastingness. 20
  O how I long to travel back,
And tread again that ancient track!
That I might once more reach that plain,
Where first I left my glorious train;
From whence the enlightened spirit sees
That shady city of palm trees.
But ah! my soul with too much stay
Is drunk, and staggers in the way!
Some men a forward motion love,
But I by backward steps would move; 30
And when this dust falls to the urn,
In that state I came, return.

From THE WORLD

I saw Eternity the other night,
Like a great ring of pure and endless light,
All calm, as it was bright;

And round beneath it Time in hours, days,
  years, 4
  Driven by the spheres
Like a vast shadow moved; in which the
  world
  And all her train were hurled.

THE TIMBER

Sure thou didst flourish once; and many
  springs,
  Many bright mornings, much dew, many
  showers,
Pass'd o'er thy head; many light hearts and
  wings,
  Which now are dead, lodged in thy living
  bowers. 4

And still a new succession sings and flies;
  Fresh groves grow up, and their green
  branches shoot
Towards the old and still enduring skies, 7
  While the low violet thrives at their root.

But thou beneath the sad and heavy line
  Of death dost waste, all senseless, cold, and
  dark;
Where not so much as dreams of light may
  shine, 11
  Nor any thought of greenness, leaf, or bark.

And yet — as if some deep hate and dissent,
  Bred in thy growth betwixt high winds and
  thee,
Were still alive — thou dost great storms resent
  Before they come, and know'st how near
  they be. 16

Else all at rest thou liest, and the fierce breath
  Of tempests can no more disturb thy ease;
But this thy strange resentment after death
  Means only those who broke in life thy
  peace. 20

THE RESTORATION

JOHN DRYDEN (1631–1700)

From STANZAS ON OLIVER CROMWELL

And now 'tis time; for their officious haste
  Who would before have borne him to the
    sky,
Like eager Romans, ere all rites were past,
  Did let too soon the sacred eagle fly.   4

Though our best notes are treason to his fame
  Joined with the loud applause of public
    voice,
Since Heaven what praise we offer to his name
  Hath rendered too authentic by its choice; 8

Though in his praise no arts can liberal be,
  Since they, whose Muses have the highest
    flown,
Add not to his immortal memory,
  But do an act of friendship to their own; 12

Yet 'tis our duty and our interest too
  Such monuments as we can build to raise,
Lest all the world prevent [1] what we should do,
  And claim a title in him by their praise. 16

How shall I then begin or where conclude
  To draw a fame so truly circular?
For in a round what order can be shewed,
  Where all the parts so equal-perfect are? 20

His grandeur he derived from Heaven alone,
  For he was great, ere Fortune made him so;
And wars, like mists that rise against the sun,
  Made him but greater seem, not greater
    grow.   24

No borrowed bays his temples did adorn,
  But to our crown he did fresh jewels bring;
Nor was his virtue poisoned, soon as born,
  With the too early thoughts of being king. 28

*   *   *   *   *   *   *

[1] anticipate

From ABSALOM AND ACHITOPHEL

*   *   *   *   *   *   *

Of these the false Achitophel [1] was first, 150
A name to all succeeding ages curst:
For close [2] designs and crooked counsels fit,
Sagacious, bold, and turbulent of wit, [3]
Restless, unfixed in principles and place,
In power unpleased, impatient of disgrace: 155
A fiery soul, which, working out its way,
Fretted the pigmy body to decay
And o'er-informed [4] the tenement of clay.
A daring pilot in extremity,
Pleased with the danger, when the waves went
  high,
He sought the storms; but, for a calm unfit,
Would steer too nigh the sands to boast his
  wit.   162
Great wits are sure to madness near allied
And thin partitions do their bounds divide;
Else, why should he, with wealth and honour
  blest,
Refuse his age the needful hours of rest? 166
Punish a body which he could not please,
Bankrupt of life, yet prodigal of ease?
And all to leave what with his toil he won
To that unfeathered two-legg'd thing, a son. 170

*   *   *   *   *   *   *

A numerous host of dreaming saints succeed
Of the true old enthusiastic breed: 530
'Gainst form and order they their power em-
  ploy,
Nothing to build and all things to destroy.
But far more numerous was the herd of such
Who think too little and who talk too much.
These out of mere instinct, they knew not
  why,
Adored their fathers' God and property, 536
And by the same blind benefit of Fate
The Devil and the Jebusite [5] did hate:
Born to be saved even in their own despite,
Because they could not help believing right. 540

[1] the Earl of Shaftesbury [2] secret [3] intellect.
[4] overfilled [5] their enemies, the Catholics

Such were the tools; but a whole Hydra [1] more
Remains of sprouting heads too long to score.
Some of their chiefs were princes of the land;
In the first rank of these did Zimri [2] stand,
A man so various that he seemed to be 545
Not one, but all mankind's epitome:
Stiff in opinions, always in the wrong,
Was everything by starts and nothing long;
But in the course of one revolving moon
Was chymist, [3] fiddler, statesman, and buffoon;
Then all for women, painting, rhyming, drinking, 551
Besides ten thousand freaks that died in thinking.
Blest madman, who could every hour employ
With something new to wish or to enjoy!
Railing and praising were his usual themes, 555
And both, to show his judgment, in extremes:
So over violent or over civil
That every man with him was God or Devil.
In squandering wealth was his peculiar art;
Nothing went unrewarded but desert. 560
Beggared by fools whom still he found [4] too late,
He had his jest, and they had his estate.
He laughed himself from Court; then sought relief
By forming parties, but could ne'er be chief:
For spite of him, the weight of business fell 565
On Absalom and wise Achitophel;
Thus wicked but in will, of means bereft,
He left not faction, but of that was left.

* * * * * * *

FROM THE HIND AND THE PANTHER [5]

A milk-white Hind, immortal and unchanged,
Fed on the lawns and in the forest ranged;
Without unspotted, innocent within,
She feared no danger, for she knew no sin.
Yet had she oft been chased with horns and hounds 5
And Scythian [6] shafts, and many wingèd wounds
Aimed at her heart; was often forced to fly,
And doomed to death, though fated not to die.
Not so her young; for their unequal line
Was hero's make, half human, half divine. 10

[1] a fabulous monster with a hundred heads, killed by Hercules [2] the Duke of Buckingham, whom Dryden hated personally [3] alchemist [4] found out [5] *For the churches symbolized by the beasts see the Notes.* [6] a general term for barbarians

Their earthly mould obnoxious was to fate,
The immortal part assumed immortal state.
Of these a slaughtered army lay in blood,
Extended o'er the Caledonian [1] wood,
Their native walk; whose vocal blood arose 15
And cried for pardon on their perjured foes.
Their fate was fruitful, and the sanguine seed,
Endued with souls, increased the sacred breed.
So captive Israel multiplied in chains,
A numerous exile, and enjoyed her pains. 20
With grief and gladness mixed, their mother viewed
Her martyred offspring and their race renewed;
Their corps to perish, but their kind to last,
So much the deathless plant the dying fruit surpassed. 24
Panting and pensive now she ranged alone,
And wandered in the kingdoms once her own.
The common hunt, though from their rage restrained
By sovereign power, her company disdained,
Grinned as they passed, and with a glaring eye
Gave gloomy signs of secret enmity. 30
'Tis true she bounded by and tripped so light,
They had not time to take a steady sight;
For truth has such a face and such a mien
As to be loved needs only to be seen.
The bloody Bear, an Independent beast 35
Unlicked to form, [2] in groans her hate expressed.
Among the timorous kind the quaking Hare
Professed neutrality, but would not swear.
Next her the buffoon Ape, as atheists use, [3] 39
Mimicked all sects and had his own to choose;
Still when the Lion looked, his knees he bent,
And paid at church a courtier's compliment.
The bristled Baptist Boar, impure as he,
But whitened with the foam of sanctity,
With fat pollutions filled the sacred place, 45
And mountains levelled in his furious race:
So first rebellion founded was in grace.
But, since the mighty ravage which he made
In German forests [4] had his guilt betrayed,
With broken tusks and with a borrowed name,
He shunned the vengeance and concealed the shame, 51
So lurked in sects unseen. With greater guile
False Reynard fed on consecrated spoil;
The graceless beast by Athanasius first
Was chased from Nice, then by Socinus nursed,

[1] Scottish [2] *Bear cubs are said to be shapeless lumps until licked into shape by the mother bear.* [3] are accustomed [4] at Münster

His impious race their blasphemy renewed, 56
And nature's king through nature's optics
    viewed;
Reversed they viewed him lessened to their
    eye,
Nor in an infant could a God descry.
New swarming sects to this obliquely tend, 60
Hence they began, and here they all will end.

* * * * * * *

But if they think at all, 'tis sure no higher 316
Than matter put in motion may aspire;
Souls that can scarce ferment their mass of
    clay,
So drossy, so divisible are they
As would but serve pure bodies for allay,[1] 320
Such souls as shards[2] produce, such beetle
    things
As only buzz to heaven with evening wings,
Strike in the dark, offending but by chance,
Such are the blindfold blows of ignorance.
They know not beings, and but hate a name;
To them the Hind and Panther are the same.

ALEXANDER'S FEAST; OR, THE POWER OF MUSIC

A SONG IN HONOUR OF ST. CECILIA'S DAY, 1697

'Twas at the royal feast for Persia won
        By Philip's warlike son:
    Aloft in awful state
    The godlike hero sate
        On his imperial throne; 5
His valiant peers were placed around;
Their brows with roses and with myrtles
    bound:
(So should desert in arms be crowned.)
The lovely Thais, by his side,
Sate like a blooming Eastern bride, 10
In flower of youth and beauty's pride.
        Happy, happy, happy pair!
            None but the brave,
            None but the brave,
        None but the brave deserves the fair.

CHORUS

    Happy, happy, happy pair!
        None but the brave,
        None but the brave,
    None but the brave deserves the fair.

[1] alloy   [2] dung

        Timotheus,[1] placed on high 20
        Amid the tuneful quire,
With flying fingers touched the lyre:
    The trembling notes ascend the sky,
    And heavenly joys inspire.
The song began from Jove,[2] 25
Who left his blissful seats above,
    (Such is the power of mighty love)
A dragon's fiery form belied[3] the god:
Sublime on radiant spires[4] he rode,
When he to fair Olympia[5] pressed; 30
    And while he sought her snowy breast,
Then round her slender waist he curled,
And stamped an image of himself, a sovereign
    of the world.
The listening crowd admire the lofty sound,
A present deity, they shout around; 35
A present deity, the vaulted roofs rebound:
        With ravished ears
        The monarch hears,
        Assumes the god,
        Affects to nod, 40
    And seems to shake the spheres.

CHORUS

        With ravished ears
        The monarch hears,
        Assumes the god,
        Affects to nod, 45
    And seems to shake the spheres.

The praise of Bacchus then the sweet musician
        sung,
    Of Bacchus ever fair, and ever young.
    The jolly god in triumph comes;
    Sound the trumpets, beat the drums; 50
        Flushed with a purple grace
        He shows his honest face:
Now give the hautboys breath; he comes, he
    comes.
    Bacchus, ever fair and young,
        Drinking joys did first ordain; 55
    Bacchus' blessings are a treasure,
    Drinking is the soldier's pleasure;
        Rich the treasure,
        Sweet the pleasure,
    Sweet is pleasure after pain. 60

[1] a celebrated Athenian musician (d. 357 B.C.),
said to have improved the cithara by adding one
string to it [2] fabled to have been Alexander's
father [3] disguised [4] uplifted in shining spirals
[5] Olympias, mother of Alexander

*CHORUS

Bacchus' blessings are a treasure,
Drinking is the soldier's pleasure;
Rich the treasure,
Sweet the pleasure,
Sweet is pleasure after pain.   65

Soothed with the sound the king grew vain;
Fought all his battles o'er again;
And thrice he routed all his foes, and thrice
he slew the slain.
The master saw the madness rise,
His glowing cheeks, his ardent eyes;   70
And while he heaven and earth defied,
Changed his hand, and checked his pride.
, He chose a mournful Muse,
Soft pity to infuse;
He sung Darius[1] great and good,   75
By too severe a fate,
Fallen, fallen, fallen, fallen,
Fallen from his high estate,
And weltering in his blood;
Deserted at his utmost need   80
By those his former bounty fed;
On the bare earth exposed he lies,
With not a friend to close his eyes.
With downcast looks the joyless victor sate,
Revolving in his altered soul   85
The various turns of chance below:
And, now and then, a sigh he stole,
And tears began to flow.

CHORUS

Revolving in his altered soul
The various turns of chance below;   90
And, now and then, a sigh he stole,
And tears began to flow.

The mighty master smiled to see
That love was in the next degree;
'Twas but a kindred-sound to move   95
For pity melts the mind to love.
Softly sweet, in Lydian measures,
Soon he soothed his soul to pleasures.
War, he sung, is toil and trouble;
Honour but an empty bubble;   100
Never ending, still beginning,
Fighting still, and still destroying:
If the world be worth thy winning,
Think, O think it worth enjoying:
Lovely Thais sits beside thee,   105
Take the good the gods provide thee.

[1] whom Alexander had conquered

The many rend the skies with loud applause:
So Love was crowned, but Music won the
cause.
The prince, unable to conceal his pain,
Gazed on the fair   110
Who caused his care,
And sighed and looked, sighed and looked,
Sighed and looked, and sighed again;
At length, with love and wine at once op-
pressed,
The vanquished victor sunk upon her breast.

CHORUS

The prince, unable to conceal his pain,
Gazed on the fair   117
Who caused his care,
And sighed and looked, sighed and looked,
Sighed and looked, and sighed again;   120
At length, with love and wine at once op-
pressed,
The vanquished victor sunk upon her breast.

Now strike the golden lyre again;
A louder yet, and yet a louder strain.
Break his bands of sleep asunder   125
And rouse him, like a rattling peal of
thunder.
Hark, hark, the horrid sound
Has raised up his head;
As awaked from the dead,
And, amazed, he stares around. 130
"Revenge, revenge!" Timotheus cries;
"See the Furies arise;
See the snakes that they rear,
How they hiss in their hair,
And the sparkles that flash from their
eyes?   135
Behold a ghastly band,
Each a torch in his hand!
Those are Grecian ghosts, that in battle were
slain,
And unburied remain
Inglorious on the plain: 140
Give the vengeance due
To the valiant crew.
Behold how they toss their torches on high,
How they point to the Persian abodes,
And glittering temples of their hostile gods."
The princes applaud with a furious joy; 146
And the king seized a flambeau with zeal to
destroy;
Thais led the way,
To light him to his prey,   149
And, like another Helen, fired another Troy.

CHORUS

And the king seized a flambeau with zeal to
    destroy;
. Thais led the way,
    To light him to his prey,   153
And, like another Helen, fired another Troy.

    Thus long ago,
  Ere heaving bellows learned to blow,
    While organs yet were mute,
    Timotheus, to his breathing flute
    And sounding lyre,
Could swell the soul to rage, or kindle soft
    desire.   160
  At last divine Cecilia[1] came,
  Inventress of the vocal frame;
The sweet enthusiast, from her sacred store,
  Enlarged the former narrow bounds,
  And added length to solemn sounds,   165
With Nature's mother-wit, and arts unknown
    before.
  Let old Timotheus yield the prize,
    Or both divide the crown:
  He raised a mortal to the skies;
    She drew an angel down.[2]   170

GRAND CHORUS

  At last divine Cecilia came,
  Inventress of the vocal frame;
The sweet enthusiast, from her sacred store,
  Enlarged the former narrow bounds,
  And added length to solemn sounds,   175
With Nature's mother-wit, and arts unknown
    before.
  Let old Timotheus yield the prize,
    Or both divide the crown:
  He raised a mortal to the skies;
    She drew an angel down.   180

LINES PRINTED UNDER THE EN-GRAVED PORTRAIT OF MILTON

(In Tonson's folio edition of the Paradise Lost, 1688)

Three poets,[3] in three distant ages born,
Greece, Italy, and England did adorn.
The first in loftiness of thought surpassed,

[1] St. Cecilia, the patron saint of musicians and, according to legend, the inventor of the organ — the "vocal frame," as Dryden calls it [2] *An angel came to hear her play.* [3] Homer, Vergil, and Milton

The next in majesty, in both the last.
The force of Nature could no farther go;
To make a third she joined the former two.

FROM AN ESSAY OF DRAMATIC POESY

  *   *   *   *   *   *   *

  This moderation of Crites, as it was pleasing to all the company, so it put an end to that dispute; which Eugenius, who seemed to have the better of the argument, would urge no farther. But Lisideius, after he had acknowledged himself of Eugenius his opinion concerning the ancients, yet told him, he had forborne, till his discourse were ended, to ask him, why he preferred the English plays above those of other nations? and whether we ought not to submit our stage to the exactness of our next neighbours?

  Though, said Eugenius, I am at all times ready to defend the honour of my country against the French, and to maintain, we are as well able to vanquish them with our pens, as our ancestors have been with their swords; yet, if you please, added he, looking upon Neander, I will commit this cause to my friend's management; his opinion of our plays is the same with mine: and besides, there is no reason, that Crites and I, who have now left the stage,[1] should reënter so suddenly upon it; which is against the laws of comedy.

  If the question had been stated, replied Lisideius, who had writ best, the French or English, forty years ago, I should have been of your opinion, and adjudged the honour to our own nation; but since that time, (said he, turning towards Neander,) we have been so long together bad Englishmen, that we had not leisure to be good poets. Beaumont, Fletcher, and Jonson, (who were only capable of bringing us to that degree of perfection which we have,) were just then leaving the world; as if in an age of so much horror, wit, and those milder studies of humanity, had no farther business among us. But the muses, who ever follow peace, went to plant in another country: it was then that the great Cardinal of Richelieu began to take them into his protection; and that, by his encouragement, Corneille, and some other Frenchmen, reformed their theatre, which before was as

[1] *i.e.,* ceased from discussion

much below ours, as it now surpasses it and the rest of Europe. But because Crites, in his discourse for the ancients, has prevented me, by observing many rules of the stage, which the moderns have borrowed from them, I shall only, in short, demand of you, whether you are not convinced that of all nations the French have observed them? In the unity of time you find them so scrupulous, that it yet remains a dispute among their poets, whether the artificial day of twelve hours, more or less, be not meant by Aristotle, rather than the natural one of twenty-four; and consequently, whether all plays ought not to be reduced into that compass. This I can testify, that in all their dramas writ within these last twenty years and upwards, I have not observed any that have extended the time to thirty hours. In the unity of place they are full as scrupulous; for many of their critics limit it to that very spot of ground where the play is supposed to begin; none of them exceed the compass of the same town or city.

The unity of action in all their plays is yet more conspicuous; for they do not burden them with under-plots, as the English do: which is the reason why many scenes of our tragi-comedies carry on a design that is nothing of kin to the main plot; and that we see two distinct webs in a play, like those in ill-wrought stuffs; and two actions, that is, two plays, carried on together, to the confounding of the audience; who, before they are warm in their concernments for one part, are diverted to another; and by that means espouse the interest of neither. From hence likewise it arises, that the one half of our actors are not known to the other. They keep their distances, as if they were Montagues and Capulets, and seldom begin an acquaintance till the last scene of the fifth act, when they are all to meet upon the stage. There is no theatre in the world has anything so absurd as the English tragi-comedy; it is a drama of our own invention, and the fashion of it is enough to proclaim it so; here a course of mirth, there another of sadness and passion, and a third of honour and a duel: thus, in two hours and a half we run through all the fits of Bedlam. The French affords you as much variety on the same day, but they do it not so unseasonably, or *mal à propos*, as we: our poets present you the play and the farce together; and our stages still retain some-

what of the original civility[1] of the Red Bull:[2]

Atque ursum et pugiles media inter carmina poscunt.[3]

The end of tragedies or serious plays, says Aristotle, is to beget admiration, compassion, or concernment; but are not mirth and compassion things incompatible? and is it not evident, that the poet must of necessity destroy the former by intermingling of the latter? that is, he must ruin the sole end and object of his tragedy, to introduce somewhat that is forced into it, and is not of the body of it. Would you not think that physician mad, who, having prescribed a purge, should immediately order you to take restringents?

But to leave our plays, and return to theirs. I have noted one great advantage they have had in the plotting of their tragedies; that is, they are always grounded upon some known history: according to that of Horace, *Ex noto fictum carmen sequar;*[4] and in that they have so imitated the ancients, that they have surpassed them. For the ancients, as was observed before, took for the foundation of their plays some poetical fiction, such as under that consideration could move but little concernment in the audience, because they already knew the event of it. But the French goes farther:

Atque ita mentitur, sic veris falsa remiscet,
Primo ne medium, medio ne discrepet imum.[5]

He so interweaves truth with probable fiction, that he puts a pleasing fallacy upon us, mends the intrigues of fate, and dispenses with the severity of history, to reward that virtue which has been rendered to us there unfortunate. Sometimes the story has left the success so doubtful, that the writer is free, by the privilege of a poet, to take that which of two or more relations will best suit with his design: as for example, in the death of Cyrus, whom Justin[6] and some others report to have perished in the Scythian war, but Xenophon

---

[1] *Spoken ironically.* [2] one of the older theatres of London [3] And in the midst of the poems they call for the bears and the boxers. [4] On a known fact I base a feigned song. [5] He so mixes false with true that the middle may not disagree with the beginning nor the end with the middle. [6] a Roman historian

affirms to have died in his bed of extreme old age. Nay more, when the event is past dispute, even then we are willing to be deceived, and the poet, if he contrives it with appearance of truth, has all the audience of his party; at least during the time his play is acting: so naturally we are kind to virtue, when our own interest is not in question, that we take it up as the general concernment of mankind. On the other side, if you consider the historical plays of Shakespeare, they are rather so many chronicles of kings, or the business many times of thirty or forty years, cramped into a representation of two hours and a half; which is not to imitate or paint nature, but rather to draw her in miniature, to take her in little; to look upon her through the wrong end of a perspective,[1] and receive her images not only much less, but infinitely more imperfect than the life: this, instead of making a play delightful, renders it ridiculous:

Quodcumque ostendis mihi sic, incredulus odi.[2]

For the spirit of man cannot be satisfied but with truth, or at least verisimility; and a poem is to contain, if not τὰ ἔτυμα,[3] yet ἐτύμοισιν ὁμοῖα,[4] as one of the Greek poets has expressed it.

Another thing in which the French differ from us and from the Spaniards, is, that they do not embarrass, or cumber themselves with too much plot; they only represent so much of a story as will constitute one whole and great action sufficient for a play: we, who undertake more, do but multiply adventures; which, not being produced from one another, as effects from causes, but barely following, constitute many actions in the drama, and consequently make it many plays.

But by pursuing closely one argument, which is not cloyed with many turns, the French have gained more liberty for verse, in which they write: they have leisure to dwell on a subject which deserves it; and to represent the passions, (which we have acknowledged to be the poet's work,) without being hurried from one thing to another, as we are in the plays of Calderon,[5] which we have seen lately upon our theatres, under the name of Spanish plots. I have taken notice but of

one tragedy of ours, whose plot has that uniformity and unity of design in it, which I have commended in the French; and that is "Rollo,"[1] or rather, under the name of Rollo, the story of Bassianus and Geta in Herodian:[2] there indeed the plot is neither large nor intricate, but just enough to fill the minds of the audience, not to cloy them. Besides, you see it founded upon the truth of history, — only the time of the action is not reduceable to the strictness of the rules; and you see in some places a little farce mingled, which is below the dignity of the other parts; and in this all our poets are extremely peccant: even Ben Jonson himself, in "Sejanus" and "Catiline," has given us this olio of a play, this unnatural mixture of comedy and tragedy, which to me sounds just as ridiculously as the history of David with the merry humours of Goliath. In "Sejanus" you may take notice of the scene betwixt Livia and the physician, which is a pleasant satire upon the artificial helps of beauty: in "Catiline" you may see the parliament of women; the little envies of them to one another; and all that passes betwixt Curio and Fulvia: scenes admirable in their kind, but of an ill mingle with the rest.

But I return again to the French writers, who, as I have said, do not burden themselves too much with plot, which has been reproached to them by an ingenious person of our nation as a fault; for he says, they commonly make but one person considerable in a play; they dwell on him, and his concernments, while the rest of the persons are only subservient to set him off. If he intends this by it, — that there is one person in the play who is of greater dignity than the rest, he must tax, not only theirs, but those of the ancients, and, which he would be loth to do, the best of ours; for it is impossible but that one person must be more conspicuous in it than any other, and consequently the greatest share in the action must devolve on him. We see it so in the management of all affairs; even in the most equal aristocracy, the balance cannot be so justly poised, but some one will be superior to the rest, either in parts, fortune, interest, or the consideration of some glorious exploit; which will reduce the greatest part of business into his hands.

---

[1] telescope [2] Whatever you show me thus, I disbelieve and hate. [3] true things [4] things resembling truth [5] a famous Spanish dramatist

[1] *The Bloody Brother, or Rollo Duke of Normandy*, a play by Fletcher and others [2] a Greek writer of the history of Rome from 180–238

But, if he would have us to imagine, that in exalting one character the rest of them are neglected, and that all of them have not some share or other in the action of the play, I desire him to produce any of Corneille's tragedies, wherein every person (like so many servants in a well-governed family) has not some employment, and who is not necessary to the carrying on of the plot, or at least to your understanding it.

There are indeed some protatic[1] persons in the ancients, whom they make use of in their plays, either to hear, or give the relation:[2] but the French avoid this with great address, making their narrations only to, or by such, who are some way interested in the main design. And now I am speaking of relations, I cannot take a fitter opportunity to add this in favour of the French, that they often use them with better judgment and more à propos than the English do. Not that I commend narrations in general, — but there are two sorts of them; one, of those things which are antecedent to the play, and are related to make the conduct of it more clear to us; but it is a fault to choose such subjects for the stage as will force us on that rock, because we see they are seldom listened to by the audience, and that is many times the ruin of the play; for, being once let pass without attention, the audience can never recover themselves to understand the plot; and indeed it is somewhat unreasonable, that they should be put to so much trouble, as, that to comprehend what passes in their sight, they must have recourse to what was done, perhaps, ten or twenty years ago.

But there is another sort of relations, that is, of things happening in the action of the play, and supposed to be done behind the scenes; and this is many times both convenient and beautiful: for, by it the French avoid the tumult to which we are subject in England, by representing duels, battles, and the like; which renders our stage too like the theatres where they fight prizes. For what is more ridiculous than to represent an army with a drum and five men behind it; all which, the hero of the other side is to drive in before him? or to see a duel fought, and one slain with two or three thrusts of the foils, which we know are so blunted, that we might give a man

an hour to kill another in good earnest with them?

I have observed, that in all our tragedies the audience cannot forbear laughing when the actors are to die; it is the most comic part of the whole play. All passions may be lively represented on the stage, if to the well-writing of them the actor supplies a good commanded voice, and limbs that move easily, and without stiffness; but there are many actions which can never be imitated to a just height: dying especially is a thing which none but a Roman gladiator could naturally perform on the stage, when he did not imitate, or represent, but do it; and therefore it is better to omit the representation of it.

* * * * * * *

I shall grant Lisideius, without much dispute, a great part of what he has urged against us; for I acknowledge, that the French contrive their plots more regularly, and observe the laws of comedy, and decorum of the stage, (to speak generally,) with more exactness than the English. Farther, I deny not but he has taxed us justly in some irregularities of ours, which he has mentioned; yet, after all, I am of opinion, that neither of our faults, nor their virtues, are considerable enough to place them above us.

For the lively imitation of nature being in the definition of a play, those which best fulfil that law, ought to be esteemed superior to the others. 'Tis true, those beauties of the French poesy are such as will raise perfection higher where it is, but are not sufficient to give it where it is not: they are indeed the beauties of a statue, but not of a man, because not animated with the soul of poesy, which is imitation of humour and passions: and this Lisideius himself, or any other, however biassed to their party, cannot but acknowledge, if he will either compare the humours of our comedies, or the characters of our serious plays, with theirs. He who will look upon theirs which have been written till these last ten years, or thereabouts, will find it an hard matter to pick out two or three passable humours amongst them. Corneille himself, their arch-poet, what has he produced except "The Liar,"[1] and you know how it was cried up in France; but when it came upon the English stage, though well translated,

[1] introductory [2] narration of events not shown on the stage

AE

[1] *Le Menteur*

and that part of Dorant acted to so much advantage as I am confident it never received in its own country, the most favourable to it would not put it in competition with many of Fletcher's or Ben Jonson's. In the rest of Corneille's comedies you have little humour; he tells you himself, his way is, first to show two lovers in good intelligence with each other; in the working up of the play, to embroil them by some mistake, and in the latter end to clear it, and reconcile them.

But of late years Molière, the younger Corneille,[1] Quinault,[2] and some others, have been imitating afar off the quick turns and graces of the English stage. They have mixed their serious plays with mirth, like our tragi-comedies, since the death of Cardinal Richelieu, which Lisideius, and many others, not observing, have commended that in them for a virtue, which they themselves no longer practise. Most of their new plays are, like some of ours, derived from the Spanish novels. There is scarce one of them without a veil,[3] and a trusty Diego,[4] who drolls much after the the rate of the "Adventures."[5] But their humours, if I may grace them with that name, are so thin sown, that never above one of them comes up in any play. I dare take upon me to find more variety of them in some one play of Ben Jonson's, than in all theirs together: as he who has seen the "Alchemist," "The Silent Woman," or "Bartholomew Fair," cannot but acknowledge with me.

I grant the French have performed what was possible on the ground-work of the Spanish plays; what was pleasant before, they have made regular: but there is not above one good play to be writ on all those plots; they are too much alike to please often, which we need not the experience of our own stage to justify. As for their new way of mingling mirth with serious plot, I do not, with Lisideius, condemn the thing, though I cannot approve their manner of doing it. He tells us, we cannot so speedily recollect ourselves after a scene of great passion and concernment, as to pass to another of mirth and humour, and to enjoy it with any relish: but why should he imagine the soul of man

more heavy than his senses? Does not the eye pass from an unpleasant object to a pleasant, in a much shorter time than is required to this? and does not the unpleasantness of the first commend the beauty of the latter? The old rule of logic might have convinced him, that contraries, when placed near, set off each other. A continued gravity keeps the spirit too much bent; we must refresh it sometimes, as we bait in a journey, that we may go on with greater ease. A scene of mirth, mixed with tragedy, has the same effect upon us which our music has betwixt the acts; which we find a relief to us from the best plots and language of the stage, if the discourses have been long. I must therefore have stronger arguments, ere I am convinced that compassion and mirth in the same subject destroy each other; and in the meantime, cannot but conclude, to the honour of our nation, that we have invented, increased, and perfected, a more pleasant way of writing for the stage, than was ever known to the ancients or moderns of any nation, which is tragi-comedy.

And this leads me to wonder why Lisideius and many others should cry up the barrenness of the French plots, above the variety and copiousness of the English. Their plots are single, they carry on one design, which is pushed forward by all the actors, every scene in the play contributing and moving towards it. Our plays, besides the main design, have underplots, or by-concernments, of less considerable persons and intrigues, which are carried on with the motion of the main plot: as they say the orb of the fixed stars, and those of the planets, though they have motions of their own, are whirled about by the motion of the *primum mobile*,[1] in which they are contained. That similitude expresses much of the English stage; for if contrary motions may be found in nature to agree; if a planet can go east and west at the same time; — one way by virtue of his own motion, the other by the force of the first mover;[2] — it will not be difficult to imagine how the under-plot, which is only different, not contrary to the great design, may naturally be conducted along with it.

Eugenius has already shown us, from the confession of the French poets, that the

---

[1] Thomas, younger brother of Pierre Corneille
[2] Philippe Quinault, the creator of lyric tragedy
[3] nun   [4] servant   [5] *The Adventures of Five Hours*, a play translated by Sir Samuel Tuke from Calderon

[1] See the note on Milton's *Hymn on the Nativity*, l. 48.   [2] primum mobile

unity of action is sufficiently preserved, if all the imperfect actions of the play are conducing to the main design; but when those petty intrigues of a play are so ill ordered, that they have no coherence with the other, I must grant that Lisideius has reason to tax that want of due connection; for coördination in a play is as dangerous and unnatural as in a state. In the meantime he must acknowledge, our variety, if well ordered, will afford a greater pleasure to the audience.

* * * * * * *

I hope I have already proved in this discourse, that though we are not altogether so punctual[1] as the French, in observing the laws of comedy, yet our errors are so few, and little, and those things wherein we excel them so considerable, that we ought of right to be preferred before them. But what will Lisideius say, if they themselves 'acknowledge they are too strictly bounded by those laws, for breaking which he has blamed the English? I will allege Corneille's words, as I find them in the end of his Discourse of the three Unities: *Il est facile aux speculatifs d'estre severes*, etc. "It is easy for speculative persons to judge severely; but if they would produce to public view ten or twelve pieces of this nature, they would perhaps give more latitude to the rules than I have done, when, by experience, they had known how much we are limited and constrained by them, and how many beauties of the stage they banished from it." To illustrate a little what he has said : — by their servile observations of the unities of time and place, and integrity of scenes, they have brought on themselves that dearth of plot, and narrowness of imagination, which may be observed in all their plays. How many beautiful accidents might naturally happen in two or three days, which cannot arrive with any probability in the compass of twenty-four hours? There is time to be allowed also for maturity of design, which amongst great and prudent persons, such as are often represented in tragedy, cannot, with any likelihood of truth, be brought to pass at so short a warning. Farther, by tying themselves strictly to the unity of place, and unbroken scenes, they are forced many times to omit some beauties which cannot be shown

where the act began; but might, if the scene were interrupted, and the stage cleared for the persons to enter in another place; and therefore the French poets are often forced upon absurdities: for if the act begins in a chamber, all the persons in the play must have some business or other to come thither, or else they are not to be shown that act; and sometimes their characters are very unfitting to appear there: as suppose it were the king's bed-chamber, yet the meanest man in the tragedy must come and despatch his business there, rather than in the lobby, or court-yard, (which is fitter for him,) for fear the stage should be cleared, and the scenes broken. Many times they fall by it into a greater inconvenience; for they keep their scenes unbroken, and yet change the place; as in one of their newest plays, where the act begins in the street. There a gentleman is to meet his friend; he sees him with his man, coming out from his father's house; they talk together, and the first goes out: the second, who is a lover, has made an appointment with his mistress; she appears at the window, and then we are to imagine the scene lies under it. This gentleman is called away, and leaves his servant with his mistress: presently her father is heard from within; the young lady is afraid the serving-man should be discovered, and thrusts him into a place of safety, which is supposed to be her closet. After this, the father enters to the daughter, and now the scene is in a house: for he is seeking from one room to another for this poor Philipin,[1] or French Diego, who is heard from within, drolling and breaking many a miserable conceit on the subject of his sad condition. In this ridiculous manner the play goes forward, the stage being never empty all the while: so that the street, the window, the two houses, and the closet, are made to walk about, and the persons to stand still. Now, what, I beseech you, is more easy than to write a regular French play, or more difficult than to write an irregular English one, like those of Fletcher, or of Shakespeare?

If they content themselves, as Corneille did, with some flat design, which, like an ill riddle, is found out ere it be half proposed, such plots we can make every way regular as easily as they; but whenever they endeavour to rise to any quick turns and counter-turns of

----

[1] exact

[1] a conventional name for a servant

plot, as some of them have attempted, since Corneille's plays have been less in vogue, you see they write as irregularly as we, though they cover it more speciously. Hence the reason is perspicuous, why no French plays, when translated, have, or ever can succeed on the English stage. For, if you consider the plots, our own are fuller of variety; if the writing, ours are more quick and fuller of spirit; and therefore 'tis a strange mistake in those who decry the way of writing plays in verse, as if the English therein imitated the French. We have borrowed nothing from them; our plots are weaved in English looms: we endeavour therein to follow the variety and greatness of characters, which are derived to us from Shakespeare and Fletcher; the copiousness and well-knitting of the intrigues we have from Jonson; and for the verse itself we have English precedents of elder date than any of Corneille's plays. Not to name our old comedies before Shakespeare, which were all writ in verse of six feet, or Alexandrines, such as the French now use, — I can show in Shakespeare, many scenes of rhyme together, and the like in Ben Jonson's tragedies: in "Catiline" and "Sejanus" sometimes thirty or forty lines, — I mean besides the chorus, or the monologues; which, by the way, showed Ben no enemy to this way of writing, especially if you read his "Sad Shepherd," which goes sometimes on rhyme, sometimes on blank verse, like an horse who eases himself on trot and amble. You find him likewise commending Fletcher's pastoral of "The Faithful Shepherdess," which is for the most part rhyme, though not refined to that purity to which it hath since been brought. And these examples are enough to clear us from a servile imitation of the French.

But to return whence I have digressed: I dare boldly affirm these two things of the English drama; — First, that we have many plays of ours as regular as any of theirs, and which, besides, have more variety of plot and characters; and, secondly, that in most of the irregular plays of Shakespeare or Fletcher, (for Ben Jonson's are for the most part regular), there is a more masculine fancy, and greater spirit in the writing, than there is in any of the French. I could produce even in Shakespeare's and Fletcher's works, some plays which are almost exactly formed; as the "Merry Wives of Windsor," and "The Scornful Lady":[1] but, because (generally speaking) Shakespeare, who writ first, did not perfectly observe the laws of comedy, and Fletcher, who came nearer to perfection, yet through carelessness made many faults; I will take the pattern of a perfect play from Ben Jonson, who was a careful and learned observer of the dramatic laws, and from all his comedies I shall select "The Silent Woman;" of which I will make a short examen, according to those rules which the French observe.

As Neander was beginning to examine "The Silent Woman," Eugenius, earnestly regarding him: I beseech you, Neander, said he, gratify the company, and me in particular, so far as, before you speak of the play, to give us a character of the author; and tell us frankly your opinion, whether you do not think all writers, both French and English, ought to give place to him?

I fear, replied Neander, that, in obeying your commands, I shall draw some envy on myself. Besides, in performing them, it will be first necessary to speak somewhat of Shakespeare and Fletcher, his rivals in poesy; and one of them, in my opinion, at least his equal, perhaps his superior.

To begin then with Shakespeare. He was the man who of all modern, and perhaps ancient poets, had the largest and most comprehensive soul. All the images of nature were still present to him, and he drew them not laboriously, but luckily: when he describes anything, you more than see it, you feel it too. Those who accuse him to have wanted learning, give him the greater commendation: he was naturally learned; he needed not the spectacles of books to read nature; he looked inwards, and found her there. I cannot say he is everywhere alike; were he so, I should do him injury to compare him with the greatest of mankind. He is many times flat, insipid; his comic wit degenerating into clenches,[2] his serious swelling into bombast. But he is always great, when some great occasion is presented to him: no man can say, he ever had a fit subject for his wit, and did not then raise himself as high above the rest of poets,

Quantum lenta solent inter viburna cupressi.[3]

---

[1] by Fletcher and Beaumont　[2] comic "gags" [3] As do the tall cypresses above the laggard shrubs.

The consideration of this made Mr. Hales of Eton say, that there was no subject of which any poet ever writ, but he would produce it much better done in Shakespeare; and however others are now generally preferred before him, yet the age wherein he lived, which had contemporaries with him, Fletcher and Jonson, never equalled them to him in their esteem: and in the last king's court, when Ben's reputation was at highest, Sir John Suckling, and with him the greater part of the courtiers, set our Shakespeare far above him.

Beaumont and Fletcher, of whom I am next to speak, had, with the advantage of Shakespeare's wit, which was their precedent, great natural gifts, improved by study; Beaumont especially being so accurate a judge of plays, that Ben Jonson, while he lived, submitted all his writings to his censure, and 'tis thought, used his judgment in correcting, if not contriving, all his plots. What value he had for him, appears by the verses he writ to him; and therefore I need speak no farther of it. The first play that brought Fletcher and him in esteem, was their "Philaster"; for before that, they had written two or three very unsuccessfully: as the like is reported of Ben Jonson, before he writ "Every Man in his Humour." Their plots are generally more regular than Shakespeare's, especially those which were made before Beaumont's death; and they understood and imitated the conversation of gentlemen much better; whose wild debaucheries, and quickness of wit in repartees, no poet before them could paint as they have done. Humour,[1] which Ben Jonson derived from particular persons, they made it not their business to describe: they represented all the passions very lively, but above all, love. I am apt to believe the English language in them arrived to its highest perfection; what words have since been taken in, are rather superfluous than ornamental. Their plays are now the most pleasant and frequent entertainments of the stage; two of theirs being acted through the year for one of Shakespeare's or Jonson's: the reason is, because there is a certain gaiety in their comedies, and pathos in their more serious plays, which suits generally with all men's humours. Shakespeare's language is likewise a little

obsolete, and Ben Jonson's wit comes short of theirs.

As for Jonson, to whose character I am now arrived, if we look upon him while he was himself, (for his last plays were but his dotages,) I think him the most learned and judicious writer which any theater ever had. He was a most severe judge of himself, as well as others. One cannot say he wanted wit, but rather that he was frugal of it. In his works you find little to retrench or alter. Wit and language, and humour also in some measure, we had before him; but something of art was wanting to the drama, till he came. He managed his strength to more advantage than any who preceded him. You seldom find him making love in any of his scenes, or endeavouring to move the passions; his genius was too sullen and saturnine to do it gracefully, especially when he knew he came after those who had performed both to such an height. Humour was his proper sphere; and in that he delighted most to represent mechanic people.[1] He was deeply conversant in the ancients, both Greek and Latin, and he borrowed boldly from them: there is scarce a poet or historian among the Roman authors of those times, whom he has not translated in "Sejanus" and "Catiline." But he has done his robberies so openly, that one may see he fears not to be taxed by any law. He invades authors like a monarch; and what would be theft in other poets, is only victory in him. With the spoils of these writers he so represents old Rome to us, in its rites, ceremonies, and customs, that if one of their poets had written either of his tragedies, we had seen less of it than in him. If there was any fault in his language, it was, that he weaved it too closely and laboriously, in his comedies especially: perhaps too, he did a little too much Romanize our tongue, leaving the words which he translated almost as much Latin as he found them: wherein, though he learnedly followed their language, he did not enough comply with the idiom of ours. If I would compare him with Shakespeare, I must acknowledge him the more correct poet, but Shakespeare the greater wit.[2] Shakespeare was the Homer, or father of our dramatic poets; Jonson was the Virgil, the pattern of elaborate writing; I admire him, but I love Shakespeare. To conclude of him;

---

[1] a natural or affected peculiarity of thought or action

[1] tradespeople   [2] genius

as he has given us the most correct plays, so in the precepts which he has laid down in his "Discoveries," we have as many and profitable rules for perfecting the stage, as any wherewith the French can furnish us.

SAMUEL PEPYS (1633-1703)

FROM HIS DIARY

September 1st. (Lord's day.) Last night being very rainy, [the water] broke into my house, the gutter being stopped, and spoiled all my ceilings almost. At church in the morning. After dinner we were very merry with Sir W. Pen[1] about the loss of his tankard, though all but a cheate, and he do not yet understand it; but the tankard was stole by Sir W. Batten, and the letter, as from the thief, wrote by me, which makes very good sport. Captain Holmes and I by coach to White Hall; in our way, I found him by discourse to be a great friend of my Lord's,[2] and he told me there was a many did seek to remove him; but they were old seamen, such as Sir J. Minnes, but he would name no more, though he do believe Sir W. Batten is one of them that do envy him, but he says he knows that the King do so love him, and the Duke of York too, that there is no fear of him. He seems to be very well acquainted with the king's mind, and with all the several factions at Court, and spoke all with so much frankness, that I do take him to be my Lord's good friend, and one able to do him great service, being a cunning fellow, and one, by his own confession to me, that can put on two several faces, and look his enemies in the face with as much love as his friends. But, good God! what an age is this, and what a world is this! that a man cannot live without playing the knave and dissimulation.

2d. Mr. Pickering and I to Westminster Hall[3] again, and there walked an houre or two talking, and, though he be a fool, yet he keeps much company, and will tell all he sees or hears, and so a man may understand what the common talk of the town is. And I find that

there are endeavours to get my Lord out of play at sea, which I believe Mr. Coventry[1] and the Duke[2] do think will make them more absolute; but I hope for all this, they will not be able to do it. My wife tells me that she met at Change[3] with my young ladies of the Wardrobe,[4] and there helped them to buy things, and also with Mr. Somerset, who did give her a bracelet of rings, which did a little trouble me, though I know there is no hurt yet in it, but only for fear of further acquaintance.

3d. Dined at home, and then with my wife to the Wardrobe, where my Lady's child was christened, my Lord Crewe and his lady, and my Lady Montagu, my Lord's mother-in-law, were the witnesses, and named Catherine, the Queen elect's name; but to my and all our trouble, the Parson of the parish christened her, and did not sigħ the child with the sign of the cross. After that was done, we had a very fine banquet.

4th. My wife come to me to Whitehall,[5] and we went and walked a good while in St. James's Parke to see the brave alterations.

5th. Put my mother and Pall[6] into the wagon, and saw them going presently — Pall crying exceedingly. To my uncle Fenner's to dinner, in the way meeting a French footman with feathers, who was in quest of my wife, and spoke with her privately, but I could not tell what it was, only my wife promised to go to some place to-morrow morning, which do trouble my mind how to know whither it was. My wife and I to the fair, and I showed her the Italians dancing the ropes, and the women that do strange tumbling tricks.

6th. I went to the Theatre, and saw "Elder Brother"[7] acted; meeting here with Sir J. Askew, Sir Theophilus Jones, and another knight, with Sir W. Pen, we to the Ship taverne, and there staid, and were merry till late at night.

7th. Having appointed the young ladies at the Wardrobe to go with them to the play to-day, my wife and I took them to the Theatre, where we seated ourselves close by the King,

---

[1] an English admiral and commissioner of the Admiralty, father of the founder of Pennsylvania [2] Edward Montagu, earl of Sandwich, general of the English fleet [3] the parliament building

[1] Sir William Coventry, M.P., later a commissioner of the Admiralty [2] the Duke of York, Lord High Admiral [3] the Royal Exchange, where there were many fine shops [4] The Earl of Sandwich had been assigned official residence at the King's Wardrobe; the young ladies belonged to his family. [5] the royal palace [6] his sister Paulina [7] a play by Fletcher

and Duke of York, and Madame Palmer,[1] which was great content; and, indeed, I can never enough admire her beauty. And here was "Bartholomew Fayre,"[2] with the puppet-showe, acted to-day, which had not been these forty years, it being so satyrical against Puritanism, they durst not till now, which is strange they should already dare to do it, and the King to countenance it, but I do never a whit like it the better for the puppets, but rather the worse. Thence home with the ladies, it being by reason of our staying a great while for the King's coming, and the length of the play, near nine o'clock before it was done.

8th. (Lord's day.) To church, and coming home again, found our new mayd Doll asleep, that she could not hear to let us in, so that we were fain to send a boy in at a window to open the door to us. Begun to look over my accounts, and, upon the whole, I do find myself, by what I can yet see, worth near 600l, for which God be blessed.

9th. To Salisbury Court play-house, where was acted the first time, "'Tis pity she's a W—e,"[3] a simple play, and ill acted, only it was my fortune to sit by a most pretty and ingenious lady, which pleased me much. To the Dolphin, to drink the 30s. that we got the other day of Sir W. Pen about his tankard. Here was Sir R. Slingsby, Holmes, Captain Allen, Mr. Turner, his wife and daughter, my Lady Batten, and Mrs. Martha, &c., and an excellent company of fiddlers; so we exceeding merry till late; and then we begun to tell Sir W. Pen the business, but he had been drinking to-day, and so is almost gone, that we could not make him understand it, which caused us more sport.

11th. To Dr. Williams, who did carry me into his garden, where he hath abundance of grapes: and he did show me how a dog that he hath do kill all the cats that come thither to kill his pigeons, and do afterwards bury them; and do it with so much care that they shall be quite covered; that if the tip of the tail hangs out, he will take up the cat again, and dig the hole deeper, which is very strange; and he tells me, that he do believe he hath killed above 100 cats. Home to my house to dinner, where I found my wife's brother Balty

as fine as hands could make him, and his servant, a Frenchman, to wait on him, and come to have my wife visit a young lady which he is a servant[1] to, and have hope to trepan,[2] and get for his wife. I did give way for my wife to go with him. Walking through Lincoln's Inn Fields, observed at the Opera a new play, "Twelfth Night," was acted there, and the King there: so I, against my own mind and resolution, could not forbear to go in, which did make the play seem a burthen to me; and I took no pleasure at all in it: and so, after it was done, went home with my mind troubled for my going thither, after my swearing to my wife that I would never go to a play without her. My wife was with her brother to see his mistress[3] to-day, and says she is young, rich, and handsome, but not likely for him to get.

12th. To my Lady's to dinner at the Wardrobe; and in my way upon the Thames, I saw the King's new pleasure-boat that is come now for the King to take pleasure in above bridge, and also two Gundaloes,[4] that are lately brought, which are very rich and fine. Called at Sir W. Batten's, and there hear that Sir W. Pen do take our jest of the tankard very ill, which I am sorry for.

13th. I was sent for by my uncle Fenner to come and advise about the burial of my aunt, the butcher,[5] who died yesterday. Thence to the Wardrobe, where I found my wife, and thence she and I to the water to spend the afternoon in pleasure, and so we went to old George's,[6] and there eat as much as we would of a hot shoulder of mutton, and so to boat again and home.

14th. Before we had dined comes Sir R. Slingsby, and his lady, and a great deal of company, to take my wife and I out by barge, to show them the King's and Duke's yachts. We had great pleasure, seeing all four yachts, viz., these two, and the two Dutch ones.

15th. (Lord's day.) To my aunt Kite's in the morning, to help my uncle Fenner to put things in order against anon for the burial. After sermon, with my wife to the burial of my aunt Kite, where, besides us and my uncle Fenner's family, there was none of any quality, but poor and rascally people. So we went to church with the corps, and there had ser-

---

[1] mistress of the King, later created Duchess of Cleveland [2] a comedy by Ben Jonson [3] a tragedy by John Ford

[1] suitor [2] ensnare [3] sweetheart [4] two gondolas, presented to the King by the Duke of Venice [5] the butcher's wife [6] a tavern

vice read at the grave, and back again with Pegg Kite, who will be, I doubt, a troublesome carrion to us executors, but if she will not be ruled, I shall fling up my executorship.

16th. Word is brought me from my brother's, that there is a fellow come from my father out of the country, on purpose to speak with me, and he made a story how he had lost his letter, but he was sure it was for me to come into the country, which I believed, but I afterwards found that it was a rogue that did use to play such tricks to get money of people, but he got none of me. Letters from my father informing me of the court,[1] and that I must come down and meet him at Impington, which I presently resolved to do.

17th. Got up, telling my wife of my journey, and she got me to hire her a horse to go along with me. So I went to my Lady's, and of Mr. Townsend did borrow a very fine side-saddle for my wife, and so, after all things were ready, she and I took coach to the end of the towne towards Kingsland, and there got upon my horse, and she upon her pretty mare that I hired for her, and she rides very well. By the mare at one time falling, she got a fall, but no harm; so we got to Ware, and there supped, and went to bed.

18th. Up early, and begun our march: the way about Puckridge very bad, and my wife, in the very last dirty place of all, got a fall, but no hurt, though some dirt. At last, she begun, poor wretch, to be tired, and I to be angry at it, but I was to blame; for she is a very good companion as long as she is well. In the afternoon, we got to Cambridge, where I left my wife at my cozen Angier's, while I went to Christ's College, and there found my brother in his chamber, and talked with him, and so to the barber's, and then to my wife again, and remounted for Impington, where my uncle received me and my wife very kindly.

*   *   *   *   *   *   *

22d. (Lord's day.) To church, where we had common prayer, and a dull sermon by one Mr. Case, who yet I heard sing very well.

23d. We took horse, and got early to Baldwick, where there was a fair, and we put in, and eat a mouthful of porke, which they made us pay 14*d.* for, which vexed me much. And

so away to Stevenage, and staid till a shower was over, and so rode easily to Welling. We supped well, and had two beds in the room, and so lay single.

24th. We rose, and set forth, but found a most sad alteration in the roade, by reason of last night's rains, they being now all dirty and washy, though not deep. So we rode easily through, and only drinking at Holloway, at the sign of a woman with cakes in one hand, and a pot of ale in the other,[1] which did give good occasion of mirth, resembling her to the maid that served us, we got home very timely and well, and finding there all well, and letters from sea, that speak of my Lord's being well; and his Action, though not considerable of any side, at Algiers.

25th. Sir W. Pen told me that I need not fear any reflection upon my Lord for their ill success at Argier, for more could not be done. Meeting Sir R. Slingsby in St. Martin's Lane, he and I in his coach through the Mewes, which is the way that now all coaches are forced to go, because of a stop at Charing Crosse, by reason of digging of a drayne there to clear the streets. To my Lord Crewe's, and dined with him, where I was used with all imaginable kindness both from him and her. And I see that he is afraid my Lord's reputacon will a little suffer in common talk by this late successe; but there is no help for it now. The Queen of England, as she is now owned and called, I hear, doth keep open court, and distinct at Lisbone. To the Theatre, and saw "The Merry Wives of Windsor" ill done.

26th. With my wife by coach to the Theatre, to show her "King and no King,"[2] it being very well done.

27th. At noon, met my wife at the Wardrobe; and there dined, where we found Captain Country, my little Captain that I loved, who carried me to the Sound,[3] with some grapes and millons [4] from my Lord at Lisbone, the first that ever I saw; but the grapes are rare things. In the afternoon comes Mr. Edward Montagu, by appointment this morning, to talk with my Lady and me about the provisions fit to be bought and sent to my Lord

---

[1] the manorial court under which Pepys held some of his copyhold estates

[1] the original of the sign called Mother Redcap [2] a play by Beaumont and Fletcher [3] Pepys had accompanied Sir Edward Montagu on his voyage to the Sound (a narrow passage between Sweden and the Danish island of Zealand) in 1658. [4] melons

along with him. And told us, that we need not trouble ourselves how to buy them, for the King would pay for all, and that he would take care to get them: which put my Lady and me into a great deal of ease of mind. Here we stayed and supped too; and, after my wife had put up some of the grapes in a basket for to be sent to the King, we took coach and home, where we found a hamper of millons sent to me also.

28th. Sir W. Pen and his daughter, and I and my wife, to the Theatre, and there saw "Father's own Son,"[1] a very good play, and the first time I ever saw it.

29th. (Lord's day.) What at dinner and supper I drink, I know not how, of my own accord, so much wine, that I was even almost foxed, and my head ached all night; so home and to bed, without prayers, which I never did yet, since I come to the house, of a Sunday night: I being now so out of order that I durst not read prayers, for fear of being perceived by my servants in what case I was.

SAMUEL BUTLER (1612–1680)

HUDIBRAS

PART I. FROM CANTO I

We grant, altho' he had much wit,
H' was very shy of using it,
As being loath to wear it out;
And therefore bore it not about,
Unless on holidays or so,　　　　　　　　　50
As men their best apparel do.
Beside, 'tis known he could speak Greek
As naturally as pigs squeak;
That Latin was no more difficile,
Than to a blackbird 'tis to whistle:
Being rich in both, he never scanted
His bounty unto such as wanted;
But much of either would afford
To many that had not one word.
For Hebrew roots, altho' they're found
To flourish most in barren ground,　　　　60
He had such plenty as sufficed
To make some think him circumcised:
And truly so perhaps he was,
'Tis many a pious Christian's case.
　He was in logic a great critic,
Profoundly skill'd in analytic:

He could distinguish, and divide
A hair 'twixt south and south-west side;
On either which he would dispute,
Confute, change hands, and still confute.　70
He'd undertake to prove, by force
Of argument, a man's no horse;
He'd prove a buzzard is no fowl,
And that a lord may be an owl,
A calf an alderman, a goose a justice,
And rooks committee-men and trustees.
He'd run in debt by disputation,
And pay with ratiocination.
All this by syllogism, true
In mood and figure, he would do.　　　　80
　For rhetoric, he could not ope
His mouth, but out there flew a trope;
And when he happen'd to break off
I' th' middle of his speech, or cough,
H' had hard words ready to show why,
And tell what rules he did it by;
Else, when with greatest art he spoke,
You'd think he talk'd like other folk:
For all a rhetorician's rules
Teach nothing but to name his tools.　　90
But, when he pleased to show't, his speech
In loftiness of sound was rich;
A Babylonish dialect,
Which learnèd pedants much affect;
It was a party-colour'd dress
Of patch'd and piebald languages:
'Twas English cut on Greek and Latin,
Like fustian heretofore on satin;
It had an odd promiscuous tone,
As if h' had talk'd three parts in one;　100
Which made some think, when he did gabble,
Th' had heard three labourers of Babel,
Or Cerberus himself pronounce
A leash of languages at once.

*　　*　　*　　*　　*　　*　　*

　Beside, he was a shrewd philosopher,
And had read every text and gloss over;
Whate'er the crabbed'st author hath,
He understood b' implicit faith;　　　130
Whatever sceptic could inquire for,
For every why he had a wherefore;
Knew more than forty of them do,
As far as words and terms could go;
All which he understood by rote,
And, as occasion served, would quote;
No matter whether right or wrong,
They might be either said or sung,
His notions fitted things so well,
That which was which he could not tell,　140
But oftentimes mistook the one

For th' other, as great clerks have done.
He could reduce all things to acts,
And knew their natures by abstracts;
Where Entity and Quiddity,
The ghosts of defunct bodies, fly;
Where truth in person does appear,
Like words congeal'd in northern air.
He knew what's what, and that's as high
As metaphysic wit can fly. 　　　　　150

JOHN OLDHAM (1653–1683)

FROM A SATIRE DISSUADING FROM POETRY

'Tis so, 'twas ever so, since heretofore
The blind old bard, with dog and bell before,
Was fain to sing for bread from door to door:
The needy muses all túrn'd Gipsies then, 159
And, of the begging-trade, e'er since have
　been:

*　　*　　*　　*　　*　　*　　*

My own hard usage here I need not press
Where you have ev'ry day before your face
Plenty of fresh resembling instances:
Great Cowley's muse the same ill treatment
　had,
Whose verse shall live forever to upbraid 171
Th' ungrateful world, that left such worth
　unpaid.
Waller himself may thank inheritance
For what he else had never got by sense.
On Butler who can think without just rage,
The glory, and the scandal of the age?
Fair stood his hopes, when first he came to
　town,
Met, ev'ry where, with welcomes of renown,
Courted, caress'd by all, with wonder read,
And promises of princely favour fed; 　　180
But what reward for all had he at last,
After a life in dull expectance pass'd?
The wretch, at summing up his misspent days,
Found nothing left, but poverty, and praise:
Of all his gains by verse he could not save
Enough to purchase flannel, and a grave:
Reduc'd to want, he, in due time, fell sick,
Was fain to die, and be interr'd on tick;
And well might bless the fever that was sent,
To rid him hence, and his worse fate prevent.
　You've seen what fortune other poets share;
View next the factors of the theatre: 　　192
That constant mart, which all the year does
　hold,

Where staple wit is barter'd, bought, and
　sold.
Here trading scriblers for their maintenance,
And livelihood, trust to a lott'ry-chance.
But who his parts would in the service spend,
Where all his hopes on vulgar breath depend?
Where ev'ry sot, for paying half a crown,[1]
Has the prerogative to cry him down. 　　200
Sedley indeed may be content with fame,
Nor care, should an ill-judging audience
　damn;
But Settle, and the rest, that write for pence,
Whose whole estate's an ounce or two of
　brains,
Should a thin house on the third day appear,
Must starve, or live in tatters all the year.
And what can we expect that's brave and
　great,
From a poor needy wretch, that writes to eat?
Who the success of the next play must wait
For lodging, food, and clothes, and whose
　chief care 　　　　　　　　　　　　210
Is how to spunge for the next meal, and
　where?

JOHN LOCKE (1632–1704)

FROM OF THE CONDUCT OF THE UNDERSTANDING

4. *Of Practice and Habits.* — We are born
with faculties and powers capable almost of
anything, such at least as would carry us
further than can easily be imagined: but it
is only the exercise of those · powers which
gives us ability and skill in anything, and leads
us towards perfection.

A middle-aged ploughman will scarce ever
be brought to the carriage and language of a
gentleman, though his body be as well-pro-
portioned, and his joints as supple, and his
natural parts not any way inferior. The legs
of a dancing-master and the fingers of a
musician fall as it were naturally, without
thought or pains, into regular and admirable
motions. Bid them change their parts, and
they will in vain endeavour to produce like
motions in the members not used to them,
and it will require length of time and long
practice to attain but some degrees of a like
ability. What incredible and astonishing ac-

---

[1] the price of a good seat

tions do we find rope-dancers and tumblers bring their bodies to! Not but that sundry in almost all manual arts are as wonderful; but I name those which the world takes notice of for such, because on that very account they give money to see them. All these admired motions, beyond the reach and almost conception of unpractised spectators, are nothing but the mere effects of use and industry in men whose bodies have nothing peculiar in them from those of the amazed lookers-on.

As it is in the body, so it is in the mind: practice makes it what it is; and most even of those excellencies which are looked on as natural endowments, will be found, when examined into more narrowly, to be the product of exercise, and to be raised to that pitch only by repeated actions. Some men are remarked for pleasantness in raillery; others for apologues and apposite diverting stories. This is apt to be taken for the effect of pure nature, and that the rather because it is not got by rules, and those who excel in either of them never purposely set themselves to the study of it as an art to be learnt. But yet it is true, that at first some lucky hit, which took with somebody and gained him commendation, encouraged him to try again, inclined his thoughts and endeavours that way, till at last he insensibly got a facility in it, without perceiving how; and that is attributed wholly to nature which was much more the effect of use and practice. I do not deny that natural disposition may often give the first rise to it, but that never carries a man far without use and exercise, and it is practice alone that brings the powers of the mind, as well as those of the body, to their perfection. Many a good poetic vein is buried under a trade, and never produces anything for want of improvement. We see the ways of discourse and reasoning are very different, even concerning the same matter, at court and in the university. And he that will go but from Westminster-hall[1] to the Exchange will find a different genius and turn in their ways of talking; and yet one cannot think that all whose lot fell in the city were born with different parts[2] from those who were bred at the university or inns of court.

To what purpose all this but to show that the difference so observable in men's understandings and parts does not arise so much from their natural faculties as acquired habits. He would be laughed at that should go about to make a fine dancer out of a country hedger at past fifty. And he will not have much better success who shall endeavour at that age to make a man reason well, or speak handsomely, who has never been used to it, though you should lay before him a collection of all the best precepts of logic or oratory. Nobody is made anything by hearing of rules or laying them up in his memory; practice must settle the habit of doing without reflecting on the rule; and you may as well hope to make a good painter or musician extempore, by a lecture and instruction in the arts of music and painting, as a coherent thinker or a strict reasoner by a set of rules showing him wherein right reasoning consists.

This being so that defects and weakness in men's understanding, as well as other faculties, come from want of a right use of their own minds, I am apt to think the fault is generally mislaid upon nature, and there is often a complaint of want of parts when the fault lies in want of a due improvement of them. We see men frequently dexterous and sharp enough in making a bargain who, if you reason with them about matters of religion, appear perfectly stupid.

JOHN BUNYAN (1628-1688)

From THE PILGRIM'S PROGRESS

THE FIGHT WITH APOLLYON

Then I saw in my dream that these good companions, when Christian was gone to the bottom of the hill, gave him a loaf of bread, a bottle of wine, and a cluster of raisins; and then he went on his way.

But now, in this Valley of Humiliation, poor Christian was hard put to it; for he had gone but a little way, before he espied a foul fiend coming over the field to meet him; his name is Apollyon. Then did Christian begin to be afraid, and to cast in his mind whether to go back or to stand his ground. But he considered again that he had no armour for his back; and, therefore, thought that to turn the back to him might give him the greater advantage, with ease to pierce him with his darts. Therefore he resolved to venture and stand his ground; for, thought he, had I no more in mine eye than the saving of my life, it would be the best way to stand.

So he went on, and Apollyon met him. Now the monster was hideous to behold; he was clothed with scales, like a fish (and they are his pride), he had wings like a dragon, feet like a bear, and out of his belly came fire and smoke, and his mouth was as the mouth of a lion. When he was come up to Christian, he beheld him with a disdainful countenance, and thus began to question with him.

Apol. Whence come you? and whither are you bound?

Chr. I am come from the City of Destruction, which is the place of all evil, and am going to the City of Zion.

Apol. By this I perceive thou art one of my subjects, for all that country is mine, and I am the prince and god of it. How is it, then, that thou hast run away from thy king? Were it not that I hope thou mayest do me more service, I would strike thee now, at one blow, to the ground.

Chr. I was born, indeed, in your dominions, but your service was hard, and your wages such as a man could not live on, "for the wages of sin is death;" therefore, when I was come to years, I did as other considerate persons do, look out, if, perhaps, I might mend myself.

Apol. There is no prince that will thus lightly lose his subjects, neither will I as yet lose thee; but since thou complainest of thy service and wages, be content to go back; what our country will afford, I do here promise to give thee.

Chr. But I have let myself to another, even to the King of princes; and how can I, with fairness, go back with thee?

Apol. Thou hast done in this according to the proverb, 'Changed a bad for a worse;' but it is ordinary for those that have professed themselves his servants, after a while to give him the slip, and return again to me. Do thou so too, and all shall be well.

Chr. I have given him my faith, and sworn my allegiance to him; how, then, can I go back from this, and not be hanged as a traitor?

Apol. Thou didst the same to me, and yet I am willing to pass by all, if now thou wilt yet turn again and go back.

Chr. What I promised thee was in my nonage; and, besides, I count the Prince under whose banner now I stand is able to absolve me; yea, and to pardon also what I did as to my compliance with thee; and be-

sides, O thou destroying Apollyon! to speak truth, I like his service, his wages, his servants, his government, his company, and country, better than thine; and, therefore, leave off to persuade me further; I am his servant, and I will follow him.

Apol. Consider again, when thou art in cool blood, what thou art like to meet with in the way that thou goest. Thou knowest that, for the most part, his servants come to an ill end, because they are transgressors against me and my ways. How many of them have been put to shameful deaths! and, besides, thou countest his service better than mine, whereas he never came yet from the place where he is to deliver any that served him out of their hands; but as for me, how many times, as all the world very well knows, have I delivered, either by power or fraud, those that have faithfully served me, from him and his, though taken by them; and so I will deliver thee.

Chr. His forbearing at present to deliver them is on purpose to try their love, whether they will cleave to him to the end; and as for the ill end thou sayest they come to, that is most glorious in their account; for, for present deliverance, they do not much expect it, for they stay for their glory, and then they shall have it, when their Prince comes in his and the glory of the angels.

Apol. Thou hast already been unfaithful in thy service to him; and how dost thou think to receive wages of him?

Chr. Wherein, O Apollyon! have I been unfaithful to him?

Apol. Thou didst faint at first setting out, when thou wast almost choked in the Gulf of Despond; thou didst attempt wrong ways to be rid of thy burden, whereas thou shouldest have stayed till thy Prince had taken it off; thou didst sinfully sleep, and lose thy choice thing; thou wast, also, almost persuaded to go back, at the sight of the lions; and when thou talkest of thy journey, and of what thou hast heard and seen, thou art inwardly desirous of vain-glory in all that thou sayest or doest.

Chr. All this is true, and much more which thou hast left out; but the Prince, whom I serve and honour, is merciful, and ready to forgive; but, besides, these infirmities possessed me in thy country, for there I sucked them in; and I have groaned under them, been sorry for them, and have obtained pardon of my Prince.

Apol. Then Apollyon broke out into a grievous rage, saying, I am an enemy to this Prince; I hate his person, his laws, and people; I am come out on purpose to withstand thee.

Chr. Apollyon, beware what you do; for I am in the king's highway, the way of holiness, therefore take heed to yourself.

Apol. Then Apollyon straddled quite over the whole breadth of the way, and said, I am void of fear in this matter: prepare thyself to die; for I swear by my infernal den, that thou shalt go no further; here will I spill[1] thy soul.

And with that he threw a flaming dart at his breast; but Christian had a shield in his hand, with which he caught it, and so prevented the danger of that.

Then did Christian draw; for he saw it was time to bestir him: and Apollyon as fast made at him, throwing darts as thick as hail; by the which, notwithstanding all that Christian could do to avoid it, Apollyon wounded him in his head, his hand, and foot. This made Christian give a little back; Apollyon, therefore, followed his work amain, and Christian again took courage, and resisted as manfully as he could. This sore combat lasted for above half a day, even till Christian was almost quite spent; for you must know, that Christian, by reason of his wounds, must needs grow weaker and weaker.

Then Apollyon, espying his opportunity, began to gather up close to Christian, and wrestling with him, gave him a dreadful fall; and with that, Christian's sword flew out of his hand. Then said Apollyon, I am sure of thee now. And with that he had almost pressed him to death; so that Christian began to despair of life: but as God would have it, while Apollyon was fetching of his last blow, thereby to make a full end of this good man, Christian nimbly stretched out his hand for his sword, and caught it, saying, "Rejoice not against me, O mine enemy: when I fall, I shall arise;" and with that gave him a deadly thrust, which made him give back, as one that had received his mortal wound. Christian perceiving that, made at him again, saying; "Nay, in all these things we are more than conquerors, through him that loved us." And with that Apollyon spread forth his dragon's wings, and sped him away, that Christian for a season saw him no more.

In this combat no man can imagine, unless he had seen and heard as I did, what yelling and hideous roaring Apollyon made all the time of the fight — he spake like a dragon; and, on the other side, what sighs and groans burst from Christian's heart. I never saw him all the while give so much as one pleasant look, till he perceived he had wounded Apollyon with his two-edged sword; then, indeed, he did smile, and look upward; but it was the dreadfulest sight that ever I saw.

VANITY FAIR

Then I saw in my dream, that when they were got out of the wilderness, they presently saw a town before them, and the name of that town is Vanity; and at the town there is a fair kept, called Vanity Fair: it is kept all the year long; it beareth the name of Vanity Fair, because the town where it is kept is lighter than vanity; and also because all that is there sold, or that cometh thither, is vanity. As is the saying of the wise, "All that cometh is vanity."

This fair is no new-erected business, but a thing of ancient standing; I will show you the original[1] of it.

Almost five thousand years agone, there were pilgrims walking to the Celestial City as these two honest persons are: and Beelzebub, Apollyon, and Legion, with their companions, perceiving by the path that the pilgrims made, that their way to the city lay through this town of Vanity, they contrived here to set up a fair; a fair wherein should be sold all sorts of vanity, and that it should last all the year long; therefore at this fair are all such merchandise sold, as houses, lands, trades, places, honours, preferments, titles, countries, kingdoms, lusts, pleasures, and delights of all sorts, as whores, bawds, wives, husbands, children, masters, servants, lives, blood, bodies, souls, silver, gold, pearls, precious stones, and what not.

And, moreover, at this fair there is at all times to be seen juggling, cheats, games, plays, fools, apes, knaves, and rogues, and that of every kind.

Here are to be seen too, and that for nothing, thefts, murders, adulteries, false swearers, and that of a blood-red colour.

And as in other fairs of less moment, there are the several rows and streets, under their

---

[1] destroy

[1] origin

proper names, where such and such wares are vended; so here likewise you have the proper places, rows, streets (viz. countries and kingdoms), where the wares of this fair are soonest to be found. Here is the Britain Row, the French Row, the Italian Row, the Spanish Row, the German Row, where several sorts of vanities are to be sold. But, as in other fairs, some one commodity is as the chief of all the fair, so the ware of Rome and her merchandise is greatly promoted in this fair; only our English nation, with some others, have taken a dislike thereat.

Now, as I said, the way to the Celestial City lies just through this town where this lusty fair is kept; and he that will go to the City, and yet not go through this town, must needs "go out of the world." The Prince of princes himself, when here, went through this town to his own country, and that upon a fair day too; yea, and as I think, it was Beelzebub, the chief lord of this fair, that invited him to buy of his vanities; yea, would have made him lord of the fair, would he but have done him reverence as he went through the town. Yea, because he was such a person of honour, Beelzebub had him from street to street, and showed him all the kingdoms of the world in a little time, that he might if possible, allure the Blessed One to cheapen[1] and buy some of his vanities; but he had no mind to the merchandise, and therefore left the town, without laying out so much as one farthing upon these vanities. This fair, therefore, is an ancient thing, of long standing, and a very great fair. Now these Pilgrims, as I said, must needs go through this fair. Well, so they did; but, behold, even as they entered into the fair, all the people in the fair were moved, and the town itself as it were in a hubbub about them; and that for several reasons; for —

First, The pilgrims were clothed with such kind of raiment as was diverse from the raiment of any that traded in that fair. The people, therefore, of the fair, made a great gazing upon them: some said they were fools, some they were bedlams,[2] and some they are outlandish men.[3]

Secondly, And as they wondered at their apparel, so they did likewise at their speech; for few could understand what they said; they naturally spoke the language of Canaan, but they that kept the fair were the men of this world; so that, from one end of the fair to the other, they seemed barbarians each to the other.

Thirdly, But that which did not a little amuse the merchandisers was, that these pilgrims set very light by all their wares; they cared not so much as to look upon them; and if they called upon them to buy, they would put their fingers in their ears, and cry, "Turn away mine eyes from beholding vanity," and look upwards, signifying that their trade and traffic was in heaven.

One chanced mockingly, beholding the carriage of the men, to say unto them, "What will ye buy?" But they, looking gravely upon him, answered, "We buy the truth." At that there was an occasion taken to despise the men the more: some mocking, some taunting, some speaking reproachfully, and some calling upon others to smite them. At last things came to a hubbub, and great stir in the fair, insomuch that all order was confounded. Now was word presently brought to the great one of the fair, who quickly came down, and deputed some of his most trusty friends to take these men into examination, about whom the fair was almost overturned. So the men were brought to examination; and they that sat upon them, asked them whence they came, whither they went, and what they did there in such an unusual garb? The men told them, that they were pilgrims and strangers in the world, and that they were going to their own country, which was the heavenly Jerusalem; and that they had given no occasion to the men of the town, nor yet to the merchandisers, thus to abuse them, and to let[1] them in their journey, except it was, for that, when one asked them what they would buy, they said they would buy the truth. But they that were appointed to examine them did not believe them to be any other than bedlams and mad, or else such as came to put all things into a confusion in the fair. Therefore they took them and beat them, and besmeared them with dirt, and then put them into the cage, that they might be made a spectacle to all the men of the fair. There, therefore, they lay for some time, and were made the objects of any man's sport, or malice, or revenge, the great ones of the fair laughing still at all that befell them. But the men being patient, and not rendering railing

---

[1] bargain for   [2] lunatics   [3] foreigners

[1] hinder

for railing, but contrariwise, blessing, and giving good words for bad, and kindness for injuries done, some men in the fair that were more observing, and less prejudiced than the rest, began to check and blame the baser sort for their continual abuses done by them to the men; they, therefore, in angry manner, let fly at them again, counting them as bad as the men in the cage, and telling them that they seemed confederates, and should be made partakers of their misfortunes. The other replied, that for aught they could see, the men were quiet, and sober, and intended nobody any harm; and that there were many that traded in their fair, that were more worthy to be put into the cage, yea, and pillory too, than were the men that they had abused. Thus, after divers words had passed on both sides, the men behaving themselves all the while very wisely and soberly before them, they fell to some blows among themselves, and did harm one to another. Then were these two poor men brought before their examiners again, and there charged as being guilty of the late hubbub that had been in the fair. So they beat them pitifully, and hanged irons upon them, and led them in chains up and down the fair, for an example and a terror to others, lest any should speak in their behalf, or join themselves unto them. But Christian and Faithful behaved themselves yet more wisely, and received the ignominy and shame that was cast upon them, with so much meekness and patience, that it won to their side, though but few in comparison of the rest, several of the men in the fair. This put the other party yet into greater rage, insomuch that they concluded the death of these two men. Wherefore they threatened, that the cage nor irons should serve their turn, but that they should die, for the abuse they had done, and for deluding the men of the fair.

MINOR LYRISTS

SONG

Love still has something of the sea,
    From whence his Mother rose;
No time his slaves from love can free,
    Nor give their thoughts repose.

They are becalm'd in clearest days,   5
    And in rough weather tost;
They wither under cold delays,
    Or are in tempests lost.

One while they seem to touch the port,
    Then straight into the main [1]   10
Some angry wind in cruel sport
    Their vessel drives again.

At first disdain and pride they fear,
    Which, if they chance to 'scape,
Rivals and falsehood soon appear   15
    In a more dreadful shape.

By such degrees to joy they come,
    And are so long withstood,
So slowly they receive the sum,
    It hardly does them good.   20

'Tis cruel to prolong a pain;
    And to defer a bliss,
Believe me, gentle Hermione,
    No less inhuman is.

An hundred thousand oaths your fears   25
    Perhaps would not remove,
And if I gazed a thousand years,
    I could no deeper love.
              — SIR CHARLES SEDLEY (1639?–1701)

TO CELIA

Not, Celia, that I juster am,
    Or better than the rest;
For I would change each hour like them
    Were not my heart at rest.

But I am tied to very thee   5
    By every thought I have;
Thy face I only care to see,
    Thy heart I only crave.

All that in woman is adored
    In thy dear self I find;   10
For the whole sex can but afford
    The handsome and the kind.

Why then should I seek further store
    And still make love anew?
When change itself can give no more,   15
    'Tis easy to be true.
              — SIR CHARLES SEDLEY (1639?–1701)

[1] open sea

LOVE AND LIFE

All my past life is mine no more;
　The flying hours are gone,
Like transitory dreams given o'er
Whose images are kept in store
　By memory alone.　　　　　　5

The time that is to come is not;
　How can it then be mine?
The present moment's all my lot;
And that, as fast as it is got,
　Phillis, is only thine.　　　　10

Then talk not of inconstancy,
　False hearts, and broken vows;
If I by miracle can be
This live-long minute true to thee,
　'Tis all that Heaven allows.
　　—JOHN WILMOT, EARL OF ROCHESTER
　　　(1647-1680)

EPITAPH ON CHARLES II

Here lies our Sovereign Lord the King,
　Whose word no man relies on,
Who never said a foolish thing,
　Nor ever did a wise one.
　　—JOHN WILMOT, EARL OF ROCHESTER
　　　(1647-1680)

THE ENCHANTMENT

I did but look and love awhile,
　'Twas but for one half-hour;
Then to resist I had no will,
　And now I have no power.

To sigh and wish is all my ease;
　Sighs which do heat impart
Enough to melt the coldest ice,
　Yet cannot warm your heart.

O would your pity give my heart
　One corner of your breast,　　　10
'Twould learn of yours the winning art
　And quickly steal the rest.
　　—THOMAS OTWAY (1652-1685)

TO HIS MISTRESS

Why dost thou shade thy lovely face? O
　why
Does that eclipsing hand of thine deny
The sunshine of the Sun's enlivening eye?　3

Without thy light what light remains in me?
Thou art my life; my way, my light's in thee;
I live, I move, and by thy beams I see.　　6

Thou art my life — if thou but turn away,
My life's a thousand deaths. Thou art my
　way —
Without thee, Love, I travel not but stray.　9

My light thou art — without thy glorious
　sight
My eyes are darken'd with eternal night.
My Love, thou art my way, my life, my light.

Thou art my way; I wander if thou fly.　　13
Thou art my light; if hid, how blind am I!
Thou art my life; if thou withdraw'st, I die.

My eyes are dark and blind, I cannot see:
To whom or whither should my darkness flee,
But to that light? — and who's that light
　but thee?　　　　　　　　　　　18

If I have lost my path, dear lover, say,
Shall I still wander in a doubtful way?　　20
Love, shall a lamb of Israel's sheepfold stray?

My path is lost, my wandering steps do stray;
I cannot go, nor can I safely stay;　　　23
Whom should I seek but thee, my path, my
　way?

And yet thou turn'st thy face away and fly'st
　me!
And yet I sue for grace and thou deny'st me!
Speak, art thou angry, Love, or only try'st
　me?　　　　　　　　　　　　27

Thou art the pilgrim's path, the blindman's
　eye,
The dead man's life. On thee my hopes rely:
If I but them remove, I surely die.　　　30

Dissolve thy sunbeams, close thy wings and
　stay!
See, see how I am blind, and dead, and stray!
— O thou art my life, my light, my way!　33

Then work thy will! If passion bid me flee,
My reason shall obey, my wings shall be
Stretch'd out no farther than from me to
　thee!　　　　　　　　　　　　36
　　—JOHN WILMOT, EARL OF ROCHESTER
　　　(1647-1680)

THE CLASSICAL AGE

DANIEL DEFOE (1661?–1731)

FROM AN ESSAY UPON PROJECTS

AN ACADEMY FOR WOMEN

I have often thought of it as one of the most barbarous customs in the world, considering us as a civilized and a Christian country, that we deny the advantages of learning to women. We reproach the sex every day with folly and impertinence, while I am confident, had they the advantages of education equal to us, they would be guilty of less than ourselves.

One would wonder, indeed, how it should happen that women are conversible at all, since they are only beholding to natural parts for all their knowledge. Their youth is spent to teach them to stitch and sew or make baubles. They are taught to read, indeed, and perhaps to write their names or so, and that is the height of a woman's education. And I would but ask any who slight the sex for their understanding, what is a man (a gentleman, I mean) good for that is taught no more?

I need not give instances, or examine the character of a gentleman with a good estate, and of a good family, and with tolerable parts, and examine what figure he makes for want of education.

The soul is placed in the body like a rough diamond, and must be polished, or the lustre of it will never appear: and 'tis manifest that as the rational soul distinguishes us from brutes, so education carries on the distinction and makes some less brutish than others. This is too evident to need any demonstration. But why then should women be denied the benefit of instruction? If knowledge and understanding had been useless additions to the sex, God Almighty would never have given them capacities, for He made nothing needless. Besides, I would ask such what they can see in ignorance that they should think it a necessary ornament to a woman?

or how much worse is a wise woman than a fool? or what has the woman done to forfeit the privilege of being taught? Does she plague us with her pride and impertinence? Why did we not let her learn, that she might have had more wit? Shall we upbraid women with folly, when 'tis only the error of this inhuman custom that hindered them being made wiser?

The capacities of women are supposed to be greater and their senses quicker than those of the men; and what they might be capable of being bred to is plain from some instances of female wit,[1] which this age is not without; which upbraids us with injustice, and looks as if we denied women the advantages of education for fear they should vie with the men in their improvements.

To remove this objection, and that women might have at least a needful opportunity of education in all sorts of useful learning, I propose the draught of an Academy for that purpose.

I know 'tis dangerous to make public appearances of the sex. They are not either to be confined or exposed; the first will disagree with their inclinations, and the last with their reputations, and therefore it is somewhat difficult; and I doubt a method proposed by an ingenious lady[2] in a little book called *Advice to the Ladies*, would be found impracticable, for, saving my respect to the sex, the levity, which perhaps is a little peculiar to them, at least in their youth, will not bear the restraint; and I am satisfied nothing but the height of bigotry can keep up a nunnery. Women are extravagantly desirous of going to heaven, and will punish their pretty bodies to get thither; but nothing else will do it, and even in that case sometimes it falls out that nature will prevail.

When I talk, therefore, of an academy for women, I mean both the model, the teaching, and the government different from what is proposed by that ingenious lady, for whose

---

· [1] intelligence   [2] Mary Astell

proposal I have a very great esteem, and also a great opinion of her wit; different, too, from all sorts of religious confinement, and, above all, from vows of celibacy.

Wherefore the academy I propose should differ but little from public schools, wherein such ladies as were willing to study should have all the advantages of learning suitable to their genius.

But since some severities of discipline more than ordinary would be absolutely necessary to preserve the reputation of the house, that persons of quality and fortune might not be afraid to venture their children thither, I shall venture to make a small scheme by way of essay.

The house I would have built in a form by itself, as well as in a place by itself. The building should be of three plain fronts, without any jettings or bearing-work, that the eye might at a glance see from one coin [1] to the other; the gardens walled in the same triangular figure, with a large moat, and but one entrance.

When thus every part of the situation was contrived as well as might be for discovery, and to render intriguing dangerous, I would have no guards, no eyes, no spies set over the ladies, but shall expect them to be tried by the principles of honor and strict virtue.

* * * * * * *

In this house, the persons who enter should be taught all sorts of breeding suitable to both their genius and their quality; and in particular music and dancing, which it would be cruelty to bar the sex of, because they are their darlings; but besides this, they should be taught languages, as particularly French and Italian; and I would venture the injury of giving a woman more tongues than one.

They should, as a particular study, be taught all the graces of speech and all the necessary air of conversation, which our common education is so defective in that I need not expose it. They should be brought to read books, and especially history, and so to read as to make them understand the world, and be able to know and judge of things when they hear of them.

To such whose genius would lead them to it I would deny no sort of learning; but the chief thing in general is to cultivate the under-

standings of the sex, that they may be capable of all sorts of conversation; that, their parts and judgments being improved, they may be as profitable in their conversation as they are pleasant.

Women, in my observation, have little or no difference in them, but as they are or are not distinguished by education. Tempers indeed may in some degree influence them, but the main distinguishing part is their breeding.

The whole sex are generally quick and sharp. I believe I may be allowed to say generally so, for you rarely see them lumpish and heavy when they are children, as boys will often be. If a woman be well bred, and taught the proper management of her natural wit, she proves generally very sensible and retentive; and without partiality, a woman of sense and manners is the finest and most delicate part of God's creation, the glory of her Maker, and the great instance of His singular regard to man, His darling creature, to whom He gave the best gift either God could bestow or man receive. And 'tis the sordidest piece of folly and ingratitude in the world to withhold from the sex the due lustre which the advantages of education give to the natural beauty of their minds.

A woman well bred and well taught, furnished with the additional accomplishments of knowledge and behavior, is a creature without comparison; her society is the emblem of sublimer enjoyments; her person is angelic and her conversation heavenly; she is all softness and sweetness, peace, love, wit, and delight. She is every way suitable to the sublimest wish, and the man that has such a one to his portion has nothing to do but to rejoice in her and be thankful.

On the other hand, suppose her to be the very same woman, and rob her of the benefit of education, and it follows thus: —

If her temper be good, want of education makes her soft and easy. Her wit, for want of teaching, makes her impertinent and talkative. Her knowledge, for want of judgment and experience, makes her fanciful and whimsical. If her temper be bad, want of breeding makes her worse, and she grows haughty, insolent, and loud. If she be passionate, want of manners makes her termagant and a scold, which is much at one with lunatic. If she be proud, want of discretion (which still is breeding) makes her conceited, fantastic,

[1] corner

and ridiculous. And from these she degenerates to be turbulent, clangorous, noisy, nasty, and the devil.

Methinks mankind for their own sakes — since, say what we will of the women, we all think fit at one time or other to be concerned with them — should take some care to breed [1] them up to be suitable and serviceable, if they expected no such thing as delight from them. Bless us! what care do we take to breed up a good horse and to break him well! and what a value do we put upon him when it is done, and all because he should be fit for our use! and why not a woman? Since all her ornaments and beauty without suitable behavior is a cheat in nature, like the false tradesman, who puts the best of his goods uppermost, that the buyer may think the rest are of the same goodness.

Beauty of the body, which is the women's glory, seems to be now unequally bestowed, and Nature, or rather Providence, to lie under some scandal about it, as if 'twas given a woman for a snare to men, and so made a kind of a she-devil of her; because, they say, exquisite beauty is rarely given with wit, more rarely with goodness of temper, and never at all with modesty. And some, pretending to justify the equity of such a distribution, will tell us 'tis the effect of the justice of Providence in dividing particular excellencies among all His creatures, share and share alike, as it were, that all might for something or other be acceptable to one another, else some would be despised.

I think both these notions false, and yet the last, which has the show of respect to Providence, is the worst, for it supposes Providence to be indigent and empty, as if it had not wherewith to furnish all the creatures it had made, but was fain to be parsimonious in its gifts, and distribute them by piecemeal for fear of being exhausted.

If I might venture my opinion against an almost universal notion, I would say most men mistake the proceedings of Providence in this case, and all the world at this day are mistaken in their practice about it. And because the assertion is very bold, I desire to explain myself.

That Almighty First Cause which made us all is certainly the fountain of excellence, as it is of being, and by an invisible influence

could have diffused equal qualities and perfections to all the creatures it has made, as the sun does its light, without the least ebb or diminution to Himself, and has given indeed to every individual sufficient to the figure His providence had designed him in the world.

* * * * * * *

But to come closer to the business, the great distinguishing difference which is seen in the world between men and women is in their education, and this is manifested by comparing it with the difference between one man or woman and another.

And herein it is that I take upon me to make such a bold assertion that all the world are mistaken in their practice about women; for I cannot think that God Almighty ever made them so delicate, so glorious creatures, and furnished them with such charms, so agreeable and so delightful to mankind, with souls capable of the same accomplishments with men, and all to be only stewards of our houses, cooks, and slaves.

Not that I am for exalting the female government in the least; but, in short, I would have men take women for companions, and educate them to be fit for it. A woman of sense and breeding will scorn as much to encroach upon the prerogative of the man as a man of sense will scorn to oppress the weakness of the woman. But if the women's souls were refined and improved by teaching, that word would be lost; to say, the *weakness of the sex* as to judgment, would be nonsense, for ignorance and folly would be no more found among women than men. I remember a passage which I heard from a very fine woman; she had wit and capacity enough, an extraordinary shape and face, and a great fortune, but had been cloistered up all her time, and, for fear of being stolen, had not had the liberty of being taught the common necessary knowledge of women's affairs; and when she came to converse in the world, her natural wit made her so sensible of the want of education, that she gave this short reflection on herself: — "I am ashamed to talk with my very maids," says she, "for I don't know when they do right or wrong. I had more need go to school than be married."

I need not enlarge on the loss the defect of education is to the sex, nor argue the benefit of the contrary practice; 'tis a thing will be more easily granted than remedied. This

----

[1] train, educate

chapter is but an essay at the thing, and I refer the practice to those happy days, if ever they shall be, when men shall be wise enough to mend it.

JONATHAN SWIFT (1667–1745)

From A TALE OF A TUB

SECTION II

Once upon a time there was a man who had three sons by one wife and all at a birth, neither could the midwife tell certainly which was the eldest. Their father died while they were young, and upon his death-bed, calling the lads to him, spoke thus:

"Sons, because I have purchased[1] no estate, nor was born to any, I have long considered of some good legacies to bequeath you, and at last, with much care as well as expense, have provided each of you (here they are) a new coat. Now, you are to understand that these coats have two virtues contained in them; one is, that with good wearing they will last you fresh and sound as long as you live; the other is, that they will grow in the same proportion with your bodies, lengthening and widening of themselves, so as to be always fit. Here, let me see them on you before I die. So, very well! Pray, children, wear them clean and brush them often. You will find in my will[2] (here it is) full instructions in every particular concerning the wearing and management of your coats, wherein you must be very exact to avoid the penalties I have appointed for every transgression or neglect, upon which your future fortunes will entirely depend. I have also commanded in my will that you should live together in one house like brethren and friends, for then you will be sure to thrive and not otherwise."

Here the story says this good father died, and the three sons went all together to seek their fortunes.

I shall not trouble you with recounting what adventures they met for the first seven years, any farther than by taking notice that they carefully observed their father's will and kept their coats in very good order; that they travelled through several countries, encountered a reasonable quantity of giants, and slew certain dragons.

Being now arrived at the proper age for producing themselves, they came up to town and fell in love with the ladies, but especially three, who about that time were in chief reputation, the Duchess d'Argent,[1] Madame de Grands-Titres,[2] and the Countess d'Orgueil.[3] On their first appearance, our three adventurers met with a very bad reception, and soon with great sagacity guessing out the reason, they quickly began to improve in the good qualities of the town. They wrote, and rallied,[4] and rhymed, and sung, and said, and said nothing; they drank, and fought, and slept, and swore, and took snuff; they went to new plays on the first night, haunted the chocolate-houses, beat the watch; they bilked hackney-coachmen, ran in debt with shopkeepers, and lay with their wives; they killed bailiffs, kicked fiddlers downstairs, ate at Locket's,[5] loitered at Will's;[6] they talked of the drawing-room[7] and never came there; dined with lords they never saw; whispered a duchess and spoke never a word; exposed the scrawls of their laundress for billet-doux of quality; came ever just from court and were never seen in it; attended the levee[8] sub dio;[9] got a list of peers by heart in one company, and with great familiarity retailed them in another. Above all, they constantly attended those committees of Senators[10] who are silent in the House and loud in the coffee-house, where they nightly adjourn to chew the cud of politics, and are encompassed with a ring of disciples who lie in wait to catch up their droppings. The three brothers had acquired forty other qualifications of the like stamp too tedious to recount, and by consequence were justly reckoned the most accomplished persons in town. But all would not suffice, and the ladies aforesaid continued still inflexible. To clear up which difficulty, I must, with the reader's good leave and patience, have recourse to some points of weight which the authors of that age have not sufficiently illustrated.

For about this time it happened a sect arose whose tenets obtained and spread very far, especially in the grand monde,[11] and among

---

[1] Duchess Money　[2] Madame Great Titles
[3] Countess Pride　[4] jested　[5] a famous tavern　[6] a fashionable coffee-house　[7] reception at court　[8] an informal reception at court　[9] in the open air, i.e., they stayed away　[10] members of the House of Commons　[11] fashionable world

---

[1] procured　　[2] the New Testament

everybody of good fashion. They worshipped a sort of idol,[1] who, as their doctrine delivered, did daily create men by a kind of manufactory operation. This idol they placed in the highest parts of the house on an altar erected about three feet. He was shown in the posture of a Persian emperor sitting on a superficies with his legs interwoven under him. This god had a goose for his ensign, whence it is that some learned men pretend to deduce his original from Jupiter Capitolinus.[2] At his left hand, beneath the altar, Hell seemed to open and catch at the animals the idol was creating, to prevent which, certain of his priests hourly flung in pieces of the uninformed mass or substance, and sometimes whole limbs already enlivened, which that horrid gulf insatiably swallowed, terrible to behold. The goose was also held a subaltern divinity, or *Deus minorum gentium*,[3] before whose shrine was sacrificed that creature[4] whose hourly food is human gore, and who is in so great renown abroad for being the delight and favourite of the Egyptian Cercopithecus.[5] Millions of these animals were cruelly slaughtered every day to appease the hunger of that consuming deity. The chief idol was also worshipped as the inventor of the yard and the needle, whether as the god of seamen, or on account of certain other mystical attributes, hath not been sufficiently cleared.

The worshippers of this deity had also a system of their belief which seemed to turn upon the following fundamental. They held the universe to be a large suit of clothes which invests everything; that the earth is invested by the air; the air is invested by the stars; and the stars are invested by the *Primum Mobile*.[6] Look on this globe of earth, you will find it to be a very complete and fashionable dress. What is that which some call land but a fine coat faced with green, or the sea but a waistcoat of water-tabby?[7] Proceed to the particular works of the creation, you will find how curious journeyman Nature hath been to trim up the vegetable beaux; observe how sparkish a periwig adorns the head of a

beech, and what a fine doublet of white satin is worn by the birch. To conclude from all, what is man himself but a microcoat,[1] or rather a complete suit of clothes with all its trimmings? As to his body there can be no dispute, but examine even the acquirements of his mind, you will find them all contribute in their order towards furnishing out an exact dress. To instance no more, is not religion a cloak, honesty a pair of shoes worn out in the dirt, self-love a surtout, vanity a shirt, and conscience a pair of breeches.

* * * * * * *

These *postulata*[2] being admitted, it will follow in due course of reasoning that those beings which the world calls improperly suits of clothes are in reality the most refined species of animals, or, to proceed higher, that they are rational creatures or men. For is it not manifest that they live, and move, and talk, and perform all other offices of human life? Are not beauty, and wit, and mien, and breeding their inseparable proprieties? In short, we see nothing but them, hear nothing but them. Is it not they who walk the streets, fill up Parliament-, coffee-, play-, bawdy-houses? It is true, indeed, that these animals, which are vulgarly called suits of clothes or dresses, do according to certain compositions receive different appellations. If one of them be trimmed up with a gold chain, and a red gown, and a white rod, and a great horse, it is called a Lord Mayor; if certain ermines and furs be placed in a certain position, we style them a Judge, and so an apt conjunction of lawn and black satin we entitle a Bishop.

Others of these professors, though agreeing in the main system, were yet more refined upon certain branches of it; and held that man was an animal compounded of two dresses, the natural and the celestial suit, which were the body and the soul; that the soul was the outward, and the body the inward clothing; that the latter was *ex traduce*,[3] but the former of daily creation and circumfusion. This last they proved by Scripture,[4] because in them we live, and move, and have our being: as likewise by philosophy, because they are all in all, and all in every part. Besides, said they, separate these two, and you

---

[1] a tailor [2] *alluding to the story that Rome was saved by the cackling of geese* [3] a god of the lesser peoples [4] lice [5] the monkey [6] In the Ptolemaic system of astronomy, the hollow sphere inclosing the universe and moving all things with itself. [7] watered silk

[1] *a play on the term "microcosm" (little world), applied to man by philosophers* [2] assumptions [3] from the original stock [4] *Acts* xvii : 28

will find the body to be only a senseless unsavoury carcass. By all which it is manifest
that the outward dress must needs be the soul.

To this system of religion were tagged
several subaltern doctrines, which were entertained with great vogue; as particularly the
faculties of the mind were deduced by the
learned among them in this manner: embroidery was sheer wit, gold fringe was agreeable conversation, gold lace was repartee, a
huge long periwig was humour, and a coat full
of powder[1] was very good raillery. All which
required abundance of finesse and delicatesse
to manage with advantage, as well as a strict
observance after time and fashions.

I have with much pains and reading collected out of ancient authors this short summary of a body of philosophy and divinity
which seems to have been composed by a vein
and race of thinking very different from any
other systems, either ancient or modern. And
it was not merely to entertain or satisfy the
reader's curiosity, but rather to give him light
into several circumstances of the following
story, that, knowing the state of dispositions
and opinions in an age so remote, he may
better comprehend those great events which
were the issue of them. I advise, therefore,
the courteous reader to peruse with a world of
application, again and again, whatever I have
written upon this matter. And so leaving
these broken ends, I carefully gather up the
chief thread of my story, and proceed.

These opinions, therefore, were so universal,
as well as the practices of them, among the
refined part of court and town, that our three
brother adventurers, as their circumstances
then stood, were strangely at a loss. For, on
the one side, the three ladies they addressed
themselves to (whom we have named already)
were ever at the very top of the fashion, and
abhorred all that were below it but the breadth
of a hair. On the other side, their father's
will was very precise, and it was the main
precept in it, with the greatest penalties annexed, not to add to or diminish from their
coats one thread without a positive command
in the will. Now the coats their father had
left them were, it is true, of very good cloth,
and besides, so neatly sewn you would swear
they were all of a piece, but, at the same time,
very plain, with little or no ornament; and it
happened that before they were a month in

town great shoulder-knots[1] came up. Straight
all the world was shoulder-knots; no approaching the ladies' *ruelles*[2] without the quota
of shoulder-knots. "That fellow," cries one,
"has no soul: where is his shoulder-knot?"
Our three brethren soon discovered their
want by sad experience, meeting in their
walks with forty mortifications and indignities.
If they went to the play-house, the door-
keeper showed them into the twelve-penny
gallery.[3] If they called a boat, says a water-
man, "I am first sculler."[4] If they stepped
into the "Rose" to take a bottle,[5] the drawer
would cry, "Friend, we sell no ale." If they
went to visit a lady, a footman met them at
the door with "Pray, send up your message."
In this unhappy case they went immediately
to consult their father's will, read it over and
over, but not a word of the shoulder-knot.
What should they do? What temper should
they find? Obedience was absolutely necessary, and yet shoulder-knots appeared extremely requisite. After much thought,
one of the brothers, who happened to be more
book-learned than the other two, said he had
found an expedient. "It is true," said he,
"there is nothing here in this will, *totidem
verbis*,[6] making mention of shoulder-knots,
but I dare conjecture we may find them *in-
clusive*, or *totidem syllabis*."[7] This distinction
was immediately approved by all; and so
they fell again to examine the will. But their
evil star had so directed the matter that the
first syllable was not to be found in the whole
writing; upon which disappointment, he who
found the former evasion took heart, and said,
"Brothers, there is yet hopes; for though
we cannot find them *totidem verbis* nor *totidem
syllabis*, I dare engage we shall make them out
tertio modo[8] or *totidem literis*."[9] This discovery was also highly commended, upon
which they fell once more to the scrutiny, and
soon picked out S, H, O, U, L, D, E, R, when
the same planet, enemy to their repose, had
wonderfully contrived that a K was not to
be found. Here was a weighty difficulty!
But the distinguishing brother (for whom
we shall hereafter find a name), now his hand

---

[1] *Men of fashion powdered their hair.*

[1] knots of gold or silver lace [2] morning recep-
tions [3] *Good seats cost two shillings and a half.*
[4] *Scullers were unfashionable; fashion demanded a
"pair of oars."* [5] of wine [6] in exactly those words
[7] in those very syllables [8] in a third way [9] in those
very letters

was in, proved by a very good argument that K was a modern illegitimate letter, unknown to the learned ages, nor anywhere to be found in ancient manuscripts. "It is true," said he, "the word *Calendae* had in Q. V. C.[1] been sometimes writ with a K, but erroneously, for in the best copies it is ever spelled with a C; and by consequence it was a gross mistake in our language to spell 'knot with a K,' but that from henceforward he would take care it should be writ with a C. Upon this all further difficulty vanished; shoulder-knots were made clearly out to be *jure paterno*,[2] and our three gentlemen swaggered with as large and as flaunting ones as the best.

But as human happiness is of a very short duration, so in those days were human fashions, upon which it entirely depends. Shoulder-knots had their time, and we must now imagine them in their decline, for a certain lord came just from Paris with fifty yards of gold lace upon his coat, exactly trimmed after the court fashion of that month. In two days all mankind appeared closed up in bars of gold lace. Whoever durst peep abroad without his complement of gold lace was as scandalous as a ——, and as ill received among the women. What should our three knights do in this momentous affair? They had sufficiently strained a point already in the affair of shoulder-knots. Upon recourse to the will, nothing appeared there but *altum silentium*.[3] That of the shoulder-knots was a loose, flying, circumstantial point, but this of gold lace seemed too considerable an alteration without better warrant. It did *aliquo modo essentiae adhaerere*,[4] and therefore required a positive precept. But about this time it fell out that the learned brother aforesaid had read "Aristotelis Dialectica,"[5] and especially that wonderful piece *de Interpretatione*, which has the faculty of teaching its readers to find out a meaning in everything but itself, like commentators on the Revelations, who proceed[6] prophets without understanding a syllable of the text. "Brothers," said he, "you are to be informed that of wills, *duo sunt genera*,[7] nuncupatory[8] and scriptory,[9]

that in the scriptory will here before us there is no precept or mention about gold lace, *conceditur*,[1] but *si idem affirmetur de nuncupatorio negatur*.[2] For, brothers, if you remember, we heard a fellow say when we were boys that he heard my father's man say that he heard my father say that he would advise his sons to get gold lace on their coats as soon as ever they could procure money to buy it." "That is very true," cries the other. "I remember it perfectly well," said the third. And so, without more ado, they got the largest gold lace in the parish, and walked about as fine as lords.

A while after, there came up all in fashion a pretty sort of flame-coloured satin for linings, and the mercer brought a pattern of it immediately to our three gentlemen. "And please your worships," said he, "my Lord C—— and Sir J. W. had linings out of this very piece last night; it takes wonderfully, and I shall not have a remnant left enough to make my wife a pin-cushion by to-morrow morning at ten o'clock." Upon this they fell again to rummage the will, because the present case also required a positive precept, the lining being held by orthodox writers to be of the essence of the coat. After long search they could fix upon nothing to the matter in hand, except a short advice in their father's will to take care of fire and put out their candles before they went to sleep. This, though a good deal for the purpose, and helping very far towards self-conviction, yet not seeming wholly of force to establish a command, and being resolved to avoid further scruple, as well as future occasion for scandal, says he that was the scholar, "I remember to have read in wills of a codicil annexed, which is indeed a part of the will, and what it contains hath equal authority with the rest. Now I have been considering of this same will here before us, and I cannot reckon it to be complete for want of such a codicil. I will therefore fasten one in its proper place very dexterously. I have had it by me some time; it was written by a dog-keeper of my grandfather's, and talks a great deal, as good luck would have it, of this very flame-coloured satin." The project was immediately approved by the other two; an old parchment scroll was tagged on according

---

[1] certain old Mss. [2] by paternal authority [3] absolute silence [4] it belonged in a manner to the essential meaning [5] Aristotle's treatise on reasoning [6] set up as, undertake to be [7] there are two kinds [8] oral [9] written

[1] it is admitted [2] but if the same is affirmed of a nuncupatory will, we deny it.

to art, in the form of a codicil annexed, and the satin bought and worn.

Next winter a player, hired for the purpose by the Corporation of Fringemakers, acted his part in a new comedy, all covered with silver fringe, and according to the laudable custom gave rise to that fashion. Upon which the brothers, consulting their father's will, to their great astonishment found these words : "Item, I charge and command my said three sons to wear no sort of silver fringe upon or about their said coats," etc., with a penalty in case of disobedience too long here to insert. However, after some pause, the brother so often mentioned for his erudition, who was well skilled in criticism, had found in a certain author, which he said should be nameless, that the same word which in the will is called fringe does also signify a broom-stick, and doubtless ought to have the same interpretation in this paragraph. This another of the brothers disliked, because of that epithet silver, which could not, he humbly conceived, in propriety of speech be reasonably applied to a broom-stick; but it was replied upon him that this epithet was understood in a mythological and allegorical sense. However, he objected again why their father should forbid them to wear a broom-stick on their coats, a caution that seemed unnatural and impertinent; upon which he was taken up short, as one that spoke irreverently of a mystery which doubtless was very useful and significant, but ought not to be over-curiously pried into or nicely reasoned upon. And in short, their father's authority being now considerably sunk, this expedient was allowed to serve as a lawful dispensation for wearing their full proportion of silver fringe.

A while after was revived an old fashion, long antiquated, of embroidery with Indian figures of men, women, and children. Here they had no occasion to examine the will. They remembered but too well how their father had always abhorred this fashion; that he made several paragraphs on purpose, importing his utter detestation of it and bestowing his everlasting curse to his sons whenever they should wear it. For all this, in a few days they appeared higher in the fashion than anybody else in the town. But they solved the matter by saying that these figures were not at all the same with those that were formerly worn and were meant in the will; besides, they did not wear them in that sense,

as forbidden by their father, but as they were a commendable custom, and of great use to the public. That these rigorous clauses in the will did therefore require some allowance and a favourable interpretation, and ought to be understood *cum grano salis*.[1]

But fashions perpetually altering in that age, the scholastic brother grew weary of searching further evasions and solving everlasting contradictions. Resolved, therefore, at all hazards to comply with the modes of the world, they concerted matters together, and agreed unanimously to lock up their father's will in a strong-box, brought out of Greece or Italy (I have forgot which), and trouble themselves no farther to examine it, but only refer to its authority whenever they thought fit. In consequence whereof, a while after it grew a general mode to wear an infinite number of points,[2] most of them tagged with silver ; upon which the scholar pronounced *ex cathedra* [3] that points were absolutely *jure paterno*,[4] as they might very well remember, It is true, indeed, the fashion prescribed somewhat more than were directly named in the will; however, that they, as heirs-general of their father, had power to make and add certain clauses for public emolument, though not deducible *todidem verbis* from the letter of the will, or else *multa absurda sequerentur*.[5] This was understood for canonical, and therefore on the following Sunday they came to church all covered with points.

The learned brother so often mentioned was reckoned the best scholar in all that or the next street to it ; insomuch, as having run something behindhand with the world, he obtained the favour from a certain lord to receive him into his house and to teach his children. A while after the lord died, and he, by long practice upon his father's will, found the way of contriving a deed of conveyance of that house to himself and his heirs ; upon which he took possession, turned the young squires out, and received his brothers in their stead.[6] . . . . .

---

[1] with a grain of salt　[2] laces used instead of buttons to fasten clothing　[3] officially　[4] in accordance with paternal law　[5] many absurd consequences would follow　[6] *For the symbolic meanings of the objects and events that figure in this satire, see the Notes at the end of this volume.*

From A MODEST PROPOSAL FOR PREVENTING THE CHILDREN OF POOR PEOPLE IN IRELAND FROM BEING A BURDEN TO THEIR PARENTS OR COUNTRY, AND FOR MAKING THEM BENEFICIAL TO THE PUBLIC

It is a melancholy object to those who walk through this great town,[1] or travel in the country, when they see the streets, the roads, and cabin-doors, crowded with beggars of the female sex, followed by three, four, or six children, all in rags, and importuning every passenger[2] for an alms. These mothers, instead of being able to work for their honest livelihood, are forced to employ all their time in strolling to beg sustenance for their helpless infants: who, as they grow up, either turn thieves for want of work, or leave their dear native country to fight for the Pretender in Spain, or sell themselves to the Barbadoes.[3]

I think it is agreed by all parties, that this prodigious number of children in the arms, or on the backs, or at the heels of their mothers, and frequently of their fathers, is, in the present deplorable state of the kingdom, a very great additional grievance; and, therefore, whoever could find out a fair, cheap, and easy method of making these children sound, useful members of the commonwealth, would deserve so well of the public, as to have his statue set up for a preserver of the nation.

But my intention is very far from being confined to provide only for the children of professed beggars; it is of a much greater extent, and shall take in the whole number of infants at a certain age, who are born of parents in effect[4] as little able to support them as those who demand our charity in the streets.

As to my own part, having turned my thoughts for many years upon this important subject, and maturely weighed the several schemes of our projectors, I have always found them grossly mistaken in their computation. It is true, a child, just born, may be supported by its mother's milk for a solar year, with little other nourishment; at most, not above the value of two shillings, which the mother may certainly get, or the value in scraps, by her lawful occupation of begging; and it is exactly at one year old that I propose to provide for them in such a manner, as, instead of being a charge upon their parents or the parish, or wanting food and raiment for the rest of their lives, they shall, on the contrary, contribute to the feeding, and partly to the clothing, of many thousands.

* * * * * * *

The number of souls in this kingdom being usually reckoned one million and a half, of these I calculate there may be about two hundred thousand couple whose wives are breeders; from which number I subtract thirty thousand couple, who are able to maintain their own children, (although I apprehend there cannot be so many, under the present distresses of the kingdom); but this being granted, there will remain a hundred and seventy thousand breeders. I again subtract fifty thousand, for those women who miscarry, or whose children die by accident or disease within the year. There only remain a hundred and twenty thousand children of poor parents annually born. The question therefore is, How this number shall be reared and provided for? which, as I have already said, under the present situation of affairs, is utterly impossible by all the methods hitherto proposed. For we can neither employ them in handicraft or agriculture; we neither build houses (I mean in the country), nor cultivate land: they can very seldom pick up a livelihood by stealing, till they arrive at six years old, except where they are of towardly parts;[1] although I confess they learn the rudiments much earlier; during which time they can, however, be properly looked upon only as probationers; as I have been informed by a principal gentleman in the county of Cavan, who protested to me, that he never knew above one or two instances under the age of six, even in a part of the kingdom so renowned for the quickest proficiency in that art.

I am assured by our merchants, that a boy or a girl before twelve years old is no saleable commodity;[2] and even when they come to this age they will not yield above three pounds or three pounds and half-a-crown at most, on the exchange; which cannot turn to account either to the parents or kingdom, the charge

---

[1] Dublin [2] passer-by [3] *Many poor persons sold themselves to go as servants to the Barbadoes and other English colonies.* [4] in reality

[1] precocious ability [2] *Poor parents often sold their children as bond-servants.*

of nutriment and rags having been at least four times that value.

I shall now, therefore, humbly propose my own thoughts, which I hope will not be liable to the least objection.

I have been assured by a very knowing American of my acquaintance in London, that a young healthy child, well nursed, is, at a year old, a most delicious, nourishing, and wholesome food, whether stewed, roasted, baked, or boiled; and I make no doubt that it will equally serve in fricasee or a ragout.

I do therefore humbly offer it to public consideration, that of the hundred and twenty thousand children already computed, twenty thousand may be reserved for breed. . . . That the remaining hundred thousand may, at a year old, be offered in sale to the persons of quality and fortune through the kingdom; always advising the mother to let them suck plentifully in the last month, so as to render them plump and fat for a good table. A child will make two dishes at an entertainment for friends; and when the family dines alone, the fore or hind quarter will make a reasonable dish, and, seasoned with a little pepper or salt, will be very good boiled on the fourth day, especially in winter.

I have reckoned, upon a medium, that a child just born will weigh twelve pounds, and in a solar year, if tolerably nursed, will increase to twenty-eight pounds.

I grant this food will be somewhat dear, and therefore very proper for landlords, who, as they have already devoured most of the parents, seem to have the best title to the children.

* * * * * * *

I have already computed the charge of nursing a beggar's child (in which list I reckon all cottagers, labourers, and four-fifths of the farmers) to be about two shillings per annum, rags included; and I believe no gentleman would repine to give ten shillings for the carcass of a good fat child, which, as I have said, will make four dishes of excellent nutritive meat, when he has only some particular friend, or his own family, to dine with him. Thus the squire will learn to be a good landlord, and grow popular among his tenants; the mother will have eight shillings net profit, and be fit for work till she produces another child.

Those who are more thrifty (as I must con-

fess the times require) may flay the carcass; the skin of which, artificially[1] dressed, will make admirable gloves for ladies, and summer-boots for fine gentlemen.

As to our city of Dublin, shambles may be appointed for this purpose in the most convenient parts of it, and butchers we may be assured will not be wanting; although I rather recommend buying the children alive, then dressing them hot from the knife, as we do roasting pigs.

* * * * * * *

SIR RICHARD STEELE
(1672–1729)

THE TATLER

NO. 95. NOVEMBER 17, 1709

Interea dulces pendent circum oscula nati,
Casta pudicitiam servat domus.[2]
— Virg. *Georg.* ii. 523.

There are several persons who have many pleasures and entertainments in their possession, which they do not enjoy. It is, therefore, a kind and good office to acquaint them with their own happiness, and turn their attention to such instances of their good fortune as they are apt to overlook. Persons in the married state often want such a monitor; and pine away their days, by looking upon the same condition in anguish and murmur, which carries with it in the opinion of others a complication[3] of all the pleasures of life, and a retreat from its inquietudes.

I am led into this thought by a visit I made an old friend, who was formerly my schoolfellow. He came to town last week with his family for the winter, and yesterday morning sent me word his wife expected me to dinner. I am, as it were, at home at that house, and every member of it knows me for their well-wisher. I cannot indeed express the pleasure it is, to be met by the children with so much joy as I am when I go thither. The boys and girls strive who shall come first, when they think it is I that am knocking at the door; and that child which loses the race to

---

[1] skilfully [2] Meanwhile his sweet children hang upon his kisses and his chaste home is the abode of virtue. [3] mixture

me runs back again to tell the father it is Mr. Bickerstaff. This day I was led in by a pretty girl, that we all thought must have forgot me; for the family has been out of town these two years. Her knowing me again was a mighty subject with us, and took up our discourse at the first entrance. After which, they began to rally[1] me upon a thousand little stories they heard in the country, about my marriage to one of my neighbour's daughters. Upon which the gentleman, my friend, said, "Nay, if Mr. Bickerstaff marries a child of any of his old companions, I hope mine shall have the preference; there is Mrs. Mary is now sixteen, and would make him as fine a widow as the best of them. But I know him too well; he is so enamoured with the very memory of those who flourished in our youth, that he will not so much as look upon the modern beauties. I remember, old gentleman, how often you went home in a day to refresh your countenance and dress when Teraminta reigned in your heart. As we came up in the coach, I repeated to my wife some of your verses on her." With such reflections on little passages[2] which happened long ago, we passed our time, during a cheerful and elegant meal. After dinner, his lady left the room, as did also the children. As soon as we were alone, he took me by the hand; "Well, my good friend," says he, "I am heartily glad to see thee; I was afraid you would never have seen all the company that dined with you to-day again. Do not you think the good woman of the house a little altered since you followed her from the playhouse, to find out who she was, for me?" I perceived a tear fall down his cheek, as he spoke, which moved me not a little. But, to turn the discourse, I said, "She is not indeed quite that creature she was, when she returned me the letter I carried from you; and told me, 'she hoped, as I was a gentleman, I would be employed no more to trouble her, who had never offended me; but would be so much the gentleman's friend, as to dissuade him from a pursuit, which he could never succeed in.' You may remember, I thought her in earnest; and you were forced to employ your cousin Will, who made his sister get acquainted with her, for you. You cannot expect her to be for ever fifteen." "Fifteen!" replied my good friend: "Ah! you little understand, you that

have lived a bachelor, how great, how exquisite a pleasure there is, in being really beloved! It is impossible, that the most beauteous face in nature should raise in me such pleasing ideas, as when I look upon that excellent woman. That fading in her countenance is chiefly caused by her watching with me, in my fever. This was followed by a fit of sickness, which had like to have carried her off last winter. I tell you sincerely, I have so many obligations to her, that I cannot, with any sort of moderation, think of her present state of health. But as to what you say of fifteen, she gives me every day pleasures beyond what I ever knew in the possession of her beauty, when I was in the vigour of youth. Every moment of her life brings me fresh instances of her complacency to my inclinations, and her prudence in regard to my fortune. Her face is to me much more beautiful than when I first saw it; there is no decay in any feature, which I cannot trace, from the very instant it was occasioned by some anxious concern for my welfare and interests. Thus, at the same time, methinks, the love I conceived towards her for what she was, is heightened by my gratitude for what she is. The love of a wife is as much above the idle passion commonly called by that name, as the loud laughter of buffoons is inferior to the elegant mirth of gentlemen. Oh! she is an inestimable jewel. In her examination of her household affairs, she shows a certain fearfulness to find a fault, which makes her servants obey her like children; and the meanest we have has an ingenuous shame for an offence, not always to be seen in children in other families. I speak freely to you, my old friend; ever since her sickness, things that gave me the quickest joy before, turn now to a certain anxiety. As the children play in the next room, I know the poor things by their steps, and am considering what they must do, should they lose their mother in their tender years. The pleasure I used to take in telling my boy stories of battles, and asking my girl questions about the disposal of her baby,[1] and the gossiping of it, is turned into inward reflection and melancholy."

He would have gone on in this tender way, when the good lady entered, and with an inexpressible sweetness in her countenance told us, "she had been searching her closet for

[1] joke [2] events   [1] doll

something very good, to treat such an old friend as I was." Her husband's eyes sparkled with pleasure at the cheerfulness of her countenance; and I saw all his fears vanish in an instant. The lady observing something in our looks which showed we had been more serious than ordinary, and seeing her husband receive her with great concern under a forced cheerfulness, immediately guessed at what we had been talking of; and applying herself to me, said, with a smile, "Mr. Bickerstaff, do not believe a word of what he tells you, I shall still live to have you for my second, as I have often promised you, unless he takes more care of himself than he has done since his coming to town. You must know, he tells me that he finds London is a much more healthy place than the country; for he sees several of his old acquaintance and school-fellows are here young fellows with fair full-bottomed periwigs.[1] I could scarce keep him in this morning from going out open-breasted."[2] My friend, who is always extremely delighted with her agreeable humour, made her sit down with us. She did it with that easiness which is peculiar to women of sense; and to keep up the good humour she had brought in with her, turned her raillery upon me. "Mr. Bickerstaff, you remember you followed me one night from the play-house; suppose you should carry me thither to-morrow night, and lead me into the front box." This put us into a long field of discourse about the beauties, who were mothers to the present, and shined in the boxes twenty years ago. I told her, "I was glad she had transferred so many of her charms, and I did not question but her eldest daughter was within half-a-year of being a toast."

We were pleasing ourselves with this fantastical preferment of the young lady, when on a sudden we were alarmed with the noise of a drum, and immediately entered my little godson to give me a point of war.[3] His mother, between laughing and chiding, would have put him out of the room; but I would not part with him so. I found, upon conversation with him, though he was a little noisy in his mirth, that the child had excellent parts,[4] and was a great master of all the learning on the

other side eight years old. I perceived him a very great historian in Æsop's Fables: but he frankly declared to me his mind, "that he did not delight in that learning, because he did not believe they were true;" for which reason I found he had very much turned his studies, for about a twelvemonth past, into the lives and adventures of Don Belianis of Greece,[1] Guy of Warwick,[2] the Seven Champions,[3] and other historians of that age. I could not but observe the satisfaction the father took in the forwardness of his son; and that these diversions might turn to some profit, I found the boy had made remarks, which might be of service to him during the course of his whole life. He would tell you the mismanagements of John Hickerthrift,[4] find fault with the passionate temper in Bevis of Southampton,[5] and loved St. George for being the champion of England;[6] and by this means had his thoughts insensibly moulded into the notions of discretion, virtue, and honour. I was extolling his accomplishments, when the mother told me, that the little girl who led me in this morning was in her way a better scholar than he. "Betty," said she, "deals chiefly in fairies and sprights; and sometimes in a winter-night will terrify the maids with her accounts, until they are afraid to go up to bed."

I sat with them until it was very late, sometimes in merry, sometimes in serious discourse, with this particular pleasure, which gives the only true relish to all conversation, a sense that every one of us liked each other. I went home, considering the different conditions of a married life and that of a bachelor; and I must confess it struck me with a secret concern, to reflect, that whenever I go off I shall leave no traces behind me. In this pensive mood I returned to my family; that is to say, to my maid, my dog, and my cat, who only can be the better or worse for what happens to me.

[1] hero of a Spanish romance translated into English in 1598 [2] a legendary English hero, who killed a giant [3] St. George of England, St. Andrew of Scotland, St. Patrick of Ireland, St. David of Wales, etc. [4] a nursery-tale hero, like Jack the Giant Killer [5] hero of a very popular semi-religious mediæval romance. [6] These heroes of the earlier romances had become in the eighteenth century the subjects of chap-books for children and the common people.

[1] such as only young men wore [2] with his coat unbuttoned, like a young gallant [3] a signal on a drum or trumpet [4] abilities

THE TATLER

NO. 167. MAY 4, 1710

Segnius irritant animos demissa per aures,
Quam quae sunt oculis submissa fidelibus.[1] — Hor.

From my own Apartment, May 2.

Having received notice, that the famous actor, Mr. Betterton, was to be interred this evening in the cloisters near Westminster Abbey, I was resolved to walk thither, and see the last office done to a man whom I had always very much admired, and from whose action I had received more strong impressions of what was great and noble in human nature, than from the arguments of the most solid philosophers, or the descriptions of the most charming poets I had ever read. As the rude and untaught multitude are no way wrought upon more effectually than by seeing public punishments and executions; so men of letters and education feel their humanity most forcibly exercised, when they attend the obsequies of men who had arrived at any perfection in liberal accomplishments. Theatrical action is to be esteemed as such, except it be objected, that we cannot call that an art which cannot be attained by art. Voice, stature, motion, and other gifts, must be very bountifully bestowed by nature, or labour and industry will but push the unhappy endeavourer in that way, the farther off his wishes.

Such an actor as Mr. Betterton ought to be recorded with the same respect as Roscius among the Romans. The greatest orator has thought fit to quote his judgment, and celebrate his life. Roscius was the example to all that would form themselves into proper and winning behaviour. His action was so well adapted to the sentiments he expressed, that the youth of Rome thought they only wanted to be virtuous to be as graceful in their appearance as Roscius. The imagination took a lovely impression of what was great and good; and they who never thought of setting up for the art of imitation, became themselves inimitable characters.

There is no human invention so aptly calculated for the forming a free-born people as that of a theatre. Tully reports, that the celebrated player of whom I am speaking, used frequently to say, "The perfection of an actor is only to become what he is doing." Young men, who are too inattentive to receive lectures, are irresistibly taken with performances. Hence it is, that I extremely lament the little relish the gentry of this nation have at present for the just and noble representations in some of our tragedies. The operas, which are of late introduced, can leave no trace behind them that can be of service beyond the present moment. To sing and to dance, are accomplishments very few have any thoughts of practising; but to speak justly, and move gracefully, is what every man thinks he does perform, or wishes he did.

I have hardly a notion, that any performer of antiquity could surpass the action of Mr. Betterton in any of the occasions in which he has appeared on our stage. The wonderful agony which he appeared in, when he examined the circumstance of the handkerchief in Othello; the mixture of love that intruded upon his mind, upon the innocent answers Desdemona makes, betrayed in his gesture such a variety and vicissitude of passions, as would admonish a man to be afraid of his own heart, and perfectly convince him, that it is to stab it, to admit that worst of daggers, jealousy. Whoever reads in his closet[1] this admirable scene, will find that he cannot, except he has as warm an imagination as Shakespeare himself, find any but dry, incoherent, and broken sentences: but a reader that has seen Betterton act it, observes there could not be a word added; that longer speeches had been unnatural, nay, impossible, in Othello's circumstances. The charming passage in the same tragedy, where he tells the manner of winning the affection of his mistress, was urged with so moving and graceful an energy, that while I walked in the Cloisters, I thought of him with the same concern as if I waited for the remains of a person who had in real life done all that I had seen him represent. The gloom of the place, and faint lights before the ceremony appeared, contributed to the melancholy disposition I was in; and I began to be extremely afflicted, that Brutus and Cassius had any difference; that Hotspur's gallantry was so unfortunate; and that the mirth and good humour of Falstaff

---

[1] Things told move us less than those seen by our own faithful eyes.

[1] private room

could not exempt him from the grave. Nay, this occasion in me, who look upon the distinctions amongst men to be merely scenical, raised reflections upon the emptiness of all human perfection and greatness in general; and I could not but regret, that the sacred heads which lie buried in the neighbourhood of this little portion of earth in which my poor old friend is deposited, are returned to dust as well as he, and that there is no difference in the grave between the imaginary and the real monarch. This made me say of human life itself with Macbeth:

> To-morrow, to-morrow, and to-morrow,
> Creeps in a stealing pace from day to day,
> To the last moment of recorded time!
> And all our yesterdays have lighted fools
> To the eternal night! Out, out, short candle!
> Life's but a walking shadow, a poor player
> That struts and frets his hour upon the stage,
> And then is heard no more.

The mention I have here made of Mr. Betterton, for whom I had, as long as I have known anything, a very great esteem and gratitude for the pleasure he gave me, can do him no good; but it may possibly be of service to the unhappy woman he has left behind him, to have it known, that this great tragedian was never in a scene half so moving, as the circumstances of his affairs created at his departure. His wife after the cohabitation of forty years in the strictest amity, has long pined away with a sense of his decay, as well in his person as his little fortune; and, in proportion to that, she has herself decayed both in her health and reason. Her husband's death, added to her age and infirmities, would certainly have determined[1] her life, but that the greatness of her distress has been her relief, by a present deprivation of her senses. This absence of reason is her best defence against sorrow, poverty, and sickness. I dwell upon this account so distinctly, in obedience to a certain great spirit, who hides her name, and has by letter applied to me to recommend to her some object of compassion, from whom she may be concealed.

This, I think, is a proper occasion for exerting such heroic generosity; and as there is an ingenuous shame in those who have known better fortune to be reduced to receive obligations, as well as a becoming pain in the truly

[1] ended

generous to receive thanks; in this case both these delicacies are preserved; for the person obliged is as incapable of knowing her benefactress, as her benefactress is unwilling to be known by her.

THE TATLER

NO. 264. DECEMBER 16, 1710

Favete linguis.[1] — HOR. *Od.* iii. 2. 2.

Boccalini,[2] in his "Parnassus," indicts a laconic writer for speaking that in three words which he might have said in two, and sentences him for his punishment to read over all the words of Guicciardini.[3] This Guicciardini is so very prolix and circumstantial in his writings, that I remember our countryman, Doctor Donne, speaking of that majestic and concise manner in which Moses has described the creation of the world, adds, "that if such an author as Guicciardini were to have written on such a subject, the world itself would not have been able to have contained the books that gave the history of its creation."

I look upon a tedious talker, or what is generally known by the name of a story-teller, to be much more insufferable than even a prolix writer. An author may be tossed out of your hand, and thrown aside when he grows dull and tiresome; but such liberties are so far from being allowed towards your orators in common conversation, that I have known a challenge sent a person for going out of the room abruptly, and leaving a man of honour in the midst of a dissertation. This evil is at present so very common and epidemical, that there is scarce a coffee-house[4] in town that has not some speakers belonging to it, who utter their political essays, and draw parallels out of Baker's "Chronicle"[5] to almost every part of her majesty's reign. It was said of two ancient authors, who had very different beauties in their style, "that if you took a word from one of them, you only spoiled his eloquence; but if you took a word from the other, you spoiled his sense." I have often applied the first part of this criticism to several of these coffee-house speakers whom I

[1] Spare speech   [2] an Italian critic, who wrote in 1612   [3] an Italian historian of the sixteenth century   [4] See Macaulay's account, p. 516.   [5] an old-fashioned history of England, pub. 1641

have at present in my thoughts, though the character that is given to the last of those authors, is what I would recommend to the imitation of my loving countrymen. But it is not only public places of resort, but private clubs and conversations over a bottle, that are infested with this loquacious kind of animal, especially with that species which I comprehend under the name of a story-teller. I would earnestly desire these gentlemen to consider, that no point of wit or mirth at the end of a story can atone for the half hour that has been lost before they come at it. I would likewise lay it home to their serious consideration, whether they think that every man in the company has not a right to speak as well as themselves? and whether they do not think they are invading another man's property, when they engross the time which should be divided equally among the company to their own private use?

What makes this evil the much greater in conversation is, that these humdrum companions seldom endeavour to wind up their narrations into a point of mirth or instruction, which might make some amends for the tediousness of them; but think they have a right to tell anything that has happened within their memory. They look upon matter of fact to be a sufficient foundation for a story, and give us a long account of things, not because they are entertaining or surprising, but because they are true.

My ingenious kinsman, Mr. Humphry Wagstaff, used to say, "the life of man is too short for a story-teller."

Methusalem might be half an hour in telling what o'clock it was: but as for us post-diluvians, we ought to do everything in haste; and in our speeches, as well as actions, remember that our time is short. A man that talks for a quarter of an hour together in company, if I meet him frequently, takes up a great part of my span. A quarter of an hour may be reckoned the eight-and-fortieth part of a day, a day the three hundred and sixtieth part of a year, and a year the threescore and tenth part of life. By this moral arithmetic, supposing a man to be in the talking world one third part of the day, whoever gives another a quarter of an hour's hearing, makes him a sacrifice of more than the four hundred thousandth part of his conversable life.

I would establish but one great general rule to be observed in all conversation, which is this, "that men should not talk to please themselves, but those that hear them." This would make them consider, whether what they speak be worth hearing; whether there be either wit or sense in what they are about to say; and, whether it be adapted to the time when, the place where, and the person to whom, it is spoken.

For the utter extirpation of these orators and story-tellers, which I look upon as very great pests of society, I have invented a watch which divides the minute into twelve parts, after the same manner that the ordinary watches are divided into hours: and will endeavour to get a patent,[1] which shall oblige every club or company to provide themselves with one of these watches, that shall lie upon the table as an hour-glass is often placed near the pulpit, to measure out the length of a discourse.

I shall be willing to allow a man one round of my watch, that is, a whole minute, to speak in; but if he exceeds that time, it shall be lawful for any of the company to look upon the watch, or to call him down to order.

Provided, however, that if any one can make it appear he is turned of threescore, he may take two, or, if he pleases, three rounds of the watch without giving offence. Provided, also, that this rule be not construed to extend to the fair sex, who shall still be at liberty to talk by the ordinary watch that is now in use. I would likewise earnestly recommend this little automaton, which may be easily carried in the pocket without any incumbrance, to all such as are troubled with this infirmity of speech, that upon pulling out their watches, they may have frequent occasion to consider what they are doing, and by that means cut the thread of the story short, and hurry to a conclusion. I shall only add, that this watch, with a paper of directions how to use it, is sold at Charles Lillie's.

I am afraid a Tatler will be thought a very improper paper to censure this humour of being talkative; but I would have my readers know that there is a great difference between *tattle* and *loquacity*, as I shall show at large in a following lucubration; it being my design to throw away a candle[2] upon that subject, in order to explain the whole art of tattling in all its branches and subdivisions.

[1] a royal order [2] *i.e.* burn it in composing an essay

THE SPECTATOR

NO. 11.   MARCH 13, 1711

Dat veniam corvis, vexat censura columbas.[1]
— Juv. *Sat.* ii. 63.

Arietta is visited by all persons of both sexes, who have any pretence to wit and gallantry. She is in that time of life which is neither affected with the follies of youth, nor infirmities of age; and her conversation is so mixed with gaiety and prudence, that she is agreeable both to the young and the old. Her behaviour is very frank, without being in the least blameable: and as she is out of the track of any amorous or ambitious pursuits of her own, her visitants entertain her with accounts of themselves very freely, whether they concern their passions or their interests. I made her a visit this afternoon, having been formerly introduced to the honour of her acquaintance by my friend Will Honeycomb, who has prevailed upon her to admit me sometimes into her assembly, as a civil inoffensive man. I found her accompanied with one person only, a common-place talker, who, upon my entrance, arose, and after a very slight civility sat down again; then, turning to Arietta, pursued his discourse, which I found· was upon the old topic of constancy in love. He went on with great facility in repeating what he talks every day of his life; and with the ornaments of insignificant laughs and gestures, enforced his arguments by quotations out of plays and songs, which allude to the perjuries of the fair, and the general levity of women. Methought he strove to shine more than ordinarily in his talkative way, that he might insult my silence, and distinguish himself before a woman of Arietta's taste, and understanding. She had often an inclination to interrupt him, but could find no opportunity, till the larum ceased of itself, which it did not till he had repeated and murdered the celebrated story of the Ephesian Matron.[2]

Arietta seemed to regard this piece of raillery as an outrage done to her sex; as indeed I have always observed that women, whether out of a nicer regard to their honour, or what other reason I cannot tell, are more sensibly touched with those general aspersions which are cast upon their sex, than men are by what is said of theirs.

When she had a little recovered herself from the serious anger she was in, she replied in the following manner:

"Sir, when I consider how perfectly new all you have said on this subject is, and that the story you have given us is not quite two thousand years old, I cannot but think it a piece of presumption to dispute it with you; but your quotations put me in mind of the fable of the lion and the man. The man walking with that noble animal, showed him, in the ostentation of human superiority, a sign of a man killing a lion. Upon which, the lion said very justly, 'We lions are none of us painters, else we could show a hundred men killed by lions for one lion killed by a man.' You men are writers, and can represent us women as unbecoming as you please in your works, while we are unable to return the injury. You have twice or thrice observed in your discourse, that hypocrisy is the very foundation of our education; and that an ability to dissemble our affections is a professed part of our breeding. These and such other reflections are sprinkled up and down the writings of all ages, by authors, who leave behind them memorials of their resentment against the scorn of particular women, in invectives against the whole sex. Such a writer, I doubt not, was the celebrated Petronius, who invented the pleasant aggravations of the frailty of the Ephesian lady; but when we consider this question between the sexes, which has been either a point of dispute or raillery ever since there were men and women, let us take facts from plain people, and from such as have not either ambition or capacity to embellish their narrations with any beauties of imagination. I was the other day amusing myself with Ligon's Account of Barbadoes;[1] and, in answer to your well-wrought tale, I will give you, (as it dwells upon my memory) out of that honest traveller, in his fifty-fifth page, the history of Inkle and Yarico.

"'Mr. Thomas Inkle, of London, aged twenty years, embarked in the Downs,[2] on the good ship called the Achilles, bound for the West Indies, on the 16th of June, 1647, in

---

[1] Censure spares the crows and attacks the doves.   [2] A story of an easily consoled widow, told by Petronius, a Latin writer of the first century.

[1] pub. 1657   [2] a roadstead for ships off the east coast of Kent

order to improve his fortune by trade and merchandise. Our adventurer was the third son of an eminent citizen, who had taken particular care to instil into his mind an early love of gain, by making him a perfect master of numbers,[1] and consequently giving him a quick view of loss and advantage, and preventing the natural impulses of his passions, by prepossession towards his interests. With a mind thus turned, young Inkle had a person every way agreeable, a ruddy vigour in his countenance, strength in his limbs, with ringlets of fair hair loosely flowing on his shoulders. It happened, in the course of the voyage, that the Achilles, in some distress, put into a creek on the main [2] of America, in search of provisions. The youth, who is the hero of my story, among others went on shore on this occasion. From their first landing they were observed by a party of Indians, who hid themselves in the woods for that purpose. The English unadvisedly marched a great distance from the shore into the country, and were intercepted by the natives, who slew the greatest number of them. Our adventurer escaped among others, by flying into a forest. Upon his coming into a remote and pathless part of the wood, he threw himself, tired and breathless, on a little hillock, when an Indian maid rushed from a thicket behind him. After the first surprise they appeared mutually agreeable to each other. If the European was highly charmed with the limbs, features, and wild graces of the naked American; the American was no less taken with the dress, complexion, and shape of an European, covered from head to foot. The Indian grew immediately enamoured of him, and consequently solicitous for his preservation. She therefore conveyed him to a cave, where she gave him a delicious repast of fruits, and led him to a stream to slake his thirst. In the midst of these good offices, she would sometimes play with his hair, and delight in the opposition of its colour to that of her fingers; then open his bosom, then laugh at him for covering it. She was, it seems, a person of distinction, for she every day came to him in a different dress, of the most beautiful shells, bugles,[3] and bredes.[4] She likewise brought him a great many spoils, which her other lovers had presented to her, so that his cave was richly adorned with all the spotted skins of

[1] arithmetic [2] mainland [3] beads [4] braided work

AE

beasts, and most parti-coloured feathers of fowls, which that world afforded. To make his confinement more tolerable, she would carry him in the dusk of the evening, or by the favour of moonlight, to unfrequented groves and solitudes, and show him where to lie down in safety, and sleep amidst the falls of waters and melody of nightingales. Her part was to watch and hold him awake in her arms, for fear of her countrymen, and wake him on occasions to consult his safety. In this manner did the lovers pass away their time, till they had learned a language of their own, in which the voyager communicated to his mistress how happy he should be to have her in his country, where she should be clothed in such silks as his waistcoat was made of, and be carried in houses drawn by horses, without being exposed to wind or weather. All this he promised her the enjoyment of, without such fears and alarms as they were there tormented with. In this tender correspondence these lovers lived for several months, when Yarico, instructed by her lover, discovered a vessel on the coast, to which she made signals; and in the night, with the utmost joy and satisfaction, accompanied him to a ship's crew of his countrymen bound to Barbadoes. When a vessel from the main arrives in that island, it seems the planters come down to the shore, where there is an immediate market of the Indians and other slaves, as with us of horses and oxen.

"'To be short, Mr. Thomas Inkle, now coming into English territories, began seriously to reflect upon his loss of time, and to weigh with himself how many days' interest of his money he had lost during his stay with Yarico. This thought made the young man very pensive, and careful what account he should be able to give his friends of his voyage. Upon which consideration, the prudent and frugal young man sold Yarico to a Barbadian merchant; notwithstanding that the poor girl, to incline him to commiserate her condition, told him that she was with child by him: but he only made use of that information, to rise in his demands upon the purchaser.'"

I was so touched with this story (which I think should be always a counterpart to the Ephesian Matron) that I left the room with tears in my eyes, which a woman of Arietta's good sense did, I am sure, take for greater applause than any compliments I could make her.

JOSEPH ADDISON (1672–1719)

FROM THE CAMPAIGN, A POEM TO HIS GRACE THE DUKE OF MARLBOROUGH

But, O my muse, what numbers wilt thou
find
To sing the furious troops in battle joined!
Methinks I hear the drum's tumultuous
sound
The victor's shouts and dying groans confound,
The dreadful burst of cannon rend the skies,
And all the thunder of the battle rise!
'Twas then great Marlborough's mighty soul
was proved.
That, in the shock of charging hosts unmoved,
Amidst confusion, horror, and despair,   281
Examined all the dreadful scenes of war;
In peaceful thought the field of death sur-
veyed,
To fainting squadrons sent the timely aid,
Inspired repulsed battalions to engage,
And taught the doubtful battle where to rage.
So when an angel by divine command
With rising tempests shakes a guilty land,
Such as of late o'er pale Britannia past,[1]
Calm and serene he drives the furious blast;
And, pleased the Almighty's orders to per-
form,   291
Rides in the whirlwind, and directs the storm.
But see the haughty household-troops[2] ad-
vance!
The dread of Europe, and the pride of France.
The war's whole art each private soldier
knows,
And with a general's love of conquest glows;
Proudly he marches on, and, void of fear,
Laughs at the shaking of the British spear:
Vain insolence! with native freedom brave,
The meanest Briton scorns the highest slave.

HYMN

The spacious firmament on high,
With all the blue ethereal sky,
And spangled heavens, a shining frame,
Their great Original proclaim.
Th' unwearied Sun from day to day   5
Does his Creator's power display;

[1] in November, 1703   [2] the royal guard of
France

And publishes to every land
The work of an Almighty hand.

Soon as the evening shades prevail,
The Moon takes up the wondrous tale;   10
And nightly to the listening Earth
Repeats the story of her birth:
Whilst all the stars that round her burn,
And all the planets in their turn,
Confirm the tidings as they roll,   15
And spread the truth from pole to pole.

What though in solemn silence all
Move round the dark terrestrial ball;
What though no real voice nor sound
Amidst their radiant orbs be found?   20
In Reason's ear they all rejoice,
And utter forth a glorious voice;
Forever singing as they shine,
"The Hand that made us is divine."

THE SPECTATOR

NO. 10. MONDAY, MARCH 12, 1711

*Non aliter quam qui adverso vix flumine lembum
Remigiis subigit: si brachia forte remisit,
Atque illum in praeceps prono rapit alveus amni.*[1]
— VIRG.

It is with much satisfaction that I hear this
great city inquiring day by day after these my
papers, and receiving my morning lectures
with a becoming seriousness and attention.
My publisher tells me, that there are already
three thousand of them distributed every day:
So that if I allow twenty readers to every
paper, which I look upon as a modest computation, I may reckon about threescore thousand disciples in London and Westminster,
who I hope will take care to distinguish themselves from the thoughtless herd of their
ignorant and unattentive brethren. Since I
have raised to myself so great an audience, I
shall spare no pains to make their instruction
agreeable, and their diversion useful. For
which reasons I shall endeavour to enliven
morality with wit, and to temper wit with
morality, that my readers may, if possible,

[1] So the boat's brawny crew the current stem,
    And, slow advancing, struggle with the stream;
    But if they slack their hands or cease to strive,
    Then down the flood with headlong haste they
       drive. — DRYDEN.

both ways find their account in the speculation of the day. And to the end that their virtue and discretion may not be short, transient, intermitting starts of thoughts, I have resolved to refresh their memories from day to day, till I have recovered them out of that desperate state of vice and folly into which the age is fallen. The mind that lies fallow but a single day, sprouts up in follies that are only to be killed by a constant and assiduous culture. It was said of Socrates, that he brought philosophy down from heaven, to inhabit among men; and I shall be ambitious to have it said of me, that I have brought philosophy out of closets and libraries, schools and colleges, to dwell in clubs and assemblies, at tea-tables and in coffee-houses.

I would therefore in a very particular manner recommend these my speculations to all well-regulated families, that set apart an hour in every morning for tea and bread and butter; and would earnestly advise them for their good to order this paper to be punctually served up, and to be looked upon as a part of the tea equipage.

Sir Francis Bacon observes, that a well-written book, compared with its rivals and antagonists, is like Moses's serpent, that immediately swallowed up and devoured those of the Egyptians. I shall not be so vain as to think, that where the Spectator appears, the other public prints will vanish; But shall leave it to my reader's consideration, whether, Is it not much better to be let into the knowledge of one's self, than to hear what passes in Muscovy or Poland; and to amuse ourselves with such writings as tend to the wearing out of ignorance, passion, and prejudice, than such as naturally conduce to inflame hatreds, and make enmities irreconcilable?

In the next place, I would recommend this paper to the daily perusal of those gentlemen whom I cannot but consider as my good brothers and allies, I mean the fraternity of Spectators, who live in the world without having anything to do in it; and either by the affluence of their fortunes, or laziness of their dispositions, have no other business with the rest of mankind, but to look upon them. Under this class of men are comprehended all contemplative tradesmen,[1] titular physicians,[2] Fellows of the Royal-society,[3] Templars[4] that

---

[1] retired merchants [2] physicians who do not practice [3] dilettante scientists [4] lawyers

are not given to be contentious, and statesmen that are out of business; in short, every one that considers the world as a theatre, and desires to form a right judgment of those who are the actors on it.

There is another set of men that I must likewise lay a claim to, whom I have lately called the blanks of society, as being altogether unfurnished with ideas, till the business and conversation of the day has supplied them. I have often considered these poor souls with an eye of great commiseration, when I have heard them asking the first man they have met with, whether there was any news stirring? and by that means gathering together materials for thinking. These needy persons do not know what to talk of, till about twelve a clock in the morning; for by that time they are pretty good judges of the weather, know which way the wind sits, and whether the Dutch mail be come in. As they lie at the mercy of the first man they meet, and are grave or impertinent all the day long, according to the notions which they have imbibed in the morning, I would earnestly entreat them not to stir out of their chambers till they have read this paper, and do promise them that I will daily instil into them such sound and wholesome sentiments, as shall have a good effect on their conversation for the ensuing twelve hours.

But there are none to whom this paper will be more useful, than to the female world. I have often thought there has not been sufficient pains taken in finding out proper employments and diversions for the fair ones. Their amusements seem contrived for them, rather as they are women, than as they are reasonable creatures; and are more adapted to the sex than to the species. The toilet is their great scene of business, and the right adjusting of their hair the principal employment of their lives. The sorting of a suit of ribbons is reckoned a very good morning's work; and if they make an excursion to a mercer's or a toy-shop, so great a fatigue makes them unfit for any thing else all the day after. Their more serious occupations are sewing and embroidery, and their greatest drudgery the preparation of jellies and sweetmeats. This, I say, is the state of ordinary women; though I know there are multitudes of those of a more elevated life and conversation, that move in an exalted sphere of knowledge and virtue, that join all the beauties of the mind to the ornaments of dress, and inspire a kind of awe and respect, as well as love, into their male beholders. I hope to encrease the number of these by publishing this daily paper, which I shall always endeavour to make an innocent if not an improving entertainment, and by that means at least divert the minds of my female readers from greater trifles. At the same time, as I would fain give some finishing touches to those which are already the most beautiful pieces in human nature, I shall endeavour to point out all those imperfections that are the blemishes, as well as those virtues which are the embellishments of the sex. In the meanwhile I hope these my gentle readers, who have so much time on their hands, will not grudge throwing away a quarter of an hour in a day on this paper, since they may do it without any hindrance to business.

I know several of my friends and well-wishers are in great pain for me, lest I should not be able to keep up the spirit of a paper which I oblige myself to furnish every day: But to make them easy in this particular, I will promise them faithfully to give it over as soon as I grow dull. This I know will be matter of great raillery to the small Wits; who will frequently put me in mind of my promise, desire me to keep my word, assure me that it is high time to give over, with many other little pleasantries of the like nature, which men of a little smart genius cannot forbear throwing out against their best friends, when they have such a handle given them of being witty. But let them remember that I do hereby enter my caveat against this piece of raillery.

THOUGHTS IN WESTMINSTER ABBEY

NO. 26. FRIDAY, MARCH 30, 1711

Pallida mors aequo pulsat pede pauperum tabernas
  Regumque turres, O beate Sexti.
Vitae summa brevis spem nos vetat inchoare longam,
  Jam te premet nox, fabulaeque manes,
Et domus exilis Plutonia.[1]

— Hor. i. *Od.* iv. 13.

[1] With equal foot, rich friend, impartial fate
  Knocks at the cottage, and the palace gate:
  Life's span forbids thee to extend thy cares,
  And stretch thy hopes beyond thy years:
  Night soon will seize, and you must quickly go
  To story'd ghosts, and Pluto's house below.

When I am in a serious humour, I very often walk by myself in Westminster Abbey; where the gloominess of the place, and the use to which it is applied, with the solemnity of the building, and the condition of the people who lie in it, are apt to fill the mind with a kind of melancholy, or rather thoughtfulness, that is not disagreeable. I yesterday passed a whole afternoon in the churchyard, the cloisters, and the church, amusing myself with the tombstones and inscriptions that I met with in those several regions of the dead. Most of them recorded nothing else of the buried person, but that he was born upon one day, and died upon another: the whole history of his life being comprehended in those two circumstances that are common to all mankind. I could not but look upon these registers of existence, whether of brass or marble, as a kind of satire upon the departed persons; who left no other memorial of them, but that they were born, and that they died. They put me in mind of several persons mentioned in the battles of heroic poems, who have sounding names given them, for no other reason but that they may be killed, and are celebrated for nothing but being knocked on the head.

" Γλαῦκόν τε Μεδόντα τε Θερσιλοχόν τε." [1]
— Hom.

"Glaucumque, Medontaque, Thersilochumque."
— Virg.

The life of these men is finely described in Holy Writ by "the path of an arrow," which is immediately closed up and lost.

Upon my going into the church, I entertained myself with the digging of a grave; and saw in every shovel-full of it that was thrown up, the fragment of a bone or skull intermixed with a kind of fresh mouldering earth, that some time or other had a place in the composition of an human body. Upon this I began to consider with myself, what innumerable multitudes of people lay confused together under the pavement of that ancient cathedral; how men and women, friends and enemies, priests and soldiers, monks and prebendaries, were crumbled amongst one another, and blended together in the same common mass; how beauty, strength, and youth, with old age, weakness, and deformity,

[1] " Glaucus, and Medon, and Thersilochus."

lay undistinguished in the same promiscuous heap of matter.

After having thus surveyed this great magazine of mortality, as it were in the lump, I examined it more particularly by the accounts which I found on several of the monuments which are raised in every quarter of that ancient fabric. Some of them were covered with such extravagant epitaphs, that if it were possible for the dead person to be acquainted with them, he would blush at the praises which his friends have bestowed on him. There are others so excessively modest, that they deliver the character of the person departed in Greek or Hebrew, and by that means are not understood once in a twelvemonth. In the poetical quarter, I found there were poets who had no monuments, and monuments which had no poets. I observed, indeed, that the present war had filled the church with many of these uninhabited monuments, which had been erected to the memory of persons whose bodies were, perhaps, buried in the plains of Blenheim, or in the bosom of the ocean.

I could not but be very much delighted with several modern epitaphs, which are written with great elegance of expression and justness of thought, and therefore do honour to the living as well as to the dead. As a foreigner is very apt to conceive an idea of the ignorance or politeness of a nation from the turn of their public monuments and inscriptions, they should be submitted to the perusal of men of learning and genius before they are put in execution. Sir Cloudesley Shovel's[1] monument has very often given me great offence. Instead of the brave, rough, English admiral, which was the distinguishing character of that plain, gallant man, he is represented on his tomb by the figure of a beau, dressed in a long periwig, and reposing himself upon velvet cushions under a canopy of state. The inscription is answerable to the monument; for, instead of celebrating the many remarkable actions he had performed in the service of his country, it acquaints us only with the manner of his death, in which it was impossible for him to reap any honour. The Dutch, whom we are apt to despise for want of genius, show an infinitely greater taste of antiquity and politeness in their buildings and works of this nature, than what we meet with in those of our own country. The monuments of their admirals, which have been erected at the public expense, represent them like themselves, and are adorned with rostral[1] crowns and naval ornaments, with beautiful festoons of sea-weed, shells, and coral.

But to return to our subject. I have left the repository of our English kings for the contemplation of another day, when I shall find my mind disposed for so serious an amusement. I know that entertainments of this nature are apt to raise dark and dismal thoughts in timorous minds and gloomy imaginations; but for my own part, though I am always serious, I do not know what it is to be melancholy; and can therefore take a view of nature in her deep and solemn scenes, with the same pleasure as in her most gay and delightful ones. By this means I can improve myself with those objects, which others consider with terror. When I look upon the tombs of the great, every emotion of envy dies in me; when I read the epitaphs of the beautiful, every inordinate desire goes out; when I meet with the grief of parents upon a tomb-stone, my heart melts with compassion: when I see the tomb of the parents themselves, I consider the vanity of grieving for those whom we must quickly follow. When I see kings lying by those who deposed them, when I consider rival wits placed side by side, or the holy men that divided the world with their contests and disputes, I reflect with sorrow and astonishment on the little competitions, factions, and debates of mankind. When I read the several dates of the tombs, of some that died yesterday, and some six hundred years ago, I consider that great day when we shall all of us be contemporaries, and make our appearance together.

THE HEAD-DRESS

NO. 98. FRIDAY, JUNE 22, 1711

Tanta est quaerendi cura decoris.[2]
— Juv. *Sat.* vi. 500.

There is not so variable a thing in nature as a lady's head-dress. Within my own memory I have known it rise and fall above thirty

---

[1] Drowned at sea, 1707

[1] a crown adorned with figures of prows of ships
[2] So studiously their persons they adorn.

degrees. About ten years ago it shot up to a very great height, insomuch that the female part of our species were much taller than the men. The women were of such an enormous stature, that "we appeared as grasshoppers before them;"[1] at present the whole sex is in a manner dwarfed, and shrunk into a race of beauties that seems almost another species. I remember several ladies, who were once very near seven foot high, that at present want some inches of five. How they came to be thus curtailed I cannot learn. Whether the whole sex be at present under any penance which we know nothing of; or whether they have cast their head-dresses in order to surprise us with something in that kind which shall be entirely new; or whether some of the tallest of the sex, being too cunning for the rest, have contrived this method to make themselves appear sizeable, is still a secret; though I find most are of opinion, they are at present like trees new lopped and pruned, that will certainly sprout up and flourish with greater heads than before. For my own part, as I do not love to be insulted by women who are taller than myself, I admire the sex much more in their present humiliation, which has reduced them to their natural dimensions, than when they had extended their persons and lengthened themselves out into formidable and gigantic figures. I am not for adding to the beautiful edifices of nature, nor for raising any whimsical superstructure upon her plans: I must therefore repeat it, that I am highly pleased with the coiffure now in fashion, and think it shows the good sense which at present very much reigns among the valuable part of the sex. One may observe that women in all ages have taken more pains than men to adorn the outside of their heads; and indeed I very much admire,[2] that those female architects who raise such wonderful structures out of ribands, lace, and wire, have not been recorded for their respective inventions. It is certain there have been as many orders in these kinds of building, as in those which have been made of marble. Sometimes they rise in the shape of a pyramid, sometimes like a tower, and sometimes like a steeple. In Juvenal's time the building grew by several orders and stories, as he has very humorously described it:

"Tot premit ordinibus, tot adhuc compagibus altum
Aedificat caput: Andromachen a fronte videbis;
Post minor est: aliam credas."[1]

— Juv. *Sat.* vi. 501.

But I do not remember in any part of my reading, that the head-dress aspired to as great an extravagance as in the fourteenth century; when it was built up in a couple of cones or spires, which stood so excessively high on each side of the head, that a woman, who was but a Pigmy without her head-dress, appeared like a Colossus upon putting it on. Monsieur Paradin[2] says, "That these old-fashioned fontanges[3] rose an ell above the head; that they were pointed like steeples; and had long loose pieces of crape fastened to the tops of them, which were curiously fringed, and hung down their backs like streamers."

The women might possibly have carried this Gothic building much higher, had not a famous monk, Thomas Conecte[4] by name, attacked it with great zeal and resolution. This holy man travelled from place to place to preach down this monstrous commode; and succeeded so well in it, that, as the magicians sacrificed their books to the flames upon the preaching of an apostle, many of the women threw down their head-dresses in the middle of his sermon, and made a bonfire of them within sight of the pulpit. He was so renowned, as well for the sanctity of his life as his manner of preaching, that he had often a congregation of twenty thousand people; the men placing themselves on the one side of his pulpit, and the women on the other, that appeared (to use the similitude of an ingenious writer) like a forest of cedars with their heads reaching to the clouds. He so warmed and animated the people against this monstrous ornament, that it lay under a kind of persecution; and, whenever it appeared in public, was pelted down by the rabble, who flung stones at the persons that wore it. But notwithstanding this prodigy vanished while the preacher was among them, it began to ap-

---

[1] "With curls on curls they build her head before,
And mount it with a formidable tower:
A giantess she seems; but look behind,
And then she dwindles to the pigmy kind."

[2] a French historian of England (1510–1590)
[3] a kind of headdress   [4] a Carmelite friar, burned in 1434

---

[1] Cf. *Numbers* xiii : 33   [2] wonder

pear again some months after his departure, or, to tell it in Monsieur Paradin's own words, "the women, that like snails in a fright had drawn in their horns, shot them out again as soon as the danger was over." This extravagance of the women's head-dresses in that age is taken notice of by Monsieur d'Argentre [1] in his History of Bretagne, and by other historians, as well as the person I have here quoted.

It is usually observed, that a good reign is the only proper time for the making of laws against the exorbitance of power; in the same manner an excessive head-dress may be attacked the most effectually when the fashion is against it. I do therefore recommend this paper to my female readers by way of prevention.

I would desire the fair sex to consider how impossible it is for them to add anything that can be ornamental to what is already the masterpiece of nature. The head has the most beautiful appearance, as well as the highest station, in a human figure. Nature has laid out all her art in beautifying the face; she has touched it with vermillion, planted in it a double row of ivory, made it the seat of smiles and blushes, lighted it up and enlivened it with the brightness of the eyes, hung it on each side with the curious organs of sense, giving it airs and graces that cannot be described, and surrounded it with such a flowing shade of hair as sets all its beauties in the most agreeable light. In short, she seems to have designed the head as the cupola to the most glorious of her works; and when we load it with such a pile of supernumerary ornaments, we destroy the symmetry of the human figure, and foolishly contrive to call off the eye from great and real beauties, to childish gewgaws, ribands, and bone-lace.

THE VISION OF MIRZA

NO. 159. SATURDAY, SEPTEMBER 1, 1711

Omnem, quae nunc obducta tuenti
Mortales hebetat visus tibi, et humida circum
Caligat, nubem eripiam [2] . . .

— VIRG. *Aen.* ii. 604.

[1] a French writer of the sixteenth century

[2] The cloud, which, intercepting the clear light,
Hangs o'er thy eyes, and blunts thy mortal sight,
I will remove . . .

When I was at Grand Cairo, I picked up several Oriental manuscripts, which I have still by me. Among others I met with one entitled "The Visions of Mirza," which I have read over with great pleasure. I intend to give it to the public when I have no other entertainment for them; and shall begin with the first vision, which I have translated word for word as follows:

"On the fifth day of the moon, which according to the custom of my forefathers I always keep holy, after having washed myself, and offered up my morning devotions, I ascended the high hills of Bagdad, in order to pass the rest of the day in meditation and prayer. As I was here airing myself on the tops of the mountains, I fell into a profound contemplation on the vanity of human life; and passing from one thought to another, 'surely,' said I, 'man is but a shadow, and life a dream.' Whilst I was thus musing, I cast my eyes towards the summit of a rock that was not far from me, where I discovered one in the habit of a shepherd, with a musical instrument in his hand. As I looked upon him he applied it to his lips, and began to play upon it. The sound of it was exceedingly sweet, and wrought into a variety of tunes that were inexpressibly melodious, and altogether different from anything I had ever heard. They put me in mind of those heavenly airs that are played to the departed souls of good men upon their first arrival in Paradise, to wear out the impressions of their last agonies, and qualify them for the pleasures of that happy place. My heart melted away in secret raptures.

"I had been often told that the rock before me was the haunt of a Genius; and that several had been entertained with music who had passed by it, but never heard that the musician had before made himself visible. When he had raised my thoughts by those transporting airs which he played to taste the pleasures of his conversation, as I looked upon him like one astonished, he beckoned to me, and by the waving of his hand directed me to approach the place where he sat. I drew near with that reverence which is due to a superior nature; and as my heart was entirely subdued by the captivating strains I had heard, I fell down at his feet and wept. The Genius smiled upon me with a look of compassion and affability that familiarized him to my imagination, and at once dispelled all the fears and apprehensions with which I approached him. He lifted me from the ground, and taking me by the hand, 'Mirza,' said he, 'I have heard thee in thy soliloquies; follow me.'

"He then led me to the highest pinnacle of the rock, and placing me on the top of it, 'Cast thy eyes eastward,' said he, 'and tell me what thou seest.' 'I see,' said I, 'a huge valley, and a prodigious tide of water rolling through it.' 'The valley that thou seest,' said he, 'is the Vale of Misery, and the tide of water that thou seest is part of the great Tide of Eternity.' 'What is the reason,' said I, 'that the tide I see rises out of a thick mist at one end, and again loses itself in a thick mist at the other?' 'What thou seest,' said he, 'is that portion of eternity which is called time, measured out by the sun, and reaching from the beginning of the world to its consummation. Examine now,' said he, 'this sea that is bounded with darkness at both ends, and tell me what thou discoverest in it.' 'I see a bridge,' said I, 'standing in the midst of the tide.' 'The bridge thou seest,' said he, 'is Human Life: consider it attentively.' Upon a more leisurely survey of it, I found that it consisted of three score and ten entire arches, with several broken arches, which added to those that were entire, made up the number about an hundred. As I was counting the arches, the Genius told me that this bridge consisted at first of a thousand arches; but that a great flood swept away the rest, and left the bridge in the ruinous condition I now beheld it. 'But tell me farther,' said he, 'what thou discoverest on it.' 'I see multitudes of people passing over it,' said I, 'and a black cloud hanging on each end of it.' As I looked more attentively, I saw several of the passengers dropping through the bridge into the great tide that flowed underneath it; and upon farther examination, perceived there were innumerable trap-doors that lay concealed in the bridge, which the passengers no sooner trod upon, but they fell through them into the tide, and immediately disappeared. These hidden pit-falls were set very thick at the entrance of the bridge, so that throngs of people no sooner broke through the cloud, but many of them fell into them. They grew thinner towards the middle, but multiplied and lay closer together towards the end of the arches that were entire.

"There were indeed some persons, but their number was very small, that continued a kind of hobbling march on the broken arches, but fell through one after another, being quite tired and spent with so long a walk.

"I passed some time in the contemplation of this wonderful structure, and the great variety of objects which it presented. My heart was filled with a deep melancholy to see several dropping unexpectedly in the midst of mirth and jollity, and catching at everything that stood by them to save themselves. Some were looking up towards the heavens, in a thoughtful posture, and in the midst of a speculation stumbled and fell out of sight. Multitudes were very busy in the pursuit of bubbles that glittered in their eyes and danced before them; but often when they thought themselves within the reach of them, their footing failed and down they sunk. In this confusion of objects, I observed some with scimitars in their hands, who ran to and fro upon the bridge, thrusting several persons on trap-doors which did not seem to lie in their way, and which they might have escaped had they not been thus forced upon them.

"The Genius seeing me indulge myself on this melancholy prospect, told me I had dwelt long enough upon it. 'Take thine eyes off the bridge,' said he, 'and tell me if thou yet seest anything thou dost not comprehend.' Upon looking up, 'What mean,' said I, 'those great flights of birds that are perpetually hovering about the bridge, and settling upon it from time to time? I see vultures, harpies, ravens, cormorants, and among many other feathered creatures several little winged boys, that perch in great numbers upon the middle arches.' 'These,' said the Genius, 'are Envy, Avarice, Superstition, Despair, Love, with the like cares and passions that infest human life.'

"I here fetched a deep sigh. 'Alas,' said I, 'Man was made in vain! how is he given away to misery and mortality! tortured in life, and swallowed up in death!' The Genius being moved with compassion towards me, bid me quit so uncomfortable a prospect. 'Look no more,' said he, 'on man in the first stage of his existence, in his setting out for eternity; but cast thine eye on that thick mist into which the tide bears the several generations of mortals that fall into it.' I directed my sight as I was ordered, and (whether or no the good Genius strengthened it with any supernatural force, or dissipated part of the mist that was before too thick for the eye to penetrate) I saw the valley opening at the farther end, and spreading forth into an immense ocean, that had a huge rock of adamant running through the midst of it, and dividing it into two equal parts. The clouds still rested on one half of it, insomuch that I could discover nothing in it; but the other appeared to me a vast ocean planted with innumerable islands, that were covered with fruits and flowers, and interwoven with a thousand little shining seas that ran among them. I could see persons dressed in glorious habits with garlands upon their heads, passing among the trees, lying down by the sides of fountains, or resting on beds of flowers; and could hear a confused harmony of singing birds, falling waters, human voices, and musical instruments. Gladness grew in me upon the discovery of so delightful a scene. I wished for the wings of an eagle, that I might fly away to those happy seats; but the Genius told me there was no passage to them except through the gates of death that I saw opening every moment upon the bridge. 'The islands,' said he, 'that lie so fresh and green before thee, and with which the whole face of the ocean appears spotted as far as thou canst see, are more in number than the sands on the sea-shore: there are myriads of islands behind those which thou here discoverest, reaching farther than thine eye, or even thine imagination can extend itself. These are the mansions of good men after death, who, according to the degree and kinds of virtue in which they excelled, are distributed among these several islands, which abound with pleasures of different kinds and degrees, suitable to the relishes and perfections of those who are settled in them: every island is a paradise accommodated to its respective inhabitants. Are not these, O Mirza, habitations worth contending for? Does life appear miserable that gives thee opportunities of earning such a reward? Is death to be feared that will convey thee to so happy an existence? Think not man was made in vain, who has such an eternity reserved for him.' I gazed with inexpressible pleasure on these happy islands. At length, said I, 'Show me now, I beseech thee, the secrets that lie hid under those dark clouds which cover the ocean on the other side of the rock of adamant.' The Genius making me no answer, I turned me about to address myself to him a second time, but I found that he had left me;

I then turned again to the vision which I had been so long contemplating; but instead of the rolling tide, the arched bridge, and the happy islands, I saw nothing but the long hollow valley of Bagdad, with oxen, sheep, and camels grazing upon the sides of it."

HILPA AND SHALUM

NO. 584. MONDAY, AUGUST 23, 1714

Hic gelidi fontes, hic mollia prata, Lycori,
Hic nemus, hic toto tecum consumerer aevo.[1]
— VIRG. *Ecl.* x. 42.

Hilpa was one of the hundred and fifty daughters of Zilpah, of the race of Cohu, by whom some of the learned think is meant Cain. She was exceedingly beautiful; and, when she was but a girl of three score and ten years of age, received the addresses of several who made love to her. Among these were two brothers, Harpath and Shalum. Harpath, being the first-born, was master of that fruitful region which lies at the foot of Mount Tirzah, in the southern parts of China. Shalum (which is to say the planter in the Chinese language) possessed all the neighboring hills, and that great range of mountains which goes under the name of Tirzah. Harpath was of a haughty contemptuous spirit; Shalum was of a gentle disposition, beloved both by God and man.

It is said, that among the antediluvian women, the daughters of Cohu had their minds wholly set upon riches; for which reason the beautiful Hilpa preferred Harpath to Shalum, because of his numerous flocks and herds that covered all the low country which runs along the foot of Mount Tirzah, and is watered by several fountains and streams breaking out of the sides of that mountain.

Harpath made so quick a despatch of his courtship, that he married Hilpa in the hundredth year of her age; and, being of an insolent temper, laughed to scorn his brother Shalum for having pretended to the beautiful Hilpa, when he was master of nothing but a

[1] Come see what pleasures in our plains abound;
The woods, the fountains, and the flow'ry ground,
Here I could live, and love, and die, with only you.

long chain of rocks and mountains. This so much provoked Shalum, that he is said to have cursed his brother in the bitterness of his heart, and to have prayed that one of his mountains might fall upon his head if ever he came within the shadow of it.

From this time forward Harpath would never venture out of the valleys, but came to an untimely end in the two hundred and fiftieth year of his age, being drowned in a river as he attempted to cross it. This river is called to this day, from his name who perished in it, the river Harpath: and, what is very remarkable, issues out of one of those mountains which Shalum wished might fall upon his brother, when he cursed him in the bitterness of his heart.

Hilpa was in the hundred and sixtieth year of her age at the death of her husband, having brought him but fifty children before he was snatched away, as has been already related. Many of the antediluvians made love to the young widow; though no one was thought so likely to succeed in her affections as her first lover Shalum, who renewed his court to her about ten years after the death of Harpath; for it was not thought decent in those days that a widow should be seen by a man within ten years after the decease of her husband.

Shalum falling into a deep melancholy, and resolving to take away that objection which had been raised against him when he made his first addresses to Hilpa, began, immediately after her marriage with Harpath, to plant all that mountainous region which fell to his lot in the division of this country. He knew how to adapt every plant to its proper soil, and is thought to have inherited many traditional secrets of that art from the first man. This employment turned at length to his profit as well as to his amusement; his mountains were in a few years shaded with young trees, that gradually shot up into groves, woods, and forests, intermixed with walks, and lawns, and gardens; insomuch that the whole region, from a naked and desolate prospect, began now to look like a second Paradise. The pleasantness of the place, and the agreeable disposition of Shalum, who was reckoned one of the mildest and wisest of all who lived before the flood, drew into it multitudes of people, who were perpetually employed in the sinking of wells, the digging of trenches, and the hollowing of trees, for the better distribution of water through every part of this spacious plantation.

The habitations of Shalum looked every year more beautiful in the eyes of Hilpa, who, after the space of seventy autumns, was wonderfully pleased with the distant prospect of Shalum's hills, which were then covered with innumerable tufts of trees and gloomy scenes, that gave a magnificence to the place, and converted it into one of the finest landscapes the eye of man could behold.

The Chinese record a letter which Shalum is said to have written to Hilpa in the eleventh year of her widowhood. I shall here translate it, without departing from that noble simplicity of sentiment and plainness of manners which appears in the original.

Shalum was at the time one hundred and eighty years old, and Hilpa one hundred and seventy.

"SHALUM, MASTER OF MOUNT TIRZAH, TO HILPA, MISTRESS OF THE VALLEYS

" *In the 788th year of the creation.*

"What have I not suffered, O thou daughter of Zilpah, since thou gavest thyself away in marriage to my rival! I grew weary of the light of the sun, and have been ever since covering myself with woods and forests. These threescore and ten years have I bewailed the loss of thee on the top of Mount Tirzah, and soothed my melancholy among a thousand gloomy shades of my own raising. My dwellings are at present as the garden of God; every part of them is filled with fruits, and flowers, and fountains. The whole mountain is perfumed for thy reception. Come up into it, O my beloved, and let us people this spot of the new world with a beautiful race of mortals; let us multiply exceedingly among these delightful shades, and fill every quarter of them with sons and daughters. Remember, O thou daughter of Zilpah, that the age of man is but a thousand years; that beauty is the admiration but of a few centuries. It flourishes as a mountain oak, or as a cedar on the top of Tirzah, which in three or four hundred years will fade away, and never be thought of by posterity, unless a young wood springs from its roots. Think well on this, and remember thy neighbour in the mountains."

Having here inserted this letter, which I look upon as the only antediluvian billet-doux now extant, I shall in my next paper give the answer to it, and the sequel of this story.

NO. 585. WEDNESDAY, AUGUST 25, 1714

*Ipsi laetitia voces ad sidera jactant
Intonsi montes: ipsae jam carmina rupes,
Ipsa sonant arbusta.*[1]
— VIRG. *Ecl.* v. 62.

THE SEQUEL OF THE STORY OF SHALUM AND HILPA

The letter inserted in my last had so good an effect upon Hilpa, that she answered in less than a twelvemonth, after the following manner:

"HILPA, MISTRESS OF THE VALLEYS, TO SHALUM, MASTER OF MOUNT TIRZAH

"*In the 789th year of the creation.*

"What have I to do with thee, O Shalum? Thou praisest Hilpa's beauty, but art thou not secretly enamoured with the verdure of her meadows? Art thou not more affected with the prospect of her green valleys, than thou wouldest be with the sight of her person? The lowings of my herds and the bleatings of my flocks make a pleasant echo in thy mountains, and sound sweetly in thy ears. What though I am delighted with the wavings of thy forests, and those breezes of perfumes which flow from the top of Tirzah, are these like the riches of the valley?

"I know thee, O Shalum; thou art more wise and happy than any of the sons of men. Thy dwellings are among the cedars; thou searchest out the diversity of soils, thou understandest the influences of the stars, and markest the change of seasons. Can a woman appear lovely in the eyes of such a one? Disquiet me not, O Shalum; let me alone, that I may enjoy those goodly possessions which are fallen to my lot. Win me not by thy enticing words. May thy trees increase and multiply! mayest thou add wood to wood, and shade to shade! but tempt not Hilpa to destroy thy solitude, and make thy retirement populous."

The Chinese say that a little time afterwards she accepted of a treat in one of the neighbouring hills to which Shalum had in-

vited her. This treat lasted for two years, and is said to have cost Shalum five hundred antelopes, two thousand ostriches, and a thousand tun of milk; but what most of all recommended it, was that variety of delicious fruits and potherbs, in which no person then living could any way equal Shalum.

He treated her in the bower which he had planted amidst the wood of nightingales. The wood was made up of such fruit-trees and plants as are most agreeable to the several kinds of singing-birds; so that it had drawn into it all the music of the country, and was filled from one end of the year to the other with the most agreeable concert in season.

He showed her every day some beautiful and surprising scene in this new region of woodlands; and, as by this means he had all the opportunities he could wish for, of opening his mind to her, he succeeded so well, that upon her departure she made him a kind of promise, and gave him her word to return him a positive answer in less than fifty years.

She had not been long among her own people in the valleys, when she received new overtures, and at the same time a most splendid visit from Mishpach, who was a mighty man of old, and had built a great city, which he called after his own name. Every house was made for at least a thousand years, nay, there were some that were leased out for three lives; so that the quantity of stone and timber consumed in this building is scarce to be imagined by those who live in the present age of the world. This great man entertained her with the voice of musical instruments which had been lately invented,[1] and danced before her to the sound of the timbrel. He also presented her with several domestic utensils wrought in brass and iron, which had been newly found out [2] for the conveniency of life. In the meantime Shalum grew very uneasy with himself, and was sorely displeased at Hilpa for the reception which she had given to Mishpach, insomuch that he never wrote to her or spoke of her during a whole revolution of Saturn; [3] but, finding that this intercourse went no farther than a visit, he again renewed his addresses to her; who, during his long silence, is said very often to have cast a wishing eye upon Mount Tirzah.

Her mind continued wavering about twenty

[1] The mountain tops unshorn, the rocks rejoice;
The lowly shrubs partake of human voice.

[1] Cf. *Genesis* iv: 21 [2] *Genesis* iv: 22 [3] nearly thirty years

years longer between Shalum and Mishpach; for though her inclinations favoured the former, her interest pleaded very powerfully for the other. While her heart was in this unsettled condition, the following accident happened, which determined her choice. A high tower of wood that stood in the city of Mishpach having caught fire by a flash of lightning, in a few days reduced the whole town to ashes. Mishpach resolved to rebuild the place, whatever it should cost him: and, having already destroyed all the timber of the country, he was forced to have recourse to Shalum, whose forests were now two hundred years old. He purchased these woods with so many herds of cattle and flocks of sheep, and with such a vast extent of fields and pastures, that Shalum was now grown more wealthy than Mishpach; and therefore appeared so charming in the eyes of Zilpah's daughter, that she no longer refused him in marriage. On the day in which he brought her up into the mountains he raised a most prodigious pile of cedar, and of every sweet smelling wood, which reached above three hundred cubits in height; he also cast into the pile bundles of myrrh and sheaves of spikenard, enriching it with every spicy shrub, and, making it fat with the gums of his plantations. This was the burnt-offering which Shalum offered in the day of his espousals: the smoke of it ascended up to heaven, and filled the whole country with incense and perfume.

·

MATTHEW PRIOR (1664–1721)

TO A CHILD OF QUALITY FIVE YEARS OLD

Lords, knights, and 'squires, the numerous band,
  That wear the fair Miss Mary's fetters,
Were summoned by her high command,
  To show their passions by their letters. 4

My pen among the rest I took,
  Lest those bright eyes that cannot read
Should dart their kindling fires, and look
  The power they have to be obeyed. 8

Nor quality, nor reputation,
  Forbid me yet my flame to tell,

Dear Five-years-old befriends my passion,
  And I may write till she can spell. 12

For, while she makes her silk-worms beds
  With all the tender things I swear;
Whilst all the house my passion reads,
  In papers round her baby's hair; 16

She may receive and own my flame,
  For, though the strictest prudes should know it,
She'll pass for a most virtuous dame,
  And I for an unhappy poet. 20

Then too, alas! when she shall tear
  The lines some younger rival sends;
She'll give me leave to write, I fear,
  And we shall still continue friends. 24

For, as our different ages move,
  'Tis so ordained, (would Fate but mend it!)
That I shall be past making love,
  When she begins to comprehend it. 28

THE REMEDY WORSE THAN THE DISEASE

I sent for Ratcliffe; was so ill,
  That other doctors gave me over:
He felt my pulse, prescribed his pill,
  And I was likely to recover. 4

But when the wit began to wheeze,
  And wine had warm'd the politician,
Cured yesterday of my disease,
  I died last night of my physician. 8

TO HIS SOUL

TRANSLATED FROM THE LATIN OF HADRIAN

Poor little, pretty, fluttering thing,
  Must we no longer live together?
And dost thou prune thy trembling wing, 3
  To take thy flight thou know'st not whither?

Thy humorous vein, thy pleasing folly
  Lie all neglected, all forgot:
And pensive, wavering, melancholy,
  Thou dread'st and hop'st thou know'st not what. 8

ALEXANDER POPE (1688–1744)

AN ESSAY ON CRITICISM

FROM PART I

'Tis hard to say, if greater want of skill
Appear in writing or in judging ill;
But, of the two, less dangerous is th' offence
To tire our patience, than mislead our sense.
Some few in that, but numbers err in this,   5
Ten censure wrong for one who writes amiss;
A fool might once himself alone expose,
Now one in verse makes many more in prose.
　'Tis with our judgments as our watches, none
Go just alike, yet each believes his own.   10
In poets as true genius is but rare,
True taste as seldom is the critic's share;
Both must alike from Heaven derive their light,
These born to judge, as well as those to write.
Let such teach others who themselves excel,
And censure freely who have written well.   16
Authors are partial to their wit,[1] 'tis true,
But are not critics to their judgment too?

* * * * * * *

　First follow Nature, and your judgment frame
By her just standard, which is still the same:
Unerring Nature, still divinely bright,   70
One clear, unchanged, and universal light,
Life, force, and beauty, must to all impart,
At once the source, and end, and test of Art.
Art from that fund each just supply provides,
Works without show, and without pomp presides: 75
In some fair body thus th' informing soul
With spirits feeds, with vigour fills the whole,
Each motion guides, and every nerve sustains;
Itself unseen, but in th' effects, remains.
Some, to whom Heaven in wit has been profuse,   80
Want as much more, to turn it to its use;
For wit and judgment often are at strife,
Though meant each other's aid, like man and wife.
'Tis more to guide than spur the Muse's steed;
Restrain his fury, than provoke his speed;   85

---

[1] creative power

The winged courser, like a generous horse,
Shows most true mettle when you check his course.
Those rules of old discovered, not devised,
Are Nature still, but Nature methodized;
Nature, like liberty, is but restrained   90
By the same laws which first herself ordained.

* * * * * * *

　You, then, whose judgment the right course would steer,
Know well each ancient's proper character;
His fable, subject, scope in every page;   120
Religion, country, genius of his age:
Without all these at once before your eyes,
Cavil you may, but never criticise.
Be Homer's works your study and delight,
Read them by day, and meditate by night;
Thence form your judgment, thence your maxims bring,   126
And trace the Muses upward to their spring.
Still with itself compared, his text peruse;
And let your comment be the Mantuan Muse.[1]
　When first young Maro[1] in his boundless mind   130
A work t' outlast immortal Rome designed,
Perhaps he seemed above the critic's law,
And but from nature's fountains scorned to draw:
But when t' examine every part he came,
Nature and Homer were, he found, the same.
Convinced, amazed, he checks the bold design;   136
And rules as strict his laboured work confine,
As if the Stagirite[2] o'erlooked each line.
Learn hence for ancient rules a just esteem;
To copy nature is to copy them.   140
　Some beauties yet no precepts can declare,
For there's a happiness as well as care.
Music resembles poetry, in each
Are nameless graces which no methods teach,
And which a master-hand alone can reach.
If, where the rules not far enough extend,
(Since rules were made but to promote their end)   147
Some lucky license answer to the full
Th' intent proposed, that license is a rule.
Thus Pegasus, a nearer way to take,   150
May boldly deviate from the common track;
From vulgar bounds with brave disorder part,
And snatch a grace beyond the reach of art,
Which without passing through the judgment, gains

---

[1] Vergil   [2] Aristotle

The heart, and all its end at once attains. 155
In prospects thus, some objects please our
    eyes,
Which out of nature's common order rise,
The shapeless rock, or hanging precipice.
Great wits sometimes may gloriously offend,
And rise to faults true critics dare not mend.
But tho' the ancients thus their rules invade,
(As kings dispense with laws themselves have
    made)   162
Moderns, beware ! or if you must offend
Against the precept, ne'er transgress its end ;
Let it be seldom and compelled by need ; 165
And have, at least, their precedent to plead.
The critic else proceeds without remorse,
Seizes your fame, and puts his laws in force.
I know there are, to whose presumptuous
    thoughts   169
Those freer beauties, e'en in them, seem faults.
Some figures monstrous and misshaped ap-
    pear,
Considered singly, or beheld too near,
Which, but proportioned to their light or
    place,
Due distance reconciles to form and grace.
A prudent chief not always must display 175
His powers in equal ranks, and fair array,
But with th' occasion and the place comply,
Conceal his force, nay, seem sometimes to
    fly.
Those oft are stratagems which errors seem,
Nor is it Homer nods, but we that dream. 180

From PART II

Others for language all their care express,
And value books, as women, men, for dress :
Their praise is still,[1] — the style is excellent ;
The sense, they humbly take upon content.
Words are like leaves ; and where they most
    abound,
Much fruit of sense beneath is rarely found.
False eloquence, like the prismatic glass, 311
Its gaudy colours spreads on every place ;
The face of nature we no more survey,
All glares alike, without distinction gay :
But true expression, like th' unchanging sun,
Clears and improves whate'er it shines upon,
It gilds all objects, but it alters none.   317
Expression is the dress of thought, and still
Appears more decent, as more suitable ;
A vile conceit in pompous words expressed,
Is like a clown in regal purple dressed :   321

For different styles with different subjects sort,
As several garbs with country, town, and
    court.
Some by old words to fame have made pre-
    tence,
Ancients in phrase, mere moderns in their
    sense ;   325
Such laboured nothings, in so strange a style,
Amaze th' unlearn'd, and make the learnèd
    smile.
Unlucky, as Fungoso [1] in the play,
These sparks with awkward vanity display
What the fine gentleman wore yesterday ; 330
And but so mimic ancient wits at best,
As apes our grandsires, in their doublets
    dressed.
In words, as fashions, the same rule will hold ;
Alike fantastic, if too new, or old :
Be not the first by whom the new are tried,
Nor yet the last to lay the old aside.   336
But most by numbers [2] judge a poet's song ;
And smooth or rough, with them, is right or
    wrong :
In the bright Muse though thousand charms
    conspire,   339
Her voice is all these tuneful fools admire ;
Who haunt Parnassus but to please their ear,
Not mend their minds ; as some to church
    repair,
Not for the doctrine, but the music there.
These equal syllables alone require,
Tho' oft the ear the open vowels tire ;   345
While expletives their feeble aid do join,
And ten low words oft creep in one dull line :
While they ring round the same unvaried
    chimes,
With sure returns of still expected rhymes ;
Where'er you find "the cooling western
    breeze,"   350
In the next line, it "whispers through the
    trees ;"
If crystal streams "with pleasing murmurs
    creep,"
The reader's threatened (not in vain) with
    "sleep :"
Then, at the last and only couplet fraught
With some unmeaning thing they call a
    thought,   355
A needless Alexandrine ends the song,
That, like a wounded snake, drags its slow
    length along.

---

[1] always

[1] In Jonson's *Every Man out of his Humour*
he unsuccessfully attempts to ape the fashionable.
[2] metre

Leave such to tune their own dull rhymes, and
    know
What's roundly smooth or languishingly slow;
And praise the easy vigour of a line,   360
Where Denham's strength, and Waller's
    sweetness join.
True ease in writing comes from art, not
    chance,
As those move easiest who have learned to
    dance.
'Tis not enough no harshness gives offence,
The sound must seem an echo to the sense.
Soft is the strain when Zephyr gently blows,
And the smooth stream in smoother numbers
    flows;   367
But when loud surges lash the sounding shore,
The hoarse, rough verse should like the tor-
    rent roar.
When Ajax strives some rock's vast weight to
    throw,   370
The line too labours, and the words move
    slow;
Not so, when swift Camilla scours the plain,
Flies o'er th' unbending corn, and skims along
    the main.'
Hear how Timotheus' varied lays surprise,
And bid alternate passions fall and rise!   375
While, at each change, the son of Libyan Jove
Now burns with glory, and then melts with
    love;
Now his fierce eyes with sparkling fury glow,
Now sighs steal out, and tears begin to flow:
Persians and Greeks like turns of nature
    found,   380
And the world's victor stood subdued by
    sound!
The power of music all our hearts allow,
And what Timotheus was, is Dryden now.

THE RAPE OF THE LOCK

AN HEROI–COMICAL POEM

CANTO I

What dire offence from amorous causes
    springs,
What mighty contests rise from trivial things,
I sing. — This verse to Caryl, Muse! is due;
This, e'en Belinda may vouchsafe to view.
Slight is the subject, but not so the praise, 5
If she inspire, and he approve my lays.
    Say what strange motive, Goddess! could
    compel
A well-bred lord t' assault a gentle belle?

Oh, say what stranger cause, yet unexplored,
Could make a gentle belle reject a lord?   10
In tasks so bold, can little men engage,
And in soft bosoms dwells such mighty rage?
    Sol through white curtains shot a timorous
    ray,
And oped those eyes that must eclipse the day.
Now lap-dogs give themselves the rousing
    shake,   15
And sleepless lovers, just at twelve, awake.
Thrice rung the bell, the slipper knocked the
    ground,[1]
And the pressed watch [2] returned a silver
    sound.
[3] [Belinda still her downy pillow pressed,
Her guardian sylph prolonged the balmy
    rest;   20
'Twas he had summoned to her silent bed
The morning dream that hovered o'er her
    head;
A youth more glittering than a birth-night
    beau,
(That e'en in slumber caused her cheek to
    glow)
Seemed to her ear his winning lips to lay, 25
And thus in whispers said, or seemed to say:
"Fairest of mortals, thou distinguished care
Of thousand bright inhabitants of air!
If e'er one vision touched thy infant thought,
Of all the nurse and all the priest have taught,
Of airy elves by moonlight shadows seen, 31
The silver token,[4] and the circled green,[5]
Or virgins visited by angel powers,
With golden crowns and wreaths of heavenly
    flowers;[6]   34
Hear and believe! thy own importance know,
Nor bound thy narrow views to things below.
Some secret truths, from learnèd pride con-
    cealed,
To maids alone and children are revealed.
What though no credit doubting wits may
    give?
The fair and innocent shall still believe.   40
Know, then, unnumbered spirits round thee fly,
The light militia of the lower sky,
These, though unseen, are ever on the wing,
Hang o'er the box, and hover round the Ring.[7]
Think what an equipage thou hast in air, 45
And view with scorn two pages and a chair.[8]

---

[1] to summon a servant [2] a repeater [3] *The
lines between brackets were not in the first version
of the poem.* [4] a fairy gift [5] where fairies danced
[6] as St. Cecilia was [7] a fashionable drive in
Hyde Park [8] a sedan chair

As now your own, our beings were of old,
And once enclosed in woman's beauteous
    mould;
Thence, by a soft transition, we repair
From earthly vehicles to these of air.   50
Think not, when woman's transient breath is
    fled,
That all her vanities at once are dead;
Succeeding vanities she still regards,
And though she plays no more, o'erlooks the
    cards.
Her joy in gilded chariots, when alive,   55
And love of ombre,[1] after death survive.
For when the fair in all their pride expire,
To their first elements their souls retire:
The sprites of fiery termagants in flame
Mount up, and take a salamander's name. 60
Soft yielding minds to water glide away,
And sip, with nymphs, their elemental tea.
The graver prude sinks downward to a gnome,
In search of mischief still on earth to roam.
The light coquettes in sylphs aloft repair, 65
And sport and flutter in the fields of air.
  "Know further yet: whoever fair and chaste
Rejects mankind, is by some sylph embraced;
For spirits, freed from mortal laws, with ease
Assume what sexes and what shapes they
    please.   70
What guards the purity of melting maids,
In courtly balls, and midnight masquerades,
Safe from the treacherous friend, the daring
    spark,[2]
The glance by day, the whisper in the dark,
When kind occasion prompts their warm de-
    sires,   75
When music softens, and when dancing fires?
'Tis but their sylph, the wise celestials know,
Though honour is the word with men below.
Some nymphs there are, too conscious of their
    face,[3]
For life predestined to the gnomes' embrace.
These swell their prospects and exalt their
    pride,   81
When offers are disdained, and love denied:
Then gay ideas crowd the vacant brain,
While peers, and dukes, and all their sweeping
    train,
And garters, stars, and coronets [4] appear, 85
And in soft sounds 'Your Grace' salutes their
    ear.
'Tis these that early taint the female soul,
Instruct the eyes of young coquettes to roll,

Teach infant cheeks a bidden blush to know,
And little hearts to flutter at a beau.   90
  "Oft when the world imagine women stray,
The sylphs through mystic mazes guide their
    way,
Through all the giddy circle they pursue,
And old impertinence expel by new.
What tender maid but must a victim fall 95
To one man's treat, but for another's ball?
When Florio speaks, what virgin could with-
    stand,
If gentle Damon did not squeeze her hand?
With varying vanities, from every part,
They shift the moving toyshop of their heart;
Where wigs with wigs, with sword-knots
    sword-knots strive,   101
Beaux banish beaux, and coaches coaches drive.
This erring mortals levity may call;
Oh, blind to truth! the sylphs contrive it all.
  "Of these am I, who thy protection claim,
A watchful sprite, and Ariel is my name. 106
Late, as I ranged the crystal wilds of air,
In the clear mirror of thy ruling star
I saw, alas! some dread event impend,
Ere to the main [1] this morning sun descend,
But Heaven reveals not what, or how, or
    where.   111
Warned by the sylph, O pious maid, beware!
This to disclose is all thy guardian can:
Beware of all, but most beware of man!"
  He said; when Shock, who thought she
    slept too long,   115
Leaped up, and waked his mistress with his
    tongue.
'Twas then, Belinda, if report say true,
Thy eyes first opened on a billet-doux;
Wounds, charms, and ardours were no sooner
    read,
But all the vision vanished from thy head.
  And now, unveiled, the toilet stands dis-
    played,   121
Each silver vase in mystic order laid.
First, robed in white, the nymph intent adores,
With head uncovered, the cosmetic powers.
A heavenly image in the glass appears, 125
To that she bends, to that her eyes she rears;
Th' inferior priestess,[2] at her altar's side,
Trembling begins the sacred rites of pride.
Unnumbered treasures ope at once, and here
The various offerings of the world appear;
From each she nicely culls with curious toil,
And decks the goddess with the glittering
    spoil.   132

---

[1] a game of cards [2] beau [3] beauty [4] symbols
of rank

[1] the ocean   [2] her maid

This casket India's glowing gems unlocks,
And all Arabia breathes from yonder box.
The tortoise here and elephant unite,   135
Transformed to combs, the speckled, and the
  white.
Here files of pins extend their shining rows,
Puffs, powders, patches, bibles, billets-doux
Now awful beauty puts on all its arms;
The fair each moment rises in her charms, 140
Repairs her smiles, awakens every grace,
And calls forth all the wonders of her face;
Sees by degrees a purer blush arise,
And keener lightnings quicken in her eyes.
The busy sylphs surround their darling care,
These set the head,[1] and those divide the hair,
Some fold the sleeve, whilst others plait the
  gown;   147
And Betty's praised for labours not her own.

CANTO II

Not with more glories, in th' ethereal plain,
The sun first rises o'er the purpled main,] [2]
Than, issuing forth, the rival of his beams
Launched on the bosom of the silver Thames.
Fair nymphs, and well-dressed youths around
  her shone,   5
But every eye was fixed on her alone.
On her white breast a sparkling cross she wore,
Which Jews might kiss, and infidels adore.
Her lively looks a sprightly mind disclose,
Quick as her eyes, and as unfixed as those; 10
Favours to none, to all she smiles extends;
Oft she rejects, but never once offends.
Bright as the sun, her eyes the gazers strike,
And, like the sun, they shine on all alike.
Yet graceful ease, and sweetness void of
  pride,   15
Might hide her faults, if belles had faults to
  hide;
If to her share some female errors fall,
Look on her face, and you'll forget 'em all.
  This nymph, to the destruction of man-
  kind,
Nourished two locks, which graceful hung be-
  hind   20
In equal curls, and well conspired to deck
With shining ringlets the smooth ivory neck.
Love in these labyrinths his slaves detains,
And mighty hearts are held in slender chains.
With hairy springes we the birds betray,   25
Slight lines of hair surprise the finny prey,

Fair tresses man's imperial race ensnare,
And beauty draws us with a single hair.
  Th' adventurous baron [1] the bright locks ad-
  mired;
He saw, he wished, and to the prize aspired.
Resolved to win, he meditates the way,   31
By force to ravish, or by fraud betray;
For when success a lover's toil attends,
Few ask, if fraud or force attained his ends.
  For this, ere Phœbus rose, he had implored
Propitious Heaven, and every power adored,
But chiefly Love; to Love an altar built,
Of twelve vast French romances, neatly gilt.
There lay three garters, half a pair of gloves,
And all the trophies of his former loves;   40
With tender billets-doux he lights the pyre,
And breathes three amorous sighs to raise the
  fire.
Then prostrate falls, and begs with ardent
  eyes
Soon to obtain, and long possess the prize.
The powers gave ear, and granted half his
  prayer;   45
The rest the winds dispersed in empty air.
  [2][But now secure the painted vessel glides,
The sunbeams trembling on the floating
  tides;
While melting music steals upon the sky,
And softened sounds along the waters die; 50
Smooth flow the waves, the zephyrs gently
  play,
Belinda smiled, and all the world was gay.
All but the sylph — with careful thoughts
  oppressed,
Th' impending woe sat heavy on his breast.
He summons straight his denizens of air;   55
The lucid squadrons round the sails repair;
Soft o'er the shrouds aërial whispers breathe,
That seemed but zephyrs to the train beneath.
Some to the sun their insect wings unfold,
Waft on the breeze, or sink in clouds of gold;
Transparent forms, too fine for mortal sight,
Their fluid bodies half dissolved in light.
Loose to the wind their airy garments flew,
Thin glittering textures of the filmy dew,
Dipt in the richest tincture of the skies,   65
Where light disports in ever-mingling dyes,
While every beam new transient colours
  flings,
Colours that change whene'er they wave their
  wings.
Amid the circle, on the gilded mast,

---

[1] head-dress   [2] *Here ends the first addition to the
original version.*
AE

[1] Lord Petre   [2] *Here begins the second addition to the original version.*

Superior by the head, was Ariel placed;   70
His purple pinions opening to the sun,
He raised his azure wand, and thus begun:
  "Ye sylphs and sylphids, to your chief give
      ear!
Fays, fairies, genii, elves, and demons, hear!
Ye know the spheres, and various tasks as-
      signed   75
By laws eternal to th' aërial kind.
Some in the fields of purest æther play,
And bask and whiten in the blaze of day.
Some guide the course of wandering orbs on
      high,
Or roll the planets through the boundless
      sky.
Some less refined, beneath the moon's pale
      light   81
Pursue the stars that shoot athwart the
      night,
Or suck the mists in grosser air below,
Or dip their pinions in the painted bow,
Or brew fierce tempests on the wintry main,
Or o'er the glebe distil the kindly rain;   86
Others on earth o'er human race preside,
Watch all their ways, and all their actions
      guide:
Of these the chief the care of nations own,
And guard with arms divine the British
      throne.
  "Our humbler province is to tend the fair,
Not a less pleasing, though less glorious care;
To save the powder from too rude a gale,
Nor let th' imprisoned essences exhale;
To draw fresh colours from the vernal flowers;
To steal from rainbows, ere they drop in
      showers,   96
A brighter wash; to curl their waving hairs,
Assist their blushes, and inspire their airs;
Nay, oft in dreams, invention we bestow,
To change a flounce, or add a furbelow. 100
  "This day, black omens threat the brightest
      fair
That e'er deserved a watchful spirit's care;
Some dire disaster, or by force, or sleight;
But what, or where, the fates have wrapped in
      night.
Whether the nymph shall break Diana's law,
Or some frail china jar receive a flaw;   106
Or stain her honour, or her new brocade;
Forget her prayers, or miss a masquerade;
Or lose her heart, or necklace, at a ball;
Or whether Heaven has doomed that Shock
      must fall.   110
Haste, then, ye spirits! to your charge repair;
The fluttering fan be Zephyretta's care;

The drops [1] to thee, Brillante, we consign;
And, Momentilla, let the watch be thine;
Do thou, Crispissa, tend her favourite lock;
Ariel himself shall be the guard of Shock. 116
To fitly chosen sylphs, of special note,
We trust th' important charge, the petticoat:
Oft have we known that seven-fold fence to
      fail,
Though stiff with hoops, and armed with ribs
      of whale;   120
Form a strong line about the silver bound,
And guard the wide circumference around.
  "Whatever spirit, careless of his charge,
His post neglects, or leaves the fair at large,
Shall feel sharp vengeance soon o'ertake his
      sins,   125
Be stopped in vials, or transfixed with pins;
Or plunged in lakes of bitter washes lie,
Or wedged whole ages in a bodkin's eye;
Gums and pomatums shall his flight restrain,
While clogged he beats his silken wings in
      vain;   130
Or alum styptics with contracting power
Shrink his thin essence like a rivelled [2] flower;
Or, as Ixion fixed, the wretch shall feel
The giddy motion of the whirling mill,[3]
In fumes of burning chocolate shall glow, 135
And tremble at the sea that froths below!"
  He spoke; the spirits from the sails de-
      scend;
Some, orb in orb, around the nymph extend;
Some thrid the mazy ringlets of her hair;
Some hang upon the pendants of her ear; 140
With beating hearts the dire event they wait,
Anxious, and trembling for the birth of fate.][4]

Canto III

Close by those meads, forever crowned with
      flowers,
Where Thames with pride surveys his rising
      towers,
There stands a structure of majestic frame,
Which from the neighbouring Hampton [5] takes
      its name.
Here Britain's statesmen oft the fall foredoom
Of foreign tyrants and of nymphs at home; 6
Here thou, great Anna! whom three realms
      obey,
Dost sometimes counsel take — and some-
      times tea.

---

[1] ear-rings [2] withered [3] chocolate mill. [4] *Here
ends the second addition to the original version.*
[5] Hampton Court

Hither the heroes and the nymphs resort,
To taste awhile the pleasures of a court; 10
In various talk th' instructive hours they
  passed,
Who gave the ball, or paid the visit last;
One speaks the glory of the British Queen,
And one describes a charming Indian screen;
A third interprets motions, looks, and eyes;
At every word a reputation dies. 16
Snuff,[1] or the fan, supply each pause of chat,
With singing, laughing, ogling, and all that.

  Meanwhile, declining from the noon of day,
The sun obliquely shoots his burning ray; 20
The hungry judges soon the sentence sign,
And wretches hang that jurymen may dine;
The merchant from th' Exchange returns in
  peace,
And the long labours of the toilet cease.
[2][Belinda now, whom thirst of fame invites, 25
Burns to encounter two adventurous knights,
At ombre singly to decide their doom;
And swells her breast with conquests yet to
  come.
Straight the three bands prepare in arms to
  join,
Each band the number of the sacred nine.[3] 30
Soon as she spreads her hand, th' aërial guard
Descend, and sit on each important card:
First, Ariel perched upon a Matadore,
Then each, according to the rank they bore;
For sylphs, yet mindful of their ancient race,
Are, as when women, wondrous fond of place.

  Behold, four kings in majesty revered,
With hoary whiskers and a forky beard;
And four fair queens whose hands sustain a
  flower,
The expressive emblem of their softer power;
Four knaves in garbs succinct, a trusty band,
Caps on their heads, and halberts in their
  hand; 42
And parti-coloured troops, a shining train,
Draw forth to combat on the velvet plain.

  The skilful nymph reviews her force with
  care: 45
Let spades be trumps! she said, and trumps
  they were.
Now moved to war her sable Matadores,
In show like leaders of the swarthy Moors.
Spadillio[4] first, unconquerable lord!
Led off two captive trumps, and swept the
  board. 50

As many more Manillio[1] forced to yield
And marched a victor from the verdant field.
Him Basto[2] followed, but his fate more hard
Gained but one trump and one plebeian card.
With his broad sabre next, a chief in years,
The hoary majesty of spades appears, 56
Puts forth one manly leg, to sight revealed,
The rest, his many-coloured robe concealed.
The rebel knave, who dares his prince engage,
Proves the just victim of his royal rage. 60
E'en mighty Pam,[3] that kings and queens o'er-
  threw,
And mowed down armies in the fights of Loo,[4]
Sad chance of war! now destitute of aid,
Falls undistinguished by the victor spade!

  Thus far both armies to Belinda yield; 65
Now to the baron fate inclines the field.
His warlike Amazon her host invades,
The imperial consort of the crown of spades;
The club's black tyrant first her victim died,
Spite of his haughty mien, and barbarous
  pride. 70
What boots the regal circle on his head,
His giant limbs, in state unwieldy spread;
That long behind he trails his pompous robe,
And, of all monarchs, only grasps the globe?

  The baron now his diamonds pours apace;
Th' embroidered king who shows but half his
  face, 76
And his refulgent queen, with powers com-
  bined,
Of broken troops an easy conquest find.
Clubs, diamonds, hearts, in wild disorder seen,
With throngs promiscuous strew the level
  green.[5] 80
Thus when dispersed a routed army runs,
Of Asia's troops, and Afric's sable sons,
With like confusion different nations fly,
Of various habit, and of various dye,
The pierced battalions disunited fall, 85
In heaps on heaps; one fate o'erwhelms them
  all.

  The knave of diamonds tries his wily arts,
And wins (oh shameful chance!) the queen of
  hearts.
At this the blood the virgin's cheek forsook,
A livid paleness spreads o'er all her look; 90
She sees, and trembles at th' approaching ill,
Just in the jaws of ruin, and codille.[6]

---

[1] Snuff was then fashionable. [2] Here begins the third addition. [3] the Muses [4] ace of spades, the highest trump

[1] deuce of spades, the next highest [2] ace of clubs, third trump. These three are called "matadores." [3] knave of clubs [4] another game, in which Pam is the highest card [5] the card table [6] a term signifying the defeat of the single player

And now (as oft in some distempered state)
On one nice trick depends the general fate.
An ace of hearts steps forth; the king unseen
Lurked in her hand, and mourned his captive
    queen :   96
He springs to vengeance with an eager pace,
And falls like thunder on the prostrate ace.
The nymph exulting fills with shouts the sky ;
The walls, the woods, and long canals reply.
Oh thoughtless mortals ! ever blind to fate,
Too soon dejected, and too soon elate.   102
Sudden, these honours shall be snatched away,
And cursed forever this victorious day.] [1]
  For lo ! the board with cups and spoons is
    crowned,   105
The berries [2] crackle, and the mill turns round ;
On shining altars of Japan [3] they raise
The silver lamp ; the fiery spirits blaze :
From silver spouts the grateful liquors glide,
While China's earth [4] receives the smoking tide :.
At once they gratify their scent and taste, 111
And frequent cups prolong the rich repast.
Straight hover round the fair her airy band ;
Some, as she sipped, the fuming liquor fanned,
Some o'er her lap their careful plumes dis-
    played,   115
Trembling, and conscious of the rich brocade.
Coffee (which makes the politician wise,
And see through all things with his half-shut
    eyes)
Sent up in vapours to the baron's brain
New stratagems the radiant lock to gain. 120
Ah, cease, rash youth ! desist ere 'tis too late,
Fear the just gods, and think of Scylla's fate !
Changed to a bird, and sent to flit in air,
She dearly pays for Nisus' injured hair ! [5]
  But when to mischief mortals bend their
    will,   125
How soon they find fit instruments of ill !
Just then Clarissa drew with tempting grace
A two-edged weapon from her shining case :
So ladies in romance assist their knight, 129
Present the spear, and arm him for the fight.
He takes the gift with reverence, and extends
The little engine on his fingers' ends ;
This just behind Belinda's neck he spread,
As o'er the fragrant steams she bends her
    head.
[6] [Swift to the lock a thousand sprites repair,
A thousand wings, by turns, blow back the
    hair ;   135

And thrice they twitched the diamond in her
    ear ;
Thrice she looked back, and thrice the foe
    drew near.
Just in that instant, anxious Ariel sought
The close recesses of the virgin's thought ; 140
As on the nosegay in her breast reclined,
He watched th' ideas rising in her mind,
Sudden he viewed, in spite of all her art,
An earthly lover lurking at her heart.
Amazed, confused, he found his power ex-
    pired,   145
Resigned to fate, and with a sigh retired.] [1]
  The peer now spreads the glittering forfex [2]
    wide,
T' inclose the lock ; now joins it, to divide.
[3] [E'en then, before the fatal engine closed, .
A wretched sylph too fondly interposed ; 150
Fate urged the shears, and cut the sylph in
    twain,
(But airy substance soon unites again).] [4]
The meeting points the sacred hair dissever
From the fair head, forever, and forever !
  Then flashed the living lightning from her
    eyes,   155
And screams of horror rend th' affrighted
    skies.
Not louder shrieks to pitying Heaven are cast,
When husbands, or when lap-dogs breathe
    their last ;
Or when rich China vessels, fallen from high,
In glittering dust and painted fragments lie !
"Let wreaths of triumph now my temples
    twine,"   161
The victor cried ; "the glorious prize is mine !
While fish in streams, or birds delight in air,
Or in a coach and six the British fair,
As long as Atalantis [5] shall be read, 165
Or the small pillow grace a lady's bed,
While visits shall be paid on solemn days,
When numerous wax-lights in bright order
    blaze,
While nymphs take treats, or assignations
    give,
So long my honour, name, and praise shall
    live !   170
What Time would spare, from steel receives its
    date,
And monuments, like men, submit to fate !
Steel could the labour of the gods destroy,
And strike to dust th' imperial towers of Troy ;

---

[1] *Here ends the third addition.* [2] coffee-berries
[3] japanned tables [4] porcelain [5] Cf. Gayley, p.
219. [6] *Here begins the fourth addition.*

[1] *Here ends the fourth addition.* [2] scissors [3] *Here
begins the fifth addition.* [4] *Here ends the fifth addition.* [5] a scandalous book of the time

Steel could the works of mortal pride con-
found,   175
And hew triumphal arches to the ground.
What wonder then, fair nymph! thy hairs
    should feel,
The conquering force of unresisted steel?"

Canto IV

But anxious cares the pensive nymph op-
    pressed,
And secret passions laboured in her breast.
Not youthful kings in battle seized alive,
Not scornful virgins who their charms survive,
Not ardent lovers robbed of all their bliss,   5
Not ancient ladies when refused a kiss,
Not tyrants fierce that unrepenting die,
Not Cynthia when her manteau's pinned
    awry,
E'er felt such rage, resentment, and despair,
As thou, sad virgin, for thy ravished hair. 10
[1] [For, that sad moment, when the sylphs with-
    drew
And Ariel weeping from Belinda flew,
Umbriel, a dusky, melancholy sprite,
As ever sullied the fair face of light,   14
Down to the central earth, his proper scene,
Repaired to search the gloomy cave of Spleen.[2]
Swift on his sooty pinions flits the gnome,
And in a vapour reached the dismal dome.
No cheerful breeze this sullen region knows,
The dreaded east is all the wind that blows.
Here in a grotto, sheltered close from air, 21
And screened in shades from day's detested
    glare,
She sighs forever on her pensive bed,
Pain at her side, and Megrim[3] at her head.
  Two handmaids wait the throne, alike in
    place,
But differing far in figure and in face.   26
Here stood Ill-nature like an ancient maid,
Her wrinkled form in black and white ar-
    rayed;
With store of prayers, for mornings, nights,
    and noons
Her hand is filled; her bosom with lampoons.
There Affectation, with a sickly mien,   31
Shows in her cheek the roses of eighteen,
Practised to lisp, and hang the head aside,
Faints into airs, and languishes with pride,
On the rich quilt sinks with becoming woe, 35
Wrapped in a gown, for sickness, and for show.

The fair ones feel such maladies as these,
When each new night-dress gives a new dis-
    ease.
  A constant vapour o'er the palace flies; 39
Strange phantoms rising as the mists arise;
Dreadful, as hermit's dreams in haunted
    shades,
Or bright, as visions of expiring maids.
Now glaring fiends, and snakes on rolling
    spires,
Pale spectres, gaping tombs, and purple fires;
Now lakes of liquid gold, Elysian scenes, 45
And crystal domes, and angels in machines.[1]
  Unnumbered throngs on every side are
    seen,
Of bodies changed to various forms by Spleen.
Here living tea-pots stand, one arm held out,
One bent; the handle this, and that the spout.
A pipkin there, like Homer's tripod,[2] walks; 51
Here sighs a jar, and there a goose-pie talks;
Men prove with child, as powerful fancy
    works,
And maids, turned bottles, call aloud for corks.
  Safe passed the gnome through this fantastic
    band,   55
A branch of healing spleenwort in his hand.
Then thus addressed the power: "Hail, way-
    ward queen!
Who rule the sex, to fifty from fifteen:
Parent of vapours[3] and of female wit;
Who give th' hysteric, or poetic fit;   60
On various tempers act by various ways,
Make some take physic, others scribble plays;
Who cause the proud their visits to delay,
And send the godly in a pet to pray.   64
A nymph there is, that all thy power disdains,
And thousands more in equal mirth main-
    tains,
But oh! if e'er thy gnome could spoil a grace,
Or raise a pimple on a beauteous face,
Like citron-waters[4] matrons' cheeks inflame,
Or change complexions at a losing game;   70
If e'er with airy horns I planted heads,
Or rumpled petticoats, or tumbled beds,
Or caused suspicion when no soul was rude,
Or discomposed the head-dress of a prude,
Or e'er to costive lap-dog gave disease,   75
Which not the tears of brightest eyes could
    ease:

---

[1] *Here begins the sixth addition.*   [2] hysteria
[3] headache

[1] stage devices for lowering gods or angels
from the sky   [2] In the *Iliad*, xviii, 373 ff.,
Hephaistos is represented as making tripods that
could walk.   [3] hypochondria   [4] a liquor distilled
from citron rinds.

Hear me, and touch Belinda with chagrin,
That single act gives half the world the
    spleen."
    The goddess with a discontented air
Seems to reject him, though she grants his
    prayer.   80
A wondrous bag with both her hands she
    binds,
Like that where once Ulysses held the winds;[1]
There she collects the force of female lungs,
Sighs, sobs, and passions, and the war of
    tongues.
A vial next she fills with fainting fears,   85
Soft sorrows, melting griefs, and flowing tears.
The gnome rejoicing bears her gifts away,
Spreads his black wings, and slowly mounts to
    day.
    Sunk in Thalestris' arms the nymph he
    found,
Her eyes dejected and her hair unbound.   90
Full o'er their heads the swelling bag he rent,
And all the furies issued at the vent.][2]
Belinda burns with more than mortal ire,
And fierce Thalestris fans the rising fire.
"O wretched maid!" she spread her hands,
    and cried,   95
(While Hampton's echoes, "Wretched maid!"
    replied)
"Was it for this you took such constant care
The bodkin,[3] comb, and essence to prepare?
For this your locks in paper durance bound,
For this with torturing irons wreathed
    around?   100
For this with fillets strained your tender head,
And bravely bore the double loads of lead?[4]
Gods! shall the ravisher display your hair,
While the fops envy, and the ladies stare!
Honour forbid! at whose unrivalled shrine
Ease, pleasure, virtue, all our sex resign. 106
Methinks already I your tears survey,
Already hear the horrid things they say,
Already see you a degraded toast,
And all your honour in a whisper lost!   110
How shall I, then, your helpless fame defend?
'Twill then be infamy to seem your friend!
And shall this prize, th' inestimable prize,
Exposed through crystal to the gazing eyes,
And heightened by the diamond's circling
    rays,
On that rapacious hand forever blaze?   116
Sooner shall grass in Hyde Park Circus[5] grow,

And wits take lodgings in the sound of Bow:[1]
Sooner let earth, air, sea, to chaos fall,
Men, monkeys, lap-dogs, parrots, perish
    all!"   120
    She said; then raging to Sir Plume repairs,
And bids her beau demand the precious hairs
(Sir Plume, of amber snuff-box justly vain,
And the nice conduct of a clouded[2] cane).
With earnest eyes, and round unthinking face,
He first the snuff-box opened, then the case,
And thus broke out — "My lord, why, what
    the devil?   127
Zounds! damn the lock! 'fore Gad, you must
    be civil!
Plague on't! 'tis, past a jest — nay, prithee
    pox!
Give her the hair," he spoke, and rapped his
    box.   130
"It grieves me much," replied the peer again,
"Who speaks so well should ever speak in
    vain.
But by this lock, this sacred lock, I swear.
(Which never more shall join its parted hair;
Which never more its honours shall renew, 135
Clipped from the lovely head where late it
    grew)
That while my nostrils draw the vital air,
This hand, which won it, shall forever wear."
He spoke, and speaking, in proud triumph
    spread
The long-contended honours of her head. 140
    [3][But Umbriel, hateful gnome! forbears not
    so;
He breaks the vial whence the sorrows flow.][3]
Then see! the nymph in beauteous grief ap-
    pears,
Her eyes half languishing, half drowned in
    tears;
On her heaved bosom hung her drooping head,
Which, with a sigh, she raised; and thus she
    said: 146
"Forever curs'd be this detested day,
Which snatched my best, my favourite curl
    away!
Happy! ah, ten times happy had I been,
If Hampton Court these eyes had never seen!
Yet am not I the first mistaken maid,   151
By love of courts to numerous ills betrayed.
Oh, had I rather unadmired remained
In some lone isle or distant northern land;
Where the gilt chariot never marks the way,

---

[1] Cf. the *Odyssey*, x, 20.   [2] *Here ends the sixth
addition.*   [3] Cf. v, 95.   [4] for curling the hair
[5] the Ring, cf. i, 44

[1] the bells of St. Mary-le-bow, in the older and
unfashionable part of London   [2] mottled, cf. *Tatler*,
No. 103.   [3-3] *The seventh addition.*

Where none learn ombre, none e'er taste
   bohea !¹   156
There kept my charms concealed from mortal
   eye,
Like roses, that in deserts bloom and die.
What moved my mind with youthful lords to
   roam ?   159
Oh, had I stayed, and said my prayers at
   home !
'Twas this, the morning omens seemed to tell :
Thrice from my trembling hand the patch-
   box² fell ;
The tottering china shook without a wind ;
Nay, Poll³ sat mute, and Shock⁴ was most un-
   kind !
A sylph, too, warned me of the threats of fate,
In mystic visions, now believed too late !   166
See the poor remnants of these slighted hairs !
My hands shall rend what e'en thy rapine
   spares ;
These in two sable ringlets taught to break,
Once gave new beauties to the snowy neck ;
The sister lock now sits uncouth, alone,   171
And in its fellow's fate foresees its own ;
Uncurled it hangs, the fatal shears demands,
And tempts once more, thy sacrilegious
   hands.

CANTO V

She said : the pitying audience melt in tears.
But Fate and Jove had stopped the baron's
   ears.
In vain Thalestris with reproach assails,
For who can move when fair Belinda fails ?
Not half so fixed the Trojan⁵ could remain,   5
While Anna begged and Dido raged in vain.
⁶[Then grave Clarissa graceful waved her fan ;
Silence ensued, and thus the nymph began :
  "Say, why are beauties praised and hon-
   oured most,
The wise man's passion, and the vain man's
   toast ?   10
Why decked with all that land and sea afford,
Why angels called, and angel-like adored ?
Why round our coaches crowd the white-
   gloved beaux,
Why bows the side-box from its inmost rows ?
How vain are all these glories, all our pains, 15
Unless good sense preserve what beauty gains ;

¹ a kind of tea ² for patches see the *Spectator*,
No. 81.   ³ the parrot   ⁴ the lap-dog   ⁵ Æneas, *cf.*
Æneid, iv, 296–440 ⁶ *Bracketed lines were not in
the original version.*

That men may say, when we the front-box
   grace,
'Behold the first in virtue as in face !'
Oh ! if to dance all night, and dress all day,
Charmed the small-pox, or chased old age
   away,
Who would not scorn what housewife's cares
   produce,   21
Or who would learn one earthly thing of use ?
To patch, nay ogle, might become a saint,
Nor could it sure be such a sin to paint.
But since, alas ! frail beauty must decay ;   25
Curled or uncurled, since locks will turn to
   grey ;
Since painted, or not painted, all shall fade,
And she who scorns a man must die a maid ;
What then remains but well our power to use,
And keep good humour still, whate'er we lose ?
And trust me, dear ! good humour can prevail,
When airs, and flights, and screams, and scold-
   ing fail.   32
Beauties in vain their pretty eyes may roll ;
Charms strike the sight, but merit wins the
   soul."
  So spoke the dame, but no applause ensued ;
Belinda frowned, Thalestris called her prude.]
"To arms, to arms !" the fierce virago¹ cries,
And swift as lightning to the combat flies. 38
All side in parties, and begin th' attack ;
Fans clap, silks rustle, and tough whalebones
   crack ;   40
Heroes' and heroines' shouts confus'dly rise,
And bass and treble voices strike the skies.
No common weapons in their hands are found,
Like gods they fight, nor dread a mortal
   wound.
  So when bold Homer makes the gods en-
   gage,   45
And heavenly breasts with human passions
   rage ;
'Gainst Pallas, Mars ; Latona, Hermes arms ;
And all Olympus rings with loud alarms :
Jove's thunder roars, Heaven trembles all
   around,
Blue Neptune storms, the bellowing deeps re-
   sound :   50
Earth shakes her nodding towers, the ground
   gives way,
And the pale ghosts start at the flash of day !
  ²[Triumphant Umbriel on a sconce's³ height
Clapped his glad wings, and sat to view the
   fight ;

¹ Thalestris ² *Bracketed lines were not in the
original version.*   ³ candlestick

Propped on their bodkin spears, the sprites
survey   55
The growing combat, or assist the fray.]
   While through the press enraged Thalestris
flies,
And scatters death around from both her eyes,
A beau and witling perished in the throng,
One died in metaphor, and one in song.   60
"O cruel nymph! a living death I bear,"[1]
Cried Dapperwit, and sunk beside his chair.
A mournful glance Sir Fopling upwards cast,
"Those eyes are made so killing"[2] — was his
last.
Thus on Mæander's[3] flowery margin lies   65
Th' expiring swan, and as he sings he dies.
   When bold Sir Plume had drawn Clarissa
down,
Chloe stepped in and killed him with a frown;
She smiled to see the doughty hero slain,
But, at her smile, the beau revived again.   70
   Now Jove suspends his golden scales in air,
Weighs the men's wits against the lady's
hair;
The doubtful beam long nods from side to
side;
At length the wits mount up, the hairs sub-
side.
   See, fierce Belinda on the Baron flies,   75
With more than usual lightning in her eyes;
Nor feared the chief th' unequal fight to try,
Who sought no more than on his foe to die.
But this bold lord with manly strength
endued,
She with one finger and a thumb subdued: 80
Just where the breath of life his nostrils drew,
A charge of snuff the wily virgin threw;
[4][The gnomes direct, to every atom just,
The pungent grains of titillating dust.]
Sudden, with starting tears each eye o'er-
flows,   85
And the high dome re-echoes to his nose.
   "Now meet thy fate," incensed Belinda
cried,
And drew a deadly bodkin from her side.
[4][(The same, his ancient personage to deck, 89
Her great great grandsire wore about his neck,
In three seal-rings; which after, melted down,
Formed a vast buckle for his widow's gown;
Her infant grandame's whistle next it grew,
The bells she jingled, and the whistle blew;

Then in a bodkin graced her mother's hairs,
Which long she wore, and now Belinda wears.)]
   "Boast not my fall," he cried, "insulting
foe!   97
Thou by some other shalt be laid as low;
Nor think to die dejects my lofty mind:
All that I dread is leaving you behind!   100
Rather than so, ah, let me still survive,
And burn in Cupid's flames — but burn
alive."
   "Restore the lock!" she cries; and all
around
"Restore the lock!" the vaulted roofs rebound.
Not fierce Othello in so loud a strain   105
Roared for the handkerchief that caused his
pain.
But see how oft ambitious aims are crossed,
And chiefs contend till all the prize is lost!
The lock, obtained with guilt, and kept with
pain,
In every place is sought, but sought in vain:
With such a prize no mortal must be blessed,
So Heaven decrees! with Heaven who can
contest?   112
   Some thought it mounted to the lunar
sphere,
Since all things lost on earth are treasured there.
There heroes' wits are kept in ponderous vases,
And beaux' in snuff-boxes and tweezer cases;
There broken vows and death-bed alms are
found,   117
And lovers' hearts with ends of riband bound,
The courtier's promises, and sick man's
prayers,
The smiles of harlots, and the tears of heirs,
Cages for gnats, and chains to yoke a flea,121
Dried butterflies, and tomes of casuistry.
   But trust the Muse — she saw it upward
rise,
Though marked by none but quick, poetic
eyes:
(So Rome's great founder to the heavens with-
drew,   125
To Proculus[1] alone confessed in view)
A sudden star, it shot through liquid air,
And drew behind a radiant trail of hair.
Not Berenice's locks[2] first rose so bright,
The heavens bespangling with dishevelled
light.

---

[1] This is the "metaphor."   [2] From a song in the
opera Camilla.   [3] a winding river in Asia Minor,
frequented by swans, cf. Ovid, Epist. vii, 1, 2
[4] Bracketed lines were not in the original version.

[1] Cf. Livy, I, 6   [2] The wife of Ptolemy Euergetes
dedicated her hair for the safe return of her husband; upon its disappearance the astronomer Conon
reported that it had been changed to the constellation
Coma Berenices.

[1][The sylphs behold it kindling as it flies, 131
And pleased pursue its progress through the skies.]
This the beau monde shall from the Mall [2]
survey,
And hail with music its propitious ray.
[1][This the blest lover shall for Venus take, 135
And send up vows from Rosamonda's lake.[2]]
This Partridge [3] soon shall view in cloudless skies,
When next he looks through Galileo's eyes; [4]
And hence th' egregious wizard shall foredoom
The fate of Louis and the fall of Rome. 140
  Then cease, bright nymph! to mourn thy ravished hair,
Which adds new glory to the shining sphere!
Not all the tresses that fair head can boast,
Shall draw such envy as the lock you lost.
For, after all the murders of your eye, 145
When, after millions slain, yourself shall die;
When those fair suns shall set, as set they must,
And all those tresses shall be laid in dust: 148
This lock, the Muse shall consecrate to fame,
And 'midst the stars inscribe Belinda's name.

From ELOÏSA TO ABELARD

In these deep solitudes and awful cells,
Where heavenly-pensive contemplation dwells,
And ever-musing melancholy reigns,
What means this tumult in a vestal's veins?
Why rove my thoughts beyond this last retreat? 5
Why feels my heart its long-forgotten heat?
Yet, yet I love! — from Abelard it came,
And Eloïsa yet must kiss the name.
  Dear fatal name! rest ever unrevealed,
Nor pass these lips in holy silence sealed! 10
Hide it, my heart, within that close disguise,
Where mixed with God's, his loved idea lies!
Oh, write it not, my hand — the name appears
Already written — wash it out, my tears!
In vain lost Eloïsa weeps and prays; 15
Her heart still dictates, and her hand obeys.
  Relentless walls! whose darksome round contains
Repentant sighs, and voluntary pains:

[1] *Bracketed lines were not in the original version.* [2] in St. James' Park. [3] an almanac maker ridiculed by Swift [4] a telescope, cf. *Par. Lost*, I, 288

Ye rugged rocks! which holy knees have worn;
Ye grots and caverns shagg'd with horrid thorn! 20
Shrines! where their vigils pale-eyed virgins keep,
And pitying saints, whose statues learn to weep!
Though cold like you, unmoved and silent grown,
I have not yet forgot myself to stone.
All is not Heaven's while Abelard has part,25
Still rebel nature holds out half my heart;
Nor prayers nor fasts its stubborn pulse restrain,
Nor tears, for ages taught to flow in vain.
  Soon as thy letters trembling I unclose,
That well-known name awakens all my woes.
Oh, name forever sad! forever dear! 31
Still breathed in sighs, still ushered with a tear.
I tremble too, where'er my own I find;
Some dire misfortune follows close behind.
Line after line my gushing eyes o'erflow, 35
Led through a sad variety of woe:
Now warm in love, now withering in my bloom,
Lost in a convent's solitary gloom!
There stern religion quenched th' unwilling flame, 39
There died the best of passions, love and fame.
  Yet write, oh! write me all, that I may join
Griefs to thy griefs, and echo sighs to thine.
Nor foes nor fortune take this power away;
And is my Abelard less kind than they?
Tears still are mine, and those I need not spare, 45
Love but demands what else were shed in prayer;
No happier task these faded eyes pursue;
To read and weep is all they now can do.
  Then share thy pain, allow that sad relief;
Ah, more than share it, give me all thy grief.
Heaven first taught letters for some wretch's aid, 51
Some banished lover, or some captive maid;
They live, they speak, they breathe what love inspires,
Warm from the soul, and faithful to its fires,
The virgin's wish without her fears impart, 55
Excuse the blush, and pour out all the heart,
Speed the soft intercourse from soul to soul,
And waft a sigh from Indus to the Pole.
  Thou know'st how guiltless first I met thy flame,

When love approached me under friendship's
   name;   60
My fancy formed thee of angelic kind,
Some emanation of th' all-beauteous Mind.
Those smiling eyes, attempering every ray,
Shone sweetly lambent with celestial day.
Guiltless I gazed; Heaven listened while you
   sung;   65
And truths divine came mended[1] from that
   tongue.
From lips like those what precept failed to
   move?
Too soon they taught me 'twas no sin to love;
Back through the paths of pleasing sense I
   ran,
Nor wished an angel whom I loved a man. 70
Dim and remote the joys of saints I see;
Nor envy them that Heaven I lose for thee.

   *   *   *   *   *   *   *

How happy is the blameless vestal's lot!
The world forgetting, by the world forgot:
Eternal sunshine of the spotless mind!
Each prayer accepted, and each wish resigned;
Labour and rest, that equal periods keep; 211
"Obedient slumbers that can wake and
   weep;"[2]
Desires composed, affections ever even;
Tears that delight, and sighs that waft to
   Heaven.
Grace shines around her with serenest beams,
And whispering angels prompt her golden
   dreams.
For her th' unfading rose of Eden blooms, 217
And wings of seraphs shed divine perfumes;
For her the Spouse prepares the bridal ring;
For her white virgins hymenæals sing; 220
To sounds of heavenly harps she dies away,
And melts in visions of eternal day.
  Far other dreams my erring soul employ,
Far other raptures, of unholy joy.   224
When at the close of each sad, sorrowing day,
Fancy restores what vengeance snatched
   away,
Then conscience sleeps, and leaving nature
   free
All my loose soul unbounded springs to thee.
O curs'd, dear horrors of all-conscious night!
How glowing guilt exalts the keen delight! 230
Provoking demons all restraint remove,
And stir within me every source of love.
I hear thee, view thee, gaze o'er all thy
   charms,

   [1] improved   [2] *Quoted from Crashaw.*

And round thy phantom glue my clasping
   arms.
I wake: — no more I hear, no more I view;
The phantom flies mé, as unkind as you. 236
I call aloud; it hears not what I say:
I stretch my empty arms; it glides away.
To dream once more I close my willing eyes;
Ye soft illusions, dear deceits, arise!   240
Alas, no more! methinks we wandering go
Through dreary wastes, and weep each other's
   woe,
Where round some mouldering tower pale ivy
   creeps,
And low-browed rocks hang nodding o'er the
   deeps.   244
Sudden you mount, you beckon from the
   skies;
Clouds interpose, waves roar, and winds arise.
I shriek, start up, the same sad prospect find,
And wake to all the griefs I left behind.

From AN ESSAY ON MAN

BOOK I

Awake, my St. John! leave all meaner things
To low ambition, and the pride of kings.
Let us (since life can little more supply
Than just to look about us and to die)
Expatiate free o'er all this scene of man; 5
A mighty maze! but not without a plan;
A wild, where weeds and flowers promiscuous
   shoot;
Or garden, tempting with forbidden fruit.
Together let us beat this ample field,
Try what the open, what the covert yield; 10
The latent tracts, the giddy heights, explore
Of all who blindly creep, or sightless soar;
Eye nature's walks, shoot folly as it flies,
And catch the manners living as they rise;
Laugh where we must, be candid where we
   can;   15
But vindicate the ways of God to man.
  I. Say first, of God above, or man below,
What can we reason, but from what we know?
Of man, what see we but his station here
From which to reason or to which refer? 20
Through worlds unnumbered though the
   God be known,
'Tis ours to trace him only in our own.
He, who through vast immensity can pierce,
See worlds on worlds compose one universe,
Observe how system into system runs, 25
What other planets circle other suns,
What varied being peoples every star,

May tell why Heaven has made us as we are.
But of this frame the bearings, and the ties,
The strong connections, nice dependencies, 30
Gradations just, has thy pervading soul
Looked through? or can a part contain the
    whole?
  Is the great chain, that draws all to agree,
And drawn supports, upheld by God, or thee?
  II. Presumptuous man! the reason wouldst
    thou find,   35
Why formed so weak, so little, and so blind?
First, if thou canst, the harder reason guess,
Why formed no weaker, blinder, and no less?
Ask of thy mother earth, why oaks are made
Taller or stronger than the weeds they shade?
Or ask of yonder argent fields above,   41
Why Jove's satellites[1] are less than Jove.
  Of systems possible, if 'tis confessed
That wisdom infinite must form the best,
Where all must full or not coherent be,   45
And all that rises, rise in due degree;
Then, in the scale of reasoning life, 'tis plain,
There must be, somewhere, such a rank as
    man:
And all the question (wrangle e'er so long)
Is only this, if God has placed him wrong? 50
  Respecting man, whatever wrong we call,
May, must be right, as relative to all.
In human works, though laboured on with
    pain,
A thousand movements scarce one purpose
    gain;
In God's, one single can its end produce; 55
Yet serves to second too some other use.
So man, who here seems principal alone,
Perhaps acts second to some sphere unknown,
Touches some wheel, or verges to some goal;
'Tis but a part we see, and not a whole.   60

*   *   *   *   *   *   *

  Then say not man's imperfect, Heaven in
    fault;
Say rather, man's as perfect as he ought: 70
His knowledge measured to his state and
    place,
His time a moment, and a point his space.
If to be perfect in a certain sphere,
What matter, soon or late, or here or there?
The blest to-day is as completely so,   75
As who began a thousand years ago.
  III. Heaven from all creatures hides the
    book of fate,
All but the page prescribed, their present state:

From brutes what men, from men what spirits
    know:
Or who could suffer being here below?   80
The lamb thy riot dooms to bleed to-day,
Had he thy reason, would he skip and play?
Pleased to the last, he crops the flowery food,
And licks the hand just raised to shed his
    blood.
Oh, blindness to the future! kindly given, 85
That each may fill the circle marked by
    Heaven:
Who sees with equal eye, as God of all,
A hero perish, or a sparrow fall,
Atoms or systems into ruin hurled,
And now a bubble burst, and now a world. 90
  Hope humbly then; with trembling pinions
    soar;
Wait the great teacher Death; and God
    adore.
What future bliss, he gives not thee to know,
But gives that hope to be thy blessing now.
Hope springs eternal in the human breast: 95
Man never is, but always to be blest.
The soul, uneasy and confined from home,
Rests and expatiates in a life to come.
  Lo, the poor Indian! whose untutored mind
Sees God in clouds, or hears him in the wind;
His soul, proud science never taught to stray
Far as the solar walk, or milky way;   102
Yet simple nature to his hope has given,
Behind the cloud-topped hill, an humbler
    Heaven;
Some safer world in depths of woods em-
    braced,   105
Some happier island in the watery waste,
Where slaves once more their native land be-
    hold,
No fiends torment, no Christians thirst for gold.
To be, contents his natural desire,
He asks no angel's wing, no seraph's fire; 110
But thinks, admitted to that equal sky,
His faithful dog shall bear him company.

*   *   *   *   *   *   *

  VII. Far as creation's ample range extends,
The scale of sensual,[1] mental power ascends.
Mark how it mounts, to man's imperial race,
From the green myriads in the peopled grass:
What modes of sight betwixt each wide ex-
    treme,   211
The mole's dim curtain, and the lynx's beam:
Of smell, the headlong lioness between
And hound sagacious on the tainted green:

Of hearing, from the life that fills the flood,
To that which warbles through the vernal
    wood: 216
The spider's touch, how exquisitely fine !
Feels at each thread, and lives along the line :
In the nice[1] bee, what sense so subtly true
From poisonous herbs extracts the healing
    dew?   220
How instinct varies in the grovelling swine,
Compared, half-reasoning elephant, with
    thine !
'Twixt that and reason, what a nice barrier,
Forever separate, yet forever near !
Remembrance and reflection how allied ;   225
What thin partitions sense from thought
    divide :
And middle natures, how they long to join,
Yet never pass th' insuperable line !
Without this just gradation, could they be
Subjected, these to those, or all to thee?   230
The powers of all subdued by thee alone,
Is not thy reason all these powers in one?

*   *   *   *   *   *   *

All are but parts of one stupendous whole,
Whose body nature is, and God the soul ;
That, changed through all, and yet in all the
    same ;
Great in the earth, as in th' ethereal frame ;[2]
Warms in the sun, refreshes in the breeze, 271
Glows in the stars, and blossoms in the trees,
Lives through all life, extends through all ex-
    tent,
Spreads undivided, operates unspent ;
Breathes in our soul, informs our mortal part,
As full, as perfect, in a hair as heart ;   276
As full, as perfect, in vile man that mourns,
As the rapt seraph[3] that adores and burns :
To him no high, no low, no great, no small ;
He fills, he bounds, connects, and equals all.
    X. Cease then, nor order imperfection
    name :   281
Our proper bliss depends on what we blame.
Know thy own point : this kind, this due
    degree
Of blindness, weakness, Heaven bestows on
    thee.
Submit. — In this, or any other sphere,   285
Secure to be as blest as thou canst bear :
Safe in the hand of one disposing Power,
Or in the natal, or the mortal hour.
All nature is but art, unknown to thee ;

[1] discriminating   [2] the heavens   [3] angels of
flame

All chance, direction, which thou canst not
    see ;
All discord, harmony not understood ;   291
All partial evil, universal good :
And, spite of pride, in erring reason's spite,
One truth is clear, Whatever is, is right.

EPISTLE TO DR. ARBUTHNOT

P. Shut, shut the door, good John ![1] fatigued,
    I said?
Tie up the knocker, say I'm sick, I'm dead.
The Dog-star rages ! nay, 'tis past a doubt,
All Bedlam,[2] or Parnassus,[3] is let out :
Fire in each eye, and papers in each hand,   5
They rave, recite, and madden round the land.
    What walls can guard me, or what shades
    can hide?
They pierce my thickets, through my grot
    they glide ;
By land, by water, they renew the charge,
They stop the chariot, and they board the
    barge.   10
No place is sacred, not the church is free ;
E'en Sunday shines no Sabbath day to me :
Then from the Mint[4] walks forth the man of
    rhyme,
Happy to catch me just at dinner-time.
    Is there a parson, much bemused in beer,15
A maudlin poetess, a rhyming peer,
A clerk, foredoomed his father's soul to cross,
Who pens a stanza, when he should engross?
Is there, who, locked from ink and paper,
    scrawls
With desperate charcoal round his darkened
    walls?
All fly to Twit'nam[5] and in humble strain   21
Apply to me, to keep them mad or vain.
Arthur, whose giddy son neglects the laws,
Imputes to me and my damn'd works the
    cause :
Poor Cornus sees his frantic wife elope,   25
And curses wit, and poetry, and Pope.
    Friend to my life ![6] (which did not you pro-
    long,
The world had wanted many an idle song)

[1] Pope's servant   [2] a hospital for lunatics
[3] figuratively the abode of poets   [4] a place in
which insolvent debtors lived, free from arrest;
on Sundays they could go anywhere without fear
of arrest   [5] Pope's villa at Twickenham, famous
for its romantic garden and grotto   [6] Dr. Arbuthnot

What drop or nostrum can this plague re-
move?
Or which must end me, a fool's wrath or love?
A dire dilemma! either way I'm sped: 31
If foes, they write, if friends, they read me
dead.
Seized and tied down to judge, how wretched
I!
Who can't be silent, and who will not lie.

* * * * * * *

Why did I write? what sin to me unknown
Dipped me in ink, my parents', or my own?
As yet a child, nor yet a fool to fame, 127
I lisped in numbers,[1] for the numbers came.
I left no calling for this idle trade,
No duty broke, no father disobeyed. 130
The Muse[2] but served to ease some friend,
not wife,
To help me through this long disease, my life,
To second, Arbuthnot! thy art and care,
And teach the being you preserved, to bear.
But why then publish? Granville the polite,
And knowing Walsh, would tell me I could
write; 136
Well-natured Garth inflamed with early
praise,
And Congreve loved, and Swift endured my
lays;
The courtly Talbot, Somers, Sheffield, read;
E'en mitred Rochester would nod the head,
And St. John's self (great Dryden's friends
before) 141
With open arms received one poet more.
Happy my studies, when by these approved!
Happier their author, when by these beloved!
From these the world will judge of men and
books, 145
Not from the Burnets, Oldmixons, and
Cookes.
Soft were my numbers; who could take
offence
While pure description held the place of sense?
Like gentle Fanny's was my flowery theme,
A painted mistress, or a purling stream. 150
Yet then did Gildon draw his venal quill; —
I wished the man a dinner, and sat still.
Yet then did Dennis rave in furious fret;
I never answered — I was not in debt.
If want provoked, or madness made them
print, 155
I waged no war with Bedlam or the Mint.
Did some more sober critic come aboard;

---

¹ verses   ² poetry

If wrong, I smiled; if right, I kissed the rod.
Pains, reading, study, are their just pretence,
And all they want is spirit, taste, and sense.
Commas and points they set exactly right, 161
And 'twere a sin to rob them of their mite;
Yet ne'er one sprig of laurel graced these
ribalds,
From slashing Bentley down to piddling
Tibbalds.
Each wight, who reads not, and but scans and
spells, 165
Each word-catcher, that lives on syllables,
E'en such small critics some regard may claim,
Preserved in Milton's or in Shakespeare's
name.
Pretty! in amber to observe the forms 169
Of hairs, or straws, or dirt, or grubs, or worms!
The things, we know, are neither rich nor rare,
But wonder how the devil they got there.
Were others angry: I excused them too;
Well might they rage, I gave them but their
due.
A man's true merit 'tis not hard to find; 175
But each man's secret standard in his mind, —
That casting-weight pride adds to emptiness, —
This, who can gratify? for who can guess?
The bard whom pilfered Pastorals renown,
Who turns a Persian tale for half a crown, 180
Just writes to make his barrenness appear,
And strains from hard-bound brains, eight lines
a year;
He, who still wanting, though he lives on theft,
Steals much, spends little, yet has nothing
left;
And he, who now to sense, now nonsense
leaning, 185
Means not, but blunders round about a mean-
ing;
And he, whose fustian's so sublimely bad,
It is not poetry, but prose run mad:
All these, my modest satire bade translate, 189
And owned that nine such poets made a Tate.
How did they fume, and stamp, and roar, and
chafe!
And swear, not Addison himself was safe.
Peace to all such! but were there one whose
fires
True genius kindles, and fair fame inspires;
Blessed with each talent and each art to
please, 195
And born to write, converse, and live with
ease:
Should such a man, too fond to rule alone,
Bear, like the Turk, no brother near the
throne, 198

View him with scornful, yet with jealous eyes
And hate for arts that caused himself to rise;
Damn with faint praise, assent with civil leer,
And without sneering, teach the rest to sneer;
Willing to wound, and yet afraid to strike,
Just hint a fault, and hesitate dislike;
Alike reserved to blame, or to commend, 205
A timorous foe, and a suspicious friend;
Dreading e'en fools, by flatterers besieged,
And so obliging, that he ne'er obliged;
Like Cato, give his little senate laws,
And sit attentive to his own applause; 210
While wits and Templars every sentence raise,
And wonder with a foolish face of praise—
Who but must laugh, if such a man there be?
Who would not weep, if Atticus were he!

*　*　*　*　*　*　*

THE DUNCIAD

FROM BOOK IV

O Muse! relate (for you can tell alone;
Wits have short memories, and dunces none)
Relate, who first, who last resigned to rest,
Whose heads she partly, whose completely,
　　blest; 622
What charms could faction, what ambition
　　lull,
The venal quiet, and entrance the dull;
Till drowned was sense, and shame, and right,
　　and wrong — 625
O sing, and hush the nations with thy song!

In vain, in vain — the all-composing hour
Resistless falls: the Muse obeys the power.
She comes! she comes! the sable throne behold
Of Night primeval and of Chaos old! 630
Before her, Fancy's gilded clouds decay,
And all its varying rainbows die away.
Wit shoots in vain its momentary fires,
The meteor drops, and in a flash expires.
As one by one, at dread Medea's strain,[1] 635
The sickening stars fade off th' ethereal plain;
As Argus' eyes, by Hermes' wand oppressed,
Closed one by one to everlasting rest:[2]
Thus at her felt approach, and secret might,
Art after art goes out, and all is night. 640
See skulking Truth to her old cavern fled,
Mountains of casuistry heaped o'er her head!
Philosophy, that leaned on Heaven before,
Shrinks to her second cause, and is no more.

[1] Cf. the incantations of Medea, as told by
Gower. [2] See the story in Gayley, pp. 92–94.

Physic of Metaphysic begs defence, 645
And Metaphysic calls for aid on Sense!
See Mystery to Mathematics fly!
In vain! they gaze, turn giddy, rave, and die.
Religion blushing veils her sacred fires,
And unawares Morality expires. 650
Nor public flame, nor private, dares to shine;
Nor human spark is left, nor glimpse divine!
Lo! thy dread empire, Chaos! is restored;
Light dies before thy uncreating word:
Thy hand, great Anarch! lets the curtain
　　fall; 655
And universal darkness buries all.

THE ILIAD

FROM BOOK VI

The chief replied: "That post shall be my
　　care, 560
Not that alone, but all the works of war.
How would the sons of Troy, in arms re-
　　nown'd,
And Troy's proud dames, whose garments
　　sweep the ground,
Attaint the lustre of my former name,
Should Hector basely quit the field of fame?
My early youth was bred to martial pains,
My soul impels me to th' embattled plains:
Let me be foremost to defend the throne,
And guard my father's glories and my own.
Yet come it will, the day decreed by fates,
(How my heart trembles while my tongue
　　relates!) 571
The day when thou, imperial Troy! must
　　bend,
And see thy warriors fall, thy glories end.
And yet no dire presage so wounds my mind,
My mother's death, the ruin of my kind,
Not Priam's hoary hairs defil'd with gore,
Not all my brothers gasping on the shore,
As thine, Andromache! Thy griefs I dread:
I see thee trembling, weeping, captive led,
In Argive[1] looms our battles to design, 580
And woes of which so large a part was thine!
To bear the victor's hard commands, or bring
The weight of waters from Hyperia's spring!
There, while you groan beneath the load of
　　life,
They cry, 'Behold the mighty Hector's wife!'
Some haughty Greek, who lives thy tears to
　　see,
Embitters all thy woes by naming me.

[1] Grecian

The thoughts of glory past and present shame,
A thousand griefs, shall waken at the name!
May I lie cold before that dreadful day,   590
Press'd with a load of monumental clay!
Thy Hector, wrapp'd in everlasting sleep,
Shall neither hear thee sigh, nor see thee
    weep."
    Thus having spoke, th' illustrious chief of
        Troy
Stretch'd his fond arms to clasp the lovely boy.
The babe clung crying to his nurse's breast,
Scar'd at the dazzling helm and nodding crest.
With secret pleasure each fond parent smil'd,
And Hector hasted to relieve his child;   599
The glittr'ing terrors from his brows unbound,
And plac'd the beaming helmet on the ground.
Then kiss'd the child, and, lifting high in
    air,
Thus to the gods preferr'd a father's pray'r:
    "O thou! whose glory fills th' ethereal
        throne,
And all ye deathless pow'rs! protect my son!
Grant him, like me, to purchase just renown,
To guard the Trojans, to defend the crown,
Against his country's foes the war to wage,
And rise the Hector of the future age!
So when, triumphant from successful toils, 610
Of heroes slain he bears the reeking spoils,
Whole hosts may hail him with deserv'd
    acclaim,
And say, 'This chief transcends his father's
    fame':
While pleas'd, amidst the gen'ral shouts of
    Troy,
His mother's conscious heart o'erflows with
    joy."
    He spoke, and fondly gazing on her charms,
Restor'd the pleasing burthen to her arms;
Soft on her fragrant breast the babe she laid,
Hush'd to repose, and with a smile survey'd.
The troubled pleasure soon chastis'd by fear,
She mingled with the smile a tender tear. 621
The soften'd chief with kind compassion
    view'd,
And dried the falling drops, and thus pur-
    sued:
    "Andromache! my soul's far better part,
Why with untimely sorrows heaves thy
    heart?
No hostile hand can antedate my doom,
Till fate condemns me to the silent tomb.
Fix'd is the term to all the race of earth,
And such the hard condition of our birth.
No force can then resist, no flight can save;
All sink alike, the fearful and the brave. 631

No more — but hasten to thy tasks at home,
There guide the spindle, and direct the loom;
Me glory summons to the martial scene,
The field of combat is the sphere for men.
Where heroes war, the foremost place I claim,
The first in danger as the first in fame."

JOHN GAY (1685–1732)

THE HARE WITH MANY FRIENDS

Friendship, like love, is but a name,
Unless to one you stint the flame.
The child whom many fathers share,
Hath seldom known a father's care.
'Tis thus in friendship; who depend
On many rarely find a friend.   6
    A Hare, who, in a civil way,
Complied with everything, like Gay,
Was known by all the bestial train,
Who haunt the wood, or graze the plain.
Her care was, never to offend,
And every creature was her friend.   12
    As forth she went at early dawn,
To taste the dew-besprinkled lawn,
Behind she hears the hunter's cries,
And from the deep-mouthed thunder flies.
She starts, she stops, she pants for breath;
She hears the near advance of death;   18
She doubles, to mislead the hound,
And measures back her mazy round:
Till, fainting in the public way,
Half dead with fear she gasping lay.
What transport in her bosom grew,
When first the Horse appeared in view!   24
"Let me," says she, "your back ascend,
And owe my safety to a friend.
You know my feet betray my flight;
To friendship every burden's light."
The Horse replied: "Poor honest Puss,
It grieves my heart to see thee thus;
Be comforted; relief is near,
For all your friends are in the rear."   32
    She next the stately Bull implored;
And thus replied the mighty lord,
"Since every beast alive can tell
That I sincerely wish you well,
I may, without offence, pretend,
To take the freedom of a friend;   38
Love calls me hence; a favourite cow
Expects me near yon barley-mow:
And when a lady's in the case,
You know, all other things give place.

To leave you thus might seem unkind;
But see, the Goat is just behind."
  The Goat remarked her pulse was high,
Her languid head, her heavy eye;
"My back," says he, "may do you harm;
The Sheep's at hand, and wool is warm." 48
  The Sheep was feeble, and complained
His sides a load of wool sustained:
Said he was slow, confessed his fears,
For hounds eat sheep as well as hares. 52
  She now the trotting Calf addressed,
To save from death a friend distressed.
"Shall I," says he, "of tender age,
In this important care engage?
Older and abler passed you by;
How strong are those, how weak am I!
Should I presume to bear you hence,
Those friends of mine may take offence.
Excuse me, then. You know my heart.
But dearest friends, alas, must part! 62
How shall we all lament! Adieu!
For see, the hounds are just in view."

BLACK-EYED SUSAN

All in the Downs [1] the fleet was moored,
  The streamers waving in the wind,
When Black-eyed Susan came aboard,
  "Oh! where shall I my true love find?
Tell me, ye jovial sailors, tell me true, 5
If my sweet William sails among the crew?"

William, who high upon the yard
  Rocked with the billow to and fro,
Soon as her well-known voice he heard
  He sighed, and cast his eyes below: 10
The cord slides swiftly through his glowing
    hands
And, quick as lightning, on the deck he
    stands.

So the sweet lark, high poised in air,
  Shuts close his pinions to his breast —
If chance his mate's shrill call he hear — 15
  And drops at once into her nest.
The noblest captain in the British fleet
Might envy William's lips those kisses sweet.

"O Susan, Susan, lovely dear,
  My vows shall ever true remain; 20
Let me kiss off that falling tear;
  We only part to meet again.

        [1] Cf. above, p. 260 b, note 2.

Change as ye list, ye winds! my heart shall be
The faithful compass that still points to thee.

"Believe not what the landsmen say, 25
  Who tempt with doubts thy constant mind;
They'll tell thee, sailors, when away,
  In every port a mistress find;
Yes, yes, believe them when they tell thee so,
For thou art present wheresoe'er I go. 30

"If to fair India's coast we sail,
  Thy eyes are seen in diamonds bright;
Thy breath is Afric's spicy gale,
  Thy skin is ivory so white.
Thus every beauteous object that I view, 35
Wakes in my soul some charm of lovely Sue.

"Though battle call me from thy arms,
  Let not my pretty Susan mourn;
Though cannons roar, yet safe from harms,
  William shall to his dear return. 40
Love turns aside the balls that round me fly,
Lest precious tears should drop from Susan's
    eye."

The boatswain gave the dreadful word;
  The sails their swelling bosom spread;
No longer must she stay aboard; 45
  They kissed — she sighed — he hung his
    head.
Her lessening boat unwilling rows to land,
"Adieu!" she cries, and waved her lily hand.

EDWARD YOUNG (1683–1765)

From THE COMPLAINT, OR NIGHT THOUGHTS

NIGHT I

MAN

How poor, how rich, how abject, how august,
How complicate, how wonderful, is man!
How passing wonder He who made him such!
Who centred in our make such strange ex-
    tremes, 70
From different natures marvellously mixed!
Connection exquisite of distant worlds!
Distinguished link in being's endless chain!
Midway from nothing to the Deity!
A beam ethereal, sullied, and absorpt!
Though sullied and dishonoured, still divine!
Dim miniature of greatness absolute!

An heir of glory! a frail child of dust!
Helpless immortal! insect infinite!
A worm! a god! — I tremble at myself, 80
And in myself am lost! At home a stranger,
Thought wanders up and down, surprised,
    aghast,
And wondering at her own. How reason
    reels!
O, what a miracle to man is man!
Triumphantly distressed! What joy! what
    dread!
Alternately transported and alarmed!
What can preserve my life? or what destroy?
An angel's arm can't snatch me from the
    grave;
Legions of angels can't confine me there.

PROCRASTINATION

By nature's law, what may be, may be now;
There's no prerogative in human hours. 371
In human hearts what bolder thought can
    rise
Than man's presumption on to-morrow's
    dawn?
Where is to-morrow? In another world.
For numbers this is certain; the reverse
Is sure to none; and yet on this 'perhaps,'
This 'peradventure,' infamous for lies,
As on a rock of adamant, we build
Our mountain hopes, spin our eternal schemes,
As[1] we the fatal sisters[2] could out-spin, 380
And big with life's futurities, expire.
Not e'en Philander[3] had bespoke his shroud,
Nor had he cause; a warning was denied:
How many fall as sudden, not as safe;
As sudden, though for years admonish'd
    home!
Of human ills the last extreme beware;

[1] as if [2] the Fates [3] Young's son-in-law,
Mr. Temple, who had died two years before
AE

Beware, Lorenzo,[1] a slow sudden death.
How dreadful that deliberate surprise!
Be wise to-day; 'tis madness to defer;
Next day the fatal precedent will plead; 390
Thus on, till wisdom is push'd out of life.
Procrastination is the thief of time;
Year after year it steals, till all are fled,
And to the mercies of a moment leaves
The vast concerns of an eternal scene.
If not so frequent, would not this be strange?
That 'tis so frequent, this is stranger still.
    Of man's miraculous mistakes this bears
The palm, "That all men are about to live,
Forever on the brink of being born."   400
All pay themselves the compliment to think
They one day shall not drivel: and their
    pride
On this reversion takes up ready praise;
At least, their own; their future selves ap-
    plaud;
How excellent that life they ne'er will lead.
Time lodg'd in their own hands is folly's
    vails;[2]
That lodg'd in fate's to wisdom they consign.
The thing they can't but purpose, they post-
    pone.
'Tis not in folly not to scorn a fool,
And scarce in human wisdom to do more. 410
All promise is poor dilatory man,
And that through every stage: when young,
    indeed,
In full content we sometimes nobly rest,
Unanxious for ourselves; and only wish,
As duteous sons our fathers were more wise.
At thirty man suspects himself a fool,
Knows it at forty and reforms his plan;
At fifty chides his infamous delay,
Pushes his prudent purpose to resolve;
In all the magnimimity of thought   420
Resolves; and re-resolves; then dies the same.

[1] probably the Duke of Wharton [2] folly's
perquisite

THE TRANSITION

LADY WINCHILSEA (1661-1720)

A NOCTURNAL REVERIE

In such a night, when every louder wind
Is to its distant cavern safe confin'd,
And only gentle zephyr fans his wings,
And lonely Philomel, still waking, sings;
Or from some tree, fam'd for the owl's delight,
She, hollowing clear, directs the wand'rer right;
In such a night, when passing clouds give place,
Or thinly vail the Heav'ns mysterious face;
When in some river, overhung with green,
The waving moon and trembling leaves are seen;   10
When freshen'd grass now bears itself upright,
And makes cool banks to pleasing rest invite,
Whence springs the woodbind and the bramble-rose,
And where the sleepy cowslip shelter'd grows;
Whilst now a paler hue the foxglove takes,
Yet chequers still with red the dusky brakes;
When scatter'd glow-worms, but in twilight fine,
Show trivial beauties watch their hour to shine,
Whilst Salisb'ry [1] stands the test of every light
In perfect charms and perfect virtue bright; 20
When odours which declin'd repelling day
Thro' temp'rate air uninterrupted stray;
When darken'd groves their softest shadows wear,
And falling waters we distinctly hear;
When thro' the gloom more venerable shows
Some ancient fabric, awful in repose,
While sunburnt hills their swarthy looks conceal
And swelling haycocks thicken up the vale;
When the loos'd horse now, as his pasture leads,
Comes slowly grazing thro' th' adjoining meads,   30

Whose stealing pace, and lengthen'd shade we fear,
Till torn up forage in his teeth we hear;
When nibbling sheep at large pursue their food,
And unmolested kine re-chew the cud;
When curlews cry beneath the village-walls,
And to her straggling brood the partridge calls;
Their shortliv'd jubilee the creatures keep,
Which but endures whilst tyrant-man does sleep;
When a sedate content the spirit feels,
And no fierce light disturb, whilst it reveals;
But silent musings urge the mind to seek   41
Something too high for syllables to speak;
Till the free soul to a compos'dness charm'd,
Finding the elements of rage disarm'd,
O'er all below a solemn quiet grown,
Joys in th' inferior world and thinks it like her own:
In such a night let me abroad remain
Till morning breaks and all's confus'd again;
Our cares, our toils, our clamours are renew'd,
Or pleasures, seldom reach'd, again pursu'd. 50

ROBERT BLAIR (1699-1746)

FROM THE GRAVE

While some affect the sun, and some the shade,
Some flee the city, some the hermitage,
Their aims as various as the roads they take
In journeying through life; the task be mine
To paint the gloomy horrors of the tomb;
Th' appointed place of rendezvous, where all
These travellers meet. Thy succours I implore,
Eternal King! whose potent arm sustains
The keys of hell and death. — The Grave, dread thing!   9
Men shiver when thou'rt nam'd: Nature, appall'd,
Shakes off her wonted firmness. — Ah! how dark

Thy long-extended realms, and rueful wastes!
Where nought but silence reigns, and night,
    dark night,
Dark as was chaos, ere the infant sun
Was roll'd together, or had tried his beams
Athwart the gloom profound. — The sickly
    taper
By glimmering through thy low-brow'd misty
    vaults,
(Furr'd round with mouldy damps and ropy
    slime)
Lets fall a supernumerary horror,
And only serves to make thy night more
    irksome.   20
Well do I know thee by thy trusty yew,
Cheerless, unsocial plant! that loves to dwell
Midst skulls and coffins, epitaphs and worms:
Where light-heel'd ghosts, and visionary
    shades,
Beneath the wan cold moon (as fame reports)
Embodied, thick, perform their mystic rounds.
No other merriment, dull tree! is thine.
    See yonder hallow'd fane; — the pious work
Of names once fam'd, now dubious or forgot,
And buried midst the wreck of things which
    were; ·   30
There lie interr'd the more illustrious dead.
The wind is up: hark! how it howls! Me-
    thinks
Till now I never heard a sound so dreary:
Doors creak, and windows clap, and night's
    foul bird,
Rook'd[1] in the spire, screams loud: the gloomy
    aisles,
Black-plaster'd, and hung round with shreds
    of 'scutcheons
And tatter'd coats of arms, send back the
    sound
Laden with heavier airs, from the low vaults,
The mansions of the dead. — Rous'd from
    their slumbers,
In grim array the grisly spectres rise,   40
Grin horrible, and, obstinately sullen,
Pass and repass, hush'd as the foot of night.
Again the screech-owl shrieks: ungracious
    sound!
I'll hear no more; it makes one's blood run
    chill.
    Quite round the pile, a row of reverend
    elms,
(Coeval near with that) all ragged show,
Long lash'd by the rude winds. Some rift half
    down

Their branchless trunks; others so thin a-top,
That scarce two crows could lodge in the same
    tree.
Strange things, the neighbours say, have
    happen'd here: 50
Wild shrieks have issued from the hollow
    tombs:
Dead men have come again, and walk'd
    about;
And the great bell has toll'd, unrung, un-
    touch'd.
(Such tales their cheer, at wake or gossiping,
When it draws near the witching time of
    night.)
    Oft in the lone church-yard at night I've
    seen,
By glimpse of moonshine chequering through
    the trees,
The school-boy, with his satchel in his hand,
Whistling aloud to bear his courage up,
And lightly tripping o'er the long flat stones,
(With nettles skirted, and with moss o'er-
    grown,)   61
That tell in homely phrase who lie below.
Sudden he starts, and hears, or thinks he
    hears,
The sound of something purring at his heels;
Full fast he flies, and dares not look behind
    him,
Till out of breath he overtakes his fellows;
Who gather round, and wonder at the tale
Of horrid apparition, tall and ghastly,
That walks at dead of night, or takes his
    stand
O'er some new-open'd grave; and (strange to
    tell!)   70
Evanishes at crowing of the cock.
    The new-made widow, too, I've sometimes
    'spied,
Sad sight! slow moving o'er the prostrate
    dead:
Listless, she crawls along in doleful black,
Whilst bursts of sorrow gush from either
    eye,
Fast falling down her now untasted cheek:
Prone on the lowly grave of the dear man
She drops; whilst busy, meddling memory,
In barbarous succession musters up   79
The past endearments of their softer hours,
Tenacious of its theme. Still, still she thinks
She sees him, and indulging the fond thought,
Clings yet more closely to the senseless turf,
Nor heeds the passenger who looks that way.

* * * * * * *

---

[1] perched, as roosting

JAMES THOMSON (1700–1748)

THE SEASONS

A SNOW SCENE

From Winter

The keener tempests come: and fuming
    dun
From all the livid east, or piercing north,
Thick clouds ascend — in whose capacious
    womb
A vapoury deluge lies, to snow congealed.
Heavy they roll their fleecy world along;
And the sky saddens with the gathered storm.
Through the hushed air the whitening shower
    descends,
At first thin wavering; till at last the flakes
Fall broad, and wide, and fast, dimming the
    day   231
With a continual flow. The cherished fields
Put on their winter-robe of purest white.
'Tis brightness all; save where the new snow
    melts
Along the mazy current. Low, the woods
Bow their hoar head; and, ere the languid sun
Faint from the west emits his evening ray,
Earth's universal face, deep-hid and chill,
Is one wild dazzling waste, that buries wide
The works of man. Drooping, the labourer-
    ox   240
Stands covered o'er with snow, and then de-
    mands
The fruit of all his toil. The fowls of heaven,
Tamed by the cruel season, crowd around
The winnowing store, and claim the little boon
Which Providence assigns them. One alone,
The redbreast, sacred to the household gods,
Wisely regardful of the embroiling sky,
In joyless fields and thorny thickets leaves
His shivering mates, and pays to trusted man
His annual visit. Half-afraid, he first   250
Against the window beats; then, brisk,
    alights
On the warm hearth; then, hopping o'er the
    floor,
Eyes all the smiling family askance,
And pecks, and starts, and wonders where he
    is —
Till, more familiar grown, the table-crumbs
Attract his slender feet. The foodless wilds
Pour forth their brown inhabitants. The
    hare,
Though timorous of heart, and hard beset

By death in various forms, dark snares, and
    dogs,
And more unpitying men, the garden seeks,
Urged on by fearless want. The bleating
    kind   261
Eye the black heaven, and next the glistening
    earth
With looks of dumb despair; then, sad dis-
    persed,
Dig for the withered herb through heaps of
    snow.

*   *   *   *   *   *   *

THE SHEEP–WASHING

From Summer

Or rushing thence, in one diffusive band,
They drive the troubled flocks, by many a dog
Compelled, to where the mazy-running brook
Forms a deep pool; this bank abrupt and
    high,
And that, fair-spreading in a pebbled shore.
Urged to the giddy brink, much is the toil,
The clamour much, of men, and boys, and
    dogs,
Ere the soft, fearful people to the flood
Commit their woolly sides. And oft the
    swain,
On some impatient seizing, hurls them in: 380
Emboldened then, nor hesitating more,
Fast, fast, they plunge amid the flashing wave,
And panting labour to the farther shore.
Repeated this, till deep the well-washed fleece
Has drunk the flood, and from his lively
    haunt
The trout is banished by the sordid stream;
Heavy and dripping, to the breezy brow
Slow move the harmless race; where, as they
    spread
Their swelling treasures to the sunny ray,
Inly disturbed, and wondering what this wild
Outrageous tumult means, their loud com-
    plaints   391
The country fill — and, tossed from rock to
    rock,
Incessant bleatings run around the hills.
At last, of snowy white, the gathered flocks
Are in the wattled pen innumerous pressed,
Head above head; and ranged in lusty rows
The shepherds sit, and whet the sounding
    shears.
The housewife waits to roll her fleecy stores,
With all her gay-drest maids attending round.
One, chief, in gracious dignity enthroned, 400

Shines o'er the rest, the pastoral queen, and
    rays
Her smiles, sweet-beaming, on her shepherd-
    king;
While the glad circle round them yield their
    souls
To festive mirth, and wit that knows no gall.
Meantime, their joyous task goes on apace:
Some mingling stir the melted tar, and some,
Deep on the new-shorn vagrant's heaving side,
To stamp his master's cypher ready stand;
Others the unwilling wether drag along; 409
And, glorying in his might, the sturdy boy
Holds by the twisted horns the indignant ram.
Behold where bound, and of its robe bereft,
By needy man, that all-depending lord,
How meek, how patient, the mild creature
    lies!
What softness in its melancholy face,
What dumb complaining innocence appears!
Fear not, ye gentle tribes, 'tis not the knife
Of horrid slaughter that is o'er you waved;
No, 'tis the tender swain's well-guided shears,
Who having now, to pay his annual care, 420
Borrowed your fleece, to you a cumbrous load,
Will send you bounding to your hills again.

THE COMING OF THE RAIN

FROM SPRING

At first a dusky wreath they seem to rise,
Scarce staining ether; but by fast degrees,
In heaps on heaps, the doubling vapour sails
Along the loaded sky, and mingling deep, 150
Sits on the horizon round, a settled gloom:
Not such as wintry storms on mortals shed,
Oppressing life; but lovely, gentle, kind,
And full of every hope and every joy,
The wish of Nature. Gradual sinks the
    breeze
Into a perfect calm; that not a breath
Is heard to quiver through the closing woods,
Or rustling turn the many twinkling leaves
Of aspen tall. The uncurling floods, diffused
In glassy breadth, seem through delusive
    lapse
Forgetful of their course. 'Tis silence all, 161
And pleasing expectation. Herds and flocks
Drop the dry sprig, and, mute-imploring, eye
The fallen verdure. Hushed in short suspense
The plumy people streak their wings with oil,
To throw the lucid moisture trickling off;
And wait the approaching sign to strike, at
    once,

Into the general choir. Even mountains,
    vales,
And forests seem, impatient, to demand
The promised sweetness. Man superior
    walks 170
Amid the glad creation, musing praise,
And looking lively gratitude. At last,
The clouds consign their treasures to the
    fields;
And, softly shaking on the dimpled pool
Prelusive drops, let all their moisture flow,
In large effusion, o'er the freshened world.

STORM IN HARVEST

FROM AUTUMN

Defeating oft the labours of the year,
The sultry south collects a potent blast.
At first, the groves are scarcely seen to stir
Their trembling tops, and a still murmur runs
Along the soft-inclining fields of corn;
But as the aërial tempest fuller swells,
And in one mighty stream, invisible,
Immense, the whole excited atmosphere
Impetuous rushes o'er the sounding world,
Strained to the root, the stooping forest pours
A rustling shower of yet untimely leaves. 321
High-beat, the circling mountains eddy in,
From the bare wild, the dissipated storm,
And send it in a torrent down the vale.
Exposed, and naked, to its utmost rage,
Through all the sea of harvest rolling round,
The billowy plain floats wide; nor can evade,
Though pliant to the blast, its seizing force —
Or whirled in air, or into vacant chaff 329
Shook waste. And sometimes too a burst of
    rain,
Swept from the black horizon, broad, descends
In one continuous flood. Still over head
The mingling tempest weaves its gloom, and
    still
The deluge deepens; till the fields around
Lie sunk, and flatted, in the sordid wave.
Sudden, the ditches swell; the meadows
    swim.
Red, from the hills, innumerable streams
Tumultuous roar; and high above its banks
The river lift; before whose rushing tide,
Herds, flocks, and harvests, cottages, and
    swains, 340
Roll mingled down: all that the winds had
    spared,
In one wild moment ruined; the big hopes,
And well-earned treasures of the painful year.

Fled to some eminence, the husbandman,
Helpless, beholds the miserable wreck
Driving along; his drowning ox at once
Descending, with his labours scattered round,
He sees; and instant o'er his shivering thought
Comes Winter unprovided, and a train
Of clamant children dear.   Ye masters, then,
Be mindful of the rough laborious hand   351
That sinks you soft in elegance and ease;
Be mindful of those limbs, in russet[1] clad,
Whose toil to yours is warmth and graceful
    pride;
And, oh, be mindful of that sparing board
Which covers yours with luxury profuse,
Makes your glass sparkle, and your sense
    rejoice!
Nor cruelly demand what the deep rains
And all-involving winds have swept away.

From THE CASTLE OF INDOLENCE

In lowly dale, fast by a river's side   10
With woody hill o'er hill encompassed
    round,
A most enchanting wizard did abide,
Than whom a fiend more fell is nowhere
    found.
It was, I ween, a lovely spot of ground;
And there a season atween June and May,
Half prankt with spring, with summer half
    imbrowned,
A listless climate made, where, sooth to say,
No living wight could work, ne cared for play.

Was nought around but images of rest:
Sleep-soothing groves, and quiet lawns be-
    tween;   20
And flowery beds, that slumbrous influence
    kest,[2]
From poppies breathed; and beds of pleas-
    ant green,
Where never yet was creeping creature seen.
Meantime unnumbered glittering streamlets
    played,
And hurlèd everywhere their waters sheen;
That, as they bickered through the sunny
    glade,
Though restless still themselves, a lulling mur-
    mur made.

Joined to the prattle of the purling rills,
Were heard the lowing herds along the vale,

And flocks loud-bleating from the distant
    hills,   30
And vacant shepherds piping in the dale:
And now and then sweet Philomel would
    wail,
Or stock-doves plain[1] amid the forest deep,
That drowsy rustled to the sighing gale;
And still a coil[2] the grasshopper did keep:
Yet all the sounds yblent inclinèd all to sleep.

Full in the passage of the vale, above,
A sable, silent, solemn forest stood;
Where nought but shadowy forms were seen
    to move,
As Idless[3] fancied in her dreaming mood:
And up the hills, on either side, a wood   41
Of blackening pines, aye waving to and fro,
Sent forth a sleepy horror through the
    blood;
And where this valley winded out below,
The murmuring main was heard, and scarcely
    heard, to flow.

A pleasing land of drowsy-head it was:
Of dreams that wave before the half-shut
    eye;
And of gay castles in the clouds that pass,
Forever flushing round a summer-sky.
There eke the soft delights, that witchingly
Instil a wanton sweetness through the
    breast,   51
And the calm pleasures, always hovered
    nigh;
But whate'er smackt of noyance, or unrest,
Was far, far off expelled from this delicious
    nest.

The landscape such, inspiring perfect ease,
Where Indolence (for so the wizard hight)
Close-hid his castle mid embowering trees,
That half shut out the beams of Phœbus
    bright,
And made a kind of checkered day and
    night.
Meanwhile, unceasing at the massy gate, 60
Beneath a spacious palm, the wicked wight
Was placed; and to his lute, of cruel fate
And labour harsh, complained, lamenting
    man's estate.

Thither continual pilgrims crowded still,
From all the roads of earth that pass there
    by:

---

[1] undyed homespun   [2] cast   [1] complain   [2] disturbance   [3] Idleness

For, as they chanced to breathe on neigh-
    bouring hill,
The freshness of this valley smote their eye,
And drew them ever and anon more nigh;
Till clustering round the enchanter false
    they hung,
Ymolten with his syren melody;   70
While o'er the enfeebling lute his hand he
    flung,
And to the trembling chords these tempting
    verses sung:

"Behold! ye pilgrims of this earth, behold!
See all but man with unearned pleasure gay:
See her bright robes the butterfly unfold,
Broke from her wintry tomb in prime of
    May!
What youthful bride can equal her array?
Who can with her for easy pleasure vie?
From mead to mead with gentle wing to
    stray,
From flower to flower on balmy gales to
    fly,   80
Is all she has to do beneath the radiant sky.

"Behold the merry minstrels of the morn,
The swarming songsters of the careless[1]
    grove;
Ten thousand throats that, from the flower-
    ing thorn,
Hymn their good God, and carol sweet of
    love,
Such grateful kindly raptures them emove![2]
They neither plough, nor sow; ne,[3] fit for
    flail,
E'er to the barn the nodding sheaves they
    drove;
Yet theirs each harvest dancing in the gale,
Whatever crowns the hill, or smiles along the
    vale.   90

"Outcast of Nature, man! the wretched
    thrall
Of bitter-dropping sweat, of sweltry pain,
Of cares that eat away the heart with gall,
And of the vices, an inhuman train,
That all proceed from savage thirst of gain:
For when hard-hearted Interest first began
To poison earth, Astræa[4] left the plain;
Guile, Violence, and Murder, seized on man,
And, for soft milky streams, with blood the
    rivers ran.   99

[1] care-free [2] move [3] nor [4] the goddess of justice, who in the Golden Age dwelt among men

"Come, ye who still the cumbrous load of
    life
Push hard up-hill; but as the farthest
    steep
You trust to gain, and put an end to strife,
Down thunders back the stone with mighty
    sweep,
And hurls your labours to the valley deep,
Forever vain: come, and, withouten fee,
I in oblivion will your sorrows steep,
Your cares, your toils; will steep you in a
    sea
Of full delight: O come, ye weary wights, to
    me!

"With me, you need not rise at early dawn,
To pass the joyless day in various stounds;[1]
Or louting[2] low, on upstart Fortune fawn,
And sell fair Honour for some paltry
    pounds;   112
Or through the city take your dirty rounds,
To cheat, and dun, and lie, and visit pay,
Now flattering base, now giving secret
    wounds;
Or prowl in courts of law for human prey,
In venal senate thieve, or rob on broad high-
    way.

"No cocks, with me, to rustic labour call,
From village on to village sounding clear;
To tardy swain no shrill-voiced matrons
    squall;   120
No dogs, no babes, no wives, to stun your
    ear;
No hammers thump; no horrid blacksmith
    sear;
Ne noisy tradesman your sweet slumbers
    start
With sounds that are a misery to hear;
But all is calm, — as would delight the
    heart
Of Sybarite of old, — all Nature, and all Art.

*   *   *   *   *   *   *

"The best of men have ever loved repose:
They hate to mingle in the filthy fray;
Where the soul sours, and gradual rancour
    grows,
Embittered more from peevish day to day,
Even those whom Fame has lent her fairest
    ray,
The most renowned of worthy wights of
    yore,   150

[1] griefs   [2] bowing

From a base world at last have stolen away:
So Scipio, to the soft Cumæan shore [1]
Retiring, tasted joy he never knew before.

"But if a little exercise you choose,
Some zest for ease, 'tis not forbidden here.
Amid the groves you may indulge the
    Muse,
Or tend the blooms, and deck the vernal
    year;
Or, softly stealing, with your watery gear, [2]
Along the brooks, the crimson-spotted fry
You may delude; the whilst, amused, you
    hear   160
Now the hoarse stream, and now the
    Zephyr's sigh,
Attunèd to the birds, and woodland melody.

"O grievous folly! to heap up estate,
Losing the days you see beneath the sun;
When, sudden, comes blind unrelenting
    Fate,
And gives the untasted portion you have
    won,
With ruthless toil and many a wretch un-
    done,
To those who mock you gone to Pluto's
    reign,
There with sad ghosts to pine, and shadows
    dun;
But sure it is of vanities most vain,   170
To toil for what you here untoiling may
    obtain."

RULE, BRITANNIA

From ALFRED, A MASQUE

When Britain first, at Heaven's command,
    Arose from out the azure main,
This was the charter of the land,
    And guardian angels sang this strain:
        Rule, Britannia, rule the waves!
        Britons never will be slaves!

The nations not so blest as thee,
    Must in their turns to tyrants fall,
Whilst thou shalt flourish great and free,
    The dread and envy of them all.   10
        Rule, Britannia, etc.

[1] Scipio Africanus, the elder, retired from the
intrigues of Rome to his country place near
Cumæ on the Italian coast.   [2] fishing tackle

Still more majestic shalt thou rise,
    More dreadful from each foreign stroke;
As the loud blast that tears the skies,
    Serves but to root thy native oak.
        Rule, Britannia, etc.

Thee haughty tyrants ne'er shall tame;
    All their attempts to bend thee down
Will but arouse thy generous flame,
    But work their woe and thy renown.   20
        Rule, Britannia, etc.

To thee belongs the rural reign;
    Thy cities shall with commerce shine;
All thine shall be the subject main, [1]
    And every shore it circles thine.
        Rule, Britannia, etc.

The Muses, still [2] with freedom found,
    Shall to thy happy coast repair;
Blest isle, with matchless beauty crowned,
    And manly hearts to guard the fair!   30
        Rule, Britannia, etc.

JOHN DYER (1700?–1758)

From GRONGAR HILL [3]

Silent Nymph, with curious eye,
Who, the purple evening, lie
On the mountain's lonely van, [4]
Beyond the noise of busy man,
Painting fair the form of things,
While the yellow linnet sings;
Or the tuneful nightingale
Charms the forest with her tale;
Come with all thy various hues,
Come, and aid thy sister Muse;   10
Now while Phœbus riding high
Gives lustre to the land and sky!
Grongar Hill invites my song,
Draw the landskip [5] bright and strong;
Grongar, in whose mossy cells
Sweetly musing Quiet dwells;
Grongar, in whose silent shade,
For the modest Muses made,
So oft I have, the evening still,
At the fountain of a rill,   20
Sate upon a flowery bed,
With my hand beneath my head;

[1] ocean   [2] always   [3] a hill in southwest Wales
[4] peak   [5] cf. L'Allegro, l. 70

While strayed my eyes o'er Towy's[1] flood,
Over mead, and over wood,
From house to house, from hill to hill,
'Till Contemplation had her fill.
   About his chequered sides I wind,
And leave his brooks and meads behind,
And groves, and grottoes where I lay,
And vistas shooting beams of day :   30
Wide and wider spreads the vale ;
As circles on a smooth canal :
The mountains round, unhappy fate !
Sooner or later, of all height,
Withdraw their summits from the skies,
And lessen as the others rise :
Still the prospect wider spreads,
Adds a thousand woods and meads,
Still it widens, widens still,
And sinks the newly-risen hill.   40
   Now, I gain the mountain's brow,
What a landskip lies below !
No clouds, no vapours intervene,
But the gay, the open scene
Does the face of nature show,
In all the hues of heaven's bow !
And, swelling to embrace the light,
Spreads around beneath the sight.
   Old castles on the cliffs arise,
Proudly towering in the skies ;   50
Rushing from the woods, the spires
Seem from hence ascending fires ;
Half his beams Apollo sheds
On the yellow mountain-heads,
Gilds the fleeces of the flocks,
And glitters on the broken rocks.
   Below me trees unnumbered rise,
Beautiful in various dyes :
The gloomy pine, the poplar blue,
The yellow beach, the sable yew,   60
The slender fir, that taper grows,
The sturdy oak with broad-spread boughs ;
And beyond the purple grove,
Haunt of Phillis, queen of love,
Gaudy as the opening dawn,
Lies a long and level lawn
On which a dark hill, steep and high,
Holds and charms the wandering eye.
Deep are his feet in Towy's flood,
His sides are cloth'd with waving wood,   70
And ancient towers crown his brow,
That cast an awful look below ;
Whose ragged walls the ivy creeps,
And with her arms from falling keeps ;

[1] a river that flows into Carmarthen Bay in southwest Wales

So both a safety from the wind
On mutual dependence find.

DAVID MALLET (1705–1765)

WILLIAM AND MARGARET

'Twas at the silent solemn hour,
  When night and morning meet ;
In glided Margaret's grimly ghost,
  And stood at William's feet.   4

Her face was like an April morn
  Clad in a wintry cloud ;
And clay-cold was her lily hand
  That held her sable shroud.   8

So shall the fairest face appear,
  When youth and years are flown :
Such is the robe that kings must wear,
  When death has reft their crown.   12

Her bloom was like the springing flower,
  That sips the silver dew ;
The rose was budded in her cheek,
  Just opening to the view.   16

But love had, like the canker-worm,
  Consumed her early prime ;
The rose grew pale, and left her cheek,
  She died before her time.   20

"Awake !" she cried, "thy true love calls,
  Come from her midnight grave :
Now let thy pity hear the maid
  Thy love refused to save.   24

"This is the dark and dreary hour
  When injured ghosts complain ;
When yawning graves give up their dead,
  To haunt the faithless swain.   28

"Bethink thee, William, of thy fault,
  Thy pledge and broken oath !
And give me back my maiden vow,
  And give me back my troth.   32

"Why did you promise love to me,
  And not that promise keep ?
Why did you swear my eyes were bright,
  Yet leave those eyes to weep ?   36

"How could you say my face was fair,
  And yet that face forsake ?

How could you win my virgin heart,
  Yet leave that heart to break?   40

"Why did you say my lip was sweet,
  And make the scarlet pale?
And why did I, young, witless maid!
  Believe the flattering tale?   44

"That face, alas! no more is fair,
  Those lips no longer red:
Dark are my eyes, now closed in death,
  And every charm is fled.   48

"The hungry worm my sister is;
  This winding-sheet I wear:
And cold and weary lasts our night,
  Till that last morn appear.   52

"But hark! the cock has warned me hence;
  A long and last adieu!
Come see, false man, how low she lies,
  Who died for love of you."   56

The lark sung loud; the morning smiled
  With beams of rosy red:
Pale William quaked in every limb,
  And raving left his bed.   60

He hied him to the fatal place
  Where Margaret's body lay;
And stretched him on the green-grass turf
  That wrapt her breathless clay.   64

And thrice he called on Margaret's name,
  And thrice he wept full sore;
Then laid his cheek to her cold grave,
  And word spake never more!

      68

SAMUEL JOHNSON (1709–1784)

CONGREVE

William Congreve descended from a family in Staffordshire, of so great antiquity that it claims a place among the few that extend their line beyond the Norman Conquest; and was the son of William Congreve, second son of Richard Congreve, of Congreve and Stratton. He visited, once at least, the residence of his ancestors; and, I believe, more places than one are still shown, in groves and gardens, where he is related to have written his "Old Bachelor."

Neither the time nor place of his birth are certainly known; if the inscription upon his monument be true, he was born in 1672. For the place; it was said by himself, that he owed his nativity to England, and by every body else that he was born in Ireland. Southern mentioned him with sharp censure, as a man that meanly disowned his native country. The biographers assign his nativity to Bardsa, near Leeds in Yorkshire, from the account given by himself, as they suppose, to Jacob.[1]

To doubt whether a man of eminence has told the truth about his own birth, is, in appearance, to be very deficient in candour; yet nobody can live long without knowing that falsehoods of convenience or vanity, falsehoods from which no evil immediately visible ensues, except the general degradation of human testimony, are very lightly uttered, and once uttered are sullenly supported. Boileau, who desired to be thought a rigorous and steady moralist, having told a petty lie to Lewis XIV, continued it afterwards by false dates; "thinking himself obliged *in honour*," says his admirer, "to maintain what, when he said it, was so well received."

Wherever Congreve was born, he was educated first at Kilkenny, and afterwards at Dublin, his father having some military employment that stationed him in Ireland: but, after having passed through the usual preparatory studies, as may be reasonably supposed, with great celerity and success, his father thought it proper to assign him a profession, by which something might be gotten; and about the time of the Revolution sent him, at the age of sixteen, to study law in the Middle Temple,[2] where he lived for several years, but with very little attention to Statutes or Reports.

His disposition to become an author appeared very early, as he very early felt that force of imagination, and possessed that copiousness of sentiment, by which intellectual pleasure can be given. His first performance was a novel, called "Incognita, or Love and Duty reconciled:" it is praised by the biographers, who quote some part of the Preface, that is, indeed, for such a time of life, uncommonly judicious. I would rather praise it than read it.

His first dramatic labour was "The Old Bachelor;" of which he says, in his defence

[1] Giles Jacob, compiler of the *Poetical Register*, an account of poets   [2] in London

against Collier,[1] "that the comedy was written, as several know, some years before it was acted. When I wrote it, I had little thoughts of the stage; but did it to amuse myself in a slow recovery from a fit of sickness. Afterwards, through my indiscretion, it was seen, and in some little time more it was acted; and I, through the remainder of my indiscretion, suffered myself to be drawn into the prosecution of a difficult and thankless study, and to be involved in a perpetual war with knaves and fools."

There seems to be a strange affectation in authors of appearing to have done every thing by chance. "The Old Bachelor" was written for amusement in the languor of convalescence. Yet it is apparently composed with great elaborateness of dialogue, and incessant ambition of wit. The age of the writer considered, it is indeed a very wonderful performance; for, whenever written, it was acted (1693) when he was not more than twenty-one years old; and was then recommended by Mr. Dryden, Mr. Southern,[2] and Mr. Maynwaring.[3] Dryden said that he never had seen such a first play; but they found it deficient in some things requisite to the success of its exhibition, and by their greater experience fitted it for the stage. Southern used to relate of one comedy, probably of this, that, when Congreve read it to the players, he pronounced it so wretchedly, that they had almost rejected it; but they were afterwards so well persuaded of its excellence, that, for half a year before it was acted, the manager allowed its author the privilege of the house.

Few plays have ever been so beneficial to the writer; for it procured him the patronage of Halifax,[4] who immediately made him one of the commissioners for licensing coaches, and soon after gave him a place in the pipe-office,[5] and another in the customs of six hundred pounds a year. Congreve's conversation must surely have been at least equally pleasing with his writings.

Such a comedy, written at such an age, requires some consideration. As the lighter species of dramatic poetry professes the imitation of common life, of real manners, and

daily incidents, it apparently presupposes a familiar knowledge of many characters, and exact observation of the passing world; the difficulty therefore is, to conceive how this knowledge can be obtained by a boy.

But if "The Old Bachelor" be more nearly examined, it will be found to be one of those comedies which may be made by a mind vigorous and acute, and furnished with comic characters by the perusal of other poets, without much actual commerce with mankind. The dialogue is one constant reciprocation of conceits, or clash of wit, in which nothing flows necessarily from the occasion or is dictated by nature. The characters both of men and women are either fictitious and artificial, as those of Heartwell and the Ladies; or easy and common, as Wittol a tame idiot, Bluff a swaggering coward, and Fondlewife a jealous puritan; and the catastrophe arises from a mistake not very probably produced, by marrying a woman in a mask.

Yet this gay comedy, when all these deductions are made, will still remain the work of very powerful and fertile faculties; the dialogue is quick and sparkling, the incidents such as seize the attention, and the wit so exuberant that it "o'er-informs its tenement."[1]

Next year he gave another specimen of his abilities in "The Double Dealer," which was not received with equal kindness. He writes to his patron the lord Halifax a dedication, in which he endeavours to reconcile the reader to that which found few friends among the audience. These apologies are always useless: "de gustibus non est disputandum;"[2] men may be convinced, but they cannot be pleased, against their will. But, though taste is obstinate, it is very variable: and time often prevails when arguments have failed.

Queen Mary conferred upon both those plays the honour of her presence; and when she died soon after, Congreve testified his gratitude by a despicable effusion of elegiac pastoral; a composition in which all is unnatural, and yet nothing is new.

In another year (1695) his prolific pen produced "Love for Love;" a comedy of nearer alliance to life, and exhibiting more real manners than either of the former. The character of Foresight[3] was then common. Dryden calculated nativities; both Cromwell and

[1] Jeremy Collier; see below [2] a well-known dramatist [3] a Templar and influential man of letters [4] George Savile, Marquis of Halifax [5] a government office in which records called pipe-rolls were kept

[1] cf. *Absalom and Achitophel*, l. 74 [2] tastes are not a subject for argument [3] an astrologer

King William had their lucky days; and Shaftesbury himself, though he had no religion, was said to regard predictions. The Sailor is not accounted very natural, but he is very pleasant.

With this play was opened the New Theatre, under the direction of Betterton the tragedian; where he exhibited two years afterwards (1687) "The Mourning Bride," a tragedy, so written as to show him sufficiently qualified for either kind of dramatic poetry.

In this play, of which, when he afterwards revised it, he reduced the versification to greater regularity, there is more bustle than sentiment; the plot is busy and intricate, and the events take hold on the attention; but, except a very few passages, we are rather amused with noise, and perplexed with stratagem, than entertained with any true delineation of natural characters. This, however, was received with more benevolence than any other of his works, and still continues to be acted and applauded.

But whatever objections may be made either to his comic or tragic excellence, they are lost at once in the blaze of admiration, when it is remembered that he had produced these four plays before he had passed his twenty-fifth year, before other men, even such as are sometime to shine in eminence, have passed their probation of literature, or presume to hope for any other notice than such as is bestowed on diligence and inquiry. Among all the efforts of early genius which literary history records, I doubt whether any one can be produced that more surpasses the common limits of nature than the plays of Congreve.

About this time began the long-continued controversy between Collier and the poets. In the reign of Charles the First the Puritans had raised a violent clamour against the drama, which they considered as an entertainment not lawful to Christians, an opinion held by them in common with the church of Rome; and Prynne published "Histriomastix," a huge volume, in which stage-plays were censured. The outrages and crimes of the Puritans brought afterwards their whole system of doctrine into disrepute, and from the Restoration the poets and players were left at quiet; for to have molested them would have had the appearance of tendency to puritanical malignity.

This danger, however, was worn away by time; and Collier, a fierce and implacable

Nonjuror,[1] knew that an attack upon the theatre would never make him suspected for a Puritan; he therefore (1698) published "A short View of the Immorality and Profaneness of the English Stage," I believe with no other motive than religious zeal and honest indignation. He was formed for a controvertist; with sufficient learning; with diction vehement and pointed, though often vulgar and incorrect; with unconquerable pertinacity; with wit in the highest degree keen and sarcastic; and with all those powers, exalted and invigorated by just confidence in his cause.

Thus qualified, and thus incited, he walked out to battle, and assailed at once most of the living writers, from Dryden to D'Urfey.[2] His onset was violent; those passages, which, while they stood single had passed with little notice, when they were accumulated and exposed together, excited horror; the wise and the pious caught the alarm; and the nation wondered why it had so long suffered irreligion and licentiousness to be openly taught at the public charge.

Nothing now remained for the poets but to resist or fly. Dryden's conscience, or his prudence, angry as he was, withheld him from the conflict: Congreve and Vanbrugh attempted answers. Congreve, a very young man, elated with success, and impatient of censure, assumed an air of confidence and security. His chief artifice of controversy is to retort upon his adversary his own words; he is very angry, and, hoping to conquer Collier with his own weapons, allows himself in the use of every term of contumely and contempt; but he has the sword without the arm of Scanderbeg; he has his antagonist's coarseness, but not his strength. Collier replied; for contest was his delight, he was not to be frighted from his purpose or his prey.

The cause of Congreve was not tenable; whatever glosses he might use for the defence or palliation of single passages, the general tenor and tendency of his plays must always be condemned. It is acknowledged, with universal conviction, that the perusal of his works will make no man better; and that their ultimate effect is to represent pleasure in alliance with vice, and to relax those obligations by which life ought to be regulated.

---

[1] one who in 1689 refused to swear allegiance to William and Mary as king and queen [2] Tom D'Urfey, a disreputable writer

The stage found other advocates, and the dispute was protracted through ten years: but at last Comedy grew more modest; and Collier lived to see the reward of his labour in the reformation of the theatre.

Of the powers by which this important victory was achieved, a quotation from "Love for Love," and the remark upon it, may afford a specimen:

"*Sir Samps.* Sampson's a very good name; for your Sampsons were strong dogs from the beginning.

"*Angel.* Have a care — If you remember, the strongest Sampson of your name pull'd an old house over his head at last."

Here you have the Sacred History burlesqued; and Sampson once more brought into the house of Dagon, to make sport for the Philistines.

Congreve's last play was "The Way of the World;" which, though as he hints in his dedication it was written with great labour and much thought, was received with so little favour, that, being in a high degree offended and disgusted, he resolved to commit his quiet and his fame no more to the caprices of an audience.

From this time his life ceased to the public; he lived for himself and for his friends; and among his friends was able to name every man of his time whom wit and elegance had raised to reputation. It may be therefore reasonably supposed that his manners were polite, and his conversation pleasing.

He seems not to have taken much pleasure in writing, as he contributed nothing to the Spectator, and only one paper to the Tatler, though published by men with whom he might be supposed willing to associate; and though he lived many years after the publication of his "Miscellaneous Poems," yet he added nothing to them, but lived on in literary indolence; engaged in no controversy, contending with no rival, neither soliciting flattery by public commendations, nor provoking enmity by malignant criticism, but passing his time among the great and splendid, in the placid enjoyment of his fame and fortune.

Having owed his fortune to Halifax, he continued always of his patron's party, but, as it seems, without violence or acrimony; and his firmness was naturally esteemed, as his abilities were reverenced. His security therefore was never violated; and when, upon the extrusion of the Whigs, some intercession was used lest Congreve should be displaced, the earl of Oxford made this answer:

"Non obtusa adeo gestamus pectora Poeni,
   Nec tam aversus equos Tyria sol jungit ab urbe."[1]

He that was thus honoured by the adverse party might naturally expect to be advanced when his friends returned to power, and he was accordingly made secretary for the island of Jamaica; a place, I suppose, without trust or care, but which, with his post in the customs, is said to have afforded him twelve hundred pounds a year.

His honours were yet far greater than his profits. Every writer mentioned him with respect; and, among other testimonies to his merit, Steele made him the patron of his Miscellany, and Pope inscribed to him his translation of the Iliad.

But he treated the Muses with ingratitude; for, having long conversed familiarly with the great, he wished to be considered rather as a man of fashion than of wit; and, when he received a visit from Voltaire, disgusted him by the despicable foppery of desiring to be considered not as an author but a gentleman; to which the Frenchman replied, "that, if he had been only a gentleman, he should not have come to visit him."

In his retirement he may be supposed to have applied himself to books; for he discovers more literature than the poets have commonly attained. But his studies were in his latter days obstructed by cataracts in his eyes, which at last terminated in blindness. This melancholy state was aggravated by the gout, for which he sought relief by a journey to Bath; but, being overturned in his chariot, complained from that time of a pain in his side, and died at his house in Surrey-street in the Strand, Jan. 29, 1728-9. Having lain in state in the Jerusalem-chamber,[2] he was buried in Westminster-abbey, where a monument is erected to his memory by Henrietta, duchess of Marlborough, to whom, for reasons either not known or not mentioned, he bequeathed a legacy of about ten thousand pounds; the accumulation of attentive parsimony, which though to her superfluous and useless, might have given great assistance to the ancient family from which he descended,

---

[1] We Carthaginians bear not such blunted souls, nor does the sun averse from our city yoke his steeds. [2] Cf. 2 *Henry IV*, Act iv, sc. v.

at that time, by the imprudence of his relation, reduced to difficulties and distress.

Congreve has merit of the highest kind; he is an original writer, who borrowed neither the models of his plot nor the manner of his dialogue. Of his plays I cannot speak distinctly; for since I inspected them many years have passed; but what remains upon my memory is, that his characters are commonly fictitious and artificial, with very little of nature, and not much of life. He formed a peculiar idea of comic excellence, which he supposed to consist in gay remarks and unexpected answers; but that which he endeavoured, he seldom failed of performing. His scenes exhibit not much of humour, imagery, or passion; his personages are a kind of intellectual gladiators; every sentence is to ward or strike; the contest of smartness is never intermitted; his wit is a meteor playing to and fro with alternate coruscations. His comedies have therefore, in some degree, the operation of tragedies; they surprise rather than divert, and raise admiration oftener than merriment. But they are the works of a mind replete with images, and quick in combination.

Of his miscellaneous poetry I cannot say any thing very favourable. The powers of Congreve seem to desert him when he leaves the stage, as Antaeus[1] was no longer strong than when he could touch the ground. It cannot be observed without wonder, that a mind so vigorous and fertile in dramatic compositions should on any other occasion discover nothing but impotence and poverty. He has in these little pieces neither elevation of fancy, selection of language, nor skill in versification; yet, if I were required to select from the whole mass of English poetry the most poetical paragraph, I know not what I could prefer to an exclamation in "The Mourning Bride":

Alm. It was a fancy'd noise; for all is hush'd.
Leo. It bore the accent of a human voice.
Alm. It was thy fear, or else some transient wind
Whistling through hollows of this vaulted aisle:
We'll listen —
Leo. Hark!
Alm. No, all is hush'd and still as death. — 'Tis dreadful!
How reverend is the face of this tall pile,
Whose ancient pillars rear their marble heads,

[1] Cf. Gayley, p. 238.

To bear aloft its arch'd and ponderous roof,
By its own weight made steadfast and immoveable,
Looking tranquillity! It strikes an awe
And terror on my aching sight; the tombs
And monumental caves of death look cold,
And shoot a chillness to my trembling heart.
Give me thy hand, and let me hear thy voice;
Nay, quickly speak to me, and let me hear
Thy voice — my own affrights me with its echoes.

He who reads these lines enjoys for a moment the powers of a poet; he feels what he remembers to have felt before; but he feels it with great increase of sensibility; he recognizes a familiar image, but meets it again amplified and expanded, embellished with beauty, and enlarged with majesty.

Yet could the author, who appears here to have enjoyed the confidence of Nature, lament the death of queen Mary in lines like these:

The rocks are cleft, and new-descending rills
Furrow the brows of all the impending hills.
The water-gods to floods their rivulets turn,
And each, with streaming eyes, supplies his wanting urn.
The Fauns forsake the woods, the Nymphs the grove,
And round the plain in sad distractions rove:
In prickly brakes their tender limbs they tear,
And leave on thorns their locks of golden hair.
With their sharp nails, themselves the Satyrs wound,
And tug their shaggy beards, and bite with grief the ground.
Lo Pan himself, beneath a blasted oak,
Dejected lies, his pipe in pieces broke.
See Pales[1] weeping too, in wild despair,
And to the piercing winds her bosom bare.
And see yon fading myrtle, where appears
The Queen of Love, all bath'd in flowing tears;
See how she wrings her hands, and beats her breast,
And tears her useless girdle from her waist!
Hear the sad murmurs of her sighing doves!
For grief they sigh, forgetful of their loves.

And, many years after, he gave no proof that time had improved his wisdom or his wit; for, on the death of the marquis of Blandford, this was his song:

And now the winds, which had so long been still,
Began the swelling air with sighs to fill!
The water nymphs, who motionless remain'd,
Like images of ice, while she complain'd,
Now loos'd their streams; as when descending rains

[1] goddess of pasturage and cattle

Roll the steep torrents headlong o'er the plains.
The prone creation, who so long had gaz'd,
Charm'd with her cries, and at her griefs amaz'd,
Began to roar and howl with horrid yell,
Dismal to hear, and terrible to tell !
Nothing but groans and sighs were heard around,
And Echo multiplied each mournful sound.

In both these funeral poems, when he has
yelled out many *syllables* of senseless *dolour*,
he dismisses his reader with senseless consolation : from the grave of Pastora[1] rises a light
that forms a star ; and where Amaryllis[2] wept
for Amyntas,[3] from every tear sprung up a
violet.

But William is his hero, and of William he
will sing :

The hovering winds on downy wings shall wait
    around,
And catch, and waft to foreign lands, the flying
    sound.

It cannot but be proper to show what they
shall have to catch and carry :

'Twas now when flowery lawns the prospect made,
And flowing brooks beneath a forest shade,
A lowing heifer, loveliest of the herd,
Stood feeding by ; while two fierce bulls prepar'd
Their armed heads for fight, by fate of war to
    prove
The victor worthy of the fair-one's love ;
Unthought presage of what met next my view ;
For soon the shady scene withdrew.
And now, for woods and fields, and springing
    flowers,
Behold a town arise, bulwark'd with walls and lofty
    towers ;
Two rival armies all the plain o'erspread,
Each in battalia rang'd, and shining arms array'd ;
With eager eyes beholding both from far
Namur, the prize and mistress of the war.

The "Birth of the Muse" is a miserable
fiction. One good line it has, which was borrowed from Dryden. The concluding verses
are these :

This said, no more remain'd. Th' etherial host
Again impatient crowd the crystal coast.
The Father, now, within his spacious hands
Encompass'd all the mingled mass of seas and
    lands ;
And, having heav'd aloft the ponderous sphere,
He launch'd the world to float in ambient air.

[1] Queen Mary [2] the Marchioness of Blandford
[3] the Marquis of Blandford

Of his irregular poems, that to Mrs. Arabella Hunt seems to be the best : his ode for
St. Cecilia's Day, however, has some lines
which Pope had in his mind when he wrote
his own.

His imitations of Horace are feebly para-
phrastical, and the additions which he makes
are of little value. He sometimes retains
what were more properly omitted, as when
he talks of *vervain* and *gums* to propitiate
Venus.

Of his translations, the satire of Juvenal
was written very early, and may therefore
be forgiven though it have not the massi-
ness and vigour of the original. In all his
versions strength and sprightliness are wanting : his Hymn to Venus, from Homer, is
perhaps the best. His lines are weakened
with expletives, and his rhymes are frequently
imperfect.

His petty poems are seldom worth the cost
of criticism ; sometimes the thoughts are false,
and sometimes common. In his verses on
Lady Gethin, the latter part is in imitation of
Dryden's ode on Mrs. Killigrew ; and Doris,
that has been so lavishly flattered by Steele,
has indeed some lively stanzas, but the expression might be mended ; and the most striking
part of the character had been already shown
in "Love for Love." His "Art of Pleasing"
is founded on a vulgar, but perhaps impracticable principle, and the staleness of the
sense is not concealed by any novelty of illustration or elegance of diction.

This tissue of poetry, from which he seems
to have hoped a lasting name, is totally neglected, and known only as appended to his
plays.

While comedy or while tragedy is regarded,
his plays are likely to be read ; but, except
what relates to the stage, I know not that he
has ever written a stanza that is sung, or a
couplet that is quoted. The general character
of his "Miscellanies" is, that they show little
wit, and little virtue.

Yet to him it must be confessed, that we
are indebted for the correction of a national
error, and for the cure of our Pindaric madness. He first taught the English writers that
Pindar's odes were regular ; and though certainly he had not the fire requisite for the
higher species of lyric poetry, he has shown
us, that enthusiasm has its rules, and that in
mere confusion there is neither grace nor
greatness.

ESSAY FROM THE RAMBLER

NO. 69.　TUESDAY, NOVEMBER 13, 1750

Flet quoque, ut in speculo rugas adspexit aniles,
Tyndaris; et secum, cur sit bis rapta, requirit.
Tempus edax rerum, tuque invidiosa vetustas
Omnia destruitis; vitiataque dentibus aevi
Paulatim lenta consumitis omnia morte.[1] — OVID.

An old Greek epigrammatist, intending to show the miseries that attend the last stage of man, imprecates upon those who are so foolish as to wish for long life, the calamity of continuing to grow old from century to century. He thought that no adventitious or foreign pain was requisite; that decrepitude itself was an epitome of whatever is dreadful; and nothing could be added to the curse of age, but that it should be extended beyond its natural limits.

The most indifferent or negligent spectator can indeed scarcely retire without heaviness of heart, from a view of the last scenes of the tragedy of life, in which he finds those, who in the former parts of the drama, were distinguished by opposition of conduct, contrariety of designs, and dissimilitude of personal qualities, all involved in one common distress, and all struggling with affliction which they cannot hope to overcome.

The other miseries, which waylay our passage through the world, wisdom may escape, and fortitude may conquer: by caution and circumspection we may steal along with very little to obstruct or incommode us; by spirit and vigour we may force a way, and reward the vexation of contest by the pleasures of victory. But a time must come when our policy and bravery shall be equally useless; when we shall all sink into helplessness and sadness, without any power of receiving solace from the pleasures that have formerly delighted us, or any prospect of emerging into a second possession of the blessings that we have lost.

[1] The dreadful wrinkles when poor Helen spy'd,
　Ah! why this second rape? — with tears she
　　cry'd.
　Time, thou devourer, and thou envious age,
　Who all destroy with keen corroding rage,
　Beneath your jaws, whate'er have pleas'd or
　　please,　　　　　．
　Must sink, consum'd by swift or slow degrees.
　　　　　　　　　　　　— ELPHINSTON.

The industry of man has, indeed, not been wanting in endeavours to procure comforts for these hours of dejection and melancholy, and to gild the dreadful gloom with artificial light. The most usual support of old age is wealth. He whose possessions are large, and whose chests are full, imagines himself always fortified against invasions on his authority. If he has lost all other means of government, if his strength and his reason fail him, he can at last alter his will; and therefore all that have hopes must likewise have fears, and he may still continue to give laws to such as have not ceased to regard their own interest.

This is, indeed, too frequently the citadel of the dotard, the last fortress to which age retires, and in which he makes the stand against the upstart race that seizes his domains, disputes his commands, and cancels his prescriptions. But here, though there may be safety, there is no pleasure; and what remains is but a proof that more was once possessed.

Nothing seems to have been more universally dreaded by the ancients than orbity, or want of children; and, indeed, to a man who has survived all the companions of his youth, all who have participated his pleasures and his cares, have been engaged in the same events, and filled their minds with the same conceptions, this full-peopled world is a dismal solitude. He stands forlorn and silent, neglected or insulted, in the midst of multitudes animated with hopes which he cannot share and employed in business which he is no longer able to forward or retard; nor can he find any to whom his life or his death are of importance, unless he has secured some domestic gratifications, some tender employments, and endeared himself to some whose interest and gratitude may unite them to him.

So different are the colours of life as we look forward to the future, or backward to the past; and so different the opinions and sentiments which this contrariety of appearance naturally produces, that the conversation of the old and young ends generally with contempt or pity on either side. To a young man entering the world with fulness of hope, and ardour of pursuit, nothing is so unpleasing as the cold caution, the faint expectations, the scrupulous diffidence, which experience and disappointments certainly infuse; and the old wonders in his turn that the world never can grow wiser, that neither precepts, nor testimonies can cure boys of their credulity and sufficiency; and that no one can be convinced that snares are laid for him, till he finds himself entangled.

Thus one generation is always the scorn and wonder of the other, and the notions of the old and young are like liquors of different gravity and texture which never can unite. The spirits of youth sublimed by health, and volatilised by passion, soon leave behind them the phlegmatic sediment of weariness and deliberation, and burst out in temerity and enterprise. The tenderness therefore which nature infuses, and which long habits of beneficence confirm, is necessary to reconcile such opposition; and an old man must be a father to bear with patience those follies and absurdities which he will perpetually imagine himself to find in the schemes and expectations, the pleasures and the sorrows, of those who have not yet been hardened by time, and chilled by frustration.

Yet it may be doubted, whether the pleasure of seeing children ripening into strength, be not overbalanced by the pain of seeing some fall in their blossom, and others blasted in their growth; some shaken down with storms, some tainted with cankers, and some shrivelled in the shade; and whether he that extends his care beyond himself, does not multiply his anxieties more than his pleasures, and weary himself to no purpose, by superintending what he cannot regulate.

But, though age be to every order of human beings sufficiently terrible, it is particularly to be dreaded by fine ladies, who have had no other end or ambition than to fill up the day and the night with dress, diversions, and flattery, and who, having made no acquaintance with knowledge, or with business, have constantly caught all their ideas from the current prattle of the hour, and been indebted for all their happiness to compliments and treats. With these ladies, age begins early, and very often lasts long; it begins when their beauty fades, when their mirth loses its sprightliness, and their motion its ease. From that time all which gave them joy vanishes from about them; they hear the praises bestowed on others, which used to swell their bosoms with exultation. They visit the seats of felicity, and endeavour to continue the habit of being delighted. But pleasure is only received when we believe that we give it in return. Neglect and petulance inform them that their power and their value are past;

AE

and what then remains but a tedious and comfortless uniformity of time, without any motion of the heart, or exercise of the reason?

Yet, however age may discourage us by its appearance from considering it in prospect, we shall all by degrees certainly be old; and therefore we ought to inquire what provision can be made against that time of distress? what happiness can be stored up against the winter of life? and how we may pass our latter years with serenity and cheerfulness?

If it has been found by the experience of mankind, that not even the best seasons of life are able to supply sufficient gratifications, without anticipating uncertain felicities, it cannot surely be supposed that old age, worn with labours, harassed with anxieties, and tortured with diseases, should have any gladness of its own, or feel any satisfaction from the contemplation of the present. All the comfort that can now be expected must be recalled from the past, or borrowed from the future; the past is very soon exhausted, all the events or actions of which the memory can afford pleasure are quickly recollected; and the future lies beyond the grave, where it can be reached only by virtue and devotion.

Piety is the only proper and adequate relief of decaying man. He that grows old without religious hopes, as he declines into imbecility, and feels pains and sorrows incessantly crowding upon him, falls into a gulf of bottomless misery, in which every reflection must plunge him deeper, and where he finds only new gradations of anguish, and precipices of horror.

From LONDON

By numbers here from shame or censure free
All crimes are safe, but hated poverty.　155
This, only this, the rigid law pursues;
This, only this, provokes the snarling muse.
The sober trader at a tatter'd cloak
Wakes from his dream, and labours for a joke;
With brisker air the silken courtiers gaze, 160
And turn the varied taunt a thousand ways.
Of all the griefs that harass the distress'd,
Sure the most bitter is a scornful jest;
Fate never wounds more deep the gen'rous heart,　.
Than when a blockhead's insult points the dart.　.　165
　Has heaven reserv'd, in pity to the poor,
No pathless waste, or undiscover'd shore?
No secret island in the boundless main?

No peaceful desert yet unclaim'd by Spain?
Quick let us rise, the happy seats explore, 170
And bear oppression's insolence no more.
This mournful truth is ev'ry where confess'd:
Slow rises worth, by poverty depress'd;
But here more slow, where all are slaves to
   gold,
Where looks are merchandise, and smiles are
   sold;   175
Where won by bribes, by flatteries implor'd,
The groom retails the favours of his lord.
  But hark! th' affrighted crowd's tumultu-
   ous cries
Roll through the streets, and thunder to the
   skies.
Rais'd from some pleasing dream of wealth
   and pow'r,   180
Some pompous palace, or some blissful bow'r,
Aghast you start, and scarce with aching sight
Sustain the approaching fire's tremendous
   light;
Swift from pursuing horrors take your way,
And leave your little All to flames a prey; 185
Then thro' the world a wretched vagrant
   roam,
For where can starving merit find a home?
In vain your mournful narrative disclose,
While all neglect, and most insult your woes.

FROM THE VANITY OF HUMAN
WISHES

Let observation, with extensive view,
Survey mankind, from China to Peru;
Remark each anxious toil, each eager strife,
And watch the busy scenes of crowded life:
Then say how hope and fear, desire and hate, 5
O'erspread with snares the clouded maze of
   fate,
Where wav'ring man, betray'd by vent'rous
   pride
To tread the dreary paths without a guide,
As treach'rous phantoms in the mist delude,
Shuns fancied ills, or chases airy good;   10
How rarely reason guides the stubborn choice,
Rules the bold hand, or prompts the suppliant
   voice;
How nations sink, by darling schemes op-
   press'd,
When Vengeance listens to the fool's request.
Fate wings with ev'ry wish th' afflictive dart,
Each gift of nature and each grace of art; 16
With fatal heat impetuous courage glows,
With fatal sweetness elocution flows,

Impeachment stops the speaker's pow'rful
   breath,
And restless fire precipitates on death.   20
  But scarce observ'd, the knowing and the
   bold
Fall in the gen'ral massacre of gold;
Wide-wasting pest! that rages unconfin'd,
And crowds with crimes the records of man-
   kind;
For gold his sword the hireling ruffian draws,
For gold the hireling judge distorts the
   laws: 26
Wealth heap'd on wealth nor truth nor safety
   buys;
The dangers gather as the treasures rise.

*   *   *   *   *   *

On what foundation stands the warrior's
   pride,
How just his hopes, let Swedish Charles[1] de-
   cide:
A frame of adamant, a soul of fire,
No dangers fright him, and no labours tire;
O'er love, o'er fear, extends his wide domain,
Unconquer'd lord of pleasure and of pain; 196
No joys to him pacific sceptres yield, —
War sounds the trump, he rushes to the field;
Behold surrounding kings their pow'rs com-
   bine,
And one capitulate, and one resign: 200
Peace courts his hand, but spreads her charms
   in vain;
"Think nothing gain'd," he cries, "till naught
   remain,
On Moscow's walls till Gothic[2] standards fly,
And all be mine beneath the polar sky."
The march begins in military state,   205
And nations on his eye suspended wait;
Stern Famine guards the solitary coast,
And Winter barricades the realms of Frost:
He comes; nor want nor cold his course
   delay; —
Hide, blushing Glory, hide Pultowa's day: 210
The vanquish'd hero leaves his broken bands,
And shows his miseries in distant lands;
Condemn'd a needy supplicant to wait,
While ladies interpose and slaves debate.
But did not Chance at length her error mend?
Did no subverted empire mark his end?   216
Did rival monarchs give the fatal wound?
Or hostile millions press him to the ground?
His fall was destin'd to a barren strand,
A petty fortress, and a dubious hand.   220

[1] Charles XII   [2] here = Swedish

He left the name, at which the world grew
    pale,
To point a moral, or adorn a tale.

*   * .   *   *   *   *   *

    But grant, the virtues of a temp'rate prime [1]
Bless with an age exempt from scorn or crime;
An age that melts with unperceiv'd decay,
And glides in modest innocence away;
Whose peaceful day Benevolence endears, 295
Whose night congratulating Conscience
    cheers;
The gen'ral fav'rite as the gen'ral friend:
Such age there is, and who shall wish its end?
    Yet ev'n on this her load Misfortune flings,
To press the weary minutes' flagging wings,
New sorrow rises as the day returns,   301
A sister sickens, or a daughter mourns.
Now kindred Merit fills the sable bier,
Now lacerated Friendship claims a tear.
Year chases year, decay pursues decay, 305
Still drops some joy from with'ring life away;
New forms arise, and diff'rent views engage,
Superfluous lags the vet'ran on the stage,
Till pitying Nature signs the last release,
And bids afflicted worth retire to peace. 310
    But few there are whom hours like these
    await,
Who set unclouded in the gulphs of Fate.
From Lydia's monarch [2] should the search
    descend,
By Solon caution'd to regard his end, 314
In life's last scene what prodigies surprise —
Fears of the brave, and follies of the wise!
From Marlb'rough's eyes the streams of do-
    tage flow,
And Swift expires a driv'ler and a show.

*   *   *   *   *   *   *

    Where then shall Hope and Fear their
    objects find?
Must dull Suspense corrupt the stagnant
    mind?
Must helpless man, in ignorance sedate, 345
Roll darkling down the torrent of his fate?
Must no dislike alarm, no wishes rise,
No cries invoke the mercies of the skies? —
Enquirer, cease; petitions yet remain,
Which heav'n may hear; nor deem religion
    vain.
                    350
Still raise for good the supplicating voice,
But leave to heav'n the measure and the
    choice;

      [1] youth   [2] Crœsus

Safe in his pow'r, whose eyes discern afar
The secret ambush of a specious pray'r.
Implore his aid, in his decisions rest, 355
Secure, whate'er he gives, he gives the best.
Yet when the sense of sacred presence fires,
And strong devotion to the skies aspires,
Pour forth thy fervours for a healthful
    mind,
Obedient passions, and a will resign'd; 360
For love, which scarce collective man can
    fill;
For patience, sov'reign o'er transmuted ill;
For faith, that, panting for a happier seat,
Counts death kind Nature's signal of retreat:
These goods for man the laws of heav'n
    ordain;   365
These goods He grants, who grants the pow'r
    to gain;
With these celestial Wisdom calms the
    mind,
And makes the happiness she does not find.

WILLIAM SHENSTONE
(1714–1763)

WRITTEN AT AN INN AT HENLEY

To thee, fair freedom! I retire
    From flattery, cards, and dice, and din;
Nor art thou found in mansions higher
    Than the low cot, or humble inn.   4

'Tis here with boundless pow'r I reign;
    And every health which I begin,
Converts dull port to bright champagne;
    Such freedom crowns it, at an inn.   8

I fly from pomp, I fly from plate!
    I fly from falsehood's specious grin!
Freedom I love, and form I hate,
    And choose my lodgings at an inn.   12

Here, waiter! take my sordid ore,
    Which lacqueys else might hope to win;
It buys, what courts have not in store;
    It buys me freedom at an inn.   16

Whoe'er has travell'd life's dull round,
    Where'er his stages may have been,
May sigh to think he still has found
    The warmest welcome, at an inn.   20

From THE SCHOOL–MISTRESS

IN IMITATION OF SPENSER

Ah me ! full sorely is my heart forlorn,
To think how modest worth neglected lies ;
While partial fame doth with her blasts
    adorn
Such deeds alone, as pride and pomp dis-
    guise ;
Deeds of ill sort, and mischievous emprize :
Lend me thy clarion, goddess ! let me try
To sound the praise of merit, ere it dies ;
Such as I oft have chaunced to espy,
Lost in the dreary shades of dull obscurity.   9

In ev'ry village mark'd with little spire,
Embow'r'd in trees, and hardly known to
    fame,
There dwells, in lowly shed, and mean attire,
A matron old, whom we school-mistress
    name ;
Who boasts unruly brats with birch to
    tame ;
They grieven sore, in piteous durance pent,
Aw'd by the pow'r of this relentless dame ;
And oft-times, on vagaries idly bent,
For unkempt hair, or talk unconn'd, are sorely
    shent.[1]   18

And all in sight doth rise a birchen tree,
Which learning near her little dome did
    stow ;
Whilom a twig of small regard to see,
Tho' now so wide its waving branches flow ;
And work the simple vassals mickle woe ;
For not a wind might curl the leaves that
    blew,
But their limbs shudder'd, and their pulse
    beat low ;
And as they look'd they found their horror
    grew,
And shap'd it into rods, and tingled at the
    view.   27

*   *   *   *   *   *   *

A russet stole was o'er her shoulders thrown ;
A russet kirtle fenc'd the nipping air ;
'Twas simple russet,[2] but it was her own ;
'Twas her own country bred the flock so
    fair ;
'Twas her own labour did the fleece pre-
    pare ;

And, sooth to say, her pupils, rang'd around,
Thro' pious awe, did term it passing rare ;
For they in gaping wonderment abound,
And think, no doubt, she been the greatest
    wight on ground.   72

Albeit ne flatt'ry did corrupt her truth,
Ne pompous title did debauch her ear ;
Goody, good-woman, gossip, n'aunt,[1] for-
    sooth,
Or dame, the sole additions[2] she did hear ;
Yet these she challeng'd, these she held
    right dear :
Ne would esteem him act as mought behove,
Who should not honour'd eld with these
    revere :
For never title yet so mean could prove,
But there was eke a mind which did that title
    love.   81

One ancient hen she took delight to feed,
The plodding pattern of the busy dame ;
Which, ever and anon, impell'd by need,
Into her school, begirt with chickens, came ;
Such favour did her past deportment claim :
And, if neglect had lavish'd on the ground
Fragment of bread, she[3] would collect the
    same ;
For well she[3] knew, and quaintly could ex-
    pound,
What sin it were to waste the smallest crumb
    she found.   90

*   *   *   *   *   *   *

In elbow chair, like that of Scottish stem
By the sharp tooth of cank'ring eld defac'd,
In which, when he receives his diadem,
Our sov'reign prince and liefest liege is
    plac'd,
The matron sate ; and some with rank she
    grac'd,
(The source of children's and of courtier's
    pride !)
Redress'd affronts, for vile affronts there
    pass'd ;
And warn'd them not the fretful to deride,
But love each other dear, whatever them be-
    tide.   144

Right well she knew each temper to descry ;
To thwart the proud, and the submiss[4] to
    raise ;

---

[1] put to shame   [2] undyed homespun

[1] mine aunt ; cf. nuncle in *King Lear*, I, iv, 117
[2] titles   [3] the hen   [4] submissive

Some with vile copper prize[1] exalt on high,
And some entice with pittance small of
praise;
And other some with baleful sprig she 'frays:
Ev'n absent, she the reins of pow'r doth
hold,
While with quaint arts the giddy crowd she
sways; 151
Forewarn'd, if little bird their pranks be-
hold,
'Twill whisper in her ear, and all the scene
unfold. 153

Lo, now with state she utters the command!
Eftsoons the urchins to their tasks repair;
Their books of stature small they take in
hand,
Which with pellucid horn secured are,[2]
To save from finger wet the letters fair:
The work so gay, that on their back is seen,
St. George's high atchievements does de-
clare;
On which thilk wight[3] that has y-gazing been
Kens the forth-coming rod, unpleasing sight,
I ween! 162

Ah, luckless he, and born beneath the beam
Of evil star! it irks me whilst I write!
As erst the bard[4] by Mulla's silver stream,
Oft, as he told of deadly dolorous plight,
Sigh'd as he sung, and did in tears indite.
For brandishing the rod, she doth begin
To loose the brogues,[5] the stripling's late
delight!
And down they drop; appears his dainty
skin,
Fair as the furry coat of whitest ermilin. 171

O ruthful scene! when from a nook obscure,
His little sister doth his peril see:
All playful as she sate, she grows demure;
She finds full soon her wonted spirits flee;
She meditates a pray'r to set him free:
Nor gentle pardon could this dame deny,
(If gentle pardon could with dames agree)
To her sad grief that swells in either eye,
And wrings her so that all for pity she could
die. 180

No longer can she now her shrieks command;
And hardly she forbears thro' aweful fear,

To rushen forth, and, with presumptuous
hand,
To stay harsh justice in its mid career.
On thee she calls, on thee, her parent dear!
(Ah! too remote to ward the shameful
blow!)
She sees no kind domestic visage near,
And soon a flood of tears begins to flow;
And gives a loose at last to unavailing woe.

* * * * * * *

The other tribe, aghast, with sore dismay,
Attend, and conn their tasks with mickle
care: 191
By turns, astony'd, ev'ry twig survey,
And, from their fellow's hateful wounds,
beware;
Knowing, I wist,[1] how each the same may
share;
'Till fear has taught them a performance
meet,
And to the well-known chest the dame re-
pair;
Whence oft with sugar'd cates she doth 'em
greet,
And ginger-bread y-rare; now, certes, doubly
sweet! 207

* * * * * * *

THOMAS GRAY (1716–1771)

AN ODE

ON A DISTANT PROSPECT OF ETON COLLEGE

Ye distant spires, ye antique towers,
　That crown the watry glade,
Where grateful Science still adores
　Her Henry's[2] holy Shade;
And ye, that from the stately brow　　　5
Of Windsor's heights th' expanse below
　Of grove, of lawn, of mead survey,
Whose turf, whose shade, whose flowers among
Wanders the hoary Thames along
　His silver-winding way.　　　10

Ah, happy hills, ah, pleasing shade,
　Ah, fields belov'd in vain,
Where once my careless childhood stray'd,
　A stranger yet to pain!

----

[1] a penny　[2] hornbooks　[3] that person　[4] Edmund Spenser　[5] breeches

[1] certainly　[2] Henry VI, the founder of Eton

I feel the gales, that from ye blow,   15
A momentary bliss bestow,
  As waving fresh their gladsome wing,
My weary soul they seem to sooth,
And, redolent of joy and youth,
  To breathe a second spring.   20

Say, Father Thames, for thou hast seen
  Full many a sprightly race
Disporting on thy margent green
  The paths of pleasure trace,
Who foremost now delight to cleave   25
With pliant arm thy glassy wave?
  The captive linnet which enthrall?
What idle progeny succeed
To chase the rolling circle's speed,
  Or urge the flying ball?   30

While some on earnest business bent
  Their murm'ring labours ply
'Gainst graver hours, that bring constraint
  To sweeten liberty:
Some bold adventurers disdain   35
The limits of their little reign,
  And unknown regions dare descry:
Still as they run they look behind,
They hear a voice in every wind,
  And snatch a fearful joy.   40

Gay hope is theirs by fancy fed,
  Less pleasing when possest;
The tear forgot as soon as shed,
  The sunshine of the breast:
Theirs buxom health of rŏsy hue,   45
Wild wit, invention ever-new,
  And lively cheer of vigour born;
The thoughtless day, the easy night,
The spirits pure, the slumbers light,
  That fly th' approach of morn.   50

Alas, regardless of their doom,
  The little victims play!
No sense have they of ills to come,
  Nor care beyond to-day:
Yet see how all around 'em wait   55
The Ministers of human fate,
  And black Misfortune's baleful train!
Ah, shew them where in ambush stand
To seize their prey the murth'rous band!
  Ah, tell them, they are men!   60

These[1] shall the fury[2] Passions tear,
  The vultures of the mind,

      [1] *dir. obj.*   [2] *a noun epithet*

Disdainful Anger, pallid Fear,
  And Shame that skulks behind;
Or pining Love shall waste their youth,   65
Or Jealousy with rankling tooth,
  That inly gnaws the secret heart,
And Envy wan, and faded Care,
Grim-visag'd comfortless Despair,
  And Sorrow's piercing dart.   70

Ambition this[1] shall tempt to rise,
  Then whirl the wretch from high,
To bitter Scorn a sacrifice,
  And grinning Infamy.
The stings of Falsehood those shall try,   75
And hard Unkindness' alter'd eye,
  That mocks the tear it forc'd to flow;
And keen Remorse with blood defil'd,
And moody Madness laughing wild
  Amid severest woe.   80

Lo, in the vale of years beneath
  A griesly troop are seen,
The painful family of Death,
  More hideous than their Queen:
This racks the joints, this fires the veins,   85
That every labouring sinew strains,
  Those in the deeper vitals rage:
Lo, Poverty, to fill the band,
That numbs the soul with icy hand,
  And slow-consuming Age.   90

To each his suff'rings: all are men,
  Condemn'd alike to groan,
The tender for another's pain;
  Th' unfeeling for his own.
Yet ah! why should they know their fate? 95
Since sorrow never comes too late,
  And happiness too swiftly flies.
Thought would destroy their paradise.
No more; where ignorance is bliss,
  'Tis folly to be wise.   100

      [1] *this one*

ELEGY

WRITTEN IN A COUNTRY CHURCH-YARD

The Curfew tolls the knell of parting day,
  The lowing herd wind slowly o'er the lea,
The plowman homeward plods his weary way,
  And leaves the world to darkness and to me.

Now fades the glimmering landscape on the
   sight, 5
And all the air¹ a solemn stillness holds,
Save where the beetle wheels his droning flight,
   And drowsy tinklings lull the distant folds;²

Save that from yonder ivy-mantled tow'r
   The moping owl does to the moon complain
Of such, as wand'ring near her secret bow'r, 11
   Molest her ancient solitary reign.

Beneath those rugged elms, that yew-tree's
   shade,
Where heaves the turf in many a mould'ring
   heap,
Each in his narrow cell for ever laid, 15
   The rude Forefathers of the hamlet sleep.

The breezy call of incense-breathing Morn,
   The swallow twitt'ring from the straw-built³
   shed,
The cock's shrill clarion, or the echoing horn,⁴
   No more shall rouse them from their lowly
   bed. 20

For them no more the blazing hearth shall
   burn,
   Or busy housewife ply her evening care:
No children run to lisp their sire's return,
   Or climb his knees the envied kiss to share.

Oft did the harvest to their sickle yield, 25
   Their furrow oft the stubborn glebe has
   broke;
How jocund did they drive their team afield!
   How bow'd the woods beneath their sturdy
   stroke!

Let not Ambition mock their useful toil,
   Their homely joys, and destiny obscure; 30
Nor Grandeur hear with a disdainful smile,
   The short and simple annals of the poor.

The boast of heraldry, the pomp of pow'r,
   And all that beauty, all that wealth e'er
   gave,
Awaits alike th' inevitable hour.⁵ 35
   The paths of glory lead but to the grave.

Nor you, ye Proud, impute to These the fault,
   If Mem'ry o'er their Tomb no Trophies
   raise,

¹ dir. obj. ² sheep folds ³ thatched ⁴ of the
hunters ⁵ subject

Where thro' the long-drawn aisle and fretted
   vault
   The pealing anthem swells the note of praise.

Can storied urn or animated bust 41
   Back to its mansion call the fleeting breath?
Can Honour's voice provoke¹ the silent dust,
   Or Flatt'ry sooth² the dull cold ear of
   Death?

Perhaps in this neglected spot is laid 45
   Some heart once pregnant with celestial fire;
Hands, that the rod of empire might have
   sway'd,
   Or wak'd to extasy the living lyre.

But Knowledge to their eyes her ample page
   Rich with the spoils of time did ne'er unroll;
Chill Penury repress'd their noble rage, 51
   And froze the genial current of the soul.

Full many a gem of purest ray serene,
   The dark unfathom'd caves of ocean bear:
Full many a flower is born to blush unseen, 55
   And waste its sweetness on the desert air.

Some village-Hampden, that with dauntless
   breast
   The little Tyrant of his fields withstood;
Some mute inglorious Milton here may rest,
   Some Cromwell guiltless of his country's
   blood. 60

Th' applause of list'ning senates to command,
   The threats of pain and ruin to despise,
To scatter plenty o'er a smiling land,
   And read their hist'ry in a nation's eyes,

Their lot forbade: nor circumscrib'd alone 65
   Their growing virtues, but their crimes con-
   fin'd;
Forbade to wade through slaughter to a throne,
   And shut the gates of mercy on mankind,

The struggling pangs of conscious truth to hide,
   To quench the blushes of ingenuous shame,
Or heap the shrine of Luxury and Pride 71
   With incense kindled at the Muse's flame.

Far from the madding crowd's ignoble strife,
   Their sober wishes never learn'd to stray;
Along the cool sequester'd vale of life 75
   They kept the noiseless tenor of their way.

¹ to call forth to action ² humor by assenting

Yet ev'n these bones from insult to protect,
Some frail memorial still erected nigh,
With uncouth rhymes and shapeless sculpture
deck'd,
Implores the passing tribute of a sigh. 80

Their name, their years, spelt by th' unletter'd
Muse,
The place of fame and elegy supply:
And many a holy text around she strews,
That teach the rustic moralist to die.

For who to dumb Forgetfulness a prey, 85
This pleasing anxious being e'er resign'd,
Left the warm precincts of the cheerful day,
Nor cast one longing ling'ring look behind?

On some fond breast the parting soul relies,
Some pious drops the closing eye requires;
Ev'n from the tomb the voice of Nature
cries, 91
Ev'n in our Ashes live their wonted Fires.

For thee, who mindful of th' unhonour'd Dead
Dost in these lines their artless tale relate;
If chance,[1] by lonely contemplation led, 95
Some kindred Spirit shall inquire thy fate,

Haply some hoary-headed Swain may say,
"Oft have we seen him at the peep of dawn
Brushing with hasty steps the dews away,
To meet the sun upon the upland lawn. 100

"There at the foot of yonder nodding beech
That wreathes its old fantastic roots so high,
His listless length at noontide would he stretch,
And pore upon the brook that babbles by.

"Hard by yon wood, now smiling as in scorn,
Mutt'ring his wayward fancies he would
rove, 106
Now drooping, woeful wan, like one forlorn,
Or craz'd with care, or cross'd in hopeless
love.

"One morn I miss'd him on the custom'd hill,
Along the heath and near his fav'rite tree,
Another came; nor yet beside the rill, 111
Nor up the lawn, nor at the wood was he;

"The next, with dirges due in sad array
Slow thro' the church-way path we saw him
borne.

[1] if perchance

Approach and read (for thou can'st read) the
lay, 115
Grav'd on the stone beneath yon aged
thorn."

THE EPITAPH

Here rests his head upon the lap of Earth
A Youth to Fortune and to Fame unknown.
Fair Science frown'd not on his humble birth,
And Melancholy mark'd him for her own. 120

Large was his bounty, and his soul sincere,
Heav'n did a recompense as largely send:
He gave to Mis'ry all he had, a tear,
He gain'd from Heav'n ('twas all he wish'd) a
friend.

No farther seek his merits to disclose, 125
Or draw his frailties from their dread abode,
(There they alike in trembling hope repose)
The bosom of his Father and his God.

THE PROGRESS OF POESY

A PINDARIC ODE

I

THE STROPHE

Awake, Æolian[1] lyre, awake,
And give to rapture all thy trembling strings.
From Helicon's[2] harmonious springs
A thousand rills their mazy progress take:
The laughing flowers, that round them blow,
Drink life and fragrance as they flow. 6
Now the rich stream of music winds along
Deep, majestic, smooth, and strong,
Thro' verdant vales, and Ceres' golden reign:[3]
Now rolling down the steep amain, 10
Headlong, impetuous, see it pour:
The rocks, and nodding groves rebellow to the
roar.

THE ANTISTROPHE

Oh! Sovereign of the willing soul,
Parent of sweet and solemn-breathing airs,
Enchanting shell![4] the sullen Cares, 15
And frantic Passions hear thy soft control.

[1] Pindaric, for so Pindar called his poetry
[2] Aganippe and Hippocrene, the fountains of the
Muses at the foot of Mt. Helicon   [3] fields of grain
[4] the lyre

On Thracia's hills the Lord of War,[1]
Has curb'd the fury of his car,
And dropp'd his thirsty lance at thy command.
Perching on the scept'red hand   20
Of Jove, thy magic lulls the feather'd king[2]
With ruffled plumes, and flagging wing:
Quench'd in dark clouds of slumber lie
The terror of his beak, and light'nings of his
    eye.

THE EPODE

Thee the voice, the dance, obey,   25
Temper'd to thy warbled lay.
O'er Idalia's[3] velvet-green
The rosy-crownèd Loves are seen
On Cytherea's day
With antic Sports, and blue-eyed Pleasures, 30
Frisking light in frolic measures;
Now pursuing, now retreating,
Now in circling troops they meet:
To brisk notes in cadence beating
Glance their many-twinkling feet.   35
Slow melting strains their Queen's approach
    declare:
Where'er she turns the Graces homage pay.
With arms sublime, that float upon the air,
In gliding state she wins her easy way:
O'er her warm cheek, and rising bosom, move
The bloom of young Desire, and purple light
    of Love.   41

II

THE STROPHE

Man's feeble race what Ills await,
Labour, and Penury, the racks of Pain,
Disease, and Sorrow's weeping train,
And Death, sad refuge from the storms of
    Fate!   45
The fond complaint, my Song, disprove,
And justify the laws of Jove.
Say, has he giv'n in vain the heav'nly
    Muse?
Night, and all her sickly dews,
Her Spectres wan, and Birds of boding cry, 50
He gives to range the dreary sky:
Till down the eastern cliffs afar
Hyperion's[4] march they spy, and glitt'ring
    shafts of war.

[1] Mars, who was especially worshipped in
Thrace [2] Jove's eagle [3] a town in Cyprus containing a temple of Venus [4] the sun's

THE ANTISTROPHE

In climes beyond the solar road,[1]
Where shaggy forms o'er ice-built mountains
    roam,   55
The Muse has broke the twilight-gloom
To cheer the shiv'ring Native's dull abode.
And oft, beneath the od'rous shade
Of Chili's boundless forests laid,
She deigns to hear the savage Youth repeat
In loose numbers wildly sweet   61
Their feather-cinctured Chiefs, and dusky
    Loves.
Her track, where'er the Goddess roves,
Glory pursue, and generous Shame,
Th' unconquerable Mind, and Freedom's holy
    flame.   65

THE EPODE

Woods, that wave o'er Delphi's steep,[2]
Isles, that crown th' Ægean deep,
Fields, that cool Ilissus laves,
Or where Mæander's amber waves
In lingering Lab'rinths creep,   70
How do your tuneful Echoes languish,
Mute, but to the voice of Anguish?
Where each old poetic Mountain
Inspiration breath'd around:
Ev'ry shade and hallow'd Fountain   75
Murmur'd deep a solemn sound:
Till the sad Nine[3] in Greece's evil hour
Left their Parnassus for the Latian plains.[4]
Alike they scorn the pomp of tyrant-Power,
And coward Vice, that revels in her chains.
When Latium had her lofty spirit lost,   81
They sought, O Albion![5] next thy sea-encircled
    coast.

III

THE STROPHE

Far from the sun and summer-gale,
In thy[6] green lap was Nature's Darling[7]
    laid,
What time, where lucid Avon stray'd,   85
To Him the mighty Mother did unveil
Her awful face: The dauntless Child
Stretch'd forth his little arms, and smiled.
This pencil take (she said) whose colours clear
Richly paint the vernal year: 90

[1] the path of the sun [2] *This and the following
are places celebrated in Greek poetry.* [3] the Muses
[4] Italy [5] England [6] *i.e.* England's [7] Shakespeare

Thine too these golden keys, immortal Boy!
This can unlock the gates of Joy;
Of Horror that, and thrilling Fears,
Or ope the sacred source of sympathetic Tears.

THE ANTISTROPHE

Nor second He,[1] that rode sublime   95
Upon the seraph-wings of Ecstasy,
The secrets of th' Abyss to spy.
He pass'd the flaming bounds of Place and
    Time:
The living Throne, the sapphire-blaze,
Where Angels tremble, while they gaze,   100
He saw; but blasted with excess of light,
Closed his eyes in endless night.
Behold, where Dryden's less presumptuous
    car,
Wide o'er the fields of Glory bear
Two Coursers[2] of ethereal race,   105
With necks in thunder cloth'd, and long-
    resounding pace.

THE EPODE

Hark, his hands the lyre explore!
Bright-eyed Fancy hovering o'er
Scatters from her pictur'd urn
Thoughts that breathe, and words that burn.
But ah! 'tis heard no more ——   111
O Lyre divine, what daring Spirit
Wakes thee now? tho' he inherit
Nor the pride, nor ample pinion,
That the Theban Eagle[3] bear   115
Sailing with supreme dominion
Thro' the azure deep of air:
Yet oft before his infant eyes would run
Such forms, as glitter in the Muse's ray
With orient hues, unborrow'd of the Sun: 120
Yet shall he mount, and keep his distant way
Beyond the limits of a vulgar fate,
Beneath the Good how far — but far above
    the Great.

THE FATAL SISTERS

AN ODE

(FROM THE NORSE TONGUE)

Now the storm begins to lower,
(Haste, the loom of hell prepare,)
Iron-sleet of arrowy shower
Hurtles in the darken'd air.

Glitt'ring lances are the loom,   5
Where the dusky warp we strain,
Weaving many a soldier's doom,
Orkney's woe, and Randver's bane.[1]

See the griesly texture grow,
('Tis of human entrails made,)   10
And the weights,[2] that play below,
Each a gasping warrior's head.

Shafts for shuttles, dipt in gore,
Shoot the trembling cords along.
Sword, that once a monarch bore,   15
Keep the tissue close and strong.

Mista black, terrific maid,
Sangrida, and Hilda[3] see,
Join the wayward work to aid:
'Tis the woof of victory.   20

Ere the ruddy sun be set,
Pikes must shiver, javelins sing,
Blade with clattering buckler meet,
Hauberk crash, and helmet ring.

(Weave the crimson web of war)   25
Let us go, and let us fly,
Where our friends the conflict share,
Where they triumph, where they die.

As the paths of fate we tread,
Wading thro' th' ensanguin'd field: 30
Gondula, and Geira,[4] spread
O'er the youthful king your shield.

We the reins to slaughter give,
Ours to kill, and ours to spare:
Spite of danger he shall live.   35
(Weave the crimson web of war.)

They, whom once the desert-beach
Pent within its bleak domain,
Soon their ample sway shall stretch
O'er the plenty of the plain.   40

Low the dauntless earl is laid,
Gor'd with many a gaping wound:
Fate demands a nobler head;
Soon a king shall bite the ground.

[1] Milton   [2] the heroic couplet   [3] Pindar

[1] death [2] weights of the loom [3] *These three are
valkyries,* i.e. *goddesses of battle.* [4] *These two are
valkyries.*

Long his loss shall Eirin[1] weep, 45
Ne'er again his likeness see;
Long her strains in sorrow steep,
Strains of immortality.

Horror covers all the heath,
Clouds of carnage blot the sun. 50
Sisters, weave the web of death;
Sisters, cease, the work is done,

Hail the task, and hail the hands!
Songs of joy and triumph sing!
Joy to the victorious bands; 55
Triumph to the younger king.

Mortal, thou that hear'st the tale,
Learn the tenor of our song.
Scotland, thro' each winding vale
'Far and wide the notes prolong. 60

Sisters, hence with spurs of speed:
Each her thundering falchion wield;
Each bestride her sable steed.
Hurry, hurry to the field.

WILLIAM COLLINS (1721–1759)

A SONG FROM SHAKESPEARE'S CYMBELYNE

*Sung by Guiderus and Arviragus over Fidelè,
Supposed to be Dead* [2]

To fair Fidelè's grassy tomb
Soft maids and village hinds shall bring
Each op'ning sweet, of earliest bloom,
And rifle all the breathing spring.

No wailing ghost shall dare appear, 5
To vex with shrieks this quiet grove;
But shepherd lads assemble here,
And melting virgins own their love.

No wither'd witch shall here be seen,
No goblins lead their nightly crew; 10
The female fays shall haunt the green,
And dress thy grave with pearly dew.

The redbreast oft at ev'ning hours
Shall kindly lend his little aid,
With hoary moss, and gather'd flow'rs, 15
To deck the ground where thou art laid.

[1] Ireland   [2] Cf. *Cymbeline*, IV, ii, 215–29

When howling winds, and beating rain,
In tempests shake the sylvan cell,
Or midst the chase on ev'ry plain,
The tender thought on thee shall dwell, 20

Each lonely scene shall thee restore,
For thee the tear be duly shed:
Belov'd, till life could charm no more;
And mourn'd, till Pity's self be dead.

ODE

WRITTEN IN THE BEGINNING OF THE YEAR 1746

How sleep the brave who sink to rest
By all their country's wishes blest!
When Spring, with dewy fingers cold,
Returns to deck their hallow'd mold,
She there shall dress a sweeter sod 5
Than Fancy's feet have ever trod.

By fairy hands their knell is rung,
By forms unseen their dirge is sung;
There Honour comes, a pilgrim grey,
To bless the turf that wraps their clay; 10
And Freedom shall awhile repair,
To dwell a weeping hermit there!

ODE TO EVENING

If ought of oaten stop, or pastoral song,
May hope, chaste Eve,[1] to sooth thy modest
    ear,
Like thy own solemn springs,
Thy springs and dying gales,

O nymph reserv'd, while now the bright-
    hair'd sun 5
Sits in yon western tent, whose cloudy skirts
With brede ethereal wove,
O'erhang his wavy bed:

Now air is hush'd, save where the weak-ey'd
    bat,
With short shrill shriek, flits by on leathern
    wing, 10
Or where the beetle winds
His small but sullen horn,

As oft he rises 'midst the twilight path,
Against the pilgrim borne in heedless hum:

[1] Evening

Now teach me, maid [1] compos'd   15
To breathe some soften'd strain,

Whose numbers, stealing thro' thy dark'ning
    vale
May not unseemly with its stillness suit,
As, musing slow, I hail
    Thy genial lov'd return !   20

For when thy folding-star [2] arising shews
His paly circlet, at his warning lamp
    The fragrant Hours, and elves
    Who slept in flow'rs the day,

And many a nymph who wreaths her brows
    with sedge,   25
And sheds the fresh'ning dew, and, lovelier
    still,
    The pensive Pleasures sweet,
    Prepare thy shadowy car.

Then lead, calm vot'ress, where some sheety
    lake
Cheers the lone heath, or some time-hallow'd
    pile   30
    Or upland fallows grey
    Reflect its last cool gleam.

But when chill blust'ring winds, or driving
    rain,
Forbid my willing feet, be mine the hut
    That from the mountain's side   35
    Views wilds, and swelling floods,

And hamlets brown, and dim-discover'd
    spires,
And hears their simple bell, and marks o'er
    all
    Thy dewy fingers draw
    The gradual dusky veil.   40

While Spring shall pour his show'rs, as oft he
    wont,
And bathe thy breathing tresses, meekest
    Eve ;
    While Summer loves to sport
    Beneath thy ling'ring light ;

While sallow Autumn fills thy lap with leaves ;
Or Winter, yelling thro' the troublous air,   46
    Affrights thy shrinking train,
    And rudely rends thy robes ;

[1] Evening [2] the evening star, the signal for
folding flocks

So long, sure-found beneath the sylvan shed,
Shall Fancy, Friendship, Science, rose-lipp'd
    Health,   50
    Thy gentlest influence own,
    And hymn thy fav'rite name !

THE PASSIONS

AN ODE TO MUSIC

When Music, heav'nly maid, was young,
While yet in early Greece she sung,
The Passions oft, to hear her shell,[1]
Throng'd around her magic cell, .
Exulting, trembling, raging, fainting,   5
Possest beyond the Muse's painting ;
By turns they felt the glowing mind
Disturb'd, delighted, rais'd, refin'd :
Till once, 'tis said, when all were fir'd,
Fill'd with fury, rapt, inspir'd,   10
From the supporting myrtles round
They snatch'd her instruments of sound ;
And as they oft had heard apart
Sweet lessons of her forceful art,
Each, for madness rul'd the hour,   15
Would prove his own expressive pow'r.

First Fear his hand, its skill to try,
    Amid the chords bewilder'd laid,
And back recoil'd, he knew not why,
    Ev'n at the sound himself had made.   20

Next Anger rush'd ; his eyes, on fire,
    In lightnings own'd his secret stings ;
In one rude clash he struck the lyre,
    And swept with hurried hand the strings.

With woful measures wan Despair   25
    Low sullen sounds his grief beguil'd ;
A solemn, strange, and mingled air ;
    'Twas sad by fits, by starts 'twas wild.

But thou, O Hope, with eyes so fair,
    What was thy delightful measure ?   30
Still it whisper'd promis'd pleasure,
    And bade the lovely scenes at distance hail !
Still would her touch the strain prolong,
    And from the rocks, the woods, the vale,
She call'd on Echo still thro' all the song ;   35
    And where her sweetest theme she chose,
A soft responsive voice was heard at ev'ry close,
And Hope enchanted smil'd, and wav'd her
    golden hair.

[1] the lyre, cf. *Progress of Poesy*, ll. 13–15

And longer had she sung, — but with a
  frown
    Revenge impatient rose ;   40
He threw his blood-stain'd sword in thunder
  down
    And with a with'ring look
  The war-denouncing trumpet took,
And blew a blast so loud and dread,
Were ne'er prophetic sounds so full of woe. 45
    And ever and anon he beat
    The doubling drum with furious heat ;
  And tho' sometimes, each dreary pause be-
    tween,
    Dejected Pity, at his side,
    Her soul-subduing voice applied,   50
Yet still he kept his wild unalter'd mien,
While each strain'd ball of sight seem'd burst-
  ing from his head.

Thy numbers, Jealousy, to nought were fix'd,
Sad proof of thy distressful state ;
Of diff'ring themes the veering song was
  mix'd,
  And now it courted Love, now raving call'd
    on Hate.   56

With eyes uprais'd, as one inspir'd,
Pale Melancholy sate retir'd,
And from her wild sequester'd seat,
In notes by distance made more sweet, 60
Pour'd thro' the mellow horn her pensive
  soul :
  And, dashing soft from rocks around,
  Bubbling runnels join'd the sound ;
Thro' glades and glooms the mingled measure
  stole :
  Or o'er some haunted stream with fond
    delay   65
    Round an holy calm diffusing,
    Love of peace and lonely musing,
  In hollow murmurs died away.

But oh, how alter'd was its sprightlier tone,
When Cheerfulness, a nymph of healthiest
  hue,
  Her bow across her shoulder flung,   71
  Her buskins [1] gemm'd with morning dew,
Blew an inspiring air, that dale and thicket
  rung,
  The hunter's call to faun and dryad known !
  The oak-crown'd sisters,[2] and their chaste-
    ey'd queen,   •   75

Satyrs, and sylvan boys, were seen,
Peeping from forth their alleys green ;
Brown Exercise rejoic'd to hear,
  And Sport leapt up and seiz'd his beechen
    spear.

Last came Joy's ecstatic trial.   80
He, with viny crown advancing,
  First to the lively pipe his hand addrest ;
But soon he saw the brisk awak'ning viol,
  Whose sweet entrancing voice he lov'd the
    best.
    They would have thought, who heard the
      strain,   85
    They saw in Tempe's vale [1] her native
      maids
    Amidst the vestal sounding shades,
To some unwearied minstrel dancing,
While, as his flying fingers kiss'd the strings,
  Love fram'd with Mirth a gay fantastic
    round ;   90
  Loose were her tresses seen, her zone un-
    bound,
  And he, amidst his frolic play,
  As if he would the charming air repay,
Shook thousand odours from his dewy wings.

O Music, sphere-descended [2] maid,   95
Friend of Pleasure, Wisdom's aid,
Why, goddess, why, to us denied,
Lay'st thou thy ancient lyre aside ?
As in that lov'd Athenian bow'r
You learn'd an all-commanding pow'r,   100
Thy mimic soul, O nymph endear'd,
Can well recall what then it heard.
Where is thy native simple heart,
Devote to Virtue, Fancy, Art ?
Arise as in that elder time,   105
Warm, energic, chaste, sublime !
Thy wonders, in that godlike age,
Fill thy recording sister's [3] page. —
'Tis said, and I believe the tale,
Thy humblest reed could more prevail, 110
Had more of strength, diviner rage,
Than all which charms this laggard age,
Ev'n all at once together found,
Cæcilia's mingled world of sound.
O bid our vain endeavours cease,   115
Revive the just designs of Greece,   ꟾ
Return in all thy simple state,
Confirm the tales her sons relate !

[1] Cf., below, note on Keats' *Ode on a Grecian
Urn*, l. 7   [2] heaven-descended   [3] Clio, the Muse
of history

[1] boots   [2] nymphs of the "chaste-eyed queen"
Diana

THOMAS WARTON (1728–1790)

SONNET IV

WRITTEN AT STONEHENGE

Thou noblest monument of Albion's isle!
Whether by Merlin's aid from Scythia's shore,
To Amber's fatal plain [1] Pendragon [2] bore,
Huge frame of giant-hands, the mighty pile,
T'entomb his Britons slain by Hengist's [3]
    guile:
Or Druid priests, sprinkled with human gore,
Taught 'mid thy massy maze their mystic
    lore:
Or Danish chiefs, enrich'd with savage spoil,
To Victory's idol vast, an unhewn shrine,
Rear'd the rude heap: or, in thy hallow'd
    round,   10
Repose the kings of Brutus' genuine line;
Or here those kings in solemn state were
    crown'd:
Studious to trace thy wondrous origine,
We muse on many an ancient tale renown'd.

OLIVER GOLDSMITH
(1728–1774)

LETTERS FROM A CITIZEN OF THE WORLD TO HIS FRIENDS IN THE EAST

LETTER XXI

THE CHINESE GOES TO SEE A PLAY

The English are as fond of seeing plays acted as the Chinese; but there is a vast difference in the manner of conducting them. We play our pieces in the open air, the English theirs under cover; we act by daylight, they by the blaze of torches. One of our plays continues eight or ten days successively; an English piece seldom takes up above four hours in the representation.

My companion in black, with whom I am now beginning to contract an intimacy, introduced me a few nights ago to the playhouse, where we placed ourselves conveniently at the foot of the stage. As the curtain was not

---

[1] near Salisbury   [2] Uther Pendragon, father of King Arthur   [3] leader of the Saxons

---

drawn before my arrival, I had an opportunity of observing the behaviour of the spectators, and indulging those reflections which novelty generally inspires.

The rich in general were placed in the lowest seats, and the poor rose above them in degrees proportioned to their poverty. The order of precedence seemed here inverted; those who were undermost all the day, now enjoyed a temporary eminence, and became masters of the ceremonies. It was they who called for the music, indulging every noisy freedom, and testifying all the insolence of beggary in exaltation.

They who held the middle region seemed not so riotous as those above them, nor yet so tame as those below: to judge by their looks, many of them seemed strangers there as well as myself. They were chiefly employed, during this period of expectation, in eating oranges, reading the story of the play, or making assignations.

Those who sat in the lowest rows, which are called the pit, seemed to consider themselves as judges of the merit of the poet and the performers; they were assembled partly to be amused, and partly to show their taste; appearing to labour under that restraint which an affectation of superior discernment generally produces. My companion, however, informed me, that not one in a hundred of them knew even the first principles of criticism; that they assumed the right of being censors because there was none to contradict their pretensions; and that every man who now called himself a connoisseur, became such to all intents and purposes.

Those who sat in the boxes appeared in the most unhappy situation of all. The rest of the audience came merely for their own amusement; these, rather to furnish out a part of the entertainment themselves. I could not avoid considering them as acting parts in dumb show — not a courtesy or nod, that was not all the result of art; not a look nor a smile that was not designed for murder. Gentlemen and ladies ogled each other through spectacles; for, my companion observed, that blindness was of late become fashionable; all affected indifference and ease, while their hearts at the same time burned for conquest. Upon the whole, the lights, the music, the ladies in their gayest dresses, the men with cheerfulness and expectation in their looks, all conspired to make a most agreeable picture, and to fill a heart that sympathises at human happiness with inexpressible serenity.

The expected time for the play to begin at last arrived; the curtain was drawn, and the actors came on. A woman, who personated a queen, came in curtseying to the audience, who clapped their hands upon her appearance. Clapping of hands is, it seems, the manner of applauding in England; the manner is absurd, but every country, you know, has its peculiar absurdities. I was equally surprised, however, at the submission of the actress, who should have considered herself as a queen, as at the little discernment of the audience who gave her such marks of applause before she attempted to deserve them. Preliminaries between her and the audience being thus adjusted, the dialogue was supported between her and a most hopeful youth, who acted the part of her confidant. They both appeared in extreme distress, for it seems the queen had lost a child some fifteen years before, and still kept its dear resemblance next her heart, while her kind companion bore a part in her sorrows.

Her lamentations grew loud; comfort is offered, but she detests the very sound: she bids them preach comfort to the winds. Upon this her husband comes in, who, seeing the queen so much afflicted, can himself hardly refrain from tears, or avoid partaking in the soft distress. After thus grieving through three scenes, the curtain dropped for the first act.

"Truly," said I to my companion, "these kings and queens are very much disturbed at no very great misfortune: certain I am, were people of humbler stations to act in this manner, they would be thought divested of common sense." I had scarcely finished this observation, when the curtain rose, and the king came on in a violent passion. His wife had, it seems, refused his proffered tenderness, had spurned his royal embrace, and he seemed resolved not to survive her fierce disdain. After he had thus fretted, and the queen had fretted through the second act, the curtain was let down once more.

"Now," says my companion, "you perceive the king to be a man of spirit; he feels at every pore: one of your phlegmatic sons of clay would have given the queen her own way, and let her come to herself by degrees; but the king is for immediate tenderness, or instant death: death and tenderness are leading

passions of every modern buskined hero; this moment they embrace, and the next stab, mixing daggers and kisses in every period."

I was going to second his remarks, when my attention was engrossed by a new object; a man came in balancing a straw upon his nose, and the audience were clapping their hands, in all the raptures of applause. "To what purpose," cried I, "does this unmeaning figure make his appearance? is he a part of the plot?" — "Unmeaning do you call him?" replied my friend in black; "this is one of the most important characters of the whole play; nothing pleases the people more than seeing a straw balanced: there is a good deal of meaning in the straw: there is something suited to every apprehension in the sight; and a fellow possessed of talents like these is sure of making his fortune."

The third act now began with an actor who came to inform us that he was the villain of the play, and intended to show strange things before all was over. He was joined by another who seemed as much disposed for mischief as he: their intrigues continued through this whole division. "If that be a villain," said I, "he must be a very stupid one to tell his secrets without being asked; such soliloquies of late are never admitted in China."

The noise of clapping interrupted me once more; a child of six years old was learning to dance on the stage, which gave the ladies and mandarines infinite satisfaction. "I am sorry," said I, "to see the pretty creature so early learning so very bad a trade; dancing being, I presume, as contemptible here as in China." — "Quite the reverse," interrupted my companion; "dancing is a very reputable and genteel employment here; men have a greater chance for encouragement from the merit of their heels than their heads. One who jumps up and flourishes his toes three times before he comes to the ground, may have three hundred a year; he who flourishes them four times, gets four hundred; but he who arrives at five is inestimable, and may demand what salary he thinks proper. The female dancers, too, are valued for this sort of jumping and crossing; and it is a cant word amongst them, that she deserves most who shows highest. But the fourth act is begun; let us be attentive."

In the fourth act the queen finds her long

lost child, now grown up into a youth of smart parts and great qualifications; wherefore she wisely considers that the crown will fit his head better than that of her husband, whom she knows to be a driveller. The king discovers her design, and here comes on the deep distress: he loves the queen, and he loves the kingdom; he resolves, therefore, in order to possess both, that her son must die. The queen exclaims at his barbarity, is frantic with rage, and at length, overcome with sorrow, falls into a fit; upon which the curtain drops, and the act is concluded.

"Observe the art of the poet," cries my companion. "When the queen can say no more, she falls into a fit. While thus her eyes are shut, while she is supported in the arms of Abigail,[1] what horrors do we not fancy! We feel it in every nerve: take my word for it, that fits are the true *aposiopesis*[2] of modern tragedy."

The fifth act began, and a busy piece it was. Scenes shifting, trumpets sounding, mobs hallooing, carpets spreading, guards bustling from one door to another; gods, demons, daggers, racks, and ratsbane. But whether the king was killed, or the queen was drowned, or the son was poisoned, I have absolutely forgotten.

When the play was over, I could not avoid observing, that the persons of the drama appeared in as much distress in the first act as the last. "How is it possible," said I, "to sympathise with them through five long acts? Pity is but a short lived passion. I hate to hear an actor mouthing trifles. Neither startings, strainings, nor attitudes, affect me, unless there be cause: after I have been once or twice deceived by those unmeaning alarms, my heart sleeps in peace, probably unaffected by the principal distress. There should be one great passion aimed at by the actor as well as the poet; all the rest should be subordinate, and only contribute to make that the greater; if the actor, therefore, exclaims upon every occasion, in the tones of despair, he attempts to move us too soon; he anticipates the blow, he ceases to affect, though he gains our applause."

I scarce perceived that the audience were almost all departed; wherefore, mixing with the crowd, my companion and I got into the

street, where, essaying a hundred obstacles from coach-wheels and palanquin poles, like birds in their flight through the branches of a forest, after various turnings, we both at length got home in safety.   Adieu.

THE DESERTED VILLAGE

Sweet Auburn! loveliest village of the plain;
Where health and plenty cheered the labour-
    ing swain,
Where smiling spring its earliest visit paid,
And parting summer's lingering blooms de-
    layed:
Dear lovely bowers of innocence and ease,   5
Seats of my youth, when every sport could
    please,
How often have I loitered o'er thy green,
Where humble happiness endeared each
    scene!
How often have I paused on every charm,
The sheltered cot, the cultivated farm,   10
The never-failing brook, the busy mill,
The decent church that topt the neighbouring
    hill,
The hawthorn bush, with seats beneath the
    shade
For talking age and whispering lovers made!
How often have I blest the coming day,   15
When toil remitting lent its turn to play,
And all the village train, from labour free,
Led up their sports beneath the spreading
    tree,
While many a pastime circled in the shade, 19
The young contending as the old surveyed;
And many a gambol frolicked o'er the ground,
And sleights of art, and feats of strength went
    round.
And still, as each repeated pleasure tired,
Succeeding sports the mirthful band inspired;
The dancing pair that simply sought renown
By holding out to tire each other down;   26
The swain mistrustless of his smutted face,
While secret laughter tittered round the
    place;
The bashful virgin's side-long looks of love,
The matron's glance that would those looks
    reprove: 30
These were thy charms, sweet village! sports
    like these,
With sweet succession, taught even toil to
    please:
These round thy bowers their cheerful influ-
    ence shed:

---

[1] her maid   [2] as a figure of rhetoric, a sudden termination before a speech is really completed

These were thy charms — but all these charms
are fled.
Sweet smiling village, loveliest of the lawn,
Thy sports are fled, and all thy charms with-
drawn;   36
Amidst thy bowers the tyrant's hand is seen
And desolation saddens all thy green:
One only master grasps the whole domain,
And half a tillage stints thy smiling plain. 40
No more thy glassy brook reflects the day,
But, choked with sedges, works its weedy
way;
Along the glades, a solitary guest,
The hollow sounding bittern guards its nest;
Amidst thy desert walks the lapwing flies, 45
And tires their echoes with unvaried cries;
Sunk are thy bowers in shapeless ruin all,
And the long grass o'ertops the mouldering
wall;
And trembling, shrinking from the spoiler's
hand,
Far, far away thy children leave the land. 50
Ill fares the land, to hastening ills a prey,
Where wealth accumulates, and men decay:
Princes and lords may flourish, or may fade;
A breath can make them, as a breath has
made: 54
But a bold peasantry, their country's pride,
When once destroyed, can never be supplied.
A time there was, ere England's griefs
began,
When every rood of ground maintained its
man;
For him light labour spread her wholesome
store,
Just gave what life required, but gave no
more: 60
His best companions, innocence and health;
And his best riches, ignorance of wealth.
But times are altered; trade's unfeeling
train
Usurp the land and dispossess the swain; 64
Along the lawn, where scattered hamlets
rose,
Unwieldy wealth and cumbrous pomp repose,
And every want to opulence allied,
And every pang that folly pays to pride.
These gentle hours that plenty bade to bloom,
Those calm desires that asked but little room,
Those healthful sports that graced the peace-
ful scene,   71
Lived in each look, and brightened all the
green;
These, far departing, seek a kinder shore,
And rural mirth and manners are no more.

Sweet Auburn! parent of the blissful hour,
Thy glades forlorn confess the tyrant's power.
Here, as I take my solitary rounds   77
Amidst thy tangling walks and ruined grounds,
And, many a year elapsed, return to view
Where once the cottage stood, the hawthorn
grew,   80
Remembrance wakes with all her busy train,
Swells at my breast, and turns the past to
pain.
In all my wanderings round this world of
care,
In all my griefs — and God has given my
share —   84
I still had hopes, my latest hours to crown,
Amidst these humble bowers to lay me down;
To husband out life's taper at the close,
And keep the flame from wasting by repose:
I still had hopes, for pride attends us still,
Amidst the swains to show my book-learned
skill,   90
Around my fire an evening group to draw,
And tell of all I felt, and all I saw;
And, as an hare whom hounds and horns
pursue
Pants to the place from whence at first she
flew,
I still had hopes, my long vexations past, 95
Here to return — and die at home at last.
O blest retirement, friend to life's decline,
Retreats from care, that never must be mine,
How happy he who crowns in shades like these
A youth of labour with an age of ease;   100
Who quits a world where strong temptations
try,
And, since 'tis hard to combat, learns to fly!
For him no wretches, born to work and weep,
Explore the mine or tempt the dangerous
deep;
No surly porter stands in guilty state,   105
To spurn imploring famine from the gate;
But on he moves to meet his latter end,
Angels around befriending Virtue's friend;
Bends to the grave with unperceived decay,
While resignation gently slopes the way; 110
And, all his prospects brightening to the last,
His heaven commences ere the world be past!
Sweet was the sound, when oft at evening's
close
Up yonder hill the village murmur rose.   114
There, as I passed with careless steps and slow,
The mingling notes came softened from below;
The swain responsive as the milk-maid sung,
The sober herd that lowed to meet their
young,

The noisy geese that gabbled o'er the pool,
The playful children just let loose from school,
The watch-dog's voice that bayed the whis-
   pering wind,   121
And the loud laugh that spoke the vacant [1]
   mind ; —
These all in sweet confusion sought the shade,
And filled each pause the nightingale had
   made.
But now the sounds of population fail,   125
No cheerful murmurs fluctuate in the gale,
No busy steps the grass-grown foot-way tread,
For all the bloomy flush of life is fled.
All but yon widowed, solitary thing,
That feebly bends beside the plashy spring :
She, wretched matron, forced in age, for
   bread,   131
To strip the brook with mantling cresses
   spread,
To pick her wintry faggot from the thorn,
To seek her nightly shed, and weep till morn ;
She only left of all the harmless train,   135
The sad historian of the pensive plain.
   Near yonder copse, where once the garden
   smiled,
And still where many a garden flower grows
   wild ;
There, where a few torn shrubs the place dis-
   close,
The village preacher's modest mansion rose.
A man he was to all the country dear,   141
And passing rich with forty pounds a year ;
Remote from towns he ran his godly race,
Nor e'er had changed, nor wished to change
   his place ;
Unpractised he to fawn, or seek for power, 145
By doctrines fashioned to the varying hour ;
Far other aims his heart had learned to prize,
More skilled to raise the wretched than to rise.
His house was known to all the vagrant train ;
He chid their wanderings but relieved their
   pain :   150
The long-remembered beggar was his guest,
Whose beard descending swept his aged
   breast ;
The ruined spendthrift, now no longer proud,
Claimed kindred there, and had his claims
   allowed ;
The broken soldier, kindly bade to stay,   155
Sat by the fire, and talked the night away,
Wept o'er his wounds or, tales of sorrow done,
Shouldered his crutch and showed how fields
   were won.

             [1] unoccupied by care

Pleased with his guests, the good man learned
   to glow,
And quite forgot their vices in their woe ; 160
Careless their merits or their faults to scan,
His pity gave ere charity began.
   Thus to relieve the wretched was his pride,
And e'en his failings leaned to Virtue's side ;
But in his duty prompt at every call,   165
He watched and wept, he prayed and felt for
   all ;
And, as a bird each fond endearment tries
To tempt its new-fledged offspring to the skies,
He tried each art, reproved each dull delay,
Allured to brighter worlds, and led the way.
   Beside the bed where parting life was laid,
And sorrow, guilt, and pain by turns dis-
   mayed,   172
The reverend champion stood. At his control
Despair and anguish fled the struggling soul ;
Comfort came down the trembling wretch to
   raise,   175
And his last faltering accents whispered
   praise.
   At church, with meek and unaffected grace,
His looks adorned the venerable place ;
Truth from his lips prevailed with double sway,
And fools, who came to scoff, remained to
   pray.   180
The service past, around the pious man,
With steady zeal, each honest rustic ran ;
Even children followed with endearing wile,
And plucked his gown to share the good man's
   smile.   184
His ready smile a parent's warmth exprest ;
Their welfare pleased him, and their cares dis-
   trest :
To them his heart, his love, his griefs were
   given,
But all his serious thoughts had rest in heaven.
As some tall cliff that lifts its awful form,
Swells from the vale, and midway leaves the
   storm,   190
Tho' round its breast the rolling clouds are
   spread,
Eternal sunshine settles on its head.
   Beside yon straggling fence that skirts the
   way,
With blossom'd furze unprofitably gay,
There, in his noisy mansion, skill'd to rule,
The village master taught his little school.
A man severe he was, and stern to view ; 197
I knew him well, and every truant knew ;
Well had the boding tremblers learned to
   trace
The day's disasters in his morning face ;   200

Full well they laughed with counterfeited glee
At all his jokes, for many a joke had he;
Full well the busy whisper circling round
Conveyed the dismal tidings when he frowned.
Yet he was kind, or, if severe in aught,   205
The love he bore to learning was in fault;
The village all declared how much he knew:
'Twas certain he could write, and cipher too;
Lands he could measure, terms and tides pre-
     sage,   209
And even the story ran that he could gauge;
In arguing, too, the parson owned his skill,
For, even tho' vanquished, he could argue
     still;
While words of learned length and thunder-
     ing sound
Amazed the gazing rustics ranged around;
And still they gazed, and still the wonder
     grew,   215
That one small head could carry all he knew.
     But past is all his fame. The very spot
Where many a time he triumphed is forgot.
Near yonder thorn, that lifts its head on high,
Where once the sign-post caught the passing
     eye,   220
Low lies that house where nut-brown draughts
     inspired,
Where graybeard mirth and smiling toil re-
     tired,
Where village statesmen talked with looks pro-
     found,
And news much older than their ale went
     round.
Imagination fondly stoops to trace   225
The parlour splendours of that festive place:
The white-washed wall, the nicely sanded
     floor,
The varnished clock that clicked behind the
     door;
The chest contrived a double debt to pay,
A bed by night, a chest of drawers by day;
The pictures placed for ornament and use,
The twelve good rules,[1] the royal game of
     goose;[2]   232
The hearth, except when winter chill'd the
     day,
With aspen boughs and flowers and fennel
     gay;
While broken tea-cups, wisely kept for show,
Ranged o'er the chimney, glistened in a row.
     Vain transitory splendours! could not all
Reprieve the tottering mansion from its fall?

[1] a card containing maxims of conduct attributed to Charles I   [2] a game much like Parchesi

Obscure it sinks, nor shall it more impart
An hour's importance to the poor man's heart.
Thither no more the peasant shall repair   241
To sweet oblivion of his daily care;
No more the farmer's news, the barber's tale,
No more the woodman's ballad shall prevail;
No more the smith his dusky brow shall clear,
Relax his ponderous strength, and lean to
     hear;   246
The host himself no longer shall be found
Careful to see the mantling bliss[1] go round;
Nor the coy maid, half willing to be prest,
Shall kiss the cup to pass it to the rest.   250
     Yes! let the rich deride, the proud disdain,
These simple blessings of the lowly train;
To me more dear, congenial to my heart,
One native charm, than all the gloss of art.
Spontaneous joys, where Nature has its play,
The soul adopts, and owns their first born
     sway;   256
Lightly they frolic o'er the vacant mind,
Unenvied, unmolested, unconfined.
But the long pomp, the midnight masquerade,
With all the freaks of wanton wealth ar-
     rayed —   260
In these, ere triflers half their wish obtain,
The toiling pleasure sickens into pain;
And, e'en while fashion's brightest arts decoy,
The heart distrusting asks if this be joy.
     Ye friends to truth, ye statesmen who
     survey   265
The rich man's joy increase, the poor's decay,
'Tis yours to judge, how wide the limits stand
Between a splendid and an happy land.
Proud swells the tide with loads of freighted
     ore,   269
And shouting Folly hails them from her
     shore;
Hoartls e'en beyond the miser's wish abound,
And rich men flock from all the world around.
Yet count our gains! This wealth is but a
     name   274
That leaves our useful products still the same.
Not so the loss. The man of wealth and
     pride
Takes up a space that many poor supplied;
Space for his lake, his park's extended bounds,
Space for his horses, equipage, and hounds:
The robe that wraps his limbs in silken sloth
Has robbed the neighbouring fields of half
     their growth;   280
His seat,[2] where solitary sports are seen,
Indignant spurns the cottage from the green:

[1] i.e., foaming ale   [2] great house

Around the world each needful product flies,
For all the luxuries the world supplies;[1]
While thus the land adorned for pleasure all
In barren splendour feebly waits the fall. 286
    As some fair female unadorned and plain,
Secure to please while youth confirms her reign,
Slights every borrowed charm that dress supplies,
Nor shares with art the triumph of her eyes;
But when those charms are past, for charms are frail, 291
When time advances, and when lovers fail,
She then shines forth, solicitous to bless,
In all the glaring impotence of dress.
Thus fares the land by luxury betrayed: 295
In nature's simplest charms at first arrayed,
But verging to decline, its splendours rise,
Its vistas strike, its palaces surprise;
While, scourged by famine from the smiling land 299
The mournful peasant leads his humble band,
And while he sinks, without one arm to save,
The country blooms — a garden and a grave.
    Where then, ah! where, shall poverty reside,
To 'scape the pressure of contiguous pride?
If to some common's fenceless limits strayed
He drives his flock to pick the scanty blade,
Those fenceless fields the sons of wealth divide,
And even the bare-worn common[2] is denied.
    If to the city sped — what waits him there?
To see profusion that he must not share; 310
To see ten thousand baneful arts combined
To pamper luxury, and thin mankind;
To see those joys the sons of pleasure know
Extorted from his fellow-creature's woe. 314
Here while the courtier glitters in brocade,
There the pale artist[3] plies the sickly trade;
Here while the proud their long-drawn pomps display,
There the black gibbet glooms beside the way.
The dome where pleasure holds her midnight reign 319
Here, richly deckt, admits the gorgeous train:
Tumultuous grandeur crowds the blazing square,
The rattling chariots clash, the torches glare.
Sure scenes like these no troubles e'en annoy!
Sure these denote one universal joy!
Are these thy serious thoughts? — Ah, turn thine eyes 325

[1] *i.e.*, useful products are exchanged for luxuries   [2] a field in which all villagers were entitled to pasture their cattle free   [3] artisan

Where the poor houseless shivering female lies.
She once, perhaps, in village plenty blest,
Has wept at tales of innocence distrest;
Her modest looks the cottage might adorn,
Sweet as the primrose peeps beneath the thorn: 330
Now lost to all; her friends, her virtue fled,
Near her betrayer's door she lays her head,
And, pinch'd with cold, and shrinking from the shower,
With heavy heart deplores that luckless hour,
When idly first, ambitious of the town, 335
She left her wheel and robes of country brown.
    Do thine, sweet Auburn, — thine, the loveliest train, —
Do thy fair tribes participate her pain?
Even now, perhaps, by cold and hunger led,
At proud men's doors they ask a little bread!
    Ah, no! To distant climes, a dreary scene,
Where half the convex world intrudes between,
Through torrid tracts with fainting steps they go,
Where wild Altama[1] murmurs to their woe.
Far different there from all that charm'd before, 345
The various terrors of that horrid shore;
Those blazing suns that dart a downward ray,
And fiercely shed intolerable day;
Those matted woods, where birds forget to sing,
But silent bats in drowsy clusters cling; 350
Those poisonous fields with rank luxuriance crowned,
Where the dark scorpion gathers death around;
Where at each step the stranger fears to wake
The rattling terrors of the vengeful snake;
Where crouching tigers wait their hapless prey, 355
And savage men more murderous still than they;
While oft in whirls the mad tornado flies,
Mingling the ravaged landscape with the skies.
Far different these from every former scene,
The cooling brook, the grassy vested green, 360
The breezy covert of the warbling grove, 361
That only sheltered thefts of harmless love.
    Good Heaven! what sorrows gloom'd that parting day,
That called them from their native walks away;

[1] the Altamaha river, in Georgia

When the poor exiles, every pleasure past,
Hung round the bowers, and fondly looked
their last,   366
And took a long farewell, and wished in vain
For seats like these beyond the western main,
And shuddering still to face the distant deep,
Returned and wept, and still returned to weep.
The good old sire the first prepared to go   371
To new found worlds, and wept for others' woe;
But for himself, in conscious virtue brave,
He only wished for worlds beyond the grave.
His lovely daughter, lovelier in her tears,   375
The fond companion of his helpless years,
Silent went next, neglectful of her charms,
And left a lover's for a father's arms.
With louder plaints the mother spoke her
woes,
And blest the cot where every pleasure rose,
And kist her thoughtless babes with many a
tear   381
And claspt them close, in sorrow doubly dear,
Whilst her fond husband strove to lend relief
In all the silent manliness of grief.
  O luxury! thou curst by Heaven's decree,
How ill exchanged are things like these for
thee!   386
How do thy potions, with insidious joy,
Diffuse their pleasure only to destroy!
Kingdoms by thee, to sickly greatness grown,
Boast of a florid vigour not their own.   390
At every draught more large and large they
grow,
A bloated mass of rank unwieldy woe;
Till sapped their strength, and every part un-
sound,
Down, down, they sink, and spread a ruin
round.
   Even now the devastation is begun,   395
And half the business of destruction done;
Even now, methinks, as pondering here I
stand,
I see the rural virtues leave the land.
Down where yon anchoring vessel spreads the
sail,
That idly waiting flaps with every gale,   400
Downward they move, a melancholy band,
Pass from the shore, and darken all the strand.
Contented toil, and hospitable care,
And kind connubial tenderness, are there;
And piety with wishes placed above,   405
And steady loyalty, and faithful love.
And thou, sweet Poetry, thou loveliest maid,
Still first to fly where sensual joys invade;
Unfit in these degenerate times of shame   409
To catch the heart, or strike for honest fame;

Dear charming nymph, neglected and decried,
My shame in crowds, my solitary pride;
Thou source of all my bliss, and all my woe,
That found'st me poor at first, and keep'st me
so;   .   414
Thou guide by which the nobler arts excel,
Thou nurse of every virtue, fare thee well!
Farewell, and oh! where'er thy voice be tried,
On Torno's cliffs,[1] or Pambamarca's side,[2]
Whether where equinoctial fervours glow,
Or winter wraps the polar world in snow,   420
Still let thy voice, prevailing over time,
Redress the rigours of the inclement clime;
Aid slighted truth with thy persuasive strain;
Teach erring man to spurn the rage of gain;
Teach him, that states of native strength
possest,
Tho' very poor, may still be very blest;   426
That trade's proud empire hastes to swift
decay,
As ocean sweeps the laboured mole away;
While self-dependent power can time defy,
As rocks resist the billows and the sky.[3]   430

From RETALIATION

*   *   *   *   *   *   *

   At a dinner so various, at such a repast,
Who'd not be a glutton, and stick to the last?
Here, waiter, more wine, let me sit while I'm
able,
Till all my companions sink under the table;
Then, with chaos and blunders encircling my
head,   21
Let me ponder, and tell what I think of the
dead.
Here lies the good Dean,[4] reunited to earth,
Who mix'd reason with pleasure, and wisdom
with mirth.
If he had any faults, he has left us in doubt,
At least in six weeks I could not find them
out;
Yet some have declared, and it can't be
denied them,
That Slyboots was cursedly cunning to hide
them.
Here lies our good Edmund,[5] whose genius
was such,   29
We scarcely can praise it, or blame it too much;   •

[1] on the boundary between Russia and Sweden
[2] a mountain in Ecuador   [3] *Lines 427–30 were
added by Dr. Johnson.*   [4] Dr. Barnard, Dean of
Derry   [5] Edmund Burke

Who, born for the universe, narrow'd his
  mind,
And to party gave up what was meant for
  mankind:
Though fraught with all learning, yet strain-
  ing his throat
To persuade Tommy Townshend [1] to lend him
  a vote;
Who, too deep for his hearers, still went on
  refining,
And thought of convincing, while they
  thought of dining;
Tho' equal to all things, for all things unfit;
Too nice [2] for a statesman, too proud for a wit;
For a patriot too cool; for a drudge diso-
  bedient;
And too fond of the right to pursue the expe-
  dient.   40
In short, 'twas his fate, unemploy'd or in
  place, Sir,
To eat mutton cold, and cut blocks with a
  razor.

*   *   *   *   *   *   *

Here Cumberland [3] lies, having acted his
  parts,
The Terence of England, the mender of
  hearts;
A flattering painter, who made it his care
To draw men as they ought to be, not as they
  are.
His gallants are all faultless, his women
  divine,
And Comedy wonders at being so fine;
Like a tragedy-queen he has dizen'd her out,
Or rather like tragedy giving a rout.
His fools have their follies so lost in a crowd
Of virtues and feelings, that folly grows
  proud;   70
And coxcombs, alike in their failings alone,
Adopting his portraits, are pleased with their
  own.
Say, where has our poet this malady caught?
Or wherefore his characters thus without
  fault?
Say, was it, that vainly directing his view
To find out men's virtues, and finding them
  few,
Quite sick of pursuing each troublesome elf,
He grew lazy at last, and drew from himself?

*   *   *   *   *   *   *

Here lies David Garrick,[1] describe him who
  can?
An abridgment of all that was pleasant in
  man;
As an actor, confest without rival to shine;
As a wit, if not first, in the very first line;
Yet with talents like these, and an excellent
  heart,
The man had his failings, a dupe to his art;
Like an ill-judging beauty his colours he
  spread,
And beplaster'd with rouge his own natural
  red.   100
On the stage he was natural, simple, affecting,
'Twas only that when he was off he was act-
  ing;
With no reason on earth to go out of his way,
He turn'd and he varied full ten times a day:
Tho' secure of our hearts, yet confoundedly
  sick
If they were not his own by finessing and
  trick;
He cast off his friends as a huntsman his pack,
For he knew when he pleased he could whistle
  them back.
Of praise a mere glutton, he swallow'd what
  came,   109
And the puff of a dunce he mistook it for fame;
Till his relish grown callous, almost to disease,
Who pepper'd the highest was surest to please.
But let us be candid, and speak out our mind:
If dunces applauded, he paid them in kind.
Ye Kenricks, ye Kellys, and Woodfalls so
  grave,[2]
What a commerce was yours, while you got
  and you gave!
How did Grub Street [3] re-echo the shouts that
  you raised,
When he was be-Roscius'd,[4] and you were be-
  praised!
But peace to his spirit, wherever it flies,
To act as an angel, and mix with the skies!
Those poets who owe their best fame to his
  skill,   121
Shall still be his flatterers, go where he will;
Old Shakespeare receive him with praise and
  with love,
And Beaumonts and Bens [5] be his Kellys
  above.

*   *   *   *   *   *   *

[1] the greatest actor of his day [2] dramatists
and critics of the time [3] where hack-writers lived
[4] Roscius was the greatest comic actor of ancient
Rome. [5] Ben Jonson and the like

[1] a member of Parliament [2] fastidious [3] Richard
Cumberland, dramatist

Here Reynolds[1] is laid, and to tell you my
   mind,
He has not left a wiser or better behind.
His pencil was striking, resistless, and grand;
His manners were gentle, complying, and
   bland;
Still born to improve us in every part,   141
His pencil our faces, his manners our heart.
To coxcombs averse, yet most civilly steering,
When they judged without skill he was still[2]
   hard of hearing;
When they talk'd of their Raphaels, Correg-
   gios and stuff,
He shifted his trumpet,[3] and only took snuff.

*   *   *   *   *   *   *

EDMUND BURKE (1729–1797)

FROM SPEECH ON THE NABOB OF ARCOT'S DEBTS

*   *   *   *   *   *   *

The great fortunes made in India, in the beginnings of conquest, naturally excited an emulation in all the parts and through the whole succession of the Company's service. But in the Company it gave rise to other sentiments. They did not find the new channels of acquisition flow with equal riches to them. On the contrary, the high flood-tide of private emolument was generally in the lowest ebb of their affairs. They began also to fear that the fortune of war might take away what the fortune of war had given. Wars were accordingly discouraged by repeated injunctions and menaces: and that the servants might not be bribed into them by the native princes, they were strictly forbidden to take any money whatsoever from their hands. But vehement passion is ingenious in resources. The Company's servants were not only stimulated, but better instructed by the prohibition. They soon fell upon a contrivance which answered their purposes far better than the methods which were forbidden: though in this also they violated an ancient, but they thought, an abrogated order. They reversed their proceedings. Instead of receiving presents, they made loans. Instead of carrying on wars in their own name, they contrived an authority,

at once irresistible and irresponsible, in whose name they might ravage at pleasure; and being thus freed from all restraint, they indulged themselves in the most extravagant speculations of plunder. The cabal[1] of creditors who have been the object of the late bountiful grant from his Majesty's ministers, in order to possess themselves, under the name of creditors and assignees, of every country in India, as fast as it should be conquered, inspired into the mind of the Nabob of Arcot[2] (then a dependent on the Company of the humblest order) a scheme of the most wild and desperate ambition that I believe ever was admitted into the thoughts of a man so situated. First, they persuaded him to consider himself as a principal member in the political system of Europe. In the next place, they held out to him, and he readily imbibed, the idea of the general empire of Hindostan. As a preliminary to this undertaking, they prevailed on him to propose a tripartite division of that vast country: one part to the Company; another to the Mahrattas;[3] and the third to himself. To himself he reserved all the southern part of the great peninsula, comprehended under the general name of the Deccan.

On this scheme of their servants, the Company was to appear in the Carnatic[4] in no other light than as a contractor for the provision of armies, and the hire of mercenaries for his use and under his direction. This disposition was to be secured by the Nabob's putting himself under the guaranty of France, and, by the means of that rival nation, preventing the English forever from assuming an equality, much less a superiority, in the Carnatic. In pursuance of this treasonable project, (treasonable on the part of the English,) they extinguished the Company as a sovereign power in that part of India; they withdrew the Company's garrisons out of all the forts and strongholds of the Carnatic; they declined to receive the ambassadors from foreign courts, and remitted them to the Nabob of Arcot; they fell upon, and totally destroyed, the oldest ally of the Company, the king of Tanjore,[5] and plundered the country to the

---

[1] Sir Joshua Reynolds, the most famous English painter of the time [2] always [3] ear-trumpet

[1] conspiracy [2] a city west and a little south of Madras [3] a warlike race of western and central India [4] a district on the eastern coast of India, now a part of the province of Madras [5] a state southwest of Madras

amount of near five millions sterling; one after another, in the Nabob's name, but with English force, they brought into a miserable servitude all the princes and great independent nobility of a vast country. In proportion to these treasons and violences, which ruined the people, the fund of the Nabob's debt grew and flourished.

Among the victims to this magnificent plan of universal plunder, worthy of the heroic avarice of the projectors, you have all heard (and he has made himself to be well remembered) of an Indian chief called Hyder Ali Khan. This man possessed the western, as the Company, under the name of the Nabob of Arcot, does the eastern division of the Carnatic. It was among the leading measures in the design of this cabal (according to their own emphatic language) to *extirpate* this Hyder Ali. They declared the Nabob of Arcot to be his sovereign, and himself to be a rebel, and publicly invested their instrument with the sovereignty of the kingdom of Mysore.[1] But their victim was not of the passive kind. They were soon obliged to conclude a treaty of peace and close alliance with this rebel, at the gates of Madras. Both before and since that treaty, every principle of policy pointed out this power as a natural alliance; and on his part it was courted by every sort of amicable office. But the cabinet council of English creditors would not suffer their Nabob of Arcot to sign the treaty, nor even to give to a prince at least his equal the ordinary titles of respect and courtesy. From that time forward, a continued plot was carried on within the divan,[2] black and white, of the Nabob of Arcot, for the destruction of Hyder Ali. As to the outward members of the double, or rather treble government of Madras, which had signed the treaty, they were always prevented by some overruling influence (which they do not describe, but which cannot be misunderstood) from performing what justice and interest combined so evidently to enforce.

When at length Hyder Ali found that he had to do with men who either would sign no convention, or whom no treaty and no signature could bind, and who were the determined enemies of human intercourse itself, he decreed to make the country possessed by these in-

corrigible and predestinated criminals a memorable example to mankind. He resolved, in the gloomy recesses of a mind capacious of such things, to leave the whole Carnatic an everlasting monument of vengeance, and to put perpetual desolation as a barrier between him and those against whom the faith which holds the moral elements of the world together was no protection. He became at length so confident of his force, so collected in his might, that he made no secret whatsoever of his dreadful resolution. Having terminated his disputes with every enemy and every rival, who buried their mutual animosities in their common detestation against the creditors of the Nabob of Arcot, he drew from every quarter whatever a savage ferocity could add to his new rudiments in the arts of destruction; and compounding all the materials of fury, havoc, and desolation into one black cloud, he hung for a while on the declivities of the mountains. Whilst the authors of all these evils were idly and stupidly gazing on this menacing meteor, which blackened all their horizon, it suddenly burst, and poured down the whole of its contents upon the plains of the Carnatic. Then ensued a scene of woe, the like of which no eye had seen, no heart conceived, and which no tongue can adequately tell. All the horrors of war before known or heard of were mercy to that new havoc. A storm of universal fire blasted every field, consumed every house, destroyed every temple. The miserable inhabitants, flying from their flaming villages, in part were slaughtered; others, without regard to sex, to age, to the respect of rank or sacredness of function, fathers torn from children, husbands from wives, enveloped in a whirlwind of cavalry, and amidst the goading spears of drivers, and the trampling of pursuing horses, were swept into captivity in an unknown and hostile land. Those who were able to evade this tempest fled to the walled cities; but escaping from fire, sword, and exile, they fell into the jaws of famine.

The alms of the settlement, in this dreadful exigency, were certainly liberal; and all was done by charity that private charity could do: but it was a people in beggary; it was a nation which stretched out its hands for food. For months together, these creatures of sufferance, whose very excess and luxury in their most plenteous days had fallen short of the allowance of our austerest fasts, silent, patient,

[1] a state west of Madras [2] council of government

resigned, without sedition or disturbance, almost without complaint, perished by an hundred a day in the streets of Madras; every day seventy at least laid their bodies in the streets or on the glacis[1] of Tanjore, and expired of famine in the granary of India. I was going to awake your justice towards this unhappy part of our fellow-citizens, by bringing before you some of the circumstances of this plague of hunger: of all the calamities which beset and waylay the life of man, this comes the nearest to our heart, and is that wherein the proudest of us all feels himself to be nothing more than he is: but I find myself unable to manage it with decorum; these details are of a species of horror so nauseous and disgusting, they are so degrading to the sufferers and to the hearers, they are so humiliating to human nature itself, that, on better thoughts, I find it more advisable to throw a pall over this hideous object, and to leave it to your general conceptions.

For eighteen months, without intermission, this destruction raged from the gates of Madras to the gates of Tanjore; and so completely did these masters in their art, Hyder Ali and his more ferocious son, absolve themselves of their impious vow, that, when the British armies traversed, as they did, the Carnatic for hundreds of miles in all directions, through the whole line of their march they did not see one man, not one woman, not one child, not one four-footed beast of any description whatever. One dead, uniform silence reigned over the whole region. With the inconsiderable exceptions of the narrow vicinage of some few forts, I wish to be understood as speaking literally. I mean to produce to you more than three witnesses, above all exception, who will support this assertion in its full extent. That hurricane of war passed through every part of the central provinces of the Carnatic. Six or seven districts to the north and to the south (and these not wholly untouched) escaped the general ravage.

The Carnatic is a country not much inferior in extent to England. Figure to yourself, Mr. Speaker, the land in whose representative chair you sit; figure to yourself the form and fashion of your sweet and cheerful country from Thames to Trent, north and south, and from the Irish to the German Sea, east and west, emptied and embowelled (may God avert the omen of our crimes!) by so accomplished a desolation. Extend your imagination a little further, and then suppose your ministers taking a survey of these scenes of waste and desolation. What would be your thoughts, if you should be informed that they were computing how much had been the amount of the excises, how much the customs, how much the land and malt tax, in order that they should charge (take it in the most favourable light) for public service, upon the relics of the satiated vengeance of relentless enemies, the whole of what England had yielded in the most exuberant seasons of peace and abundance? What would you call it? To call it tyranny sublimed into madness would be too faint an image; yet this very madness is the principle upon which the ministers at your right hand have proceeded in their estimate of the revenues of the Carnatic, when they were providing, not supply for the establishments of its protection, but rewards for the authors of its ruin.

Every day you are fatigued and disgusted with this cant, "The Carnatic is a country that will soon recover, and become instantly as prosperous as ever." They think they are talking to innocents, who will believe, that, by sowing of dragons' teeth, men may come up ready grown and ready armed.[1] They who will give themselves the trouble of considering (for it requires no great reach of thought, no very profound knowledge) the manner in which mankind are increased, and countries cultivated, will regard all this raving as it ought to be regarded. In order that the people, after a long period of vexation and plunder, may be in a condition to maintain government, government must begin by maintaining them. Here the road to economy lies not through receipt, but through expense; and in that country Nature has given no short cut to your object. Men must propagate, like other animals, by the mouth. Never did oppression light the nuptial torch; never did extortion and usury spread out the genial bed. Does any of you think that England, so wasted, would, under such a nursing attendance, so rapidly and cheaply recover? But he is meanly acquainted with either England or India who does not know that England would a thousand times sooner

---

[1] a sloping bank in a fortification

[1] Cf. footnote on p. 210, above

resume population, fertility, and what ought to be the ultimate secretion from both, revenue, than such a country as the Carnatic.

The Carnatic is not by the bounty of Nature a fertile soil. The general size of its cattle is proof enough that it is much otherwise. It is some days since I moved that a curious and interesting map, kept in the India house, should be laid before you. The India House is not yet in readiness to send it; I have therefore brought down my own copy, and there it lies for the use of any gentleman who may think such a matter worthy of his attention. It is, indeed, a noble map, and of noble things; but it is decisive against the golden dreams and sanguine speculations of avarice run mad. In addition to what you know must be the case in every part of the world, (the necessity of a previous provision of habitation, seed, stock, capital,) that map will show you that the uses of the influences of Heaven itself are in that country a work of art. The Carnatic is refreshed by few or no living brooks or running streams, and it has rain only at a season; but its product of rice exacts the use of water subject to perpetual command. This is the national bank of the Carnatic, on which it must have a perpetual credit, or it perishes irretrievably. For that reason, in the happier times of India, a number, almost incredible, of reservoirs have been made in chosen places throughout the whole country: they are formed, for the greater part, of mounds of earth and stones, with sluices of solid masonry; the whole constructed with admirable skill and labour, and maintained at a mighty charge. In the territory contained in that map alone, I have been at the trouble of reckoning the reservoirs, and they amount to upwards of eleven hundred, from the extent of two or three acres to five miles in circuit. From these reservoirs currents are occasionally drawn over the fields, and these watercourses again call for a considerable expense to keep them properly scoured and duly levelled. Taking the district in that map as a measure, there cannot be in the Carnatic and Tanjore fewer than ten thousand of these reservoirs of the larger and middling dimensions, to say nothing of those for domestic services, and the use of religious purification. These are not the enterprises of your power, nor in a style of magnificence suited to the taste of your minister. These are the monuments of real kings, who were the fathers of their people, — testa-

tors to a posterity which they embraced as their own. These are the grand sepulchres built by ambition, — but by the ambition of an insatiable benevolence, which, not contented with reigning in the dispensation of happiness during the contracted term of human life, had strained, with all the reachings and graspings of a vivacious mind, to extend the dominion of their bounty beyond the limits of Nature, and to perpetuate themselves through generations of generations, the guardians, the protectors, the nourishers of mankind.

Long before the late invasion, the persons who are objects of the grant of public money now before you had so diverted the supply of the pious funds of culture and population, that everywhere the reservoirs were fallen into a miserable decay. But after those domestic enemies had provoked the entry of a cruel foreign foe into the country, he did not leave it, until his revenge had completed the destruction begun by their avarice. Few, very few indeed, of these magazines of water that are not either totally destroyed, or cut through with such gaps as to require a serious attention and much cost to reëstablish them, as the means of present subsistence to the people and of future revenue to the state.

What, Sir, would a virtuous and enlightened ministry do, on the view of the ruins of such works before them? — on the view of such a chasm of desolation as that which yawned in the midst of those countries, to the north and south, which still bore some vestiges of cultivation? They would have reduced all their most necessary establishments; they would have suspended the justest payments; they would have employed every shilling derived from the producing to reanimate the powers of the unproductive parts. While they were performing this fundamental duty, whilst they were celebrating these mysteries of justice and humanity, they would have told the corps of fictitious creditors, whose crimes were their claims, that they must keep an awful distance, — that they must silence their inauspicious tongues, — that they must hold off their profane, unhallowed paws from this holy work; they would have proclaimed, with a voice that should make itself heard, that on every country the first creditor is the plough, — that this original, indefeasible claim supersedes every other demand.

This is what a wise and virtuous ministry

would have done and said. This, therefore, is what our minister could never think of saying or doing. A ministry of another kind would have first improved the country, and have thus laid a solid foundation for future opulence and future force. But on this grand point of the restoration of the country there is not one syllable to be found in the correspondence of our ministers, from the first to the last; they felt nothing for a land desolated by fire, sword, and famine: their sympathies took another direction; they were touched with pity for bribery, so long tormented with a fruitless itching of its palms; their bowels yearned for usury, that had long missed the harvest of its returning months; they felt for peculation, which had been for so many years raking in the dust of an empty treasury; they were melted into compassion for rapine and oppression, licking their dry, parched, unbloody jaws. These were the objects of their solicitude. These were the necessities for which they were studious to provide. . . .

FROM REFLECTIONS ON THE REVOLUTION IN FRANCE

' *   *   *   *   *   *   *

It is now sixteen or seventeen years since I saw the queen of France, then the Dauphiness,[1] at Versailles; and surely never lighted on this orb, which she hardly seemed to touch, a more delightful vision. I saw her just above the horizon, decorating and cheering the elevated sphere she just began to move in, — glittering like the morning-star, full of life and splendour and joy. Oh! what a revolution! and what an heart must I have, to contemplate without emotion that elevation and that fall! Little did I dream, when she added titles of veneration to those of enthusiastic, distant, respectful love, that she should ever be obliged to carry the sharp antidote against disgrace concealed in that bosom! little did I dream that I should have lived to see such disasters fallen upon her in a nation of gallant men, in a nation of men of honour, and of cavaliers! I thought ten thousand swords must have leaped from their scabbards to avenge even a look that threatened her with insult. But the age of chivalry is gone. That of sophisters, economists, and

[1] wife of the crown prince

calculators has succeeded; and the glory of Europe is extinguished forever. Never, never more, shall we behold that generous loyalty to rank and sex, that proud submission, that dignified obedience, that subordination of the heart, which kept alive, even in servitude itself, the spirit of an exalted freedom! The unbought grace of life, the cheap defence of nations, the nurse of manly sentiment and heroic enterprise, is gone! It is gone, that sensibility of principle, that chastity of honour, which felt a stain like a wound, which inspired courage whilst it mitigated ferocity, which ennobled whatever it touched, and under which vice itself lost half its evil by losing all its grossness!

The mixed system of opinion and sentiment had its origin in the ancient chivalry; and the principle, though varied in its appearance by the varying state of human affairs, subsisted and influenced through a long succession of generations, even to the time we live in. If it should ever be totally extinguished, the loss, I fear, will be great. It is this which has given its character to modern Europe. It is this which has distinguished it under all its forms of government, and distinguished it to its advantage, from the states of Asia, and possibly from those states which flourished in the most brilliant periods of the antique world. It was this, which, without confounding ranks, had produced a noble equality, and handed it down through all the gradations of social life. It was this opinion which mitigated kings into companions, and raised private men to be fellows with kings. Without force or opposition, it subdued the fierceness of pride and power; it obliged sovereigns to submit to the soft collar of social esteem, compelled stern ·authority to submit to elegance, and gave a domination, vanquisher of laws, to be subdued by manners.

But now all is to be changed. All the pleasing illusions which made power gentle and obedience liberal, which harmonised the different shades of life, and which by a bland assimilation incorporated into politics the sentiments which beautify and soften private society, are to be dissolved by this new conquering empire of light and reason. All the decent drapery of life is to be rudely torn off. All the superadded ideas, furnished from the wardrobe of a moral imagination, which the heart owns and the understanding ratifies, as necessary to cover the defects of our naked,

shivering nature, and to raise it to dignity in
our own estimation, are to be exploded as a
ridiculous, absurd, and antiquated fashion.

* * * * * * *

WILLIAM COWPER (1731–1800)

THE TASK

From BOOK I

There often wanders one, whom better days
Saw better clad, in cloak of satin trimmed 535
With lace, and hat with splendid riband bound.
A serving-maid was she, and fell in love
With one who left her, went to sea, and died.
Her fancy followed him through foaming waves
To distant shores, and she would sit and weep
At what a sailor suffers; fancy too, 541
Delusive most where warmest wishes are,
Would oft anticipate his glad return,
And dream of transports she was not to know.
She heard the doleful tidings of his death, 545
And never smiled again. And now she roams
The dreary waste; there spends the livelong
day,
And there, unless when charity forbids,
The livelong night. A tattered apron hides,
Worn as a cloak, and hardly hides, a gown 550
More tattered still; and both but ill conceal
A bosom heaved with never-ceasing sighs.
She begs an idle pin of all she meets,
And hoards them in her sleeve; but needful
food,
Though pressed with hunger oft, or comelier
clothes, 555
Though pinched with cold, asks never. —
Kate is crazed.
I see a column of slow-rising smoke
O'ertop the lofty wood that skirts the wild.
A vagabond and useless tribe there eat
Their miserable meal. A kettle, slung 560
Between two poles upon a stick transverse,
Receives the morsel; flesh obscene of dog,
Or vermin, or, at best, of cock purloined
From his accustomed perch. Hard-faring
race!
They pick their fuel out of every hedge, 565
Which, kindled with dry leaves, just saves un-
quenched
The spark of life. The sportive wind blows
wide
Their fluttering rags, and shows a tawny skin,
The vellum of the pedigree they claim.

Great skill have they in palmistry, and more
To conjure clean away the gold they touch,
Conveying worthless dross into its place; 572
Loud when they beg, dumb only when they
steal.
Strange! that a creature rational, and cast
In human mould, should brutalize by choice
His nature, and, though capable of arts 576
By which the world might profit and himself,
Self banished from society, prefer
Such squalid sloth to honourable toil!
Yet even these, though, feigning sickness oft,
They swathe the forehead, drag the limping
limb, 581
And vex their flesh with artificial sores,
Can change their whine into a mirthful note
When safe occasion offers; and with dance,
And music of the bladder and the bag,[1] 585
Beguile their woes, and make the woods re-
sound.
Such health and gaiety of heart enjoy
The houseless rovers of the sylvan world;
And breathing wholesome air, and wandering
much,
Need other physic none to heal the effects 590
Of loathsome diet, penury, and cold.

* * * * * * *

From BOOK II

Oh for a lodge in some vast wilderness,[2]
Some boundless contiguity of shade,
Where rumour of oppression and deceit,
Of unsuccessful or successful war,
Might never reach me more! My ear is
pained, 5
My soul is sick with every day's report
Of wrong and outrage with which earth is filled.
There is no flesh in man's obdurate heart,
It does not feel for man; the natural bond
Of brotherhood is severed as the flax 10
That falls asunder at the touch of fire.
He finds his fellow guilty of a skin
Not coloured like his own, and, having power
To enforce the wrong, for such a worthy cause
Dooms and devotes him as his lawful prey. 15
Lands intersected by a narrow frith
Abhor each other. Mountains interposed
Make enemies of nations who had else
Like kindred drops been mingled into one.
Thus man devotes his brother, and destroys;
And worse than all, and most to be deplored,
As human nature's broadest, foulest blot, 22

---

[1] bagpipe   [2] Cf. *Jeremiah*, ix: 2

Chains him, and tasks him, and exacts his
sweat
With stripes that Mercy, with a bleeding
heart,
Weeps when she sees inflicted on a beast. 25
Then what is man? And what man seeing
this,
And having human feelings, does not blush
And hang his head, to think himself a man?
I would not have a slave to till my ground,
To carry me, to fan me while I sleep, 30
And tremble when I wake, for all the wealth
That sinews bought and sold have ever earned.
No: dear as freedom is, and in my heart's
Just estimation prized above all price,
I had much rather be myself the slave 35
And wear the bonds, than fasten them on him.
We have no slaves at home. — Then why
abroad?
And they themselves once ferried o'er the
wave
That parts us, are emancipate and loosed.
Slaves cannot breathe in England;[1] if their
lungs 40
Receive our air, that moment they are free,
They touch our country, and their shackles
fall.
That's noble, and bespeaks a nation proud
And jealous of the blessing. Spread it then,
And let it circulate through every vein
Of all your empire; that where Britain's
power
Is felt, mankind may feel her mercy too. 47

* * * * * * *

FROM BOOK V

'Tis morning; and the sun with ruddy orb
Ascending, fires the horizon: while the clouds
That crowd away before the driving wind,
More ardent as the disk emerges more,
Resemble most some city in a blaze, 5
Seen through the leafless wood. His slanting
ray
Slides ineffectual down the snowy vale,
And tinging all with his own rosy hue,
From every herb and every spiry blade
Stretches a length of shadow o'er the field. 10
Mine, spindling into longitude immense,
In spite of gravity, and sage remark
That I myself am but a fleeting shade,

[1] the decision of Chief Justice Lord Mansfield,
June 22, 1772

Provokes me to a smile. With eye askance
I view the muscular proportioned limb 15
Transformed to a lean shank. The shapeless
pair,
As they designed to mock me, at my side
Take step for step; and as I near approach
The cottage, walk along the plastered wall,
Preposterous sight! the legs without the man.
The verdure of the plain lies buried deep 21
Beneath the dazzling deluge; and the bents[1]
And coarser grass, upspearing o'er the rest,
Of late unsightly and unseen, now shine
Conspicuous, and in bright apparel clad, 25
And fledged with icy feathers, nod superb.
The cattle mourn in corners where the fence
Screens them, and seem half-petrified to sleep
In unrecumbent sadness. There they wait
Their wonted fodder, not like hungering man,
Fretful if unsupplied, but silent, meek, 31
And patient of the slow-paced swain's delay.
He from the stack carves out the accustomed
load,
Deep-plunging, and again deep-plunging oft,
His broad keen knife into the solid mass; 35
Smooth as a wall the upright remnant stands,
With such undeviating and even force
He severs it away: no needless care
Lest storms should overset the leaning pile
Deciduous, or its own unbalanced weight. 40
Forth goes the woodman, leaving unconcerned
The cheerful haunts of man, to wield the axe
And drive the wedge in yonder forest drear,
From morn to eve his solitary task.
Shaggy, and lean, and shrewd, with pointed
ears 45
And tail cropped short, half lurcher[2] and half
cur,
His dog attends him. Close behind his heel
Now creeps he slow; and now with many a
frisk
Wide scampering, snatches up the drifted snow
With ivory teeth, or ploughs it with his snout;
Then shakes his powdered coat, and barks for
joy. 51
Heedless of all his pranks, the sturdy churl
Moves right toward the mark; nor stops for
aught,
But now and then with pressure of his thumb
To adjust the fragrant charge of a short tube
That fumes beneath his nose: the trailing
cloud 56
Streams far behind him, scenting all the air.

[1] wiry grass [2] a cross between greyhound
and sheep-dog, keen both of sight and of scent

Now from the roost, or from the neighbouring
          pale,
Where, diligent to catch the first faint gleam
Of smiling day, they gossiped side by side, 60
Come trooping at the housewife's well-known
          call
The feathered tribes domestic.   Half on wing,
And half on foot, they brush the fleecy flood,
Conscious, and fearful of too deep a plunge.
The sparrows peep, and quit the sheltering
          eaves   65
To seize the fair occasion.   Well they eye
The scattered grain, and thievishly resolved
To escape the impending famine, often scared
As oft return, a pert voracious kind.   69
Clean riddance quickly made, one only care
Remains to each, the search of sunny nook,
Or shed impervious to the blast.   Resigned
To sad necessity, the cock foregoes
His wonted strut, and wading at their head
With well-considered steps, seems to resent 75
His altered gait and stateliness retrenched.

* * * * * * *

ON THE LOSS OF THE ROYAL
GEORGE

Toll for the brave !
    The brave that are no more !
All sunk beneath the wave,
    Fast by their native shore !

Eight hundred of the brave,   5
    Whose courage well was tried,
Had made the vessel heel,
    And laid her on her side.

A land-breeze shook the shrouds,
    And she was overset ;   10
Down went the Royal George,
    With all her crew complete.

Toll for the brave !
    Brave Kempenfelt [1] is gone ;
His last sea-fight is fought ;   15
    His work of glory done.

It was not in the battle ;
    No tempest gave the shock ;
She sprang no fatal leak ;
    She ran upon no rock.   20

[1] rear-admiral of the fleet

His sword was in its sheath ;
    His fingers held the pen,
When Kempenfelt went down
    With twice four hundred men.

Weigh the vessel up,   25
    Once dreaded by our foes !
And mingle with our cup
    The tears that England owes.

Her timbers are yet sound,
    And she may float again   30
Full charged with England's thunder,
    And plough the distant main.

But Kempenfelt is gone,
    His victories are o'er ;
And he and his eight hundred   35
    Shall plough the wave no more.

ON THE RECEIPT OF MY MOTHER'S
PICTURE

Oh that those lips had language ! Life has
          passed
With me but roughly since I heard thee last.
Those lips are thine — thy own sweet smile I
          see,
The same that oft in childhood solaced me ;
Voice only fails, else how distinct they say,
"Grieve not, my child, chase all thy fears
          away !"
The meek intelligence of those dear eyes
(Bless'd be the art that can immortalise,
The art that baffles Time's tyrannic claim
To quench it) here shines on me still the same.
    Faithful remembrancer of one so dear,   11
O welcome guest, though unexpected here !
Who bidst me honour with an artless song,
Affectionate, a mother lost so long,[1]
I will obey, not willingly alone,
But gladly, as the precept were her own :
And, while that face renews my filial grief,
Fancy shall weave a charm for my relief,
Shall steep me in Elysian reverie,
A momentary dream that thou art she.   20
    My mother ! when I learnt that thou wast
          dead [2]
Say, wast thou conscious of the tears I shed,
Hovered thy spirit o'er thy sorrowing son,
Wretch even then, life's journey just begun ?

[1] fifty-two years   [2] He was only six when she
died.

Perhaps thou gavest me, though unfelt, a kiss:
Perhaps a tear, if souls can weep in bliss —
Ah, that maternal smile! It answers — Yes.
I heard the bell tolled on thy burial day,
I saw the hearse that bore thee slow away,
And turning from my nursery window, drew
A long, long sigh, and wept a last adieu! 31
But was it such? — It was. — Where thou art gone
Adieus and farewells are a sound unknown.
May I but meet thee on that peaceful shore,
The parting word shall pass my lips no more!
Thy maidens, grieved themselves at my concern,
Oft gave me promise of thy quick return.
What ardently I wished I long believed,
And, disappointed still, was still deceived.
By expectation every day beguiled,   40
Dupe of *to-morrow* even from a child.
Thus many a sad to-morrow came and went,
Till, all my stock of infant sorrow spent,
I learned at last submission to my lot;
But, though I less deplored thee, ne'er forgot.
Where once we dwelt our name is heard no
    more,
Children not thine have trod my nursery floor;
And where the gardener Robin, day by day,
Drew me to school along the public way,
Delighted with my bauble coach, and wrapped
In scarlet mantle warm, and velvet capped,
'Tis now become a history little known, 52
That once we called the pastoral house[1] our
    own.
Short-lived possession! but the record fair
That memory keeps, of all thy kindness there,
Still outlives many a storm that has effaced
A thousand other themes less deeply traced.
Thy nightly visits to my chamber made,
That thou mightst know me safe and warmly
    laid;
Thy morning bounties ere I left my home, 60
The biscuit, or confectionary plum;
The fragrant waters on my cheeks bestowed
By thy own hand, till fresh they shone and
    glowed;
All this, and more endearing still than all,
Thy constant flow of love, that knew no fall,
Ne'er roughened by those cataracts and brakes
That humour interposed too often makes;
All this still legible in memory's page,
And still to be so to my latest age,
Adds joy to duty, makes me glad to pay 70
Such honours to thee as my numbers may;

[1] the rectory

Perhaps a frail memorial, but sincere,
Not scorned in heaven, though little noticed
    here.
    Could Time, his flight reversed, restore the
        hours,
When, playing with thy vesture's tissued
    flowers,
The violet, the pink, and jassamine,
I pricked them into paper with a pin
(And thou wast happier than myself the while,
Wouldst softly speak, and stroke my head and
    smile),
Could those few pleasant days again appear,
Might one wish bring them, would I wish them
    here?   81
I would not trust my heart — the dear delight
Seems so to be desired, perhaps I might. —
But no — what here we call our life is such,
So little to be loved, and thou so much,
That I should ill requite thee to constrain
Thy unbound spirit into bonds again.
    Thou, as a gallant bark from Albion's coast
(The storms all weathered and the ocean
    crossed)
Shoots into port at some well-havened isle, 90
Where spices breathe, and brighter seasons
    smile,
There sits quiescent on the floods that show
Her beauteous form reflected clear below,
While airs impregnated with incense play
Around her, fanning light her streamers gay;
So thou, with sails how swift! hast reached
    the shore,
"Where tempests never beat nor billows roar."
And thy loved consort on the dangerous tide
Of life long since has anchored by thy side.
But me, scarce hoping to attain that rest, 100
Always from port withheld, always distressed —
Me howling blasts drive devious, tempest tost,
Sails ripped, seams opening wide, and compass lost,
And day by day some current's thwarting
    force
Sets me more distant from a prosperous course.
Yet, oh, the thought that thou art safe, and
    he!
That thought is joy, arrive what may to me.
My boast is not, that I deduce my birth
From loins enthroned and rulers of the earth;
But higher far my proud pretensions rise —
The son of parents passed into the skies! 111
And now, farewell — Time unrevoked has run
His wonted course, yet what I wished is
    done.

By contemplation's help, not sought in vain,
I seem to have lived my childhood o'er again ;
To have renewed the joys that once were
          mine,
Without the sin of violating thine :
And, while the wings of Fancy still are free,
And I can view this mimic show of thee,   119
Time has but half succeeded in his theft —
Thyself removed, thy power to soothe me left.

JAMES MACPHERSON (?)

(1736–1796)

THE POEMS OF OSSIAN

FROM CATH–LODA[1]

DUAN III

Whence is the stream of years? Whither
do they roll along? Where have they hid, in
mist, their many coloured sides?

I look unto the times of old, but they seem
dim to Ossian's eyes, like reflected moonbeams
on a distant lake. Here rise the red beams
of war ! There, silent, dwells a feeble race !
They mark no years with their deeds, as slow
they pass along. Dweller between the
shields ! thou that awakest the failing soul !
descend from thy wall, harp of Cona,[2] with thy
voices three ! Come with that which kindles
the past : rear the forms of old, on their own
dark-brown years !

U-thorno, hill of storms, I behold my race
on thy side. Fingal is bending in night over
Duth-maruno's tomb. Near him are the steps
of his heroes, hunters of the boar. By Turthor's stream the host of Lochlin[3] is deep in
shades. The wrathful kings[4] stood on two
hills : they looked forward from their bossy
shields. They looked forward to the stars
of night, red wandering in the west. Cruth-
loda[5] bends from high, like a formless meteor
in clouds. He sends abroad the winds, and
marks them with his signs. Starno foresaw
that Morven's king[6] was not to yield in war.

He twice struck the tree in wrath. He
rushed before his son. He hummed a surly
song, and heard his hair in wind. Turned

from one another, they stood, like two oaks,
which different winds had bent ; each hangs
over his own loud rill, and shakes his boughs
in the course of blasts.

"Annir,"[1] said Starno of lakes, "was a fire
that consumed of old. He poured death from
his eyes along the striving fields. His joy was
in the fall of men. Blood to him was a summer stream, that brings joy to the withered
vales, from its own mossy rock. He came
forth to the lake Luth-cormo, to meet the tall
Corman-trunar, he from Urlor of streams,
dweller of battle's wing.

"The chief of Urlor had come to Gormal
with his dark-bosomed ships. He saw the
daughter of Annir, white-armed Foina-bragal.
He saw her ! Nor careless rolled her eyes on
the rider of stormy waves. She fled to his
ship in darkness, like a moonbeam through a
nightly veil. Annir pursued along the deep ;
he called the winds of heaven. Nor alone was
the king ! Starno was by his side. Like
U-thorno's young eagle, I turned my eyes on
my father.

"We rushed into roaring[2] Urlor. With his
people came tall Corman-trunar. We fought ;
but the foe prevailed. In his wrath my
father stood. He lopped the young trees with
his sword. His eyes rolled red in his rage.
I marked the soul of the king, and I retired
in night. From the field I took a broken helmet ; a shield that was pierced with steel ;
pointless was the spear in my hand. I went
to find the foe.

"On a rock sat tall Corman-trunar beside
his burning oak ; and near him beneath a tree,
sat deep-bosomed Foina-bragal. I threw my
broken shield before her. I spoke the words
of peace. 'Beside his rolling sea lies Annir of
many lakes. The king was pierced in battle ;
and Starno is to raise his tomb.[3] Me, a son of
Loda,[4] he sends to white-handed Foina, to bid
her send a lock from her hair, to rest with her
father in earth. And thou, king of roaring
Urlor, let the battle cease, till Annir receive
the shell[5] from fiery-eyed Cruth-loda.'[6]

"Bursting into tears, she rose, and tore a lock
from her hair ; a lock, which wandered in the
blast, along her heaving breast. Corman-
trunar gave the shell,[7] and bade me rejoice

---

[1] the Battle of Loda [2] the home of Ossian
[3] Norway [4] Starno, king of Lochlin, or Norway,
and Swaran, his son and heir [5] Odin, chief god
of the Norsemen [6] Fingal (of Scotland)

[1] father of Starno [2] because of its many
streams [3] This was untrue. [4] He was disguised.
[5] Shells were used as drinking-cups. [6] i.e., in Val-
halla, the heaven of heroes [7] offered drink

before him. I rested in the shade of night, and hid my face in my helmet deep. Sleep descended on the foe. I rose, like a stalking ghost. I pierced the side of Corman-trunar. Nor did Foina-brugal escape. She rolled her white bosom in blood.

"Why, then, daughter of heroes, didst thou wake my rage?

"Morning rose. The foe were fled, like the departure of mist. Annir struck his bossy shield. He called his dark-haired son. I came, streaked with wandering blood: thrice rose the shout of the king, like the bursting forth of a squall of wind from a cloud by night. We rejoiced three days above the dead, and called the hawks of heaven. They came from all their winds to feast on Annir's foes.

"Swaran, Fingal is alone in his hill of night. Let thy spear pierce the king in secret; like Annir, my soul shall rejoice."

"Son of Annir," said Swaran, "I shall not slay in shades: I move forth in light: the hawks rush from all their winds. They are wont to trace my course: it is not harmless through war."

Burning rose the rage of the king.[1] He thrice raised his gleaming spear. But, starting, he spared his son, and rushed into the night. By Turthor's stream, a cave is dark, the dwelling of Corban-cargla.[2] There he laid the helmet of kings, and called the maid of Lulan; but she was distant far in Loda's resounding hall.[3]

Swelling in his rage, he strode to where Fingal lay alone. The king was laid on his shield, on his own secret hill.

Stern hunter of shaggy boars! no feeble maid is laid before thee. No boy on his ferny bed, by Turthor's murmuring stream. Here is spread the couch of the mighty, from which they rise to deeds of death! Hunter of shaggy boars, awaken not the terrible!

Starno came murmuring on. Fingal arose in arms. "Who art thou, son of night!" Silent he threw the spear. They mixed their gloomy strife. The shield of Starno fell, cleft in twain. He is bound to an oak. The early beam arose. It was then Fingal beheld the king. He rolled awhile his silent eyes. He thought of other days, when white-bosomed

---

[1] Starno   [2] the maid of Lulan, beloved by Starno, but in love with Swaran   [3] i.e., she was dead

AE

Agandecca[1] moved like the music of songs. He loosed the thong from his hands. "Son of Annir," he said, "retire. Retire to Gormal of shells;[2] a beam that was set returns. I remember thy white-bosomed daughter; dreadful king, away! Go to thy troubled dwelling, cloudy foe of the lovely. Let the stranger shun thee, thou gloomy in the hall!"

A tale of the times of old!

JAMES BOSWELL (1740-1795)

THE LIFE OF SAMUEL JOHNSON, LL.D.

FROM CHAPTER XIII (1763)

* * * * * * *

He talked very contemptuously of Churchill's[3] poetry, observing, that "it had a temporary currency, only from its audacity of abuse, and being filled with living names, and that it would sink into oblivion." I ventured to hint that he was not quite a fair judge, as Churchill had attacked him violently.[4] Johnson: "Nay, Sir, I am a very fair judge. He did not attack me violently till he found I did not like his poetry; and his attack on me shall not prevent me from continuing to say what I think of him, from an apprehension that it may be ascribed to resentment. No, Sir, I called the fellow a blockhead at first, and I will call him a blockhead still. However, I will acknowledge that I have a better opinion of him now than I once had; for he has shown more fertility than I expected. To be sure, he is a tree that cannot produce good fruit: he only bears crabs. But, Sir, a tree that produces a great many crabs, is better than a tree which produces only a few."

In this depreciation of Churchill's poetry, I could not agree with him. It is very true that the greatest part of it is upon the topics of the day, on which account, as it brought him great fame and profit at the time, it must

---

[1] daughter of Starno and sweetheart of Fingal, killed long before by her father for revealing to Fingal a plot against his life   [2] the castle of Starno, where drink was dispensed liberally   [3] Charles Churchill (1731-64), then in considerable repute as a poet   [4] He satirized Johnson as credulous in his poem *The Ghost.*

proportionably slide out of the public attention, as other occasional objects succeed. But Churchill had extraordinary vigour both of thought and expression. His portraits of the players will ever be valuable to the true lovers of the drama ; and his strong caricatures of several eminent men of his age, will not be forgotten by the curious. Let me add, that there are in his works many passages which are of a general nature ; and his "Prophecy of Famine" is a poem of no ordinary merit. It is, indeed, falsely injurious to Scotland ; but therefore, may be allowed a greater share of invention.

Bonnell Thornton had just published a burlesque "Ode on St. Cecilia's day," [1] adapted to the ancient British music, viz., the saltbox, the Jew's-harp, the marrow-bones and cleaver, the hum-strum, or hurdy-gurdy, etc. Johnson praised its humour, and seemed much diverted with it. He repeated the following passage :

"In strains more exalted the salt-box shall join,
And clattering and battering and clapping combine ;
With a rap and a tap, while the hollow side sounds,
Up and down leaps the flap, and with rattling rebounds."

*   *   *   *   *   *   *

On Tuesday, the 5th of July, I again visited Johnson. He told me he had looked into the poems of a pretty voluminous writer, Mr. (now Dr.) John Ogilvie, one of the Presbyterian ministers of Scotland, which had lately come out, but could find no thinking in them. Boswell : "Is there not imagination in them, Sir ?" Johnson : "Why, Sir, there is in them what *was* imagination, but it is no more imagination in *him*, than sound is sound in the echo. And his diction too is not his own. We have long ago seen *white-robed innocence* and *flower-bespangled meads*."

Talking of London, he observed, "Sir, if you wish to have a just notion of the magnitude of this city, you must not be satisfied with seeing its great streets and squares, but must survey the innumerable little lanes and courts. It is not in the showy evolutions of buildings, but in the multiplicity of human habitations which are crowded together, that

the wonderful immensity of London consists." — I have often amused myself with thinking how different a place London is to different people. They, whose narrow minds are contracted to the consideration of some one particular pursuit, view it only through that medium. A politician thinks of it merely as the seat of government in its different departments ; a grazier, as a vast market for cattle ; a mercantile man, as a place where a prodigious deal of business is done upon 'Change ; a dramatic enthusiast, as the grand scene of theatrical entertainments ; a man of pleasure, as an assemblage of taverns, and the great emporium for ladies of easy virtue. But the intellectual man is struck with it, as comprehending the whole of human life in all its variety, the contemplation of which is inexhaustible.

On Wednesday, July 6, he was engaged to sup with me at my lodgings in Downing-street, Westminster. But on the preceding night my landlord having behaved very rudely to me and some company who were with me, I had resolved not to remain another night in his house. I was exceedingly uneasy at the awkward appearance I supposed I should make to Johnson and the other gentlemen whom I had invited, not being able to receive them at home, and being obliged to order supper at the Mitre. I went to Johnson in the morning, and talked of it as of a serious distress. He laughed, and said, "Consider, Sir, how insignificant this will appear a twelvemonth hence." Were this consideration to be applied to most of the little vexatious incidents of life, by which our quiet is too often disturbed, it would prevent many painful sensations. I have tried it frequently with good effect. "There is nothing," continued he, "in this mighty misfortune ; nay, we shall be better at the Mitre." I told him that I had been at Sir John Fielding's office, complaining of my landlord, and had been informed that though I had taken my lodgings for a year, I might, upon proof of his bad behaviour, quit them when I pleased, without being under an obligation to pay rent for any longer time than while I possessed them. The fertility of Johnson's mind could show itself even upon so small a matter as this. "Why, Sir," said he, "I suppose this must be the law, since you have been told so in Bow-street.[1] But if your landlord

---

[1] It was set to music by Dr. Burney, and performed at Ranelagh in masks.

[1] police headquarters

could hold you to your bargain, and the lodgings should be yours for a year, you may certainly use them as you think fit. So, Sir, you may quarter two life-guardsmen upon him; or you may send the greatest scoundrel you can find into your apartments; or you may say that you want to make some experiments in natural philosophy, and may burn a large quantity of asafœtida in his house."

I had as my guests this evening at the Mitre Tavern, Dr. Johnson, Dr. Goldsmith, Mr. Thomas Davies, Mr. Eccles, an Irish gentleman, for whose agreeable company I was obliged to Mr. Davies, and the Rev. Mr. John Ogilvie, who was desirous of being in company with my illustrious friend, while I, in my turn, was proud to have the honour of showing one of my countrymen upon what easy terms Johnson permitted me to live with him.

Goldsmith, as usual, endeavoured with too much eagerness to *shine* and disputed very warmly with Johnson against the well-known maxim of the British constitution, "the king can do no wrong;" affirming, that "what was morally false could not be politically true; and as the king might, in the exercise of his regal power, command and cause the doing of what was wrong, it certainly might be said, in sense and in reason, that he could do wrong." Johnson: "Sir, you are to consider that in our constitution, according to its true principles, the king is the head, he is supreme; he is above everything, and there is no power by which he can be tried. Therefore, it is, Sir, that we hold the king can do no wrong; that whatever may happen to be wrong in government may not be above our reach by being ascribed to majesty. Redress is always to be had against oppression by punishing the immediate agents. The king, though he should command, cannot force a judge to condemn a man unjustly; therefore it is the judge whom we prosecute and punish. Political institutions are formed upon the consideration of what will most frequently tend to the good of the whole, although now and then exceptions may occur. Thus it is better in general that a nation should have a supreme legislative power, although it may at times be abused. And then, Sir, there is this consideration, that *if the abuse be enormous, nature will rise up, and claiming her original rights, overturn a corrupt political system.*" I mark this animated sentence with peculiar pleasure, as

a noble instance of that truly dignified spirit of freedom which ever glowed in his heart, though he was charged with slavish tenets by superficial observers, because he was at all times indignant against that false patriotism, that pretended love of freedom, that unruly restlessness which is inconsistent with the stable authority of any good government.

This generous sentiment, which he uttered with great fervour, struck me exceedingly, and stirred my blood to that pitch of fancied resistance, the possibility of which I am glad to keep in mind, but to which I trust I never shall be forced.

"Great abilities," said he, "are not requisite for an historian; for in historical composition all the greatest powers of the human mind are quiescent. He has facts ready to his hand, so there is no exercise of invention. Imagination is not required in any high degree; only about as much as is used in the lower kinds of poetry. Some penetration, accuracy, and colouring, will fit a man for the task, if he can give the application which is necessary."

"'Bayle's Dictionary'[1] is a very useful work for those to consult who love the biographical part of literature, which is what I love most."

Talking of the eminent writers in Queen Anne's reign, he observed, "I think Dr. Arbuthnot[2] the first man among them. He was the most universal genius, being an excellent physician, a man of deep learning, and a man of much humour. Mr. Addison was, to be sure, a great man; his learning was not profound, but his morality, his humour, and his elegance of writing set him very high."

Mr. Ogilvie was unlucky enough to choose for the topic of his conversation the praises of his native country. He began with saying, that there was very rich land around Edinburgh. Goldsmith, who had studied physic there, contradicted this, very untruly, with a sneering laugh. Disconcerted a little by this, Mr. Ogilvie then took a new ground, where, I suppose, he thought himself perfectly safe; for he observed, that Scotland had a great many noble wild prospects. Johnson: "I believe, Sir, you have a great many. Norway,

[1] Dictionnaire historique et critique (1696) by Pierre Bayle, a French philosopher and critic; especially through the English translation of the Dictionary his sceptical views had great influence in England in the eighteenth century. [2] Cf. Pope's *Epistle to Dr. Arbuthnot*, p. 288, above

too, has noble wild prospects; and Lapland is remarkable for prodigious noble wild prospects. But, Sir, let me tell you, the noblest prospect which a Scotchman ever sees, is the high-road that leads him to England!" This unexpected and pointed sally produced a roar of applause. After all, however, those who admire the rude grandeur of nature cannot deny it to Caledonia.

On Saturday, July 9, I found Johnson surrounded with a numerous levee, but have not preserved any part of his conversation. On the 14th we had another evening by ourselves at the Mitre. It happened to be a very rainy night; I made some commonplace observations on the relaxation of nerves and depression of spirits which such weather occasioned; adding, however, that it was good for the vegetable creation. Johnson, who, as we have already seen, denied that the temperature of the air had any influence on the human frame, answered, with a smile of ridicule, "Why, yes, Sir, it is good for vegetables, and for the animals who eat those vegetables, and for the animals who eat those animals." This observation of his, aptly enough introduced a good supper and I soon forgot, in Johnson's company, the influence of a moist atmosphere.

Feeling myself now quite at ease as his companion, though I had all possible reverence for him, I expressed a regret that I could not be so easy with my father, though he was not much older than Johnson, and certainly, however respectable, had not more learning and greater abilities to depress me. I asked him the reason of this. Johnson: "Why, Sir, I am a man of the world. I live in the world, and I take, in some degree, the colour of the world as it moves along. Your father is a judge in a remote part of the island, and all his notions are taken from the old world. Besides, Sir, there must always be a struggle between a father and son, while one aims at power and the other at independence." I said, I was afraid my father would force me to be a lawyer. Johnson: "Sir, you need not be afraid of his forcing you to be a laborious practising lawyer; that is not in his power. For, as the proverb says, 'One man may lead a horse to the water, but twenty cannot make him drink.' He may be displeased that you are not what he wishes you to be; but that displeasure will not go far. If he insists only on your having as much law as is necessary

for a man of property, and then endeavours to get you into parliament, he is quite in the right."

He enlarged very convincingly upon the excellence of rhyme over blank verse in English poetry. I mentioned to him that Dr. Adam Smith,[1] in his lectures upon composition, when I studied under him in the College of Glasgow, had maintained the same opinion strenuously, and I repeated some of his arguments. Johnson: "Sir, I was once in company with Smith, and we did not take to each other; but had I known that he loved rhyme as much as you tell me he does, I should have hugged him."

Talking of those who denied the truth of Christianity, he said, "It is always easy to be on the negative side. If a man were now to deny that there is salt upon the table, you could not reduce him to an absurdity. Come, let us try this a little further. I deny that Canada is taken, and I can support my denial by pretty good arguments. The French are a much more numerous people than we; and it is not likely that they would allow us to take it. 'But the ministry have assured us, in all the formality of the Gazette, that it is taken.' — Very true. But the ministry have put us to an enormous expense by the war in America, and it is their interest to persuade us that we have got something for our money. — 'But the fact is confirmed by thousands of men who were at the taking of it.' — Ay, but these men have still more interest in deceiving us. They don't want that you should think the French have beat them, but that they have beat the French. Now suppose you should go over and find that it really is taken, that would only satisfy yourself; for when you come home we will not believe you. We will say, you have been bribed. — Yet, Sir, notwithstanding all these plausible objections, we have no doubt that Canada is really ours. Such is the weight of common testimony. How much stronger are the evidences of the Christian religion?"

"Idleness is a disease which must be combated; but I would not advise a rigid adherence to a particular plan of study. I myself have never persisted in any plan for two days together. A man ought to read just as inclination leads him; for what he reads as a task will do him little good. A young man

[1] author of the famous *Wealth of Nations*

should read five hours in a day, and so may acquire a great deal of knowledge."

To a man of vigorous intellect and ardent curiosity like his own, reading without a regular plan may be beneficial; though even such a man must submit to it, if he would attain a full understanding of any of the sciences.

To such a degree of unrestrained frankness had he now accustomed me that in the course of this evening I talked of the numerous reflections which had been thrown out against him, on account of his having accepted a pension from his present Majesty. "Why, Sir," said he, with a hearty laugh, "it is a mighty foolish noise that they make. I have accepted of a pension as a reward which has been thought due to my literary merit; and now that I have this pension, I am the same man in every respect that I have ever been; I retain the same principles. It is true, that I cannot now curse (smiling) the house of Hanover; nor would it be decent for me to drink King James's health in the wine that King George gives me money to pay for. But, Sir, I think that the pleasure of cursing the house of Hanover, and drinking King James's health, are amply overbalanced by three hundred pounds a year."

* * * * * * *

It will be observed, that when giving me advice as to my travels, Dr. Johnson did not dwell upon cities, and palaces, and pictures, and shows, and Arcadian scenes. He was of Lord Essex's opinion, who advises his kinsman, Roger Earl of Rutland, "rather to go a hundred miles to speak with one wise man, then five miles to see a fair town."[1]

I described to him an impudent fellow from Scotland, who affected to be a savage, and railed at all established systems. Johnson: "There is nothing surprising in this, Sir. He wants to make himself conspicuous. He would tumble in a hog-sty, as long as you looked at him and called to him to come out. But let him alone, never mind him, and he'll soon give it over."

I added that the same person maintained that there was no distinction between virtue and vice. Johnson: "Why, Sir, if the fellow does not think as he speaks, he is lying; and I see not what honour he can propose to himself from having the character of a liar. But

[1] in a letter dated Jan. 4, 1596

if he does really think that there is no distinction between virtue and vice, why, Sir, when he leaves our houses let us count our spoons."

Sir David Dalrymple, now one of the judges of Scotland by the title of Lord Hailes, had contributed much to increase my high opinion of Johnson, on account of his writings, long before I attained to a personal acquaintance with him; I, in return, had informed Johnson of Sir David's eminent character for learning and religion; and Johnson was so much pleased, that at one of our evening meetings he gave him for his toast. I at this time kept up a very frequent correspondence with Sir David; and I read to Dr. Johnson to-night the following passage from the letter which I had last received from him:

It gives me pleasure to think that you have obtained the friendship of Mr. Samuel Johnson. He is one of the best moral writers which England has produced. At the same time, I envy you the free and undisguised converse with such a man. May I beg you to present my best respects to him, and to assure him of the veneration which I entertain for the author of the 'Rambler' and of 'Rasselas'? Let me recommend this last work to you; with the 'Rambler' you certainly are acquainted. In 'Rasselas' you will see a tenderhearted operator, who probes the wound only to heal it. Swift, on the contrary, mangles human nature. He cuts and slashes as if he took pleasure in the operation, like the tyrant who said, *Ita feri ut se sentiat emori.*[1]

Johnson seemed to be much gratified by this just and well-turned compliment.

He recommended to me to keep a journal of my life, full and unreserved. He said it would be a very good exercise, and would yield me great satisfaction when the particulars were faded from my remembrance. I was uncommonly fortunate in having had a previous coincidence of opinion with him upon this subject, for I had kept such a journal for some time; and it was no small pleasure to me to have this to tell him, and to receive his approbation. He counselled me to keep it private, and said I might surely have a friend who would burn it in case of my death. From this habit I have been enabled to give the world so many anecdotes, which would otherwise have been lost to posterity. I mentioned that I was afraid I put into my journal

[1] Strike in such a way that he may feel the pangs of death

too many little incidents. Johnson: "There is nothing, Sir, too little for so little a creature as man. It is by studying little things that we attain the great art of having as little misery and as much happiness as possible."

Next morning Mr. Dempster happened to call on me, and was so much struck even with the imperfect account which I gave him of Dr. Johnson's conversation, that to his honour be it recorded, when I complained that drinking port and sitting up late with him affected my nerves for some time after, he said, "One had better be palsied at eighteen than not keep company with such a man."

On Tuesday, July 18, I found tall Sir Thomas Robinson sitting with Johnson. Sir Thomas said, that the King of Prussia valued himself upon three things; upon being a hero, a musician, and an author. Johnson: "Pretty well, Sir, for one man. As to his being an author, I have not looked at his poetry; but his prose is poor stuff. He writes just as you may suppose Voltaire's footboy to do, who has been his amanuensis. He has such parts as the valet might have, and about as much of the colouring of the style as might be got by transcribing his works." When I was at Ferney, I repeated this to Voltaire, in order to reconcile him somewhat to Johnson, whom he, in affecting the English mode of expression, had previously characterised as "a superstitious dog"; but after hearing such a criticism on Frederick the Great, with whom he was then on bad terms, he exclaimed, "An honest fellow!"

But I think the criticism much too severe; for the "Memoirs of the House of Brandenburgh" are written as well as many works of that kind. His poetry, for the style of which he himself makes a frank apology, "*jargonnant un François barbare*,"[1] though fraught with pernicious ravings of infidelity, has in many places, great animation, and in some a pathetic tenderness.

Upon this contemptuous animadversion on the King of Prussia, I observed to Johnson, "It would seem then, Sir, that much less parts are necessary to make a king, than to make an author: for the King of Prussia is confessedly the greatest king now in Europe, yet you think he makes a very poor figure as an author."

Mr. Levett this day showed me Dr. John-

[1] using a barbarous kind of French

son's library, which was contained in two garrets over his chambers, where Lintot, son of the celebrated bookseller of that name, had formerly his warehouse. I found a number of good books, but very dusty and in great confusion. The floor was strewed with manuscript leaves, in Johnson's own handwriting, which I beheld with a degree of veneration, supposing they perhaps might contain portions of the "Rambler," or of "Rasselas." I observed an apparatus for chemical experiments, of which Johnson was all his life very fond. The place seemed to be very favourable for retirement and meditation. Johnson told me, that he went up thither without mentioning it to his servant when he wanted to study, secure from interrruption; for he would not allow his servant to say he was not at home when he really was. "A servant's strict regard for truth," said he, "must be weakened by such a practice. A philosopher may know that it is merely a form of denial; but few servants are such nice distinguishers. If I accustom a servant to tell a lie for *me*, have I not reason to apprehend that he will tell many lies for *himself?*" I am, however, satisfied that every servant, of any degree of intelligence, understands saying his master is not at home, not at all as the affirmation of a fact, but as customary words, intimating that his master wishes not to be seen; so that there can be no bad effect from it.

Mr. Temple, now vicar of St. Gluvias, Cornwall, who had been my intimate friend for many years, had at this time chambers in Farrar's-buildings, at the bottom of Inner Temple-lane, which he kindly lent me upon my quitting my lodgings, he being to return to Trinity Hall, Cambridge. I found them particularly convenient for me, as they were so near Dr. Johnson's.

On Wednesday, July 20, Dr. Johnson, Mr. Dempster, and my uncle, Dr. Boswell, who happened to be now in London, supped with me at these chambers. Johnson: "Pity is not natural to man. Children are always cruel. Savages are always cruel. Pity is acquired and improved by the cultivation of reason. We may have uneasy sensations from seeing a creature in distress, without pity: for we have not pity unless we wish to relieve them. When I am on my way to dine with a friend, and finding it late, have bid the coachman make haste, if I happen to attend when he whips his horses, I may feel unpleasantly that the animals are put to pain, but I do not wish him to desist. No, Sir, I wish him to drive on."

Mr. Alexander Donaldson, bookseller of Edinburgh, had for some time opened a shop in London, and sold his cheap editions of the most popular English books, in defiance of the supposed common-law right of *Literary Property*. Johnson, though he concurred in the opinion which was afterwards sanctioned by a judgment of the House of Lords, that there was no such right, was at this time very angry that the booksellers of London, for whom he uniformly professed much regard, should suffer from an invasion of what they had ever considered to be secure; and he was loud and violent against Mr. Donaldson. "He is a fellow who takes advantage of the law to injure his brethren; for, notwithstanding that the statute secures only fourteen years of exclusive right, it has always been understood by the *trade*, that he who buys the copyright of a book from the author obtains a perpetual property; and upon that belief, numberless bargains are made to transfer that property after the expiration of the statutory term. Now, Donaldson, I say, takes advantage here, of people who have really an equitable title from usage; and if we consider how few of the books, of which they buy the property, succeed so well as to bring profit, we should be of opinion that the term of fourteen years is too short; it should be sixty years." Dempster: "Donaldson, Sir, is anxious for the encouragement of literature. He reduces the price of books, so that poor students may buy them." Johnson (laughing): "Well, Sir, allowing that to be his motive, he is no better than Robin Hood, who robbed the rich in order to give to the poor."

It is remarkable, that when the great question concerning Literary Property came to be ultimately tried before the supreme tribunal of this country, in consequence of the very spirited exertions of Mr. Donaldson, Dr. Johnson was zealous against a perpetuity; but he thought that the term of the exclusive right of authors should be considerably enlarged. He was then for granting a hundred years.

The conversation now turned upon Mr. David Hume's[1] style. Johnson: "Why, Sir,

his style is not English; the structure of his sentences is French. Now the French structure and the English structure may, in the nature of things, be equally good. But if you allow that the English language is established, he is wrong. My name might originally have been Nicholson, as well as Johnson; but were you to call me Nicholson now, you would call me very absurdly."

Rousseau's treatise on the inequality of mankind was at this time a fashionable topic. It gave rise to an observation by Mr. Dempster, that the advantages of fortune and rank were nothing to a wise man, who ought to value only merit. Johnson: "If man were a savage, living in the woods by himself, this might be true; but in civilised society we all depend upon each other and our happiness is very much owing to the good opinion of mankind. Now, Sir, in civilised society, external advantages make us more respected. A man with a good coat upon his back meets with a better reception than he who has a bad one. Sir, you may analyse this and say what is there in it? But that will avail you nothing, for it is part of a general system. Pound St. Paul's church into atoms, and consider any single atom; it is, to be sure, good for nothing; but put all these atoms together and you have St. Paul's church. So it is with human felicity, which is made up of many ingredients, each of which may be shown to be very insignificant. In civilised society personal merit will not serve you so much as money will. Sir, you may make the experiment. Go into the street and give one man a lecture on morality and another a shilling, and see which will respect you most. If you wish only to support nature, Sir William Petty[1] fixes your allowance at three pounds a year; but as times are much altered, let us call it six pounds. This sum will fill your belly, shelter you from the weather, and even get you a strong lasting coat, supposing it to be made of good bull's hide. Now, Sir, all beyond this is artificial, and is desired in order to obtain a greater degree of respect from our fellow-creatures. And, Sir, if six hundred pounds a year procure a man more consequence, and, of course, more happiness than six pounds a year, the same proportion will hold as to six thousand, and so on, as far as opulence can be carried. Perhaps he who has a large fortune may not be

---

[1] the Scottish philosopher and historian

[1] an English writer on economics (1623-87)

so happy as he who has a small one; but that must proceed from other causes than from his having the large fortune: for, *caeteris paribus*,[1] he who is rich in a civilised society must be happier than he who is poor; as riches, if properly used, (and it is a man's own fault if they are not,) must be productive of the highest advantages. Money, to be sure, of itself is of no use: for its only use is to part with it. Rousseau, and all those who deal in paradoxes, are led away by a childish desire of novelty. When I was a boy I used always to choose the wrong side of a debate, because most ingenious things, that is to say, most new things, could be said upon it. Sir, there is nothing for which you may not muster up more plausible arguments than those which are urged against wealth and other external advantages. Why, now, there is stealing: why should it be thought a crime? When we consider by what unjust methods property has been often acquired, and that what was unjustly got it must be unjust to keep, where is the harm in one man's taking the property of another from him? Besides, Sir, when we consider the bad use that many people make of their property, and how much better use the thief may make of it, it may be defended as a very allowable practice. Yet, Sir, the experience of mankind has discovered stealing to be so very bad a thing that they make no scruple to hang a man for it. When I was running about this town a very poor fellow, I was a great arguer for the advantages of poverty; but I was, at the same time, very sorry to be poor. Sir, all the arguments which are brought to represent poverty as no evil, show it to be evidently a great evil. You never find people labouring to convince you that you may live very happily upon a plentiful fortune. — So you hear people talking how miserable a king must be, and yet they all wish to be in his place."

It was suggested that kings must be unhappy, because they are deprived of the greatest of all satisfactions, easy and unreserved society. Johnson: "This is an illfounded notion. Being a king does not exclude a man from such society. Great kings have always been social. The King of Prussia, the only great king at present, is very social. Charles the Second, the last king of England who was a man of parts, was social; and our Henrys and Edwards were all social."

Mr. Dempster having endeavoured to maintain that intrinsic merit *ought* to make the only distinction among mankind, Johnson: "Why, Sir, mankind have found that this cannot be. How shall we determine the proportion of intrinsic merit? Were that to be the only distinction amongst mankind, we should soon quarrel about the degrees of it. Were all distinctions abolished, the strongest would not long acquiesce, but would endeavour to obtain a superiority by their bodily strength. But, Sir, as subordination is very necessary for society, and contentions for superiority very dangerous, mankind, that is to say, all civilised nations, have settled it upon a plain invariable principle. A man is born to hereditary rank; or his being appointed to certain offices gives him a certain rank. Subordination tends greatly to human happiness. Were we all upon an equality, we should have no other enjoyment than mere animal pleasure."

I said, I considered distinction or rank to be of so much importance in civilised society, that if I were asked on the same day to dine with the first duke in England, and with the first man in Britain for genius, I should hesitate which to prefer. Johnson: "To be sure, Sir, if you were to dine only once, and it were never to be known where you dined, you would choose rather to dine with the first man for genius; but to gain most respect, you should dine with the first duke in England. For nine people in ten that you meet with, would have a higher opinion of you for having dined with a duke; and the great genius himself would receive you better, because you had been with the great duke."

He took care to guard himself against any possible suspicion that his settled principles of reverence for rank and respect for wealth were at all owing to mean or interested motives; for he asserted his own independence as a literary man. "No man," said he, "who ever lived by literature, has lived more independently than I have done." He said he had taken longer time than he needed to have done in composing his Dictionary.[1] He received our compliments upon that great work with complacency, and told us that the Acad-

---

[1] other things being equal

[1] published in 1755; it soon became and long remained the standard for English

emy *della Crusca*[1] could scarcely believe that it was done by one man.

* * * * * * *

At night, Mr. Johnson and I supped in a private room at the Turk's Head coffee-house, in the Strand. "I encourage this house," said he, "for the mistress of it is a good civil woman, and has not much business."

"Sir, I love the acquaintance of young people; because, in the first place, I don't like to think myself growing old. In the next place, young acquaintances must last longest, if they do last; and then, Sir, young men have more virtue than old men; they have more generous sentiments in every respect. I love the young dogs of this age; they have more wit and humour and knowledge of life than we had; but then the dogs are not so good scholars. Sir, in my early years I read very hard. It is a sad reflection, but a true one, that I knew almost as much at eighteen as I do now. My judgment, to be sure, was not so good, but I had all the facts. I remember very well when I was at Oxford, an old gentleman said to me, 'Young man, ply your book diligently now, and acquire a stock of knowledge; for when years come upon you, you will find that poring upon books will be but an irksome task.'"

This account of his reading, given by himself in plain words, sufficiently confirms what I have already advanced upon the disputed question as to his application. It reconciles any seeming inconsistency in his way of talking upon it at different times; and shows that idleness and reading hard were with him relative terms, the import of which, as used by him, must be gathered from a comparison with what scholars of different degrees of ardour and assiduity have been known to do. And let it be remembered that he was now talking spontaneously, and expressing his genuine sentiments; whereas at other times he might be induced from his spirit of contradiction, or more properly from his love of argumentative contest, to speak lightly of his own application to study. It is pleasing to consider that the old gentleman's gloomy prophecy as to the irksomeness of books to men of an advanced age, which is too often fulfilled, was so far from being verified in Johnson, that his ardour

for literature never failed, and his last writings had more ease and vivacity than any of his earlier productions.

He mentioned to me now, for the first time, that he had been distressed by melancholy, and for that reason had been obliged to fly from study and meditation, to the dissipating variety of life. Against melancholy he recommended constant occupation of mind, a great deal of exercise, moderation in eating and drinking, and especially to shun drinking at night. He said melancholy people were apt to fly to intemperance for relief, but that it sunk them much deeper in misery. He observed, that labouring men who work hard, and live sparingly, are seldom or never troubled with low spirits.

* * * * * * *

He said Dr. Joseph Warton was a very agreeable man, and his "Essay on the Genius and Writings of Pope" a very pleasing book. I wondered that he delayed so long to give us the continuation of it. Johnson: "Why, Sir, I suppose he finds himself a little disappointed in not having been able to persuade the world to be of his opinion as to Pope."

We have now been favoured with the concluding volume, in which, to use a parliamentary expression, he has *explained*, so as not to appear quite so adverse to the opinion of the world, concerning Pope, as was at first thought; and we must all agree that his work is a most valuable accession to English literature.

A writer of deserved eminence being mentioned, Johnson said, "Why, Sir, he is a man of good parts, but being originally poor, he has got a love of mean company and low jocularity; a very bad thing, Sir. To laugh is good, and to talk is good. But you ought no more to think it enough if you laugh, than you are to think it enough if you talk. You may laugh in as many ways as you talk; and surely *every* way of talking that is practised cannot be esteemed."

I spoke of Sir James Macdonald as a young man of most distinguished merit, who united the highest reputation at Eton and Oxford, with the patriarchal spirit of a great Highland chieftain. I mentioned that Sir James had said to me, that he had never seen Mr. Johnson, but he had a great respect for him, though at the same time it was mixed with some degree of terror. Johnson: "Sir, if he were

---

[1] a Florentine literary society which published a large dictionary of the Italian language

to be acquainted with me, it might lessen both."

* * * * * * *

He maintained that a boy at school was the happiest of human beings. I supported a different opinion, from which I have never yet varied, that a man is happier; and I enlarged upon the anxiety and sufferings which are endured at school. Johnson: "Ah, Sir, a boy's being flogged is not so severe as a man's having the hiss of the world against him. Men have a solicitude about fame; and the greater share they have of it, the more afraid they are of losing it." I silently asked myself, "Is it possible that the great Samuel Johnson really entertains any such apprehension, and is not confident that his exalted fame is established upon a foundation never to be shaken?"

He this evening drank a bumper to Sir David Dalrymple, "as a man of worth, a scholar, and a wit." "I have," said he, "never heard of him, except from you; but let him know my opinion of him: for as he does not show himself much in the world, he should have the praise of the few who hear of him."

On Tuesday, July 26, I found Mr. Johnson alone. It was a very wet day, and I again complained of the disagreeable effects of such weather. Johnson: "Sir, this is all imagination, which physicians encourage; for man lives in air as a fish lives in water; so that if the atmosphere press heavy from above, there is an equal resistance from below. To be sure, bad weather is hard upon people who are obliged to be abroad; and men cannot labour so well in the open air in bad weather as in good; but, Sir, a smith, or a tailor, whose work is within doors, will surely do as much in rainy weather as in fair. Some very delicate frames, indeed, may be affected by wet weather; but not common constitutions."

We talked of the education of children; and I asked him what he thought was best to teach them first. Johnson: "Sir, it is no matter what you teach them first, any more than what leg you shall put into your breeches first. Sir, you may stand disputing which is best to put in first, but in the meantime your breech is bare. Sir, while you are considering which of two things you should teach your child first, another boy has learned them both."

On Thursday, July 28, we again supped in private at the Turk's Head coffee-house. Johnson: "Swift has a higher reputation than he deserves. His excellence is strong sense; for his humour, though very well, is not remarkably good. I doubt whether the 'Tale of a Tub' be his; for he never owned it, and it is much above his usual manner."

"Thomson,[1] I think, had as much of the poet about him as most writers. Everything appeared to him through the medium of his favourite pursuit. He could not have viewed those two candles burning but with a poetical eye."

"Has not —— a great deal of wit, Sir?" Johnson: "I do not think so, Sir. He is, indeed, continually attempting wit, but he fails. And I have no more pleasure in hearing a man attempting wit and failing, than in seeing a man trying to leap over a ditch and tumbling into it."

He laughed heartily when I mentioned to him a saying of his concerning Mr. Thomas Sheridan,[2] which Foote[3] took a wicked pleasure to circulate. "Why, Sir, Sherry is dull, naturally dull; but it must have taken him a great deal of pains to become what we now see him. Such an excess of stupidity, Sir, is not in Nature." — "So," said he, "I allowed him all his own merit."

He now added, "Sheridan cannot bear me. I bring his declamation to a point. I ask him a plain question, 'What do you mean to teach?' Besides, Sir, what influence can Mr. Sheridan have upon the language of this great country, by his narrow exertions? Sir, it is burning a farthing candle at Dover, to show light at Calais."

* * * * * * *

Next day, Sunday, July 3, I told him I had been that morning at a meeting of the people called Quakers, where I had heard a woman preach. Johnson: "Sir, a woman's preaching is like a dog's walking on his hind legs. It is not done well; but you are surprised to find it done at all."

On Tuesday, August 2, (the day of my departure from London having been fixed for

[1] author of *The Seasons*, etc. [2] an Irishman who acted, taught elocution, and published a pronouncing dictionary of the English language — father of Richard Brinsley Sheridan, the brilliant orator and dramatist [3] Samuel Foote (1720-77), a popular actor and dramatist

the 5th,) Dr. Johnson did me the honour to pass a part of the morning with me at my chambers. He said, "that he always felt an inclination to do nothing." I observed, that it was strange to think that the most indolent man in Britain had written the most laborious work, "The English Dictionary."

* * * * * * *

JUNIUS

LETTER XV

TO HIS GRACE THE DUKE OF GRAFTON

July 8, 1769.

My Lord,

If nature had given you an understanding qualified to keep pace with the wishes and principles of your heart, she would have made you, perhaps, the most formidable minister that ever was employed under a limited monarch to accomplish the ruin of a free people. When neither the feelings of shame, the reproaches of conscience, nor the dread of punishment, form any bar to the designs of a minister, the people would have too much reason to lament their condition, if they did not find some resource in the weakness of his understanding. We owe it to the bounty of Providence, that the completest depravity of the heart is sometimes strangely united with a confusion of the mind which counteracts the most favourite principles, and makes the same man treacherous without art, and a hypocrite without deceiving. The measures, for instance, in which your Grace's activity has been chiefly exerted, as they were adopted without skill, should have been conducted with more than common dexterity. But truly, my Lord, the execution has been as gross as the design. By one decisive step you have defeated all the arts of writing. You have fairly confounded the intrigues of opposition, and silenced the clamours of faction. A dark, ambiguous system might require and furnish the materials of ingenious illustration; and, in doubtful measures, the virulent exaggeration of party must be employed to rouse and engage the passions of the people. You have now brought the merits of your administration to an issue on which every Englishman of the narrowest capacity may determine for himself. It is not an alarm to the passions, but a calm appeal to the judgment of the people upon their own most essential interests. A more experienced minister would not have hazarded a direct invasion of the first principles of the constitution before he had made some progress in subduing the spirit of the people. With such a cause as yours, my Lord, it is not sufficient that you have the court at your devotion unless you can find means to corrupt or intimidate the jury. The collective body of the people form that jury, and from their decision there is but one appeal.

Whether you have talents to support you at a crisis of such difficulty and danger should long since have been considered. Judging truly of your disposition, you have, perhaps, mistaken the extent of your capacity. Good faith and folly have so long been received for synonymous terms, that the reverse of the proposition has grown into credit, and every villain fancies himself a man of abilities. It is the apprehension of your friends, my Lord, that you have drawn some hasty conclusion of this sort, and that a partial reliance upon your moral character has betrayed you beyond the depth of your understanding. You have now carried things too far to retreat. You have plainly declared to the people what they are to expect from the continuance of your administration. It is time for your Grace to consider what you also may expect in return from their spirit and their resentment.

Since the accession of our most gracious sovereign to the throne we have seen a system of government which may well be called a reign of experiments. Parties of all denominations have been employed and dismissed. The advice of the ablest men in this country has been repeatedly called for and rejected; and when the royal displeasure has been signified to a minister, the marks of it have usually been proportioned to his abilities and integrity. The spirit of the favourite[1] had some apparent influence upon every administration: and every set of ministers preserved an appearance of duration, as long as they submitted to that influence. But there were certain services to be performed for the favourite's security, or to gratify his resentments, which your predecessors in office had the wisdom or the virtue not to undertake. The moment this refractory spirit was discovered their disgrace was determined. Lord

[1] the Earl of Bute

Chatham, Mr. Grenville, and Lord Rockingham have successively had the honour to be dismissed for preferring their duty as servants of the public to those compliances which were expected from their station. A submissive administration was at last gradually collected from the deserters of all parties, interests, and connections; and nothing remained but to find a leader for these gallant well-disciplined troops. Stand forth, my Lord, for thou art the man. Lord Bute found no resource of dependence or security in the proud, imposing superiority of Lord Chatham's abilities, the shrewd, inflexible judgment of Mr. Grenville, nor in the mild but determined integrity of Lord Rockingham. His views and situation required a creature void of all these properties; and he was forced to go through every division, resolution, composition, and refinement of political chemistry, before he happily arrived at the *caput mortuum*[1] of vitriol in your Grace. Flat and insipid in your retired state, but, brought into action, you become vitriol again. Such are the extremes of alternate indolence or fury which have governed your whole administration. Your circumstances with regard to the people soon becoming desperate, like other honest servants you determined to involve the best of masters in the same difficulties with yourself. We owe it to your Grace's well-directed labours, that your sovereign has been persuaded to doubt of the affections of his subjects, and the people to suspect the virtues of their sovereign, at a time when both were unquestionable. You have degraded the royal dignity into a base, dishonourable competition with Mr. Wilkes,[2] nor had you abilities to carry even this last contemptible triumph over a private man, without the grossest violation of the fundamental laws of the constitution and rights of the people. But these are rights, my Lord, which you can no more annihilate than you can the soil to which they are annexed. The question no longer turns upon points of national honour and security abroad, or on the degrees of expedience and propriety of measures at home. It was not inconsistent that you should abandon the cause of liberty in another country,[3] which you had persecuted

in your own; and in the common arts of domestic corruption, we miss no part of Sir Robert Walpole's system except his abilities. In this humble imitative line you might long have proceeded, safe and contemptible. You might, probably, never have risen to the dignity of being hated, and even have been despised with moderation. But it seems you meant to be distinguished, and, to a mind like yours, there was no other road to fame but by the destruction of a noble fabric, which you thought had been too long the admiration of mankind. The use you have made of the military force introduced an alarming change in the mode of executing the laws. The arbitrary appointment of Mr. Luttrell[1] invades the foundation of the laws themselves, as it manifestly transfers the right of legislation from those whom the people have chosen to those whom the people have rejected. With a succession of such appointments we may soon see a House of Commons collected, in the choice of which the other towns and counties of England will have as little share as the devoted county of Middlesex.

Yet, I trust, your Grace will find that the people of this country are neither to be intimidated by violent measures, nor deceived by refinements. When they see Mr. Luttrell seated in the House of Commons by mere dint of power, and in direct opposition to the choice of a whole county, they will not listen to those subtleties by which every arbitrary exertion of authority is explained into the law and privilege of parliament. It requires no persuasion of argument, but simply the evidence of the senses, to convince them that to transfer the right of election from the collective to the representative body of the people contradicts all those ideas of a House of Commons which they have received from their forefathers, and which they have already, though vainly perhaps, delivered to their children. The principles on which this violent measure has been defended, have added scorn to injury, and forced us to feel that we are not only oppressed but insulted.

With what force, my Lord, with what protection, are you prepared to meet the united detestation of the people of England? The city of London has given a generous example

---

[1] *literally*, dead head; *here*, lifeless residue
[2] John Wilkes, a worthless profligate, but a vigorous champion of popular rights and constitutional methods [3] America

[1] Appointed by the House of Commons to the seat to which Wilkes had been elected by the County of Middlesex.

to the kingdom in what manner a king of this country ought to be addressed; and I fancy, my Lord, it is not yet in your courage to stand between your sovereign and the addresses of his subjects. The injuries you have done this country are such as demand not only redress but vengeance. In vain shall you look for protection to that venal vote which you have already paid for — another must be purchased; and to save a minister, the House of Commons must declare themselves not only independent of their constituents, but the determined enemies of the constitution. Consider, my Lord, whether this be an extremity to which their fears will permit them to advance, or, if *their* protection should fail you, how far you are authorised to rely upon the sincerity of those smiles which a pious court lavishes without reluctance upon a libertine by profession. It is not, indeed, the least of the thousand contradictions which attend you, that a man, marked to the world by the grossest violation of all ceremony and decorum, should be the first servant of a court in which prayers are morality and kneeling is religion. Trust not too far to appearances by which your predecessors have been deceived, though they have not been injured. Even the best of princes may at last discover that this is a contention in which everything may be lost but nothing can be gained; and, as you became minister by accident, were adopted without choice, trusted without confidence, and continued without favour, be assured that, whenever an occasion presses, you will be discarded without even the forms of regret. You will then have reason to be thankful if you are permitted to retire to that seat of learning[1] which, in contemplation of the system of your life, the comparative purity of your manners with those of their high steward, and a thousand other recommending circumstances, has chosen you to encourage the growing virtue of their youth, and to preside over their education. Whenever the spirit of distributing prebends and bishoprics shall have departed from you, you will find that learned seminary perfectly recovered from the delirium of an installation, and, what in truth it ought to be, once more a peaceful scene of slumber and thoughtless meditation. The venerable tutors of the university will no

longer distress your modesty by proposing you for a pattern to their pupils. The learned dulness of declamation will be silent; and even the venal muse, though happiest in fiction, will forget your virtues. Yet, for the benefit of the succeeding age, I could wish that your retreat might be deferred until your morals shall happily be ripened to that maturity of corruption at which the worst examples cease to be contagious.

Junius.

THOMAS CHATTERTON
(1752–1770)

BRISTOWE TRAGEDIE;
OR, THE DETHE OF SYR CHARLES BAWDIN

The feathered songster chaunticleer
    Han wounde[1] hys bugle horne,
And tolde the earlie villager
    The commynge of the morne: 4

Kynge Edwarde[2] sawe the ruddie streakes
    Of lyghte eclypse the greie;
And herde the raven's crokynge throte
    Proclayme the fated daie.   8

"Thou'rt ryghte," quod he, "for, by the Godde
That syttes enthron'd on hyghe!
Charles Bawdin, and hys fellowes twaine,
    To-daie shall surelie die."   12

Thenne wythe a jugge of nappy ale
    Hys knyghtes dydd onne hymm waite;
"Goe tell the traytour, thatt to-daie
    Hee leaves thys mortall state."   16

Sir Canterlone thenne bendedd lowe,
    With harte brymm-fulle of woe;
Hee journey'd to the castle-gate,
    And to Syr Charles dydd goe.   20

Butt whenne hee came, hys children twaine,
    And eke hys lovynge wyfe,
Wythe brinie tears dydd wett the floore,
    For goode Syr Charleses lyfe.   24

[1] Grafton was elected Chancellor of the University of Cambridge in 1768.

[1] has sounded   [2] Edward IV

"O goode Syr Charles!" sayd Canterlone,
"Badde tydyngs I doe brynge."
"Speke boldlie, manne," sayd brave Syr
Charles,
"Whatte says the traytor kynge?"　28

"I greeve to telle; before yonne Sonne
Does fromme the welkinn flye,
Hee hathe uppon hys honour sworne,
Thatt thou shalt surelie die."　32

"Wee all must die," quod brave Syr Charles;
"Of thatte I'm not affearde;
Whatte bootes to lyve a little space?
Thanke Jesu, I'm prepar'd:　36

"Butt telle thye kynge, for myne hee's not,
I'de sooner die to-daie
Thanne lyve hys slave, as manie are,
Though I shoulde lyve for aie."　40

Thenne Canterlone hee dydd goe out,
To telle the maior[1] straite
To gett all thynges ynne redyness
For goode Syr Charleses fate.　44

Thenne Maisterr Canynge saughte the kynge,
And felle down onne hys knee;
"I'm come," quod hee, "unto your grace
To move your clemencye."　48

Thenne quod the kynge, "Youre tale speke
out,
You have been much oure friende;
Whatever youre request may bee,
Wee wylle to ytte attende."　52

"My nobile leige! alle my request
Ys for a nobile knyghte,
Who, though may hap hee has donne
wronge,
Hee thoughte ytte stylle was ryghte:　56

"He has a spouse and children twaine,
Alle rewyn'd are for aie;
Yff that you are resolved to lett
Charles Bawdin die to-dai."　60

"Speke not of such a traytour vile,"
The kynge ynn furie sayde;
"Before the evening starre doth sheene,[2]
Bawdin shall loose hys hedde:　64

---

[1] William Canynge, mayor of Bristol in 1461.
[2] shine

"Justice does loudlie for hym calle,
And hee shalle have hys meede:
Speke, maister Canynge! Whatte thynge else
Att present doe you neede?"　68

"My nobile leige!" goode Canynge sayde,
"Leave justice to our Godde,
And laye the yronne rule asyde;
Be thyne the olyve rodde.　72

"Was Godde to serche our hertes and reines,
The best were synners grete;
Christ's vicarr only knowes ne[1] synne,
Ynne alle thys mortall state.　76

"Lett mercie rule thyne infante reigne,
'Twylle faste[2] thye crowne fulle sure;
From race to race thye familie
Alle sov'reigns shall endure:　80

"But yff wythe bloode and slaughter thou
Beginne thy infante reigne,
Thy crowne upponne thy childrennes brows
Wylle never long remayne."　84

"Canynge, awaie! thys traytour vile
Has scorn'd my power and mee;
Howe canst thou then for such a manne
Entreate my clemencye?"　88

"My nobile leige! the trulie brave
Wylle val'rous actions prize;
Respect a brave and nobile mynde,
Although ynne enemies."　92

"Canynge, awaie! By Godde ynne Heav'n
That dydd mee beinge gyve,
I wylle nott taste a bitt of breade
Whilst thys Syr Charles dothe lyve.　96

"By Marie, and alle Seinctes ynne Heav'n,
Thys sunne shall be hys laste,"
Thenne Canynge dropt a brinie teare,
And from the presence paste.　100

With herte brymm-fulle of gnawynge grief,
Hee to Syr Charles dydd goe,
And sat hymm downe uponne a stoole,
And teares beganne to flowe.　104

"Wee all must die," quod brave Syr Charles;
"Whatte bootes ytte howe or whenne;
Dethe ys the sure, the certaine fate
Of all wee mortall menne.　108

---

[1] no　　　[2] fasten

"Saye why, my friende, thie honest soul
  Runns overr att thyne eye;
Is ytte for my most welcome doome
  Thatt thou dost child-lyke crye?"   112

Quod godlie Canynge, "I doe weepe,
  Thatt thou soe soone must dye,
And leave thy sonnes and helpless wyfe;
  'Tys thys thatt wettes myne eye."   116

"Thenne drie the tears thatt out thyne eye
  From godlie fountaines sprynge;
Dethe I despise, and alle the power
  Of Edwarde, traytour kynge.   120

"Whan through the tyrant's welcom means
  I shall resigne my lyfe,
The Godde I serve wylle soone provyde
  For bothe mye sonnes and wyfe.   124

"Before I sawe the lyghtsome sunne,
  Thys was appointed mee;
Shall mortall manne repyne or grudge
  What Godde ordeynes to bee?   128

"Howe oft ynne battaile have I stoode,
  Whan thousands dy'd arounde;
Whan smokynge streemes of crimson bloode
  Imbrew'd the fatten'd grounde: 132

"Howe dydd I knowe thatt ev'ry dart,
  That cutte the airie waie,
Myghte nott fynde passage toe my harte,
  And close myne eyes for aie?   136

"And shall I nowe, forr feere of dethe,
  Looke wanne and bee dysmayde?
Ne! fromm my herte flie childyshe feere,
  Bee alle the manne display'd.   140

"Ah! goddelyke Henrie![1] Godde forefende,[2]
  And guarde thee and thye sonne,
Yff 'tis hys wylle; but yff 'tis nott,
  Why thenne hys wylle bee donne.   144

"My honest friende, my faulte has beene
  To serve Godde and mye prynce;
And thatt I no tyme-server am,
  My dethe wylle soone convynce.   148

"Ynne Londonne citye was I borne,
  Of parents of grete note;
My fadre dydd a nobile armes
  Emblazon onne hys cote: 152

[1] Henry VI, imprisoned by Edward IV   [2] defend

"I make ne[1] doubte butt hee ys gone
  Where soone I hope to goe;
Where wee for ever shall bee blest,
  From oute the reech of woe.   156

"Hee taughte mee justice and the laws
  Wyth pitie to unite;
And eke hee taughte mee howe to knowe
  The wronge cause fromm the ryghte: 160

"Hee taughte mee wyth a prudent hande
  To feede the hungrie poore,
Ne lett mye sarvants dryve awaie
  The hungrie fromme my doore: 164

"And none can saye butt alle mye lyfe
  I have hys wordyes kept;
And summ'd the actyonns of the daie
  Eche nyghte before I slept.   168

"I have a spouse, goe aske of her
  Yff I defyl'd her bedde?
I have a kynge, and none can laie
  Black treason onne my hedde.   172

"Ynne Lent, and onne the holie eve,
  Fromm fleshe I dydd refrayne;
Whie should I thenne appeare dismay'd
  To leave thys worlde of payne?   176

"Ne, hapless Henrie! I rejoyce,
  I shall ne[2] see thye dethe;
Moste willynglie ynne thye just cause
  Doe I resign my brethe.   180

"Oh, fickle people! rewyn'd[3] londe!
  Thou wylt kenne peace ne moe;
Whyle Richard's sonnes[4] exalt themselves,
  Thye brookes wythe bloude wylle flowe.   184

"Saie, were ye tyr'd of godlie peace,
  And godlie Henrie's reigne,
Thatt you dyd choppe[5] your easie daies
  For those of bloude and peyne?   188

"Whatte though I onne a sledde be drawne,
  And mangled by a hynde,
I doe defye the traytor's pow'r,
  Hee can ne harm my mynd;   192

[1] no [2] not [3] ruined [4] Edward IV and Richard, Duke of Gloucester (later Richard III) [5] exchange

"Whatte though, uphoisted onne a pole,
　　Mye lymbes shall rotte ynne ayre,
And ne ryche monument of brasse
　　Charles Bawdin's name shall bear;　196

"Yett ynne the holie booke above,
　　Whyche tyme can't eate awaie,
There wythe the sarvants of the Lord
　　Mye name shall lyve for aie.　　200

"Thenne welcome dethe! for lyfe eterne
　　I leave thys mortall lyfe:
Farewell vayne world, and alle that's deare,
　　Mye sonnes and lovynge wyfe!　　204

"Nowe dethe as welcome to mee comes,
　　As e'er the moneth of Maie;
Nor woulde I even wyshe to lyve,
　　Wyth my dere wyfe to staie."　　208

Quod Canynge, "'Tys a goodlie thynge
　　To bee prepar'd to die;
And from thys world of peyne and grefe
　　To Godde ynne heav'n to flie."　　212

And nowe the belle began to tolle,
　　And claryonnes to sound;
Syr Charles hee herde the horses feete
　　A prauncyng onne the grounde:　216

And just before the officers
　　His lovynge wyfe came ynne,
Weepynge unfeignèd teeres of woe,
　　Wythe loude and dysmalle dynne.　220

"Sweet Florence! nowe I praie forbere,
　　Ynn quiet lett mee die;
Praie Godde thatt ev'ry Christain soule
　　Maye looke onne dethe as I.　　224

"Sweet Florence! why these brinie teers?
　　Theye washe my soule awaie,
And almost make mee wyshe for lyfe,
　　Wyth thee, sweete dame, to staie.　228

"'Tys butt a journie I shalle goe
　　Untoe the lande of blysse;
Nowe, as a proofe of husbande's love,
　　Receive thys holie kysse."　　232

Thenne Florence, fault'ring ynne her saie,[1]
　　Tremblynge these wordyes spoke,
"Ah, cruele Edwarde! bloudie kynge!
　　Mye herte ys welle nyghe broke:　236

　　　　　[1] speech

"Ah, sweete Syr Charles! why wylt thou
　　goe,
　　Wythoute thye lovynge wyfe?
The cruelle axe thatt cuttes thy necke,
　　Ytte eke shall ende mye lyfe."　　240

And nowe the officers came ynne
　　To brynge Syr Charles awaie,
Whoe turnèd toe hys lovynge wyfe,
　　And thus to her dydd saie:　　244

"I goe to lyfe, and nott to dethe;
　　Truste thou ynne Godde above,
And teache thy sonnes to feare the Lorde,
　　And ynne theyre hertes hym love:　248

"Teache them to runne the nobile race
　　Thatt I theyre fader runne;
Florence! shou'd dethe thee take — adieu!
　　Yee officers leade onne."　　252

Thenne Florence rav'd as anie madde,
　　And dydd her tresses tere;
"Oh staie, mye husbande, lorde, and lyfe!"
　　Syr Charles thenne dropt a teare.　256

'Tyll tyrèdd[1] oute wythe ravynge loude,
　　Shee fellen onne the flore;
Syr Charles exerted alle hys myghte,
　　And march'd fromm oute the dore.　260

Uponne a sledde hee mounted thenne,
　　Wythe lookes full brave and swete;
Lookes thatt enshone[2] ne more concern
　　Thanne anie ynne the strete.　　264

Before hym went the council-menne,
　　Ynne scarlett robes and golde,
And tassils spanglynge ynne the sunne,
　　Muche glorious to beholde:　　268

The Freers of Seincte Augustyne next
　　Appearèd to the syghte,
Alle cladd ynne homelie russett weedes,
　　Of godlie monkysh plyghte:[3]　272

Ynne diffraunt partes a godlie psaume
　　Moste sweetlie theye dydd chaunt;
Behynde theyre backes syx mynstrelles
　　came,
　　Who tun'd the strunge bataunt.[4]　276

　　[1] tired　[2] showed　[3] style　[4] a mythical instrument (due to Chatterton's misunderstanding of
an ancient word)

Thenne fyve-and-twentye archers came;
  Echone the bowe dydd bende,
From rescue of Kynge Henries friends
  Syr Charles forr to defend.   280

Bolde as a lyon came Syr Charles,
  Drawne onne a cloth-layde sledde,
Bye two blacke stedes ynne trappynges white,
  Wyth plumes uponne theyre hedde: 284

Behynde hym five-and-twenty moe
  Of archers stronge and stoute,
Wyth bended bowe echone ynne hande,
  Marchèd ynne goodlie route;   288

Seincte Jameses Freers marchèd next,
  Echone hys parte dydd chaunt;
Behynde theyre backes syx mynstrelles came,
  Who tun'd the strunge bataunt: 292

Thenne came the maior and eldermenne,
  Ynne clothe of scarlett deck't;
And theyre attendynge menne echone,
  Lyke easterne princes trickt: 296

And after them, a multitude
  Of citizens dydd thronge;
The wyndowes were alle fulle of heddes,
  As hee dydd passe alonge.   300

And whenne hee came to the hyghe crosse,
  Syr Charles dydd turne and saie,
"O thou, thatt savest manne fromme synne,
  Washe mye soule clean thys daie!"   304

Att the grete mynster wyndowe sat
  The kynge ynne myckle[1] state,
To see Charles Bawdin goe alonge
  To hys most welcom fate.   308

Soone as the sledde drewe nyghe enowe,
  Thatt Edwarde hee myghte heare,
The brave Syr Charles hee dydd stande uppe,
  And thus hys wordes declare: 312

"Thou seest me, Edwarde! traytour vile!
  Expos'd to infamie;
Butt bee assur'd, disloyall manne!
  I'm greaterr nowe thanne thee.   316

"Bye foule proceedyngs, murdre, bloude,
  Thou wearest nowe a crowne;
And hast appoynted mee to die,
  By power nott thyne owne.   320

[1] great

AE

"Thou thynkest I shall die to-daie;
  I have beene dede 'till nowe,
And soone shall lyve to weare a crowne
  For aie uponne my browe: 324

"Whylst thou, perhapps, for som few yeares,
  Shalt rule thys fickle lande,
To lett them knowe howe wyde the rule
  'Twixt kynge and tyrant hande: 328

"Thye pow'r unjust, thou traytour slave!
  Shall falle onne thye owne hedde" —
Fromm out of hearyng of the kynge
  Departed thenne the sledde.   332

Kynge Edwarde's soule rush'd to hys face,
  Hee turn'd hys hedde awaie,
And to hys broder Gloucester
  Hee thus dydd speke and saie: 336

"To hym that soe much dreaded dethe
  Ne ghastlie terrors brynge,
Beholde the manne! hee spake the truthe,
  Hee's greater thanne a kynge!"   340

"Soe let hym die!" Duke Richarde sayde;
  "And maye echone oure foes
Bende downe theyre neckes to bloudie axe
  And feede the carryon crowes."   344

And nowe the horses gentlie drewe
  Syr Charles uppe the hyghe hylle;
The axe dydd glysterr ynne the sunne,
  His pretious bloude to spylle.   348

Syrr Charles dydd uppe the scaffold goe,
  As uppe a gilded carre
Of victorye, bye val'rous chiefs
  Gayn'd ynne the bloudie warre: 352

And to the people hee dyd saie,
  "Beholde you see mee dye,
For servynge loyally mye kynge,
  Mye kynge most ryghtfullie.   356

"As longe as Edwarde rules thys land,
  Ne quiet you wylle knowe:
Your sonnes and husbandes shalle bee slayne
  And brookes wythe bloude shall flowe.   360

"You leave youre goode and lawfulle kynge,
  Whenne ynne adversitye;
Lyke mee, untoe the true cause stycke,
  And for the true cause dye."   364

Thenne hee, wyth preestes, uponne hys knees,
  A prayer to Godde dyd make,
Beseechynge hym unto hymselfe
  Hys partynge soule to take.   368

Thenne, kneelynge downe, hee layd hys hedde
  Most seemlie onne the blocke;
Whyche fromme hys bodie fayre at once
  The able heddes-manne stroke: 372

And oute the bloude beganne to flowe,
  And rounde the scaffolde twyne;
And teares, enow to washe 't awaie,
  Dydd flowe fromme each mann's eyne. 376

The bloudie axe hys bodie fayre
  Ynnto foure partes cutte;
And ev'rye parte, and eke hys hedde,
  Uponne a pole was putte.   380

One parte dydd rotte onne Kynwulph-hylle,
  One onne the mynster-tower,
And one from off the castle-gate
  The crowen [1] dydd devoure;   384

The other onne Seyncte Powle's goode gate,
  A dreery spectacle;
Hys hedde was plac'd onne the hyghe crosse,
  Ynne hyghe-streete most nobile.   388

Thus was the ende of Bawdin's fate:
  Godde prosper longe oure kynge,
And grante hee maye, wyth Bawdin's soule,
  Ynne heav'n Godd's mercie synge! 392

THE ACCOUNTE OF W. CANYNGES FEAST [2]

Thorowe the halle the belle han sounde;
Byelecoyle doe the grave beseeme;
The ealdermenne doe sytte arounde,
Ande snoffelle oppe the cheorte steeme
Lyche asses wylde ynne desarte waste   5
Swotelye the morneynge ayre doe taste.

Syche coyne thie ate; the minstrels plaie,
The dynne of angelles doe theie keepe;
Heie stylle; the guestes ha ne to saie,
Butte nodde yer thankes ande falle aslape 10
Thos echone daie bee I to deene,
Gyf Rowley, Iscamm, or Tyb Gorges be ne
  seene.

[1] crows [2] *For a translation of this absurd jargon
see the* Notes.

GEORGE CRABBE (1754–1832)

From TALES

TALE X — THE LOVER'S JOURNEY

On either side
Is level fen, a prospect wild and wide,
With dikes on either hand by ocean's self
  supplied:
Far on the right the distant sea is seen,
And salt the springs that feed the marsh
  between.
Beneath an ancient bridge the straitened flood
Rolls through its sloping banks of slimy mud;
Near it a sunken boat resists the tide,   111
That frets and hurries to th' opposing side;
The rushes sharp, that on the borders grow,
Bend their brown flow'rets to the stream
  below,
Impure in all its course, in all its progress
  slow:
Here a grave Flora scarcely deigns to bloom,
Nor wears a rosy blush, nor sheds perfume:
The few dull flowers that o'er the place are
  spread
Partake the nature of their fenny bed;
Here on its wiry stem, in rigid bloom,   120
Grows the salt lavender that lacks perfume:
Here the dwarf sallows creep, the septfoil
  harsh,
And the soft slimy mallow of the marsh;
Low on the ear the distant billows sound,
And just in view appears their stony bound;
No hedge nor tree conceals the glowing sun;
Birds, save a wat'ry tribe, the district shun,
Nor chirp among the reeds where bitter waters
  run.

* * * * * * *

Again, the country was enclosed, a wide
And sandy road has banks on either side;
Where, lo! a hollow on the left appeared,
And there a gipsy tribe their tent had reared;
'Twas open spread, to catch the morning sun,
And they had now their early meal begun,
When two brown boys just left their grassy
  seat,
The early traveller with their prayers to greet:
While yet Orlando held his pence in hand,
He saw their sister on her duty stand;   150
Some twelve years old, demure, affected, sly,
Prepared the force of early powers to try;
Sudden a look of languor he descries,
And well-feigned apprehension in her eyes;

Trained but yet savage, in her speaking face
He marked the features of her vagrant race;
When a light laugh and roguish leer ex-
    pressed
The vice implanted in her youthful breast:
Forth from the tent her elder brother came,
Who seemed offended, yet forbore to blame
The young designer, but could only trace 161
The looks of pity in the traveller's face:
Within, the father, who from fences nigh
Had brought the fuel for the fire's supply,
Watched now the feeble blaze, and stood de-
    jected by.
On ragged rug, just borrowed from the bed,
And by the hand of coarse indulgence fed,
In dirty patchwork negligently dressed,
Reclined the wife, an infant at her breast;
In her wild face some touch of grace re-
    mained,
Of vigour palsied and of beauty stained; 171
Her bloodshot eyes on her unheeding mate
Were wrathful turned, and seemed her wants
    to state,
Cursing his tardy aid — her mother there
With gipsy-state engrossed the only chair;
Solemn and dull her look; with such she
    stands,
And reads the milk-maid's fortune in her
    hands,
Tracing the lines of life; assumed through
    years,
Each feature now the steady falsehood wears;
With hard and savage eye she views the
    food,
And grudging pinches their intruding brood;
Last in the group, the worn-out grandsire
    sits
Neglected, lost, and living but by fits: 183
Useless, despised, his worthless labours done,
And half protected by the vicious son,
Who half supports him; he with heavy
    glance
Views the young ruffians who around him
    dance;
And, by the sadness in his face, appears
To trace the progress of their future years:
Through what strange course of misery, vice,
    deceit, 190
Must wildly wander each unpractised cheat!
What shame and grief, what punishment and
    pain,
Sport of fierce passions, must each child sus-
    tain —
Ere they like him approach their latter end,
Without a hope, a comfort, or a friend!

WILLIAM BLAKE (1757–1827)

FROM SONGS OF INNOCENCE

INTRODUCTION

Piping down the valleys wild,
    Piping songs of pleasant glee,
On a cloud I saw a child,
    And he laughing said to me: 4

"Pipe a song about a Lamb!"
    So I piped with merry cheer.
"Piper, pipe that song again;"
    So I piped: he wept to hear. 8

"Drop thy pipe, thy happy pipe;
    Sing thy songs of happy cheer!"
So I sung the same again,
    While he wept with joy to hear. 12

"Piper, sit thee down and write
    In a book, that all may read."
So he vanished from my sight;
    And I plucked a hollow reed, 16

And I made a rural pen,
    And I stained the water clear,
And I wrote my happy songs
    Every child may joy to hear. 20

FROM SONGS OF EXPERIENCE

THE CLOD AND THE PEBBLE

"Love seeketh not itself to please,
    Nor for itself hath any care,
But for another gives its ease,
    And builds a heaven in hell's despair." 4

So sung a little clod of clay,
    Trodden with the cattle's feet,
But a pebble of the brook
    Warbled out these metres meet: 8

"Love seeketh only Self to please,
    To bind another to its delight,
Joys in another's loss of ease,
    And builds a hell in heaven's despite." 12

THE SICK ROSE

O Rose, thou art sick!
　The invisible worm,
　That flies in the night,
　　In the howling storm,　　　　4

Has found out thy bed
　Of crimson joy,
And his dark secret love
　Does thy life destroy.　　　　8

THE TIGER

Tiger, tiger, burning bright
In the forests of the night,
What immortal hand or eye
Could frame thy fearful symmetry?　　4

In what distant deeps or skies
Burnt the fire of thine eyes?
On what wings dare he aspire?
What the hand dare seize the fire?　　8

And what shoulder and what art
Could twist the sinews of thy heart?
And, when thy heart began to beat,
What dread hand and what dread feet?　12

What the hammer? what the chain?
In what furnace was thy brain?
What the anvil? what dread grasp
Dare its deadly terrors clasp?　　　16

When the stars threw down their spears,
And watered heaven with their tears,
Did He smile His work to see?
Did He who made the lamb make thee?　20

Tiger, tiger, burning bright
In the forests of the night,
What immortal hand or eye
Dare frame thy fearful symmetry?　　24

A POISON TREE

I was angry with my friend:
I told my wrath, my wrath did end.
I was angry with my foe:
I told it not, my wrath did grow.　　4

And I watered it in fears
Night and morning with my tears,
And I sunnèd it with smiles
And with soft deceitful wiles.　　8

And it grew both day and night,
Till it bore an apple bright,
And my foe beheld it shine,
And he knew that it was mine, —　　12

And into my garden stole
When the night had veiled the pole;
In the morning, glad, I see
My foe outstretched beneath the tree.　16

FROM IDEAS OF GOOD AND EVIL

AUGURIES OF INNOCENCE

To see the world in a grain of sand,
　And a heaven in a wild flower;
Hold infinity in the palm of your hand,
　And eternity in an hour.　　　4

TWO KINDS OF RICHES

Since all the riches of all this world
　May be gifts from the devil and earthly
　　kings,
I should suspect that I worshipped the devil
　If I thanked God for worldly things.　4

The countless gold of a merry heart,
　The rubies and pearls of a loving eye,
The idle man never can bring to the mart,
　Nor the cunning hoard up in his treasury. 8

LOVE'S SECRET

Never seek to tell thy love,
　Love that never told shall be;
For the gentle wind does move
　Silently, invisibly.　　　　4

I told my love, I told my love,
　I told her all my heart,
Trembling, cold, in ghastly fears.
　Ah! she did depart!　　　　8

Soon after she was gone from me,
　A traveller came by,
Silently, invisibly:
　He took her with a sigh.　　　12

MINOR SCOTTISH POETS

THERE'S NAE LUCK ABOUT THE HOUSE [1]

And are ye sure the news is true?
　And are ye sure he's weel?
Is this a time to think of wark?
　Ye jauds,[2] fling by your wheel.　　　4
Is this the time to think of wark,
　When Colin's at the door?
Gi'e me my cloak! I'll to the quay
　And see him come ashore.　　　8

For there's nae luck about the house,
　There's nae luck ava;[3]
There's little pleasure in the house,
　When our gudeman's awa'.　　　12

Rise up and mak' a clean fireside;
　Put on the muckle pot;
Gi'e little Kate her cotton gown,
　And Jock his Sunday coat:　　　16
And mak' their shoon as black as slaes,[4]
　Their hose as white as snaw;
It's a' to please my ain gudeman,
　For he's been long awa'.　　　20

There's twa fat hens upon the bauk,[5]
　Been fed this month and mair;
Mak' haste and thraw[6] their necks about,
　That Colin weel may fare;　　　24
And mak' the table neat and clean,
　Gar[7] ilka thing look braw;
It's a' for love of my gudeman,
　For he's been long awa'.　　　28

O gi'e me down my bigonet,[8]
　My bishop satin gown,
For I maun tell the bailie's wife
　That Colin's come to town.　　　32
My Sunday's shoon they maun[9] gae on,
　My hose o' pearl blue;
'Tis a' to please my ain gudeman,
　For he's baith leal and true.　　　36

Sae true his words, sae smooth his speech,
　His breath's like caller[10] air!
His very foot has music in't,
　As he comes up the stair.　　　40

And will I see his face again?
　And will I hear him speak?
I'm downright dizzy with the thought, —
　In troth, I'm like to greet.[1]　　　44

The cauld blasts o' the winter wind,
　That thrillèd through my heart,
They're a' blawn by; I ha'e him safe,
　Till death we'll never part:　　　48
But what puts parting in my head?
　It may be far awa';
The present moment is our ain,
　The neist[2] we never saw.　　　52

Since Colin's weel, I'm weel content,
　I ha'e nae more to crave;
Could I but live to mak' him blest,
　I'm blest above the lave:[3]　　　56
And will I see his face again?
　And will I hear him speak?
I'm downright dizzy wi' the thought, —
　In troth, I'm like to greet.　　　60

— WILLIAM JULIUS MICKLE (1735–1788)

THE FLOWERS OF THE FOREST

I've heard them lilting,[4] at our ewe-milking,
Lasses a-lilting, before the dawn of day;
But now they are moaning, on ilka green loaning;[5]
The Flowers of the Forest are a' wede[6] away.

At bughts[7] in the morning nae blythe lads are scorning;[8]
The lasses are lanely, and dowie,[9] and wae;
Nae daffing,[10] nae gabbing, but sighing and sabbing,
Ilk ane lifts her leglin,[11] and hies her away.　8

In hairst,[12] at the shearing, nae youths now are jeering,
The bandsters[13] are lyart,[14] and runkled and grey;
At fair or at preaching, nae wooing, nae fleeching[15] —
The Flowers of the Forest are a' wede away.　12

At e'en, in the gloaming, nae swankies[16] are roaming
'Bout stacks wi' the lasses at bogle[17] to play;

---

[1] This poem is often wrongly ascribed to Jean Adams.　[2] jades　[3] at all　[4] sloes　[5] cross-beam　[6] twist　[7] make　[8] bonnet　[9] must　[10] fresh

[1] weep　[2] next　[3] rest　[4] singing　[5] meadow path　[6] vanished　[7] sheep-pens　[8] bantering　[9] dull　[10] jesting　[11] pail　[12] harvest　[13] binders　[14] old　[15] coaxing　[16] young men　[17] bugbear

But ilk ane sits eerie, lamenting her dearie —
The Flowers of the Forest are a' wede away. 16

Dool and wae for the order sent our lads to
 the Border!
The English, for ance, by guile wan the day;
The Flowers of the Forest, that fought aye the
 foremost,
The prime of our land, lie cauld in the clay. 20

We'll hear nae more lilting at our ewe-milking,
Women and bairns are heartless and wae;
Sighing and moaning on ilka green loaning,
The Flowers of the Forest are a' wede away. 24
    —JANE ELLIOT (1727–1805)

FROM CALLER WATER

Whan father Adie first pat [1] spade in
The bonny yeard of antient Eden
His amry [2] had nae liquor laid in,
 To fire his mou',[3]
Nor did he thole [4] his wife's upbraidin'
 For being fou.[5]   6

A caller [6] burn o' siller sheen
Ran cannily out o'er the green,
And whan our gutcher's [7] drouth had been
 To bide right sair,[8]
He loutit [9] down and drank bedeen [10]
 A dainty skair.[11]   12

His bairns a' before the flood
Had langer tack [12] o' flesh and blood,
And on mair pithy shanks they stood
 Than Noah's line,
Wha still hae been a feckless brood
 Wi' drinking wine.   18

The fuddlin' Bardies now-a-days
Rin maukin-mad [13] in Bacchus' praise,
And limp and stoiter thro' their lays
 Anacreontic,
While each his sea of wine displays
 As big's the Pontic.   24

My muse will no gang far frae hame,
Or scour a' airths [14] to hound for fame;
In troth, the jillet [15] ye might blame
 For thinking on't,

[1] put [2] cupboard [3] mouth [4] endure [5] full
[6] fresh [7] grandfather's [8] right sore to endure
[9] bent [10] quickly [11] share [12] lease [13] mad as a hare
[14] regions [15] huzzy

Whan eithly [1] she can find the theme
 Of *aqua font*.[2]   30

This is the name that doctors use
Their patients' noodles to confuse;
Wi' simples clad in terms abstruse,
 They labour still,
In kittle [3] words to gar [4] you roose [5]
 Their want o' skill.   36

But we'll hae nae sick [6] clitter-clatter,
And briefly to expound the matter,
It shall be ca'd good Caller Water,
 Than whilk,[7] I trow,
Few drogs in doctors' shops are better
 For me or you.   42
    —ROBERT FERGUSSON (1750–1774)

ROBERT BURNS (1759–1796)

SONG, — GREEN GROW THE RASHES

CHORUS. — Green grow the rashes, O!
 Green grow the rashes, O!
  The sweetest hours that e'er I spend
  Are spent amang the lasses, O.

There's nought but care on ev'ry han', 5
 In every hour that passes, O:
What signifies the life o' man,
 An' 'twere na for the lasses, O?

The war'ly [8] race may riches chase,
 An' riches still may fly them, O; 10
An' tho' at last they catch them fast,
 Their hearts can ne'er enjoy them, O.

But gie me a cannie [9] hour at e'en,
 My arms about my dearie, O;
An' war'ly cares, an' war'ly men, 15
 May a' gae tapsalteerie,[10] O.

For you sae douce,[11] ye sneer at this;
 Ye're nought but senseless asses, O:
The wisest man the warl' e'er saw,
 He dearly lov'd the lasses, O. 20

Auld Nature swears, the lovely dears
 Her noblest work she classes, O:
Her prentice han' she try'd on man,
 An' then she made the lasses, O.

[1] easily [2] *aqua fontis* = water from the spring
[3] ticklish [4] make. [5] praise [6] such [7] which [8] worldly
[9] quiet [10] topsy-turvy [11] solemn

ADDRESS TO THE DEIL

O Prince! O Chief of many thronèd pow'rs!
That led th' embattled seraphim to war. —
       — MILTON.

O thou! whatever title suit thee, —
Auld Hornie, Satan, Nick, or Clootie!
Wha in yon cavern, grim an' sootie,
    Clos'd under hatches,
Spairges [1] about the brunstane cootie [2]   5
    To scaud [3] poor wretches!

Hear me, auld Hangie, for a wee,
An' let poor damnèd bodies be;
I'm sure sma' pleasure it can gie,
    E'en to a deil,   10
To skelp [4] an' scaud poor dogs like me,
    An' hear us squeel!

Great is thy pow'r, an' great thy fame;
Far ken'd [5] an' noted is thy name;
An' tho' yon lowin heugh's [6] thy hame,[7]   15
    Thou travels far;
An' faith! thou's neither lag [8] nor lame,
    Nor blate [9] nor scaur.[10]

Whyles,[11] rangin like a roarin lion,
For prey a' holes an' corners tryin;   20
Whyles, on the strong-wing'd tempest flyin,
    Tirlin' [12] the kirks; [13]
Whyles, in the human bosom pryin,
    Unseen thou lurks.

I've heard my rev'rend grannie say,   25
In lanely [14] glens ye like to stray;
Or whare auld ruin'd castles gray
    Nod to the moon,
Ye fright the nightly wand'rer's way
    Wi' eldritch [15] croon.   30

When twilight did my grannie summon
To say her pray'rs, douce [16] honest woman,
Aft yont [17] the dike she's heard you bummin,
    Wi' eerie drone;
Or, rustlin, thro' the boortrees [18] comin,   35
    Wi' heavy groan.

Ae [19] dreary, windy, winter night,
The stars shot down wi' sklentin [20] light,

Wi' you mysel I gat a fright
    Ayont [1] the lough; [2]   40
Ye like a rash-buss [3] stood in sight
    Wi' waving sough.

The cudgel in my nieve [4] did shake,
Each bristl'd hair stood like a stake,
When wi' an eldritch,[5] stoor [6] "Quaick,
    quaick,"   45
    Amang the springs,
Awa ye squatter'd like a drake,
    On whistlin wings.

Let warlocks [7] grim an' wither'd hags
Tell how wi' you on ragweed nags   50
They skim the muirs an' dizzy crags
    Wi' wicked speed;
And in kirk-yards [8] renew their leagues,
    Owre howket [9] dead.

Thence, countra wives wi' toil an' pain   55
May plunge an' plunge the kirn [10] in vain;
For oh! the yellow treasure's taen
    By witchin skill;
An' dawtet,[11] twal-pint hawkie's [12] gaen
    As yell's [13] the bill.[14]   60

*   *   *   *   *   *   *

When thowes [15] dissolve the snawy hoord,[16]
An' float the jinglin icy-boord,
Then water-kelpies [17] haunt the foord
    By your direction,   70
An' nighted trav'lers are allur'd
    To their destruction.

And aft [18] your moss-traversing spunkies [19]
Decoy the wight that late and drunk is:
The bleezing,[20] curst, mischievous monkeys 75
    Delude his eyes,
Till in some miry slough he sunk is,
    Ne'er mair to rise.

When masons' mystic word and grip
In storms an' tempests raise you up,   80
Some cock or cat your rage maun stop,
    Or, strange to tell,
The youngest brither [21] ye wad whip
    Aff [22] straught to hell!

[1] splashes [2] brimstone tub [3] scald [4] slap
[5] known [6] flaming ravine [7] home [8] sluggish [9] shy
[10] timid [11] sometimes [12] unroofing [13] churches
[14] lonely [15] unearthly [16] grave [17] often beyond
[18] elders [19] one [20] slanting

[1] beyond [2] lake [3] rush-bush [4] fist [5] unearthly
[6] harsh [7] wizards [8] church-yards [9] dug up [10] churn
[11] petted [12] twelve-pint cow [13] dry as [14] bull
[15] thaws [16] snowy hoard [17] water-spirits [18] often
[19] will-o'-the-wisps [20] blazing [21] brother [22] off

Lang syne, in Eden's bonie yard,   85
When youthfu' lovers first were pair'd,
And all the soul of love they shar'd,
     The raptur'd hour,
Sweet on the fragrant flow'ry swaird,[1]
     In shady bow'r ;   90

Then you, ye auld sneck-drawin [2] dog !
Ye cam to Paradise incog,
And play'd on man a cursed brogue,[3]
     (Black be your fa' !)
And gied the infant warld a shog,[4]   95
     Maist [5] ruin'd a'.

D'ye mind that day, when in a bizz,[6]
Wi' reeket [7] duds and reestet gizz,[8]
Ye did present your smoutie phiz
     Mang better folk,   100
An' sklented [9] on the man of Uz [10]
     Your spitefu' joke?

An' how ye gat him i' your thrall,
An' brak him out o' house and hal',
While scabs and blotches did him gall,   105
     Wi' bitter claw,
An' lows'd [11] his ill-tongued, wicked scaul,[12]
     Was warst ava? [13]

But a' your doings to rehearse,
Your wily snares an' fechtin fierce,   110
Sin' that day Michael [14] did you pierce,
     Down to this time,
Wad ding [15] a Lallan [16] tongue, or Erse,
     In prose or rhyme.

An' now, auld Cloots,[17] I ken ye're thinkin,   115
A certain Bardie's rantin, drinkin,
Some luckless hour will send him linkin,[18]
     To your black pit ;
But faith ! he'll turn a corner jinkin,[19]
     An' cheat you yet.   120

But fare you weel, auld Nickie-ben !
O wad ye tak a thought an' men' !
Ye aiblins [20] might — I dinna ken
     Still hae a stake : [21]
I'm wae [22] to think upo' yon den,   125
     Ev'n for your sake !

---

[1] sward   [2] latch-lifting   [3] trick   [4] shock   [5] almost
[6] flurry   [7] smoked   [8] singed face   [9] directed   [10] Job
[11] loosed   [12] scold   [13] worst of all   [14] cf. Milton,
Par. Lost, VI, 326 [15] baffle [16] Lowland [17] old Hoofs
[18] tripping [19] darting [20] possibly [21] still have a
chance in the game [22] sad

From LINES TO JOHN LAPRAIK

I am nae Poet, in a sense,
But just a Rhymer like by chance,   50
An' hae to learning nae pretence ;
     Yet what the matter?
Whene'er my Muse does on me glance,
     I jingle at her.

Your critic-folk may cock their nose,   55
And say, "How can you e'er propose,
You wha ken hardly verse frae prose,
     To mak a sang?"
But, by your leave, my learned foes,
     Ye're maybe wrang.   60

What's a' your jargon o' your schools,
Your Latin names for horns an' stools?
If honest nature made you fools,
     What sairs [1] your grammars?
Ye'd better taen [2] up spades and shools,   65
     Or knappin-hammers.[3]

A set o' dull, conceited hashes [4]
Confuse their brains in college classes !
They gang in stirks [5] and come out asses,
     Plain truth to speak ;   70
An' syne [6] they think to climb Parnassus
     By dint o' Greek !

Gie me ae [7] spark o' Nature's fire,
That's a' the learnin I desire ;
Then, tho' I drudge thro' dub [8] an' mire   75
     At pleugh or cart,
My Muse, though hamely in attire,
     May touch the heart.

TO A MOUSE

ON TURNING UP HER NEST WITH THE PLOUGH, NOVEMBER, 1785

Wee, sleekit,[9] cowrin, tim'rous beastie,
Oh, what a panic's in thy breastie !
Thou need na start awa sae hasty
     Wi' bickerin [10] brattle ! [11]
I wad be laith [12] to rin an' chase thee   5
     Wi' murd'rin pattle ! [13]

---

[1] serves   [2] have taken   [3] stone breakers   [4] fools
[5] steers   [6] then   [7] one   [8] puddle   [9] sleek   [10] hurrying
[11] scamper   [12] loth   [13] paddle

I'm truly sorry man's dominion
Has broken nature's social union,
An' justifies that ill opinion
    Which makes thee startle   10
At me, thy poor earth-born companion,
    An' fellow-mortal!

I doubt na, whyles,[1] but thou may thieve:
What then? poor beastie, thou maun live!
A daimen [2] icker [3] in a thrave [4]   15
    'S a sma' request;
I'll get a blessin wi' the lave,[5]
    An' never miss 't!

Thy wee bit housie, too, in ruin!
Its silly wa's [6] the win's are strewin!   20
An' naething, now, to big [7] a new ane,
    O' foggage [8] green!
An' bleak December's winds ensuin
    Baith snell [9] an' keen!

Thou saw the fields laid bare and waste,   25
An' weary winter comin fast,
An' cozie here beneath the blast
    Thou thought to dwell,
Till crash! the cruel coulter past
    Out thro' thy cell.   30

That wee bit heap o' leaves an' stibble
Has cost thee mony a weary nibble!
Now thou's turn'd out for a' thy trouble,
    But [10] house or hald,
To thole [11] the winter's sleety dribble   35
    An' cranreuch [12] cauld!

But, Mousie, thou art no thy lane [13]
In proving foresight may be vain:
The best laid schemes o' mice an' men   40
    Gang aft a-gley,[14]
An' lea'e us nought but grief an' pain
    For promis'd joy.

Still thou art blest, compar'd wi' me!
The present only toucheth thee:
But, och! I backward cast my ee [15]   45
    On prospects drear!
An' forward, tho' I canna see,
    I guess an' fear!

[1] sometimes [2] occasional [3] ear of grain [4] twenty-four sheaves [5] rest [6] its poor walls [7] build [8] rank grass [9] piercing [10] without [11] endure [12] hoar-frost [13] lone [14] amiss [15] eye

THE COTTER'S SATURDAY NIGHT

INSCRIBED TO ROBERT AIKEN, ESQ.

Let not Ambition mock their useful toil,
  Their homely joys and destiny obscure;
Nor Grandeur hear with a disdainful smile,
  The short and simple annals of the poor.
             — GRAY.

My lov'd, my honour'd, much respected
    friend!
  No mercenary bard his homage pays;
With honest pride, I scorn each selfish end:
  My dearest meed a friend's esteem and
    praise.
To you I sing, in simple Scottish lays,   5
  The lowly train in life's sequester'd scene;
  The native feelings strong, the guileless
    ways;
What Aiken in a cottage would have been;
Ah! tho' his worth unknown, far happier
    there, I ween!

November chill blaws loud wi' angry sugh,[1]
  The short'ning winter day is near a close;
The miry beasts retreating frae the pleugh,
  The black'ning trains o' craws to their
    repose;
The toil-worn Cotter frae his labour
    goes, —
This night his weekly moil is at an end, —
  Collects his spades, his mattocks and his
    hoes,   16
Hoping the morn [2] in ease and rest to spend,
And weary, o'er the moor, his course does
    hameward bend.

At length his lonely cot appears in view,
  Beneath the shelter of an agèd tree;   20
Th' expectant wee-things, toddlin, stacher [3]
    through
  To meet their dad, wi' flichterin [4] noise
    an' glee.
His wee bit ingle,[5] blinkin bonilie,
His clean hearth-stane, his thrifty wifie's
    smile,   24
  The lisping infant prattling on his knee,
Does a' his weary kiaugh [6] and care beguile,
An' makes him quite forget his labour an' his
    toil.

[1] sound   [2] morrow   [3] stagger   [4] fluttering
[5] fire-place   [6] anxiety

Belyve,[1] the elder bairns come drappin in,
 At service out amang the farmers roun';
Some ca[2] the pleugh, some herd, some
  tentie[3] rin   30
 A cannie errand to a neibor toun:
 Their eldest hope, their Jenny, woman-
  grown,
In youthfu' bloom, love sparkling in her ee,
 Comes hame, perhaps to shew a braw[4]
  new gown,
 Or deposite her sair-won[5] penny-fee,   35
To help her parents dear, if they in hardship be.

With joy unfeign'd brothers and sisters meet,
 An' each for other's weelfare kindly
  spiers:[6]
 The social hours, swift-wing'd, unnotic'd
  fleet;
 Each tells the uncos[7] that he sees or
  hears.   40
 The parents, partial, eye their hopeful
  years;
 Anticipation forward points the view;
 The mother, wi' her needle an' her
  sheers,
 Gars[8] auld claes look amaist as weel's the
  new;
The father mixes a' wi' admonition due.   45

Their master's an' their mistress's com-
  mand
 The younkers a' are warnèd to obey;
 An' mind their labours wi' an eydent[9]
  hand,
 An' ne'er tho' out o' sight, to jauk or
  play: 49
 "An' O! be sure to fear the Lord alway,
An' mind your duty, duly, morn an' night!
 Lest in temptation's path ye gang astray,
 Implore His counsel and assisting might:
They never sought in vain that sought the
  Lord aright!"   54

But hark! a rap comes gently to the door.
 Jenny, wha kens the meaning o' the same,
Tells how a neibor lad cam o'er the moor,
 To do some errands, and convoy her
  hame.
 The wily mother sees the conscious flame
Sparkle in Jenny's ee, and flush her cheek;
 Wi' heart-struck, anxious care, inquires
  his name,   61

While Jenny hafflins[1] is afraid to speak;
Weel pleas'd the mother hears it's nae wild
  worthless rake.

Wi' kindly welcome Jenny brings him ben,[2]
 A strappin youth; he takes the mother's
  eye;
Blythe Jenny sees the visit's no ill taen;[3] 66
 The father cracks[4] of horses, pleughs, and
  kye.[5]
 The youngster's artless heart o'erflows
  wi' joy,
But, blate[6] and laithfu',[7] scarce can weel
  behave;
 The mother wi' a woman's wiles can spy
What makes the youth sae bashfu' an' sae
  grave,   71
Weel-pleas'd to think her bairn's respected
  like the lave.[8]

O happy love! where love like this is found!
 O heart-felt raptures! bliss beyond com-
  pare!
I've pacèd much this weary, mortal round,
 And sage experience bids me this declare—
 "If Heaven a draught of heavenly pleas-
  ure spare,   77
 One cordial in this melancholy vale,
'Tis when a youthful, loving, modest pair,
In other's arms breathe out the tender tale,
Beneath the milk-white thorn that scents the
  ev'ning gale."   81

Is there, in human form, that bears a heart,
 A wretch! a villain! lost to love and
  truth!
That can with studied, sly, ensnaring art
 Betray sweet Jenny's unsuspecting
  youth?   85
 Curse on his perjur'd arts! dissembling
  smooth!
Are honour, virtue, conscience, all exil'd?
 Is there no pity, no relenting ruth,
Points to the parents fondling o'er their
  child,
Then paints the ruin'd maid, and their dis-
  traction wild?   90

But now the supper crowns their simple
  board,
 The halesome parritch,[9] chief of Scotia's
  food;

---

[1] presently [2] drive [3] careful [4] fine [5] hard-won
[6] asks [7] odds and ends [8] makes [9] diligent

[1] partly [2] within [3] not ill taken [4] talks [5] cows
[6] shy [7] bashful [8] rest [9] porridge

The sowpe [1] their only hawkie [2] does afford,
  That yont [3] the hallan [4] snugly chows her
    cud.
The dame brings forth, in complimental
  mood,   95
To grace the lad, her weel-hain'd [5] kebbuck
  fell,[6]
An' aft [7] he's prest, an' aft he ca's it
  guid;
The frugal wifie, garrulous, will tell,
How 'twas a towmond [8] auld, sin' lint [9] was
  i' the bell.   99

The cheerfu' supper done, wi' serious face,
  They round the ingle form a circle wide;
The sire turns o'er with patriarchal grace
  The big ha'-bible,[10] ance his father's
    pride;
His bonnet rev'rently is laid aside,
  His lyart [11] haffets [12] wearing thin and
    bare;   105
  Those strains that once did sweet in Zion
    glide,
He wales [13] a portion with judicious care;
And, "Let us worship God," he says with
  solemn air.

They chant their artless notes in simple
  guise;
  They tune their hearts, by far the noblest
    aim: 110
Perhaps *Dundee's* wild-warbling measures
  rise,
  Or plaintive *Martyrs*, worthy of the
    name,
Or noble *Elgin* beets [14] the heaven-ward
  flame,
  The sweetest far of Scotia's holy lays.
Compar'd with these, Italian trills are
  tame;   115
The tickl'd ear no heart-felt raptures raise;
Nae unison hae they with our Creator's praise.

The priest-like father reads the sacred
  page, —
  How Abram was the friend of God on
    high;
Or Moses bade eternal warfare wage   120
  With Amalek's ungracious progeny;
Or how the royal bard did groaning lie

---

[1] milk [2] cow [3] beyond [4] partition [5] well-saved
[6] strong cheese [7] often [8] twelve-month [9] since flax
[10] hall Bible [11] gray [12] locks [13] chooses [14] incites,
kindles

Beneath the stroke of heaven's avenging
  ire;
  Or Job's pathetic plaint, and wailing cry;
Or rapt Isaiah's wild, seraphic fire;   125
Or other holy seers that tune the sacred lyre.

Perhaps the Christian volume is the
  theme, —
  How guiltless blood for guilty man was
    shed;
How He, who bore in heav'n the second
  name,
  Had not on earth whereon to lay His
    head: 130
  How His first followers and servants
    sped;
The precepts sage they wrote to many a
  land;
  How he, who lone in Patmos banishèd,
Saw in the sun a mighty angel stand,
And heard great Bab'lon's doom pronounced
  by Heav'n's command.   135

Then kneeling down to Heaven's Eternal
  King,
  The saint, the father, and the husband
    prays:
Hope "springs exulting on triumphant
  wing,"
  That thus they all shall meet in future
    days:
There ever bask in uncreated rays,   140
No more to sigh or shed the bitter tear,
  Together hymning their Creator's praise,
In such society, yet still more dear,
While circling Time moves round in an eternal
  sphere.

Compar'd with this, how poor Religion's
  pride   145
  In all the pomp of method and of art,
When men display to congregations wide
  Devotion's ev'ry grace except the heart!
The Pow'r, incens'd, the pageant will
  desert,
  The pompous strain, the sacerdotal stole;
But haply in some cottage far apart   151
May hear, well pleased, the language of the
  soul,
And in His book of life the inmates poor enrol.

Then homeward all take off their sev'ral
  way;
  The youngling cottagers retire to rest;
The parent-pair their secret homage pay,

And proffer up to Heav'n the warm re-
    quest,
That He, who stills the raven's clam'rous
    nest
And decks the lily fair in flow'ry pride,
    Would, in the way His wisdom sees the
    best,   160
For them and for their little ones provide;
But chiefly, in their hearts with grace divine
    preside.

From scenes like these old Scotia's grandeur
    springs,
    That makes her lov'd at home, rever'd
    abroad:
Princes and lords are but the breath of
    kings,   165
"An honest man's the noblest work of
    God" :[1]
    And certes, in fair Virtue's heavenly
    road,
The cottage leaves the palace far behind:
What is a lordling's pomp? a cumbrous
    load,   169
Disguising oft the wretch of human kind,
Studied in arts of hell, in wickedness refin'd !

O Scotia ! my dear, my native soil !
    For whom my warmest wish to Heaven
    is sent !
Long may thy hardy sons of rustic toil
    Be blest with health, and peace, and sweet
    content !   175
    And, oh ! may Heaven their simple lives
    prevent
From luxury's contagion, weak and vile !
Then, howe'er crowns and coronets be
    rent,
A virtuous populace may rise the while,
And stand a wall of fire around their much-
    lov'd isle.   180

O Thou ! who pour'd the patriotic tide
That stream'd thro' Wallace's undaunted
    heart,
Who dar'd to nobly stem tyrannic pride,
    Or nobly die, the second glorious part,—
(The patriot's God peculiarly thou art,
    His friend, inspirer, guardian, and reward !)
O never, never Scotia's realm desert,
But still the patriot, and the patriot-bard,
In bright succession raise, her ornament and
    guard !

[1] Quoted from Pope

ADDRESS TO THE UNCO GUID, OR THE RIGIDLY RIGHTEOUS

O ye wha are sae guid yoursel,
    Sae pious and sae holy,
Ye've nought to do but mark and tell
    Your neibour's fauts and folly !
Whase life is like a weel-gaun[1] mill,   5
    Supply'd wi' store o' water,
The heapet happer's[2] ebbing still,
    And still the clap[3] plays clatter, —

Hear me, ye venerable core,[4]
    As counsel for poor mortals,   10
That frequent pass douce[5] Wisdom's door
    For glaiket[6] Folly's portals;
I for their thoughtless, careless sakes
    Would here propone defences —
Their donsie[7] tricks, their black mistakes, 15
    Their failings and mischances.

Ye see your state wi' theirs compar'd,
    And shudder at the niffer;[8]
But cast a moment's fair regard,
    What maks the mighty differ?[9]   20
Discount what scant occasion gave,
    That purity ye pride in,
And (what's aft[10] mair than a' the lave[11])
    Your better art o' hidin.

Think, when your castigated pulse   25
    Gies now and then a wallop,
What ragings must his veins convulse
    That still eternal gallop:
Wi' wind and tide fair i' your tail,
    Right on ye scud your sea-way;   30
But in the teeth o' baith[12] to sail,
    It maks an unco[13] leeway.

See Social Life and Glee sit down,
    All joyous and unthinking,
Till, quite transmugrify'd,[14] they're grown 35
    Debauchery and Drinking:
O would they stay to calculate
    Th' eternal consequences;
Or — your more dreaded hell to state —
    Damnation of expenses !   40

Ye high, exalted, virtuous Dames,
    Tied up in godly laces,

---

[1] well-going [2] heapèd hopper is [3] clapper
[4] company [5] grave [6] giddy [7] reckless [8] exchange
[9] difference [10] often [11] rest [12] both [13] wonderful
[14] metamorphosed

Before you gie poor Frailty names,
  Suppose a change o' cases:
A dear lov'd lad, convenience snug,   45
  A treacherous inclination —
But, let me whisper i' your lug, [1]
  Ye're aiblins [2] nae temptation.

Then gently scan your brother man,
  Still gentler sister woman;   50
Tho' they may gang a kennin [3] wrang,
  To step aside is human:
One point must still be greatly dark,
  The moving Why they do it;
And just as lamely can ye mark,   55
  How far perhaps they rue it.

Who made the heart, 'tis He alone
  Decidedly can try us,
He knows each chord, its various tone,
  Each spring, its various bias: 60
Then at the balance, let's be mute,
  We never can adjust it;
What's done we partly can compute,
  But know not what's resisted.

TO A MOUNTAIN DAISY

ON TURNING ONE DOWN WITH THE PLOUGH, IN APRIL, 1786

Wee, modest, crimson-tippèd flow'r,
Thou's met me in an evil hour;
For I maun crush amang the stoure [4]
    Thy slender stem:
To spare thee now is past my pow'r,   5
    Thou bonie gem.

Alas! it's no thy neibor sweet,
The bonie lark, companion meet,
Bending thee 'mang the dewy weet
    Wi' spreckl'd breast,   10
When upward-springing, blythe, to greet
    The purpling east.

Cauld blew the bitter-biting north
Upon thy early, humble birth;
Yet cheerfully thou glinted forth   15
    Amid the storm,
Scarce rear'd above the parent-earth
    Thy tender form.

The flaunting flowers our gardens yield
High shelt'ring woods an' wa's [5] maun shield:

But thou, beneath the random bield [1]   21
        O' clod or stane,
Adorns the histie [2] stibble-field
        Unseen, alane.

There, in thy scanty mantle clad,   25
Thy snawie bosom sun-ward spread,
Thou lifts thy unassuming head
        In humble guise;
But now the share uptears thy bed,
        And low thou lies!   30

Such is the fate of artless Maid,
Sweet flow'ret of the rural shade!
By love's simplicity betray'd
        And guileless trust;
Till she, like thee, all soil'd, is laid   35
        Low i' the dust.

Such is the fate of simple Bard,
On life's rough ocean luckless starr'd!
Unskilful he to note the card
        Of prudent lore,   40
Till billows rage and gales blow hard,
        And whelm him o'er!

Such fate to suffering Worth is giv'n,
Who long with wants and woes has striv'n,
By human pride or cunning driv'n   45
        To mis'ry's brink;
Till, wrench'd of ev'ry stay but Heav'n,
        He ruin'd sink!

Ev'n thou who mourn'st the Daisy's fate,
That fate is thine — no distant date;   50
Stern Ruin's ploughshare drives elate,
        Full on thy bloom,
Till crush'd beneath the furrow's weight
        Shall be thy doom.

A BARD'S EPITAPH

Is there a whim-inspirèd fool,
Owre [3] fast for thought, owre hot for rule,
Owre blate [4] to seek, owre proud to snool? [5] —
    Let him draw near;
And owre this grassy heap sing dool, [6]   5
    And drap a tear.

Is there a bard of rustic song,
Who, noteless, steals the crowds among,

[1] ear   [2] perhaps   [3] trifle   [4] dust   [5] walls
[6] sorrow

[1] shelter   [2] dry   [3] over   [4] bashful   [5] cringe

That weekly this area throng? —
          Oh, pass not by!   10
But with a frater-feeling strong
          Here heave a sigh.

Is there a man whose judgment clear
Can others teach the course to steer,
Yet runs himself life's mad career   15
          Wild as the wave? —
Here pause — and thro' the starting tear
          Survey this grave.

The poor inhabitant below
Was quick to learn and wise to know,   20
And keenly felt the friendly glow
          And softer flame;
But thoughtless follies laid him low,
          And stain'd his name!

Reader, attend! whether thy soul   25
Soars fancy's flights beyond the pole,
Or darkling grubs this earthly hole
          In low pursuit;
Know, prudent, cautious self-control
          Is wisdom's root.   30

TAM O' SHANTER

A TALE

Of Brownyis and of Bogillis full is this buke.
          — GAWIN DOUGLAS

When chapman billies [1] leave the street,
And drouthy [2] neibors neibors meet,
As market-days are wearing late,
And folk begin to tak the gate;
While we sit bousin at the nappy, [3]   5
And gettin fou and unco [4] happy,
We think na on the lang Scots miles,
The mosses, waters, slaps, [5] and stiles,
That lie between us and our hame,
Whare sits our sulky, sullen dame,   10
Gathering her brows like gathering storm,
Nursing her wrath to keep it warm.

This truth fand honest Tam o' Shanter,
As he frae Ayr ae night did canter:
(Auld Ayr, wham ne'er a town surpasses,   15
For honest men and bonie lasses.)

O Tam! had'st thou but been sae wise
As taen thy ain wife Kate's advice!

[1] pedlers [2] thirsty [3] ale [4] marvellously [5] gaps

She tauld thee weel thou was a skellum, [1]
A bletherin, blusterin, drunken blellum; [2]   20
That frae November till October,
Ae [3] market-day thou was na sober;
That ilka [4] melder [5] wi' the miller,
Thou sat as lang as thou had siller;
That ev'ry naig [6] was ca'd [7] a shoe on,   25
The smith and thee gat roarin fou on;
That at the Lord's house, ev'n on Sunday,
Thou drank wi' Kirkton Jean till Monday.
She prophesied, that, late or soon,
Thou would be found deep drown'd in Doon;
Or catch't wi' warlocks [8] in the mirk, [9]   31
By Alloway's auld haunted kirk.

Ah, gentle dames! it gars [10] me greet, [11]
To think how mony counsels sweet,
How mony lengthened sage advices,   35
The husband frae the wife despises!

But to our tale: — Ae market night,
Tam had got planted unco right,
Fast by an ingle, [12] bleezin finely,
Wi' reamin swats [13] that drank divinely;   40
And at his elbow, Souter Johnie,
His ancient, trusty, drouthy crony:
Tam lo'ed him like a vera brither; [14]
They had been fou [15] for weeks thegither.
The night drave on wi' sangs and clatter;   45
And ay the ale was growing better:
The landlady and Tam grew gracious
Wi' secret favours, sweet, and precious:
The souter [16] tauld his queerest stories;
The landlord's laugh was ready chorus: 50
The storm without might rair and rustle,
Tam did na mind the storm a whistle.

Care, mad to see a man sae happy,
E'en drown'd himsel amang the nappy: [17]
As beés flee hame wi' lades o' treasure,   55
The minutes wing'd their way wi' pleasure;
Kings may be blest, but Tam was glorious,
O'er a' the ills o' life victorious!

But pleasures are like poppies spread,
You seize the flow'r, its bloom is shed;   60
Or like the snow falls in the river,
A moment white — then melts forever;
Or like the borealis race,
That flit ere you can point their place;

[1] wretch [2] idle-talker [3] one [4] every [5] grinding
[6] nag [7] driven [8] wizards [9] dark [10] makes [11] weep
[12] fireside [13] foaming ale [14] brother [15] full [16] cobbler [17] ale

Or like the rainbow's lovely form 65
Evanishing amid the storm.

Nae man can tether time or tide:
The hour approaches Tam maun ride, —
That hour, o' night's black arch the key-
stane,
That dreary hour he mounts his beast in; 70
And sic a night he taks the road in,
As ne'er poor sinner was abroad in.

The wind blew as 't wad blawn its last;
The rattling show'rs rose on the blast;
The speedy gleams the darkness swallow'd;
Loud, deep, and lang the thunder bellow'd ·
That night, a child might understand,
The Deil had business on his hand.

Weel mounted on his grey mare, Meg, —
A better never lifted leg, — 80
Tam skelpit [1] on thro' dub [2] and mire,
Despising wind and rain and fire;
Whiles holding fast his guid blue bonnet,
Whiles crooning o'er some auld Scots sonnet,
Whiles glowrin round wi' prudent cares, 85
Lest bogles [3] catch him unawares.
Kirk-Alloway was drawing nigh,
Whare ghaists and houlets [4] nightly cry.

By this time he was cross the ford,
Whare in the snaw the chapman smoor'd; [5]
And past the birks [6] and meikle [7] stane, 91
Whare drucken [8] Charlie brak's neck-bane; [9]
And thro' the whins,[10] and by the cairn,[11]
Whare hunters fand the murder'd bairn; [12]
And near the thorn, aboon [13] the well, 95
Whare Mungo's mither hang'd hersel.
Before him Doon pours all his floods;
The doubling storm roars thro' the woods;
The lightnings flash from pole to pole,
Near and more near the thunders roll; 100
When, glimmering thro' the groaning trees,
Kirk-Alloway seemed in a bleeze: [14]
Thro' ilka bore [15] the beams were glancing,
And loud resounded mirth and dancing.

Inspiring bold John Barleycorn! 105
What dangers thou can'st make us scorn!
Wi' tippenny [16] we fear nae evil;
Wi' usquebae [17] we'll face the devil!

The swats [1] sae ream'd [2] in Tammie's noddle,
Fair play, he car'd na deils a boddle.[3] 110
But Maggie stood right sair astonish'd,
Till, by the heel and hand admonish'd,
She ventur'd forward on the light;
And, wow! Tam saw an unco [4] sight!

Warlocks and witches in a dance; 115
Nae cotillon brent-new [5] frae France,
But hornpipes, jigs, strathspeys, and reels
Put life and mettle in their heels:
A winnock [6] bunker [7] in the east,
There sat Auld Nick in shape o' beast; 120
A towzie tyke,[8] black, grim, and large,
To gie them music was his charge;
He screw'd the pipes and gart [9] them skirl,[10]
Till roof and rafters a' did dirl.[11] —
Coffins stood round like open presses, 125
That shaw'd the dead in their last dresses;
And by some devilish cantraip [12] sleight
Each in its cauld hand held a light,
By which heroic Tam was able
To note upon the haly table 130
A murderer's banes in gibbet airns; [13]
Twa span-lang, wee, unchristen'd bairns;
A thief, new-cutted frae the rape [14] —
Wi' his last gasp his gab [15] did gape;
Five tomahawks, wi' blude red-rusted; 135
Five scymitars, wi' murder crusted;
A garter, which a babe had strangled;
A knife, a father's throat had mangled,
Whom his ain son o' life bereft —
The grey hairs yet stack to the heft; 140
Wi' mair o' horrible and awfu',
Which ev'n to name wad be unlawfu'.

As Tammie glowr'd, amaz'd and curious,
The mirth and fun grew fast and furious:
The piper loud and louder blew, 145
The dancers quick and quicker flew;
They reel'd, they set, they cross'd, they
cleekit,[16]
Till ilka carlin [17] swat [18] and reekit,[19]
And coost [20] her duddies [21] to the wark [22]
And linket at it in her sark! [23] 150

Now Tam, O Tam! had thae been queans,[24]
A' plump and strapping in their teens!

[1] ale [2] foamed [3] copper [4] marvellous [5] brand-
new [6] window [7] seat [8] shaggy cur [9] made
[10] scream [11] throb [12] tricksy [13] irons [14] rope
[15] mouth [16] clutched [17] old woman [18] sweated
[19] steamed [20] cast aside [21] clothes [22] work [23] che-
mise [24] girls

[1] clattered [2] puddle [3] goblins [4] owls [5] smothered
[6] birches [7] big [8] drunken [9] neck-bone [10] gorse
[11] pile of stones [12] child [13] above [14] blaze [15] every
crevice [16] twopenny ale [17] whiskey

Their sarks, instead o' creeshie [1] flannen,
Been snaw-white seventeen hunder linen! [2] —
Thir [3] breeks o' mine, my only pair,   155
That ance were plush, o' gude blue hair,
I wad hae gien them aff my hurdies,[4]
For ae blink o' the bonie burdies! [5]

*   *   *   *   *   *   *

But Tam ken'd what was what fu' brawlie; [6]
There was ae winsom wench and walie,[7]
That night enlisted in the core [8]   165
(Lang after ken'd on Carrick shore;
For mony a beast to dead she shot,
And perish'd mony a bonie boat,
And shook baith meikle [9] corn and bear,[10]
And kept the country-side in fear);   170
Her cutty sark [11] o' Paisley harn,[12]
That while a lassie she had worn,
In longitude tho' sorely scanty,
It was her best, and she was vauntie.[13]
Ah! little kent thy reverend grannie,   175
That sark she coft [14] for her wee Nannie,
Wi' twa pund Scots ('twas a' her riches),
Wad ever graced a dance o' witches!

But here my Muse her wing maun cow'r,
Sic flights are far beyond her pow'r;   180
To sing how Nannie lap and flang,
(A souple jad she was and strang,)
And how Tam stood like ane bewitch'd,
And thought his very een [15] enrich'd;
Even Satan glowr'd and fidg'd [16] fu' fain,[17] 185
And hotch'd [18] and blew wi' might and
     main:
Till first ae caper, syne [19] anither,
Tam tint [20] his reason a' thegither,
And roars out, "Weel done, Cutty-sark!" [21]
And in an instant all was dark: 190
And scarcely had he Maggie rallied,
When out the hellish legion sallied.

As bees bizz out wi' angry fyke,[22]
When plundering herds assail their byke; [23]
As open pussie's [24] mortal foes,   195
When, pop! she starts before their nose;
As eager runs the market-crowd,
When "Catch the thief!" resounds aloud;
So Maggie runs, the witches follow,
Wi' mony an eldritch [25] skriech and hollo. 200

Ah, Tam! ah, Tam! thou'll get thy fairin! [1]
In hell they'll roast thee like a herrin!
In vain thy Kate awaits thy comin!
Kate soon will be a woefu' woman!
Now, do thy speedy utmost, Meg,   205
And win the key-stane of the brig: [2]
There at them thou thy tail may toss,
A running stream they dare na cross.
But ere the key-stane she could make,
The fient [3] a tail she had to shake!   210
For Nannie, far before the rest,
Hard upon noble Maggie prest,
And flew at Tam wi' furious ettle; [4]
But little wist she Maggie's mettle —
Ae [5] spring brought aff her master hale,   215
But left behind her ain [6] grey tail:
The carlin [7] claught her by the rump,
And left poor Maggie scarce a stump.

Now, wha this tale o' truth shall read,
Ilk [8] man and mother's son, take heed,   220
Whene'er to drink you are inclin'd,
Or cutty-sarks run in your mind,
Think, ye may buy the joys owre [9] dear,
Remember Tam o' Shanter's mear.[10]

BONIE DOON

Ye flowery banks o' bonie Doon,
    How can ye blume sae fair?
How can ye chant, ye little birds,
    And I sae fu' o' care?

Thou'll break my heart, thou bonie bird,   5
    That sings upon the bough;
Thou minds me o' the happy days,
    When my fause luve was true.

Thou'll break my heart, thou bonie bird,
    That sings beside thy mate;   10
For sae I sat, and sae I sang,
    And wist na o' my fate.

Aft hae I rov'd by bonie Doon
    To see the wood-bine twine,
And ilka [8] bird sang o' its luve,   15
    And sae did I o' mine.

Wi' lightsome heart I pu'd a rose
    Frae aff its thorny tree;
And my fause [11] luver staw [12] my rose
    But left the thorn wi' me.   20

---

[1] greasy   [2] very fine linen   [3] these   [4] hips   [5] girls
[6] well   [7] goodly   [8] company   [9] much   [10] barley   [11] short
skirt   [12] linen   [13] proud   [14] bought   [15] eyes   [16] fidgeted
[17] eagerly   [18] squirmed   [19] then   [20] lost   [21] Short-skirt
[22] fuss   [23] hive   [24] the hare's   [25] unearthly

[1] reward   [2] bridge   [3] devil   [4] aim   [5] one   [6] own
[7] wench   [8] every   [9] over   [10] mare   [11] false   [12] stole

AE FOND KISS

Ae fond kiss, and then we sever;
Ae fareweel, and then forever!
Deep in heart-wrung tears I'll pledge thee,
Warring sighs and groans I'll wage thee.
Who shall say that Fortune grieves him,   5
While the star of hope she leaves him?
Me, nae cheerfu' twinkle lights me;
Dark despair around benights me.

I'll ne'er blame my partial fancy,
Naething could resist my Nancy;   10
But to see her was to love her;
Love but her, and love forever.
Had we never lov'd sae kindly,
Had we never lov'd sae blindly,
Never met — or never parted —   15
We had ne'er been broken-hearted.

Fare thee weel, thou first and fairest!
Fare thee weel, thou best and dearest!
Thine be ilka [1] joy and treasure,
Peace, enjoyment, love, and pleasure!   20
Ae fond kiss, and then we sever;
Ae fareweel, alas, forever!
Deep in heart-wrung tears I'll pledge thee,
Warring sighs and groans I'll wage thee!

BONIE LESLEY

O saw ye bonie Lesley
  As she gaed o'er the border?
She's gane, like Alexander,
  To spread her conquests farther.

To see her is to love her,   5
  And love but her forever;
For Nature made her what she is,
  And never made anither!

Thou art a queen, fair Lesley,
  Thy subjects, we before thee: 10
Thou art divine, fair Lesley,
  The hearts o' men adore thee.

The Deil he could na scaith [2] thee,
  Or aught that wad belang thee;
He'd look into thy bonie face,   15
  And say, "I canna wrang thee."

[1] every   [2] injure

AE

The Powers aboon will tent [1] thee;
  Misfortune sha' na steer [2] thee;
Thou'rt like themselves sae lovely,
  That ill they'll ne'er let near thee.   20

Return again, fair Lesley,
  Return to Caledonie!
That we may brag, we hae a lass
  There's nane again sae bonie.

HIGHLAND MARY

Ye banks, and braes,[3] and streams around
  The castle o' Montgomery,
Green be your woods and fair your flowers,
  Your waters never drumlie! [4]
There simmer first unfauld her robes,   5
  And there the langest tarry;
For there I took the last fareweel,
  O' my sweet Highland Mary.

How sweetly bloom'd the gay green birk,[5]
  How rich the hawthorn's blossom,   10
As underneath their fragrant shade
  I clasp'd her to my bosom!
The golden hours, on angel wings,
  Flew o'er me and my dearie;
For dear to me as light and life,   15
  Was my sweet Highland Mary.

Wi' monie a vow and lock'd embrace
  Our parting was fu' tender;
And, pledging aft to meet again,
  We tore oursels asunder;   20
But O! fell death's untimely frost,
  That nipt my flower sae early!
Now green's the sod, and cauld's the clay,
  That wraps my Highland Mary!

O pale, pale now, those rosy lips,   25
  I aft hae kiss'd sae fondly!
And closed for aye the sparkling glance,
  That dwelt on me sae kindly!
And mould'ring now in silent dust,
  That heart that lo'ed me dearly!   30
But still within my bosom's core
  Shall live my Highland Mary.

[1] tend   [2] hurt   [3] slopes   [4] muddy   [5] birch

DUNCAN GRAY

Duncan Gray came here to woo,
  Ha, ha, the wooin o't !
On blythe Yule night when we were fou,[1]
  Ha, ha, the wooin o't !
Maggie coost her head fu hiegh,   5
Look'd asklent [2] and unco skiegh,[3]
Gart [4] poor Duncan stand abiegh; [5]
  Ha, ha, the wooin o't !

Duncan fleech'd,[6] and Duncan pray'd ;
  Ha, ha, the wooin o't !   10
Meg was deaf as Ailsa Craig,[7]
  Ha, ha, the wooin o't !
Duncan sigh'd baith out and in,
Grat [8] his een [9] baith bleer't [10] and blin',
Spak o' lowpin [11] owre a linn ; [12]
  Ha, ha, the wooin o't !   15

Time and chance are but a tide,
  Ha, ha, the wooin o't !
Slighted love is sair to bide,[13]
  Ha, ha, the wooin o't !   20
"Shall I, like a fool," quoth he,
"For a haughty hizzie [14] die ?
She may gae to — France for me !"
  Ha, ha, the wooin o't !

How it comes let doctors tell,   25
  Ha, ha, the wooin o't !
Meg grew sick as he grew hale,
  Ha, ha, the wooin o't !
Something in her bosom wrings,
For relief a sigh she brings ;   30
And O ! her een, they spak sic things !
  Ha, ha, the wooin o't !

Duncan was a lad o' grace,
  Ha, ha, the wooin o't !
Maggie's was a piteous case,   35
  Ha, ha, the wooin o't !
Duncan could na be her death,
Swelling pity smoor'd [15] his wrath ;
Now they're crouse [16] and cantie [17] baith ;
  Ha, ha, the wooin o't !   40

[1] full [2] sidewise [3] wondrous shy [4] made [5] off
[6] flattered [7] a mountainous island off Ayrshire
[8] wept [9] eyes [10] bleared [11] leaping [12] water-
fall [13] hard to endure [14] lass [15] smothered
[16] bright [17] happy

SCOTS WHA HAE

Scots, wha hae wi' Wallace bled,
Scots, wham Bruce has aften led ;
Welcome to your gory bed,
  Or to victory !
Now's the day, and now's the hour ;   5
See the front o' battle lour ;
See approach proud Edward's power —
  Chains and slavery !

Wha will be a traitor knave ?
Wha can fill a coward's grave ?   10
Wha sae base as be a slave ?
  Let him turn and flee !
Wha for Scotland's king and law
Freedom's sword will strongly draw,
Freeman stand, or Freeman fa',   15
  Let him follow me !

By oppression's woes and pains
By your sons in servile chains !
We will drain our dearest veins,
  But they shall be free !   20
Lay the proud usurpers low !
Tyrants fall in every foe !
Liberty's in every blow ! —
  Let us do or die !

A MAN'S A MAN FOR A' THAT

Is there, for honest poverty,
  That hings his head, an' a' that ?
The coward slave, we pass him by,
  We dare be poor for a' that !
    For a' that, an' a' that,   5
      Our toils obscure, an' a' that ;
    The rank is but the guinea's stamp ;
    The man's the gowd [1] for a' that.

What tho' on hamely fare we dine,
  Wear hodden-gray,[2] an' a' that ;   10
Gie fools their silks, and knaves their wine,
  A man's a man for a' that.
    For a' that, an' a' that,
      Their tinsel show, an' a' that ;
    The honest man, tho' e'er sae poor,   15
      Is king o' men for a' that.

[1] gold   [2] coarse grey cloth

Ye see yon birkie,[1] ca'd a lord,
  Wha struts, an' stares, an' a' that;
Tho' hundreds worship at his word,
  He's but a coof [2] for a' that: 20
    For a' that, an' a' that,
      His riband, star, an' a' that,
    The man o' independent mind,
      He looks and laughs at a' that.

A prince can mak a belted knight,   25
  A marquis, duke, an' a' that;
But an honest man's aboon [3] his might,
  Guid faith he mauna fa' [4] that!

[1] young fellow   [2] fool   [3] above   [4] cannot
accomplish

    For a' that, an' a' that,
      Their dignities, an' a' that,   30
    The pith o' sense, an' pride o' worth,
      Are higher rank than a' that.

Then let us pray that come it may,
  As come it will for a' that,
That sense and worth, o'er a' the earth,   35
  May bear the gree,[1] an' a' that.
    For a' that, an' a' that,
      It's coming yet, for a' that,
    That man to man, the warld o'er,
      Shall brothers be for a' that.   40

[1] prize

THE ROMANTIC REVIVAL

WILLIAM WORDSWORTH
(1770–1850)

From THE PREFACE TO "LYRICAL
BALLADS"

* * * * * * *

The principal object, then, which I proposed
to myself in these Poems was to choose incidents and situations from common life, and to
relate or describe them, throughout, as far as
was possible, in a selection of language really
used by men, and, at the same time, to throw
over them a certain colouring of imagination,
whereby ordinary things should be presented
to the mind in an unusual way; and, further,
and above all, to make these incidents and
situations interesting by tracing in them,
truly though not ostentatiously, the primary
laws of our nature: chiefly, as far as regards
the manner in which we associate ideas in a
state of excitement. Low and rustic life was
generally chosen, because, in that condition,
the essential passions of the heart find a better
soil in which they can attain their maturity,
are less under restraint, and speak a plainer
and more emphatic language; because in that
condition of life our elementary feelings coexist in a state of greater simplicity, and, consequently, may be more accurately contemplated, and more forcibly communicated;
because the manners of rural life germinate
from those elementary feelings; and from the
necessary character of rural occupations, are
more easily comprehended, and are more
durable; and, lastly, because in that condition
the passions of men are incorporated with
the beautiful and permanent forms of nature.
The language, too, of these men is adopted
(purified indeed from what appears to be its
real defects, from all lasting and rational
causes of dislike or disgust) because such men
hourly communicate with the best objects
from which the best part of language is originally derived; and because, from their rank

in society and the sameness and narrow circle
of their intercourse, being less under the influence of social vanity, they convey their feelings and notions in simple and unelaborated
expressions. Accordingly, such a language,
arising out of repeated experience and regular
feelings, is a more permanent, and a far more
philosophical language, than that which is
frequently substituted for it by Poets, who
think that they are conferring honour upon
themselves and their art, in proportion as they
separate themselves from the sympathies of
men, and indulge in arbitrary and capricious
habits of expression, in order to furnish food
for fickle tastes, and fickle appetites, of their
own creation.

I cannot, however, be insensible of the present outcry against the triviality and meanness,
both of thought and language, which some of
my contemporaries have occasionally introduced into their metrical compositions; and I
acknowledge that this defect, where it exists,
is more dishonourable to the Writer's own
character than false refinement or arbitrary
innovation, though I should contend at the
same time, that it is far less pernicious in the
sum of its consequences. From such verses
the Poems in these volumes will be found distinguished at least by one mark of difference,
that each of them has a worthy *purpose*. Not
that I mean to say, I always began to write
with a distinct purpose formally conceived;
but my habits of meditation have so formed
my feelings, as that my descriptions of such
objects as strongly excite those feelings, will
be found to carry along with them a *purpose*.
If in this opinion I am mistaken, I can have
little right to the name of a Poet. For all
good poetry is the spontaneous overflow of
powerful feelings: and though this be true,
Poems to which any value can be attached
were never produced on any variety of subjects but by a man, who, being possessed of
more than usual organic sensibility, had also
thought long and deeply. For our continued
influxes of feeling are modified and directed
by our thoughts, which are indeed the repre-

sentatives of all our past feelings: and, as by contemplating the relation of these general representatives to each other we discover what is really important to men, so, by the repetition and continuance of this act, our feelings will be connected with important subjects, till at length, if we be originally possessed of much sensibility, such habits of mind will be produced, that, by observing blindly and mechanically the impulses of those habits, we shall describe objects, and utter sentiments, of such a nature, and in such connection with each other, that the understanding of the being to whom we address ourselves, if he be in a healthful state of association, must necessarily be in some degree enlightened, and his affections ameliorated.

* * * * * * *

I will not abuse the indulgence of my Reader by dwelling longer upon this subject; but it is proper that I should mention one other circumstance which distinguishes these Poems from the popular Poetry of the day; it is this, that the feeling therein developed gives importance to the action and situation, and not the action and situation to the feeling. My meaning will be rendered perfectly intelligible by referring my Reader to the Poems entitled *Poor Susan* and the *Childless Father*, particularly to the last Stanza of the latter Poem.

I will not suffer a sense of false modesty to prevent me from asserting, that I point my Reader's attention to this mark of distinction, far less for the sake of these particular Poems than from the general importance of the subject. The subject is indeed important! For the human mind is capable of being excited without the application of gross and violent stimulants; and he must have a very faint perception of its beauty and dignity who does not know this, and who does not further know, that one being is elevated above another, in proportion as he possesses this capability. It has therefore appeared to me, that to endeavour to produce or enlarge this capability is one of the best services in which, at any period, a Writer can be engaged; but this service, excellent at all times, is especially so at the present day. For a multitude of causes, unknown to former times, are now acting with a combined force to blunt the discriminating powers of the mind, and unfitting it for all voluntary exertion, to reduce it to a state of

almost savage torpor. The most effective of these causes are the great national events which are daily taking place, and the increasing accumulation of men in cities, where the uniformity of their occupations produces a craving for extraordinary incident, which the rapid communication of intelligence hourly gratifies. To this tendency of life and manners the literature and theatrical exhibitions of the country have conformed themselves. The invaluable works of our elder writers, I had almost said the works of Shakspeare and Milton, are driven into neglect by frantic novels, sickly and stupid German Tragedies, and deluges of idle and extravagant stories in verse. — When I think upon this degrading thirst after outrageous stimulation, I am almost ashamed to have spoken of the feeble effort with which I have endeavoured to counteract it; and, reflecting upon the magnitude of the general evil, I should be oppressed with no dishonourable melancholy, had I not a deep impression of certain inherent and indestructible qualities of the human mind, and likewise of certain powers in the great and permanent objects that act upon it, which are equally inherent and indestructible; and did I not further add to this impression a belief, that the time is approaching when the evil will be systematically opposed, by men of greater powers, and with far more distinguished success.

Having dwelt thus long on the subjects and aim of these Poems, I shall request the Reader's permission to apprise him of a few circumstances relating to their *style*, in order, among other reasons, that I may not be censured for not having performed what I never attempted. The Reader will find that personifications of abstract ideas rarely occur in these volumes; and, I hope, are utterly rejected as an ordinary device to elevate the style, and raise it above prose. I have proposed to myself to imitate, and, as far as is possible, to adopt the very language of men; and assuredly such personifications do not make any natural or regular part of that language. They are, indeed, a figure of speech occasionally prompted by passion, and I have made use of them as such; but I have endeavoured utterly to reject them as a mechanical device of style, or as a family language which Writers in metre seem to lay claim to by prescription. I have wished to keep my Reader in the company of flesh and blood, persuaded that by so doing I shall interest him. I am, however, well aware that others who pursue a different track may interest him likewise; I do not interfere with their claim, I only wish to prefer a different claim of my own. There will also be found in these pieces little of what is usually called poetic diction; I have taken as much pains to avoid it as others ordinarily take to produce it; this I have done for the reason already alleged, to bring my language near to the language of men, and further, because the pleasure which I have proposed to myself to impart, is of a kind very different from that which is supposed by many persons to be the proper object of poetry. I do not know how, without being culpably particular, I can give my Reader a more exact notion of the style in which I wished these poems to be written, than, by informing him that I have at all times endeavoured to look steadily at my subject, consequently, I hope that there is in these Poems little falsehood of description, and that my ideas are expressed in language fitted to their respective importance. Something I must have gained by this practice, as it is friendly to one property of all good poetry, namely, good sense; but it has necessarily cut me off from a large portion of phrases and figures of speech which from father to son have long been regarded as the common inheritance of Poets. I have also thought it expedient to restrict myself still further, having abstained from the use of many expressions, in themselves proper and beautiful, but which have been foolishly repeated by bad Poets, till such feelings of disgust are connected with them as it is scarcely possible by any art of association to overpower.

If in a poem there should be found a series of lines, or even a single line, in which the language, though naturally arranged, and according to the strict laws of metre, does not differ from that of prose, there is a numerous class of critics who, when they stumble upon these prosaisms, as they call them, imagine that they have made a notable discovery, and exult over the Poet as over a man ignorant of his own profession. Now these men would establish a canon of criticism which the Reader will conclude he must utterly reject, if he wishes to be pleased with these pieces. And it would be a most easy task to prove to him, that not only the language of a large portion of every good poem, even of the most elevated character, must necessarily, except with reference to the metre, in no respect differ from that of good prose, but likewise that some of the most interesting parts of the best poems will be found to be strictly the language of prose, when prose is well written. The truth of this assertion might be demonstrated by innumerable passages from almost all the poetical writings, even of Milton himself.

I will go further. I do not doubt that it may be safely affirmed, that there neither is, nor can be, any essential difference between the language of prose and metrical composition. We are fond of tracing the resemblance between Poetry and Painting, and, accordingly, we call them Sisters: but where shall we find bonds of connection sufficiently strict to typify the affinity betwixt metrical and prose composition? They both speak by and to the same organs; the bodies in which both of them are clothed may be said to be of the same substance, their affections are kindred, and almost identical, not necessarily differing even in degree; Poetry [1] sheds no tears "such as Angels weep" but natural and human tears; she can boast of no celestial Ichor that distinguishes her vital juices from those of prose; the same human blood circulates through the veins of them both.

If it be affirmed that rhyme and metrical arrangement of themselves constitute a distinction which overturns what I have been saying on the strict affinity of metrical language with that of prose, and paves the way for other artificial distinctions which the mind voluntarily admits, I answer that the language of such Poetry as I am recommending is, as far as is possible, a selection of the language really spoken by men; that this selection, wherever it is made with true taste and feeling, will of itself form a distinction far greater than would at first be imagined, and

---

[1] I here use the word "Poetry" (though against my own judgment) as opposed to the word "Prose," and synonymous with metrical composition. But much confusion has been introduced into criticism by this contradistinction of Poetry and Prose, instead of the more philosophical one of Poetry and Matter of Fact, or Science. The only strict antithesis to Prose is Metre: nor is this, in truth, a *strict* antithesis; because lines and passages of metre so naturally occur in writing prose, that it would be scarcely possible to avoid them, even were it desirable.

will entirely separate the composition from the vulgarity and meanness of ordinary life; and, if metre be superadded thereto, I believe that a dissimilitude will be produced altogether sufficient for the gratification of a rational mind. What other distinction would we have? Whence is it to come? And where is it to exist? Not, surely, where the Poet speaks through the mouths of his characters: it cannot be necessary here, either for elevation of style, or any of its supposed ornaments: for, if the Poet's subject be judiciously chosen, it will naturally, and upon fit occasion, lead him to passions the language of which, if selected truly and judiciously, must necessarily be dignified and variegated, and alive with metaphors and figures. I forbear to speak of an incongruity which would shock the intelligent Reader, should the Poet interweave any foreign splendour of his own with that which the passion naturally suggests: it is sufficient to say that such addition is unnecessary. And, surely, it is more probable that those passages, which with propriety abound with metaphors and figures, will have their due effect, if, upon other occasions where the passions are of a milder character, the style also be subdued and temperate.

But, as the pleasure which I hope to give by the Poems I now present to the Reader must depend entirely on just notions upon this subject, and, as it is in itself of the highest importance to our taste and moral feelings, I cannot content myself with these detached remarks. And if, in what I am about to say, it shall appear to some that my labour is unnecessary, and that I am like a man fighting a battle without enemies, I would remind such persons, that, whatever may be the language outwardly holden by men, a practical faith in the opinions which I am wishing to establish is almost unknown. If my conclusions are admitted, and carried as far as they must be carried if admitted at all, our judgments concerning the works of the greatest Poets both ancient and modern will be far different from what they are at present, both when we praise, and when we censure: and our moral feelings influencing and influenced by these judgments will, I believe, be corrected and purified.

Taking up the subject, then, upon general grounds, I ask what is meant by the word "Poet"? What is a Poet? To whom does he address himself? And what language is to be expected from him? He is a man speaking to men: a man, it is true, endued with more lively sensibility, more enthusiasm and tenderness, who has a greater knowledge of human nature, and a more comprehensive soul, than are supposed to be common among mankind; a man pleased with his own passions and volitions, and who rejoices more than other men in the spirit of life that is in him; delighting to contemplate similar volitions and passions as manifested in the goings-on of the Universe, and habitually impelled to create them where he does not find them. To these qualities he has added, a disposition to be affected more than other men by absent things as if they were present; an ability of conjuring up in himself passions, which are indeed far from being the same as those produced by real events, yet (especially in those parts of the general sympathy which are pleasing and delightful) do more nearly resemble the passions produced by real events, than anything which, from the motions of their own minds merely, other men are accustomed to feel in themselves; whence, and from practice, he has acquired a greater readiness and power in expressing what he thinks and feels, and especially those thoughts and feelings which, by his own choice, or from the structure of his own mind, arise in him without immediate external excitement.

But, whatever portion of this faculty we may suppose even the greatest Poet to possess, there cannot be a doubt but that the language which it will suggest to him, must, in liveliness and truth, fall far short of that which is uttered by men in real life, under the actual pressure of those passions, certain shadows of which the Poet thus produces, or feels to be produced, in himself.

However exalted a notion we would wish to cherish of the character of a Poet, it is obvious, that, while he describes and imitates passions, his situation is altogether slavish and mechanical, compared with the freedom and power of real and substantial action and suffering. So that it will be the wish of the Poet to bring his feelings near to those of the persons whose feelings he describes, nay, for short spaces of time, perhaps, to let himself slip into an entire delusion, and even confound and identify his own feelings with theirs; modifying only the language which is thus suggested to him by a consideration that he describes for a particular purpose, that of giving pleasure. Here, then, he will apply the principle on which I have so much insisted, namely, that of selection; on this he will depend for removing what would otherwise be painful or disgusting in the passion; he will feel that there is no necessity to trick out or to elevate nature: and, the more industriously he applies this principle, the deeper will be his faith that no words, which *his* fancy or imagination can suggest, will be to be compared with those which are the emanations of reality and truth.

But it may be said by those who do not object to the general spirit of these remarks, that, as it is impossible for the poet to produce upon all occasions language as exquisitely fitted for the passion as that which the real passion itself suggests, it is proper that he should consider himself as in the situation of a translator, who deems himself justified when he substitutes excellencies of another kind for those which are unattainable by him; and endeavours occasionally to surpass his original, in order to make some amends for the general inferiority to which he feels that he must submit. But this would be to encourage idleness and unmanly despair. Further, it is the language of men who speak of what they do not understand; who talk of Poetry as of a matter of amusement and idle pleasure; who will converse with us as gravely about a *taste* for Poetry, as they express it, as if it were a thing as indifferent as a taste for Rope-dancing, or Frontiniac [1] or Sherry. Aristotle, I have been told, hath said, that Poetry is the most philosophic of all writing: it is so: its object is truth, not individual and local, but general, and operative; not standing upon external testimony, but carried alive into the heart by passion; truth which is its own testimony, which gives strength and divinity to the tribunal to which it appeals, and receives them from the same tribunal. Poetry is the image of man and nature. The obstacles which stand in the way of the fidelity of the Biographer and Historian and of their consequent utility, are incalculably greater than those which are to be encountered by the Poet who has an adequate notion of the dignity of his art. The Poet writes under one restriction only, namely, that of the necessity of giving immediate pleasure to a human Being possessed of that information which may be expected from him, not as a lawyer, a physician, a mariner, an astronomer, or a natural philosopher, but as a Man. Except this one restriction, there is no object standing between the Poet and the image of things; between this, and the Biographer and Historian there are a thousand.

Nor let this necessity of producing immediate pleasure be considered as a degradation of the Poet's art. It is far otherwise. It is an acknowledgment of the beauty of the universe, an acknowledgment the more sincere, because it is not formal, but indirect; it is a task light and easy to him who looks at the world in the spirit of love: further, it is an homage paid to the native and naked dignity of man, to the grand elementary principle of pleasure, by which he knows, and feels, and lives, and moves. We have no sympathy but what is propagated by pleasure: I would not be misunderstood; but wherever we sympathise with pain, it will be found that the sympathy is produced and carried on by subtle combinations with pleasure. We have no knowledge, that is, no general principles drawn from the contemplation of particular facts, but what has been built up by pleasure, and exists in us by pleasure alone. The Man of Science, the Chemist and Mathematician, whatever difficulties and disgusts they may have had to struggle with, know and feel this. However painful may be the objects with which the Anatomist's knowledge is connected, he feels that his knowledge is pleasure; and where he has no pleasure he has no knowledge. What then does the Poet? He considers man and the objects that surround him as acting and reacting upon each other, so as to produce an infinite complexity of pain and pleasure; he considers man in his own nature and in his ordinary life as contemplating this with a certain quantity of immediate knowledge, with certain convictions, intuitions, and deductions, which by habit become of the nature of intuitions; he considers him as looking upon this complex scene of ideas and sensations, and finding everywhere objects that immediately excite in him sympathies which, from the necessities of his nature, are accompanied by an overbalance of enjoyment.

To this knowledge which all men carry about with them, and to these sympathies in which, without any other discipline than that of our daily life, we are fitted to take delight, the Poet principally directs his attention.

[1] a sweet wine of France

He considers man and nature as essentially adapted to each other, and the mind of man as naturally the mirror of the fairest and most interesting qualities of nature. And thus the Poet, prompted by this feeling of pleasure which accompanies him through the whole course of his studies, converses with general nature with affections akin to those, which, through labour and length of time, the Man of Science has raised up in himself, by conversing with those particular parts of nature which are the objects of his studies. The knowledge both of the Poet and the Man of Science is pleasure; but the knowledge of the one cleaves to us as a necessary part of our existence, our natural and inalienable inheritance; the other is a personal and individual acquisition, slow to come to us, and by no habitual and direct sympathy connecting us with our fellow-beings. The Man of Science seeks truth as a remote and unknown benefactor; he cherishes and loves it in his solitude: the Poet, singing a song in which all human beings join with him, rejoices in the presence of truth as our visible friend and hourly companion. Poetry is the breath and finer spirit of all knowledge; it is the impassioned expression which is in the countenance of all Science. Emphatically may it be said of the Poet, as Shakespeare hath said of man, "that he looks before and after." He is the rock of defence of human nature; an upholder and preserver, carrying everywhere with him relationship and love. In spite of difference of soil and climate, of language and manners, of laws and customs, in spite of things silently gone out of mind, and things violently destroyed, the Poet binds together by passion and knowledge the vast empire of human society, as it is spread over the whole earth, and over all time. The objects of the Poet's thoughts are everywhere; though the eyes and senses of man are, it is true, his favourite guides, yet he will follow wheresoever he can find an atmosphere of sensation in which to move his wings. Poetry is the first and last of all knowledge — it is as immortal as the heart of man. If the labours of Men of Science should ever create any material revolution, direct or indirect, in our condition, and in the impressions which we habitually receive, the Poet will sleep then no more than at present, but he will be ready to follow the steps of the Man of Science, not only in those general indirect effects, but he will be at his side, carrying sensation into the midst of the objects of the Science itself. The remotest discoveries of the Chemist, the Botanist, or Mineralogist, will be as proper objects of the Poet's art as any upon which it can be employed, if the time should ever come when these things shall be familiar to us, and the relations under which they are contemplated by the followers of these respective Sciences shall be manifestly and palpably material to us as enjoying and suffering beings. If the time should ever come when what is now called Science, thus familiarised to men, shall be ready to put on, as it were, a form of flesh and blood, the Poet will lend his divine spirit to aid the transfiguration, and will welcome the Being thus produced, as a dear and genuine inmate of the household of man. — It is not, then, to be supposed that any one, who holds that sublime notion of Poetry which I have attempted to convey, will break in upon the sanctity and truth of his pictures by transitory and accidental ornaments, and endeavour to excite admiration of himself by arts, the necessity of which must manifestly depend upon the assumed meanness of his subject.

* * * * * * *

I have said that poetry is the spontaneous overflow of powerful feelings: it takes its origin from emotion recollected in tranquillity; the emotion is contemplated, till, by a species of reaction, the tranquillity gradually disappears, and an emotion, kindred to that which was before the subject of contemplation, is gradually produced, and does itself actually exist in the mind. In this mood successful composition generally begins, and in a mood similar to this it is carried on; but the emotion of whatever kind, and in whatever degree, from various causes, is qualified by various pleasures, so that in describing any passions whatsoever, which are voluntarily described, the mind will, upon the whole, be in a state of enjoyment. Now, if Nature be thus cautious in preserving in a state of enjoyment a being thus employed, the Poet ought to profit by the lesson thus held forth to him, and ought especially to take care, that, whatever passions he communicates to his Reader, those passions, if his Reader's mind be sound and vigorous, should always be accompanied with an overbalance of pleasure. How the music of harmonious metrical language, the sense of difficulty overcome, and the blind association of pleasure which has been previously received from the works of rhyme or metre of the same or similar construction, and indistinct perception perpetually renewed of language closely resembling that of real life, and yet, in the circumstance of metre, differing from it so widely — all these imperceptibly make up a complex feeling of delight, which is of the most important use in tempering the painful feeling which will always be found intermingled with powerful descriptions of the deeper passions. This effect is always produced in pathetic and impassioned poetry; while, in lighter compositions, the ease and gracefulness with which the Poet manages his numbers are themselves confessedly a principal source of the gratification of the Reader. I might, perhaps, include all which it is *necessary* to say upon this subject, by affirming what few persons will deny, that, of two descriptions either of passions, manners, or characters, each of them equally well executed, the one in prose· and the other in verse, the verse will be read a hundred times where the prose is read once. We see that Pope, by the power of verse alone, has contrived to render the plainest common sense interesting, and even frequently to invest it with the appearance of passion.

* * * * * * *

Long as I have detained my Reader, I hope he will permit me to caution him against a mode of false criticism which has been applied to Poetry in which the language closely resembles that of life and nature. Such verses have been triumphed over in parodies of which Dr. Johnson's stanza is a fair specimen.

I put my hat upon my head
And walked into the Strand,
And there I met another man
Whose hat was in his hand.

Immediately under these lines I will place one of the most justly-admired stanzas of the "Babes in the Wood."

These pretty babes with hand in hand
Went wandering up and down;
But never more they saw the Man
Approaching from the Town.

In both these stanzas the words, and the order of the words, in no respect differ from the most unimpassioned conversation. There are words in both, for example, "the Strand," and "the Town," connected with none but the most familiar ideas; yet the one stanza we admit as admirable, and the other as a fair example of the superlatively contemptible. Whence arises this difference? Not from the metre, not from the language, not from the order of the words; but the *matter* expressed in Dr. Johnson's stanza is contemptible. The proper method of treating trivial and simple verses, ˙to which Dr. Johnson's stanza would be a fair parallelism, is not to say, This is a bad kind of poetry, or, This is not poetry; but, This wants sense; it is neither interesting in itself, nor can *lead* to anything interesting; the images neither originate in that sane state of feeling which arises out of thought, nor can excite thought or feeling in the Reader. This is the only sensible manner of dealing with such verses. Why trouble yourself about the species till you have previously decided upon the ˙genus? Why take pains to prove that an ape is not a Newton, when it is self-evident that he is not a man?

* * * * * * *

WE ARE SEVEN

———— A simple child,
That lightly draws its breath,
And feels its life in every limb,
What should it know of death?

I met a little cottage girl: 5
She was eight years old, she said;
Her hair was thick with many a curl
That clustered round her head.

She had a rustic, woodland air,
And she was wildly clad: 10
Her eyes were fair, and very fair;
— Her beauty made me glad.

"Sisters and brothers, little maid,
How many may you be?"
"How many? Seven in all," she said,   15
And wondering looked at me.

"And where are they? I pray you tell."
She answered, "Seven are we;
And two of us at Conway dwell,
And two are gone to sea.   20

"Two of us in the church-yard lie,
My sister and my brother;
And, in the church-yard cottage, I
Dwell near them with my mother."

"You say that two at Conway dwell, 25
And two are gone to sea,
Yet ye are seven! — I pray you tell,
Sweet maid, how this may be."

Then did the little maid reply,
"Seven boys and girls are we; 30
Two of us in the church-yard lie,
Beneath the church-yard tree."

"You run about, my little maid,
Your limbs they are alive;
If two are in the church-yard laid, 35
Then ye are only five."

"Their graves are green, they may be seen,"
The little maid replied,
"Twelve steps or more from my mother's
door,
And they are side by side. 40

"My stockings there I often knit,
My kerchief there I hem;
And there upon the ground I sit,
And sing a song to them.

"And often after sunset, sir, 45
When it is light and fair,
I take my little porringer,
And eat my supper there.

"The first that died was sister Jane;
In bed she moaning lay, 50
Till God released her of her pain;
And then she went away.

"So in the church-yard she was laid;
And, when the grass was dry,
Together round her grave we played, 55
My brother John and I.

"And when the ground was white with snow,
And I could run and slide,
My brother John was forced to go,
And he lies by her side." 60

"How many are you, then," said I.
"If they two are in heaven?"
Quick was the little maid's reply,
"O master! we are seven."

"But they are dead; those two are dead! 65
Their spirits are in heaven!"
'Twas throwing words away; for still
The little maid would have her will,
And said, "Nay, we are seven!"

EXPOSTULATION AND REPLY

"Why, William, on that old grey stone,
Thus for the length of half a day,
Why, William, sit you thus alone,
And dream your time away?

"Where are your books? — that light be-
queathed 5
To beings else forlorn and blind!
Up! up! and drink the spirit breathed
From dead men to their kind.

"You look round on your Mother Earth,
As if she for no purpose bore you; 10
As if you were her first-born birth,
And none had lived before you!"

One morning thus, by Esthwaite lake,
When life was sweet, I knew not why,
To me my good friend Matthew spake, 15
And thus I made reply:

"The eye — it cannot choose but see;
We cannot bid the ear be still;
Our bodies feel, where'er they be,
Against or with our will. 20

"Nor less I deem that there are Powers
Which of themselves our minds impress;
That we can feed this mind of ours
In a wise passiveness.

"Think you, 'mid all this mighty sum 25
Of things forever speaking,
That nothing of itself will come,
But we must still be seeking?

"— Then ask not wherefore, here, alone,
Conversing as I may, 30
I sit upon this old grey stone,
And dream my time away."

THE TABLES TURNED

AN EVENING SCENE ON THE SAME SUBJECT

Up! up! my friend, and quit your books;
Or surely you'll grow double:
Up! up! my friend, and clear your looks;
Why all this toil and trouble?

The sun, above the mountain's head,   5
A freshening lustre mellow
Through all the long green fields has spread,
His first sweet evening yellow.

Books! 'tis a dull and endless strife:
Come, hear the woodland linnet,   10
How sweet his music! on my life
There's more of wisdom in it.

And hark! how blithe the throstle sings!
He, too, is no mean preacher:
Come forth into the light of things,   15
Let Nature be your teacher.

She has a world of ready wealth,
Our minds and hearts to bless —
Spontaneous wisdom breathed by health,
Truth breathed by cheerfulness.   20

One impulse from a vernal wood
May teach you more of man,
Of moral evil and of good,
Than all the sages can.

Sweet is the lore which Nature brings;   25
Our meddling intellect
Misshapes the beauteous forms of things: —
We murder to dissect.

Enough of Science and of Art;
Close up those barren leaves;   30
Come forth, and bring with you a heart
That watches and receives.

LINES COMPOSED A FEW MILES ABOVE TINTERN ABBEY, ON RE-VISITING THE BANKS OF THE WYE DURING A TOUR

JULY 13, 1798

Five years have past; five summers, with the
    length
Of five long winters! and again I hear

These waters, rolling from their mountain-
    springs
With a soft inland murmur. — Once again
Do I behold these steep and lofty cliffs,   5
That on a wild secluded scene impress
Thoughts of more deep seclusion; and connect
The landscape with the quiet of the sky.
The day is come when I again repose
Here, under this dark sycamore, and view   10
These plots of cottage-ground, these orchard-
    tufts,
Which at this season, with their unripe fruits,
Are clad in one green hue, and lose themselves
'Mid groves and copses.   Once again I see
These hedgerows, hardly hedgerows, little lines
Of sportive wood run wild: these pastoral
    farms,   16
Green to the very door; and wreaths of smoke
Sent up, in silence, from among the trees!
With some uncertain notice, as might seem
Of vagrant dwellers in the houseless woods, 20
Or of some hermit's cave, where by his fire
The hermit sits alone.   These beauteous forms,
Through a long absence, have not been to me
As is a landscape to a blind man's eye:
But oft, in lonely rooms, and 'mid the din 25
Of towns and cities, I have owed to them
In hours of weariness, sensations sweet,
Felt in the blood, and felt along the heart;
And passing even into my purer mind,
With tranquil restoration: — feelings too   30
Of unremembered pleasure: such, perhaps,
As have no slight or trivial influence
On that best portion of a good man's life,
His little, nameless, unremembered acts
Of kindness and of love.   Nor less, I trust,35
To them I may have owed another gift,
Of aspect more sublime; that blessed mood,
In which the burthen of the mystery,
In which the heavy and the weary weight
Of all this unintelligible world,   40
Is lightened: — that serene and blessed mood,
In which the affections gently lead us on, —
Until, the breath of this corporeal frame
And even the motion of our human blood
Almost suspended, we are laid asleep   45
In body, and become a living soul:
While with an eye made quiet by the power
Of harmony, and the deep power of joy,
We see into the life of things.
                                If this
Be but a vain belief, yet, oh! how oft —   50
In darkness and amid the many shapes
Of joyless daylight; when the fretful stir

Unprofitable, and the fever of the world,
Have hung upon the beatings of my heart —
How oft, in spirit, have I turned to thee,   55
O sylvan Wye! thou wanderer thro' the
      woods,
How often has my spirit turned to thee!
    And now, with gleams of half-extinguished
      thought,
With many recognitions dim and faint,
And somewhat of a sad perplexity,   60
The picture of the mind revives again :
While here I stand, not only with the sense
Of present pleasure, but with pleasing thoughts
That in this moment there is life and food
For future years.   And so I dare to hope,   65
Though changed, no doubt, from what I was
      when first
I came among these hills ; when like a roe
I bounded o'er the mountains, by the sides
Of the deep rivers, and the lonely streams,
Wherever nature led : more like a man   70
Flying from something that he dreads, than
      one
Who sought the thing he loved.   For nature
      then
(The coarser pleasures of my boyish days,
And their glad animal movements all gone by)
To me was all in all. — I cannot paint   75
What then I was.   The sounding cataract
Haunted me like a passion ; the tall rock,
The mountain, and the deep and gloomy
      wood,
Their colours and their forms, were then to
      me
An appetite ; a feeling and a love,   80
That had no need of a remoter charm,
By thought supplied, nor any interest
Unborrowed from the eye. — That time is
      past,
And all its aching joys are now no more,
And all its dizzy raptures.   Not for this   85
Faint I, nor mourn, nor murmur ; other gifts
Have followed ; for such loss, I would believe,
Abundant recompense.   For I have learned
To look on nature, not as in the hour
Of thoughtless youth ; but hearing oftentimes
The still, sad music of humanity,   91
Nor harsh nor grating, though of ample power
To chasten and subdue.   And I have felt
A presence that disturbs me with the joy
Of elevated thoughts ; a sense sublime,   95
Of something far more deeply interfused,
Whose dwelling is the light of setting suns,
And the round ocean and the living air,
And the blue sky, and in the mind of man ;

A motion and a spirit, that impels   100
All thinking things, all objects of all thought,
And rolls through all things.   Therefore am I
      still
A lover of the meadows and the woods,
And mountains ; and of all that we behold
From this green earth ; of all the mighty
      world   105
Of eye, and ear, — both what they half create,
And what perceive ; well pleased to recognise
In nature and the language of the sense,
The anchor of my purest thoughts, the nurse,
The guide, the guardian of my heart, and soul
Of all my moral being.
                    Nor perchance,   111
If I were not thus taught, should I the more
Suffer my genial spirits to decay :
For thou art with me here upon the banks
Of this fair river ; thou my dearest friend,
My dear, dear friend ; and in thy voice I
      catch   116
The language of my former heart, and read
My former pleasures in the shooting lights
Of thy wild eyes.   Oh! yet a little while
May I behold in thee what I was once,   120
My dear, dear sister! and this prayer I make,
Knowing that Nature never did betray
The heart that loved her ; 'tis her privilege,
Through all the years of this our life, to lead
From joy to joy : for she can so inform   125
The mind that is within us, so impress
With quietness and beauty, and so feed
With lofty thoughts, that neither evil tongues,
Rash judgments, nor the sneers of selfish men,
Nor greetings where no kindness is, nor all
The dreary intercourse of daily life,   131
Shall e'er prevail against us, or disturb
Our cheerful faith, that all which we behold
Is full of blessings.   Therefore let the moon
Shine on thee in thy solitary walk ;   135
And let the misty mountain-winds be free
To blow against thee : and, in after years,
When these wild ecstasies shall be matured
Into a sober pleasure ; when thy mind
Shall be a mansion for all lovely forms,   140
Thy memory be as a dwelling-place
For all sweet sounds and harmonies ; oh!
      then,
If solitude, or fear, or pain, or grief,
Should be thy portion, with what healing
      thoughts
Of tender joy wilt thou remember me,   145
And these my exhortations! Nor, per-
      chance —
If I should be where I no more can hear

Thy voice, nor catch from thy wild eyes these
    gleams
Of past existence — wilt thou then forget
That on the banks of this delightful stream
We stood together; and that I, so long   151
A worshipper of Nature, hither came
Unwearied in that service: rather say
With warmer love — oh! with far deeper zeal
Of holier love. Nor wilt thou then forget, 155
That after many wanderings, many years
Of absence, these steep woods and lofty cliffs,
And this green pastoral landscape, were to me
More dear, both for themselves and for thy
    sake!

LUCY

She dwelt among the untrodden ways
    Beside the springs of Dove,
A maid whom there were none to praise
    And very few to love:

A violet by a mossy stone   5
    Half hidden from the eye!
— Fair as a star, when only one
    Is shining in the sky.

She lived unknown, and few could know
    When Lucy ceased to be;   10
But she is in her grave, and, oh,
    The difference to me!

THREE YEARS SHE GREW

Three years she grew in sun and shower,
Then Nature said, "A lovelier flower
    On earth was never sown;
This child I to myself will take;
She shall be mine, and I will make   5
    A lady of my own.

"Myself will to my darling be
Both law and impulse: and with me
    The girl, in rock and plain,
In earth and heaven, in glade and bower, 10
Shall feel an overseeing power
    To kindle or restrain.

"She shall be sportive as the fawn
That wild with glee across the lawn,
    Or up the mountain springs;   15
And hers shall be the breathing balm,
And hers the silence and the calm
    Of mute insensate things.

"The floating clouds their state shall lend
To her; for her the willow bend;   20
    Nor shall she fail to see
Even in the motions of the storm
Grace that shall mould the maiden's form
    By silent sympathy.

"The stars of midnight shall be dear   25
To her; and she shall lean her ear
    In many a secret place
Where rivulets dance their wayward round,
And beauty born of murmuring sound
    Shall pass into her face.   30

"And vital feelings of delight
Shall rear her form to stately height,
    Her virgin bosom swell;
Such thoughts to Lucy I will give
While she and I together live   35
    Here in this happy dell."

Thus Nature spake — the work was done —
How soon my Lucy's race was run!
    She died, and left to me
This heath, this calm, and quiet scene;   40
The memory of what has been,
    And never more will be.

A SLUMBER DID MY SPIRIT SEAL

A slumber did my spirit seal;
    I had no human fears;
She seemed a thing that could not feel
    The touch of earthly years.

No motion has she now, no force;   5
    She neither hears nor sees;
Rolled round in earth's diurnal course,
    With rocks, and stones, and trees.

LUCY GRAY; OR, SOLITUDE

Oft I had heard of Lucy Gray:
And, when I crossed the wild,
I chanced to see at break of day
The solitary child.

No mate, no comrade Lucy knew,   5
She dwelt on a wide moor,
— The sweetest thing that ever grew
Beside a human door!

You yet may spy the fawn at play
The hare upon the green;
But the sweet face of Lucy Gray   10
Will never more be seen.

"To-night will be a stormy night —
You to the town must go;
And take a lantern, child, to light   15
Your mother through the snow."

"That, Father! will I gladly do:
'Tis scarcely afternoon —
The minster-clock has just struck two,
And yonder is the moon!"   20

At this the father raised his hook,
And snapped a faggot-band;
He plied his work; — and Lucy took
The lantern in her hand.

Not blither is the mountain roe: 25
With many a wanton stroke
Her feet disperse the powdery snow,
That rises up like smoke.

The storm came on before its time:
She wandered up and down;   30
And many a hill did Lucy climb:
But never reached the town.

The wretched parents all that night
Went shouting far and wide;
But there was neither sound nor sight   35
To serve them for a guide.

At daybreak on a hill they stood
That overlooked the moor;
And thence they saw the bridge of wood,
A furlong from their door.   40

They wept — and, turning homeward, cried,
"In heaven we all shall meet;"
— When in the snow the mother spied
The print of Lucy's feet.

Then downwards from the steep hill's edge
They tracked the footmarks small;   46
And through the broken hawthorn hedge,
And by the long stone-wall;

And then an open field they crossed:
The marks were still the same;   50
They tracked them on, nor ever lost;
And to the bridge they came.

They followed from the snowy bank
Those footmarks, one by one,
Into the middle of the plank;   55
And further there were none!

— Yet some maintain that to this day
She is a living child;
That you may see sweet Lucy Gray
Upon the lonesome wild.   60

O'er rough and smooth she trips along,
And never looks behind;
And sings a solitary song
That whistles in the wind.

THE RECLUSE

From BOOK I

On Man, on Nature, and on Human Life,
Musing in solitude, I oft perceive
Fair trains of imagery before me rise,
Accompanied by feelings of delight
Pure, or with no unpleasing sadness mixed;   5
And I am conscious of affecting thoughts
And dear remembrances, whose presence
        soothes
Or elevates the mind, intent to weigh
The good and evil of our mortal state.   9
— To these emotions, whencesoe'er they come,
Whether from breath of outward circumstance,
Or from the soul — an impulse to herself —
I would give utterance in numerous[1] verse.
Of Truth, of Grandeur, Beauty, Love, and
        Hope,
And melancholy Fear subdued by Faith;   15
Of blessèd consolations in distress;
Of moral strength, and intellectual power;
Of joy in widest commonalty spread;
Of the individual mind that keeps her own
Inviolate retirement, subject there   20
To conscience only, and the law supreme
Of that Intelligence which governs all —
I sing: — "fit audience let me find though
        few!"[2]
    So prayed, more gaining than he asked, the
        bard —
In holiest mood. Urania,[3] I shall need   25
Thy guidance, or a greater muse, if such
Descend to earth or dwell in highest heaven!
For I must tread on shadowy ground, must
        sink

---

[1] melodious   [2] *Quoted from Milton.*   [3] *Cf.* note
on Shelley's *Adonais*, l. 12

Deep — and, aloft ascending, breathe in
　　worlds　　　　　　　　　　　　　　29
To which the heaven of heavens is but a veil.
All strength — all terror, single or in bands,
That ever was put forth in personal form —
Jehovah — with his thunder, and the choir
Of shouting angels, and the empyreal thrones —
I pass them unalarmed.　Not Chaos, not　35
The darkest pit of lowest Erebus,
Nor aught of blinder vacancy, scooped out
By help of dreams — can breed such fear and
　　awe
As falls upon us often when we look
Into our minds, into the mind of Man —　40
My haunt, and the main region of my song.
— Beauty — a living Presence of the earth,
Surpassing the most fair ideal forms
Which craft of delicate Spirits hath composed
From earth's materials — waits upon my
　　steps ;　　　　　　　　　　　　　45
Pitches her tents before me as I move,
An hourly neighbour.　Paradise, and groves
Elysian, Fortunate Fields — like those of old
Sought in the Atlantic Main — why should
　　they be
A history only of departed things,　　　50
Or a mere fiction of what never was?
For the discerning intellect of Man,
When wedded to this goodly universe
In love and holy passion, shall find these
A simple produce of the common day.　55
— I, long before the blissful hour arrives,
Would chant, in lonely peace, the spousal
　　verse
Of this great consummation : — and, by words
Which speak of nothing more than what we
　. are,
Would I arouse the sensual from their sleep 60
Of death, and win the vacant and the vain
To noble raptures ; while my voice proclaims
How exquisitely the individual mind
(And the progressive powers perhaps no less
Of the whole species) to the external world 65
Is fitted : — and how exquisitely, too —
Theme this but little heard of among men —
The external world is fitted to the mind ;
And the creation (by no lower name
Can it be called) which they with blended
　　might　　　　　　　　　　　　　70
Accomplish : — this is our high argument.[1]
— Such grateful haunts foregoing, if I oft
Must turn elsewhere — to travel near the
　　tribes

[1] great subject

And fellowships of men, and see ill sights
Of madding passions mutually inflamed ;　75
Must hear Humanity in fields and groves
Pipe solitary anguish ; or must hang
Brooding above the fierce confederate storm
Of sorrow, barricadoed evermore
Within the walls of cities — may these sounds
Have their authentic comment ; that even
　　these　　　　　　　　　　　　　81
Hearing, I be not downcast or forlorn ! —
Descend, prophetic Spirit ! that inspir'st
The human Soul of universal earth,
Dreaming on things to come ; and dost
　　possess　　　　　　　　　　　　85
A metropolitan temple in the hearts
Of mighty poets ; upon me bestow
A gift of genuine insight ; that my song
With star-like virtue in its place may shine,
Shedding benignant influence, and secure　90
Itself from all malevolent effect
Of those mutations that extend their sway
Throughout the nether sphere ! — And if with
　　this
I mix more lowly matter ; with the thing
Contemplated, describe the Mind and Man 95
Contemplating ; and who, and what he was —
The transitory being that beheld
This vision ; — when and where, and how he
　　lived ;
Be not this labour useless.　If such theme
May sort with highest objects, then — dread
　　Power !　　　　　　　　　　　　100
Whose gracious favour is the primal source
Of all illumination — may my life
Express the image of a better time,
More wise desires, and simpler manners ; —
　　nurse
My heart in genuine freedom : — all pure
　　thoughts　　　　　　　　　　　105
Be with me ; — so shall thy unfailing love
Guide, and support, and cheer me to the
　　end!

TO THE CUCKOO

O blithe New-comer! I have heard,
I hear thee and rejoice.
O Cuckoo! shall I call thee Bird,
Or but a wandering Voice?

While I am lying on the grass　　　　5
Thy twofold shout I hear,
From hill to hill it seems to pass,
At once far off, and near.

Though babbling only to the Vale,
Of sunshine and of flowers,   10
Thou bringest unto me a tale
Of visionary hours.

Thrice welcome, darling of the Spring!
Even yet thou art to me
No bird, but an invisible thing,   15
A voice, a mystery;

The same whom in my school-boy days
I listened to; that Cry
Which made me look a thousand ways
In bush, and tree, and sky.   20

To seek thee did I often rove
Through woods and on the green;
And thou wert still a hope, a love;
Still longed for, never seen.

And I can listen to thee yet;   25
Can lie upon the plain
And listen, till I do beget
That golden time again.

O blessèd Bird! the earth we pace
Again appears to be   30
An unsubstantial faery place,
That is fit home for thee!

MY HEART LEAPS UP WHEN I BEHOLD

My heart leaps up when I behold
    A rainbow in the sky:
So was it when my life began;
So is it now I am a man;
So be it when I shall grow old,   5
    Or let me die!
The Child is father of the Man;
And I could wish my days to be
Bound each to each by natural piety.

THE SOLITARY REAPER

Behold her, single in the field,
Yon solitary Highland Lass!
Reaping and singing by herself;
Stop here, or gently pass!
Alone she cuts and binds the grain   5
And sings a melancholy strain;
O listen! for the vale profound
Is overflowing with the sound.

AE

No nightingale did ever chaunt
More welcome notes to weary bands   10
Of travellers in some shady haunt,
Among Arabian sands:
A voice so thrilling ne'er was heard
In spring-time from the cuckoo-bird
Breaking the silence of the seas   15
Among the farthest Hebrides.

Will no one tell me what she sings? —
Perhaps the plaintive numbers flow
For old, unhappy, far-off things,
And battles long ago: 20
Or is it some more humble lay,
Familiar matter of to-day?
Some natural sorrow, loss, or pain,
That has been, and may be again?

Whate'er the theme, the maiden sang   25
As if her song could have no ending;
I saw her singing at her work,
And o'er the sickle bending; —
I listened, motionless and still;
And, as I mounted up the hill   30
The music in my heart I bore,
Long after it was heard no more.

SHE WAS A PHANTOM OF DELIGHT

She was a phantom of delight
When first she gleamed upon my sight;
A lovely apparition, sent
To be a moment's ornament;
Her eyes as stars of twilight fair;   5
Like twilight's, too, her dusky hair;
But all things else about her drawn
From May-time and the cheerful dawn;
A dancing shape, an image gay,
To haunt, to startle, and way-lay.   10

I saw her upon nearer view,
A spirit, yet a woman too!
Her household motions light and free,
And steps of virgin-liberty;
A countenance in which did meet   15
Sweet records, promises as sweet;
A creature not too bright or good
For human nature's daily food;
For transient sorrows, simple wiles,
Praise, blame, love, kisses, tears, and smiles.

And now I see with eye serene   21
The very pulse of the machine;
A being breathing thoughtful breath,

A traveller between life and death;
The reason firm, the temperate will,   25
Endurance, foresight, strength, and skill;
A perfect woman, nobly planned,
To warn, to comfort, and command;
And yet a spirit still, and bright
With something of angelic light.   30

I WANDERED LONELY AS A CLOUD

I wandered lonely as a cloud
That floats on high o'er vales and hills,
When all at once I saw a crowd,
A host, of golden daffodils;
Beside the lake, beneath the trees,   5
Fluttering and dancing in the breeze.

Continuous as the stars that shine
And twinkle on the milky way,
They stretched in never-ending line
Along the margin of a bay: 10
Ten thousand saw I at a glance,
Tossing their heads in sprightly dance.

The waves beside them danced; but they
Out-did the sparkling waves in glee:
A poet could not but be gay   15
In such a jocund company:
I gazed — and gazed — but little thought
What wealth the show to me had brought:

For oft, when on my couch I lie
In vacant or in pensive mood,   20
They flash upon that inward eye
Which is the bliss of solitude;
And then my heart with pleasure fills,
And dances with the daffodils.

ODE TO DUTY

Stern Daughter of the Voice of God!
O Duty! if that name thou love
Who art a light to guide, a rod
To check the erring, and reprove;
Thou, who art victory and law   5
When empty terrors overawe;
From vain temptations dost set free;
And calm'st the weary strife of frail humanity!

There are who ask not if thine eye
Be on them; who, in love and truth,   10
Where no misgiving is, rely
Upon the genial sense of youth:

Glad Hearts! without reproach or blot
Who do thy work, and know it not:
Oh! if through confidence misplaced   15
They fail, thy saving arms, dread Power!
    around them cast.

Serene will be our days and bright,
And happy will our nature be,
When love is an unerring light,
And joy its own security.   20
And they a blissful course may hold
Even now, who, not unwisely bold,
Live in the spirit of this creed;
Yet seek thy firm support, according to their
    need.

I, loving freedom, and untried;   25
No sport of every random gust,
Yet being to myself a guide,
Too blindly have reposed my trust:
And oft, when in my heart was heard
Thy timely mandate, I deferred   30
The task, in smoother walks to stray;
But thee I now would serve more strictly, if I
    may.

Through no disturbance of my soul,
Or strong compunction in me wrought,
I supplicate for thy control;   35
But in the quietness of thought:
Me this unchartered freedom tires;
I feel the weight of chance-desires:
My hopes no more must change their name,
I long for a repose that ever is the same.   40

Stern Lawgiver! yet thou dost wear
The Godhead's most benignant grace;
Nor know we anything so fair
As is the smile upon thy face:
Flowers laugh before thee on their beds   45
And fragrance in thy footing treads;
Thou dost preserve the stars from wrong;
And the most ancient heavens, through thee,
    are fresh and strong.

To humbler functions, awful Power!
I call thee: I myself commend   50
Unto thy guidance from this hour;
Oh, let my weakness have an end!
Give unto me, made lowly wise,
The spirit of self-sacrifice;
The confidence of reason give;   55
And in the light of truth thy bondman let me
    live!

PERSONAL TALK

I

I am not one who much or oft delight
To season my fireside with personal talk, —
Of friends, who live within an easy walk,
Or neighbours, daily, weekly, in my sight:
And, for [1] my chance-acquaintance, ladies bright, 5
Sons, mothers, maidens withering on the stalk,
These all wear out of me, like forms, with chalk
Painted on rich men's floors, for one feast-night.
Better than such discourse doth silence long,
Long, barren silence, square with my desire; 10
To sit without emotion, hope, or aim,
In the loved presence of my cottage fire,
And listen to the flapping of the flame,
Or kettle whispering its faint undersong.

II

"Yet life," you say, "is life; we have seen and see, 15
And with a living pleasure we describe;
And fits of sprightly malice do but bribe
The languid mind into activity.
Sound sense, and love itself, and mirth and glee
Are fostered by the comment and the gibe." 20
Even be it so; yet still among your tribe,
Our daily world's true worldings, rank not me!
Children are blest, and powerful; their world lies
More justly balanced; partly at their feet,
And part far from them: sweetest melodies 25
Are those that are by distance made more sweet;
Whose mind is but the mind of his own eyes,
He is a slave; the meanest we can meet!

III

Wings have we, — and as far as we can go,
We may find pleasure: wilderness and wood,
Blank ocean and mere sky, support that mood
Which with [2] the lofty sanctifies the low. 32
Dreams, books, are each a world; and books, we know,
Are a substantial world, both pure and good:

[1] as for   [2] by means of

Round these, with tendrils strong as flesh and blood, 35
Our pastime and our happiness will grow.
There find I personal themes, a plenteous store,
Matter wherein right voluble I am,
To which I listen with a ready ear;
Two shall be named, pre-eminently dear, —
The gentle Lady married to the Moor; 41
And heavenly Una with her milk-white Lamb.

IV

Nor can I not believe but that hereby
Great gains are mine; for thus I live remote
From evil-speaking; rancour, never sought, 45
Comes to me not; malignant truth, or lie.
Hence have I genial seasons, hence have I
Smooth passions, smooth discourse, and joyous thought:
And thus from day to day my little boat
Rocks in its harbour, lodging peaceably. 50
Blessings be with them — and eternal praise,
Who gave us nobler loves, and nobler cares —
The Poets, who on earth have made us heirs
Of truth and pure delight by heavenly lays!
Oh! might my name be numbered among theirs,
Then gladly would I end my mortal days. 56

ODE

INTIMATIONS OF IMMORTALITY FROM RECOLLECTIONS OF EARLY CHILDHOOD

I

There was a time when meadow, grove and stream,
The earth, and every common sight,
      To me did seem
      Apparelled in celestial light,
The glory and the freshness of a dream. 5
It is not now as it hath been of yore; —
      Turn wheresoe'er I may,
         By night or day,
The things which I have seen I now can see no more.

II

      The Rainbow comes and goes, 10
      And lovely is the Rose;
      The Moon doth with delight

Look round her when the heavens are bare;
　　Waters on a starry night
　　Are beautiful and fair;　　15
The sunshine is a glorious birth;
But yet I know, where'er I go,
That there hath past away a glory from the earth.

III

Now, while the birds thus sing a joyous song,
　　And while the young lambs bound　　20
　　　As to the tabor's sound,
To me alone there came a thought of grief;
A timely utterance gave that thought relief,
　　And I again am strong:　　24
The cataracts blow their trumpets from the steep;
No more shall grief of mine the season wrong;
I hear the echoes through the mountains throng,
The winds come to me from the fields of sleep,
　　And all the earth is gay:
　　　Land and sea　　30
　　Give themselves up to jollity,
　　　And with the heart of May
　　Doth every beast keep holiday; —
　　　Thou child of joy,
Shout round me, let me hear thy shouts, thou happy shepherd-boy!　　35

IV

Ye blessèd creatures, I have heard the call
　　Ye to each other make; I see
The heavens laugh with you in your jubilee:
　　My heart is at your festival,
　　My head hath its coronal,　　40
The fullness of your bliss, I feel — I feel it all.
　　Oh evil day! if I were sullen
　　While Earth herself is adorning,
　　　This sweet May-morning,
　　And the children are culling　　45
　　　On every side,
　　In a thousand valleys far and wide,
　　Fresh flowers; while the sun shines warm,
And the babe leaps up on his mother's arm —
　　I hear, I hear, with joy I hear!　　50
— But there's a tree, of many, one,
A single field which I have looked upon,
Both of them speak of something that is gone:
　　The pansy at my feet
　　Doth the same tale repeat:　　55

Whither is fled the visionary gleam?
Where is it now, the glory and the dream?

V

Our birth is but a sleep and a forgetting:
The Soul that rises with us, our life's Star,
　　Hath had elsewhere its setting,　　60
　　　And cometh from afar:
　　Not in entire forgetfulness,
　　And not in utter nakedness,
But trailing clouds of glory do we come
　　From God, who is our home:　　65
Heaven lies about us in our infancy!
Shades of the prison-house begin to close
　　Upon the growing boy,
But he beholds the light, and whence it flows,
　　He sees it in his joy;　　70
The Youth, who daily farther from the east
　　Must travel, still is Nature's priest,
　　And by the vision splendid
　　Is on his way attended;
At length the Man perceives it die away,　　75
And fade into the light of common day.

VI

Earth fills her lap with pleasures of her own;
Yearnings she hath in her own natural kind,
And, even with something of a mother's mind,
　　And no unworthy aim,　　80
　　The homely nurse doth all she can
To make her foster-child, her inmate Man,
　　Forget the glories he hath known,
And that imperial palace whence he came.　　84

VII

Behold the Child among his new-born blisses,
A six years' darling of a pigmy size!
See, where 'mid work of his own hand he lies,
Fretted by sallies of his mother's kisses,
With light upon him from his father's eyes!
See, at his feet, some little plan or chart,　　90
Some fragment from his dream of human life,
Shaped by himself with newly-learnèd art;
　　A wedding or a festival,
　　A mourning or a funeral;
　　　And this hath now his heart,　　95
　　And unto this he frames his song:
　　　Then will he fit his tongue
To dialogues of business, love, or strife;
　　But it will not be long
　　Ere this be thrown aside,　　100
　　And with new joy and pride

The little Actor cons another part;
Filling from time to time his "humorous
    stage"
With all the Persons, down to palsied Age,
That Life brings with her in her equipage; 105
    As if his whole vocation
    Were endless imitation.

VIII

Thou, whose exterior semblance doth belie
    Thy soul's immensity;   •
Thou best philosopher, who yet dost keep 110
Thy heritage, thou eye among the blind,
That, deaf and silent, read'st the eternal deep,
Haunted forever by the eternal mind, —
    Mighty prophet! Seer blest!
    On whom those truths do rest, 115
Which we are toiling all our lives to find,
In darkness lost, the darkness of the grave;
Thou, over whom thy immortality
Broods like the day, a master o'er a slave,
A presence which is not to be put by; 120
Thou little Child, yet glorious in the might
Of heaven-born freedom on thy being's height,
Why with such earnest pains dost thou pro-
    voke
The years to bring the inevitable yoke,
Thus blindly with thy blessedness at strife?
Full soon thy Soul shall have her earthly
    freight, 126
And custom lie upon thee with a weight,
Heavy as frost, and deep almost as life!

IX

    O joy! that in our embers
    Is something that doth live, 130
    That nature yet remembers
    What was so fugitive!
The thought of our past years in me doth
    breed
Perpetual benediction: not indeed 134
For that which is most worthy to be blest —
Delight and liberty, the simple creed
Of childhood, whether busy or at rest,
With new-fledged hope still fluttering in his
    breast: —
    Not for these I raise
    The song of thanks and praise; 140
    But for those obstinate questionings
    Of sense and outward things,
    Fallings from us, vanishings;
    Blank misgivings of a Creature
Moving about in worlds not realised, 145

High instincts before which our mortal nature
Did tremble like a guilty thing surprised:
    But for those first affections,
    Those shadowy recollections,
    Which, be they what they may, 150
Are yet the fountain light of all our day,
Are yet a master light of all our seeing;
Uphold us, cherish, and have power to make
Our noisy years seem moments in the being
Of the eternal Silence: truths that wake, 155
    To perish never;
Which neither listlessness, nor mad endeav-
    our,
Nor Man nor Boy,
Nor all that is at enmity with joy,
Can utterly abolish or destroy! 160
    Hence in a season of calm weather
    Though inland far we be,
Our Souls have sight of that immortal sea
    Which brought us hither,
    Can in a moment travel thither, 165
And see the Children sport upon the shore,
And hear the mighty waters rolling evermore.

X

Then sing, ye Birds, sing, sing a joyous song!
    And let the young lambs bound
    As to the tabor's sound! 170
We in thought will join your throng,
    Ye that pipe and ye that play,
    Ye that through your hearts to-day
    Feel the gladness of the May!
What though the radiance which was once so
    bright 175
Be now forever taken from my sight,
    Though nothing can bring back the hour
Of splendour in the grass, of glory in the
    flower;
    We will grieve not, rather find
    Strength in what remains behind; 180
    In the primal sympathy
    Which having been must ever be;
    In the soothing thoughts that spring
    Out of human suffering; 184
    In the faith that looks through death,
In years that bring the philosophic mind.

XI

And O ye Fountains, Meadows, Hills, and
    Groves,
Forebode not any severing of our loves!
Yet in my heart of hearts I feel your might;
I only have relinquished one delight 190

To live beneath your more habitual sway.
I love the Brooks which down their channels
　　fret,
Even more than when I tripped lightly as they;
The innocent brightness of a new-born Day
　　　　　Is lovely yet;　　　　　　195
The Clouds that gather round the setting sun
Do take a sober colouring from an eye
That hath kept watch o'er man's mortality;
Another race hath been, and other palms are
　　won.
Thanks to the human heart by which we live,
Thanks to its tenderness, its joys, and fears,
To me the meanest flower that blows can give
Thoughts that do often lie too deep for tears.

TO A SKY–LARK

Ethereal minstrel! pilgrim of the sky!
Dost thou despise the earth where cares
　　abound?
Or, while the wings aspire, are heart and eye
Both with thy nest upon the dewy ground?
Thy nest which thou canst drop into at will, 5
Those quivering wings composed, that music
　　still!

Leave to the nightingale her shady wood;
A privacy of glorious light is thine;
Whence thou dost pour upon the world a flood
Of harmony, with instinct more divine;　10
Type of the wise who soar, but never roam:
True to the kindred points of Heaven and
　　Home!

SONNETS

ON THE EXTINCTION OF THE VENE-TIAN REPUBLIC

Once did She hold the gorgeous east in fee;
And was the safeguard of the west: the worth
Of Venice did not fall below her birth,
Venice, the eldest child of Liberty.
She was a maiden city, bright and free;　5
No guile seduced, no force could violate;
And, when she took unto herself a Mate,
She must espouse the everlasting Sea.
And what if she had seen those glories fade,
Those titles vanish, and that strength decay;
Yet shall some tribute of regret be paid　10
When her long life hath reached its final day:
Men are we, and must grieve when even the
　　Shade
Of that which once was great is passed away.

TO TOUSSAINT L'OUVERTURE

Toussaint, the most unhappy man of men!
Whether the whistling rustic tend his plough
Within thy hearing, or thy head be now
Pillowed in some deep dungeon's earless
　　den;—
O miserable chieftain! where and when　5
Wilt thou find patience? Yet die not; do
　　thou
Wear rather in thy bonds a cheerful brow:
Though fallen thyself, never to rise again,
Live, and take comfort. Thou hast left be-hind
Powers that will work for thee; air, earth, and
　　skies;　　　　　　　　10
There's not a breathing of the common wind
That will forget thee; thou hast great allies;
Thy friends are exultations, agonies,
And love, and man's unconquerable mind.

SEPTEMBER, 1802, NEAR DOVER

Inland, within a hollow vale, I stood;
And saw, while sea was calm and air was clear,
The coast of France—the coast of France
　　how near!
Drawn almost into frightful neighbourhood.
I shrunk; for verily the barrier flood　5
Was like a lake, or river bright and fair,
A span of waters; yet what power is there!
What mightiness for evil and for good!
Even so doth God protect us if we be
Virtuous and wise. Winds blow, and waters
　　roll,　　　　　　　　10
Strength to the brave, and Power, and Deity;
Yet in themselves are nothing! One decree
Spake laws to them, and said that by the
　　soul
Only, the nations shall be great and free.

THOUGHT OF A BRITON ON THE SUBJUGATION OF SWITZERLAND

Two voices are there; one is of the sea,
One of the mountains; each a mighty voice:
In both from age to age thou didst rejoice,
They were thy chosen music, Liberty!
There came a tyrant, and with holy glee　5
Thou fought'st against him; but hast vainly
　　striven:
Thou from thy Alpine holds at length art
　　driven,

Where not a torrent murmurs heard by thee.
Of one deep bliss thine ear hath been bereft:
Then cleave, O cleave to that which still is
   left;   10
For, high-souled Maid, what sorrow would it
   be
That mountain floods should thunder as
   before,
And ocean bellow from his rocky shore,
And neither awful voice be heard by thee.

LONDON, 1802

Milton! thou should'st be living at this hour:
England hath need of thee: she is a fen
Of stagnant waters: altar, sword, and pen,
Fireside, the heroic wealth of hall and bower,
Have forfeited their ancient English dower   5
Of inward happiness. We are selfish men;
Oh! raise us up, return to us again;
And give us manners, virtue, freedom, power.
Thy soul was like a Star, and dwelt apart:
Thou hadst a voice whose sound was like the
   sea: 10
Pure as the naked heavens, majestic, free,
So didst thou travel on life's common way,
In cheerful godliness; and yet thy heart
The lowliest duties on herself did lay.

COMPOSED UPON WESTMINSTER BRIDGE, SEPT. 3, 1802

Earth has not anything to show more fair:
Dull would he be of soul who could pass by
A sight so touching in its majesty:
This City now doth, like a garment, wear
The beauty of the morning; silent, bare,   5
Ships, towers, domes, theatres, and temples lie
Open unto the fields, and to the sky;
All bright and glittering in the smokeless air.
Never did sun more beautifully steep
In his first splendour, valley, rock, or hill;   10
Ne'er saw I, never felt, a calm so deep!
The river glideth at his own sweet will:
Dear God! the very houses seem asleep;
And all that mighty heart is lying still!

ON THE SEA-SHORE NEAR CALAIS

It is a beauteous evening, calm and free,
The holy time is quiet as a Nun
Breathless with adoration; the broad sun
Is sinking down in its tranquillity;

The gentleness of heaven broods o'er the Sea: 5
Listen! the mighty Being is awake,
And doth with his eternal motion make
A sound like thunder — everlastingly.
Dear Child! dear Girl! that walkest with
   me here,
If thou appear untouched by solemn thought,
Thy nature is not therefore less divine: 11
Thou liest in Abraham's bosom all the year;
And worship'st at the temple's inner shrine,
God being with thee when we know it not.

THE WORLD IS TOO MUCH WITH US

The world is too much with us: late and soon,
Getting and spending, we lay waste our
   powers:
Little we see in Nature that is ours;
We have given our hearts away, a sordid boon!
This Sea that bares her bosom to the moon;   5
The winds that will be howling at all hours,
And are up-gathered now like sleeping
   flowers;
For this, for everything, we are out of tune;
It moves us not. — Great God! I'd rather be
A Pagan suckled in a creed outworn;   10
So might I, standing on this pleasant lea,
Have glimpses that would make me less
   forlorn;
Have sight of Proteus rising from the sea;
Or hear old Triton blow his wreathèd horn.

TO SLEEP

A flock of sheep that leisurely pass by,
One after one; the sound of rain, and bees
Murmuring; the fall of rivers, winds and seas,
Smooth fields, white sheets of water, and pure
   sky:
I have thought of all by turns, and yet do lie 5
Sleepless! and soon the small birds' melodies
Must hear, first uttered from my orchard
   trees;
And the first cuckoo's melancholy cry.
Even thus last night, and two nights more, I
   lay,
And could not win thee, Sleep! by any stealth:
So do not let me wear to-night away: 11
Without Thee what is all the morning's
   wealth?
Come, blessed barrier between day and day,
Dear mother of fresh thoughts and joyous
   health!

THE RIVER DUDDON

*   *   *   *   *   *   *

IV

I thought of thee, my partner and my guide,
As being past away. — Vain sympathies!
For, backward, Duddon! as I cast my eyes,
I see what was, and is, and will abide;
Still glides the Stream, and shall forever glide;
The Form remains, the Function never dies; 6
While we, the brave, the mighty, and the
    wise,
We Men, who in our morn of youth defied
The elements, must vanish; — be it so!
Enough, if something from our hands have
    power   10
To live, and act, and serve the future hour;
And if, as toward the silent tomb we go,
Through love, through hope, and faith's tran-
    scendent dower,
We feel that we are greater than we know.

MOST SWEET IT IS

Most sweet it is with unuplifted eyes
To pace the ground, if path be there or none,
While a fair region round the traveller lies
Which he forbears again to look upon;
Pleased rather with some soft ideal scene,   5
The work of Fancy, or some happy tone
Of meditation, slipping in between
The beauty coming and the beauty gone.
If Thought and Love desert us, from that day
Let us break off all commerce with the Muse:
With Thought and Love companions of our
    way,   11
Whate'er the senses take or may refuse,
The Mind's internal heaven shall shed her
    dews
Of inspiration on the humblest lay.

SCORN NOT THE SONNET

Scorn not the Sonnet; Critic, you have
    frowned,
Mindless of its just honours; with this key
Shakespeare unlocked his heart: the melody
Of this small lute gave ease to Petrarch's
    wound;
A thousand times this pipe did Tasso sound; 5
With it Camoëns soothed an exile's grief;
The Sonnet glittered a gay myrtle leaf
Amid the cypress with which Dante crowned

His visionary brow: a glow-worm lamp,
It cheered mild Spenser, called from Faery-
    land   10
To struggle through dark ways; and, when a
    damp
Fell round the path of Milton, in his hand
The Thing became a trumpet; whence he
    blew
Soul-animating strains — alas, too few!

SAMUEL   TAYLOR   COLERIDGE
(1772–1834)

BIOGRAPHIA LITERARIA

CHAP. XIV

During the first year that Mr. Wordsworth
and I were neighbours, our conversations
turned frequently on the two cardinal points
of poetry, the power of exciting the sympathy
of the reader by a faithful adherence to the
truth of nature, and the power of giving the
interest of novelty by the modifying colours
of imagination. The sudden charm, which
accidents of light and shade, which moonlight
or sunset, diffused over a known and familiar
landscape, appeared to represent the practicability of combining both. These are
the poetry of nature. The thought suggested itself (to which of us I do not recollect)
that a series of poems might be composed of
two sorts. In the one, the incidents and
agents were to be, in part at least, supernatural; and the excellence aimed at was to
consist in the interesting of the affections by
the dramatic truth of such emotions as would
naturally accompany such situations, supposing them real. And real in this sense they
have been to every human being who, from
whatever source of delusion, has at any time
believed himself under supernatural agency.
For the second class, subjects were to be
chosen from ordinary life; the characters
and incidents were to be such as will be found
in every village and its vicinity where there is
a meditative and feeling mind to seek after
them, or to notice them when they present
themselves.

In this idea originated the plan of the
"Lyrical Ballads"; in which it was agreed
that my endeavours should be directed to
persons and characters supernatural, or at

least romantic; yet so as to transfer from our inward nature a human interest and a semblance of truth sufficient to procure for these shadows of imagination that willing suspension of disbelief for the moment, which constitutes poetic faith. Mr. Wordsworth, on the other hand, was to propose to himself as his object, to give the charm of novelty to things of every day, and to excite a feeling analogous to the supernatural, by awakening the mind's attention from the lethargy of custom, and directing it to the loveliness and the wonders of the world before us; an inexhaustible treasure, but for which, in consequence of the film of familiarity and selfish solicitude, we have eyes, yet see not, ears that hear not, and hearts that neither feel nor understand.

With this view I wrote the "Ancient Mariner," and was preparing, among other poems, the "Dark Ladie," and the "Christabel," in which I should have more nearly realised my ideal than I had done in my first attempt. But Mr. Wordsworth's industry had proved so much more successful, and the number of his poems so much greater, that my compositions, instead of forming a balance, appeared rather an interpolation of heterogeneous matter. Mr. Wordsworth added two or three poems written in his own character, in the impassioned, lofty, and sustained diction which is characteristic of his genius. In this form the "Lyrical Ballads" were published; and were presented by him, as an experiment, whether subjects, which from their nature rejected the usual ornaments and extracolloquial style of poems in general, might not be so managed in the language of ordinary life as to produce the pleasurable interest which it is the peculiar business of poetry to impart. To the second edition he added a preface of considerable length; in which, notwithstanding some passages of apparently a contrary import, he was understood to contend for the extension of this style to poetry of all kinds, and to reject as vicious and indefensible all phrases and forms of style that were not included in what he (unfortunately, I think, adopting an equivocal expression) called the language of real life. From this preface, prefixed to poems in which it was impossible to deny the presence of original genius, however mistaken its direction might be deemed, arose the whole long-continued controversy. For from the conjunction of perceived power with supposed heresy I explain the inveteracy, and in some instances, I grieve to say, the acrimonious passions, with which the controversy has been conducted by the assailants.

Had Mr. Wordsworth's poems been the silly, the childish things which they were for a long time described as being; had they been really distinguished from the compositions of other poets merely by meanness of language and inanity of thought; had they indeed contained nothing more than what is found in the parodies and pretended imitations of them; they must have sunk at once, a dead weight, into the slough of oblivion, and have dragged the preface along with them. But year after year increased the number of Mr. Wordsworth's admirers. They were found, too, not in the lower classes of the reading public, but chiefly among young men of strong sensibility and meditative minds; and their admiration (inflamed perhaps in some degree by opposition) was distinguished by its intensity, I might almost say, by its religious fervour. These facts, and the intellectual energy of the author, which was more or less consciously felt, where it was outwardly and even boisterously denied, meeting with sentiments of aversion to his opinions, and of alarm at their consequences, produced an eddy of criticism, which would of itself have borne up the poems by the violence with which it whirled them round and round. With many parts of this preface, in the sense attributed to them, and which the words undoubtedly seem to authorise, I never concurred; but, on the contrary, objected to them as erroneous in principle, and as contradictory (in appearance at least) both to other parts of the same preface and to the author's own practice in the greater number of the poems themselves. Mr. Wordsworth, in his recent collection, has, I find, degraded this prefatory disquisition to the end of his second volume, to be read or not at the reader's choice. But he has not, as far as I can discover, announced any change in his poetic creed. At all events, considering it as the source of a controversy, in which I have been honoured more than I deserve by the frequent conjunction of my name with his, I think it expedient to declare, once for all, in what points I coincide with his opinions, and in what points I altogether differ. But in order to render myself intelligible, I must previously, in as few words as possible, explain my ideas, first, of a poem; and secondly, of poetry itself, in kind and in essence.

The office of philosophical disquisition consists in just distinction; while it is the privilege of the philosopher to preserve himself constantly aware that distinction is not division. In order to obtain adequate notions of any truth, we must intellectually separate its distinguishable parts; and this is the technical process of philosophy. But having so done, we must then restore them in our conceptions to the unity in which they actually coexist; and this is the result of philosophy. A poem contains the same elements as a prose composition; the difference, therefore, must consist in a different combination of them, in consequence of a different object proposed. According to the difference of the object will be the difference of the combination. It is possible that the object may be merely to facilitate the recollection of any given facts or observations by artificial arrangement; and the composition will be a poem, merely because it is distinguished from prose by metre, or by rhyme, or by both conjointly. In this, the lowest sense, a man might attribute the name of a poem to the well-known enumeration of the days in the several months:

"Thirty days hath September,
April, June, and November," etc.

and others of the same class and purpose. And as a particular pleasure is found in anticipating the recurrence of sound and quantities, all compositions that have this charm superadded, whatever be their contents, *may* be entitled poems.

So much for the superficial form. A difference of object and contents supplies an additional ground of distinction. The immediate purpose may be the communication of truths: either of truth absolute and demonstrable, as in works of science; or of facts experienced and recorded, as in history. Pleasure, and that of the highest and most permanent kind, may result from the attainment of the end; but it is not itself the immediate end. In other works the communication of pleasure may be the immediate purpose; and though truth, either moral or intellectual, ought to be the ultimate end, yet this will distinguish the character of the author, not the class to which

the work belongs. Blest indeed is that state of society, in which the immediate purpose would be baffled by the perversion of the proper ultimate end; in which no charm of diction or imagery could exempt the Bathyllus even of an Anacreon, or the Alexis of Virgil, from disgust and aversion!

But the communication of pleasure may be the immediate object of a work not metrically composed; and that object may have been in a high degree attained, as in novels and romances. Would then the mere superaddition of metre, with or without rhyme, entitle these to the name of poems? The answer is, that nothing can permanently please, which does not contain in itself the reason why it is so, and not otherwise. If metre be superadded, all other parts must be made consonant with it. They must be such as to justify the perpetual and distinct attention to each part, which an exact correspondent recurrence of accent and sound are calculated to excite. The final definition then, so deduced, may be thus worded. A poem is that species of composition, which is opposed to works of science, by proposing for its immediate object pleasure, not truth; and from all other species (having this object in common with it) it is discriminated by proposing to itself such delight from the whole, as is compatible with a distinct gratification from each component part.

Controversy is not seldom excited in consequence of the disputants attaching each a different meaning to the same word; and in few instances has this been more striking than in disputes concerning the present subject. If a man chooses to call every composition a poem, which is rhyme, or measure, or both, I must leave his opinion uncontroverted. The distinction is at least competent to characterise the writer's intention. If it were subjoined, that the whole is likewise entertaining or affecting as a tale, or as a series of interesting reflections, I of course admit this as another fit ingredient of a poem, and an additional merit. But if the definition sought for be that of a legitimate poem, I answer, it must be one the parts of which mutually support and explain each other; all in their proportion harmonising with, and supporting the purpose and known influences of metrical arrangement. The philosophic critics of all ages coincide with the ultimate judgment of all countries, in equally denying the praises of a just poem, on the one hand to a series of striking lines or distichs, each of which absorbing the whole attention of the reader to itself, disjoins it from its context, and makes it a separate whole, instead of a harmonising part; and on the other hand, to an unsustained composition, from which the reader collects rapidly the general result unattracted by the component parts. The reader should be carried forward, not merely or chiefly by the mechanical impulse of curiosity, or by a restless desire to arrive at the final solution; but by the pleasurable activity of mind excited by the attractions of the journey itself. Like the motion of a serpent, which the Egyptians made the emblem of intellectual power; or like the path of sound through the air, at every step he pauses and half recedes, and from the retrogressive movement collects the force which again carries him onward, *Praecipitandus est liber spiritus*,[1] says Petronius Arbiter most happily. The epithet, *liber*, here balances the preceding verb: and it is not easy to conceive more meaning condensed in fewer words.

But if this should be admitted as a satisfactory character of a poem, we have still to seek for a definition of poetry. The writings of Plato, and Bishop Taylor, and the *Theoria Sacra* of Burnet, furnish undeniable proofs that poetry of the highest kind may exist without metre, and even without the contra-distinguishing objects of a poem. The first chapter of Isaiah (indeed a very large proportion of the whole book) is poetry in the most emphatic sense; yet it would be not less irrational than strange to assert, that pleasure, and not truth, was the immediate object of the prophet. In short, whatever specific import we attach to the word poetry, there will be found involved in it, as a necessary consequence, that a poem of any length neither can be, nor ought to be, all poetry. Yet if a harmonious whole is to be produced, the remaining parts must be preserved in keeping with the poetry; and this can be no otherwise effected than by such a studied selection and artificial arrangement as will partake of one, though not a peculiar, property of poetry. And this again can be no other than the property of exciting a more continuous and equal attention than the language of prose aims at, whether colloquial or written.

My own conclusions on the nature of poetry, in the strictest use of the word, have been in part anticipated in the preceding disquisition on the fancy and imagination. What is poetry? is so nearly the same question with, what is a poet? that the answer to the one is involved in the solution of the other. For it is a distinction resulting from the poetic genius itself, which sustains and modifies the images, thoughts, and emotions of the poet's own mind. The poet, described in ideal perfection, brings the whole soul of man into activity, with the subordination of its faculties to each other, according to their relative worth and dignity. He diffuses a tone and spirit of unity, that blends, and (as it were) fuses, each into each, by that synthetic and magical power, to which we have exclusively appropriated the name of imagination. This power, first put in action by the will and understanding, and retained under their irremissive,[1] though gentle and unnoticed, control (*laxis effertur habenis* [2]) reveals itself in the balance or reconciliation of opposite or discordant qualities: of sameness, with difference; of the general, with the concrete; the idea, with the image; the individual, with the representative; the sense of novelty and freshness, with old and familiar objects: a more than usual state of emotion, with more than usual order; judgment ever awake and steady self-possession, with enthusiasm and feeling profound or vehement; and while it blends and harmonises the natural and the artificial, still subordinates art to nature; the manner to the matter; and our admiration of the poet to our sympathy with the poetry.

* * * * * *

KUBLA KHAN: OR, A VISION IN A DREAM

A FRAGMENT

In Xanadu did Kubla Khan
A stately pleasure-dome decree:
Where Alph, the sacred river, ran
Through caverns measureless to man
Down to a sunless sea.   5

So twice five miles of fertile ground
With walls and towers were girdled round:
And there were gardens bright with sinuous
    rills,

---

[1] The free spirit must be urged headlong.

[1] unremitting   [2] He is borne with loosened reins.

Where blossom'd many an incense-bearing tree;
And here were forests ancient as the hills,   10
Enfolding sunny spots of greenery.

But oh! that deep romantic chasm which slanted
Down the green hill athwart a cedarn cover!
A savage place! as holy and enchanted
As e'er beneath a waning moon was haunted   15
By woman wailing for her demon-lover!
And from this chasm, with ceaseless turmoil seething,
As if this earth in fast thick pants were breathing,
A mighty fountain momently was forced:
Amid whose swift half-intermitted burst   20
Huge fragments vaulted like rebounding hail,
Or chaffy grain beneath the thresher's flail:
And 'mid these dancing rocks at once and ever
It flung up momently the sacred river.
Five miles meandering with a mazy motion   25
Through wood and dale the sacred river ran,
Then reach'd the caverns measureless to man,
And sank in tumult to a lifeless ocean:
And 'mid this tumult Kubla heard from far
Ancestral voices prophesying war!   30

The shadow of the dome of pleasure
Floated midway on the waves;
Where was heard the mingled measure
From the fountain and the caves.
It was a miracle of rare device,   35
A sunny pleasure-dome with caves of ice!

A damsel with a dulcimer
In a vision once I saw:
It was an Abyssinian maid,
And on her dulcimer she play'd,   40
Singing of Mount Abora.
Could I revive within me
Her symphony and song,
To such a deep delight 'twould win me,
That with music loud and long,   45
I would build that dome in air,
That sunny dome! those caves of ice!
And all who heard should see them there,—
And all should cry, Beware! Beware!—
His flashing eyes, his floating hair!   50
Weave a circle round him thrice,
And close your eyes with holy dread,
For he on honey-dew hath fed,
And drunk the milk of Paradise

THE RIME OF THE ANCIENT MARINER

IN SEVEN PARTS

PART I

An ancient Mariner meeteth three gallants bidden to a wedding-feast, and detaineth one.

It is an ancient Mariner,
And he stoppeth one of three.
"By thy long grey beard and glittering eye,
Now wherefore stopp'st thou me?

The bridegroom's doors are open'd wide,   5
And I am next of kin;
The guests are met, the feast is set:
May'st hear the merry din."

He holds him with his skinny hand,
"There was a ship," quoth he.   10
"Hold off! unhand me, grey-beard loon!"
Eftsoons his hand dropt he.

The wedding-guest is spellbound by the eye of the old seafaring man, and constrained to hear his tale.

He holds him with his glittering eye —
The wedding-guest stood still,
And listens like a three years' child: 15
The Mariner hath his will.

The wedding-guest sat on a stone:
He cannot choose but hear;

And thus spake on that ancient man,
The bright-eyed Mariner.　　　　20

"The ship was cheer'd, the harbour clear'd,
Merrily did we drop
Below the kirk, below the hill,
Below the lighthouse top.

The sun came up upon the left,　　　25
Out of the sea came he !
And he shone bright, and on the right
Went down into the sea.

Higher and higher every day,
Till over the mast at noon —"
The wedding-guest here beat his breast,　30
For he heard the loud bassoon.

The bride hath paced into the hall,
Red as a rose is she ;
Nodding their heads before her goes　　35
The merry minstrelsy.

The wedding-guest he beat his breast,
Yet he cannot choose but hear ;
And thus spake on that ancient man,
The bright-eyed Mariner.　　　　40

"And now the storm-blast came, and he
Was tyrannous and strong :
He struck with his o'ertaking wings,
And chased us south along.

With sloping masts and dipping prow,　45
As who pursued with yell and blow
Still treads the shadow of his foe,
And forward bends his head,
The ship drove fast, loud roar'd the blast,
And southward aye we fled.　　　　50

And now there came both mist and snow,
And it grew wondrous cold ;
And ice, mast-high, came floating by,
As green as emerald ;

And through the drifts the snowy clifts　55
Did send a dismal sheen :
Nor shapes of men nor beasts we ken —
The ice was all between.

The ice was here, the ice was there,
The ice was all around :　　　　60
It crack'd and growl'd, and roar'd and howl'd,
Like noises in a swound !

The Mariner tells how the ship sailed southward with a good wind and fair weather, till it reached the Line.

The wedding-guest heareth the bridal music ; but the Mariner continueth his tale.

The ship drawn by a storm toward the south pole.

The land of ice, and of fearful sounds, where no living thing was to be seen.

Till a great
sea-bird, called
the Albatross,
came through
the snow-fog,
and was
received with
great joy and
hospitality.
At length did cross an Albatross:
Thorough the fog it came:
As if it had been a Christian soul,   65
We hail'd it in God's name.

It ate the food it ne'er had eat,
And round and round it flew.
The ice did split with a thunder-fit;
The helmsman steer'd us through!   70

And lo! the
Albatross
proveth a bird
of good omen,
and followeth
the ship as it
returned
northward,
through fog
and floating
ice.
And a good south wind sprung up behind;
The Albatross did follow,
And every day, for food or play
Came to the mariners' hollo!

In mist or cloud, on mast or shroud,   75
It perch'd for vespers nine;
Whiles all the night, through fog-smoke white,
Glimmer'd the white moon-shine."

The ancient
Mariner
inhospitably
killeth the
pious bird of
good omen.
"God save thee, ancient Mariner!
From the fiends, that plague thee thus!—   80
Why look'st thou so?"—"With my cross-bow
I shot the Albatross!

PART II

"The sun now rose upon the right:
Out of the sea came he,
Still hid in mist, and on the left   85
Went down into the sea.

And the good south wind still blew behind,
But no sweet bird did follow,
Nor any day, for food or play,
Came to the mariners' hollo!   90

His shipmates
cry out against
the ancient
Mariner, for
killing the
bird of good
luck.
And I had done a hellish thing,
And it would work 'em woe;
For all averr'd, I had kill'd the bird
That made the breeze to blow.
Ah wretch! said they, the bird to slay   95
That made the breeze to blow!

But when the
fog cleared
off, they jus-
tify the same,
and thus
make them-
selves accom-
plices in the
crime.
Nor dim nor red, like God's own head,
The glorious sun uprist:
Then all averr'd, I had kill'd the bird
That brought the fog and mist.   100
'Twas right, said they, such birds to slay,
That bring the fog and mist.

The fair breeze blew, the white foam flew,
The furrow follow'd free:
We were the first that ever burst   105
Into that silent sea.

Down dropt the breeze, the sails dropt down,
'Twas sad as sad could be;
And we did speak only to break
The silence of the sea!   110

All in a hot and copper sky,
The bloody sun, at noon,
Right up above the mast did stand,
No bigger than the moon.

Day after day, day after day,   115
We stuck, nor breath nor motion;
As idle as a painted ship
Upon a painted ocean.

Water, water, every where,
And all the boards did shrink;   120
Water, water, every where,
Nor any drop to drink.

The very deep did rot: O Christ!
That ever this should be!
Yea, slimy things did crawl with legs   125
Upon the slimy sea.

About, about, in reel and rout,
The death-fires danced at night;
The water, like a witch's oils,
Burnt green, and blue and white.   130

And some in dreams assured were
Of the spirit that plagued us so:
Nine fathom deep he had follow'd us,
From the land of mist and snow.

And every tongue, through utter drought,   135
Was wither'd at the root;
We could not speak, no more than if
We had been choked with soot.

Ah! well-a-day! what evil looks
Had I from old and young!   140
Instead of the cross, the Albatross
About my neck was hung.

Part III

"There pass'd a weary time. Each throat
Was parch'd, and glazed each eye.
A weary time! A weary time!   145
How glazed each weary eye!
When looking westward I beheld
A something in the sky.

The ancient Mariner beholdeth a sign in the element afar off.

At first it seem'd a little speck,
And then it seem'd a mist: 150
It moved and moved, and took at last
A certain shape, I wist.[1]

A speck, a mist, a shape, I wist!
And still it near'd and near'd:
As if it dodged a water-sprite,   155
It plunged and tack'd and veer'd.

At its nearer approach, it seemeth him to be a ship; and at a dear ransom he freeth his speech from the bonds of thirst.

With throats unslaked, with black lips baked,
We could nor laugh nor wail;
Through utter drought all dumb we stood!
I bit my arm, I suck'd the blood,   160
And cried, A sail! a sail!

A flash of joy;

With throats unslaked, with black lips baked,
Agape they heard me call:
Gramercy![2] they for joy did grin,
And all at once their breath drew in,   165
As[3] they were drinking all.

And horror follows. For can it be a ship *that comes onward without wind or tide?*

'See! see! (I cried) she tacks no more!
Hither, to work us weal,
Without a breeze, without a tide,
She steadies with upright keel!'   170

The western wave was all a-flame:
The day was well nigh done:
Almost upon the western wave
Rested the broad bright sun;
When that strange shape drove suddenly   175
Betwixt us and the sun.

It seemeth him but the skeleton of a ship.

And straight the sun was fleck'd with bars,
(Heaven's Mother send us grace!)
As if through a dungeon grate he peer'd,
With broad and burning face.   180

Alas! (thought I, and my heart beat loud)
How fast she nears and nears!
Are those her sails that glance in the sun,
Like restless gossameres?[4]

[1] I perceived   [2] Many thanks!   [3] as if   [4] fine cobwebs that float in the air in clear weather

Are those her ribs through which the sun   185
Did peer, as through a grate?
And is that Woman all her crew?
Is that a Death? and are there two?
Is Death that woman's mate?

Her lips were red, her looks were free,   190
Her locks were yellow as gold:
Her skin was as white as leprosy,
The night-mare Life-in-Death was she,
Who thicks man's blood with cold.

The naked hulk alongside came,   195
And the twain were casting dice;
'The game is done! I've, I've won!'
Quoth she, and whistles thrice.

The sun's rim dips; the stars rush out:
At one stride comes the dark;   200
With far-heard whisper, o'er the sea,
Off shot the spectre-bark.

We listen'd and look'd sideways up!
Fear at my heart, as at a cup,
My life-blood seem'd to sip!   205
The stars were dim, and thick the night,
The steersman's face by his lamp gleam'd white;
From the sails the dew did drip —
Till clomb above the eastern bar
The hornèd moon, with one bright star   210
Within the nether tip.

One after one, by the star-dogg'd moon,
Too quick for groan or sigh,
Each turn'd his face with a ghastly pang,
And cursed me with his eye.   215

Four times fifty living men,
(And I heard nor sigh nor groan)
With heavy thump, a lifeless lump,
They dropp'd down one by one.

The souls did from their bodies fly, —   220
They fled to bliss or woe!
And every soul, it pass'd me by,
Like the whizz of my cross-bow!"

Part IV

"I fear thee, ancient Mariner!
I fear thy skinny hand!   225
And thou art long, and lank, and brown,
As is the ribb'd sea-sand.

[marginal glosses:]

And its ribs are seen as bars on the face of the setting sun.

The spectre-woman and her death-mate, and no other on board the skeleton ship.

Like vessel, like crew!

Death, and Life-in-Death, have diced for the ship's crew, and she (the latter) winneth the ancient Mariner.

No twilight within the courts of the sun.

At the rising of the moon,

One after another,

His shipmates drop down dead.

But Life-in-Death begins her work on the ancient Mariner.

The wedding-guest feareth that a spirit is talking to him.

AE

I fear thee and thy glittering eye,
And thy skinny hand, so brown." —

But the ancient Mariner assureth him of his bodily life, and proceedeth to relate his horrible penance.

"Fear not, fear not, thou wedding-guest!　230
This body dropt not down.

Alone, alone, all, all alone,
Alone on a wide wide sea!
And never a saint took pity on
My soul in agony.　235

He despiseth the creatures of the calm,

The many men, so beautiful!
And they all dead did lie:
And a thousand thousand slimy things
Lived on; and so did I.

And envieth that *they* should live, and so many lie dead.

I look'd upon the rotting sea,　240
And drew my eyes away;
I look'd upon the rotting deck,
And there the dead men lay.

I look'd to Heaven, and tried to pray;
But or ever a prayer had gusht,　245
A wicked whisper came, and made
My heart as dry as dust.

I closed my lids, and kept them close,
And the balls like pulses beat;
For the sky and the sea, and the sea and the sky,
Lay like a load on my weary eye,　251
And the dead were at my feet.

But the curse liveth for him in the eye of the dead men.

The cold sweat melted from their limbs,
Nor rot nor reek did they:
The look with which they look'd on me　255
Had never pass'd away.

An orphan's curse would drag to hell
A spirit from on high;
But oh! more horrible than that
Is the curse in a dead man's eye!　260
Seven days, seven nights, I saw that curse,
And yet I could not die.

In his loneliness and fixedness he yearneth towards the journeying moon, and the stars that still sojourn, yet still move onward; and everywhere the blue sky belongs to them, and is their appointed rest, and their native country, and their own natural homes, which they enter unannounced, as lords that are certainly expected, and yet there is a silent joy at their arrival.

The moving moon went up the sky,
And no where did abide:
Softly she was going up,　265
And a star or two beside —

Her beams bemock'd the sultry main,
Like April hoar-frost spread;
But where the ship's huge shadow lay,
The charmèd water burnt alway　270
A still and awful red.

Beyond the shadow of the ship,
I watch'd the water-snakes:
They moved in tracks of shining white,
And when they rear'd, the elfish light   275
Fell off in hoary flakes.

By the light of the moon he beholdeth God's creatures of the great calm.

Within the shadow of the ship
I watch'd their rich attire:
Blue, glossy green, and velvet black,
They coil'd and swam; and every track   280
Was a flash of golden fire.

O happy living things! no tongue
Their beauty might declare:
A spring of love gush'd from my heart,
And I bless'd them unaware!   285
Sure my kind saint took pity on me,
And I bless'd them unaware.

Their beauty and their happiness.

He blesseth them in his heart.

The selfsame moment I could pray;
And from my neck so free
The Albatross fell off, and sank   290
Like lead into the sea.

The spell begins to break.

PART V

"Oh sleep! it is a gentle thing,
Belov'd from pole to pole!
To Mary Queen the praise be given!
She sent the gentle sleep from Heaven,   295
That slid into my soul.

The silly buckets on the deck,
That had so long remain'd,
I dreamt that they were fill'd with dew;
And when I awoke, it rain'd.   300

By grace of the holy Mother, the ancient Mariner is refreshed with rain.

My lips were wet, my throat was cold,
My garments all were dank;
Sure I had drunken in my dreams,
And still my body drank.

I moved, and could not feel my limbs: 305
I was so light — almost
I thought that I had died in sleep,
And was a blessed ghost.

And soon I heard a roaring wind:
It did not come anear;   310
But with its sound it shook the sails,
That were so thin and sere.[1]

He heareth sounds and seeth strange sights and commotions in the sky and the element.

---

[1] dry

The upper air burst into life !
And a hundred fire-flags sheen,[1]
To and fro they were hurried about;   315
And to and fro, and in and out,
The wan stars danced between.

And the coming wind did roar more loud,
And the sails did sigh like sedge;
And the rain pour'd down from one black cloud;
The moon was at its edge.   321

The thick black cloud was cleft, and still
The moon was at its side:
Like waters shot from some high crag,
The lightning fell with never a jag,   325
A river steep and wide.

The bodies of the ship's crew are inspirited, and the ship moves on;

The loud wind never reach'd the ship,
Yet now the ship moved on !
Beneath the lightning and the moon
The dead men gave a groan.   330

They groan'd, they stirr'd, they all uprose,
Nor spake, nor moved their eyes;
It had been strange, even in a dream,
To have seen those dead men rise.

The helmsman steer'd, the ship moved on;   335
Yet never a breeze up-blew;
The mariners all 'gan work the ropes,
Where they were wont to do:
They raised their limbs like lifeless tools —
We were a ghastly crew.   340

The body of my brother's son
Stood by me, knee to knee:
The body and I pull'd at one rope,
But he said nought to me."

But not by the souls of the men, nor by demons of earth or middle air, but by a blessed troop of angelic spirits, sent down by the invocation of the guardian saint.

"I fear thee, ancient Mariner !"   345
"Be calm, thou Wedding-Guest !
'Twas not those souls that fled in pain,
Which to their corses came again,
But a troop of spirits blest:

For when it dawn'd — they dropp'd their arms,
And cluster'd round the mast;   351
Sweet sounds rose slowly through their mouths,
And from their bodies pass'd.

Around, around, flew each sweet sound,
Then darted to the sun;   355
Slowly the sounds come back again,
Now mix'd, now one by one.

---

[1] beautiful

Sometimes a-dropping from the sky
I heard the skylark sing;
Sometimes all little birds that are,   360
How they seem'd to fill the sea and air
With their sweet jargoning!

And now 'twas like all instruments,
Now like a lonely flute;
And now it is an angel's song,   365
That makes the heavens be mute.

It ceased; yet still the sails made on
A pleasant noise till noon,
A noise like of a hidden brook
In the leafy month of June,   370
That to the sleeping woods all night
Singeth a quiet tune.

Till noon we quietly sail'd on,
Yet never a breeze did breathe:
Slowly and smoothly went the ship,   375
Moved onward from beneath.

Under the keel nine fathom deep,
From the land of mist and snow,
The spirit slid; and it was he
That made the ship to go.   380
The sails at noon left off their tune,
And the ship stood still also.

The lonesome spirit from the south-pole carries on the ship as far as the Line, in obedience to the angelic troop, but still requireth vengeance.

The sun, right up above the mast,
Had fix'd her to the ocean;
But in a minute she 'gan stir,   385
With a short uneasy motion —
Backwards and forwards half her length,
With a short uneasy motion.

Then like a pawing horse let go,
She made a sudden bound: 390
It flung the blood into my head,
And I fell down in a swound.

How long in that same fit I lay,
I have not to declare;
But ere my living life return'd,   395
I heard, and in my soul discern'd
Two voices in the air.

The Polar Spirit's fellow demons, the invisible inhabitants of the element, take part in his wrong; and two of them relate, one to the other, that penance long and heavy for the ancient Mariner hath been accorded to the Polar Spirit, who returneth southward.

'Is it he?' quoth one, 'is this the man?
By Him who died on cross,
With his cruel bow he laid full low   400
The harmless Albatross.

'The spirit who bideth by himself
In the land of mist and snow,

He loved the bird that loved the man
Who shot him with his bow.'   405

The other was a softer voice,
As soft as honey-dew:
Quoth he, 'The man hath penance done,
And penance more will do.'

PART VI

First Voice

'But tell me, tell me! speak again,   410
Thy soft response renewing —
What makes that ship drive on so fast?
What is the ocean doing?'

Second Voice

'Still as a slave before his lord,
The ocean hath no blast;
His great bright eye most silently   415
Up to the moon is cast —

If he may know which way to go;
For she guides him, smooth or grim.
See, brother, see! how graciously   420
She looketh down on him.'

First Voice

The Mariner
hath been cast
into a trance;
for the angelic
power causeth
the vessel to
drive north-
ward, faster
than human
life could en-
dure.

'But why drives on that ship so fast,
Without or wave or wind?'

Second Voice

'The air is cut away before,
And closes from behind.
Fly, brother, fly! more high, more high!   425
Or we shall be belated:
For slow and slow that ship will go,
When the Mariner's trance is abated.'

The super-
natural mo-
tion is
retarded;
the Mariner
awakes, and
his penance
begins anew.

I woke, and we were sailing on,   430
As in a gentle weather:
'Twas night, calm night, the moon was high;
The dead men stood together.

All stood together on the deck,
For a charnel-dungeon fitter:
All fix'd on me their stony eyes,   435
That in the moon did glitter.

The pang, the curse, with which they died,
Had never pass'd away:
I could not draw my eyes from theirs,   440
Nor turn them up to pray.

And now this spell was snapt : once more
I view'd the ocean green,
And look'd far forth, yet little saw
Of what had else been seen —   445

Like one, that on a lonesome road
Doth walk in fear and dread,
And having once turn'd round, walks on,
And turns no more his head ;
Because he knows a frightful fiend   450
Doth close behind him tread.

But soon there breathed a wind on me,
Nor sound nor motion made :
Its path was not upon the sea,
In ripple or in shade.   455

It raised my hair, it fann'd my cheek
Like a meadow-gale of spring —
It mingled strangely with my fears,
Yet it felt like a welcoming.

Swiftly, swiftly flew the ship,   460
Yet she sail'd softly too :
Sweetly, sweetly blew the breeze —
On me alone it blew.

Oh ! dream of joy ! is this indeed
The lighthouse top I see ?   465
Is this the hill ? is this the kirk ?
Is this mine own countree ?

We drifted o'er the harbour-bar,
And I with sobs did pray —
'O let me be awake, my God !   470
Or let me sleep alway.'

The harbour-bay was clear as glass,
So smoothly it was strewn !
And on the bay the moonlight lay,
And the shadow of the moon.   475

The rock shone bright, the kirk no less,
That stands above the rock :
The moonlight steep'd in silentness
The steady weathercock.

And the bay was white with silent light,   480
Till rising from the same,
Full many shapes, that shadows were,
In crimson colours came.

A little distance from the prow
Those crimson shadows were :   485
I turn'd my eyes upon the deck —
Oh, Christ ! what saw I there !

The curse is finally expiated,

And the ancient Mariner beholdeth his native country.

The angelic spirits leave the dead bodies,

And appear in their own forms of light.

Each corse lay flat, lifeless and flat,
And, by the holy rood !
A man all light, a seraph-man,   490
On every corse there stood.

This seraph-band, each waved his hand :
It was a heavenly sight !
They stood as signals to the land,
Each one a lovely light :   495

This seraph-band, each waved his hand,
No voice did they impart —
No voice ; but oh ! the silence sank
Like music on my heart.

But soon I heard the dash of oars,   500
I heard the pilot's cheer ;
My head was turn'd perforce away,
And I saw a boat appear.

The pilot, and the pilot's boy,
I heard them coming fast :   505
Dear Lord in Heaven ! it was a joy
The dead men could not blast.

I saw a third — I heard his voice :
It is the Hermit good !
He singeth loud his godly hymns   510
That he makes in the wood.
He'll shrieve my soul, he'll wash away
The Albatross's blood.

Part VII

The Hermit
of the Wood

"This Hermit good lives in that wood
Which slopes down to the sea.   515
How loudly his sweet voice he rears !
He loves to talk with marineres
That come from a far countree.

He kneels at morn, and noon, and eve —
He hath a cushion plump :   520
It is the moss that wholly hides
The rotted old oak-stump.

The skiff-boat near'd : I heard them talk,
'Why, this is strange, I trow !
Where are those lights so many and fair,   525
That signal made but now ?'

Approacheth
the ship with
wonder.

'Strange, by my faith !' the Hermit said —
'And they answer'd not our cheer !
The planks look warp'd ! and see those sails,
How thin they are and sere !   530
I never saw aught like to them,
Unless perchance it were

Brown skeletons of leaves that lag
My forest-brook along:
When the ivy-tod is heavy with snow,   535
And the owlet whoops to the wolf below
That eats the she-wolf's young.'

'Dear Lord! it hath a fiendish look —
(The pilot made reply)
I am a-fear'd' — 'Push on, push on!'   540
Said the Hermit cheerily.

The boat came closer to the ship,
But I nor spake nor stirr'd;
The boat came close beneath the ship,
And straight a sound was heard.   545

Under the water it rumbled on,   *The ship sud-*
Still louder and more dread: *denly sinketh.*
It reach'd the ship, it split the bay;
The ship went down like lead.

Stunn'd by that loud and dreadful sound,   550 *The ancient*
Which sky and ocean smote,   *Mariner is*
Like one that hath been seven days drown'd,   *saved in the*
My body lay afloat;   *pilot's boat.*
But swift as dreams, myself I found
Within the pilot's boat.   555

Upon the whirl, where sank the ship,
The boat spun round and round;
And all was still, save that the hill
Was telling of the sound.

I moved my lips — the pilot shriek'd,   560
And fell down in a fit;
The holy Hermit raised his eyes,
And pray'd where he did sit.

I took the oars: the pilot's boy,
Who now doth crazy go,   565
Laugh'd loud and long, and all the while
His eyes went to and fro.
'Ha! ha!' quoth he, 'full plain I see,
The Devil knows how to row.'

And now, all in my own countree,   570
I stood on the firm land!
The Hermit stepp'd forth from the boat,
And scarcely he could stand.

'O shrieve me, shrieve me, holy man!'   *The ancient*
The Hermit cross'd his brow.   575 *Mariner*
'Say quick,' quoth he, 'I bid thee say — *earnestly*
What manner of man art thou?'   *entreateth*
                                    the Hermit to
Forthwith this frame of mine was wrench'd *shrieve him;*
With a woeful agony,   *and the pen-*
                                      ance of life
                                      falls on him.

Which forced me to begin my tale: 580
And then it left me free.

And ever and anon throughout his future life an agony constraineth him to travel from land to land;

Since then at an uncertain hour,
That agony returns;
And till my ghastly tale is told,
This heart within me burns.   585

I pass, like night, from land to land:
I have strange power of speech;
That moment that his face I see,
I know the man that must hear me:
To him my tale I teach.   590

What loud uproar bursts from that door!
The wedding-guests are there;
But in the garden-bower the bride
And bride-maids singing are:
And hark the little vesper bell,   595
Which biddeth me to prayer!

O Wedding-Guest! this soul hath been
Alone on a wide wide sea:
So lonely 'twas, that God himself
Scarce seemèd there to be.   600

O sweeter than the marriage-feast,
'Tis sweeter far to me,
To walk together to the kirk
With a goodly company! —

To walk together to the kirk,   605
And all together pray,
While each to his great Father bends,
Old men, and babes, and loving friends,
And youths and maidens gay!

And to teach, by his own example, love and reverence to all things that God made and loveth.

Farewell, farewell! but this I tell   610
To thee, thou Wedding-Guest!
He prayeth well, who loveth well
Both man and bird and beast.

He prayeth best, who loveth best
All things both great and small;   615
For the dear God who loveth us,
He made and loveth all."

The Mariner, whose eye is bright,
Whose beard with age is hoar,
Is gone; and now the Wedding-Guest   620
Turn'd from the bridegroom's door.

He went like one that hath been stunn'd,
And is of sense forlorn:
A sadder and a wiser man
He rose the morrow morn.   625

CHRISTABEL

From PART I

'Tis the middle of night by the castle clock,
And the owls have awaken'd the crowing cock;
Tu—whit — Tu—whoo!
And hark, again! the crowing cock,
How drowsily it crew.   5
Sir Leoline, the Baron rich,
Hath a toothless mastiff bitch;
From her kennel beneath the rock
She maketh answer to the clock,   9
Four for the quarters, and twelve for the hour;
Ever and aye, by shine and shower,
Sixteen short howls, not over loud;
Some say, she sees my lady's shroud.

Is the night chilly and dark?
The night is chilly, but not dark.   15
The thin grey cloud is spread on high,
It covers but not hides the sky.
The moon is behind, and at the full;
And yet she looks both small and dull.
The night is chill, the cloud is grey: 20
'Tis a month before the month of May,
And the Spring comes slowly up this way.

The lovely lady, Christabel,
Whom her father loves so well,
What makes her in the wood so late,   25
A furlong from the castle gate?
She had dreams all yesternight
Of her own betrothèd knight;
And she in the midnight wood will pray
For the weal of her lover that's far away.   30

She stole along, she nothing spoke,
The sighs she heaved were soft and low,
And naught was green upon the oak,
But moss and rarest mistletoe:
She kneels beneath the huge oak tree,   35
And in silence prayeth she.

The lady sprang up suddenly,
The lovely lady, Christabel!
It moan'd as near as near can be,
But what it is she cannot tell. —   40
On the other side it seems to be,
Of the huge, broad-breasted, old oak tree.

The night is chill; the forest bare;
Is it the wind that moaneth bleak?
There is not wind enough in the air   45

To move away the ringlet curl
From the lovely lady's cheek —
There is not wind enough to twirl
The one red leaf, the last of its clan,
That dances as often as dance it can,   50
Hanging so light, and hanging so high,
On the topmost twig that looks up at the sky.

Hush, beating heart of Christabel!
Jesu, Maria, shield her well!
She folded her arms beneath her cloak,   55
And stole to the other side of the oak.
    What sees she there?

There she sees a damsel bright,
Drest in a silken robe of white,
That shadowy in the moonlight shone: 60
The neck that made that white robe wan,
Her stately neck, and arms were bare;
Her blue-vein'd feet unsandal'd were;
And wildly glitter'd here and there
The gems entangled in her hair.   65
I guess, 'twas frightful there to see
A lady so richly clad as she —
Beautiful exceedingly!

"Mary mother, save me now!"
Said Christabel, "and who art thou?"   70

The lady strange made answer meet,
And her voice was faint and sweet: —
"Have pity on my sore distress,
I scarce can speak for weariness:
Stretch forth thy hand, and have no fear!"   75
Said Christabel, "How camest thou here?"
And the lady, whose voice was faint and sweet
Did thus pursue her answer meet: —
"My sire is of a noble line,
And my name is Geraldine: 80
Five warriors seized me yestermorn,
Me, even me, a maid forlorn:
They choked my cries with force and fright,
And tied me on a palfrey white,
The palfrey was as fleet as wind,   85
And they rode furiously behind.
They spurr'd amain, their steeds were white:
And once we cross'd the shade of night.
As sure as Heaven shall rescue me,
I have no thought what men they be;   90
Nor do I know how long it is
(For I have lain entranced, I wis)
Since one, the tallest of the five,
Took me from the palfrey's back,
A weary woman, scarce alive.   95
Some mutter'd words his comrades spoke:
He placed me underneath this oak;

He swore they would return with haste;
Whither they went I cannot tell —
I thought I heard, some minutes past,   100
Sounds as of a castle bell.
Stretch forth thy hand," thus ended she,
"And help a wretched maid to flee."

*   *   *   *   *   *   *

ROBERT SOUTHEY (1774–1843)

THE WELL OF ST. KEYNE

A well there is in the West country,
  And a clearer one never was seen;
There is not a wife in the West country
  But has heard of the Well of St. Keyne.   4

An oak and an elm tree stand beside,
  And behind does an ash-tree grow,
And a willow from the bank above
  Droops to the water below.   8

A traveller came to the Well of St. Keyne;
  Joyfully he drew nigh,
For from cock-crow he had been travelling,
  And there was not a cloud in the sky.   12

He drank of the water so cool and clear,
  For thirsty and hot was he,
And he sat down upon the bank,
  Under the willow-tree.   16

There came a man from the house hard by
  At the well to fill his pail,
On the well-side he rested it,
  And he bade the stranger hail.   20

"Now art thou a bachelor, stranger?" quoth he,
  "For an if thou hast a wife,
The happiest draught thou hast drank this day
  That ever thou didst in thy life.   24

"Or has thy good woman, if one thou hast
  Ever here in Cornwall been?
For an if she have, I'll venture my life
  She has drunk of the Well of St. Keyne."   28

"I have left a good woman who never was
  here,"
  The stranger he made reply;
"But that my draught should be the better for
  that,
  I pray you answer me why."   32

"St. Keyne," quoth the Cornish-man, "many
  a time
  Drank of this crystal well,
And before the Angel summoned her
  She laid on the water a spell.   36

"If the Husband of this gifted well
  Shall drink before his Wife,
A happy man thenceforth is he,
  For he shall be Master for life.   40

"But if the Wife should drink of it first,
  God help the Husband then!"
The stranger stooped to the Well of St. Keyne,
  And drank of the waters again.   44

"You drank of the well, I warrant, betimes?"
  He to the Cornish-man said.
But the Cornish-man smiled as the stranger
  spake,
  And sheepishly shook his head.   48

"I hastened, as soon as the wedding was done,
  And left my wife in the porch.
But i' faith, she had been wiser than me,
  For she took a bottle to Church."

FRANCIS JEFFREY (1773–1850)

"THE WHITE DOE OF RYLSTONE"

This, we think, has the merit of being the
very worst poem we ever saw imprinted in a
quarto volume; and though it was scarcely
to be expected, we confess, that Mr. Wordsworth, with all his ambition, should so soon
have attained to that distinction, the wonder
may perhaps be diminished when we state,
that it seems to us to consist of a happy union
of all the faults, without any of the beauties,
which belong to his school of poetry. It is
just such a work, in short, as some wicked
enemy of that school might be supposed to
have devised, on purpose to make it ridiculous; and when we first took it up, we could
not help suspecting that some ill-natured
critic had actually taken this harsh method of
instructing Mr. Wordsworth, by example,
in the nature of those errors, against which
our precepts had been so often directed in
vain. We had not gone far, however, till
we felt intimately that nothing in the nature
of a joke could be so insupportably dull; —
and that this must be the work of one who

earnestly believed it to be a pattern of pathetic simplicity, and gave it out as such to the admiration of all intelligent readers. In this point of view, the work may be regarded as curious at least, if not in some degree interesting; and, at all events, it must be instructive to be made aware of the excesses into which superior understandings may be betrayed, by long self-indulgence, and the strange extravagances into which they may run, when under the influence of that intoxication which is produced by unrestrained admiration of themselves. This poetical intoxication, indeed, to pursue the figure a little farther, seems capable of assuming as many forms as the vulgar one which arises from wine; and it appears to require as delicate a management to make a man a good poet by the help of the one, as to make him a good companion by means of the other. In both cases a little mistake as to the dose or the quality of the inspiring fluid may make him absolutely outrageous, or lull him over into the most profound stupidity, instead of brightening up the hidden stores of his genius: and truly we are concerned to say, that Mr. Wordsworth seems hitherto to have been unlucky in the choice of his liquor — or of his bottle-holder. In some of his odes and ethic exhortations, he was exposed to the public in a state of incoherent rapture and glorious delirium, to which we think we have seen a parallel among the humbler lovers of jollity. In the Lyrical Ballads, he was exhibited, on the whole, in a vein of very pretty deliration; but in the poem before us, he appears in a state of low and maudlin imbecility, which would not have misbecome Master Silence[1] himself, in the close of a social day. Whether this unhappy result is to be ascribed to any adulteration of his Castalian[2] cups, or to the unlucky choice of his company over them, we cannot presume to say. It may be that he has dashed his Hippocrene[3] with too large an infusion of lake[4] water, or assisted its operation too exclusively by the study of the ancient historical ballads of "the north countrie." That there are palpable imitations of the style and manner of those venerable compositions in the work before us, is indeed undeniable; but it unfortunately happens, that while the hobbling versification, the mean diction, and flat stupidity of these models are very exactly copied, and even improved upon, in this imitation, their rude energy, manly simplicity, and occasional felicity of expression, have totally disappeared; and, instead of them, a large allowance of the author's own metaphysical sensibility, and mystical wordiness, is forced into an unnatural combination with the borrowed beauties which have just been mentioned.

SIR WALTER SCOTT (1771–1832)

THE LAY OF THE LAST MINSTREL

FROM CANTO VI

THE LAY OF ROSABELLE

O listen, listen, ladies gay!
  No haughty feat of arms I tell;
Soft is the note, and sad the lay,
  That mourns the lovely Rosabelle;   4

"Moor, moor the barge, ye gallant crew!
  And, gentle ladye, deign to stay,
Rest thee in Castle Ravensheuch,
  Nor tempt the stormy firth[1] to-day.   8

"The blackening wave is edged with white:
  To inch[2] and rock the sea-mews fly;
The fishers have heard the Water-Sprite,
  Whose screams forbode that wreck is nigh. 12

"Last night the gifted Seer did view
  A wet shroud swathed round ladye gay;
Then stay thee, Fair, in Ravensheuch:
  Why cross the gloomy firth to-day?" — 16

"'Tis not because Lord Lindesay's heir
  To-night at Roslin leads the ball,
But that my ladye-mother there
  Sits lonely in her castle-hall.   20

"'Tis not because the ring they ride,
  And Lindesay at the ring rides well,
But that my sire the wine will chide,
  If 'tis not fill'd by Rosabelle." —   24

---

[1] Cf. Shakespeare's *Henry IV*, Part II.   [2] from the Castalian fountain on Mt. Parnassus, sacred to the Muses   [3] a fountain on Mt. Helicon, sacred to the Muses   [4] a jesting allusion to Wordsworth's residence in the Lake district

[1] bay   [2] island

O'er Roslin all that dreary night
  A wondrous blaze was seen to gleam;
'Twas broader than the watch-fire's light,
  And redder than the bright moonbeam. 28

It glared on Roslin's castled rock,
  It ruddied all the copse-wood glen;
'Twas seen from Dryden's groves of oak,
  And seen from cavern'd Hawthornden. 32

Seem'd all on fire that chapel proud,
  Where Roslin's chiefs uncoffin'd lie,
Each Baron, for a sable shroud,
  Sheathed in his iron panoply. 36

Seem'd all on fire, within, around,
  Deep sacristy and altar's pale,[1]
Shone every pillar foliage-bound,
  And glimmer'd all the dead men's mail. 40

Blazed battlement and pinnet[2] high,
  Blazed every rose-carved buttress fair —
So still they blaze, when fate is nigh
  The lordly line of high St. Clair. 44

There are twenty of Roslin's barons bold
  Lie buried within that proud chapelle;
Each one the holy vault doth hold —
  But the sea holds lovely Rosabelle! 48

And each St. Clair was buried there,
  With candle, with book, and with knell;
But the sea-caves rung, and the wild winds
      sung,
  The dirge of lovely Rosabelle. 52

CHRISTMAS IN THE OLDEN TIME

From MARMION, INTRODUCTION TO CANTO VI

Heap on more wood! — the wind is chill;
But let it whistle as it will,
We'll keep our Christmas merry still.
Each age has deemed the new-born year
The fittest time for festal cheer:
Even, heathen yet, the savage Dane
At Iol[3] more deep the mead did drain;
High on the beach his galleys drew,
And feasted all his pirate crew;
Then in his low and pine-built hall,   10
Where shields and axes decked the wall,

[1] enclosure   [2] pinnacle   [3] Yule, the heathen
Christmas

They gorged upon the half-dressed steer;
Caroused in seas of sable beer;
While round, in brutal jest, were thrown
The half-gnawed rib and marrow-bone;
Or listened all, in grim delight,
While Scalds[1] yelled out the joys of fight.
Then forth in frenzy would they hie,
While wildly-loose their red locks fly;
And, dancing round the blazing pile,   20
They make such barbarous mirth the while,
As best might to the mind recall
The boisterous joys of Odin's hall.[2]
    And well our Christian sires of old
Loved when the year its course had rolled
And brought blithe Christmas back again
With all its hospitable train.
Domestic and religious rite
Gave honour to the holy night:
On Christmas eve the bells were rung;   30
On Christmas eve the mass was sung;
That only night, in all the year,
Saw the stoled priest the chalice rear.[3]
The damsel donned her kirtle sheen;
The hall was dressed with holly green;
Forth to the wood did merry-men go,
To gather in the mistletoe.
Then opened wide the baron's hall
To vassal, tenant, serf, and all;
Power laid his rod of rule aside;   40
And Ceremony doffed her pride.
The heir, with roses in his shoes,
That night might village partner choose;
The lord, underogating,[4] share
The vulgar game of "post and pair."
All hailed with uncontrolled delight,
And general voice, the happy night
That to the cottage, as the crown,
Brought tidings of salvation down.
    The fire, with well-dried logs supplied,   50
Went roaring up the chimney wide;
The huge hall-table's oaken face,
Scrubbed till it shone, the day to grace,
Bore then upon its massive board
No mark to part the squire and lord.
Then was brought in the lusty brawn,
By old blue-coated serving-man;
Then the grim boar's-head frowned on high
Crested with bays and rosemary.
Well can the green-garbed ranger tell   60
How, when, and where the monster fell;

[1] poets   [2] in the Other-world, where heroes
fought and feasted forever   [3] The Mass is not
celebrated at night except at Christmas.   [4] without loss of dignity

What dogs before his death he tore,
And all the baiting of the boar.
The wassail round, in good brown bowls,
Garnished with ribbons, blithely trowls.
There the huge sirloin reeked; hard by
Plum-porridge stood, and Christmas pie;
Nor failed old Scotland to produce,
At such high-tide, her savoury goose.
Then came the merry maskers in,   70
And carols roared with blithesome din;
If unmelodious was the song,
It was a hearty note, and strong.
Who lists may in their mumming see
Traces of ancient mystery;[1]
White skirts supplied the masquerade,
And smutted cheeks the visors made:
But, O! what maskers richly dight
Can boast of bosoms half so light!
England was merry England, when   80
Old Christmas brought his sports again.
'Twas Christmas broached the mightiest ale;
'Twas Christmas told the merriest tale;
A Christmas gambol oft could cheer
The poor man's heart through half the year.

SOLDIER, REST! THY WARFARE O'ER

From THE LADY OF THE LAKE

Soldier, rest! thy warfare o'er,
  Sleep the sleep that knows not breaking;
Dream of battled fields no more,
  Days of danger, nights of waking.
In our isle's enchanted hall,
  Hands unseen thy couch are strewing,
Fairy strains of music fall,
  Every sense in slumber dewing.
Soldier, rest! thy warfare o'er,
Dream of fighting fields no more;   10
Sleep the sleep that knows not breaking,
Morn of toil, nor night of waking.

No rude sound shall reach thine ear,
  Armour's clang, or war-steed champing,
Trump nor pibroch summon here
  Mustering clan, or squadron tramping.
Yet the lark's shrill fife may come
  At the daybreak from the fallow,
And the bittern sound his drum,
  Booming from the sedgy shallow.   20
Ruder sounds shall none be near,
Guards nor warders challenge here;
Here's no war-steed's neigh and champing,
Shouting clans or squadrons stamping.

[1] religious drama

Huntsman, rest! thy chase is done,
  While our slumbrous spells assail ye,
Dream not, with the rising sun,
  Bugles here shall sound reveille.
Sleep! the deer is in his den;
  Sleep! thy hounds are by thee lying;   30
Sleep! nor dream in yonder glen
  How thy gallant steed lay dying.
Huntsman, rest! thy chase is done;
Think not of the rising sun,
For, at dawning to assail ye,
Here no bugles sound reveille.

FITZ-JAMES AND RODERICK DHU

From THE LADY OF THE LAKE

Canto V

VIII

"Enough, I am by promise tied
To match me with this man of pride:
Twice have I sought Clan-Alpine's glen
In peace; but when I come again,
I come with banner, brand, and bow,
As leader seeks his mortal foe.
For lovelorn swain, in lady's bower,
Ne'er panted for the appointed hour,
As I, until before me stand   25
This rebel Chieftain and his band."

IX

"Have, then, thy wish!"—He whistled
    shrill,
And he was answered from the hill;
Wild as the scream of the curlew,
From crag to crag the signal flew.
Instant, through copse and heath, arose
Bonnets and spears and bended bows;
On right, on left, above, below,
Sprung up at once the lurking foe;
From shingles grey their lances start,
The bracken bush sends forth the dart,   10
The rushes and the willow wand
Are bristling into axe and brand,
And every tuft of broom gives life
To plaided warrior armed for strife.
That whistle garrisoned the glen
At once with full five hundred men,
As if the yawning hill to heaven
A subterranean host had given.
Watching their leader's beck and will,
All silent there they stood, and still.   20

Like the loose crags whose threatening mass
Lay tottering o'er the hollow pass,
As if an infant's touch could urge
Their headlong passage down the verge,
With step and weapon forward flung,
Upon the mountain-side they hung.
The Mountaineer cast glance of pride
Along Benledi's [1] living side,
Then fixed his eye and sable brow
Full on Fitz-James: [2] "How say'st thou
    now?   30
These are Clan-Alpine's warriors true;
And, Saxon, — I am Roderick Dhu!" [3]

X

Fitz-James was brave; — though to his heart
The life-blood thrilled with sudden start,
He manned himself with dauntless air,
Returned the Chief his haughty stare,
His back against a rock he bore,
And firmly placed his foot before: —
"Come one, come all! this rock shall fly
From its firm base as soon as I."
Sir Roderick marked, — and in his eyes
Respect was mingled with surprise,   10
And the stern joy which warriors feel
In foeman worthy of their steel.
Short space he stood, — then waved his hand:
Down sunk the disappearing band;
Each warrior vanished where he stood,
In broom or bracken, heath or wood:
Sunk brand and spear, and bended bow,
In osiers pale and copses low:
It seemed as if their mother Earth
Had swallowed up her warlike birth.   20
The wind's last breath had tossed in air
Pennon and plaid and plumage fair, —
The next but swept a lone hillside,
Where heath and fern were waving wide;
The sun's last glance was glinted back,
From spear and glaive, [4] from targe [5] and
    jack, [6] —
The next, all unreflected, shone
On bracken green, and cold grey stone.

XI

Fitz-James   looked   round, — yet   scarce
    believed
The witness that his sight received;

---

[1] a high mountain, north of Loch Vennachar
[2] James V, in disguise   [3] Black Roderick, chief of
Clan-Alpine   [4] sword   [5] small shield   [6] leather jacket

Such apparition well might seem
Delusion of a dreadful dream.
Sir Roderick in suspense he eyed,
And to his look the Chief replied:
"Fear naught — nay, that I need not say —
But — doubt not aught from mine array.
Thou art my guest; — I pledged my word
As far as Coilantogle ford: [1]   10
Nor would I call a clansman's brand
For aid against one valiant hand,
Though on our strife lay every vale
Rent by the Saxon from the Gael.
So move we on; — I only meant
To show the reed on which you leant,
Deeming this path you might pursue
Without a pass from Roderick Dhu."
They moved; — I said Fitz-James was brave,
As ever knight that belted glaive;   20
Yet dare not say that now his blood
Kept on its wont and tempered flood,
As, following Roderick's stride, he drew
That seeming lonesome pathway through,
Which yet, by fearful proof, was rife
With lances, that, to take his life,
Waited but signal from a guide,
So late dishonoured and defied.
Ever, by stealth, his eye sought round
The vanished guardians of the ground,   30
And still, from copse and heather deep,
Fancy saw spear and broadsword peep,
And in the plover's shrilly strain
The signal whistle heard again.
Nor breathed he free till far behind
The pass was left; for then they wind
Along a wide and level green,
Where neither tree nor tuft was seen,
Nor rush nor bush of broom was near,
To hide a bonnet or a spear.   40

XII

The Chief in silence strode before,
And reached that torrent's sounding shore,
Which, daughter of three mighty lakes, [2]
From Vennachar in silver breaks,
Sweeps through the plain, and ceaseless mines
On Bochastle [3] the mouldering lines,
Where Rome, the Empress of the world,
Of yore her eagle wings unfurled.
And here his course the Chieftain stayed,
Threw down his target and his plaid,   10

---

[1] at the east end of Loch Vennachar   [2] Lochs
Katrine, Achray, and Vennachar   [3] a moor in
which are the ruins of a Roman camp

And to the Lowland warrior said:
"Bold Saxon! to his promise just,
Vich-Alpine [1] has discharged his trust.
This murderous Chief, this ruthless man,
This head of a rebellious clan,
Hath led thee safe through watch and ward,
Far past Clan-Alpine's outmost guard.
Now, man to man, and steel to steel,
A Chieftain's vengeance thou shalt feel.
See, here, all vantageless I stand,　　20
Armed, like thyself, with single brand;
For this is Coilantogle ford,
And thou must keep thee with thy sword."

XIII

The Saxon paused: "I ne'er delayed,
When foeman bade me draw my blade;
Nay more, brave Chief, I vowed thy death:
Yet sure thy fair and generous faith,
And my deep debt for life preserved,
A better meed have well deserved:
Can naught but blood our feud atone?
Are there no means?" "No, Stranger, none!
And hear, — to fire thy flagging zeal, —
The Saxon cause rests on thy steel;　　10
For thus spoke Fate, by prophet bred
Between the living and the dead:
'Who spills the foremost foeman's life
His party conquers in the strife.'"
"Then, by my word," the Saxon said,
"The riddle is already read.
Seek yonder brake beneath the cliff, —
There lies Red Murdock,[2] stark and stiff.
Thus Fate hath solved her prophecy,
Then yield to Fate, and not to me.　　20
To James, at Stirling, let us go,
When, if thou wilt be still his foe,
Or if the King shall not agree
To grant thee grace and favour free,
I plight my honour, oath, and word,
That, to thy native strengths restored,
With each advantage shalt thou stand,
That aids thee now to guard thy land."

XIV

Dark lightning flashed from Roderick's eye:
"Soars thy presumption, then, so high,
Because a wretched kern [3] ye slew,
Homage to name to Roderick Dhu?

He yields not, he, to man nor fate!
Thou add'st but fuel to my hate: —
My clansman's blood demands revenge.
Not yet prepared? — By Heaven, I change
My thought, and hold thy valour light
As that of some vain carpet knight,　　10
Who ill deserved my courteous care,
And whose best boast is but to wear
A braid of his fair lady's hair."
"I thank thee, Roderick, for the word!
It nerves my heart, it steels my sword;
For I have sworn this braid [1] to stain
In the best blood that warms thy vein.
Now, truce, farewell! and, ruth, begone! —
Yet think not that by thee alone,
Proud Chief! can courtesy be shown;　　20
Though not from copse, nor heath, nor cairn,
Start at my whistle clansmen stern,
Of this small horn one feeble blast
Would fearful odds against thee cast.
But fear not — doubt not — which thou wilt —
We try this quarrel hilt to hilt."
Then each at once his falchion drew,
Each on the ground his scabbard threw,
Each looked to sun and stream and plain,
And what they ne'er might see again;　　30
Then, foot and point and eye opposed,
In dubious strife they darkly closed.

XV

Ill fared it then with Roderick Dhu,
That on the field his targe he threw,
Whose brazen studs and tough bull-hide
Had death so often dashed aside;
For, trained abroad his arms to wield,
Fitz-James's blade was sword and shield.
He practised every pass and ward,
To thrust, to strike, to feint, to guard;
While less expert, though stronger far,
The Gael maintained unequal war.　　10
Three times in closing strife they stood,
And thrice the Saxon blade drank blood:
No stinted draught, no scanty tide,
The gushing floods the tartans dyed.
Fierce Roderick felt the fatal drain,
And showered his blows like wintry rain;
And, as firm rock or castle-roof
Against the winter shower is proof,
The foe, invulnerable still,
Foiled his wild rage by steady skill;　　20

---

[1] the descendant of Alpine　[2] a guide who tried to betray him　[3] a foot-soldier

AE

[1] For the story of the braid and his oath, see Canto IV, xxi-xxviii.

Till, at advantage ta'en, his brand
Forced Roderick's weapon from his hand,
And, backwards borne upon the lea,
Brought the proud Chieftain to his knee.

XVI

"Now yield thee, or, by Him who made
The world, thy heart's blood dyes my blade!"
"Thy threats, thy mercy, I defy!
Let recreant yield, who fears to die."
Like adder darting from his coil,
Like wolf that dashes through the toil,
Like mountain-cat who guards her young,
Full at Fitz-James's throat he sprung;
Received, but recked not of a wound,
And locked his arms his foeman round.   10
Now, gallant Saxon, hold thine own!
No maiden's hand is round thee thrown!
That desperate grasp thy frame might feel
Through bars of brass and triple steel!
They tug! They strain! Down, down they go,
The Gael above, Fitz-James below.
The Chieftain's gripe his throat compressed,
His knee was planted in his breast;
His clotted locks he backward threw,
Across his brow his hand he drew,   20
From blood and mist to clear his sight,
Then gleamed aloft his dagger bright!
But hate and fury ill supplied
The stream of life's exhausted tide,
And all too late the advantage came,
To turn the odds of deadly game;
For, while the dagger gleamed on high,
Reeled soul and sense, reeled brain and eye.
Down came the blow! but in the heath
The erring blade found bloodless sheath.   30
The struggling foe may now unclasp
The fainting Chief's relaxing grasp;
Unwounded from the dreadful close,
But breathless all, Fitz-James arose.

CHARLES LAMB (1775–1834)

THE TWO RACES OF MEN

The human species, according to the best theory I can form of it, is composed of two distinct races, *the men who borrow*, and *the men who lend*. To these two original diversities may be reduced all those impertinent classifications of Gothic and Celtic tribes, white men, black men, red men. All the dwellers upon earth, "Parthians, and Medes,

and Elamites,"[1] flock hither, and do naturally fall in with one or other of these primary distinctions. The infinite superiority of the former, which I choose to designate as the *great race*, is discernible in their figure, port, and a certain instinctive sovereignty. The latter are born degraded. "He shall serve his brethren."[2] There is something in the air of one of this caste, lean and suspicious; contrasting with the open, trusting, generous manners of the other.

Observe who have been the greatest borrowers of all ages — Alcibiades[3] — Falstaff — Sir Richard Steele — our late incomparable Brinsley[4] — what a family likeness in all four!

What a careless, even deportment hath your borrower! what rosy gills! what a beautiful reliance on Providence doth he manifest, — taking no more thought than lilies![5] What contempt for money, — accounting it (yours and mine especially) no better than dross! What a liberal confounding of those pedantic distinctions of *meum* and *tuum*![6] or rather, what a noble simplification of language (beyond Tooke[7]), resolving these supposed opposites into one clear, intelligible pronoun adjective! — What near approaches doth he make to the primitive *community*, — to the extent of one-half of the principle at least!

He is the true taxer "who calleth all the world up to be taxed";[8] and the distance is as vast between him and *one of us*, as subsisted betwixt the Augustan Majesty[9] and the poorest obolary[10] Jew that paid it tribute-pittance at Jerusalem! — His exactions, too, have such a cheerful, voluntary air! So far removed from your sour parochial or state-gatherers, — those ink-horn varlets, who carry their want of welcome in their faces! He cometh to you with a smile, and troubleth you with no receipt; confining himself to no set season. Every day is his Candlemas, or his Feast of Holy Michael.[11] He applieth the *lene tormentum*[12] of a pleasant look to your purse, —

[1] *Acts*, ii: 9   [2] inaccurately quoted from *Genesis*, ix: 25   [3] a pupil of Socrates, celebrated for his beauty, talents, insolence, and extravagance   [4] Richard Brinsley Sheridan, dramatist, orator, and spendthrift   [5] Cf. *Matthew*, vi: 28   [6] mine and thine   [7] Horne Tooke, an English philologer (1736–1812)   [8] Cf. *Luke*, ii: 1   [9] Roman government   [10] able to pay only a halfpenny   [11] customary dates for settling debts   [12] mild torture, Horace, *Odes*, III, xxi, 13

which to that gentle warmth expands her silken leaves, as naturally as the cloak of the traveller, for which sun and wind contended! He is the true Propontic which never ebbeth![1] The sea which taketh handsomely at each man's hand. In vain the victim, whom he delighteth to honour, struggles with destiny; he is in the net. Lend therefore cheerfully, O man ordained to lend — that thou lose not in the end, with thy worldly penny, the reversion promised.[2] Combine not preposterously in thine own person the penalties of Lazarus and of Dives![3] — but, when thou seest the proper authority coming, meet it smilingly, as it were half-way. Come, a handsome sacrifice! See how light *he* makes of it! Strain not courtesies with a noble enemy.

Reflections like the foregoing were forced upon my mind by the death of my old friend, Ralph Bigod, Esq., who departed this life on Wednesday evening; dying, as he had lived, without much trouble. He boasted himself a descendant from mighty ancestors of that name, who heretofore held ducal dignities in this realm. In his actions and sentiments he belied not the stock to which he pretended. Early in life he found himself invested with ample revenues; which, with that noble disinterestedness which I have noticed as inherent in men of the *great race*, he took almost immediate measures entirely to dissipate and bring to nothing: for there is something revolting in the idea of a king holding a private purse; and the thoughts of Bigod were all regal. Thus furnished, by the very act of disfurnishment; getting rid of the cumbersome luggage of riches, more apt (as one[4] sings)

To slacken virtue, and abate her edge,
Than prompt her to do aught may merit praise,

he sets forth, like some Alexander, upon his great enterprise, "borrowing and to borrow!"

In his periegesis, or triumphant progress throughout this island, it has been calculated that he laid a tithe part of the inhabitants under contribution. I reject this estimate as greatly exaggerated: but having had the honour of accompanying my friend, divers times, in his perambulations about this vast city, I own I was greatly struck at first with the prodigious number of faces we met, who claimed a sort of respectful acquaintance with us. He was one day so obliging as to explain the phenomenon. It seems, these were his tributaries; feeders of his exchequer; gentlemen, his good friends (as he was pleased to express himself), to whom he had occasionally been beholden for a loan. Their multitudes did no way disconcert him. He rather took a pride in numbering them; and, with Comus, seemed pleased to be "stocked with so fair a herd."[1]

With such sources, it was a wonder how he contrived to keep his treasury always empty. He did it by force of an aphorism, which he had often in his mouth, that "money kept longer than three days stinks." So he made use of it while it was fresh. A good part he drank away (for he was an excellent toss-pot), some he gave away, the rest he threw away, literally tossing and hurling it violently from him — as boys do burs, or as if it had been infectious, — into ponds, or ditches, or deep holes, — inscrutable cavities of the earth: — or he would bury it (where he would never seek it again) by a river's side under some bank, which (he would facetiously observe) paid no interest — but out away from him it must go peremptorily, as Hagar's offspring[2] into the wilderness, while it was sweet. He never missed it. The streams were perennial which fed his fisc.[3] When new supplies became necessary, the first person that had the felicity to fall in with him, friend or stranger, was sure to contribute to the deficiency. For Bigod had an *Undeniable* way with him. He had a cheerful, open exterior, a quick jovial eye, a bald forehead, just touched with grey (*cana fides*).[4] He anticipated no excuse, and found none. And, waiving for a while my theory as to the *great race*, I would put it to the most untheorising reader, who may at times have disposable coin in his pocket, whether it is not more repugnant to the kindliness of his nature to refuse such a one as I am describing, than to say *no* to a poor petitionary rogue (your bastard borrower), who, by his mumping visnomy,[5] tells you that he expects nothing better; and, therefore, whose preconceived notions and expectations you do in reality so much less shock in the refusal.

---

[1] Cf. *Othello*, III, iii, 453-6 [2] Cf. *Luke*, vi: 35 [3] *i.e.*, suffer in both worlds [4] Milton, *Par. Regained*, ii, 455-6.

[1] Milton, *Comus*, ii, 151-2 [2] *Genesis*, xxi: 14 [3] treasury [4] hoary faith, *i.e.*, a sign of honesty, *Æneid*, i, 292 [5] begging countenance

When I think of this man; his fiery glow of heart; his swell of feeling; how magnificent, how *ideal* he was; how great at the midnight hour; and when I compare with him the companions with whom I have associated since, I grudge the saving of a few idle ducats, and think that I am fallen into the society of *lenders*, and *little men*.

To one like Elia,[1] whose treasures are rather cased in leather covers than closed in iron coffers, there is a class of alienators more formidable than that which I have touched upon; I mean your *borrowers of books* — those mutilators of collections, spoilers of the symmetry of shelves, and creators of odd volumes. There is Comberbatch,[2] matchless in his depredations!

That foul gap in the bottom shelf facing you, like a great eye-tooth knocked out — (you are now with me in my little back study in Bloomsbury, Reader!) — with the huge Switzer-like[3] tomes on each side (like the Guildhall giants, in their reformed posture, guardant of nothing[4]) once held the tallest of my folios, *Opera Bonaventurae*,[5] choice and massy divinity, to which its two supporters (school divinity also, but of a lesser calibre, — Bellarmine,[6] and Holy Thomas[7]) showed but as dwarfs, — itself an Ascapart![8] — *that* Comberbatch abstracted upon the faith of a theory he holds, which is more easy, I confess, for me to suffer by than to refute, namely, that "the title to property in a book" (my Bonaventure, for instance) "is in exact ratio to the claimant's powers of understanding and appreciating the same." Should he go on acting upon this theory, which of our shelves is safe?

The slight vacuum in the left-hand case — two shelves from the ceiling — scarcely distinguishable but by the quick eye of a loser — was whilom the commodious resting-place of Browne on Urn Burial. C. will hardly allege that he knows more about that treatise than I do, who introduced it to him, and was

indeed the first (of the moderns) to discover its beauties — but so have I known a foolish lover to praise his mistress in the presence of a rival more qualified to carry her off than himself. — Just below, Dodsley's dramas[1] want their fourth volume, where Vittoria Corombona[2] is! The remainder nine are as distasteful as Priam's refuse sons, when the fates *borrowed* Hector. Here stood the Anatomy of Melancholy,[3] in sober state. — There loitered the Complete Angler; quiet as in life, by some stream side. — In yonder nook, John Buncle, a widower-volume, with "eyes closed," mourns his ravished mate.[4]

One justice I must do my friend, that if he sometimes, like the sea, sweeps away a treasure, at another time, sea-like, he throws up as rich an equivalent to match it. I have a small under-collection of this nature (my friend's gatherings in his various calls), picked up, he has forgotten at what odd places, and deposited with as little memory at mine. I take in these orphans, the twice-deserted. These proselytes of the gate[5] are welcome as the true Hebrews. There they stand in conjunction; natives, and naturalised. The latter seem as little disposed to inquire out their true lineage as I am. — I charge no ware-house-room for these deodands,[6] nor shall ever put myself to the ungentlemanly trouble of advertising a sale of them to pay expenses.

To lose a volume to C. carries some sense and meaning in it. You are sure that he will make one hearty meal on your viands, if he can give no account of the platter after it. But what moved thee, wayward, spiteful K.,[7] to be so importunate to carry off with thee, in spite of tears and adjurations to thee to forbear, the Letters of that princely woman, the thrice noble Margaret Newcastle?[8] — knowing at the time, and knowing that I knew also, thou most assuredly wouldst never turn over one leaf of the illustrious folio: — what but the mere spirit of contradiction, and childish

---

[1] Lamb's pen-name　[2] the name assumed by Coleridge when he enlisted as a soldier　[3] The papal guard of Switzers was composed of tall men. [4] The figures of Gog and Magog, which once guarded the entrance, had been removed to the batk of the hall.　[5] St. Bonaventura (1221–74), a great religious writer　[6] an Italian theologian (1542–1621)　[7] Cf. p. 211, Note 2　[8] a giant in the romance of Bevis of Hampton

[1] a collection of Elizabethan plays　[2] a play by John Webster　[3] a curious and learned book by Robert Burton (1621)　[4] *The Life of John Buncle, Esq.*, a novel in two volumes, by Thomas Amory　[5] a late Rabbinical title for sojourners in Israel, cf. *Exod.*, xx: 10　[6] Used loosely for "forfeited objects"　[7] James Kenney, dramatist (1780–1849)　[8] Duchess of Newcastle (1624?–74), a talented and learned woman

love of getting the better of thy friend? —
Then, worst cut of all! to transport it with
thee to the Gallican land —

Unworthy land to harbour such a sweetness,
A virtue in which all ennobling thoughts dwelt,
Pure thoughts, kind thoughts, high thoughts, her
    sex's wonder![1]

— hadst thou not thy play-books, and books
of jests and fancies, about thee, to keep thee
merry, even as thou keepest all companies
with thy quips and mirthful. tales? Child of
the Greenroom, it was unkindly, unkindly
done of thee. Thy wife, too, that part-
French, better-part-Englishwoman! — that
she could fix upon no other treatise to bear
away, in kindly token of remembering us,
than the works of Fulke Greville, Lord Brook[2]
— of which no Frenchman, nor woman of
France, Italy, or England, was ever by nature
constituted to comprehend a tittle! *Was
there not Zimmermann[3] on Solitude?*

Reader, if haply thou art blessed with a
moderate collection, be shy of showing it; or
if thy heart overfloweth to lend them, lend
thy books; but let it be to such a one as
S. T. C.[4] — he will return them (generally
anticipating the time appointed) with usury;
enriched with annotations, tripling their value.
I have had experience. Many are these
precious Mss. of his — (in *matter* oftentimes,
and almost in *quantity* not unfrequently, vying
with the originals) in no very clerkly hand —
legible in my Daniel;[5] in old Burton; in Sir
Thomas Browne; and those abstruser cogitations of the Greville, now, alas! wandering
in Pagan lands. — I counsel thee, shut not
thy heart, nor thy library, against S. T. C.

MRS. BATTLE'S OPINIONS ON WHIST

"A clear fire, a clean hearth, and the rigour
of the game." This was the celebrated *wish*
of old Sarah Battle[6] (now with God), who,
next to her devotions, loved a good game of
whist. She was none of your lukewarm
gamesters, your half-and-half players, who
have no objection to take a hand, if you want
one to make up a rubber; who affirm that
they have no pleasure in winning; that they
like to win one game and lose another; that
they can while away an hour very agreeably
at a card-table, but are indifferent whether
they play or no; and will desire an adversary
who has slipped a wrong card, to take it up
and play another. These insufferable triflers
are the curse of a table. One of these flies
will spoil a whole pot.[1] Of such it may be
said that they do not play at cards, but only
play at playing at them.

Sarah Battle was none of that breed. She
detested them, as I do, from her heart and
soul; and would not, save upon a striking
emergency, willingly seat herself at the same
table with them. She loved a thorough-paced
partner, a determined enemy. She took, and
gave, no concessions. She hated favours.
She never made a revoke, nor ever passed it
over in her adversary without exacting the
utmost forfeiture. She fought a good fight:
cut and thrust. She held not her good sword
(her cards) "like a dancer."[2] She sat bolt
upright; and neither showed you her cards,
nor desired to see yours. All people have
their blind side — their superstitions; and I
have heard her declare, under the rose, that
Hearts was her favourite suit.

I never in my life — and I knew Sarah
Battle many of the best years of it — saw her
take out her snuff-box when it was her turn
to play; or snuff a candle in the middle of a
game; or ring for a servant, till it was fairly
over. She never introduced, or connived at,
miscellaneous conversation during its process.
As she emphatically observed, cards were
cards; and if I ever saw unmingled distaste
in her fine last-century countenance, it was at
the airs of a young gentleman of a literary
turn, who had been with difficulty persuaded
to take a hand; and who, in his excess of
candour, declared, that he thought there was
no harm in unbending the mind now and
then, after serious studies, in recreations of
that kind! She could not bear to have her
noble occupation, to which she wound up her
faculties, considered in that light. It was her
business, her duty, the thing she came into
the world to do, — and she did it. She unbent her mind afterwards — over a book.

Pope was her favourite author: his Rape
of the Lock her favourite work. She once

---

[1] apparently composed by Lamb himself   [2] Sir
Philip Sidney's friend   [3] a Swiss philosopher
(1728–95)   [4] Coleridge   [5] Samuel Daniel   [6] an
imaginary name and person

[1] Cf. *Eccles.*, x: 1   [2] Cf. *Ant. and Cleop.*, III, xi,
35–6

did me the favour to play over with me (with the cards) his celebrated game of Ombre in that poem; and to explain to me how far it agreed with, and in what points it would be found to differ from, tradrille. Her illustrations were apposite and poignant; and I had the pleasure of sending the substance of them to Mr. Bowles;[1] but I suppose they came too late to be inserted among his ingenious notes upon that author.

Quadrille,[2] she has often told me, was her first love; but whist had engaged her maturer esteem. The former, she said, was showy and specious, and likely to allure young persons. The uncertainty and quick shifting of partners — a thing which the constancy of whist abhors; the dazzling supremacy and regal investiture of Spadille[3] — absurd, as she justly observed, in the pure aristocracy of whist, where his crown and garter give him no proper power above his brother-nobility of the Aces; — the giddy vanity, so taking to the inexperienced, of playing alone;[4] above all, the overpowering attractions of a *Sans Prendre Vole*,[5] — to the triumph of which there is certainly nothing parallel or approaching, in the contingencies of whist; — all these, she would say, make quadrille a game of captivation to the young and enthusiastic. But whist was the *solider* game: that was her word. It was a long meal; not like quadrille, a feast of snatches. One of two rubbers might co-extend in duration with an evening. They gave time to form rooted friendships, to cultivate steady enmities. She despised the chance-started, capricious, and ever-fluctuating alliances of the other. The skirmishes of quadrille, she would say, reminded her of the petty ephemeral embroilments of the little Italian states, depicted by Machiavel:[6] perpetually changing postures and connections; bitter foes to-day, sugared darlings to-morrow; kissing and scratching in a breath; — but the wars of whist were comparable to the long, steady, deep-rooted, rational antipathies of the great French and English nations.

A grave simplicity was what she chiefly admired in her favourite game. There was nothing silly in it, like the nob[7] in cribbage —

nothing superfluous. No *flushes* — that most irrational of all pleas that a reasonable being can set up: — that any one should claim four by virtue of holding cards of the same mark and colour, without reference to the playing of the game, or the individual worth or pretensions of the cards themselves! She held this to be a solecism; as pitiful an ambition at cards as alliteration is in authorship. She despised superficiality, and looked deeper than the colours of things. — Suits were soldiers, she would say, and must have a uniformity of array to distinguish them: but what should we say to a foolish squire, who should claim a merit from dressing up his tenantry in red jackets, that never were to be marshalled — never to take the field? — She even wished that whist were more simple than it is; and, in my mind, would have stripped it of some appendages, which, in the state of human frailty, may be venially, and even commendably, allowed of. She saw no reason for the deciding of the trump by the turn of the card. Why not one suit always trumps? — Why two colours, when the mark of the suit would have sufficiently distinguished them without it?

"But the eye, my dear madam, is agreeably refreshed with the variety. Man is not a creature of pure reason — he must have his senses delightfully appealed to. We see it in Roman Catholic countries, where the music and the paintings draw in many to worship, whom your quaker spirit of unsensualising would have kept out. — You, yourself, have a pretty collection of paintings — but confess to me, whether, walking in your gallery at Sandham,[1] among those clear Vandykes,[2] or among the Paul Potters[3] in the ante-room, you ever felt your bosom glow with an elegant delight, at all comparable to *that* you have it in your power to experience most evenings over a well-arranged assortment of the court-cards? — the pretty antic habits, like heralds in a procession — the gay triumph-assuring scarlets — the contrasting deadly-killing sables — the 'hoary majesty of spades' — Pam in all his glory! — [4]

"All these might be dispensed with; and

---

[1] He edited Pope in 1806.   [2] a variety of ombre   [3] Cf. p. 279, n. 4   [4] Cf. p. 279, ll. 25ff.   [5] a term in quadrille for a hand able to take all the tricks   [6] a famous historian of Italy (1469-1527)   [7] the knave turned, in cribbage

[1] an imaginary mansion   [2] pictures by the famous Dutch portrait painter, Sir Anthony Vandyke (1599-1641)   [3] Paul Potter, a Dutch painter of animals (1625-54)   [4] Cf. *Rape of the Lock*, iii, 56, 61.

with their naked names upon the drab paste-board, the game might go on very well, pic-tureless; but the *beauty* of cards would be extinguished forever. Stripped of all that is imaginative in them, they must degenerate into mere gambling. Imagine a dull deal board, or drum head, to spread them on, in-stead of that nice verdant carpet[1] (next to nature's), fittest arena for those courtly com-batants to play their gallant jousts and tour-neys in! — Exchange those delicately-turned ivory markers — (work of Chinese artist, unconscious of their symbol, — or as pro-fanely slighting their true application as the arrantest Ephesian journeyman[2] that turned out those little shrines for the goddess) — exchange them for little bits of leather (our ancestors' money), or chalk and a slate!" —

The old lady, with a smile, confessed the soundness of my logic; and to her approbation of my arguments on her favourite topic that evening I have always fancied myself indebted for the legacy of a curious cribbage-board, made of the finest Sienna marble, which her maternal uncle (old Walter Plumer, whom I have elsewhere celebrated) brought with him from Florence: — this, and a trifle of five hundred pounds, came to me at her death.

The former bequest (which I do not least value) I have kept with religious care; though she herself, to confess a truth, was never greatly taken with cribbage. It was an essen-tially vulgar game, I have heard her say, — disputing with her uncle, who was very par-tial to it. She could never heartily bring her mouth to pronounce "*Go*," or "*That's a go*." She called it an ungrammatical game. The pegging teased her. I once knew her to for-feit a rubber (a five-dollar stake) because she would not take advantage of the turn-up knave, which would have given it her, but which she must have claimed by the disgrace-ful tenure of declaring "*two for his heels*." There is something extremely genteel in this sort of self-denial. Sarah Battle was a gentle-woman born.

Piquet she held the best game at the cards for two persons, though she would ridicule the pedantry of the terms — such as pique — re-pique — the capot — they savoured (she thought) of affectation. But games for two, or even three, she never greatly cared for. She loved the quadrate, or square. She would

argue thus: — Cards are warfare: the ends are gain, with glory. But cards are war, in disguise of a sport: when single adversaries encounter, the ends proposed are too palpable. By themselves, it is too close a fight; with spectators, it is not much bettered. No looker-on can be interested, except for a bet, and then it is a mere affair of money; he cares not for your luck *sympathetically*, or for your play. — Three are still worse; a mere naked war of every man against every man, as in cribbage, without league or alliance; or a rotation of petty and contradictory interests, a succession of heartless leagues, and not much more hearty infractions of them, as in tradrille.[1] — But in square games (*she meant whist*), all that is possible to be attained in card-playing is accomplished. There are the incentives of profit with honour, common to every species — though the *latter* can be but very imperfectly enjoyed in those other games, where the spectator is only feebly a partici-pator. But the parties in whist are specta-tors and principals too. They are a theatre to themselves, and a looker-on is not wanted. He is rather worse than nothing, and an im-pertinence. Whist abhors neutrality, or in-terests beyond its sphere. You glory in some surprising stroke of skill or fortune, not be-cause a cold — or even an interested — by-stander witnesses it, but because your *partner* sympathises in the contingency. You win for two. You triumph for two. Two are exalted. Two again are mortified; which divides their disgrace, as the conjunction doubles (by taking off the invidiousness) your glories. Two losing to two are better recon-ciled, than one to one in that close butchery. The hostile feeling is weakened by multiply-ing the channels. War becomes a civil game. By such reasonings as these the old lady was accustomed to defend her favourite pastime.

No inducement could ever prevail upon her to play at any game, where chance entered into the composition, *for nothing*. Chance, she would argue — and here again, admire the subtlety of her conclusion; — chance is nothing, but where something else depends upon it. It is obvious, that cannot be *glory*. What rational cause of exultation could it give to a man to turn up size[2] ace a hundred times together by himself? or before specta-tors, where no stake was depending? — Make

---

[1] Cf. *ibid.*, iii, 44, 80.　[2] Cf. *Acts*, xix: 24, 25.

[1] a variety of ombre　[2] six

a lottery of a hundred thousand tickets with
but one fortunate number — and what possible principle of our nature, except stupid
wonderment, could it gratify to gain that
number as many times successively without a
prize? Therefore she disliked the mixture of
chance in backgammon, where it was not
played for money. She called it foolish, and
those people idiots, who were taken with a
lucky hit under such circumstances. Games
of pure skill were as little to her fancy.
Played for a stake, they were a mere system
of overreaching. Played for glory, they were
a mere setting of one man's wit, — his memory, or combination-faculty rather — against
another's; like a mock-engagement at a
review, bloodless and profitless. She could
not conceive a *game* wanting the spritely
infusion of chance, the handsome excuses
of good fortune. Two people playing at
chess in a corner of a room, whilst whist was
stirring in the centre, would inspire her with
insufferable horror and ennui. Those well-
cut similitudes of Castles and Knights, the
imagery of the board, she would argue (and
I think in this case justly), were entirely
misplaced and senseless. Those hardhead
contests can in no instance ally with the fancy.
They reject form and colour. A pencil and
dry slate (she used to say) were the proper
arena for such combatants.

To those puny objectors against cards, as
nurturing the bad passions, she would retort,
that man is a gaming animal. He must be
always trying to get the better in something
or other: — that this passion can scarcely be
more safely expended than upon a game at
cards: that cards are a temporary illusion;
in truth, a mere drama; for we do but *play*
at being mightily concerned, where a few idle
shillings are at stake, yet, during the illusion,
we *are* as mightily concerned as those whose
stake is crowns and kingdoms. They are a
sort of dream-fighting; much ado; great
battling, and little bloodshed; mighty means
for disproportioned ends: quite as diverting,
and a great deal more innoxious, than many
of those more serious *games* of life, which men
play without esteeming them to be such.

With great deference to the old lady's judgment in these matters, I think I have experienced some moments in my life when playing
at cards *for nothing* has even been agreeable.
When I am in sickness, or not in the best
spirits, I sometimes call for the cards, and

play a game at piquet *for love* with my cousin
Bridget [1] — Bridget Elia.

I grant there is something sneaking in it;
but with a tooth-ache, or a sprained ankle, —
when you are subdued and humble, — you
are glad to put up with an inferior spring
of action.

There is such a thing in nature, I am convinced, as *sick whist*.

I grant it is not the highest style of man — I
deprecate the manes [2] of Sarah Battle — she
lives not, alas! to whom I should apologise.

At such times, those *terms* which my old
friend objected to, come in as something ad-
missible — I love to get a tierce or a quatorze,
though they mean nothing. I am subdued to
an inferior interest. Those shadows of winning amuse me.

That last game I had with my sweet cousin
(I capotted her) — (dare I tell thee, how
foolish I am?) — I wished it might have lasted
forever, though we gained nothing, and lost
nothing, though it was a mere shade of play:
I would be content to go on in that idle folly
for ever. The pipkin should be ever boiling,
that was to prepare the gentle lenitive to my
foot, which Bridget was doomed to apply after
the game was over: and, as I do not much
relish appliances, there it should ever bubble.
Bridget and I should be ever playing.

A CHAPTER ON EARS

I have no ear. —

Mistake me not, Reader — nor imagine that
I am by nature destitute of those exterior
twin appendages, hanging ornaments, and
(architecturally speaking) handsome volutes [3]
to the human capital. Better my mother had
never borne me. — I am, I think, rather delicately than copiously provided with those
conduits; and I feel no disposition to envy
the mule for his plenty, or the mole for her
exactness, in those ingenious labyrinthine inlets — those indispensable side-intelligencers.

Neither have I incurred, or done anything
to incur, with Defoe, that hideous disfigure-
ment, which constrained him to draw upon
assurance — to feel "quite unabashed," [4] and

---

[1] that is, his sister Mary [2] spirit [3] spiral ornaments on the capital of an Ionic pillar [4] "Earless, on high, stood unabashed Defoe," *Dunciad*,
ii, 147; but Defoe did *not* lose his ears.

at ease upon that article. I was never, I thank my stars, in the pillory; nor, if I read them aright, is it within the compass of my destiny, that I ever should be.

When therefore I say that I have no ear, you will understand me to mean — *for music*. To say that this heart never melted at the concord of sweet sounds, would be a foul self-libel. *"Water parted from the sea"*[1] never fails to move it strangely. So does *"In infancy."*[1] But they were used to be sung at her harpsichord (the old-fashioned instrument in vogue in those days) by a gentlewoman — the gentlest, sure, that ever merited the appellation — the sweetest — why should I hesitate to name Mrs. S——, once the blooming Fanny Weatheral of the Temple[2] — who had power to thrill the soul of Elia, small imp as he was, even in his long coats; and to make him glow, tremble, and blush with a passion, that not faintly indicated the dayspring of that absorbing sentiment which was afterwards destined to overwhelm and subdue his nature quite for Alice W——n.[3]

I even think that *sentimentally* I am disposed to harmony. But *organically* I am incapable of a tune. I have been practising *"God save the King"* all my life; whistling and humming of it over to myself in solitary corners; and am not yet arrived, they tell me, within many quavers of it. Yet hath the loyalty of Elia never been impeached.

I am not without suspicion, that I have an undeveloped faculty of music within me. For, thrumming, in my wild way, on my friend A.'s piano, the other morning, while he was engaged in an adjoining parlour, — on his return he was pleased to say, *"he thought it could not be the maid!"* On his first surprise at hearing the keys touched in somewhat an airy and masterful way, not dreaming of me, his suspicions had lighted on *Jenny*. But a grace, snatched from a superior refinement, soon convinced him that some being — technically perhaps deficient, but higher informed from a principle common to all the fine arts — had swayed the keys to a mood which Jenny, with all her (less cultivated) enthusiasm, could never have elicited from them. I mention this as a proof of my friend's pene-

tration, and not with any view of disparaging Jenny.

Scientifically I could never be made to understand (yet have I taken some pains) what a note in music is; or how one note should differ from another. Much less in voices can I distinguish a soprano from a tenor. Only sometimes the thorough-bass I contrive to guess at, from its being supereminently harsh and disagreeable. I tremble, however, for my misapplication of the simplest terms of *that* which I disclaim. While I profess my ignorance, I scarce know what to *say* I am ignorant of. I hate, perhaps, by misnomers. *Sostenuto* and *adagio* stand in the like relation of obscurity to me; and *Sol, Fa, Mi, Re,* is as conjuring as *Baralipton.*[1]

It is hard to stand alone in an age like this, — (constituted to the quick and critical perception of all harmonious combinations, I verily believe, beyond all preceding ages, since Jubal[2] stumbled upon the gamut,) to remain, as it were, singly unimpressible to the magic influences of an art, which is said to have such an especial stroke at soothing, elevating, and refining the passions. — Yet, rather than break the candid current of my confessions, I must avow to you that I have received a great deal more pain than pleasure from this so cried-up faculty.

I am constitutionally susceptible of noises. A carpenter's hammer, in a warm summer noon, will fret me into more than midsummer madness. But those unconnected, unset sounds are nothing to the measured malice of music. The ear is passive to those single strokes; willingly enduring stripes, while it hath no task to con. To music it cannot be passive. It will strive — mine at least will — spite of its inaptitude, to thrid the maze; like an unskilled eye painfully poring upon hieroglyphics. I have sat through an Italian Opera, till, for sheer pain, and inexplicable anguish, I have rushed out into the noisiest places of the crowded streets, to solace myself with sounds, which I was not obliged to follow, and get rid of the distracting torment of endless, fruitless, barren attention! I take refuge in the unpretending assemblage of honest common-life sounds; — and the purgatory of the Enraged Musician[3] becomes my paradise.

---

[1] Songs in *Artaxerxes*, an opera he heard when six years old — his first play   [2] Cf. Spenser's *Prothalamion*, ll. 132–5.   [3] a feigned name for the love of his youth

[1] technical term in logic   [2] the traditional inventor of musical instruments, cf. *Genesis*, iv: 21.   [3] a picture by William Hogarth (1697-1764)

I have sat at an Oratorio (that profanation
of the purposes of the cheerful playhouse)
watching the faces of the auditory in the pit
(what a contrast to Hogarth's Laughing Audience!) immovable, or affecting some faint
emotion — till (as some have said, that our
occupations in the next world will be but a
shadow of what delighted us in this) I have
imagined myself in some cold Theatre in
Hades, where some of the *forms* of the earthly
one should be kept us, with none of the
enjoyment ; or like that

> — Party in a parlour
> All silent, and all damned.[1]

Above all, those insufferable concertos, and
pieces of music, as they are called, do plague
and embitter my apprehension. — Words are
something ; but to be exposed to an endless
battery of mere sounds ; to be long a-dying ;
to lie stretched upon a rack of roses ; to keep
up languor by unintermitted effort ; to pile
honey upon sugar, and sugar upon honey, to
an interminable tedious sweetness ; to fill up
sound with feeling, and strain ideas to keep
pace with it ; to gaze on empty frames, and
be forced to make the pictures for yourself ;
to read a book, *all stops*,[2] and be obliged to
supply the verbal matter ; to invent extempore tragedies to answer to the vague gestures
of an inexplicable rambling mime [3] — these are
faint shadows of what I have undergone from
a series of the ablest-executed pieces of this
empty *instrumental music*.

I deny not, that in the opening of a concert,
I have experienced something vastly lulling
and agreeable : — afterwards followeth the
languor and the oppression. Like that dis-
appointing book in Patmos ;[4] or, like the
comings on of melancholy, described by Burton, doth music make her first insinuating
approaches : — "Most pleasant it is to such
as are melancholy given, to walk alone in
some solitary grove, betwixt wood and water,
by some brook side, and to meditate upon
some delightsome and pleasant subject, which
shall affect him most, *amabilis insania*,[5] and
mentis gratissimus error.[6] A most incomparable delight to build castles in the air, to go

smiling to themselves, acting an infinite
variety of parts, which they suppose, and
strongly imagine, they act, or that they see
done. — So delightsome these toys [1] at first,
they could spend whole days and nights without sleep, even whole years in such contem-
plations, and fantastical meditations, which
are like so many dreams, and will hardly
be drawn from them — winding and unwind-
ing themselves as so many clocks, and still
pleasing their humours, until at the last the
scene turns upon a sudden, and they being
now habitated to such meditations and solitary places, can endure no company, can think
of nothing but harsh and distasteful subjects.
Fear, sorrow, suspicion, *subrusticus pudor*,[2]
discontent, cares, and weariness of life, surprise them on a sudden, and they can think
of nothing else : continually suspecting, no
sooner are their eyes open, but this infernal
plague of melancholy seizeth on them, and
terrifies their souls, representing some dismal object to their minds ; which now, by
no means, no labour, no persuasions, they
can avoid, they cannot be rid of, they cannot
resist."

Something like this "scene turning" I have
experienced at the evening parties, at the
house of my good Catholic friend *Nov——* ;[3]
who, by the aid of a capital organ, himself
the most finished of players, converts his
drawing-room into a chapel, his week days
into Sundays, and these latter into minor
heavens.

When my friend commences upon one of
those solemn anthems, which peradventure
struck upon my heedless ear, rambling in the
side aisles of the dim Abbey, some five-and-
thirty years since, waking a new sense, and
putting a soul of old religion into my young
apprehension — (whether it be *that*, in which
the Psalmist, weary of the persecutions of
bad men, wisheth to himself dove's wings —
or *that other* which, with a like measure of so-
briety and pathos, inquireth by what means
the young man shall best cleanse his mind) —
a holy calm pervadeth me. — I am for the
time

> — rapt above earth,
> And possess joys not promised at my birth.[4]

---

[1] From a suppressed stanza of Wordsworth's
Peter Bell. [2] punctuation marks [3] a pantomim-
ist [4] Cf. *Revelation*, x : 10 [5] pleasant lunacy
[6] most delightful mental delusion

[1] trifles [2] almost clownish shame [3] Vincent
Novello, organist of the Portuguese embassy
chapel [4] By an unknown author ; quoted in
Walton's *Complete Angler*.

But when this master of the spell, not content to have laid a soul prostrate, goes on, in his power, to inflict more bliss than lies in her capacity to receive — impatient to overcome her "earthly" with his "heavenly," — still pouring in, for protracted hours, fresh waves and fresh from the sea of sound, or from that inexhausted *German* ocean,[1] above which, in triumphant progress, dolphin-seated, ride those Arions [2] *Haydn* and *Mozart*, with their attendant Tritons,[3] *Bach, Beethoven*, and a countless tribe, whom to attempt to reckon up would but plunge me again in the deeps, — I stagger under the weight of harmony, reeling to and fro at my wits' end ; — clouds, as of frankincense, oppress me — priests, altars, censers dazzle before me — the genius of *his* religion hath me in her toils — a shadowy triple tiara invests the brow of my friend, late so naked, so ingenuous — he is Pope, — and by him sits, like as in the anomaly of dreams, a she-Pope too, — tri-coroneted like himself ! — I am converted, and yet a Protestant ; — at once *malleus hereticorum*,[4] and myself grand heresiarch : or three heresies centre in my person : — I am Marcion, Ebion, and Cerinthus [5] — Gog and Magog [6] — what not ? — till the coming in of the friendly supper-tray dissipates the figment, and a draught of true Lutheran beer (in which chiefly my friend shows himself no bigot) at once reconciles me to the rationalities of a purer faith ; and restores to me the genuine unterrifying aspects of my pleasant-countenanced host and hostess.

THE OLD FAMILIAR FACES

I have had playmates, I have had companions,
In my days of childhood, in my joyful school-
  days ;
All, all are gone, the old familiar faces.

I have been laughing, I have been carousing,
Drinking late, sitting late, with my bosom
  cronies ;
All, all are gone, the old familiar faces.   6

[1] of music [2] Arion, a Greek lyric poet, is fabled to have been thrown into the sea by sailors and carried safely ashore by dolphins who had gathered to listen to his music. [3] Cf. note on Wordsworth's sonnet, *The world is too much with us*, l. 14. [4] Hammer of Heretics, title of a book by Johann Faber (1478-1541) [5] typical heresiarchs [6] Cf. *Revelation*, xx : 8

I loved a love once, fairest among women ;
Closed are her doors on me, I must not see
  her —
All, all are gone, the old familiar faces.

I have a friend,[1] a kinder friend has no man ;
Like an ingrate, I left my friend abruptly ;
Left him, to muse on the old familiar faces. 12

Ghost-like I paced round the haunts of my
  childhood,
Earth seemed a desert I was bound to traverse,
Seeking to find the old familiar faces.

Friend of my bosom,[2] thou more than a
  brother,
Why wert not thou born in my father's
  dwelling ?
So might we talk of the old familiar faces — 18

How some they have died, and some they
  have left me,
And some are taken from me ; all are departed ;
All, all are gone, the old familiar faces.

THOMAS CAMPBELL (1777-1844)

YE MARINERS OF ENGLAND

A NAVAL ODE

Ye mariners of England
That guard our native seas,
Whose flag has braved a thousand years
The battle and the breeze !
Your glorious standard launch again
To match another foe,
And sweep through the deep,
While the stormy winds do blow ;
While the battle rages loud and long,
And the stormy winds do blow.   10

The spirits of your fathers
Shall start from every wave ! —
For the deck it was their field of fame,
And Ocean was their grave :
Where Blake and mighty Nelson fell
Your manly hearts shall glow,
As ye sweep through the deep,
While the stormy winds do blow ;
While the battle rages loud and long,
And the stormy winds do blow.   20

[1] Charles Lloyd   [2] Coleridge

Britannia needs no bulwark,
No towers along the steep;
Her march is o'er the mountain waves,
Her home is on the deep.
With thunders from her native oak
She quells the floods below —
As they roar on the shore,
When the stormy winds do blow;
When the battle rages loud and long,
And the stormy winds do blow.   30

The meteor flag of England
Shall yet terrific burn,
Till danger's troubled night depart
And the star of peace return.
Then, then, ye ocean-warriors!
Our song and feast shall flow
To the fame of your name,
When the storm has ceased to blow;
When the fiery fight is heard no more,
And the storm has ceased to blow.   40

BATTLE OF THE BALTIC

Of Nelson and the North
Sing the glorious day's renown,
When to battle fierce came forth
All the might of Denmark's crown,
And her arms along the deep proudly shone;
By each gun the lighted brand
In a bold determin'd hand,
And the Prince of all the land
Led them on.   9

Like leviathans afloat
Lay their bulwarks on the brine,
While the sign of battle flew
On the lofty British line:
It was ten of April morn by the chime:
As they drifted on their path,
There was silence deep as death,
And the boldest held his breath
For a time.   18

But the might of England flushed
To anticipate the scene,
And her van the fleeter rushed
O'er the deadly space between —
"Hearts of oak," our captains cried, when
    each gun
From its adamantine lips
Spread a death-shade round the ships,
Like the hurricane eclipse
Of the sun.   27

Again! again! again!
And the havoc did not slack,
Till a feeble cheer the Dane
To our cheering sent us back; —
Their shots along the deep slowly boom: —
Then ceased — and all is wail,
As they strike the shattered sail,
Or in conflagration pale
Light the gloom.   36

Out spoke the victor then,
As he hailed them o'er the wave;
"Ye are brothers! ye are men!
And we conquer but to save;
So peace instead of death let us bring:
But yield, proud foe, thy fleet
With the crews at England's feet,
And make submission meet
To our King."   45

Then Denmark blest our chief,
That he gave her wounds repose;
And the sounds of joy and grief,
From her people wildly rose,
As death withdrew his shades from the day;
While the sun looked smiling bright
O'er a wide and woeful sight,
Where the fires of funeral light
Died away.   54

Now joy, old England, raise!
For the tidings of thy might,
By the festal cities' blaze,
While the wine cup shines in light;
And yet amidst that joy and uproar,
Let us think of them that sleep,
Full many a fathom deep,
By thy wild and stormy steep,
Elsinore!   63

Brave hearts! to Britain's pride
Once so faithful and so true,
On the deck of fame that died, —
With the gallant good Riou,[1]
Soft sigh the winds of heaven o'er their
    grave!
While the billow mournful rolls,
And the mermaid's song condoles,
Singing glory to the souls
Of the brave!   72

[1] Capt. Edward Riou, distinguished for his skill
and courage in this battle, was cut in two by a
cannon shot.

THOMAS MOORE (1779–1852)

THE TIME I'VE LOST IN WOOING

The time I've lost in wooing,
In watching and pursuing
 The light, that lies
 In woman's eyes,
Has been my heart's undoing.
Tho' Wisdom oft has sought me,
I scorn'd the lore she brought me,
 My only books
 Were woman's looks,
And folly's all they've taught me.   10

Her smile when Beauty granted,
I hung with gaze enchanted,
 Like him the Sprite,
 Whom maids by night
Oft meet in glen that's haunted.
Like him, too, Beauty won me,
But while her eyes were on me;
 If once their ray
 Was turned away,
Oh, winds could not outrun me.   20

And are those follies going?
And is my proud heart growing
 Too cold or wise
 For brilliant eyes
Again to set it glowing?
No, vain, alas! th' endeavour
From bonds so sweet to sever;
 Poor Wisdom's chance
 Against a glance
Is now as weak as ever.   30

OFT, IN THE STILLY NIGHT

Oft, in the stilly night,
 Ere Slumber's chain has bound me,
Fond Memory brings the light
 Of other days around me;
  The smiles, the tears,
  Of boyhood's years,
 The words of love then spoken;
  The eyes that shone,
  Now dimm'd and gone,
 The cheerful hearts now broken!   10
Thus, in the stilly night,
 Ere Slumber's chain has bound me,
Sad Memory brings the light
 Of other days around me.

When I remember all
 The friends, so link'd together,
I've seen around me fall,
 Like leaves in wintry weather;
  I feel like one
  Who treads alone   20
 Some banquet-hall deserted,
  Whose lights are fled,
  Whose garlands dead,
 And all but he departed!
Thus, in the stilly night,
 Ere Slumber's chain has bound me,
Sad Memory brings the light
 Of other days around me.

'TIS THE LAST ROSE OF SUMMER

'Tis the last rose of summer,
 Left blooming alone;
All her lovely companions
 Are faded and gone;
No flower of her kindred,
 No rosebud, is nigh
To reflect back her blushes,
 Or give sigh for sigh!   8

I'll not leave thee, thou lone one,
 To pine on the stem;
Since the lovely are sleeping,
 Go, sleep thou with them;
Thus kindly I scatter
 Thy leaves o'er the bed
Where thy mates of the garden
 Lie scentless and dead.   16

So soon may I follow,
 When friendships decay,
And from love's shining circle
 The gems drop away!
When true hearts lie withered,
 And fond ones are flown,
O, who would inhabit
 This bleak world alone!   24

THE HARP THAT ONCE THROUGH TARA'S HALLS

The harp that once through Tara's halls [1]
 The soul of music shed,
Now hangs as mute on Tara's walls
 As if that soul were fled.

[1] the palace of the high kings of Ireland

So sleeps the pride of former days,
　　So glory's thrill is o'er,
And hearts that once beat high for praise
　　Now feel that pulse no more !　　8

No more to chiefs and ladies bright
　　The harp of Tara swells;
The chord alone that breaks at night
　　Its tale of ruin tells.
Thus Freedom now so seldom wakes,
　　The only throb she gives
Is when some heart indignant breaks,
　　To show that still she lives.　　16

LEIGH HUNT (1784–1859)

RONDEAU

Jenny kissed me when we met,
　　Jumping from the chair she sat in;
Time, you thief, who love to get
　　Sweets into your list, put that in:
Say I'm weary, say I'm sad,　　5
　　Say that health and wealth have missed me,
Say I'm growing old, but add,
　　Jenny kissed me.

FAIRIES' SONG

We the fairies blithe and antic,
Of dimensions not gigantic,
Though the moonshine mostly keep us
Oft in orchards frisk and peep us.　　4

Stolen sweets are always sweeter;
Stolen kisses much completer;
Stolen looks are nice in chapels;
Stolen, stolen be your apples.　　8

When to bed the world are bobbing,
Then's the time for orchard-robbing;
Yet the fruit were scarce worth peeling
Were it not for stealing, stealing.　　12

THOMAS DE QUINCEY (1785–1859)

FROM CONFESSIONS OF AN ENGLISH OPIUM–EATER

INTRODUCTION TO THE PAINS OF OPIUM

If any man, poor or rich, were to say that he would tell us what had been the happiest day in his life, and the why and the wherefore, I suppose that we should all cry out, Hear him! hear him! As to the happiest day, that must be very difficult for any wise man to name; because any event, that could occupy so distinguished a place in a man's retrospect of his life, or be entitled to have shed a special felicity on any one day, ought to be of such an enduring character, as that (accidents apart) it should have continued to shed the same felicity, or one not distinguishably less, on many years together. To the happiest *lustrum*, however, or even to the happiest *year*, it may be allowed to any man to point without discountenance from wisdom. This year, in my case, reader, was the one which we have now reached; though it stood, I confess, as a parenthesis between years of a gloomier character. It was a year of brilliant water (to speak after the manner of jewellers), set, as it were, and insulated, in the gloom and cloudy melancholy of opium. Strange as it may sound, I had a little before this time descended suddenly, and without any considerable effort, from three hundred and twenty grains of opium (that is, eight thousand drops of laudanum) per day, to forty grains, or one-eighth part. Instantaneously, and as if by magic, the cloud of profoundest melancholy which rested upon my brain, like some black vapours that I have seen roll away from the summits of mountains, drew off in one day; passed off with its murky banners as simultaneously as a ship that has been stranded, and is floated off by a spring tide, —

That moveth altogether, if it move at all.[1]

Now, then, I was again happy; I now took only one thousand drops of laudanum per day, — and what was that? A latter spring had come to close up the season of youth:

---

[1] Wordsworth, *Resolution and Independence*, l. 77; *altogether* should be *all together*

my brain performed its functions as healthily as ever before. I read Kant[1] again, and again I understood him, or fancied that I did. Again my feelings of pleasure expanded themselves to all around me; and, if any man from Oxford or Cambridge, or from neither, had been announced to me in my unpretending cottage, I should have welcomed him with as sumptuous a reception as so poor a man could offer. Whatever else was wanting to a wise man's happiness, of laudanum I would have given him as much as he wished, and in a golden cup. And, by the way, now that I speak of giving laudanum away, I remember, about this time, a little incident, which I mention, because, trifling as it was, the reader will soon meet it again in my dreams, which it influenced more fearfully than could be imagined. One day a Malay knocked at my door. What business a Malay could have to transact amongst English mountains, I cannot conjecture; but possibly he was on his road to a seaport about forty miles distant.

The servant who opened the door to him was a young girl, born and bred amongst the mountains, who had never seen an Asiatic dress of any sort: his turban, therefore, confounded her not a little; and as it turned out that his attainments in English were exactly of the same extent as hers in the Malay, there seemed to be an impassable gulf fixed between all communication of ideas, if either party had happened to possess any. In this dilemma, the girl, recollecting the reputed learning of her master (and, doubtless, giving me credit for a knowledge of all the languages of the earth, besides, perhaps, a few of the lunar ones), came and gave me to understand that there was a sort of demon below, whom she clearly imagined that my art would exorcise from the house. I did not immediately go down; but when I did, the group which presented itself, arranged as it was by accident, though not very elaborate, took hold of my fancy and my eye in a way that none of the statuesque attitudes exhibited in the ballets at the opera-house, though so ostentatiously complex, had ever done. In a cottage kitchen but panelled on the wall with dark wood, that from age and rubbing resembled oak, and looking more like a rustic hall of entrance than a kitchen, stood the Malay, his turban and loose trousers of dingy white relieved upon the dark panelling; he had placed himself nearer to the girl than she seemed to relish, though her native spirit of mountain intrepidity contended with the feeling of simple awe which her countenance expressed, as she gazed upon the tiger-cat before her. And a more striking picture there could not be imagined, than the beautiful English face of the girl, and its exquisite fairness, together with her erect and independent attitude, contrasted with the sallow and bilious skin of the Malay, enamelled or veneered with mahogany by marine air, his small, fierce, restless eyes, thin lips, slavish gestures, and adorations. Half hidden by the ferocious-looking Malay, was a little child from a neighbouring cottage, who had crept in after him, and was now in the act of reverting its head and gazing upwards at the turban and the fiery eyes beneath it, whilst with one hand he caught at the dress of the young woman for protection.

My knowledge of the Oriental tongues is not remarkably extensive, being, indeed, confined to two words, — the Arabic word for barley, and the Turkish for opium (madjoon), which I have learnt from Anastasius.[1] And, as I had neither a Malay dictionary, nor even Adelung's *Mithridates*,[2] which might have helped me to a few words, I addressed him in some lines from the Iliad; considering that, of such language as I possessed, the Greek, in point of longitude, came geographically nearest to an Oriental one. He worshipped me in a devout manner, and replied in what I suppose was Malay. In this way I saved my reputation with my neighbours; for the Malay had no means of betraying the secret. He lay down upon the floor for about an hour, and then pursued his journey. On his departure, I presented him with a piece of opium. To him, as an Orientalist, I concluded that opium must be familiar, and the expression of his face convinced me that it was. Nevertheless, I was struck with some little consternation when I saw him suddenly raise his hand to his mouth, and (in the schoolboy phrase) bolt the whole, divided into three pieces, at one mouthful. The quantity was enough to kill three dragoons and their horses, and I felt some alarm for the poor creature; but what could be done? I had given him

---

[1] a profound German philosopher (1724–1804)

[1] *Anastasius: or, Memoirs of a Greek* (1819) by Thomas Hope [2] *Mithridates, oder allgemeine Sprachenkunde* (1806), by J. C. Adelung, contains specimens of many languages.

the opium in compassion for his solitary life, on recollecting that, if he had travelled on foot from London, it must be nearly three weeks since he could have exchanged a thought with any human being. I could not think of violating the laws of hospitality by having him seized and drenched with an emetic, and thus frightening him into a notion that we were going to sacrifice him to some English idol. No; there was clearly no help for it. He took his leave, and for some days I felt anxious; but, as I never heard of any Malay being found dead, I became convinced that he was used to opium, and that I must have done him the service I designed, by giving him one night of respite from the pains of wandering.

This incident I have digressed to mention, because this Malay (partly from the picturesque exhibition he assisted to frame, partly from the anxiety I connected with his image for some days) fastened afterwards upon my dreams, and brought other Malays with him worse than himself, that ran "a-muck" at me, and led me into a world of troubles. But, to quit this episode, and to return to my intercalary year of happiness. I have said already, that on a subject so important to us all as happiness, we should listen with pleasure to any man's experience or experiments, even though he were but a ploughboy, who cannot be supposed to have ploughed very deep in such an intractable soil as that of human pains and pleasures, or to have conducted his researches upon any very enlightened principles. But I, who have taken happiness, both in a solid and a liquid shape, both boiled and unboiled, both East India and Turkey, — who have conducted my experiments upon this interesting subject with a sort of galvanic battery, — and have, for the general benefit of the world, inoculated myself, as it were, with the poison of eight hundred drops of laudanum per day (just for the same reason as a French surgeon inoculated himself lately with a cancer, — an English one, twenty years ago, with plague, — and a third, I know not of what nation, with hydrophobia), — I, it will be admitted, must surely know what happiness is, if anybody does. And therefore I will here lay down an analysis of happiness; and, as the most interesting mode of communicating it, I will give it, not didactically, but wrapt up and involved in a picture of one evening, as I spent every evening during the intercalary year when laudanum, though taken daily, was to me no more than the elixir of pleasure. This done, I shall quit the subject of happiness altogether, and pass to a very different one, — the *pains of opium.*

Let there be a cottage, standing in a valley, eighteen miles from any town; no spacious valley, but about two miles long by three quarters of a mile in average width, — the benefit of which provision is, that all the families resident within its circuit will compose, as it were, one larger household, personally familiar to your eye, and more or less interesting to your affections. Let the mountains be real mountains, between three and four thousand feet high, and the cottage a real cottage, not (as a witty author has it) "a cottage with a double coach-house"; let it be, in fact (for I must abide by the actual scene), a white cottage, embowered with flowering shrubs, so chosen as to unfold a succession of flowers upon the walls, and clustering around the windows, through all the months of spring, summer, and autumn; beginning, in fact, with May roses, and ending with jasmine. Let it, however, *not* be spring, nor summer, nor autumn; but winter, in its sternest shape. This is a most important point in the science of happiness. And I am surprised to see people overlook it, and think it matter of congratulation that winter is going, or, if coming, is not likely to be a severe one. On the contrary, I put up a petition, annually, for as much snow, hail, frost, or storm of one kind or other, as the skies can possibly afford us. Surely everybody is aware of the divine pleasures which attend a winter fireside, — candles at four o'clock, warm hearth-rugs, tea, a fair tea-maker, shutters closed, curtains flowing in ample draperies on the floor, whilst the wind and rain are raging audibly without.

And at the doors and windows seem to call
As heaven and earth they would together mell;
Yet the least entrance find they none at all;
Whence sweeter grows our rest secure in massy hall.
— *Castle of Indolence.*

All these are items in the description of a winter evening which must surely be familiar to everybody born in a high latitude. And it is evident that most of these delicacies, like ice-cream, require a very low temperature of the atmosphere to produce them: they are fruits which cannot be ripened without weather stormy or inclement, in some way or other. I am not "*particular,*" as people say, whether it be snow, or black frost, or wind so strong that (as Mr. —— says) "you may lean your back against it like a post." I can put up even with rain, provided that it rains cats and dogs; but something of the sort I must have; and if I have not, I think myself in a manner ill used: for why am I called on to pay so heavily for winter, in coals, and candles, and various privations that will occur even to gentlemen, if I am not to have the article good of its kind? No: a Canadian winter, for my money; or a Russian one, where every man is but a co-proprietor with the north wind in the fee-simple of his own ears. Indeed, so great an epicure am I in this matter, that I cannot relish a winter night fully, if it be much past St. Thomas' day,[1] and have degenerated into disgusting tendencies to vernal appearances; — no, it must be divided by a thick wall of dark nights from all return of light and sunshine. From the latter weeks of October to Christmas-eve, therefore, is the period during which happiness is in season, which, in my judgment, enters the room with the tea-tray; for tea, though ridiculed by those who are naturally of coarse nerves, or are become so from wine-drinking, and are not susceptible of influence from so refined a stimulant, will always be the favourite beverage of the intellectual; and, for my part, I would have joined Dr. Johnson in a *bellum internecinum*[2] against Jonas Hanway,[3] or any other impious person who should presume to disparage it. But here, to save myself the trouble of too much verbal description, I will introduce a painter, and give him directions for the rest of the picture. Painters do not like white cottages, unless a good deal weather-stained; but, as the reader now understands that it is a winter night, his services will not be required except for the inside of the house.

Paint me, then, a room seventeen feet by twelve, and not more than seven and a half feet high. This, reader, is somewhat ambitiously styled, in my family, the drawing-room; but being contrived "a double debt to pay,"[4] it is also, and more justly, termed the library; for it happens that books are the only article of property in which I am richer than my neighbours. Of these I have about five

thousand, collected gradually since my eighteenth year. Therefore, painter, put as many as you can into this room. Make it populous with books, and, furthermore, paint me a good fire; and furniture plain and modest, befitting the unpretending cottage of a scholar. And near the fire paint me a tea-table; and (as it is clear that no creature can come to see one, such a stormy night) place only two cups and saucers on the tea-tray; and, if you know how to paint such a thing symbolically, or otherwise, paint me an eternal tea-pot, — eternal *a parte ante*, and *a parte post;*[1] for I usually drink tea from eight o'clock at night to four in the morning. And, as it is very unpleasant to make tea, or to pour it out for one's self, paint me a lovely young woman, sitting at the table. Paint her arms like Aurora's,[2] and her smiles like Hebe's;[3] — but no, dear M., not even in jest let me insinuate that thy power to illuminate my cottage rests upon a tenure so perishable as mere personal beauty; or that the witchcraft of angelic smiles lies within the empire of any earthly pencil. Pass, then, my good painter, to something more within its power; and the next article brought forward should naturally be myself, — a picture of the Opium-eater, with his "little golden receptacle of the pernicious drug"[4] lying beside him on the table. As to the opium, I have no objection to see a picture of *that*, though I would rather see the original; you may paint it, if you choose; but I apprise you that no "little" receptacle would, even in 1816, answer *my* purpose, who was at a distance from the "stately Pantheon,"[5] and all druggists (mortal or otherwise). No: you may as well paint the real receptacle, which was not of gold, but of glass, and as much like a wine-decanter as possible. Into this you may put a quart of ruby-coloured laudanum; that, and a book of German metaphysics placed by its side, will sufficiently attest my being in the neighbourhood; but as to myself, there I demur. I admit that, naturally, I ought to occupy the foreground of the picture; that being the hero of the piece, or (if you choose) the criminal at the bar, my body

---

[1] Dec. 21 or Dec. 29   [2] war to the death   [3] a violent opponent of tea, who got into conflict on the subject with Dr. Johnson, who was a great tea-drinker   [4] Cf. *The Deserted Village*, l. 229

AE

---

[1] eternal from both directions [2] the goddess of morning [3] the goddess of eternal youth [4] Such as Anastasius had [5] Cf. Wordsworth, *The Power of Music*, ll. 3, 4; De Quincey bought his first opium from a druggist near the Pantheon, who seemed to him hardly mortal.

should be had into court. This seems reasonable; but why should I confess, on this point, to a painter? or, why confess at all? If the public (into whose private ear I am confidentially whispering my confessions, and not into any painter's) should chance to have framed some agreeable picture for itself of the Opium-eater's exterior, — should have ascribed to him, romantically, an elegant person, or a handsome face, why should I barbarously tear from it so pleasing a delusion, — pleasing both to the public and to me? No: paint me, if at all, according to your own fancy; and, as a painter's fancy should teem with beautiful creations, I cannot fail, in that way, to be a gainer. And now, reader, we have run through all the ten categories[1] of my condition, as it stood about 1816–1817, up to the middle of which latter year I judge myself to have been a happy man; and the elements of that happiness I have endeavoured to place before you, in the above sketch of the interior of a scholar's library, — in a cottage among the mountains, on a stormy winter evening.

But now farewell, a long farewell, to happiness, winter or summer! farewell to smiles and laughter! farewell to peace of mind! farewell to hope and to tranquil dreams, and to the blessed consolations of sleep! For more than three years and a half I am summoned away from these; I am now arrived at an Iliad of woes: for I have now to record

THE PAINS OF OPIUM

　　　. . . as when some great painter dips
His pencil in the gloom of earthquake and eclipse.
　　　　　Shelley's *Revolt of Islam* (V. 23).

*　　*　　*　　*　　*　　*　　*

I now pass to what is the main subject of these latter confessions, to the history and journal of what took place in my dreams; for these were the immediate and proximate cause of my acutest suffering.

The first notice I had of any important change going on in this part of my physical economy, was from the re-awaking of a state of eye generally incident to childhood, or exalted states of irritability. I know not whether my reader is aware that many children, perhaps most, have a power of painting,

as it were, upon the darkness, all sorts of phantoms: in some that power is simply a mechanic affection of the eye; others have a voluntary or semi-voluntary power to dismiss or summon them; or, as a child once said to me, when I questioned him on this matter, "I can tell them to go, and they go; but sometimes they come when I don't tell them to come." Whereupon I told him that he had almost as unlimited a command over apparitions as a Roman centurion over his soldiers. In the middle of 1817, I think it was, that this faculty became positively distressing to me: at night, when I lay awake in bed, vast processions passed along in mournful pomp; friezes of never-ending stories, that to my feelings were as sad and solemn as if they were stories drawn from times before Œdipus[1] or Priam,[2] before Tyre,[3] before Memphis.[4] And, at the same time, a corresponding change took place in my dreams; a theatre seemed suddenly opened and lighted up within my brain, which presented, nightly, spectacles of more than earthly splendour. And the four following facts may be mentioned, as noticeable at this time:

I. That, as the creative state of the eye increased, a sympathy seemed to arise between the waking and the dreaming states of the brain in one point, — that whatsoever I happened to call up and to trace by a voluntary act upon the darkness was very apt to transfer itself to my dreams; so that I feared to exercise this faculty; for, as Midas turned all things to gold, that yet baffled his hopes and defrauded his human desires, so whatsoever things capable of being visually represented I did but think of in the darkness, immediately shaped themselves into phantoms of the eye; and, by a process apparently no less inevitable, when thus once traced in faint and visionary colours, like writings in sympathetic ink, they were drawn out, by the fierce chemistry of my dreams, into insufferable splendour that fretted my heart.

II. For this, and all other changes in my dreams, were accompanied by deep-seated anxiety and gloomy melancholy, such as are wholly incommunicable by words. I seemed every night to descend — not metaphorically, but literally to descend — into chasms and

---

[1] Aristotle's ten classes into which all things may be distributed

[1] King of Thebes　[2] King of Troy　[3] already famous in the time of Solomon　[4] the ancient capital of Egypt

sunless abysses, depths below depths, from which it seemed hopeless that I could ever re-ascend. Nor did I, by waking, feel that I *had* re-ascended. This I do not dwell upon; because the state of gloom which attended these gorgeous spectacles, amounting at last to utter darkness, as of some suicidal despondency, cannot be approached by words.

III. The sense of space, and in the end the sense of time, were both powerfully affected. Buildings, landscapes, etc., were exhibited in proportions so vast as the bodily eye is not fitted to receive. Space swelled, and was amplified to an extent of unutterable infinity. This, however, did not disturb me so much as the vast expansion of time. I sometimes seemed to have lived for seventy or one hundred years in one night; nay, sometimes had feelings representative of a millennium, passed in that time, or, however, of a duration far beyond the limits of any human experience.

IV. The minutest incidents of childhood, or forgotten scenes of later years, were often revived. I could not be said to recollect them; for if I had been told of them when waking, I should not have been able to acknowledge them as parts of my past experience. But placed as they were before me, in dreams like intuitions, and clothed in all their evanescent circumstances and accompanying feelings, I *recognised* them instantaneously. I was once told by a near relative of mine, that having in her childhood fallen into a river, and being on the very verge of death but for the critical assistance which reached her, she saw in a moment her whole life, in its minutest incidents, arrayed before her simultaneously as in a mirror; and she had a faculty developed as suddenly for comprehending the whole and every part. This, from some opium experiences of mine, I can believe; I have, indeed, seen the same thing asserted twice in modern books, and accompanied by a remark which I am convinced is true, namely, that the dread book of account, which the Scriptures speak of, is, in fact, the mind of each individual. Of this, at least, I feel assured, that there is no such thing as *forgetting* possible to the mind; a thousand accidents may and will interpose a veil between our present consciousness and the secret inscriptions on the mind. Accidents of the same sort will also rend away this veil; but alike, whether veiled or unveiled, the inscription remains forever; just as the stars seem to withdraw before the com-

mon light of day, whereas, in fact, we all know that it is the light which is drawn over them as a veil; and that they are waiting to be revealed, when the obscuring daylight shall have withdrawn.

Having noticed these four facts as memorably distinguishing my dreams from those of health, I shall now cite a case illustrative of the first fact; and shall then cite any others that I remember, either in their chronological order, or any other that may give them more effect as pictures to the reader.

I had been in youth, and even since, for occasional amusement, a great reader of Livy, whom I confess that I prefer, both for style and matter, to any other of the Roman historians; and I had often felt as most solemn and appalling sounds, and most emphatically representative of the majesty of the Roman people, the two words so often occurring in Livy — *Consul Romanus ;* especially when the consul is introduced in his military character. I mean to say, that the words king, sultan, regent, etc., or any other titles of those who embody in their own persons the collective majesty of a great people, had less power over my reverential feelings. I had, also, though no great reader of history, made myself minutely and critically familiar with one period of English history, namely, the period of the Parliamentary War, having been attracted by the moral grandeur of some who figured in that day, and by the many interesting memoirs which survive those unquiet times. Both these parts of my lighter reading, having furnished me often with matter of reflection, now furnished me with matter for my dreams. Often I used to see, after painting upon the blank darkness, a sort of rehearsal whilst waking, a crowd of ladies, and perhaps a festival and dances. And I heard it said, or I said to myself, "These are English ladies from the unhappy times of Charles I. These are the wives and daughters of those who met in peace, and sat at the same tables, and were allied by marriage or by blood; and yet, after a certain day in August, 1642,[1] never smiled upon each other again, nor met but in the field of battle; and at Marston Moor, at Newbury, or at Naseby,[2] cut asunder all ties of love by the cruel sabre, and washed away in blood the memory of ancient friendship."

[1] August 22, 1642, when the war began   [2] battles of the Parliamentary War

The ladies danced, and looked as lovely as the court of George IV. Yet I knew, even in my dream, that they had been in the grave for nearly two centuries. This pageant would suddenly dissolve; and, at a clapping of hands, would be heard the heart-quaking sound of *Consul Romanus;* and immediately came "sweeping by,"[1] in gorgeous paludaments,[2] Paulus or Marius,[3] girt around by a company of centurions, with the crimson tunic hoisted on a spear, and followed by the *alalagmos*[4] of the Roman legions.

Many years ago, when I was looking over Piranesi's Antiquities of Rome, Mr. Coleridge, who was standing by, described to me a set of plates by that artist, called his *Dreams*,[5] and which record the scenery of his own visions during the delirium of a fever. Some of them (I describe only from memory of Mr. Coleridge's account) represented vast Gothic halls; on the floor of which stood all sorts of engines and machinery, wheels, cables, pulleys, levers, catapults, etc., expressive of enormous power put forth, and resistance overcome. Creeping along the sides of the walls, you perceived a staircase; and upon it, groping his way upwards, was Piranesi himself. Follow the stairs a little further, and you perceive it to come to a sudden, abrupt termination, without any balustrade, and allowing no step onwards to him who had reached the extremity, except into the depths below. Whatever is to become of poor Piranesi, you suppose, at least, that his labours must in some way terminate here. But raise your eyes, and behold a second flight of stairs still higher; on which again Piranesi is perceived, by this time standing on the very brink of the abyss. Again elevate your eye, and a still more aerial flight of stairs is beheld; and again is poor Piranesi busy on his aspiring labours; and so on, until the unfinished stairs and Piranesi both are lost in the upper gloom of the hall. With the same power of endless growth and self-reproduction did my architecture proceed in dreams. In the early stage of my malady, the splendours of my dreams were indeed chiefly architectural; and I beheld such pomp of cities and palaces as was never yet beheld by the waking eye, unless in the clouds. From a great modern poet I cite the part of a passage which

describes, as an appearance actually beheld in the clouds, what in many of its circumstances I saw frequently in sleep:

> The appearance, instantaneously disclosed,
> Was of a mighty city — boldly say
> A wilderness of building, sinking far
> And self-withdrawn into a wondrous depth,
> Far sinking into splendour — without end!
> Fabric it seemed of diamond, and of gold,
> With alabaster domes and silver spires,
> And blazing terrace upon terrace, high
> Uplifted; here, serene pavilions bright,
> In avenues disposed; there towers begirt
> With battlements that on their restless fronts
> Bore stars — illumination of all gems!
> By earthly nature had the effect been wrought
> Upon the dark materials of the storm
> Now pacified; on them, and on the coves,
> And mountain-steeps and summits, whereunto
> The vapours had receded — taking there
> Their station under a cerulean sky, etc., etc.[1]

The sublime circumstance — "battlements that on their *restless* fronts bore stars" — might have been copied from my architectural dreams, for it often occurred. We hear it reported of Dryden, and of Fuseli[2] in modern times, that they thought proper to eat raw meat for the sake of obtaining splendid dreams: how much better, for such a purpose, to have eaten opium, which yet I do not remember that any poet is recorded to have done, except the dramatist Shadwell;[3] and in ancient days, Homer is, I think, rightly reputed to have known the virtues of opium.

To my architecture succeeded dreams of lakes, and silvery expanses of water: these haunted me so much, that I feared (though possibly it will appear ludicrous to a medical man) that some dropsical state or tendency of the brain might thus be making itself (to use a metaphysical word) *objective*, and the sentient organ *project* itself as its own object. For two months I suffered greatly in my head — a part of my bodily structure which had hitherto been so clear from all touch or taint of weakness (physically, I mean), that I used to say of it, as the last Lord Orford[4] said of his stomach, that it seemed likely to survive the rest of my person. Till now I had never felt

---

[1] Cf. *Il Penseroso*, l. 98. [2] military cloaks [3] two famous consuls and generals [4] noise of the war-cries [5] There was no such publication.

[1] From Wordsworth's *Excursion* [2] a Swiss painter (1741–1825), who painted many subjects from Milton's *Paradise Lost* [3] a second-rate dramatist of the Restoration period [4] Horace Walpole, a distinguished dilettante (1717–97)

a headache even, or any the slightest pain, except rheumatic pains caused by my own folly. However, I got over this attack, though it must have been verging on something very dangerous.

The waters now changed their character, — from translucent lakes, shining like mirrors, they now became seas and oceans. And now came a tremendous change, which, unfolding itself slowly like a scroll, through many months, promised an abiding torment; and, in fact, it never left me until the winding up of my case. Hitherto the human face had often mixed in my dreams, but not despotically, nor with any special power of tormenting. But now that which I have called the tyranny of the human face, began to unfold itself. Perhaps some part of my London life might be answerable for this. Be that as it may, now it was that upon the rocking waters of the ocean the human face began to appear; the sea appeared paved with innumerable faces, upturned to the heavens; faces, imploring, wrathful, despairing, surged upwards by thousands, by myriads, by generations, by centuries: my agitation was infinite, my mind tossed and surged with the ocean.

May, 1818. — The Malay has been a fearful enemy for months. I have been every night, through his means, transported into Asiatic scenes. I know not whether others share in my feelings on this point; but I have often thought that if I were compelled to forego England, and to live in China, and among Chinese manners and modes of life and scenery, I should go mad. The causes of my horror lie deep, and some of them must be common to others. Southern Asia, in general, is the seat of awful images and associations. As the cradle of the human race, it would alone have a dim and reverential feeling connected with it. But there are other reasons. No man can pretend that the wild, barbarous, and capricious superstitions of Africa, or of savage tribes elsewhere, affect him in the way that he is affected by the ancient, monumental, cruel, and elaborate religions of Indostan, etc. The mere antiquity of Asiatic things, of their institutions, histories, modes of faith, etc., is so impressive, that to me the vast age of the race and name overpowers the sense of youth in the individual. A young Chinese seems to me an antediluvian man renewed. Even Englishmen, though not bred in any knowledge of

such institutions, cannot but shudder at the mystic sublimity of *castes* that have flowed apart, and refused to mix, through such immemorial tracts of time; nor can any man fail to be awed by the names of the Ganges, or the Euphrates. It contributes much to these feelings, that Southern Asia is, and has been for thousands of years, the part of the earth most swarming with human life, the great *officina gentium*.[1] Man is a weed in those regions. The vast empires, also, into which the enormous population of Asia has always been cast, give a further sublimity to the feelings associated with all oriental names or images. In China, over and above what it has in common with the rest of Southern Asia, I am terrified by the modes of life, by the manners, and the barrier of utter abhorrence, and want of sympathy, placed between us by feelings deeper than I can analyse. I could sooner live with lunatics, or brute animals. All this, and much more than I can say, or have time to say, the reader must enter into, before he can comprehend the unimaginable horror which these dreams of oriental imagery, and mythological tortures, impressed upon me. Under the connecting feeling of tropical heat and vertical sunlights, I brought together all creatures, birds, beasts, reptiles, all trees and plants, usages and appearances, that are found in all tropical regions, and assembled them together in China or Indostan. From kindred feelings, I soon brought Egypt and all her gods under the same law. I was stared at, hooted at, grinned at, chattered at, by monkeys, by paroquets, by cockatoos. I ran into pagodas, and was fixed, for centuries, at the summit, or in secret rooms: I was the idol; I was the priest; I was worshipped; I was sacrificed. I fled from the wrath of Brama[2] through all the forests of Asia: Vishnu hated me; Seeva laid wait for me. I came suddenly upon Isis and Osiris:[3] I had done a deed, they said, which the ibis and the crocodile trembled at. I was buried, for a thousand years, in stone coffins, with mummies and sphinxes, in narrow chambers at the heart of eternal pyramids. I was kissed, with cancerous kisses, by crocodiles; and laid, confounded with all unutterable

---

[1] laboratory of the nations [2] Brahmâ, Vishnu, and Siva, Hindu deities embodying the creative, preservative, and destructive principles [3] Cf. Milton's *Hymn on the Nativity*, ll. 212, 213.

slimy things, amongst reeds and Nilotic mud.

I thus give the reader some slight abstraction of my oriental dreams, which always filled me with such amazement at the monstrous scenery, that horror seemed absorbed, for a while, in sheer astonishment. Sooner or later came a reflux of feeling that swallowed up the astonishment, and left me, not so much in terror, as in hatred and abomination of what I saw. Over every form, and threat, and punishment, and dim sightless incarceration, brooded a sense of eternity and infinity that drove me into an oppression as of madness. Into these dreams only, it was, with one or two slight exceptions, that any circumstances of physical horror entered. All before had been moral and spiritual terrors. But here the main agents were ugly birds, or snakes, or crocodiles, especially the last. The cursed crocodile became to me the object of more horror than almost all the rest. I was compelled to live with him; and (as was always the case, almost, in my dreams) for centuries. I escaped sometimes, and found myself in Chinese houses with cane tables, etc. All the feet of the tables, sofas, etc., soon became instinct with life: the abominable head of the crocodile, and his leering eyes, looked out at me, multiplied into a thousand repetitions; and I stood loathing and fascinated. And so often did this hideous reptile haunt my dreams, that many times the very same dream was broken up in the very same way: I heard gentle voices speaking to me (I hear everything when I am sleeping), and instantly I awoke: it was broad noon, and my children were standing, hand in hand, at my bedside, come to show me their coloured shoes, or new frocks, or to let me see them dressed for going out. I protest that so awful was the transition from the damned crocodile, and the other unutterable monsters and abortions of my dreams, to the sight of innocent *human* natures and of infancy, that, in the mighty and sudden revulsion of mind, I wept, and could not forbear it, as I kissed their faces.

June, 1819. *   *   *   *   *   *

I thought that it was a Sunday morning in May; that it was Easter Sunday, and as yet very early in the morning. I was standing, as it seemed to me, at the door of my own cottage. Right before me lay the very scene which could really be commanded from that situation, but exalted, as was usual, and

solemnised by the power of dreams. There were the same mountains, and the same lovely valley at their feet; but the mountains were raised to more than Alpine height, and there was interspace far larger between them of meadows and forest lawns; the hedges were rich with white roses; and no living creature was to be seen, excepting that in the green church-yard there were cattle tranquilly reposing upon the verdant graves, and particularly round about the grave of a child whom I had tenderly loved, just as I had really beheld them, a little before sunrise, in the same summer, when that child died. I gazed upon the well-known scene, and I said aloud (as I thought) to myself, "It yet wants much of sunrise; and it is Easter Sunday; and that is the day on which they celebrate the first fruits of resurrection. I will walk abroad; old griefs shall be forgotten to-day; for the air is cool and still, and the hills are high, and stretch away to heaven; and the forest glades are as quiet as the church-yard; and with the dew I can wash the fever from my forehead, and then I shall be unhappy no longer." And I turned, as if to open my garden gate; and immediately I saw upon the left a scene far different; but which yet the power of dreams had reconciled into harmony with the other. The scene was an oriental one; and there also it was Easter Sunday, and very early in the morning. And at a vast distance were visible, as a stain upon the horizon, the domes and cupolas of a great city — an image or faint abstraction, caught, perhaps, in childhood, from some picture of Jerusalem. And not a bow-shot from me, upon a stone, and shaded by Judean palms, there sat a woman; and I looked, and it was — Ann![1] She fixed her eyes upon me earnestly; and I said to her, at length, "So, then, I have found you, at last." I waited; but she answered me not a word. Her face was the same as when I saw it last, and yet, again, how different! Seventeen years ago, when the lamp-light fell upon her face, as for the last time I kissed her lips (lips, Ann, that to me were not polluted!), her eyes were streaming with tears; — her tears were now wiped away;[2] she seemed more beautiful than she was at that time, but in all other points the same, and not older. Her

[1] a poor girl who had befriended him when he ran away from school and came to London
[2] Cf. *Revelation,* vii: 17 and xxi: 4.

looks were tranquil, but with unusual solemnity of expression, and I now gazed upon her with some awe; but suddenly her countenance grew dim, and, turning to the mountains, I perceived vapours rolling between us; in a moment, all had vanished; thick darkness came on; and in the twinkling of an'eye I was far away from mountains, and by lamplight in Oxford-street, walking again with Ann — just as we walked seventeen years before, when we were both children.

As a final specimen, I cite one of a different character, from 1820.

The dream commenced with a music which now I often heard in dreams — a music of preparation and of awakening suspense; a music like the opening of the Coronation Anthem,[1] and which, like *that*, gave the feeling of a vast march, of infinite cavalcades filing off, and the tread of innumerable armies. The morning was come of a mighty day — a day of crisis and of final hope for human nature, then suffering some mysterious eclipse, and labouring in some dread extremity. Somewhere, I knew not where — somehow, I knew not how — by some beings, I knew not whom — a battle, a strife, an agony, was conducting, — was evolving like a great drama, or piece of music; with which my sympathy was the more insupportable from my confusion as to its place, its cause, its nature, and its possible issue. I, as is usual in dreams (where, of necessity, we make ourselves central to every movement), had the power, and yet had not the power, to decide it. I had the power, if I could raise myself, to will it; and yet again had not the power, for the weight of twenty Atlantics was upon me, or the oppression of inexpiable guilt. "Deeper than ever plummet sounded,"[2] I lay inactive. Then, like a chorus, the passion deepened. Some greater interest was at stake; some mightier cause than ever yet the sword had pleaded, or trumpet had proclaimed. Then came sudden alarms; hurryings to and fro; trepidations of innumerable fugitives. I knew not whether from the good cause or the bad; darkness and lights; tempest and human faces; and at last, with the sense that all was lost, female forms, and the features that were worth all the world to me, and but a moment allowed, — and

[1] The music was written in 1727 by Handel for the coronation of George II. [2] Cf. *The Tempest*, III, iii, 101.

clasped hands, and heart-breaking partings, and then — everlasting farewells! and, with a sigh, such as the caves of hell sighed when the incestuous mother uttered the abhorred name of death,[1] the sound was reverberated — everlasting farewells! and again, and yet again reverberated — everlasting farewells!

And I awoke in struggles, and cried aloud — "I will sleep no more!"

GEORGE NOEL GORDON, LORD BYRON (1788–1824)

FROM ENGLISH BARDS AND SCOTCH REVIEWERS

* * * * * * *

A man must serve his time to every trade,
Save censure — critics all are ready made.
Take hackney'd jokes from Miller,[2] got by rote,
With just enough of learning to misquote; 66
A mind well skill'd to find or forge a fault;
A turn for punning, call it Attic salt;
To Jeffrey[3] go, be silent and discreet,
His pay is just ten sterling pounds per sheet:
Fear not to lie, 'twill seem a lucky hit; 71
Shrink not from blasphemy, 'twill pass for wit:
Care not for feeling — pass your proper jest,
And stand a critic, hated yet caress'd.
   And shall we own such judgment? no — as soon
Seek roses in December, ice in June;
Hope constancy in wind, or corn in chaff,
Believe a woman, or an epitaph,
Or any other thing that's false, before
You trust in critics who themselves are sore;
Or yield one single thought to be misled 81
By Jeffrey's heart, or Lambe's[4] Bœotian head.[5]

* * * * * * *

Behold! in various throngs the scribbling crew,
For notice eager, pass in long review;
Each spurs his jaded Pegasus apace,
And rhyme and blank maintain an equal race,

[1] *Par. Lost*, II, 648–814. [2] *Joe Miller's Jestbook*, pub. 1730 and many times reprinted — proverbial for stale jokes [3] Francis Lord Jeffrey, editor of the *Edinburgh Review* [4] Byron said: "Messrs. Jeffrey and Lambe are the Alpha and Omega of the *Edinburgh Review*." [5] The Bœotians were proverbial for stupidity.

Sonnets on sonnets crowd, and ode on ode; 141
And tales of terror jostle on the road;
Immeasurable measures[1] move along;
For simpering Folly loves a varied song,
To strange mysterious Dullness still the friend,
Admires the strain she cannot comprehend.
Thus Lays of Minstrels — may they be the last!
On half-strung harps whine mournful to the blast.
While mountain spirits prate to river sprites,
That dames may listen to their sound at night;
And goblin brats of Gilpin Horner's brood,[2] 151
Decoy young border-nobles through the wood.
And skip at every step, Lord knows how high,
And frighten foolish babes, the Lord knows why;
While high-born ladies in their magic cell,
Forbidding knights to read who cannot spell,
Despatch a courier to a wizard's grave,
And fight with honest men to shield a knave.
　Next view in state, proud prancing on his roan,
The golden-crested haughty Marmion,　160
Now forging scrolls, now foremost in the fight,
Not quite a felon, yet but half a knight,
The gibbet or the field prepared to grace —
A mighty mixture of the great and base.
And think'st thou, Scott! by vain conceit-perchance,
On public taste to foist thy stale romance,
Though Murray with his Miller[3] may combine
To yield thy muse just half-a-crown per line?
No! when the sons of song descend to trade,
Their bays are sear, their former laurels fade.
Let such forego the poet's sacred name,　171
Who rack their brains for lucre, not for fame:
Low may they sink to merited contempt,
And scorn remunerate the mean attempt!
Such be their meed, such still the just reward
Of prostituted muse and hireling bard!
For this we spurn Apollo's venal son,
'And bid a long "good night to Marmion."[4]
　These are the themes that claim our plaudits now;
These are the bards to whom the muse must bow:　180

[1] A jibe at the metres of Scott, Coleridge, etc.
[2] Scott's *Lay of the Last Minstrel* was suggested by a folk-tale of a goblin called Gilpin Horner.
[3] Constable, Murray, and Miller were Scott's publishers. [4] Originally spoken with sorrow by Henry Blount on reading the death of Marmion

While Milton, Dryden, Pope, alike forgot,
Resign their hallow'd bays to Walter Scott.

*　　*　　*　　*　　*　　*　　*

With eagle pinions soaring to the skies,　195
Behold the ballad monger, Southey, rise!
To him let Camoëns,[1] Milton, Tasso,[2] yield,
Whose annual strains, like armies, take the field.
First in the ranks see Joan of Arc[3] advance,
The scourge of England, and the boast of France!　200
Though burnt by wicked Bedford for a witch,
Behold her statue placed in glory's niche,
Her fetters burst, and just released from prison,
A virgin Phœnix from her ashes risen.
Next see tremendous Thalaba[3] come on,
Arabia's monstrous, wild, and wondrous son;
Domdaniel's[4] dread destroyer, who o'erthrew
More mad magicians than the world e'er knew.
Immortal hero! all thy foes o'ercome,
Forever reign — the rival of Tom Thumb!
Since startled metre fled before thy face,　211
Well wert thou doom'd the last of all thy race!
Well might triumphant Genii bear thee hence,
Illustrious conqueror of common sense!
Now, last and greatest, Madoc[3] spreads his sails,
Cacique[5] in Mexico, and Prince in Wales;
Tells us strange tales, as other travellers do,
More old than Mandeville's, and not so true.
Oh! Southey, Southey! cease thy varied song!
A Bard may chaunt too often and too long:220
As thou art strong in verse, in mercy spare!
A fourth, alas! were more than we could bear.
But if, in spite of all the world can say,
Thou still wilt verseward plod thy weary way;
If still in Berkley ballads,[6] most uncivil,
Thou wilt devote old women to the devil,
The babe unborn thy dread intent may rue;
"God help thee," Southey, and thy readers too.
　Next comes the dull disciple of thy school,
That mild apostate from poetic rule,　230

[1] a famous Portuguese epic poet (1524–80) [2] a famous Italian epic poet (1544–95) [3] epics by Southey [4] a seminary for evil magicians held in a cave in Arabia; its destruction is the theme of Thalaba [5] chief [6] "*The Old Woman of Berkley*, a ballad by Southey, wherein an aged gentlewoman is carried away by Beelzebub, on a 'high-trotting horse.'" — Byron's note.

The simple Wordsworth, framer of a lay
As soft as evening in his favourite May;
Who warns his friend "to shake off toil and
    trouble;
And quit his books, for fear of growing
    double;"
Who, both by precept and example, shows
That prose is verse, and verse is merely prose,
Convincing all, by demonstration plain,
Poetic souls delight in prose insane;
And Christmas stories, tortured into rhyme,
Contain the essence of the true sublime: 240
Thus when he tells the tale of Betty Foy,
The idiot mother of "an idiot Boy;"
A moon-struck silly lad who lost his way,
And, like his bard, confounded night with day;
So close on each pathetic part he dwells,
And each adventure so sublimely tells,
That all who view the "idiot in his glory,"
Conceive the Bard the hero of the story.

Shall gentle Coleridge pass unnoticed here,
To turgid ode and tumid stanza dear? 250
Though themes of innocence amuse him best,
Yet still obscurity's a welcome guest.
If Inspiration should her aid refuse
To him who takes a Pixy for a Muse,[1]
Yet none in lofty numbers can surpass
The bard who soars to elegize an ass.
How well the subject suits his noble mind!
"A fellow-feeling makes us wondrous kind!"

*   *   *   *   *   *   *

CHILDE HAROLD'S PILGRIMAGE

THE FAREWELL: From CANTO I

Oh, thou! in Hellas deem'd of heavenly
    birth,
Muse! form'd or fabled at the minstrel's
    will!
Since shamed full oft by later lyres on earth,
Mine dares not call thee from thy sacred
    hill;
Yet there I've wander'd by thy vaunted
    rill;
Yes! sigh'd o'er Delphi's long-deserted
    shrine,
Where, save that feeble fountain, all is still;
Nor mote my shell awake the weary Nine 8
To grace so plain a tale — this lowly lay of
    mine.

[1] In *Songs of the Pixies;* one of the poems is
entitled *To a Young Ass.*

Whilome in Albion's isle there dwelt a youth
Who ne in virtue's ways did take delight;
But spent his days in riot most uncouth,
And vex'd with mirth the drowsy ear of
    Night.
Ah, me! in sooth he was a shameless wight,
Sore given to revel and ungodly glee;
Few earthly things found favour in his sight
Save concubines and carnal companie   17
And flaunting wassailers of high and low de-
    gree.

Childe Harold was he hight: — but whence
    his name
And lineage long, it suits me not to say;
Suffice it, that perchance they were of fame,
And had been glorious in another day:
But one sad losel soils a name for aye,
However mighty in the olden time;
Nor all that heralds rake from coffin'd clay,
Nor florid prose, nor honey'd lies of rhyme,
Can blazon evil deeds, or consecrate a crime.

Childe Harold bask'd him in the noontide
    sun,   28
Disporting there like any other fly,
Nor deem'd before his little day was done
One blast might chill him into misery.
But long ere scarce a third of his pass'd by,
Worse than adversity the Childe befell;
He felt the fullness of satiety:
Then loathed he in his native land to dwell,
Which seem'd to him more lone than Eremite's
    sad cell.   36

For he through Sin's long labyrinth had run,
Nor made atonement when he did amiss,
Had sigh'd to many, though he loved but
    one,
And that lov'd one, alas, could ne'er be his.
Ah, happy she! to 'scape from him whose
    kiss
Had been pollution unto aught so chaste;
Who soon had left her charms for vulgar
    bliss,
And spoil'd her goodly lands to gild his
    waste,
Nor calm domestic peace had ever deign'd to
    taste.   45

And now Childe Harold was sore sick at
    heart,
And from his fellow bacchanals would flee;
'Tis said, at times the sullen tear would
    start,

But Pride congeal'd the drop within his e'e;
Apart he stalk'd in joyless reverie,
And from his native land resolv'd to go,
And visit scorching climes beyond the sea:
With pleasure drugg'd, he almost long'd for
woe,
And e'en for change of scene would seek the
shades below.   54

The Childe departed from his father's hall;
It was a vast and venerable pile;
So old, it seemèd only not to fall,
Yet strength was pillar'd in each massy aisle.
Monastic dome! condemn'd to uses vile!
Where Superstition once had made her den,
Now Paphian girls were known to sing and
smile;   61
And monks might deem their time was come
agen,
If ancient tales say true, nor wrong these holy
men.

Yet ofttimes, in his maddest mirthful mood,
Strange pangs would flash along Childe
Harold's brow,
As if the memory of some deadly feud
Or disappointed passion lurk'd below:
But this none knew, nor haply cared to
know;
For his was not that open, artless soul
That feels relief by bidding sorrow flow;
Nor sought he friend to counsel or condole,
Whate'er this grief mote be, which he could
not control.   72

And none did love him — though to hall and
bower
He gather'd revellers from far and near,
He knew them flatterers of the festal hour;
The heartless parasites of present cheer.
Yea! none did love him — not his lemans
dear —
But pomp and power alone are woman's care,
And where these are light Eros finds a feere;
Maidens, like moths, are ever caught by
glare,   80
And Mammon wins his way where Seraphs
might despair.

Childe Harold had a mother — not forgot,
Though parting from that mother he did
shun:
A sister whom he loved, but saw her not
Before his weary pilgrimage begun:
If friends he had, he bade adieu to none,

Yet deem not thence his breast a breast of
steel;
Ye, who have known what 'tis to dote upon
A few dear objects, will in sadness feel
Such partings break the heart they fondly
hope to heal.   90

His house, his home, his heritage, his lands,
The laughing dames in whom he did delight,
Whose large blue eyes, fair locks, and snowy
hands,
Might shake the saintship of an anchorite,
And long had fed his youthful appetite;
His goblets brimm'd with every costly wine,
And all that mote to luxury invite,
Without a sigh he left to cross the brine,
And traverse Paynim shores, and pass Earth's
central line.

The sails were fill'd, and fair the light winds
blew,   100
As glad to waft him from his native home;
And fast the white rocks faded from his
view,
And soon were lost in circumambient foam;
And then, it may be, of his wish to roam
Repented he, but in his bosom slept   105
The silent thought, nor from his lips did
come
One word of wail, whilst others sate and
wept,
And to the reckless gales unmanly moaning
kept.

But when the sun was sinking in the sea,
He seized his harp, which he at times could
string,   110
And strike, albeit with untaught melody,
When deem'd he no strange ear was listen-
ing;
And now his fingers o'er it he did fling,
And tuned his farewell in the dim twilight,
While flew the vessel on her snowy wing,
And fleeting shores receded from his sight,
Thus to the elements he pour'd his last "Good
Night."   117

Adieu, adieu! my native shore
Fades o'er the waters blue;
The night-winds sigh, the breakers roar,
And shrieks the wild sea-mew.
Yon sun that sets upon the sea
We follow in his flight;
Farewell awhile to him and thee,
My native land — Good night!   125

A few short hours, and he will rise,
　To give the morrow birth;
And I shall hail the main and skies,
　But not my mother earth.
Deserted is my own good hall,
　Its hearth is desolate;
Wild weeds are gathering on the wall,
　My dog howls at the gate.　133

　＊　　＊　　＊　　＊　　＊　　＊　　＊

And now I'm in the world alone,
　Upon the wide, wide sea;
But why should I for others groan,
　When none will sigh for me?
Perchance my dog will whine in vain,
　Till fed by stranger hands;
But long ere I come back again
　He'd tear me where he stands.　189

With thee, my bark, I'll swiftly go
　Athwart the foaming brine;
Nor care what land thou bear'st me to,
　So not again to mine.
Welcome, welcome, ye dark blue waves!
　And when you fail my sight,
Welcome, ye deserts, and ye caves!
　My native land — Good night!　197

WATERLOO: From CANTO III

There was a sound of revelry by night,
And Belgium's capital had gather'd then
Her Beauty and her Chivalry, and bright
The lamps shone o'er fair women and brave
　men;
A thousand hearts beat happily; and when
Music arose with its voluptuous swell,
Soft eyes look'd love to eyes which spake
　again,
And all went merry as a marriage bell;
But hush! hark! a deep sound strikes like a
　rising knell!　189

Did ye not hear it? — No; 'twas but the
　wind,
Or the car rattling o'er the stony street;
On with the dance! let joy be unconfined;
No sleep till morn, when Youth and Pleas-
　ure meet
To chase the glowing Hours with flying
　feet. —
But hark! that heavy sound breaks in once
　more,
As if the clouds its echo would repeat;

And nearer, clearer, deadlier than before!
Arm! arm! it is — it is — the cannon's open-
　ing roar!　198

Within a window'd niche of that high hall
Sate Brunswick's fated chieftain; he did
　hear
That sound the first amidst the festival,
And caught its tone with Death's prophetic
　ear,
And when they smiled because he deem'd it
　near,
His heart more truly knew that peal too well
Which stretch'd his father on a bloody bier,
And roused the vengeance blood alone could
　quell.　206
He rush'd into the field, and, foremost fight-
　ing, fell.

Ah! then and there was hurrying to and
　fro,
And gathering tears, and tremblings of dis-
　tress,
And cheeks all pale, which but an hour ago
Blush'd at the praise of their own loveli-
　ness;
And there were sudden partings, such as
　press
The life from out young hearts, and chok-
　ing sighs
Which ne'er might be repeated: who could
　guess
If ever more should meet those mutual eyes,
Since upon night so sweet such awful morn
　could rise!　216

And there was mounting in hot haste: the
　steed,
The mustering squadron, and the clattering
　car,
Went pouring forward with impetuous speed,
And swiftly forming in the ranks of war;
And the deep thunder peal on peal afar;
And near, the beat of the alarming drum
Roused up the soldier ere the morning star;
While throng'd the citizens with terror
　dumb,
Or whispering with white lips — "The foe!
　They come! they come!"　225

And wild and high the "Cameron's Gather-
　ing" rose,
The war-note of Lochiel, which Albyn's hills
Have heard, and heard, too, have her Saxon
　foes;

How in the noon of night that pibroch thrills
Savage and shrill! But with the breath
 which fills
Their mountain pipe, so fill the mountaineers
With the fierce native daring which instils
The stirring memory of a thousand years,
And Evan's, Donald's fame rings in each clans-
 man's ears! 234

And Ardennes waves above them her green
 leaves,
Dewy with Nature's tear-drops, as they pass,
Grieving, if aught inanimate e'er grieves,
Over the unreturning brave, — alas!
Ere evening to be trodden like the grass
Which now beneath them, but above shall
 grow
In its next verdure, when this fiery mass
Of living valour, rolling on the foe,
And burning with high hope, shall moulder
 cold and low. 243

Last noon beheld them full of lusty life,
Last eve in Beauty's circle proudly gay,
The midnight brought the signal-sound of
 strife,
The morn the marshalling in arms — the
 day
Battle's magnificently stern array!
The thunder-clouds close o'er it, which when
 rent
The earth is cover'd thick with other clay,
Which her own clay shall cover, heap'd and
 pent,
Rider and horse — friend, foe, — in one red
 burial blent! 252

MAN AND NATURE: From CANTO III.

Lake Leman [1] woos me with its crystal face,
The mirror where the stars and mountains
 view
The stillness of their aspect in each trace
Its clear depth yields of their far height and
 hue;
There is too much of man here, to look
 through
With a fit mind the might which I behold;
But soon in me shall Loneliness renew
Thoughts hid, but not less cherish'd than
 of old,
Ere mingling with the herd had penn'd me in
 their fold. 612

[1] Lake Geneva

To fly from, need not be to hate, mankind;
All are not fit with them to stir and toil,
Nor is it discontent to keep the mind
Deep in its fountain, lest it overboil
In the hot throng, where we become the
 spoil
Of our infection, till too late and long
We may deplore and struggle with the coil,
In wretched interchange of wrong for wrong
'Midst a contentious world, striving where
 none are strong. 621

There, in a moment, we may plunge our
 years
In fatal penitence, and in the blight
Of our own soul turn all our blood to tears,
And colour things to come with hues of
 Night:
The race of life becomes a hopeless flight
To those that walk in darkness; on the sea
The boldest steer but where their ports in-
 vite,
But there are wanderers o'er Eternity
Whose bark drives on and on, and anchor'd
 ne'er shall be. 630

Is it not better, then, to be alone,
And love Earth only for its earthly sake?
By the blue rushing of the arrowy Rhone,
Or the pure bosom of its nursing lake,
Which feeds it as a mother who doth make
A fair but froward infant her own care,
Kissing its cries away as these awake; —
Is it not better thus our lives to wear,
Than join the crushing crowd, doom'd to in-
 flict or bear? 639

I live not in myself, but I become
Portion of that around me: and to me,
High mountains are a feeling, but the hum
Of human cities torture; I can see
Nothing to loathe in Nature, save to be
A link reluctant in a fleshly chain, 645
Class'd among creatures, when the soul can
 flee,
And with the sky, the peak, the heaving
 plain
Of ocean, or the stars, mingle, and not in vain.

And thus I am absorb'd, and this is life:
I look upon the peopled desert past,
As on a place of agony and strife,
Where, for some sin, to Sorrow I was cast,
To act and suffer, but remount at last
With a fresh pinion; which I feel to spring,

Though young, yet waxing vigorous as the blast
Which it would cope with, on delighted wing,
Spurning the clay-cold bonds which round our being cling. 657

And when, at length, the mind shall be all free
From what it hates in this degraded form,
Reft of its carnal life, save what shall be
Existent happier in the fly and worm, —
When elements to elements conform,
And dust is as it should be, shall I not
Feel all I see, less dazzling, but more warm?
The bodiless thought? the Spirit of each spot?
Of which, even now, I share at times the immortal lot? 666

Are not the mountains, waves, and skies, a part
Of me and of my soul, as I of them?
Is not the love of these deep in my heart
With a pure passion? should I not contemn
All objects, if compared with these? and stem
A tide of suffering rather than forego
Such feelings for the hard and worldly phlegm
Of those whose eyes are only turn'd below,
Gazing upon the ground, with thoughts which dare not glow? 675

ROME: From CANTO IV

O Rome! my country! city of the soul!
The orphans of the heart must turn to thee,
Lone mother of dead empires! and control
In their shut breasts their petty misery.
What are our woes and sufferance? Come and see
The cypress, hear the owl, and plod your way
O'er steps of broken thrones and temples, — Ye!
Whose agonies are evils of a day —
A world is at our feet as fragile as our clay. 702

The Niobe[1] of nations! there she stands,
Childless and crownless in her voiceless woe;
An empty urn within her wither'd hands,
Whose holy dust was scatter'd long ago;

[1] The children of Niobe were slain by Apollo.

The Scipios' tomb contains no ashes now;
The very sepulchres lie tenantless
Of their heroic dwellers: dost thou flow,
Old Tiber! through a marble wilderness?
Rise, with thy yellow waves, and mantle her distress. 711

The Goth, the Christian, Time, War, Flood, and Fire,
Have dealt upon the seven-hill'd city's pride:
She saw her glories star by star expire,
And up the steep barbarian monarchs ride,
Where the car[1] climb'd the Capitol; far and wide
Temple and tower went down, nor left a site: —
Chaos of ruins! who shall trace the void,
O'er the dim fragments cast a lunar light,
And say, "Here was, or is," where all is doubly night? 720

LOVE: From CANTO IV

O Love! no habitant of earth thou art —
An unseen seraph, we believe in thee, —
A faith whose martyrs are the broken heart,
But never yet hath seen, nor e'er shall see,
The naked eye, thy form, as it should be:
The mind hath made thee, as it peopled heaven,
Even with its own desiring phantasy,
And to a thought such shape and image given,
As haunts the unquench'd soul — parch'd — wearied — wrung — and riven. 1089

Of its own beauty is the mind diseased,
And fevers into false creation; — where,
Where are the forms the sculptor's soul hath seized?
In him alone. Can Nature show so fair?
Where are the charms and virtues which we dare
Conceive in boyhood and pursue as men,
The unreach'd Paradise of our despair,
Which o'er-informs the pencil and the pen,
And overpowers the page where it would bloom again? 1098

Who loves, raves — 'tis youth's frenzy — but the cure
Is bitterer still; as charm by charm unwinds

[1] chariot

Which robed our idols, and we see too sure
Nor worth nor beauty dwells from out the
   mind's
Ideal shape of such; yet still it binds
The fatal spell, and still it draws us on,
Reaping the whirlwind from the oft-sown
   winds;
The stubborn heart, its alchemy begun,
Seems ever near the prize — wealthiest when
   most undone.   1107

We wither from our youth, we gasp away —
Sick — sick; unfound the boon — unslaked
   the thirst,
Though to the last, in verge of our decay,
Some phantom lures, such as we sought at
   first —
But all too late, — so are we doubly curst,
Love, fame, ambition, avarice — 'tis the
   same —
Each idle, and all ill, and none the worst —
For all are meteors with a different name,
And Death the sable smoke where vanishes the
   flame.   1116

Few — none — find what they love or could
   have loved:
Though accident, blind contact, and the
   strong
Necessity of loving, have removed
Antipathies — but to recur, ere long,
Envenom'd with irrevocable wrong;
And Circumstance, that unspiritual god
And miscreator, makes and helps along
Our coming evils with a crutch-like rod,
Whose touch turns Hope to dust — the dust
   we all have trod.   1125

MAN AND NATURE: From CANTO IV

Oh! that the Desert were my dwelling-place
With one fair Spirit for my minister,
That I might all forget the human race,
And, hating no one, love but only her!
Ye Elements! — in whose ennobling stir
I feel myself exalted — can ye not
Accord me such a being? Do I err
In deeming such inhabit many a spot?
Though with them to converse can rarely be
   our lot.   1593

There is a pleasure in the pathless woods,
There is a rapture on the lonely shore,
There is society where none intrudes,
By the deep Sea, and music in its roar:

I love not man the less, but Nature more,
From these our interviews, in which I steal
From all I may be, or have been before,
To mingle with the Universe, and feel   1601
What I can ne'er express, yet cannot all con-
   ceal.

Roll on, thou deep and dark blue Ocean —
   roll!
Ten thousand fleets sweep over thee in vain;
Man marks the earth with ruin — his con-
   trol
Stops with the shore; — upon the watery
   plain
The wrecks are all thy deed, nor doth re-
   main
A shadow of man's ravage, save his own,
When for a moment, like a drop of rain,
He sinks into thy depths with bubbling
   groan,
Without a grave, unknell'd, uncoffin'd and
   unknown,   1611

His steps are not upon thy paths — thy
   fields
Are not a spoil for him — thou dost arise
And shake him from thee; the vile strength
   he wields
For earth's destruction thou dost all de-
   spise,
Spurning him from thy bosom to the skies,
And send'st him, shivering in thy playful
   spray,
And howling, to his Gods, where haply lies
His petty hope in some near port or bay,
And dashest him again to earth — there let
   him lay.   1620

The armaments which thunderstrike the
   walls
Of rock-built cities, bidding nations quake,
And monarchs tremble in their capitals,
The oak leviathans, whose huge ribs make
Their clay creator the vain title take
Of lord of thee, and arbiter of war;
These are thy toys, and, as the snowy
   flake,
They melt into thy yeast of waves, which
   mar
Alike the Armada's pride, or spoils of Trafal-
   gar.[1]

[1] The uninjured ships of the Armada are contrasted with those broken in the battle of Trafalgar.

Thy shores are empires, changed in all save
  thee —   1630
Assyria, Greece, Rome, Carthage, what are
  they?
Thy waters washed them power while they
  were free,
And many.a tyrant since: their shores obey
The stranger, slave or savage; their decay
Has dried up realms to deserts: — not so
  thou,
Unchangeable save to thy wild waves'
  play —
Time writes no wrinkle on thine azure
  brow —
Such as creation's dawn beheld, thou rollest
  now.

Thou glorious mirror, where the Almighty's
  form
Glasses itself in tempests: in all time, 1640
Calm or convulsed — in breeze, or gale, or
  storm,
Icing the pole, or in the torrid clime
Dark-heaving; — boundless, endless, and
  sublime —
The image of Eternity — the throne
Of the Invisible; even from out thy slime
The monsters of the deep are made; each
  zone
Obeys thee; thou goest forth, dread, fathom-
  less, alone.   1647

And I have loved thee, Ocean! and my joy
Of youthful sports was on thy breast to be
Borne, like thy bubbles, onward: from a
  boy
I wanton'd with thy breakers — they to me
Were a delight; and if the freshening sea
Made them a terror — 'twas a pleasing fear,
For I was as it were a child of thee,
And trusted to thy billows far and near,
And laid my hand upon thy mane — as I do
  here.   1656

SONNET ON CHILLON

Eternal Spirit of the chainless Mind!
  Brightest in dungeons, Liberty! thou art,
  For there thy habitation is the heart —
The heart which love of thee alone can bind;
And when thy sons to fetters are consign'd —
  To fetters, and the damp vault's dayless
    gloom,
  Their country conquers with their martyr-
    dom,

And Freedom's fame finds wings on every
  wind.
Chillon![1] thy prison is a holy place,
  And thy sad floor an altar — for 'twas trod,
Until his very steps have left a trace   11
  Worn, as if thy cold pavement were a sod,
By Bonnivard! May none those marks
  efface!
For they appeal from tyranny to God.

THE PRISONER OF CHILLON

My hair is gray, but not from years;
  Nor grew it white
  In a single night,
As men's have grown from sudden fears:
My limbs are bow'd, though not with toil,
  But rusted with a vile repose,
For they have been a dungeon's spoil,
  And mine has been the fate of those
To whom the goodly earth and air
Are bann'd, and barr'd — forbidden fare;   10
But this was for my father's faith
I suffer'd chains and courted death:
That father perish'd at the stake
For tenets he would not forsake;
And for the same his lineal race
In darkness found a dwelling-place.
We were seven — who now are one;
  Six in youth, and one in age,
Finish'd as they had begun,
  Proud of Persecution's rage;   20
One in fire, and two in field,
Their belief with blood have seal'd
Dying as their father died,
For the God their foes denied; —
Three were in a dungeon cast,
Of whom this wreck is left the last.

There are seven pillars of Gothic mould,
In Chillon's dungeon deep and old;
There are seven columns, massy and gray,
Dim with a dull imprison'd ray,   30
A sunbeam which hath lost its way,
And through the crevice and the cleft
Of the thick wall is fallen and left:
Creeping o'er the floor so damp,
Like a marsh's meteor lamp:
And in each pillar there is a ring,
  And in each ring there is a chain;
That iron is a cankering thing,
  For in these limbs its teeth remain,

---

[1] The castle of Chillon covers a huge rock at
the eastern end of Lake Geneva (Lake Leman).

With marks that will not wear away,   40
Till I have done with this new day,
Which now is painful to these eyes,
Which have not seen the sun so rise
For years — I cannot count them o'er;
I lost their long and heavy score
When my last brother droop'd and died,
And I lay living by his side.

They chain'd us each to a column stone,
And we were three — yet each alone;
We could not move a single pace,   50
We could not see each other's face,
But with that pale and livid light
That made us strangers in our sight:
And thus together — yet apart,
Fetter'd in hand, but join'd in heart,
'Twas still some solace in the dearth
Of the pure elements of earth,
To hearken to each other's speech,
And each turn comforter to each,
With some new hope, or legend old,   60
Or song heroically bold;
But even these at length grew cold.
Our voices took a dreary tone,
An echo of the dungeon-stone,
  A grating sound — not full and free,
  As they of yore were wont to be:
  It might be fancy — but to me
They never sounded like our own.

I was the eldest of the three;
  And to uphold and cheer the rest   70
  I ought to do — and did — my best,
And each did well in his degree.
  The youngest, whom my father loved,
Because our mother's brow was given
To him — with eyes as blue as heaven, —
  For him my soul was sorely moved.
And truly might it be distress'd
To see such bird in such a nest;
For he was beautiful as day —
  (When day was beautiful to me   80
  As to young eagles, being free) —
  A polar day, which will not see
A sunset till its summer's gone,
  Its sleepless summer of long light,
The snow-clad offspring of the sun:
  And thus he was as pure and bright,
And in his natural spirit gay,
With tears for naught but others' ills,
And then they flow'd like mountain rills,
Unless he could assuage the woe   90
Which he abhorr'd to view below.

The other was as pure of mind,
But form'd to combat with his kind;
Strong in his frame, and of a mood
Which 'gainst the world in war had stood,
And perish'd in the foremost rank
  With joy — but not in chains to pine:
His spirit wither'd with their clank,
  I saw it silently decline —
  And so perchance in sooth did mine;   100
But yet I forced it on to cheer
Those relics of a home so dear.
He was a hunter of the hills,
  Had follow'd there the deer and wolf;
  To him this dungeon was a gulf,
And fetter'd feet the worst of ills.
  Lake Leman lies by Chillon's walls:
A thousand feet in depth below
Its massy waters meet and flow;
Thus much the fathom line was sent   110
From Chillon's snow-white battlement,
  Which round about the wave enthralls:
A double dungeon wall and wave
Have made — and like a living grave.
Below the surface of the lake
The dark vault lies wherein we lay,
We heard it ripple night and day;
  Sounding o'er our heads it knock'd;
And I have felt the winter's spray
Wash through the bars when winds were high
And wanton in the happy sky;   121
  And then the very rock hath rock'd,
  And I have felt it shake, unshock'd,
Because I could have smiled to see
The death that would have set me free.

I said my nearer brother pined,
I said his mighty heart declined,
He loathed and put away his food:
It was not that 'twas coarse and rude,
For we were used to hunters' fare,   130
And for the like had little care:
The milk drawn from the mountain goat
Was changed for water from the moat;
Our bread was such as captives' tears
Have moisten'd many a thousand years,
Since man first pent his fellow-men
Like brutes within an iron den;
But what were these to us or him?
These wasted not his heart or limb;
My brother's soul was of that mould   140
Which in a palace had grown cold,
Had his free-breathing been denied
The range of the steep mountain's side.
But why delay the truth? — he died.
I saw, and could not hold his head,

Nor reach his dying hand — nor dead —
Though hard I strove, but strove in vain,
To rend and gnash my bonds in twain.
He died — and they unlock'd his chain
And scoop'd for him a shallow grave   150
Even from the cold earth of our cave.
I begg'd them, as a boon, to lay
His corse in dust whereon the day
Might shine — it was a foolish thought,
But then within my brain it wrought,
That even in death his free-born breast
In such a dungeon could not rest.
I might have spared my idle prayer —
They coldly laugh'd — and laid him there:
The flat and turfless earth above   160
The being we so much did love;
His empty chain above it leant,
Such murder's fitting monument!
But he, the favourite and the flower,
Most cherish'd since his natal hour,
His mother's image in fair face,
The infant love of all his race,
His martyr'd father's dearest thought,
My latest care, for whom I sought
To hoard my life, that his might be   170
Less wretched now, and one day free;
He, too, who yet had held untired
A spirit natural or inspired —
He, too, was struck, and day by day
Was wither'd on the stalk away.
O God! it is a fearful thing
To see the human soul take wing
In any shape, in any mood: —
I've seen it rushing forth in blood,
I've seen it on the breaking ocean   180
Strive with a swoll'n convulsive motion,
I've seen the sick and ghastly bed
Of Sin delirious with its dread:
But these were horrors — this was woe
Unmix'd with such, — but sure and slow:
He faded, and so calm and meek,
So softly worn, so sweetly weak,
So tearless, yet so tender, — kind,
And grieved for those he left behind;
With all the while a cheek whose bloom   190
Was as a mockery of the tomb,
Whose tints as gently sunk away
As a departing rainbow's ray —
An eye of most transparent light,
That almost made the dungeon bright,
And not a word of murmur — not
A groan o'er his untimely lot!
A little talk of better days,
A little hope my own to raise,
For I was sunk in silence — lost   200

In this last loss, of all the most:
And then the sighs he would suppress
Of fainting nature's feebleness,
More slowly drawn, grew less and less.
I listen'd, but I could not hear —
I call'd, for I was wild with fear;
I knew 'twas hopeless, but my dread
Would not be thus admonishèd;
I call'd, and thought I heard a sound —
I burst my chain with one strong bound,   210
And rush'd to him; — I found him not;
I only stirr'd in this black spot,
I only lived — *I* only drew
The accursed breath of dungeon-dew;
The last, — the sole, — the dearest link
Between me and the eternal brink
Which bound me to my failing race,
Was broken in this fatal place.
One on the earth, and one beneath —
My brothers — both had ceased to breath:
I took that hand which lay so still;   221
Alas, my own was full as chill;
I had not strength to stir or strive,
But felt that I was still alive —
A frantic feeling, when we know
That what we love shall ne'er be so.
          I know not why
          I could not die;
I had no earthly hope — but faith,
And that forbade a selfish death.   230

What next befell me then and there
I know not well — I never knew: —
First came the loss of light, and air,
          And then of darkness too:
I had no thought, no feeling — none —
Among the stones I stood a stone,
And was scarce conscious what I wist,
As shrubless crags within the mist;
For all was blank, and bleak, and gray,
It was not night — it was not day;   240
It was not even the dungeon-light,
So hateful to my heavy sight,
But vacancy absorbing space,
And fixedness, without a place:
There were no stars, — no earth, — no time, —
No check, — no change, — no good, — no
          crime, —
But silence, and a stirless breath
Which neither was of life nor death;
A sea of stagnant idleness,
Blind, boundless, mute, and motionless!   250

A light broke in upon my brain —
     It was the carol of a bird;

It ceased, and then it came again,
　　The sweetest song ear ever heard;
And mine was thankful, till my eyes
Ran over with the glad surprise,
And they that moment could not see
I was the mate of misery;
But then by dull degrees came back
My senses to their wonted track,　　260
I saw the dungeon walls and floor
Close slowly round me as before,
I saw the glimmer of the sun
Creeping as it before had done,
But through the crevice where it came
That bird was perch'd, as fond and tame,
　　And tamer than upon the tree;
A lovely bird, with azure wings,
And song that said a thousand things,
　　And seem'd to say them all for me!　　270
I never saw its like before,
I ne'er shall see its likeness more:
It seem'd, like me, to want a mate,
But was not half so desolate,
And it was come to love me when
None lived to love me so again,
And cheering from my dungeon's brink,
Had brought me back to feel and think.
I know not if it late were free,
　　Or broke its cage to perch on mine,　　280
But knowing well captivity,
　　Sweet bird, I could not wish for thine!
Or if it were, in wingèd guise,
A visitant from Paradise;
For — Heaven forgive that thought, the while
Which made me both to weep and smile —
I sometimes deem'd that it might be
My brother's soul come down to me;
But then at last away it flew,
And then 'twas mortal — well I knew,　　290
For he would never thus have flown,
And left me twice so doubly lone —
Lone, — as the corse within its shroud;
Lone, — as a solitary cloud,
A single cloud on a sunny day,
While all the rest of heaven is clear,
A frown upon the atmosphere,
That hath no business to appear
　　When skies are blue and earth is gay.

A kind of change came in my fate,　　300
My keepers grew compassionate;
I know not what had made them so,
They were inured to sights of woe;
But so it was — my broken chain
With links unfasten'd did remain,
And it was liberty to stride

Along my cell from side to side,
And up and down, and then athwart,
And tread it over every part;
And round the pillars one by one,　　310
Returning where my walk begun,
Avoiding only, as I trod,
My brothers' graves without a sod;
For if I thought with heedless tread
My step profaned their lowly bed,
My breath came gaspingly and thick,
And my crush'd heart fell blind and sick.

I made a footing in the wall,
　　It was not therefrom to escape,
For I had buried one and all　　320
Who loved me in 'a human shape;
And the whole earth would henceforth be
A wider prison unto me:
No child — no sire — no kin had I,
No partner in my misery;
I thought of this, and I was glad,
For thought of them had[1] made me mad;
But I was curious to ascend
To my barr'd windows, and to bend
Once more, upon the mountains high,　　330
The quiet of a loving eye.

I saw them — and they were the same,
They were not changed like me in frame;
I saw their thousand years of snow
On high — their wide long lake below,
And the blue Rhone in fullest flow;
I heard the torrents leap and gush
O'er channell'd rock and broken bush;
I saw the white-wall'd distant town,
And whiter sails go skimming down;　　340
And then there was a little isle,
Which in my very face did smile,
　　The only one in view:
A small green isle, it seem'd no more,
Scarce broader than my dungeon floor;
But in it there were three tall trees,
And o'er it blew the mountain breeze,
And by it there were waters flowing,
And on it there were young flowers growing,
　　Of gentle breath and hue.　　350
The fish swam by the castle wall,
And they seem'd joyous, each and all;
The eagle rode the rising blast,
Methought he never flew so fast
As then to me he seem'd to fly,
And then new tears came in my eye,
And I felt troubled — and would fain

[1] would have

I had not left my recent chain;
And when I did descend again,
The darkness of my dim abode   360
Fell on me as a heavy load;
It was as is a new-dug grave,
Closing o'er one we sought to save.
And yet my glance, too much opprest,
Had almost need of such a rest.

It might be months, or years, or days,
   I kept no count — I took no note,
I had no hope my eyes to raise,
   And clear them of their dreary mote;
At last men came to set me free,   370
   I ask'd not why, and reck'd not where;
It was at length the same to me,
Fetter'd or fetterless to be,
   I learn'd to love despair.
And thus, when they appear'd at last,
And all my bonds aside were cast,
These heavy walls to me had grown
A hermitage — and all my own!
And half I felt as they were come
To tear me from a second home: 380
With spiders I had friendship made,
And watch'd them in their sullen trade,
Had seen the mice by moonlight play,
And why should I feel less than they?
We were all inmates of one place,
And I, the monarch of each race,
Had power to kill — yet, strange to tell!
In quiet we had learn'd to dwell —
My very chains and I grew friends,
So much a long communion tends   390
To make us what we are: — even I
Regain'd my freedom with a sigh.

ODE

I

Oh Venice! Venice! when thy marble walls
   Are level with the waters, there shall be
A cry of nations o'er thy sunken halls,
   A loud lament along the sweeping sea!
If I, a northern wanderer, weep for thee,
What should thy sons do? — any thing but
   weep:
And yet they only murmur in their sleep.
In contrast with their fathers — as the
   slime,
The dull green ooze of the receding deep,
Is with the dashing of the spring-tide foam,
That drives the sailor shipless to his home,
Are they to those that were; and thus they
   creep,   12

Crouching and crab-like, through their sap-
   ping streets.
Oh! agony — that centuries should reap
No mellower harvest! Thirteen hundred years
Of wealth and glory turn'd to dust and tears;
And every monument the stranger meets,
Church, palace, pillar, as a mourner greets;
And even the Lion all subdued appears,
And the harsh sound of the barbarian drum,
With dull and daily dissonance, repeats   21
The echo of thy tyrant's voice along
The soft waves, once all musical to song,
That heaved beneath the moonlight with the
   throng
Of gondolas — and to the busy hum
Of cheerful creatures, whose most sinful deeds
Were but the overbeating of the heart,
And flow of too much happiness, which needs
The aid of age to turn its course apart
From the luxuriant and voluptuous flood   30
Of sweet sensations battling with the blood.
But these are better than the gloomy errors,
The weeds of nations in their last decay,
When vice walks forth with her unsoften'd
   terrors,
And mirth is madness, and but smiles to slay;
And hope is nothing but a false delay,
The sick man's lightning half an hour ere
   death,
When faintness, the last mortal birth of pain,
And apathy of limb, the dull beginning
Of the cold staggering race which death is
   winning,   40
Steals vein by vein and pulse by pulse away;
Yet so relieving the o'ertortured clay,
To him appears renewal of his breath,
And freedom the mere numbness of his
   chain; —
And then he talks of life, and how again
He feels his spirit soaring, albeit weak,
And of the fresher air, which he would seek;
And as he whispers knows not that he gasps,
That his thin finger feels not what it clasps,
And so the film comes o'er him — and the
   dizzy   50
Chamber swims round and round — and
   shadows busy,
At which he vainly catches, flit and gleam,
Till the last rattle chokes the strangled scream.
And all is ice and blackness, — and the earth
That which it was the moment ere our birth.

II

There is no hope for nations! Search the page
   Of many thousand years — the daily scene,

The flow and ebb of each recurring age,
  The everlasting to be which hath been,
    Hath taught us nought or little : still we
      lean   60
On things that rot beneath our weight, and
  wear
Our strength away in wrestling with the air;
For 'tis our nature strikes us down : the
  beasts
Slaughter'd in hourly hecatombs for feasts
Are of as high an order — they must go
Even where their driver goads them, though
  to slaughter.
Ye men, who pour your blood for kings as
  water,
What have they given your children in return ?
A heritage of servitude and woes,
A blindfold bondage where your hire is blows.
What ? do not yet the red-hot ploughshares
  burn,   71
O'er which you stumble in a false ordeal,
And deem this proof of loyalty the real ;
Kissing the hand that guides you to your scars,
And glorying as you tread the glowing bars?
All that your sires have left you, all that time
Bequeaths of free, and history of sublime,
Spring from a different theme ! — Ye see and
  read,
Admire and sigh, and then succumb and
  bleed !
Save the few spirits, who, despite of all,   80
And worse than all, the sudden crimes en-
  gender'd
By the down-thundering of the prison-wall,
And thirst to swallow the sweet waters
  tender'd,
Gushing from freedom's fountains — when
  the crowd,
Madden'd with centuries of drought, are loud,
And trample on each other to obtain
The cup which brings oblivion of a chain
Heavy and sore, — in which long yoked they
  plough'd
The sand, — or if there sprung the yellow
  grain,
'Twas not for them, their necks were too
  much bow'd,   90
And their dead palates chew'd the cud of
  pain : —
Yes ! the few spirits — who, despite of deeds
Which they abhor, confound not with the
  cause
Those momentary starts from Nature's laws,
Which, like the pestilence and earthquake,
  smite

But for a term, then pass, and leave the earth
With all her seasons to repair the blight
With a few summers, and again put forth
Cities and generations — fair, when free —
For, tyranny, there blooms no bud for
  thee !

III

Glory and empire ! once upon these towers
  With freedom — godlike triad ! how ye sate !
The league of mightiest nations, in those hours
  When Venice was an envy, might abate,
    But did not quench, her spirit — in her fate
All were enwrapp'd : the feasted monarchs
  knew
And loved their hostess, nor could learn
  to hate,
Although they humbled — with the kingly
  few
The many felt, for from all days and climes
She was the voyager's worship ; — even her
  crimes   110
Were of the softer order — born of love,
She drank no blood, nor fatten'd on the dead,
But gladden'd where her harmless conquests
  spread ;
For these restored the cross, that from above
Hallow'd her sheltering banners, which in-
  cessant
Flew between earth and the unholy crescent,
Which, if it waned and dwindled, earth may
  thank
The city it has clothed in chains, which clank
Now, creaking in the ears of those who owe
The name of freedom to her glorious struggles ;
Yet she but shares with them a common woe,
And call'd the "kingdom" of a conquering
  foe, —   122
But knows what all — and, most of all, we
  know —
With what set gilded terms a tyrant juggles !

IV

The name of commonwealth is past and gone
  O'er the three fractions of the groaning
    globe ;
Venice is crush'd, and Holland deigns to own
  A sceptre, and endures the purple robe ;
If the free Switzer yet bestrides alone
His chainless mountains, 'tis but for a time,
For tyranny of late is cunning grown,   131
And in its own good season tramples down
The sparkles of our ashes. One great clime,
Whose vigorous offspring by dividing ocean,

Are kept apart and nursed in the devotion
Of freedom, which their fathers fought for,
     and
Bequeath'd — a heritage of heart and hand,
And proud distinction from each other land,
Whose sons must bow them at a monarch's
     motion,
As if his senseless sceptre were a wand   140
Full of the magic of exploded science —
Still one great clime, in full and free defiance,
Yet rears her crest, unconquer'd and sublime,
Above the far Atlantic! — She has taught
Her Esau-brethren [1] that the haughty flag,
The floating fence of Albion's feebler crag,
May strike to those whose red right hands
     have bought
Rights cheaply earn'd with blood.   Still, still,
     forever
Better, though each man's life-blood were a
     river,   149
That it should flow, and overflow, than creep
Through thousand lazy channels in our veins,
Damn'd like the dull canal with locks and
     chains,
And moving, as a sick man in his sleep,
Three paces, and then faltering : — better be
Where the extinguish'd Spartans still are free,
In their proud charnel of Thermopylæ,
Than stagnate in our marsh, — or o'er the
     deep
Fly, and one current to the ocean add,
One spirit to the souls our fathers had,
One freeman more, America, to thee!   160

KNOW YE THE LAND?

Know ye the land where the cypress and
     myrtle
   Are emblems of deeds that are done in their
     clime?
Where the rage of the vulture, the love of the
     turtle,[2]
   Now melt into sorrow, now madden to
     crime?
Know ye the land of the cedar and vine,
Where the flowers ever blossom, the beams
     ever shine;
Where the light wings of Zephyr, oppress'd
     with perfume,
Wax faint o'er the gardens of Gúl [3] in her
     bloom;

   [1] Those who have sold their birth-right, Liberty.
   [2] dove   [3] the rose

Where the citron and olive are fairest of
     fruit,
And the voice of the nightingale never is
     mute :   10
Where the tints of the earth, and the hues of
     the sky,
In colour though varied, in beauty may vie,
And the purple of ocean is deepest in dye;
Where the virgins are soft as the roses they
     twine,
And all, save the spirit of man, is divine?
'Tis the clime of the East; 'tis the land of the
     Sun —
Can he smile on such deeds as his children
     have done?
Oh! wild as the accents of lovers' farewell
Are the hearts which they bear, and the tales
     which they tell.   19

SHE WALKS IN BEAUTY

She walks in beauty, like the night
   Of cloudless climes and starry skies;
And all that's best of dark and bright
   Meet in her aspect and her eyes:
Thus mellow'd to that tender light   5
   Which heaven to gaudy day denies.

One shade the more, one ray the less,
   Had half impair'd the nameless grace
Which waves in every raven tress,
   Or softly lightens o'er her face;   10
Where thoughts serenely sweet express
   How pure, how dear, their dwelling-place.

And on that cheek, and o'er that brow,
   So soft, so calm, yet eloquent,
The smiles that win, the tints that glow,
   But tell of days in goodness spent,
A mind at peace with all below,
   A heart whose love is innocent!   18

SO, WE'LL GO NO MORE A ROVING

So, we'll go no more a roving
   So late into the night,
Though the heart be still as loving,
   And the moon be still as bright.

For the sword outwears its sheath,   5
   And the soul wears out the breast,
And the heart must pause to breathe,
   And love itself have rest.

Though the night was made for loving,
    And the day returns too soon,   10
Yet we'll go no more a roving
    By the light of the moon.

CHARLES WOLFE (1791–1823)

THE BURIAL OF SIR JOHN MOORE AT CORUNNA

Not a drum was heard, not a funeral note,
    As his corse to the rampart we hurried;
Not a soldier discharged his farewell shot
    O'er the grave where our hero we buried.   4

We buried him darkly at dead of night,
    The sods with our bayonets turning;
By the struggling moonbeam's misty light,
    And the lantern dimly burning.   8

No useless coffin enclosed his breast,
    Not in sheet nor in shroud we wound him,
But he lay like a warrior taking his rest
    With his martial cloak around him.   12

Few and short were the prayers we said,
    And we spoke not a word of sorrow;
But we steadfastly gazed on the face that was
        dead,
    And we bitterly thought of the morrow.   16

We thought as we hollowed his narrow bed,
    And smoothed down his lonely pillow,
That the foe and the stranger would tread o'er
        his head,
    And we far away on the billow!   20

Lightly they'll talk of the spirit that's gone,
    And o'er his cold ashes upbraid him, —
But little he'll reck, if they let him sleep on
    In the grave where a Briton has laid him.   24

But half of our weary task was done
    When the clock struck the hour for retiring;
And we heard the distant and random gun
    That the foe was sullenly firing.   28

Slowly and sadly we laid him down,
    From the field of his fame fresh and gory;
We carved not a line, and we raised not a
        stone —
    But we left him alone with his glory.   32

PERCY BYSSHE SHELLEY
(1792–1822)

FROM ALASTOR; OR, THE SPIRIT OF SOLITUDE

Nondum amabam, et amare amabam, quærebam
    quid amarem, amans amare.[1]
        — Confess. St. August.

There was a Poet whose untimely tomb   50
No human hands with pious reverence reared,
But the charmed eddies of autumnal winds
Built o'er his mouldering bones a pyramid
Of mouldering leaves in the waste wilder-
        ness: —
A lovely youth, — no mourning maiden
        decked   55
With weeping flowers, or votive cypress
        wreath,
The lone couch of his everlasting sleep: —
Gentle, and brave, and generous, — no lorn
        bard
Breathed o'er his dark fate one melodious
        sigh:
He lived, he died, he sung, in solitude.   60
Strangers have wept to hear his passionate
        notes,
And virgins, as unknown he passed, have pined
And wasted for fond love of his wild eyes.
The fire of those soft orbs has ceased to burn,
And Silence, too enamoured of that voice,   65
Locks its mute music in her rugged cell.

By solemn vision, and bright silver dream,
His infancy was nurtured.   Every sight
And sound from the vast earth and ambient
        air,
Sent to his heart its choicest impulses.   70
The fountains of divine philosophy
Fled not his thirsting lips, and all of great,
Or good, or lovely, which the sacred past
In truth or fable consecrates, he felt
And knew.   When early youth had passed,
        he left   75
His cold fireside and alienated home
To seek strange truths in undiscovered lands.
Many a wide waste and tangled wilderness
Has lured his fearless steps; and he has
        bought
With his sweet voice and eyes, from savage
        men,   80

[1] I was not yet in love, and I was in love with
love, I was seeking what I might love, loving love.

His rest and food.   Nature's most secret steps
He like her shadow has pursued, where'er
The red volcano overcanopies
Its fields of snow and pinnacles of ice
With burning smoke, or where bitumen
    lakes   85
On black bare pointed islets ever beat
With sluggish surge, or where the secret caves
Rugged and dark, winding among the springs
Of fire and poison, inaccessible
To avarice or pride, their starry domes   90
Of diamond and of gold expand above
Numberless and immeasurable halls,
Frequent with crystal column, and clear
    shrines
Of pearl, and thrones radiant with chrysolite.
Nor had that scene of ampler majesty   95
Than gems or gold, the varying roof of heaven
And the green earth, lost in his heart its
    claims
To love and wonder; he would linger long
In lonesome vales, making the wild his home,
Until the doves and squirrels would partake
From his innocuous hand his bloodless food, 102
Lured by the gentle meaning of his looks, 102
And the wild antelope, that starts whene'er
The dry leaf rustles in the brake, suspend
Her timid steps to gaze upon a form   105
More graceful than her own.
                              His wandering step,
Obedient to high thoughts, has visited
The awful ruins of the days of old:
Athens, and Tyre, and Balbec,[1] and the waste
Where stood Jerusalem, the fallen towers 110
Of Babylon, the eternal pyramids,
Memphis and Thebes, and whatsoe'er of
    strange
Sculptured on alabaster obelisk,
Or jasper tomb, or mutilated sphinx,
Dark Æthiopia in her desert hills   115
Conceals.   Among the ruined temples there,
Stupendous columns, and wild images
Of more than man, where marble dæmons
    watch
The Zodiac's brazen mystery, and dead men
Hang their mute thoughts on the mute walls
    around,   120
He lingered, poring on memorials
Of the world's youth, through the long burn-
    ing day
Gazed on those speechless shapes, nor, when
    the moon

[1] Baalbec, an ancient Syrian city, sacred to the
worship of Baal, the sun god

Filled the mysterious halls with floating shades,
Suspended he that task, but ever gazed   1·5
And gazed, till meaning on his vacant mind
Flashed like strong inspiration, and he saw
The thrilling secrets of the birth of time.

*   *   *   *   *   *   *

HYMN TO INTELLECTUAL BEAUTY

The awful shadow of some unseen Power
    Floats though unseen amongst us, —
        visiting
    This various world with as inconstant wing
As summer winds that creep from flower to
        flower ; —
Like moonbeams that behind some piny
        mountain shower,[1]   5
        It visits with inconstant glance
        Each human heart and countenance;
Like hues and harmonies of evening, —
        Like clouds in starlight widely spread, —
        Like memory of music fled, —   10
        Like aught that for its grace may be
Dear, and yet dearer for its mystery.

Spirit of BEAUTY, that dost consecrate
    With thine own hues all thou dost shine
        upon
    Of human thought or form, — where art
        thou gone?   15
Why dost thou pass away and leave our state,
This dim vast vale of tears, vacant and
        desolate?
        Ask why the sunlight not forever
        Weaves rainbows ·o'er yon mountain
            river,
Why aught should fail and fade that once is
        shown,   20
        Why fear and dream and death and birth
        Cast on the daylight of this earth
        Such gloom, — why man has such a scope
For love and hate, despondency and hope?

No voice from some sublimer world hath ever
    To sage or poet these responses given — 26
    Therefore the names of Dæmon, Ghost, and
        Heaven,
Remain the records of their vain endeavour,
Frail spells — whose uttered charm might not
        avail to sever,
        From all we hear and all we see,   30
        Doubt, chance, and mutability.

[1] Observe that "shower" is a verb.

Thy light alone — like mist o'er mountains
  driven,
  Or music by the night wind sent,
  Through strings of some still instrument,
  Or moonlight on a midnight stream,   35
Gives grace and truth to life's unquiet dream.

Love, Hope, and Self-esteem, like clouds
  depart
  And come, for some uncertain moments
  lent.
Man were immortal, and omnipotent,   39
Didst thou, unknown and awful as thou art,
Keep with thy glorious train firm state within
  his heart.
  Thou messenger of sympathies,
  That wax and wane in lovers' eyes —
Thou — that to human thought art nourish-
  ment,
  Like darkness to a dying flame!   45
  Depart not as thy shadow came,
  Depart not — lest the grave should be,
Like life and fear, a dark reality.

While yet a boy I sought for ghosts, and sped
  Through many a listening chamber, cave
  and ruin,   50
  And starlight wood, with fearful steps
  pursuing
Hopes of high talk with the departed dead.
I called on poisonous names with which our
  youth is fed,
  I was not heard — I saw them not —·
  When musing deeply on the lot   55
Of life, at the sweet time when winds are
  wooing   ·
  All vital things that wake to bring
  News of birds and blossoming, —
  Sudden, thy shadow fell on me;
I shrieked, and clasped my hands in ecstasy!

I vowed that I would dedicate my powers 61
  To thee and thine — have I not kept the
  vow?
  With beating heart and streaming eyes,
  even now
I call the phantoms of a thousand hours
Each from his voiceless grave: they have in
  visioned bower   65
  Of studious zeal or love's delight
  Outstretched· with me the envious
  night —
They know that never joy illumed my brow
  Unlinked with hope that thou wouldst
  free

This world from its dark slavery,   70
  That thou — O awful LOVELINESS,
Wouldst give whate'er these words cannot
  express.

The day becomes more solemn and serene
  When noon is past — there is a harmony
  In autumn, and a lustre in its sky,   75
Which through the summer is not heard or
  seen,
As if it could not be, as if it had not been!
  Thus let thy power, which like the truth
  Of nature on my passive youth
Descended, to my onward life supply   80
  Its calm — to one who worships thee,
  And every form containing thee,
  Whom, SPIRIT fair, thy spells did bind
To fear himself, and love all human kind.

SONNET

OZYMANDIAS

I met a traveller from an antique land
Who said: Two vast and trunkless legs of
  stone
Stand in the desert. Near them, on the sand,
Half sunk, a shattered visage lies, whose
  frown,
And wrinkled lip, and sneer of cold command,
Tell that its sculptor well those passions read
Which yet survive, (stamped on these life-
  less things,)   7
The hand that mocked them and the heart
  that fed:
And on the pedestal these words appear:
"My name is Ozymandias, king of kings: 10
Look on my works, ye Mighty, and despair!"
Nothing beside remains. Round the decay
Of that colossal wreck, boundless and bare
The lone and level sands stretch far away.

From LINES WRITTEN AMONG THE EUGANEAN HILLS

Many a green isle needs must be
In the deep wide sea of misery,
Or the mariner, worn and wan,
Never thus could voyage on
Day and night, and night and day,   5
Drifting on his dreary way,
With the solid darkness black
Closing round his vessel's track;
Whilst, above, the sunless sky,
Big with clouds, hangs heavily,   10

And behind, the tempest fleet
Hurries on with lightning feet,
Riving sail, and cord, and plank,
Till the ship has almost drank
Death from the o'er-brimming deep;   15
And sinks down, down, like that sleep
When the dreamer seems to be
Weltering through eternity;
And the dim low line before
Of a dark and distant shore   20
Still recedes, as ever still
Longing with divided will,
But no power to seek or shun,
He is ever drifted on
O'er the unreposing wave   25
To the haven of the grave.
What if there no friends will greet;
What if there no heart will meet
His with love's impatient beat;
Wander wheresoe'er he may,   30
Can he dream before that day
To find refuge from distress
In friendship's smile, in love's caress?

   *   *   *   *   *   *   *

Lo, the sun floats up the sky
Like thought-wingèd Liberty,
Till the universal light
Seems to level plain and height;
From the sea a mist has spread,   210
And the beams of morn lie dead
On the towers of Venice now,
Like its glory long ago.
By the skirts of that gray cloud
Many-domèd Padua proud   215
Stands, a peopled solitude,
'Mid the harvest-shining plain,
Where the peasant heaps his grain
In the garner of his foe,
And the milk-white oxen slow   220
With the purple vintage strain,
Heaped upon the creaking wain,
That the brutal Celt may swill
Drunken sleep with savage will;
And the sickle to the sword   225
Lies unchanged, though many a lord,
Like a weed whose shade is poison,
Overgrows this region's foison,
Sheaves of whom are ripe to come
To destruction's harvest home: 230
Men must reap the things they sow,
Force from force must ever flow,
Or worse; but 'tis a bitter woe
That love or reason cannot change
The despot's rage, the slave's revenge.   235

Padua, thou within whose walls
Those mute guests at festivals,
Son and Mother, Death and Sin,
Played at dice for Ezzelin,
Till Death cried, "I win, I win!"   240
And Sin cursed to lose the wager,
But Death promised, to assuage her,
That he would petition for
Her to be made Vice-Emperor,
When the destined years were o'er,   245
Over all between the Po
And the eastern Alpine snow,
Under the mighty Austrian.
Sin smiled so as Sin only can,
And since that time, aye, long before,   250
Both have ruled from shore to shore.
That incestuous pair, who follow
Tyrants as the sun the swallow,
As Repentance follows Crime,
And as changes follow Time.   255

In thine halls the lamp of learning,
Padua, now no more is burning;
Like a meteor, whose wild way
Is lost over the grave of day,
It gleams betrayed and to betray: 260
Once remotest nations came
To adore that sacred flame,
When it lit not many a hearth
On this cold and gloomy earth:
Now new fires from antique light   265
Spring beneath the wide world's might;
But their spark lies dead in thee,
Trampled out by tyranny.
As the Norway woodman quells,
In the depth of piny dells,   270
One light flame among the brakes,
While the boundless forest shakes,
And its mighty trunks are torn
By the fire thus lowly born:
The spark beneath his feet is dead,   275
He starts to see the flames it fed
Howling through the darkened sky
With a myriad tongues victoriously,
And sinks down in fear: so thou,
O Tyranny, beholdest now   280
Light around thee, and thou hearest
The loud flames ascend, and fearest:
Grovel on the earth: aye, hide
In the dust thy purple pride!

Noon descends around me now: 285
'Tis the noon of autumn's glow,
When a soft and purple mist
Like a vaporous amethyst,

Or an air-dissolvèd star
Mingling light and fragrance, far   290
From the curved horizon's bound
To the point of heaven's profound,
Fills the overflowing sky ;
And the plains that silent lie
Underneath, the leaves unsodden   295
Where the infant frost has trodden
With his morning-wingèd feet,
Whose bright print is gleaming yet ;
And the red and golden vines,
Piercing with their trellised lines   300
The rough, dark-skirted wilderness ;
The dun and bladed grass no less,
Pointing from this hoary tower
In the windless air ; the flower
Glimmering at my feet ; the line   305
Of the olive-sandalled Apennine
In the south dimly islanded ;
And the Alps, whose snows are spread
High between the clouds and sun ;
And of living things each one ;   310
And my spirit which so long
Darkened this swift stream of song,
Interpenetrated lie
By the glory of the sky :
Be it love, light, harmony,   315
Odour, or the soul of all
Which from heaven like dew doth fall,
Or the mind which feeds this verse
Peopling the lone universe.
Noon descends, and after noon   320
Autumn's evening meets me soon,
Leading the infantine moon,
And that one star, which to her
Almost seems to minister
Half the crimson light she brings   325
From the sunset's radiant springs :
And the soft dreams of the morn,
(Which like wingèd winds had borne
To that silent isle, which lies
'Mid remembered agonies,   330
The frail bark of this lone being,)
Pass, to other sufferers fleeing,
And its ancient pilot, Pain,
Sits beside the helm again.

Other flowering isles must be   335
In the sea of life and agony :
Other spirits float and flee
O'er that gulph : even now, perhaps,
On some rock the wild wave wraps,
With folded wings they waiting sit   340
For my bark, to pilot it
To some calm and blooming cove,

Where for me, and those I love,
May a windless bower be built,
Far from passion, pain, and guilt,   345
In a dell 'mid lawny hills,
Which the wild sea-murmur fills,
And soft sunshine, and the sound
Of old forests echoing round,
And the light and smell divine   350
Of all flowers that breathe and shine :
We may live so happy there,
That the spirits of the air,
Envying us, may even entice
To our healing paradise   355
The polluting multitude ;
But their rage would be subdued
By that clime divine and calm,
And the winds whose wings rain balm
On the uplifted soul, and leaves   360
Under which the bright sea heaves ;
While each breathless interval
In their whisperings musical
The inspired soul supplies
With its own deep melodies,   365
And the love which heals all strife
Circling, like the breath of life,
All things in that sweet abode
With its own mild brotherhood :
They, not it, would change ; and soon   370
Every sprite beneath the moon
Would repent its envy vain,
And the earth grow young again.

ODE TO THE WEST WIND

I

O, wild West Wind, thou breath of Autumn's
      being,
Thou, from whose unseen presence the leaves
      dead
Are driven, like ghosts from an enchanter
      fleeing,

Yellow, and black, and pale, and hectic red,
Pestilence-stricken multitudes : O, thou,   5
Who chariotest to their dark wintry bed

The wingèd seeds, where they lie cold and
      low,
Each like a corpse within its grave, until
Thine azure sister of the spring shall blow

Her clarion o'er the dreaming earth, and fill 10
(Driving sweet buds like flocks to feed in air)
With living hues and odours plain and hill :

Wild Spirit, which art moving everywhere;
Destroyer and preserver; hear, O, hear!

II

Thou on whose stream, 'mid the steep sky's
    commotion,   15
Loose clouds like earth's decaying leaves are
    shed,
Shook from the tangled boughs of Heaven and
    Ocean,

Angels of rain and lightning: there are
    spread
On the blue surface of thine airy surge,
Like the bright hair uplifted from the head 20

Of some fierce Mænad, even from the dim
    verge
Of the horizon to the zenith's height,
The locks of the approaching storm. Thou
    dirge

Of the dying year, to which this closing night
Will be the dome of a vast sepulchre,   25
Vaulted with all thy congregated might

Of vapours, from whose solid atmosphere
Black rain, and fire, and hail will burst: O,
    hear!

III

Thou who didst waken from his summer
    dreams
The blue Mediterranean, where he lay,   30
Lulled by the coil of his crystalline streams,

Beside a pumice isle in Baiæ's bay,
And saw in sleep old palaces and towers
Quivering within the wave's intenser day,

All overgrown with azure moss and flowers 35
So sweet, the sense faints picturing them!
    Thou
For whose path the Atlantic's level powers

Cleave themselves into chasms, while far below
The sea-blooms and the oozy woods which
    wear
The sapless foliage of the ocean, know   40

Thy voice, and suddenly grow gray with fear,
And tremble and despoil themselves: O,
    hear!

IV

If I were a dead leaf thou mightest bear;
If I were a swift cloud to fly with thee;
A wave to pant beneath thy power, and share

The impulse of thy strength, only less free 46
Than thou, O, uncontrollable! If even
I were as in my boyhood, and could be

The comrade of thy wanderings over heaven,
As then, when to outstrip thy skiey speed 50
Scarce seemed a vision; I would ne'er have
    striven

As thus with thee in prayer in my sore need.
Oh! lift me as a wave, a leaf, a cloud!
I fall upon the thorns of life! I bleed!

A heavy weight of hours has chained and
    bowed   55
One too like thee: tameless, and swift, and
    proud.

V

Make me thy lyre, even as the forest is:
What if my leaves are falling like its own!
The tumult of thy mighty harmonies

Will take from both a deep, autumnal tone,
Sweet though in sadness. Be thou, spirit
    fierce,   61
My spirit! Be thou me, impetuous one!

Drive my dead thoughts over the universe
Like withered leaves to quicken a new birth!
And, by the incantation of this verse,   65

Scatter, as from an unextinguished hearth
Ashes and sparks, my words among mankind!
Be through my lips to unawakened earth

The trumpet of a prophecy! O, wind,
If Winter comes, can Spring be far behind? 70

THE INDIAN SERENADE

I arise from dreams of thee
In the first sweet sleep of night,
When the winds are breathing low,
And the stars are shining bright:
I arise from dreams of thee,   5
And a spirit in my feet
Hath led me — who knows how?
To thy chamber window, Sweet!

The wandering airs they faint
On the dark, the silent stream — 10
The Champak[1] odours fail
Like sweet thoughts in a dream;
The nightingale's complaint,
It dies upon her heart; —
As I must on thine, 15
O! belovèd as thou art!

O lift me from the grass!
I die! I faint! I fail!
Let thy love in kisses rain
On my lips and eyelids pale. 20
My cheek is cold and white, alas!
My heart beats loud and fast; —
Oh! press it to thine own again,
Where it will break at last.

THE CLOUD

I bring fresh showers for the thirsting flowers,
From the seas and the streams;
I bear light shade for the leaves when laid
In their noon-day dreams.
From my wings are shaken the dews that
waken 5
The sweet buds every one,
When rocked to rest on their mother's breast,
As she dances about the sun.
I wield the flail of the lashing hail,
And whiten the green plains under, 10
And then again I dissolve it in rain,
And laugh as I pass in thunder.

I sift the snow on the mountains below,
And their great pines groan aghast;
And all the night 'tis my pillow white, 15
While I sleep in the arms of the blast.
Sublime on the towers of my skiey bowers,
Lightning my pilot sits;
In a cavern under is fettered the thunder, —
It struggles and howls at fits; 20
Over earth and ocean, with gentle motion,
This pilot is guiding me,
Lured by the love of the genii that move
In the depths of the purple sea;
Over the rills, and the crags, and the hills, 25
Over the lakes and the plains,
Wherever he dream, under mountain or
stream,
The Spirit he loves remains;

[1] a tree of India, belonging to the magnolia family

And I all the while bask in heaven's blue smile,
Whilst he is dissolving in rains. 30

The sanguine sunrise, with his meteor eyes,
And his burning plumes outspread,
Leaps on the back of my sailing rack,
When the morning star shines dead,
As on the jag of a mountain crag, 35
Which an earthquake rocks and swings,
An eagle alit one moment may sit
In the light of its golden wings.
And when sunset may breathe, from the lit
sea beneath,
Its ardours of rest and of love, 40
And the crimson pall of eve may fall
From the depth of heaven above,
With wings folded I rest, on mine airy nest,
As still as a brooding dove.

That orbèd maiden with white fire laden, 45
Whom mortals call the moon,
Glides glimmering o'er my fleece-like floor,
By the midnight breezes strewn;
And wherever the beat of her unseen feet,
Which only the angels hear, 50
May have broken the woof of my tent's thin
roof,
The stars peep behind her and peer;
And I laugh to see them whirl and flee,
Like a swarm of golden bees,
When I widen the rent in my wind-built tent,
Till the calm rivers, lakes, and seas, 56
Like strips of the sky fallen through me on
high,
Are each paved with the moon and
these.

I bind the sun's throne with a burning zone,
And the moon's with a girdle of pearl;
The volcanoes are dim, and the stars reel and
swim, 61
When the whirlwinds my banner
unfurl.
From cape to cape, with a bridge-like shape,
Over a torrent sea,
Sunbeam-proof, I hang like a roof, 65
The mountains its columns be.
The triumphal arch through which I march
With hurricane, fire, and snow,
When the powers of the air are chained to my
chair,
Is the million-coloured bow; 70
The sphere-fire above its soft colours wove,
While the moist earth was laughing
below.

I am the daughter of earth and water,
    And the nursling of the sky;
I pass through the pores of the ocean and
    shores;   75
    I change, but I cannot die.
For after the rain when, with never a stain,
    The pavilion of heaven is bare,
And the winds and sunbeams with their con-
    vex gleams
    Build up the blue dome of air,   80
I silently laugh at my own cenotaph,
    And out of the caverns of rain,
Like a child from the womb, like a ghost from
    the tomb,
    I arise and unbuild it again.

TO A SKYLARK

Hail to thee, blithe spirit!
    Bird thou never wert,
That from heaven, or near it,
    Pourest thy full heart
In profuse strains of unpremeditated art.   5

Higher still and higher
    From the earth thou springest
Like a cloud of fire;
    The blue deep thou wingest,
And singing still dost soar, and soaring ever
    singest.   10

In the golden lightning
    Of the sunken sun,
O'er which clouds are brightning,
    Thou dost float and run;
Like an unbodied joy whose race is just begun.

The pale purple even   16
    Melts around thy flight;
Like a star of heaven
    In the broad day-light
Thou art unseen, but yet I hear thy shrill
    delight,   20

Keen as are the arrows
    Of that silver sphere,
Whose intense lamp narrows
    In the white dawn clear,
Until we hardly see, we feel that it is there. 25

All the earth and air
    With thy voice is loud,
As, when night is bare,
    From one lonely cloud
The moon rains out her beams, and heaven is
    overflowed.   30

What thou art we know not;
    What is most like thee?
From rainbow clouds there flow not
    Drops so bright to see
As from thy presence showers a rain of
    melody.   35

Like a poet hidden
    In the light of thought,
Singing hymns unbidden,
    Till the world is wrought
To sympathy with hopes and fears it heeded
    not: 40

Like a high-born maiden
    In a palace tower,
Soothing her love-laden
    Soul in secret hour
With music sweet as love, which overflows
    her bower: 45

Like a glow-worm golden
    In a dell of dew,
Scattering unbeholden
    Its aërial hue
Among the flowers and grass which screen it
    from the view: 50

Like a rose embowered
    In its own green leaves,
By warm winds deflowered,
    Till the scent it gives
Makes faint with too much sweet these heavy-
    wingèd thieves.   55

Sound of vernal showers
    On the twinkling grass,
Rain-awakened flowers,
    All that ever was
Joyous, and clear, and fresh, thy music doth
    surpass.   60

Teach us, sprite or bird,
    What sweet thoughts are thine;
I have never heard
    Praise of love or wine
That panted forth a flood of rapture so
    divine: 65

Chorus Hymenæal,
    Or triumphal chaunt,
Matched with thine, would be all
    But an empty vaunt,
A thing wherein we feel there is some hidden
    want.   70

What objects are the fountains
    Of thy happy strain?
What fields, or waves, or mountains?
    What shapes of sky or plain?
What love of thine own kind? what ignorance
    of pain?   75

With thy clear keen joyance
    Languor cannot be —
Shadow of annoyance
    Never came near thee:
Thou lovest — but ne'er knew love's sad
    satiety.   80

Waking or asleep,
    Thou of death must deem
Things more true and deep
    Than we mortals dream,
Or how could thy notes flow in such a crystal
    stream?   85

We look before and after
    And pine for what is not:
Our sincerest laughter
    With some pain is fraught;
Our sweetest songs are those that tell of
    saddest thought.   90

Yet if we could scorn
    Hate, and pride, and fear;
If we were things born
    Not to shed a tear,
I know not how thy joy we ever should come
    near.   95

Better than all measures
    Of delightful sound —
Better than all treasures
    That in books are found —
Thy skill to poet were, thou scorner of the
    ground!   100

Teach me half the gladness
    That thy brain must know,
Such harmonious madness
    From my lips would flow,
The world should listen then — as I am
    listening now.   105

TO ———

Music, when soft voices die,
Vibrates in the memory —
Odours, when sweet violets sicken,
Live within the sense they quicken.

Rose-leaves, when the rose is dead,   5
Are heaped for the belovèd's bed;
And so thy thoughts, when thou art gone,
Love itself shall slumber on.

ADONAIS

I weep for Adonais — he is dead!
O, weep for Adonais! though our tears
Thaw not the frost which binds so dear a
    head!
And thou, sad Hour, selected from all years
To mourn our loss, rouse thy obscure com-
    peers,   5
And teach them thine own sorrow, say:
    "With me
Died Adonais; till the Future dares
Forget the Past, his fate and fame shall be
An echo and a light unto eternity."

Where wert thou, mighty Mother, when he
    lay,   10
When thy Son lay, pierced by the shaft
    which flies
In darkness? where was lorn Urania
When Adonais died? With veilèd eyes,
'Mid listening Echoes, in her Paradise
She sate, while one, with soft enamoured
    breath,   15
Rekindled all the fading melodies,
With which, like flowers that mock the
    corse beneath,
He had adorned and hid the coming bulk of
    death.

O, weep for Adonais — he is dead!
Wake, melancholy Mother, wake and
    weep!   20
Yet wherefore? Quench within their burn-
    ing bed
Thy fiery tears, and let thy loud heart keep
Like his, a mute and uncomplaining sleep;
For he is gone, where all things wise and
    fair
Descend; — oh, dream not that the amo-
    rous Deep   25
Will yet restore him to the vital air;
Death feeds on his mute voice, and laughs at
    our despair.

Most musical of mourners, weep again!
Lament anew, Urania! — He died, —
Who was the Sire of an immortal strain,
Blind, old, and lonely, when his country's
    pride,   31

The priest, the slave, and the liberticide,
Trampled and mocked with many a loathèd
rite
Of lust and blood; he went, unterrified,
Into the gulph of death; but his clear
Sprite   35
Yet reigns o'er earth; the third among the
sons of light.

Most musical of mourners, weep anew!
Not all to that bright station dared to
climb;
And happier they their happiness who
knew,
Whose tapers yet burn through that night
of time   40
In which suns perished; others more
sublime,
Struck by the envious wrath of man or God,
Have sunk, extinct in their refulgent
prime;
And some yet live, treading the thorny road,
Which leads, through toil and hate, to Fame's
serene abode.   45

But now, thy youngest, dearest one has
perished,
The nursling of thy widowhood, who grew,
Like a pale flower by some sad maiden
cherished,
And fed with true love tears, instead of
dew;
Most musical of mourners, weep anew! 50
Thy extreme hope, the loveliest and the
last,
The bloom, whose petals, nipped before
they blew,
Died on the promise of the fruit, is waste;
The broken lily lies — the storm is overpast.

To that high Capital, where kingly Death
Keeps his pale court in beauty and decay,
He came; and bought, with price of purest
breath,   57
A grave among the eternal. — Come away!
Haste, while the vault of blue Italian day
Is yet his fitting charnel-roof! while still 60
He lies, as if in dewy sleep he lay;
Awake him not! surely he takes his fill
Of deep and liquid rest, forgetful of all ill.

He will awake no more, oh, never more! —
Within the twilight chamber spreads apace
The shadow of white Death, and at the
door   66

Invisible Corruption waits to trace
His extreme way to her dim dwelling-place;
The eternal Hunger sits, but pity and awe
Soothe her pale rage, nor dares she to deface
So fair a prey, till darkness, and the law
Of change, shall o'er his sleep the mortal
curtain draw.   72

O, weep for Adonais! — The quick Dreams,
The passion-wingèd Ministers of thought,
Who were his flocks, whom near the living
streams   75
Of his young spirit he fed, and whom he
taught
The love which was its music, wander
not, —
Wander no more, from kindling brain to
brain,
But droop there, whence they sprung; and
mourn their lot
Round the cold heart, where, after their
sweet pain,   80
They ne'er will gather strength, or find a home
again.

And one with trembling hands clasps his
cold head,
And fans him with her moonlight wings, and
cries:
"Our love, our hope, our sorrow, is not
dead;
See, on the silken fringe of his faint eyes, 85
Like dew upon a sleeping flower, there lies
A tear some Dream has loosened from his
brain."
Lost Angel of a ruined Paradise!
She knew not 'twas her own; as with no
stain
She faded, like a cloud which had outwept
its rain.   90

One from a lucid urn of starry dew
Washed his light limbs as if embalming
them;
Another clipped her profuse locks, and
threw
The wreath upon him, like an anadem,
Which frozen tears instead of pearls be-
gem;   95
Another in her wilful grief would break
Her bow and wingèd reeds, as if to stem
A greater loss with one which was more
weak;
And dull the barbèd fire against his frozen
cheek.

Another Splendour on his mouth alit,   100
That mouth, whence it was wont to draw
the breath
Which gave it strength to pierce the
guarded wit,
And pass into the panting heart beneath
With lightning and with music: the damp
death
Quenched its caress upon his icy lips;   105
And, as a dying meteor stains a wreath
Of moonlight vapour, which the cold night
clips,
It flushed through his pale limbs, and passed
to its eclipse.

And others came . . .   Desires and Adora-
tions,
Wingèd Persuasions and veiled Destinies,
Splendours, and Glooms, and glimmering
Incarnations   111
Of hopes and fears, and twilight Phantasies;
And Sorrow, with her family of Sighs,
And Pleasure, blind with tears, led by the
gleam
Of her own dying smile instead of eyes,   115
Came in slow pomp; — the moving pomp
might seem
Like pageantry of mist on an autumnal
stream.

All he had loved, and moulded into thought,
From shape, and hue, and odour, and sweet
sound,
Lamented Adonais.   Morning sought   120
Her eastern watch-tower, and her hair
unbound,
Wet with the tears which should adorn the
ground,
Dimmed the aërial eyes that kindle day;
Afar the melancholy thunder moaned,
Pale Ocean in unquiet slumber lay,   125
And the wild winds flew round, sobbing in
their dismay.

Lost Echo sits amid the voiceless mountains,
And feeds her grief with his remembered
lay,
And will no more reply to winds or fountains,
Or amorous birds perched on the young
green spray,   130
Or herdsman's horn, or bell at closing day;
Since she can mimic not his lips, more
dear

Than those for whose disdain she pined
away
Into a shadow of all sounds: — a drear
Murmur, between their songs, is all the wood-
men hear.   135

Grief made the young Spring wild, and she
threw down
Her kindling buds, as if she Autumn were,
Or they dead leaves; since her delight is
. flown,
For whom should she have waked the sullen
year?
To Phœbus was not Hyacinth so dear,   140
Nor to himself Narcissus, as to both
Thou, Adonais: wan they stand and sere
Amid the faint companions of their youth,
With dew all turned to tears; odour, to
sighing ruth.

Thy spirit's sister, the lorn nightingale,
Mourns not her mate with such melodious
pain;   146
Not so the eagle, who like thee could scale
Heaven, and could nourish in the sun's
domain
Her mighty youth with morning, doth
complain,   •
Soaring and screaming round her empty
nest,   150
As Albion wails for thee: the curse of
Cain
Light on his head who pierced thy innocent
breast,
And scared the angel soul that was its earthly
guest!

Ah, woe is me!   Winter is come and gone,
But grief returns with the revolving year;
The airs and streams renew their joyous
tone;   156
The ants, the bees, the swallows reappear;
Fresh leaves and flowers deck the dead
Seasons' bier;
The amorous birds now pair in every brake,
And build their mossy homes in field and
brere;   160
And the green lizard, and the golden snake,
Like unimprisoned flames, out of their trance
awake.

Through wood and stream and field and hill
and Ocean
A quickening life from the Earth's heart has
burst,

As it has ever done, with change and mo-
    tion,   165
From the great morning of the world when
    first
God dawned on Chaos; in its stream im-
    mersed
The lamps of Heaven flash with a softer
    light;
All baser things pant with life's sacred
    thirst;
Diffuse themselves; and spend in love's
    delight   170
The beauty and the joy of ·their renewèd
    might.

The leprous corpse touched by this spirit
    tender
Exhales itself in flowers of gentle breath;
Like incarnations of the stars, when
    splendour   174
Is changed to fragrance, they illumine death
And mock the merry worm that wakes
    beneath;
Naught we know, dies. Shall that alone
    which knows
Be as a sword consumed before the sheath
By sightless lightning? — th' intense atom
    glows
A moment, then is quenched in a most cold
    repose.   180

Alas! that all we loved of him should be,
But for our grief, as if it had not been,
And grief itself be mortal! Woe is me!
Whence are we, and why are we? of what
    scene
The actors or spectators? Great and mean
Meet massed in death, who lends what life
    must borrow.   186
As long as skies are blue, and fields are
    green,
Evening must usher night, night urge the
    morrow,
Month follow month with woe, and year wake
    year to sorrow.

He will awake no more, oh, never more!
"Wake thou," cried Misery, "childless
    Mother, rise   191
Out of thy sleep, and slake, in thy heart's
    core,
A wound more fierce than his with tears
    and sighs."
And all the Dreams that watched Urania's
    eyes,   194
AE

And all the Echoes whom their sister's song
Had held in holy silence, cried: "Arise!"
Swift as a Thought by the snake Memory
    stung,
From her ambrosial rest the fading Splendour
    sprung.

She rose like an autumnal Night, that
    springs   199
Out of the East, and follows wild and drear
The golden Day, which, on eternal wings,
Even as a ghost abandoning a bier,
Had left the Earth a corpse. Sorrow and
    fear
So struck, so roused, so rapt Urania;   204
So saddened round her like an atmosphere
Of stormy mist; so swept her on her way
Even to the mournful place where Adonais
    lay.

Out of her secret Paradise she sped,
Through camps and cities rough with
    stone, and steel,
And human hearts, which to her aëry tread
Yielding not, wounded the invisible   210
Palms of her tender feet where'er they fell:
And barbèd tongues, and thoughts more
    sharp than they,
Rent the soft Form they never could repel,
Whose sacred blood, like the young tears of
    May,   215
Paved with eternal flowers that undeserving
    way.

In the death chamber for a moment Death,
Shamed by the presence of that living
    Might,
Blushed to annihilation, and the breath
Revisited those lips, and life's pale light 220
Flashed through those limbs, so late her
    dear delight.
"Leave me not wild and drear and com-
    fortless,
As silent lightning leaves the starless night!
Leave me not!" cried Urania: her distress
Roused Death: Death rose and smiled, and
    met her vain caress.   225

"Stay yet awhile! speak to me once again;
Kiss me, so long but as a kiss may live;
And in my heartless breast and burning
    brain
That word, that kiss shall all thoughts else
    survive,
With food of saddest memory kept alive,

Now thou art dead, as if it were a part 231
Of thee, my Adonais! I would give
All that I am to be as thou now art!
But I am chained to Time, and cannot
    thence depart!

"Oh gentle child, beautiful as thou wert,
Why didst thou leave the trodden paths
    of men 236
Too soon, and with weak hands though
    mighty heart
Dare the unpastured dragon in his den?
Defenceless as thou wert, oh where was
    then
Wisdom the mirrored shield, or scorn the
    spear? 240
Or hadst thou waited the full cycle, when
Thy spirit should have filled its crescent
    sphere,
The monsters of life's waste had fled from
    thee like deer.

"The herded wolves, bold only to pursue;
The obscene ravens, clamorous o'er the
    dead; 245
The vultures to the conqueror's banner
    true,
Who feed where Desolation first has fed,
And whose wings rain contagion; — how
    they fled,
When like Apollo, from his golden bow,
The Pythian of the age one arrow sped 250
And smiled! — The spoilers tempt no
    second blow;
They fawn on the proud feet that spurn them
    lying low.

"The sun comes forth, and many reptiles
    spawn;
He sets, and each ephemeral insect then
Is gathered into death without a dawn, 255
And the immortal stars awake again;
So is it in the world of living men:
A godlike mind soars forth, in its delight
Making earth bare and veiling heaven, and
    when
It sinks, the swarms that dimmed or shared
    its light 260
Leave to its kindred lamps the spirit's awful
    night."

Thus ceased she: and the mountain shep-
    herds came,
Their garlands sere, their magic mantles
    rent;

The Pilgrim of Eternity, whose fame
Over his living head like Heaven is bent,
An early but enduring monument, 266
Came, veiling all the lightnings of his song
In sorrow; from her wilds Ierne sent
The sweetest lyrist of her saddest wrong,
And love taught grief to fall like music from
    his tongue. 270

Midst others of less note, came one frail
    Form,
A phantom among men, companionless
As the last cloud of an expiring storm
Whose thunder is its knell; he, as I guess,
Had gazed on Nature's naked loveliness,
Actæon-like, and now he fled astray 276
With feeble steps o'er the world's wilderness,
And his own thoughts, along that rugged
    way,
Pursued, like raging hounds, their father and
    their prey.

A pardlike Spirit beautiful and swift —
A Love in desolation masked; — a Power
Girt round with weakness; — it can scarce
    uplift 282
The weight of the superincumbent hour;
It is a dying lamp, a falling shower,
A breaking billow; — even whilst we speak
Is it not broken? On the withering
    flower 286
The killing sun smiles brightly; on a
    cheek
The life can burn in blood, even while the
    heart may break.

His head was bound with pansies over-
    blown,
And faded violets, white, and pied, and
    blue; 290
And a light spear topped with a cypress
    cone,
Round whose rude shaft dark ivy tresses
    grew
Yet dripping with the forest's noonday dew,
Vibrated, as the ever-beating heart
Shook the weak hand that grasped it; of
    that crew 295
He came the last, neglected and apart;
A herd-abandoned deer, struck by the hunter's
    dart.

All stood aloof, and at his partial moan
Smiled through their tears; well knew that
    gentle band

Who in another's fate now wept his own;
As, in the accents of an unknown land, 301
He sung new sorrow; sad Urania scanned
The Stranger's mien, and murmured:
"Who art thou?"
He answered not, but with a sudden hand
Made bare his branded and ensanguined
brow, 305
Which was like Cain's or Christ's — Oh!
that it should be so!

What softer voice is hushed over the dead?
Athwart what brow is that dark mantle
thrown?
What form leans sadly o'er the white death-
bed,
In mockery of monumental stone, 310
The heavy heart heaving without a moan?
If it be He, who, gentlest of the wise,
Taught, soothed, loved, honoured the de-
parted one,
Let me not vex with inharmonious sighs
The silence of that heart's accepted sacrifice.

Our Adonais has drunk poison — oh! 316
What deaf and viperous murderer could
crown
Life's early cup with such a draught of woe?
The nameless worm would now itself disown:
It felt, yet could escape the magic tone 320
Whose prelude held all envy, hate, and
wrong,
But what was howling in one breast alone,
Silent with expectation of the song,
Whose master's hand is cold, whose silver
lyre unstrung.

Live thou, whose infamy is not thy fame!
Live! fear no heavier chastisement from
me, 326
Thou noteless blot on a remembered name!
But be thyself, and know thyself to be!
And ever at thy season be thou free
To spill the venom when thy fangs o'er-
flow: 330
Remorse and Self-contempt shall cling to
thee;
Hot Shame shall burn upon thy secret
brow,
And like a beaten hound tremble thou shalt
— as now.

Nor let us weep that our delight is fled
Far from these carrion kites that scream
below; 335

He wakes or sleeps with the enduring dead;
Thou canst not soar where he is sitting now.
Dust to the dust! but the pure spirit shall
flow
Back to the burning fountain whence it
came, 339
A portion of the Eternal, which must glow
Through time and change, unquenchably
the same,
Whilst thy cold embers choke the sordid
hearth of shame.

Peace, peace! he is not dead, he doth not
sleep —
He hath awakened from the dream of
life —
'Tis we who, lost in stormy visions, keep
With phantoms an unprofitable strife, 346
And in mad trance strike with our spirit's
knife
Invulnerable nothings. — *We* decay
Like corpses in a charnel; fear and grief
Convulse us and consume us day by day,
And cold hopes swarm like worms within
our living clay. 351

He has outsoared the shadow of our night;
Envy and calumny and hate and pain,
And that unrest which men miscall delight,
Can touch him not and torture not again;
From the contagion of the world's slow
stain 356
He is secure, and now can never mourn
A heart grown cold, a head grown grey in
vain;
Nor, when the spirit's self has ceased to
burn, 359
With sparkless ashes load an unlamented urn.

He lives, he wakes — 'tis Death is dead,
not he;
Mourn not for Adonais. — Thou young
Dawn,
Turn all thy dew to splendour, for from
thee
The spirit thou lamentest is not gone;
Ye caverns and ye forests, cease to moan!
Cease ye faint flowers and fountains, and
thou Air, 366
Which like a mourning veil thy scarf hadst
thrown
O'er the abandoned Earth, now leave it
bare
Even to the joyous stars which smile on its
despair!

He is made one with Nature: there is
  heard   370
His voice in all her music, from the moan
Of thunder, to the song of night's sweet
  bird;
He is a presence to be felt and known
In darkness and in light, from herb and
  stone,
Spreading itself where'er that Power may
  move   375
Which has withdrawn his being to its own;
Which wields the world with never wearied
  love,
Sustains it from beneath, and kindles it above.

He is a portion of the loveliness
Which once he made more lovely: he doth
  bear   380
His part, while the one Spirit's plastic stress
Sweeps through the dull dense world, com-
  pelling there
All new successions to the forms they wear;
Torturing th' unwilling dross that checks
  its flight   384
To its own likeness, as each mass may bear;
And bursting in its beauty and its might
From trees and beasts and men into the
  Heaven's light.

The splendours of the firmament of time
May be eclipsed, but are extinguished not;
Like stars to their appointed height they
  climb,   390
And death is a low mist which cannot blot
The brightness it may veil. When lofty
  thought
Lifts a young heart above its mortal lair,
And love and life contend in it, for what
Shall be its earthly doom, the dead live
  there   395
And move like winds of light on dark and
  stormy air.

The inheritors of unfulfilled renown
Rose from their thrones, built beyond mor-
  tal thought,
Far in the Unapparent. Chatterton
Rose pale, his solemn agony had not   400
Yet faded from him; Sidney, as he fought
And as he fell and as he lived and loved,
Sublimely mild, a Spirit without spot,
Arose; and Lucan, by his death ap-
  proved:
Oblivion, as they rose, shrank like a thing
  reproved.   405

And many more, whose names on Earth
  are dark
But whose transmitted effluence cannot die
So long as fire outlives the parent spark,
Rose, robed in dazzling immortality.   409
"Thou art become as one of us," they cry
"It was for thee yon kingless sphere has
  long
Swung blind in unascended majesty,
Silent alone amid an Heaven of Song.
Assume thy wingèd throne, thou Vesper of
  our throng!"

Who mourns for Adonais? oh come forth,
Fond wretch! and know thyself and him
  aright.   416
Clasp with thy panting soul the pendulous
  Earth;
As from a centre, dart thy spirit's light
Beyond all worlds, until its spacious
  might
Satiate the void circumference: then
  shrink   420
Even to a point within our day and
  night;
And keep thy heart light, lest it make thee
  sink,
When hope has kindled hope, and lured thee
  to the brink.

Or go to Rome, which is the sepulchre,
O, not of him, but of our joy: 'tis
  naught   425
That ages, empires, and religions there
Lie buried in the ravage they have wrought;
For such as he can lend, — they borrow not
Glory from those who made the world their
  prey;
And he is gathered to the kings of thought
Who waged contention with their time's
  decay,   431
And of the past are all that cannot pass away.

Go thou to Rome, — at once the Paradise,
The grave, the city, and the wilderness;
And where its wrecks like shattered moun-
  tains rise,   435
And flowering weeds and fragrant copses
  dress
The bones of Desolation's nakedness
Pass, till the Spirit of the spot shall lead
Thy footsteps to a slope of green access
Where, like an infant's smile, over the dead,
A light of laughing flowers along the grass is
  spread.   441

And grey walls moulder round, on which
  dull Time
Feeds, like slow fire upon a hoary brand;
And one keen pyramid with wedge sublime,
Pavilioning the dust of him who planned
This refuge for his memory, doth stand 446
Like flame transformed to marble; and
  beneath,
A field is spread, on which a newer band
Have pitched in Heaven's smile their camp
  of death,
Welcoming him we lose with scarce extin-
  guished breath.   450

Here pause: these graves are all too young
  as yet
To have outgrown the sorrow which con-
  signed
Its charge to each; and if the seal is set,
Here, on one fountain of a mourning mind,
Break it not thou! too surely shalt thou
  find   455
Thine own well full, if thou returnest home,
Of tears and gall. From the world's bitter
  wind
Seek shelter in the shadow of the tomb.
What Adonais is, why fear we to become?

The One remains, the many change and
  pass;   460
Heaven's light forever shines, Earth's
  shadows fly;
Life, like a dome of many-coloured glass,
Stains the white radiance of Eternity,
Until Death tramples it to fragments. —
  Die,
If thou wouldst be with that which thou
  dost seek!   465
Follow where all is fled! — Rome's azure
  sky,
Flowers, ruins, statues, music, words, are
  weak
The glory they transfuse with fitting truth to
  speak.

Why linger, why turn back, why shrink,
  my Heart?
Thy hopes are gone before: from all things
  here   470
They have departed; thou shouldst now
  depart!
A light is past from the revolving year,
And man, and woman; and what still is dear
Attracts to crush, repels to make thee
  wither.

The soft sky smiles, — the low wind whispers near;   475
'Tis Adonais calls! oh, hasten thither,
No more let Life divide what Death can join
  together.

That Light whose smile kindles the Uni-
  verse,
That Beauty in which all things work and
  move,
That Benediction which the eclipsing
  Curse   480
Of birth can quench not, that sustaining
  Love
Which, through the web of being blindly
  wove
By man and beast and earth and air and
  sea,
Burns bright or dim, as each are mirrors of
The fire for which all thirst, now beams on
  me,   485
Consuming the last clouds of cold mortality.

The breath whose might I have invoked in
  song
Descends on me; my spirit's bark is driven
Far from the shore, far from the trembling
  throng   489
Whose sails were never to the tempest
  given;
The massy earth and sphered skies are
  riven!
I am borne darkly, fearfully, afar:
Whilst burning through the inmost veil of
  Heaven,
The soul of Adonais, like a star,   494
Beacons from the abode where the Eternal
  are.

FINAL CHORUS FROM HELLAS

The world's great age begins anew,
  The golden years return,
The earth doth like a snake renew
  Her winter weeds outworn:
Heaven smiles, and faiths and empires gleam,
Like wrecks of a dissolving dream.   6

A brighter Hellas rears its mountains
  From waves serener far;
A new Peneus rolls his fountains
  Against the morning-star.   10
Where fairer Tempe bloom, there sleep
Young Cyclads on a sunnier deep.

A loftier Argo cleaves the main,
　Fraught with a later prize ;
Another Orpheus sings again,　　　　　　15
　And loves, and weeps, and dies.
A new Ulysses leaves once more
Calypso for his native shore.

O, write no more the tale of Troy,
　If earth Death's scroll must be !　　　20
Nor mix with Laian rage the joy
　Which dawns upon the free :
Although a subtler Sphinx renew
Riddles of death Thebes never knew.

Another Athens shall arise,　　　　　　25
　And to remoter time
Bequeath, like sunset to the skies,
　The splendour of its prime ;
And leave, if naught so bright may live,
All earth can take or Heaven can give.　30

Saturn and Love their long repose
　Shall burst, more bright and good
Than all who fell, than One who rose,
　Than many unsubdued :
Not gold, not blood, their altar dowers,　35
But votive tears and symbol flowers.

O cease ! must hate and death return ?
　Cease ! must men kill and die ?
Cease ! drain not to its dregs the urn
　Of bitter prophecy.　　　　　　　40
The world is weary of the past,
O might it die or rest at last !

TO NIGHT

Swiftly walk o'er the western wave,
　　Spirit of Night !
　Out of the misty eastern cave,
Where all the long and lone daylight
Thou wovest dreams of joy and fear,　5
Which make thee terrible and dear, —
　　Swift be thy flight !

Wrap thy form in a mantle grey,
　　Star in-wrought !
Blind with thine hair the eyes of Day ;　10
Kiss her until she be wearied out ;
Then wander o'er city, and sea, and land,
Touching all with thine opiate wand —
　　Come, long sought !

When I arose and saw the dawn,　15
　　I sighed for thee ;

When light rode high, and the dew was gone,
And noon lay heavy on flower and tree,
And the weary Day turned to his rest,
Lingering like an unloved guest,　　　20
　　I sighed for thee.

Thy brother Death came, and cried,
　　Wouldst thou me ?
Thy sweet child Sleep, the filmy-eyed,
Murmured like a noon-tide bee,　　　25
Shall I nestle near thy side ?
Wouldst thou me ? — And I replied,
　　No, not thee !

Death will come when thou art dead,
　　Soon, too soon —　　　　　　30
Sleep will come when thou art fled ;
Of neither would I ask the boon
I ask of thee, belovèd Night —
Swift be thine approaching flight,
　　Come soon, soon !　　　　　35

TO ——

One word is too often profaned
　　For me to profane it,
One feeling too falsely disdained
　　For thee to disdain it.
One hope is too like despair　　　5
　　For prudence to smother,
And pity from thee more dear,
　　Than that from another.

I can give not what men call love,
　　But wilt thou accept not　　　10
The worship the heart lifts above
　　And the Heavens reject not, —
The desire of the moth for the star,
　　Of the night for the morrow,
The devotion to something afar　　15
　　From the sphere of our sorrow ?

JOHN KEATS (1795–1821)

ODE TO A NIGHTINGALE

My heart aches, and a drowsy numbness pains
　My sense, as though of hemlock I had
　　drunk,
Or emptied some dull opiate to the drains
　One minute past, and Lethe-wards had
　　sunk :
'Tis not through envy of thy happy lot,　5

But being too happy in thine happiness, —
  That thou, light-wingèd Dryad of the trees
    In some melodious plot
  Of beechen green, and shadows numberless,
    Singest of summer in full-throated ease.

O for a draught of vintage! that hath been
  Cool'd a long age in the deep-delvèd earth,
Tasting of Flora and the country green,
  Dance, and Provençal song, and sunburnt
    mirth!
O for a beaker full of the warm South,   15
  Full of the true, the blushful Hippocrene,
    With beaded bubbles winking at the brim,
      And purple-stainèd mouth;
  That I might drink, and leave the world
    unseen,
  And with thee fade away into the forest
    dim: 20

Fade far away, dissolve, and quite forget,
  What thou among the leaves hast never
    known,
The weariness, the fever, and the fret
  Here, where men sit and hear each other
    groan;
Where palsy shakes a few, sad, last grey hairs,
  Where youth grows pale, and spectre-thin,
    and dies;   26
    Where but to think is to be full of sorrow
      And leaden-eyed despairs,
  Where Beauty cannot keep her lustrous
    eyes,
    Or new Love pine at them beyond to-
      morrow.   30

Away! away! for I will fly to thee,
  Not charioted by Bacchus and his pards,
But on the viewless wings of Poesy,
  Though the dull brain perplexes and re-
    tards:
Already with thee! tender is the night.   35
  And haply the Queen-Moon is on her throne,
    Cluster'd around by all her starry Fays;
      But here there is no light,
  Save what from heaven is with the breezes
    blown
    Through verdurous glooms and winding
      mossy ways.   40

I cannot see what flowers are at my feet,
  Nor what soft incense hangs upon the
    boughs,
But, in embalmèd darkness, guess each sweet
  Wherewith the seasonable month endows

The grass, the thicket, and the fruit-tree wild;
  White hawthorn, and the pastoral eglan-
    tine;   46
  Fast fading violets cover'd up in leaves;
    And mid-May's eldest child,
  The coming musk-rose, full of dewy wine,
    The murmurous haunt of flies on summer
    eves.   50

Darkling I listen; and, for many a time
  I have been half in love with easeful Death,
Call'd him soft names in many a musèd rhyme,
  To take into the air my quiet breath;
Now more than ever seems it rich to die, 55
  To cease upon the midnight with no pain,
    While thou art pouring forth thy soul
    abroad
      In such an ecstasy!
  Still wouldst thou sing, and I have ears in
    vain —
    To thy high requiem become a sod.   60

Thou wast not born for death, immortal Bird!
  No hungry generations tread thee down;
The voice I hear this passing night was heard
  In ancient days by emperor and clown:
Perhaps the self-same song that found a path
  Through the sad heart of Ruth, when, sick
    for home,   66
    She stood in tears amid the alien corn;
      The same that oft-times hath
  Charm'd magic casements, opening on the
    foam
    Of perilous seas, in faery lands forlorn. 70

Forlorn! the very word is like a bell
  To toll me back from thee to my sole self!
Adieu! the fancy cannot cheat so well
  As she is fam'd to do, deceiving elf.
Adieu! adieu! thy plaintive anthem fades 75
  Past the near meadows, over the still stream,
    Up the hill-side; and now 'tis buried deep
    In the next valley-glades:
  Was it a vision, or a waking dream?   79
    Fled is that music: — Do I wake or sleep?

ODE ON A GRECIAN URN

Thou still unravish'd bride of quietness,
  Thou foster-child of silence and slow time,
Sylvan historian, who canst thus express
  A flowery tale more sweetly than our rhyme:
What leaf-fring'd legend haunts about thy
    shape   5

Of deities or mortals, or of both,
  In Tempe or the dales of Arcady?
What men or gods are these?   What maidens
    loth?
    What mad pursuit?   What struggle to
      escape?
    What pipes and timbrels?   What wild
      ecstasy?   10

Heard melodies are sweet, but those unheard
  Are sweeter; therefore, ye soft pipes, play on;
Not to the sensual ear, but, more endear'd,
  Pipe to the spirit ditties of no tone:
Fair youth, beneath the trees, thou canst not
    leave   15
Thy song, nor ever can those trees be bare;
  Bold Lover, never, never canst thou kiss,
Though winning near the goal — yet, do not
    grieve;
  She cannot fade, though thou hast not thy
    bliss,
    Forever wilt thou love, and she be fair! 20

Ah, happy, happy boughs! that cannot shed
  Your leaves, nor ever bid the Spring adieu:
And, happy melodist, unwearied,
  Forever piping songs forever new;
More happy love! more happy, happy love!
  Forever warm and still to be enjoy'd,   26
  Forever panting, and forever young;
All breathing human passion far above,
  That leaves a heart high-sorrowful and
    cloy'd,
    A burning forehead, and a parching
      tongue.   30

Who are these coming to the sacrifice?
  To what green altar, O mysterious priest,
Lead'st thou that heifer lowing at the skies,
  And all her silken flanks with garlands drest?
What little town by river or sea shore,   35
  Or mountain-built with peaceful citadel,
  Is emptied of this folk, this pious morn?
And, little town, thy streets for evermore
  Will silent be; and not a soul to tell
    Why thou art desolate, can e'er return. 40

O Attic shape! Fair attitude! with brede
  Of marble men and maidens overwrought,
With forest branches and the trodden weed;
  Thou, silent form, dost tease us out of
    thought
As doth eternity: Cold Pastoral!   45
  When old age shall this generation waste,
    Thou shalt remain, in midst of other woe

Than ours, a friend to man, to whom thou
    say'st,
  "Beauty is truth, truth beauty," — that is
    all,
    Ye know on earth, and all ye need to
      know.   50

TO AUTUMN

Season of mists and mellow fruitfulness,
  Close bosom-friend of the maturing sun;
Conspiring with him how to load and bless
  With fruit the vines that round the thatch-
    eaves run;   4
To bend with apples the moss'd cottage-trees,
  And fill all fruit with ripeness to the core;
    To swell the gourd, and plump the hazel
    shells
With a sweet kernel; to set budding more,
  And still more, later flowers for the bees,
Until they think warm days will never cease,
  For Summer has o'er-brimmed their
    clammy cells.   11

Who hath not seen thee oft amid thy store?
  Sometimes whoever seeks abroad may find
Thee sitting careless on a granary floor,
  Thy hair soft-lifted by the winnowing wind;
Or on a half-reap'd furrow sound asleep,   16
  Drows'd with the fume of poppies, while thy
    hook
    Spares the next swath and all its twinèd
    flowers:
And sometimes like a gleaner thou dost keep
  Steady thy laden head across a brook;   20
  Or by a cider-press, with patient look,
    Thou watchest the last oozings hours by
    hours.

Where are the songs of Spring?   Ay, where
    are they?
  Think not of them, thou hast thy music
    too, —
While barrèd clouds bloom the soft-dying day,
  And touch the stubble-plains with rosy hue;
Then in a wailful choir the small gnats mourn
  Among the river sallows, borne aloft
    Or sinking as the light wind lives or dies;
And full-grown lambs loud bleat from hilly
    bourn;   30
  Hedge-crickets sing; and now with treble
    soft
    The red-breast whistles from a garden-croft;
    And gathering swallows twitter in the
    skies.

ODE

Bards of Passion and of Mirth,
Ye have left your souls on earth!
Have ye souls in heaven too,
Double-lived in regions new?
Yes, and those of heaven commune   5
With the spheres of sun and moon;
With the noise of fountains wond'rous,
And the parle of voices thund'rous;
With the whisper of heaven's trees
And one another, in soft ease   10
Seated on Elysian lawns
Brows'd by none but Dian's fawns;
Underneath large bluebells tented,
Where the daisies are rose-scented,
And the rose herself has got   15
Perfume which on earth is not;
Where the nightingale doth sing
Not a senseless, trancèd thing,
But divine melodious truth;
Philosophic numbers smooth;   20
Tales and golden histories
Of heaven and its mysteries.

Thus ye live on high, and then
On the earth ye live again;
And the souls ye left behind you   25
Teach us, here, the way to find you
Where your other souls are joying,
Never slumber'd, never cloying.
Here, your earth-born souls still speak
To mortals, of their little week;   30
Of their sorrows and delights;
Of their passions and their spites;
Of their glory and their shame;
What doth strengthen and what maim.
Thus ye teach us, every day,   35
Wisdom, though fled far away.

Bards of Passion and of Mirth,
Ye have left your souls on earth!
Ye have souls in heaven too,
Double-lived in regions new!   40

LINES ON THE MERMAID TAVERN

Souls of Poets dead and gone,
What Elysium have ye known,
Happy field or mossy cavern,
Choicer than the Mermaid Tavern?
Have ye tippled drink more fine   5
Than mine host's Canary wine?
Or are fruits of Paradise

Sweeter than those dainty pies
Of venison?   O generous food!
Drest as though bold Robin Hood   10
Would, with his maid Marian,
Sup and bowse from horn and can.

I have heard that on a day
Mine host's sign-board flew away,
Nobody knew whither, till   15
An astrologer's old quill
To a sheepskin gave the story,
Said he saw you in your glory,
Underneath a new old-sign
Sipping beverage divine,   20
And pledging with contented smack
The Mermaid in the Zodiac.

Souls of Poets dead and gone,
What Elysium have ye known,
Happy field or mossy cavern,   25
Choicer than the Mermaid Tavern?

LA BELLE DAME SANS MERCI

O what can ail thee, knight-at-arms,
    Alone and palely loitering?
The sedge has wither'd from the lake,
    And no birds sing,   4

O what can ail thee, knight-at-arms,
    So haggard and so woe-begone?
The squirrel's granary is full,
    And the harvest's done.   8

I see a lily on thy brow
    With anguish moist and fever dew,
And on thy cheeks a fading rose
    Fast withereth too.   12

"I met a lady in the meads,
    Full beautiful — a faery's child;
Her hair was long, her foot was light,
    And her eyes were wild.   16

"I made a garland for her head,
    And bracelets too, and fragrant zone;
She look'd at me as she did love,
    And made sweet moan.   20

"I set her on my pacing steed,
    And nothing else saw all day long,
For sideways would she lean, and sing
    A faery's song.   24

"She found me roots of relish sweet,
  And honey wild, and manna-dew,
And sure in language strange she said —
  'I love thee true.'   28

"She took me to her elfin grot,
  And there she wept and sigh'd full sore,
And there I shut her wild, wild eyes,
  With kisses four.
                                                             32
"And there she lullèd me asleep,
  And there I dream'd — ah! woe betide! —
The latest dream I ever dream'd
  On the cold hill's side.   36

"I saw pale kings and princes too,
  Pale warriors, death-pale were they all;
They cried — 'La Belle Dame sans Merci
  Hath thee in thrall!'   40

"I saw their starved lips in the gloom,
  With horrid warning gapèd wide;
And I awoke, and found me here
  On the cold hill's side.   44

"And this is why I sojourn here,
  Alone and palely loitering,
Though the sedge is wither'd from the lake,
  And no birds sing."   48

SONNETS

THE GRASSHOPPER AND THE CRICKET

The poetry of earth is never dead:
  When all the birds are faint with the hot
    sun,
  And hide in cooling trees, a voice will run
From hedge to hedge about the new-mown
    mead;
That is the Grasshopper's — he takes the lead
  In summer luxury, — he has never done   6
  With his delights; for when tired out with
    fun
He rests at ease beneath some pleasant weed.
The poetry of earth is ceasing never:
  On a lone winter evening, when the frost   10
    Has wrought a silence, from the stove
      there shrills
The Cricket's song, in warmth increasing ever,
  And seems to one in drowsiness half lost,
    The Grasshopper's among some grassy
      hills.

ON FIRST LOOKING INTO CHAPMAN'S HOMER

Much have I travell'd in the realms of gold,
  And many goodly states and kingdoms seen;
  Round many western islands have I been
Which bards in fealty to Apollo hold.
Oft of one wide expanse had I been told   5
  That deep-brow'd Homer ruled as his
    demesne;
  Yet did I never breathe its pure serene
Till I heard Chapman speak out loud and
    bold:
Then felt I like some watcher of the skies
  When a new planet swims into his ken;   10
Or like stout Cortez when with eagle eyes
  He star'd at the Pacific — and all his men
Look'd at each other with a wild surmise —
  Silent, upon a peak in Darien.

TO SLEEP

O soft embalmer of the still midnight!
  Shutting with careful fingers and benign
Our gloom-pleased eyes, embower'd from the
    light,
  Enshaded in forgetfulness divine;
O soothest Sleep! if so it please thee, close,   5
  In midst of this thine hymn, my willing eyes,
Or wait the amen, ere thy poppy throws
  Around my bed its lulling charities;
Then save me, or the passèd day will shine
Upon my pillow, breeding many woes;   10
Save me from curious conscience, that still
    lords
  Its strength for darkness, burrowing like a
    mole;
Turn the key deftly in the oilèd wards,
  And seal the hushèd casket of my soul.

ON THE SEA

It keeps eternal whisperings around
  Desolate shores, and with its mighty swell
  Gluts twice ten thousand caverns, till the
    spell
Of Hecate leaves them their old shadowy
    sound.
Often 'tis in such gentle temper found   5
  That scarcely will the very smallest shell
  Be mov'd for days from whence it sometime
    fell,
When last the winds of heaven were unbound.

Oh, ye, who have your eye-balls vex'd and
  tir'd,
  Feast them upon the wideness of the sea; 10
  O, ye, whose ears are dinn'd with uproar
  rude,
  Or fed too much with cloying melody, —
    Sit ye near some old cavern's mouth, and
    brood
Until ye start, as if the sea-nymphs quir'd!

WHEN I HAVE FEARS

When I have fears that I may cease to be
  Before my pen has glean'd my teeming
  brain,
Before high pilèd books, in charact'ry,
  Hold like rich garners the full-ripen'd grain;
When I behold, upon the night's starr'd face, 5
  Huge cloudy symbols of a high romance,
And think that I may never live to trace
  Their shadows, with the magic hand of
  chance;
And when I feel, fair creature of an hour!
  That I shall never look upon thee more, 10
Never have relish in the faery power
  Of unreflecting love! — then on the shore
Of the wide world I stand alone, and think
Till love and fame to nothingness do sink.

BRIGHT STAR!

Bright star! would I were steadfast as thou
  art —
Not in lone splendour hung aloft the night,
And watching, with eternal lids apart,
  Like Nature's patient sleepless Eremite,
The moving waters at their priestlike task 5
  Of pure ablution round earth's human shores,
Or gazing on the new soft fallen mask
  Of snow upon the mountains and the
  moors —
No — yet still steadfast, still unchangeable,
  Pillow'd upon my fair love's ripening breast,
To feel forever its soft fall and swell, 11
  Awake forever in a sweet unrest,
Still, still to hear her tender-taken breath,
And so live ever — or else swoon to death.

ENDYMION

From BOOK I

A thing of beauty is a joy forever:
Its loveliness increases; it will never

Pass into nothingness; but still will keep
A bower quiet for us, and a sleep
Full of sweet dreams, and health, and quiet
  breathing. 5
Therefore, on every morrow, are we wreathing
A flowery band to bind us to the earth,
Spite of despondence, of the inhuman dearth
Of noble natures, of the gloomy days,
Of all the unhealthy and o'er-darkened ways
Made for our searching: yes, in spite of all, 11
Some shape of beauty moves away the pall
From our dark spirits. Such the sun, the
  moon,
Trees old and young, sprouting a shady boòn
For simple sheep; and such are daffodils 15
With the green world they live in; and clear
  rills
That for themselves a cooling covert make
'Gainst the hot season; the mid forest brake,
Rich with a sprinkling of fair musk-rose
  blooms:
And such too is the grandeur of the dooms 20
We have imagined for the mighty dead;
All lovely tales that we have heard or read:
An endless fountain of immortal drink,
Pouring unto us from the heaven's brink.

  Nor do we merely feel these essences 25
For one short hour; no, even as the trees
That whisper round a temple become soon
Dear as the temple's self, so does the moon,
The passion poesy, glories infinite,
Haunt us till they become a cheering light 30
Unto our souls, and bound to us so fast,
That, whether there be shine, or gloom o'er-
  cast,
They alway must be with us, or we die.

　*　*　*　*　*　*　*

"This river does not see the naked sky, 540
Till it begins to progress silverly
Around the western border of the wood,
Whence, from a certain spot, its winding flood
Seems at the distance like a crescent moon:
And in that nook, the very pride of June, 545
Had I been us'd to pass my weary eyes;
The rather for the sun unwilling leaves
So dear a picture of his sovereign power,
And I could witness his most kingly hour,
When he doth tighten up the golden reins, 550
And paces leisurely down amber plains
His snorting four. Now when his chariot last
Its beams against the zodiac-lion [1] cast,

[1] the zodiacal sign Leo, in which the sun
travels from July 21 to August 21

There blossom'd suddenly a magic bed
Of sacred ditamy,[1] and poppies red:　555
At which I wondered greatly, knowing well
That but one night had wrought this flowery
　spell;
And, sitting down close by, began to muse
What it might mean.

`　*　*　*　*　*　*　*

" And lo! from opening clouds, I saw emerge
The loveliest moon that ever silver'd o'er
A shell for Neptune's goblet: she did soar
So passionately bright, my dazzled soul　594
Commingling with her argent spheres did roll
Through clear and cloudy, even when she
　went
At last into a dark and vapoury tent —
Whereat, methought, the lidless-eyèd train
Of planets all were in the blue again.
To commune with those orbs, once more I
　rais'd　600
My sight right upward: but it was quite
　dazed
By a bright something, sailing down apace,
Making me quickly veil my eyes and face:
Again I look'd, and, O ye deities,
Who from Olympus watch our destinies!　605
Whence that completed form of all complete-
　ness?
Whence came that high perfection of all sweet-
　ness?
Speak, stubborn earth, and tell me where, O
　where
Hast thou a symbol of her golden hair?　609
Not oat-sheaves drooping in the western
　sun;
Not — thy soft hand, fair sister! let me shun
Such follying before thee — yet she had,
Indeed, locks bright enough to make me mad;
And they were simply gordian'd up and
　braided,
Leaving, in naked comeliness, unshaded,　615
Her pearl round ears, white neck, and orbèd
　brow;
The which were blended in, I know not how,
With such a paradise of lips and eyes,
Blush-tinted cheeks, half smiles, and faintest
　sighs,
That, when I think thereon, my spirit clings
And plays about its fancy, till the stings　621
Of human neighbourhood envenom all.
Unto what awful power shall I call?

[1] a flower of Greece, supposed to possess magical properties

To what high fane? — Ah! see her hovering
　feet,
More bluely vein'd, more soft, more whitely
　sweet　625
Than those of sea-born Venus, when she rose
From out her cradle shell.　The wind out-
　blows
Her scarf into a fluttering pavilion;
'Tis blue, and over-spangled with a million
Of little eyes, as though thou wert to shed 630
Over the darkest, lushest bluebell bed,
Handfuls of daisies." — "Endymion, how
　strange!
Dream within dream!" — "She took an airy
　range,
And then, towards me, like a very maid,
Came blushing, waning, willing, and afraid,
And press'd me by the hand: Ah! 'twas too
　much;　636
Methought I fainted at the charmèd touch,
Yet held my recollection, even as one
Who dives three fathoms where the waters run
Gurgling in beds of coral: for anon,　640
I felt upmounted in that region
Where falling stars dart their artillery forth,
And eagles struggle with the buffeting north
That balances the heavy meteor-stone; —
Felt too, I was not fearful, nor alone;　645
But lapp'd and lull'd along the dangerous sky.
Soon, as it seem'd, we left our journeying high,
And straightway into frightful eddies swoop'd;
Such as ay muster where grey time has scoop'd
Huge dens and caverns in a mountain's side:
There hollow sounds arous'd me, and I sigh'd
To faint once more by looking on my bliss —
I was distracted; madly did I kiss　653
The wooing arms which held me, and did give
My eyes at once to death: but 'twas to live,
To take in draughts of life from the gold fount
Of kind and passionate looks; to count, and
　count
The moments, by some greedy help that seem'd
A second self, that each might be redeem'd
And plunder'd of its load of blessedness.　660
Ah, desperate mortal!　I e'en dar'd to press
Her very cheek against my crownèd lip,
And, at that moment, felt my body dip
Into a warmer air: a moment more,
Our feet were soft in flowers.　There was store
Of newest joys upon that alp.　Sometimes 666
A scent of violets, and blossoming limes,
Loiter'd around us; then of honey cells,
Made delicate from all white-flower bells;
And once, above the edges of our nest,　670
An arch face peep'd, — an Oread as I guess'd.

HYPERION

A FRAGMENT

From Book I

Deep in the shady sadness of a vale
Far sunken from the healthy breath of morn,
Far from the fiery noon, and eve's one star,
Sat gray-hair'd Saturn, quiet as a stone,
Still as the silence round about his lair;   5
Forest on forest hung about his head
Like cloud on cloud.   No stir of air was there,
Not so much life as on a summer's day
Robs not one light seed from the feather'd
   grass,
But where the dead leaf fell, there did it rest.
A stream went voiceless by, still deadened
   more   11
By reason of his fallen divinity
Spreading a shade: the Naiad 'mid her reeds
Press'd her cold finger closer to her lips.

Along the margin-sand large foot-marks
   went,   15
No further than to where his feet had stray'd,
And slept there since.   Upon the sodden
   ground
His old right hand lay nerveless, listless, dead,
Unsceptred; and his realmless eyes were
   closed;
While his bow'd head seem'd list'ning to the
   Earth,   20
His ancient mother, for some comfort yet.

It seem'd no force could wake him from his
   place;
But there came one, who with a kindred hand
Touch'd his wide shoulders, after bending low
With reverence, though to one who knew it
   not.   26
She was a Goddess of the infant world;
By her in stature the tall Amazon
Had stood a pigmy's height: she would have
   ta'en
Achilles by the hair and bent his neck;
Or with a finger stay'd Ixion's wheel.   30
Her face was large as that of Memphian
   sphinx,
Pedestal'd haply in a palace court,
When sages look'd to Egypt for their lore.
But oh! how unlike marble was that face:
How beautiful, if sorrow had not made   35
Sorrow more beautiful than Beauty's self.
There was a listening fear in her regard,
As if calamity had but begun;

As if the vanward clouds of evil days
Had spent their malice, and the sullen rear   40
Was with its storèd thunder labouring up.
One hand she press'd upon that aching spot
Where beats the human heart, as if just there,
Though an immortal, she felt cruel pain:
The other upon Saturn's bended neck   45
She laid, and to the level of his ear
Leaning with parted lips, some words she
   spake
In solemn tenor and deep organ tone:
Some mourning words, which in our feeble
   tongue
Would come in these like accents; O how frail
To that large utterance of the early Gods!   51
"Saturn, look up! — though wherefore, poor
   old King?
I have no comfort for thee, no, not one:
I cannot say, 'O wherefore sleepest thou?'
For heaven is parted from thee, and the earth
Knows thee not, thus afflicted, for a God;   56
And ocean too, with all its solemn noise,
Has from thy sceptre pass'd; and all the air
Is emptied of thine hoary majesty.
Thy thunder, conscious of the new command,
Rumbles reluctant o'er our fallen house;   61
And thy sharp lightning in unpractised hands
Scorches and burns our once serene domain.
O aching time! O moments big as years!
All as ye pass swell out the monstrous truth,
And press it so upon our weary griefs   66
That unbelief has not a space to breathe.
Saturn, sleep on: — O thoughtless, why did I
Thus violate thy slumbrous solitude?
Why should I ope thy melancholy eyes?   70
Saturn, sleep on! while at thy feet I weep."

As when, upon a trancèd summer night,
Those green-rob'd senators of mighty woods,
Tall oaks, branch-charmèd by the earnest
   stars,
Dream, and so dream all night without a stir,
Save from one gradual solitary gust   76
Which comes upon the silence, and dies off,
As if the ebbing air had but one wave;
So came these words and went; the while in
   tears
She touch'd her fair large forehead to the
   ground,   80
Just where her falling hair might be outspread
A soft and silken mat for Saturn's feet.
One moon, with alteration slow, had shed
Her silver seasons four upon the night,
And still these two were postured motionless,
Like natural sculpture in cathedral cavern;   86

The frozen God still couchant on the earth,
And the sad Goddess weeping at his feet:
Until at length old Saturn lifted up
His faded eyes, and saw his kingdom gone, 90
And all the gloom and sorrow of the place,
And that fair kneeling Goddess; and then
    spake,
As with a palsied tongue, and while his beard
Shook horrid with such aspen-malady:
"O tender spouse of gold Hyperion,   95
Thea, I feel thee ere I see thy face;
Look up, and let me see our doom in it;
Look up, and tell me if this feeble shape
Is Saturn's; tell me, if thou hear'st the voice
Of Saturn; tell me, if this wrinkling brow, 100
Naked and bare of its great diadem,
Peers like the front of Saturn. Who had
    power
To make me desolate? whence came the
    strength?
How was it nurtur'd to such bursting forth,
While Fate seem'd strangled in my nervous
    grasp?   105
But it is so; and I am smother'd up,
And buried from all godlike exercise
Of influence benign on planets pale,
Of admonitions to the winds and seas,
Of peaceful sway above man's harvesting, 110
And all those acts which Deity supreme
Doth ease its heart of love in. — I am gone
Away from my own bosom: I have left
My strong identity, my real self,
Somewhere between the throne, and where I
    sit,   115
Here on this spot of earth. Search, Thea,
    search!
Open thine eyes eterne, and sphere them round
Upon all space: space starr'd, and lorn of light;
Space region'd with life-air; and barren void;
Spaces of fire, and all the yawn of hell. — 120
Search, Thea, search! and tell me, if thou seest
A certain shape or shadow, making way
With wings or chariot fierce to repossess
A heaven he lost erewhile: it must — it must
Be of ripe progress — Saturn must be King.
Yes, there must be a golden victory;   126
There must be Gods thrown down, and trum-
    pets blown
Of triumph calm, and hymns of festival
Upon the gold clouds metropolitan,
Voices of soft proclaim, and silver stir   130
Of strings in hollow shells; and there shall be
Beautiful things made new, for the surprise
Of the sky-children; I will give command:
Thea! Thea! Thea! where is Saturn?"

THE EVE OF ST. AGNES

St. Agnes' Eve — Ah, bitter chill it was!
The owl, for all his feathers, was a-cold;
The hare limp'd trembling through the
    frozen grass,
And silent was the flock in woolly fold:
Numb were the Beadsman's fingers, while
    he told   5
His rosary, and while his frosted breath,
Like pious incense from a censer old,
Seem'd taking flight for heaven, without a
    death,
Past the sweet Virgin's picture, while his
    prayer he saith.   9

His prayer he saith, this patient, holy
    man;
Then takes his lamp, and riseth from his
    knees,
And back returneth, meagre, barefoot,
    wan,
Along the chapel aisle by slow degrees:
The sculptured dead, on each side, seem to
    freeze,
Emprison'd in black, purgatorial rails: 15
Knights, ladies, praying in dumb orat'ries,
He passeth by; and his weak spirit fails,
To think how they may ache in icy hoods and
    mails.

Northward he turneth through a little door,
And scarce three steps, ere Music's golden
    tongue   20
Flatter'd to tears this agèd man and poor;
But no — already had his deathbell rung;
The joys of all his life were said and sung:
His was harsh penance on St. Agnes' Eve:
Another way he went, and soon among   25
Rough ashes sat he for his soul's reprieve,
And all night kept awake, for sinners' sake to
    grieve.

That ancient Beadsman heard the prelude
    soft;
And so it chanc'd, for many a door was wide
From hurry to and fro. Soon, up aloft, 30
The silver, snarling trumpets 'gan to chide:
The level chambers, ready with their pride,
Were glowing to receive a thousand guests:
The carvèd angels, ever eager-eyed,
Star'd, where upon their heads the cornice
    rests,   35
With hair blown back, and wings put cross-
    wise on their breasts.

At length burst in the argent revelry,
With plume, tiara, and all rich array,
Numerous as shadows haunting fairily
The brain, new stuff'd, in youth, with
    triumphs gay   40
Of old romance. These let us wish away,
And turn, sole-thoughted, to one Lady there,
Whose heart had brooded, all that wintry
    day,
On love, and winged St. Agnes' saintly care,
As she had heard old dames full many times
    declare.   45

They told her how, upon St. Agnes' Eve,
Young virgins might have visions of delight,
And soft adorings from their loves receive
Upon the honeyed middle of the night,
If ceremonies due they did aright;   50
As, supperless to bed they must retire,
And couch supine their beauties, lily white;
Nor look behind, nor sideways, but require
Of Heaven with upward eyes for all that they
    desire.

Full of this whim was thoughtful Madeline:
The music, yearning like a God in pain, 56
She scarcely heard: her maiden eyes divine,
Fix'd on the floor, saw many a sweeping
    train
Pass by — she heeded not at all: in vain
Came many a tiptoe, amorous cavalier, 60
And back retir'd; not cool'd by high dis-
    dain,
But she saw not: her heart was otherwhere:
She sigh'd for Agnes' dreams, the sweetest of
    the year.

She danc'd along with vague, regardless
    eyes,
Anxious her lips, her breathing quick and
    short: 65
The hallowed hour was near at hand: she
    sighs
Amid the timbrels, and the thronged resort
Of whisperers in anger, or in sport;
'Mid looks of love, defiance, hate, and scorn,
Hoodwink'd[1] with fairy fancy; all amort,[2] 70
Save to St. Agnes and her lambs unshorn,
And all the bliss to be before to-morrow morn.

So, purposing each moment to retire,
She linger'd still. Meantime, across the
    moors,

Had come young Porphyro, with heart on
    fire   75
For Madeline. Beside the portal doors,
Buttress'd from moonlight, stands he, and
    implores
All saints to give him sight of Madeline,
But for one moment in the tedious hours,
That he might gaze and worship all unseen;
Perchance speak, kneel, touch, kiss — in sooth
    such things have been.   81

He ventures in: let no buzzed whisper tell:
All eyes be muffled, or a hundred swords
Will storm his heart, Love's fev'rous citadel:
For him, those chambers held barbarian
    hordes,   85
Hyena foemen, and hot-blooded lords,
Whose very dogs would execrations howl
Against his lineage: not one breast affords
Him any mercy, in that mansion foul,
Save one old beldame, weak in body and in
    soul.   90

Ah, happy chance! the aged creature came,
Shuffling along with ivory-headed wand,
To where he stood, hid from the torch's
    flame,
Behind a broad hall-pillar, far beyond 94
The sound of merriment and chorus bland:
He startled her; but soon she knew his face,
And grasp'd his fingers in her palsied hand,
Saying, "Mercy, Porphyro! hie thee from
    this place;
They are all here to-night, the whole blood-
    thirsty race!

"Get hence! get hence! there's dwarfish
    Hildebrand;   100
He had a fever late, and in the fit
He curs'd thee and thine, both house and
    land:
Then there's that old Lord Maurice, not a
    whit
More tame for his grey hairs — Alas me!
    flit!
Flit like a ghost away." — "Ah, Gossip[1]
    dear,   105
We're safe enough; here in this armchair
    sit,
And tell me how" — "Good Saints! not
    here, not here;
Follow me, child, or else these stones will be
    thy bier."

[1] blinded   [2] dead

[1] godmother

He follow'd through a lowly archèd way,
Brushing the cobwebs with his lofty plume;
And as she mutter'd "Well-a — well-a-
    day!"   111
He found him in a little moonlight room,
Pale, lattic'd, chill, and silent as a tomb.
"Now tell me where is Madeline," said he,
"O tell me, Angela, by the holy loom 115
Which none but secret sisterhood may see,
When they St. Agnes' wool are weaving
    piously."

"St. Agnes! Ah! it is St. Agnes' Eve —
Yet men will murder upon holy days:
Thou must hold water in a witch's sieve, 120
And be liege-lord of all the Elves and Fays,
To venture so: it fills me with amaze
To see thee, Porphyro! — St. Agnes' Eve!
God's help! my lady fair the conjurer plays
This very night: good angels her deceive!
But let me laugh awhile, I've mickle time to
    grieve."   126

Feebly she laugheth in the languid moon,
While Porphyro upon her face doth look,
Like puzzled urchin on an aged crone
Who keepeth clos'd a wond'rous riddle-book,
As spectacled she sits in chimney nook. 131
But soon his eyes grew brilliant, when she
    told
His lady's purpose; and he scarce could
    brook[1]
Tears, at the thought of those enchantments
    cold,
And Madeline asleep in lap of legends old. 135

Sudden a thought came like a full-blown rose,
Flushing his brow, and in his painèd heart
Made purple riot: then doth he propose
A stratagem, that makes the beldame[2] start:
"A cruel man and impious thou art: 140
Sweet lady, let her pray, and sleep, and
    dream
Alone with her good angels, far apart
From wicked men like thee. Go, go! — I
    deem
Thou canst not surely be the same that thou
    didst seem."   144

"I will not harm her, by all saints I swear,"
Quoth Porphyro: "O may I ne'er find grace
When my weak voice shall whisper its last
    prayer,

1 hold back   2 old woman

If one of her soft ringlets I displace,
Or look with ruffian passion in her face:
Good Angela, believe me by these tears;
Or I will, even in a moment's space,   151
Awake, with horrid shout, my foemen's ears,
And beard them, though they be more fang'd
    than wolves and bears."

"Ah! why wilt thou affright a feeble soul?
A poor, weak, palsy-stricken, churchyard
    thing, —   155
Whose passing-bell[1] may ere the midnight
    toll;
Whose prayers for thee, each morn and
    evening,
Were never miss'd." — Thus plaining,[2] doth
    she bring
A gentler speech from burning Porphyro;
So woeful, and of such deep sorrowing, 160
That Angela gives promise she will do
Whatever he shall wish, betide her weal or woe.

Which was, to lead him, in close secrecy,
Even to Madeline's chamber, and there hide
Him in a closet, of such privacy   165
That he might see her beauty unespied,
And win perhaps that night a peerless bride,
While legioned fairies pac'd the coverlet,
And pale enchantment held her sleepy-eyed.
Never on such a night have lovers met, 170
Since Merlin paid his Demon all the monstrous
    debt.[3]

"It shall be as thou wishest," said the dame:
"All cates[4] and dainties shall be stored there
Quickly on this feast-night: by the tam-
    bour frame
Her own lute thou wilt see: no time to spare,
For I am slow and feeble, and scarce dare
On such a catering trust my dizzy head. 177
Wait here, my child, with patience; kneel
    in prayer
The while. Ah! thou must needs the lady
    wed,
Or may I never leave my grave among the
    dead."   180

So saying, she hobbled off with busy fear.
The lover's endless minutes slowly pass'd;
The dame return'd, and whisper'd in his ear

1 bell rung when one is dying   2 lamenting
3 Merlin the Magician, of Arthurian romance, was
deceived and bespelled by Vivien, his mistress,
cf. Tennyson's *Merlin and Vivien*.   4 delicacies

To follow her; with agèd eyes aghast
From fright of dim espial. Safe at last, 185
Through many a dusky gallery, they gain
The maiden's chamber, silken, hushed, and
   chaste;
Where Porphyro took covert, pleas'd amain.[1]
His poor guide hurried back with agues in her
   brain.

Her falt'ring hand upon the balustrade, 190
Old Angela was feeling for the stair,
When Madeline, St. Agnes' charmèd maid,
Rose, like a missioned spirit, unaware:
With silver taper's light, and pious care,
She turn'd, and down the agèd gossip led
To a safe level matting. Now prepare, 196
Young Porphyro, for gazing on that bed;
She comes, she comes again, like ring-dove
   fray'd and fled.

Out went the taper as she hurried in; 199
Its little smoke, in pallid moonshine, died:
She closed the door, she panted all akin
To spirits of the air, and visions, wide:
No uttered syllable, or, woe betide!
But to her heart, her heart was voluble,
Paining with eloquence her balmy side; 205
As though a tongueless nightingale should
   swell
Her throat in vain, and die, heart-stifled, in
   her dell.

A casement high and triple-arched there was,
All garlanded with carven imag'ries
Of fruits, and flowers, and bunches of knot-
   grass,   210
And diamonded with panes of quaint device,
Innumerable of stains and splendid dyes,
As are the tiger-moth's deep-damasked
   wings;
And in the midst, 'mong thousand herald-
   ries,
And twilight saints, and dim emblazonings,
A shielded scutcheon blush'd with blood of
   queens and kings.   216

Full on this casement shone the wintry
   moon,
And threw warm gules[2] on Madeline's fair
   breast,
As down she knelt for heaven's grace and
   boon;
Rose-bloom fell on her hands, together prest,

And on her silver cross soft amethyst, 221
And on her hair a glory, like a saint:
She seem'd a splendid angel, newly drest,
Save wings, for heaven: — Porphyro grew
   faint:
She knelt, so pure a thing, so free from mortal
   taint.   225

Anon his heart revives: her vespers done,
Of all its wreathèd pearls her hair she frees;
Unclasps her warmèd jewels one by one;
Loosens her fragrant bodice; by degrees
Her rich attire creeps rustling to her knees:
Half-hidden, like a mermaid in sea-weed,
Pensive awhile she dreams awake, and sees,
In fancy, fair St. Agnes in her bed, 233
But dares not look behind, or all the charm is
   fled.

Soon, trembling in her soft and chilly nest,
In sort of wakeful swoon, perplex'd she
   lay,   236
Until the poppied warmth of sleep oppress'd
Her soothèd limbs, and soul fatigued away;
Flown, like a thought, until the morrow-
   day;
Blissfully haven'd both from joy and pain;
Clasp'd like a missal where swart Paynims
   pray;[1]   241
Blinded alike from sunshine and from rain,
As though a rose should shut, and be a bud
   again.

Stol'n to this paradise, and so entranced,
Prophyro gazed upon her empty dress, 245
And listen'd to her breathing, if it chanc'd
To wake into a slumberous tenderness;
Which when he heard, that minute did he
   bless,
And breath'd himself: then from the closet
   crept,
Noiseless as fear[2] in a wide wilderness, 250
And over the hush'd carpet, silent, stept,
And 'tween the curtains peep'd, where, lo! —
   how fast she slept.

Then by the bedside, where the faded moon
Made a dim, silver twilight, soft he set 254
A table, and, half anguish'd, threw thereon
A cloth of woven crimson, gold, and jet: —
O for some drowsy Morphean amulet!
The boisterous, midnight, festive clarion,

---

[1] greatly   [2] red color

[1] A mass-book would not be opened by devout
pagans. [2] i.e., a person in fear

AE

The kettle-drum, and far-heard clarionet,
Affray his ears, though but in dying tone : —
The hall door shuts again, and all the noise is
    gone.   261

And still she slept an azure-lidded sleep,
In blanchèd linen, smooth, and lavender'd,
While he from forth the closet brought a heap
Of candied apple, quince, and plum, and
    gourd ;   265
With jellies soother [1] than the creamy curd,
And lucent syrups, tinct with cinnamon ;
Manna and dates, in argosy transferr'd
From Fez ; and spicèd dainties, every one,
From silken Samarcand to cedared Lebanon.

These delicates he heap'd with glowing hand
On golden dishes and in baskets bright
Of wreathèd silver : sumptuous they stand
In the retirèd quiet of the night,   274
Filling the chilly room with perfume light.—
"And now, my love, my seraph fair, awake!
Thou art my heaven, and I thine eremite :
Open thine eyes, for meek St. Agnes' sake,
Or I shall drowse beside thee, so my soul doth
    ache."   279

Thus whispering, his warm, unnervèd arm
Sank in her pillow.   Shaded was her dream
By the dusk curtains : — 'twas a midnight
    charm
Impossible to melt as icèd stream :
The lustrous salvers in the moonlight gleam ;
Broad golden fringe upon the carpet lies :
It seem'd he never, never could redeem   286
From such a steadfast spell his lady's eyes ;
So mus'd awhile, entoil'd in woofèd phantasies.

Awakening up, he took her hollow lute, —
Tumultuous, — and, in chords that tender-
    est be,   290
He play'd an ancient ditty, long since mute,
In Provence call'd, "La belle dame sans
    merci," [2]
Close to her ear touching the melody ; —
Wherewith disturb'd, she utter'd a soft
    moan :
He ceased — she panted quick — and sud-
    denly   295
Her blue affrayèd eyes wide open shone :
Upon his knees he sank, pale as smooth-sculp-
    tured stone.

[1] smoother   [2] Cf. Keats' poem with the same
title.

Her eyes were open, but she still beheld,
Now wide awake, the vision of her sleep :
There was a painful change, that night
    expell'd   300
The blisses of her dream so pure and deep,
At which fair Madeline began to weep,
And moan forth witless words with many a
    sigh ;
While still her gaze on Porphyro would keep ;
Who knelt, with joinèd hands and piteous
    eye,   305
Fearing to move or speak, she look'd so dream-
    ingly.

"Ah, Porphyro !" said she, " but even now
Thy voice was at sweet tremble in mine ear
Made tunable with every sweetest vow ;
And those sad eyes were spiritual and clear :
How chang'd thou art ! how pallid, chill, and
    drear !   311
Give me that voice again, my Porphyro,
Those looks immortal, those complainings
    dear !
Oh leave me not in this eternal woe,
For if thou diest, my Love, I know not where
    to go."

Beyond a mortal man impassion'd far
At these voluptuous accents, he arose,
Ethereal, flushed, and like a throbbing star
Seen 'mid the sapphire heaven's deep repose ;
Into her dream he melted, as the rose   320
Blendeth its odour with the violet, —
Solution sweet : meantime the frost-wind
    blows
Like Love's alarum, pattering the sharp sleet
Against the window-panes ; St. Agnes' moon
    hath set.

'Tis dark : quick pattereth the flaw-blown
    sleet :   325
"This is no dream, my bride, my Madeline !"
'Tis dark : the icèd gusts still rave and beat :
"No dream, alas ! alas ! and woe is mine !
Porphyro will leave me here to fade and
    pine. —
Cruel ! what traitor could thee hither bring ?
I curse not, for my heart is lost in thine,   331
Though thou forsakest a deceivèd thing ; —
A dove forlorn and lost with sick unprunèd
    wing."

"My Madeline ! sweet dreamer ! lovely
    bride !
Say, may I be for aye thy vassal blest ?   335

Thy beauty's shield, heart-shaped and
   vermeil dyed?
Ah, silver shrine, here will I take my rest
After so many hours of toil and quest,
A famished pilgrim,—sav'd by miracle. 339
Though I have found, I will not rob thy nest
Saving of thy sweet self; if thou think'st
   well
To trust, fair Madeline, to no rude infidel.

"Hark! 'tis an elfin-storm from fairy land,
Of haggard seeming, but a boon indeed: 344
Arise — arise! the morning is at hand; —
The bloated wassailers will never heed: —
Let us away, my love, with happy speed;
There are no ears to hear, or eyes to see, —
Drown'd all in Rhenish and the sleepy mead:
Awake! arise! my love, and fearless be, 350
For o'er the southern moors I have a home for
   thee."

She hurried at his words, beset with fears,
For there were sleeping dragons all around,
At glaring watch, perhaps, with ready
   spears —
Down the wide stairs a darkling way they
   found. —   355
In all the house was heard no human sound.
A chain-drooped lamp was flickering by
   each door;
The arras, rich with horseman, hawk, and
   hound,   358
Flutter'd in the besieging wind's uproar;
And the long carpets rose along the gusty floor.

They glide, like phantoms, into the wide
   hall;
Like phantoms, to the iron porch they glide;
Where lay the Porter, in uneasy sprawl,
With a huge empty flagon by his side:
The wakeful bloodhound rose, and shook
   his hide,   365
But his sagacious eye an inmate owns:
By one, and one, the bolts full easy slide: —
The chains lie silent on the footworn
   stones; —
The key turns, and the door upon its hinges
   groans.

And they are gone: ay, ages long ago 370
These lovers fled away into the storm.
That night the Baron dreamt of many a woe,
And all his warrior-guests, with shade and
   form
Of witch, and demon, and large coffin-worm,
Were long be-nightmar'd. Angela the old

Died palsy-twitch'd, with meagre face
   deform;   376
The Beadsman, after thousand avès told,
For aye unsought for slept among his ashes
   cold.

WALTER SAVAGE LANDOR
(1775–1864)

ÆSOP AND RHODOPÈ

SECOND CONVERSATION

Æsop. And so, our fellow-slaves are given
to contention on the score of dignity?

Rhodopè. I do not believe they are much
addicted to contention: for, whenever the
good Xanthus hears a signal of such misbe-
haviour, he either brings a scourge into the
midst of them or sends our lady to scold them
smartly for it.

Æsop. Admirable evidence against their
propensity!

Rhodopè. I will not have you find them out
so, nor laugh at them.

Æsop. Seeing that the good Xanthus and
our lady are equally fond of thee, and always
visit thee both together, the girls, however
envious, cannot well or safely be arrogant, but
must of necessity yield the first place to thee.

Rhodopè. They indeed are observant of the
kindness thus bestowed upon me: yet they
afflict me by taunting me continually with
what I am unable to deny.

Æsop. If it is true, it ought little to trouble
thee; if untrue, less. I know, for I have
looked into nothing else of late, no evil can
thy heart have admitted: a sigh of thine before the gods would remove the heaviest that
could fall on it. Pray tell me what it may be.
Come, be courageous; be cheerful. I can
easily pardon a smile if thou impleadest me of
curiosity.

Rhodopè. They remark to me that enemies
or robbers took them forcibly from their parents . . . and that . . . and that . . .

Æsop. Likely enough: what then? Why
desist from speaking? why cover thy face
with thy hair and hands? Rhodopè!
Rhodopè! dost thou weep moreover?

Rhodopè. It is so sure!

Æsop. Was the fault thine?

Rhodopè. O that it were! . . . if there was
any.

Æsop. While it pains thee to tell it, keep thy silence; but when utterance is a solace, then impart it.

Rhodopè. They remind me (oh! who could have had the cruelty to relate it?) that my father, my own dear father . . .

Æsop. Say not the rest: I know it: his day was come.

Rhodopè. . . . sold me, sold me. You start: you did not at the lightning last night, nor at the rolling sounds above. And do you, generous Æsop! do you also call a misfortune a disgrace?

Æsop. If it is, I am among the most disgraceful of men. Didst thou dearly love thy father?

Rhodopè. All loved him. He was very fond of me.

Æsop. And yet sold thee! sold thee to a stranger!

Rhodopè. He was the kindest of all kind fathers, nevertheless. Nine summers ago, you may have heard perhaps, there was a grievous famine in our land of Thrace.

Æsop. I remember it perfectly.

Rhodopè. O poor Æsop! and were you too famishing in your native Phrygia?

Æsop. The calamity extended beyond the narrow sea that separates our countries. My appetite was sharpened; but the appetite and the wits are equally set on the same grindstone.

Rhodopè. I was then scarcely five years old: my mother died the year before: my father sighed at every funeral, but he sighed more deeply at every bridal, song. He loved me because he loved her who bore me: and yet I made him sorrowful whether I cried or smiled. If ever I vexed him, it was because I would not play when he told me, but made him, by my weeping, weep again.

Æsop. And yet he could endure to lose thee! he, thy father! Could any other? could any who lives on the fruits of the earth, endure it? O age, that art incumbent over me! blessed be thou; thrice blessed! Not that thou stillest the tumults of the heart, and promisest eternal calm, but that, prevented by thy beneficence, I never shall experience this only intolerable wretchedness.

Rhodopè. Alas! alas!

Æsop. Thou art now happy, and shouldst not utter that useless exclamation.

Rhodopè. You said something angrily and vehemently when you stepped aside. Is it not enough that the handmaidens doubt the kindness of my father? Must so virtuous and so wise a man as Æsop blame him also?

Æsop. Perhaps he is little to be blamed; certainly he is much to be pitied.

Rhodopè. Kind heart! on which mine must never rest!

Æsop. Rest on it for comfort and for counsel when they fail thee: rest on it, as the deities on the breast of mortals, to console and purify it.

Rhodopè. Could I remove any sorrow from it, I should be contented.

Æsop. Then be so; and proceed in thy narrative.

Rhodopè. Bear with me a little yet. My thoughts have overpowered my words, and now themselves are overpowered and scattered.

Forty-seven days ago (this is only the forty-eighth since I beheld you first) I was a child; I was ignorant, I was careless.

Æsop. If these qualities are signs of childhood, the universe is a nursery.

Rhodopè. Affliction, which makes many wiser, had no such effect on me. But reverence and love (why should I hesitate at the one avowal more than at the other?) came over me, to ripen my understanding.

Æsop. O Rhodopè! we must loiter no longer upon this discourse.

Rhodopè. Why not?

Æsop. Pleasant is yonder beanfield, seen over the high papyrus when it waves and bends: deep laden with the sweet heaviness of its odour is the listless air that palpitates dizzily above it: but Death is lurking for the slumberer beneath its blossoms.

Rhodopè. You must not love then! . . . but may not I?

Æsop. We will . . . but . . .

Rhodopè. *We!* O sound that is to vibrate on my breast forever! O hour! happier than all other hours since time began! O gracious Gods! who brought me into bondage!

Æsop. Be calm, be composed, be circumspect. We must hide our treasure that we may not lose it.

Rhodopè. I do not think that you can love me; and I fear and tremble to hope so. Ah, yes; you have said you did. But again you only look at me, and sigh as if you repented.

Æsop. Unworthy as I may be of thy fond regard, I am not unworthy of thy fullest confidence: why distrust me?

Rhodopè. Never will I . . . never, never.

To know that I possess your love, surpasses all other knowledge, dear as is all that I receive from you. I should be tired of my own voice if I heard it on aught beside: and, even yours is less melodious in any other sound than *Rhodopè*.

Æsop. Do such little girls learn to flatter?

Rhodopè. Teach me how to speak, since you could not teach me how to be silent.

Æsop. Speak no longer of me, but of thyself; and only of things that never pain thee.

Rhodopè. Nothing can pain me now.

Æsop. Relate thy story then, from infancy.

Rhodopè. I must hold your hand: I am afraid of losing you again.

Æsop. Now begin. Why silent so long?

Rhodopè. I have dropped all memory of what is told by me and what is untold.

Æsop. Recollect a little. I can be patient with this hand in mine.

Rhodopè. I am not certain that yours is any help to recollection.

Æsop. Shall I remove it?

Rhodopè. O! now I think I can recall the whole story. What did you say? did you ask any question?

Æsop. None, excepting what thou hast answered.

Rhodopè. Never shall I forget the morning when my father, sitting in the coolest part of the house, exchanged his last measure of grain for a chlamys of scarlet cloth fringed with silver. He watched the merchant out of the door, and then looked wistfully into the corn-chest. I, who thought there was something worth seeing, looked in also, and, finding it empty, expressed my disappointment, not thinking however about the corn. A faint and transient smile came over his countenance at the sight of mine. He unfolded the chlamys, stretched it out with both hands before me, and then cast it over my shoulders. I looked down on the glittering fringe and screamed with joy. He then went out; and I know not what flowers he gathered, but he gathered many; and some he placed in my bosom, and some in my hair. But I told him with captious pride, first that I could arrange them better, and again that I would have only the white. However, when he had selected all the white, and I had placed a few of them according to my fancy, I told him (rising in my slipper) he might crown me with the remainder. The splendour of my apparel gave me a sensation of authority. Soon as

the flowers had taken their station on my head, I expressed a dignified satisfaction at the taste displayed by my father, just as if I could have seen how they appeared! But he knew that there was at least as much pleasure as pride in it, and perhaps we divided the latter (alas! not both) pretty equally. He now took me into the market-place, where a concourse of people was waiting for the purchase of slaves. Merchants came and looked at me; some commending, others disparaging; but all agreeing that I was slender and delicate, that I could not live long, and that I should give much trouble. Many would have bought the chlamys, but there was something less salable in the child and flowers.

Æsop. Had thy features been coarse and thy voice rustic, they would all have patted thy cheeks and found no fault in thee.

Rhodopè. As it was, every one had bought exactly such another in time past, and been a loser by it. At these speeches I perceived the flowers tremble slightly on my bosom, from my father's agitation. Although he scoffed at them, knowing my healthiness, he was troubled internally, and said many short prayers, not very unlike imprecations, turning his head aside. Proud was I, prouder than ever, when at last several talents were offered for me, and by the very man who in the beginning had undervalued me the most, and prophesied the worst of me. My father scowled at him, and refused the money. I thought he was playing a game, and began to wonder what it could be, since I never had seen it played before. Then I fancied it might be some celebration because plenty had returned to the city, insomuch that my father had bartered the last of the corn he hoarded. I grew more and more delighted at the sport. But soon there advanced an elderly man, who said gravely, "Thou hast stolen this child: her vesture alone is worth above a hundred drachmas. Carry her home again to her parents, and do it directly, or Nemesis[1] and the Eumenides[2] will overtake thee." Knowing the estimation in which my father had always been holden by his fellow-citizens, I laughed again, and pinched his ear. He, although naturally choleric, burst forth into no resentment at these reproaches, but said calmly, "I think I know thee by name, O

---

[1] the goddess who avenges wrongs [2] the Furies, who also are regarded as avengers

guest! Surely thou art Xanthus the Samian. Deliver this child from famine."

Again I laughed aloud and heartily; and, thinking it was now my part of the game, I held out both my arms and protruded my whole body towards the stranger. He would not receive me from my father's neck, but he asked me with benignity and solicitude if I was hungry: at which I laughed again, and more than ever: for it was early in the morning, soon after the first meal, and my father had nourished me most carefully and plentifully in all the days of the famine. But Xanthus, waiting for no answer, took out of a sack, which one of his slaves carried at his side, a cake of wheaten bread and a piece of honey-comb, and gave them to me. I held the honey-comb to my father's mouth, thinking it the most of a dainty. He dashed it to the ground; but, seizing the bread, he began to devour it ferociously. This also I thought was in play; and I clapped my hands at his distortions. But Xanthus looked on him like one afraid, and smote the cake from him, crying aloud, "Name the price." My father now placed me in his arms, naming a price much below what the other had offered, saying, "The gods are ever with thee, O Xanthus; therefore to thee do I consign my child." But while Xanthus was counting out the silver, my father seized the cake again, which the slave had taken up and was about to replace in the wallet. His hunger was exasperated by the taste and the delay. Suddenly there arose much tumult. Turning round in the old woman's bosom who had received me from Xanthus, I saw my beloved father struggling on the ground, livid and speechless. The more violent my cries, the more rapidly they hurried me away; and many were soon between us. Little was I suspicious that he had suffered the pangs of famine long before: alas! and he had suffered them for me. Do I weep while I am telling you they ended? I could not have closed his eyes; I was too young; but I might have received his last breath; the only comfort of an orphan's bosom. Do you now think him blamable, O Æsop?

Æsop. It was sublime humanity: it was for-bearance and self-denial which even the immortal gods have never shown us. He could endure to perish by those torments which alone are both acute and slow; he could number the steps of death and miss not one: but he could never see thy tears, nor let thee see his. O weakness above all fortitude! Glory to the man who rather bears a grief corroding his breast, than permits it to prowl beyond, and to prey on the tender and compassionate! Women commiserate the brave, and men the beautiful. The dominion of Pity has usually this extent, no wider. Thy father was exposed to the obloquy not only of the malicious, but also of the ignorant and thoughtless, who condemn in the unfortunate what they applaud in the prosperous. There is no shame in poverty or in slavery, if we neither make ourselves poor by our improvidence nor slaves by our venality. The lowest and highest of the human race are sold: most of the intermediate are also slaves, but slaves who bring no money in the market.

Rhodopè. Surely the great and powerful are never to be purchased: are they?

Æsop. It may be a defect in my vision, but I cannot see greatness on the earth. What they tell me is great and aspiring, to me seems little and crawling. Let me meet thy question with another. What monarch gives his daughter for nothing? Either he receives stone walls and unwilling cities in return, or he barters her for a parcel of spears and horses and horsemen, waving away from his declining and helpless age young joyous life, and trampling down the freshest and the sweetest memories. Midas[1] in the highth of prosperity would have given his daughter to Lycaon,[2] rather than to the gentlest, the most virtuous, the most intelligent of his subjects. Thy father threw wealth aside, and, placing thee under the protection of Virtue, rose up from the house of Famine to partake in the festivals of the Gods.

Release my neck, O Rhodopè! for I have other questions to ask of thee about him.

Rhodopè. To hear thee converse on him in such a manner, I can do even that.

Æsop. Before the day of separation was he never sorrowful? Did he never by tears or silence reveal the secret of his soul?

Rhodopè. I was too infantine to perceive or imagine his intention. The night before I became the slave of Xanthus, he sat on the edge of my bed. I pretended to be asleep: he moved away silently and softly. I saw him collect in the hollow of his hand the crumbs I

[1] the type of avarice [2] a king of Arcadia noted for his impiety

had wasted on the floor, and then eat them, and then look if any were remaining. I thought he did so out of fondness for me, remembering that, even before the famine, he had often swept up off the table the bread I had broken, and had made me put it between his lips. I would not dissemble very long, but said:

"Come, now you have wakened me, you must sing me asleep again, as you did when I was little."

He smiled faintly at this, and, after some delay, when he had walked up and down the chamber, thus began:

"I will sing to thee one song more, my wakeful Rhodopè! my chirping bird! over whom is no mother's wing! That it may lull thee asleep, I will celebrate no longer, as in the days of wine and plenteousness, the glory of Mars, guiding in their invisibly rapid onset the dappled steeds of Rhæsus.[1] What hast thou to do, my little one, with arrows tired of clustering in the quiver? How much quieter is thy pallet than the tents which whitened the plain of Simöis![2] What knowest thou about the river Eurotas?[3] What knowest thou about its ancient palace, once trodden by assembled Gods, and then polluted by the Phrygian? What knowest thou of perfidious men or of sanguinary deeds?

"Pardon me, O goddess[4] who presidest in Cythera! I am not irreverent to thee, but ever grateful. May she upon whose brow I lay my hand, praise and bless thee for evermore!

"Ah, yes! continue to hold up above the coverlet those fresh and rosy palms clasped together: her benefits have descended on thy beauteous head, my child! The Fates also have sung, beyond thy hearing, of pleasanter scenes than snow-fed Hebrus;[5] of more than dim grottos and sky-bright waters. Even now a low murmur swells upward to my ear: and not from the spindle comes the sound, but from those who sing slowly over it, bending all three their tremulous heads together. I wish thou couldst hear it; for seldom are their voices so sweet. Thy pillow intercepts the song perhaps: lie down again, lie down, my Rhodopè! I will repeat what they are saying:

"'Happier shalt thou be, nor less glorious, than even she,[1] the truly beloved, for whose return to the distaff and the lyre the portals of Tænarus flew open. In the woody dells of Ismarus, and when she bathed among the swans of Strymon, the nymphs called her Eurydicè. Thou shalt behold that fairest and that fondest one hereafter. But first thou must go unto the land of the lotos, where famine never cometh, and where alone the works of man are immortal.'

"O my child! the undeceiving Fates have uttered this. Other powers have visited me, and have strengthened my heart with dreams and visions. We shall meet again, my Rhodopè, in shady groves and verdant meadows, and we shall sit by the side of those who loved us."

He was rising: I threw my arms about his neck, and, before I would let him go, I made him promise to place me, not by the side, but between them: for I thought of her who had left us. At that time there were but two, O Æsop.

You ponder: you are about to reprove my assurance in having thus repeated my own praises. I would have omitted some of the words, only that it might have disturbed the measure and cadences, and have put me out. They are the very words my dearest father sang; and they are the last: yet, shame upon me! the nurse (the same who stood listening near, who attended me into this country) could remember them more perfectly: it is from her I have learnt them since; she often sings them, even to herself.

Æsop. So shall others. There is much both in them and in thee to render them memorable.

Rhodopè. Who flatters now?

Æsop. Flattery often runs beyond Truth, in a hurry to embrace her; but not here. The dullest of mortals, seeing and hearing thee, would never misinterpret the prophecy of the Fates.

If, turning back, I could overpass the vale of years, and could stand on the mountain-top, and could look again far before me at the bright ascending morn, we would enjoy the prospect together; we would walk along the summit hand in hand, O Rhodopè, and we would only sigh at last when we found ourselves below with others.

---

[1] A Thracian hero; Rhodopè was from Thrace.
[2] a river near Troy   [3] a river near Sparta   [4] Venus
[5] Cf. *Lycidas*, l. 63.

[1] Eurydicè; for her story, see Gayley's *Classic Myths*, pp. 185–8.

ROSE AYLMER

Ah, what avails the sceptred race,
    Ah, what the form divine!
What every virtue, every grace!
    Rose Aylmer, all were thine.
Rose Aylmer, whom these wakeful eyes
    May weep, but never see,
A night of memories and of sighs
    I consecrate to thee.

A FIESOLAN IDYL

Here, where precipitate Spring with one light
        bound
Into hot Summer's lusty arms expires,
And where go forth at morn, at eve, at night,
Soft airs that want the lute to play with 'em,
And softer sighs that know not what they
        want,
Aside a wall, beneath an orange-tree,
Whose tallest flowers could tell the lowlier
        ones
Of sights in Fiesole right up above,
While I was gazing a few paces off
At what they seem'd to show me with their
        nods,   10
Their frequent whispers and their pointing
        shoots,
A gentle maid came down the garden-steps
And gathered the pure treasure in her lap.
I heard the branches rustle, and stepp'd forth
To drive the ox away, or mule, or goat,
Such I believed it must be.   How could I
Let beast o'erpower them? when hath wind or
        rain
Borne hard upon weak plant that wanted me,
And I (however they might bluster round)
Walk'd off? 'Twere most ungrateful: for
        sweet scents   20
Are the swift vehicles of still sweeter thoughts,
And nurse and pillow the dull memory
That would let drop without them her best
        stores.
They bring me tales of youth and tones of love,
And 'tis and ever was my wish and way
To let all flowers live freely, and all die
(Whene'er their Genius bids their souls de-
        part)
Among their kindred in their native place.
I never pluck the rose; the violet's head
Hath shaken with my breath upon its bank   30
And not reproach'd me; the ever-sacred cup
Of the pure lily hath between my hands

Felt safe, unsoil'd, nor lost one grain of gold.
I saw the light that made the glossy leaves
More glossy; the fair arm, the fairer cheek
Warmed by the eye intent on its pursuit;
I saw the foot that, although half-erect
From its grey slipper, could not lift her up
To what she wanted: I held down a branch
And gather'd her some blossoms; since their
        hour   40
Was come, and bees had wounded them, and
        flies
Of harder wing were working their way thro'
And scattering them in fragments under foot.
So crisp were some, they rattled unevolved,
Others, ere broken off, fell into shells,
For such appear the petals when detach'd,
Unbending, brittle, lucid, white like snow,
And like snow not seen through, by eye or
        sun:
Yet every one her gown received from me
Was fairer than the first. I thought not so, 50
But so she praised them to reward my care.
I said, "You find the largest." "This in-
        deed,"
Cried she, "is large and sweet." She held one
        forth,
Whether for me to look at or to take
She knew not, nor did I; but taking it
Would best have solved (and this she felt) her
        doubt.
I dared not touch it; for it seemed a part
Of her own self; fresh, full, the most mature
Of blossoms, yet a blossom; with a touch
To fall, and yet unfallen. She drew back   60
The boon she tender'd, and then finding not
The ribbon at her waist to fix it in,
Dropp'd it, as loth to drop it, on the rest.

TO ROBERT BROWNING

There is delight in singing, though none hear
Beside the singer; and there is delight
In praising, though the praiser sit alone
And see the prais'd far off him, far above.
Shakespeare is not our poet, but the world's,
Therefore on him no speech! and brief for
        thee,
Browning! Since Chaucer was alive and hale,
No man hath walk'd along our roads with step
So active, so inquiring eye, or tongue
So varied in discourse. But warmer climes 10
Give brighter plumage, stronger wing: the
        breeze
Of Alpine highths thou playest with, borne on

Beyond Sorrento and Amalfi,[1] where
The Siren waits thee, singing song for song.

WHY

Why do our joys depart
For cares to seize the heart?
I know not. Nature says,
Obey; and Man obeys.
I see, and know not why,
Thorns live and roses die.

ON HIS SEVENTY–FIFTH BIRTHDAY

I strove with none, for none was worth my
    strife,
  Nature I loved, and next to Nature, Art;
I warmed both hands before the fire of life,
  It sinks, and I am ready to depart.

ON DEATH

Death stands above me, whispering low
  I know not what into my ear:
Of his strange language all I know
  Is, there is not a word of fear.

THOMAS HOOD (1798–1845)

THE SONG OF THE SHIRT

With fingers weary and worn,
  With eyelids heavy and red,
A woman sat, in unwomanly rags,
  Plying her needle and thread —
Stitch! stitch! stitch!
  In poverty, hunger, and dirt,
And still with a voice of dolorous pitch
  She sang the "Song of the Shirt."   8

"Work! work! work!
  While the cock is crowing aloof!
And work — work — work,
  Till the stars shine through the roof!
It's Oh! to be a slave
Along with the barbarous Turk,
Where woman has never a soul to save,
  If this is Christian work!   16

[1] Towns of southern Italy, whither Browning
was going.

"Work — work — work,
  Till the brain begins to swim;
Work — work — work,
  Till the eyes are heavy and dim!
Seam, and gusset, and band,
  Band, and gusset, and seam,
Till over the buttons I fall asleep,
  And sew them on in a dream!   24

"Oh, Men, with Sisters dear!
  Oh, Men, with Mothers and Wives!
It is not linen you're wearing out
  But human creatures' lives!
Stitch — stitch — stitch,
  In poverty, hunger, and dirt,
Sewing at once, with a double thread,
  A Shroud as well as a Shirt.   32

"But why do I talk of Death?
  That Phantom of grisly bone,
I hardly fear its terrible shape,
  It seems so like my own —
It seems so like my own,
  Because of the fasts I keep;
Oh, God! that bread should be so dear,
  And flesh and blood so cheap!   40

"Work — work — work!
  My labour never flags;
And what are its wages? A bed of straw,
  A crust of bread — and rags.
That shatter'd roof — this naked floor —
  A table — a broken chair —
And a wall so blank, my shadow I thank
  For sometimes falling there!   48

"Work — work — work!
  From weary chime to chime,
Work — work — work,
  As prisoners work for crime!
Band, and gusset, and seam,
  Seam, and gusset, and band,
Till the heart is sick, and the brain benumb'd,
  As well as the weary hand.   56

"Work — work — work,
  In the dull December light,
And work — work — work,
  When the weather is warm and bright —
While underneath the eaves
  The brooding swallows cling
As if to show me their sunny backs
  And twit me with the spring.   64

"Oh! but to breathe the breath
  Of the cowslip and primrose sweet —
With the sky above my head,
  And the grass beneath my feet;
For only one short hour
  To feel as I used to feel,
Before I knew the woes of want
  And the walk that costs a meal.   72

"Oh! but for one short hour!
  A respite however brief!
No blessèd leisure for Love or Hope,
  But only time for Grief!
A little weeping would ease my heart,
  But in their briny bed
My tears must stop, for every drop
  Hinders needle and thread!"   80

With fingers weary and worn,
  With eyelids heavy and red,
A woman sat, in unwomanly rags,
  Plying her needle and thread —
Stitch! stitch! stitch!
  In poverty, hunger, and dirt,
And still with a voice of dolorous pitch, —
Would that its tone could reach the Rich! —
  She sang this "Song of the Shirt!"   89

RUTH

She stood breast-high amid the corn,
Clasped by the golden light of morn,
  Like the sweetheart of the sun,
  Who many a glowing kiss had won.   4

On her cheek an autumn flush,
Deeply ripen'd; — such a blush
  In the midst of brown was born,
  Like red poppies grown with corn.   8

Round her eyes her tresses fell,
Which were blackest none could tell,
  But long lashes veiled a light,
  That had else been all too bright.   12

And her hat, with shady brim,
Made her tressy forehead dim; —
  Thus she stood amid the stooks,
  Praising God with sweetest looks.   16

Sure, I said, Heav'n did not mean,
Where I reap thou should'st but glean;
  Lay thy sheaf adown and come,
  Share my harvest and my home.   20

WINTHROP MACKWORTH PRAED (1802–1839)

THE BELLE OF THE BALL-ROOM

Years — years ago, — ere yet my dreams
  Had been of being wise or witty, —
Ere I had done with writing themes,
  Or yawned o'er this infernal Chitty [1]; —
Years — years ago, — while all my joy
  Was in my fowling-piece and filly, —
In short, while I was yet a boy,
  I fell in love with Laura Lily.   8

I saw her at the County Ball:
  There, when the sounds of flute and fiddle
Gave signal sweet in that old hall
  Of hands across and down the middle,
Hers was the subtlest spell by far
  Of all that set young hearts romancing;
She was our queen, our rose, our star;   15
  And then she danced — O Heaven, her
    dancing!

Dark was her hair, her hand was white;
  Her voice was exquisitely tender;
Her eyes were full of liquid light;
  I never saw a waist so slender!
Her every look, her every smile,
  Shot right and left a score of arrows;
I thought 'twas Venus from her isle,   23
  And wondered where she'd left her sparrows.

She talked, — of politics or prayers, —
  Of Southey's prose or Wordsworth's son-
    nets, —
Of danglers — or of dancing bears,
  Of battles — or the last new bonnets,
By candlelight, at twelve o'clock,
  To me it mattered not a tittle;
If those bright lips had quoted Locke,[2]   31
  I might have thought they murmured Little.[3]

Through sunny May, through sultry June,
  I loved her with a love eternal;
I spoke her praises to the moon,
  I wrote them to the Sunday Journal:
My mother laughed; I soon found out
  That ancient ladies have no feeling:
My father frowned; but how should gout
  See any happiness in kneeling?   40

[1] a writer on law   [2] a philosopher, cf. p. 238
[3] a pseudonym of Thomas Moore, writer of love
songs

She was the daughter of a Dean,
  Rich, fat, and rather apoplectic;
She had one brother, just thirteen,
  Whose colour was extremely hectic;
Her grandmother for many a year
  Had fed the parish with her bounty;
Her second cousin was a peer,
  And Lord Lieutenant of the County.   48

But titles, and the three per cents,
  And mortgages, and great relations,
And India bonds, and tithes, and rents,
  Oh, what are they to love's sensations?
Black eyes, fair forehead, clustering locks —
  Such wealth, such honours, Cupid chooses;
He cares as little for the Stocks,
  As Baron Rothschild for the Muses.   56

She sketched; the vale, the wood, the beach,
  Grew lovelier from her pencil's shading:
She botanised; I envied each
  Young blossom in her boudoir fading:
She warbled Handel; [1] it was grand;
  She made the Catalani [2] jealous:
She touched the organ; I could stand
  For hours and hours to blow the bellows.   64

She kept an album, too, at home,
  Well filled with all an album's glories;
Paintings of butterflies, and Rome,
  Patterns for trimmings, Persian stories;
Soft songs to Julia's cockatoo,
  Fierce odes to Famine and to Slaughter;
And autographs of Prince Leboo, [3]
  And recipes for elder-water.   72

And she was flattered, worshipped, bored;
  Her steps were watched, her dress was noted,
Her poodle dog was quite adored,
  Her sayings were extremely quoted;
She laughed, and every heart was glad,
  As if the taxes were abolished;
She frowned, and every look was sad,
  As if the Opera were demolished.   80

She smiled on many, just for fun, —
  I knew that there was nothing in it;
I was the first — the only one
  Her heart had thought of for a minute. —
I knew it, for she told me so,
  In phrase which was divinely moulded;

[1] Handel's music was popular in England at this time   [2] an Italian prima donna   [3] Prince Le Beau, a distinguished Belgian diplomat

She wrote a charming hand, — and oh!
  How sweetly all her notes were folded!   88

Our love was like most other loves; —
  A little glow, a little shiver,
A rose-bud, and a pair of gloves,
  And "Fly not yet" — upon the river;
Some jealousy of some one's heir,
  Some hopes of dying broken-hearted;
A miniature, a lock of hair,
  The usual vows, — and then we parted.   96

We parted; months and years rolled by;
  We met again four summers after:
Our parting was all sob and sigh;
  Our meeting was all mirth and laughter:
For in my heart's most secret cell
  There had been many other lodgers;
And she was not the ball-room's belle,
  But only — Mrs. Something Rogers!   104

THOMAS LOVELL BEDDOES
(1803–1849)

FROM DEATH'S JEST-BOOK

SONG

Old Adam, the carrion crow,
  The old crow of Cairo;
He sat in the shower, and let it flow
  Under his tail and over his crest;
  And through every feather
  Leaked the wet weather;
And the bough swung under his nest;
  For his beak it was heavy with marrow.
  Is that the wind dying? O no;
  It's only two devils, that blow
  Through a murderer's bones, to and fro,
    In the ghosts' moonshine.   12

Ho! Eve, my grey carrion wife,
  When we have supped on kings' marrow,
Where shall we drink and make merry our life?
  Our nest it is Queen Cleopatra's skull,
    'Tis cloven and cracked,
    And battered and hacked,
  But with tears of blue eyes it is full:
Let us drink then, my raven of Cairo.
  Is that the wind dying? O no;
  It's only two devils, that blow
  Through a murderer's bones, to and fro,
    In the ghosts' moonshine.   24

DREAM–PEDLARY

If there were dreams to sell,
  What would you buy?
Some cost a passing bell;
  Some a light sigh,
That shakes from Life's fresh crown
Only a rose-leaf down.
If there were dreams to sell,
Merry and sad to tell,
And the crier rang the bell,
  What would you buy?   10

A cottage lone and still,
  With bowers nigh,
Shadowy, my woes to still,
  Until I die.
Such pearl from Life's fresh crown
Fain would I shake me down.
Were dreams to have at will,
This would best heal my ill,
  This would I buy.   19

But there were dreams to sell
  Ill didst thou buy;
Life is a dream, they tell,
  Waking, to die.

Dreaming a dream to prize,
Is wishing ghosts to rise;
And, if I had the spell
To call the buried well,
  Which one would I?   28

If there are ghosts to raise,
  What shall I call,
Out of hell's murky haze,
  Heaven's blue pall?
Raise my loved long-lost boy
To lead me to his joy. —
There are no ghosts to raise;
Out of death lead no ways;
  Vain is the call.   37

Know'st thou not ghosts to sue,
  No love thou hast.
Else lie, as I will do,
  And breathe thy last.
So out of Life's fresh crown
Fall like a rose-leaf down.
Thus are the ghosts to woo;
Thus are all dreams made true,
  Ever to last!   46

THE VICTORIAN AGE

THOMAS CARLYLE (1795–1881)

SARTOR RESARTUS

BOOK II, CHAPTER VII

THE EVERLASTING NO

Under the strange nebulous envelopment, wherein our Professor has now shrouded himself, no doubt but his spiritual nature is nevertheless progressive, and growing: for how can the "Son of Time," in any case, stand still? We behold him, through those dim years, in a state of crisis, of transition: his mad Pilgrimings, and general solution into aimless Discontinuity, what is all this but a mad Fermentation; wherefrom, the fiercer it is, the clearer product will one day evolve itself?

Such transitions are ever full of pain: thus the Eagle when he moults is sickly; and, to attain his new beak, must harshly dash-off the old one upon rocks. What Stoicism soever our Wanderer, in his individual acts and motions, may affect, it is clear that there is a hot fever of anarchy and misery raving within; coruscations of which flash out: as, indeed, how could there be other? Have we not seen him disappointed, bemocked of Destiny, through long years? All that the young heart might desire and pray for has been denied; nay, as in the last worst instance, offered and then snatched away. Ever an "excellent Passivity"; but of useful, reasonable Activity, essential to the former as Food to Hunger, nothing granted: till at length, in this wild Pilgrimage, he must forcibly seize for himself an Activity, though useless, unreasonable. Alas, his cup of bitterness, which had been filling drop by drop, ever since the first "ruddy morning" in the Hinterschlag Gymnasium,[1] was at the very lip; and then with that poison-drop, of the Towgood-and-Blumine[1] business, it runs over, and even hisses over in a deluge of foam.

He himself says once, with more justice than originality: "Man is, properly speaking, based upon Hope, he has no other possession but Hope; this world of his is emphatically the Place of Hope." What then was our Professor's possession? We see him, for the present, quite shut-out from Hope; looking not into the golden orient, but vaguely all around into a dim copper firmament, pregnant with earthquake and tornado.

Alas, shut-out from Hope, in a deeper sense than we yet dream of! For, as he wanders wearisomely through this world, he has now lost all tidings of another and higher. Full of religion, or at least of religiosity, as our Friend has since exhibited himself, he hides not that, in those days, he was wholly irreligious: "Doubt had darkened into Unbelief," says he; "shade after shade goes grimly over your soul, till you have the fixed, starless, Tartarean black." To such readers as have reflected, what can be called reflecting, on man's life, and happily discovered, in contradiction to much Profit-and-Loss Philosophy, speculative and practical, that Soul is *not* synonymous with Stomach; who understand, therefore, in our Friend's words, "that, for man's well-being, Faith is properly the one thing needful; how, with it, Martyrs, otherwise weak, can cheerfully endure the shame and the cross; and without it, Worldlings puke-up their sick existence, by suicide, in the midst of luxury": to such, it will be clear that, for a pure moral nature, the loss of his religious Belief was the loss of everything. Unhappy young man! All wounds, the crush of long-continued Destitution, the stab of false Friendship, and of false Love, all wounds in thy so genial heart, would have healed again, had not its life-warmth been withdrawn. Well might he exclaim, in his wild way: "Is there no God,

---

[1] Smite-behind Highschool (Annan Academy, where Carlyle went to school)

[1] Towgood, a friend of Teufelsdröckh's; Blumine (from *Ger.* Blume, *a flower*), the girl whom both loved

then; but at best an absentee God, sitting idle, ever since the first Sabbath, at the outside of his Universe, and *seeing* it go? Has the word Duty no meaning; is what we call Duty no divine Messenger and Guide, but a false earthly Fantasm, made-up of Desire and Fear, of emanations from the Gallows and from Doctor Graham's Celestial Bed?[1] Happiness of an approving Conscience! Did not Paul of Tarsus, whom admiring men have since named Saint, feel that *he* was 'the chief of sinners,' and Nero of Rome, jocund in spirit (*wohlgemuth*), spend much of his time in fiddling? Foolish Wordmonger, and Motive-grinder, who in thy Logic-mill hast an earthly mechanism for the Godlike itself, and wouldst fain grind me out Virtue ·from the husks of Pleasure, — I tell thee, Nay! To the unregenerate Prometheus Vinctus[2] of a man, it is ever the bitterest aggravation of his wretchedness that he is conscious of Virtue, that he feels himself the victim not of suffering only, but of injustice. What then? Is the heroic inspiration we name Virtue but some Passion; some bubble of the blood, bubbling in the direction others *profit* by? I know not: only this I know, if what thou namest Happiness be our true aim, then are we all astray. With Stupidity and sound digestion man may front much. But what, in these dull unimaginative days are the terrors of Conscience to the diseases of the Liver! Not on Morality, but on Cookery, let us build our stronghold: there brandishing our frying-pan, as censer, let us offer sweet incense to the Devil, and live at ease on the fat things *he* has provided for his Elect!"

Thus has the bewildered Wanderer to stand, as so many have done, shouting question after question into the Sibyl-cave[3] of Destiny, and receive no Answer but an Echo. It is all a grim Desert, this once-fair world of his; wherein is heard only the howling of wild-beasts, or the shrieks of despairing, hate-filled men; and no Pillar of Cloud by day, and no Pillar of Fire by night,[4] any longer guides the Pilgrim. To such length has the spirit of Inquiry carried him. "But what boots it (*was thut's*)?" cries he; "it is but the common lot in this era. Not having come to spiritual majority prior to the *Siècle de Louis Quinze*,[1] and not being born purely a Loghead (*Dummkopf*), thou hadst no other outlook. The whole world is, like thee, sold to Unbelief; their old Temples of the Godhead, which for long have not been rainproof, crumble down; and men ask now: Where is the Godhead; our eyes never saw him?"

Pitiful enough were it, for all these wild utterances, to call our Diogenes[2] wicked. Unprofitable servants as we all are, perhaps at no era of his life was he more decisively the Servant of Goodness, the Servant of God, than even now when doubting God's existence. "One circumstance I note," says he: "after all the nameless woe that Inquiry, which for me, what it is not always, was genuine Love of Truth, had wrought me, I nevertheless still loved Truth, and would bate no jot of my allegiance to her. 'Truth!' I cried, 'though the Heavens crush me for following her: no Falsehood! though a whole celestial Lubberland[3] were the price of Apostasy.' In conduct it was the same. Had a divine Messenger from the clouds, or miraculous Handwriting on the wall, convincingly proclaimed to me *This thou shalt do*, with what passionate readiness, as I often thought, would I have done it, had it been leaping into the infernal Fire. Thus, in spite of all Motive-grinders, and Mechanical Profit-and-Loss Philosophies, with the sick ophthalmia and hallucination they had brought on, was the Infinite nature of Duty still dimly present to me: living without God in the world, of God's light I was not utterly bereft; if my as yet sealed eyes, with their unspeakable longing, could nowhere see Him, nevertheless in my heart He was present, and His heaven-written Law still stood legible and sacred there."

Meanwhile, under all these tribulations, and temporal and spiritual destitutions, what must the Wanderer, in his silent soul, have endured! "The painfullest feeling," writes he, "is that of your own Feebleness (*Unkraft*); ever as the English Milton says, to be weak is the true misery. And yet of your Strength there is and can be no clear feeling, save by what you have prospered in, by what you have

---

[1] the invention of a quack for curing sterility
[2] Prometheus Bound — the victim of the wrath of Zeus because he stole fire from heaven for mankind　　[3] visited by Aeneas (*Aeneid*, VI, 36 ff.)
[4] Cf. *Exodus*, xiii : 21, 22

[1] Age of Louis XV, the age of scepticism　[2] an eccentric Greek philosopher　[3] the fabulous land of the lazy, where food grew ready cooked on the trees and the vines flowed with wine

done. Between vague wavering Capability and fixed indubitable Performance, what a difference! A certain inarticulate Self-consciousness dwells dimly in us; which only our Works can render articulate and decisively discernible. Our Works are the mirror wherein the spirit first sees its natural lineaments. Hence, too, the folly of that impossible Precept, *Know thyself;* till it be translated into this partially possible one, *Know what thou canst work at.*

"But for me, so strangely unprosperous had I been, the net-result of my Workings amounted as yet simply to — Nothing. How then could I believe in my Strength, when there was as yet no mirror to see it in? Ever did this agitating, yet, as I now perceive, quite frivolous question, remain to me insoluble: Hast thou a certain Faculty, a certain Worth, such even as the most have not; or art thou the completest Dullard of these modern times? Alas! the fearful Unbelief is unbelief in yourself; and how could I believe? Had not my first, last Faith in myself, when even to me the Heavens seemed laid open, and I dared to love, been all-too cruelly belied? The speculative Mystery of Life grew ever more mysterious to me; neither in the practical Mystery had I made the slightest progress, but been everywhere buffeted, foiled, and contemptuously cast out. A feeble unit in the middle of a threatening Infinitude, I seemed to have nothing given me but eyes, whereby to discern my own wretchedness. Invisible yet impenetrable walls, as of Enchantment, divided me from all living: was there, in the wide world, any true bosom I could press trustfully to mine? O Heaven, No, there was none! I kept a lock upon my lips: why should I speak much with that shifting variety of so-called Friends, in whose withered, vain and too-hungry souls, Friendship was but an incredible tradition? In such cases, your resource is to talk little, and that little mostly from the Newspapers. Now when I look back, it was a strange isolation I then lived in. The men and women around me, even speaking with me, were but Figures: I had, practically, forgotten that they were alive, that they were not merely automatic. In the midst of their crowded streets, and assemblages, I walked solitary; and (except as it was my own heart, not another's, that I kept devouring) savage also, as the tiger in his jungle. Some comfort it

would have been, could I, like a Faust, have fancied myself tempted and tormented of the Devil; for a Hell, as I imagine, without Life, though only diabolic Life, were more frightful: but in our age of Down-pulling and Disbelief, the very Devil has been pulled down, you cannot so much as believe in a Devil. To me the Universe was all void of Life, of Purpose, of Volition, even of Hostility: it was one huge, dead, immeasurable Steam-engine, rolling on, in its dead indifference, to grind me limb from limb. O, the vast gloomy, solitary Golgotha,[1] and Mill of Death! Why was the Living banished thither companionless, conscious? Why, if there is no Devil; nay, unless the Devil is your God?"

A prey incessantly to such corrosions, might not, moreover, as the worst aggravation to them, the iron constitution even of a Teufelsdröckh threaten to fail? We conjecture that he has known sickness; and, in spite of his locomotive habits, perhaps sickness of the chronic sort. Hear this, for example: "How beautiful to die of broken-heart, on Paper! Quite another thing in practice; every window of your Feeling, even of your Intellect, as it were, begrimed and mud-bespattered, so that no pure ray can enter; a whole Drugshop in your inwards; the foredone soul drowning slowly in quagmires of Disgust!"

Putting all which external and internal miseries together, may we not find in the following sentences, quite in our Professor's still vein, significance enough? "From Suicide a certain aftershine (*Nachschein*) of Christianity withheld me: perhaps also a certain indolence of character; for, was not that a remedy I had at any time within reach? Often, however, was there a question present to me: Should some one now, at the turning of that corner, blow thee suddenly out of Space, into the other World, or other No-world, by pistol-shot, — how were it? On which ground, too, I have often, in sea-storms and sieged cities and other death-scenes, exhibited an imperturbability, which passed, falsely enough, for courage."

"So had it lasted," concludes the Wanderer, "so had it lasted, as in bitter protracted Death-agony, through long years. The heart within me, unvisited by any heavenly dewdrop, was smouldering in sulphurous, slow-consuming fire. Almost since earliest memory I had shed

---

[1] Place of skulls

no tear; or once only when I, murmuring half-audibly, recited Faust's Deathsong, that wild *Selig der den er im Siegesglanze findet* (Happy whom *he* finds in Battle's splendour), and thought that of this last Friend even I was not forsaken, that Destiny itself could not doom me not to die. Having no hope, neither had I any definite fear, were it of Man or of Devil: nay, I often felt as if it might be solacing, could the Arch-Devil himself, though in Tartarean terrors, but rise to me, that I might tell him a little of my mind. And yet, strangely enough, I lived in a continual, indefinite, pining fear; tremulous, pusillanimous, apprehensive of I knew not what: it seemed as if all things in the Heavens above and the Earth beneath would hurt me; as if the Heavens and the Earth were but boundless jaws of a devouring monster, wherein I, palpitating, waited to be devoured.

"Full of such humour, and perhaps the miserablest man in the whole French Capital or Suburbs, was I, one sultry Dog-day, after much perambulation, toiling along the dirty little *Rue Saint-Thomas de l'Enfer*, among civic rubbish enough, in a close atmosphere, and over pavements hot as Nebuchadnezzar's Furnace; whereby doubtless my spirits were little cheered; when, all at once, there rose a Thought in me, and I asked myself: 'What *art* thou afraid of? Wherefore, like a coward, dost thou forever pip and whimper, and go cowering and trembling? Despicable biped! what is the sum-total of the worst that lies before thee? Death? Well, Death; and say the pangs of Tophet too, and all that the Devil and Man may, will, or can do against thee! Hast thou not a heart; canst thou not suffer whatsoever it be; and, as a Child of Freedom, though outcast, trample Tophet itself under thy feet, while it consumes thee? Let it come, then; I will meet it and defy it!' And as I so thought, there rushed like a stream of fire over my whole soul; and I shook base Fear away from me forever. I was strong of unknown strength; a spirit, almost a god. Ever from that time, the temper of my misery was changed: not Fear or whining Sorrow was it, but Indignation and grim fire-eyed Defiance.

"Thus had the Everlasting No (*das ewige Nein*) pealed authoritatively through all the recesses of my Being, of my Me; and then was it that my whole Me stood up, in native God-created majesty, and with emphasis recorded its Protest. Such a Protest, the most important transaction in Life, may that same Indignation and Defiance, in a psychological point of view, be fitly called. The Everlasting No had said: 'Behold, thou art fatherless, outcast, and the Universe is mine (the Devil's)'; to which my whole Me now made answer: '*I* am not thine, but Free, and forever hate thee!'

"It is from this hour that I incline to date my Spiritual New-birth, or Baphometic[1] Fire-baptism; perhaps I directly thereupon began to be a Man."

CHAPTER VIII

CENTRE OF INDIFFERENCE

Though, after this "Baphometic Fire-baptism" of his, our Wanderer signifies that his Unrest was but increased; as, indeed, "Indignation and Defiance," especially against things in general, are not the most peaceable inmates; yet can the Psychologist surmise that it was no longer a quite hopeless Unrest; that henceforth it had at least a fixed centre to revolve round. For the fire-baptised soul, long so scathed and thunder-riven, here feels its own Freedom, which feeling is its Baphometic Baptism: the citadel of its whole kingdom it has thus gained by assault; and will keep inexpugnable; outwards from which the remaining dominions, not indeed without hard battling, will doubtless by degrees be conquered and pacificated. Under another figure, we might say, if in that great moment, in the *Rue Saint-Thomas de l'Enfer*, the old inward Satanic School was not yet thrown out of doors, it received peremptory judicial notice to quit; — whereby, for the rest, its howl-chantings, Ernulphus-cursings,[2] and rebellious gnashings of teeth, might, in the meanwhile, become only the more tumultuous, and difficult to keep secret.

Accordingly, if we scrutinise these Pilgrimings well, there is perhaps discernible henceforth a certain incipient method in their madness. Not wholly as a Spectre does Teufelsdröckh now storm through the world; at worst as a spectre-fighting Man, nay who will

[1] originally connected with mysterious rites attributed to the Templars; here, spiritually illuminating [2] elaborate and voluminous cursings, cf. *Tristram Shandy*, bk. iii, ch. xi

one day be a Spectre-queller. If pilgriming restlessly to so many "Saints' Wells,"[1] and ever without quenching of his thirst, he nevertheless finds little secular wells, whereby from time to time some alleviation is ministered. In a word, he is now, if not ceasing, yet intermitting to "eat his own heart"; and clutches round him outwardly on the Not-Me for wholesomer food. Does not the following glimpse exhibit him in a much more natural state?

"Towns also and Cities, especially the ancient, I failed not to look upon with interest. How beautiful to see thereby, as through a long vista, into the remote Time; to have, as it were, an actual section of almost the earliest Past brought safe into the Present, and set before your eyes! There, in that old City, was a live ember of Culinary Fire put down, say only two-thousand years ago; and there, burning more or less triumphantly, with such fuel as the region yielded, it has burnt, and still burns, and thou thyself seest the very smoke thereof. Ah! and the far more mysterious live ember of Vital Fire was then also put down there; and still miraculously burns and spreads; and the smoke and ashes thereof (in these Judgment-Halls and Church-yards), and its bellows-engines (in these Churches), thou still seest; and its flame, looking out from every kind countenance, and every hateful one, still warms thee or scorches thee.

"Of Man's Activity and Attainment the chief results are aeriform, mystic, and preserved in Tradition only: such are his Forms of of Government, with the Authority they rest on; his Customs, or Fashions both of Cloth-Habits and of Soul-Habits; much more his collective stock of Handicrafts, the whole Faculty he has acquired of manipulating Nature: all these things, as indispensable and priceless as they are, cannot in any way be fixed under lock and key, but must flit, spirit-like, on impalpable vehicles, from Father to Son; if you demand sight of them, they are nowhere to be met with. Visible Ploughmen and Hammermen there have been, ever from Cain and Tubalcain[2] downwards: but where does your accumulated Agricultural, Metallurgic, and other Manufacturing Skill lie warehoused? It transmits itself on

the atmospheric air, on the sun's rays (by Hearing and Vision); it is a thing aeriform, impalpable, of quite spiritual sort. In like manner, ask me not, Where are the Laws; where is the Government? In vain wilt thou go to Schönbrunn,[1] to Downing Street,[2] to the Palais Bourbon:[3] thou findest nothing there, but brick or stone houses, and some bundles of Papers tied with tape. Where, then, is that same cunningly-devised or mighty Government of theirs to be laid hands on? Everywhere, yet nowhere: seen only in its works, this too is a thing aeriform, invisible; or if you will, mystic and miraculous. So spiritual (*geistig*) is our whole daily Life: all that we do springs out of Mystery, Spirit, invisible Force; only like a little Cloud-image, or Armida's Palace,[4] air-built, does the Actual body itself forth from the great mystic Deep.

"Visible and tangible products of the Past, again, I reckon-up to the extent of three: Cities, with their Cabinets and Arsenals; then tilled Fields, to either or to both of which divisions Roads with their Bridges may belong; and thirdly — Books. In which third truly, the last-invented, lies a worth far surpassing that of the two others. Wondrous indeed is the virtue of a true Book. Not like a dead city of stones, yearly crumbling, yearly needing repair; more like a tilled field, but then a spiritual field: like a spiritual tree, let me rather say, it stands from year to year, and from age to age (we have Books that already number some hundred-and-fifty human ages); and yearly comes its new produce of leaves (Commentaries, Deductions, Philosophical, Political Systems; or were it only Sermons, Pamphlets, Journalistic Essays), every one of which is talismanic and thaumaturgic, for it can persuade men. O thou who art able to write a Book, which once in the two centuries or oftener there is a man gifted to do, envy not him whom they name City-builder, and inexpressibly pity him whom they name Conqueror or City-burner! Thou too art a Conqueror and Victor; but of the true sort, namely over the Devil: thou too hast built what will outlast all marble and metal,

[1] a palace near Vienna, the seat of the Austrian government [2] a street in London, where the chief government offices are [3] in Paris, now the Chamber of Deputies [4] Bower of Bliss in which the sorceress Armida holds the knight Rinaldo enchanted, in Tasso's *Jerusalem Delivered*

[1] where people go to be cured of disease by miracle [2] Cf. *Genesis*, iv: 22

AE

and be a wonder-bringing City of the Mind, a Temple and Seminary and Prophetic Mount, whereto all kindreds of the Earth will pilgrim. — Fool! why journeyest thou wearisomely, in thy antiquarian fervour, to gaze on the stone pyramids of Geeza or the clay ones of Sacchara?[1] These stand there, as I can tell thee, idle and inert, looking over the Desert, foolishly enough, for the last three-thousand years: but canst thou not open thy Hebrew Bible, then, or even Luther's Version thereof?"

No less satisfactory is his sudden appearance not in Battle, yet on some Battle-field; which, we soon gather, must be that of Wagram:[2] so that here, for once, is a certain approximation to distinctness of date. Omitting much, let us impart what follows:

"Horrible enough! A whole Marchfeld[3] strewed with shell-splinters, cannon-shot, ruined tumbrils, and dead men and horses; stragglers still remaining not so much as buried. And those red mould heaps: ay, there lie the Shells of Men, out of which all the Life and Virtue has been blown; and now they are swept together, and crammed-down out of sight, like blown Egg-shells! — Did Nature, when she bade the Donau[4] bring down his mould-cargoes from the Carinthian and Carpathian Heights, and spread them out here into the softest, richest level, — intend thee, O Marchfeld, for a corn-bearing Nursery, whereon her children might be nursed; or for a Cockpit, wherein they might the more commodiously be throttled and tattered? Were thy three broad highways, meeting here from the ends of Europe, made for Ammunition-wagons, then? Were thy Wagrams and Stillfrieds[5] but so many ready-built Case-mates, wherein the house of Hapsburg might batter with artillery, and with artillery be battered? König Ottokar, amid yonder hillocks, dies under Rodolf's[6] truncheon; here Kaiser Franz[7] falls a-swoon under Napoleon's: within which five centuries, to omit the others, how has thy breast, fair Plain, been defaced and defiled! The greensward is torn-up and trampled-down; man's fond care of it, his fruit-trees, hedge-rows, and pleasant dwellings, blown-away with gunpowder; and the kind seed-field lies a desolate, hideous Place of Skulls. — Nevertheless, Nature is at work; neither shall these Powder-Devilkins with their utmost devilry gainsay her: but all that gore and carnage will be shrouded-in, absorbed into manure; and next year the Marchfeld will be green, nay greener. Thrifty un-wearied Nature, ever out of our great waste educing some little profit of thy own, — how dost thou, from the very carcass of the Killer, bring Life for the Living![1]

"What, speaking in quite unofficial language, is the net-purport and upshot of war? To my own knowledge, for example, there dwell and toil, in the British village of Dumdrudge,[2] usually some five-hundred souls. From these, by certain 'Natural Enemies' of the French, there are successively selected, during the French war, say thirty able-bodied men: Dumdrudge, at her own expense, has suckled and nursed them; she has, not without difficulty and sorrow, fed them up to manhood, and even trained them to crafts, so that one can weave, another build, another hammer, and the weakest can stand under thirty stone avoirdupois. Nevertheless, amid much weeping and swearing, they are selected; all dressed in red; and shipped away, at the public charges, some two-thousand miles, or say only to the south of Spain; and fed there till wanted. And now to that same spot in the south of Spain, are thirty similar French artisans, from a French Dumdrudge, in like manner wending: till at length, after infinite effort, the two parties come into actual juxtaposition; and Thirty stands fronting Thirty, each with a gun in his hand. Straightway the word 'Fire!' is given: and they blow the souls out of one another; and in place of sixty brisk useful craftsmen, the world has sixty dead carcasses, which it must bury, and anew shed tears for. Had these men any quarrel? Busy as the Devil is, not the smallest! They lived far enough apart; were the entirest strangers; nay, in so wide a Universe, there was even unconsciously, by Commerce, some mutual helpfulness between them. How then? Simpleton! their Governors had fallen-out; and, instead of shoot-

---

[1] Ghizeh or Gizeh, and Sakkara, in Egypt [2] in Austria, fought in 1809 [3] the plain of Wagram [4] Danube [5] a village near Wagram [6] Ottocar, king of Bohemia was defeated in this plain by Rudolf of Hapsburg, 1278. [7] Francis I of Austria, defeated here by Napoleon

[1] Cf. *Judges*, xiv : 8, 14 [2] a fictitious name = dumb drudge

ing one another, had the cunning to make these poor blockheads shoot. — Alas, so is it in Deutschland, and hitherto in all other lands; still as of old, 'what devilry soever Kings do, the Greeks must pay the piper!'[1] — In that fiction of the English Smollett, it is true, the final Cessation of War is perhaps prophetically shadowed forth; where the two Natural Enemies, in person, take each a Tobacco-pipe, filled with Brimstone; light the same, and smoke in one another's faces till the weaker gives in: but from such predicted Peace-Era, what blood-filled trenches, and contentious centuries, may still divide us!"

Thus can the Professor, at least in lucid intervals, look away from his own sorrows, over the many-coloured world, and pertinently enough note what is passing there. We may remark, indeed, that for the matter of spiritual culture, if for nothing else, perhaps few periods of his life were richer than this. Internally, there is the most momentous instructive Course of Practical Philosophy, with Experiments, going on; towards the right comprehension of which his Peripatetic habits, favourable to Meditation, might help him rather than hinder. Externally, again, as he wanders to and fro, there are, if for the longing heart little substance, yet for the seeing eye sights enough: in these so boundless Travels of his, granting that the Satanic School was even partially kept down, what an incredible knowledge of our Planet, and its Inhabitants and their Works, that is to say, of all knowable things, might not Teufelsdröckh acquire!

"I have read in most Public Libraries," says he, "including those of Constantinople and Samarcand: in most Colleges, except the Chinese Mandarin ones, I have studied, or seen that there was no studying. Unknown languages have I oftenest gathered from their natural repertory, the Air, by my organ of Hearing; Statistics, Geographics, Topographics came, through the Eye, almost of their own accord. The ways of Man, how he seeks food, and warmth, and protection for himself, in most regions, are ocularly known to me. Like the great Hadrian,[2] I meted-out

much of the terraqueous Globe with a pair of Compasses that belonged to myself only.

"Of great Scenes, why speak? Three summer days, I lingered reflecting, and composing (*dichtete*), by the Pine-chasms of Vaucluse;[1] and in that clear lakelet moistened my bread. I have sat under the Palm-trees of Tadmor; smoked a pipe among the ruins of Babylon. The great Wall of China I have seen; and can testify that it is of gray brick, coped and covered with granite, and shows only secondrate masonry. — Great events, also, have not I witnessed? Kings sweated-down (*ausgemergelt*) into Berlin-and-Milan Customhouse-Officers; the World well won, and the World well lost; oftener than once a hundred-thousand individuals shot (by each other) in one day. All kindreds and peoples and nations dashed together, and shifted and shovelled into heaps, that they might ferment there, and in time unite. The birth-pangs of Democracy, wherewith convulsed Europe was groaning in cries that reached Heaven, could not escape me.

"For great Men I have ever had the warmest predilection; and can perhaps boast that few such in this era have wholly escaped me. Great Men are the inspired (speaking and acting) Texts of that divine Book of Revelations, whereof a Chapter is completed from epoch to epoch, and by some named History; to which inspired Texts your numerous talented men, and your innumerable untalented men, are the better or worse exegetic Commentaries, and wagonload of too-stupid, heretical or orthodox, weekly Sermons. For my study, the inspired Texts themselves! Thus did not I, in very early days, having disguised me as a tavern-waiter, stand behind the field-chairs, under that shady Tree at Treisnitz[2] by the Jena Highway; waiting upon the great Schiller and greater Goethe; and hearing what I have not forgotten. For —"

— But at this point the Editor recalls his principle of caution, some time ago laid down, and must suppress much. Let not the sacredness of Laurelled, still more, of Crowned Heads, be tampered with. Should we, at a future day, find circumstances altered, and the time come for Publication, then may these glimpses into the privacy of the Illustrious be conceded; which for the present were little

---

[1] "They who dance must pay the piper," and Horace, *Epist.* I, ii, 14: "Quicquid delirant reges, plectuntur Achivi." [2] The emperor Hadrian, at the head of his army, paced out on foot the circle of his empire, as Carlyle says elsewhere.

[1] where Petrarch lived for a time, near Avignon
[2] correctly, Triesnitz, where the poets used to meet

better than treacherous, perhaps traitorous Eavesdroppings. Of Lord Byron, therefore, of Pope Pius,[1] Emperor Tarakwang,[2] and the "White Water-roses" (Chinese Carbonari[3]) with their mysteries, no notice here! Of Napoleon himself we shall only, glancing from afar, remark that Teufelsdröckh's relation to him seems to have been of very varied character. At first we find our poor Professor on the point of being shot as a spy; then taken into private conversation, even pinched on the ear, yet presented with no money; at last indignantly dismissed, almost thrown out of doors, as an "Ideologist." "He himself," says the Professor, "was among the completest Ideologists, at least Ideopraxists[4]: in the Idea (*in der Idee*) he lived, moved, and fought. The man was a Divine Missionary, though unconscious of it; and preached, through the cannon's throat, that great doctrine, *La carrière ouverte aux talens* (The Tools to him that can handle them), which is our ultimate Political Evangel, wherein alone can Liberty lie. Madly enough he preached, it is true, as Enthusiasts and first Missionaries are wont, with imperfect utterance, amid much frothy rant; yet as articulately perhaps as the case admitted. Or call him, if you will, an American Backwoodsman, who had to fell unpenetrated forests, and battle with innumerable wolves, and did not entirely forbear strong liquor, rioting, and even theft; whom, notwithstanding, the peaceful Sower will follow, and, as he cuts the boundless harvest, bless."

More legitimate and decisively authentic is Teufelsdröckh's appearance and emergence (we know not well whence) in the solitude of the North Cape, on that June Midnight. He has a "light-blue Spanish cloak" hanging round him, as his "most commodious, principal, indeed sole upper-garment"; and stands there, on the World-promontory, looking over the infinite Brine, like a little blue Belfry (as we figure), now motionless indeed, yet ready, if stirred, to ring quaintest changes.

"Silence as of death," writes he; "for Midnight, even in the Arctic latitudes, has its character: nothing but the granite cliffs ruddy-tinged, the peaceable gurgle of that slow-heaving Polar Ocean, over which in the utmost

North the great Sun hangs low and lazy, as if he too were slumbering. Yet is his cloud-couch wrought of crimson and cloth-of-gold; yet does his light stream over the mirror of waters, like a tremulous fire-pillar, shooting downwards to the abyss, and hide itself under my feet. In such moments, Solitude also is invaluable; for who would speak, or be looked on, when behind him lies all Europe and Africa, fast asleep, except the watchmen; and before him the silent Immensity, and Palace of the Eternal, whereof our Sun is but a porch-lamp?

"Nevertheless, in this solemn moment, comes a man, or monster, scrambling from among the rock-hollows; and, shaggy, huge as the Hyperborean Bear, hails me in Russian speech: most probably, therefore, a Russian Smuggler. With courteous brevity, I signify my indifference to contraband-trade, my humane intentions, yet strong wish to be private. In vain: the monster, counting doubtless on his superior stature, and minded to make sport for himself, or perhaps profit, were it with murder, continues to advance; ever assailing me with his importunate train-oil breath; and now has advanced, till we stand both on the verge of the rock, the deep Sea rippling greedily down below. What argument will avail? On the thick Hyperborean, cherubic reasoning, seraphic eloquence were lost. Prepared for such extremity, I, deftly enough, whisk aside one step; draw out, from my interior reservoirs, a sufficient Birmingham Horse-pistol, and say, 'Be so obliging as retire, Friend (*Erziehe sich zurück, Freund*), and with promptitude!' This logic even the Hyperborean understands: fast enough, with apologetic, petitionary growl, he sidles off; and, except for suicidal as well as homicidal purposes, need not return.

"Such I hold to be the genuine use of Gunpowder: that it makes all men alike tall. Nay, if thou be cooler, cleverer than I, if thou have more *Mind*, though all but no *Body* whatever, then canst thou kill me first, and art the taller. Hereby, at last, is the Goliath powerless, and the David resistless; savage Animalism is nothing, inventive Spiritualism is all.

"With respect to Duels, indeed, I have my own ideas. Few things, in this so surprising world, strike me with more surprise. Two little visual Spectra of men, hovering with insecure enough cohesion in the midst of the Unfathomable, and to dissolve therein, at any rate, very soon, — make pause at the distance

---

[1] Pius VII, died 1823 [2] Taou-Kwang, began to reign in 1820 [3] a secret society in Italy, working for a republic, in the early part of the nineteenth century [4] those who put ideas into practice

of twelve paces asunder; whirl round; and, simultaneously by the cunningest mechanism, explode one another into Dissolution; and off-hand become Air, and Non-extant! Deuce on it (*verdammt*), the little spitfires! — Nay, I think with old Hugo von Trimberg:[1] 'God must needs laugh outright, could such a thing be, to see his wondrous Manikins here below.'"

But amid these specialities, let us not forget the great generality, which is our chief quest here: How prospered the inner man of Teufelsdröckh under so much outward shifting? Does Legion[2] still lurk in him, though re-pressed, or has he exorcised that Devil's Brood? We can answer that the symptoms continue promising. Experience is the grand spiritual Doctor; and with him Teufelsdröckh has now been long a patient, swallowing many a bitter bolus. Unless our poor Friend belong to the numerous class of Incurables, which seems not likely, some cure will doubtless be effected. We should rather say that Legion, or the Satanic School, was now pretty well extirpated and cast out, but next to nothing introduced in its room; whereby the heart remains, for the while, in a quiet but no comfortable state.

"At length, after so much roasting," thus writes our Autobiographer, "I was what you might name calcined. Pray only that it be not rather, as is the more frequent issue, re-duced to a *caput-mortuum!*[3] But in any case, by mere dint of practice, I had grown familiar with many things. Wretchedness was still wretched; but I could now partly see through it, and despise it. Which highest mortal, in this inane Existence, had I not found a Shadow-hunter or Shadow-hunted; and, when I looked through his brave garnitures, miser-able enough? Thy wishes have all been sniffed aside, thought I: but what, had they even been all granted! Did not the Boy Alexander[4] weep because he had not two Planets to conquer; or a whole Solar System; or after that, a whole Universe? *Ach Gott*, when I gazed into these Stars, have they not looked-down on me as if with pity, from their serene spaces; like Eyes glistening with heavenly tears over the little lot of man! Thousands of human generations, all as noisy as our own, have been swallowed-up of Time, and there remains no wreck of them any more;

and Arcturus and Orion and Sirius and the Pleiades are still shining in their courses, clear and young, as when the Shepherd[1] first noted them in the plain of Shinar. Pshaw! what is this paltry little Dog-cage[2] of an Earth; what art thou that sittest whining there? Thou art still Nothing, Nobody: true; but who, then, is Something, Somebody? For thee the Family of Man has no use; it rejects thee; thou art wholly as a dissevered limb: so be it; perhaps it is better so!"

Too-heavy-laden Teufelsdröckh! Yet surely his bands are loosening; one day he will hurl the burden far from him, and bound forth free and with a second youth.

"This," says our Professor, "was the Centre of Indifference I had now reached; through which whoso travels from the Negative Pole to the Positive must necessarily pass."

CHAPTER IX

THE EVERLASTING YEA

"Temptations in the Wilderness!" ex-claims Teufelsdröckh: "Have we not all to be tried with such? Not so easily can the old Adam, lodged in us by birth, be dispossessed. Our Life is compassed round with Necessity; yet is the meaning of Life itself no other than Freedom, than Voluntary Force: thus have we a warfare; in the beginning, especially, a hard-fought battle. For the God-given man-date, *Work thou in Welldoing*, lies mysteriously written, in Promethean[3] Prophetic Characters, in our hearts; and leaves us no rest, night or day, till it be deciphered and obeyed; till it burn forth, in our conduct, a visible, acted Gospel of Freedom. And as the clay-given mandate, *Eat thou and be filled*, at the same time persuasively proclaims itself through every nerve, — must there not be a confusion, a contest, before the better Influence can become the upper?

"To me nothing seems more natural than that the Son of Man, when such God-given mandate first prophetically stirs within him, and the Clay must now be vanquished or van-quish, — should be carried of the spirit into

---

[1] a thirteenth century German poet and moral-ist [2] Cf. *Mark*, v : 9 [3] worthless remains [4] Alex-ander the Great

[1] Cf. *Job*, ix : 9; Babylonian shepherds (in the plain of Shinar) were regarded as the first astronomers. [2] a wheel like a squirrel-cage [3] perhaps, like Prometheus, full of love for the human race

grim Solitudes, and there fronting the Tempter do grimmest battle with him; defiantly setting him at naught, till he yield and fly. Name it as we choose: with or without visible Devil, whether in the natural Desert of rocks and sands, or in the populous moral Desert of selfishness and baseness, — to such Temptation are we all called. Unhappy if we are not! Unhappy if we are but Half-men, in whom that divine handwriting has never blazed forth, all-subduing, in true sun-splendour; but quivers dubiously amid meaner lights: or smoulders, in dull pain, in darkness, under earthly vapours! — Our Wilderness is the wide World in an Atheistic Century; our Forty Days are long years of suffering and fasting: nevertheless, to these also comes an end. Yes, to me also was given, if not Victory, yet the consciousness of Battle, and the resolve to persevere therein while life or faculty is left. To me also, entangled in the enchanted forests, demon-peopled, doleful of sight and of sound, it was given, after weariest wanderings, to work out my way into the higher sunlit slopes — of that Mountain which has no summit, or whose summit is in Heaven only!"[1]

He says elsewhere, under a less ambitious figure; as figures are, once for all, natural to him: "Has not thy Life been that of most sufficient men (*tüchtigen Männer*) thou hast known in this generation? An outflush of foolish young Enthusiasm, like the first fallow-crop, wherein are as many weeds as valuable herbs: this all parched away, under the Droughts of practical and spiritual Unbelief, as Disappointment, in thought and act, often-repeated gave rise to Doubt, and Doubt gradually settled into Denial! If I have had a second-crop, and now see the perennial greensward, and sit under umbrageous cedars, which defy all Drought (and Doubt); herein too, be the Heavens praised, I am not without examples, and even exemplars."

So that, for Teufelsdröckh also, there has been a "glorious revolution": these mad shadow-hunting and shadow-hunted Pilgrimings of his were but some purifying "Temptation in the Wilderness," before his apostolic work (such as it was) could begin; which Temptation is now happily over, and the Devil once more worsted! Was "that high moment in the *Rue de l'Enfer*," then, properly the turn-

ing-point of the battle; when the Fiend said, *Worship me, or be torn in shreds;* and was answered valiantly with an *A page Satana?*[1] — Singular Teufelsdröckh, would thou hadst told thy singular story in plain words! But it is fruitless to look there, in those Paper-bags, for such. Nothing but innuendoes, figurative crotchets: a typical Shadow, fitfully wavering, prophetico-satiric; no clear logical Picture. "How paint to the sensual eye," asks he once, "what passes in the Holy-of-Holies of Man's Soul; in what words, known to these profane times, speak even afar-off of the unspeakable?" We ask in turn: Why perplex these times, profane as they are, with needless obscurity, by omission and by commission? Not mystical only is our Professor, but whimsical; and involves himself, now more than ever, in eye-bewildering *chiaroscuro*. Successive glimpses, here faithfully imparted, our more gifted readers must endeavour to combine for their own behoof.

He says: "The hot Harmattan[2] wind had raged itself out; its howl went silent within me; and the long-deafened soul could now hear. I paused in my wild wanderings; and sat me down to wait, and consider; for it was as if the hour of change drew nigh. I seemed to surrender, to renounce utterly, and say: Fly, then, false shadows of Hope; I will chase you no more, I will believe you no more. And ye too, haggard spectres of Fear, I care not for you; ye too are all shadows and a lie. Let me rest here: for I am way-weary and life-weary; I will rest here, were it but to die: to die or to live is alike to me; alike insignificant." — And again: "Here, then, as I lay in that Centre of Indifference, cast, doubtless by benignant upper Influence, into a healing sleep, the heavy dreams rolled gradually away, and I awoke to a new Heaven and a new Earth. The first preliminary moral Act, Annihilation of Self (*Selbsttödtung*), had been happily accomplished; and my mind's eyes were now unsealed, and its hands ungyved."

Might we not also conjecture that the following passage refers to his Locality, during this same "healing sleep"; that his Pilgrim-staff lies cast aside here, on "the high table-land"; and indeed that the repose is already taking wholesome effect on him? If it were

---

[1] an allusion to the mountain seen in Dante's *Divina Commedia*

[1] "Away, Satan!"   [2] a terrible wind on the coast of Guinea

not that the tone, in some parts, has more of riancy,[1] even of levity, than we could have expected! However, in Teufelsdröckh, there is always the strangest Dualism: light dancing, with guitar-music, will be going on in the forecourt, while by fits from within comes the faint whimpering of woe and wail. We transcribe the piece entire:

"Beautiful it was to sit there, as in my skyey Tent, musing and meditating; on the high table-land, in front of the Mountains; over me, as roof, the azure Dome, and around me, for walls, four azure-flowing curtains, — namely, of the Four azure Winds, on whose bottom-fringes also I have seen gilding. And then to fancy the fair Castles, that stood sheltered in these Mountain hollows; with their green flower-lawns, and white dames and damosels, lovely enough: or better still, the straw-roofed Cottages, wherein stood many a Mother baking bread, with her children round her: — all hidden and protectingly folded-up in the valley-folds; yet there and alive, as sure as if I beheld them. Or to see, as well as fancy, the nine Towns and Villages, that lay round my mountain-seat, which, in still weather, were wont to speak to me (by their steeple-bells) with metal tongue; and, in almost all weather, proclaimed their vitality by repeated Smoke-clouds; whereon, as on a culinary horologue,[2] I might read the hour of the day. For it was the smoke of cookery, as kind housewives at morning, midday, eventide, were boiling their husbands' kettles; and ever a blue pillar rose up into the air, successively or simultaneously, from each of the nine, saying, as plainly as smoke could say: Such and such a meal is getting ready here. Not uninteresting! For you have the whole Borough, with all its love-makings and scandal-mongeries, contentions and contentments, as in miniature, and could cover it all with your hat. — If, in my wide Wayfarings, I had learned to look into the business of the World in its details, here perhaps was the place for combining it into general propositions, and deducing inferences therefrom.

"Often also could I see the black Tempest marching in anger through the distance: round some Schreckhorn,[3] as yet grim-blue, would the eddying vapour gather, and there tumultuously eddy, and flow down like a mad witch's hair; till, after a space, it vanished, and, in the clear sunbeam, your Schreckhorn stood smiling grim-white, for the vapour had held snow. How thou fermentest and elaboratest in thy great fermenting-vat and laboratory of an Atmosphere, of a World, O Nature! — Or what is Nature? Ha! why do I not name thee God? Art thou not the 'Living Garment of God?'[1] O Heavens, is it, in very deed, He, then, that ever speaks through thee; that lives and loves in thee, that lives and loves in me?

"Fore-shadows, call them rather fore-splendours, of that Truth, and Beginning of Truths, fell mysteriously over my soul. Sweeter than Dayspring to the Shipwrecked in Nova Zembla; ah, like the mother's voice to her little child that strays bewildered, weeping, in unknown tumults; like soft streamings of celestial music to my too-exasperated heart, came that Evangel. The Universe is not dead and demoniacal, a charnel-house with spectres; but godlike, and my Father's!

"With other eyes, too, could I now look upon my fellow man: with an infinite Love, an infinite Pity. Poor, wandering, wayward man! Art thou not tried, and beaten with stripes, even as I am? Ever, whether thou bear the royal mantle or the beggar's gabardine, art thou not so weary, so heavy-laden; and thy Bed of Rest is but a Grave. O my Brother, my Brother, why cannot I shelter thee in my bosom, and wipe away all tears from thy eyes! — Truly, the din of many-voiced Life, which, in this solitude, with the mind's organ, I could hear, was no longer a maddening discord, but a melting one; like inarticulate cries, and sobbings of a dumb creature, which in the ear of Heaven are prayers. The poor Earth, with her poor joys, was now my needy Mother, not my cruel Stepdame; Man, with his so mad Wants and so mean Endeavours, had become the dearer to me; and even for his sufferings and his sins, I now first named him Brother. Thus was I standing in the porch of that 'Sanctuary of Sorrow'; by strange, steep ways, had I too been guided thither; and ere long its sacred gates would open, and the 'Divine Depth of Sorrow' lie disclosed to me."

The Professor says, he here first got eye on the Knot that had been strangling him, and

---

[1] spirit of laughter [2] horologe, clock [3] peak of terror; here generic for mountain

[1] from Goethe's *Faust:* "der Gottheit lebendiges Kleid"

straightway could unfasten it, and was free. "A vain interminable controversy," writes he, "touching what is at present called Origin of Evil, or some such thing, arises in every soul, since the beginning of the world; and in every soul, that would pass from idle Suffering into actual Endeavouring, must first be put an end to. The most, in our time, have to go content with a simple, incomplete enough Suppression of this controversy; to a few, some Solution of it is indispensable. In every new era, too, such Solution comes-out in different terms; and ever the Solution of the last era has become obsolete, and is found unserviceable. For it is man's nature to change his Dialect from century to century; he cannot help it though he would. The authentic *Church-Catechism* of our present century has not yet fallen into my hands: meanwhile, for my own private behoof, I attempt to elucidate the matter so. Man's Unhappiness, as I construe, comes of his Greatness; it is because there is an Infinite in him, which with all his cunning he cannot quite bury under the Finite. Will the whole Finance Ministers and Upholsterers and Confectioners of modern Europe undertake, in joint-stock company, to make one Shoeblack *happy?* They cannot accomplish it, above an hour or two: for the Shoeblack also has a Soul quite other than his Stomach; and would require, if you consider it, for his permanent satisfaction and saturation, simply this allotment, no more, and no less: *God's infinite Universe altogether to himself*, therein to enjoy infinitely, and fill every wish as fast as it rose. Oceans of Hochheimer,[1] a Throat like that of Ophiuchus:[2] speak not of them; to the infinite Shoeblack they are as nothing. No sooner is your ocean filled, than he grumbles that it might have been of better vintage. Try him with half of a Universe, of an Omnipotence, he sets to quarrelling with the proprietor of the other half, and declares himself the most maltreated of men. — Always there is a black spot in our sunshine: it is even, as I said, the *Shadow of Ourselves*.

"But the whim we have of Happiness is somewhat thus. By certain valuations, and averages, of our own striking, we come upon some sort of average terrestrial lot; this we fancy belongs to us by nature, and of indefeasible right. It is simple payment of our wages, of our deserts; requires neither thanks nor complaint; only such *overplus* as there may be do we account Happiness; any *deficit* again is Misery. Now consider that we have the valuation of our deserts ourselves, and what a fund of Self-conceit there is in each of us, — do you wonder that the balance should so often dip the wrong way, and many a Blockhead cry: See there, what a payment; was ever worthy gentleman so used! — I tell thee, Blockhead, it all comes of thy Vanity; of what thou *fanciest* those same deserts of thine to be. Fancy that thou deservest to be hanged (as is most likely), thou wilt feel it happiness to be only shot: fancy that thou deservest to be hanged in a hair-halter, it will be a luxury to die in hemp.

"So true it is, what I then said, that *the Fraction of Life can be increased in value not so much by increasing your Numerator as by lessening your Denominator.* Nay, unless my Algebra deceive me, *Unity* itself divided by *Zero* will give *Infinity.* Make thy claim of wages a zero, then; thou hast the world under thy feet. Well did the Wisest of our time[1] write: 'It is only with Renunciation (*Entsagen*) that Life, properly speaking, can be said to begin.'

"I asked myself: What is this that, ever since earliest years, thou hast been fretting and fuming, and lamenting and self-tormenting, on account of? Say it in a word: is it not because thou art not *happy?* Because the Thou (sweet gentleman) is not sufficiently honoured, nourished, soft-bedded, and lovingly cared-for? Foolish soul! What Act of Legislature was there that *thou* shouldst be Happy? A little while ago thou hadst no right to *be* at all. What if thou wert born and predestined not to be Happy, but to be Unhappy! Art thou nothing other than a Vulture, then, that fliest through the Universe seeking after somewhat to *eat;* and shrieking dolefully because carrion enough is not given thee? Close thy *Byron;* open thy *Goethe.*"

"*Es leuchtet mir ein*, I see a glimpse of it!" cries he elsewhere: "there is in man a Higher than Love of Happiness: he can do without Happiness, and instead thereof find Blessedness! Was it not to preach-forth this same Higher that sages and martyrs, the Poet and the Priest, in all times, have spoken and suffered; bearing testimony, through life and

---

[1] hock, a Rhine wine   [2] an ancient constellation, also called Serpentarius, the serpent-bearer

[1] Goethe

through death, of the Godlike that is in Man, and how in the Godlike only has he Strength and Freedom? Which God-inspired Doctrine art thou also honoured to be taught; O Heavens! and broken with manifold merciful Afflictions, even till thou become contrite, and learn it! O, thank thy Destiny for these; thankfully bear what yet remain: thou hadst need of them; the Self in thee needed to be annihilated. By benignant fever-paroxysms is Life rooting out the deep-seated chronic Disease, and triumphs over Death. On the roaring billows of Time, thou art not engulfed, but borne aloft into the azure of Eternity. Love not Pleasure; love God. This is the *Everlasting Yea*, wherein all contradiction is solved: wherein whoso walks and works, it is well with him."

And again: "Small is it that thou canst trample the Earth with its injuries under thy feet, as old Greek Zeno[1] trained thee: thou canst love the Earth while it injures thee, and even because it injures thee; for this a Greater than Zeno was needed, and he too was sent. Knowest thou that '*Worship of Sorrow*'? The Temple thereof, founded some eighteen centuries ago, now lies in ruins, overgrown with jungle, the habitation of doleful creatures: nevertheless, venture forward; in a low crypt, arched out of falling fragments, thou findest the Altar still there, and its sacred Lamp perennially burning."

Without pretending to comment on which strange utterances, the Editor will only remark, that there lies beside them much of a still more questionable character; unsuited to the general apprehension; nay, wherein he himself does not see his way. Nebulous disquisitions on Religion, yet not without bursts of splendour; on the "perennial continuance of Inspiration"; on Prophecy; that there are "true Priests," as well as Baal-Priests, in our own day": with more of the like sort. We select some fractions, by way of finish to this farrago.

"Cease, my much-respected Herr von Voltaire," thus apostrophises the Professor: "shut thy sweet voice; for the task appointed thee seems finished. Sufficiently hast thou demonstrated this proposition, considerable or otherwise: That the Mythus of the Christian Religion looks not in the eighteenth century as it did in the eighth. Alas, were thy six-

and-thirty quartos, and the six-and-thirty thousand other quartos and folios, and flying sheets or reams, printed before and since on the same subject, all needed to convince us of so little! But what next? Wilt thou help us to embody the divine Spirit of that Religion in a new Mythus, in a new vehicle and vesture, that our Souls, otherwise too like perishing, may live? What! thou hast no faculty in that kind? Only a torch for burning, no hammer for building? Take our thanks, then, and — thyself away.

"Meanwhile what are antiquated Mythuses to me? Or is the God present, felt in my own heart, a thing which Herr von Voltaire will dispute out of me; or dispute into me? To the '*Worship of Sorrow*' ascribe what origin and genesis thou pleasest, *has* not that Worship originated, and been generated; is it not *here*? Feel it in thy heart, and then say whether it is of God! This is Belief; all else is Opinion, — for which latter whoso will, let him worry and be worried."

"Neither," observes he elsewhere, "shall ye tear-out one another's eyes, struggling over 'Plenary Inspiration,'[1] and such-like: try rather to get a little even Partial Inspiration, each of you for himself. One Bible I know, of whose Plenary Inspiration doubt is not so much as possible; nay with my own eyes I saw the God's-Hand writing it: thereof all other Bibles are but Leaves, — say, in Picture-Writing to assist the weaker faculty."

Or to give the wearied reader relief, and bring it to an end, let him take the following perhaps more intelligible passage:

"To me, in this our life," says the Professor, "which is an internecine warfare with the Time-spirit, other warfare seems questionable. Hast thou in any way a Contention with thy brother, I advise thee, think well what the meaning thereof is. If thou gauge it to the bottom, it is simply this: 'Fellow, see! thou art taking more than thy share of Happiness in the world, something from *my* share: which, by the Heavens, thou shalt not; nay, I will fight thee rather.' — Alas, and the whole lot to be divided is such a beggarly matter, truly a 'feast of shells,' for the substance has been spilled out: not enough to quench one Appetite; and the collective human species clutching at them! — Can we not, in all such cases,

[1] a stoic philosopher

[1] that which excludes all defects in the expression of it

rather say: 'Take it, thou too-ravenous individual; take that pitiful additional fraction of a share, which I reckoned mine, but which thou so wantest; take it with a blessing: would to Heaven I had enough for thee !' — If Fichte's *Wissenschaftslehre*[1] be, 'to a certain extent, Applied Christianity,' surely to a still greater extent, so is this. We have here not a Whole Duty of Man, yet a Half Duty, namely, the Passive half: could we but do it, as we can demonstrate it !

"But indeed Conviction, were it never so excellent, is worthless till it convert itself into Conduct. Nay, properly Conviction is not possible till then; inasmuch as all Speculation is by nature endless, formless, a vortex amid vortices: only by a felt indubitable certainty of Experience does it find any centre to revolve round, and so fashion itself into a system. Most true is it, as a wise man teaches us, that 'Doubt of any sort cannot be removed except by Action.' On which ground, too, let him who gropes painfully in darkness or uncertain light, and prays vehemently that the dawn may ripen into day, lay this other precept well to heart, which to me was of invaluable service: '*Do the Duty which lies nearest thee,*' which thou knowest to be a Duty ! Thy second Duty will already have become clearer.

"May we not say, however, that the hour of Spiritual Enfranchisement is even this: When your Ideal World, wherein the whole man has been dimly struggling and inexpressibly languishing to work, becomes revealed and thrown open; and you discover, with amazement enough, like the Lothario in *Wilhelm Meister*,[2] that your 'America is here or nowhere'? The Situation that has not its Duty, its Ideal, was never yet occupied by man. Yes, here, in this poor, miserable, hampered, despicable Actual, wherein thou even now standest, here or nowhere is thy Ideal: work it out therefrom; and working, believe, live, be free. Fool ! the Ideal is in thyself, the impediment too is in thyself: thy Condition is but the stuff thou art to shape that same Ideal out of: what matters whether such stuff be of this sort or that, so the Form thou give it be heroic, be poetic? O thou that

pinest in the imprisonment of the Actual, and criest bitterly to the gods for a kingdom wherein to rule and create, know this of a truth: the thing thou seekest is already with thee, 'here or nowhere,' couldst thou only see !

"But it is with man's Soul as it was with Nature: the beginning of Creation is—Light. Till the eye have vision, the whole members are in bonds. Divine moment, when over the tempest-tost Soul, as once over the wild-weltering Chaos, it is spoken: Let there be light ! Ever to the greatest that has felt such moment, is it not miraculous and God-announcing; even as, under simpler figures, to the simplest and least. The mad primeval Discord is hushed; the rudely-jumbled conflicting elements bind themselves into separate Firmaments: deep silent rock-foundations are built beneath; and the skyey vault with its everlasting Luminaries above: instead of a dark wasteful Chaos, we have a blooming, fertile, Heaven-encompassed World.

"I too could now say to myself: Be no longer a Chaos, but a World, or even Worldkin.[1] Produce ! Produce ! Were it but the pitifullest infinitesimal fraction of a Product, produce it, in God's name ! 'Tis the utmost thou hast in thee: out with it, then. Up, up ! Whatsoever thy hand findeth to do, do it with thy whole might. Work while it is called Today; for the Night cometh, wherein no man can work."

THOMAS BABINGTON, LORD MACAULAY (1800–1859)

THE HISTORY OF ENGLAND

VOLUME I
From Chapter III

I intend, in this chapter, to give a description of the state in which England was at the time when the crown passed from Charles the Second to his brother. Such a description, composed from scanty and dispersed materials, must necessarily be very imperfect. Yet it may perhaps correct some false notions which would make the subsequent narrative unintelligible or uninstructive.

If we would study with profit the history of our ancestors, we must be constantly on our

---

[1] the chief work of the German metaphysician Fichte, of which the full title is, in English: *Fundamental Principles of the Whole Theory of Science*   [2] a novel by Goethe

[1] little world

guard against that delusion which the well-known names of families, places, and offices naturally produce, and must never forget that the country of which we read was a very different country from that in which we live.

* * * * * * *

Could the England of 1685 be, by some magical process, set before our eyes, we should not know one landscape in a hundred or one building in ten thousand. The country gentleman would not recognise his own fields. The inhabitant of the town would not recognise his own street. Everything has been changed but the great features of nature, and a few massive and durable works of human art. We might find out Snowdon and Windermere, the Cheddar Cliffs and Beachy Head. We might find out here and there a Norman minster, or a castle which witnessed the wars of the Roses. But, with such rare exceptions, everything would be strange to us. Many thousands of square miles which are now rich corn land and meadow, intersected by green hedgerows, and dotted with villages and pleasant country seats, would appear as moors overgrown with furze, or fens abandoned to wild ducks. We should see straggling huts built of wood and covered with thatch, where we now see manufacturing towns and seaports renowned to the farthest ends of the world. The capital itself would shrink to dimensions not much exceeding those of its present suburb on the south of the Thames.[1] Not less strange to us would be the garb and manners of the people, the furniture and the equipages, the interior of the shops and dwellings. Such a change in the state of a nation seems to be at least as well entitled to the notice of a historian as any change of the dynasty or of the ministry.

One of the first objects of an inquirer, who wishes to form a correct notion of the state of a community at a given time, must be to ascertain of how many persons that community then consisted. Unfortunately the population of England in 1685 cannot be ascertained with perfect accuracy. For no great state had then adopted the wise course of periodically numbering the people. All men were left to conjecture for themselves; and, as they generally conjectured without examining facts, and under the influence of strong passions and prejudices, their guesses were often ludicrously absurd. Even intelligent Londoners ordinarily talked of London as containing several millions of souls. It was confidently asserted by many that, during the thirty-five years which had elapsed between the accession of Charles the First and the Restoration, the population of the City had increased by two millions. Even while the ravages of the plague and fire were recent, it was the fashion to say that the capital still had a million and a half of inhabitants. Some persons, disgusted by these exaggerations, ran violently into the opposite extreme. Thus Isaac Vossius, a man of undoubted parts and learning, strenuously maintained that there were only two millions of human beings in England, Scotland, and Ireland taken together.

We are not, however, left without the means of correcting the wild blunders into which some minds were hurried by national vanity and others by a morbid love of paradox. There are extant three computations which seem to be entitled to peculiar attention. They are entirely independent of each other: they proceed on different principles; and yet there is little difference in the results.

* * * * * * *

Of these three estimates, framed without concert by different persons from different sets of materials, the highest, which is that of King, does not exceed the lowest, which is that of Finlaison,[1] by one twelfth. We may, therefore, with confidence pronounce that, when James the Second reigned, England contained between five million and five million five hundred thousand inhabitants. On the very highest supposition she then had less than one third of her present population, and less than three times the population which is now collected in her gigantic capital.

* * * * * * *

We should be much mistaken if we pictured to ourselves the squires of the seventeenth century as men bearing a close resemblance to their descendants, the country members and chairmen of quarter sessions with whom we are familiar. The modern country gentleman generally receives a liberal education, passes from a distinguished school to a distinguished college, and has ample opportunity to become

---

[1] Southwark

[1] Gregory King (1648–1712) and John Finlaison (1783–1860), English statisticians

an excellent scholar. He has generally seen something of foreign countries. A considerable part of his life has generally been passed in the capital; and the refinements of the capital follow him into the country. There is perhaps no class of dwellings so pleasing as the rural seats of the English gentry. In the parks and pleasure grounds, nature, dressed yet not disguised by art, wears her most alluring form. In the buildings, good sense and good taste combine to produce a happy union of the comfortable and the graceful. The pictures, the musical instruments, the library, would in any other country be considered as proving the owner to be an eminently polished and accomplished man. A country gentleman who witnessed the Revolution was probably in receipt of about a fourth part of the rent which his acres now yield to his posterity. He was, therefore, as compared with his posterity, a poor man, and was generally under the necessity of residing, with little interruption, on his estate. To travel on the Continent, to maintain an establishment in London, or even to visit London frequently, were pleasures in which only the great proprietors could indulge. It may be confidently affirmed that of the squires whose names were then in the Commissions of Peace and Lieutenancy not one in twenty went to town once in five years, or had ever in his life wandered so far as Paris. Many lords of manors had received an education differing little from that of their menial servants. The heir of an estate often passed his boyhood and youth at the seat of his family with no better tutors than grooms and gamekeepers, and scarce attained learning enough to sign his name to a Mittimus.[1] If he went to school and to college, he generally returned before he was twenty to the seclusion of the old hall, and there, unless his mind were very happily constituted by nature, soon forgot his academical pursuits in rural business and pleasures. His chief serious employment was the care of his property. He examined samples of grain, handled pigs, and, on market days, made bargains over a tankard with drovers and hop merchants. His chief pleasures were commonly derived from field sports and from an unrefined sensuality. His language and pronunciation were such as we should now expect to hear only from the most ignorant clowns. His oaths, coarse jests, and

[1] a writ of commitment to prison

scurrilous terms of abuse, were uttered with the broadest accent of his province. It was easy to discern, from the first words which he spoke, whether he came from Somersetshire or Yorkshire. He troubled himself little about decorating his abode, and, if he attempted decoration, seldom produced anything but deformity. The litter of a farmyard gathered under the windows of his bedchamber, and the cabbages and gooseberry bushes grew close to his hall door. His table was loaded with coarse plenty; and guests were cordially welcomed to it. But, as the habit of drinking to excess was general in the class to which he belonged, and as his fortune did not enable him to intoxicate large assemblies daily with claret or canary, strong beer was the ordinary beverage. The quantity of beer consumed in those days was indeed enormous. For beer then was to the middle and lower classes, not only all that beer now is, but all that wine, tea, and ardent spirits now are. It was only at great houses, or on great occasions, that foreign drink was placed on the board. The ladies of the house, whose business it had commonly been to cook the repast, retired as soon as the dishes had been devoured, and left the gentlemen to their ale and tobacco. The coarse jollity of the afternoon was often prolonged till the revellers were laid under the table.

It was very seldom that the country gentleman caught glimpses of the great world; and what he saw of it tended rather to confuse than to enlighten his understanding. His opinions respecting religion, government, foreign countries and former times, having been derived, not from study, from observation, or from conversation with enlightened companions, but from such traditions as were current in his own small circle, were the opinions of a child. He adhered to them, however, with the obstinacy which is generally found in ignorant men accustomed to be fed with flattery. His animosities were numerous and bitter. He hated Frenchmen and Italians, Scotchmen and Irishmen, Papists and Presbyterians, Independents and Baptists, Quakers and Jews. Towards London and Londoners he felt an aversion which more than once produced important political effects. His wife and daughter were in tastes and acquirements below a housekeeper or a still-room maid of the present day. They stitched and spun, brewed gooseberry wine, cured marigolds,[1] and made the crust for the venison pasty.

From this description it might be supposed that the English esquire of the seventeenth century did not materially differ from a rustic miller or alehouse keeper of our time. There are, however, some important parts of his character still to be noted, which will greatly modify this estimate. Unlettered as he was and unpolished, he was still in some most important points a gentleman. He was a member of a proud and powerful aristocracy, and was distinguished by many both of the good and of the bad qualities which belong to aristocrats. His family pride was beyond that of a Talbot or a Howard.[2] He knew the genealogies and coats of arms of all his neighbours, and could tell which of them had assumed supporters[3] without any right, and which of them were so unfortunate as to be great-grandsons of aldermen. He was a magistrate, and, as such, administered gratuitously to those who dwelt around him a rude patriarchal justice, which, in spite of innumerable blunders and of occasional acts of tyranny, was yet better than no justice at all. He was an officer of the trainbands; and his military dignity, though it might move the mirth of gallants who had served a campaign in Flanders, raised his character in his own eyes and in the eyes of his neighbours. Nor indeed was his soldiership justly a subject of derision. In every county there were elderly gentlemen who had seen service which was no child's play. One had been knighted by Charles the First, after the battle of Edgehill. Another still wore a patch over the scar which he had received at Naseby. A third had defended his old house till Fairfax had blown in the door with a petard. The presence of these old Cavaliers, with their old swords and holsters, and with their old stories about Goring and Lunsford,[4] gave to the musters of militia an earnest and warlike aspect which would otherwise have been wanting. Even those country gentlemen who were too young to have themselves ex-

[1] used for making conserves, for flavoring soups, and for coloring cheese   [2] two of the most distinguished families of the nobility   [3] a term in heraldry for figures supporting an escutcheon, cf. the lion and the unicorn that support the shield of Great Britain   [4] noted persons of the Parliamentary War

changed blows with the cuirassiers of the Parliament had, from childhood, been surrounded by the traces of recent war, and fed with stories of the martial exploits of their fathers and uncles. Thus the character of the English esquire of the seventeenth century was compounded of two elements which we seldom or never find united. His ignorance and uncouthness, his low tastes and gross phrases, would, in our time, be considered as indicating a nature and a breeding thoroughly plebeian. Yet he was essentially a patrician, and had, in large measure, both the virtues and the vices which flourish among men set from their birth in high place, and used to respect themselves and to be respected by others. It is not easy for a generation accustomed to find chivalrous sentiments only in company with liberal studies and polished manners to image to itself a man with the deportment, the vocabulary, and the accent of a carter, yet punctilious on matters of genealogy and precedence, and ready to risk his life rather than see a stain cast on the honour of his house. It is, however, only by thus joining together things seldom or never found together in our own experience that we can form a just idea of that rustic aristocracy which constituted the main strength of the armies of Charles the First, and which long supported, with strange fidelity, the interest of his descendants.

* * * * * * *

Whoever examines the maps of London which were published toward the close of the reign of Charles the Second will see that only the nucleus of the present capital then existed. The town did not, as now, fade by imperceptible degrees into the country. No long avenues of villas, embowered in lilacs and laburnums, extended from the great centre of wealth and civilisation almost to the boundaries of Middlesex and far into the heart of Kent and Surrey. In the east, no part of the immense line of warehouses and artificial lakes which now stretches from the Tower to Blackwall had even been projected. On the west, scarcely one of those stately piles of building which are inhabited by the noble and wealthy was in existence; and Chelsea, which is now peopled by more than forty thousand human beings, was a quiet country village with about a thousand inhabitants. On the north, cattle fed, and sportsmen wandered with dogs and guns, over the site of the borough of Marylebone, and over far the greater part of the space now covered by the boroughs of Finsbury and of the Tower Hamlets. Islington was almost a solitude; and poets loved to contrast its silence and repose with the din and turmoil of the monster London. On the south the capital is now connected with its suburb by several bridges, not inferior in magnificence and solidity to the noblest works of the Cæsars. In 1685, a single line of irregular arches, overhung by piles of mean and crazy houses, and garnished, after a fashion worthy of the naked barbarians of Dahomy, with scores of mouldering heads, impeded the navigation of the river.

Of the metropolis, the City, properly so called, was the most important division. At the time of the Restoration it had been built, for the most part, of wood and plaster; the few bricks that were used were ill baked; the booths where goods were exposed to sale projected far into the streets, and were overhung by the upper stories. A few specimens of this architecture may still be seen in those districts which were not reached by the great fire. That fire had, in a few days, covered a space of less than a square mile with the ruins of eighty-nine churches and of thirteen thousand houses. But the City had risen again with a celerity which had excited the admiration of neighbouring countries. Unfortunately, the old lines of the streets had been to a great extent preserved; and those lines, originally traced in an age when even princesses performed their journeys on horseback, were often too narrow to allow wheeled carriages to pass each other with ease, and were therefore ill adapted for the residence of wealthy persons in an age when a coach and six was a fashionable luxury. The style of building was, however, far superior to that of the City which had perished. The ordinary material was brick, of much better quality than had formerly been used. On the sites of the ancient parish churches had arisen a multitude of new domes, towers, and spires which bore the mark of the fertile genius of Wren. In every place save one the traces of the great devastation had been completely effaced. But the crowds of workmen, the scaffolds, and the masses of hewn stone were still to be seen where the noblest of Protestant temples was slowly rising on the ruins of the old Cathedral of Saint Paul.

*   *   *   *   *   *   *

He who then rambled to what is now the gayest and most crowded part of Regent Street found himself in a solitude, and was sometimes so fortunate as to have a shot at a woodcock. On the north the Oxford road ran between hedges. Three or four hundred yards to the south were the garden walls of a few great houses which were considered as quite out of town. On the west was a meadow renowned for a spring from which, long afterwards, Conduit Street was named. On the east was a field not to be passed without a shudder by any Londoner of that age. There, as in a place far from the haunts of men, had been dug, twenty years before, when the great plague was raging, a pit into which the dead carts had nightly shot corpses by scores. It was popularly believed that the earth was deeply tainted with infection, and could not be disturbed without imminent risk to human life. No foundations were laid there till two generations had passed without any return of the pestilence, and till the ghastly spot had long been surrounded by buildings.

We should greatly err if we were to suppose that any of the streets and squares then bore the same aspect as at present. The great majority of the houses, indeed, have, since that time, been wholly, or in great part, rebuilt. If the most fashionable parts of the capital could be placed before us such as they then were, we should be disgusted by their squalid appearance, and poisoned by their noisome atmosphere.

In Covent Garden a filthy and noisy market was held close to the dwellings of the great. Fruit women screamed, carters fought, cabbage stalks and rotten apples accumulated in heaps at the thresholds of the Countess of Berkshire and of the Bishop of Durham.

The centre of Lincoln's Inn Fields was an open space where the rabble congregated every evening, within a few yards of Cardigan House and Winchester House, to hear mountebanks harangue, to see bears dance, and to set dogs at oxen. Rubbish was shot in every part of the area. Horses were exercised there. The beggars were as noisy and importunate as in the worst governed cities of the Continent.

A Lincoln's Inn mumper[1] was a proverb. The whole fraternity knew the arms and liveries of every charitably disposed grandee in the neighbourhood, and, as soon as his lordship's coach and six appeared, came hopping and crawling in crowds to persecute him. These disorders lasted, in spite of many accidents, and of some legal proceedings, till, in the reign of George the Second, Sir Joseph Jekyll, Master of the Rolls, was knocked down and nearly killed in the middle of the square. Then at length palisades were set up, and a pleasant garden laid out.

Saint James's Square was a receptacle for all the offal and cinders, for all the dead cats and dead dogs of Westminster. At one time a cudgel player kept the ring there. At another time an impudent squatter settled himself there, and built a shed for rubbish under the windows of the gilded saloons in which the first magnates of the realm, Norfolk, Ormond, Kent, and Pembroke, gave banquets and balls. It was not till these nuisances had lasted through a whole generation, and till much had been written about them, that the inhabitants applied to Parliament for permission to put up rails, and to plant trees.

When such was the state of the region inhabited by the most luxurious portion of society, we may easily believe that the great body of the population suffered what would now be considered as insupportable grievances. The pavement was detestable: all foreigners cried shame upon it. The drainage was so bad that in rainy weather the gutters soon became torrents. Several facetious poets have commemorated the fury with which these black rivulets roared down Snow Hill and Ludgate Hill, bearing to Fleet Ditch a vast tribute of animal and vegetable filth from the stalls of butchers and green-grocers. This flood was profusely thrown to right and left by coaches and carts. To keep as far from the carriage road as possible was therefore the wish of every pedestrian. The mild and timid gave the wall. The bold and athletic took it. If two roisterers met, they cocked their hats in each other's faces, and pushed each other about till the weaker was shoved towards the kennel. If he was a mere bully he sneaked off, muttering that he should find a time. If he was pugnacious, the

[1] beggar

encounter probably ended in a duel behind Montague House.

The houses were not numbered. There would indeed have been little advantage in numbering them; for of the coachmen, chairmen, porters, and errand boys of London, a very small proportion could read. It was necessary to use marks which the most ignorant could understand. The shops were therefore distinguished by painted or sculptured signs, which gave a gay and grotesque aspect to the streets. The walk from Charing Cross to Whitechapel lay through an endless succession of Saracens' Heads, Royal Oaks, Blue Bears, and Golden Lambs, which disappeared when they were no longer required for the direction of the common people.

* * * * * * *

We may easily imagine what, in such times, must have been the state of the quarters of London which were peopled by the outcasts of society. Among those quarters one had attained a scandalous preëminence. On the confines of the City and the Temple had been founded, in the thirteenth century, a House of Carmelite Friars, distinguished by their white hoods. The precinct of this house had, before the Reformation, been a sanctuary for criminals, and still retained the privilege of protecting debtors from arrest. Insolvents consequently were to be found in every dwelling, from cellar to garret. Of these a large proportion were knaves and libertines, and were followed to their asylum by women more abandoned than themselves. The civil power was unable to keep order in a district swarming with such inhabitants; and thus Whitefriars became the favourite resort of all who wished to be emancipated from the restraints of the law. Though the immunities legally belonging to the place extended only to cases of debt, cheats, false witnesses, forgers, and highwaymen found refuge there. For amidst a rabble so desperate no peace officer's life was in safety. At the cry of "Rescue," bullies with swords and cudgels, and termagant hags with spits and broomsticks, poured forth by hundreds; and the intruder was fortunate if he escaped back into Fleet Street, hustled, stripped, and pumped upon. Even the warrant of the Chief-justice of England could not be executed without the help of a company of musketeers. Such relics of the barbarism of the darkest ages were to be found within a short walk of the chambers[1] where Somers[2] was studying history and law, of the chapel[3] where Tillotson was preaching, of the coffee-house[4] where Dryden was passing judgment on poems and plays, and of the hall where the Royal Society was examining the astronomical system of Isaac Newton.

*   *   *   *   *   *   *

The coffee-house must not be dismissed with a cursory mention. It might, indeed, at that time have been not improperly called a most important political institution. No Parliament had sat for years. The municipal council of the city had ceased to speak the sense of the citizens. Public meetings, harangues, resolutions, and the rest of the modern machinery of agitation had not yet come into fashion. Nothing resembling the modern newspaper existed. In such circumstances the coffee-houses were the chief organs through which the public opinion of the metropolis vented itself.

The first of these establishments had been set up, in the time of the Commonwealth, by a Turkey merchant, who had acquired among the Mahometans a taste for their favourite beverage. The convenience of being able to make appointments in any part of the town, and of being able to pass evenings socially at a very small charge, was so great that the fashion spread fast. Every man of the upper or middle class went daily to his coffee-house to learn the news and to discuss it. Every coffee-house had one or more orators to whose eloquence the crowd listened with admiration, and who soon became, what the journalists of our time have been called, a fourth Estate of the realm. The court had long seen with uneasiness the growth of this new power in the state. An attempt had been made, during Danby's administration,[5] to close the coffee-houses. But men of all parties missed their usual places of resort so much that there was a

universal outcry. The government did not venture, in opposition to a feeling so strong and general, to enforce a regulation of which the legality might well be questioned. Since that time ten years had elapsed, and during those years the number and influence of the coffee-houses had been constantly increasing. Foreigners remarked that the coffee-house was that which especially distinguished London from all other cities; that the coffee-house was the Londoner's home, and that those who wished to find a gentleman commonly asked, not whether he lived in Fleet Street or Chancery Lane, but whether he frequented the Grecian or the Rainbow. Nobody was excluded from these places who laid down his penny at the bar. Yet every rank and profession, and every shade of religious and political opinion, had its own headquarters. There were houses near Saint James's Park where fops congregated, their heads and shoulders covered with black or flaxen wigs, not less ample than those which are now worn by the Chancellor and by the Speaker of the House of Commons. The wig came from Paris; and so did the rest of the fine gentleman's ornaments, his embroidered coat, his fringed gloves, and the tassels which upheld his pantaloons. The conversation was in that dialect which, long after it had ceased to be spoken in fashionable circles, continued, in the mouth of Lord Foppington,[1] to excite the mirth of theatres. The atmosphere was like that of a perfumer's shop. Tobacco in any other form than that of richly scented snuff was held in abomination. If any clown, ignorant of the usages of the house, called for a pipe, the sneers of the whole assembly and the short answers of the waiters soon convinced him that he had better go somewhere else. Nor, indeed, would he have had far to go. For, in general, the coffee-rooms reeked with tobacco like a guard-room; and strangers sometimes expressed their surprise that so many people should leave their own firesides to sit in the midst of eternal fog and stench. Nowhere was the smoking more constant than at Will's. That celebrated house, situated between Covent Garden and Bow Street,

---

[1] in the Middle Temple [2] Lord Somers, made lord chancellor in 1697 [3] Lincoln's Inn chapel, where Tillotson preached until he became Archbishop of Canterbury in 1691 [4] Will's coffee-house, cf. below, p. 517 [5] Danby was lord treasurer, 1673-8

[1] a popular personification of foppery, in Vanbrugh's comedy *The Relapse* (1697), Cibber's *The Careless Husband* (1704), and Sheridan's *A Trip to Scarborough* (1777)

was sacred to polite letters. There the talk was about poetical justice and the unities of place and time. There was a faction for Perrault and the moderns, a faction for Boileau and the ancients. One group debated whether Paradise Lost ought not to have been in rhyme. To another an envious poetaster demonstrated that Venice Preserved[1] ought to have been hooted from the stage. Under no roof was a greater variety of figures to be seen. There were earls in stars and garters, clergymen in cassocks and bands, pert Templars, sheepish lads from the Universities, translators and index-makers in ragged coats of frieze. The great press was to get near the chair where John Dryden sat. In winter that chair was always in the warmest nook by the fire; in summer it stood in the balcony. To bow to the Laureate, and to hear his opinion of Racine's last tragedy or of Bossu's treatise on epic poetry, was thought a privilege. A pinch from his snuffbox was an honour sufficient to turn the head of a young enthusiast. There were coffee-houses where the first medical men might be consulted. Dr. John Radcliffe, who, in the year 1685, rose to the largest practice in London, came daily, at the hour when the Exchange was full, from his house in Bow Street, then a fashionable part of the capital, to Garraway's, and was to be found, surrounded by surgeons and apothecaries, at a particular table. There were Puritan coffee-houses where no oath was heard, and where lank-haired men discussed election and reprobation through their noses; Jew coffee-houses where dark-eyed money changers from Venice and from Amsterdam greeted each other; and popish coffee-houses where, as good Protestants believed, Jesuits planned, over their cups, another great fire, and cast silver bullets to shoot the King.

These gregarious habits had no small share in forming the character of the Londoner of that age. He was, indeed, a different being from the rustic Englishman. There was not then the intercourse which now exists between the two classes. Only very great men were in the habit of dividing the year between town and country. Few esquires came to the capital thrice in their lives. Nor was it yet the practice of all citizens in easy circumstances to breathe the fresh air of

the fields and woods during some weeks of every summer. A cockney in a rural village was stared at as much as if he had intruded into a kraal of Hottentots. On the other hand, when the lord of a Lincolnshire or Shropshire manor appeared in Fleet Street, he was as easily distinguished from the resident population as a Turk or a Lascar. His dress, his gait, his accent, the manner in which he gazed at the shops, stumbled into the gutters, ran against the porters, and stood under the waterspouts, marked him out as an excellent subject for the operations of swindlers and banterers. Bullies jostled him into the kennel. Hackney coachmen splashed him from head to foot. Thieves explored with perfect security the huge pockets of his horseman's coat, while he stood entranced by the splendour of the Lord Mayor's show. Money droppers, sore from the cart's tail, introduced themselves to him, and appeared to him the most honest friendly gentlemen that he had ever seen. Painted women, the refuse of Lewkner Lane and Whetstone Park, passed themselves on him for countesses and maids of honour. If he asked his way to Saint James's, his informants sent him to Mile End. If he went into a shop, he was instantly discerned to be a fit purchaser of everything that nobody else would buy, of second-hand embroidery, copper rings, and watches that would not go. If he rambled into any fashionable coffee-house, he became a mark for the insolent derision of fops and the grave waggery of Templars. Enraged and mortified, he soon returned to his mansion, and there, in the homage of his tenants and the conversation of his boon companions, found consolation for the vexations and humiliations which he had undergone. There he was once more a great man, and saw nothing above himself except when at the assizes he took his seat on the bench near the judge, or when at the muster of the militia he saluted the Lord Lieutenant.

---

[1] a tragedy by Otway (1682)

AE

JOHN HENRY, CARDINAL NEWMAN (1801–1890)

FROM THE IDEA OF A UNIVERSITY

DISCOURSE VI

KNOWLEDGE VIEWED IN RELATION TO LEARNING

3

I suppose the *primâ-facie* view which the public at large would take of a University, considering it as a place of Education, is nothing more or less than a place for acquiring a great deal of knowledge on a great many subjects. Memory is one of the first developed of the mental faculties; a boy's business when he goes to school is to learn, that is, to store up things in his memory. For some years his intellect is little more than an instrument for taking in facts, or a receptacle for storing them; he welcomes them as fast as they come to him; he lives on what is without; he has his eyes ever about him; he has a lively susceptibility of impressions; he imbibes information of every kind; and little does he make his own in a true sense of the word, living rather upon his neighbours all around him. He has opinions, religious, political, and literary, and, for a boy, is very positive in them and sure about them; but he gets them from his schoolfellows, or his masters, or his parents, as the case may be. Such as he is in his other relations, such also is he in his school exercises; his mind is observant, sharp, ready, retentive; he is almost passive in the acquisition of knowledge. I say this in no disparagement of the idea of a clever boy. Geography, chronology, history, language, natural history, he heaps up the matter of these studies as treasures for a future day. It is the seven years of plenty with him: he gathers in by handfuls, like the Egyptians,[1] without counting; and though, as time goes on, there is exercise for his argumentative powers in the Elements of Mathematics, and for his taste in the Poets and Orators, still, while at school, or at least, till quite the last years of his time, he acquires, and little more; and when he is leaving for the University, he is mainly the creature of for-

eign influences and circumstances, and made up of accidents, homogeneous or not, as the case may be. Moreover, the moral habits, which are a boy's praise, encourage and assist this result; that is, diligence, assiduity, regularity, despatch, persevering application; for these are the direct conditions of acquisition, and naturally lead to it. Acquirements, again, are emphatically producible, and at a moment; they are a something to show, both for master and scholar; an audience, even though ignorant themselves of the subjects of an examination, can comprehend when questions are answered and when they are not. Here again is a reason why mental culture is in the minds of men identified with the acquisition of knowledge.

The same notion possesses the public mind, when it passes on from the thought of a school to that of a University: and with the best of reasons so far as this, that there is no true culture without acquirements, and that philosophy presupposes knowledge. It requires a great deal of reading, or a wide range of information, to warrant us in putting forth our opinions on any serious subject; and without such learning the most original mind may be able indeed to dazzle, to amuse, to refute, to perplex, but not to come to any useful result or any trustworthy conclusion. There are indeed persons who profess a different view of the matter, and even act upon it. Every now and then you will find a person of vigorous or fertile mind, who relies upon his own resources, despises all former authors, and gives the world, with the utmost fearlessness, his views upon religion, or history, or any other popular subject. And his works may sell for a while; he may get a name in his day; but this will be all. His readers are sure to find on the long run that his doctrines are mere theories, and not the expression of facts, that they are chaff instead of bread, and then his popularity drops as suddenly as it rose.

Knowledge then is the indispensable condition of expansion of mind, and the instrument of attaining to it; this cannot be denied, it is ever to be insisted on; I begin with it as a first principle; however, the very truth of it carries men too far, and confirms to them the notion that it is the whole of the matter. A narrow mind is thought to be that which contains little knowledge; and an enlarged mind, that which holds a great deal; and what

---

[1] cf. *Genesis*, xli: 49

seems to put the matter beyond dispute is, the fact of the great number of studies which are pursued in a University, by its very profession. Lectures are given on every kind of subject; examinations are held; prizes awarded. There are moral, metaphysical, physical Professors; Professors of languages, of history, of mathematics, of experimental science. Lists of questions are published, wonderful for their range and depth, variety and difficulty; treatises are written, which carry upon their very face the evidence of extensive reading or multifarious information; what then is wanting for mental culture to a person of large reading and scientific attainments? what is grasp of mind but acquirement? where shall philosophical repose be found, but in the consciousness and enjoyment of large intellectual possessions?

And yet this notion is, I conceive, a mistake, and my present business is to show that it is one, and that the end of a Liberal Education is not mere knowledge, or knowledge considered in its *matter;* and I shall best attain my object, by actually setting down some cases, which will be generally granted to be instances of the process of enlightenment or enlargement of mind, and others which are not, and thus, by the comparison, you will be able to judge, for yourselves, Gentlemen, whether Knowledge, that is, acquirement, is after all the real principle of the enlargement, or whether that principle is not rather something beyond it.

4

For instance, let a person, whose experience has hitherto been confined to the more calm and unpretending scenery of these islands, whether here[1] or in England, go for the first time into parts where physical nature puts on her wilder and more awful forms, whether at home or abroad, as into mountainous districts; or let one, who has ever lived in a quiet village, go for the first time to a great metropolis, — then I suppose he will have a sensation which perhaps he never had before. He has a feeling not in addition or increase of former feelings, but of something different in its nature. He will perhaps be borne forward, and find for a time that he has lost his bearings. He

[1] in Ireland

has made a certain progress, and he has a consciousness of mental enlargement; he does not stand where he did, he has a new centre, and a range of thoughts to which he was before a stranger.

Again, the view of the heavens which the telescope opens upon us, if allowed to fill and possess the mind, may almost whirl it round and make it dizzy. It brings in a flood of ideas, and is rightly called an intellectual enlargement, whatever is meant by the term.

And so again, the sight of beasts of prey and other foreign animals, their strangeness, the originality (if I may use the term) of their forms and gestures and habits and their variety and independence of each other, throw us out of ourselves into another creation, and as if under another Creator, if I may so express the temptation which may come on the mind. We seem to have new faculties, or a new exercise for our faculties, by this addition to our knowledge; like a prisoner, who, having been accustomed to wear manacles or fetters, suddenly finds his arms and legs free.

Hence Physical Science generally, in all its departments, as bringing before us the exuberant riches and resources, yet the orderly course, of the Universe, elevates and excites the student, and at first, I may say, almost takes away his breath, while in time it exercises a tranquillising influence upon him.

Again, the study of history is said to enlarge and enlighten the mind, and why? because, as I conceive, it gives it a power of judging of passing events, and of all events, and a conscious superiority over them, which before it did not possess.

And in like manner, what is called seeing the world, entering into active life, going into society, travelling, gaining acquaintance with the various classes of the community, coming into contact with the principles and modes of thought of various parties, interests, and races, their views, aims, habits and manners, their religious creeds and forms of worship, — gaining experience how various yet how alike men are, how low-minded, how bad, how opposed, yet how confident in their opinions; all this exerts a perceptible influence upon the mind, which it is impossible to mistake, be it good or be it bad, and is popularly called its enlargement.

And then again, the first time the mind

comes across the arguments and speculations of unbelievers, and feels what a novel light they cast upon what he has hitherto accounted sacred; and still more, if it gives in to them and embraces them, and throws off as so much prejudice what it has hitherto held, and, as if waking from a dream, begins to realise to its imagination that there is now no such thing as law and the transgression of law, that sin is a phantom, and punishment a bugbear, that it is free to sin, free to enjoy the world and the flesh; and still further, when it does enjoy them, and reflects that it may think and hold just what it will, that "the world is all before it where to choose," [1] and what system to build up as its own private persuasion; when this torrent of wilful thoughts rushes over and inundates it, who will deny that the fruit of the tree of knowledge, or what the mind takes for knowledge, has made it one of the gods, with a sense of expansion and elevation, — an intoxication in reality, still, so far as the subjective state of the mind goes, an illumination? Hence the fanaticism of individuals or nations, who suddenly cast off their Maker. Their eyes are opened; and, like the judgment-stricken king in the Tragedy,[2] they see two suns, and a magic universe, out of which they look back upon their former state of faith and innocence with a sort of contempt and indignation, as if they were then but fools, and the dupes of imposture.

On the other hand, Religion has its own enlargement, and an enlargement, not of tumult, but of peace. It is often remarked of uneducated persons, who have hitherto thought little of the unseen world, that, on their turning to God, looking into themselves, regulating their hearts, reforming their conduct, and meditating on death and judgment, heaven and hell, they seem to become, in point of intellect, different beings from what they were. Before, they took things as they came, and thought no more of one thing than another. But now every event has a meaning; they have their own estimate of whatever happens to them; they are mindful of times and seasons, and compare the present

with the past; and the world, no longer dull, monotonous, unprofitable, and hopeless, is a various and complicated drama, with parts and an object, and an awful moral.

5

Now from these instances, to which many more might be added, it is plain, first, that the communication of knowledge certainly is either a condition or the means of that sense of enlargement or enlightenment, of which at this day we hear so much in certain quarters: this cannot be denied; but next, it is equally plain, that such communication is not the whole of the process. The enlargement consists, not merely in the passive reception into the mind of a number of ideas hitherto unknown to it, but in the mind's energetic and simultaneous action upon and towards and among those new ideas, which are rushing in upon it. It is the action of a formative power, reducing to order and meaning the matter of our acquirements; it is a making the objects of our knowledge subjectively our own, or, to use a familiar word, it is a digestion of what we receive, into the substance of our previous state of thought; and without this no enlargement is said to follow. There is no enlargement, unless there be a comparison of ideas one with another, as they come before the mind, and a systematising of them. We feel our minds to be growing and expanding *then*, when we not only learn, but refer what we learn to what we know already. It is not the mere addition to our knowledge that is the illumination; but the locomotion, the movement onwards, of that mental centre, to which both what we know, and what we are learning, the accumulating mass of our acquirements, gravitates. And therefore a truly great intellect, and recognised to be such by the common opinion of mankind, such as the intellect of Aristotle, or of St. Thomas, or of Newton, or of Goethe, (I purposely take instances within and without the Catholic pale, when I would speak of the intellect as such), is one which takes a connected view of old and new, past and present, far and near, and which has an insight into the influence of all these one on another; without which there is no whole, and no centre. It possesses the knowledge, not only of things, but also of their mutual and true relations; knowl-

---

[1] cf. *Par. Lost*, XII, 646   [2] In the *Bacchæ* of Euripides (ll. 918–9) Pentheus, King of Thebes, smitten with madness for defying the god Dionysus, says: "Lo, I seem to see two suns and a double Thebes, the seven-gated city."

edge, not merely considered as acquirement, but as philosophy.

Accordingly, when this analytical, distributive, harmonising process is away, the mind experiences no enlargement, and is not reckoned as enlightened or comprehensive, whatever it may add to its knowledge. For instance, a great memory, as I have already said, does not make a philosopher, any more than a dictionary can be called a grammar. There are men who embrace in their minds a vast multitude of ideas, but with little sensibility about their real relations towards each other. These may be antiquarians, annalists, naturalists; they may be learned in the law; they may be versed in statistics; they are most useful in their own place; I should shrink from speaking disrespectfully of them; still, there is nothing in such attainments to guarantee the absence of narrowness of mind. If they are nothing more than well-read men, or men of information, they have not what specially deserves the name of culture of mind, or fulfils the type of Liberal Education.

In like manner, we sometimes fall in with persons who have seen much of the world, and of the men who, in their day, have played a conspicuous part in it, but who generalise nothing, and have no observation, in the true sense of the word. They abound in information in detail, curious and entertaining, about men and things; and, having lived under the influence of no very clear or settled principles, religious or political, they speak of every one and everything, only as so many phenomena, which are complete in themselves, and lead to nothing, not discussing them, or teaching any truth, or instructing the hearer, but simply talking. No one would say that these persons, well informed as they are, had attained to any great culture of intellect or to philosophy.

The case is the same still more strikingly where the persons in question are beyond dispute men of inferior powers and deficient education. Perhaps they have been much in foreign countries, and they receive, in a passive, otiose, unfruitful way, the various facts which are forced upon them there. Seafaring men, for example, range from one end of the earth to the other; but the multiplicity of external objects which they have encountered forms no symmetrical and consistent picture upon their imagination; they see

the tapestry of human life, as it were, on the wrong side, and it tells no story. They sleep, and they rise up, and they find themselves, now in Europe, now in Asia; they see visions of great cities and wild regions; they are in the marts of commerce, or amid the islands of the South; they gaze on Pompey's Pillar,[1] or on the Andes; and nothing which meets them carries them forward or backward, to any idea beyond itself. Nothing has a drift or relation; nothing has a history or a promise. Everything stands by itself, and comes and goes in its turn, like the shifting scenes of a show, which leave the spectator where he was. Perhaps you are near such a man on a particular occasion, and expect him to be shocked or perplexed at something which occurs; but one thing is much the same to him as another, or, if he is perplexed, it is as not knowing what to say, whether it is right to admire, or to ridicule, or to disapprove, while conscious that some expression of opinion is expected from him; for in fact he has no standard of judgment at all, and no landmarks to guide him to a conclusion. Such is mere acquisition, and, I repeat, no one would dream of calling it philosophy.

6

Instances, such as these, confirm, by the contrast, the conclusion I have already drawn from those which preceded them. That only is true enlargement of mind which is the power of viewing many things at once as one whole, of referring them severally to their true place in the universal system, of understanding their respective values, and determining their mutual dependence. Thus is that form of Universal Knowledge, of which I have on a former occasion spoken, set up in the individual intellect, and constitutes its perfection. Possessed of this real illumination, the mind never views any part of the extended subject-matter of Knowledge without recollecting that it is but a part, or without the associations which spring from this recollection. It makes everything in some sort lead to everything else; it would communicate the image of the whole to every separate portion, till that whole becomes in

---

[1] a beautiful column in Alexandria, Egypt, falsely connected with Pompey, really erected in honor of the Emperor Diocletian

imagination like a spirit, everywhere pervading and penetrating its component parts,
and giving them one definite meaning. Just
as our bodily organs, when mentioned, recall
their function in the body, as the word
"creation" suggests the Creator, and "subjects" a sovereign, so, in the mind of the
Philosopher, as we are abstractedly conceiving
of him, the elements of the physical and
moral world, sciences, arts, pursuits, ranks,
offices, events, opinions, individualities, are
all viewed as one, with correlative functions,
and as gradually by successive combinations
converging, one and all, to the true centre.

To have even a portion of this illuminative
reason and true philosophy is the highest
state to which nature can aspire, in the way
of intellect; it puts the mind above the
influence of chance and necessity, above
anxiety, suspense, unsettlement, and superstition, which is the lot of the many. Men,
whose minds are possessed with some one
object, take exaggerated views of its importance, are feverish in the pursuit of it, make
it the measure of things which are utterly
foreign to it, and are startled and despond
if it happens to fail them. They are ever
in alarm or in transport. Those on the other
hand who have no object or principle whatever to hold by, lose their way, every step
they take. They are thrown out, and do not
know what to think or say, at every fresh
juncture; they have no view of persons, or
occurrences, or facts, which come suddenly
upon them, and they hang upon the opinion
of others, for want of internal resources.
But the intellect, which has been disciplined
to the perfection of its powers, which knows,
and thinks while it knows, which has learned
to leaven the dense mass of facts and events
with the elastic force of reason, such an intellect cannot be partial, cannot be exclusive,
cannot be impetuous, cannot be at a loss,
cannot but be patient, collected, and majesti-
cally calm, because it discerns the end in every
beginning, the origin in every end, the law
in every interruption, the limit in each delay;
because it ever knows where it stands, and
how its path lies from one point to another.
It is the τετράγωνος[1] of the Peripatetic,

and has the "nil admirari"[1] of the
Stoic, —

Felix qui potuit rerum cognoscere causas,
Atque metus omnes, et inexorabile fatum
Subjecit pedibus, strepitumque Acherontis avari.[2]

There are men who, when in difficulties, originate at the moment vast ideas or dazzling
projects; who, under the influence of excitement, are able to cast a light, almost as if
from inspiration, on a subject or course of
action which comes before them; who have
a sudden presence of mind equal to any emergency, rising with the occasion, and an undaunted magnanimous bearing, and an energy
and keenness which is but made intense by
opposition. This is genius, this is heroism;
it is the exhibition of a natural gift, which
no culture can teach, at which no Institution
can aim; here, on the contrary, we are concerned, not with mere nature, but with training and teaching. That perfection of the
Intellect, which is the result of Education,
and its *beau idéal*, to be imparted to individuals in their respective measures, is the
clear, calm, accurate vision and comprehension of all things, as far as the finite mind
can embrace them, each in its place, and with
its own characteristics upon it. It is almost
prophetic from its knowledge of history;
it is almost heart-searching from its knowledge
of human nature; it has almost supernatural
charity from its freedom from littleness and
prejudice; it has almost the repose of faith,
because nothing can startle it; it has almost the beauty and harmony of heavenly
contemplation, so intimate is it with the
eternal order of things and the music of the
spheres.

[1] The Stoic philosophy (so called because its
founder Zeno taught in a porch) is phrased by
Horace in "nil admirari," meaning "to be dazzled
by nothing" or "to be without emotion." This, he
says, is the only way to win happiness and retain
it (*Epist.* I. 6. 1).   [2] Fortunate is he who is able
to understand things in their real nature and can
trample upon fears of all sorts and inexorable
fate and the noise of greedy Acheron.

Vergil, *Georgics*, II, 490-2.

[1] "four-square" — a term applied to the ideal
man by Aristotle, founder of the Peripatetic
school of philosophy (so called because he lec-
tured in the shady walks of the Lyceum)

ALFRED, LORD TENNYSON
(1809–1892).

THE LADY OF SHALOTT

PART I

On either side the river lie
Long fields of barley and of rye,
That clothe the wold and meet the sky;
And thro' the field the road runs by
    To many-tower'd Camelot;
And up and down the people go,
Gazing where the lilies blow
Round an island there below,
    The island of Shalott. 9

Willows whiten, aspens quiver,
Little breezes dusk and shiver
Thro' the wave that runs forever
By the island in the river
    Flowing down to Camelot.
Four grey walls, and four grey towers,
Overlook a space of flowers,
And the silent isle imbowers
    The Lady of Shalott. 18

By the margin, willow-veil'd,
Slide the heavy barges trail'd
By slow horses; and unhail'd
The shallop flitteth silken-sail'd
    Skimming down to Camelot:
But who hath seen her wave her hand?
Or at the casement seen her stand?
Or is she known in all the land,
    The Lady of Shalott? 27

Only reapers, reaping early
In among the bearded barley,
Hear a song that echoes cheerly
From the river winding clearly,
    Down to tower'd Camelot:
And by the moon the reaper weary,
Piling sheaves in uplands airy,
Listening, whispers, "'Tis the fairy
    Lady of Shalott." 36

PART II

There she weaves by night and day
A magic web with colours gay.
She has heard a whisper say,
A curse is on her if she stay
    To look down to Camelot.

She knows not what the curse may be,
And so she weaveth steadily,
And little other care hath she,
    The Lady of Shalott. 45

And moving thro' a mirror clear
That hangs before her all the year,
Shadows of the world appear.
There she sees the highway near
    Winding down to Camelot:
There the river eddy whirls,
And there the surly village-churls,
And the red cloaks of market girls,
    Pass onward from Shalott. 54

Sometimes a troop of damsels glad,
An abbot on an ambling pad,
Sometimes a curly shepherd-lad,
Or long-hair'd page in crimson clad,
    Goes by to tower'd Camelot;
And sometimes thro' the mirror blue
The knights come riding two and two:
She hath no loyal knight and true,
    The Lady of Shalott. 63

But in her web she still delights
To weave the mirror's magic sights,
For often thro' the silent nights
A funeral, with plumes and lights
    And music, went to Camelot:
Or when the moon was overhead,
Came two young lovers lately wed;
"I am half sick of shadows," said
    The Lady of Shalott. 72

PART III

A bow-shot from her bower-eaves,
He rode between the barley-sheaves,
The sun came dazzling thro' the leaves,
And flamed upon the brazen greaves
    Of bold Sir Lancelot.
A red-cross knight forever kneel'd
To a lady in his shield,
That sparkled on the yellow field,
    Beside remote Shalott. 81

The gemmy bridle glitter'd free,
Like to some branch of stars we see
Hung in the golden Galaxy.
The bridle bells rang merrily
    As he rode down to Camelot:
And from his blazon'd baldric slung
A mighty silver bugle hung,
And as he rode his armour rung,
    Beside remote Shalott. 90

All in the blue unclouded weather
Thick-jewell'd shone the saddle-leather,
The helmet and the helmet-feather
Burn'd like one burning flame together,
    As he rode down to Camelot.
As often thro' the purple night,
Below the starry clusters bright,
Some bearded meteor trailing light,
    Moves over still Shalott.   99

His broad clear brow in sunlight glow'd;
On burnish'd hooves his war-horse strode;
From underneath his helmet flow'd
His coal-black curls as on he rode,
    As he rode down to Camelot.
From the bank and from the river
He flash'd into the crystal mirror,
"Tirra lirra," by the river
    Sang Sir Lancelot.   108

She left the web, she left the loom,
She made three paces thro' the room,
She saw the water-lily bloom,
She saw the helmet and the plume,
    She look'd down to Camelot.
Out flew the web and floated wide;
The mirror crack'd from side to side;
"The curse is come upon me," cried
    The Lady of Shalott.   117

PART IV

In the stormy east-wind straining,
The pale yellow woods were waning,
The broad stream in his banks complaining,
Heavily the low sky raining,
    Over tower'd Camelot;
Down she came and found a boat
Beneath a willow left afloat,
And round about the prow she wrote
    The Lady of Shalott.   126

And down the river's dim expanse
Like some bold seer in a trance,
Seeing all his own mischance —
With a glassy countenance
    Did she look to Camelot.
And at the closing of the day
She loosed the chain, and down she lay;
The broad stream bore her far away,
    The Lady of Shalott.   135

Lying, robed in snowy white,
That loosely flew to left and right —

The leaves upon her falling light —
Thro' the noises of the night
    She floated down to Camelot:
And as the boat-head wound along
The willowy hills and fields among,
They heard her singing her last song,
    The Lady of Shalott.   144

Heard a carol, mournful, holy,
Chanted loudly, chanted lowly,
Till her blood was frozen slowly,
And her eyes were darken'd wholly,
    Turn'd to tower'd Camelot.
For ere she reach'd upon the tide
The first house by the water-side,
Singing in her song she died,
    The Lady of Shalott.   153

Under tower and balcony,
By garden-wall and gallery,
A gleaming shape she floated by,
Dead-pale between the houses high,
    Silent into Camelot.
Out upon the wharfs they came,
Knight and burgher, lord and dame,
And round the prow they read her name,
    The Lady of Shalott.   162

Who is this? and what is here?
And in the lighted palace near
Died the sound of royal cheer;
And they cross'd themselves for fear,
    All the knights at Camelot:
But Lancelot mused a little space;
He said, "She has a lovely face;
God in his mercy lend her grace,
    The Lady of Shalott."   171

A DREAM OF FAIR WOMEN

I read, before my eyelids dropt their shade,[1]
  "The Legend of Good Women," long ago
Sung by the morning-star of song, who made
    His music heard below;   4

Dan[2] Chaucer, the first warbler, whose sweet
  breath
Preluded those melodious bursts that fill
The spacious times of great Elizabeth
    With sounds that echo still.   8

---

[1] *i.e.,* before I fell asleep   [2] not a name but a
title of respect, like the Spanish *Don,* from Latin
dominus

And, for a while, the knowledge of his art
  Held me above the subject, as strong gales
Hold swollen clouds from raining, tho' my
    heart,
  Brimful of those wild tales,   12

Charged both mine eyes with tears. In every
    land
  I saw, wherever light illumineth,
Beauty and anguish walking hand in hand
  The downward slope to death.   16

Those far-renownèd brides of ancient song
  Peopled the hollow dark, like burning stars,
And I heard sounds of insult, shame, and
    wrong,
  And trumpets blown for wars;   20

And clattering flints batter'd with clanging
    hoofs;
  And I saw crowds in column'd sanctuaries;
And forms that pass'd at windows and on roofs
  Of marble palaces;   24

Corpses across the threshold; heroes tall
  Dislodging pinnacle and parapet
Upon the tortoise[1] creeping to the wall;
  Lances in ambush set;   28

And high shrine-doors burst thro' with heated
    blasts
  That run before the fluttering tongues of
    fire;
White surf wind-scatter'd over sails and masts,
  And ever climbing higher;   32

Squadrons and squares of men in brazen plates,
  Scaffolds, still sheets of water, divers woes,
Ranges of glimmering vaults with iron grates,
  And hush'd seraglios.   36

So shape chased shape as swift as, when to land
  Bluster the winds and tides the self-same
    way,
Crisp foam-flakes scud along the level sand,
  Torn from the fringe of spray.   40

I started once, or seem'd to start in pain,
  Resolved on noble things, and strove to
    speak,
As when a great thought strikes along the brain,
  And flushes all the cheek.   44

[1] a close formation of troops protected by
overlapping their shields above their heads

And once my arm was lifted to hew down
  A cavalier from off his saddle-bow,
That bore a lady from a leaguer'd town;
  And then, I know not how,   48

All those sharp fancies, by down-lapsing
    thought
  Stream'd onward, lost their edges, and did
    creep,
Roll'd on each other, rounded, smooth'd, and
    brought
  Into the gulfs of sleep.   52

At last methought that I had wander'd far
  In an old wood: fresh-wash'd in coolest
    dew
The maiden splendours of the morning star
  Shook in the steadfast blue.   56

Enormous elm-tree-boles did stoop and lean
  Upon the dusky brushwood underneath
Their broad curved branches, fledged with
    clearest green,
  New from its silken sheath.   60

The dim red morn had died, her journey
    done,
  And with dead lips smiled at the twilight
    plain,
Half-fall'n across the threshold of the sun,
  Never to rise again.   64

There was no motion in the dumb dead air,
  Not any song of bird or sound of rill;
Gross darkness of the inner sepulchre
  Is not so deadly still   68

As that wide forest. Growths of jasmine
    turn'd
  Their humid arms festooning tree to tree,
And at the root thro' lush green grasses
    burn'd
  The red anemone.   72

I knew the flowers, I knew the leaves, I knew
  The tearful glimmer of the languid dawn
On those long, rank, dark wood-walks
    drench'd in dew,
  Leading from lawn to lawn.   76

The smell of violets, hidden in the green,
  Pour'd back into my empty soul and
    frame
The times when I remember to have been
  Joyful and free from blame.   80

And from within me a clear undertone
  Thrill'd thro' mine ears in that unblissful
    clime,
"Pass freely thro': the wood is all thine own,
  Until the end of time."   84

At length I saw a lady [1] within call,
  Stiller than chisell'd marble, standing
    there;
A daughter of the gods, divinely tall,
  And most divinely fair.   88

Her loveliness with shame and with surprise
  Froze my swift speech: she, turning on my
    face
The star-like sorrows of immortal eyes,
  Spoke slowly in her place.   92

"I had great beauty: ask thou not my name:
  No one can be more wise than destiny.
Many drew swords and died. Where'er I
    came
  I brought calamity."   96

"No marvel, sovereign lady: in fair field
  Myself for such a face had boldly died,"
I answer'd free; and turning I appeal'd
  To one that stood beside.[2]   100

But she, with sick and scornful looks averse,
  To her full height her stately stature draws;
"My youth," she said, "was blasted with a
    curse:
  This woman was the cause.   104

"I was cut off from hope in that sad place,
  Which men call'd Aulis in those iron years:
My father [3] held his hand upon his face;
  I, blinded with my tears,   108

"Still strove to speak: my voice was thick
    with sighs
  As in a dream. Dimly I could descry
The stern black-bearded kings with wolfish
    eyes,
  Waiting to see me die.   112

"The high masts flicker'd as they lay afloat;
  The crowds, the temples, waver'd, and the
    shore;
The bright death quiver'd at the victim's
    throat;
  Touch'd; and I knew no more."   116

Whereto the other with a downward brow:
  "I would the white cold heavy-plunging
    foam,
Whirl'd by the wind, had roll'd me deep below
  Then when I left my home."   120

Her slow full words sank thro' the silence
    drear,
  As thunder-drops fall on a sleeping sea:
Sudden I heard a voice that cried, "Come
    here,
  That I may look on thee."   124

I turning saw, throned on a flowery rise,
  One sitting on a crimson scarf unroll'd;[1]
A queen, with swarthy cheeks and bold black
    eyes,
  Brow-bound with burning gold.   128

She, flashing forth a haughty smile, began:
  "I govern'd men by change, and so I sway'd
All moods. 'Tis long since I have seen a man.
  Once, like the moon, I made   132

"The ever-shifting currents of the blood
  According to my humour ebb and flow.
I have no men to govern in this wood: 136
  That makes my only woe.

"Nay—yet it chafes me that I could not bend
  One will; nor tame and tutor with mine eye
That dull cold-blooded Cæsar. Prythee,
    friend,
  Where is Mark Antony?

"The man, my lover, with whom I rode sub-
    lime
  On Fortune's neck: we sat as God by God:
The Nilus would have risen before his time
  And flooded at our nod.   144

"We drank the Libyan Sun to sleep, and lit
  Lamps which out-burn'd Canopus.[2] O my
    life
In Egypt! O the dalliance and the wit,
  The flattery and the strife,   148

"And the wild kiss, when fresh from war's
    alarms,
  My Hercules, my Roman Antony,
My mailèd Bacchus leapt into my arms,
  Contented there to die!   152

[1] Cleopatra [2] a star in the southern constellation Argo

[1] Helen of Troy [2] Iphigenia [3] Agamemnon

"And there he died: and when I heard my
   name
   Sigh'd forth with life, I would not brook[1]
   my fear
Of the other:[2] with a worm I balk'd his fame.
   What else was left? look here!"   156

(With that she tore her robe apart, and half
   The polish'd argent of her breast to sight
Laid bare. Thereto she pointed with a laugh,
   Showing the aspick's bite.)   160

"I died a Queen. The Roman soldier found
   Me lying dead, my crown about my brows,
A name forever! — lying robed and crown'd,
   Worthy a Roman spouse."   164

Her warbling voice, a lyre of widest range
   Struck by all passion, did fall down and
   glance
From tone to tone, and glided thro' all change
   Of liveliest utterance.   168

When she made pause I knew not for delight:
   Because with sudden motion from the
   ground
She rais'd her piercing orbs, and fill'd with
   light
   The interval of sound.   172

Still with their fires Love tipt his keenest
   darts;
As once they drew into two burning rings
All beams of Love, melting the mighty hearts
   Of captains and of kings.   176

Slowly my sense undazzled. Then I heard
   A noise of some one[3] coming thro' the lawn,
And singing clearer than the crested bird[4]
   That claps his wings at dawn.   180

"The torrent brooks of hallow'd Israel
   From craggy hollows pouring, late and soon,
Sound all night long, in falling thro' the dell,
   Far-heard beneath the moon.   184

"The balmy moon of blessèd Israel
   Floods all the deep-blue gloom with beams
   divine:
All night the splinter'd crags that wall the dell
   With spires of silver shine."   188

[1] endure   [2] Octavius, who conquered Antony
[3] Jephthah's daughter, cf. *Judges*, ix   [4] the
lark

As one that museth where broad sunshine laves
   The lawn by some cathedral, thro' the door
Hearing the holy organ rolling waves
   Of sound on roof and floor   192

Within, and anthem sung, is charm'd and tied
   To where he stands, — so stood I, when that
   flow
Of music left the lips of her that died
   To save her father's vow;   196

The daughter of the warrior Gileadite;
   A maiden pure; as when she went along
From Mizpeh's tower'd gate with welcome
   light,
   With timbrel and with song.   200

My words leapt forth: "Heaven heads the
   count of crimes
With that wild oath." She render'd answer
   high:
"Not so, nor once alone; a thousand times
   I would be born and die.   204

"Single I grew, like some green plant, whose
   root
Creeps to the garden water-pipes beneath,
Feeding the flower; but ere my flower to fruit
   Changed, I was ripe for death.   208

"My God, my land, my father — these did
   move
Me from my bliss of life, that Nature gave,
Lower'd softly with a threefold cord of love
   Down to a silent grave.   212

"And I went mourning, 'No fair Hebrew boy
   Shall smile away my maiden blame among
The Hebrew mothers' — emptied of all joy,
   Leaving the dance and song,   216

"Leaving the olive-gardens far below,
   Leaving the promise of my bridal bower,
The valleys of grape-loaded vines that glow
   Beneath the battled tower.   220

"The light white cloud swam over us. Anon
   We heard the lion roaring from his den;
We saw the large white stars rise one by one,
   Or, from the darken'd glen,   224

"Saw God divide the night with flying flame,
   And thunder on the everlasting hills.
I heard Him, for He spake, and grief became
   A solemn scorn of ills.   228

"When the next moon was roll'd into the sky,
  Strength came to me that equall'd my desire.
How beautiful a thing it was to die
  For God and for my sire!   232

"It comforts me in this one thought to dwell,
  That I subdued me to my father's will;
Because the kiss he gave me, ere I fell,
  Sweetens the spirit still.   236

"Moreover it is written that my race
  Hew'd Ammon, hip and thigh, from Aroer
On Arnon unto Minneth." Here her face
  Glow'd as I look'd at her.   240

She lock'd her lips: she left me where I stood:
  "Glory to God," she sang, and passed afar,
Thridding the sombre boskage of the wood,
  Toward the morning-star.   244

Losing her carol I stood pensively,
  As one that from a casement leans his head,
When midnight bells cease ringing suddenly,
  And the old year is dead.   248

"Alas! alas!" a low voice, full of care,
  Murmur'd beside me. "Turn and look on
    me:
I am that Rosamond,[1] whom men call fair,
  If what I was I be.   252

"Would I had been some maiden coarse and
    poor!
  O me, that I should ever see the light!
Those dragon eyes of anger'd Eleanor
  Do hunt me, day and night."   256

She ceased in tears, fallen from hope and trust:
  To whom the Egyptian: "O, you tamely
    died!
You should have clung to Fulvia's[2] waist, and
    thrust
  The dagger thro' her side."   260

With that sharp sound the white dawn's creep-
    ing beams,
  Stol'n to my brain, dissolved the mystery
Of folded sleep. The captain of my dreams
  Ruled in the eastern sky.   264

Morn broaden'd on the borders of the dark,
  Ere I saw her, who clasp'd in her last trance

[1] loved by Henry II of England, whose queen
was Eleanor of Aquitaine [2] Antony's wife

Her murder'd father's head,[1] or Joan of Arc,
  A light of ancient France;   268

Or her[2] who knew that Love can vanquish
    Death,
  Who kneeling with one arm about her king,
Drew forth the poison with her balmy breath,
  Sweet as new buds in Spring.   272

No memory labours longer from the deep
  Gold-mines of thought to lift the hidden ore
That glimpses, moving up, than I from sleep
  To gather and tell o'er   276

Each little sound and sight. With what dull
    pain
  Compass'd, how eagerly I sought to strike
Into that wondrous track of dreams again!
  But no two dreams are like.   280

As when a soul laments, which hath been blest,
  Desiring what is mingled with past years,
In yearnings that can never be exprest
  By sighs or groans or tears;   284

Because all words, tho' cull'd with choicest art,
  Failing to give the bitter of the sweet,
Wither beneath the palate, and the heart
  Faints, faded by its heat.   288

MORTE D'ARTHUR

So all day long the noise of battle roll'd
Among the mountains by the winter sea;
Until King Arthur's table, man by man,
Had fallen in Lyonness[3] about their Lord,
King Arthur: then, because his wound was
    deep,
The bold Sir Bedivere uplifted him,
Sir Bedivere, the last of all his knights,
And bore him to a chapel nigh the field,
A broken chancel with a broken cross,
That stood on a dark strait of barren land. 10
On one side lay the Ocean, and on one
Lay a great water, and the moon was full.
  Then spake King Arthur to Sir Bedivere:
"The sequel of to-day unsolders all
The goodliest fellowship of famous knights
Whereof this world holds record. Such a sleep

[1] Margaret, daughter of Sir Thomas More
[2] Eleanor of Castile, wife of Edward I of England
[3] supposed to lie between Cornwall and the Scilly
Isles, now submerged, but cf. Layamon's *Brut*

They sleep — the men I loved. I think that we
Shall nevermore, at any future time,
Delight our souls with talk of knightly deeds,
Walking about the gardens and the halls   20
Of Camelot,[1] as in the days that were.
I perish by this people which I made, —
Tho' Merlin [2] sware that I should come again
To rule once more — but let what will be, be,
I am so deeply smitten thro' the helm
That without help I cannot last till morn.
Thou therefore take my brand Excalibur,
Which was my pride: for thou rememberest how
In those old days, one summer noon, an arm
Rose up from out the bosom of the lake,   30
Clothed in white samite, mystic, wonderful,
Holding the sword — and how I row'd across
And took it, and have worn it like a king:
And, wheresoever I am sung or told
In aftertime, this also shall be known:
But now delay not: take Excalibur,
And fling him far into the middle mere:[3]
Watch what thou seest, and lightly bring me word."
    To him replied the bold Sir Bedivere:
"It is not meet, Sir King, to leave thee thus,
Aidless, alone, and smitten thro' the helm. 41
A little thing may harm a wounded man.
Yet I thy hest will all perform at full,
Watch what I see, and lightly bring thee word."
    So saying, from the ruin'd shrine he stept
And in the moon athwart the place of tombs,
Where lay the mighty bones of ancient men,
Old knights, and over them the sea-wind sang
Shrill, chill, with flakes of foam. He, stepping down
By zig-zag paths, and juts of pointed rock, 50
Came on the shining levels of the lake.
    There drew he forth the brand Excalibur,
And o'er him, drawing it, the winter moon,
Brightening the skirts of a long cloud, ran forth
And sparkled keen with frost against the hilt:
For all the haft twinkled with diamond sparks,
Myriads of topaz-lights, and jacinth-work
Of subtlest jewellery. He gazed so long
That both his eyes were dazzled, as he stood,
This way and that dividing the swift mind, 60
In act to throw: but at the last it seem'd
Better to leave Excalibur conceal'd
There in the many-knotted water-flags,

That whistled stiff and dry about the marge.
So strode he back slow to the wounded King.
    Then spake King Arthur to Sir Bedivere:
"Hast thou perform'd my mission which I gave?
What is it thou hast seen? or what hast heard?"
    And answer made the bold Sir Bedivere:
"I heard the ripple washing in the reeds, 70
And the wild water lapping on the crag."
    To whom replied King Arthur, faint and pale:
"Thou hast betray'd thy nature and thy name,
Not rendering true answer, as beseem'd
Thy fealty, nor like a noble knight:
For surer sign had follow'd, either hand,
Or voice, or else a motion of the mere.
This is a shameful thing for men to lie.
Yet now, I charge thee, quickly go again,
As thou art lief [1] and dear, and do the thing 80
I bade thee, watch, and lightly bring me word."
    Then went Sir Bedivere the second time
Across the ridge, and paced beside the mere,
Counting the dewy pebbles, fix'd in thought;
But when he saw the wonder of the hilt,
How curiously and strangely chased, he smote
His palms together, and he cried aloud:
    "And if indeed I cast the brand away,
Surely a precious thing, one worthy note,
Should thus be lost forever from the earth, 90
Which might have pleased the eyes of many men.
What good should follow this, if this were done?
What harm, undone? deep harm to disobey,
Seeing obedience is the bond of rule.
Were it well to obey then, if a king demand
An act unprofitable, against himself?
The King is sick, and knows not what he does.
What record, or what relic of my lord
Should be to aftertime, but empty breath 99
And rumours of a doubt? but were this kept,
Stored in some treasure-house of mighty kings,
Some one might show it at a joust of arms,
Saying, 'King Arthur's sword, Excalibur,
Wrought by the lonely maiden of the Lake.
Nine years she wrought it, sitting in the deeps
Upon the hidden bases of the hills.'
So might some old man speak in the aftertime
To all the people, winning reverence.
But now much honour and much fame were lost."

---

[1] King Arthur's capital [2] cf. Layamon's *Brut*,
p. 8, above [3] the middle of the lake

[1] beloved

So spake he clouded with his own conceit,[1]
And hid Excalibur the second time,   111
And so strode back slow to the wounded
      King.
   Then spoke King Arthur, breathing heavily :
"What is it thou hast seen ? or what hast
      heard ?"
   And answer made the bold Sir Bedivere :
"I heard the water lapping on the crag,
And the long ripple washing in the reeds."
   To whom replied King Arthur, much in
      wrath :
"Ah, miserable and unkind, untrue,
Unknightly, traitor-hearted ! Woe is me !
Authority forgets a dying king,   121
Laid widow'd of the power in his eye
That bow'd the will. I see thee what thou
      art,
For thou, the latest-left of all my knights,
In whom should meet the offices of all,
Thou wouldst betray me for the precious hilt ;
Either from lust of gold, or like a girl
Valuing the giddy pleasure of the eyes.
Yet, for a man may fail in duty twice,
And the third time may prosper, get thee
      hence :
But, if thou spare to fling Excalibur,   131
I will arise and slay thee with my hands."
   Then quickly rose Sir Bedivere, and ran,
And, leaping down the ridges lightly, plunged
Among the bulrush-beds, and clutch'd the
      sword,
And strongly wheel'd and threw it. The great
      brand
Made lightnings in the splendour of the moon,
And flashing round and round, and whirl'd in
      an arch,
Shot like a streamer of the northern morn,[2]
Seen where the moving isles of winter [3] shock
By night, with noises of the northern sea. 141
So flash'd and fell the brand Excalibur :
But ere he [4] dipt the surface, rose an arm
Clothed in white samite, mystic, wonderful,
And caught him by the hilt, and brandish'd
      him
Three times, and drew him under in the mere.
And lightly went the other to the King.
   Then spoke King Arthur, drawing thicker
      breath :
"Now see I by thine eyes that this is done.
Speak out : what is it thou hast heard, or
      seen ?"

[1] idea [2] Aurora Borealis [3] ice-bergs [4] Excalibur,
cf. ll. 145, etc.

   And answer made the bold Sir Bedivere : 151
"Sir King, I closed mine eyelids, lest the gems
Should blind my purpose, for I never saw,
Nor shall see, here or elsewhere, till I die,
Not tho' I live three lives of mortal men,
So great a miracle as yonder hilt.
Then with both hands I flung him, wheeling
      him ;
But when I look'd again, behold an arm,
Clothed in white samite, mystic, wonderful,
That caught him by the hilt, and brandish'd
      him   160
Three times, and drew him under in the mere."
   And answer made King Arthur, breathing
      hard :
"My end draws nigh ; 'tis time that I were
      gone.
Make broad thy shoulders to receive my
      weight,
And bear me to the margin ; yet I fear
My wound hath taken cold, and I shall die."
   So saying, from the pavement he half rose,
Slowly, with pain, reclining on his arm,
And looking wistfully with wide blue eyes
As in a picture. Him Sir Bedivere   170
Remorsefully regarded thro' his tears,
And would have spoken, but he found not
      words,
Then took with care, and kneeling on one knee,
O'er both his shoulders drew the languid
      hands,
And rising bore him thro' the place of tombs.
   But, as he walk'd, King Arthur panted hard,
Like one that feels a nightmare on his bed
When all the house is mute. So sigh'd the
      King,
Muttering and murmuring at his ear, "Quick,
      quick !
I fear it is too late, and I shall die."   180
But the other swiftly strode from ridge to
      ridge,
Clothed with his breath, and looking, as he
      walk'd,
Larger than human on the frozen hills.
He heard the deep behind him, and a cry
Before. His own thought drove him, like a
      goad.
Dry clash'd his harness in the icy caves
And barren chasms, and all to left and right
The bare black cliff clang'd round him, as he
      based
His feet on juts of slippery crag that rang
Sharp-smitten with the dint of armèd heels —
And on a sudden, lo ! the level lake,   191
And the long glories of the winter moon.

Then saw they how there hove a dusky
    barge,
Dark as a funeral scarf from stem to stern,
Beneath them; and descending they were
    ware
That all the decks were dense with stately
    forms
Black-stoled, black-hooded, like a dream — by
    these
Three Queens with crowns of gold — and
    from them rose
A cry that shiver'd to the tingling stars,
And, as it were one voice, an agony   200
Of lamentation, like a wind, that shrills
All night in a waste land, where no one comes,
Or hath come, since the making of the world.
    Then murmur'd Arthur, "Place me in the
    barge,"
And to the barge they came. There those
    three Queens
Put forth their hands, and took the King, and
    wept.
But she, that rose the tallest of them all
And fairest, laid his head upon her lap,
And loosed the shatter'd casque, and chafed
    his hands,
And call'd him by his name, complaining loud,
And dropping bitter tears against his brow
Striped with dark blood: for all his face was
    white   212
And colourless, and like the wither'd moon
Smote by the fresh beam of the springing
    east;
And all his greaves and cuisses dash'd with
    drops
Of onset; and the light and lustrous curls —
That made his forehead like a rising sun
High from the dais-throne — were parch'd
    with dust;
Or, clotted into points and hanging loose,
Mix'd with the knightly growth that fringed
    his lips.   220
So like a shatter'd column lay the King;
Not like that Arthur who, with lance in rest,
From spur to plume a star of tournament,
Shot thro' the lists at Camelot, and charged
Before the eyes of ladies and of kings.
    Then loudly cried the bold Sir Bedivere:
"Ah! my Lord Arthur, whither shall I go?
Where shall I hide my forehead and my eyes?
For now I see the true old times are dead,
When every morning brought a noble chance,
And every chance brought out a noble knight.
Such times have been not since the light that
    led   232

The holy Elders [1] with the gift of myrrh.
But now the whole Round Table is dissolved
Which was an image of the mighty world;
And I, the last, go forth companionless,
And the days darken round me, and the
    years,
Among new men, strange faces, other minds."
    And slowly answered Arthur from the
    barge:
"The old order changeth, yielding place to
    new,
And God fulfils Himself in many ways,   241
Lest one good custom should corrupt the
    world.
Comfort thyself: what comfort is in me?
I have lived my life, and that which I have
    done
May He within Himself make pure! but thou,
If thou shouldst never see my face again,
Pray for my soul. More things are wrought
    by prayer
Than this world dreams of. Wherefore, let
    thy voice
Rise like a fountain for me night and day.
For what are men better than sheep or goats
That nourish a blind life within the brain,
If, knowing God, they lift not hands of prayer
Both for themselves and those who call them
    friend?   253
For so the whole round earth is every way
Bound by gold chains about the feet of God.
But now farewell. I am going a long way
With these thou seest — if indeed I go —
(For all my mind is clouded with a doubt)
To the island-valley of Avilion;
Where falls not hail, or rain, or any snow,   260
Nor ever wind blows loudly; but it lies
Deep-meadow'd, happy, fair with orchard-
    lawns
And bowery hollows crown'd with summer sea,
Where I will heal me of my grievous wound."
    So said he, and the barge with oar and sail
Moved from the brink, like some full-breasted
    swan
That, fluting a wild carol ere her death, [2]
Ruffles her pure cold plume, and takes the
    flood
With swarthy webs. Long stood Sir Bedivere
Revolving many memories, till the hull   270
Look'd one black dot against the verge of
    dawn,
And on the mere the wailing died away.

[1] the Wise Men of the East   [2] The swan is
fabled to sing just before dying.

ULYSSES

It little profits that an idle king,
By this still hearth, among these barren crags,
Match'd with an agèd wife,[1] I mete and dole
Unequal laws unto a savage race,
That hoard, and sleep, and feed, and know not me.
I cannot rest from travel: I will drink
Life to the lees: all times I have enjoy'd
Greatly, have suffer'd greatly, both with those
That loved me, and alone; on shore, and when
Thro' scudding drifts the rainy Hyades[2]   10
Vext the dim sea; I am become a name;
For always roaming with a hungry heart
Much have I seen and known; cities of men,
And manners, climates, councils, governments,
Myself not least, but honour'd of them all;
And drunk delight of battle with my peers,
Far on the ringing plains of windy Troy.
I am a part of all that I have met.
Yet all experience is an arch where-thro'
Gleams that untravell'd world, whose margin fades   20
Forever and forever when I move.
How dull it is to pause, to make an end,
To rust unburnish'd, not to shine in use!
As tho' to breathe were life.   Life piled on life
Were all too little, and of one to me
Little remains: but every hour is saved
From that eternal silence, something more,
A bringer of new things; and vile it were
For some three suns to store and hoard myself,
And this grey spirit yearning in desire   30
To follow knowledge like a sinking star,
Beyond the utmost bound of human thought.
This is my son, mine own Telemachus,
To whom I leave the sceptre and the isle[3] —
Well-loved of me, discerning to fulfil
This labour, by slow prudence to make mild
A rugged people, and thro' soft degrees
Subdue them to the useful and the good.
Most blameless is he, centred in the sphere
Of common duties, decent not to fail   40
In offices of tenderness, and pay
Meet adoration to my household gods,
When I am gone.   He works his work, I mine.
There lies the port; the vessel puffs her sail:
There gloom the dark broad seas.   My mariners,

[1] Penelope, who for twenty years awaited his return from Troy [2] a cluster of stars in Taurus, supposed to presage rain [3] Ithaca

Souls that have toil'd, and wrought, and thought with me —
That ever with a frolic welcome took
The thunder and the sunshine, and opposed
Free hearts, free foreheads — you and I are old;
Old age hath yet his honour and his toil;   50
Death closes all: but something ere the end,
Some work of noble note, may yet be done,
Not unbecoming men that strove with Gods.
The lights begin to twinkle from the rocks:
The long day wanes: the slow moon climbs: the deep
Moans round with many voices.   Come, my friends,
'Tis not too late to seek a newer world.
Push off, and sitting well in order smite
The sounding furrows; for my purpose holds
To sail beyond the sunset, and the baths   60
Of all the western stars, until I die.
It may be that the gulfs will wash us down:
It may be we shall touch the Happy Isles,[1]
And see the great Achilles, whom we knew.
Tho' much is taken, much abides; and tho'
We are not now that strength which in old days
Moved earth and heaven; that which we are, we are;
One equal temper of heroic hearts,
Made weak by time and fate, but strong in will
To strive, to seek, to find, and not to yield.   70

LOCKSLEY HALL

Comrades, leave me here a little, while as yet 'tis early morn:
Leave me here, and when you want me, sound upon the bugle-horn.

'Tis the place, and all around it, as of old, the curlews call,
Dreary gleams about the moorland flying over Locksley Hall;

Locksley Hall, that in the distance overlooks the sandy tracts,
And the hollow ocean-ridges roaring into cataracts.

[1] islands supposed by the ancients to lie west of Gibraltar and to be the abode of the blest

Many a night from yonder ivied casement, ere
   I went to rest,
Did I look on great Orion sloping slowly to
   the West.

Many a night I saw the Pleiads, rising thro'
   the mellow shade,
Glitter like a swarm of fire-flies tangled in a
   silver braid.   10

Here about the beach I wander'd, nourishing
   a youth sublime
With the fairy tales of science, and the long
   result of Time;

When the centuries behind me like a fruitful
   land reposed;
When I clung to all the present for the promise
   that it closed:

When I dipt into the future far as human eye
   could see;
Saw the Vision of the world, and all the wonder that would be. —

In the Spring a fuller crimson comes upon the
   robin's breast;
In the Spring the wanton lapwing gets himself
   another crest;

In the Spring a livelier iris changes on the
   burnish'd dove;
In the Spring a young man's fancy lightly
   turns to thoughts of love.   20

Then her cheek was pale and thinner than
   should be for one so young,
And her eyes on all my motions with a mute
   observance hung.

And I said, "My cousin Amy, speak, and
   speak the truth to me,
Trust me, cousin, all the current of my being
   sets to thee."

On her pallid cheek and forehead came a colour
   and a light,
As I have seen the rosy red flushing in the
   northern night.

And she turn'd — her bosom shaken with a
   sudden storm of sighs —
All the spirit deeply dawning in the dark of
   hazel eyes —

Saying, "I have hid my feelings, fearing they
   should do me wrong";
Saying, "Dost thou love me, cousin?" weeping, "I have loved thee long."   30

Love took up the glass [1] of Time, and turn'd it
   in his glowing hands;
Every moment, lightly shaken, ran itself in
   golden sands.

Love took up the harp of Life, and smote on
   all the chords with might;
Smote the chord of Self, that, trembling,
   pass'd in music out of sight.

Many a morning on the moorland did we hear
   the copses ring,
And her whisper throng'd my pulses with the
   fullness of the Spring.

Many an evening by the waters did we watch
   the stately ships,
And our spirits rush'd together at the touching of the lips.

O my cousin, shallow-hearted! O my Amy,
   mine no more!
O the dreary, dreary moorland! O the barren,
   barren shore!   40

Falser than all fancy fathoms, falser than all
   songs have sung,
Puppet to a father's threat, and servile to a
   shrewish tongue!

Is it well to wish thee happy? — having
   known me — to decline
On a range of lower feelings and a narrower
   heart than mine!

Yet it shall be: thou shalt lower to his level
   day by day,
What is fine within thee growing coarse to sympathise with clay.

As the husband is, the wife is: thou art mated
   with a clown,
And the grossness of his nature will have
   weight to drag thee down.

He will hold thee, when his passion shall have
   spent its novel force,
Something better than his dog, a little dearer
   than his horse.   50

[1] hourglass

What is this? his eyes are heavy; think not
    they are glazed with wine.
Go to him: it is thy duty: kiss him: take his
    hand in thine.

It may be my lord is weary, that his brain is
    overwrought;
Soothe him with thy finer fancies, touch him
    with thy lighter thought.

He will answer to the purpose, easy things to
    understand —
Better thou wert dead before me, tho' I slew
    thee with my hand!

Better thou and I were lying, hidden from the
    heart's disgrace,
Roll'd in one another's arms, and silent in a
    last embrace.

Cursed be the social wants that sin against
    the strength of youth!
Cursed be the social lies that warp us from
    the living truth!   60

Cursed be the sickly forms that err from honest
    Nature's rule!
Cursed be the gold that gilds the straiten'd
    forehead of the fool!

Well — 'tis well that I should bluster! —
    Hadst thou less unworthy proved —
Would to God — for I had loved thee more
    than ever wife was loved.

Am I mad, that I should cherish that which
    bears but bitter fruit?
I will pluck it from my bosom, tho' my heart
    be at the root.

Never, tho' my mortal summers to such length
    of years should come
As the many-winter'd crow that leads the
    clanging rookery home.

Where is comfort? in division of the records
    of the mind?
Can I part her from herself, and love her, as
    I knew her, kind?   70

I remember one that perish'd:[1] sweetly did
    she speak and move:
Such a one do I remember, whom to look at
    was to love.

[1] *i.e.*, one who is dead to him

Can I think of her as dead, and love her for
    the love she bore?
No — she never loved me truly: love is love
    for evermore.

Comfort? comfort scorn'd of devils! this is
    truth the poet sings,
That a sorrow's crown of sorrow is remember-
    ing happier things.[1]

Drug thy memories, lest thou learn it, lest thy
    heart be put to proof,
In the dead unhappy night, and when the rain
    is on the roof.

Like a dog, he hunts in dreams, and thou art
    staring at the wall,
Where the dying night-lamp flickers, and the
    shadows rise and fall.   80

Then a hand shall pass before thee, pointing
    to his drunken sleep,
To thy widow'd marriage-pillows, to the tears
    that thou wilt weep.

Thou shalt hear the "Never, never," whisper'd
    by the phantom years,
And a song from out the distance in the ring-
    ing of thine ears;

And an eye shall vex thee, looking ancient
    kindness on thy pain.
Turn thee, turn thee on thy pillow: get thee
    to thy rest again.

Nay, but Nature brings thee solace; for a
    tender voice will cry.
'Tis a purer life than thine; a lip to drain thy
    trouble dry.

Baby lips will laugh me down: my latest rival
    brings thee rest.
Baby fingers, waxen touches, press me from
    the mother's breast.   90

O, the child too clothes the father with a dear-
    ness not his due.
Half is thine and half is his: it will be worthy
    of the two.

O, I see thee old and formal, fitted to thy petty
    part,
With a little hoard of maxims preaching down
    a daughter's heart.

[1] See Notes on *Dream of Fair Women*, ll. 73–6

"They were dangerous guides the feelings —
    she herself was not exempt —
Truly, she herself had suffer'd". — Perish in
    thy self-contempt !

Overlive it — lower yet — be happy ! where-
    fore should I care?
I myself must mix with action, lest I wither
    by despair.

What is that which I should turn to, lighting
    upon days like these?
Every door is barr'd with gold, and opens but
    to golden keys.   100

Every gate is throng'd with suitors, all the
    markets overflow.
I have but an angry fancy; what is that
    which I should do?

I had been content to perish, falling on the foe-
    man's ground,
When the ranks are roll'd in vapour, and the
    winds are laid with sound.

But the jingling of the guinea helps the hurt
    that Honour feels,
And the nations do but murmur, snarling at
    each other's heels.

Can I but relive in sadness? I will turn that
    earlier page.
Hide me from thy deep emotion, O thou won-
    drous Mother-Age !

Make me feel the wild pulsation that I felt
    before the strife,
When I heard my days before me, and the
    tumult of my life;   110

Yearning for the large excitement that the
    coming years would yield,
Eager-hearted as a boy when first he leaves
    his father's field,

And at night along the dusky highway near
    and nearer drawn,
Sees in heaven the light of London flaring like
    a dreary dawn;

And his spirit leaps within him to be gone
    before him then,
Underneath the light he looks at, in among
    the throngs of men:

Men, my brothers, men the workers, ever
    reaping something new :
That which they have done but earnest of the
    things that they shall do:

For I dipt into the future, far as human eye
    could see,
Saw the Vision of the world, and all the won-
    der that would be;   120

Saw the heavens fill with commerce, argosies
    of magic sails,
Pilots of the purple twilight, dropping down
    with costly bales;

Heard the heavens fill with shouting, and there
    rain'd a ghastly dew
From the nations' airy navies grappling in the
    central blue;

Far along the world-wide whisper of the south-
    wind rushing warm,
With the standards of the peoples plunging
    thro' the thunder-storm;

Till the war-drum throbb'd no longer, and the
    battle-flags were furl'd
In the Parliament of man, the Federation of
    the world.

There the common sense of most shall hold a
    fretful realm in awe,
And the kindly earth shall slumber, lapt in
    universal law.   130

So I triumph'd ere my passion sweeping thro'
    me left me dry,
Left me with the palsied heart, and left me
    with the jaundiced eye;

Eye, to which all order festers, all things here
    are out of joint :
Science moves, but slowly slowly, creeping on
    from point to point :

Slowly comes a hungry people, as a lion creep-
    ing nigher,
Glares at one that nods and winks behind a
    slowly-dying fire.

Yet I doubt not thro' the ages one increasing
    purpose runs,
And the thoughts of men are widen'd with the
    process of the suns.

What is that to him that reaps not harvest of
    his youthful joys,
Tho' the deep heart of existence beat forever
    like a boy's?   140

Knowledge comes, but wisdom lingers, and I
    linger on the shore,
And the individual withers, and the world is
    more and more.

Knowledge comes, but wisdom lingers, and he
    bears a laden breast,
Full of sad experience, moving toward the
    stillness of his rest.

Hark, my merry comrades call me, sounding
    on the bugle-horn,
They to whom my foolish passion were a tar-
    get for their scorn:

Shall it not be scorn to me to harp on such a
    moulder'd string?
I am shamed thro' all my nature to have loved
    so slight a thing.

Weakness to be wroth with weakness!
    woman's pleasure, woman's pain —
Nature made them blinder motions bounded
    in a shallower brain: 150

Woman is the lesser man, and all thy passions,
    match'd with mine,
Are as moonlight unto sunlight, and as water
    unto wine —

Here at least, where nature sickens, nothing.
    Ah, for some retreat
Deep in yonder shining Orient, where my life
    began to beat;

Where in wild Mahratta-battle[1] fell my father
    evil-starr'd; —
I was left a trampled orphan, and a selfish
    uncle's ward.

Or to burst all links of habit — there to wan-
    der far away,
On from island unto island at the gateways of
    the day.

Larger constellations burning, mellow moons
    and happy skies,
Breadths of tropic shade and palms in cluster,
    knots of Paradise.   160

[1] See above, p. 331, n. 3.

Never comes the trader, never floats an Euro-
    pean flag,
Slides the bird o'er lustrous woodland, swings
    the trailer from the crag;

Droops the heavy-blossom'd bower, hangs the
    heavy-fruited tree —
Summer isles of Eden lying in dark-purple
    spheres of sea.

There methinks would be enjoyment more
    than in this march of mind,
In the steamship, in the railway, in the
    thoughts that shake mankind.

There the passions cramp'd no longer shall
    have scope and breathing space;
I will take some savage woman, she shall rear
    my dusky race.

Iron jointed, supple-sinew'd, they shall dive,
    and they shall run,
Catch the wild goat by the hair, and hurl their
    lances in the sun;   170

Whistle back the parrot's call, and leap the
    rainbows of the brooks,
Not with blinded eyesight poring over miser-
    able books —

Fool, again the dream, the fancy! but I know
    my words are wild,
But I count the grey barbarian lower than the
    Christian child.

I, to herd with narrow foreheads, vacant of our
    glorious gains,
Like a beast with lower pleasures, like a beast
    with lower pains!

Mated with a squalid savage — what to me
    were sun or clime?
I the heir of all the ages, in the foremost files
    of time —

I that rather held it better men should perish
    one by one,
Than that earth should stand at gaze like
    Joshua's moon in Ajalon![1]   180

Not in vain the distance beacons. Forward,
    forward let us range,
Let the great world spin forever down the
    ringing grooves of change.

[1] *Joshua*, x : 12, 13.

Thro' the shadow of the globe we sweep into
   the younger day:
Better fifty years of Europe than a cycle of
   Cathay.[1]

Mother-Age (for mine I knew not), help me as
   when life begun:
Rift the hills, and roll the waters, flash the
   lightnings, weigh the Sun.

O, I see the crescent promise of my spirit hath
   not set.
Ancient founts of inspiration well thro' all my
   fancy yet.

Howsoever these things be, a long farewell to
   Locksley Hall!
Now for me the woods may wither, now for
   me the roof-tree fall.   190

Comes a vapour from the margin, blackening
   over heath and holt,
Cramming all the blast before it, in its breast
   a thunderbolt.

Let it fall on Locksley Hall, with rain or hail,
   or fire or snow;
For the mighty wind arises, roaring seaward,
   and I go.

ST. AGNES' EVE

Deep on the convent-roof the snows
   Are sparkling to the moon:
My breath to heaven like vapour goes:
   May my soul follow soon!
The shadows of the convent-towers
   Slant down the snowy sward,   6
Still creeping with the creeping hours
   That lead me to my Lord:
Make Thou my spirit pure and clear
   As are the frosty skies,
Or this first snowdrop of the year
   That in my bosom lies.   12

As these white robes are soil'd and dark,
   To yonder shining ground;
As this pale taper's earthly spark,
   To yonder argent round;
So shows my soul before the Lamb,
   My spirit before Thee;   18
So in mine earthly house I am,
   To that I hope to be.

[1] China

Break up the heavens, O Lord! and far,
   Thro' all yon starlight keen,
Draw me, Thy bride, a glittering star,
   In raiment white and clean.   24

He lifts me to the golden doors;
   The flashes come and go;
All heaven bursts her starry floors,
   And strows her lights below,
And deepens on and up! the gates
   Roll back, and far within   30
For me the Heavenly Bridegroom waits,
   To make me pure of sin.
The sabbaths of Eternity,
   One sabbath deep and wide —
A light upon the shining sea —
   The Bridegroom with His bride!   36

SIR GALAHAD

My good blade carves the casques of men,
   My tough lance thrusteth sure,
My strength is as the strength of ten,
   Because my heart is pure.
The shattering trumpet shrilleth high,
   The hard brands shiver on the steel,
The splinter'd spear-shafts crack and fly,
   The horse and rider reel:
They reel, they roll in clanging lists,
   And when the tide of combat stands,   10
Perfume and flowers fall in showers,
   That lightly rain from ladies' hands.

How sweet are looks that ladies bend
   On whom their favours fall!
For them I battle till the end,
   To save from shame and thrall:
But all my heart is drawn above,
   My knees are bow'd in crypt and shrine:
I never felt the kiss of love,
   Nor maiden's hand in mine.   20
More bounteous aspects on me beam,
   Me mightier transports move and thrill;
So keep I fair thro' faith and prayer
   A virgin heart in work and will.

When down the stormy crescent goes,
   A light before me swims,
Between dark stems the forest glows,
   I hear a noise of hymns:
Then by some secret shrine I ride;
   I hear a voice but none are there;   30
The stalls are void, the doors are wide,
   The tapers burning fair.

Fair gleams the snowy altar-cloth,
The silver vessels sparkle clean,
The shrill bell rings, the censer swings,
And solemn chants resound between.

Sometimes on lonely mountain-meres
I find a magic bark;
I leap on board: no helmsman steers:
I float till all is dark.
A gentle sound, an awful light!   40
Three angels bear the holy Grail:
With folded feet, in stoles of white,
On sleeping wings they sail.
Ah, blessed vision! blood of God!
My spirit beats her mortal bars,
As down dark tides the glory slides,
And star-like mingles with the stars.

When on my goodly charger borne
Thro' dreaming towns I go,
The cock crows ere the Christmas morn,   50
The streets are dumb with snow.
The tempest crackles on the leads,
And, ringing, springs from brand and mail;
But o'er the dark a glory spreads,
And gilds the driving hail.
I leave the plain, I climb the height;
No branchy thicket shelter yields;
But blessed forms in whistling storms
Fly o'er waste fens and windy fields.   60

A maiden knight — to me is given
Such hope, I know not fear;
I yearn to breathe the airs of heaven
That often meet me here.
I muse on joy that will not cease,
Pure spaces clothed in living beams,
Pure lilies of eternal peace,
Whose odours haunt my dreams;
And, stricken by an angel's hand,
This mortal armour that I wear,   70
This weight and size, this heart and eyes,
Are touch'd, are turn'd to finest air.

The clouds are broken in the sky,
And thro' the mountain-walls
A rolling organ-harmony
Swells up, and shakes and falls.
Then move the trees, the copses nod,
Wings flutter, voices hover clear:
"O just and faithful knight of God!
Ride on! the prize is near."   80
So pass I hostel, hall, and grange;
By bridge and ford, by park and pale,
All-arm'd I ride, whate'er betide,
Until I find the holy Grail.

BREAK, BREAK, BREAK

Break, break, break,
On thy cold grey stones, O Sea!
And I would that my tongue could utter
The thoughts that arise in me.   4

O well for the fisherman's boy,
That he shouts with his sister at play!
O well for the sailor lad,
That he sings in his boat on the bay!   8

And the stately ships go on
To their haven under the hill;
But O for the touch of a vanish'd hand,
And the sound of a voice that is still!   12

Break, break, break,
At the foot of thy crags, O Sea!
But the tender grace of a day that is dead
Will never come back to me.   16

WAGES

Glory of warrior, glory of orator, glory of song,
Paid with a voice flying by to be lost on an
endless sea —
Glory of Virtue, to fight, to struggle, to right
the wrong —
Nay, but she aim'd not at glory, no lover of
glory she: 4
Give her the glory of going on, and still to be.

The wages of sin is death: if the wages of Virtue be dust,
Would she have heart to endure for the life
of the worm and the fly?
She desires no isles of the blest, no quiet seats
of the just,
To rest in a golden grove, or to bask in a
summer sky: 9
Give her the wages of going on, and not to die.

THE HIGHER PANTHEISM

The sun, the moon, the stars, the seas, the
hills and the plains —
Are not these, O Soul, the Vision of Him who
reigns?

Is not the Vision He? tho' He be not that
which He seems?
Dreams are true while they last, and do we not
live in dreams?   4

Earth, these solid stars, this weight of body
and limb,
Are they not sign and symbol of thy division
from Him?

Dark is the world to thee: thyself art the
reason why;
For is He not all but thou, that hast power
to feel "I am I"?   8

Glory about thee, without thee; and thou ful-
fillest thy doom
Making Him broken gleams, and a stifled
splendour and gloom.

Speak to Him thou for He hears, and Spirit
with Spirit can meet —
Closer is He than breathing, and nearer than
hands and feet.   12

God is law, say the wise; O Soul, and let us
rejoice,
For if He thunder by law the thunder is yet
His voice.

Law is God, say some: no God at all, says the
fool;
For all we have power to see is a straight staff
bent in a pool;   16

And the ear of man cannot hear, and the eye
of man cannot see;
But if we could see and hear, this Vision —
were it not He?

From MAUD

XXII

Come into the garden, Maud,
  For the black bat, night, has flown,
Come into the garden, Maud,
  I am here at the gate alone;
And the woodbine spices are wafted abroad,
  And the musk of the rose is blown.   6

For a breeze of morning moves,
  And the planet of Love is on high,
Beginning to faint in the light that she loves
  On a bed of daffodil sky,
To faint in the light of the sun she loves,
  To faint in his light, and to die.   12

All night have the roses heard
  The flute, violin, bassoon;

All night has the casement jessamine stirr'd
  To the dancers dancing in tune;
Till a silence fell with the waking bird,
  And a hush with the setting moon.   18

I said to the lily, "There is but one
  With whom she has heart to be gay.
When will the dancers leave her alone?
  She is weary of dance and play."
Now half to the setting moon are gone,
  And half to the rising day;
Low on the sand and loud on the stone
  The last wheel echoes away.   26

I said to the rose, "The brief night goes
  In babble and revel and wine.
O young lord-lover, what sighs are those,
  For one that will never be thine?
But mine, but mine," so I sware to the rose,
  "For ever and ever, mine."   32

And the soul of the rose went into my blood,
  As the music clash'd in the hall;
And long by the garden lake I stood,
  For I heard your rivulet fall
From the lake to the meadow and on to the
    wood,
  Our wood, that is dearer than all;   38

From the meadow your walks have left so
    sweet
  That whenever a March-wind sighs
He sets the jewel-print of your feet
  In violets blue as your eyes,
To the woody hollows in which we meet
  And the valleys of Paradise.   44

The slender acacia would not shake
  One long milk-bloom on the tree;
The white lake-blossom fell into the lake
  As the pimpernel [1] dozed on the lea;
But the rose was awake all night for your sake,
  Knowing your promise to me;
The lilies and roses were all awake,
  They sigh'd for the dawn and thee.   52

Queen rose of the rosebud garden of girls,
  Come hither, the dances are done,
In gloss of satin and glimmer of pearls,
  Queen lily and rose in one;
Shine out, little head, sunning over with curls,
  To the flowers, and be their sun.   58

[1] probably the scarlet pimpernel, a flower of the
primrose family

There has fallen a splendid tear
  From the passion-flower at the gate.
She is coming, my dove, my dear;
  She is coming, my life, my fate;
The red rose cries, "She is near, she is near;"
  And the white rose weeps, "She is late;"
The larkspur listens, "I hear, I hear;"
  And the lily whispers, "I wait."   66

She is coming, my own, my sweet;
  Were it ever so airy a tread,
My heart would hear her and beat,
  Were it earth in an earthy bed;
My dust would hear her and beat,
  Had I lain for a century dead;
Would start and tremble under her feet,
  And blossom in purple and red.   74

From IN MEMORIAM

PROEM

Strong Son of God, immortal Love,
  Whom we, that have not seen thy face,
  By faith, and faith alone, embrace,
Believing where we cannot prove;   4

Thine are these orbs of light and shade;
  Thou madest Life in man and brute;
  Thou madest Death; and lo, thy foot
Is on the skull which thou hast made.   8

Thou wilt not leave us in the dust:
  Thou madest man, he knows not why,
  He thinks he was not made to die;
And thou hast made him: thou art just.   12

Thou seemest human and divine,
  The highest, holiest manhood, thou:
  Our wills are ours, we know not how;
Our wills are ours, to make them thine.   16

Our little systems have their day;
  They have their day and cease to be:
  They are but broken lights of thee,
And thou, O Lord, art more than they.   20

We have but faith: we cannot know;
  For knowledge is of things we see;
  And yet we trust it comes from thee,
A beam in darkness: let it grow.   24

Let knowledge grow from more to more,
  But more of reverence in us dwell;
  That mind and soul, according well,
May make one music as before,   28

But vaster. We are fools and slight;
  We mock thee when we do not fear:
  But help thy foolish ones to bear;
Help thy vain worlds to bear thy light.   32

Forgive what seem'd my sin in me;
  What seem'd my worth since I began;
  For merit lives from man to man,
And not from man, O Lord, to thee.   36

Forgive my grief for one removed,
  Thy creature, whom I found so fair.
  I trust he lives in thee, and there
I find him worthier to be loved.   40

Forgive these wild and wandering cries,
  Confusions of a wasted youth;
  Forgive them where they fail in truth,
And in thy wisdom make me wise.   44

I

I held it truth, with him who sings
  To one clear harp in divers tones,[1]
  That men may rise on stepping-stones
Of their dead selves to higher things.   4

But who shall so forecast the years
  And find in loss a gain to match?
  Or reach a hand thro' time to catch
The far-off interest of tears?   8

Let Love clasp Grief lest both be drown'd,
  Let darkness keep her raven gloss:
  Ah, sweeter to be drunk with loss,
To dance with death, to beat the ground,   12

Than that the victor Hours should scorn
  The long result of love, and boast,
  "Behold the man that loved and lost,
But all he was is overworn."   16

XXVII

I envy not in any moods
  The captive void of noble rage,
  The linnet born within the cage,
That never knew the summer woods: 4

I envy not the beast that takes
  His license in the field of time,
  Unfetter'd by the sense of crime,
To whom a conscience never wakes;   8

[1] Tennyson said he meant Goethe.

Nor, what may count itself as blest,
  The heart that never plighted troth
  But stagnates in the weeds of sloth;
Nor any want-begotten rest.   12

I hold it true, whate'er befall;
  I feel it, when I sorrow most;
  'Tis better to have loved and lost
Than never to have loved at all.   16

XXXI

When Lazarus left his charnel-cave,
  And home to Mary's house return'd,
  Was this demanded — if he yearn'd
To hear her weeping by his grave?   4

"Where wert thou, brother, those four days?"
  There lives no record of reply,
  Which telling what it is to die
Had surely added praise to praise.   8

From every house the neighbours met,
  The streets were fill'd with joyful sound,
  A solemn gladness even crown'd
The purple brows of Olivet.   12

Behold a man raised up by Christ!
  The rest remaineth unreveal'd;
  He told it not; or something seal'd
The lips of that Evangelist.   16

XXXII

Her eyes are homes of silent prayer,
  Nor other thought her mind admits
  But, he was dead, and there he sits,
And He that brought him back is there.   4

Then one deep love doth supersede
  All other, when her ardent gaze
  Roves from the living brother's face,
And rests upon the Life indeed.   8

All subtle thought, all curious fears,
  Borne down by gladness so complete,
  She bows, she bathes the Saviour's feet
With costly spikenard and with tears.   12

Thrice blest whose lives are faithful prayers,
  Whose loves in higher love endure;
  What souls possess themselves so pure,
Or is there blessedness like theirs?   16

LIV

Oh yet we trust that somehow good
  Will be the final goal of ill,
  To pangs of nature, sins of will,
Defects of doubt, and taints of blood;   4

That nothing walks with aimless feet;
  That not one life shall be destroy'd,
  Or cast as rubbish to the void,
When God hath made the pile complete;   8

That not a worm is cloven in vain;
  That not a moth with vain desire
  Is shrivell'd in a fruitless fire,
Or but subserves another's gain.   12

Behold, we know not anything;
  I can but trust that good shall fall
  At last — far off — at last, to all,
And every winter change to spring.   16

So runs my dream; but what am I?
  An infant crying in the night:
  An infant crying for the light:
And with no language but a cry.   20

LVII

Peace; come away: the song of woe
  Is after all an earthly song:
  Peace; come away: we do him wrong
To sing so wildly: let us go.   4

Come; let us go: your cheeks are pale;
  But half my life I leave behind:
  Methinks my friend is richly shrined;
But I shall pass; my work will fail.   8

Yet in these ears, till hearing dies,
  One set slow bell will seem to toll
  The passing of the sweetest soul
That ever look'd with human eyes.   12

I hear it now, and o'er and o'er,
  Eternal greetings to the dead;
  And "Ave,[1] Ave, Ave," said,
"Adieu, adieu" for evermore.   16

XCVI

You say, but with no touch of scorn,
  Sweet-hearted, you, whose light-blue eyes
  Are tender over drowning flies,
You tell me, doubt is Devil-born.   4

[1] *Ave* (the Latin word of greeting) is dissyllabic.

I know not: one indeed I knew
  In many a subtle question versed,
  Who touch'd a jarring lyre at first,
But ever strove to make it true: 8

Perplext in faith, but pure in deeds,
  At last he beat his music out.
  There lives more faith in honest doubt,
Believe me, than in half the creeds. 12

He fought his doubts and gather'd strength,
  He would not make his judgment blind,
  He faced the spectres of the mind
And laid them: thus he came at length 16

To find a stronger faith his own;
  And Power was with him in the night,
  Which makes the darkness and the light,
And dwells not in the light alone, 20

But in the darkness and the cloud,
  As over Sinai's peaks of old,
  While Israel made their gods of gold,
Altho' the trumpet blew so loud. 24

CVI

Ring out, wild bells, to the wild sky,
  The flying cloud, the frosty light:
  The year is dying in the night;
Ring out, wild bells, and let him die. 4

Ring out the old, ring in the new,
  Ring, happy bells, across the snow:
  The year is going, let him go;
Ring out the false, ring in the true. 8

Ring out the grief that saps the mind,
  For those that here we see no more;
  Ring out the feud of rich and poor,
Ring in redress to all mankind. 12

Ring out a slowly dying cause,
  And ancient forms of party strife;
  Ring in the nobler modes of life,
With sweeter manners, purer laws. 16

Ring out the want, the care, the sin,
  The faithless coldness of the times;
  Ring out, ring out my mournful rhymes,
But ring the fuller minstrel in. 20

Ring out false pride in place and blood,
  The civic slander and the spite;
  Ring in the love of truth and right,
Ring in the common love of good. 24

Ring out old shapes of foul disease;
  Ring out the narrowing lust of gold;
  Ring out the thousand wars of old,
Ring in the thousand years of peace. 28

Ring in the valiant man and free,
  The larger heart, the kindlier hand;
  Ring out the darkness of the land,
Ring in the Christ that is to be. 32

CXXX

Thy voice is on the rolling air;
  I hear thee where the waters run;
  Thou standest in the rising sun,
And in the setting thou art fair. 4

What art thou then? I cannot guess;
  But tho' I seem in star and flower
  To feel thee some diffusive power,
I do not therefore love thee less: 8

My love involves the love before;
  My love is vaster passion now;
  Tho' mix'd with God and Nature thou,
I seem to love thee more and more. 12

Far off thou art, but ever nigh;
  I have thee still, and I rejoice;
  I prosper, circled with thy voice;
I shall not lose thee tho' I die. 16

From THE EPILOGUE

And rise, O moon, from yonder down,
  Till over down and over dale
  All night the shining vapour sail
And pass the silent-lighted town, 112

The white-faced halls, the glancing rills,
  And catch at every mountain head,
  And o'er the friths that branch and spread
Their sleeping silver thro' the hills; 116

And touch with shade the bridal doors,
  With tender gloom the roof, the wall;
  And breaking let the splendour fall
To spangle all the happy shores 120

By which they rest, and ocean sounds,
  And, star and system rolling past,
  A soul shall draw from out the vast
And strike his being into bounds,   124

And, moved thro' life of lower phase,
  Result in man, be born and think,
  And act and love, a closer link
Betwixt us and the crowning race   128

Of those that, eye to eye, shall look
  On knowledge; under whose command
  Is Earth and Earth's, and in their hand
Is Nature like an open book;   132

No longer half-akin to brute,
  For all we thought and loved and did,
  And hoped, and suffer'd, is but seed
Of what in them is flower and fruit;   136

Whereof the man, that with me trod
  This planet, was a noble type
  Appearing ere the times were ripe,
That friend of mine who lives in God, 140

That God, which ever lives and loves,
  One God, one law, one element,
  And one far-off divine event,
To which the whole creation moves.   144

SIR JOHN FRANKLIN

ON THE CENOTAPH IN WESTMINSTER ABBEY

Not here! the white North has thy bones;
      and thou,
  Heroic sailor-soul,
Art passing on thine happier voyage now
  Toward no earthly pole.   4

TO DANTE

WRITTEN AT REQUEST OF THE FLORENTINES

King, that hast reign'd six hundred years, and
      grown
In power, and ever growest! since thine own
Fair Florence honouring thy nativity,
Thy Florence now the crown of Italy,
Hath sought the tribute of a verse from me,
I, wearing but the garland of a day,   6
Cast at thy feet one flower that fades away.

THE SILENT VOICES

When the dumb Hour, clothed in black,
Brings the Dreams about my bed,
Call me not so often back,
Silent Voices of the dead,
Toward the lowland ways behind me,
And the sunlight that is gone!
Call me rather, silent voices,
Forward to the starry track
Glimmering up the heights beyond me
On, and always on!   10

MERLIN AND THE GLEAM

I

O young Mariner,
You from the haven
Under the sea-cliff,
You that are watching
The gray Magician
With eyes of wonder,
I am Merlin,
And I am dying,
I am Merlin
Who follow The Gleam.   10

II

Mighty the Wizard
Who found me at sunrise
Sleeping, and woke me
And learn'd me Magic!
Great the Master,
And sweet the Magic,
When over the valley,
In early summers,
Over the mountain,
On human faces,   20
And all around me,
Moving to melody,
Floated The Gleam.

III

Once at the croak of a Raven who crost it,
A barbarous people,
Blind to the magic,
And deaf to the melody,
Snarl'd at and cursed me.
A demon vext me,
The light retreated,   30
The landskip darken'd,
The melody deaden'd,
The Master whisper'd
"Follow The Gleam."

IV

Then to the melody,
Over a wilderness
Gliding, and glancing at
Elf of the woodland,
Gnome of the cavern,
Griffin and Giant,   40
And dancing of Fairies
In desolate hollows,
And wraiths of the mountain,
And rolling of dragons
By warble of water,
Or cataract music
Of falling torrents,
Flitted The Gleam.

V

Down from the mountain
And over the level,   50
And streaming and shining on
Silent river,
Silvery willow,
Pasture and plowland,
Horses and oxen,
Innocent maidens,
Garrulous children,
Homestead and harvest,
Reaper and gleaner,
And rough-ruddy faces   60
Of lowly labour,
Slided The Gleam. —

VI

Then, with a melody
Stronger and statelier,
Led me at length
To the city and palace
Of Arthur the king;
Touch'd at the golden
Cross of the churches,
Flash'd on the Tournament,   70
Flicker'd and bicker'd
From helmet to helmet,
And last on the forehead
Of Arthur the blameless
Rested The Gleam.

VII

Clouds and darkness
Closed upon Camelot;

Arthur had vanish'd
I knew not whither,
The king who loved me,   80
And cannot die;
For out of the darkness
Silent and slowly
The Gleam, that had waned to a wintry
    glimmer
On icy fallow
And faded forest,
Drew to the valley
Named of the shadow,
And slowly brightening
Out of the glimmer,   90
And slowly moving again to a melody
Yearningly tender,
Fell on the shadow,
No longer a shadow,
But clothed with The Gleam.

VIII

And broader and brighter
The Gleam flying onward,
Wed to the melody,
Sang thro' the world;
And slower and fainter,   100
Old and weary,
But eager to follow,
I saw, whenever
In passing it glanced upon
Hamlet or city,
That under the Crosses
The dead man's garden,
The mortal hillock,
Would break into blossom;
And to the land's   110
Last limit I came —
And can no longer,
But die rejoicing,
For thro' the Magic
Of Him the Mighty,
Who taught me in childhood,
There on the border
Of boundless Ocean,
And all but in Heaven
Hovers The Gleam.   120

IX

Not of the sunlight,
Not of the moonlight,
Not of the starlight !
O young Mariner,

Down to the haven,
Call your companions,
Launch your vessel,
And crowd your canvas,
And, ere it vanishes   130
Over the margin,
After it, follow it,
Follow The Gleam.

CROSSING THE BAR

Sunset and evening star,
  And one clear call for me !
And may there be no moaning of the bar,
  When I put out to sea,   4

But such a tide as moving seems asleep,
  Too full for sound and foam,
When that which drew from out the boundless
    deep
  Turns again home.   8

Twilight and evening bell,
  And after that the dark !
And may there be no sadness of farewell,
  When I embark ;   12

For tho' from out our bourne of Time and
    Place
  The flood may bear me far,
I hope to see my Pilot face to face
  When I have crost the bar.   16

ELIZABETH BARRETT BROWN-
ING (1806-1861)

SONNETS FROM THE PORTUGUESE

I

I thought once how Theocritus had sung
Of the sweet years, the dear and wished-for
    years,
Who each one in a gracious hand appears
To bear a gift for mortals, old or young:
And, as I mused it in his antique tongue,
I saw in gradual vision through my tears,
The sweet, sad years, the melancholy years,
Those of my own life, who by turns had flung
A shadow across me.   Straightway I was
    'ware,
So weeping, how a mystic Shape did move 10

Behind me, and drew me backward by the
    hair ;
And a voice said in mastery while I strove,
"Guess now who holds thee ?" — "Death !"
    I said.   But there,
The silver answer rang : "Not Death, but
    Love."

VII

The face of all the world is changed, I think,
Since first I heard the footsteps of thy soul
Move still, oh, still, beside me ; as they stole
Betwixt me and the dreadful outer brink
Of obvious death, where I who thought to sink
Was caught up into love and taught the whole
Of life in a new rhythm.   The cup of dole[1]
God gave for baptism, I am fain[2] to drink,
And praise its sweetness, Sweet, with thee
    anear.
The name of country, heaven, are changed
    away
For where thou art or shalt be, there or here ;
And this — this lute and song — loved yester-
    day,   12
(The singing angels know) are only dear,
Because thy name moves right in what they
    say.

XIV

If thou must love me, let it be for nought
Except for love's sake only.   Do not say,
"I love her for her smile — her look — her way
Of speaking gently, — for a trick of thought
That falls in well with mine, and certes brought
A sense of pleasant ease on such a day ;" —
For these things in themselves, Belovèd, may
Be changed, or change for thee, — and love so
    wrought,
May be unwrought so.   Neither love me for
Thine own dear pity's wiping my cheeks dry :
A creature might forget to weep, who bore 11
Thy comfort long, and lose thy love thereby.
But love me for love's sake, that evermore
Thou may'st love on through love's eternity.

XVII

My poet, thou canst touch on all the notes
God set between His After and Before,
And strike up and strike off the general roar
Of the rushing worlds a melody that floats

---

[1] sorrow   [2] glad

In a serene air purely. Antidotes
Of medicated music, answering for
Mankind's forlornest uses, thou canst pour
From thence into their ears. God's will
    devotes
Thine to such ends and mine to wait on thine !
How, Dearest, wilt thou have me for most use?
A hope, to sing by gladly? — or a fine   11
Sad memory, with thy songs to interfuse?
A shade, in which to sing — of palm or pine?
A grave on which to rest from singing? —
    Choose.

XX

Belovèd, my Belovèd, when I think
That thou wast in the world a year ago,
What time I sate alone here in the snow
And saw no footprint, heard the silence sink
No moment at thy voice, — but link by link
Went counting all my chains as if that so
They never could fall off at any blow
Struck by thy possible hand, — why, thus I
    drink
Of life's great cup of wonder. Wonderful,
Never to feel thee thrill the day or night   10
With personal act or speech, — nor ever cull
Some prescience of thee with the blossoms
    white
Thou sawest growing ! Atheists are as dull,
Who cannot guess God's presence out of sight.

XXI

Say over again and yet once over again
That thou dost love me. Though the word
    repeated
Should seem "a cuckoo-song,"[1] as thou dost
    treat it,
Remember never to the hill or plain,
Valley and wood, without her cuckoo-strain,
Comes the fresh Spring in all her green com-
    pleted !
Belovèd, I, amid the darkness greeted
By a doubtful spirit-voice, in that doubt's
    pain
Cry, "Speak once more, thou lovest !" Who
    can fear
Too many stars, though each in heaven shall
    roll —   10
Too many flowers, though each shall crown
    the year ?
Say thou dost love me, love me, love me —
    toll

[1] a constant repetition of the same few notes

The silver iterance ! — only minding, Dear,
To love me also in silence, with thy soul.

XXII

When our two souls stand up erect and strong,
Face to face, silent, drawing nigh and nigher,
Until the lengthening wings break into fire
At either curvèd point, — What bitter wrong
Can the earth do to us, that we should not
    long
Be here contented ? Think. In mounting
    higher,
The angels would press on us, and aspire
To drop some golden orb of perfect song
Into our deep, dear silence. Let us stay
Rather on earth, Belovèd, — where the unfit,
Contrarious moods of men recoil away   11
And isolate pure spirits, and permit
A place to stand and love in for a day,
With darkness and the death-hour rounding it.

XXVIII

My letters all dead paper, mute and white !
And yet they seem alive and quivering
Against my tremulous hands which loose the
    string
And let them drop down on my knee to-night.
This said, he wished to have me in his sight
Once, as a friend ; this fixed a day in spring
To come and touch my hand — a simple thing,
Yet I wept for it ! — this — the paper's
    light —
Said, "*Dear*, I love thee"; and I sank and
    quailed
As if God's future thundered on my past : 10
This said, "I am thine" — and so its ink has
    paled
With lying at my heart that beat too fast :
And this — O Love, thy words have ill
    availed,
If, what this said, I dared repeat at last !

XLIII

How do I love thee ? Let me count the ways.
I love thee to the depth and breadth and
    height
My soul can reach, when feeling out of sight
For the ends of Being and Ideal Grace.
I love thee to the level of everyday's
Most quiet need, by sun and candlelight.
I love thee freely, as men strive for Right ;

I love thee purely, as they turn from Praise;
I love thee with the passion put to use
In my old griefs, and with my childhood's
    faith;   10
I love thee with a love I seemed to lose
With my lost saints, — I love thee with the
    breath,
Smiles, tears, of all my life! — and, if God
    choose,
I shall but love thee better after death.

THE CRY OF THE CHILDREN

Do ye hear the children weeping, O my
    brothers,
    Ere the sorrow comes with years?
They are leaning their young heads against
    their mothers,
    And *that* cannot stop their tears.
The young lambs are bleating in the meadows:
    The young birds are chirping in the nest;
The young fawns are playing with the shadows;
    The young flowers are blowing toward
        the west —
But the young, young children, O my brothers,
    They are weeping bitterly!   10
They are weeping in the playtime of the
    others,
    In the country of the free.

Do you question the young children in their
    sorrow,
    Why their tears are falling so?
The old man may weep for his to-morrow
    Which is lost in Long Ago;
The old tree is leafless in the forest,
    The old year is ending in the frost,
The old wound, if stricken, is the sorest,
    The old hope is hardest to be lost: 20
But the young, young children, O my brothers,
    Do you ask them why they stand
Weeping sore before the bosoms of their
    mothers,
    In our happy Fatherland?

They look up with their pale and sunken
    faces,
    And their looks are sad to see,
For the man's hoary anguish draws and
    presses
    Down the cheeks of infancy;
"Your old earth," they say, "is very dreary,
    Our young feet," they say, "are very
    weak!

Few paces have we taken, yet are weary — 31
    Our grave-rest is very far to seek:
Ask the agèd why they weep, and not the
    children,
    For the outside earth is cold,
And we young ones stand without, in our
    bewildering,
    And the graves are for the old:
"True," say the children, "it may happen
    That we die before our time:
Little Alice died last year, her grave is shapen
    Like a snowball, in the rime.   40
We looked into the pit prepared to take her:
    Was no room for any work in the close
    clay!
From the sleep wherein she lieth none will
    wake her
    Crying, 'Get up, little Alice! it is day.'
If you listen by that grave, in sun and shower,
    With your ear down, little Alice never
    cries;
Could we see her face, be sure we should not
    know her,
    For a smile has time for growing in her
    eyes:
And merry go her moments, lulled and stilled
    in
    The shroud by the kirk-chime.   50
It is good when it happens," say the children,
    "That we die before our time."

Alas, alas, the children! they are seeking
    Death in life as best to have:
They are binding up their hearts away from
    breaking,
    With a cerement from the grave.
Go out, children, from the mine and from
    the city,
    Sing out, children, as the little thrushes
    do;
Pluck your handfuls of the meadow-cowslips
    pretty,
    Laugh aloud, to feel your fingers let them
    through!   60
But they answer, "Are your cowslips of the
    meadows
    Like our weeds anear the mine?
Leave us quiet in the dark of the coal-shadows,
    From your pleasures fair and fine!

"For oh," say the children, "we are weary,
    And we cannot run or leap;
If we cared for any meadows, it were merely
    To drop down in them and sleep.

Our knees tremble sorely in the stooping,
    We fall upon our faces, trying to go ; 70
And, underneath our heavy eyelids drooping,
    The reddest flower would look as pale as
      snow.
For, all day, we drag our burden tiring,
    Through the coal-dark, underground ;
Or, all day, we drive the wheels of iron
    In the factories, round and round.

"For, all day, the wheels are droning,
    turning ;
    Their wind comes in our faces,
Till our hearts turn, our heads, with pulses
    burning,
    And the walls turn in their places : 80
Turns the sky in the high window, blank and
    reeling,
    Turns the long light that drops adown
      the wall,
Turn the black flies that crawl along the
    ceiling :
    All are turning, all the day, and we with
      all.
And all day the iron wheels are droning :
    And sometimes we could pray,
'O ye wheels,' (breaking out in a mad moan-
    ing)
    'Stop ! be silent for to-day !'"

Ay, be silent ! Let them hear each other
    breathing
    For a moment, mouth to mouth ! 90
Let them touch each other's hands, in a fresh
    wreathing
    Of their tender human youth !
Let them feel that this cold metallic motion
    Is not all the life God fashions or
      reveals :
Let them prove their living souls against the
    notion
    That they live in you, or under you, O
      wheels !
Still, all day, the iron wheels go onward,
    Grinding life down from its mark ;
And the children's souls, which God is calling
    sunward,
    Spin on blindly in the dark. 100

Now tell the poor young children, O my
    brothers,
    To look up to Him and pray ;
So the blessed One who blesseth all the
    others,
    Will bless them another day.

They answer, "Who is God that He should
    hear us,
    While the rushing of the iron wheels is
      stirred ?
When we sob aloud, the human creatures
    near us
    Pass by, hearing not, or answer not a
      word.
And we hear not (for the wheels in their
    resounding)
    Strangers speaking at the door : 110
Is it likely God, with angels singing round Him,
    Hears our weeping any more ?

"Two words, indeed, of praying we remember ;
    And at midnight's hour of harm,
'Our Father,' looking upward in the chamber,
    We say softly for a charm.
We know no other words, except 'Our Father,'
    And we think that, in some pause of
      angels' song,
God may pluck them with the silence sweet to
    gather,
    And hold both within His right hand
      which is strong. 120
'Our Father !' If He heard us, He would
    surely
    (For they call Him good and mild)
Answer, smiling down the steep world very
    purely,
    'Come and rest with me, my child.'

"But no !" say the children, weeping faster,
    "He is speechless as a stone :
And they tell us, of His image is the master
    Who commands us to work on.
Go to !" say the children, — "Up in Heaven,
    Dark, wheel-like, turning clouds are all
      we find : 130
Do not mock us ; grief has made us unbeliev-
    ing :
    We look up for God, but tears have made
      us blind."
Do you hear the children weeping and dis-
    proving,
    O my brothers, what ye preach ?
For God's possible is taught by His world's
    loving,
    And the children doubt of each.

And well may the children weep before you !
    They are weary ere they run ;
They have never seen the sunshine, nor the
    glory
    Which is brighter than the sun : 140

They know the grief of man, without its
    wisdom;
  They sink in man's despair, without its
    calm;
And slaves, without the liberty in Christdom,
  Are martyrs, by the pang without the
    palm:
Are worn as if with age, yet unretrievingly
  The harvest of its memories cannot
    reap, —
Are orphans of the earthly love and heav-
    enly.
    Let them weep! let them weep!

They look up with their pale and sunken
    faces,
  And their look is dread to see,   150
For they mind you of their angels in high
    places,
  With eyes turned on Deity.
"How long," they say, "how long, O cruel
    nation,
  Will you stand, to move the world, on a
    child's heart, —
Stifle down with a mailed heel its palpitation,
  And tread onward to your throne amid
    the mart?
Our blood splashes upward, O gold-heaper,
  And your purple shows your path!
But the child's sob in the silence curses deeper
  Than the strong man in his wrath." 160

A MUSICAL INSTRUMENT

What was he doing, the great god Pan,[1]
  Down in the reeds by the river?
Spreading ruin and scattering ban,
Splashing and paddling with hoofs of a goat,
And breaking the golden lilies afloat
  With the dragon-fly on the river?   6

He tore out a reed, the great god Pan,
  From the deep cool bed of the river,
The limpid water turbidly ran,
And the broken lilies a-dying lay,
And the dragon-fly had fled away,
  Ere he brought it out of the river.   12

High on the shore sat the great god Pan,
  While turbidly flowed the river,
And hacked and hewed as a great god can

[1] the goat-footed god, traditional inventor of
the shepherd's flute

With his hard bleak steel at the patient reed,
Till there was not a sign of the leaf indeed
  To prove it fresh from the river.   18

He cut it short, did the great god Pan,
  (How tall it stood in the river!),
Then drew the pith, like the heart of a man,
Steadily from the outside ring,
And notched the poor dry empty thing
  In holes as he sat by the river.   24

"This is the way," laughed the great god Pan,
  (Laughed while he sat by the river)
"The only way since gods began
To make sweet music, they could succeed."
Then dropping his mouth to a hole in the
    reed,
  He blew in power by the river.   30

Sweet, sweet, sweet, O Pan!
  Piercing sweet by the river!
Blinding sweet, O great god Pan!
The sun on the hill forgot to die,
And the lilies revived, and the dragon-fly
  Came back to dream on the river.   36

Yet half a beast is the great god Pan
  To laugh, as he sits by the river,
Making a poet out of a man:
The true gods sigh for the cost and pain —
For the reed which grows never more again
  As the reed with the reeds of the river.   42

ROBERT BROWNING (1812–1889)

CAVALIER TUNES

I. MARCHING ALONG

Kentish Sir Byng stood for his King,
Bidding the crop-headed[1] Parliament swing:
And, pressing a troop unable to stoop
And see the rogues flourish and honest folk
    droop,
Marched them along, fifty-score strong,
Great-hearted gentlemen, singing this song. 6

God for King Charles! Pym[2] and such carles
To the Devil that prompts 'em their treason-
    ous parles!

[1] short-haired, Roundheads   [2] Pym, Hampden,
Hazelrig, Fiennes, and Sir Harry Vane the
younger were prominent Parliamentarians.

Cavaliers, up! Lips from the cup,
Hands from the pasty, nor bite take nor sup
Till you're —
  CHORUS. — Marching along, fifty-score
        strong,
        Great-hearted gentlemen, sing-
        ing this song.   12

Hampden to hell, and his obsequies' knell
Serve [1] Hazelrig, Fiennes, and young Harry as
  well!
England, good cheer! Rupert [2] is near!
Kentish and loyalists, keep we not here,
  CHO. — Marching along, fifty-score strong,
        Great-hearted gentlemen, singing
        this song?   18

Then, God for King Charles! Pym and his
  snarls
To the Devil that pricks on such pestilent
  carles!
Hold by the right, you double your might;
So, onward to Nottingham,[3] fresh for the fight,
  CHO. — March we along, fifty-score strong,
        Great-hearted gentlemen, singing
        this song!   24

II. GIVE A ROUSE

King Charles, and who'll do him right now?
King Charles, and who's ripe for fight now?
Give a rouse: here's, in hell's despite now,
King Charles!   4

Who gave me the goods that went since?
Who raised me the house that sank once?
Who helped me to gold I spent since?
Who found me in wine you drank once?   8
  CHO. — King Charles, and who'll do him
        right now?
      King Charles, and who's ripe for
        fight now?
      Give a rouse: here's, in hell's
        despite now,
      King Charles!   12

To whom used my boy George quaff else,
By the old fool's side that begot him?
For whom did he cheer and laugh else,
While Noll's [4] damned troopers shot him?   16

[1] Let it serve [2] Prince Rupert, nephew of King
Charles and commander of his cavalry [3] where
the King's troops assembled in 1642 [4] Oliver
Cromwell

  CHO. — King Charles, and who'll do him
        right now?
      King Charles, and who's ripe for
        fight now?
      Give a rouse: here's, in hell's
        despite now,
      King Charles!   20

"HOW THEY BROUGHT THE GOOD NEWS FROM GHENT TO AIX"

(16—)

I sprang to the stirrup, and Joris, and he;
I galloped, Dirck galloped, we galloped all
  three;
"Good speed!" cried the watch, as the gate-
  bolts undrew;
"Speed!" echoed the wall to us galloping
  through;
Behind shut the postern, the lights sank
  to rest,
And into the midnight we galloped abreast. 6

Not a word to each other; we kept the great
  pace
Neck by neck, stride by stride, never changing
  our place;
I turned in my saddle and made its girths
  tight,
Then shortened each stirrup, and set the
  pique [1] right,
Rebuckled the check-strap, chained slacker
  the bit,
Nor galloped less steadily Roland a whit. 12

'Twas moonset at starting; but while we
  drew near
Lokeren, the cocks crew and twilight dawned
  clear;
At Boom, a great yellow star came out to see;
At Düffeld, 'twas morning as plain as could
  be;
And from Mecheln church-steeple we heard
  the half-chime,   17
So Joris broke silence with, "Yet there is
  time!"

At Aershot, up leaped of a sudden the sun,
And against him the cattle stood black every
  one,
To stare through the mist at us galloping past,
And I saw my stout galloper Roland at last,

[1] pommel

With resolute shoulders, each butting away 23
The haze, as some bluff river headland its
  spray:

And his low head and crest, just one sharp
  ear bent back
For my voice, and the other pricked out on
  his track;
And one eye's black intelligence, — ever that
  glance
O'er its white edge at me, his own master,
  askance!
And the thick heavy spume-flakes which aye
  and anon
His fierce lips shook upwards in galloping on.

By Hasselt, Dirck groaned; and cried Joris,
  "Stay spur!   31
Your Roos galloped bravely, the fault's not
  in her,
We'll remember at Aix" — for one heard the
  quick wheeze
Of her chest, saw the stretched neck and
  staggering knees,
And sunk tail, and horrible heave of the flank,
As down on her haunches she shuddered and
  sank.   36

So, we were left galloping, Joris and I,
Past Looz and past Tongres, no cloud in the
  sky;
The broad sun above laughed a pitiless laugh,
'Neath our feet broke the brittle bright stubble
  like chaff;
Till over by Dalhem a dome-spire sprang
  white,
And "Gallop," gasped Joris, "for Aix is in
  sight!"   42

"How they'll greet us!" — and all in a
  moment his roan
Rolled neck and croup over, lay dead as a
  stone;
And there was my Roland to bear the whole
  weight
Of the news which alone could save Aix from
  her fate,
With his nostrils like pits full of blood to the
  brim,   47
And with circles of red for his eye-sockets' rim.

Then I cast loose my buffcoat, each holster
  let fall,
Shook off both my jack-boots, let go belt and
  all,

Stood up in the stirrup, leaned, patted his ear,
Called my Roland his pet-name, my horse
  without peer;
Clapped my hands, laughed and sang, any
  noise, bad or good,   53
Till at length into Aix Roland galloped and
  stood.

And all I remember is — friends flocking
  round
As I sat with his head 'twixt my knees on the
  ground;
And no voice but was praising this Roland of
  mine,
As I poured down his throat our last measure
  of wine,
Which (the burgesses voted by common
  consent)
Was no more than his due who brought good
  news from Ghent.   60

SONG

Nay but you, who do not love her,
  Is she not pure gold, my mistress?
Holds earth aught — speak truth — above
  her?
  Aught like this tress, see, and this tress,
And this last fairest tress of all,
So fair, see, ere I let it fall?   6

Because you spend your lives in praising;
  To praise, you search the wide world over:
Then why not witness, calmly gazing,
  If earth holds aught — speak truth —
  above her?
Above this tress, and this, I touch
But cannot praise, I love so much!   12

EVELYN HOPE

Beautiful Evelyn Hope is dead!
  Sit and watch by her side an hour.
That is her book-shelf, this her bed;
  She plucked that piece of geranium-flower,
Beginning to die too, in the glass;
  Little has yet been changed, I think:
The shutters are shut, no light may pass
  Save two long rays through the hinge's
  chink.   8

Sixteen years old when she died!
  Perhaps she had scarcely heard my name;

It was not her time to love; beside,
  Her life had many a hope and aim,
Duties enough and little cares,
  And now was quiet, now astir,
Till God's hand beckoned unawares, —
  And the sweet white brow is all of her. 16

Is it too late then, Evelyn Hope?
  What, your soul was pure and true,
The good stars met in your horoscope,
  Made you of spirit, fire and dew —
And, just because I was thrice as old
  And our paths in the world diverged so wide,
Each was naught to each, must I be told?
  We were fellow mortals, naught beside? 24

No, indeed! for God above
  Is great to grant, as mighty to make,
And creates the love to reward the love:
  I claim you still, for my own love's sake!
Delayed it may be for more lives yet,
  Through worlds I shall traverse, not a few:
Much is to learn, much to forget
  Ere the time be come for taking you. 32

But the time will come, — at last it will,
  When, Evelyn Hope, what meant (I shall say)
In the lower earth, in the years long still,
  That body and soul so pure and gay?
Why your hair was amber, I shall divine,
  And your mouth of your own geranium's
    red —
And what you would do with me, in fine,
  In the new life come in the old one's stead.

I have lived (I shall say) so much since then,
  Given up myself so many times, 42
Gained me the gains of various men,
  Ransacked the ages, spoiled the climes;
Yet one thing, one, in my soul's full scope,
  Either I missed or itself missed me:
And I want and find you, Evelyn Hope!
  What is the issue? let us see! 48

I loved you, Evelyn, all the while!
  My heart seemed full as it could hold;
There was place and to spare for the frank
    young smile,
  And the red young mouth, and the hair's
    young gold.
So hush, — I will give you this leaf to keep:
  See, I shut it inside the sweet cold hand!
There, that is our secret: go to sleep! 55
  You will wake, and remember, and under-
    stand.

HOME–THOUGHTS, FROM ABROAD

Oh, to be in England
Now that April's there,
And whoever wakes in England
Sees, some morning, unaware,
That the lowest boughs and the brush-wood
    sheaf
Round the elm-tree bole are in tiny leaf,
While the chaffinch sings on the orchard bough
In England — now!
And after April, when May follows, 9
And the whitethroat builds, and all the
    swallows!
Hark, where my blossomed pear-tree in the
    hedge
Leans to the field and scatters on the clover
Blossoms and dewdrops — at the bent spray's
    edge —
That's the wise thrush; he sings each song
    twice over,
Lest you should think he never could recapture
  The first fine careless rapture!
And though the fields look rough with hoary
    dew,
All will be gay when noontide wakes anew
The buttercups, the little children's dower 19
— Far brighter than this gaudy melon-flower!

From Saul

XVII

"I have gone the whole round of creation:
    I saw and I spoke;
I, a work of God's hand for that purpose, re-
    ceived in my brain
And pronounced on the rest of his handwork
    — returned him again 110
His creation's approval or censure: I spoke
    as I saw:
I report, as a man may of God's work — all's
    love, yet all's law.
Now I lay down the judgeship he lent me.
    Each faculty tasked
To perceive him, has gained an abyss, where
    a dewdrop was asked.
Have I knowledge? confounded it shrivels at
    Wisdom laid bare.
Have I forethought? how purblind, how
    blank, to the Infinite Care!
Do I task any faculty highest, to image suc-
    cess?
I but open my eyes, — and perfection, no
    more and no less,

In the kind I imagined, full-fronts me, and
    God is seen God
In the star, in the stone, in the flesh, in the
    soul and the clod.   120
And thus looking within and around me, I
    ever renew
(With that stoop of the soul which in bending
    upraises it too)
The submission of man's nothing-perfect to
    God's all-complete,
As by each new obeisance in spirit, I climb to
    his feet.
Yet with all this abounding experience, this
    deity known,
I shall dare to discover some province, some
    gift of my own.
There's a faculty pleasant to exercise, hard to
    hoodwink,
I am fain to keep still in abeyance, (I laugh
    as I think)
Lest, insisting to claim and parade in it, wot
    ye, I worst
E'en the Giver in one gift. — Behold, I could
    love if I durst!   130
But I sink the pretension as fearing a man
    may o'ertake
God's own speed in the one way of love: I
    abstain for love's sake.
— What, my soul? see thus far and no
    farther? when doors great and small,
Nine-and-ninety flew ope at our touch, should
    the hundredth appall?
In the least things have faith, yet distrust in
    the greatest of all?
Do I find love so full in my nature, God's
    ultimate gift,
That I doubt his own love can compete with
    it? Here, the parts shift?
Here, the creature surpass the Creator, —
    the end, what Began?
Would I fain in my impotent yearning do
    all for this man,
And dare doubt he alone shall not help him,
    who yet alone can?   140
Would it ever have entered my mind, the
    bare will, much less power,
To bestow on this Saul what I sang of, the
    marvellous dower
Of the life he was gifted and filled with? to
    make such a soul,
Such a body, and then such an earth for
    insphering the whole?
And doth it not enter my mind (as my warm
    tears attest)

These good things being given, to go on, and
    give one more, the best?
Ay, to save and redeem and restore him, main-
    tain at the height
This perfection, — succeed with life's day-
    spring, death's minute of night?
Interpose at the difficult minute, snatch Saul
    the mistake,
Saul the failure, the ruin he seems now, —
    and bid him awake   150
From the dream, the probation, the prelude,
    to find himself set
Clear and safe in new light and new life, —
    a new harmony yet
To be run, and continued, and ended — who
    knows? — or endure!
The man taught enough by life's dream, of
    the rest to make sure;
By the pain-throb, triumphantly winning in-
    tensified bliss,
And the next world's reward and repose, by
    the struggles in this.

XVIII

"I believe it! 'Tis thou, God, that givest, 'tis
    I who receive:
In the first is the last, in thy will is my power
    to believe.
All's one gift: thou canst grant it moreover,
    as prompt to my prayer
As I breathe out this breath, as I open these
    arms to the air.   160
From thy will stream the worlds, life and
    nature, thy dread Sabaoth:[1]
I will? — the mere atoms despise me! Why
    am I not loth
To look that, even that in the face too? Why
    is it I dare
Think but lightly of such impuissance?
    What stops my despair?
This; — 'tis not what man Does which exalts
    him, but what man Would do!
See the King — I would help him but cannot,
    the wishes fall through.
Could I wrestle to raise him from sorrow,
    grow poor to enrich,
To fill up his life, starve my own out, I would
    — knowing which,
I know that my service is perfect. Oh, speak
    through me now!
Would I suffer for him that I love? So
    wouldst thou — so wilt thou!   170

[1] armies

So shall crown thee the topmost, ineffablest,
    uttermost crown —
And thy love fill infinitude wholly, nor leave
    up nor down
One spot for the creature to stand in! It is
    by no breath,
Turn of eye, wave of hand, that salvation joins
    issue with death!
As thy Love is discovered almighty, almighty
    be proved
Thy power, that exists with and for it, of
    being Beloved!
He who did most, shall bear most; the strong-
    est shall stand the most weak.
'Tis the weakness in strength, that I cry for!
    my flesh, that I seek
In the Godhead! I seek and I find it. O Saul,
    it shall be
A Face like my face that receives thee; a
    Man like to me,   180
Thou shalt love and be loved by, forever: a
    Hand like this hand
Shall throw open the gates of new life to
    thee! See the Christ stand!"

SONG

MY STAR

All that I know
    Of a certain star
Is, it can throw
    (Like the angled spar)
Now a dart of red,
    Now a dart of blue;
Till my friends have said
    They would fain see, too,
My star that dartles the red and the blue!
Then it stops like a bird: like a flower, hangs
    furled: 10
    They must solace themselves with the
    Saturn above it.
What matter to me if their star is a world?
    Mine has opened its soul to me; therefore
    I love it.

MY LAST DUCHESS

FERRARA

That's my last Duchess painted on the wall,
Looking as if she were alive. I call
That piece a wonder, now: Fra Pandolf's
    hands
Worked busily a day, and there she stands.

Will't please you sit and look at her? I said
"Fra Pandolf" by design, for never read
Strangers like you that pictured countenance,
The depth and passion of its earnest glance,
But to myself they turned (since none puts by
The curtain I have drawn for you, but I)   10
And seemed as they would ask me, if they
    durst,
How such a glance came there; so, not the
    first
Are you to turn and ask thus. Sir, 'twas not
Her husband's presence only, called that spot
Of joy into the Duchess' cheek: perhaps
Fra Pandolf chanced to say, "Her mantle laps
Over my lady's wrist too much," or "Paint
Must never hope to reproduce the faint
Half-flush that dies along her throat:" such
    stuff
Was courtesy, she thought, and cause enough
For calling up that spot of joy. She had   21
A heart — how shall I say? — too soon made
    glad,
Too easily impressed: she liked whate'er
She looked on, and her looks went every-
    where.
Sir, 'twas all one! My favour at her breast,
The dropping of the daylight in the West,
The bough of cherries some officious fool
Broke in the orchard for her, the white mule
She rode with round the terrace — all and
    each
Would draw from her alike the approving
    speech,
Or blush, at least. She thanked men, —
    good! but thanked   31
Somehow — I know not how — as if she
    ranked
My gift of a nine-hundred-years-old name
With anybody's gift. Who'd stoop to blame
This sort of trifling? Even had you skill
In speech — (which I have not) — to make
    your will
Quite clear to such an one, and say, "Just
    this
Or that in you disgusts me; here you miss,
Or there exceed the mark" — and if she let
Herself be lessoned so, nor plainly set   40
Her wits to yours, forsooth, and made excuse
— E'en then would be some stooping; and I
    choose
Never to stoop. Oh sir, she smiled, no doubt,
Whene'er I passed her; but who passed with-
    out
Much the same smile? This grew; I gave
    commands;

Then all smiles stopped together. There she
    stands
As if alive. Will't please you rise? We'll
    meet
The company below, then. I repeat,
The Count your master's known munificence
Is ample warrant that no just pretence   50
Of mine for dowry will be disallowed;
Though his fair daughter's self, as I avowed
At starting, is my object. Nay, we'll go
Together down, sir. Notice Neptune,
    though,
Taming a sea-horse, thought a rarity,
Which Claus of Innsbruck cast in bronze for
    me!

A GRAMMARIAN'S FUNERAL

SHORTLY AFTER THE REVIVAL OF LEARNING IN EUROPE

Let us begin and carry up this corpse,
    Singing together.
Leave we the common crofts, the vulgar
    thorpes
    Each in its tether
Sleeping safe on the bosom of the plain,
    Cared-for till cock-crow:
Look out if yonder be not day again
    Rimming the rock-row!
That's the appropriate country; there, man's
    thought,
    Rarer, intenser,   10
Self-gathered for an outbreak, as it ought,
    Chafes in the censer.
Leave we the unlettered plain its herd and
    crop;
    Seek we sepulture
On a tall mountain, cited to the top,
    Crowded with culture!
All the peaks soar, but one the rest excels;
    Clouds overcome it;
No! yonder sparkle is the citadel's
    Circling its summit.   20
Thither our path lies; wind we up the
    heights;
    Wait ye the warning?
Our low life was the level's and the night's;
    He's for the morning.
Step to a tune, square chests, erect each
    head,
    'Ware the beholders!
This is our master, famous, calm and dead,
    Borne on our shoulders.

Sleep, crop and herd! sleep, darkling thorpe
    and croft,
    Safe from the weather!   30
He, whom we convoy to his grave aloft,
    Singing together,
He was a man born with thy face and throat,
    Lyric Apollo!
Long he lived nameless: how should Spring
    take note
    Winter would follow?
Till lo, the little touch, and youth was gone!
    Cramped and diminished,
Moaned he, "New measures, other feet anon!
    My dance is finished"?   40
No, that's the world's way: (keep the moun-
    tain-side,
    Make for the city!)
He knew the signal, and stepped on with pride
    Over men's pity;
Left play for work, and grappled with the
    world
    Bent on escaping:
"What's in the scroll," quoth he, "thou
    keepest furled?
    Show me their shaping,
Theirs who most studied man, the bard and
    sage, —
    Give!" — So, he gowned him,   50
Straight got by heart that book to its last
    page:
    Learnèd, we found him.
Yea, but we found him bald too, eyes like
    lead,
    Accents uncertain:
"Time to taste life," another would have
    said,
    "Up with the curtain!"
This man said rather, "Actual life comes
    next?
    Patience a moment!
Grant I have mastered learning's crabbed text,
    Still there's the comment.   60
Let me know all! Prate not of most or least,
    Painful or easy!
Even to the crumbs I'd fain eat up the feast,
    Ay, nor feel queasy."
Oh, such a life as he resolved to live,
    When he had learned it,
When he had gathered all books had to give!
    Sooner, he spurned it.
Image the whole, then execute the parts —
    Fancy the fabric   70
Quite, ere you build, ere steel strike fire from
    quartz,
    Ere mortar dab brick!

(Here's the town-gate reached : there's the
　　market-place
　　Gaping before us.)
Yea, this in him was the peculiar grace
　　(Hearten our chorus !)
That before living he'd learn how to live —
　　No end to learning :
Earn the means first — God surely will con-
　　trive
　　Use for our earning.　　　　　　　　　80
Others mistrust and say, "But time escapes :
　　Live now or never !"
He said, "What's time? Leave Now for dogs
　　and apes !
　　Man has Forever."
Back to his book then : deeper drooped his
　　head :
　　Calculus[1] racked him :
Leaden before, his eyes grew dross of lead :
　　Tussis[2] attacked him.
"Now, master, take a little rest !" — not he !
　　(Caution redoubled,　　　　　　　　90
Step two abreast, the way winds narrowly !)
　　Not a whit troubled,
Back to his studies, fresher than at first,
　　Fierce as a dragon
He (soul-hydroptic with a sacred thirst)[3]
　　Sucked at the flagon.
Oh, if we draw a circle premature,
　　Heedless of far gain,
Greedy for quick returns of profit, sure
　　Bad is our bargain !　　　　　　　　100
Was it not great ? did not he throw on God,
　　(He loves the burthen) —
God's task to make the heavenly period
　　Perfect the earthen ?
Did not he magnify the mind, show clear
　　Just what it all meant ?
He would not discount life, as fools do here,
　　Paid by instalment.
He ventured neck or nothing — heaven's
　　success
　　Found, or earth's failure :　　　　　110
"Wilt thou trust death or not ?" He an-
　　swered "Yes !
　　Hence with life's pale lure !"
That low man seeks a little thing to do,
　　Sees it and does it :
This high man, with a great thing to pursue,
　　Dies ere he knows it.
That low man goes on adding one to one,
　　His hundred's soon hit :

This high man, aiming at a million,
　　Misses an unit.　　　　　　　　　　120
That, has the world here — should he need the
　　next,
　　Let the world mind him !
This, throws himself on God, and unperplexed
　　Seeking shall find him.
So, with the throttling hands of death at strife,
　　Ground he at grammar ;
Still, through the rattle, parts of speech were
　　rife :
　　While he could stammer
He settled *Hoti's* business — let it be ! —
　　Properly based *Oun* —　　　　　　130
Gave us the doctrine of the enclitic *De*,[1]
　　Dead from the waist down.
Well, here's the platform, here's the proper
　　place ;
　　Hail to your purlieus,
All ye highfliers of the feathered race,
　　Swallows and curlews !
Here's the top-peak ; the multitude below
　　Live, for they can, there :
This man decided not to Live but Know —
　　Bury this man there ?　　　　　　140
Here — here's his place, where meteors shoot,
　　clouds form,
　　Lightnings are loosened,
Stars come and go ! Let joy break with the
　　storm,
　　Peace let the dew send !
Lofty designs must close in like effects :
　　Loftily lying,
Leave him — still loftier than the world suspects
　　Living and dying.

"CHILDE[2] ROLAND TO THE DARK TOWER CAME"

(See Edgar's song in *Lear*)

My first thought was, he lied in every word,
　　That hoary cripple, with malicious eye
　　Askance to watch the working of his lie
On mine, and mouth scarce able to afford
Suppression of the glee, that pursed and scored
　　Its edge, at one more victim gained thereby.

What else should he be set for, with his staff ? 7
　　What, save to waylay with his lies, ensnare
　　All travellers who might find him posted
　　there,

---

[1] the stone　[2] a cough　[3] thirsty like one who
has dropsy

[1] minute but difficult problems of Greek
grammar　[2] a young knight

And ask the road? I guessed what skull-like
  laugh
Would break, what crutch 'gin write my
  epitaph
For pastime in the dusty thoroughfare, 12

If at his counsel I should turn aside
  Into that ominous tract which, all agree,
  Hides the Dark Tower. Yet acquiescingly
I did turn as he pointed: neither pride
Nor hope rekindling at the end descried, 17
So much as gladness that some end might be.

For, what with my whole world-wide wander-
  ing,
  What with my search drawn out through
  years, my hope
  Dwindled into a ghost not fit to cope
With that obstreperous joy success would
  bring, —
I hardly tried now to rebuke the spring
My heart made, finding failure in its scope.

As when a sick man very near to death 25
  Seems dead indeed, and feels begin and end
  The tears, and takes the farewell of each
  friend,
And hears one bid the other go, draw breath
Freelier outside, ("since all is o'er," he saith,
  "And the blow fallen no grieving can
  amend;") 30

While some discuss if near the other graves
  Be room enough for this, and when a day
  Suits best for carrying the corpse away,
With care about the banners, scarves and
  staves:
And still the man hears all, and only craves 35
  He may not shame such tender love and
  stay.

Thus, I had so long suffered in this quest,
  Heard failure prophesied so oft, been writ
  So many times among "The Band" — to
  wit,
The knights who to the Dark Tower's search
  addressed 40
Their steps — that just to fail as they, seemed
  best,
  And all the doubt was now — should I be
  fit?

So, quiet as despair, I turned from him,
  That hateful cripple, out of his highway
  Into the path he pointed. All the day 45

Had been a dreary one at best, and dim
Was settling to its close, yet shot one grim
  Red leer to see the plain catch its estray.

For mark! no sooner was I fairly found
  Pledged to the plain, after a pace or two,
  Than, pausing to throw backward a last
  view
O'er the safe road, 'twas gone; grey plain all
  round:
Nothing but plain to the horizon's bound.
  I might go on; naught else remained to do.

So, on I went. I think I never saw 55
  Such starved ignoble nature; nothing
  throve:
  For flowers — as well expect a cedar grove!
But cockle, spurge, according to their law
Might propagate their kind, with none to
  awe, 59
  You'd think: a burr had been a treasure
  trove.

No! penury, inertness and grimace,
  In some strange sort, were the land's por-
  tion. "See
  Or shut your eyes," said Nature peevishly,
"It nothing skills:[1] I cannot help my case:
'Tis the Last Judgment's fire must cure this
  place,
  Calcine its clods and set my prisoners free."

If there pushed any ragged thistle-stalk 67
  Above its mates, the head was chopped; the
  bents[2]
  Were jealous else. What made those holes
  and rents
In the dock's harsh swarth leaves, bruised as
  to balk
All hope of greenness? 'tis a brute must
  walk
  Pashing their life out, with a brute's intents.

As for the grass, it grew as scant as hair 73
  In leprosy; thin dry blades pricked the
  mud
  Which underneath looked kneaded up with
  blood.
One stiff blind horse, his every bone a-stare,
Stood stupefied, however he came there: 77
  Thrust out past service from the devil's
  stud!

[1] it makes no difference [2] the old stalks of
weeds or grass

Alive? he might be dead for aught I know,
  With that red gaunt and colloped[1] neck
    a-strain,
  And shut eyes underneath the rusty mane;
Seldom went such grotesqueness with such
    woe;
I never saw a brute I hated so;
  He must be wicked to deserve such pain. 84

I shut my eyes and turned them on my heart.
  As a man calls for wine before he fights,
  I asked one draught of earlier, happier sights,
Ere fitly I could hope to play my part.
  Think first, fight afterwards — the soldier's
    art:
  One taste of the old time sets all to rights. 90

Not it! I fancied Cuthbert's reddening face
  Beneath its garniture of curly gold,
  Dear fellow, till I almost felt him fold
An arm in mine to fix me to the place,
  That way he used. Alas, one night's disgrace!
  Out went my heart's new fire and left it
    cold. 96

Giles then, the soul of honour — there he
    stands
  Frank as ten years ago when knighted first.
  What honest man should dare (he said) he
    durst.
Good — but the scene shifts — faugh! what
    hangman hands
  Pin to his breast a parchment? His own
    bands
  Read it. Poor traitor, spit upon and curst!

Better this present than a past like that; 103
  Back therefore to my darkening path again!
  No sound, no sight as far as eye could strain.
Will the night send a howlet or a bat?
  I asked: when something on the dismal flat
  Came to arrest my thoughts and change
    their train. 108

A sudden little river crossed my path
  As unexpected as a serpent comes.
  No sluggish tide congenial to the glooms;
This, as it frothed by, might have been a bath
For the fiend's glowing hoof — to see the
    wrath
  Of its black eddy bespate[2] with flakes and
    spumes.

So petty yet so spiteful! All along,   115
  Low scrubby alders kneeled down over it;
  Drenched willows flung them headlong in a
    fit
Of mute despair, a suicidal throng:
The river which had done them all the wrong,
  Whate'er that was, rolled by, deterred no
    whit.

Which, while I forded, — good saints, how I
    feared   121
  To set my foot upon a dead man's cheek,
  Each step, or feel the spear I thrust to seek
For hollows, tangled in his hair or beard!
— It may have been a water-rat I speared,
  But, ugh! it sounded like a baby's shriek.

Glad was I when I reached the other bank. 127
  Now for a better country. Vain presage!
  Who were the strugglers, what war did they
    wage,
Whose savage trample thus could pad the
    dank
Soil to a plash? Toads in a poisoned tank,
  Or wild cats in a red-hot iron cage —   132

The fight must so have seemed in that fell
    cirque.
  What penned them there, with all the plain
    to choose?
  No footprint leading to that horrid mews,
None out of it. Mad brewage set to work
Their brains, no doubt, like galley-slaves the
    Turk
  Pits for his pastime, Christians against Jews.

And more than that — a furlong on — why,
    there!   139
  What bad use was that engine for, that
    wheel,
  Or brake, not wheel — that harrow fit to
    reel
Men's bodies out like silk? with all the air[1]
Of Tophet's tool,[2] on earth left unaware, 143
  Or brought to sharpen its rusty teeth of
    steel.

Then came a bit of stubbed ground, once a
    wood,
  Next a marsh, it would seem, and now
    mere earth
  Desperate and done with: (so a fool finds
    mirth,

---

[1] Used of the folds or ridges of the horse's
withered neck.   [2] bespattered

[1] look   [2] an instrument of hell

Makes a thing and then mars it, till his mood
Changes and off he goes!) within a rood —
Bog, clay and rubble, sand and stark black
    dearth.   150

Now blotches rankling, coloured gay and grim,
    Now patches where some leanness of the
        soil's
    Broke into moss or substances like boils;
Then came some palsied oak, a cleft in him
Like a distorted mouth that splits its rim
    Gaping at death, and dies while it recoils

And just as far as ever from the end!   157
    Naught in the distance but the evening,
        naught
    To point my footstep further! At the
        thought,
A great black bird, Apollyon's bosom-friend,
Sailed past, nor beat his wide wing dragon-
        penned [1]
    That brushed my cap — perchance the
        guide I sought.   162

For, looking up, aware I somehow grew,
    'Spite of the dusk, the plain had given place
    All round to mountains — with such name
        to grace
Mere ugly heights and heaps now stolen in
        view.
How thus they had surprised me, — solve it,
        you!
    How to get from them was no clearer case.

Yet half I seemed to recognise some trick   169
    Of mischief happened to me, God knows
        when —
    In a bad dream perhaps. Here ended, then,
Progress this way. When, in the very nick
Of giving up, one time more, came a click   173
    As when a trap shuts — you're inside the
        den!

Burningly it came on me all at once,
    This was the place! those two hills on the
        right,
    Crouched like two bulls locked horn in horn
        in fight;
While to the left, a tall scalped mountain . . .
        Dunce,
Dotard, a-dozing at the very nonce,[2]
    After a life spent training for the sight!   180

What in the midst lay but the Tower itself?
    The round squat turret, blind as the fool's
        heart,
    Built of brown stone, without a counterpart
In the whole world. The tempest's mocking
        elf
Points to the shipman thus the unseen shelf
He strikes on, only when the timbers start.

Not see? because of night perhaps? — why,
        day   187
    Came back again for that! before it left,
    The dying sunset kindled through a cleft:
The hills, like giants at a hunting, lay,
Chin upon hand, to see the game at bay, —
    "Now stab and end the creature — to the
        heft!"   192

Not hear? when noise was everywhere! it
        tolled
    Increasing like a bell. Names in my ears,
    Of all the lost adventurers my peers, —
How such a one was strong, and such was bold,
And such was fortunate, yet each of old
    Lost, lost! one moment knelled the woe of
        years.   198

There they stood, ranged along the hillsides,
        met
    To view the last of me, a living frame
    For one more picture! in a sheet of flame
I saw them and I knew them all. And yet
Dauntless the slug-horn to my lips I set,
    And blew. "*Childe Roland to the Dark
        Tower came.*"   204

FRA LIPPO LIPPI

I am poor brother Lippo, by your leave!
You need not clap your torches to my face.
Zooks,[1] what's to blame? you think you see a
        monk!
What, 'tis past midnight, and you go the
        rounds,
And here you catch me at an alley's end
Where sportive ladies leave their doors ajar?
The Carmine's my cloister: hunt it up,
Do, — harry out, if you must show your zeal,
Whatever rat, there, haps on his wrong hole,
And nip each softling of a wee white mouse,   10
Weke, weke, that's crept to keep him company!
Aha, you know your betters! Then, you'll take

---

[1] provided with dragon feathers; cf. p. 240
[2] critical moment

[1] a mincing oath

Your hand away that's fiddling on my throat,
And please to know me likewise.   Who am I?
Why, one, sir, who is lodging with a friend
Three streets off — he's a certain . . . how
    d'ye call?
Master — a . . . Cosimo of the Medici,[1]
I' the house that caps the corner.   Boh! you
    were best!
Remember and tell me, the day you're hanged,
How you affected such a gullet's-gripe!   20
But you, sir,[2] it concerns you that your knaves
Pick up a manner nor discredit you:
Zooks, are we pilchards, that they sweep the
    streets
And count fair prize what comes into their
    net?
He's Judas to a tittle, that man is!
Just such a face!   Why, sir, you make amends.
Lord, I'm not angry!   Bid your hangdogs go
Drink out this quarter-florin to the health
Of the munificent House that harbours me
(And many more beside, lads! more beside!)
And all's come square again.   I'd like his face —
His, elbowing on his comrade in the door   32
With the pike and lantern, — for the slave
    that holds
John Baptist's head a-dangle by the hair
With one hand ("Look you, now," as who
    should say)
And his weapon in the other, yet unwiped!
It's not your chance to have a bit of chalk,
A wood-coal or the like? or you should see!
Yes, I'm the painter, since you style me so.
What, brother Lippo's doings, up and down,
You know them and they take you? like
    enough!   41
I saw the proper twinkle in your eye —
'Tell you, I liked your looks at very first.
Let's sit and set things straight now, hip to
    haunch.
Here's spring come, and the nights one makes
    up bands
To roam the town and sing out carnival,
And I've been three weeks shut within my
    mew,
A-painting for the great man, saints and saints
And saints again.   I could not paint all
    night —   49
Ouf!   I leaned out of window for fresh air.
There came a hurry of feet and little feet,
A sweep of lute-strings, laughs, and whifts of
    song, —

[1] Cosimo de' Medici, the leading citizen of
Florence [2] the leader of the band of watchmen

Flower o' the broom,
Take away love, and our earth is a tomb!
Flower o' the quince,
I let Lisa go, and what good in life since?
Flower o' the thyme — and so on.   Round they
    went.[1]
Scarce had they turned the corner when a
    titter
Like the skipping of rabbits by moonlight, —
    three slim shapes,
And a face that looked up . . . zooks, sir,
    flesh and blood,   60
That's all I'm made of!   Into shreds it went,
Curtain and counterpane and coverlet,
All the bed-furniture — a dozen knots,
There was a ladder!   Down I let myself,
Hands and feet, scrambling somehow, and so
    dropped,
And after them.   I came up with the fun
Hard by Saint Laurence,[2] hail fellow, well
    met, —
Flower o' the rose,
If I've been merry, what matter who knows?
And so as I was stealing back again   70
To get to bed and have a bit of sleep
Ere I rise up to-morrow and go work
On Jerome[3] knocking at his poor old breast
With his great round stone to subdue the
    flesh,
You snap me of the sudden.   Ah, I see!
Though your eye twinkles still, you shake your
    head —
Mine's shaved — a monk, you say — the
    sting's in that!
If Master Cosimo announced himself,
Mum's the word naturally; but a monk!
Come, what am I a beast for? tell us, now!   80
I was a baby when my mother died
And father died and left me in the street.
I starved there, God knows how, a year or two
On fig-skins, melon-parings, rinds and shucks,
Refuse and rubbish.   One fine frosty day,
My stomach being empty as your hat,
The wind doubled me up and down I went.
Old Aunt Lapaccia trussed[4] me with one hand,
(Its fellow was a stinger as I knew)
And so along the wall, over the bridge,   90
By the straight cut to the convent.   Six words
    there,
While I stood munching my first bread that
    month:

[1] *i.e.*, they sang in turn [2] the famous church
of San Lorenzo [3] an ascetic, and one of the four
greatest church fathers [4] seized

"So, boy, you're minded," quoth the good fat father,
Wiping his own mouth, 'twas refection-time,—
"To quit this very miserable world?
Will you renounce" . . . "the mouthful of bread?" thought I;
"By no means!" Brief, they made a monk of me;
I did renounce the world, its pride and greed,
Palace, farm, villa, shop, and banking-house,
Trash, such as these poor devils of Medici 100
Have given their hearts to — all at eight years old.
Well, sir, I found in time, you may be sure,
'Twas not for nothing — the good bellyful,
The warm serge and the rope that goes all round,
And day-long blessed idleness beside!
"Let's see what the urchin's fit for" — that came next.
Not overmuch their way, I must confess.
Such a to-do! They tried me with their books;
Lord, they'd have taught me Latin in pure waste!
Flower o' the clove, 110
All the Latin I construe is "amo," I love!
But, mind you, when a boy starves in the streets
Eight years together, as my fortune was,
Watching folk's faces to know who will fling
The bit of half-stripped grape-bunch he desires,
And who will curse or kick him for his pains,—
Which gentleman processional[1] and fine,
Holding a candle to the Sacrament,
Will wink and let him lift a plate and catch
The droppings of the wax to sell again, 120
Or holla for the Eight[2] and have him whipped,
How say I? — nay, which dog bites, which lets drop
His bone from the heap of offal in the street,—
Why, soul and sense of him grow sharp alike,
He learns the look of things, and none the less
For admonition from the hunger-pinch.
I had a store of such remarks, be sure,
Which, after I found leisure, turned to use.
I drew men's faces on my copy-books,
Scrawled them within the antiphonary's[3] marge, 130
Joined-legs and arms to the long music-notes,
Found eyes and nose and chin for A's and B's,

And made a string of pictures of the world
Betwixt the ins and outs of verb and noun,
On the wall, the bench, the door.   The monks looked black.
"Nay," quoth the Prior, "turn him out, d'ye say?
In no wise.   Lose a crow and catch a lark.
What if at last we get our man of parts,
We Carmelites, like those Camaldolese[1] 139
And Preaching Friars,[2] to do our church up fine
And put the front on it that ought to be!"
And hereupon he bade me daub away.
Thank you! my head being crammed, the walls a blank,
Never was such prompt disemburdening.
First, every sort of monk, the black and white,
I drew them, fat and lean: then, folk at church,
From good old gossips waiting to confess
Their cribs[3] of barrel-droppings, candle-ends,—
To the breathless fellow at the altar-foot,
Fresh from his murder, safe and sitting there
With the little children round him in a row 151
Of admiration, half for his beard and half
For that white anger of his victim's son
Shaking a fist at him with one fierce arm,
Signing himself with the other because of Christ
(Whose sad face on the cross sees only this
After the passion of a thousand years)
Till some poor girl, her apron o'er her head,
(Which the intense eyes looked through) came at eve
On tiptoe, said a word, dropped in a loaf, 160
Her pair of earrings and a bunch of flowers
(The brute took growling), prayed, and so was gone.
I painted all, then cried "'Tis ask and have;
Choose, for more's ready!" — laid the ladder flat,
And showed my covered bit of cloister-wall.
The monks closed in a circle and praised loud
Till checked, taught what to see and not to see,
Being simple bodies, — "That's the very man!
Look at the boy who stoops to pat the dog!
That woman's like the Prior's niece who comes
To care about his asthma: it's the life!" 171
But there my triumph's straw-fire flared and funked;
Their betters took their turn to see and say:

---

[1] walking in procession with the Sacrament
[2] the magistrates   [3] book of antiphons or responsive songs

[1] Benedictine monks at Camaldoli   [2] Dominicans; their painter was Fra Angelico   [3] thefts

The Prior and the learned pulled a face
And stopped all that in no time. "How?
　　what's here?
Quite from the mark of painting, bless us all!
Faces, arms, legs, and bodies like the true
As much as pea and pea! it's devil's-game!
Your business is not to catch men with show,
With homage to the perishable clay,　　180
But lift them over it, ignore it all,
Make them forget there's such a thing as flesh.
Your business is to paint the souls of men —
Man's soul, and it's a fire, smoke . . . no, it's
　　not . . .
It's vapour done up like a new-born babe —
(In that shape when you die it leaves your
　　mouth)
It's . . . well, what matters talking, it's the
　　soul!
Give us no more of body than shows soul!
Here's Giotto,[1] with his Saint a-praising
　　God,
That sets us praising, — why not stop with
　　him?　　190
Why put all thoughts of praise out of our head
With wonder at lines, colours, and what not?
Paint the soul, never mind the legs and arms!
Rub all out, try at it a second time.
Oh, that white smallish female with the
　　breasts,
She's just my niece . . . Herodias,[2] I would
　　say, —
Who went and danced and got men's heads
　　cut off!
Have it all out!" Now, is this sense, I ask?
A fine way to paint soul, by painting body
So ill, the eye can't stop there, must go further
And can't fare worse! Thus, yellow does for
　　white　　201
When what you put for yellow's simply black,
And any sort of meaning looks intense
When all beside itself means and looks naught.
Why can't a painter lift each foot in turn,
Left foot and right foot, go a double step,
Make his flesh liker and his soul more like,
Both in their order? Take the prettiest face,
The Prior's niece . . . patron-saint — is it so
　　pretty
You can't discover if it means hope, fear,　　210
Sorrow or joy? won't beauty go with these?
Suppose I've made her eyes all right and blue,
Can't I take breath and try to add life's flash,

And then add soul and heighten them three-
　　fold?
Or say there's beauty with no soul at all —
(I never saw it — put the case the same —)
If you get simple beauty and naught else,
You get about the best thing God invents:
That's somewhat: and you'll find the soul you
　　have missed,
Within yourself, when you return him thanks.
"Rub all out!" Well, well, there's my life,
　　in short,　　221
And so the thing has gone on ever since.
I'm grown a man no doubt, I've broken
　　bounds:
You should not take a fellow eight years old
And make him swear to never kiss the girls.
I'm my own master, paint now as I please —
Having a friend, you see, in the Corner-house!
Lord, it's fast holding by the rings in front —
Those great rings serve more purposes than
　　just
To plant a flag in, or tie up a horse!　　230
And yet the old schooling sticks, the old grave
　　eyes
Are peeping o'er my shoulder as I work,
The heads shake still — "It's art's decline,
　　my son!
You're not of the true painters, great and old:
Brother Angelico's[1] the man, you'll find;
Brother Lorenzo[2] stands his single peer:
Fag on at flesh, you'll never make the third!"
Flower o' the pine,
You keep your mistr . . . manners, and I'll
　　stick to mine!
I'm not the third, then: bless us, they must
　　know!　　240
Don't you think they're the likeliest to know,
They with their Latin? So, I swallow my
　　rage,
Clench my teeth, suck my lips in tight, and
　　paint
To please them — sometimes do and some-
　　times don't;
For, doing most, there's pretty sure to come
A turn, some warm eve finds me at my
　　saints —
A laugh, a cry, the business of the world —
(*Flower o' the peach,*
Death for us all, and his own life for each!)　　249
And my whole soul revolves, the cup runs over,
The world and life's too big to pass for a dream,

[1] the first great Italian painter (1276?-1337)
[2] The Prior's memory is at fault, cf. *Matt.*
xiv: 6.

[1] Giovanni da Fiesole, called Fra Angelico
from his fondness for painting angels [2] Lorenzo
Monaco, of Sienna

And I do these wild things in sheer despite,
And play the fooleries you catch me at,
In pure rage! The old mill-horse, out at grass
After hard years, throws up his stiff heels so,
Although the miller does not preach to him
The only good of grass is to make chaff.
What would men have? Do they like grass or
no —
May they or mayn't they? all I want's the
thing
Settled forever one way. As it is, 260
You tell too many lies and hurt yourself:
You don't like what you only like too much.
You do like what, if given you at your word,
You find abundantly detestable.
For me, I think I speak as I was taught;
I always see the garden and God there
A-making man's wife: and, my lesson learned,
The value and significance of flesh,
I can't unlearn ten minutes afterwards.

You understand me: I'm a beast, I know.
But see, now — why, I see as certainly 271
As that the morning-star's about to shine,
What will hap some day. We've a youngster
here
Comes to our convent, studies what I do,
Slouches and stares and lets no atom drop:
His name is Guidi[1] — he'll not mind the
monks —
They call him Hulking Tom,[2] he lets them
talk —
He picks my practice up — he'll paint apace,
I hope so — though I never live so long,
I know what's sure to follow. You be judge!
You speak no Latin more than I, belike; 281
However you're my man, you've seen the world
— The beauty and the wonder and the power,
The shapes of things, their colours, lights and
shades,
Changes, surprises, — and God made it all!
— For what? Do you feel thankful, ay or no,
For this fair town's face, yonder river's line,
The mountain round it and the sky above,
Much more the figures of man, woman, child,
These are the frame to? What's it all about?
To be passed over, despised? or dwelt upon,
Wondered at? oh, this last of course! — you
say. 292
But why not do as well as say, — paint these
Just as they are, careless what comes of it?
God's works — paint any one, and count it
crime

[1] Tommaso Guidi (1401-28) [2] Masaccio

To let a truth slip. Don't object, "His works
Are here already; nature is complete:
Suppose you reproduce her — (which you
can't)
There's no advantage! you must beat her,
then."
For, don't you mark? we're made so that we
love 300
First when we see them painted, things we
have passed
Perhaps a hundred times nor cared to see;
And so they are better, painted — better to us,
Which is the same thing. Art was given for
that;
God uses us to help each other so,
Lending our minds out. Have you noticed,
now,
Your cullion's hanging face! A bit of chalk,
And trust me but you should, though! How
much more,
If I drew higher things with the same truth!
That were to take the Prior's pulpit-place, 310
Interpret God to all of you! Oh, oh,
It makes me mad to see what men shall do
And we in our graves! This world's no blot
for us,
Nor blank; it means intensely, and means
good:
To find its meaning is my meat and drink.
"Ay, but you don't so instigate to prayer!"
Strikes in the Prior: "when your meaning's
plain
It does not say to folk — remember matins,
Or, mind you fast next Friday!" Why, for
this
What need of art at all? A skull and bones,
Two bits of stick nailed crosswise, or, what's
best, 321
A bell to chime the hour with, does as well.
I painted a Saint Laurence[1] six months since
At Prato,[2] splashed the fresco in fine style:
"How looks my painting, now the scaffold's
down?"
I ask a brother: "Hugely," he returns —
"Already not one phiz of your three slaves
Who turn the Deacon off his toasted side,[3]
But's scratched and prodded to our heart's
content,
The pious people have so eased their own 330
With coming to say prayers there in a rage:
We get on fast to see the bricks beneath.

[1] a martyr who was broiled on a gridiron
[2] twelve miles west of Florence [3] He asked to
be turned over, as one side was "done."

Expect another job this time next year,
For pity and religion grow i' the crowd —
Your painting serves its purpose!" Hang the
    fools!

— That is — you'll not mistake an idle word
Spoke in a huff by a poor monk, God wot,
Tasting the air this spicy night which turns
The unaccustomed head like Chianti wine!
Oh, the church knows! don't misreport me,
    now!   340
It's natural a poor monk out of bounds
Should have his apt word to excuse himself:
And hearken how I plot to make amends.
I have bethought me: I shall paint a piece
. . . There's for you! Give me six months,
    then go, see
Something in Sant' Ambrogio's![1] Bless the
    nuns!
They want a cast o' my office. I shall paint
God in the midst, Madonna and her babe,
Ringed by a bowery, flowery angel-brood,
Lilies and vestments and white faces, sweet
As puff on puff of grated orris-root   351
When ladies crowd to Church at midsummer.
And then i' the front, of course a saint or
    two —
Saint John,[2] because he saves the Florentines,
Saint Ambrose, who puts down in black and
    white
The convent's friends and gives them a long
    day,
And Job, I must have him there past mistake,
The man of Uz (and Us without the z,
Painters who need his patience). Well, all
    these
Secured at their devotion, up shall come   360
Out of a corner when you least expect,
As one by a dark stair into a great light,
Music and talking, who but Lippo! I! —
Mazed, motionless, and moonstruck — I'm
    the man!
Back I shrink — what is this I see and
    hear?
I, caught up with my monk's-things by mis-
    take,
My old serge gown and rope that goes all
    round,
I, in this presence, this pure company!
Where's a hole, where's a corner for escape?
Then steps a sweet, angelic slip of a thing   370

[1] a convent dedicated to St. Ambrose (340? –
397), one of the four greatest church fathers
[2] John the Baptist, patron saint of Florence

Forward, puts out a soft palm — "Not so
    fast!"
— Addresses the celestial presence, "nay —
He made you and devised you, after all,
Though he's none of you! Could Saint John
    there draw —
His camel-hair made up a painting-brush?
We come to brother Lippo for all that,
Iste perfecit opus!"[1] So, all smile —
I shuffle sideways with my blushing face
Under the cover of a hundred wings   379
Thrown like a spread of kirtles when you're
    gay
And play hot cockles, all the doors being shut,
Till, wholly unexpected, in there pops
The hothead husband! Thus I scuttle off
To some safe bench behind, not letting go
The palm of her, the little lily thing
That spoke the good word for me in the nick,
Like the Prior's niece . . . Saint Lucy, I
    would say.
And so all's saved for me, and for the church
A pretty picture gained. Go, six months
    hence!
Your hand, sir, and good-by: no lights, no
    lights!   390
The street's hushed, and I know my own way
    back,
Don't fear me! There's the grey beginning.
    Zooks!

ONE WORD MORE

TO E. B. B.

LONDON, SEPTEMBER, 1855

I

There they are, my fifty men and women
Naming me the fifty poems finished!
Take them, Love, the book and me together;
Where the heart lies, let the brain lie also.

II

Rafael made a century of sonnets,
Made and wrote them in a certain volume
Dinted with the silver-pointed pencil
Else he only used to draw Madonnas:
These, the world might view — but one, the
    volume.
Who that one, you ask? Your heart instructs
    you.

[1] "He painted the picture."

Did she live and love it all her lifetime? 11
Did she drop, his lady of the sonnets,
Die, and let it drop beside her pillow
Where it lay in place of Rafael's glory,
Rafael's cheek so duteous and so loving —
Cheek, the world was wont to hail a painter's,
Rafael's cheek, her love had turned a poet's?

III

You and I would rather read that volume,
(Taken to his beating bosom by it)
Lean and list the bosom-beats of Rafael, 20
Would we not? than wonder at Madonnas —
Her, San Sisto [1] names, and Her, Foligno, [2]
Her, that visits Florence in a vision, [3]
Her, that's left with lilies in the Louvre [4] —
Seen by us and all the world in circle.

IV

You and I will never read that volume.
Guido Reni, [5] like his own eye's apple
Guarded long the treasure-book and loved it.
Guido Reni dying, all Bologna
Cried, and the world cried too, "Ours, the
    treasure!" 30
Suddenly, as rare things will, it vanished.

V

Dante once prepared to paint an angel:
Whom to please? You whisper "Beatrice." [6]
While he mused and traced it and retraced it,
(Peradventure with a pen corroded
Still by drops of that hot ink he dipped for,
When, his left-hand i' the hair o' the wicked, [7]
Back he held the brow and pricked its stigma,
Bit into the live man's flesh for parchment,
Loosed him, laughed to see the writing rankle,
Let the wretch go festering through Flor-
    ence) —
Dante, who loved well because he hated,
Hated wickedness that hinders loving,
Dante standing, studying his angel, —
In there broke the folk of his Inferno.

---

[1] the Sistine Madonna, now in Dresden [2] the
Madonna di Foligno, now in the Vatican at Rome
[3] the Madonna del Granduca, representing her as
appearing to a votary in a vision [4] In the Louvre
at Paris, the Madonna called La Belle Jardinière
is seated in a garden. [5] a Florentine painter
(1575–1642) [6] Beatrice Portinari, Dante's ideal
love [7] cf. *Inferno*, xxxii, 97

AE

Says he — "Certain people of importance"
(Such he gave his daily dreadful line to)
"Entered and would seize, forsooth, the poet."
Says the poet — "Then I stopped my paint-
    ing."

VI

You and I would rather see that angel, 50
Painted by the tenderness of Dante,
Would we not? — than read a fresh Inferno.

VII

You and I will never see that picture.
While he mused on love and Beatrice,
While he softened o'er his outlined angel,
In they broke, those "people of importance:"
We and Bice [1] bear the loss forever.

VIII

What of Rafael's sonnets, Dante's picture?
This: no artist lives and loves, that longs
    not
Once, and only once, and for one only, 60
(Ah, the prize!) to find his love a language
Fit and fair and simple and sufficient —
Using nature that's an art to others,
Not, this one time, art that's turned his
    nature.
Ay, of all the artists living, loving,
None but would forego his proper dowry, —
Does he paint? he fain would write a poem, —
Does he write? he fain would paint a picture,
Put to proof art alien to the artist's,
Once, and only once, and for one only, 70
So to be the man and leave the artist,
Gain the man's joy, miss the artist's sorrow.

IX

Wherefore? Heaven's gift takes earth's
    abatement!
He who smites the rock and spreads the
    water, [2]
Bidding drink and live a crowd beneath him,
Even he, the minute makes immortal,
Proves, perchance, but mortal in the minute,
Desecrates, belike, the deed in doing.
While he smites, how can he but remember,
So he smote before, in such a peril, 80
When they stood and mocked — "Shall smit-
    ing help us?"

---

[1] diminutive of Beatrice [2] Moses, cf. *Num.* xx.

When they drank and sneered — "A stroke is
    easy!"
When they wiped their mouths and went their
    journey,
Throwing him for thanks — "But drought
    was pleasant."
Thus old memories mar the actual triumph;
Thus the doing savours of disrelish;
Thus achievement lacks a gracious somewhat;
O'er-importuned brows becloud the mandate,
Carelessness or consciousness — the gesture.
For he bears an ancient wrong about him, 90
Sees and knows again those phalanxed faces,
Hears, yet one time more, the 'customed prel-
    ude —
"How shouldst thou of all men, smite, and
    save us?"
Guesses what is like to prove the sequel —
"Egypt's flesh-pots[1] — nay, the drought was
    better."

X

Oh, the crowd must have emphatic warrant!
Theirs, the Sinai-forehead's cloven brilliance,[2]
Right-arm's rod-sweep, tongue's imperial fiat.
Never dares the man put off the prophet.

XI

Did he love one face from out the thousands,
(Were she Jethro's daughter,[3] white and
    wifely,   101
Were she but the Æthiopian bondslave,)[4]
He would envy yon dumb patient camel,
Keeping a reserve of scanty water
Meant to save his own life in the desert;
Ready in the desert to deliver
(Kneeling down to let his breast be opened)
Hoard and life together for his mistress.

XII

I shall never, in the years remaining,
Paint you pictures, no, nor carve you statues,
Make you music that should all-express me;
So it seems: I stand on my attainment.   112
This of verse alone, one life allows me;
Verse and nothing else have I to give you.
Other heights in other lives, God willing:
All the gifts from all the heights, your own,
    Love!

---

[1] cf. *Exodus* xvi : 3   [2] *Exodus* xxxiv : 29   [3] *Exodus*
ii : 21   [4] *Numbers* xii : 1

XIII

Yet a semblance of resource avails us —
Shade so finely touched, love's sense must
    seize it.
Take these lines, look lovingly and nearly,
Lines I write the first time and the last time.
He who works in fresco, steals a hair-brush,
Curbs the liberal hand, subservient proudly,
Cramps his spirit, crowds its all in little, 123
Makes a strange art of an art familiar,
Fills his lady's missal-marge[1] with flowerets.
He who blows through bronze, may breathe
    through silver,
Fitly serenade a slumbrous princess.
He who writes, may write for once as I do.

XIV

Love, you saw me gather men and women,
Live or dead or fashioned by my fancy,   130
Enter each and all, and use their service,
Speak from every mouth, — the speech, a
    poem.
Hardly shall I tell my joys and sorrows,
Hopes and fears, belief and disbelieving:
I am mine and yours — the rest be all men's,
Karshish, Cleon, Norbert, and the fifty.[2]
Let me speak this once in my true person,
Not as Lippo, Roland, or Andrea,
Though the fruit of speech be just this sen-
    tence:
Pray you, look on these my men and women,
Take and keep my fifty poems finished;   141
Where my heart lies, let my brain lie also!
Poor the speech; be how I speak, for all
    things.

XV

Not but that you know me! Lo, the moon's
    self!
Here in London, yonder late in Florence,
Still we find her face, the thrice-transfigured.
Curving on a sky imbrued with colour,
Drifted over Fiesole by twilight,
Came she, our new crescent of a hair's-
    breadth.
Full she flared it, lamping Samminiato,[3] 150
Rounder 'twixt the cypresses and rounder,
Perfect till the nightingales applauded.
Now, a piece of her old self, impoverished,

---

[1] The margins of missals and other service
books were often filled with beautiful pictures of
flowers, birds, etc.   [2] Characters in Browning's
Men and Women   [3] a mountain near Florence

Hard to greet, she traverses the house-roofs,
Hurries with unhandsome thrift of silver,
Goes dispiritedly, glad to finish.

XVI

What, there's nothing in the moon noteworthy?
Nay: for if that moon could love a mortal,
Use, to charm him (so to fit a fancy),
All her magic ('tis the old sweet mythos[1]),   160
She would turn a new side to her mortal,
Side unseen of herdsman, huntsman, steers-
    man —
Blank to Zoroaster on his terrace,
Blind to Galileo on his turret,
Dumb to Homer, dumb to Keats — him, even!
Think, the wonder of the moonstruck mor-
    tal —
When she turns round, comes again in heaven,
Opens out anew for worse or better!
Proves she like some portent of an iceberg
Swimming full upon the ship it founders,   170
Hungry with huge teeth of splintered crystals?
Proves she as the paved work of a sapphire
Seen by Moses[2] when he climbed the moun-
    tain?
Moses, Aaron, Nadab and Abihu
Climbed and saw the very God, the Highest,
Stand upon the paved work of a sapphire.
Like the bodied heaven in his clearness
Shone the stone, the sapphire of that paved
    work,
When they ate and drank and saw God also!

XVII

What were seen? None knows, none ever
    shall know.   180
Only this is sure — the sight were other,
Not the moon's same side, born late in
    Florence,
Dying now impoverished here in London.
God be thanked, the meanest of his creatures
Boasts two soul-sides, one to face the world
    with,
One to show a woman when he loves her!

XVIII

This I say of me, but think of you, Love!
This to you — yourself my moon of poets!

[1] the myth of Endymion, beloved of the moon
goddess [2] *Exodus* xxiv: 10

Ah, but that's the world's side, there's the
    wonder,
Thus they see you, praise you, think they
    know you!   190
There, in turn I stand with them and praise
    you —
Out of my own self, I dare to phrase it.
But the best is when I glide from out them,
Cross a step or two of dubious twilight,
Come out on the other side, the novel
Silent silver lights and darks undreamed of,
Where I hush and bless myself with silence.

XIX

Oh, their Rafael of the dear Madonnas,
Oh, their Dante of the dread Inferno,   199
Wrote one song — and in my brain I sing it,
Drew one angel — borne, see, on my bosom!
                                    — R. B.

ABT VOGLER

AFTER HE HAS BEEN EXTEMPORISING
UPON THE MUSICAL INSTRUMENT
OF HIS INVENTION

Would that the structure brave, the manifold
    music I build,
    Bidding my organ obey, calling its keys to
        their work,
Claiming each slave of the sound, at a touch,
    as when Solomon willed
    Armies of angels that soar, legions of demon
        that lurk,
Man, brute, reptile, fly, — alien of end and of
    aim,
    Adverse, each from the other heaven-high,
        hell-deep removed, —
Should rush into sight at once as he named the
    ineffable Name,
    And pile him a palace straight, to pleasure
        the princess he loved!   8

Would it might tarry like his, the beautiful
    building of mine,
    This which my keys in a crowd pressed and
        importuned to raise!
Ah, one and all, how they helped, would dis-
    part now and now combine,
    Zealous to hasten the work, heighten their
        master his praise!
And one would bury his brow with a blind
    plunge down to hell,

Burrow awhile and build, broad on the roots
  of things,
Then up again swim into sight, having based
  me my palace well,
  Founded it, fearless of flame, flat on the
    nether springs.   16

And another would mount and march, like the
  excellent minion he was,
Ay, another and yet another, one crowd but
  with many a crest,
Raising my rampired walls of gold as transpar-
  ent as glass,
  Eager to do and die, yield each his place to
    the rest:
For higher still and higher (as a runner tips
  with fire,
  When a great illumination surprises a festal
    night —
Outlined round and round Rome's dome from
  space to spire)
  Up, the pinnacled glory reached, and the
    pride of my soul was in sight.   24

In sight? Not half!. for it seemed, it was
  certain, to match man's birth,
  Nature in turn conceived, obeying an
    impulse as I;
And the emulous heaven yearned down, made
  effort to reach the earth,
  As the earth had done her best, in my pas-
    sion, to scale the sky:
Novel splendours burst forth, grew familiar
  and dwelt with mine,
  Not a point nor peak but found and fixed
    its wandering star;
Meteor-moons, balls of blaze: and they did
  not pale nor pine,
  For earth had attained to heaven, there was
    no more near nor far.   32

Nay more; for there wanted not who walked
  in the glare and glow,
  Presences plain in the place; or, fresh from
    the Protoplast,[1]
Furnished for ages to come, when a kindlier
  wind should blow,
  Lured now to begin and live, in a house to
    their liking at last;
Or else the wonderful Dead who have passed
  through the body and gone,
  But were back once more to breathe in an
    old world worth their new:

What never had been, was now; what was, as
  it shall be anon;
  And what is, — shall I say, matched both?
    for I was made perfect too.   40

All through[1] my keys that gave their sounds to
  a wish of my soul,
All through my soul that praised as its wish
  flowed visibly forth,
All through music and me! For think, had I
  painted the whole,
  Why, there it had stood, to see, nor the
    process so wonder-worth:
Had I written the same, made verse — still,
  effect proceeds from cause,
  Ye know why the forms are fair, ye hear
    how the tale is told;
It is all triumphant art, but art in obedience
  to laws,
  Painter and poet are proud in the artist-list
    enrolled: —   48

But here is the finger of God, a flash of the will
  that can,
  Existent behind all laws, that made them
    and, lo, they are!
And I know not if, save in this, such gift be
  allowed to man,
  That out of three sounds he frame, not a
    fourth sound, but a star.
Consider it well: each tone of our scale in
  itself is naught:
  It is everywhere in the world — loud, soft,
    and all is said:
Give it to me to use! I mix it with two in my
  thought:
  And there! Ye have heard and seen: con-
    sider and bow the head!   56

Well, it is gone at last, the palace of music I
  reared;
  Gone! and the good tears start, the praises
    that come too slow;
For one is assured at first, one scarce can say
  that he feared,
  That he even gave it a thought, the gone
    thing was to go.
Never to be again! But many more of the
  kind
  As good, nay, better perchance: is this your
    comfort to me?
To me, who must be saved because I cling
  with my mind

---

[1] Creator   [1] by means of

To the same, same self, same love, same
    God : ay, what was, shall be.   64

Therefore to whom turn I but to thee, the inef-
    fable Name ?
Builder and maker, thou, of houses not
    made with hands !
What, have fear of change from thee who art
    ever the same ?
    Doubt that thy power can fill the heart that
      thy power expands ?
There shall never be one lost good ! What
    was, shall live as before ;
    The evil is null, is naught, is silence imply-
      ing sound ;
What was good shall be good, with, for evil, so
    much good more ;
    On the earth the broken arcs ; in the heaven
      a perfect round.   72

All we have willed or hoped or dreamed of good
    shall exist ;
    Not its semblance, but itself ; no beauty,
      nor good, nor power
Whose voice has gone forth, but each survives
    for the melodist
    When eternity affirms the conception of an
      hour.
The high that proved too high, the heroic for
    earth too hard,
    The passion that left the ground to lose
      itself in the sky,
Are music sent up to God by the lover and the
    bard ;
    Enough that he heard it once : we shall hear
      it by and by.   80

And what is our failure here but a triumph's
    evidence
    For the fullness of the days ? Have we with-
      ered or agonized ?
Why else was the pause prolonged but that
    singing might issue thence ?
    Why rushed the discords in, but that har-
      mony should be prized ?
Sorrow is hard to bear, and doubt is slow to
    clear,
    Each sufferer says his say, his scheme of the
      weal and woe :
But God has a few of us whom he whispers in
    the ear ;
    The rest may reason and welcome : 'tis we
      musicians know.   88

Well, it is earth with me ; silence resumes her
    reign :
    I will be patient and proud, and soberly ac-
      quiesce.
Give me the keys, I feel for the common
    chord again,
    Sliding by semitones till I sink to the minor,
      — yes,
And I blunt it into a ninth, and I stand on
    alien ground,
    Surveying awhile the heights I rolled from
      into the deep ;
Which, hark, I have dared and done, for my
    resting-place is found,
    The C Major of this life : so, now I will
      try to sleep.   96

RABBI BEN EZRA

Grow old along with me !
The best is yet to be,
The last of life, for which the first was made :
Our times are in his hand
Who saith, "A whole I planned,
Youth shows but half ; trust God : see all, nor
    be afraid !"   6

Not that, amassing flowers,
Youth sighed, "Which rose make ours,
Which lily leave and then as best recall ?"
Not that, admiring stars,
It yearned, "Nor Jove, nor Mars ;
Mine be some figured flame which blends,
    transcends them all !"   12

Not for such hopes and fears
Annulling youth's brief years,
Do I remonstrate : folly wide the mark !
Rather I prize the doubt
Low kinds exist without,   17
Finished and finite clods, untroubled by a
    spark.

Poor vaunt of life indeed,
Were man but formed to feed
On joy, to solely seek and find and feast :
Such feasting ended, then
As sure an end to men ;
Irks care[1] the crop-full bird ? Frets doubt[1] the
    maw-crammed beast ?   24

Rejoice we are allied
To that which doth provide

[1] Subject of the verb.

And not partake, effect and not receive !
A spark disturbs our clod ;
Nearer we hold of God
Who gives, than of his tribes that take, I must
    believe.   30

Then, welcome each rebuff
That turns earth's smoothness rough,
Each sting that bids nor sit nor stand but go !
Be our joys three-parts pain !
Strive, and hold cheap the strain ;
Learn, nor account the pang ; dare, never
    grudge the throe !   36

For thence, — a paradox
Which comforts while it mocks, —
Shall life succeed in that it seems to fail :
What I aspired to be,
And was not, comforts me :
A brute I might have been, but would not
    sink i' the scale.   42

What is he but a brute
Whose flesh has soul to suit,
Whose spirit works lest arms and legs want
    play ?
To man, propose this test —
Thy body at its best,
How far can that project thy soul on its lone
    way ?   48

Yet gifts should prove their use :
I own the Past profuse
Of power each side, perfection every turn :
Eyes, ears took in their dole,
Brain treasured up the whole ;
Should not the heart beat once "How good to
    live and learn" ?   54

Not once beat "Praise be thine !
I see the whole design,
I, who saw power, see now love perfect too :
Perfect I call thy plan :
Thanks that I was a man !
Maker, remake, complete, — I trust what
    thou shalt do" ?   60

For pleasant is this flesh ;
Our soul, in its rose-mesh
Pulled ever to the earth, still yearns for rest :
Would we some prize might hold
To match those manifold
Possessions of the brute, — gain most, as we
    did best !   66

Let us not always say,
"Spite of this flesh to-day
I strove, made head, gained ground upon the
    whole !"
As the bird wings and sings,
Let us cry, "All good things
Are ours, nor soul helps flesh more, now, than
    flesh helps soul !"   72

Therefore I summon age
To grant youth's heritage,
Life's struggle having so far reached its term :
Thence shall I pass, approved
A man, for aye removed
From the developed brute ; a god, though in
    the germ.   78

And I shall thereupon
Take rest, ere I be gone
Once more on my adventure brave and new :
Fearless and unperplexed,
When I wage battle next,
What weapons to select, what armour to in-
    due.[1]   84

Youth ended, I shall try
My gain or loss thereby ;
Leave the fire ashes, what survives is gold :
And I shall weigh the same,
Give life its praise or blame :
Young, all lay in dispute ; I shall know, being
    old.   90

For note, when evening shuts,
A certain moment cuts
The deed off, calls the glory from the grey :
A whisper from the west
Shoots — "Add this to the rest,
Take it and try its worth : here dies another
    day."   96

So, still within this life,
Though lifted o'er its strife,
Let me discern, compare, pronounce at last,
"This rage was right i' the main,
That acquiescence vain :
The Future I may face now I have proved the
    Past."   102

For more is not reserved
To man, with soul just nerved
To act to-morrow what he learns to-day :
Here, work enough[2] to watch

    [1] put on   [2] *i.e.*, it is work enough

The Master work, and catch
Hints of the proper craft, tricks of the tool's
 true play.   108

As it was better, youth
Should strive, through acts uncouth,
Toward making, than repose on aught found
 made:
So, better, age, exempt
From strife, should know, than tempt
Further. Thou waitedst age: wait death nor
 be afraid!   114

Enough now, if the Right
And Good and Infinite
Be named here, as thou callest thy hand thine
 own,
With knowledge absolute,
Subject to no dispute
From fools that crowded youth, nor let thee
 feel alone.   120

Be there, for once and all,
Severed great minds from small,
Announced to each his station in the Past!
Was I, the world arraigned,
Were they, my soul disdained,
Right? Let age speak the truth and give us
 peace at last!   126

Now, who shall arbitrate?
Ten men love what I hate,
Shun what I follow, slight what I receive;
Ten, who in ears and eyes
Match me: we all surmise,
They this thing, and I that: whom shall my
 soul believe?   132

Not on the vulgar mass
Called "work," must sentence pass,
Things done, that took the eye and had the
 price;
O'er which, from level stand,
The low world laid its hand,
Found straightway to its mind, could value in
 a trice: 138

But all, the world's coarse thumb
And finger failed to plumb,
So passed in making up the main account;
All instincts immature,
All purposes unsure,
That weighed not as his work, yet swelled the
 man's amount: 144

Thoughts hardly to be packed
Into a narrow act,
Fancies that broke through language and es-
 caped;
All I could never be,
All, men ignored in me,
This, I was worth to God, whose wheel the
 pitcher shaped.[1]   150

Ay, note that Potter's wheel,
That metaphor! and feel
Why time spins fast, why passive lies our
 clay, —
Thou, to whom fools propound,
When the wine makes its round,
"Since life fleets, all is change; the Past gone,
 seize to-day!"   156

Fool! All that is, at all,
Lasts ever, past recall;
Earth changes, but thy soul and God stand
 sure:
What entered into thee,
That was, is, and shall be:
Time's wheel runs back or stops: Potter and
 clay endure.   162

He fixed thee 'mid this dance
Of plastic circumstance,
This Present, thou, forsooth, wouldst fain
 arrest:
Machinery just meant
To give thy soul its bent,
Try thee and turn thee forth, sufficiently im-
 pressed.   168

What though the earlier grooves,
Which ran the laughing loves
Around thy base, no longer pause and press?
What though, about thy rim,
Skull-things in order grim   173
Grow out, in graver mood, obey the sterner
 stress?

Look not thou down but up!
To uses of a cup,
The festal board, lamp's flash and trumpet's
 peal,
The new wine's foaming flow,
The Master's lips aglow!
Thou, heaven's consummate cup, what needst
 thou with earth's wheel?   180

[1] cf. *Jeremiah* xviii : 2–6; *Isaiah* xlv : 9; *Romans* ix : 21.

But I need, now as then,
Thee, God, who mouldest men;
And since, not even while the whirl was worst,
Did I — to the wheel of life,
With shapes and colours rife,
Bound dizzily — mistake my end, to slake thy
    thirst: 186

So, take and use thy work:
Amend what flaws may lurk,
What strain o' the stuff, what warpings past
    the aim!
My times be in thy hand!
Perfect the cup as planned!
Let age approve of youth, and death complete
    the same!   192

APPARITIONS

Such a starved bank of moss
    Till, that May-morn,
Blue ran the flash across:
    Violets were born!

Sky — what a scowl of cloud
    Till, near and far,
Ray on ray split the shroud:
    Splendid, a star!

World — how it walled about
    Life with disgrace   10
Till God's own smile came out:
    That was thy face!

WANTING IS — WHAT?

Wanting is — what?
Summer redundant,
Blueness abundant,
— Where is the blot?
Beamy the world, yet a blank all the same,
— Framework which waits for a picture to
    frame:
What of the leafage, what of the flower?
Roses embowering with naught they em-
    bower!
Come then, complete incompletion, O comer,
Pant through the blueness, perfect the sum-
    mer!   10
    Breathe but one breath
    Rose-beauty above,
    And all that was death
    Grows life, grows love,
    Grows love!

NEVER THE TIME AND THE PLACE

Never the time and the place
    And the loved one all together!
This path — how soft to pace!
    This May — what magic weather!
Where is the loved one's face?
In a dream that loved one's face meets mine,
    But the house is narrow, the place is bleak,
Where, outside, rain and wind combine
    With a furtive ear, if I strive to speak,
    With a hostile eye at my flushing cheek, 10

With a malice that marks each word, each sign!
O enemy sly and serpentine,
    Uncoil thee from the waking man!
        Do I hold the Past
        Thus firm and fast,
    Yet doubt if the Future hold I can?
This path so soft to pace shall lead
Through the magic of May to herself indeed!
Or narrow if needs the house must be,
Outside are the storms and strangers: we —
Oh, close, safe, warm sleep I and she, 21
— I and she!

THE EPILOGUE TO ASOLANDO

At the midnight in the silence of the sleep-time,
    When you set your fancies free,
Will they pass to where — by death, fools
    think, imprisoned —
Low he lies who once so loved you, whom you
    loved so,
        — Pity me?   5

Oh to love so, be so loved, yet so mistaken!
    What had I on earth to do
With the slothful, with the mawkish, the un-
    manly?
Like the aimless, helpless, hopeless, did I drivel
        — Being — who?   10

One who never turned his back but marched
    breast forward,
    Never doubted clouds would break,
Never dreamed, though right were worsted,
    wrong would triumph,
Held we fall to rise, are baffled to fight better,
    Sleep to wake.   15

No, at noonday in the bustle of man's work-
    time
    Greet the unseen with a cheer!

Bid him forward, breast and back as either
    should be,
"Strive and thrive!" cry "Speed, — fight on,
    fare ever
        There as here!"   20

WILLIAM MAKEPEACE THACK-
ERAY (1811–1863)

THE ENGLISH HUMOURISTS

STERNE

Roger Sterne, Sterne's father, was the second
son of a numerous race, descendants of
Richard Sterne, Archbishop of York, in the
reign of Charles II; and children of Simon
Sterne and Mary Jaques, his wife, heiress of
Elvington, near York. Roger was an ensign
in Colonel Hans Hamilton's regiment, and
engaged in Flanders in Queen Anne's wars.
He married the daughter of a noted sutler, —
"N. B., he was in debt to him," his son writes,
pursuing the paternal biography — and
marched through the world with his companion; she following the regiment and bringing many children to poor Roger Sterne. The
Captain was an irascible but kind and simple
little man, Sterne says, and he informs us that
his sire was run through the body at Gibraltar,
by a brother officer, in a duel which arose out
of a dispute about a goose. Roger never entirely recovered from the effects of this ren-
contre, but died presently at Jamaica, whither
he had followed the drum.

Laurence, his second child, was born at
Clonmel, in Ireland, in 1713, and travelled
for the first ten years of his life, on his father's
march, from barrack to transport, from Ireland to England.

One relative of his mother's took her and
her family under shelter for ten months at
Mullingar; another collateral descendant of
the Archbishop's housed them for a year at his
castle near Carrickfergus. Larry Sterne was
put to school at Halifax in England, finally
was adopted by his kinsman of Elvington, and
parted company with his father, the Captain,
who marched on his path of life till he met the
fatal goose which closed his career. The most
picturesque and delightful parts of Laurence
Sterne's writings we owe to his recollections of
the military life. Trim's montero cap, and
Le Fevre's sword, and dear Uncle Toby's ro-
quelaure[1] are doubtless reminiscences of the
boy, who had lived with the followers of William and Marlborough, and had beat time with
his little feet to the fifes of Ramillies[2] in Dublin
barrack-yard, or played with the torn flags
and halberds of Malplaquet[3] on the parade-
ground at Clonmel.

Laurence remained at Halifax school till
he was eighteen years old. His wit and cleverness appear to have acquired the respect of
his master here; for when the usher[4] whipped
Laurence for writing his name on the newly
whitewashed schoolroom ceiling, the peda-
gogue in chief rebuked the understrapper, and
said that the name should never be effaced,
for Sterne was a boy of genius, and would
come to preferment.

His cousin, the Squire of Elvington, sent
Sterne to Jesus College, Cambridge, where he
remained some years, and, taking orders,[5] got,
through his uncle's interest, the living[6] of Sut-
ton and a prebendal stall[7] at York. Through
his wife's connections he got the living of Still-
ington. He married her in 1741, having
ardently courted the young lady for some
years previously. It was not until the young
lady fancied herself dying, that she made
Sterne acquainted with the extent of her liking
for him. One evening when he was sitting
with her, with an almost broken heart to see
her so ill (the Reverend Mr. Sterne's heart
was a good deal broken in the course of his
life), she said — "My dear Laurey, I never
can be yours, for I verily believe I have not
long to live; but I have left you every shilling
of my fortune;" a generosity which overpowered Sterne. She recovered: and so they
were married, and grew heartily tired of each
other before many years were over. "Nescio
quid est materia cum me," Sterne writes to
one of his friends (in dog-Latin, and very sad
dog-Latin too); "sed sum fatigatus et aegrotus de mea uxore plus quam unquam:" which
means, I am sorry to say, "I don't know what
is the matter with me; but I am more tired
and sick of my wife than ever."

This to be sure was five-and-twenty years
after Laurey had been overcome by her generosity, and she by Laurey's love. Then he
wrote to her of the delights of marriage, say-

---

[1] See *Tristram Shandy*. [2] a battle in 1706
[3] a battle in 1709 [4] assistant teacher [5] becoming
a clergyman [6] income as rector [7] income for
occasional services at the cathedral

ing, "We will be as merry and as innocent as our first parents in Paradise, before the arch-fiend entered that indescribable scene. The kindest affections will have room to expand in our retirement: let the human tempest and hurricane rage at a distance, the desolation is beyond the horizon of peace. My L. has seen a polyanthus blow in December? — Some friendly wall has sheltered it from the biting wind. No planetary influence shall reach us but that which presides and cherishes the sweetest flowers. The gloomy family of care and distrust shall be banished from our dwelling, guarded by thy kind and tutelar deity. We will sing our choral songs of gratitude and rejoice to the end of our pilgrimage. Adieu, my L. Return to one who languishes for thy society! — As I take up my pen, my poor pulse quickens, my pale face glows, and tears are trickling down on my paper as I trace the word L."

And it is about this woman, with whom he finds no fault but that she bores him, that our philanthropist writes, "Sum fatigatus et aegrotus" — *Sum mortaliter in amore*[1] with somebody else! That fine flower of love, that polyanthus over which Sterne snivelled so many tears, could not last for a quarter of a century!

Or rather it could not be expected that a gentleman with such a fountain at command should keep it to *arroser*[2] one homely old lady, when a score of younger and prettier people might be refreshed from the same gushing source. It was in December 1767, that the Reverend Laurence Sterne, the famous Shandean,[3] the charming Yorick,[4] the delight of the fashionable world, the delicious divine for whose sermons the whole polite world was subscribing, the occupier of Rabelais's easy-chair, only fresh stuffed and more elegant than when in the possession of the cynical old curate of Meudon,[5] — the more than rival of the Dean of Saint Patrick's,[6] wrote the above-quoted respectable letter to his friend in London: and it was in April of the same year that he was pouring out his fond heart to Mrs. Elizabeth Draper, wife of "Daniel Draper, Esquire, Councillor of Bombay, and, in 1775, chief of

the factory of Surat — a gentleman very much respected in that quarter of the globe."

"I got thy letter last night, Eliza," Sterne writes, "on my return from Lord Bathurst's, where I dined" — (the letter has this merit in it, that it contains a pleasant reminiscence of better men than Sterne, and introduces us to a portrait of a kind old gentleman) — "I got thy letter last night, Eliza, on my return from Lord Bathurst's; and where I was heard — as I talked of thee an hour without intermission — with so much pleasure and attention, that the good old Lord toasted your health three different times; and now he is in his 85th year, says he hopes to live long enough to be introduced as a friend to my fair Indian disciple, and to see her eclipse all other Nabobesses as much in wealth as she does already in exterior and, what is far better" (for Sterne is nothing without his morality), "in interior merit. This nobleman is an old friend of mine. You know he was always the protector of men of wit and genius, and has had those of the last century, Addison, Steele, Pope, Swift, Prior, &c., always at his table. The manner in which his notice began of me was as singular as it was polite. He came up to me one day as I was at the Princess of Wales's Court, and said, 'I want to know you, Mr. Sterne, but it is fit you also should know who it is that wishes this pleasure. You have heard of an old Lord Bathurst, of whom your Popes and Swifts have sung and spoken so much? I have lived my life with geniuses of that cast; but have survived them; and, despairing ever to find their equals, it is some years since I have shut up my books and closed my accounts; but you have kindled a desire in me of opening them once more before I die: which I now do: so go home and dine with me.' This nobleman, I say, is a prodigy, for he has all the wit and promptness of a man of thirty; a disposition to be pleased, and a power to please others, beyond whatever I knew; added to which a man of learning, courtesy, and feeling.

"He heard me talk of thee, Eliza, with uncommon satisfaction — for there was only a third person, *and of sensibility*, with us: and a most sentimental[1] afternoon, till nine o'clock have we passed! But thou, Eliza, wert the star that conducted and enlivened the discourse! And when I talked not of thee, still

---

[1] I am mortally in love   [2] sprinkle   [3] creator of Tristram Shandy   [4] a name assumed by Sterne in *Tristram Shandy* from *Hamlet*, V, i, 198   [5] François Rabelais, a famous French satirist (1495?–1553)   [6] Swift

[1] *i.e.*, indulging in fine sentiments

didst thou fill my mind, and warm every thought I uttered, for I am not ashamed to acknowledge I greatly miss thee. Best of all good girls! the sufferings I have sustained all night in consequence of thine, Eliza, are beyond the power of words. . . . And so thou hast fixed thy Bramin's portrait over thy writing-desk, and wilt consult it in all doubts and difficulties? — Grateful and good girl! Yorick smiles contentedly over all thou dost: his picture does not do justice to his own complacency. I am glad your shipmates are friendly beings" (Eliza was at Deal, going back to the Councillor at Bombay, and indeed it was high time she should be off). "You could least dispense with what is contrary to your own nature, which is soft and gentle, Eliza; it would civilise savages — though pity were it thou shouldst be tainted with the office. Write to me, my child, thy delicious letters. Let them speak the easy carelessness of a heart that opens itself anyhow, everyhow. Such, Eliza, I write to thee!" (The artless rogue, of course he did!) "And so I should ever love thee, most artlessly, most affectionately, if Providence permitted thy residence in the same section of the globe: for I am all that honour and affection can make me 'Thy Bramin.'"

The Bramin continues addressing Mrs. Draper until the departure of the *Earl of Chatham* Indiaman from Deal, on the 3rd of April 1767. He is amiably anxious about the fresh paint for Eliza's cabin; he is uncommonly solicitous about her companions on board: —

"I fear the best of your shipmates are only genteel by comparison with the contrasted crew with which thou beholdest them. So was — you know who — from the same fallacy which was put upon your judgment when — but I will not mortify you!"

"You know who" was, of course, Daniel Draper, Esquire, of Bombay — a gentleman very much respected in that quarter of the globe, and about whose probable health our worthy Bramin writes with delightful candour:

"I honour you, Eliza, for keeping secret some things which, if explained, had been a panegyric on yourself. There is a dignity in venerable affliction which will not allow it to appeal to the world for pity or redress. Well have you supported that character, my amiable, my philosophical friend! And, indeed, I begin to think you have as many virtues as my Uncle Toby's widow. Talking of widows — pray, Eliza, if ever you are such, do not think of giving yourself to some wealthy Nabob, because I design to marry you myself. My wife cannot live long, and I know not the woman I should like so well for her substitute as yourself. 'Tis true I am ninety-five in constitution, and you but twenty-five; but what I want in youth, I will make up in wit and good-humour. Not Swift so loved his Stella, Scarron his Maintenon, or Waller his Saccharissa. Tell me, in answer to this, that you approve and honour the proposal."

Approve and honour the proposal! The coward was writing gay letters to his friends this while, with sneering allusions to this poor foolish *Bramine*.[1] Her ship was not out of the Downs and the charming Sterne was at the "Mount Coffee-house," with a sheet of gilt-edged paper before him, offering that precious treasure his heart to Lady P——, asking whether it gave her pleasure to see him unhappy? whether it added to her triumph that her eyes and lips had turned a man into a fool? — quoting the Lord's Prayer, with a horrible baseness of blasphemy, as a proof that he had desired not to be led into temptation, and swearing himself the most tender and sincere fool in the world. It was from his home at Coxwold, that he wrote the Latin Letter, which, I suppose, he was ashamed to put into English. I find in my copy of the Letters that there is a note of, I can't call it admiration, at Letter 112, which seems to announce that there was a No. 3 to whom the wretched wornout old scamp was paying his addresses; and the year after, having come back to his lodgings in Bond Street, with his "Sentimental Journey" to launch upon the town, eager as ever for praise and pleasure — as vain, as wicked, as witty, as false as he had ever been, death at length seized the feeble wretch, and on the 18th of March 1768, that "bale of cadaverous goods," as he calls his body, was consigned to Pluto. In his last letter there is one sign of grace — the real affection with which he entreats a friend to be a guardian to his daughter Lydia. All his letters to her are artless, kind, affectionate, and *not* sentimental; as a hundred pages in his writings are beautiful, and full, not of surprising humour merely, but of genuine love and kindness. A perilous trade, indeed, is that of a man who

[1] feminine of **Brahmin** (invented by Sterne)

has to bring his tears and laughter, his recollections, his personal griefs and joys, his private thoughts and feelings to market, to write them on paper, and sell them for money. Does he exaggerate his grief, so as to get his reader's pity for a false sensibility? feign indignation, so as to establish a character for virtue? elaborate repartees, so that he may pass for a wit? steal from other authors, and put down the theft to the credit side of his own reputation for ingenuity and learning? feign originality? affect benevolence or misanthropy? appeal to the gallery gods with claptraps and vulgar baits to catch applause?

How much of the pain and emphasis is necessary for the fair business of the stage, and how much of the rant and rouge is put on for the vanity of the actor? His audience trusts him: can he trust himself? How much was deliberate calculation and imposture — how much was false sensibility — and how much true feeling? Where did the lie begin, and did he know where? and where did the truth end in the art and scheme of this man of genius, this actor, this quack? Some time since, I was in the company of a French actor who began after dinner, and at his own request, to sing French songs of the sort called *des chansons grivoises*,[1] and which he performed admirably, and to the dissatisfaction of most persons present. Having finished these, he commenced a sentimental ballad — it was so charmingly sung that it touched all persons present, and especially the singer himself, whose voice trembled, whose eyes filled with emotion, and who was snivelling and weeping quite genuine tears by the time his own ditty was over. I suppose Sterne had this artistical sensibility; he used to blubber perpetually in his study, and finding his tears infectious, and that they brought him a great popularity, he exercised the lucrative gift of weeping: he utilised it, and cried on every occasion. I own that I don't value or respect much the cheap dribble of those fountains. He fatigues me with his perpetual disquiet and his uneasy appeals to my risible or sentimental faculties. He is always looking in my face, watching his effect, uncertain whether I think him an impostor or not; posture-making, coaxing, and imploring me. "See what sensibility I have — own now that I'm very clever — do cry now, you can't resist this." The humour of

Swift and Rabelais, whom he pretended to succeed, poured from them as naturally as song does from a bird; they lose no manly dignity with it, but laugh their hearty great laugh out of their broad chests as nature bade them. But this man — who can make you laugh, who can make you cry too — never lets his reader alone, or will permit his audience repose: when you are quiet, he fancies he must rouse you, and turns over head and heels, or sidles up and whispers a nasty story. The man is a great jester, not a great humourist. He goes to work systematically and of cold blood; paints his face, puts on his ruff and motley clothes, and lays down his carpet and tumbles on it.

For instance, take the "Sentimental Journey," and see in the writer the deliberate propensity to make points and seek applause. He gets to "Dessein's Hotel," he wants a carriage to travel to Paris, he goes to the inn-yard, and begins what the actors call "business" at once. There is that little carriage (the *désobligeante*[1]).

"Four months had elapsed since it had finished its career of Europe in the corner of Monsieur Dessein's coach-yard, and having sallied out thence but a vamped-up business at first, though it had been twice taken to pieces on Mont Cenis, it had not profited much by its adventures, but by none so little as the standing so many months unpitied in the corner of Monsieur Dessein's coach-yard. Much, indeed, was not to be said for it — but something might — and when a few words will rescue misery out of her distress, I hate the man who can be a churl of them."

Le tour est fait![2] Paillasse[3] has tumbled! Paillasse has jumped over the *désobligeante*, cleared it, hood and all, and bows to the noble company. Does anybody believe that this is a real Sentiment? that this luxury of generosity, this gallant rescue of Misery — out of an old cab, is genuine feeling? It is as genuine as the virtuous oratory of Joseph Surface[4] when he begins, "The man who," etc., etc., and wishes to pass off for a saint with his credulous, good-humoured dupes.

Our friend purchases the carriage: after turning that notorious old monk to good ac-

---

[1] indecent songs

[1] the disobliging (because it seated only one person)   [2] "The trick has been done."   [3] the clown   [4] the hypocrite in Sheridan's *School for Scandal*

count, and effecting (like a soft and good-natured Paillasse as he was, and very free with his money when he had it) an exchange of snuff-boxes with the old Franciscan, jogs out of Calais; sets down in immense figures on the credit side of his account the sous he gives away to the Montreuil beggars; and, at Nampont, gets out of the chaise and whimpers over that famous dead donkey, for which any sentimentalist may cry who will. It is agreeably and skilfully done — that dead jackass: like Monsieur de Soubise's [1] cook on the campaign, Sterne dresses it, and serves it up quite tender and with a very piquant sauce. But tears and fine feelings, and a white pocket-handkerchief, and funeral sermon, and horses and feathers, and a procession of mutes,[2] and a hearse with a dead donkey inside! Psha, mountebank! I'll not give thee one penny more for that trick, donkey and, all!

This donkey had appeared once before with signal effect. In 1765, three years before the publication of the "Sentimental Journey," the seventh and eighth volumes of "Tristram Shandy" were given to the world, and the famous Lyons donkey makes his entry in those volumes (pp. 315, 316): —

"'Twas by a poor ass, with a couple of large panniers at his back, who had just turned in to collect eleemosynary turnip-tops and cabbage-leaves, and stood dubious, with his two forefeet at the inside of the threshold, and with his two hinder feet towards the street, as not knowing very well whether he was to go in or no.

"Now 'tis an animal (be in what hurry I may) I cannot bear to strike: there is a patient endurance of suffering wrote so unaffectedly in his looks and carriage which pleads so mightily for him, that it always disarms me, and to that degree that I do not like to speak unkindly to him: on the contrary, meet him where I will, whether in town or country, in cart or under panniers, whether in liberty or bondage, I have ever something civil to say to him on my part; and, as one word begets another (if he has as little to do as I), I generally fall into conversation with him; and surely never is my imagination so busy as in framing responses from the etchings of his

---

[1] The Prince de Soubise, defeated in the decisive battle of Rossbach, regarded a good cook as more essential to a general than any other official.
[2] hired mourners

countenance; and where those carry me not deep enough, in flying from my own heart into his, and seeing what is natural for an ass to think — as well as a man, upon the occasion. In truth, it is the only creature of all the classes of beings below me with whom I can do this. . . . With an ass I can commune forever.

"'Come, Honesty,' said I, seeing it was impracticable to pass betwixt him and the gate, 'art thou for coming in or going out?'

"The ass twisted his head round to look up the street.

"'Well!' replied I, 'we'll wait a minute for thy driver.'

"He turned his head thoughtfully about, and looked wistfully the opposite way.

"'I understand thee perfectly,' answered I: 'if thou takest a wrong step in this affair, he will cudgel thee to death. Well! a minute is but a minute; and if it saves a fellow-creature a drubbing, it shall not be set down as ill spent.'

"He was eating the stem of an artichoke as this discourse went on, and, in the little peevish contentions between hunger and unsavouriness, had dropped it out of his mouth half-a-dozen times, and had picked it up again. 'God help thee, Jack!' said I, 'thou hast a bitter breakfast on't — and many a bitter day's labour, and many a bitter blow, I fear, for its wages! 'Tis all, all bitterness to thee — whatever life is to others! And now thy mouth, if one knew the truth of it, is as bitter, I dare say, as soot' (for he had cast aside the stem), 'and thou hast not a friend perhaps in all this world that will give thee a macaroon.' In saying this, I pulled out a paper of 'em, which I had just bought, and gave him one; and at this moment that I am telling it, my heart smites me that there was more of pleasantry in the conceit of seeing *how* an ass would eat a macaroon than of benevolence in giving him one, which presided in the act.

"When the ass had eaten his macaroon, I pressed him to come in. The poor beast was heavy loaded — his legs seemed to tremble under him — he hung rather backwards, and, as I pulled at his halter, it broke in my hand. He looked up pensive in my face: 'Don't thrash me with it; but if you will you may.' 'If I do,' said I, 'I'll be d—.'"

A critic who refuses to see in this charming description wit, humour, pathos, a kind nature speaking, and a real sentiment, must be hard indeed to move and to please. A page or two farther we come to a description not less beautiful — a landscape and figures, deliciously painted by one who had the keenest enjoyment and the most tremulous sensibility: —

"'Twas in the road between Nismes and Lunel,[1] where is the best Muscatto wine[2] in all France: the sun was set, they had done their work: the nymphs had tied up their hair afresh, and the swains were preparing for a carousal. My mule made a dead point.[3] ''Tis the pipe and tambourine,' said I — 'I never will argue a point with one of your family as long as I live;' so leaping off his back, and kicking off one boot into this ditch and t'other into that, 'I'll take a dance,' said I, 'so stay you here.'

"A sunburnt daughter of labour rose up from the group to meet me as I advanced towards them; her hair, which was of a dark chestnut approaching to a black, was tied up in a knot, all but a single tress.

"'We want a cavalier,' said she, holding out both her hands, as if to offer them. 'And a cavalier you shall have,' said I, taking hold of both of them. 'We could not have done without you,' said she, letting go one hand, with self-taught politeness, and leading me up with the other.

"A lame youth, whom Apollo had recompensed with a pipe, and to which he had added a tambourine of his own accord, ran sweetly over the prelude, as he sat upon the bank. 'Tie me up this tress instantly,' said Nannette, putting a piece of string into my hand. It taught me to forget I was a stranger. The whole knot fell down — we had been seven years acquainted. The youth struck the note upon the tambourine, his pipe followed, and off we bounded.

"The sister of the youth — who had stolen her voice from heaven — sang alternately with her brother. 'Twas a Gascoigne roundelay: 'Viva la joia, fidon la tristessa.'[4] The nymphs joined in unison, and their swains an octave below them.

"Viva la joia was in Nannette's lips, viva la joia in her eyes. A transient spark of amity shot across the space betwixt us. She looked amiable. Why could I not live and end my days thus? 'Just Disposer of our joys and sorrows!' cried I, 'why could not a man sit

down in the lap of content here, and dance, and sing, and say his prayers, and go to heaven with this nut-brown maid?' Capriciously did she bend her head on one side, and dance up insidious. 'Then 'tis time to dance off,' quoth I.''

And with this pretty dance and chorus, the volume artfully concludes. Even here one can't give the whole description. There is not a page in Sterne's writing but has something that were better away, a latent corruption — a hint, as of an impure presence.

Some of that dreary *double entendre*[1] may be attributed to freer times and manners than ours, but not all. The foul satyr's eyes leer out of the leaves constantly: the last words the famous author wrote were bad and wicked — the last lines the poor stricken wretch penned were for pity and pardon. I think of these past writers and of one who lives amongst us now, and am grateful for the innocent laughter and the sweet and unsullied page which the author of "David Copperfield" gives to my children.

ARTHUR HUGH CLOUGH
(1819–1861)

QUA CURSUM VENTUS[2]

As ships, becalmed at eve, that lay
  With canvas drooping, side by side,
Two towers of sail at dawn of day
  Are scarce long leagues apart descried; 4

When fell the night, upsprung the breeze,
  And all the darkling hours they plied,
Nor dreamt but each the self-same seas
  By each was cleaving, side by side: 8

E'en so — but why the tale reveal
  Of those, whom year by year unchanged,
Brief absence joined anew to feel,
  Astounded, soul from soul estranged? 12

At dead of night their sails were filled,
  And onward each rejoicing steered —
Ah, neither blame, for neither willed, 15
  Or wist, what first with dawn appeared!

---

[1] in Provence, where such scenes are characteristic [2] muscatel wine [3] stopped like a pointer dog [4] "Long live joy, down with sadness."

[1] "double meaning," suggesting an indecent idea [2] Whithersoever the wind directs the course.

To veer, how vain ! On, onward strain,
  Brave barks ! In light, in darkness too,
Through winds and tides one compass
    guides —
  To that, and your own selves, be true. 20

But O blithe breeze ; and O great seas,
  Though ne'er, that earliest parting past,
On your wide plain they join again,
  Together lead them home at last. 24

One port, methought, alike they sought,
  One purpose hold where'er they fare, —
O bounding breeze, O rushing seas !
  At last, at last, unite them there ! 28

WITH WHOM IS NO VARIABLENESS, NEITHER SHADOW OF TURNING[1]

  It fortifies my soul to know
  That, though I perish, Truth is so :
  That, howsoe'er I stray and range,
  Whate'er I do, Thou dost not change.
  I steadier step when I recall
  That, if I slip, Thou dost not fall.

EASTER DAY

I

NAPLES, 1849

Through the great sinful streets of Naples as
    I past,
  With fiercer heat than flamed above my
      head
My heart was hot within me ; till at last
  My brain was lightened when my tongue
      had said —
    Christ is not risen ! 5

    Christ is not risen, no —
    He lies and moulders low ;
      Christ is not risen !

What though the stone were rolled away, and
    though
  The grave found empty there ? — 10
    If not there, then elsewhere ;
If not where Joseph laid Him first, why then
  Where other men

Translaid Him after, in some humbler clay.
  Long ere to-day 15
Corruption that sad perfect work hath done,
Which here she scarcely, lightly had begun :
  The foul engendered worm
Feeds on the flesh of the life-giving form
Of our most Holy and Anointed One. 20
    He is not risen, no —
    He lies and moulders low ;
      Christ is not risen.

What if the women, ere the dawn was grey,
  Saw one or more great angels, as they say 25
(Angels, or Him himself) ? Yet neither there,
    nor then,
Nor afterwards, nor elsewhere, nor at all,
Hath He appeared to Peter or the Ten ;[1]
Nor, save in thunderous terror, to blind Saul ;
Save in an after Gospel and late Creed, 30
    He is not risen, indeed, —
      Christ is not risen !

Or, what if e'en, as runs a tale, the Ten
  Saw, heard, and touched, again and yet
      again ?
What if at Emmaüs' inn, and by Capernaüm's
    Lake,
  Came One, the bread that brake — 36
Came One that spake as never mortal spake,
And with them ate, and drank, and stood, and
    walked about ?
  Ah, "some" did well to "doubt" ![2]
Ah ! the true Christ, while these things came
    to pass, 40
Nor heard, nor spake, nor walked, nor lived,
    alas !
    He was not risen, no —
    He lay and mouldered low,
      Christ was not risen !

* * * * * * *

As circulates in some great city crowd 45
A rumour changeful, vague, importunate, and
    loud,
From no determined centre, or of fact
    Or authorship exact,
    Which no man can deny
    Nor verify ; 50
  So spread the wondrous fame ;
    He all the same
  Lay senseless, mouldering, low :
He was not risen, no —
    Christ was not risen. 55

---

[1] *James* i : 17

[1] apostles   [2] cf. *Matt.* xxviii : 17

Ashes to ashes, dust to dust;
As of the unjust, also of the just —
    Yea, of that Just One, too!
This is the one sad Gospel that is true —
        Christ is not risen!   60

Is He not risen, and shall we not rise?
    Oh, we unwise!
What did we dream, what wake we to dis-
        cover?
Ye hills, fall on us, and ye mountains, cover!
    In darkness and great gloom   65
Come ere we thought it is *our* day of doom;
From the cursed world, which is one tomb,
        Christ is not risen!

Eat, drink, and play, and think that this is
        bliss:
There is no heaven but this;   70
    There is no hell,
Save earth, which serves the purpose doubly
        well,
    Seeing it visits still
With equalest apportionment of ill
Both good and bad alike, and brings to one
        same dust   75
    The unjust and the just
    With Christ, who is not risen.

Eat, drink, and die, for we are souls bereaved:
    Of all the creatures under heaven's wide
        cope
We are most hopeless, who had once most
        hope,
And most beliefless, that had most believed.
    Ashes to ashes, dust to dust;   82
    As of the unjust, also of the just —
        Yea, of that Just One too!
It is the one sad Gospel that is true —
        Christ is not risen!   86

Weep not beside the tomb,
Ye women, unto whom
He was great solace while ye tended Him;
Ye who with napkin o'er the head   90
And folds of linen round each wounded limb
Laid out the Sacred Dead;
And thou that bar'st Him in thy wondering
        womb;
Yea, Daughters of Jerusalem, depart,
Bind up as best ye may your own sad bleed-
        ing heart: 95
Go to your homes, your living children tend,
    Your earthly spouses love;
    Set your affections *not* on things above,

Which moth and rust corrupt, which quickliest
        come to end:
Or pray, if pray ye must, and pray, if pray ye
        can,   100
For death; since dead is He whom ye deemed
        more than man,
    Who is not risen: no —
    But lies and moulders low —
        Who is not risen.

Ye men of Galilee!   105
Why stand ye looking up to heaven, where
        Him ye ne'er may see,
Neither ascending hence, nor returning hither
        again?
Ye ignorant and idle fishermen!
Hence to your huts, and boats, and inland
        native shore,
And catch not men, but fish;   110
    Whate'er things ye might wish,
Him neither here nor there ye e'er shall meet
        with more.
Ye poor deluded youths, go home,
Mend the old nets ye left to roam,
Tie the split oar, patch the torn sail: 115
    It was indeed an "idle tale" —
        He was not risen!

And, oh, good men of ages yet to be,
Who shall believe *because* ye did not see —
    Oh, be ye warned, be wise!   120
    No more with pleading eyes,
    And sobs of strong desire,
Unto the empty vacant void aspire,
Seeking another and impossible birth
That is not of your own, and only mother
        earth.   125
But if there is no other life for you,
Sit down and be content, since this must even
        do:
        He is not risen!

One look, and then depart,
    Ye humble and ye holy men of heart; 130
And ye! ye ministers and stewards of a Word
Which ye would preach, because another
        heard —
Ye worshippers of that ye do not know,
Take these things hence and go: —
        He is not risen!   135

Here, on our Easter Day
We rise, we come, and lo! we find Him not,
Gardener nor other, on the sacred spot:
Where they have laid Him there is none to say;

No sound, nor in, nor out — no word   140
Of where to seek the dead or meet the living
    Lord.
There is no glistering of an angel's wings,
There is no voice of heavenly clear behest:
Let us go hence, and think upon these things
    In silence, which is best.   145
    Is He not risen? No —
    But lies and moulders low?
      Christ is not risen?

EASTER DAY

II

So in the sinful streets, abstracted and alone,
I with my secret self held communing of mine
    own.
  So in the southern city spake the tongue
Of one that somewhat overwildly sung,
But in a later hour I sat and heard
Another voice that spake — another graver
    word.
Weep not, it bade, whatever hath been said,
Though He be dead, He is not dead.
    In the true creed
    He is yet risen indeed;   10
      Christ is yet risen.

Weep not beside His tomb,
Ye women unto whom
He was great comfort and yet greater grief;
Nor ye, ye faithful few that wont with Him
    to roam,
Seek sadly what for Him ye left, go hopeless to
    your home;
Nor ye despair, ye sharers yet to be of their
    belief;
    Though He be dead, He is not dead,
    Nor gone, though fled,
    Not lost, though vanishèd;   20
    Though He return not, though
    He lies and moulders low;
    In the true creed
    He is yet risen indeed;
      Christ is yet risen.

Sit if ye will, sit down upon the ground,
Yet not to weep and wail, but calmly look
    around.
    Whate'er befell,
    Earth is not hell;
Now, too, as when it first began,   30
Life is yet life, and man is man.

AE

For all that breathe beneath the heaven's high
    cope,
Joy with grief mixes, with despondence hope.
Hope conquers cowardice, joy grief:
Or at least, faith unbelief.
    Though dead, not dead;
    Not gone, though fled;
    Not lost, though vanishèd.
    In the great gospel and true creed,
    He is yet risen indeed;   40
      Christ is yet risen.

"PERCHÈ PENSA? PENSANDO S'INVECCHIA"[1]

To spend uncounted years of pain,
Again, again, and yet again,
In working out in heart and brain
    The problem of our being here;
To gather facts from far and near,
Upon the mind to hold them clear,
And, knowing more may yet appear,
Unto one's latest breath to fear,
The premature result to draw —
Is this the object, end, and law,   10
    And purpose of our being here?

SAY NOT THE STRUGGLE NOUGHT AVAILETH

Say not the struggle nought availeth,
    The labour and the wounds are vain,
The enemy faints not, nor faileth,
    And as things have been they remain.   4

If hopes were dupes, fears may be liars;
    It may be, in yon smoke concealed,
Your comrades chase e'en now the fliers,
    And, but for you, possess the field.   8

For while the tired waves, vainly breaking,
    Seem here no painful inch to gain,
Far back, through creeks and inlets making,
    Comes silent, flooding in, the main.   12

And not by eastern windows only,
    When daylight comes, comes in the light,
In front, the sun climbs slow, how slowly,
    But westward, look, the land is bright.   16

[1] "Why think? By thinking one grows old"

JOHN RUSKIN (1819–1900)

THE STONES OF VENICE

VOL. II. CHAP. IV.

ST. MARK'S

§ X. And now I wish that the reader, before I bring him into St. Mark's Place, would imagine himself for a little time in a quiet English cathedral town, and walk with me to the west front of its cathedral. Let us go together up the more retired street, at the end of which we can see the pinnacles of one of the towers, and then through the low gray gateway, with its battlemented top and small latticed window in the centre, into the inner private-looking road or close, where nothing goes in but the carts of the tradesmen who supply the bishop and the chapter, and where there are little shaven grass-plots, fenced in by neat rails, before old-fashioned groups of somewhat diminutive and excessively trim houses, with little oriel and bay windows jutting out here and there, and deep wooden cornices and eaves painted cream colour and white, and small porches to their doors in the shape of cockle-shells, or little, crooked, thick, indescribable wooden gables warped a little on one side; and so forward till we come to larger houses, also old-fashioned, but of red brick, and with gardens behind them, and fruit walls, which show here and there, among the nectarines, the vestiges of an old cloister arch or shaft, and looking in front on the cathedral square itself, laid out in rigid divisions of smooth grass and gravel walk, yet not uncheerful, especially on the sunny side where the canons' children are walking with their nurserymaids. And so, taking care not to tread on the grass, we will go along the straight walk to the west front, and there stand for a time, looking up at its deep-pointed porches and the dark places between their pillars where there were statues once, and where the fragments, here and there, of a stately figure are still left, which has in it the likeness of a king, perhaps indeed a king on earth, perhaps a saintly king long ago in heaven; and so, higher and higher up to the great mouldering wall of rugged sculpture and confused arcades, shattered, and gray, and grisly with heads of dragons and mocking fiends, worn by the rain and swirling winds into yet unseemlier shape, and coloured on their stony scales by the deep russet-orange lichen, melancholy gold; and so, higher still, to the bleak towers, so far above that the eye loses itself among the bosses of their traceries, though they are rude and strong, and only sees, like a drift of eddying black points, now closing, now scattering, and now settling suddenly into invisible places among the bosses and flowers, the crowd of restless birds that fill the whole square with that strange clangour of theirs, so harsh and yet so soothing, like the cries of birds on a solitary coast between the cliffs and sea.

§ XI. Think for a little while of that scene, and the meaning of all its small formalisms, mixed with its serene sublimity. Estimate its secluded, continuous, drowsy felicities, and its evidence of the sense and steady performance of such kind of duties as can be regulated by the cathedral clock; and weigh the influence of those dark towers on all who have passed through the lonely square at their feet for centuries, and on all who have seen them rising far away over the wooded plain, or catching on their square masses the last rays of the sunset, when the city at their feet was indicated only by the mist at the bend of the river. And then let us quickly recollect that we are in Venice, and land at the extremity of the Calle Lunga San Moisè, which may be considered as there answering to the secluded street that led us to our English cathedral gateway.

§ XII. We find ourselves in a paved alley, some seven feet wide where it is widest, full of people, and resonant with cries of itinerant salesmen — a shriek in their beginning, and dying away into a kind of brazen ringing, all the worse for its confinement between the high houses of the passage along which we have to make our way. Over-head an inextricable confusion of rugged shutters, and iron balconies and chimney flues pushed out on brackets to save room, and arched windows with projecting sills of Istrian stone, and gleams of green leaves here and there where a fig-tree branch escapes over a lower wall from some inner cortile,[1] leading the eye up to the narrow stream of blue sky high over all. On each side, a row of shops, as densely set as may be, occupying, in fact, intervals between the square stone shafts, about eight feet high,

---

[1] courtyard

which carry the first floors: intervals of which one is narrow and serves as a door; the other is, in the more respectable shops, wainscotted to the height of the counter and glazed above, but in those of the poorer tradesmen left open to the ground, and the wares laid on benches and tables in the open air, the light in all cases entering at the front only, and fading away in a few feet from the threshold into a gloom which the eye from without cannot penetrate, but which is generally broken by a ray or two from a feeble lamp at the back of the shop, suspended before a print of the Virgin. The less pious shopkeeper sometimes leaves his lamp unlighted, and is contented with a penny print; the more religious one has his print coloured and set in a little shrine with a gilded or figured fringe, with perhaps a faded flower or two on each side, and his lamp burning brilliantly. Here at the fruiterer's, where the dark-green water-melons are heaped upon the counter like cannon balls, the Madonna has a tabernacle of fresh laurel leaves; but the pewterer next door has let his lamp out, and there is nothing to be seen in his shop but the dull gleam of the studded patterns on the copper pans, hanging from his roof in the darkness. Next comes a "Vendita Frittole e Liquori,"[1] where the Virgin, enthroned in a very humble manner beside a tallow candle on a back shelf, presides over certain ambrosial morsels of a nature too ambiguous to be defined or enumerated. But a few steps farther on, at the regular wine-shop of the calle,[2] where we are offered "Vino Nostrani a Soldi 28.32,"[3] the Madonna is in great glory, enthroned above ten or a dozen large red casks of three-year-old vintage, and flanked by goodly ranks of bottles of Maraschino, and two crimson lamps; and for the evening, when the gondoliers will come to drink out, under her auspices, the money they have gained during the day, she will have a whole chandelier.

§ XIII. A yard or two farther, we pass the hostelry of the Black Eagle, and, glancing as we pass through the square door of marble, deeply moulded, in the outer wall, we see the shadows of its pergola of vines resting on an ancient well, with a pointed shield carved on its side; and so presently emerge on the bridge and Campo San Moisè, whence to the entrance into St. Mark's Place, called the Bocca di Piazza (mouth of the square), the Venetian character is nearly destroyed, first by the frightful façade of San Moisè, which we will pause at another time to examine, and then by the modernising of the shops as they near the piazza, and the mingling with the lower Venetian populace of lounging groups of English and Austrians.[1] We will push fast through them into the shadow of the pillars at the end of the "Bocca di Piazza," and then we forget them all; for between those pillars there opens a great light, and, in the midst of it, as we advance slowly, the vast tower of St. Mark seems to lift itself visibly forth from the level field of chequered stones; and, on each side, the countless arches prolong themselves into ranged symmetry, as if the rugged and irregular houses that pressed together above us in the dark alley had been struck back into sudden obedience and lovely order, and all their rude casements and broken walls had been transformed into arches charged with goodly sculpture, and fluted shafts of delicate stone.

§ XIV. And well may they fall back, for beyond those troops of ordered arches there rises a vision out of the earth, and all the great square seems to have opened from it in a kind of awe, that we may see it far away — a multitude of pillars and white domes, clustered into a long low pyramid of coloured light; a treasure-heap, it seems, partly of gold, and partly of opal and mother-of-pearl, hollowed beneath into five great vaulted porches, ceiled with fair mosaic, and beset with sculpture of alabaster, clear as amber and delicate as ivory — sculpture fantastic and involved, of palm leaves and lilies, and grapes and pomegranates, and birds clinging and fluttering among the branches, all twined together into an endless network of buds and plumes; and, in the midst of it, the solemn forms of angels, sceptred, and robed to the feet, and leaning to each other across the gates, their figures indistinct among the gleaming of the golden ground through the leaves beside them, interrupted and dim, like the morning light as it faded back among the branches of Eden, when first its gates were angel-guarded long ago. And round the walls of the porches there are set pillars of variegated stones,

<hr/>

[1] shop for cakes and drinks [2] street [3] wine of the district at 28.32 pence

[1] At the time Ruskin was writing Venice belonged to Austria.

jasper and porphyry, and deep-green serpentine spotted with flakes of snow, and marbles, that half refuse and half yield to the sunshine, Cleopatra-like, "their bluest veins to kiss"[1] — the shadow, as it steals back from them, revealing line after line of azure undulation, as a receding tide leaves the waved sand; their capitals rich with interwoven tracery, rooted knots of herbage, and drifting leaves of acanthus and vine, and mystical signs, all beginning and ending in the Cross; and above them, in the broad archivolts, a continuous chain of language and of life — angels, and the signs of heaven, and the labours of men, each in its appointed season upon the earth; and above these, another range of glittering pinnacles, mixed with white arches edged with scarlet flowers — a confusion of delight, amidst which the breasts of the Greek horses are seen blazing in their breadth of golden strength, and the St. Mark's Lion, lifted on a blue field covered with stars, until at last, as if in ecstasy, the crests of the arches break into a marble foam, and toss themselves far into the blue sky in flashes and wreaths of sculptured spray, as if the breakers on the Lido[2] shore had been frost-bound before they fell, and the sea-nymphs had inlaid them with coral and amethyst.

Between that grim cathedral of England and this, what an interval! There is a type of it in the very birds that haunt them; for, instead of the restless crowd, hoarse-voiced and sable-winged, drifting on the bleak upper air, the St. Mark's porches are full of doves, that nestle among the marble foliage, and mingle the soft iridescence of, their living plumes, changing at every motion, with the tints, hardly less lovely, that have stood unchanged for seven hundred years.

§ XV. And what effect has this splendour on those who pass beneath it? You may walk from sunrise to sunset, to and fro, before the gateway of St. Mark's, and you will not see an eye lifted to it, nor a countenance brightened by it. Priest and layman, soldier and civilian, rich and poor, pass by it alike regardlessly. Up to the very recesses of the porches, the meanest tradesmen of the city push their counters; nay, the foundations of its pillars are themselves the seats — not "of

them that sell doves"[1] for sacrifice, but of the vendors of toys and caricatures. Round the whole square in front of the church there is almost a continuous line of cafés, where the idle Venetians of the middle classes lounge, and read empty journals; in its centre the Austrian bands play during the time of vespers, their martial music jarring with the organ notes — the march drowning the miserere, and the sullen crowd thickening round them — a crowd, which, if it had its will, would stiletto every soldier that pipes to it. And in the recesses of the porches, all day long, knots of men of the lowest classes, unemployed and listless, lie basking in the sun like lizards; and unregarded children — every heavy glance of their young eyes full of desperation and stony depravity, and their throats hoarse with cursing — gamble, and fight, and snarl, and sleep, hour after hour, clashing their bruised centesimi[2] upon the marble ledges of the church porch. And the images of Christ and His angels look down upon it continually.

From THE CROWN OF WILD OLIVE

PREFACE

Twenty years ago, there was no lovelier piece of lowland scenery in South England, nor any more pathetic in the world, by its expression of sweet human character and life, than that immediately bordering on the sources of the Wandle,[3] and including the lower moors of Addington, and the villages of Beddington and Carshalton, with all their pools and streams. No clearer or diviner waters ever sang with constant lips of the hand which "giveth rain from heaven";[4] no pastures ever lightened in spring time with more passionate blossoming; no sweeter homes ever hallowed the heart of the passer-by with their pride of peaceful gladness — fain-hidden — yet full-confessed. The place remains, or, until a few months ago, remained, nearly unchanged in its larger features; but, with deliberate mind I say, that I have never seen anything so ghastly in its inner tragic meaning, — not in

---

[1] cf. *Ant. and Cleo.*, II, v, 29   [2] a stretch of sandy islets separating the Lagoon of Venice from the Gulf of Venice

[1] cf. *Matt.* xxi : 12, *Mark* xi : 15   [2] coins worth about one-fifth of a cent   [3] a river that rises in Surrey a few miles south of London   [4] cf. *Job* v : 10

Pisan Maremma,[1] — not by Campagna[2] tomb, — not by the sand-isles of the Torcellan shore,[3] — as the slow stealing of aspects of reckless, indolent, animal neglect, over the delicate sweetness of that English scene : nor is any blasphemy or impiety — any frantic saying or godless thought — more appalling to me, using the best power of judgment I have to discern its sense and scope, than the insolent defilings of those springs by the human herds that drink of them. Just where the welling of stainless water, trembling and pure, like a body of light, enters the pool of Carshalton, cutting itself a radiant channel down to the gravel, through warp of feathery weeds, all waving, which it traverses with its deep threads of clearness, like the chalcedony in moss-agate, starred here and there with white grenouillette ;[4] just in the very rush and murmur of the first spreading currents, the human wretches of the place cast their street and house foulness ; heaps of dust and slime, and broken shreds of old metal, and rags of putrid clothes ; they having neither energy to cart it away, nor decency enough to dig it into the ground, thus shed into the stream, to diffuse what venom of it will float and melt, far away, in all places where God meant those waters to bring joy and health. And, in a little pool, behind some houses farther in the village, where another spring rises, the shattered stones of the well, and of the little fretted channel which was long ago built and traced for it by gentler hands, lie scattered, each from each, under a ragged bank of mortar, and scoria ;[5] and bricklayers' refuse, on one side, which the clean water nevertheless chastises to purity ; but it cannot conquer the dead earth beyond ; and there, circled and coiled under festering scum, the stagnant edge of the pool effaces itself into a slope of black slime, the accumulation of indolent years. Half-a-dozen men, with one day's work, could cleanse those pools, and trim the flowers about their banks, and make every breath of summer air above them rich with cool balm ; and every glittering wave medicinal, as if it ran, troubled of angels, from the porch of Bethesda.[6] But that day's work is never given, nor will be ; nor will any joy be possible to heart of man, for

evermore, about those wells of English waters.

When I last left them, I walked up slowly through the back streets of Croydon,[1] from the old church to the hospital ; and, just on the left, before coming up to the crossing of the High Street, there was a new public-house built. And the front of it was built in so wise manner, that a recess of two feet was left below its front windows, between them and the street-pavement — a recess too narrow for any possible use (for even if it had been occupied by a seat, as in old time it might have been, everybody walking along the street would have fallen over the legs of the reposing wayfarers). But, by way of making this two feet depth of freehold land more expressive of the dignity of an establishment for the sale of spirituous liquors, it was fenced from the pavement by an imposing iron railing, having four or five spearheads to the yard of it, and six feet high ; containing as much iron and iron-work, indeed, as could well be put into the space ; and by this stately arrangement, the little piece of dead ground within, between wall and street, became a protective receptacle of refuse ; cigar ends, and oyster shells, and the like, such as an open-handed English street-populace, habitually scatters from its presence, and was thus left, unsweepable by any ordinary methods. Now the iron bars which, uselessly (or in great degree worse than uselessly), enclosed this bit of ground, and made it pestilent, represented a quantity of work which would have cleansed the Carshalton pools three times over ; — of work partly cramped and deadly, in the mine ; partly fierce and exhaustive, at the furnace, partly foolish and sedentary, of ill-taught students making bad designs : work from the beginning to the last fruits of it, and in all the branches of it, venomous, deathful, and miserable. Now, how did it come to pass that this work was done instead of the other ; that the strength and life of the English operative were spent in defiling ground, instead of redeeming it ; and in producing an entirely (in that place) valueless piece of metal, which can neither be eaten nor breathed, instead of medicinal fresh air, and pure water?

There is but one reason for it, and at present a conclusive one, — that the capitalist can charge percentage on the work in the one case,

---

[1] a desolate marsh near Pisa   [2] a plain near Rome   [3] near Venice   [4] water crowfoot   [5] slag
[6] cf. *John* v : 2–4

[1] a suburb of London

and cannot in the other. If, having certain
funds for supporting labour at my disposal, I
pay men merely to keep my ground in order,
my money is, in that function, spent once for
all; but if I pay them to dig iron out of my
ground, and work it, and sell it, I can charge
rent for the ground, and percentage both on
the manufacture and the sale, and make my
capital profitable in these three by-ways.
The greater part of the profitable investment
of capital, in the present day, is in operations
of this kind, in which the public is persuaded
to buy something of no use to it, on production, or sale, of which, the capitalist may
charge percentages; the said public remaining
all the while under the persuasion that the
percentages, thus obtained are real national
gains, whereas, they are merely filchings
out of partially light pockets, to swell heavy
ones.

Thus, the Croydon publican buys the iron
railing, to make himself more conspicuous to
drunkards. The public-housekeeper on the
other side of the way presently buys another
railing, to out-rail him with. Both are, as to
their *relative* attractiveness to customers of
taste, just where they were before; but they
have lost the price of the railings; which they
must either themselves finally lose, or make
their aforesaid customers of taste pay, by raising the price of their beer, or adulterating it.
Either the publicans, or their customers, are
thus poorer by precisely what the capitalist
has gained; and the value of the work itself,
meantime, has been lost, to the nation; the
iron bars in that form and place being wholly
useless. It is this mode of taxation of the poor
by the rich which is referred to in the text, in
comparing the modern acquisitive power of
capital with that of the lance and sword; the
only difference being that the levy of blackmail in old times was by force, and is now by
cozening. The old rider and reiver[1] frankly
quartered himself on the publican for the
night; the modern one merely makes his lance
into an iron spike, and persuades his host to
buy it. One comes as an open robber, the
other as a cheating peddler; but the result, to
the injured person's pocket, is absolutely the
same. Of course many useful industries
mingle with, and disguise the useless ones;
and in the habits of energy aroused by the
struggle, there is a certain direct good. It is

[1] robber

far better to spend four thousand pounds in
making a good gun, and then to blow it to
pieces, than to pass life in idleness. Only do
not let it be called "political economy."
There is also a confused notion in the minds
of many persons, that the gathering of the
property of the poor into the hands of the rich
does no ultimate harm; since, in whosesoever
hands it may be, it must be spent at last, and
thus, they think, return to the poor again.
This fallacy has been again and again exposed;
but grant the plea true, and the same apology
may, of course, be made for blackmail, or any
other form of robbery. It might be (though
practically it never is) as advantageous for the
nation that the robber should have the spending of the money he extorts, as that the person robbed should have spent it. But this is
no excuse for the theft. If I were to put a
turnpike on the road where it passes my own
gate, and endeavour to exact a shilling from
every passenger, the public would soon do
away with my gate, without listening to any
plea on my part that "it was as advantageous
to them, in the end, that I should spend their
shillings, as that they themselves should."
But if, instead of outfacing them with a turnpike, I can only persuade them to come in and
buy stones, or old iron, or any other useless
thing, out of my ground, I may rob them to
the same extent, and be, moreover, thanked
as a public benefactor, and promoter of commercial prosperity. And this main question
for the poor of England — for the poor of all
countries — is wholly omitted in every common treatise on the subject of wealth. Even
by the labourers themselves, the operation of
capital is regarded only in its effect on their
immediate interests; never in the far more
terrific power of its appointment of the kind
and the object of labour. It matters little,
ultimately, how much a labourer is paid for
making anything; but it matters fearfully
what the thing is, which he is compelled to
make. If his labour is so ordered as to produce food, and fresh air, and fresh water, no
matter that his wages are low; — the food and
fresh air and water will be at last there; and
he will at last get them. But if he is paid to
destroy food and fresh air, or to produce iron
bars instead of them, — the food and air will
finally *not* be there, and he will *not* get them,
to his great and final inconvenience. So that,
conclusively, in political as in household
economy the great question is, not so much

what money you have in your pocket, as what you will buy with it, and do with it.

I have been long accustomed, as all men engaged in work of investigation must be, to hear my statements laughed at for years, before they are examined or believed; and I am generally content to wait the public's time. But it has not been without displeased surprise that I have found myself totally unable, as yet, by any repetition, or illustration, to force this plain thought into my readers' heads — that the wealth of nations, as of men, consists in substance, not in ciphers; and that the real good of all work, and of all commerce, depends on the final worth of the thing you make, or get by it. This is a practical enough statement, one would think: but the English public has been so possessed by its modern school of economists with the notion that Business is always good, whether it be busy in mischief or in benefit; and that buying and selling are always salutary, whatever the intrinsic worth of what you buy or sell, — that it seems impossible to gain so much as a patient hearing for any inquiry respecting the substantial result of our eager modern labours. I have never felt more checked by the sense of this impossibility than in arranging the heads of the following three lectures, which, though delivered at considerable intervals of time, and in different places, were not prepared without reference to each other. Their connection would, however, have been made far more distinct, if I had not been prevented, by what I feel to be another great difficulty in addressing English audiences, from enforcing, with any decision, the common, and to me, the most important, part of their subjects. I chiefly desired (as I have just said) to question my hearers — operatives, merchants, and soldiers, as to the ultimate meaning of the *business* they had in hand; and to know from them what they expected or intended their manufacture to come to, their selling to come to, and their killing to come to. That appeared the first point needing determination before I could speak to them with any real utility or effect. "You craftsmen — salesmen — swordsmen,— do but tell me clearly what you want; then, if I can say anything to help you, I will; and if not, I will account to you as I best may for my inability." But in order to put this question into any terms, one had first of all to face the difficulty just spoken of — to me for the present insuperable, — the difficulty of know-

ing whether to address one's audience as believing, or not believing, in any other world than this. For if you address any average modern English company as believing in an Eternal life, and endeavour to draw any conclusions, from this assumed belief, as to their present business, they will forthwith tell you that what you say is very beautiful, but it is not practical. If, on the contrary, you frankly address them as unbelievers in Eternal life, and try to draw any consequences from that unbelief, — they immediately hold you for an accursed person, and shake off the dust from their feet at you. And the more I thought over what I had got to say, the less I found I could say it, without some reference to this intangible or intractable part of the subject. It made all the difference, in asserting any principle of war, whether one assumed that a discharge of artillery would merely knead down a certain quantity of red clay into a level line, as in a brick field; or whether, out of every separately Christian-named portion of the ruinous heap, there went out, into the smoke and dead-fallen air of battle, some astonished condition of soul, unwillingly released. It made all the difference, in speaking of the possible range of commerce, whether one assumed that all bargains related only to visible property — or whether property, for the present invisible, but nevertheless real, was elsewhere purchasable on other terms. It made all the difference, in addressing a body of men subject to considerable hardship, and having to find some way out of it — whether one could confidently say to them, "My friends, — you have only to die, and all will be right;" or whether one had any secret misgiving that such advice was more blessed to him that gave, than to him that took it. And therefore the deliberate reader will find, throughout these lectures, a hesitation in driving points home, and a pausing short of conclusions which he will feel I would fain have come to; hesitation which arises wholly from this uncertainty of my hearers' temper. For I do not now speak, nor have I ever spoken, since the time of first forward youth, in any proselyting temper, as desiring to persuade any one of what, in such matters, I thought myself; but, whomsoever I venture to address, I take for the time his creed as I find it; and endeavour to push it into such vital fruit as it seems capable of. Thus, it is a creed with a great part of the existing English people, that they are in possession of a book which tells them, straight from the lips of God, all they ought to do, and need to know. I have read that book, with as much care as most of them, for some forty years; and am thankful that, on those who trust it, I can press its pleadings. My endeavour has been uniformly to make them trust it more deeply than they do; trust it, not in their own favourite verses only, but in the sum of all; trust it not as a fetich or talisman, which they are to be saved by daily repetitions of; but as a Captain's order, to be heard and obeyed at their peril. I was always encouraged by supposing my hearers to hold such belief. To these, if to any, I once had hope of addressing, with acceptance, words which insisted on the guilt of pride, and the futility of avarice; from these, if from any, I once expected ratification of a political economy, which asserted that the life was more than the meat, and the body than raiment;[1] and these, it once seemed to me, I might ask, without accusation of fanaticism, not merely in doctrine of the lips, but in the bestowal of their heart's treasure, to separate themselves from the crowd of whom it is written, "After all these things do the Gentiles seek."[2]

It cannot, however, be assumed, with any semblance of reason, that a general audience is now wholly, or even in majority, composed of these religious persons. A large portion must always consist of men who admit no such creed; or who, at least, are inaccessible to appeals founded on it. And as, with the so-called Christian, I desired to plead for honest declaration and fulfilment of his belief in life, — with the so-called infidel, I desired to plead for an honest declaration and fulfilment of his belief in death. The dilemma is inevitable. Men must either hereafter live, or hereafter die; fate may be bravely met, and conduct wisely ordered, on either expectation; but never in hesitation between ungrasped hope, and unconfronted fear. We usually believe in immortality, so far as to avoid preparation for death; and in mortality, so far as to avoid preparation for anything after death. Whereas, a wise man will at least hold himself prepared for one or other of two events, of which one or other is inevitable; and will have all things in order, for his sleep, or in readiness, for his awakening.

Nor have we any right to call it an ignoble judgment, if he determine to put them in order, as for sleep. A brave belief in life is indeed an enviable state of mind, but, as far as I can discern, an unusual one. I know few Christians so convinced of the splendour of the rooms in their Father's house, as to be happier when their friends are called to those mansions, than they would have been if the Queen had sent for them to live at court: nor has the Church's most ardent "desire to depart, and be with Christ,"[1] ever cured it of the singular habit of putting on mourning for every person summoned to such departure. On the contrary, a brave belief in death has been assuredly held by many not ignoble persons, and it is a sign of the last depravity in the Church itself, when it assumes that such a belief is inconsistent with either purity of character, or energy of hand. The shortness of life is not, to any rational person, a conclusive reason for wasting the space of it which may be granted him; nor does the anticipation of death to-morrow suggest, to any one but a drunkard, the expediency of drunkenness to-day. To teach that there is no device in the grave,[2] may indeed make the deviceless person more contented in his dulness; but it will make the deviser only more earnest in devising: nor is human conduct likely, in every case, to be purer, under the conviction that all its evil may in a moment be pardoned, and all its wrong-doing in a moment redeemed; and that the sigh of repentance, which purges the guilt of the past, will waft the soul into a felicity which forgets its pain, — than it may be under the sterner, and to many not unwise minds more probable, apprehension, that "what a man soweth that shall he also reap,"[3] — or others reap, — when he, the living seed of pestilence, walketh no more in darkness, but lies down therein.

But to men whose feebleness of sight, or bitterness of soul, or the offence given by the conduct of those who claim higher hope, may have rendered this painful creed the only possible one, there is an appeal to be made, more secure in its ground than any which can be addressed to happier persons. I would fain, if I might offencelessly, have spoken to them as if none others heard; and have said thus: Hear me, you dying men, who will soon be deaf forever. For these others, at your right

[1] *Matt.* vi : 25   [2] *Matt.* vi : 32   [1] *Philipp.* i : 23   [2] *Eccl.* ix : 10   [3] *Galat.* vi : 7

hand and your left, who look forward to a state of infinite existence, in which all their errors will be overruled, and all their faults forgiven; for these, who, stained and blackened in the battle-smoke of mortality, have but to dip themselves for an instant in the font of death, and to rise renewed of plumage, as a dove that is covered with silver, and her feathers like gold;[1] for these, indeed, it may be permissible to waste their numbered moments, through faith in a future of innumerable hours; to these, in their weakness, it may be conceded that they should tamper with sin which can only bring forth fruit of righteousness, and profit by the iniquity which, one day, will be remembered no more. In them, it may be no sign of hardness of heart to neglect the poor, over whom they know their Master is watching; and to leave those to perish temporarily, who cannot perish eternally. But, for you, there is no such hope, and therefore no such excuse. This fate, which you ordain for the wretched, you believe to be all their inheritance; you may crush them, before the moth,[2] and they will never rise to rebuke you; — their breath, which fails for lack of food, once expiring, will never be recalled to whisper against you a word of accusing; — they and you, as you think, shall lie down together in the dust, and the worms cover you;[3] — and for them there shall be no consolation, and on you no vengeance, — only the question murmured above your grave: "Who shall repay him what he hath done?" Is it therefore easier for you in your heart to inflict the sorrow for which there is no remedy? Will you take, wantonly, this little all of his life from your poor brother, and make his brief hours long to him with pain? Will you be readier to the injustice which can never be redressed; and niggardly of mercy which you *can* bestow but once, and which, refusing, you refuse forever? I think better of you, even of the most selfish, than that you would do this, well understood. And for yourselves, it seems to me, the question becomes not less grave, in these curt limits. If your life were but a fever fit, — the madness of a night, whose follies were all to be forgotten in the dawn, it might matter little how you fretted away the sickly hours, — what toys you snatched at, or let fall, — what visions you followed wistfully with the deceived eyes

of sleepless phrenzy. Is the earth only an hospital? Play, if you care to play, on the floor of the hospital den. Knit its straw into what crowns please you; gather the dust of it for treasure, and die rich in that, clutching at the black motes in the air with your dying hands; — and yet, it may be well with you. But if this life be no dream, and the world no hospital; if all the peace and power and joy you can ever win, must be won now; and all fruit of victory gathered here, or never; — will you still, throughout the puny totality of your life, weary yourselves in the fire for vanity?[1] If there is no rest which remaineth for you, is there none you might presently take? was this grass of the earth made green for your shroud only, not for your bed? and can you never lie down *upon* it, but only *under* it? The heathen, to whose creed you have returned, thought not so. They knew that life brought its contest, but they expected from it also the crown of all contest: No proud one! no jewelled circlet flaming through Heaven above the height of the unmerited throne; only some few leaves of wild olive, cool to the tired brow, through a few years of peace. It should have been of gold, they thought; but Jupiter was poor; this was the best the god could give them. Seeking a greater than this, they had known it a mockery. Not in war, not in wealth, not in tyranny, was there any happiness to be found for them — only in kindly peace, fruitful and free. The wreath was to be of *wild* olive, mark you: — the tree that grows carelessly; tufting the rocks with no vivid bloom, no verdure of branch; only with soft snow of blossom, and scarcely fulfilled fruit, mixed with gray leaf and thornset stem; no fastening of diadem for you but with such sharp embroidery! But this, such as it is, you may win while yet you live; type of gray honour and sweet rest. Free-heartedness, and graciousness, and undisturbed trust, and requited love, and the sight of the peace of others, and the ministry to their pain; — these, and the blue sky above you, and the sweet waters and flowers of the earth beneath; and mysteries and presences, innumerable, of living things, — these may yet be here your riches; untormenting and divine; serviceable for the life that now is; nor, it may be, without promise of that which is to come.[2]

---

[1] *Ps.* lxviii : 13   [2] cf. *Job* iv : 19   [3] cf. *Job* xxi : 26

[1] *Hab.* ii : 13   [2] 1 *Tim.* iv : 8

FREDERICK LOCKER–LAMPSON
(1821–1895)

TO MY GRANDMOTHER

Suggested by a picture by Mr. Romney

This Relative of mine,
Was she seventy-and-nine
　　When she died?
By the canvas may be seen
How she look'd at seventeen,
　　As a bride.

Beneath a summer tree
Her maiden reverie
　　Has a charm;
Her ringlets are in taste;　　10
What an arm! and what a waist
　　For an arm!

With her bridal-wreath, bouquet,
Lace farthingale,[1] and gay
　　Falbala,[2] —
If Romney's touch be true,
What a lucky dog were you,
　　Grandpapa!

Her lips are sweet as love;
They are parting! Do they move?
　　Are they dumb?　　21
Her eyes are blue, and beam
Beseechingly, and seem
　　To say, "Come!"

What funny fancy slips
From atween these cherry lips?
　　Whisper me,
Fair Sorceress in paint,
What canon[3] says I mayn't
　　Marry thee?　　30

That good-for-nothing Time
Has a confidence sublime!
　　When I first
Saw this Lady, in my youth,
Her winters had, forsooth,
　　Done their worst.

Her locks, as white as snow,
Once shamed the swarthy crow;
　　By-and-by

That fowl's avenging sprite　　40
Set his cruel foot for spite
　　Near her eye.

Her rounded form was lean,
And her silk was bombazine;
　　Well I wot
With her needles would she sit,
And for hours would she knit, —
　　Would she not?

Ah perishable clay!
Her charms had dropt away　　50
　　One by one;
But if she heaved a sigh
With a burthen, it was, "Thy
　　Will be done."

In travail, as in tears,
With the fardel[1] of her years
　　Overprest,
In mercy she was borne
Where the weary and the worn
　　Are at rest.　　60

Oh, if you now are there,
And sweet as once you were,
　　Grandmamma,
This nether world agrees
You'll all the better please
　　Grandpapa.

THE UNREALISED IDEAL

My only Love is always near, —
　　In country or in town,
I see her twinkling feet, I hear
　　The whisper of her gown.

She foots it ever fair and young,　　5
　　Her locks are tied in haste,
And one is o'er her shoulder flung,
　　And hangs below her waist.

She ran before me in the meads;
　　And down this world-worn track　　10
She leads me on; but while she leads,
　　She never gazes back.

And yet her voice is in my dreams,
　　To witch me more and more;
That wooing voice! Ah me, it seems　　15
　　Less near me than of yore.

[1] a contrivance like a hoopskirt　[2] furbelow,
flounce　[3] ecclesiastical law

[1] burden

Lightly I sped when hope was high,
    And youth beguiled the chase;
I follow — follow still; but I
    Shall never see her Face.   20

SIDNEY DOBELL (1824–1874)

AMERICA

I

Men say, Columbia, we shall hear thy guns.
But in what tongue shall be thy battle-cry?
Not that our sires did love in years gone by,
When all the Pilgrim Fathers were little sons
In merrie homes of Englaunde? Back, and
    see
Thy satchel'd ancestor! Behold, he runs
To mine, and, clasp'd, they tread the equal lea
To the same village-school, where side by side
They spell "our Father." Hard by, the twin-
    pride
Of that grey hall whose ancient oriel gleams
Thro' yon baronial pines, with looks of light
Our sister-mothers sit beneath one tree.   12
Meanwhile our Shakespeare wanders past and
    dreams
His Helena and Hermia. Shall we fight?

II

Nor force nor fraud shall sunder us! O ye
Who north or south, on east or western land,
Native to noble sounds, say truth for truth,
Freedom for freedom, love for love, and God
For God; O ye who in eternal youth
Speak with a living and creative flood
This universal English, and do stand
Its breathing book; live worthy of that grand
Heroic utterance — parted, yet a whole,   9
Far, yet unsevered, — children brave and free
Of the great Mother-tongue, and ye shall be
Lords of an Empire wide as Shakespeare's
    soul,
Sublime as Milton's immemorial theme,
And rich as Chaucer's speech, and fair as
    Spenser's dream.

MATTHEW ARNOLD (1822–1888)

FROM CULTURE AND ANARCHY

SWEETNESS AND LIGHT

The disparagers of culture make its motive curiosity; sometimes, indeed, they make its motive mere exclusiveness and vanity. The culture which is supposed to plume itself on a smattering of Greek and Latin is a culture which is begotten by nothing so intellectual as curiosity; it is valued either out of sheer vanity and ignorance or else as an engine of social and class distinction, separating its holder, like a badge or title, from other people who have not got it. No serious man would call this *culture*, or attach any value to it, as culture, at all. To find the real ground for the very different estimate which serious people will set upon culture, we must find some motive for culture in the terms of which may lie a real ambiguity; and such a motive the word *curiosity* gives us.

I have before now pointed out that we English do not, like the foreigners, use this word in a good sense as well as in a bad sense. With us the word is always used in a somewhat disapproving sense. A liberal and intelligent eagerness about the things of the mind may be meant by a foreigner when he speaks of curiosity, but with us the word always conveys a certain notion of frivolous and unedifying activity. In the *Quarterly Review*, some little time ago, was an estimate of the celebrated French critic, M. Sainte-Beuve, and a very inadequate estimate it in my judgment was. And its inadequacy consisted chiefly in this: that in our English way it left out of sight the double sense really involved in the word *curiosity*, thinking enough was said to stamp M. Sainte-Beuve with blame if it was said that he was impelled in his operations as a critic by curiosity, and omitting either to perceive that M. Sainte-Beuve himself, and many other people with him, would consider that this was praiseworthy and not blameworthy, or to point out why it ought really to be accounted worthy of blame and not of praise. For as there is a curiosity about intellectual matters which is futile, and merely a disease, so there is certainly a curiosity, — a desire after the things of the mind simply for their own sakes and for the pleasure of seeing them as they are, — which is, in an intelligent being, natural and laudable. Nay, and the very desire to see things as they are implies a balance and regulation of mind which is not often attained without fruitful effort, and which is the very opposite of the blind and diseased impulse of mind which is what we mean to blame when we blame curiosity. Montesquieu[1] says: "The first motive which ought to impel us to study is the desire to augment the excellence of our nature, and to render an intelligent being yet more intelligent." This is the true ground to assign for the genuine scientific passion, however manifested, and for culture, viewed simply as a fruit of this passion; and it is a worthy ground, even though we let the term *curiosity* stand to describe it.

But there is of culture another view, in which not solely the scientific passion, the sheer desire to see things as they are, natural and proper in an intelligent being, appears as the ground of it. There is a view in which all the love of our neighbour, the impulses toward action, help, and beneficence, the desire for removing human error, clearing human confusion, and diminishing human misery, the noble aspiration to leave the world better and happier than we found it, — motives eminently such as are called social, — come in as part of the grounds of culture, and the main and preëminent part. Culture is then properly described not as having its origin in curiosity, but as having its origin in the love of perfection; it is *a study of perfection*. It moves by the force, not merely or primarily of the scientific passion for pure knowledge, but also of the moral and social passion for doing good. As, in the first view of it, we took for its worthy motto Montesquieu's words: "To render an intelligent being yet more intelligent!" so, in the second view of it, there is no better motto which it can have than these words of Bishop Wilson:[2] "To make reason and the will of God prevail!"

Only, whereas the passion for doing good is apt to be overhasty in determining what reason and the will of God say, because its turn is for acting rather than thinking and it wants to be beginning to act; and whereas it is apt to take its own conceptions, which proceed from its own state of development and share in all the imperfections and immaturities of this, for a basis of action; what distinguishes culture is, that it is possessed by the scientific passion as well as by the passion of doing good; that it demands worthy notions of reason and the will of God, and does not readily suffer its own crude conceptions to substitute themselves for them. And knowing that no action or institution can be salutary and stable which is not based on reason and the will of God, it is not so bent on acting and instituting, even with the great aim of diminishing human error and misery ever before its thoughts, but that it can remember that acting and instituting are of little use, unless we know how and what we ought to act and to institute.

This culture is more interesting and more far-reaching than that other, which is founded solely on the scientific passion for knowing. But it needs times of faith and ardour, times when the intellectual horizon is opening and widening all round us, to flourish in. And is not the close and bounded intellectual horizon within which we have long lived and moved now lifting up, and are not new lights finding free passage to shine in upon us? For a long time there was no passage for them to make their way in upon us, and then it was of no use to think of adapting the world's action to them. Where was the hope of making reason and the will of God prevail among people who had a routine which they had christened reason and the will of God, in which they were inextricably bound, and beyond which they had no power of looking? But now the iron force of adhesion to the old routine, — social, political, religious — has wonderfully yielded; the iron force of exclusion of all which is new has wonderfully yielded. The danger now is, not that people should obstinately refuse to allow anything but their old routine to pass for reason and the will of God, but either that they should allow some novelty or other to pass for these too easily, or else that they should underrate the importance of them altogether, and think it enough to follow action for its own sake, without troubling themselves to make reason and the will of God prevail therein. Now, then, is the moment for culture to be of service, culture which believes in making reason and the will of God prevail, believes in perfection, is the study and pursuit of perfection, and is no longer debarred, by a rigid invincible exclusion of whatever is new, from getting

---

[1] a French philosopher (1689–1755), author of the famous *L'esprit des lois* [2] Thomas Wilson (1663–1755), Bishop of Sodor and Man

acceptance for its ideas, simply because they are new.

The moment this view of culture is seized, the moment it is regarded not solely as the endeavour to see things as they are, to draw towards a knowledge of the universal order which seems to be intended and aimed at in the world, and which it is a man's happiness to go along with or his misery to go counter to, — to learn, in short, the will of God, — the moment, I say, culture is considered not merely as the endeavour to *see* and *learn* this, but as the endeavour, also, to make it *prevail*, the moral, social, and beneficent character of culture becomes manifest. The mere endeavour to see and learn the truth for our own personal satisfaction is indeed a commencement for making it prevail, a preparing the way for this, which always serves this, and is wrongly, therefore, stamped with blame absolutely in itself and not only in its caricature and degeneration. But perhaps it has got stamped with blame, and disparaged with the dubious title of curiosity, because in comparison with this wider endeavour of such great and plain utility it looks selfish, petty, and unprofitable.

And religion, the greatest and most important of the efforts by which the human race has manifested its impulse to perfect itself, — religion, that voice of the deepest human experience, — does not only enjoin and sanction the aim which is the great aim of culture, the aim of setting ourselves to ascertain what perfection is and to make it prevail; but also, in determining generally in what human perfection consists, religion comes to a conclusion identical with that which culture, — culture seeking the determination of this question through *all* the voices of human experience which have been heard upon it, of art, science, poetry, philosophy, history, as well as of religion, in order to give a greater fulness and certainty to its solution, — likewise reaches. Religion says: *The kingdom of God is within you;* and culture, in like manner, places human perfection in an *internal* condition, in the growth and predominance of our humanity proper, as distinguished from our animality. It places it in the ever-increasing efficacy and in the general harmonious expansion of those gifts of thought and feeling, which make the peculiar dignity, wealth, and happiness of human nature. As I have said on a former occasion: "It is in making endless additions to itself, in the endless expansion of its powers, in endless growth in wisdom and beauty, that the spirit of the human race finds its ideal. To reach this ideal, culture is an indispensable aid, and that is the true value of culture." Not a having and a resting, but a growing and a becoming, is the character of perfection as culture conceives it; and here, too, it coincides with religion.

And because men are all members of one great whole, and the sympathy which is in human nature will not allow one member to be indifferent to the rest or to have a perfect welfare independent of the rest, the expansion of our humanity, to suit the idea of perfection which culture forms, must be a *general* expansion. Perfection, as culture conceives it, is not possible while the individual remains isolated. The individual is required, under pain of being stunted and enfeebled in his own development if he disobeys, to carry others along with him in his march towards perfection, to be continually doing all he can to enlarge and increase the volume of the human stream sweeping thitherward. And here, once more, culture lays on us the same obligation as religion, which says, as Bishop Wilson has admirably put it, that "to promote the kingdom of God is to increase and hasten one's own happiness."

But, finally, perfection, — as culture from a thorough disinterested study of human nature and human experience learns to conceive it, — is a harmonious expansion of *all* the powers which make the beauty and worth of human nature, and is not consistent with the over-development of any one power at the expense of the rest. Here culture goes beyond religion, as religion is generally conceived by us.

If culture, then, is a study of perfection, and of harmonious perfection, general perfection, and perfection which consists in becoming something rather than in having something, in an inward condition of the mind and spirit, not in an outward set of circumstances, — it is clear that culture, instead of being the frivolous and useless thing which Mr. Bright,[1] and Mr. Frederic Harrison,[2] and many other Liberals are apt to call it, has a very important function to fulfil for mankind. And this

[1] John Bright (1811–89), English Liberal statesman and orator   [2] (b. 1831), essayist and leader of the Positivist philosophy in England

function is particularly important in our modern world, of which the whole civilisation is, to a much greater degree than the civilisation of Greece and Rome, mechanical and external, and tends constantly to become more so. But above all in our own country has culture a weighty part to perform, because here that mechanical character, which civilisation tends to take everywhere, is shown in the most eminent degree. Indeed nearly all the characters of perfection, as culture teaches us to fix them, meet in this country with some powerful tendency which thwarts them and sets them at defiance. The idea of perfection as an *inward* condition of the mind and spirit is at variance with the mechanical and material civilisation in esteem with us, and nowhere, as I have said, so much in esteem as with us. The idea of perfection as a *general* expansion of the human family is at variance with our strong individualism, our hatred of all limits to the unrestrained swing of the individual's personality, our maxim of "every man for himself." Above all, the idea of perfection as a *harmonious* expansion of human nature is at variance with our want of flexibility, with our inaptitude for seeing more than one side of a thing, with our intense energetic absorption in the particular pursuit we happen to be following. So culture has a rough task to achieve in this country. Its preachers have, and are likely long to have, a hard time of it, and they will much oftener be regarded, for a great while to come, as elegant or spurious Jeremiahs than as friends and benefactors. That, however, will not prevent their doing in the end good service if they persevere. And, meanwhile, the mode of action they have to pursue, and the sort of habits they must fight against, ought to be made quite clear for every one to see, who may be willing to look at the matter attentively and dispassionately.

Faith in machinery is, I said, our besetting danger; often in machinery most absurdly disproportioned to the end which this machinery, if it is to do any good at all, is to serve; but always in machinery, as if it had a value in and for itself. What is freedom but machinery? what is population but machinery? what is coal but machinery? what are railroads but machinery? what is wealth but machinery? what are, even, religious organisations but machinery? Now almost every voice in England is accustomed to speak of

these things as if they were precious ends in themselves, and therefore had some of the characters of perfection indisputably joined to them. I have before now noticed Mr. Roebuck's stock argument for proving the greatness and happiness of England as she is, and for quite stopping the mouths of all gainsayers. Mr. Roebuck is never weary of reiterating this argument of his, so I do not know why I should be weary of noticing it. "May not every man in England say what he likes?" — Mr. Roebuck perpetually asks; and that, he thinks, is quite sufficient, and when every man may say what he likes, our aspirations ought to be satisfied. But the aspirations of culture, which is the study of perfection, are not satisfied, unless what men say, when they may say what they like, is worth saying, — has good in it, and more good than bad. In the same way the *Times*, replying to some foreign strictures on the dress, looks, and behaviour of the English abroad, urges that the English ideal is that every one should be free to do and to look just as he likes. But culture indefatigably tries, not to make what each raw person may like the rule by which he fashions himself; but to draw ever nearer to a sense of what is indeed beautiful, graceful, and becoming, and to get the raw person to like that.

And in the same way with respect to railroads and coal. Every one must have observed the strange language current during the late discussions as to the possible failure of our supplies of coal. Our coal, thousands of people were saying, is the real basis of our national greatness; if our coal runs short, there is an end of the greatness of England. But what *is* greatness? — culture makes us ask. Greatness is a spiritual condition worthy to excite love, interest, and admiration; and the outward proof of possessing greatness is that we excite love, interest, and admiration. If England were swallowed up by the sea to-morrow, which of the two, a hundred years hence, would most excite the love, interest, and admiration of mankind, — would most, therefore, show the evidences of having possessed greatness, — the England of the last twenty years, or the England of Elizabeth, of a time of splendid spiritual effort, but when our coal, and our industrial operations depending on coal, were very little developed? Well, then, what an unsound habit of mind it must be which makes us talk of things like coal or iron as constituting the greatness of England, and how salutary a friend is culture, bent on seeing things as they are, and thus dissipating delusions of this kind and fixing standards of perfection that are real!

Wealth, again, that end to which our prodigious works for material advantage are directed, — the commonest of commonplaces tells us how men are always apt to regard wealth as a precious end in itself; and certainly they have never been so apt thus to regard it as they are in England at the present time. Never did people believe anything more firmly than nine Englishmen out of ten at the present day believe that our greatness and welfare are proved by our being so very rich. Now, the use of culture is that it helps us, by means of its spiritual standard of perfection, to regard wealth as but machinery, and not only to say as a matter of words that we regard wealth as but machinery, but really to perceive and feel that it is so. If it were not for this purging effect wrought upon our minds by culture, the whole world, the future as well as the present, would inevitably belong to the Philistines.[1] The people who believe most that our greatness and welfare are proved by our being very rich, and who most give their lives and thoughts to becoming rich, are just the very people whom we call Philistines. Culture says: "Consider these people, then, their way of life, their habits, their manners, the very tones of their voice; look at them attentively; observe the literature they read, the things which give them pleasure, the words which come forth out of their mouths, the thoughts which make the furniture of their minds: would any amount of wealth be worth having with the condition that one was to become just like these people by having it?" And thus culture begets a dissatisfaction which is of the highest possible value in stemming the common tide of men's thoughts in a wealthy and industrial community, and which saves the future, as one may hope, from being vulgarised, even if it cannot save the present.

Population, again, and bodily health and vigour, are things which are nowhere treated in such an unintelligent, misleading, exaggerated way as in England. Both are really machinery; yet how many people all around us do we see rest in them and fail to look beyond them! Why, one has heard people, fresh from reading certain articles of the Times on the Registrar-General's returns of marriages and births in this country, who would talk of our large English families in quite a solemn strain, as if they had something in itself beautiful, elevating, and meritorious in them; as if the British Philistine would have only to present himself before the Great Judge with his twelve children, in order to be received among the sheep as a matter of right!

But bodily health and vigour, it may be said, are not to be classed with wealth and population as mere machinery; they have a more real and essential value. True; but only as they are more intimately connected with a perfect spiritual condition than wealth or population are. The moment we disjoin them from the idea of a perfect spiritual condition, and pursue them, as we do pursue them, for their own sake and as ends in themselves, our worship of them becomes as mere worship of machinery, as our worship of wealth or population, and as unintelligent and vulgarising a worship as that is. Every one with anything like an adequate idea of human perfection has distinctly marked this subordination to higher and spiritual ends of the cultivation of bodily vigour and activity. "Bodily exercise profiteth little; but godliness is profitable unto all things," says the author of the Epistle to Timothy. And the utilitarian Franklin says just as explicitly: — "Eat and drink such an exact quantity as suits the constitution of thy body, *in reference to the services of the mind.*" But the point of view of culture, keeping the mark of human perfection simply and broadly in view, and not assigning to this perfection, as religion or utilitarianism assigns to it, a special and limited character, this point of view, I say, of culture is best given by these words of Epictetus:[1] — "It is a sign of ἀφυΐα," says he, — that is, of a nature not finely tempered, — "to give yourselves up to things which relate to the body; to make, for instance, a great fuss about exercise, a great fuss about eating, a great fuss about drinking, a great fuss about walking, a great fuss about riding. All these things ought to be done merely by the way:

---

[1] those who have no interest beyond "the main chance," enemies of ideas and art

[1] a Roman Stoic philosopher, author of many famous maxims of conduct

the formation of the spirit and character must be our real concern." This is admirable; and, indeed, the Greek word εὐφυΐα, a finely tempered nature, gives exactly the notion of perfection as culture brings us to conceive it; a harmonious perfection, a perfection in which the characters of beauty and intelligence are both present, which unites "the two noblest of things," — as Swift, who of one of the two, at any rate, had himself all too little, most happily calls them in his *Battle of the Books*, — "the two noblest of things, *sweetness and light.*" The εὐφυής is the man who tends towards sweetness and light; the ἀφυής, on the other hand, is our Philistine. The immense spiritual significance of the Greeks is due to their having been inspired with this central and happy idea of the essential character of human perfection; and Mr. Bright's misconception of culture, as a smattering of Greek and Latin, comes itself, after all, from this wonderful significance of the Greeks having affected the very machinery of our education, and is in itself a kind of homage to it.

In thus making sweetness and light to be characters of perfection, culture is of like spirit with poetry, follows one law with poetry. Far more than on our freedom, our population, and our industrialism, many amongst us rely upon our religious organisations to save us. I have called religion a yet more important manifestation of human nature than poetry, because it has worked on a broader scale for perfection, and with greater masses of men. But the idea of beauty and of a human nature perfect on all its sides, which is the dominant idea of poetry, is a true and invaluable idea, though it has not yet had the success that the idea of conquering the obvious faults of our animality, and of a human nature perfect on the moral side, — which is the dominant idea of religion, — has been enabled to have; and it is destined, adding to itself the religious idea of a devout energy, to transform and govern the other.

The best art and poetry of the Greeks, in which religion and poetry are one, in which the idea of beauty and of a human nature perfect on all sides adds to itself a religious and devout energy, and works in the strength of that, is on this account of such surpassing interest and instructiveness for us, though it was, — as, having regard to the Greeks themselves, we must own, — a premature attempt, an attempt which for success needed the moral and religious fibre in humanity to be more braced and developed than it had yet been. But Greece did not err in having the idea of beauty, harmony, and complete human perfection, so present and paramount. It is impossible to have this idea too present and paramount; only, the moral fibre must be braced too. And we, because we have braced the moral fibre, are not on that account in the right way, if at the same time the idea of beauty, harmony, and complete human perfection, is wanting or misapprehended amongst us; and evidently it *is* wanting or misapprehended at present. And when we rely as we do on our religious organisations, which in themselves do not and cannot give us this idea, and think we have done enough if we make them spread and prevail, then, I say, we fall into our common fault of overvaluing machinery.

* * * * * * *

The impulse of the English race towards moral development and self-conquest has nowhere so powerfully manifested itself as in Puritanism. Nowhere has Puritanism found so adequate an expression as in the religious organisation of the Independents.[1] The modern Independents have a newspaper, the *Nonconformist*, written with great sincerity and ability. The motto, the standard, the profession of faith which this organ of theirs carries aloft, is: "The Dissidence of Dissent and the Protestantism of the Protestant religion."[2] There is sweetness and light, and an ideal of complete harmonious human perfection! One need not go to culture and poetry to find language to judge it. Religion, with its instinct for perfection, supplies language to judge it, language, too, which is in our mouths every day. "Finally, be of one mind, united in feeling," says St. Peter. There is an ideal which judges the Puritan ideal: "The Dissidence of Dissent and the Protestantism of the Protestant religion!" And religious organisations like this are what people believe in, rest in, would give their lives for! Such, I say, is the wonderful virtue of even the beginnings of perfection, of having conquered even the plain faults of our animality, that the religious organisation which has helped us to do it can seem to us something precious, salutary, and

---

[1] *i.e.*, Congregationalists [2] Quoted from Burke's speech on *Conciliation*.

to be propagated, even when it wears such a brand of imperfection on its forehead as this. And men have got such a habit of giving to the language of religion a special application, of making it a mere jargon, that for the condemnation which religion itself passes on the shortcomings of their religious organisations they have no ear; they are sure to cheat themselves and to explain this condemnation away. They can only be reached by the criticism which culture, like poetry, speaking a language not to be sophisticated, and resolutely testing these organisations by the ideal of a human perfection complete on all sides, applies to them.

But men of culture and poetry, it will be said, are again and again failing, and failing conspicuously, in the necessary first stage to a harmonious perfection, in the subduing of the great obvious faults of our animality, which it is the glory of these religious organisations to have helped us to subdue. True, they do often so fail. They have often been without the virtues as well as the faults of the Puritan; it has been one of their dangers that they so felt the Puritan's faults that they too much neglected the practice of his virtues. I will not, however, exculpate them at the Puritan's expense. They have often failed in morality, and morality is indispensable. And they have been punished for their failure, as the Puritan has been rewarded for his performance. They have been punished wherein they erred; but their ideal of beauty, of sweetness and light, and a human nature complete on all its sides, remains the true ideal of perfection still; just as the Puritan's ideal of perfection remains narrow and inadequate, although for what he did well he has been richly rewarded. Notwithstanding the mighty results of the Pilgrim Fathers' voyage, they and their standard of perfection are rightly judged when we figure to ourselves Shakspeare or Virgil, — souls in whom sweetness and light, and all that in human nature is most humane, were eminent, — accompanying them on their voyage, and think what intolerable company Shakspeare and Virgil would have found them! In the same way let us judge the religious organisations which we see all around us. Do not let us deny the good and the happiness which they have accomplished; but do not let us fail to see clearly that their idea of human perfection is narrow and inadequate, and that the Dissidence of Dissent and the Protestantism of the Protestant religion will never bring

humanity to its true goal. As I said with regard to wealth: Let us look at the life of those who live in and for it, — so I say with regard to the religious organisations. Look at the life imaged in such a newspaper as the *Nonconformist*, — a life of jealousy of the Establishment, disputes, tea-meetings, openings of chapels, sermons; and then think of it as an ideal of a human life completing itself on all sides, and aspiring with all its organs after sweetness, light, and perfection!

Another newspaper, representing, like the *Nonconformist*, one of the religious organisations of this country, was a short time ago giving an account of the crowd at Epsom on the Derby[1] day, and of all the vice and hideousness which was to be seen in that crowd; and then the writer turned suddenly round upon Professor Huxley,[2] and asked him how he proposed to cure all this vice and hideousness without religion. I confess I felt disposed to ask the asker this question: and how do you propose to cure it with such a religion as yours? How is the ideal of a life so unlovely, so unattractive, so incomplete, so narrow, so far removed from a true and satisfying ideal of human perfection, as is the life of your religious organisation as you yourself reflect it, to conquer and transform all this vice and hideousness? Indeed, the strongest plea for the study of perfection as pursued by culture, the clearest proof of the actual inadequacy of the idea of perfection held by the religious organisations, — expressing, as I have said, the most wide-spread effort which the human race has yet made after perfection, — is to be found in the state of our life and society with these in possession of it, and having been in possession of it I know not how many hundred years. We are all of us included in some religious organisation or other; we all call ourselves, in the sublime and aspiring language of religion which I have before noticed, *children of God*. Children of God; — it is an immense pretension! — and how are we to justify it? By the works which we do, and the words which we speak. And the work which we collective children of God do, our grand centre of life, our *city* which we have builded for us to dwell in, is London! London, with its unutterable external hideousness, and with its internal canker of *publicc*

<hr>

[1] an annual race for three-year-olds   [2] a biologist and agnostic (1825-95)

egestas, privatim opulentia,[1] — to use the words which Sallust puts into Cato's mouth about Rome, — unequalled in the world! The word, again, which we children of God speak, the voice which most hits our collective thought, the newspaper with the largest circulation in England, nay, with the largest circulation in the whole world, is the *Daily Telegraph!* I say that when our religious organisations, — which I admit to express the most considerable effort after perfection that our race has yet made, — land us in no better result than this, it is high time to examine carefully their idea of perfection, and to see whether it does not leave out of account sides and forces of human nature which we might turn to great use; whether it would not be more operative if it were more complete. And I say that the English reliance on our religious organisations and on their ideas of human perfection just as they stand, is like our reliance on freedom, on muscular Christianity, on population, on coal, on wealth, — mere belief in machinery, and unfruitful; and that it is wholesomely counteracted by culture, bent on seeing things as they are, and on drawing the human race onwards to a more complete, a harmonious perfection.

Culture, however, shows its single-minded love of perfection, its desire simply to make reason and the will of God prevail, its freedom from fanaticism, by its attitude towards all this machinery, even while it insists that it is machinery. Fanatics, seeing the mischief men do themselves by their blind belief in some machinery or other, — whether it is wealth and industrialism, or whether it is the cultivation of bodily strength and activity, or whether it is a religious organisation, — oppose with might and main the tendency to this or that political and religious organisation, or to games and athletic exercises, or to wealth and industrialism, and try violently to stop it. But the flexibility which sweetness and light give, and which is one of the rewards of culture pursued in good faith, enables a man to see that a tendency may be necessary, and even, as a preparation for something in the future, salutary, and yet that the generations or individuals who obey this tendency are sacrificed to it, that they fall short of the hope of perfection by following it; and that its

mischiefs are to be criticised, lest it should take too firm a hold and last after it has served its purpose.

Mr. Gladstone well pointed out, in a speech at Paris, — and others have pointed out the same thing, — how necessary is the present great movement towards wealth and industrialism, in order to lay broad foundations of material well-being for the society of the future. The worst of these justifications is, that they are generally addressed to the very people engaged, body and soul, in the movement in question; at all events, that they are always seized with the greatest avidity by these people, and taken by them as quite justifying their life; and that thus they tend to harden them in their sins. Now, culture admits the necessity of the movement towards fortune-making and exaggerated industrialism, readily allows that the future may derive benefit from it; but insists, at the same time, that the passing generations of industrialists, — forming, for the most part, the stout main body of Philistinism, — are sacrificed to it. In the same way, the result of all the games and sports which occupy the passing generation of boys and young men may be the establishment of a better and sounder physical type for the future to work with. Culture does not set itself against the games and sports; it congratulates the future, and hopes it will make a good use of its improved physical basis; but it points out that our passing generation of boys and young men is, meantime, sacrificed. Puritanism was perhaps necessary to develop the moral fibre of the English race, Nonconformity to break the yoke of ecclesiastical domination over men's minds and to prepare the way for freedom of thought in the distant future; still, culture points out that the harmonious perfection of generations of Puritans and Nonconformists has been, in consequence, sacrificed. Freedom of speech may be necessary for the society of the future, but the young lions[1] of the *Daily Telegraph* in the meanwhile are sacrificed. A voice for every man in his country's government may be necessary for the society of the future, but meanwhile Mr. Beales[2] and Mr. Bradlaugh[3] are sacrificed.

---

[1] "public want and private wealth," quoted from Sallust's *Catiline*, lii

[1] Arnold's term for the editorial writers of the *Telegraph*　[2] Edmond Beales, M.P., an active advocate of reforms　[3] Charles Bradlaugh, a radical lecturer and writer, later a member of Parliament

Oxford, the Oxford of the past, has many faults; and she has heavily paid for them in defeat, in isolation, in want of hold upon the modern world. Yet we in Oxford, brought up amidst the beauty and sweetness of that beautiful place, have not failed to seize one truth, — the truth that beauty and sweetness are essential characters of a complete human perfection. When I insist on this, I am all in the faith and tradition of Oxford. I say boldly that this our sentiment for beauty and sweetness, our sentiment against hideousness and rawness, has been at the bottom of our attachment to so many beaten causes, of our opposition to so many triumphant movements. And the sentiment is true, and has never been wholly defeated, and has shown its power even in its defeat. We have not won our political battles, we have not carried our main points, we have not stopped our adversaries' advance, we have not marched victoriously with the modern world; but we have told silently upon the mind of the country, we have prepared currents of feeling which sap our adversaries' position when it seems gained, we have kept up our own communications with the future. Look at the course of the great movement which shook Oxford to its centre some thirty years ago! It was directed, as any one who reads Dr. Newman's *Apology*[1] may see, against what in one word may be called "Liberalism." Liberalism prevailed; it was the appointed force to do the work of the hour; it was necessary, it was inevitable that it should prevail. The Oxford movement was broken, it failed; our wrecks are scattered on every shore: —

Quae regio in terris nostri non plena laboris? [2]

But what was it, this liberalism, as Dr. Newman saw it, and as it really broke the Oxford movement? It was the great middle-class liberalism, which had for the cardinal points of its belief the Reform Bill of 1832, and local self-government, in politics; in the social sphere, free-trade, unrestricted competition, and the making of large industrial fortunes; in the religious sphere, the Dissidence of Dissent and the Protestantism of the Protestant religion. I do not say that other and more intelligent forces than this were not

opposed to the Oxford movement: but this was the force which really beat it; this was the force which Dr. Newman felt himself fighting with; this was the force which till only the other day seemed to be the paramount force in this country, and to be in possession of the future; this was the force whose achievements fill Mr. Lowe[1] with such inexpressible admiration, and whose rule he was so horror-struck to see threatened. And where is this great force of Philistinism now? It is thrust into the second rank, it is become a power of yesterday, it has lost the future. A new power has suddenly appeared, a power which it is impossible yet to judge fully, but which is certainly a wholly different force from middle-class liberalism; different in its cardinal points of belief, different in its tendencies in every sphere. It loves and admires neither the legislation of middle-class Parliaments, nor the local self-government of middle-class vestries, nor the unrestricted competition of middle-class industrialists, nor the Dissidence of middle-class Dissent and the Protestantism of middle-class Protestant religion. I am not now praising this new force, or saying that its own ideals are better; all I say is, that they are wholly different. And who will estimate how much the currents of feeling created by Dr. Newman's movement, the keen desire for beauty and sweetness which it nourished, the deep aversion it manifested to the hardness and vulgarity of middle-class liberalism, the strong light it turned on the hideous and grotesque illusions of middle-class Protestantism, — who will estimate how much all these contributed to swell the tide of secret dissatisfaction which has mined the ground under self-confident liberalism of the last thirty years, and has prepared the way for its sudden collapse and supersession? It is in this manner that the sentiment of Oxford for beauty and sweetness conquers, and in this manner long may it continue to conquer!

* * * * * *

Culture is always assigning to system-makers and systems a smaller share in the bent of human destiny than their friends like. A current in people's minds sets towards new ideas; people are dissatisfied with their old

---

[1] J. H. Newman (later Cardinal), *Apologia pro Vita Sua* [2] "What region in the world is not filled with the tale of our woe?"

[1] Robert Lowe (afterwards Lord Sherbrooke), a bitter opponent of Disraeli's Reform Bill

narrow stock of Philistine ideas, Anglo-Saxon ideas, or any other; and some man, some Bentham [1] or Comte,[2] who has the real merit of having early and strongly felt and helped the new current, but who brings plenty of narrowness and mistakes of his own into his feeling and help of it, is credited with being the author of the whole current, the fit person to be entrusted with its regulation and to guide the human race.

The excellent German historian of the mythology of Rome, Preller, relating the introduction at Rome under the Tarquins [3] of the worship of Apollo, the god of light, healing, and reconciliation, will have us observe that it was not so much the Tarquins who brought to Rome the new worship of Apollo, as a current in the mind of the Roman people which set powerfully at that time towards a new worship of this kind, and away from the old run of Latin and Sabine [4] religious ideas. In a similar way, culture directs our attention to the natural current there is in human affairs, and to its continual working, and will not let us rivet our faith upon any one man and his doings. It makes us see not only his good side, but also how much in him was of necessity limited and transient; nay, it even feels a pleasure, a sense of an increased freedom and of an ampler future, in so doing.

I remember, when I was under the influence of a mind to which I feel the greatest obligations, the mind of a man who was the very incarnation of sanity and clear sense, a man the most considerable, it seems to me, whom America has yet produced, — Benjamin Franklin, — I remember the relief with which, after long feeling the sway of Franklin's imperturbable common-sense, I came upon a project of his for a new version of the Book of Job, to replace the old version, the style of which, says Franklin, has become obsolete, and thence less agreeable. "I give," he continues, "a few verses, which may serve as a sample of the kind of version I would recommend." We all recollect the famous verse

in our translation: "Then Satan answered the Lord and said: 'Doth Job fear God for nought?'" Franklin makes this: "Does your Majesty imagine that Job's good conduct is the effect of mere personal attachment and affection?" I well remember how, when first I read that, I drew a deep breath of relief, and said to myself: "After all, there is a stretch of humanity beyond Franklin's victorious good sense!" So, after hearing Bentham cried loudly up as the renovator of modern society, and Bentham's mind and ideas proposed as the rulers of our future, I open the *Deontology*.[1] There I read: "While Xenophon was writing his history and Euclid teaching geometry, Socrates and Plato were talking nonsense under pretence of talking wisdom and morality. This morality of theirs consisted in words; this wisdom of theirs was the denial of matters known to every man's experience." From the moment of reading that, I am delivered from the bondage of Bentham! the fanaticism of his adherents can touch me no longer. I feel the inadequacy of his mind and ideas for supplying the rule of human society, for perfection.

Culture tends always thus to deal with the men of a system, of disciples, of a school; with men like Comte, or the late Mr. Buckle, or Mr. Mill.[2] However much it may find to admire in these personages, or in some of them, it nevertheless remembers the text: "Be not ye called Rabbi!" and it soon passes on from any Rabbi. But Jacobinism loves a Rabbi; it does not want to pass on from its Rabbi in pursuit of a future and still unreached perfection; it wants its Rabbi and his ideas to stand for perfection, that they may with the more authority recast the world; and for Jacobinism, therefore, culture, — eternally passing onwards and seeking, — is an impertinence and an offence. But culture, just because it resists this tendency of Jacobinism to impose on us a man with limitations and errors of his own along with the true ideas of which he is the organ, really does the world and Jacobinism itself a service.

So, too, Jacobinism, in its fierce hatred of the past and of those whom it makes liable for the sins of the past, cannot away with the inexhaustible indulgence proper to culture, the consideration of circumstances, the severe

---

[1] Jeremy Bentham (1748–1832), founder of Utilitarianism, the doctrine that virtue consists in acting for the greatest happiness of the greatest number [2] Auguste Comte (1798–1857), founder of Positivism, the doctrine that only the verifiable facts of existence are to be attended to in philosophy [3] mythical kings of Rome [4] a race incorporated with the Romans

[1] "The theory of what is proper" [2] rationalistic philosophers

judgment of actions joined to the merciful judgment of persons. "The man of culture is in politics," cries Mr. Frederic Harrison, "one of the poorest mortals alive !" Mr. Frederic Harrison wants to be doing business, and he complains that the man of culture stops him with a "turn for small fault-finding, love of selfish ease, and indecision in action." Of what use is culture, he asks, except for "a critic of new books or a professor of *belles lettres*"? Why, it is of use because, in presence of the fierce exasperation which breathes, or rather, I may say, hisses through the whole production in which Mr. Frederic Harrison asks that question, it reminds us that the perfection of human nature is sweetness and light. It is of use because, like religion, — that other effort after perfection, — it testifies that, where bitter envying and strife are, there is confusion and every evil work.

The pursuit of perfection, then, is the pursuit of sweetness and light. He who works for sweetness and light, works to make reason and the will of God prevail. He who works for machinery, he who works for hatred, works only for confusion. Culture looks beyond machinery, culture hates hatred; culture has one great passion, the passion for sweetness and light. It has one even yet greater ! — the passion for making them *prevail*. It is not satisfied till we *all* come to a perfect man ; it knows that the sweetness and light of the few must be imperfect until the raw and unkindled masses of humanity are touched with sweetness and light. If I have not shrunk from saying that we must work for sweetness and light, so neither have I shrunk from saying that we must have a broad basis, must have sweetness and light for as many as possible. Again and again I have insisted how those are the happy moments of humanity, how those are the marking epochs of a people's life, how those are the flowering times for literature and art and all the creative power of genius, when there is a *national* glow of life and thought, when the whole of society is in the fullest measure permeated by thought, sensible to beauty, intelligent and alive. Only it must be *real* thought and *real* beauty ; *real* sweetness and *real* light. Plenty of people will try to give the masses, as they call them, an intellectual food prepared and adapted in the way they think proper for the actual condition of the masses. The ordinary popular literature is an example of this way of working on the masses. Plenty of people will try to indoctrinate the masses with the set of ideas and judgments constituting the creed of their own profession or party. Our religious and political organisations give an example of this way of working on the masses. I condemn neither way ; but culture works differently. It does not try to teach down to the level of inferior classes ; it does not try to win them for this or that sect of its own, with ready-made judgments and watchwords. It seeks to do away with classes ; to make the best that has been thought and known in the world current everywhere ; to make all men live in an atmosphere of sweetness and light, where they may use ideas, as it uses them itself, freely, — nourished, and not bound by them.

This is the *social idea ;* and the men of culture are the true apostles of equality. The great men of culture are those who have had a passion for diffusing, for making prevail, for carrying from one end of society to the other, the best knowledge, the best ideas of their time ; who have laboured to divest knowledge of all that was harsh, uncouth, difficult, abstract, professional, exclusive ; to humanise it, to make it efficient outside the clique of the cultivated and learned, yet still remaining the *best* knowledge and thought of the time, and a true source, therefore, of sweetness and light. Such a man was Abelard[1] in the Middle Ages, in spite of all his imperfections ; and thence the boundless emotion and enthusiasm which Abelard excited. Such were Lessing[2] and Herder[3] in Germany, at the end of the last century ; and their services to Germany were in this way inestimably precious. Generations will pass, and literary monuments will accumulate, and works far more perfect than the works of Lessing and Herder will be produced in Germany ; and yet the names of these two men will fill a German with a reverence and enthusiasm such as the names of the most gifted masters will hardly awaken. And why ? Because they *humanised* knowledge ; because they broadened the basis of life and intelligence ; because they worked powerfully to diffuse sweetness and light, to make reason and the will of God prevail. With Saint

[1] Pierre Abelard (1079–1142), a brilliant teacher and philosopher [2] G. E. Lessing (1729–1781), famous German dramatist and critic [3] J. G. von Herder (1744–1803), poet and critic

Augustine they said: "Let us not leave thee alone to make in the secret of thy knowledge, as thou didst before the creation of the firmament, the division of light from darkness; let the children of thy spirit, placed in their firmament, make their light shine upon the earth, mark the division of night and day, and announce the revolution of the times; for the old order is passed, and the new arises; the night is spent, the day is come forth; and thou shalt. crown the year with thy blessing, when thou shalt send forth labourers into thy harvest sown by other hands than theirs; when thou shalt send forth new labourers to new seedtimes, whereof the harvest shall be not yet."

SHAKESPEARE

Others abide our question. Thou art free.
We ask and ask: Thou smilest and art still,
Out-topping knowledge. For the loftiest hill
That to the stars uncrowns his majesty,
Planting his steadfast footsteps in the sea,
Making the Heaven of Heavens his dwelling-place,
Spares but the cloudy border of his base
To the foil'd searching of mortality:
And thou, who didst the stars and sunbeams know,
Self-school'd, self-scann'd, self-honour'd, self-secure,   10
Didst walk on Earth unguess'd at. Better so!
All pains the immortal spirit must endure,
All weakness that impairs, all griefs that bow,
Find their sole voice in that victorious brow.

THE FORSAKEN MERMAN

Come, dear children, let us away;
  Down and away below.
Now my brothers call from the bay;
Now the great winds shorewards blow;
Now the salt tides seawards flow;   5
Now the wild white horses play,
Champ and chafe and toss in the spray.
    Children dear, let us away.
    This way, this way.

Call her once before you go.   10
  Call once yet.
In a voice that she will know:
  "Margaret! Margaret!"

Children's voices should be dear
(Call once more) to a mother's ear:
Children's voices, wild with pain.
    Surely she will come again.
Call her once and come away.
    This way, this way.
"Mother dear, we cannot stay."   20
The wild white horses foam and fret.
    Margaret! Margaret!

Come, dear children, come away down.
    Call no more.
One last look at the white-wall'd town,   25
And the little grey church on the windy shore.
    Then come down.
She will not come though you call all day.
    Come away, come away.

Children dear, was it yesterday   30
We heard the sweet bells over the bay?
    In the caverns where we lay,
    Through the surf and through the swell
The far-off sound of a silver bell?
Sand-strewn caverns, cool and deep,
Where the winds are all asleep;
Where the spent lights quiver and gleam;
Where the salt weed sways in the stream;
Where the sea-beasts, rang'd all round,
Feed in the ooze of their pasture-ground;   40
Where the sea-snakes coil and twine,
Dry their mail and bask in the brine;
Where great whales come sailing by,
Sail and sail, with unshut eye,
Round the world forever and aye?   45
    When did music come this way?
    Children dear, was it yesterday?

    Children dear, was it yesterday
    (Call yet once) that she went away?
    Once she sate with you and me,   50
    On a red gold throne in the heart of the sea,
    And the youngest sate on her knee.
She comb'd its bright hair, and she tended it well,
When down swung the sound of the far-off bell.
She sigh'd, she look'd up through the clear green sea.
She said: "I must go, for my kinsfolk pray
In the little grey church on the shore to-day.
'Twill be Easter-time in the world — ah me!
And I lose my poor soul, Merman, here with thee."
I said: "Go up, dear heart, through the waves.

Say thy prayer, and come back to the kind sea-
    caves."   61
    She smil'd, she went up through the surf
      in the bay.
    Children dear, was it yesterday?

    Children dear, were we long alone?
"The sea grows stormy, the little ones moan.
Long prayers," I said, "in the world they say.
Come," I said, and we rose through the surf in
    the bay.
We went up the beach, by the sandy down
Where the sea-stocks bloom, to the white-
    wall'd town.
Through the narrow pav'd streets, where all
    was still,   70
To the little grey church on the windy hill.
From the church came a murmur of folk at
    their prayers,
But we stood without in the cold blowing airs.
We climb'd on the graves, on the stones, worn
    with rains,
And we gaz'd up the aisle through the small
    leaded panes.
    She sate by the pillar; we saw her clear:
    "Margaret, hist! come quick, we are here.
    Dear heart," I said, "we are long alone.
    The sea grows stormy, the little ones
      moan."
But, ah, she gave me never a look,   80
For her eyes were seal'd to the holy book.
Loud prays the priest; shut stands the door.
Come away, children, call no more.
Come away, come down, call no more.

    Down, down, down.
    Down to the depths of the sea.
She sits at her wheel in the humming town,
    Singing most joyfully.
Hark, what she sings; "O joy, O joy,
For the humming street, and the child with
    its toy.
For the priest, and the bell, and the holy well.
    For the wheel where I spun,   92
    And the blessed light of the sun."
And so she sings her fill,
Singing most joyfully,
Till the shuttle falls from her hand,
And the whizzing wheel stands still.
She steals to the window, and looks at the
    sand;
And over the sand at the sea;
And her eyes are set in a stare;   100
And anon there breaks a sigh,
And anon there drops a tear,

From a sorrow-clouded eye,
And a heart sorrow-laden,
    A long, long sigh.
For the cold strange eyes of a little Mermaiden
And the gleam of her golden hair.

Come away, away, children.
Come, children, come down.
The salt tide rolls seaward.   110
Lights shine in the town.
She will start from her slumber
When gusts shake the door;
She will hear the winds howling,
Will hear the waves roar.
We shall see, while above us
The waves roar and whirl,
A ceiling of amber,
A pavement of pearl.
Singing, "Here came a mortal,   120
But faithless was she.
And alone dwell forever
The kings of the sea."

But, children, at midnight,
When soft the winds blow;
When clear falls the moonlight;
When spring-tides are low;
When sweet airs come seaward
From heaths starr'd with broom;
And high rocks throw mildly   130
On the blanch'd sands a gloom:
Up the still, glistening beaches,
Up the creeks we will hie;
Over banks of bright seaweed
The ebb-tide leaves dry,
We will gaze, from the sand-hills,
At the white, sleeping town;
At the church on the hill-side —
    And then come back down.
Singing, "There dwells a lov'd one,   140
But cruel is she.
She left lonely forever
The kings of the sea."

TO MARGUERITE

IN RETURNING A VOLUME OF THE LETTERS OF ORTIS[1]

Yes! in the sea of life enisl'd,[2]
With echoing straits between us thrown,

[1] *The Last Letters of Jacopo Ortis*, a popular
sentimental romance (1797) by Ugo Foscolo, an
Italian poet and novelist   [2] confined to islands

Dotting the shoreless watery wild,
We mortal millions live *alone*.
The islands feel the enclasping flow,
And then their endless bounds they know. 6

But when the moon their hollows lights,
And they are swept by balms of spring,
And in their glens, on starry nights,
The nightingales divinely sing;
And lovely notes, from shore to shore,
Across the sounds and channels pour — 12

Oh! then a longing like despair
Is to their farthest caverns sent;
For surely once, they feel, we were
Parts of a single continent!
Now round us spreads the watery plain —
Oh might our marges meet again! 18

Who order'd, that their longing's fire
Should be, as soon as kindled, cool'd?
Who renders vain their deep desire? —
A God, a God their severance rul'd!
And bade betwixt their shores to be
The unplumb'd, salt, estranging sea. 24

MORALITY

We cannot kindle when we will
The fire that in the heart resides,
The spirit bloweth and is still,
In mystery our soul abides:
But tasks in hours of insight will'd
Can be through hours of gloom fulfill'd. 6

With aching hands and bleeding feet
We dig and heap, lay stone on stone;
We bear the burden and the heat
Of the long day, and wish 'twere done.
Not till the hours of light return,
All we have built do we discern. 12

Then, when the clouds are off the soul,
When thou dost bask in Nature's eye,
Ask, how *she* view'd thy self-control,
Thy struggling task'd morality —
Nature, whose free, light, cheerful air,
Oft made thee, in thy gloom, despair. 18

And she, whose censure thou dost dread,
Whose eye thou wert afraid to seek,
See, on her face a glow is spread,
A strong emotion on her cheek.
"Ah child," she cries, "that strife divine —
Whence was it, for it is not mine? 24

"There is no effort on *my* brow —
I do not strive, I do not weep.
I rush with the swift spheres, and glow
In joy, and, when I will, I sleep. —
Yet that severe, that earnest air
I saw, I felt it once — but where? 30

"I knew not yet the gauge of Time,
Nor wore the manacles of Space.
I felt it in some other clime —
I saw it in some other place.
— 'Twas when the heavenly house I trod,
And lay upon the breast of God." 36

THE FUTURE

A wanderer is man from his birth.
He was born in a ship
On the breast of the River of Time.
Brimming with wonder and joy
He spreads out his arms to the light,
Rivets his gaze on the banks of the stream.

As what he sees is, so have his thoughts been.
Whether he wakes
Where the snowy mountainous pass
Echoing the screams of the eagles 10
Hems in its gorges the bed
Of the new-born clear-flowing stream:

Whether he first sees light
Where the river in gleaming rings
Sluggishly winds through the plain:
Whether in sound of the swallowing sea: —
As is the world on the banks
So is the mind of the man.

Vainly does each as he glides
Fable and dream 20
Of the lands which the River of Time
Had left ere he woke on its breast,
Or shall reach when his eyes have been
clos'd.
Only the tract where he sails
He wots of: only the thoughts,
Rais'd by the objects he passes, are his.

Who can see the green Earth any more
As she was by the sources of Time?
Who imagines her fields as they lay
In the sunshine, unworn by the plough? 30
Who thinks as they thought,
The tribes who then liv'd on her breast,
Her vigorous primitive sons?

What girl
Now reads in her bosom as clear
As Rebekah read, when she sate
At eve by the palm-shaded well?[1]
Who guards in her breast
As deep, as pellucid a spring
Of feeling, as tranquil, as sure?   40

What Bard,
At the height of his vision, can deem
Of God, of the world, of the soul,
With a plainness as near,
As flashing as Moses felt,
When he lay in the night by his flock
On the starlit Arabian waste?[2]
Can rise and obey
The beck of the Spirit like him?

This tract which the River of Time   50
Now flows through with us, is the Plain.
Gone is the calm of its earlier shore.
Border'd by cities and hoarse
With a thousand cries is its stream.
And we on its breast, our minds
Are confused as the cries which we hear,
Changing and shot as the sights which we
    see.

And we say that repose has fled
Forever the course of the River of Time.
That cities will crowd to its edge   60
In a blacker incessanter line;
That the din will be more on its banks,
Denser the trade on its stream,
Flatter the plain where it flows,
    Fiercer the sun overhead;
That never will those on its breast
See an ennobling sight,
Drink of the feeling of quiet again.

But what was before us we know not,
And we know not what shall succeed.   70

Haply, the River of Time,
As it grows, as the towns on its marge
Fling their wavering lights
On a wider, statelier stream —
May acquire, if not the calm
Of its early mountainous shore,
    Yet a solemn peace of its own.

And the width of the waters, the hush
Of the grey expanse where he floats,

[1] cf. *Genesis* xxiv   [2] cf. *Exodus* iii

Freshening its current and spotted with foam
As it draws to the Ocean, may strike   81
Peace to the soul of the man on its breast:
    As the pale waste widens around him —
As the banks fade dimmer away —
As the stars come out, and the night-wind
Brings up the stream
Murmurs and scents of the infinite Sea.

SOHRAB AND RUSTUM

AN EPISODE

And the first grey of morning fill'd the east,
And the fog rose out of the Oxus[1] stream.
But all the Tartar camp along the stream
Was hush'd, and still the men were plunged in
    sleep:
Sohrab alone, he slept not: all night long
He had lain wakeful, tossing on his bed;
But when the grey dawn stole into his tent,
He rose, and clad himself, and girt his sword,
And took his horseman's cloak, and left his
    tent,
And went abroad into the cold wet fog,   10
Through the dim camp to Peran-Wisa's[2] tent.
    Through the black Tartar tents he pass'd,
        which stood
Clustering like bee-hives on the low flat strand
Of Oxus, where the summer floods o'erflow
When the sun melts the snows in high Pamere:[3]
Through the black tents he pass'd, o'er that
    low strand,
And to a hillock came, a little back
From the stream's brink, the spot where first
    a boat,
Crossing the stream in summer, scrapes the
    land.
The men of former times had crown'd the top
With a clay fort: but that was fall'n; and
    now   21
The Tartars built there Peran-Wisa's tent,
A dome of laths, and o'er it felts were spread.
And Sohrab came there, and went in, and
    stood
Upon the thick-pil'd carpets in the tent,
And found the old man sleeping on his bed
Of rugs and felts, and near him lay his arms.
And Peran-Wisa heard him, though the step

[1] the great river now called Amu Daria, flowing
between Afghanistan and Bokhara and emptying
into the Aral Sea   [2] leader of the Tartars   [3] the
plateau of Pamir (16,000 ft. high), where the Oxus
has its source

Was dull'd; for he slept light, an old man's
　　sleep;　　　　　　　　　　　　　　29
And he rose quickly on one arm, and said: —
"Who art thou? for it is not yet clear dawn.
Speak! is there news, or any night alarm?"
　　But Sohrab came to the bedside, and said:
"Thou know'st me, Peran-Wisa: it is I.
The sun is not yet risen, and the foe
Sleep; but I sleep not; all night long I lie
Tossing and wakeful, and I come to thee.
For so did King Afrasiab[1] bid me seek
Thy counsel, and to heed thee as thy son,
In Samarcand, before the army march'd;
And I will tell thee what my heart desires.　41
Thou know'st if, since from Ader-baijan[2] first
I came among the Tartars, and bore arms,
I have still serv'd Afrasiab well, and shown,
At my boy's years, the courage of a man.
This too thou know'st, that, while I still bear on
The conquering Tartar ensigns through the
　　world,
And beat the Persians back on every field,
I seek one man, one man, and one alone —　49
Rustum, my father; who, I hop'd, should
　　greet,
Should one day greet, upon some well-fought
　　field
His not unworthy, not inglorious son.
So I long hop'd, but him I never find.
Come then, hear now, and grant me what I ask.
Let the two armies rest to-day: but I
Will challenge forth the bravest Persian lords
To meet me, man to man: if I prevail,
Rustum will surely hear it; if I fall —
Old man, the dead need no one, claim no kin.
Dim is the rumour of a common[3] fight,　60
Where host meets host, and many names are
　　sunk:
But of a single combat Fame speaks clear."
　　He spoke: and Peran-Wisa took the hand
Of the young man in his, and sigh'd, and
　　said: —
"O Sohrab, an unquiet heart is thine!
Canst thou not rest among the Tartar chiefs,
And share the battle's common chance with us
Who love thee, but must press forever first,
In single fight incurring single risk,
To find a father thou hast never seen?　70
Or, if indeed this one desire rules all,
To seek out Rustum — seek him not through
　　fight:
Seek him in peace, and carry to his arms,

O Sohrab, carry an unwounded son!
But far hence seek him, for he is not here.
For now it is not as when I was young,
When Rustum was in front of every fray:
But now he keeps apart, and sits at home,
In Seïstan,[1] with Zal, his father old.
Whether that his own mighty strength at last
Feels the abhorr'd approaches of old age;　81
Or in some quarrel with the Persian King.
　　There go! — Thou wilt not? Yet my
　　heart forebodes
Danger or death awaits thee on this field.
Fain would I know thee safe and well, though
　　lost
To us: fain therefore send thee hence, in
　　peace
To seek thy father, not seek single fights
In vain: — but who can keep the lion's cub
From ravening? and who govern Rustum's
　　son?
Go: I will grant thee what thy heart desires."
　　So said he, and dropp'd Sohrab's hand, and
　　left　　　　　　　　　　　　　　91
His bed, and the warm rugs whereon he lay,
And o'er his chilly limbs his woollen coat
He pass'd, and tied his sandals on his feet,
And threw a white cloak round him, and he
　　took
In his right hand a ruler's staff, no sword;
And on his head he placed his sheep-skin cap,
Black, glossy, curl'd, the fleece of Kara-Kul;[2]
And rais'd the curtain of his tent, and call'd
His herald to his side, and went abroad.　100
　　The sun, by this, had risen, and clear'd the
　　fog
From the broad Oxus and the glittering sands:
And from their tents the Tartar horsemen fil'd
Into the open plain; so Haman bade;
Haman, who next to Peran-Wisa rul'd
The host, and still was in his lusty prime.
From their black tents, long files of horse, they
　　stream'd:
As when, some grey November morn, the files
In marching order spread, of long-neck'd
　　cranes,
Stream over Casbin,[3] and the southern slopes
Of Elburz, from the Aralian[4] estuaries,　111
Or some frore[5] Caspian reed-bed, southward
　　bound

[1] king of the Tartars　[2] the northwest province
of Persia, west of the Caspian Sea　[3] general

[1] a district in southwestern Afghanistan, bordering on Persia　[2] a district of Bokhara noted for
sheep, near the city of Bokhara　[3] Kasbin, a city
south of the Caspian Sea and the Elburz Mountains　[4] belonging to the Aral Sea　[5] frozen

For the warm Persian sea-board: so they
stream'd.
The Tartars of the Oxus, the King's guard,
First, with black sheep-skin caps and with
long spears ; ·
Large men, large steeds; who from Bokhara
come
And Khiva, and ferment the milk of mares.[1]
Next the more temperate Toorkmuns [2] of the
south,
The Tukas,[3] and the lances of Salore,   119
And those from Attruck [4] and the Caspian
sands ;
Light men, and on light steeds, who only drink
The acrid milk of camels, and their wells.
And then a swarm of wandering horse, who
came
From far, and a more doubtful service own'd ;
The Tartars of Ferghana, from the banks
Of the Jaxartes,[5] men with scanty beards
And close-set skull-caps; and those wilder
hordes
Who roam o'er Kipchak and the northern
waste,
Kalmuks and unkemp'd Kuzzaks,[6] tribes who
stray
Nearest the Pole, and wandering Kirghizzes,
Who come on shaggy ponies from Pamere. 131
These all fil'd out from camp into the plain.
    And on the other side the Persians form'd:
First a light cloud of horse, Tartars they
seem'd,
The Ilyats of Khorassan: [7] and behind,
The royal troops of Persia, horse and foot,
Marshal'd battalions bright in burnish'd steel.
    But Peran-Wisa with his herald came,
Threading the Tartar squadrons to the front,
And with his staff kept back the foremost
ranks.
And when Ferood, who led the Persians, saw
That Peran-Wisa kept the Tartars back,   142
He took his spear, and to the front he came,
And check'd his ranks, and fix'd them where
they stood.
And the old Tartar came upon the sand
Betwixt the silent hosts, and spake, and
said : —

[1] to make kumiss, an intoxicating drink
[2] Turcomans   [3] the Tekke-Turcomans from Merv
[4] the river Atrek, which flows into the Caspian
Sea (at the southeast corner)   [5] now the Syr
Daria, which rises in northern Pamir and flows
into the Aral Sea   [6] Cossacks   [7] a desert district
in northeastern Persia

"Ferood, and ye, Persians and Tartars,
hear !
Let there be truce between the hosts to-day.
But choose a champion from the Persian lords
To fight our champion Sohrab, man to man."
    As, in the country, on a morn in June,   151
When the dew glistens on the pearlèd ears,
A shiver runs through the deep corn [1] for
joy —
So, when they heard what Peran-Wisa said,
A thrill through all the Tartar squadrons ran
Of pride and hope for Sohrab, whom they
lov'd.
    But as a troop of peddlers, from Cabool,[2]
Cross underneath the Indian Caucasus,[3]
That vast sky-neighboring mountain of milk
snow ;   159
Winding so high, that, as they mount, they
pass
Long flocks of travelling birds dead on the
snow,
Chok'd by the air, and scarce can they them-
selves
Slake their parch'd throats with sugar'd mul-
berries —
In single file they move, and stop their breath,
For fear they should dislodge the o'erhanging
snows —
So the pale Persians held their breath with
fear.
    And to Ferood his brother Chiefs came up
To counsel : Gudurz and Zoarrah came,
And Feraburz, who rul'd the Persian host
Second, and was the uncle of the King :   170
These came and counsell'd ; and then Gudurz
said : —
    "Ferood, shame bids us take their challenge
up,
Yet champion have we none to match this
youth.
He has the wild stag's foot, the lion's heart.
But Rustum came last night ; aloof he sits
And sullen, and has pitched his tents apart :
Him will I seek, and carry to his ear
The Tartar challenge, and this young man's
name.
Haply he will forget his wrath, and fight.   179
Stand forth the while, and take their chal-
lenge up."
    So spake he ; and Ferood stood forth and
said :
"Old man, be it agreed as thou hast said."

[1] grain, not Indian corn   [2] Kabul   [3] the Hindu-
Kush Mountains

Let Sohrab arm, and we will find a man."
  He spoke; and Peran-Wisa turn'd, and
      strode
Back through the opening squadrons to his
      tent.
But through the anxious Persians Gudurz ran,
And cross'd the camp which lay behind, and
      reach'd,
Out on the sands beyond it, Rustum's tents.
Of scarlet cloth they were, and glittering gay,
Just pitch'd: the high pavilion in the midst
Was Rustum's, and his men lay camp'd
      around.   191
And Gudurz enter'd Rustum's tent, and found
Rustum: his morning meal was done, but still
The table stood beside him, charg'd with food;
A side of roasted sheep, and cakes of bread,
And dark green melons; and there Rustum
      sate
Listless, and held a falcon on his wrist,   197
And play'd with it; but Gudurz came and
      stood
Before him; and he look'd, and saw him
      stand;
And with a cry sprang up, and dropp'd the
      bird,
And greeted Gudurz with both hands, and
      said: —
  "Welcome! these eyes could see no better
      sight.
What news? but sit down first, and eat and
      drink."
  But Gudurz stood in the tent door, and
      said: —
"Not now: a time will come to eat and drink,
But not to-day: to-day has other needs.
The armies are drawn out, and stand at gaze:
For from the Tartars is a challenge brought
To pick a champion from the Persian lords
To fight their champion — and thou know'st
      his name —   210
Sohrab men call him, but his birth is hid.
O Rustum, like thy might is this young man's!
He has the wild stag's foot, the lion's heart.
And he is young, and Iran's Chiefs are old,
Or else too weak; and all eyes turn to thee.
Come down and help us, Rustum, or we lose."
He spoke: but Rustum answer'd with a smile:
"Go to! if Iran's Chiefs are old, then I
Am older: if the young are weak, the King
Errs strangely: for the King, for Kai Khosroo,
Himself is young, and honours younger men,
And lets the agèd moulder to their graves. 222
Rustum he loves no more, but loves the
      young —

The young may rise at Sohrab's vaunts, not I.
For what care I, though all speak Sohrab's
      fame?
For would that I myself had such a son,
And not that one slight helpless girl I have,
A son so fam'd, so brave, to send to war,
And I to tarry with the snow-hair'd Zal,[1]
My father, whom the robber Afghans vex, 230
And clip his borders short, and drive his herds,
And he has none to guard his weak old age.
There would I go, and hang my armour up,
And with my great name fence that weak old
      man,
And spend the goodly treasures I have got,
And rest my age, and hear of Sohrab's fame,
And leave to death the hosts of thankless kings,
And with these slaughterous hands draw
      sword no more."   238
  He spoke, and smiled; and Gudurz made
      reply:
"What then, O Rustum, will men say to this,
When Sohrab dares our bravest forth, and
      seeks
Thee most of all, and thou, whom most he
      seeks,
Hidest thy face?   Take heed, lest men should
      say,
'Like some old miser, Rustum hoards his
      fame,
And shuns to peril it with younger men.'"
And, greatly mov'd, then Rustum made reply:
"O Gudurz, wherefore dost thou say such
      words?
Thou knowest better words than this to say.
What is one more, one less, obscure or fam'd,
Valiant or craven, young or old, to me?   250
Are not they mortal, am not I myself?
But who for men of nought would do great
      deeds?
Come, thou shall see how Rustum hoards his
      fame.
But I will fight unknown, and in plain arms;
Let not men say of Rustum, he was match'd
In single fight with any mortal man."
  He spoke and frown'd; and Gudurz turn'd,
      and ran   257
Back quickly through the camp in fear and joy,
Fear at his wrath, but joy that Rustum came.
But Rustum strode to his tent door, and call'd

---

[1] Zal was at this time old, but according to tradition he was born with snow-white hair, on which
account his father cast him out on the Elburz
Mountains, where he was miraculously preserved
by a griffin, cf. ll. 676–9.

His followers in, and bade them bring his arms,
And clad himself in steel: the arms he chose
Were plain, and on his shield was no device,
Only his helm was rich, inlaid with gold,
And from the fluted spine atop, a plume
Of horsehair wav'd, a scarlet horsehair plume.
So arm'd, he issued forth; and Ruksh, his horse,
Follow'd him, like a faithful hound, at heel,
Ruksh, whose renown was nois'd through all the earth,
The horse, whom Rustum on a foray once 270
Did in Bokhara by the river find
A colt beneath its dam, and drove him home,
And rear'd him; a bright bay, with lofty crest;
Dight with a saddle-cloth of broider'd green
Crusted with gold, and on the ground were work'd
All beasts of chase, all beasts which hunters know:
So follow'd, Rustum left his tents, and cross'd
The camp, and to the Persian host appear'd.
And all the Persians knew him, and with shouts
Hail'd; but the Tartars knew not who he was.
And dear as the wet diver to the eyes 281
Of his pale wife who waits and weeps on shore,
By sandy Bahrein,[1] in the Persian Gulf,
Plunging all day into the blue waves, at night,
Having made up his tale[2] of precious pearls,
Rejoins her in their hut upon the sands —
So dear to the pale Persians Rustum came.

And Rustum to the Persian front advanc'd,
And Sohrab arm'd in Haman's tent, and came.
And as afield the reapers cut a swathe 290
Down through the middle of a rich man's corn,
And on each side are squares of standing corn,
And in the midst a stubble, short and bare;
So on each side were squares of men, with spears
Bristling, and in the midst, the open sand.
And Rustum came upon the sand, and cast
His eyes towards the Tartar tents, and saw
Sohrab come forth, and ey'd him as he came.

As some rich woman, on a winter's morn,
Eyes through her silken curtains the poor drudge 300
Who with numb blacken'd fingers makes her fire —
At cock-crow on a starlit winter's morn,
When the frost flowers the whiten'd window-panes —

And wonders how she lives, and what the thoughts
Of that poor drudge may be; so Rustum ey'd
The unknown adventurous Youth, who from afar
Came seeking Rustum, and defying forth
All the most valiant chiefs: long he perus'd
His spirited air, and wonder'd who he was.
For very young he seem'd, tenderly rear'd;
Like some young cypress, tall, and dark, and straight, 311
Which in a queen's secluded garden throws
Its slight dark shadow on the moonlit turf,
By midnight, to a bubbling fountain's sound—
So slender Sohrab seem'd, so softly rear'd.
And a deep pity enter'd Rustum's soul
As he beheld him coming; and he stood,
And beckon'd to him with his hand, and said:
"O thou young man, the air of Heaven is soft,
And warm, and pleasant; but the grave is cold.
Heaven's air is better than the cold dead grave.
Behold me: I am vast, and clad in iron, 322
And tried; and I have stood on many a field
Of blood, and I have fought with many a foe:
Never was that field lost, or that foe sav'd.
O Sohrab, wherefore wilt thou rush on death?
Be govern'd: quit the Tartar host, and come
To Iran, and be as my son to me,
And fight beneath my banner till I die.
There are no youths in Iran brave as thou."
So he spake, mildly: Sohrab heard his voice, 331
The mighty voice of Rustum; and he saw
His giant figure planted on the sand,
Sole, like some single tower, which a chief
Has builded on the waste in former years
Against the robbers; and he saw that head,
Streak'd with its first grey hairs: hope fill'd his soul;
And he ran forwards and embrac'd his knees,
And clasp'd his hand within his own and said: —
"Oh, by thy father's head! by thine own soul! 340
Art thou not Rustum? Speak! art thou not he?"
But Rustum ey'd askance the kneeling youth,
And turn'd away, and spoke to his own soul:—
"Ah me, I muse what this young fox may mean.
False, wily, boastful, are these Tartar boys.
For if I now confess this thing he asks,

And hide it not, but say, 'Rustum is here,'
He will not yield indeed, nor quit our foes,
But he will find some pretext not to fight,
And praise my fame, and proffer courteous
    gifts,
A belt or sword perhaps, and go his way.   351
And on a feast day, in Afrasiab's hall,
In Samarcand, he will arise and cry:
'I challeng'd once, when the two armies camp'd
Beside the Oxus, all the Persian lords
To cope with me in single fight; but they
Shrank; only Rustum dar'd: then he and I
Chang'd gifts, and went on equal terms away.'
So will he speak, perhaps, while men applaud.
Then were the chiefs of Iran sham'd through
    me."
    And then he turn'd, and sternly spake
    aloud: —
"Rise! wherefore dost thou vainly question
    thus
Of Rustum? I am here, whom thou hast
    call'd
By challenge forth: make good thy vaunt, or
    yield.   364
Is it with Rustum only thou wouldst fight?
Rash boy, men look on Rustum's face and flee.
For well I know, that did great Rustum stand
Before thy face this day, and were reveal'd,
There would be then no talk of fighting more.
But being what I am, I tell thee this;   370
Do thou record it in thine inmost soul:
Either thou shalt renounce thy vaunt, and
    yield;
Or else thy bones shall strew this sand, till
    winds
Bleach them, or Oxus with his summer floods,
Oxus in summer wash them all away."
    He spoke: and Sohrab answer'd, on his
    feet: —
"Art thou so fierce? Thou wilt not fright me
    so.
I am no girl, to be made pale by words.
Yet this thou hast said well, did Rustum stand
Here on this field, there were no fighting then.
But Rustum is far hence, and we stand here.
Begin: thou art more vast, more dread than
    I,   382
And thou art prov'd, I know, and I am
    young —
But yet Success sways with the breath of
    Heaven.
And though thou thinkest that thou knowest
    sure
Thy victory, yet thou canst not surely know.
For we are all, like swimmers in the sea,

Pois'd on the top of a huge wave of Fate,
Which hangs uncertain to which side to fall.
And whether it will heave us up to land,   390
Or whether it will roll us out to sea,
Back out to sea, to the deep waves of death,
We know not, and no search will make us
    know:
Only the event will teach us in its hour."
    He spoke; and Rustum answer'd not, but
    hurl'd
His spear: down from the shoulder, down it
    came,
As on some partridge in the corn a hawk
That long has tower'd in the airy clouds
Drops like a plummet: Sohrab saw it come,
And sprang aside, quick as a flash: the spear
Hiss'd, and went quivering down into the
    sand,   401
Which it sent flying wide:—then Sohrab threw
In turn, and full struck Rustum's shield:
    sharp rang,
The iron plates rang sharp, but turn'd the
    spear.
And Rustum seiz'd his club, which none but he
Could wield: an unlopp'd trunk it was, and
    huge,
Still rough; like those which men in treeless
    plains
To build them boats fish from the flooded
    rivers,
Hyphasis or Hydaspes,[1] when, high up
By their dark springs, the wind in winter-time
Has made in Himalayan forests wrack,   411
And strewn the channels with torn boughs;
    so huge
The club which Rustum lifted now, and struck
One stroke; but again Sohrab sprang aside
Lithe as the glancing snake, and the club came
Thundering to earth, and leapt from Rustum's
    hand.
And Rustum follow'd his own blow, and fell
To his knees, and with his fingers clutch'd the
    sand:
And now might Sohrab have unsheath'd his
    sword,
And pierc'd the mighty Rustum while he lay
Dizzy, and on his knees, and chok'd with
    sand: 421
But he look'd on, and smil'd, nor bar'd his
    sword,
But courteously drew back, and spoke, and
    said: —

[1] rivers which rise in the highlands of Kashmir
and flow into the Indus

"Thou strik'st too hard: that club of thine will float
Upon the summer-floods, and not my bones.
But rise, and be not wroth; not wroth am I:
No, when I see thee, wrath forsakes my soul.
Thou say'st thou art not Rustum: be it so.
Who art thou then, that canst so touch my soul?
Boy as I am, I have seen battles too;   430
Have waded foremost in their bloody waves,
And heard their hollow roar of dying men;
But never was my heart thus touch'd before.
Are they from Heaven, these softenings of the heart?
O thou old warrior, let us yield to Heaven!
Come, plant we here in earth our angry spears,
And make a truce, and sit upon this sand,
And pledge each other in red wine, like friends,
And thou shalt talk to me of Rustum's deeds.
There are enough foes in the Persian host   440
Whom I may meet, and strike, and feel no pang;
Champions enough Afrasiab has, whom thou
Mayst fight; fight them, when they confront thy spear.
But oh, let there be peace 'twixt thee and me!"
  He ceas'd: but while he spake, Rustum had risen,
And stood erect, trembling with rage: his club
He left to lie, but had regain'd his spear,
Whose fiery point now in his mail'd right-hand
Blaz'd bright and baleful, like that autumn Star,
The baleful sign of fevers:[1] dust had soil'd 450
His stately crest, and dimm'd his glittering arms.
His breast heav'd; his lips foam'd; and twice his voice
Was chok'd with rage: at last these words broke way: —
  "Girl! Nimble with thy feet, not with thy hands!
Curl'd minion, dancer, coiner of sweet words!
Fight; let me hear thy hateful voice no more!
Thou art not in Afrasiab's gardens now
With Tartar girls, with whom thou art wont to dance;
But on the Oxus sands, and in the dance
Of battle, and with me, who make no play 460
Of war: I fight it out, and hand to hand.
Speak not to me of truce, and pledge, and wine!
Remember all thy valour: try thy feints

And cunning: all the pity I had is gone:
Because thou hast sham'd me before both the hosts
With thy light skipping tricks, and thy girl's wiles."
  He spoke; and Sohrab kindled at his taunts,
And he too drew his sword: at once they rush'd
Together, as two eagles on one prey
Come rushing down together from the clouds,
One from the east, one from the west: their shields 471
Dash'd with a clang together, and a din
Rose, such as that the sinewy woodcutters
Make often in the forest's heart at morn,
Of hewing axes, crashing trees: such blows
Rustum and Sohrab on each other hail'd.
And you would say that sun and stars took part
In that unnatural[1] conflict; for a cloud
Grew suddenly in Heaven, and dark'd the sun
Over the fighters' heads; and a wind rose 480
Under their feet, and moaning swept the plain,
And in a sandy whirlwind wrapp'd the pair.
In gloom they twain were wrapp'd, and they alone;
For both the on-looking hosts on either hand
Stood in broad daylight, and the sky was pure,
And the sun sparkled on the Oxus stream.
But in the gloom they fought, with bloodshot eyes
And labouring breath; first Rustum struck the shield 488
Which Sohrab held stiff out: the steel-spik'd spear
Rent the tough plates, but fail'd to reach the skin,
And Rustum pluck'd it back with angry groan.
Then Sohrab with his sword smote Rustum's helm,
Nor clove its steel quite through; but all the crest
He shore[2] away, and that proud horsehair plume,
Never till now defil'd, sank to the dust;
And Rustum bow'd his head; but then the gloom
Grew blacker: thunder rumbled in the air,
And lightnings rend the cloud; and Ruksh, the horse,
Who stood at hand, utter'd a dreadful cry:
No horse's cry was that, most like the roar 500

[1] The belief that the stars caused epidemics was universal in ancient times.

[1] because between father and son [2] sheared, cut

Of some pain'd desert lion, who all day
Has trail'd the hunter's javelin in his side,
And comes at night to die upon the sand : —
The two hosts heard that cry, and quak'd for
    fear,
And Oxus curdled as it cross'd his stream.
But Sohrab heard, and quail'd not, but rush'd
    on,
And struck again ; and again Rustum bow'd
His head ; but this time all the blade, like
    glass,
Sprang in a thousand shivers on the helm,
And in his hand the hilt remain'd alone.   510
Then Rustum rais'd his head ; his dreadful
    eyes
Glar'd, and he shook on high his menacing
    spear,
And shouted, "Rustum !" Sohrab heard that
    shout,
And shrank amaz'd : back he recoil'd one step,
And scann'd with blinking eyes the advancing
    Form :
And then he stood bewilder'd ; and he dropp'd
His covering shield, and the spear pierc'd his
    side.
He reel'd, and staggering back, sunk to the
    ground.
And then the gloom dispers'd, and the wind
    fell,
And the bright sun broke forth, and melted all
The cloud ; and the two armies saw the pair ;
Saw Rustum standing, safe upon his feet, 522
And Sohrab, wounded, on the bloody sand.
    Then with a bitter smile, Rustum began : —
"Sohrab, thou thoughtest in thy mind to kill
A Persian lord this day, and strip his corpse,
And bear thy trophies to Afrasiab's tent.
Or else that the great Rustum would come
    down
Himself to fight, and that thy wiles would
    move
His heart to take a gift, and let thee go.   530
And then that all the Tartar host would praise
Thy courage or thy craft, and spread thy fame,
To glad thy father in his weak old age.
Fool ! thou art slain, and by an unknown
    man !
Dearer to the red jackals shalt thou be,
Than to thy friends, and to thy father old."
    And, with a fearless mien, Sohrab replied :—
"Unknown thou art ; yet thy fierce vaunt is
    vain.
Thou dost not slay me, proud and boastful
    man !
No ! Rustum slays me, and this filial heart.

For were I match'd with ten such men as thou,
And I were he who till to-day I was,   542
They should be lying here, I standing there.
But that belovèd name unnerv'd my arm —
That name, and something, I confess, in thee,
Which troubles all my heart, and made my
    shield
Fall ; and thy spear transfix'd an unarm'd foe.
And now thou boastest, and insult'st my fate.
But hear thou this, fierce Man, tremble to
    hear !   549
The mighty Rustum shall avenge my death !
My father, whom I seek through all the world,
He shall avenge my death, and punish thee !"
    As when some hunter in the spring hath
    found
A breeding eagle sitting on her nest,
Upon the craggy isle of a hill-lake,
And pierc'd her with an arrow as she rose,
And follow'd her to find her where she fell
Far off ; — anon her mate comes winging back
From hunting, and a great way off descries
His huddling young left sole ; at that, he
    checks
His pinion, and with short uneasy sweeps 561
Circles above his eyry, with loud screams
Chiding his mate back to her nest ; but she
Lies dying, with the arrow in her side,
In some far stony gorge out of his ken,
A heap of fluttering feathers : never more
Shall the lake glass her, flying over it ;
Never the black and dripping precipices
Echo her stormy scream as she sails by : —
As that poor bird flies home, nor knows his
    loss —
So Rustum knew not his own loss, but stood
Over his dying son, and knew him not.   572
    But, with a cold, incredulous voice, he
    said : —
"What prate is this of fathers and revenge?
The mighty Rustum never had a son."
    And, with a failing voice, Sohrab replied : —
"Ah yes, he had ! and that lost son am I.
Surely the news will one day reach his ear,
Reach Rustum, where he sits, and tarries long,
Somewhere, I know not where, but far from
    here ;
And pierce him like a stab, and make him leap
To arms, and cry for vengeance upon thee.
Fierce Man, bethink thee, for an only son !
What will that grief, what will that vengeance
    be !   584
Oh, could I live, till I that grief had seen !
Yet him I pity not so much, but her,
My mother, who in Ader-baijan dwells

With that old King, her father, who grows grey
With age, and rules over the valiant Koords.
Her most I pity, who no more will see   590
Sohrab returning from the Tartar camp,
With spoils and honour, when the war is done.
But a dark rumour will be bruited up,
From tribe to tribe, until it reach her ear;
And then will that defenceless woman learn
That Sohrab will rejoice her sight no more;
But that in battle with a nameless foe,
By the far distant Oxus, he is slain."

He spoke; and as he ceas'd he wept aloud,
Thinking of her he left, and his own death.   600
He spoke; but Rustum listen'd, plung'd in thought.
Nor did he yet believe it was his son
Who spoke, although he call'd back names he knew;
For he had had sure tidings that the babe,
Which was in Ader-baijan born to him,
Had been a puny girl, no boy at all:
So that sad mother sent him word, for fear
Rustum should take the boy, to train in arms;
And so he deem'd that either Sohrab took,
By a false boast, the style of Rustum's son;
Or that men gave it him, to swell his fame.
So deem'd he; yet he listen'd, plung'd in thought;   612
And his soul set to grief, as the vast tide
Of the bright rocking Ocean sets to shore
At the full moon: tears gathered in his eyes
For he remember'd his own early youth,
And all its bounding rapture; as, at dawn,
The Shepherd from his mountain-lodge descries
A far bright City, smitten by the sun,
Through many rolling clouds;—so Rustum saw
His youth; saw Sohrab's mother, in her bloom;   621
And that old King, her father, who lov'd well
His wandering guest, and gave him his fair child
With joy; and all the pleasant life they led,
They three, in that long-distant summertime—
The castle, and the dewy woods, and hunt
And hound, and morn on those delightful hills
In Ader-baijan. And he saw that Youth,
Of age and looks to be his own dear son,
Piteous and lovely, lying on the sand,   630
Like some rich hyacinth, which by the scythe
Of an unskilful gardener has been cut,
Mowing the garden grass-plots near its bed,

And lies, a fragrant tower of purple bloom,
On the mown, dying grass;—so Sohrab lay,
Lovely in death, upon the common sand.
And Rustum gaz'd on him with grief, and said:—
"O Sohrab, thou indeed art such a son
Whom Rustum, wert thou his, might well have lov'd!
Yet here thou errest, Sohrab, or else men   640
Have told thee false;—thou art not Rustum's son.
For Rustum had no son: one child he had—
But one—a girl: who with her mother now
Plies some light female task, nor dreams of us—
Of us she dreams not, nor of wounds, nor war."

But Sohrab answer'd him in wrath; for now
The anguish of the deep-fix'd spear grew fierce,
And he desired to draw forth the steel,
And let the blood flow free, and so to die;
But first he would convince his stubborn foe—
And, rising sternly on one arm, he said:—   651
"Man, who art thou who dost deny my words?
Truth sits upon the lips of dying men,
And Falsehood, while I liv'd, was far from mine.
I tell thee, prick'd upon this arm I bear
That seal which Rustum to my mother gave,
That she might prick it on the babe she bore."

He spoke: and all the blood left Rustum's cheeks;
And his knees totter'd, and he smote his hand,
Against his breast, his heavy mailèd hand,   660
That the hard iron corslet clank'd aloud:
And to his heart he press'd the other hand
And in a hollow voice he spake, and said:—
"Sohrab, that were a proof which could not lie.
If thou shew this, then art thou Rustum's son."
Then, with weak hasty fingers, Sohrab loos'd
His belt, and near the shoulder bar'd his arm,
And shew'd a sign in faint vermilion points
Prick'd: as a cunning workman, in Pekin,
Pricks with vermilion some clear porcelain vase,
An emperor's gift—at early morn he paints,
And all day long, and, when night comes, the lamp   672
Lights up his studious forehead and thin hands:—
So delicately prick'd the sign appear'd
On Sohrab's arm, the sign of Rustum's seal.

AE

It was that Griffin, which of old rear'd Zal,
Rustum's great father, whom they left to die,
A helpless babe, among the mountain rocks.
Him that kind Creature found, and rear'd, and
    lov'd —
Then Rustum took it for his glorious sign.
And Sohrab bar'd that figure on his arm, 681
And himself scann'd it long with mournful
    eyes,
And then he touch'd it with his hand and
    said : —
  "How say'st thou? Is that sign the proper
    sign
Of Rustum's son, or of some other man's?"
  He spoke: but Rustum gaz'd, and gaz'd,
    and stood
Speechless; and then he utter'd one sharp
    cry —
"O Boy — thy Father!" — and his voice
    chok'd there.
And then a dark cloud pass'd before his eyes,
And his head swam, and he sank down to
    earth.   690
But Sohrab crawl'd to where he lay, and cast
His arms about his neck, and kiss'd his lips,
And with fond faltering fingers strok'd his
    cheeks,
Trying to call him back to life: and life
Came back to Rustum, and he op'd his eyes,
And they stood wide with horror; and he
    seiz'd
In both his hands the dust which lay around,
And threw it on his head, and smirch'd his
    hair,
His hair, and face, and beard, and glittering
    arms:
And strong convulsive groanings shook his
    breast,
And his sobs chok'd him; and he clutch'd his
    sword,   701
To draw it, and forever let life out.
But Sohrab saw his thought, and held his
    hands,
And with a soothing voice he spoke, and
    said : —
  "Father, forbear: for I but meet to-day
The doom that at my birth was written down
In Heaven, and thou art Heaven's unconscious
    hand.
Surely my heart cried out that it was thou,
When first I saw thee; and thy heart spoke
    too,
I know it: but Fate trod those promptings
    down   710
Under its iron heel; Fate, Fate engag'd

The strife, and hurl'd me on my father's spear.
But let us speak no more of this : I find
My father; let me feel that I have found.
Come, sit beside me on this sand, and take
My head betwixt thy hands, and kiss my
    cheeks,
And wash them with thy tears, and say : 'My
    son !'
Quick ! quick ! for number'd are my sands of
    life,
And swift; for like the lightning to this field
I came, and like the wind I go away —   720
Sudden, and swift, and like a passing wind.
But it was writ in Heaven that this should be."
  So said he: and his voice releas'd the heart
Of Rustum, and his tears broke forth; he cast
His arms round his son's neck, and wept aloud,
And kiss'd him. And awe fell on both the
    hosts
When they saw Rustum's grief: and Ruksh,
    the horse,
With his head bowing to the ground, and mane
Sweeping the dust, came near, and in mute
    woe
First to the one, then to the other mov'd 730
His head, as if inquiring what their grief
Might mean; and from his dark, compassion-
    ate eyes
The big warm tears roll'd down, and cak'd the
    sand.
But Rustum chid him with stern voice, and
    said : —
  "Ruksh, now thou grievest; but, O Ruksh,
    thy feet
Should then have rotted on their nimble joints,
When first they bore thy Master to this field."
  But Sohrab look'd upon the horse and
    said : —
"Is this then Ruksh? How often, in past
    days,   739
My mother told me of thee, thou brave Steed !
My terrible father's terrible horse; and said,
That I should one day find thy lord and thee.
Come, let me lay my hand upon thy mane.
O Ruksh, thou art more fortunate than I;
For thou hast gone where I shall never go,
And snuff'd the breezes of my father's home.
And thou hast trod the sands of Seïstan,
And seen the River of Helmund, and the Lake
Of Zirrah; and the aged Zal himself
Has often strok'd thy neck, and given thee
    food,
Corn in a golden platter soak'd with wine, 751
And said — 'O Ruksh ! bear Rustum well !' —
    but I

Have never known my grandsire's furrow'd
    face,
Nor seen his lofty house in Seïstan,
Nor slak'd my thirst at the clear Helmund
    stream :
But lodg'd among my father's foes, and seen
Afrasiab's cities only, Samarcand,
Bokhara, and lone Khiva in the waste,
And the black Toorkmun tents ; and only
    drunk
The desert rivers, Moorghab and Tejend, 760
Kohik, and where the Kalmuks feed their
    sheep,
The northern Sir ;[1] and this great Oxus
    stream —
The yellow Oxus, by whose brink I die."
    And, with a heavy groan, Rustum re-
    plied : —
"Oh that its waves were flowing over me !
Oh that I saw its grains of yellow silt
Roll tumbling in the current o'er my head !"
    And, with a grave mild voice, Sohrab re-
    plied : —
"Desire not that, my father : thou must live.
For some are born to do great deeds, and live,
As some are born to be obscur'd, and die. 771
Do thou the deeds I die too young to do,
And reap a second glory in thine age.
Thou art my father, and thy gain is mine.
But come : thou seest this great host of men
Which follow me ; I pray thee, slay not these :
Let me entreat for them : what have they
    done ?
They follow'd me, my hope, my fame, my star.
Let them all cross the Oxus back in peace.
But me thou must bear hence, not send with
    them,
But carry me with thee to Seïstan,   781
And place me on a bed, and mourn for me,
Thou, and the snow-hair'd Zal, and all thy
    friends.
And thou must lay me in that lovely earth,
And heap a stately mound above my bones,
And plant a far-seen pillar over all :
That so the passing horseman on the waste
May see my tomb a great way off, and say —
'Sohrab, the mighty Rustum's son, lies there,
Whom his great father did in ignorance kill'
And I be not forgotten in my grave."   791
    And, with a mournful voice, Rustum re-
    plied : —
"Fear not ; as thou hast said, Sohrab, my son,
So shall it be ; for I will burn my tents,

[1] Syr Daria, cf. l. 129

And quit the host, and bear thee hence with
    me,
And carry thee away to Seïstan,
And place thee on a bed, and mourn for thee,
With the snow-headed Zal, and all my friends.
And I will lay thee in that lovely earth,
And heap a stately mound above thy bones,
And plant a far-seen pillar over all :   801
And men shall not forget thee in thy grave.
And I will spare thy host : yea, let them go :
Let them all cross the Oxus back in peace.
What should I do with slaying any more ?
For would that all whom I have ever slain
Might be once more alive ; my bitterest foes,
And they who were call'd champions in their
    time,
And through whose death I won that fame I
    have ;
And I were nothing but a common man, 810
A poor, mean soldier, and without renown ;
So thou mightest live too, my Son, my Son !
Or rather would that I, even I myself,
Might now be lying on this bloody sand,
Near death, and by an ignorant stroke of thine,
Not thou of mine ; and I might die, not thou ;
And I, not thou, be borne to Seïstan ;
And Zal might weep above my grave, not
    thine ;
And say — 'O son, I weep thee not too sore,
For willingly, I know, thou met'st thine end.'
But now in blood and battles was my youth,
And full of blood and battles is my age ; 822
And I shall never end this life of blood."
    Then, at the point of death, Sohrab re-
    plied : —
"A life of blood indeed, thou dreadful Man !
But thou shalt yet have peace ; only not now ;
Not yet : but thou shalt have it on that day,
When thou shalt sail in a high-masted Ship,
Thou and the other peers of Kai Khosroo,
Returning home over the salt blue sea,
From laying thy dear Master in his grave."
    And Rustum gazed on Sohrab's face, and
    said : —   832
"Soon be that day, my Son, and deep that sea !
Till then, if Fate so wills, let me endure."
    He spoke ; and Sohrab smil'd on him, and
    took
The spear, and drew it from his side, and eased
His wound's imperious anguish : but the blood
Came welling from the open gash, and life
Flow'd with the stream : all down his cold
    white side
The crimson torrent pour'd, dim now and
    soil'd,

Like the soil'd tissue of white violets   841
Left, freshly gather'd, on their native bank,
By romping children, whom their nurses call
From the hot fields at noon: his head droop'd
    low,
His limbs grew slack; motionless, white, he
    lay —
White, with eyes clos'd; only when heavy
    gasps,
Deep, heavy gasps, quivering through all his
    frame,
Convuls'd him back to life, he open'd them,
And fix'd them feebly on his father's face:
Till now all strength was ebb'd, and from his
    limbs
Unwillingly the spirit fled away,   851
Regretting the warm mansion which it left,
And youth and bloom, and this delightful
    world.
    So, on the bloody sand, Sohrab lay dead.
And the great Rustum drew his horseman's
    cloak
Down o'er his face, and sate by his dead son.
As those black granite pillars, once high-rear'd
By Jemshid[1] in Persepolis, to bear
His house, now, 'mid their broken flights of
    steps,
Lie prone, enormous, down the mountain
    side —   860
So in the sand lay Rustum by his son.
    And night came down over the solemn
    waste,
And the two gazing hosts, and that sole pair,
And darken'd all; and a cold fog, with night,
Crept from the Oxus.   Soon a hum arose,
As of a great assembly loosed, and fires
Began to twinkle through the fog: for now
Both armies moved to camp, and took their
    meal:
The Persians took it on the open sands
Southward; the Tartars by the river marge:
And Rustum and his son were left alone.   871
    But the majestic River floated on,
Out of the mist and hum of that low land,
Into the frosty starlight, and there mov'd,
Rejoicing, through the hush'd Chorasmian[2]
    waste,
Under the solitary moon: he flow'd
Right for the Polar Star, past Orgunjè,[3]

[1] a mythical king who reigned 700 years; the
black granite pillars found at Persepolis in Persia
are called the ruins of his throne   [2] Chorasmia
on the Oxus was once the seat of a great empire.
[3] a village on the Oxus

Brimming, and bright, and large: then sands
    begin
To hem his watery march, and dam his
    streams,
And split his currents; that for many a league
The shorn and parcell'd Oxus strains along
Through beds of sand and matted rushy isles—
Oxus, forgetting the bright speed he had   883
In his high mountain cradle in Pamere,
A foil'd circuitous wanderer: — till at last
The long'd-for dash of waves is heard, and
    wide
His luminous home of waters opens, bright
And tranquil, from whose floor the new-bath'd
    stars
Emerge, and shine upon the Aral Sea.

. PHILOMELA

Hark! ah, the Nightingale![1]
The tawny-throated!
Hark! from that moonlit cedar what a burst!
What triumph! hark — what pain!

O Wanderer from a Grecian shore,
Still, after many years, in distant lands,
Still nourishing in thy bewilder'd brain
That wild, unquench'd, deep-sunken, old-
    world pain —

      Say, will it never heal?
      And can this fragrant lawn   10
      With its cool trees, and night,
      And the sweet, tranquil Thames,
      And moonshine, and the dew,
      To thy rack'd heart and brain
        Afford no balm?

    Dost thou to-night behold
Here, through the moonlight on this English
    grass,
The unfriendly palace in the Thracian wild?
    Dost thou again peruse
With hot cheeks and sear'd eyes   20
The too clear web, and thy dumb Sister's
    shame?
    Dost thou once more assay
Thy flight, and feel come over thee,
Poor Fugitive, the feathery change
Once more, and once more seem to make re-
    sound

[1] Cf. the other nightingale poems in this volume
and the story of Philomela in Gayley's *Classic
Myths*, p. 258.

With love and hate, triumph and agony,
Lone Daulis, and the high Cephissian vale?
Listen, Eugenia —
How thick the bursts come crowding through
    the leaves!
Again — thou hearest!   30
Eternal Passion!
Eternal Pain!

THE SCHOLAR GIPSY

Go, for they call you, Shepherd, from the hill;
  Go, Shepherd, and untie the wattled cotes:[1]
  No longer leave thy wistful flock unfed,
  Nor let thy bawling fellows rack their
    throats,
  Nor the cropp'd grasses shoot another
    head.
    But when the fields are still,
  And the tired men and dogs all gone to rest,
  And only the white sheep are sometimes
    seen
    Cross and recross the strips of moon-
      blanch'd green;   9
  Come, Shepherd, and again renew the quest.

Here, where the reaper was at work of late,
  In this high field's dark corner, where he
    leaves
  His coat, his basket, and his earthen
    cruse,[2]
  And in the sun all morning binds the sheaves,
  Then here, at noon, comes back his stores
    to use;
    Here will I sit and wait,
  While to my ear from uplands far away 17
  The bleating of the folded flocks is borne;
  With distant cries of reapers in the corn—
    All the live murmur of a summer's day.

Screen'd is this nook o'er the high, half-reap'd
    field,
  And here till sun-down, Shepherd, will I be.
    Through the thick corn,[3] the scarlet
      poppies peep,
  And round green roots and yellowing stalks
    I see
    Pale blue convolvulus in tendrils creep:
    And air-swept lindens yield
  Their scent, and rustle down their perfum'd
    showers

Of bloom on the bent grass where I am
    laid,
  And bower me from the August sun with
    shade;   29
  And the eye travels down to Oxford's towers.

And near me on the grass lies Glanvil's book[1]—
  Come, let me read the oft-read tale again,
  The story of that Oxford scholar poor,
  Of pregnant parts and quick inventive brain,
  Who, tired of knocking at Preferment's
    door,
    One summer morn forsook
  His friends, and went to learn the Gipsy lore,
  And roam'd the world with that wild
    brotherhood,
  And came, as most men deem'd, to little
    good,   39
  But came to Oxford and his friends no more.

But once, years after, in the country lanes,
  Two scholars whom at college erst he knew
    Met him, and of his way of life enquir'd.
  Whereat he answer'd, that the Gipsy crew,
    His mates, had arts to rule as they desir'd
    The workings of men's brains;
  And they can bind them to what thoughts
    they will:
  "And I," he said, "the secret of their art,
  When fully learn'd, will to the world
    impart: 49
  But it needs happy moments for this skill."

This said, he left them, and return'd no more,
  But rumours hung about the country side
    That the lost Scholar long was seen to
    stray,
  Seen by rare glimpses, pensive and tongue-
    tied,
    In hat of antique shape, and cloak of grey,
    The same the Gipsies wore.
Shepherds had met him on the Hurst[2] in
    spring:
  At some lone alehouse in the Berkshire
    moors,
  On the warm ingle bench,[3] the smock-
    frock'd boors[4]
Had found him seated at their entering. 60

[1] sheepfolds built of woven boughs: the gates
were tied up [2] water-jug [3] grain

[1] *The Vanity of Dogmatizing*, by Joseph Glanvil
(1661), contains the story on which this poem
is based. [2] Cumner Hurst, a hill southwest of
Oxford [3] bench in the chimney-corner [4] farm-
laborers in smock-frocks (outer garments like
shirts or blouses)

But, 'mid their drink and clatter, he would fly:
And I myself seem half to know thy looks,
  And put the shepherds, Wanderer, on thy
    trace;
And boys who in lone wheatfields scare the
  rooks
  I ask if thou hast pass'd their quiet place;
    Or in my boat I lie
Moor'd to the cool bank in the summer
  heats,
'Mid wide grass meadows which the sun-
  shine fills,
  And watch the warm green-muffled
    Cumner hills,
And wonder if thou haunt'st their shy
  retreats.   70

For most, I know, thou lov'st retired ground.
Thee, at the ferry, Oxford riders blithe,
  Returning home on summer nights, have
    met
Crossing the stripling Thames at Bab-lock-
  hithe,[1]
  Trailing in the cool stream thy fingers wet,
    As the slow punt[2] swings round:
And leaning backwards in a pensive dream,
And fostering in thy lap a heap of flowers
Pluck'd in shy fields and distant wood-
  land bowers,
  And thine eyes resting on the moonlit
    stream.   80

And then they land, and thou art seen no more.
Maidens who from the distant hamlets come
To dance[3] around the Fyfield elm in May,
Oft through the darkening fields have seen
  thee roam,
  Or cross a stile into the public way.
Oft thou hast given them store
Of flowers — the frail-leaf'd, white anem-
  one —
  Dark bluebells drench'd with dews of
    summer eves —
  And purple orchises with spotted leaves—
But none has words she can report of
  thee.   90

And, above Godstow Bridge,[4] when hay-time's
  here
In June, and many a scythe in sunshine
  flames,

Men who through those wide fields of
  breezy grass
Where black-wing'd swallows haunt the
  glittering Thames,
  To bathe in the abandon'd lasher[1] pass,
  Have often pass'd thee near
Sitting upon the river bank o'ergrown:
  Mark'd thine outlandish garb, thy figure
    spare,
  Thy dark vague eyes, and soft abstracted
    air;
But, when they came from bathing, thou
  wert gone.   100

At some lone homestead in the Cumner hills,
  Where at her open door the housewife darns,
  Thou hast been seen, or hanging on a gate
To watch the threshers in the mossy barns.
  Children, who early range these slopes and
    late
  For cresses from the rills,
Have known thee watching, all an April day,
  The springing pastures and the feeding
    kine;
  And mark'd thee, when the stars come
    out and shine,
Through the long dewy grass move slow
  away.   110

In Autumn, on the skirts of Bagley Wood —
  Where most the gipsies by the turf-edg'd
    way
  Pitch their smok'd tents, and every bush
    you see
With scarlet patches tagg'd and shreds of
  grey,
  Above the forest-ground called Thessaly—
  The blackbird picking food
Sees thee, nor stops his meal, nor fears at
  all;
So often has he known thee past him stray,
Rapt, twirling in thy hand a wither'd
  spray,
And waiting for the spark from Heaven
  to fall.   120

And once, in winter, on the causeway chill
  Where home through flooded fields foot-
    travellers go,
  Have I not pass'd thee on the wooden
    bridge
Wrapt in thy cloak and battling with the
  snow,

[1] a village four miles from Oxford   [2] a kind of
boat much used on the Thames   [3] the Maypole
dance   [4] two miles above Oxford

[1] the pool of slack water below a dam

Thy face towards Hinksey[1] and its wintry
  ridge?
And thou hast climbed the hill,
And gain'd the white brow of the Cumner
  range,
Turn'd once to watch, while thick the
  snowflakes fall,
The line of festal light in Christ-Church[2]
  hall —
Then sought thy straw in some sequester'd
  grange.   130

But what — I dream! Two hundred years
  are flown
Since first thy story ran through Oxford
  halls,
And the grave Glanvil did the tale inscribe
That thou wert wander'd from the studious
  walls
To learn strange arts, and join a Gipsy
  tribe:
And thou from earth art gone
Long since, and in some quiet churchyard
  laid;
Some country nook, where o'er thy un-
  known grave
Tall grasses and white flowering nettles
  wave —
Under a dark red-fruited yew-tree's
  shade.   140

— No, no, thou hast not felt the lapse of
  hours.
For what wears out the life of mortal men?
  'Tis that from change to change their
  being rolls:
'Tis that repeated shocks, again, again,
Exhaust the energy of strongest souls,
And numb the elastic powers.
Till having us'd our nerves with bliss and
  teen,[3]
And tir'd upon a thousand schemes our
  wit,
To the just-pausing Genius we remit
Our worn-out life, and are — what we
  have been.   150

Thou hast not liv'd, why should'st thou perish,
  so?
Thou hadst *one* aim, *one* business, *one* desire:
Else wert thou long since number'd with
  the dead —

[1] a neighboring village [2] one of the largest
and richest colleges of Oxford [3] sorrow

Else hadst thou spent, like other men, thy
  fire.
The generations of thy peers are fled,
And we ourselves shall go;
But thou possessest an immortal lot,
And we imagine thee exempt from age
And living as thou liv'st on Glanvil's page,
Because thou hadst — what we, alas, have
  not!   160

For early didst thou leave the world, with
  powers
Fresh, undiverted to the world without,
Firm to their mark, not spent on other
  things;
Free from the sick fatigue, the languid
  doubt,
Which much to have tried, in much been
  baffled, brings.
O Life unlike to ours!
Who fluctuate idly without term or scope,
Of whom each strives, nor knows for what
  he strives,
And each half lives a hundred different
  lives;
Who wait like thee, but not, like thee, in
  hope.   170

Thou waitest for the spark from Heaven: and
  we,
Light half-believers of our casual creeds,
Who never deeply felt, nor clearly will'd,
Whose insight never has borne fruit in deeds,
Whose vague resolves never have been
  fulfill'd;
For whom each year we see
Breeds new beginnings, disappointments
  new;
Who hesitate and falter life away,
And lose to-morrow the ground won to-
  day —
Ah, do not we, Wanderer, await it too? 180

Yes, we await it, but it still delays,
And then we suffer; and amongst us One,
Who most has suffer'd, takes dejectedly
His seat upon the intellectual throne;
And all his store of sad experience he
Lays bare of wretched days;
Tells us his misery's birth and growth and
  signs,
And how the dying spark of hope was fed,
And how the breast was sooth'd, and how
  the head,
And all his hourly varied anodynes.   100

This for our wisest : and we others pine,
And wish the long unhappy dream would
  end,
  And waive all claim to bliss, and try to
    bear ;
  With close-lipp'd Patience for our only
    friend,
  Sad Patience, too near neighbour to De-
    spair :
  But none has hope like thine.
Thou through the fields and through the
  woods dost stray,   197
  Roaming the country side, a truant boy,
  Nursing thy project in unclouded joy,
And every doubt long blown by time away.

O born in days when wits were fresh and clear,
And life ran gaily as the sparkling Thames ;
  Before this strange disease of modern life,
  With its sick hurry, its divided aims,
  Its heads o'ertax'd, its palsied hearts, was
    rife —
  Fly hence, our contact fear !
  Still fly, plunge deeper in the bowering
    wood !
  Averse, as Dido did with gesture stern
  From her false friend's[1] approach in Hades
    turn,   209
Wave us away, and keep thy solitude.

Still nursing the unconquerable hope,
  Still clutching the inviolable shade,
  With a free outward impulse brushing
    through,
  By night, the silver'd branches of the
    glade —
  Far on the forest skirts, where none pur-
    sue,
  On some mild pastoral slope   216
Emerge, and resting on the moonlit pales,
  Freshen thy flowers, as in former years,
  With dew, or listen with enchanted ears,
From the dark dingles,[2] to the nightingales.

But fly our paths, our feverish contact fly !
For strong the infection of our mental strife,
  Which, though its gives no bliss, yet spoils
    for rest ;
  And we should win thee from thy own fair
    life,
  Like us distracted, and like us unblest.
  Soon, soon thy cheer would die,

¹ Æneas, cf. Æneid, VI, 450–71, or Gayley,
p. 348   ² small wooded valleys

Thy hopes grow timorous, and unfix'd thy
  powers,
  And thy clear aims be cross and shifting
    made :
  And then thy glad perennial youth would
    fade,   229
Fade, and grow old at last and die like ours.

Then fly our greetings, fly our speech and
  smiles !
— As some grave Tyrian trader, from the
  sea,
  Descried at sunrise an emerging prow
Lifting the cool-hair'd creepers[1] stealthily,
  The fringes of a southward-facing brow
    Among the Ægean isles ;
And saw the merry Grecian coaster come,
  Freighted with amber grapes, and Chian
    wine,[2]
  Green bursting figs, and tunnies steep'd
    in brine ;
And knew the intruders on his ancient
  home,   240
The young light-hearted Masters of the waves ;
  And snatch'd his rudder, and shook out
    more sail,
  And day and night held on indignantly
O'er the blue Midland[3] waters with the gale,
  Betwixt the Syrtes[4] and soft Sicily,
    To where the Atlantic raves
Outside the Western Straits ;[5] and unbent
  sails
  There, where down cloudy cliffs, through
    sheets of foam,   248
  Shy traffickers, the dark Iberians[6] come ;
And on the beach undid his corded bales.

THE LAST WORD

Creep into thy narrow bed,
Creep, and let no more be said !
Vain thy onset ! all stands fast.
Thou thyself must break at last.   4

Let the long contention cease !
Geese are swans, and swans are geese.
Let them have it how they will !
Thou art tired ; best be still.   8

¹ vines hanging down from a cliff over the sea
² wine of Chios, a Greek island   ³ Mediterranean
⁴ the gulfs of Sidra and Gabes on the north coast
of Africa   ⁵ the Straits of Gibraltar   ⁶ a race in-
habiting the Spanish peninsula and, at this time,
parts of the British Islands

They out-talk'd thee, hiss'd thee, tore thee!
Better men fared thus before thee;
Fired their ringing shot and pass'd,
Hotly charged — and sank at last.   12

Charge once more, then, and be dumb!
Let the victors, when they come,
When the forts of folly fall,
Find thy body by the wall.   16

EDWARD FITZGERALD
(1809–1883)

From THE RUBAIYAT OF OMAR KHAYYAM

VII

Come, fill the Cup, and in the fire of Spring
Your Winter-garment of Repentance fling:
    The Bird of Time has but a little way
To flutter — and the Bird is on the Wing.

VIII

Whether at Naishápúr[1] or Babylon,[2]
Whether the Cup with sweet or bitter run,
    The Wine of Life keeps oozing drop by
    drop,
The Leaves of Life keep falling one by one.

IX

Each Morn a thousand Roses brings, you
    say;
Yes, but where leaves the Rose of Yesterday?
    And this first Summer month that brings
    the Rose
Shall take Jamshyd[3] and Kaikobád[4] away.

*   *   *   *   *   *   *

XII

A Book of Verses underneath the Bough,
A Jug of Wine, a Loaf of Bread — and Thou
    Beside me singing in the Wilderness —
Oh, Wilderness were Paradise enow!

[1] an ancient city in northeast Persia   [2] in
southwest Persia   [3] cf. note on *Sohrab and
Rustum*, l. 858   [4] a predecessor of Kai Kosru,
cf. *Sohrab and Rustum*, l. 220

XIII

Some for the Glories of This World; and some
Sigh for the Prophet's Paradise to come;
    Ah, take the Cash, and let the Credit go,
Nor heed the rumble of a distant Drum!

*   *   *   *   *   *   *

XVI

The Worldly Hope men set their Hearts upon
Turns Ashes — or it prospers; and anon,
    Like Snow upon the Desert's dusty Face,
Lighting a little hour or two — was gone.

XVII

Think, in this batter'd Caravanserai
Whose Portals are alternate Night and Day,
    How Sultán after Sultán with his Pomp
Abode his destin'd Hour, and went his way.

XVIII

They say the Lion and the Lizard keep
The Courts where Jamshyd gloried and drank
    deep:
    And Bahrám, that great Hunter — the Wild
    Ass
Stamps o'er his Head, but cannot break his
    Sleep.

*   *   *   *   *   *   *

XXIV

Ah, make the most of what we yet may spend,
Before we too into the Dust descend;
    Dust into Dust, and under Dust, to lie,
Sans Wine, sans Song, sans Singer, and — sans
    End!

*   *   *   *   *   *   *

XXVII

Myself when young did eagerly frequent
Doctor and Saint, and heard great argument
    About it and about: but evermore
Came out by the same door where in I went.

XXVIII

With them the seed of Wisdom did I sow,
And with mine own hand wrought to make it
    grow;
    And this was all the Harvest that I reap'd—
"I came like Water, and like Wind I go."

XXIX

Into this Universe, and WHY not knowing
Nor WHENCE, like Water willy-nilly flowing;
    And out of it, as Wind along the Waste,
I know not WHITHER, willy-nilly blowing.

XXX

What, without asking, hither hurried WHENCE?
And, without asking, WHITHER hurried hence!
    Oh, many a Cup of this forbidden Wine
Must drown the memory of that insolence!

XXXI

Up from Earth's Centre through the Seventh
    Gate
I rose, and on the Throne of Saturn[1] sate,
    And many a Knot unravel'd by the Road;
But not the Master-knot of Human Fate.

XXXII

There was the Door to which I found no Key;
There was the Veil through which I could not
    see:
    Some little talk awhile of ME and THEE
There was — and then no more of THEE and
    ME.[2]

* * * * * * *

XLIX

Would you that spangle of Existence spend
About THE SECRET — quick about it, Friend!
    A Hair perhaps divides the False and
    True —
And upon what, prithee, does life depend?

L

A Hair perhaps divides the False and True;
Yes; and a single Alif[3] were the clue —
    Could you but find it — to the Treasure-
    house,
And peradventure to THE MASTER too;

[1] In the old astronomy Saturn is lord of the
seventh sphere or heaven. [2] the individual personalities being absorbed in the absolute One
[3] the vowel *a*, represented by a minute symbol, the
presence or absence of which would change the
meaning of a word

LI

Whose secret Presence, through Creation's
    veins
Running Quicksilver-like eludes your pains;
    Taking all shapes from Máh to Máhi;[1] and
They change and perish all — but He remains;

LII

A moment guess'd — then back behind the
    Fold
Immerst of Darkness round the Drama roll'd
    Which, for the Pastime of Eternity,
He doth Himself contrive, enact, behold.

* * * * * * *

LXVI

I sent my Soul through the Invisible
Some letter of that After-life to spell:
    And by and by my Soul return'd to me,
And answer'd, "I Myself am Heav'n and
    Hell:"

LXVII

Heav'n but the Vision of fulfill'd Desire,
And Hell the Shadow from a Soul on fire,
    Cast on the Darkness into which Ourselves,
So late emerg'd from, shall so soon expire.

LXVIII

We are no other than a moving row
Of Magic Shadow-shapes that come and go
    Round with the Sun-illumin'd Lantern[2] held
In Midnight by the Master of the Show;

LXIX

But helpless Pieces of the Game He plays
Upon this Checker-board of Nights and Days;
    Hither and thither moves, and checks, and
    slays,
And one by one back in the Closet lays.

LXX

The Ball no question makes of Ayes and Noes,
But Right or Left as strikes the Player goes;
    And He that toss'd you down into the Field,
He knows about it all — HE knows — HE
    knows!

[1] from fish to moon [2] a crude sort of moving
picture show made by a revolving cylinder with
figures painted on its translucent sides and a
candle at the centre

LXXI

The Moving Finger writes; and, having writ,
Moves on: nor all your Piety nor Wit
  Shall lure it back to cancel half a Line
Nor all your Tears wash out a Word of it.

*   *   *   *   *   *

XCVI

Yet Ah, that Spring should vanish with the
    Rose!
That Youth's sweet-scented manuscript should
    close!
  The Nightingale that in the branches sang,
Ah whence, and whither flown again, who
    knows!

XCVII

Would but the Desert of the Fountain yield
One glimpse — if dimly, yet indeed, reveal'd,
  To which the fainting Traveller might
    spring,
As springs the trampled herbage of the field!

XCVIII

Would but some wingèd Angel ere too late
Arrest the yet unfolded Roll of Fate,
  And make the stern Recorder otherwise
Enregister, or quite obliterate!

XCIX

Ah Love! could you and I with Him conspire
To grasp this sorry Scheme of Things entire,
  Would not we shatter it to bits — and then
Re-mould it nearer to the Heart's desire!

COVENTRY PATMORE
(1823–1896)

FROM THE ANGEL IN THE HOUSE

BOOK I, CANTO III. PRELUDES
I. THE LOVER

He meets, by heavenly chance express,
  The destined maid; some hidden hand
Unveils to him that loveliness
  Which others cannot understand.
His merits in her presence grow,   5
  To match the promise in her eyes,

And round her happy footsteps blow
  The authentic airs of Paradise.
For joy of her he cannot sleep,
  Her beauty haunts him all the night;   10
It melts his heart, it makes him weep
  For wonder, worship, and delight.
O, paradox of love, he longs,
  Most humble when he most aspires,
To suffer scorn and cruel wrongs   15
  From her he honours and desires.
Her graces make him rich, and ask
  No guerdon; this imperial style
Affronts him; he disdains to bask,
  The pensioner of her priceless smile.   20
He prays for some hard thing to do,
  Some work of fame and labour immense,
To stretch the languid bulk and thew
  Of love's fresh-born magnipotence.
No smallest boon were bought too dear,   25
  Though bartered for his love-sick life;
Yet trusts he, with undaunted cheer,
  To vanquish heaven, and call her Wife.
He notes how queens of sweetness still
  Neglect their crowns, and stoop to mate;
How, self-consign'd with lavish will,   31
  They ask but love proportionate;
How swift pursuit by small degrees,
  Love's tactic, works like miracle;
How valour, clothed in courtesies,   35
  Brings down the loftiest citadel;
And therefore, though he merits not
  To kiss the braid upon her skirt,
His hope discouraged ne'er a jot,
  Out-soars all possible desert.   40

BOOK I, CANTO VIII. PRELUDES
I. LIFE OF LIFE

What's that, which, ere I spake, was gone:
  So joyful and intense a spark,
That, whilst o'erhead the wonder shone,
  The day, before but dull, grew dark?
I do not know; but this I know,   5
  That, had the splendour lived a year,
The truth that I some heavenly show
  Did see, could not be now more clear.
This know I too: might mortal breath
  Express the passion then inspired,   10
Evil would die a natural death,
  And nothing transient be desired;
And error from the soul would pass,
  And leave the senses pure and strong
As sunbeams. But the best, alas,   15
  Has neither memory nor tongue!

II. The Revelation

An idle poet, here and there,
　　Looks round him; but, for all the rest,
The world, unfathomably fair,
　　Is duller than a witling's jest.
Love wakes men, once a life-time each;　5
　　They lift their heavy lids and look;
And, lo, what one sweet page can teach,
　　They read with joy, then shut the book.
And some give thanks, and some blaspheme,
　　And most forget; but, either way,　10
That and the Child's unheeded dream
　　Is all the light of all their day.

III. The Spirit's Epochs

Not in the crises of events,
　　Of compass'd hopes, or fears fulfill'd,
Or acts of gravest consequence,
　　Are life's delight and depth reveal'd.
The day of days was not the day;　5
　　That went before, or was postponed;
The night Death took our lamp away
　　Was not the night on which we groaned.
I drew my bride, beneath the moon,
　　Across my threshold; happy hour!　10
But, ah, the walk that afternoon
　　We saw the water-flags in flower!

From THE UNKNOWN EROS

THE TOYS

My little Son, who look'd from thoughtful
　　eyes
And moved and spoke in quiet grown-up wise,
Having my law the seventh time disobey'd,
I struck him, and dismiss'd
With hard words and unkiss'd, —　5
His Mother, who was patient, being dead.
Then, fearing lest his grief should hinder sleep,
　　I visited his bed,
But found him slumbering deep,
With darken'd eyelids, and their lashes yet　10
From his late sobbing wet.
And I, with moan,
Kissing away his tears, left others of my own;
For, on a table drawn beside his head,
　　He had put, within his reach,　15
A box of counters and a red-vein'd stone,
A piece of glass abraded by the beach,
And six or seven shells,
A bottle of bluebells,

And two French copper coins, ranged there
　　with careful art,　20
To comfort his sad heart.
So when that night I pray'd
To God, I wept, and said:
"Ah, when at last we lie with trancèd breath,
　　Not vexing Thee in death,　25
And Thou rememberest of what toys
We made our joys,
How weakly understood
Thy great commanded good,
Then, fatherly not less　30
Than I whom Thou hast moulded from the
　　clay,
Thou'lt leave Thy wrath, and say,
'I will be sorry for their childishness.'"

DANTE GABRIEL ROSSETTI
(1828–1882)

THE BLESSED DAMOZEL

The blessed damozel[1] leaned out
　　From the gold bar of Heaven;
Her eyes were deeper than the depth
　　Of waters stilled at even;
She had three lilies in her hand,
　　And the stars in her hair were seven.　6

Her robe, ungirt from clasp to hem,
　　No wrought flowers did adorn,
But a white rose of Mary's gift,
　　For service meetly worn;
Her hair that lay along her back
　　Was yellow like ripe corn.　12

Herseemed[2] she scarce had been a day
　　One of God's choristers;
The wonder was not yet quite gone
　　From that still look of hers;
Albeit, to them she left, her day
　　Had counted as ten years.　18

(To one, it is ten years of years.
　　. . . Yet now, and in this place,
Surely she leaned o'er me — her hair
　　Fell all about my face. . . .
Nothing: the autumn fall of leaves.
　　The whole year sets apace.)　24

It was the rampart of God's house
　　That she was standing on;

[1] lady　　[2] It seemed to her

By God built over the sheer depth
  The which is Space begun;
So high, that looking downward thence
  She scarce could see the sun.   30

It lies in Heaven, across the flood
  Of ether, as a bridge.
Beneath, the tides of day and night
  With flame and darkness ridge
The void, as low as where this earth
  Spins like a fretful midge.   36

Around her, lovers, newly met
  'Mid deathless love's acclaims,
Spoke evermore among themselves
  Their heart-remembered names;
And the souls mounting up to God
  Went by her like thin flames.   42

And still she bowed herself and stooped
  Out of the circling charm;
Until her bosom must have made
  The bar she leaned on warm,
And the lilies lay as if asleep
  Along her bended arm.   48

From the fixed place of Heaven she saw
  Time like a pulse shake fierce
Through all the worlds.   Her gaze still strove
  Within the gulf to pierce
Its path; and now she spoke as when
  The stars sang in their spheres.   54

The sun was gone now; the curled moon
  Was like a little feather
Fluttering far down the gulf; and now
  She spoke through the still weather.
Her voice was like the voice the stars
  Had when they sang together.[1]   60

(Ah sweet! Even now, in that bird's song,
  Strove not her accents there,
Fain to be hearkened? When those bells
  Possessed the mid-day air,
Strove not her steps to reach my side
  Down all the echoing stair?)   66

"I wish that he were come to me,
  For he will come," she said.
"Have I not prayed in Heaven? — on earth,
  Lord, Lord, has he not pray'd?
Are not two prayers a perfect strength?
  And shall I feel afraid?   72

[1] Cf. note on Milton's *Hymn on the Nativity*,
l. 119.

"When round his head the aureole clings,
  And he is clothed in white,
I'll take his hand and go with him
  To the deep wells of light;
As unto a stream we will step down,
  And bathe there in God's sight.   78

"We two will stand beside that shrine,
  Occult, withheld, untrod,
Whose lamps are stirred continually
  With prayer sent up to God;
And see our old prayers, granted, melt
  Each like a little cloud.   84

"We two will lie i' the shadow of
  That living mystic tree
Within whose secret growth the Dove[1]
  Is sometimes felt to be,
While every leaf that His plumes touch
  Saith His Name audibly.   90

"And I myself will teach to him,
  I myself, lying so,
The songs I sing here; which his voice
  Shall pause in, hushed and slow,
And find some knowledge at each pause,
  Or some new thing to know."   96

(Alas! We two, we two, thou say'st!
  Yea, one wast thou with me
That once of old.   But shall God lift
  To endless unity
The soul whose likeness with thy soul
  Was but its love for thee?)   102

"We too," she said, "will seek the groves
  Where the lady Mary is,
With her five handmaidens, whose names
  Are five sweet symphonies,
Cecily, Gertrude, Magdalen,
  Margaret and Rosalys.   108

"Circlewise sit they, with bound locks
  And foreheads garlanded;
Into the fine cloth white like flame
  Weaving the golden thread,
To fashion the birth-robes for them
  Who are just born, being dead.   114

"He shall fear, haply, and be dumb:
  Then will I lay my cheek
To his, and tell about our love,
  Not once abashed or weak:

[1] the Holy Ghost

And the dear Mother will approve
    My pride, and let me speak.   120

"Herself shall bring us, hand in hand,
    To Him round whom all souls
Kneel, the clear-ranged unnumbered heads
    Bowed with their aureoles:
And angels meeting us shall sing
    To their citherns and citoles.[1]   126

"There will I ask of Christ the Lord
    Thus much for him and me: —
Only to live as once on earth
    With Love, only to be,
As then awhile, forever now
    Together, I and he."   132

She gazed and listened and then said,
    Less sad of speech than mild, —
"All this is when he comes." She ceased.
    The light thrilled towards her, fill'd
With angels in strong level flight.
    Her eyes prayed, and she smil'd.   138

(I saw her smile.) But soon their path
    Was vague in distant spheres:
And then she cast her arms along
    The golden barriers,
And laid her face between her hands,
    And wept. (I heard her tears.)   144

SISTER HELEN

"Why did you melt your waxen man,
    Sister Helen?
To-day is the third since you began."
    "The time was long, yet the time ran,
        Little brother."
    (O Mother, Mary Mother,
Three days to-day, between Hell and Heaven!) 7

"But if you have done your work aright,
    Sister Helen,
You'll let me play, for you said I might."
"Be very still in your play to-night,
    Little brother." 12
    (O Mother, Mary Mother,
Third night, to-night, between Hell and Heaven!)

"You said it must melt ere vesper-bell,
    Sister Helen;
If now it be molten, all is well."

[1] ancient musical instruments

"Even so, — nay, peace! you cannot tell,
        Little brother."
    (O Mother, Mary Mother,
What is this, between Hell and Heaven?)   21

"Oh the waxen knave was plump to-day,
        Sister Helen;
How like dead folk he has dropped away!"
"Nay now, of the dead what can you say, 25
        Little brother?"
    (O Mother, Mary Mother,
What of the dead, between Hell and Heaven?)

"See, see, the sunken pile of wood,
        Sister Helen,
Shines through the thinned wax red as
    blood!"
"Nay now, when looked you yet on blood, 32
        Little brother?"
    (O Mother, Mary Mother,
How pale she is, between Hell and Heaven!)

"Now close your eyes, for they're sick and sore,
        Sister Helen,
And I'll play without the gallery door."
"Aye, let me rest, — I'll lie on the floor,
        Little brother."40
    (O Mother, Mary Mother,
What rest to-night between Hell and Heaven?)

"Here high up in the balcony,
        Sister Helen,
The moon flies face to face with me."
"Aye, look and say whatever you see,
        Little brother."47
    (O Mother, Mary Mother,
What sight to-night, between Hell and Heaven?)

"Outside it's merry in the wind's wake,
        Sister Helen;
In the shaken trees the chill stars shake." 52
"Hush, heard you a horse-tread as you spake,
        Little brother?"
    (O Mother, Mary Mother,
What sound to-night, between Hell and Heaven?)

"I hear a horse-tread, and I see,
        Sister Helen,
Three horsemen that ride terribly."
"Little brother, whence come the three,
        Little brother?"
    (O Mother, Mary Mother,
Whence should they come, between Hell and
    Heaven?)   63

"They come by the hill-verge from Boyne Bar,
    Sister Helen,
And one draws nigh, but two are afar."
"Look, look, do you know them who they are,
    Little brother?"68
   (*O Mother, Mary Mother,*
Who should they be, between Hell and Heaven?)

"Oh, it's Keith of Eastholm rides so fast,
    Sister Helen,
For I know the white mane on the blast."
"The hour has come, has come at last,
    Little brother!"
   (*O Mother, Mary Mother,*
Her hour at last, between Hell and Heaven!) 77

"He has made a sign and called Halloo!
    Sister Helen,
And he says that he would speak with you."
"Oh tell him I fear the frozen dew,
    Little brother." 82
   (*O Mother, Mary Mother,*
Why laughs she thus, between Hell and Heaven?)

"The wind is loud, but I hear him cry,
    Sister Helen,
That Keith of Ewern's like to die."
"And he and thou, and thou and I,
    Little brother."89
   (*O Mother, Mary Mother,*
And they and we, between Hell and Heaven!)

"Three days ago, on his marriage-morn,
    Sister Helen,
He sickened, and lies since then forlorn."
"For bridegroom's side is the bride a thorn,
    Little brother?"
   (*O Mother, Mary Mother,*
Cold bridal cheer, between Hell and Heaven!) 98

"Three days and nights he has lain abed,
    Sister Helen,
And he prays in torment to be dead." 101
"The thing may chance, if he have prayed,
    Little brother!"
   (*O Mother, Mary Mother,*
If he have prayed, between Hell and Heaven!)

"But he has not ceased to cry to-day,
    Sister Helen,
That you should take your curse away." 108
"*My* prayer was heard, — he need but pray,
    Little brother!"
   (*O Mother, Mary Mother,*
Shall God not hear, between Hell and Heaven?)

"But he says, till you take back your ban,
    Sister Helen,
His soul would pass, yet never can."
"Nay then, shall I slay a living man,
    Little brother?"
   (*O Mother, Mary Mother,*
A living soul, between Hell and Heaven!) 119

"But he calls forever on your name,
    Sister Helen,
And says that he melts before a flame."
"My heart for his pleasure fared the same,
    Little brother."
   (*O Mother, Mary Mother,*
Fire at the heart, between Hell and Heaven!) 126

"Here's Keith of Westholm riding fast,
    Sister Helen,
For I know the white plume on the blast."
"The hour, the sweet hour I forecast, 130
    Little brother!"
   (*O Mother, Mary Mother,*
Is the hour sweet, between Hell and Heaven?)

"He stops to speak, and he stills his horse,
    Sister Helen;
But his words are drowned in the wind's
    course."   136
"Nay hear, nay hear, you must hear perforce,
    Little brother!"
   (*O Mother, Mary Mother,*
What word now heard, between Hell and Heaven?)

"Oh, he says that Keith of Ewern's cry,
    Sister Helen,
Is ever to see you ere he die."
"In all that his soul sees, there am I, 144
    Little brother!"
   (*O Mother, Mary Mother,*
The soul's one sight, between Hell and Heaven!)

"He sends a ring and a broken coin,
    Sister Helen,
And bids you mind the banks of Boyne."
"What else he broke will he ever join, 151
    Little brother?"
   (*O Mother, Mary Mother,*
No, never joined, between Hell and Heaven!)

"He yields you these and craves full fain,
    Sister Helen,
You pardon him in his mortal pain."
"What else he took will he give again,
    Little brother?"
   (*O Mother, Mary Mother,*
Not twice to give, between Hell and Heaven!) 161

"He calls your name in an agony,
    Sister Helen,
That even dead Love must weep to see."
"Hate, born of Love, is blind as he, 165
    Little brother!"
   (*O Mother, Mary Mother,*
Love turned to hate, between Hell and Heaven!)

"Oh it's Keith of Keith now that rides fast,
    Sister Helen,
For I know the white hair on the blast."
"The short, short hour will soon be past, 172
    Little brother!"
   (*O Mother, Mary Mother,*
Will soon be past, between Hell and Heaven!)

"He looks at me and he tries to speak,
    Sister Helen,
But oh! his voice is sad and weak!"
"What here should the mighty Baron seek,
    Little brother!"
   (*O Mother, Mary Mother,*
Is this the end, between Hell and Heaven?) 182

"Oh his son still cries, if you forgive,
    Sister Helen,
The body dies, but the soul shall live."
"Fire shall forgive me as I forgive,
    Little brother!"
   (*O Mother, Mary Mother,*
As she forgives, between Hell and Heaven!) 189

"Oh he prays you, as his heart would rive,
    Sister Helen,
To save his dear son's soul alive."
"Fire cannot slay it, it shall thrive,
    Little brother!"
   (*O Mother, Mary Mother,*
Alas, alas, between Hell and Heaven!) 196

"He cries to you, kneeling in the road,
    Sister Helen,
To go with him for the love of God!"
"The way is long to his son's abode, 200
    Little brother."
   (*O Mother, Mary Mother,*
The way is long, between Hell and Heaven!)

"A lady's here, by a dark steed brought,
    Sister Helen,
So darkly clad, I saw her not."
"See her now or never see aught, 207
    Little brother!"
   (*O Mother, Mary Mother,*
What more to see, between Hell and Heaven!)

"Her hood falls back, and the moon shines fair,
    Sister Helen,
On the Lady of Ewern's golden hair." 213
"Blest hour of my power and her despair,
    Little brother!"
   (*O Mother, Mary Mother,*
Hour blest and bann'd, between Hell and Heaven!)

"Pale, pale her cheeks, that in pride did glow,
    Sister Helen, 219
'Neath the bridal-wreath three days ago."
"One morn for pride and three days for woe,
    Little brother!"
   (*O Mother, Mary Mother,*
Three days, three nights, between Hell and Heaven!)

"Her clasped hands stretch from her bending head,
    Sister Helen; 226
With the loud wind's wail her sobs are wed."
"What wedding-strains hath her bridal-bed,
    Little brother?"
   (*O Mother, Mary Mother,*
What strain but death's between Hell and Heaven?)

"She may not speak, she sinks in a swoon,
    Sister Helen,—
She lifts her lips and gasps on the moon." 234
"Oh! might I but hear her soul's blithe tune,
    Little brother!"
   (*O Mother, Mary Mother,*
Her woe's dumb cry, between Hell and Heaven!)

"They've caught her to Westholm's saddle-bow,
    Sister Helen,
And her moonlit hair gleams white in its flow."
"Let it turn whiter than winter snow, 242
    Little brother!"
   (*O Mother, Mary Mother,*
Woe-withered gold, between Hell and Heaven!)

"O Sister Helen, you heard the bell,
    Sister Helen!
More loud than the vesper-chime it fell."
"No vesper-chime, but a dying knell,
    Little brother!"
   (*O Mother, Mary Mother,*
His dying knell, between Hell and Heaven!) 252

"Alas! but I fear the heavy sound,
    Sister Helen;

Is it in the sky or in the ground?"
"Say, have they turned their horses round,
            Little brother?"
        (*O Mother, Mary Mother,*
What would she more, between Hell and
Heaven?)   259

"They have raised the old man from his knee,
            Sister Helen,
And they ride in silence hastily."
"More fast the naked soul doth flee,   263
            Little brother!"
        (*O Mother, Mary Mother,*
The naked soul, between Hell and Heaven!) 266

"Flank to flank are the three steeds gone,
            Sister Helen,
But the lady's dark steed goes alone."
"And lonely her bridegroom's soul hath flown,
            Little brother."
        (*O Mother, Mary Mother,*
The lonely ghost, between Hell and Heaven!) 273

"Oh the wind is sad in the iron chill,
            Sister Helen,
And weary sad they look by the hill."
"But he and I are sadder still,
            Little brother!"
        (*O Mother, Mary Mother,*
Most sad of all, between Hell and Heaven!) 280

"See, see, the wax has dropped from its place,
            Sister Helen,
And the flames are winning up apace!"
"Yet here they burn but for a space,
            Little brother!"
        (*O Mother, Mary Mother,*
Here for a space, between Hell and Heaven!) 287

"Ah! what white thing at the door has cross'd,
            Sister Helen,
Ah! what is this that sighs in the frost?"
"A soul that's lost as mine is lost,   291
            Little brother!"
        (*O Mother, Mary Mother,*
Lost, lost, all lost, between Hell and Heaven!)

THE BALLAD OF DEAD LADIES

(FROM FRANÇOIS VILLON)[1]

Tell me now in what hidden way is
Lady Flora the lovely Roman?

[1] Cf. Stevenson's essay, pp. 662 ff.

AE

Where's Hipparchia, and where is Thaïs,
    Neither of them the fairer woman?
Where is Echo, beheld of no man,
    Only heard on river and mere, —
    She whose beauty was more than human? . . .
But where are the snows of yester-year?   8

Where's Héloise, the learned nun,
    For whose sake Abeillard, I ween,
Lost manhood and put priesthood on?
    (From Love he won such dule and teen!)
And where, I pray you, is the Queen
    Who willed that Buridan should steer
    Sewed in a sack's mouth down the Seine? . . .
But where are the snows of yester-year?   16

White Queen Blanche, like a queen of lilies,
    With a voice like any mermaiden, —
Bertha Broadfoot, Beatrice, Alice,
    And Ermengarde the lady of Maine, —
    And that good Joan whom Englishmen
At Rouen doomed and burned her there, —
    Mother of God, where are they then? . . .
But where are the snows of yester-year?   24

Nay, never ask this week, fair lord,
    Where they are gone, nor yet this year,
Except with this for an overword,[1] —
    "But where are the snows of yester-year?"

FRANCESCA DA RIMINI

(FROM DANTE)[2]

*   *   *   *   *   *   *

When I made answer, I began: "Alas!
    How many sweet thoughts and how much
        desire
Led these two onward to the dolorous pass!"
    Then turned to them, as who would fain
        inquire,
And said: "Francesca, these thine agonies
    Wring tears for pity and grief that they in-
        spire: —
But tell me, — in the season of sweet sighs,
    When and what way did Love instruct you
        so
That he in your vague longings made you
        wise?"   9
    Than she to me: "There is no greater woe
Then the remembrance brings of happy days
    In Misery; and this thy guide[3] doth know.

[1] refrain   [2] *Inferno*, v, 112-42   [3] Vergil; no
special passage, but his general experience is meant

But if the first beginnings to retrace
  Of our sad love can yield thee solace here,
So will I be as one that weeps and says.
  One day we read, for pastime and sweet
    cheer,
Of Lancelot,[1] how he found Love tyrannous:
  We were alone and without any fear.
Our eyes were drawn together, reading thus,
  Full oft, and still our cheeks would pale and
    glow;   20
But one sole point it was that conquered us.
  For when we read of that great lover, how
He kissed the smile which he had longed to
    win, —
  Then he whom nought can sever from me
    now
Forever, kissed my mouth, all quivering.
  A Galahalt[2] was the book, and he that writ:
Upon that day we read no more therein."
  At the tale told, while one soul uttered it,
The other wept: a pang so pitiable
  That I was seized, like death, in swooning-
    fit,   30
And even as a dead body falls, I fell.

ON REFUSAL OF AID BETWEEN NATIONS

Not that the earth is changing, O my God!
  Nor that the seasons totter in their walk, —
  Not that the virulent ill of act and talk
Seethes ever as a winepress ever trod, —
Not therefore are we certain that the rod
  Weighs in thine hand to smite thy world;
    though now
  Beneath thine hand so many nations bow,
So many kings: — not therefore, O my God! —
But because Man is parcelled out in men
  To-day; because, for any wrongful blow, 10
  No man not stricken asks, "I would be
    told
Why thou dost thus:" but his heart whispers
    then,
  "He is he, I am I." By this we know
  That the earth falls asunder, being old.

THE SONNET

A Sonnet is a moment's monument, —
  Memorial from the Soul's eternity
  To one dead deathless hour. Look that it be,

Whether for lustral rite or dire portent,
Of its own arduous fulness reverent:
  Carve it in ivory or in ebony,
  As Day or Night may rule; and let Time
    see
Its flowering crest impearled and orient.
A Sonnet is a coin: its face reveals
  The soul, — its converse, to what Power
    'tis due: —   10
Whether for tribute to the august appeals
  Of Life, or dower in Love's high retinue,
It serve; or, 'mid the dark wharf's cavernous
    breath,
In Charon's[1] palm it pay the toll to Death.

LOVE–SIGHT

When do I see thee most, belovèd one?
  When in the light the spirits of mine eyes
  Before thy face, their altar, solemnize
The worship of that Love through thee made
    known?
Or when in the dusk hours, (we two alone,)
  Close-kissed and eloquent of still replies
  Thy twilight-hidden glimmering visage lies,
And my soul only sees thy soul its own?
O love, my love! if I no more should see
Thyself, nor on the earth the shadow of thee,
  Nor image of thine eyes in any spring, — 11
How then should sound upon Life's darkening
    slope
The ground-whirl of the perished leaves of
    Hope,
  The wind of Death's imperishable wing?

LOVE–SWEETNESS

Sweet dimness of her loosened hair's downfall
  About thy face; her sweet hands round thy
    head
  In gracious fostering union garlanded;
Her tremulous smiles; her glances' sweet recall
Of love; her murmuring sighs memorial;
  Her mouth's culled sweetness by thy kisses
    shed
  On cheeks and neck and eyelids, and so led
Back to her mouth which answers there for
    all: —
What sweeter than these things, except the
    thing

---

[1] the lover of Guinevere, King Arthur's queen
[2] i.e., the book brought them together as he did
Launcelot and Guinevere

[1] the ferryman who in Greek mythology conveyed the spirits of the dead across the river Styx
to Hades

In lacking which all these would lose their
  sweet : —   10
The confident heart's still fervour : the
  swift beat,
And soft subsidence of the spirit's wing,
Then when it feels, in cloud-girt wayfaring,
  The breath of kindred plumes against its
    feet?

MID-RAPTURE

Thou lovely and belovèd, thou my love;
  Whose kiss seems still the first; whose
    summoning eyes,
  Even now, as for our love-world's new sun-
    rise,
Shed very dawn; whose voice, attuned above
All modulation of the deep-bowered dove,
  Is like a hand laid softly on the soul;
  Whose hand is like a sweet voice to control
Those worn tired brows it hath the keeping
  of : —
What word can answer to thy word, — what
  gaze
  To thine, which now absorbs within its
    sphere   10
  My worshipping face, till I am mirrored
    there
Light-circled in a heaven of deep-drawn rays?
  What clasp, what kiss mine inmost heart
    can prove,
  O lovely and belovèd, O my love?

SOUL-LIGHT

What other woman could be loved like you,
  Or how of you should love possess his fill?
  After the fulness of all rapture, still, —
As at the end of some deep avenue
A tender glamour of day, — there comes to
  view
  Far in your eyes a yet more hungering
    thrill, —
  Such fire as Love's soul-winnowing hands
    distil
Even from his inmost ark of light and dew.
And as the traveller triumphs with the sun,
  Glorying in heat's mid-height, yet startide
    brings
Wonder new-born, and still fresh transport
  springs   11
  From limpid lambent hours of day begun; —
  Even so, through eyes and voice, your soul
    doth move
My soul with changeful light of infinite love.

KNOWN IN VAIN

As two whose love, first foolish, widening
  scope,
  Knows suddenly, to music high and soft,
  The Holy of holies; who because they
    scoff'd
Are now amazed with shame, nor dare to
  cope
With the whole truth aloud, lest heaven should
  ope;
  Yet, at their meetings, laugh not as they
    laugh'd
  In speech; nor speak, at length; but sitting
    oft
Together, within hopeless sight of hope
For hours are silent : — So it happeneth
  When Work and Will awake too late, to
    gaze   10
After their life sailed by, and hold their
  breath.
  Ah! who shall dare to search through what
    sad maze
  Thenceforth their incommunicable ways
Follow the desultory feet of Death?

THE LANDMARK

Was *that* the landmark? What, — the foolish
  well
  Whose wave, low down, I did not stoop to
    drink,
  But sat and flung the pebbles from its
    brink
In sport to send its imaged skies pell-mell,
(And mine own image, had I noted well!) —
  Was that my point of turning? — I had
    thought
  The stations of my course should rise un-
    sought,
As altar-stone or ensigned citadel.
But lo! the path is missed, I must go back,
  And thirst to drink when next I reach the
    spring   10
Which once I stained, which since may have
  grown black.
  Yet though no light be left nor bird now
    sing
  As here I turn, I'll thank God, hastening,
That the same goal is still on the same
  track.

THE CHOICE

I

Eat thou and drink; to-morrow thou shalt
  die.
  Surely the earth, that's wise being very old,
  Needs not our help. Then loose me, love,
  and hold
Thy sultry hair up from my face; that I
May pour for thee this golden wine, brim-
  high,
  Till round the glass thy fingers glow like
  gold.
  We'll drown all hours: thy song, while
  hours are toll'd,
Shall leap, as fountains veil the changing sky.
Now kiss, and think that there are really
  those,
  My own high-bosomed beauty, who increase
  Vain gold, vain lore, and yet might choose
  our way!   11
    Through many years they toil; then on
    a day
  They die not, — for their life was death, —
  but cease;
And round their narrow lips the mould falls
  close.

II

Watch thou and fear; to-morrow thou shalt
  die.
  Or art thou sure thou shalt have time for
  death?
  Is not the day which God's word promiseth
To come man knows not when? In yonder
  sky,
Now while we speak, the sun speeds forth:
  can I
  Or thou assure him of his goal? God's
  breath
Even at this moment haply quickeneth
The air to a flame; till spirits, always nigh
Though screened and hid, shall walk the day-
  light here.
    And dost thou prate of all that man shall
    do?
    Canst thou, who hast but plagues, pre-
    sume to be   11
    Glad in his gladness that comes after
    thee?
Will *his* strength slay *thy* worm in Hell?
  Go to:
Cover thy countenance, and watch, and fear.

III

Think thou and act; to-morrow thou shalt
  die.
  Outstretch'd in the sun's warmth upon the
  shore,
  Thou say'st: "Man's measured path is all
  gone o'er;
Up all his years, steeply, with strain and sigh,
Man clomb until he touched the truth;
  and I,
  Even I, am he whom it was destined for."
  How should this be? Art thou then so
  much more
Than they who sowed, that thou shouldst reap
  thereby?
Nay, come up hither. From this wave-
  washed mound
  Unto the furthest flood-brim look with me;
  Then reach on with thy thought till it be
  drown'd.   11
    Miles and miles distant though the last line
    be,
  And though thy soul sail leagues and leagues
  beyond, —
  Still, leagues beyond those leagues, there is
  more sea.

VAIN VIRTUES

What is the sorriest thing that enters Hell?
  None of the sins, — but this and that fair
  deed
  Which a soul's sin at length could supersede.
These yet are virgins, whom death's timely
  knell
Might once have sainted; whom the fiends
  compel
  Together now, in snake-bound shuddering
  sheaves
  Of anguish, while the pit's pollution leaves
Their refuse maidenhood abominable.
Night sucks them down, the tribute of the
  pit,
  Whose names, half entered in the book of
  Life,
    Were God's desire at noon. And as their
    hair   11
And eyes sink last, the Torturer deigns no
  whit
  To gaze, but, yearning, waits his destined
  wife,
    The Sin still blithe on earth that sent
    them there.

LOST DAYS

The lost days of my life until to-day,
  What were they, could I see them on the
    street
  Lie as they fell? Would they be ears of
    wheat
Sown once for food but trodden into clay?
Or golden coins squandered and still to-pay?
  Or drops of blood dabbling the guilty feet?
  Or such spilt water as in dreams must cheat
The undying throats of Hell, athirst alway?
I do not see them here; but after death
  God knows I know the faces I shall see,   10
Each one a murdered self, with low last breath.
  "I am thyself, — what hast thou done to
    me?"
"And I — and I — thyself," (lo! each one
    saith,)
  "And thou thyself to all eternity!"

A SUPERSCRIPTION

Look in my face; my name is Might-have-
    been;
  I am also called No-more, Too-late, Fare-
    well;
Unto thine ear I hold the dead-sea shell
Cast up thy Life's foam-fretted feet between;
Unto thine eyes the glass where that is seen
  Which had Life's form and Love's, but by
    my spell
  Is now a shaken shadow intolerable,
Of ultimate things unuttered the frail screen.
Mark me, how still I am! But should there
    dart
  One moment through thy soul the soft sur-
    prise   10
  Of that winged Peace which lulls the breath
    of sighs, —
Then shalt thou see me smile, and turn apart
Thy visage to mine ambush at thy heart,
  Sleepless with cold commemorative eyes.

THE ONE HOPE

When vain desire at last and vain regret
  Go hand in hand to death, and all is vain,
  What shall assuage the unforgotten pain
And teach the unforgetful to forget?
Shall Peace be still a sunk stream long un-
    met, —
  Or may the soul at once in a green plain
  Stoop through the spray of some sweet life-
    fountain

And cull the dew-drenched flowering amulet?
Ah! when the wan soul in that golden air
  Between the scriptured petals softly blown
  Peers breathless for the gift of grace un-
    known, —   11
Ah! let none other alien spell soe'er
But only the one Hope's one name be there, —
  Not less nor more, but even that word alone.

WILLIAM MORRIS (1834-1896)

THE EARTHLY PARADISE

Of Heaven or Hell I have no power to sing,
I cannot ease the burden of your fears,
Or make quick-coming death a little thing,
Or bring again the pleasure of past years,
Nor for my words shall ye forget your tears,
Or hope again for aught that I can say,
The idle singer of an empty day.   7

But rather, when aweary of your mirth,
From full hearts still unsatisfied ye sigh,
And, feeling kindly unto all the earth,
Grudge every minute as it passes by,
Made the more mindful that the sweet days
    die —
— Remember me a little then, I pray,
The idle singer of an empty day.   14

The heavy trouble, the bewildering care
That weighs us down who live and earn our
    bread,
These idle verses have no power to bear;
So let me sing of names rememberèd,
Because they, living not, can ne'er be dead,
Or long time take their memory quite away
From us poor singers of an empty day.   21

Dreamer of dreams, born out of my due
    time,
Why should I strive to set the crooked straight?
Let it suffice me that my murmuring rhyme
Beats with light wing against the ivory gate,[1]
Telling a tale not too importunate
To those who in the sleepy region stay,
Lulled by the singer of an empty day.   28

Folk say, a wizard to a northern king
At Christmas-tide such wondrous things did
    show,

[1] the gate of false dreams; cf. Æneid, VI,
895-6

That through one window men beheld the spring,
And through another saw the summer glow,
And through a third the fruited vines a-row,
While still, unheard, but in its wonted way,
Piped the drear wind of that December day.

So with this Earthly Paradise it is, 36
If ye will read aright, and pardon me,
Who strive to build a shadowy isle of bliss
Midmost the beating of the steely sea,[1]
Where tossed about all hearts of men must be;
Whose ravening monsters mighty men shall slay,
Not the poor singer of an empty day. 42

PROLOGUE

Forget six counties overhung with smoke,
Forget the snorting steam and piston stroke,
Forget the spreading of the hideous town;
Think rather of the pack-horse on the down,
And dream of London, small, and white, and clean,
The clear Thames bordered by its gardens green;
Think, that below bridge the green lapping waves
Smite some few keels that bear Levantine staves,
Cut from the yew wood on the burnt-up hill,
And pointed jars that Greek hands toiled to fill, 10
And treasured scanty spice from some far sea,
Florence gold cloth, and Ypres napery,
And cloth of Bruges, and hogsheads of Guienne;
While nigh the thronged wharf Geoffrey Chaucer's pen
Moves over bills of lading — mid such times
Shall dwell the hollow puppets of my rhymes.

*   *   *   *   *   *   *

THE LADY OF THE LAND

It happened once, some men of Italy
Midst the Greek Islands went a sea-roving,
And much good fortune had they on the sea:
Of many a man they had the ransoming,
And many a chain they gat, and goodly thing;
And midst their voyage to an isle they came,
Whereof my story keepeth not the name. 7

[1] of modern life

Now though but little was there left to gain,
Because the richer folk had gone away,
Yet since by this of water they were fain
They came to anchor in a land-locked bay,
Whence in a while some went ashore to play,
Going but lightly armed in twos or threes,
For midst that folk they feared no enemies. 14

And of these fellows that thus went ashore,
One was there who left all his friends behind;
Who going inland ever more and more,
And being left quite alone, at last did find
A lonely valley sheltered from the wind,
Wherein, amidst an ancient cypress wood,
A long-deserted ruined castle stood. 21

The wood, once ordered in fair grove and glade,
With gardens overlooked by terraces,
And marble-pavèd pools for pleasure made,
Was tangled now, and choked with fallen trees;
And he who went there, with but little ease
Must stumble by the stream's side, once made meet
For tender women's dainty wandering feet. 28

The raven's croak, the low wind choked and drear,
The baffled stream, the grey wolf's doleful cry,
Were all the sounds that mariner could hear,
As through the wood he wandered painfully;
But as unto the house he drew anigh,
The pillars of a ruined shrine he saw,
The once fair temple of a fallen law. 35

No image was there left behind to tell
Before whose face the knees of men had bowed;
An altar of black stone, of old wrought well,
Alone beneath a ruined roof now showed
The goal whereto the folk were wont to crowd,
Seeking for things forgotten long agò,
Praying for heads long ages laid a-low. 42

Close to the temple was the castle-gate,
Doorless and crumbling; there our fellow turned,
Trembling indeed at what might chance to wait
The prey entrapped, yet with a heart that burned
To know the most of what might there be learned,
And hoping somewhat too, amid his fear,
To light on such things as all men hold dear.

Noble the house was, nor seemed built for
  war, 50
But rather like the work of other days,
When men, in better peace than now they are,
Had leisure on the world around to gaze,
And noted well the past times' changing ways;
And fair with sculptured stories it was
  wrought,
By lapse of time unto dim ruin brought. 56

Now as he looked about on all these things,
And strove to read the mouldering histories,
Above the door an image with wide wings,
Whose unclad limbs a serpent seemed to seize,
He dimly saw, although the western breeze,
And years of biting frost and washing rain,
Had made the carver's labour well-nigh vain.

But this, though perished sore, and worn
  away, 64
He noted well, because it seemed to be,
After the fashion of another day,
Some great man's badge of war, or armoury;[1]
And round it a carved wreath he seemed to
  see:
But taking note of these things, at the last
The mariner beneath the gateway passed. 70

And there a lovely cloistered court he
  found,
A fountain in the midst o'erthrown and dry,
And in the cloister briers twining round
The slender shafts; the wondrous imagery
Outworn by more than many years gone by;
Because the country people, in their fear
Of wizardry, had wrought destruction here;

And piteously these fair things had been
  maimed; 78
There stood great Jove, lacking his head of
  might,
Here was the archer, swift Apollo, lamed;
The shapely limbs of Venus hid from sight
By weeds and shards; Diana's ankles light
Bound with the cable of some coasting ship;
And rusty nails through Helen's maddening
  lip. 84

Therefrom unto the chambers did he pass,
And found them fair still, midst of their decay,
Though in them now no sign of man there was,
And everything but stone had passed away
That made them lovely in that vanished day;

---

[1] coat of arms

Nay, the mere walls themselves would soon be
  gone 90
And nought be left but heaps of mouldering
  stone.

But he, when all the place he had gone o'er,
And with much trouble clomb the broken stair,
And from the topmost turret seen the shore
And his good ship drawn up at anchor there,
Came down again, and found a crypt most fair
Built wonderfully beneath the greatest hall,
And there he saw a door within the wall, 98

Well-hinged, close shut; nor was there in
  that place
Another on its hinges, therefore he
Stood there and pondered for a little space,
And thought, "Perchance some marvel I shall
  see,
For surely here some dweller there must be,
Because this door seems whole, and new, and
  sound,
While nought but ruin I can see around." 105

So with that word, moved by a strong
  desire,
He tried the hasp, that yielded to his hand,
And in a strange place, lit as by a fire
Unseen but near, he presently did stand;
And by an odorous breeze his face was fanned,
As though in some Arabian plain he stood,
Anigh the border of a spice-tree wood. 112

He moved not for awhile, but looking round,
He wondered much to see the place so fair,
Because, unlike the castle above ground,
No pillager or wrecker had been there;
It seemed that time had passed on otherwhere,
Nor laid a finger on this hidden place,
Rich with the wealth of some forgotten race.

With hangings, fresh as when they left the
  loom, 120
The walls were hung a space above the head,
Slim ivory chairs were set about the room,
And in one corner was a dainty bed,
That seemed for some fair queen apparellèd;
And marble was the worst stone of the floor,
That with rich Indian webs was covered o'er.

The wanderer trembled when he saw all this,
Because he deemed by magic it was wrought;
Yet in his heart a longing for some bliss, 129
Whereof the hard and changing world knows
  nought,

Arose and urged him on, and dimmed the
    thought
That there perchance some devil lurked to slay
The heedless wanderer from the light of day.

Over against him was another door   134
Set in the wall; so, casting fear aside,
With hurried steps he crossed the varied floor,
And there again the silver latch he tried
And with no pain the door he opened wide,
And entering the new chamber cautiously
The glory of great heaps of gold could see.

Upon the floor uncounted medals lay,   141
Like things of little value; here and there
Stood golden caldrons, that might well out-
    weigh
The biggest midst an emperor's copper-ware,
And golden cups were set on tables fair,
Themselves of gold; and in all hollow things
Were stored great gems, worthy the crowns
    of kings.   147

The walls and roof with gold were overlaid,
And precious raiment from the wall hung
    down;
The fall of kings that treasure might have
    stayed,
Or gained some longing conqueror great re-
    nown,
Or built again some god-destroyed old town;
What wonder, if this plunderer of the sea
Stood gazing at it long and dizzily?   154

But at the last his troubled eyes and dazed
He lifted from the glory of that gold,
And then the image, that well-nigh erased
Over the castle-gate he did behold,
Above a door well wrought in colored gold
Again he saw; a naked girl with wings
Enfolded in a serpent's scaly rings.   161

And even as his eyes were fixed on it
A woman's voice came from the other side,
And through his heart strange hopes began to
    flit
That in some wondrous land he might abide
Not dying, master of a deathless bride,   166
So o'er the gold which now he scarce could see
He went, and passed this last door eagerly.

Then in a room he stood wherein there was
A marble bath, whose brimming water yet
Was scarcely still; a vessel of green glass
Half full of odorous ointment was there set

Upon the topmost step that still was wet,
And jewelled shoes and women's dainty gear,
Lay cast upon the varied pavement near. 175

In one quick glance these things his eyes
    did see,
But speedily they turned round to behold
Another sight, for throned on ivory
There sat a woman, whose wet tresses rolled
On to the floor in waves of gleaming gold, 180
Cast back from such a form as, erewhile shown
To one poor shepherd, lighted up Troy town.[1]

Naked she was, the kisses of her feet   183
Upon the floor a dying path had made
From the full bath unto her ivory seat;
In her right hand, upon her bosom laid,
She held a golden comb, a mirror weighed
Her left hand down, aback her fair head lay
Dreaming awake of some long vanished day.

Her eyes were shut, but she seemed not to
    sleep,   190
Her lips were murmuring things unheard and
    low,
Or sometimes twitched as though she needs
    must weep
Though from her eyes the tears refused to flow,
And oft with heavenly red her cheek did glow,
As if remembrance of some half-sweet shame
Across the web of many memories came.   196

There stood the man, scarce daring to draw
    breath
For fear the lovely sight should fade away;
Forgetting heaven, forgetting life and death,
Trembling for fear lest something he should
    say
Unwitting, lest some sob should yet betray
His presence there, for to his eager eyes
Already did the tears begin to rise.   203

But as he gazed, she moved, and with a sigh
Bent forward, dropping down her golden head;
"Alas, alas! another day gone by,
Another day and no soul come," she said.
"Another year, and still I am not dead!"
And with that word once more her head she
    raised,   209
And on the trembling man with great eyes
    gazed.

[1] Helen's, shown to Paris, who abducted her,
brought on the war that ended in the burning of
Troy.

Then he imploring hands to her did reach,
And toward her very slowly 'gan to move
And with wet eyes her pity did beseech,
And seeing her about to speak, he strove   214
From trembling lips to utter words of love;
But with a look she stayed his doubtful feet,
And made sweet music as their eyes did meet.

For now she spoke in gentle voice and clear,
Using the Greek tongue that he knew full
    well;
"What man art thou, that thus hast wandered
    here,   220
And found this lonely chamber where I dwell?
Beware, beware! for I have many a spell;
If greed of power and gold have led thee on,
Not lightly shall this untold wealth be won.

"But if thou com'st here, knowing of my
    tale,   225
In hope to bear away my body fair,
Stout must thine heart be, nor shall that
    avail
If thou a wicked soul in thee dost bear;
So once again I bid thee to beware,
Because no base man things like this may see,
And live thereafter long and happily."   231

"Lady," he said, "in Florence is my home,
And in my city noble is my name;
Neither on peddling voyage am I come,
But, like my fathers, bent to gather fame;
And though thy face has set my heart a-flame
Yet of thy story nothing do I know,
But here have wandered heedlessly enow.

"But since the sight of thee mine eyes did
    bless,   239
What can I be but thine? what wouldst thou
    have?
From those thy words, I deem from some
    distress
By deeds of mine thy dear life I might save;
O then, delay not! if one ever gave
His life to any, mine I give to thee;
Come, tell me what the price of love must be?

"Swift death, to be with thee a day and
    night   246
And with the earliest dawning to be slain?
Or better, a long year of great delight,
And many years of misery and pain?
Or worse, and this poor hour for all my gain?
A sorry merchant am I on this day,
E'en as thou willest so must I obey."   252

She said, "What brave words! nought
    divine am I,
But an unhappy and unheard-of maid
Compelled by evil fate and destiny
To live, who long ago should have been laid
Under the earth within the cypress shade.
Hearken awhile, and quickly shalt thou know
What deed I pray thee to accomplish now.

"God grant indeed thy words are not for
    nought!   260
Then shalt thou save me, since for many a day
To such a dreadful life I have been brought:
Nor will I spare with all my heart to pay
What man soever takes my grief away;
Ah! I will love thee, if thou lovest me
But well enough my saviour now to be.   266

"My father lived a many years agone
Lord of this land, master of all cunning,
Who ruddy gold could draw from out grey
    stone,
And gather wealth from many an uncouth
    thing;
He made the wilderness rejoice and sing,
And such a leech he was that none could say
Without his word what soul should pass away.

"Unto Diana such a gift he gave,   274
Goddess above, below, and on the earth,
That I should be her virgin and her slave
From the first hour of my most wretched
    birth;
Therefore my life had known but little mirth
When I had come unto my twentieth year
And the last time of hallowing drew anear.   280

"So in her temple had I lived and died
And all would long ago have passed away,
But ere that time came, did strange things
    betide,
Whereby I am alive unto this day;
Alas, the bitter words that I must say!
Ah! can I bring my wretched tongue to tell
How I was brought unto this fearful hell?   287

"A queen I was, what gods I knew I loved,
And nothing evil was there in my thought,
And yet by love my wretched heart was moved
Until to utter ruin I was brought!
Alas! thou sayest our gods were vain and
    nought;
Wait, wait, till thou hast heard this tale of
    mine,   293
Then shalt thou think them devilish or divine.

"Hearken! in spite of father and of vow
I loved a man; but for that sin I think
Men had forgiven me — yea, yea, even thou;
But from the gods the full cup must I drink,
And into misery unheard of sink,   299
Tormented, when their own names are forgot,
And men must doubt if e'er they lived or not.

"Glorious my lover was unto my sight,
Most beautiful, — of love we grew so fain
That we at last agreed, that on a night   304
We should be happy, but that[1] he were slain
Or shut in hold; and neither joy nor pain
Should else forbid that hoped-for time to be;
So came the night that made a wretch of me.

"Ah! well do I remember all that night,
When through the window shone the orb of
June,   310
And by the bed flickered the taper's light,
Whereby I trembled, gazing at the moon:
Ah me! the meeting that we had, when soon
Into his strong, well-trusted arms I fell,
And many a sorrow we began to tell.   315

"Ah me! what parting on that night we
had!
I think the story of my great despair
A little while might merry folk make sad;
For, as he swept away my yellow hair
To make my shoulder and my bosom bare,
I raised mine eyes, and shuddering could be-
hold
A shadow cast upon the bed of gold: 322

"Then suddenly was quenched my hot
desire
And he untwined his arms; the moon so pale
A while ago, seemed changed to blood and fire,
And yet my limbs beneath me did not fail,
And neither had I strength to cry or wail,
But stood there helpless, bare, and shivering,
With staring eyes still fixed upon the thing. 329

"Because the shade that on the bed of gold
The changed and dreadful moon was throwing
down
Was of Diana, whom I did behold,
With knotted hair, and shining girt-up gown,
And on the high white brow, a deadly frown
Bent upon us, who stood scarce drawing
breath,
Striving to meet the horrible sure death. 336

"No word at all the dreadful goddess said,
But soon across my feet my lover lay,
And well indeed I knew that he was dead;
And would that I had died on that same day!
For in a while the image turned away,
And without words my doom I understood,
And felt a horror change my human blood. 343

"And there I fell, and on the floor I lay
By the dead man, till daylight came on me,
And not a word thenceforward could I say
For three years; till of grief and misery,
The lingering pest,[1] the cruel enemy,
My father and his folk were dead and gone,
And in this castle I was left alone: 350

"And then the doom foreseen upon me fell,
For Queen Diana did my body change
Into a fork-tongued dragon, flesh and fell,[2]
And through the island nightly do I range,
Or in the green sea mate with monsters strange,
When in the middle of the moonlit night
The sleepy mariner I do affright.   357

"But all day long upon this gold I lie
Within this place, where never mason's hand
Smote trowel on the marble noisily;
Drowsy I lie, no folk at my command,
Who once was called the Lady of the Land;
Who might have bought a kingdom with a
kiss,   363
Yea, half the world with such a sight as this."

And therewithal, with rosy fingers light,
Backward her heavy-hanging hair she threw,
To give her naked beauty more to sight;
But when, forgetting all the things he knew,
Maddened with love unto the prize he drew,
She cried, "Nay, wait! for wherefore wilt
thou die,
Why should we not be happy, thou and I? 371

"Wilt thou not save me? once in every year
This rightful form of mine that thou dost see
By favour of the goddess have I here
From sunrise unto sunset given me,
That some brave man may end my misery.
And thou — art thou not brave? can thy
heart fail,   377
Whose eyes e'en now are weeping at my tale?

"Then listen! when this day is overpast,
A fearful monster shall I be again,

---

[1] unless

[1] plague   [2] skin

And thou mayst be my saviour at the last;
Unless, once more, thy words are nought and
vain.
If thou of love and sovereignty art fain,
Come thou next morn, and when thou seest
here
A hideous dragon, have thereof no fear, 385

"But take the loathsome head up in thine
hands,
And kiss it, and be master presently
Of twice the wealth that is in all the lands
From Cathay[1] to the head of Italy;
And master also, if it pleaseth thee,
Of all thou praisest as so fresh and bright,
Of what thou callest crown of all delight. 392

"Ah! with what joy then shall I see again
The sunlight on the green grass and the trees,
And hear the clatter of the summer rain,
And see the joyous folk beyond the seas.
Ah, me! to hold my child upon my knees,
After the weeping of unkindly tears, 398
And all the wrongs of these four hundred years.

"Go now, go quick! leave this grey heap
of stone;
And from thy glad heart think upon thy way,
How I shall love thee — yea, love thee alone,
That bringest me from dark death unto day;
For this shall be thy wages and thy pay;
Unheard-of wealth, unheard-of love is near,
If thou hast heart a little dread to bear." 406

Therewith she turned to go; but he cried out,
"Ah! wilt thou leave me then without one kiss,
To slay the very seeds of fear and doubt,
That glad to-morrow may bring certain bliss?
Hast thou forgotten how love lives by this,
The memory of some hopeful close embrace,
Low whispered words within some lonely
place?" 413

But she, when his bright glittering eyes she
saw,
And burning cheeks, cried out, "Alas, alas!
Must I be quite undone, and wilt thou draw
A worse fate on me than the first one was?
O haste thee from this fatal place to pass!
Yet, ere thou goest, take this, lest thou
shouldst deem
Thou hast been fooled by some strange mid-
day dream." 420

So saying, blushing like a new-kissed maid,
From off her neck a little gem she drew,
That, 'twixt those snowy rose-tinged hillocks
laid,
The secrets of her glorious beauty knew; 424
And ere he well perceived what she would do,
She touched his hand, the gem within it lay,
And, turning, from his sight she fled away.

Then at the doorway where her rosy heel
Had glanced and vanished, he awhile did
stare, 429
And still upon his hand he seemed to feel
The varying kisses of her fingers fair;
Then turned he toward the dreary crypt and
bare,
And dizzily throughout the castle passed,
Till by the ruined fane he stood at last. 434

Then weighing still the gem within his hand,
He stumbled backward through the cypress
wood,
Thinking the while of some strange lovely
land,
Where all his life should be most fair and good
Till on the valley's wall of hills he stood, 439
And slowly thence passed down unto the bay
Red with the death of that bewildering day.

The next day came, and he, who all the
night
Had ceaselessly been turning in his bed,
Arose and clad himself in armour bright,
And many a danger he remembered;
Storming of towns, lone sieges full of dread,
That with renown his heart had borne him
through
And this thing seemed a little thing to do. 448

So on he went, and on the way he thought
Of all the glorious things of yesterday,
Nought of the price whereat they must be
bought,
But ever to himself did softly say,
"No roaming now, my wars are passed away;
No long dull days devoid of happiness,
When such a love my yearning heart shall
bless." 455

Thus to the castle did he come at last,
But when unto the gateway he drew near,
And underneath its ruined archway passed
Into a court, a strange noise did he hear,
And through his heart there shot a pang of
fear; 460

[1] China

Trembling, he gat his sword into his hand,
And midmost of the cloisters took his stand.

But for a while that unknown noise in-
   creased,
A rattling, that with strident roars did blend,
And whining moans; but suddenly it ceased,
A fearful thing stood at the cloister's end,
And eyed him for a while, then 'gan to wend
Adown the cloisters, and began again   468
That rattling, and the moan like fiends in pain.

And as it came on towards him, with its
   teeth
The body of a slain goat did it tear,
The blood whereof in its hot jaws did seethe,
And on its tongue he saw the smoking hair;
Then his heart sank, and standing trembling
   there,
Throughout his mind wild thoughts and fearful
   ran,
"Some fiend she was," he said, "the bane[1] of
   man."   476

Yet he abode her still, although his blood
Curdled within him: the thing dropped the
   goat,
And creeping on, came close to where he stood,
And raised its head to him, and wrinkled
   throat,
Then he cried out and wildly at her smote,
Shutting his eyes, and turned and from the
   place   482
Ran swiftly, with a white and ghastly face.

But little things rough stones and tree-
   trunks seemed,
And if he fell, he rose and ran on still;
No more he felt his hurts than if he dreamed,
He made no stay for valley or steep hill,
Heedless he dashed through many a foaming
   rill,
Until he came unto the ship at last   489
And with no word into the deep hold passed.

Meanwhile the dragon, seeing him clean
   gone,
Followed him not, but crying horribly,
Caught up within her jaws a block of stone
And ground it into powder, then turned she,
With cries that folk could hear far out at sea,
And reached the treasure set apart of old,
To brood above the hidden heaps of gold.   497

[1] destroyer

Yet was she seen again on many a day
By some half-waking mariner, or herd,
Playing amid the ripples of the bay,
Or on the hills making all things afeard,
Or in the wood, that did that castle gird,
But never any man again durst go   503
To seek her woman's form, and end her woe.

As for the man, who knows what things he
   bore?
What mournful faces peopled the sad night,
What wailings vexed him with reproaches sore,
What images of that nigh-gained delight!
What dreamed caresses from soft hands and
   white,
Turning to horrors ere they reached the best:
What struggles vain, what shame, what huge
   unrest?   511

No man he knew, three days he lay and
   raved,
And cried for death, until a lethargy
Fell on him, and his fellows thought him
   saved;
But on the third night he awoke to die;
And at Byzantium doth his body lie
Between two blossoming pomegranate trees,
Within the churchyard of the Genoese.   518

ALGERNON CHARLES SWIN-BURNE (1837–1909)

CHORUS FROM ATALANTA IN CALYDON

When the hounds of spring are on winter's
   traces,
   The mother of months in meadow or plain
Fills the shadows and windy places
   With lisp of leaves and ripple of rain;
And the brown bright nightingale amorous
Is half assuaged for Itylus,[1]
For the Thracian ships and the foreign faces,
   The tongueless vigil, and all the pain.   8

Come with bows bent and with emptying of
   quivers,
   Maiden most perfect, lady of light,
With a noise of winds and many rivers,
   With a clamour of waters, and with might;

[1] cf. the nightingale poems in this volume and
the note on Sidney's *The Nightingale*.

Bind on thy sandals, O thou most fleet,
Over the splendour and speed of thy feet;
For the faint east quickens, the wan west
    shivers,
    Round the feet of the day and the feet of
        the night.   16

Where shall we find her, how shall we sing to
    her,
    Fold our hands round her knees, and cling?
Oh that man's heart were as fire and could
    spring to her,
    Fire, or the strength of the streams that
        spring!
For the stars and the winds are unto her
As raiment, as songs of the harp-player;
For the risen stars and the fallen cling to her
    And the southwest-wind and the west-wind
        sing.   24

For winter's rains and ruins are over,
    And all the season of snows and sins;
The days dividing lover and lover,
    The light that loses, the night that wins;
And time remember'd is grief forgotten,
And frosts are slain and flowers begotten,
And in green underwood and cover
    Blossom by blossom the spring begins.   32

The full streams feed on flower of rushes,
    Ripe grasses trammel a travelling foot,
The faint fresh flame of the young year flushes
    From leaf to flower and flower to fruit;
And fruit and leaf are as gold and fire,
And the oat[1] is heard above the lyre,
And the hoofèd heel of a satyr crushes
    The chestnut-husk at the chestnut-root. 40

And Pan[2] by noon and Bacchus[3] by night,
    Fleeter of foot than the fleet-foot kid,
Follows with dancing and fills with delight
    The Mænad[4] and the Bassarid;[4]
And soft as lips that laugh and hide,
The laughing leaves of the trees divide,
And screen from seeing and leave in sight
    The god pursuing, the maiden hid.   48

The ivy falls with the Bacchanal's[4] hair
    Over her eyebrows hiding her eyes;
The wild vine slipping down leaves bare
    Her bright breast shortening into sighs;

[1] reed pipe [2] god of wild life [3] god of wine
[4] women worshippers of Bacchus

The wild vine slips with the weight of its
    leaves,
But the berried ivy catches and cleaves
To the limbs that glitter, the feet that scare
    The wolf that follows, the fawn that flies. 56

THE GARDEN OF PROSERPINE[1]

Here, where the world is quiet;
    Here, where all trouble seems
Dead winds' and spent waves' riot
    In doubtful dreams of dreams;
I watch the green field growing
For reaping folk and sowing,
For harvest-time and mowing,
    A sleepy world of streams.   8

I am tired of tears and laughter,
    And men that laugh and weep;
Of what may come hereafter
    For men that sow to reap:
I am weary of days and hours,
Blown buds of barren flowers,
Desires and dreams and powers
    And everything but sleep.   16

Here life has death for neighbour,
    And far from eye or ear
Wan waves and wet winds labour,
    Weak ships and spirits steer;
They drive adrift, and whither
They wot not who make thither;
But no such winds blow hither,
    And no such things grow here.   24

No growth of moor or coppice,
    No heather-flower or vine,
But bloomless buds of poppies,
    Green grapes of Proserpine,[2]
Pale beds of blowing rushes,
Where no leaf blooms or blushes
Save this whereout she crushes
    For dead men deadly wine.   32

Pale, without name or number,
    In fruitless fields of corn,
They bow themselves and slumber
    All night till light is born;
And like a soul belated,
In hell and heaven unmated,

[1] the wife of Pluto, god of the infernal regions;
she was the daughter of Ceres, goddess of harvests
[2] Proserpine, as queen of Hades

By cloud and mist abated
  Comes out of darkness morn.   40

Though one were strong as seven,
  He too with death shall dwell,
Nor wake with wings in heaven,
  Nor weep for pains in hell;
Though one were fair as roses,
  His beauty clouds and closes;
And well though love reposes,
  In the end it is not well.   48

Pale, beyond porch and portal,
  Crowned with calm leaves, she stands
Who gathers all things mortal
  With cold immortal hands;
Her languid lips are sweeter
Than love's who fears to greet her
To men that mix and meet her
  From·many times and lands.   56

She waits for each and other,
  She waits for all men born;
Forgets the earth her mother,
  The life of fruits and corn;
And spring and seed and swallow
Take wing for her and follow
Where summer song rings hollow
  And flowers are put to scorn.   64

There go the loves that wither,
  The old loves with wearier wings;
And all dead years draw thither,
  And all disastrous things;
Dead dreams of days forsaken,
Blind buds that snows have shaken,
Wild leaves that winds have taken,
  Red strays of ruined springs.   72

We are not sure of sorrow,
  And joy was never sure;
To-day will die to-morrow;
  Time stoops to no man's lure;
And love, grown faint and fretful,
With lips but half regretful
Sighs, and with eyes forgetful
  Weeps that no loves endure.   80

From too much love of living,
  From hope and fear set free,
We thank with brief thanksgiving
  Whatever gods may be
That no life lives forever;
That dead men rise up never;
That even the weariest river
  Winds somewhere safe to sea.   88

Then star nor sun shall waken,
  Nor any change of light:
Nor sound of waters shaken,
  Nor any sound or sight:
Nor wintry leaves nor vernal,
Nor days nor things diurnal;
Only the sleep eternal
  In an eternal night.
                                        96

ITYLUS[1]

Swallow, my sister, O sister swallow,
  How can thine heart be full of the spring?
  A thousand summers are over and dead.
What hast thou found in the spring to follow?
  What hast thou found in thy heart to sing?
    What wilt thou do when the summer is
      shed?   6

O swallow, sister, O fair swift swallow,
  Why wilt thou fly after spring to the south,
  The soft south whither thine heart is set?
Shall not the grief of the old time follow?
  Shall not the song thereof cleave to thy
    mouth?
    Hast thou forgotten ere I forget?   12

Sister, my sister, O fleet sweet swallow,
  Thy way is long to the sun and the
    south;
  But I, fulfill'd of my heart's desire,
Shedding my song upon height, upon hollow,
  From tawny body and sweet small mouth
    Feed the heart of the night with fire.   18

I the nightingale all spring through,
  O swallow, sister, O changing swallow,
    All spring through till the spring be done,
Clothed with the light of the night on the
    dew,
  Sing, while the hours and the wild birds
    follow,   23
    Take flight and follow and find the sun.

Sister, my sister, O soft light swallow,
  Though all things feast in the spring's guest-
    chamber,
    How hast thou heart to be glad thereof
      yet?
For where thou fliest I shall not follow,
  Till life forget and death remember,
    Till thou remember and I forget.   30

[1] cf. note on Sidney's *The Nightingale*

Swallow, my sister, O singing swallow,
  I know not how thou hast heart to sing.
    Hast thou the heart? is it all past over?
Thy lord the summer is good to follow,
  And fair the feet of thy lover the spring:
    But what wilt thou say to the spring thy
      lover? 36

O swallow, sister, O fleeting swallow,
  My heart in me is a molten ember
    And over my head the waves have met.
But thou wouldst tarry or I would follow
  Could I forget or thou remember,
    Couldst thou remember and I forget. 42

O sweet stray sister, O shifting swallow,
  The heart's division divideth us.
    Thy heart is light as a leaf of a tree;
But mine goes forth among sea-gulfs hollow
  To the place of the slaying of Itylus,
    The feast of Daulis, the Thracian sea. 48

O swallow, sister, O rapid swallow,
  I pray thee sing not a little space.
    Are not the roofs and the lintels wet?
The woven web[1] that was plain to follow,
  The small slain body, the flower-like face,
    Can I remember if thou forget? 54

O sister, sister, thy first-begotten!
  The hands that cling and the feet that follow,
    The voice of the child's blood crying yet,
Who hath remember'd me? who hath forgotten?
  Thou hast forgotten, O summer swallow,
    But the world shall end when I forget. 60

ÉTUDE RÉALISTE[2]

I

A baby's feet, like sea-shells pink,
  Might tempt, should heaven see meet,
An angel's lips to kiss, we think,
  A baby's feet. 4

Like rose-hued sea-flowers toward the heat
  They stretch and spread and wink
Their ten soft buds that part and meet. 7

No flower-bells that expand and shrink
  Gleam half so heavenly sweet
As shine on life's untrodden brink
  A baby's feet. 11

[1] containing the story of Procne's wrongs
[2] study from life

II

A baby's hands, like rosebuds furled
  Whence yet no leaf expands,
Ope if you touch, though close upcurled,
  A baby's hands. 4

Then, fast as warriors grip their brands
  When battle's bolt is hurled,
They close, clenched hard like tightening
  bands. 7

No rosebuds yet by dawn impearled
  Match, even in loveliest lands,
The sweetest flowers in all the world —
  A baby's hands. 11

III

A baby's eyes, ere speech begin,
  Ere lips learn words or sighs,
Bless all things bright enough to win
  A baby's eyes. 4

Love, while the sweet thing laughs and lies,
  And sleep flows out and in,
Sees perfect in them Paradise. 7

Their glance might cast out pain and sin,
  Their speech make dumb the wise,
By mute glad godhead felt within
  A baby's eyes. 11

THE SALT OF THE EARTH

If childhood were not in the world,
  But only men and women grown;
No baby-locks in tendrils curled,
  No baby-blossoms blown; 4

Though men were stronger, women fairer,
  And nearer all delights in reach,
And verse and music uttered rarer
  Tones of more godlike speech; 8

Though the utmost life of life's best hours
  Found, as it cannot now find, words;
Though desert sands were sweet as flowers,
  And flowers could sing like birds, 12

But children never heard them, never
  They felt a child's foot leap and run;
This were a drearier star than ever
  Yet looked upon the sun. 16

SONNETS

ON LAMB'S SPECIMENS OF DRAMATIC POETS

If all the flowers of all the fields on earth
　By wonder-working summer were made one,
　Its fragrance were not sweeter in the sun,
Its treasure-house of leaves were not more
　worth
Than those wherefrom thy light of musing
　mirth
　Shone, till each leaf whereon thy pen would
　run
　Breathed life, and all its breath was benison.
Beloved beyond all names of English birth,
More dear than mightier memories; gentlest
　name
That ever clothed itself with flower-sweet
　fame,
Or linked itself with loftiest names of old　11
　By right and might of loving; I, that am
Less than the least of those within thy fold,
　Give only thanks for them to thee, Charles
　Lamb.

HOPE AND FEAR

Beneath the shadow of dawn's aërial cope,
　With eyes enkindled as the sun's own
　sphere,
　Hope from the front of youth in godlike
　cheer
Looks Godward, past the shades where blind
　·　men grope
Round the dark door that prayers nor dreams
　can ope,
　And makes for joy the very darkness dear
　That gives her wide wings play; nor dreams
　that fear
At noon may rise and pierce the heart of
　hope.
Then, when the soul leaves off to dream and
　yearn,
May truth first purge her eyesight to discern
　What once being known leaves time no
　power to appal;　11
Till youth at last, ere yet youth be not,
　learn
　The kind wise word that falls from years
　that fall —
　"Hope thou not much, and fear thou not
　at all."

AFTER SUNSET

If light of life outlive the set of sun
　That men call death and end of all things,
　then
　How should not that which life held best for
　men
And proved most precious, though it seem
　undone
By force of death and woful victory won,
　Be first and surest of revival, when
　Death shall bow down to life arisen again?
So shall the soul seen be the self-same one
That looked and spake with even such lips
　and eyes
As love shall doubt not then to recognise,　10
　And all bright thoughts and smiles of all
　time past
Revive, transfigured, but in spirit and sense
None other than we knew, for evidence
　That love's last mortal word was not his
　last.

GEORGE MEREDITH (1828–1909)

LOVE IN THE VALLEY

Under yonder beech-tree single on the green-
　sward,
　Couch'd with her arms behind her golden
　head,
Knees and tresses folded to slip and ripple idly,
　Lies my young love sleeping in the shade.
Had I the heart to slide an arm beneath her,
　Press her parting lips as her waist I gather
　slow,
Waking in amazement she could not but em-
　brace me:
　Then would she hold me and never let me
　go?　8

·　·　·　·　·　·　·　·

Shy as the squirrel and wayward as the swal-
　low,
　Swift as the swallow along the river's light
Circleting the surface to meet his mirror'd
　winglets,
　Fleeter she seems in her stay than in her
　flight.
Shy as the squirrel that leaps among the pine-
　tops,
　Wayward as the swallow overhead at set of
　sun,

She whom I love is hard to catch and conquer,
Hard, but oh the glory of the winning were
she won!   16

When her mother tends her before the laugh-
ing mirror,
Tying up her laces, looping up her hair,
Often she thinks, were this wild thing wedded,
More love should I have, and much less care.
When her mother tends her before the lighted
mirror,
Loosening her laces, combing down her
curls,
Often she thinks, were this wild thing wedded,
I should miss but one for many boys and
girls.   24

.   .   .   .

Heartless she is as the shadow in the meadows
Flying to the hills on a blue and breezy noon.
No, she is athirst and drinking up her wonder:
Earth to her is young as the slip of the new
moon.
Deals she an unkindness, 'tis but her rapid
measure,
Even as in a dance; and her smile can heal
no less:
Like the swinging May-cloud that pelts the
flowers with hailstones
Off a sunny border, she was made to bruise
and bless.   32

Lovely are the curves of the white owl sweeping
Wavy in the dusk lit by one large star.
Lone on the fir-branch, his rattle-note unvaried,
Brooding o'er the gloom, spins the brown
evejar.[1]
Darker grows the valley, more and more forgetting:
So were it with me if forgetting could be
will'd.
Tell the grassy hollow that holds the bubbling
well-spring,
Tell it to forget the source that keeps it
fill'd.   40

.   .   .   .

Stepping down the hill with her fair companions,
Arm in arm, all against the raying West,

---

[1] a bird similar to the whippoorwill

AE

Boldly she sings, to the merry tune she
marches,
Brave is her shape, and sweeter unpossess'd.
Sweeter, for she is what my heart first awaking
Whisper'd the world was; morning light is
she.
Love that so desires would fain keep her
changeless;
Fain would fling the net, and fain have her
free.   48

Happy happy time, when the white star hovers
Low over dim fields fresh with bloomy dew,
Near the face of dawn, that draws athwart the
darkness,
Threading it with colour, like yewberries
the yew.
Thicker crowd the shades as the grave East
deepens
Glowing, and with crimson a long cloud
swells.
Maiden still the morn is; and strange she is,
and secret;
Strange her eyes; her cheeks are cold as cold
sea-shells.   56

.   .   .   .

Sunrays, leaning on our southern hills and
lighting
Wild cloud-mountains that drag the hills
along,
Oft ends the day of your shifting brilliant
laughter
Chill as a dull face frowning on a song.
Ay, but shows the South-West a ripple-
feather'd bosom
Blown to silver while the clouds are shaken
and ascend
Scaling the mid-heavens as they stream, there
comes a sunset   63
Rich, deep like love in beauty without end.

When at dawn she sighs, and like an infant
to the window
Turns grave eyes craving light, released
from dreams,
Beautiful she looks, like a white water-lily
Bursting out of bud in havens of the streams.
When from bed she rises clothed from neck to
ankle
In her long nightgown sweet as boughs of
May,
Beautiful she looks, like a tall garden-lily 71
Pure from the night, and splendid for the day.

.   .   .   .

Mother of the dews, dark eye-lash'd twilight,
  Low-lidded twilight, o'er the valley's brim,
Rounding on thy breast sings the dew-
    delighted skylark,
  Clear as though the dew-drops had their
    voice in him,
Hidden where the rose-flush drinks the rayless
    planet,
  Fountain-full he pours the spraying foun-
    tain-showers.
Let me hear her laughter, I would have her
    ever
  Cool as. dew in twilight, the lark above the
    flowers.   80

All the girls are out with their baskets for the
    primrose;
  Up lanes, woods through, they troop in
    joyful bands.
My sweet leads: she knows not why, but now
    she loiters,
  Eyes the bent anemones, and hangs her
    hands.
Such a look will tell that the violets are peep-
    ing,
  Coming the rose: and unaware a cry
Springs in her bosom for odours and for colour,
  Covert and the nightingale; she knows not
    why.   88

. . . .

Kerchief'd head and chin she darts between
    her tulips,
  Streaming like a willow grey in arrowy
    rain:
Some bend beaten cheek to gravel, and their
    angel
  She will be; she lifts them, and on she
    speeds again.
Black the driving raincloud breasts the iron
    gateway:
  She is forth to cheer a neighbour lacking
    mirth.
So when sky and grass met rolling dumb for
    thunder   95
  Saw I once a white dove, sole light of earth.

Prim little scholars are the flowers of her
    garden,
  Train'd to stand in rows, and asking if they
    please.
I might love them well but for loving more the
    wild ones:
  O my wild ones! they tell me more than
    these.

You, my wild one, you tell of honied field-rose,
  Violet, blushing eglantine in life; and even
    as they,
They by the wayside are earnest of your good-
    ness,
  You are of life's, on the banks that line the
    way.   104

. . . .

Peering at her chamber the white crowns the
    red rose,
  Jasmine winds the porch with stars two and
    three.
Parted is the window; she sleeps; the starry
    jasmine
  Breathes a falling breath that carries
    thoughts of me.
Sweeter unpossess'd, have I said of her my
    sweetest?
  Not while she sleeps: while she sleeps the
    jasmine breathes,
Luring her to love; she sleeps; the starry
    jasmine
  Bears me to her pillow under white rose-
    wreaths.   112

Yellow with birdfoot-trefoil are the grass-
    glades;
  Yellow with cinquefoil of the dew-grey leaf;
Yellow with stonecrop; the moss-mounds are
    yellow;
  Blue-neck'd the wheat sways, yellowing to
    the sheaf.
Green-yellow, bursts from the copse the laugh-
    ing yaffle; [1]
  Sharp as a sickle is the edge of shade and
    shine:
Earth in her heart laughs looking at the
    heavens,
  Thinking of the harvest: I look and think
    of mine.   120

. . . .

This I may know: her dressing and un-
    dressing
  Such a change of light shows as when the
    skies in sport
Shift from cloud to moonlight; or edging over
    thunder
  Slips a ray of sun; or sweeping into port
White sails furl; or on the ocean borders
  White sails lean along the waves leaping
    green.

[1] the green woodpecker

Visions of her shower before me, but from
  eyesight
    Guarded she would be like the sun were she
      seen. 128

Front door and back of the moss'd old farm-
  house
    Open with the morn, and in a breezy link
Freshly sparkles garden to stripe-shadow'd
  orchard,
    Green across a rill where on sand the min-
      nows wink.
Busy in the grass the early sun of summer
    Swarms, and the blackbird's mellow fluting
      notes
Call my darling up with round and roguish
  challenge:
    Quaintest, richest carol of all the singing
      throats! 136

Cool was the woodside; cool as her white
  dairy
    Keeping sweet the cream-pan; and there
      the boys from school,
Cricketing below, rush'd brown and red with
  sunshine;
    O the dark translucence of the deep-eyed
      cool!
Spying from the farm, herself she fetch'd a
  pitcher
    Full of milk, and tilted for each in turn the
      beak.
Then a little fellow, mouth up and on tiptoe,
    Said, "I will kiss you": she laugh'd and
      lean'd her cheek. 144

Doves of the fir-wood walling high our red roof
    Through the long noon coo, crooning
      through the coo.
Loose droop the leaves, and down the sleepy
  roadway
    Sometimes pipes a chaffinch; loose droops
      the blue.
Cows flap a slow tail knee-deep in the river,
    Breathless, given up to sun and gnat and fly.
Nowhere is she seen; and if I see her nowhere,
    Lightning may come, straight rains and
      tiger sky. 152

O the golden sheaf, the rustling treasure-
  armful!
·O the nutbrown tresses nodding interlaced!
O the treasure-tresses one another over

Nodding! O the girdle slack about the
  waist!
Slain are the poppies that shot their random
  scarlet
    Quick amid the wheat-ears: wound about
      the waist,
Gather'd, see these brides of Earth one blush
  of ripeness! 159
O the nutbrown tresses nodding interlaced!

Large and smoky red the sun's cold disk drops,
    Clipp'd by naked hills, on violet shaded
      snow:
Eastward large and still lights up a bower of
  moonrise,
    Whence at her leisure steps the moon aglow.
Nightlong on black print-branches our beech-
  tree
    Gazes in this whiteness: nightlong could I.
Here may life on death or death on life be
  painted.
    Let me clasp her soul to know she cannot
      die! 168

Gossips count her faults; they scour a narrow
  chamber
    Where there is no window, read not heaven
      or her.
"When she was a tiny," one agèd woman
  quavers,
    Plucks at my heart and leads me by the ear.
Faults she had once as she learn'd to run and
  tumbled:
    Faults of feature some see, beauty not
      complete.
Yet, good gossips, beauty that makes holy
    Earth and air, may have faults from head
      to feet. 176

Hither she comes; she comes to me; she
  lingers,
    Deepens her brown eyebrows, while in new
      surprise
High rise the lashes in wonder of a stranger;
    Yet am I the light and living of her eyes.
Something friends have told her fills her heart
  to brimming,
    Nets her in her blushes, and wounds her,
      and tames. —
Sure of her haven, O like a dove alighting,
    Arms up, she dropp'd: our souls were in our
      names. 184

Soon will she lie like a white frost sunrise.
   Yellow oats and brown wheat, barley pale
      as rye,
Long since your sheaves have yielded to the
      thresher,
   Felt the girdle loosen'd, seen the tresses fly.
Soon will she lie like a blood-red sunset.
   Swift with the to-morrow, green-wing'd
      Spring!
Sing from the South-west, bring her back the
      truants,
   Nightingale and swallow, song and dipping
      wing.   192

Soft new beech-leaves, up to beamy April
   Spreading bough on bough a primrose
      mountain, you
Lucid in the moon, raise lilies to the skyfields,
   Youngest green transfused in silver shining
      through;
Fairer than the lily, than the wild white
      cherry:
   Fair as in image my seraph love appears
Borne to me by dreams when dawn is at my
      eye-lids: 199
   Fair as in the flesh she swims to me on tears.

· · · · · · · ·

Could I find a place to be alone with heaven,
   I would speak my heart out: heaven is my
      need.
Every woodland tree is flushing like the dog-
      wood,
   Flashing like the whitebeam,[1] swaying like
      the reed.
Flushing like the dogwood crimson in October;
   Streaming like the flag-reed South-west
      blown;
Flashing as in gusts the sudden-lighted white-
      beam: 207
   All seem to know what is for heaven alone.

JUGGLING JERRY

Pitch here the tent, while the old horse grazes:
   By the old hedge-side we'll halt a stage.
It's nigh my last above the daisies:
   My next leaf'll be man's blank page.
Yes, my old girl! and it's no use crying:
   Juggler, constable, king, must bow.
One that outjuggles all's been spying
   Long to have me, and he has me now.   8

[1] a European tree with white flowers and orange-
red fruits

We've travelled times to this old common:
   Often we've hung our pots in the gorse.
We've had a stirring life, old woman!
   You, and I, and the old grey horse.
Races, and fairs, and royal occasions,
   Found us coming to their call:
Now they'll miss us at our stations:
   There's a Juggler outjuggles all!   16

Up goes the lark, as if all were jolly!
   Over the duck-pond the willow shakes.
Easy to think that grieving's folly,
   When the hand's firm as driven stakes!
Ay, when we're strong, and braced, and
      manful,
   Life's a sweet fiddle: but we're a batch
Born to become the Great Juggler's han'ful:
   Balls he shies up, and is safe to catch.   24

Here's where the lads of the village cricket:
   I was a lad not wide from here:
Couldn't I whip off the bale[1] from the
      wicket?
Like an old world those days appear!
Donkey, sheep, geese and thatched ale-house
      — I know them!
They are old friends of my halts, and seem,
   Somehow, as if kind thanks I owe them: 31
   Juggling don't hinder the heart's esteem.

Juggling's no sin, for we must have victual:
   Nature allows us to bait for the fool.
Holding one's own makes us juggle no little;
   But, to increase it, hard juggling's the rule.
You that are sneering at my profession,
   Haven't you juggled a vast amount?   38
There's the Prime Minister, in one Session,
   Juggles more games than my sins'll count.

I've murdered insects with mock thunder:
   Conscience, for that, in men don't quail.
I've made bread from the bump of wonder:
   That's my business, and there's my tale.
Fashion and rank all praised the professor:
   Ay! and I've had my smile from the Queen:
Bravo, Jerry! she meant: God bless her!
   Ain't this a sermon on that scene?   48

I've studied men from my topsy-turvy
   Close, and, I reckon, rather true.
Some are fine fellows: some, right scurvy:
   Most, a dash between the two.

[1] the cross-piece on a cricket wicket; Jerry
means he was a good bowler

But it's a woman, old girl, that makes me
    Think more kindly of the race:
And it's a woman, old girl, that shakes me
    When the Great Juggler I must face.   59

We two were married, due and legal:
    Honest we've lived since we've been one.
Lord! I could then jump like an eagle:
    You danced bright as a bit o' the sun.
Birds in a May-bush we were! right merry!
    All night we kiss'd, we juggled all day.
Joy was the heart of Juggling Jerry!   63
    Now from his old girl he's juggled away.

It's past parsons to console us:
    No, nor no doctor fetch for me:
I can die without my bolus;
    Two of a trade, lass, never agree!
Parson and Doctor! — don't they love rarely,
    Fighting the devil in other men's fields!
Stand up yourself and match him fairly:
    Then see how the rascal yields!   72

I, lass, have lived no gipsy, flaunting
    Finery while his poor helpmate grubs:
Coin I've stored, and you won't be wanting:
    You sha'n't beg from the troughs and tubs.
Nobly you've stuck to me, though in his
        kitchen
    Many a Marquis would hail you Cook!
Palaces you could have ruled and grown rich
        in,
    But your old Jerry you never forsook.   80

Hand up the chirper![1] ripe ale winks in it;
    Let's have comfort and be at peace.
Once a stout draught made me light as a linnet.
    Cheer up! the Lord must have his lease.
May be — for none see in that black hollow —
    It's just a place where we're held in pawn,
And, when the Great Juggler makes as to
        swallow,
    It's just the sword-trick — I ain't quite
        gone.   88

Yonder came smells of the gorse, so nutty,
    Gold-like and warm: it's the prime of May.
Better than mortar, brick, and putty,
    Is God's house on a blowing day.
Lean me more up the mound; now I feel it:
    All the old heath-smells! Ain't it strange?
There's the world laughing, as if to conceal it!
    But He's by us, juggling the change.   96

[1] cheering cup

I mind it well, by the sea-beach lying,
    Once — it's long gone — when two gulls we
        beheld,
Which, as the moon got up, were flying
    Down a big wave that sparked and swelled.
Crack went a gun: one fell: the second
    Wheeled round him twice, and was off for
        new luck: 102
There in the dark her white wing beckon'd: —
    Drop me a kiss — I'm the bird dead-struck!

BELLEROPHON[1]

Maimed, beggared, grey; seeking an alms;
        with nod
Of palsy doing task of thanks for bread;
    Upon the stature of a god,
He whom the Gods have struck bends low his
        head.

Weak words he has, that slip the nerveless
        tongue
Deformed, like his great frame: a broken arc:
    Once radiant as the javelin flung
Right at the centre breastplate of his mark.

Oft pausing on his white-eyed inward look,
Some undermountain narrative he tells,   10
    As gapped by Lykian[2] heat the brook
Cut from the source that in the upland swells.

The cottagers who dole him fruit and crust,
With patient inattention hear him prate:
    And comes the snow, and comes the dust,
Comes the old wanderer, more bent of late.

A crazy beggar grateful for a meal
Has ever of himself a world to say.
    For them he is an ancient wheel   19
Spinning a knotted thread the livelong day.

He cannot, nor do they, the tale connect;
For never singer in the land has been
    Who him for theme did not reject:
Spurned of the hoof that sprang the Hippo-
    crene.[3]

[1] In his youth he bridled and rode the winged
horse Pegasus and slew the monster Chimæra.
He was reported to have been killed in attempting
to fly to heaven. [2] Lykia (or Lycia), a mountainous region in Asia Minor where Bellerophon
killed Chimæra [3] the fountain struck out on
Mt. Helicon by the hoof of Pegasus

Albeit a theme of flame to bring them straight
The snorting white-winged brother of the
    wave,[1]
    They hear him as a thing by fate
Cursed in unholy babble to his grave.

As men that spied the wings, that heard the
    snort,
Their sires have told; and of a martial prince
    Bestriding him; and old report   31
Speaks of a monster slain by one long since.

There is that story of the golden bit
By Goddess [2] given to tame the lightning steed:
    A mortal who could mount, and sit
Flying, and up Olympus midway speed.

He rose like the loosed fountain's utmost leap;
He played the star at span of heaven right o'er
    Men's heads; they saw the snowy steep,
Saw the winged shoulders: him they saw not
    more.   40

He fell: and says the shattered man, "I fell":
And sweeps an arm the height an eagle wins;
    And in his breast a mouthless well
Heaves the worn patches of his coat of skins.

Lo, this is he in whom the surgent springs
Of recollections richer than our skies
    To feed the flow of tuneful strings,
Show but a pool of scum for shooting flies. 48

LUCIFER IN STARLIGHT

On a starred night Prince Lucifer uprose.
Tired of his dark dominion, swung the fiend
Above the rolling ball in cloud part screened,
Where sinners hugged their spectre of repose.
Poor prey to his hot fit of pride were those.
And now upon his western wing he leaned,
Now his huge bulk o'er Afric's sands careened,
Now the black planet shadowed Arctic snows.
Soaring through wider zones that pricked his
    scars
With memory of the old revolt from Awe,   10
He reached a middle height, and at the stars,
Which are the brain of heaven, he looked, and
    sank.
Around the ancient track marched, rank on
    rank,
The army of unalterable law.

[1] The horse was a gift to mortals from Neptune,
god of the sea.   [2] Minerva

ASK, IS LOVE DIVINE

Ask, is Love divine,
    Voices all are, Ay.
Question for the sign,
    There's a common sigh.   4

Would we through our years
    Love forego,
Quit of scars and tears?
    Ah, but no, no, no!   8

SONG OF THE SONGLESS

They have no song, the sedges dry,
And still they sing.
It is within my breast they sing,
As I pass by.
Within my breast they touch a spring,
They wake a sigh.   6
There is but sound of sedges dry;
In me they sing.

DIRGE IN WOODS

A wind sways the pines,
    And below
Not a breath of wild air;
Still as the mosses that glow
On the flooring and over the lines
Of the roots here and there.
The pine-tree drops its dead;
They are quiet as under the sea.
Overhead, overhead
Rushes life in a race,   10
As the clouds the clouds chase:
    And we go,
And we drop like the fruits of the tree,
    Even we,
    Even so.

CHRISTINA ROSSETTI
(1830–1894)

THE BRIDE-SONG
From THE PRINCE'S PROGRESS

Too late for love, too late for joy!
    Too late! too late!
You loitered on the road too long,
    You trifled at the gate:
The enchanted dove upon her branch
    Died without a mate;

The enchanted princess in her tower
  Slept, died, behind the grate;
Her heart was starving all this while
  You made it wait.   10

Ten years ago, five years ago,
  One year ago, —
Even then you had arrived in time,
  Though somewhat slow;
Then you had known her living face,
  Which now you cannot know:
The frozen fountain would have leaped,
  The buds gone on to blow,
The warm south wind would have awaked
  To melt the snow.   20

Is she fair now as she lies?
  Once she was fair;
Meet queen for any kingly king,
  With gold-dust on her hair.
Now these are poppies in her locks,
  White poppies she must wear;
Must wear a veil to shroud her face
  And the want graven there:
Or is the hunger fed at length,
  Cast off the care?   30

We never saw her with a smile
  Or with a frown;
Her bed seemed never soft to her,
  Though tossed of down;
She little heeded what she wore,
  Kirtle, or wreath, or gown;
We think her white brows often ached
  Beneath her crown,
Till silvery hairs showed in her locks
  That used to be so brown.   40

We never heard her speak in haste:
  Her tones were sweet,
And modulated just so much
  As it was meet:
Her heart sat silent through the noise
  And concourse of the street.
There was no hurry in her hands,
  No hurry in her feet;
There was no bliss drew nigh to her,
  That she might run to greet.   50

You should have wept her yesterday,
  Wasting upon her bed:
But wherefore should you weep to-day
  That she is dead?
Lo, we who love weep not to-day,
  But crown her royal head.

Let be these poppies that we strew,
  Your roses are too red:
Let be these poppies, not for you
  Cut down and spread.   60

A BIRTHDAY

My heart is like a singing bird
  Whose nest is in a watered shoot;
My heart is like an apple-tree
  Whose boughs are bent with thick-set fruit;
My heart is like a rainbow shell
  That paddles in a halcyon sea;
My heart is gladder than all these
  Because my love is come to me.   8

Raise me a dais of silk and down;
  Hang it with vair [1] and purple dyes;
Carve it in doves and pomegranates,
  And peacocks with a hundred eyes;
Work it in gold and silver grapes,
  In leaves and silver fleur-de-lys;
Because the birthday of my life
  Is come, my love is come to me.   16

SONG

When I am dead, my dearest,
  Sing no sad songs for me;
Plant thou no roses at my head,
  Nor shady cypress-tree:
Be the green grass above me
  With showers and dewdrops wet;
And if thou wilt, remember,
  And if thou wilt, forget.   8

I shall not see the shadows,
  I shall not feel the rain;
I shall not hear the nightingale
  Sing on, as if in pain:
And dreaming through the twilight
  That doth not rise nor set,
Haply I may remember,
  And haply may forget.   16

THE FIRST DAY

I wish I could remember that first day,
First hour, first moment of your meeting
      me,
  If bright or dim the season, it might be

---

[1] a fur much esteemed in ancient times

Summer or Winter for aught I can say;
So unrecorded did it slip away,
So blind was I to see and to foresee,
So dull to mark the budding of my tree
That would not blossom yet for many a
May.
If only I could recollect it, such
A day of days! I let it come and go   10
As traceless as a thaw of bygone snow;
It seemed to mean so little, meant so much;
If only now I could recall that touch,
First touch of hand in hand — Did one but
know!

REMEMBER

Remember me when I am gone away,
Gone far away into the silent land;
When you can no more hold me by the
hand,
Nor I half turn to go, yet turning stay.
Remember me when no more, day by day,
You tell me of our future that you planned:
Only remember me; you understand
It will be late to counsel then or pray.
Yet if you should forget me for a while   9
And afterwards remember, do not grieve:
For if the darkness and corruption leave
A vestige of the thoughts that once I had,
Better by far you should forget and smile
Than that you should remember and be sad.

REST

O Earth, lie heavily upon her eyes;
Seal her sweet eyes weary of watching,
Earth;
Lie close around her; leave no room for
mirth
With its harsh laughter, nor for sound of
sighs.
She hath no questions, she hath no replies,
Hushed in and curtained with a blessèd
dearth
Of all that irked her from the hour of birth;
With stillness that is almost Paradise.
Darkness more clear than noonday holdeth
her,
Silence more musical than any song;   10
Even her very heart has ceased to stir:
Until the morning of Eternity
Her rest shall not begin nor end, but be;
And when she wakes she will not think it
long.

THE LOWEST PLACE

Give me the lowest place: not that I dare
Ask for that lowest place, but Thou hast
died
That I might live and share
Thy glory by Thy side.   4

Give me the lowest place: or if for me
That lowest place too high, make one more
low
Where I may sit and see
My God and love Thee so.   8

JAMES THOMSON (1834–1882)

From THE CITY OF DREADFUL NIGHT

As I came through the desert thus it was,
As I came through the desert: All was black,
In heaven no single star, on earth no track;
A brooding hush without a stir or note,
The air so thick it clotted in my throat;
And thus for hours; then some enormous things
Swooped past with savage cries and clanking
wings:
But I strode on austere;
No hope could have no fear.   176

As I came through the desert thus it was,
As I came through the desert: Eyes of fire
Glared at me throbbing with a starved desire;
The hoarse and heavy and carnivorous breath
Was hot upon me from deep jaws of death;
Sharp claws, swift talons, fleshless fingers cold
Plucked at me from the bushes, tried to hold:
But I strode on austere;
No hope could have no fear.   185

As I came through the desert thus it was,
As I came through the desert: Lo you, there,
That hillock burning with a brazen glare;
Those myriad dusky flames with points a-glow
Which writhed and hissed and darted to and
fro;
A Sabbath of the Serpents, heaped pell-mell
For Devil's roll-call and some fête of Hell:
Yet I strode on austere;
No hope could have no fear.   194

As I came through the desert thus it was,
As I came through the desert: Meteors ran
And crossed their javelins on the black sky-
span;

The zenith opened to a gulf of flame,
The dreadful thunderbolts jarred earth's fixed
    frame;
The ground all heaved in waves of fire that
    surged
And weltered round me sole there unsub-
    merged:
        Yet I strode on austere;
        No hope could have no fear. 203

As I came through the desert thus it was,
As I came through the desert: Air once more,
And I was close upon a wild sea-shore;
Enormous cliffs arose on either hand,
The deep tide thundered up a league-broad
    strand;
White foambelts seethed there, wan spray
    swept and flew;
The sky broke, moon and stars and clouds and
    blue:
        And I strode on austere;
        No hope could have no fear. 212

As I came through the desert thus it was,
As I came through the desert: On the left
The sun arose and crowned a broad crag-cleft;
There stopped and burned out black, except a
    rim,
A bleeding eyeless socket, red and dim;
Whereon the moon fell suddenly south-west,
And stood above the right-hand cliffs at rest:
        Still I strode on austere;
        No hope could have no fear. 221

As I came through the desert thus it was,
As I came through the desert: From the
    right
A shape came slowly with a ruddy light;
A woman with a red lamp in her hand,
Bareheaded and barefooted on that strand;
O desolation moving with such grace!
O anguish with such beauty in thy face!
        I fell as on my bier,
        Hope travailed with such fear. 230

As I came through the desert thus it was,
As I came through the desert: I was twain,
Two selves distinct that cannot join again;
One stood apart and knew but could not stir,
And watched the other stark in swoon and
    her;
And she came on, and never turned aside,
Between such sun and moon and roaring tide:
        And as she came more near
        My soul grew mad with fear. 239

As I came through the desert thus it was,
As I came through the desert: Hell is mild
And piteous matched with that accursèd wild;
A large black sign was on her breast that
    bowed,
A broad black band ran down her snow-white
    shroud;
That lamp she held was her own burning
    heart,
Whose blood-drops trickled step by step
    apart:
        The mystery was clear;
        Mad rage had swallowed fear. 248

As I came through the desert thus it was,
As I came through the desert: By the sea
She knelt and bent above that senseless me;
Those lamp-drops fell upon my white brow
    there,
She tried to cleanse them with her tears and
    hair;
She murmured words of pity, love, and woe,
She heeded not the level rushing flow:
        And mad with rage and fear,
        I stood stonebound so near. 257

As I came through the desert thus it was,
As I came through the desert: When the tide
Swept up to her there kneeling by my side,
She clasped that corpse-like me, and they
    were borne
Away, and this vile me was left forlorn;
I know the whole sea cannot quench that
    heart,
Or cleanse that brow, or wash those two
    apart:
        They love; their doom is drear,
        Yet they nor hope nor fear;
        But I, what do I here? 267

From SUNDAY UP THE RIVER

XV

Give a man a horse he can ride,
  Give a man a boat he can sail;
And his rank and wealth, his strength and
    health,
  On sea nor shore shall fail. 4

Give a man a pipe he can smoke,
  Give a man a book he can read;
And his home is bright with a calm delight,
  Though the room be poor indeed. 8

Give a man a girl he can love,
  As I, O my Love, love thee;
And his heart is great with the pulse of Fate,
  At home, on land, on sea.   12

ART

II

If you have a carrier-dove
  That can fly over land and sea;
And a message for your Love,
  "Lady, I love but thee!"   4

And this dove will never stir
  But straight from her to you,
And straight from you to her;
  As you know and she knows too.   8

Will you first ensure, O sage,
  Your dove that never tires
With your message in a cage,
  Though a cage of golden wires?   12

Or will you fling your dove:
  "Fly, darling, without rest,
Over land and sea to my Love,
  And fold your wings in her breast?"   16

WALTER PATER (1839–1894)

FROM STYLE

*   *   *   *   *   *   *

What, then, did Flaubert[1] understand by beauty, in the art he pursued with so much fervour, with so much self-command? Let us hear a sympathetic commentator: —

"Possessed of an absolute belief that there exists but one way of expressing one thing, one word to call it by, one adjective to qualify, one verb to animate it, he gave himself to superhuman labour for the discovery, in every phrase, of that word, that verb, that epithet. In this way, he believed in some mysterious harmony of expression, and when a true word seemed to him to lack euphony still went on seeking another, with invincible patience, certain that he had not yet got hold of the *unique* word. . . . A   thousand   preoccupations would beset him at the same moment, always with this desperate certitude fixed in his spirit: Among all the expressions in the world, all forms and turns of expression, there is but *one* — one form, one mode — to express what I want to say."

The one word for the one thing, the one thought, amid the multitude of words, terms, that might just do: the problem of style was there! — the unique word, phrase, sentence, paragraph, essay, or song, absolutely proper to the single mental presentation or vision within. In that perfect justice, over and above the many contingent and removable beauties with which beautiful style may charm us, but which it can exist without, independent of them yet dexterously availing itself of them, omnipresent in good work, in function at every point, from single epithets to the rhythm of a whole book, lay the specific, indispensable, very intellectual, beauty of literature, the possibility of which constitutes it a fine art.

One seems to detect the influence of a philosophic idea there, the idea of a natural economy, of some preëxistent adaptation, between a relative, somewhere in the world of thought, and its correlative, somewhere in the world of language — both alike, rather, somewhere in the mind of the artist, desiderative, expectant, inventive — meeting each other with the readiness of "soul and body reunited," in Blake's[1] rapturous design; and, in fact, Flaubert was fond of giving his theory philosophical expression.

"There are no beautiful thoughts," he would say, "without beautiful forms, and conversely. As it is impossible to extract from a physical body the qualities which really constitute it — colour, extension, and the like — without reducing it to a hollow abstraction, in a word, without destroying it; just so it is impossible to detach the form from the idea, for the idea only exists by virtue of the form."

All the recognised flowers, the removable ornaments of literature (including harmony and ease in reading aloud, very carefully considered by him) counted certainly; for these too are part of the actual value of what one says. But still, after all, with Flaubert, the search, the unwearied research, was not for the smooth, or winsome, or forcible word, as

---

[1] Gustave Flaubert (1821–80), a French novelist, noted for his ideas on the art of writing.

[1] William Blake, poet and engraver

such, as with false Ciceronians,[1] but quite simply and honestly for the word's adjustment to its meaning. The first condition of this must be, of course, to know yourself, to have ascertained your own sense exactly. Then, if we suppose an artist, he says to the reader, — I want you to see precisely what I see. Into the mind sensitive to "form," a flood of random sounds, colours, incidents, is ever penetrating from the world without, to become, by sympathetic selection, a part of its very structure, and, in turn, the visible vesture and expression of that other world it sees so steadily within, nay, already with a partial conformity thereto, to be refined, enlarged, corrected, at a hundred points; and it is just there, just at those doubtful points that the function of style, as tact or taste, intervenes. The unique term will come more quickly to one than another, at one time than another, according also to the kind of matter in question. Quickness and slowness, ease and closeness alike, have nothing to do with the artistic character of the true word found at last. As there is a charm of ease, so there is also a special charm in the signs of discovery, of effort and contention towards a due end, as so often with Flaubert himself — in the style which has been pliant, as only obstinate, durable metal can be, to the inherent perplexities and recusancy of a certain difficult thought.

If Flaubert had not told us, perhaps we should never have guessed how tardy and painful his own procedure really was, and after reading his confession may think that his almost endless hesitation had much to do with diseased nerves. Often, perhaps, the felicity supposed will be the product of a happier, a more exuberant nature than Flaubert's. Aggravated, certainly, by a morbid physical condition, that anxiety in "seeking the phrase," which gathered all the other small *ennuis* of a really quiet existence into a kind of battle, was connected with his lifelong contention against facile poetry, facile art — art, facile and flimsy; and what constitutes the true artist is not the slowness or quickness of the process, but the absolute success of the result.

* * * * * * *

[1] those who regard Cicero's style as the only correct model

Coming slowly or quickly, when it comes, as it came with so much labour of mind, but also with so much lustre, to Gustave Flaubert, this discovery of the word will be, like all artistic success and felicity, incapable of strict analysis: effect of an intuitive condition of mind, it must be recognised by like intuition on the part of the reader, and a sort of immediate sense. In every one of those masterly sentences of Flaubert there was, below all mere contrivance, shaping and afterthought, by some happy instantaneous concourse of the various faculties of the mind with each other, the exact apprehension of what was *needed* to carry the meaning. And that it fits with absolute justice will be a judgment of immediate sense in the appreciative reader. We all feel this in what may be called inspired translation. Well! all language involves translation from inward to outward. In literature, as in all forms of art, there are the absolute and the merely relative or accessory beauties; and precisely in that exact proportion of the term to its purpose is the absolute beauty of style, prose or verse. All the good qualities, the beauties, of verse also, are such, only as precise expression.

In the highest as in the lowliest literature, then, the one indispensable beauty is, after all, truth: — truth to bare fact in the latter, as to some personal sense of fact, diverted somewhat from men's ordinary sense of it, in the former; truth there as accuracy, truth here as expression, that finest and most intimate form of truth, the *vraie vérité*. And what an eclectic principle this really is! employing for its one sole purpose — that absolute accordance of expression to idea — all other literary beauties and excellences whatever: how many kinds of style it covers, explains, justifies, and at the same time safeguards! Scott's facility, Flaubert's deeply pondered evocation of "the phrase," are equally good art. Say what you have to say, what you have a will to say, in the simplest, the most direct and exact manner possible, with no surplusage: — there, is the justification of the sentence so fortunately born, "entire, smooth, and round," that it needs no punctuation, and also (that is the point!) of the most elaborate period, if it be right in its elaboration. Here is the office of ornament: here also the purpose of restraint in ornament. As the exponent of truth, that austerity (the beauty, the function, of which in literature

Flaubert understood so well) becomes not the correctness or purism of the mere scholar, but a security against the otiose, a jealous exclusion of what does not really tell towards the pursuit of relief, of life and vigour in the portraiture of one's sense. License again, the making free with rule, if it be indeed, as people fancy, a habit of genius, flinging aside or transforming all that opposes the liberty of beautiful production, will be but faith to one's own meaning. The seeming baldness of *Le Rouge et Le Noir*[1] is nothing in itself; the wild ornament of *Les Misérables*[2] is nothing in itself; and the restraint of Flaubert, amid a real natural opulence, only redoubled beauty — the phrase so large and so precise at the same time, hard as bronze, in service to the more perfect adaptation of words to their matter. Afterthoughts, retouchings, finish, will be of profit only so far as they too really serve to bring out the original, initiative, generative, sense in them.

In this way, according to the well-known saying,[3] "The style is the man," complex or simple, in his individuality, his plenary sense of what he really has to say, his sense of the world; all cautions regarding style arising out of so many natural scruples as to the medium through which alone he can expose that inward sense of things, the purity of this medium, its laws or tricks of refraction: nothing is to be left there which might give conveyance to any matter save that. Style in all its varieties, reserved or opulent, terse, abundant, musical, stimulant, academic, so long as each is really characteristic or expressive, finds thus its justification, the sumptuous good taste of Cicero being as truly the man himself, and not another, justified, yet insured inalienably to him, thereby, as would have been his portrait by Raffaelle,[4] in full consular splendour, on his ivory chair.

A relegation, you may say perhaps — a relegation of style to the subjectivity, the mere caprice, of the individual, which must soon transform it into mannerism. Not so! since there is, under the conditions supposed, for those elements of the man, for every lineament of the vision within, the one word, the one acceptable word, recognisable by the sensitive, by others "who have intelligence" in the matter, as absolutely as ever anything can be in the evanescent and delicate region of human language. The style, the manner, would be the man, not in his unreasoned and really uncharacteristic caprices, involuntary or affected, but in absolutely sincere apprehension of what is most real to him. But let us hear our French guide again. —

"Styles," says Flaubert's commentator, "*Styles*, as so many peculiar moulds, each of which bears the mark of a particular writer, who is to pour into it the whole content of his ideas, were no part of his theory. What he believed in was *Style:* that is to say, a certain absolute and unique manner of expressing a thing, in all its intensity and colour. For him the *form* was the work itself. As in living creatures, the blood, nourishing the body, determines its very contour and external aspect, just so, to his mind, the *matter*, the basis, in a work of art, imposed, necessarily, the unique, the just expression, the measure, the rhythm — the *form* in all its characteristics."

If the style be the man, in all the colour and intensity of a veritable apprehension, it will be in a real sense "impersonal."

I said, thinking of books like Victor Hugo's *Les Misérables*, that prose literature was the characteristic art of the nineteenth century, as others, thinking of its triumphs since the youth of Bach,[1] have assigned that place to music. Music and prose literature are, in one sense, the opposite terms of art; the art of literature presenting to the imagination, through the intelligence, a range of interests, as free and various as those which music presents to it through sense. And certainly the tendency of what has been here said is to bring literature too under those conditions, by conformity to which music takes rank as the typically perfect art. If music be the ideal of all art whatever, precisely because in music it is impossible to distinguish the form from the substance or matter, the subject from the expression, then, literature, by finding its specific excellence in the absolute correspondence of the term to its import, will be but fulfilling the condition of all artistic quality in things everywhere, of all good art.

---

[1] a famous novel by Stendhal (Henri Beyle, 1783–1842), whom Flaubert greatly admired [2] by Victor Hugo (1802–85) [3] by the celebrated French naturalist, Buffon (1707–88) [4] cf. note on Browning's *One Word More*, l. 5

[1] Johann Sebastian Bach (1685–1750), one of the greatest of modern composers of music

Good art, but not necessarily great art; the distinction between great art and good art depending immediately, as regards literature at all events, not on its form, but on the matter. Thackeray's *Esmond*, surely, is greater art than *Vanity Fair*, by the greater dignity of its interests. It is on the quality of the matter it informs or controls, its compass, its variety, its alliance to great ends, or the depth of the note of revolt, or the largeness of hope in it, that the greatness of literary art depends, as *The Divine Comedy*, *Paradise Lost*, *Les Misérables*, *The English Bible*, are great art. Given the conditions I have tried to explain as constituting good art; — then, if it be devoted further to the increase of men's happiness, to the redemption of the oppressed, or the enlargement of our sympathies with each other, or to such presentment of new or old truth about ourselves and our relation to the world as may ennoble and fortify us in our sojourn here, or immediately, as with Dante, to the glory of God, it will be also great art; if, over and above those qualities I summed up as mind and soul — that colour and mystic perfume, and that reasonable structure, it has something of the soul of humanity in it, and finds its logical, its architectural place, in the great structure of human life.

FROM THE CHILD IN THE HOUSE

As Florian Deleal walked, one hot afternoon, he overtook by the wayside a poor aged man, and, as he seemed weary with the road, helped him on with the burden which he carried, a certain distance. And as the man told his story, it chanced that he named the place, a little place in the neighbourhood of a great city, where Florian had passed his earliest years, but which he had never since seen, and, the story told, went forward on his journey comforted. And that night, like a reward for his pity, a dream of that place came to Florian, a dream which did for him the office of the finer sort of memory, bringing its object to mind with a great clearness, yet, as sometimes happens in dreams, raised a little above itself, and above ordinary retrospect. The true aspect of the place, especially of the house there in which he had lived as a child, the fashion of its doors, its hearths, its windows, the very scent upon the air of it, was with him in sleep for a season; only, with tints more musically blent on wall and floor, and some finer light and shadow running in and out along its curves and angles, and with all its little carvings daintier. He awoke with a sigh at the thought of almost thirty years which lay between him and that place, yet with a flutter of pleasure still within him at the fair light, as if it were a smile, upon it. And it happened that this accident of his dream was just the thing needed for the beginning of a certain design he then had in view, the noting, namely, of some things in the story of his spirit — in that process of brain-building by which we are, each one of us, what we are. With the image of the place so clear and favourable upon him, he fell to thinking of himself therein, and how his thoughts had grown up to him. In that half-spiritualised house he could watch the better, over again, the gradual expansion of the soul which had come to be there — of which indeed, through the law which makes the material objects about them so large an element in children's lives, it had actually become a part; inward and outward being woven through and through each other into one inextricable texture — half, tint and trace and accident of homely colour and form, from the wood and the bricks; half, mere soul-stuff, floated thither from who knows how far. In the house and garden of his dream he saw a child moving, and could divide the main streams at least of the winds that had played on him, and study so the first stage in that mental journey.

The *old house*, as when Florian talked of it afterwards he always called it (as all children do, who can recollect a change of home, soon enough but not too soon to mark a period in their lives), really was an old house; and an element of French descent in its inmates — descent from Watteau,[1] the old court-painter, one of whose gallant pieces still hung in one of the rooms — might explain, together with some other things, a noticeable trimness and comely whiteness about everything there — the curtains, the couches, the paint on the walls with which the light and shadow played

[1] Jean Antoine Watteau (1684–1721), a celebrated French painter of elegant and graceful shepherds and shepherdesses (courtiers in disguise)

so delicately; might explain also the tolerance of the great poplar in the garden, a tree most often despised by English people, but which French people love, having observed a certain fresh way its leaves have of dealing with the wind, making it sound, in never so slight a stirring of the air, like running water.

The old-fashioned, low wainscoting went round the rooms, and up the staircase with carved balusters and shadowy angles, landing half-way up at a broad window, with a swallow's nest below the sill, and the blossom of an old pear-tree showing across it in late April, against the blue, below which the perfumed juice of the find of fallen fruit in autumn was so fresh. At the next turning came the closet which held on its deep shelves the best china. Little angel faces and reedy flutings stood out round the fireplace of the children's room. And on the top of the house, above the large attic, where the white mice ran in the twilight — an infinite, unexplored wonderland of childish treasures, glass beads, empty scent-bottles still sweet, thrums[1] of coloured silks, among its lumber — a flat space of roof, railed round, gave a view of the neighbouring steeples; for the house, as I said, stood near a great city, which sent up heavenwards, over the twisting weathervanes, not seldom, its beds of rolling cloud and smoke, touched with storm or sunshine. But the child of whom I am writing did not hate the fog, because of the crimson lights which fell from it sometimes upon the chimneys, and the whites which gleamed through its openings, on summer mornings, on turret or pavement. For it is false to suppose that a child's sense of beauty is dependent on any choiceness or special fineness, in the objects which present themselves to it, though this indeed comes to be the rule with most of us in later life; earlier, in some degree, we see inwardly; and the child finds for itself, and with unstinted delight, a difference for the sense, in those whites and reds through the smoke on very homely buildings, and in the gold of the dandelions at the roadside, just beyond the houses, where not a handful of earth is virgin and untouched, in the lack of better ministries to its desire of beauty.

This house then stood not far beyond the gloom and rumours of the town, among high garden-walls, bright all summer-time with Golden-rod, and brown-and-golden Wall-flower — *Flos Parietis*, as the children's Latin-reading father taught them to call it, while he was with them. Tracing back the threads of his complex spiritual habit, as he was used in after years to do, Florian found that he owed to the place many tones of sentiment afterwards customary with him, certain inward lights under which things most naturally presented themselves to him. The coming and going of travellers to the town along the way, the shadow of the streets, the sudden breath of the neighbouring gardens, the singular brightness of bright weather there, its singular darknesses which linked themselves in his mind to certain engraved illustrations in the old big Bible at home, the coolness of the dark, cavernous shops round the great church, with its giddy winding stair up to the pigeons and the bells — a citadel of peace in the heart of the trouble — all this acted on his childish fancy, so that ever afterwards the like aspects and incidents never failed to throw him into a well-recognized imaginative mood, seeming, actually to have become a part of the texture of his mind. Also, Florian could trace home to this point a pervading preference in himself for a kind of comeliness and dignity, an *urbanity* literally, in modes of life, which he connected with the pale people of towns, and which made him susceptible to a kind of exquisite satisfaction in the trimness and well-considered grace of certain things and persons he afterwards met with, here and there, in his way through the world.

So the child of whom I am writing lived on there quietly; things without thus ministering to him, as he sat daily at the window with the birdcage hanging below it, and his mother taught him to read, wondering at the ease with which he learned, and at the quickness of his memory. The perfume of the little flowers of the lime-tree fell through the air upon them like rain; while time seemed to move ever more slowly to the murmur of the bees in it, till it almost stood still on June afternoons. How insignificant, at the moment, seem the influences of the sensible things which are tossed and fall and lie about us, so, or so, in the environment of early childhood. How indelibly, as we afterwards discover, they affect us; with what capricious attractions and associations

---

[1] short lengths

they figure themselves on the white paper,[1] the smooth wax, of our ingenuous souls, as "with lead in the rock forever,"[2] giving form and feature, and as it were assigned house-room in our memory, to early experiences of feeling and thought, which abide with us ever afterwards, thus, and not otherwise. The realities and passions, the rumours of the greater world without, steal in upon us, each by its own special little passage-way, through the wall of custom about us; and never afterwards quite detach themselves from this or that accident, or trick, in the mode of their first entrance to us. Our susceptibilities, the discovery of our powers, manifold experiences — our various experiences of the coming and going of bodily pain, for instance — belong to this or the other well-remembered place in the material habitation — that little white room with the window across which the heavy blossoms could beat so peevishly in the wind, with just that particular catch or throb, such a sense of teasing in it, on gusty mornings; and the early habitation thus gradually becomes a sort of material shrine or sanctuary of sentiment; a system of visible symbolism interweaves itself through all our thoughts and passions; and irresistibly, little shapes, voices, accidents — the angle at which the sun in the morning fell on the pillow — become parts of the great chain wherewith we are bound.

Thus far, for Florian, what all this had determined was a peculiarly strong sense of home — so forcible a motive with all of us — prompting to us our customary love of the earth, and the larger part of our fear of death, that revulsion we have from it, as from something strange, untried, unfriendly; though lifelong imprisonment, they tell you, and final banishment from home is a thing bitterer still; the looking forward to but a short space, a mere childish *goûter*[3] and dessert of it, before the end, being so great a resource of effort to pilgrims and wayfarers, and the soldier in distant quarters, and lending, in lack of that, some power of solace to the thought of sleep in the home churchyard, at least — dead cheek by dead cheek, and with the rain soaking in upon one from above.

So powerful is this instinct, and yet accidents like those I have been speaking of so mechanically determine it; its essence being indeed the early familiar, as constituting our ideal, or typical conception, of rest and security. Out of so many possible conditions, just this for you and that for me, brings ever the unmistakable realisation of the delightful *chez soi;*[1] this for the Englishman, for me and you, with the closely-drawn white curtain and the shaded lamp; that, quite other, for the wandering Arab, who folds his tent every morning, and makes his sleeping-place among haunted ruins, or in old tombs.

With Florian then the sense of home became singularly intense, his good fortune being that the special character of his home was in itself so essentially home-like. As after many wanderings I have come to fancy that some parts of Surrey and Kent are, for Englishmen, the true landscape, true home-countries, by right, partly, of a certain earthy warmth in the yellow of the sand below their gorse-bushes, and of a certain gray-blue mist after rain, in the hollows of the hills there, welcome to fatigued eyes, and never seen farther south; so I think that the sort of house I have described, with precisely those proportions of red-brick and green, and with a just perceptible monotony in the subdued order of it, for its distinguishing note, is for Englishmen at least typically home-like. And so for Florian that general human instinct was reinforced by this special home-likeness in the place his wandering soul had happened to light on, as, in the second degree, its body and earthly tabernacle; the sense of harmony between his soul and its physical environment became, for a time at least, like perfectly played music, and the life led there singularly tranquil and filled with a curious sense of self-possession. The love of security, of an habitually undisputed standing-ground or sleeping-place, came to count for much in the generation and correcting of his thoughts, and afterwards as a salutary principle of restraint in all his wanderings of spirit. The wistful yearning towards home, in absence from it, as the shadows of evening deepened, and he followed in thought what was doing there from hour to hour, interpreted to him much of a yearning and regret he experienced afterwards, towards he knew not what, out of

---

[1] The comparison of the infant mind to a sheet of blank paper ready to be written upon, originated with the philosopher John Locke; it is practically the same as Aristotle's figure of a smooth wax tablet.   [2] cf. *Job*, xix: 24   [3] taste

[1] "homey-ness"

strange ways of feeling and thought in which, from time to time, his spirit found itself alone; and in the tears shed in such absences there seemed always to be some soul-subduing foretaste of what his last tears might be.

And the sense of security could hardly have been deeper, the quiet of the child's soul being one with the quiet of its home, a place "enclosed" and "sealed." But upon this assured place, upon the child's assured soul which resembled it, there came floating in from the larger world without, as at windows left ajar unknowingly, or over the high garden walls, two streams of impressions, the sentiments of beauty and pain — recognitions of the visible, tangible, audible, loveliness of things, as a very real and somewhat tyrannous element in them — and of the sorrow of the world, of grown people and children and animals, as a thing not to be put by in them. From this point he could trace two predominant processes of mental change in him — the growth of an almost diseased sensibility to the spectacle of suffering, and, parallel with this, the rapid growth of a certain capacity of fascination by bright colour and choice form — the sweet curvings, for instance, of the lips of those who seemed to him comely persons, modulated in such delicate unisons to the things they said or sang, — marking early the activity in him of a more than customary sensuousness, "the lust of the eye,"[1] as the Preacher says, which might lead him, one day, how far! Could he have foreseen the weariness of the way! In music sometimes the two sorts of impressions came together, and he would weep, to the surprise of older people. Tears of joy too the child knew, also to older people's surprise; real tears, once, of relief from long-strung, childish expectation, when he found returned at evening, with new roses in her cheeks, the little sister who had been to a place where there was a wood, and brought back for him a treasure of fallen acorns, and black crow's feathers, and his peace at finding her again near him mingled all night with some intimate sense of the distant forest, the rumour of its breezes, with the glossy blackbirds aslant and the branches lifted in them, and of the perfect nicety of the little cups that fell. So those two elementary apprehensions of the tenderness and of the colour in things grew apace in him, and were seen

by him afterwards to send their roots back into the beginnings of life.

Let me note first some of the occasions of his recognition of the element of pain in things — incidents, now and again, which seemed suddenly to awake in him the whole force of that sentiment which Goethe has called the *Weltschmerz*,[1] and in which the concentrated sorrow of the world seemed suddenly to lie heavy upon him. A book lay in an old book-case, of which he cared to remember one picture — a woman sitting, with hands bound behind her, the dress, the cap, the hair, folded with a simplicity which touched him strangely, as if not by her own hands, but with some ambiguous care at the hands of others — Queen Marie Antoinette, on her way to execution — we all remember David's[2] drawing, meant merely to make her ridiculous. The face that had been so high had learned to be mute and resistless; but out of its very resistlessness, seemed now to call on men to have pity, and forbear; and he took note of that, as he closed the book, as a thing to look at again, if he should at any time find himself tempted to be cruel. Again he would never quite forget the appeal in the small sister's face, in the garden under the lilacs, terrified at a spider lighted on her sleeve. He could trace back to the look then noted a certain mercy conceived always for people in fear, even of little things, which seemed to make him, though but for a moment, capable of almost any sacrifice of himself. Impressible, susceptible persons, indeed, who had had their sorrows, lived about him; and this sensibility was due in part to the tacit influence of their presence, enforcing upon him habitually the fact that there are those who pass their days, as a matter of course, in a sort of "going quietly." Most poignantly of all he could recall, in unfading minutest circumstance, the cry on the stair, sounding bitterly through the house, and struck into his soul forever, of an aged woman, his father's sister, come now to announce his death in distant India; how it seemed to make the aged woman like a child again; and, he knew not why, but this fancy was full of pity to him. There were the little sorrows of the dumb animals too — of the white angora, with a dark tail like an ermine's, and a face like a flower, who fell into a linger-

---

[1] cf. *I John*, ii: 16

[1] world-sorrow [2] Jacques Louis David (1748–1825), a French historical painter

ing sickness, and became quite delicately human in its valetudinarianism, and came to have a hundred different expressions of voice — how it grew worse and worse, till it began to feel the light too much for it, and at last, after one wild morning of pain, the little soul flickered away from the body, quite worn to death already, and now but feebly retaining it.

So he wanted another pet; and as there were starlings about the place, which could be taught to speak, one of them was caught, and he meant to treat it kindly; but in the night its young ones could be heard crying after it, and the responsive cry of the mother-bird towards them; and at last, with the first light, though not till after some debate with himself, he went down and opened the cage, and saw a sharp bound of the prisoner up to her nestlings; and therewith came the sense of remorse, — that he too was become an accomplice in moving, to the limit of his small power, the springs and handles of that great machine in things, constructed so ingeniously to play pain-fugues[1] on the delicate nerve-work of living creatures.

I have remarked how, in the process of our brain-building, as the house of thought in which we live gets itself together, like some airy bird's-nest of floating thistle-down and chance straws, compact at last, little accidents have their consequence; and thus it happened that, as he walked one evening, a garden gate, usually closed, stood open; and lo! within, a great red hawthorn in full flower, embossing heavily the bleached and twisted trunk and branches, so aged that there were but few green leaves thereon — a plumage of tender, crimson fire out of the heart of the dry wood. The perfume of the tree had now and again reached him, in the currents of the wind, over the wall, and he had wondered what might be behind it, and was now allowed to fill his arms with the flowers — flowers enough for all the old blue-china pots along the chimney-piece, making fête[2] in the children's room. Was it some periodic moment in the expansion of soul within him, or mere trick of heat in the heavily-laden summer air? But the beauty of the thing struck home to him feverishly; and in dreams all night he loitered along a magic roadway of crimson flowers, which seemed to open ruddily in thick, fresh masses about his

feet, and fill softly all the little hollows in the banks on either side. Always afterwards, summer by summer, as the flowers came on, the blossom of the red hawthorn still seemed to him absolutely the reddest of all things; and the goodly crimson, still alive in the works of old Venetian masters or old Flemish tapestries, called out always from afar the recollection of the flame in those perishing little petals, as it pulsed gradually out of them, kept long in the drawers of an old cabinet. Also then, for the first time, he seemed to experience a passionateness in his relation to fair outward objects, an inexplicable excitement in their presence, which disturbed him, and from which he half longed to be free. A touch of regret or desire mingled all night with the remembered presence of the red flowers, and their perfume in the darkness about him; and the longing for some undivined, entire possession of them was the beginning of a revelation to him, growing ever clearer, with the coming of the gracious summer guise of fields and trees and persons in each succeeding year, of a certain, at times seemingly exclusive, predominance in his interests, of beautiful physical things, a kind of tyranny of the sense over him.

In later years he came upon philosophies which occupied him much in the estimate of the proportion of the sensuous and the ideal elements in human knowledge, the relative parts they bear in it; and, in his intellectual scheme, was led to assign very little to the abstract thought, and much to its sensible vehicle or occasion. Such metaphysical speculation did but reinforce what was instinctive in his way of receiving the world, and for him, everywhere, that sensible vehicle or occasion became, perhaps only too surely, the necessary concomitant of any perception of things, real enough to be of any weight or reckoning, in his house of thought. There were times when he could think of the necessity he was under of associating all thoughts to touch and sight, as a sympathetic link between himself and actual, feeling, living objects; a protest in favour of real men and women against mere gray, unreal abstractions; and he remembered gratefully how the Christian religion, hardly less than the religion of the ancient Greeks, translating so much of its spiritual verity into things that may be seen, condescends in part to sanction this infirmity, if so it be, of our human existence, wherein the

---

[1] elaborately interwoven compositions of pain
[2] festival

AE

world of sense is so much with us, and welcomed this thought as a kind of keeper and sentinel over his soul therein. But certainly, he came more and more to be unable to care for, or think of soul but as in an actual body, or of any world but that wherein are water and trees, and where men and women look, so or so, and press actual hands. It was the trick even his pity learned, fastening those who suffered in anywise to his affections by a kind of sensible attachments. He would think of Julian, fallen into incurable sickness, as spoiled in the sweet blossom of his skin like pale amber, and his honey-like hair; of Cecil, early dead, as cut off from the lilies, from golden summer days, from women's voices; and then what comforted him a little was the thought of the turning of the child's flesh to violets in the turf above him. And thinking of the very poor, it was not the things which most men care most for that he yearned to give them; but fairer roses, perhaps, and power to taste quite as they will, at their ease and not task-burdened, a certain desirable, clear light in the new morning, through which sometimes he had noticed them, quite unconscious of it, on their way to their early toil.

* * * * * * *

ROBERT LOUIS STEVENSON
(1850–1894)

FRANÇOIS VILLON, STUDENT, POET, AND HOUSEBREAKER

Perhaps one of the most curious revolutions in literary history is the sudden bull's-eye light cast by M. Longnon on the obscure existence of François Villon. His book is not remarkable merely as a chapter of biography exhumed after four centuries. To readers of the poet it will recall, with a flavour of satire, that characteristic passage in which he bequeaths his spectacles — with a humorous reservation of the case — to the hospital for blind paupers known as the Fifteen-Score. Thus equipped, let the blind paupers go and separate the good from the bad in the cemetery of the Innocents! For his own part the poet can see no distinction. Much have the dead people made of their advantages. What does it matter now that they have lain in state beds and nour-

ished portly bodies upon cakes and cream! Here they all lie, to be trodden in the mud; the large estate and the small, sounding virtue and adroit or powerful vice, in very much the same condition; and a bishop not to be distinguished from a lamplighter with even the strongest spectacles.

Such was Villon's cynical philosophy. Four hundred years after his death, when surely all danger might be considered at an end, a pair of critical spectacles have been applied to his own remains; and though he left behind him a sufficiently ragged reputation from the first, it is only after these four hundred years that his delinquencies have been finally tracked home, and we can assign him to his proper place among the good or wicked. It is a staggering thought, and one that affords a fine figure of the imperishability of men's acts, that the stealth of the private inquiry office can be carried so far back into the dead and dusty past. We are not so soon quit of our concerns as Villon fancied. In the extreme of dissolution, when not so much as a man's name is remembered, when his dust is scattered to the four winds, and perhaps the very grave and the very graveyard where he was laid to rest have been forgotten, desecrated, and buried under populous towns, — even in this extreme let an antiquary fall across a sheet of manuscript, and the name will be recalled, the old infamy will pop out into daylight like a toad out of a fissure in the rock, and the shadow of the shade of what was once a man will be heartily pilloried by his descendants. A little while ago and Villon was almost totally forgotten; then he was revived for the sake of his verses; and now he is being revived with a vengeance in the detection of his misdemeanours. How unsubstantial is this projection of a man's existence, which can lie in abeyance for centuries and then be brushed up again and set forth for the consideration of posterity by a few dips in an antiquary's inkpot! This precarious tenure of fame goes a long way to justify those (and they are not few) who prefer cakes and cream in the immediate present.

A WILD YOUTH

François de Montcorbier, *alias* François des Loges, *alias* François Villon, *alias* Michel Mouton, Master of Arts in the University of Paris, was born in that city in the summer of

1431. It was a memorable year for France on other and higher considerations. A great-hearted girl and a poor-hearted boy made, the one her last, the other his first appearance on the public stage of that unhappy country. On the 30th of May the ashes of Joan of Arc were thrown into the Seine, and on the 2d of December our Henry Sixth made his Joyous Entry dismally enough into disaffected and depopulating Paris. Sword and fire still ravaged the open country. On a single April Saturday twelve hundred persons, besides children, made their escape out of the starving capital. The hangman, as is not uninteresting to note in connection with Master Francis, was kept hard at work in 1431; on the last of April and on the 4th of May alone, sixty-two bandits swung from Paris gibbets. A more confused or troublous time it would have been difficult to select for a start in life. Not even a man's nationality was certain; for the people of Paris there was no such thing as a Frenchman. The English were the English indeed, but the French were only the Armagnacs, whom, with Joan of Arc at their head, they had beaten back from under their ramparts not two years before. Such public sentiment as they had centred about their dear Duke of Burgundy, and the dear Duke had no more urgent business than to keep out of their neighbourhood. . . . At least, and whether he liked it or not, our disreputable troubadour was tubbed and swaddled as a subject of the English crown.

We hear nothing of Villon's father except that he was poor and of mean extraction. His mother was given piously,[1] which does not imply very much in an old Frenchwoman, and quite uneducated. He had an uncle, a monk in an abbey at Angers, who must have prospered beyond the family average, and was reported to be worth five or six hundred crowns. Of this uncle and his money-box the reader will hear once more. In 1448 Francis became a student of the University of Paris; in 1450 he took the degree of Bachelor, and in 1452 that of Master of Arts. His *bourse*, or the sum paid weekly for his board, was of the amount of two sous. Now two sous was about the price of a pound of salt butter in the bad times of 1417; it was the price of half-a-pound in the worse times of 1419; and in 1444, just four years before Villon joined the University, it seems to have been taken as the average wage for a day's manual labour. In short, it cannot have been a very profuse allowance to keep a sharp-set lad in breakfast and supper for seven mortal days; and Villon's share of the cakes and pastry and general good cheer, to which he is never weary of referring, must have been slender from the first.

The educational arrangements of the University of Paris were, to our way of thinking, somewhat incomplete. Worldly and monkish elements were presented in a curious confusion, which the youth might disentangle for himself. If he had an opportunity, on the one hand, of acquiring much hair-drawn divinity and a taste for formal disputation, he was put in the way of much gross and flaunting vice upon the other. The lecture room of a scholastic doctor was sometimes under the same roof with establishments of a very different and peculiarly unedifying order. The students had extraordinary privileges, which by all accounts they abused extraordinarily. And while some condemned themselves to an almost sepulchral regularity and seclusion, others fled the schools, swaggered in the street "with their thumbs in their girdle," passed the night in riot, and behaved themselves as the worthy forerunners of Jehan Frollo in the romance of *Notre Dame de Paris*.[1] Villon tells us himself that he was among the truants, but we hardly needed his avowal. The burlesque erudition in which he sometimes indulged implies no more than the merest smattering of knowledge; whereas his acquaintance with blackguard haunts and industries could only have been acquired by early and consistent impiety and idleness. He passed his degrees, it is true; but some of us who have been to modern universities will make their own reflections on the value of the test. As for his three pupils, Colin Laurent, Girard Gossouyn, and Jehan Marceau — if they were really his pupils in any serious sense — what can we say but God help them! And sure enough, by his own description, they turned out as ragged, rowdy, and ignorant as was to be looked for from the views and manners of their rare preceptor.

At some time or other, before or during his university career, the poet was adopted by

---

[1] of pious tendencies

[1] by Victor Hugo

Master Guillaume de Villon, chaplain of Saint Benoît-le-Bétourné near the Sorbonne. From him he borrowed the surname by which he is known to posterity. It was most likely from his house, called the *Porte Rouge*,[1] and situated in a garden in the cloister of Saint Benoît, that Master Francis heard the bell of the Sorbonne[2] ring out the Angelus[3] while he was finishing his *Small Testament* at Christmastide in 1456. Toward this benefactor he usually gets credit for a respectable display of gratitude. But with his trap and pitfall style of writing, it is easy to make too sure. His sentiments are about as much to be relied on as those of a professional beggar; and in this, as in so many other matters, he comes toward us whining and piping the eye,[4] and goes off again with a whoop and his finger to his nose. Thus, he calls Guillaume de Villon his "more than father," thanks him with a great show of sincerity for having helped him out of many scrapes, and bequeaths him his portion of renown. But the portion of renown which belonged to a young thief, distinguished (if, at the period when he wrote this legacy, he was distinguished at all) for having written some more or less obscene and scurrilous ballads, must have been little fitted to gratify the self-respect or increase the reputation of a benevolent ecclesiastic. The same remark applies to a subsequent legacy of the poet's library, with specification of one work which was plainly neither decent nor devout. We are thus left on the horns of a dilemma. If the chaplain was a godly, philanthropic personage, who had tried to graft good principles and good behaviour on this wild slip of an adopted son, these jesting legacies would obviously cut him to the heart. The position of an adopted son toward his adoptive father is one full of delicacy; where a man lends his name he looks for great consideration. And this legacy of Villon's portion of renown may be taken as the mere fling of an unregenerate scapegrace who has wit enough to recognise in his own shame the readiest weapon of offence against a prosy benefactor's feelings. The gratitude of Master Francis figures, on this reading, as a frightful *minus* quantity. If, on the other hand, those jests were given and taken in good humour, the whole relation

between the pair degenerates into the unedifying complicity of a debauched old chaplain and a witty and dissolute young scholar. At this rate the house with the red door may have rung with the most mundane minstrelsy; and it may have been below its roof that Villon, through a hole in the plaster, studied, as he tells us, the leisures of a rich ecclesiastic.

It was, perhaps, of some moment in the poet's life that he should have inhabited the cloister of Saint Benoît. Three of the most remarkable among his early acquaintances are Catherine de Vauselles, for whom he entertained a short-lived affection and an enduring and most unmanly resentment; Regnier de Montigny, a young blackguard of good birth; and Colin de Cayeux, a fellow with a marked aptitude for picking locks. Now we are on a foundation of mere conjecture, but it is at least curious to find that two of the canons of Saint Benoît answered respectively to the names of Pierre de Vaucel and Etienne de Montigny, and that there was a householder called Nicolas de Cayeux in a street — the Rue des Poirées — in the immediate neighbourhood of the cloister. M. Longnon is almost ready to identify Catherine as the niece of Pierre; Regnier as the nephew of Etienne, and Colin as the son of Nicolas. Without going so far, it must be owned that the approximation of names is significant. As we go on to see the part played by each of these persons in the sordid melodrama of the poet's life, we shall come to regard it as even more notable. Is it not Clough who has remarked that, after all, everything lies in juxtaposition?[1] Many a man's destiny has been settled by nothing apparently more grave than a pretty face on the opposite side of the street and a couple of bad companions round the corner.

Catherine de Vauselles (or de Vaucel — the change is within the limits of Villon's license) had plainly delighted in the poet's conversation; near neighbours or not, they were much together; and Villon made no secret of his court, and suffered himself to believe that his feeling was repaid in kind. This may have been an error from the first, or he may have estranged her by subsequent misconduct or temerity. One can easily imagine Villon an impatient wooer. One thing, at least, is sure: that the affair terminated in a manner bitterly

[1] Red Door   [2] a college of the University   [3] a summons to a devotional service   [4] pretending to weep

[1] cf. his *Amours de Voyage*

humiliating to Master Francis. In presence of his lady-love, perhaps under her window and certainly with her connivance, he was unmercifully thrashed by one Noë le Joly — beaten, as he says himself, like dirty linen on the washing-board. It is characteristic that his malice had notably increased between the time when he wrote the *Small Testament* immediately on the back of the occurrence, and the time when he wrote the *Large Testament* five years after. On the latter occasion nothing is too bad for his "damsel with the twisted nose," as he calls her. She is spared neither hint nor accusation, and he tells his messenger to accost her with the vilest insults. Villon, it is thought, was out of Paris when these amenities escaped his pen; or perhaps the strong arm of Noë le Joly would have been again in requisition. So ends the love story, if love story it may properly be called. Poets are not necessarily fortunate in love; but they usually fall among more romantic circumstances and bear their disappointment with a better grace.

The neighbourhood of Regnier de Montigny and Colin de Cayeux was probably more influential on his after life than the contempt of Catherine. For a man who is greedy of all pleasures, and provided with little money and less dignity of character, we may prophesy a safe and speedy voyage downward. Humble or even truckling virtue may walk unspotted in this life. But only those who despise the pleasures can afford to despise the opinion of the world. A man of a strong, heady temperament, like Villon, is very differently tempted. His eyes lay hold on all provocations greedily, and his heart flames up at a look into imperious desire; he is snared and broached to by anything and everything, from a pretty face to a piece of pastry in a cookshop window; he will drink the rinsing of the wine cup, stay the latest at the tavern party; tap at the lit windows, follow the sound of singing, and beat the whole neighbourhood for another reveller, as he goes reluctantly homeward: and grudge himself every hour of sleep as a black empty period in which he cannot follow after pleasure. Such a person is lost if he have not dignity, or, failing that, at least pride, which is its shadow and in many ways its substitute. Master Francis, I fancy, would follow his own eager instincts without much spiritual struggle. And we soon find him fallen among thieves in sober, literal earnest,

and counting as acquaintances the most disreputable people he could lay his hands on: fellows who stole ducks in Paris Moat; sergeants of the criminal court, and archers of the watch; blackguards who slept at night under the butchers' stalls, and for whom the aforesaid archers peered about carefully with lanterns; Regnier de Montigny, Colin de Cayeux, and their crew, all bound on a favouring breeze toward the gallows; the disorderly abbess of Port Royal, who went about at fair time with soldiers and thieves, and conducted her abbey on the queerest principles; and most likely Perette Mauger, the great Paris receiver of stolen goods, not yet dreaming, poor woman! of the last scene of her career when Henry Cousin, executor of the high justice, shall bury her, alive and most reluctant, in front of the new Montigny gibbet. Nay, our friend soon began to take a foremost rank in this society. He could string off verses, which is always an agreeable talent; and he could make himself useful in many other ways. The whole ragged army of Bohemia, and whosoever loved good cheer without at all loving to work and pay for it, are addressed in contemporary verses as the "Subjects of François Villon." He was a good genius to all hungry and unscrupulous persons; and became the hero of a whole legendary cycle of tavern tricks and cheateries. At best, these were doubtful levities, rather too thievish for a schoolboy, rather too gamesome for a thief. But he would not linger long in this equivocal border land. He must soon have complied with his surroundings. He was one who would go where the cannikin clinked, not caring who should pay; and from supping in the wolves' den, there is but a step to hunting with the pack. And here, as I am on the chapter of his degradation, I shall say all I mean to say about its darkest expression, and be done with it for good. Some charitable critics see no more than a *jeu d'esprit*, a graceful and trifling exercise of the imagination, in the grimy ballad of Fat Peg (*Grosse Margot*). I am not able to follow these gentlemen to this polite extreme. Out of all Villon's works that ballad stands forth in flaring reality, gross and ghastly, as a thing written in a contraction of disgust. M. Longnon shows us more and more clearly at every page that we are to read our poet literally, that his names are the names of real persons, and the events he chronicles were actual events. But even if the tendency of criticism had run the other way, this ballad would have gone far to prove itself. I can well understand the reluctance of worthy persons in this matter; for of course it is unpleasant to think of a man of genius as one who held, in the words of Marina to Boult —

"A place, for which the pained'st fiend
Of hell would not in reputation change."[1]

But beyond this natural unwillingness, the whole difficulty of the case springs from a highly virtuous ignorance of life. Paris now is not so different from the Paris of then; and the whole of the doings of Bohemia are not written in the sugar-candy pastorals of Murger.[2] It is really not at all surprising that a young man of the fifteenth century, with a knack of making verses, should accept his bread upon disgraceful terms. The race of those who do is not extinct; and some of them to this day write the prettiest verses imaginable. . . . After this, it were impossible for Master Francis to fall lower: to go and steal for himself would be an admirable advance from every point of view, divine or human.

And yet it is not as a thief, but as a homicide, that he makes his first appearance before angry justice. On June 5, 1455, when he was about twenty-four, and had been Master of Arts for a matter of three years, we behold him for the first time quite definitely. Angry justice had, as it were, photographed him in the act of his homicide; and M. Longnon, rummaging among old deeds, has turned up the negative and printed it off for our instruction. Villon had been supping — copiously we may believe — and sat on a stone bench in front of the Church of Saint Benoît, in company with a priest called Gilles and a woman of the name of Isabeau. It was nine o'clock, a mighty late hour for the period, and evidently a fine summer's night. Master Francis carried a mantle, like a prudent man, to keep him from the dews (serain), and had a sword below it dangling from his girdle. So these three dallied in front of St. Benoît, taking their pleasure (pour soy esbatre). Suddenly there arrived upon the scene a priest, Philippe Chermoye or Sermaise, also with sword and cloak, and accompanied by one

Master Jehan le Mardi. Sermaise, according to Villon's account, which is all we have to go upon, came up blustering and denying God; as Villon rose to make room for him upon the bench, thrust him rudely back into his place; and finally drew his sword and cut open his lower lip, by what I should imagine was a very clumsy stroke. Up to this point, Villon professes to have been a model of courtesy,· even of feebleness; and the brawl, in his version, reads like the fable of the wolf and the lamb. But now the lamb was roused; he drew his sword, stabbed Sermaise in the groin, knocked him on the head with a big stone, and then, leaving him to his fate, went away to have his own lip doctored by a barber[1] of the name of Fouquet. In one version, he says that Gilles, Isabeau, and Le Mardi ran away at the first high words, and that he and Sermaise had it out alone; in another, Le Mardi is represented as returning and wresting Villon's sword from him: the reader may please himself. Sermaise was picked up, lay all that night in the prison of Saint Benoît, where he was examined by an official of the Châtelet[2] and expressly pardoned Villon, and died on the following Saturday in the Hôtel Dieu.[3]

This, as I have said, was in June. Not before January of the next year could Villon extract a pardon from the king; but while his hand was in, he got two. One is for "François des Loges, alias (auterment dit) de Villon"; and the other runs in the name of François de Montcorbier. Nay, it appears there was a further complication; for in the narrative of the first of these documents, it is mentioned that he passed himself off upon Fouquet, the barber-surgeon, as one Michel Mouton. M. Longnon has a theory that this unhappy accident with Sermaise was the cause of Villon's subsequent irregularities; and that up to that moment he had been the pink of good behaviour. But the matter has to my eyes a more dubious air. A pardon necessary for Des Loges and another for Montcorbier? and these two the same person? and one or both of them known by the alias of Villon, however honestly come by? and lastly, in the heat of the moment, a fourth name thrown out with an assured countenance? A ship is not to be trusted that sails under so many colours.

[1] Pericles, IV, vi, 173-4 [2] Henri Murger (1822-1861), who celebrated the Bohemian life of Paris in Scènes de la vie de Bohème

[1] In those days barbers were surgeons for minor operations. [2] the city prison [3] a hospital

This is not the simple bearing of innocence. No — the young master was already treading crooked paths; already, he would start and blench at a hand upon his shoulder, with the look we know so well in the face of Hogarth's Idle Apprentice;[1] already, in the blue devils,[2] he would see Henry Cousin, the executor of high justice, going in dolorous procession toward Montfaucon, and hear the wind and the birds crying around Paris gibbet.

A Gang of Thieves

In spite of the prodigious number of people who managed to get hanged, the fifteenth century was by no means a bad time for criminals. A great confusion of parties and great dust of fighting favoured the escape of private housebreakers and quiet fellows who stole ducks in Paris Moat. Prisons were leaky; and as we shall see, a man with a few crowns in his pocket and perhaps some acquaintance among the officials, could easily slip out and become once more a free marauder. There was no want of a sanctuary where he might harbour until troubles blew by; and accomplices helped each other with more or less good faith. Clerks,[3] above all, had remarkable facilities for a criminal way of life; for they were privileged, except in cases of notorious incorrigibility, to be plucked from the hands of rude secular justice and tried by a tribunal of their own. In 1402, a couple of thieves, both clerks of the University, were condemned to death by the Provost of Paris. As they were taken to Montfaucon, they kept crying "high and clearly" for their benefit of clergy,[4] but were none the less pitilessly hanged and gibbeted. Indignant Alma Mater interfered before the king; and the Provost was deprived of all royal offices, and condemned to return the bodies and erect a great stone cross, on the road from Paris to the gibbet, graven with the effigies of these two holy martyrs. We shall hear more of the benefit of clergy; for after this the reader will not be surprised to meet with thieves in the shape of tonsured clerks, or even priests and monks.

To a knot of such learned pilferers our poet certainly belonged; and by turning over a few more of M. Longnon's negatives, we shall get a clear idea of their character and doings. Montigny and De Cayeux are names already known; Guy Tabary, Petit-Jehan, Dom Nicolas, little Thibault, who was both clerk and goldsmith, and who made picklocks and melted plate for himself and his companions — with these the reader has still to become acquainted. Petit-Jehan[1] and De Cayeux were handy fellows and enjoyed a useful preeminence in honour of their doings with the picklock. "*Dictus des Cahyeus est fortis operator crochetorum,*" says Tabary's interrogation, "*sed dictus Petit-Jehan, ejus socius, est forcius operator.*"[2] But the flower of the flock was little Thibault; it was reported that no lock could stand before him; he had a persuasive hand; let us salute capacity wherever we may find it. Perhaps the term *gang* is not quite properly applied to the persons whose fortunes we are now about to follow; rather they were independent malefactors, socially intimate, and occasionally joining together for some serious operation, just as modern stock jobbers form a syndicate for an important loan. Nor were they at all particular to any branch of misdoing. They did not scrupulously confine themselves to a single sort of theft, as I hear is common among modern thieves. They were ready for anything, from pitch-and-toss[3] to manslaughter. Montigny, for instance, had neglected neither of these extremes, and we find him accused of cheating at games of hazard[4] on the one hand, and on the other of the murder of one Thevenin Pensete in a house by the Cemetery of St. John. If time had only spared us some particulars, might not this last have furnished us with the matter of a grisly winter's tale?

At Christmas-time in 1456, readers of Villon will remember that he was engaged on the *Small Testament.*[5] About the same period, *circa festum nativitatis Domini,*[6] he took part in a memorable supper at the Mule Tavern, in front of the Church of St. Mathurin.

---

[1] The Industrious and the Idle Apprentice are shown in a series of pictures by William Hogarth (1697-1764), a great English caricaturist and satirist. [2] when in low spirits [3] men of education [4] the right of demanding a trial before an ecclesiastical court instead of a secular court

[1] Little-John [2] The said des Cahyeus is a great artist with picklocks, but the said Petit-Jehan, his 'pal,' is a greater. [3] a game like matching pennies [4] craps [5] The 'testament,' or 'will,' was a popular form of literary composition [6] about Christmas

Tabary, who seems to have been very much Villon's creature, had ordered the supper in the course of the afternoon. He was a man who had had troubles in his time and languished in the Bishop of Paris's prisons on a suspicion of picking locks; confiding, convivial, not very astute — who had copied out a whole improper romance with his own right hand. This supper-party was to be his first introduction to De Cayeux and Petit-Jehan, which was probably a matter of some concern to the poor man's muddy wits; in the sequel, at least, he speaks of both with an undisguised respect, based on professional inferiority in the matter of picklocks. Dom Nicolas, a Picardy monk, was the fifth and last at table. When supper had been despatched and fairly washed down, we may suppose, with white Baigneux or red Beaune, which were favourite wines among the fellowship, Tabary was solemnly sworn over to secrecy on the night's performances; and the party left the Mule and proceeded to an unoccupied house belonging to Robert de Saint-Simon. This, over a low wall, they entered without difficulty. All but Tabary took off their upper garments; a ladder was found and applied to the high wall which separated Saint-Simon's house from the court of the College of Navarre; the four fellows in their shirt sleeves (as we might say) clambered over in a twinkling; and Master Guy Tabary remained alone beside the overcoats. From the court the burglars made their way into the vestry of the chapel, where they found a large chest, strengthened with iron bands and closed with four locks. One of these locks they picked, and then, by levering up the corner, forced the other three. Inside was a small coffer, of walnut wood, also barred with iron, but fastened with only three locks, which were all comfortably picked by way of the keyhole. In the walnut coffer — a joyous sight by our thieves' lantern — were five hundred crowns of gold. There was some talk of opening the aumries,[1] where, if they had only known, a booty eight or nine times greater lay ready to their hand; but one of the party (I have a humorous suspicion it was Dom Nicolas, the Picardy monk) hurried them away. It was ten o'clock when they mounted the ladder; it was about midnight before Tabary beheld them coming back. To him they gave ten

crowns, and promised a share of a two-crown dinner on the morrow; whereat we may suppose his mouth watered. In course of time, he got wind of the real amount of their booty and understood how scurvily he had been used; but he seems to have borne no malice. How could he, against such superb operators as Petit-Jehan and De Cayeux; or a person like Villon, who could have made a new improper romance out of his own head, instead of merely copying an old one with mechanical right hand?

The rest of the winter was not uneventful for the gang. First they made a demonstration against the Church of St. Mathurin after chalices,[1] and were ignominiously chased away by barking dogs. Then Tabary fell out with Casin Chollet, one of the fellows who stole ducks in Paris Moat, who subsequently became a sergeant of the Châtelet and distinguished himself by misconduct, followed by imprisonment and public castigation, during the wars of Louis Eleventh. The quarrel was not conducted with a proper regard to the king's peace, and the pair publicly belaboured each other until the police stepped in, and Master Tabary was cast once more into the prisons of the Bishop. While he still lay in durance, another job was cleverly executed by the band in broad daylight, at the Augustine Monastery. Brother Guillaume Coiffier was beguiled by an accomplice to St. Mathurin to say mass; and during his absence, his chamber was entered and five or six hundred crowns in money and some silver plate successfully abstracted. A melancholy man was Coiffier on his return! Eight crowns from this adventure were forwarded by little Thibault to the incarcerated Tabary; and with these he bribed the jailer and reappeared in Paris taverns. Some time before or shortly after this, Villon set out for Angers, as he had promised in the *Small Testament*. The object of this excursion was not merely to avoid the presence of his cruel mistress or the strong arm of Noë le Joly, but to plan a deliberate robbery on his uncle the monk. As soon as he had properly studied the ground, the others were to go over in force from Paris — picklocks and all — and away with my uncle's strongbox! This throws a comical sidelight on his own accusation against his relatives, that they had "forgotten natural duty" and

---

[1] closets

[1] cups used for sacramental wine

disowned him because he was poor. A poor relation is a distasteful circumstance at the best, but a poor relation who plans deliberate robberies against those of his blood, and trudges hundreds of weary leagues to put them into execution, is surely a little on the wrong side of toleration. The uncle at Angers may have been monstrously undutiful; but the nephew from Paris was upsides with him.

On the 23d April, that venerable and discreet person, Master Pierre Marchand, Curate and Prior of Paray-le-Monial, in the diocese of Chartres, arrived in Paris and put up at the sign of the Three Chandeliers, in the Rue de la Huchette. Next day, or the day after, as he was breakfasting at the sign of the Arm-chair, he fell into talk with two customers, one of whom was a priest and the other our friend Tabary. The idiotic Tabary became mighty confidential as to his past life. Pierre Marchand, who was an acquaintance of Guillaume Coiffier's and had sympathised with him over his loss, pricked up his ears at the mention of picklocks, and led on the transcriber of improper romances from one thing to another, until they were fast friends. For picklocks the Prior of Paray professed a keen curiosity; but Tabary, upon some late alarm, had thrown all his into the Seine. Let that be no difficulty, however, for was there not little Thibault, who could make them of all shapes and sizes, and to whom Tabary, smelling an accomplice, would be only too glad to introduce his new acquaintance? On the morrow, accordingly, they met; and Tabary, after having first wet his whistle at the Prior's expense, led him to Notre Dame[1] and presented him to four or five "young companions," who were keeping sanctuary[2] in the church. They were all clerks, recently escaped, like Tabary himself, from the episcopal prisons. Among these we may notice Thibault, the operator, a little fellow of twenty-six, wearing long hair behind. The Prior expressed, through Tabary, his anxiety to become their accomplice and altogether such as they were (*de leur sorte et de leurs complices*). Mighty polite they showed themselves, and made him many fine speeches in return. But for all that, perhaps because they had longer heads than Tabary, perhaps because it is less easy to wheedle men in a body, they kept obstinately to generali-

ties and gave him no information as to their exploits, past, present, or to come. I suppose Tabary groaned under this reserve; for no sooner were he and the Prior out of the church than he fairly emptied his heart to him, gave him full details of many hanging matters in the past, and explained the future intentions of the band. The scheme of the hour was to rob another Augustine monk, Robert de la Porte, and in this the Prior agreed to take a hand, with simulated greed. Thus, in the course of two days, he had turned this wine-skin of a Tabary inside out. For a while longer the farce was carried on; the Prior was introduced to Petit-Jehan, whom he describes as a little, very smart man of thirty, with a black beard and a short jacket; an appointment was made and broken in the de la Porte affair; Tabary had some breakfast at the Prior's charge and leaked out more secrets under the influence of wine and friendship; and then all of a sudden, on the 17th of May, an alarm sprang up, the Prior picked up his skirts and walked quietly over to the Châtelet to make a deposition, and the whole band took to their heels and vanished out of Paris and the sight of the police.

Vanish as they like, they all go with a clog about their feet. Sooner or later, here or there, they will be caught in the fact, and ignominiously sent home. From our vantage of four centuries afterward, it is odd and pitiful to watch the order in which the fugitives are captured and dragged in.

Montigny was the first. In August of that same year, he was laid by the heels on many grievous counts; sacrilegious robberies, frauds, incorrigibility, and that bad business about Thevenin Pensete in the house by the Cemetery of St. John. He was reclaimed by the ecclesiastical authorities as a clerk; but the claim was rebutted on the score of incorrigibility, and ultimately fell to the ground; and he was condemned to death by the Provost of Paris. It was a very rude hour for Montigny, but hope was not yet over. He was a fellow of some birth; his father had been king's pantler;[1] his sister, probably married to some one about the Court, was in the family way, and her health would be endangered if the execution was proceeded with. So down comes Charles the Seventh with letters of mercy, commuting the penalty to a year in a dungeon on bread

[1] the cathedral   [2] staying in the church, where they could not be arrested

[1] in charge of the pantry

and water, and a pilgrimage to the shrine of St. James in Galicia. Alas! the document was incomplete; it did not contain the full tale of Montigny's enormities; it did not recite that he had been denied benefit of clergy, and it said nothing about Thevenin Pensete. Montigny's hour was at hand. Benefit of clergy, honourable descent from king's pantler, sister in the family way, royal letters of commutation — all were of no avail. He had been in prison in Rouen, in Tours, in Bordeaux, and four times already in Paris; and out of all these he had come scathless; but now he must make a little excursion as far as Montfaucon with Henry Cousin, executor of high justice. There let him swing among the carrion crows.

About a year later, in July, 1458, the police laid hands on Tabary. Before the ecclesiastical commissary he was twice examined, and, on the latter occasion, put to the question[1] ordinary and extraordinary. What a dismal change from pleasant suppers at the Mule, where he sat in triumph with expert operators and great wits! He is at the lees of life, poor rogue; and those fingers which once transcribed improper romances are now agonisingly stretched upon the rack. We have no sure knowledge, but we may have a shrewd guess of the conclusion. Tabary, the admirer, would go the same way as those whom he admired.

The last we hear of is Colin de Cayeux. He was caught in autumn 1460, in the great Church of St. Leu d'Esserens, which makes so fine a figure in the pleasant Oise valley between Creil and Beaumont. He was reclaimed by no less than two bishops; but the Procureur[2] for the Provost held fast by incorrigible Colin. 1460 was an ill-starred year: for justice was making a clean sweep of "poor and indigent persons, thieves, cheats, and lockpickers," in the neighbourhood of Paris; and Colin de Cayeux, with many others, was condemned to death and hanged.

VILLON AND THE GALLOWS

Villon was still absent on the Angers expedition when the Prior of Paray sent such a bombshell among his accomplices; and the dates of his return and arrest remain undiscoverable. M. Campaux plausibly enough

opined for the autumn of 1457, which would make him closely follow on Montigny, and the first of those denounced by the Prior to fall into the toils. We may suppose, at least, that it was not long thereafter; we may suppose him competed for between lay and clerical Courts; and we may suppose him alternately pert and impudent, humble and fawning, in his defence. But at the end of all supposing, we come upon some nuggets of fact. For first, he was put to the question by water.[1] He who had tossed off so many cups of white Baigneux or red Beaune, now drank water through linen folds, until his bowels were flooded and his heart stood still. After so much raising of the elbow, so much outcry of fictitious thirst, here at last was enough drinking for a lifetime. Truly, of our pleasant vices, the gods make whips to scourge us.[2] And secondly he was condemned to be hanged. A man may have been expecting a catastrophe for years, and yet find himself unprepared when it arrives. Certainly, Villon found, in this legitimate issue of his career, a very staggering and grave consideration. Every beast, as he says, clings bitterly to a whole skin. If everything is lost, and even honour, life still remains; nay, and it becomes, like the ewe lamb in Nathan's parable,[3] as dear as all the rest. "Do you fancy," he asks, in a lively ballad, "that I had not enough philosophy under my hood to cry out: 'I appeal'? If I had made any bones about the matter, I should have been planted upright in the fields, by the St. Denis Road" — Montfaucon being on the way to St. Denis. An appeal to Parliament, as we saw in the case of Colin de Cayeux, did not necessarily lead to an acquittal or a commutation; and while the matter was pending, our poet had ample opportunity to reflect on his position. Hanging is a sharp argument, and to swing with many others on the gibbet adds a horrible corollary for the imagination. With the aspect of Montfaucon he was well acquainted; indeed, as the neighbourhood appears to have been sacred to junketing and nocturnal picnics of wild young men and women, he had probably studied it under all varieties of hour and weather. And now, as he lay in prison waiting the mortal push, these different aspects crowded back on his imagination with a

---

[1] put through 'the third degree' [2] deputy

[1] recently called 'the water-cure' [2] cf. *King Lear*, V, iii, 170-1 [3] *II Samuel*, xii : 3

new and startling significance; and he wrote a ballad, by way of epitaph for himself and his companions, which remains unique in the annals of mankind. It is, in the highest sense, a piece of his biography: —

La pluye nous a debuez et lavez,[1]
Et le soleil dessechez et noirciz;
Pies, corbeaulx, nous ont les yeux cavez,
Et arrachez la barbe et les sourcilz.
Jamais, nul temps, nous ne sommes rassis;
Puis çà, puis là, comme le vent varie,
A son plaisir sans cesser nous charie,
Plus becquetez d'oiseaulx que dez a couldre.
Ne soyez donc de nostre confrairie,
Mais priez Dieu que tous nous vueille absouldre.

Here is some genuine thieves' literature after so much that was spurious; sharp as an etching, written with a shuddering soul. There is an intensity of consideration in the piece that shows it to be the transcript of familiar thoughts. It is the quintessence of many a doleful nightmare on the straw, when he felt himself swing helpless in the wind, and saw the birds turn about him, screaming and menacing his eyes.

And, after all, the Parliament changed his sentence into one of banishment; and to Roussillon, in Dauphiny, our poet must carry his woes without delay. Travellers between Lyons and Marseilles may remember a station on the line, some way below Vienne, where the Rhone fleets seaward between vine-clad hills. This was Villon's Siberia. It would be a little warm in summer perhaps, and a little cold in winter in that draughty valley between two great mountain fields; but what with the hills, and the racing river, and the fiery Rhone wines, he was little to be pitied on

[1] The rain hath scoured us and washed us clean,
And the sun hath blackened and scorched us dry;
Magpies and crows at our eyes have been
And have plucked out our beards and the brows from the eye;
Never — no moment — at rest we lie,
But sway and swing as the wind doth blow,
Unceasingly driven at his will to and fro;
No thimble so pecked as each bird-pecked face.
Be not of our brotherhood, ye below,
But pray God pardon us all, of his grace!

the conditions of his exile. Villon, in a remarkably bad ballad, written in a breath, heartily thanked and fulsomely belauded the Parliament; the *envoi*,[1] like the proverbial postscript of a lady's letter, containing the pith of his performance in a request for three days' delay to settle his affairs and bid his friends farewell. He was probably not followed out of Paris, like Antoine Fradin, the popular preacher, another exile of a few years later, by weeping multitudes; but I dare say one or two rogues of his acquaintance would keep him company for a mile or so on the south road, and drink a bottle with him before they turned. For banished people, in those days, seem to have set out on their own responsibility, in their own guard, and at their own expense. It was no joke to make one's way from Paris to Roussillon alone and penniless in the fifteenth century. Villon says he left a rag of his tails on every bush. Indeed, he must have had many a weary tramp, many a slender meal, and many a to-do with blustering captains of the Ordonnance. But with one of his light fingers, we may fancy that he took as good as he gave; for every rag of his tail, he would manage to indemnify himself upon the population in the shape of food, or wine, or ringing money; and his route would be traceable across France and Burgundy by housewives and inn-keepers lamenting over petty thefts, like the track of a single human locust. A strange figure he must have cut in the eyes of the good country people: this ragged, blackguard city poet, with a smack of the Paris student, and a smack of the Paris street arab, posting along the highways, in rain or sun, among the green fields and vineyards.[2] For himself, he had no taste for rural loveliness; green fields and vineyards would be mighty indifferent to Master Francis; but he would often have his tongue in his cheek at the simplicity of rustic dupes, and often, at city gates, he might stop to contemplate the gibbet with its swinging bodies, and hug himself on his escape.

How long he stayed at Roussillon, how far he became the protégé of the Bourbons, to whom

[1] the short stanza (usually of four lines) ending a ballade and containing a direct address to the person for whom it was written; see Chaucer's ballades or Rossetti's translation from Villon
[2] More sombre but perhaps not less tuneful than Autolycus.

that town belonged, or when it was that he
took part, under the auspices of Charles of
Orleans,[1] in a rhyming tournament to be referred to once again in the pages of the present
volume, are matters that still remain in darkness, in spite of M. Longnon's diligent rummaging among archives. When we next find
him, in summer 1461, alas! he is once more in
durance : this time at Méun-sur-Loire, in the
prisons of Thibault d'Aussigny, Bishop of
Orleans. He had been lowered in a basket
into a noisome pit, where he lay, all summer,
gnawing hard crusts and railing upon fate.
His teeth, he says, were like the teeth of a
rake : a touch of haggard portraiture all the
more real for being excessive and burlesque,
and all the more proper to the man for being a
caricature of his own misery. His eyes were
"bandaged with thick walls." It might blow
hurricanes overhead ; the lightning might leap
in high heaven ; but no word of all this
reached him in his noisome pit. "Il n'entre,
ou gist, n'escler ni tourbillon."[2] Above all, he
was fevered with envy and anger at the freedom of others ; and his heart flowed over into
curses as he thought of Thibault d'Aussigny,
walking the streets in God's sunlight, and blessing people with extended fingers. So much
we find sharply lined in his own poems. Why
he was cast again into prison — how he had
again managed to shave the gallows — this
we know not, nor, from the destruction of
authorities, are we ever likely to learn. But
on October 2d, 1461, or some day immediately
preceding, the new King, Louis Eleventh,
made his joyous entry into Méun. Now it
was a part of the formality on such occasions
for the new King to liberate certain prisoners ;
and so the basket was let down into Villon's
pit, and hastily did Master Francis scramble
in, and was most joyfully hauled up, and shot
out, blinking and tottering, but once more a
free man, into the blessed sun and wind. Now
or never is the time for verses! Such a happy
revolution would turn the head of a stocking-
weaver, and set him jingling rhymes. And
so — after a voyage to Paris, where he finds
Montigny and De Cayeux clattering their
bones upon the gibbet, and his three pupils
roystering in Paris streets, "with their thumbs

under their girdles," — down sits Master
Francis to write his *Large Testament*, and
perpetuate his name in a sort of glorious
ignominy.

THE LARGE TESTAMENT

Of this capital achievement and, with it,
of Villon's style in general, it is here the place
to speak. The *Large Testament* is a hurly-
burly of cynical and sentimental reflections
about life, jesting legacies to friends and enemies, and, interspersed among these many
admirable ballades, both serious and absurd.
With so free a design, no thought that occurred
to him would need to be dismissed without
expression ; and he could draw at full length
the portrait of his own bedevilled soul, and of
the bleak and blackguardly world which was
the theatre of his exploits and sufferings.
If the reader can conceive something between
the slap-dash inconsequence of Byron's *Don
Juan* and the racy humorous gravity and
brief noble touches that distinguish the ver-
nacular poems of Burns, he will have formed
some idea of Villon's style. To the latter
writer — except in the ballades, which are
quite his own, and can be paralleled from no
other language known to me — he bears a
particular resemblance. In common with
Burns, he has a certain rugged compression,
a brutal vivacity of epithet, a homely vigour,
a delight in local personalities, and an interest
in many sides of life, that are often despised
and passed over by more effete and cultured
poets. Both also, in their strong, easy,
colloquial way, tend to become difficult and
obscure ; the obscurity in the case of Villon
passing at times into the absolute darkness of
cant language. They are perhaps the only
two great masters of expression who keep
sending their readers to a glossary.

"Shall we not dare to say of a thief," asks
Montaigne,[1] "that he has a handsome leg"?
It is a far more serious claim that we have to
put forward in behalf of Villon. Beside that
of his contemporaries, his writing, so full of
colour, so eloquent, so picturesque, stands out
in an almost miraculous isolation. If only
one or two of the chroniclers could have taken
a leaf out of his book, history would have
been a pastime, and the fifteenth century as
present to our minds as the age of Charles

---

[1] a prince and poet who had been a prisoner
in England from 1415 to 1440; Stevenson has
an essay on him [2] There enters not, where he
lies, lightning-flash nor whirlwind.

[1] a delightful French essayist (1533–1592)

Second. This gallows-bird was the one great writer of his age and country, and initiated modern literature for France. Boileau,[1] long ago, in the period of perukes and snuff-boxes, recognised him as the first articulate poet in the language; and if we measure him, not by priority of merit, but living duration of influence, not on a comparison with obscure forerunners, but with great and famous successors, we shall install this ragged and disreputable figure in a far higher niche in glory's temple than was ever dreamed of by the critic. It is, in itself, a memorable fact that, before 1542, in the very dawn of printing, and while modern France was in the making, the works of Villon ran through seven different editions. Out of him flows much of Rabelais;[2] and through Rabelais, directly and indirectly, a deep, permanent, and growing inspiration. Not only his style, but his callous pertinent way of looking upon the sordid and ugly sides of life, becomes every day a more specific feature in the literature of France. And only the other year, a work of some power appeared in Paris, and appeared with infinite scandal, which owed its whole inner significance and much of its outward form to the study of our rhyming thief.[3]

The world to which he introduces us is, as before said, blackguardly and bleak. Paris swarms before us, full of famine, shame, and death; monks and the servants of great lords hold high wassail upon cakes and pastry; the poor man licks his lips before the baker's window; people with patched eyes sprawl all night under the stall; chuckling Tabary transcribes an improper romance; barebosomed lasses and ruffling students swagger in the streets; the drunkard goes stumbling homeward; the graveyard is full of bones; and away on Montfaucon, Colin de Cayeux and Montigny hang draggled in the rain. Is there nothing better to be seen than sordid misery and worthless joys? Only where the poor old mother of the poet kneels in church below painted windows, and makes tremulous supplication to the Mother of God.

In our mixed world, full of green fields and happy lovers, where not long before, Joan of Arc had led one of the highest and noblest lives in the whole story of mankind, this was all worth chronicling that our poet could perceive. His eyes were indeed sealed with his own filth. He dwelt all his life in a pit more noisome than the dungeon at Méun. In the moral world, also, there are large phenomena not recognisable out of holes and corners. Loud winds blow, speeding home deep-laden ships and sweeping rubbish from the earth; the lightning leaps and cleans the face of heaven; high purposes and brave passions shake and sublimate men's spirits; and meanwhile, in the narrow dungeon of his soul, Villon is mumbling crusts and picking vermin.

Along with this deadly gloom of outlook, we must take another characteristic of his work: its unrivalled insincerity. I can give no better similitude of this quality than I have given already: that he comes up with a whine, and runs away with a whoop and his finger to his nose. His pathos is that of a professional mendicant who should happen to be a man of genius; his levity that of a bitter street arab, full of bread. On a first reading, the pathetic passages preoccupy the reader, and he is cheated out of an alms in the shape of sympathy. But when the thing is studied the illusion fades away: in the transitions, above all, we can detect the evil, ironical temper of the man; and instead of a flighty work, where many crude but genuine feelings tumble together for the mastery as in the lists of tournament, we are tempted to think of the *Large Testament* as of one long-drawn epical grimace, pulled by a merry-andrew,[1] who has found a certain despicable eminence over human respect and human affections by perching himself astride upon the gallows. Between these two views, at best, all temperate judgments will be found to fall; and rather, as I imagine, toward the last.

There were two things on which he felt with perfect and, in one case, even threatening sincerity.

The first of these was an undisguised envy of those richer than himself. He was forever drawing a parallel, already exemplified from his own words, between the happy life of the well-to-do and the miseries of the poor. Burns, too proud and honest not to work, continued through all reverses to sing of

---

[1] Nicholas Boileau-Despreaux (1636–1711), the leading critic of the classical age in France
[2] François Rabelais (1490?–1553), a great prose satirist   [3] Perhaps Albert Glatigny's *L'Illustre Brezacier* (1873).

[1] clown

poverty with a light, defiant note. Béranger[1] waited till he was himself beyond the reach of want, before writing the *Old Vagabond* or *Jacques*. Samuel Johnson, although he was very sorry to be poor, "was a great arguer for the advantages of poverty" in his ill days.[2] Thus it is that brave men carry their crosses, and smile with the fox burrowing in their vitals.[3] But Villon, who had not the courage to be poor with honesty, now whiningly implores our sympathy, now shows his teeth upon the dung-heap with an ugly snarl. He envies bitterly, envies passionately. Poverty, he protests, drives men to steal, as hunger makes the wolf sally from the forest. The poor, he goes on, will always have a carping word to say, or, if that outlet be denied, nourish rebellious thoughts. It is a calumny on the noble army of the poor. Thousands in a small way of life, ay, and even in the smallest go through life with tenfold as much honour and dignity and peace of mind, as the rich gluttons whose dainties and state-beds awakened Villon's covetous temper. And every morning's sun sees thousands who pass whistling to their toil. But Villon was the "mauvais pauvre":[4] defined by Victor Hugo, and, in its English expression, so admirably stereotyped by Dickens. He was the first wicked sans-culotte.[5] He is the man of genius with the mole-skin cap.[6] He is mighty pathetic and beseeching here in the street, but I would not go down a dark road with him for a large consideration.

The second of the points on which he was genuine and emphatic was common to the middle ages; a deep and somewhat snivelling conviction of the transitory nature of this life and the pity and horror of death. Old age and the grave, with some dark and yet half-sceptical terror of an after-world — these were ideas that clung about his bones like a disease. An old ape, as he says, may play all the tricks in its repertory, and none of them will tickle an audience into good humour. "Tousjours vieil synge est desplaisant."[7] It is not the old jester who receives most recognition at a tavern party, but the young fellow, fresh and handsome, who knows the new

slang, and carries off his vice with a certain air. Of this, as a tavern jester himself, he would be pointedly conscious. As for the women with whom he was best acquainted, his reflections on their old age, in all their harrowing pathos, shall remain in the original for me. Horace[1] has disgraced himself to something the same tune; but what Horace throws out with an ill-favoured laugh, Villon dwells on with an almost maudlin whimper.

It is in death that he finds his truest inspiration; in the swift and sorrowful change that overtakes beauty; in the strange revolution by which great fortunes and renowns are diminished to a handful of churchyard dust; and in the utter passing away of what was once lovable and mighty. It is in this that the mixed texture of his thought enables him to reach such poignant and terrible effects, and to enhance pity with ridicule, like a man cutting capers to a funeral march. It is in this, also, that he rises out of himself into the higher spheres of art. So, in the ballade by which he is best known, he rings the changes on names that once stood for beautiful and queenly women, and are now no more than letters and a legend. "Where are the snows of yester year?" runs the burden.[2] And so, in another not so famous, he passes in review the different degrees of bygone men, from the holy Apostles and the golden Emperor of the East, down to the heralds, pursuivants, and trumpeters, who also bore their part in the world's pageantries and ate greedily at great folks' tables: all this to the refrain of "So much carry the winds away!" Probably, there was some melancholy in his mind for a yet lower grade, and Montigny and Colin de Cayeux clattering their bones on Paris gibbet. Alas, and with so pitiful an experience of life, Villon can offer us nothing but terror and lamentation about death! No one has ever more skilfully communicated his own disenchantment; no one ever blown a more ear-piercing note of sadness. This unrepentant thief can attain neither to Christian confidence, nor to the spirit of the bright Greek saying, that whom the gods love die early. It is a poor heart, and a poorer age, that cannot accept the conditions of life with some heroic readiness.

*   *   *   *   *   *   *

---

[1] a famous French song-writer (1780–1857) [2] cf. p. 348 a, above [3] Like the Spartan boy in the well-known story. [4] vicious pauper [5] radical revolutionist [6] Such caps are common in the slums of London. [7] An old ape is always tiresome.

[1] the famous Roman satirist (65–8 B.C.) [2] cf. p. 629, above

The date of the *Large Testament* is the last date in the poet's biography. After having achieved that admirable and despicable performance, he disappears into the night from whence he came. How or when he died, whether decently in bed or trussed up to a gallows, remains a riddle for foolhardy commentators. It appears his health had suffered in the pit at Méun; he was thirty years of age and quite bald; with the notch in his under lip where Sermaise had struck him with the sword, and what wrinkles the reader may imagine. In default of portraits, this is all I have been able to piece together, and perhaps even the baldness should be taken as a figure of his destitution. A sinister dog, in all likelihood, but with a look in his eye, and the loose flexile mouth that goes with wit and an overweening sensual temperament. Certainly the sorriest figure on the rolls of fame.

NOTES[1]

INTRODUCTORY

That there is little literature in English that is of high quality between the Norman Conquest and the middle of the fourteenth century is not surprising if we remember the social conditions of the country. Scholars in England, as in the rest of Europe at that time, wrote and spoke and read Latin. Most books of learning, therefore, whether sacred or profane, — histories, scientific, philosophical, religious, and literary treatises, etc., — were written in Latin. The language of the upper classes was French. The French literature of the continent was accessible to them, and many of the most interesting literary works in Old French — romances, plays, legends of saints, religious songs, love songs, and political satires — were written in England by persons whose native language was French. This continued until the fourteenth century, when, as we learn from many evidences, the upper classes began to give up French; see the picturesque account of this given by Trevisa, p. 71 of this book. The history of literature in England is therefore in this period a very different thing from the history of English literature, and we cannot judge of the literary ability, tastes, or culture of Englishmen from 1066 to 1350 without taking into account what they read and wrote in Latin and French as well as in English.

During all this time the principal works written in English were such as were supposed to be of practical interest to those who could not read Latin or French: sermons, religious treatises, poems of sacred or secular history, didactic poems, and the like. Some works of entertainment were produced for those who understood English only, but as parchment was very expensive, few of

these were written down, the usual way of publishing them being to recite them.

Another fact must be taken into consideration in studying the literary culture of England in the Middle Ages. Only a small part of the writings which once existed have come down to us. A large portion of mediæval literature has perished by the ordinary decay and accidents natural to the passage of so long a time; but there have been also some special agencies of destruction. Chief among them was the disestablishment of the monasteries in England by Henry VIII. He did not, to be sure, order the destruction of the manuscripts; but no care was taken to preserve them, and many were destroyed by ignorant zealots, while many were wantonly used for the vilest purposes. What happened may be read in Dr. Gasquet's *Henry the VIII and the English Monasteries* or in John Bale's *Leyland's New Year's Gift to King Henry VIII*. Bale, who was a learned scholar of that time, says: " Never had we bene offended for the losse of our lybraryes, beynge so many in nombre, and in so desolate places for the more parte, yf the chiefe monumentes and most notable workes of our excellent wryters had bene reserved. . . . But to destroye all without consyderacyon is, and wyll be unto England for ever, a moste horryble infamy amonge the grave senyours of other nacyons. A greate nombre of them whych purchased those superstycyouse mansyons [*i.e.*, the monasteries] reserved of those lybrarye bokes . . . some to scoure theyr candel-styckes and some to rubbe their bootes. Some they solde to the grossers and sope sellers, and some they sent over see to the bokebynders, not in small nombre, but at times whole shyppes full, to the wonderynge of the foren nacyons. . . . I knowe a merchaunt man, whych shall at thys tyme be namelesse, that boughte the contentes of two noble lybraryes for xl shyllynges pryce, a shame it is to be spoken. This stuffe hathe he occupyed [*i.e.*, used] in the stede of graye paper [wrapping paper] by the space of more than X. yeares, and yet he hath store ynough for as many yeares to come."

---

[1] For convenience of reference, page numbers are given throughout. For the poetical selections, line numbers are also given; for the prose selections, *a* or *b* is added to the page number, when necessary, to indicate whether the passage discussed is in the first or the second column.

THE PRONUNCIATION OF MIDDLE ENGLISH

Even those students who do not try to read the original text of the Middle English selections should try to pronounce some parts of the poems, at least, in order to obtain a sense of the verse effects.

The pronunciation of Middle English changed considerably between the beginning and the end of the period and there were many differences between the different dialects at the same time. Besides this, we assume that as great differences existed then between different individuals as exist now in the pronunciation of Modern English. Therefore only very rough approximations to the actual sounds can be suggested; but such a conventional system will enable the reader to get some idea of the fuller tones of ancient English and to maintain in his reading a uniform and unbroken poetic feeling.

The following sounds are commonly given for Chaucer's English and may be used for Middle English in general:

VOWELS

long *a* as in *father*.
short *a* as in *Florida*.
long *e* (or *ee*, *ie*) as in *fête*, or *fate*.
short *e* as in *met*.
long *i* (or *y*) as in *machine*.
long *o* (or *oo*) as in *note; oo* is never pronounced like *oo* in *boot*.
short *o* as in *not*.
ou as *oo* in *boot*; but occasionally like *ō* + *oo*.
long *u* as French *u* or German *ü*.
short *u* the same, but short.
short *u* and short *o* also often have the sound of *u* in *full;* this is in words which have in modern English the vowel sound of *sun*, *son*, *but*, *wonder*, etc.; *u* is never pronounced like *u* in *but*.

DIPHTHONGS

ai, *ay* originally like *i* in *pine;* in Chaucer's time like *ē* + *i* or *ey* in *they*.
au, *aw* like *ou* in *house*, but occasionally like *au* in *fraud*.
ei, *ey* = *ē* + *i* or *ey* in *they*.
eu, *ew* = *ē* + *oo* with emphasis on the *ē*.
oi, *oy* as in *noise*, *boy*.

CONSONANTS

As in modern English, with the following exceptions:

ch always as in *such*.
f, when between vowels, like *v*.
gh like German *ch*.
r was trilled.

There were no silent letters. The *k* in *knoweth*, the *l* in *folk*, the *g* in *gnawe* were sounded. Unaccented final *e* was pronounced like *e* in German *Gabe* or *meine;* but in verse when followed by a word beginning with a vowel or a weak *h* (such as *his*, *hire*, *him*, *habbe*, *have*, *hadde*, *honour*, *hour*) it was not sounded at all.

A few additional letters which are used in the early texts will be noticed as they occur.

EARLY MIDDLE ENGLISH

THE ANGLO-SAXON CHRONICLE

Pages 1 f. *The Anglo-Saxon Chronicle* belongs for the most part, of course, to the history of English literature before the Norman Conquest; but the later records, especially those of the Peterborough version, from which our selection is taken, are of great importance for the study of modern English prose. The Chronicle seems to have been begun in the reign of Alfred the Great, perhaps in consequence of his efforts for the education of his people. It exists in six versions, differing more or less from one another both as to the events recorded and the period of time covered, but together forming, in a manner, a single work. The early entries, beginning with 60 B.C., were compiled from various sources and are, for the most part, very meager and uninteresting. Here are the complete records for two years: "An. DCCLXXII. Here (that is, in this year) Bishop Milred died." "An. DCCLXXIII. Here a red cross appeared in the sky after sunset; and in this year the Mercians and the men of Kent fought at Otford; and wondrous serpents were seen in the land of the South-Saxons." For long, weary stretches of years, there are, with the notable exception of the vivid account of the death of Cynewulf, few more exciting entries than these. Even when great events are recorded, there is no effort to tell how or why they occurred, no attempt to produce an interesting narrative. In the time of King Alfred, however, a change appears, and, though the records still have the character of annals rather than of history, the narrative is often very detailed and interesting, especially in regard to the long and fierce contest with the Danes.

After the Norman Conquest, one version of

the Chronicle, that kept by the monks of Peter-borough, contains entries of the greatest importance both for the history of the times and for the state of the English language then. The latest of these entries is for the year 1154, when the turbulent reign of the weak Stephen was followed by the strong and peaceful administration of Henry II. The selection we have chosen is from the entry for 1137, and gives a startling picture of the terrors of the time. But although the account is true, it would be a mistake to infer from it, as some have done, that civilization had perished in England. Not only were the monks of Peterborough at this very time rebuilding their beautiful monastery and other men erecting churches and cathedrals of wonderful beauty in other parts of England, it was in these very years that literature flourished with extraordinary vigor. The great stories of King Arthur and Merlin the Magician first appear in literature in King Stephen's reign. It may well give one a shock, at least of surprise, to learn that Geoffrey of Monmouth, who introduced these stories into literature, dedicated one of his books to the very Alexander, bishop of Lincoln, mentioned in l. 12 and the other to Robert earl of Gloucester, King Stephen's half-brother and bitterest enemy.

The most notable things about this passage, considered as English prose, are its simplicity and straightforwardness and its strong resemblance to modern English in sentence structure and word order. These features are probably to be accounted for by the fact that, though the writer doubtless understood Latin, he did not feel that he was producing literature, but only making a plain record of facts, and consequently did not attempt the clumsy artificialities so often produced by those who tried to imitate Latin prose in English.

Pronunciation. In addition to the usual symbols of sounds (see p. 678), the following require special attention in this section:

æ like long *e* in *there: gære*, p. 1, l. 1, *under-gæton*, l. 16, *wæron*, l. 21, *ævric*, l. 22, *agænes*, l. 23, *dæies*, p. 2, l. 1, *uuæren*, l. 4, *nævre*, l. 4, *hæved*, l. 10, *gæde*, l. 11, *hærnes* l. 11.

æ like short *a: æt*, p. 1, l. 10.

æ like long *a: ælle*, p. 1, l. 14.

au like *aw* in *saw: saule*, p. 1, l. 8.

eo = *ē* + *ō: eom*, p. 1, l. 4, *heolden*, l. 20, *heom*, p. 2, ll. 2, 6.

c and *cc* like *tch: micel*, p. 1, l. 6, *ævric*, l. 22, *rice*, l. 22; *uurecce*, l. 25, *wrecce*, p. 2, l. 17.

g like *y: gære*, p. 1, l. 1, *get* (pr. *yet*), l. 5, *gæde*, p. 2, l. 11.

i like *y: iafen* (pr. *yaven*), p. 1, l. 14.

sc like *sh: sculde*, p. 1, l. 3, *biscop*, l. 11.

u and *uu* like *w: suikes*, p. 1, l. 15, *suoren*, l. 19, *suencten*, l. 24, *suythe*, l. 25; *uuenden*, p. 1, l. 3, *uurecce*, l. 25, *uuaren*, l. 27, *uuæren*, p. 2, l. 4, *uurythen*, l. 10, *uuerse*, l. 19.

POEMA MORALE

Pp. 2 ff. This is the first important English poem after the Norman Conquest. It consists of a large number (about 400 lines) of moral and religious precepts embodying the author's philosophy of life, and was evidently written for the purpose of inculcating right living in all who read or heard it. As the short specimen given here shows, the questions of life, present and future, are treated in a spirit of selfish prudence, and the sentiment most frequently and powerfully appealed to is that of self-preservation. The spirit of the author is a sincere but hard and narrow Christianity, untouched by the tenderness of personal affection for Jesus or of concern for one's friends and fellow-men notable in the best work of Richard Rolle, Thomas de Hales, or even the dull but lovable Orrm. The author has, however, much skill in language and versification, and at times the vigor and vividness of his work is undeniable. The poem must have been very popular in its day, as all peoples in the early stages of development are fond of proverbial sayings and similar forms of practical wisdom. Several copies of it, made in various parts of England, have come down to us.

The verse is the seven-stressed line known as the septenarius, or septenary. The rhythm seems to me trochaic, or falling. The line naturally falls into two parts rhythmically: one of four stresses and one of three. The weak final *e* is always pronounced except before a vowel sound. Every line, therefore, ends in a weak syllable, and an extra syllable often occurs at the cæsura (*i.e.*, the metrical pause within the line). Many lines also have a weak syllable at the beginning before the first stress (see ll. 2, 3, 8, 10, etc.).

Pronunciation. The following require special notice:

a like *a* in *name: fale*, l. 10.

æ like long *e* in *there: wælde*, l. 2, *i-læd*, l. 5, *ær*, ll. 13, 17, *ærwe*, l. 19, *æie*, l. 20, *æch*, l. 27, *ævrich*, l. 32.

æ like short *a: æm*, l. 1, *scæl*, l. 21. *thænne*, l. 22,

ea like short *a: sceal*, ll. 26, 35.

ea like long *a* in *father: eald*, l. 4.

eo like short *o: eom*, l. 4, *weorde*, l. 3, *weorche*, l. 11.

eo like long *e* in *fête: i-beon*, ll. 3, 28, *beo*, ll. 4, 26, 28, *beoth*, l. 19, *i-seon*, l. 18, *seowen*, l. 22, *heovene*, l. 27, *seovene*, l. 28, *leovre*, l. 29, *freond*, l. 30.

u like *ü* or short *i: dude*, l. 2, *unnut*, l. 5, *a-gult*, l. 11, *buth*, l. 23, *for-yut*, l. 25, *uvele*, l. 26, *sulf*, ll. 29, 40, *sulfne*, l. 33, *wulleth*, l. 34, *wule*, l. 39.

h like German *ch: ah*, l. 2.

sc like *sh: scæl*, l. 21, *sculen*, l. 22, *sceal*, ll. 26, 35, *scolde*, l. 37.

sc like *s: sclawen*, l. 37.

ORRM

The Orrmulum

Pp. 4 f. *The Orrmulum* is interesting almost solely because the author was a theorist about English spelling. He devised a system of his own for representing the pronunciation as exactly as possible and carried it out with much skill and consistency throughout his long poem of 20,000 lines. As scholars are now greatly interested in learning how English was pronounced in early ages, Orrm's work is of the highest value. As literature, it hardly deserves consideration. It was not intended to be a poem in the modern sense. It was written in verse because verse then seemed the proper form for anything that aspired to be literature. The author merely wished to present to his countrymen an English version of the Gospels read in the services of the church throughout the year, accompanied by explanations which should make clear their whole meaning, figurative as well as literal.

It is perhaps the most tedious book in existence. This arises in large part from its excessive explicitness. Orrm is not content to express an idea simply and clearly once but must repeat it again and again; and in his anxiety that there shall be no mistake as to his meaning, instead of using pronouns to refer to matters already mentioned, he repeats at each recurrence of an object or an idea all that he has previously said about it. Although he was doubtless by nature a dull man, this peculiarity of his style seems intentional and due to his belief in the dulness of his readers; for the Dedication, addressed to his brother Walter, is free from this repetition and, though entirely lacking in charm, is simple and straightforward in style. His poem seems not to have been altogether unprovoked, for it was written at the request of his brother Walter; but there is no evidence that it met with any appreciation, for the single copy that has been preserved seems to be that written by the author himself. In spite of his dulness, however, the gentleness and amiability of Orrm and his real love of God and his fellowmen are manifest in all his work.

In his time the old system of spelling English was being abandoned, partly because the language had changed so greatly that the spelling no longer fitted the pronunciation, and partly because most of the copyists had been trained in spelling French and had difficulty in adapting the French system to English words. There must have been much discussion of spelling and more than one phonetic system was probably devised, but Orrm's is the only one of any individual character that has come down to us.

The verse of the Orrmulum is the septenarius, for the lines as printed are to be taken in pairs. It differs from the verse of the *Poema Morale* in having an iambic, or rising, rhythm and in being monotonously regular.

ll. 7–10. Orrm tells us that both he and his brother Walter were Augustinian canons, that is, members of an order whose function it was to read the services of the Church. One or both of them may have been attached to the Cathedral of Lincoln; at any rate, the language of Orrm points to that district.

Pronunciation. In the *Orrmulum* every vowel followed by a doubled consonant in the same syllable is short; all other vowels are long; thus the first vowel in *broþer*, l. 1, *flæshess*, l. 2, *lernenn*, l. 20, is long; both vowels in *aflterr*, l. 2, *Ennglissh*, l. 19, *wirrkenn*, l. 24, are short. In a few instances there is a mark of length or of shortness (see ll. 6, 7, 37, 44).

The symbol " þ " has the sound of *th* in *thin*, *thank*. The symbol " ȝ " may be pronounced like *y* in *yet*, but it should be made rougher and stronger than that sound.

LAYAMON

The Brut

Pp. 5 ff. Layamon, the author of *The Brut*, was a man of much greater ability than Orrm. His work is a versified chronicle or history of Britain from the destruction of Troy to 689 A.D. It is based mainly upon a similar French poem, the *Roman de Brut*, by Wace; but Layamon added much from oral traditions known to him, especially about King Arthur. The merits of the poem at its best are those of a lively and picturesque narrative, rapid, simple, and vigorous, with much of the spirit of the older English epic. The versification also, though not precisely that of the older epic, is thoroughly national. Rhyme occurs now and then, and may be due to French influence; but, as it is used, it gives rather the effect of the occasional rhymes in the later old English heroic poems, like the *Battle of Maldon*, and is probably a native development.

To us of the present day the most interesting parts of Layamon are those which deal with the story of King Lear, the coming of Hengist and Horsa, and, above all, the wars and death of King Arthur. *The Brut* contains about 30,000 lines and exists in two versions, one of about 1200 A.D., from which our selection is taken, and another of fifty years later, a sort of modernization made necessary by the rapid change of the language in those days.

Layamon's name is traditionally spelled with a *y*, but the sound originally was a voiced spirant guttural, more like *g* than *y*. Both *a*'s are sounded like *a* in *father*. As the voiced spirant guttural does not occur in modern English, the name may be pronounced either " La'-ga-mon " or " La'ya-mon."

Layamon was a priest who lived at Arley on the Severn, about 20 miles west and a little south of Birmingham. His dialect was therefore very different from that of Orrm.

The battle between Arthur and his traitorous son Modred is perhaps in modern times the most famous episode of Arthurian story. The exact location of this legendary battle cannot be determined. Layamon says it occurred in Cornwall at Camelford on the river *Tambre*. The river Tamar is still the boundary between Cornwall and Devonshire. A place called Camelford, identified with the Camelot of other forms of the Arthurian legend, still exists, but it is twenty miles from the river. It is, however, near Tintagel, which is famous in Arthurian story.

Uther (l. 28609) is Arthur's father, Uther Pendragon. *Argante* is not mentioned elsewhere. Some other versions of the story tell of three queens who received Arthur; Malory gives their names.

The story as told by Malory (p. 85) and by Tennyson (p. 528) should be read along with this.

Pronunciation. See the general notes on pronunciation and the special remarks on *Poema Morale*. Note further *sceort* (pr. *short*), l. 28624, *sceoven* (pr. *shŏven*), l. 28625; *habbeoth* (pr. *hăvĕth*), l. 28607; *sceone* (pr. *shaynè*), l. 28613, *eovste* (pr. *ayvstĕ*), l. 28629; *seothe* (pr. *sĭththĕ*), l. 28618; *wulle* (pr. *willĕ*), l. 28610, *wunne* (pr. *winnĕ*),

l. 28621, *Bruttes* (pr. *Brittes*), l. 28572, *Brutten* (pr. *Britten*), l. 28620; *uthen* (pr. to rhyme with Mod. Eng. *heathen*), l. 28625.

THE ANCREN RIWLE

P. 8. *The Ancren Riwle*, as its name indicates, is a treatise for the guidance and instruction of some nuns. We learn from the book itself that it was written, at their special request, for three young women of gentle birth, — " daughters of one father and one mother," who had forsaken the world for the life of religious contemplation and meditation.

There has been some discussion as to the author; he is thought by some to have been Richard Poore, or Le Poor, bishop successively of Chichester, Salisbury, and Durham, who was born at Tarrent, and whose heart was buried there after his death in 1237. But this view is probably incorrect, as the nunnery at Tarrent was a large one, while the women for whom this book was written lived alone. At any rate, the author was evidently a man in whom learning and no little knowledge of the world were combined with a singularly sweet simplicity, which has often been taken for naïveté. His learning appears abundantly in his familiarity with the writings of the great Church Fathers and the classical Latin authors who were known in his day; his knowledge of the world appears partly in his sagacious counsels as to the more serious temptations of a nun's life, and partly in his adaptation of courtly romantic motives to spiritual themes; while the sweet simplicity of his character is constantly and lovably revealed in the tone of all that he says — even in its sly and charming humor — and in his solicitude about infinite petty details, which are individually insignificant, to be sure, but mean much for the delicacy and peace of life. Of the eight parts or books into which the work is divided only two are devoted to external, material matters, the other six to the inner life; and this proportion is a true indication of the comparative values which the good counselor sets upon these things. The style, for all the learning displayed, is simple and direct, with few traces of Latin sentence structure or word order — a fact due perhaps to the nature and destination of the book no less than to the character of the author.

There are versions in French and Latin. The French seems to have been the original, and the English and Latin to have been translated from it. The impounding of stray cattle (l. 9) is still practised in many country towns and villages.

KING HORN

Pp. 9 ff. This is one of the earliest and best of the metrical romances — a kind of literature which then filled the place now occupied by the novel. Ancient romances, like early novels, usually begin at the beginning. In our first selection, this part of his subject has been treated with artistic brevity by the author and made essential to the story itself. The rest of the story tells how Horn and his companions were received by Ailmar, king of Westerness; how the king's daughter Rymenhild falls in love with Horn and woos him; how their love is betrayed by Fikenhild and Horn is banished; how, after seven years of adventure in Ireland, he returns just in time to rescue Rymenhild from a forced marriage, marries her himself, and immediately sets out for his own country, where he rescues his mother and avenges his father; how during this absence his old comrade Fikenhild seizes and carries off Rymenhild; and how Horn, with some of his followers, disguised as minstrels, enters the castle, kills the traitor and his men, and rewards his faithful followers.

Our second selection gives a part of the story of Rymenhild's wooing of Horn, whose royal descent is unknown to her. The return of Horn from Ireland is told in modified form in the ballad of *Hind Horn* (p. 83).

The narrative is full of incident, is well constructed, thoroughly motived, and told with rapidity and directness. The poem contains 1568 lines and, judging from the number of versions, was very popular.

My translation of this poem is very unsatisfactory. The original is in verses of three or four stresses; the lines of three stresses usually end in a weak syllable. It is very difficult, if not entirely impossible, to secure this effect in a long poem in modern English. In the case of this translation it could be done only by disregarding the matter and tone of the original and introducing ideas entirely alien to the simple and almost bald narrative. But I have tried to retain the 3- or 4-stress movement throughout. The poem was not intended for reading but for recitation to a musical accompaniment. If the reader will kindly recall the manner in which he used to recite in sing-song with strong stresses,

> Lit'-tle Tom'-my Tuck'-er
> Sang' for' his sup'-per,

he will get the movement of the original and will perhaps be able to produce a passable rhythm in the lines of the translation.

NICHOLAS DE GUILDFORD (?)
The Owl and the Nightingale

Pp. 14 ff. *The Owl and the Nightingale* is a work of very different character from any of the preceding. It is poetry in the modern sense of the term and deserves a very high rank when tested by the best standards of modern taste. The strife between the Owl and the Nightingale is in itself such a theme as existed by the hundred in mediæval literature. Strifes and debates, indeed, formed a special literary type, found in every language cultivated in Western Europe. There were strifes between Summer and Winter, between Youth and Age, between Water and Wine; debates as to whether a soldier or a scholar is the better lover, as to whether women are an evil or a good, as to any subject having, or seeming to have, two sides. Only a few of them rise to any considerable dignity or beauty or force. One, *The Debate between the Body and the Soul*, is among the most powerful religious poems of that age and is almost as impressive to-day as when it was first written, though some of its themes have since been worn threadbare. What especially distinguishes *The Owl and the Nightingale* is the astonishing dramatic sympathy of the author. The grief and indignation of the Owl at the failure of the world to recognize the beauty of his song are set forth with the same imaginative simplicity and candor as is the Nightingale's confidence in her own superiority. Such sympathetic imaginative power, such psychological subtlety, and such humor as are shown in this poem and in Chaucer are rare even in these days when machine-made sympathy and subtlety have been put within the reach of the least endowed. The author's name is unknown; it has been supposed to be Nicholas de Guildford, because towards the end of the poem the birds agree to leave the decision of the strife between them to Master Nicholas of Guildford, who is described as very skilful in music. But obviously Master Nicholas is more probably not the author, but some friend of his. The poem contains 1794 lines.

As King Alfred was famed for his wisdom it was natural that many proverbs should be ascribed to him. A collection of them (709 lines) is preserved from the beginning of the thirteenth century. Most of them are very good and some are picturesquely and even poetically expressed. They are published by Dr. R. Morris in *An Old English Miscellany* and reprinted in part, in Morris and Skeat's *Specimens of Early English*, Part I. This collection does not contain the proverb quoted in ll. 351–352, but there may have been other collections.

CURSOR MUNDI

Pp. 17 f. *Cursor Mundi* is a versified account of biblical history from the Creation to the time of Solomon and from the birth of the Virgin Mary to her Assumption, ending with the Final Judgment. In subject-matter and in the organization of it, *Cursor Mundi* resembles the great dramatic cycles of the Middle Ages; so much so, indeed, that it has been supposed to be the source of some of these plays. The poem is very long, about 25,000 lines, and seems to have been very widely read. The specimen given here exhibits its merits fairly and may serve to show us one of the most agreeable forms in which our ancestors received their knowledge of Bible history. The story here related is, of course, not from any of the canonical books of the Bible, but from the apocryphal gospel of Matthew.

THOMAS DE HALES
A LUVE RON

Pp. 19 f. Thomas de Hales was a Franciscan friar, known to us by an affectionate message to him in a letter from the famous Adam de Marisco. It is therefore probable that the date ascribed to his poem should be about 1250. It is certain that he lived before the order of friars had been corrupted by the intrusion of designing and unscrupulous men, and while it still retained the purity and enthusiasm of its great founder. Thomas was a man of great learning, but the sweetness and passionate simplicity of this little poem are not unworthy of the fine spirit of St. Francis himself. The subject of the poem and the circumstances of its composition as given in the first stanza, it may be noted, indicate the nearness of the friars to the people, — that familiar and homely interest in all the affairs of old and young which gave them their tremendous opportunities for good and for evil in the thirteenth and fourteenth centuries.

In the title of the poem, "Ron" (pronounced Rōōn) means a "charm or incantation"; it is derived from the name, *rūn*, given to ancient Teutonic letters, which were used in magic.

The poem contains 25 stanzas. Those omitted are as good as those given here, but they develop the same theme and contain few new ideas.

With stanzas 9 and 10 compare the *Ubi sunt* poem (p. 23) and the Latin college song *Ubi sunt qui ante nos In mundo fuere?*

Amadas and Idoyne (l. 67) were a pair of lovers almost as famous in the Middle Ages as Tristram and Iseult.

MIDDLE ENGLISH LYRICS

Pp. 21 ff. The three little *Lyrics* brought together here are among the best of the multitudinous lyrics of the age. Many of them have been preserved for us in manuscripts, many others are alluded to or quoted in snatches by chroniclers or writers of narrative poems, and many more must have perished entirely, either through loss of the manuscripts or because they were never written down. Enough remain to prove that the ancient fame of "Merrie England" for song was well deserved and to show that the poetical gifts of mediæval Englishmen are to be studied not in dull didactic poem or prosy rhymed chronicle, but in poems written in the spirit of free and joyous artistry. Better known than any of those given here is the charming *Cuckoo-song*, composed about 1250, of which the music as well as the words has come down to us. Of our selections the first and second are songs of springtime and love, and hardly require any comment, though it may be interesting to compare the second with the Earl of Surrey's treatment of the same theme on page 100. The third is an extract from a longer poem, but is a unit in itself and is one of the best lyrical expressions of a theme made famous to the Middle Ages by St. Bernard of Clairvaux and to all ages by François Villon (see Rossetti's translation of Villon's ballade, p. 629).

THE AGE OF CHAUCER
WILLIAM LANGLAND (?)
PIERS THE PLOWMAN

Pp. 24 ff. The poems which go under the name of Langland were, I think, the work of several distinct and very different men. One of these men wrote the Prologue and the first eight passus, or cantos, of the A-text (1800 lines) about 1362. The poem became very popular and was continued by another man who carried it on to about the middle of the twelfth passus and left it unfinished. A certain John But then finished it by a hasty and absurd account of the sudden death of the author. About 1377 another writer, equal to the first in picturesqueness of phrasing and vividness of detail, but deficient in power of consecutive thought and constructive ability, revised the whole poem composed by the first two writers, neglecting the passus containing the death of the author. His method of revision was to leave practically unchanged what he found written but to make numerous insertions, expanding suggestions of the original, and numerous additions, developing themes untouched by the earlier writers. The work as he left it is called the B-text. Fifteen or twenty years later a man of greater learning than any of the others and of a more orderly and systematic habit of mind than the author of the B-text, but of much less poetic ability — a pedant, in fact — revised the B-text, rearranging, inserting, and adding. The poem as he left it is called the C-text. The moral earnestness, the satirical power, the picturesque phrasing of the poem have long been recognized, but, until recently, when it was suggested that it was not all the work of one man, the poem was charged with vagueness, obscurity, formlessness. Now it appears that we ought to read and criticise the different parts separately; and if we do so, we find that the work of the first author (the first half of the A-text) is as clear as it is picturesque, that one need never be at a loss as to its meaning or the relation of its parts, and that its author was a man of remarkable constructive and organizing power. Confusion and uncertainty do not enter until his work has received the well-meant and powerful but inartistic insertions and additions of others. His work may be seen in the first selection. That of the writer of the B-text is seen at its very best, and free from its usual defects, in the second selection, which constitutes his first insertion in the poem as he found it.

As a whole, the series of poems is divided into two main sections: the first called the *Vision of William concerning Piers the Plowman;* and the second called *Do-well, Do-better, and Do-best.* Each section contains several visions. All are devoted to satire of the abuses reigning in all classes of society. The authors are not reformers in the sense of wishing to set forth new ideas or theories; they are conservatives, who hold that the evils of their time arise from neglect of the good ideals of the past, and who wish to restore the good conditions that existed in former times. Even the warnings addressed to the king betray no sense of conscious innovation. The figure of Piers the Plowman as the typical honest laborer — the only aspect in which he appears in the A-text — made a great impression upon the minds of the

discontented peasants and their leaders, and his name and those of Do-well, Do-better, and Do-best — which were emphasized later — became rallying cries for the Peasants' Revolt of 1381. In the sixteenth century *Piers the Plowman* was much read by the religious reformers and was regarded — like the works of Chaucer and Wiclif — as anti-Catholic. But the authors of the poems did not intend to attack the Church or Society, but only the abuses that had grown up in both.

The first selection (p. 24) presents a vision of "a field full of folk," representative of the world in general with its diversified interests and occupations. It will be observed that the author does not depict the world as altogether given over to evil practices, as is sometimes stated. He sees not only wasters but honest laborers, and not only lying and worthless palmers and pilgrims but also devout nuns and hermits, who observe the rules of religion and worship God sincerely.

The second selection (p. 28) is a fable, introduced into the Prologue abruptly and without motivation by the author of the B-text. As the whole thing is a dream, this may be artistically justified. At any rate, it is one of the most picturesque and effective pieces of writing in the whole group of poems. It is supposed to have been written in 1377 when the old king Edward III, who had fallen into the hands of evil and corrupt counsellors, was lying ill, and his successor to the throne was Richard, the eight-year old son of the Black Prince. The conservatism of the author is shown in the fact that although he shares the anger and disgust with which the Commons regard their once beloved and admired monarch, he fears the change that will come when the old cat dies and the kitten becomes ruler. It is possible, however, that the poem was written later, after the death of Edward, and that the "old cat" is John of Gaunt, Duke of Lancaster, who was in actual control of the government for several years.

The verse of both selections is the Old English alliterative verse, modified somewhat by the changes which the language had undergone since the Conquest. For several reasons, it seems probable that the use of this verse in the fourteenth century was due, not to a revival of the old form, but to a continuation of it throughout the centuries. It is very unlikely that there was any one in the fourteenth century who could read Old English (Anglo-Saxon) verse. Popular verse of this form may have existed in the north and west of England during the preceding centuries with very little chance of being committed to writing (see p. 677, above): the period of its reappearance in written literature is precisely that at which the upper classes were abandoning the use of French (see Trevisa, p. 71, above); and the differences between this alliterative verse and the older form are just such as might be expected if the verse had existed continuously, changing as the language changed.

The structure of this verse is simple. Each line is divided into two half-lines, each having two principal stresses. The half-lines are bound together by alliteration of the stressed syllables; that is, these syllables begin with similar sounds. In the standard line, both of the stressed syllables in the first half-line and the first stressed syllable in the second begin alike; but all sorts of variations from the standard occur.

SIR JOHN MANDEVILLE (?)

THE VOIAGE AND TRAVAILE OF SIR JOHN MAUNDEVILE, KT.

Pp. 30 ff. *The Voiage and Travaile of Sir John Maundevile, Kt.* is one of the greatest and most successful literary impostures ever perpetrated. It seems first to have been issued about 1371 in French, from which it was very soon translated into Latin, English, and many other languages. Its popularity was enormous, as is attested by the immense number of Mss. which have come down to us, and by the frequency with which it has been reprinted ever since 1475, the date of the first printed edition. Incredible as are many of the stories it contains, the apparent simplicity and candor of the author, his careful distinction between what he himself had seen and what he reported only on hearsay, his effort to avoid all exaggeration even in his most absurd statements, gained ready belief for his preposterous fabrications, and this was confirmed by the fact that some of the statements which at first seemed most incredible — such as the roundness of the earth — were actually true and were proved to be so by the discoveries of the fifteenth and sixteenth centuries.

The book was really compiled from many sources, principally the travels of William of Boldensele, a German traveler of the previous century, and Friar Odoric of Pordenone, an Italian who visited Asia in 1316–1320, the *Speculum Historiale* of Vincent of Beauvais, a great mediæval compilation of history and legend, and Pliny's *Natural History*, that great storehouse of the marvelous.

As to the identity of the author, he is now believed to have been one Jean de Bourgogne, an Englishman who fled from England after the execution of his lord, John baron de Mowbray, in 1322, but it is not certainly known whether Mandeville or Bourgogne was his real name. Two witnesses of the sixteenth century record having seen at Liège a tomb to the memory of Dominus Johannes de Mandeville, on which was an epitaph giving the date of his death as Nov. 17, 1371, and some verses declaring him to have been the English Ulysses. In any event, the book is one of the most fascinating books of marvels ever written, and the English version, although a translation, is of the highest importance for the history of English prose.

The story told in Chapter IV is the source of William Morris' fine poem, *The Lady of the Land* (pp. 634 ff.). Mandeville merely narrates the legend, Morris vizualizes the scene and all the occurrences, and transmits his vision to his readers.

JOHN WICLIF

THE GOSPEL OF MATHEW

Pp. 34 ff. Of John Wyclif no account is necessary here. Whatever may have been his own part in the translations of the Bible which go under his name, these translations are of great importance for the history of English prose style. The same selection (the fifth chapter of St. Matthew) has therefore been given from both the earlier and the later versions. The differences between them are very striking and instructive. In order to afford opportunity for further study of the gradual development of the matchless style of the Authorized Version of the English Bible, the same chapter is given from Tyndale's version (p. 96). Both the Authorized and the Revised versions are so easily accessible that it seems unnecessary to print the same chapter from them, but they should not be neglected in the comparison.

SYR GAWAYN AND THE GRENE KNYGHT

Pp. 37 ff. The author of *Syr Gawayn and the Grene Knyght* (p. 37) and *Pearl* (p. 46) — if these poems are really by the same author, as is usually supposed — was not merely a writer of great natural powers but a careful and conscious artist. It is supposed that *Gawayn* was written while the author was still occupied with worldly thoughts and interests and that *Pearl* and two (or three) other religious poems were composed after his conversion to a serious religious life; and this is a very reasonable supposition if the poems be the work of one man.

Gawayn belongs to the number of metrical romances dealing with the knights of the Round Table and their adventures, but in one important respect it is very different from most of them. They are, as a rule, the work of authors who had little qualification for their task beyond a certain ease in narration and versification and a retentive memory. The author of *Gawayn*, however, does not merely repeat a story which he has heard or read; he uses the materials of tradition as freely as Tennyson or Arnold or Swinburne or any other modern artist, and displays a power of construction, a skill in climax, a sense of pictorial effect, fairly comparable with theirs. All this can be seen in the brief episode here given, which has been chosen, not because it is better than many others, but because it is self-explanatory. The interest of the reader is maintained unflaggingly throughout the 2550 lines of the poem.

The situation presented in our extract is as follows: King Arthur, the greatest of the kings of Britain, with the knights and ladies of his court, is celebrating the Christmas season. It is New Year's Day and all have attended service in the royal chapel and are seated in the banquet hall, where all "dainties" are served in double portions. The others ate; but Arthur, who was young and somewhat "wild of mood," would never eat on such festival days until he had either witnessed some adventure or heard some wonderful tale. Suddenly there rode in at the hall-door a gigantic knight, clothed in green and riding a green horse. He had long green hair and a green beard as big as a bush. All the trappings of his horse were green, with gold ornaments. He wore no armor and carried no shield or spear. In his right hand he had a branch of holly and in his left a huge battle-axe. The axe was as keen as a razor; the shaft was bound with iron and wound with a green lace that ended in tassels, or buttons, of green. He saluted no one but looked about haughtily and cried: "Where is the head of this company? I wish to see him and speak with him." At this point our selection begins. It contains the whole account of the occurrences in Arthur's hall.

The rest of the poem tells of the adventures of Gawain in the fulfilment of his promise: his search for the Green Chapel, his entertainment at a great castle, where his loyalty is tested thrice, and his meeting with the Green Knight on the morning of the next New Year's Day at the mysterious chapel.

The story is clearly derived from a Celtic tale of the Other-world, and it possesses in no small degree that power of natural magic which Matthew Arnold noted as the most eminent characteristic of Celtic poetry. Three modern English versions of it are accessible, two by Miss Jessie L. Weston: a condensed prose version in *Arthurian Romances Unrepresented in Malory*, Vol. I; and one in verse in *Romance, Vision and Satire;* and another prose version by E. J. B. Kirtlan.

PEARL

Pp. 46 ff. *Pearl* (1212 lines), though entirely different in subject and tone and manner, is equally admirable. It seems to give the experience of a father who has lost a beloved little daughter, his "Pearl," and who, a few years later, falling asleep in his arbor, sees her in a vision, not as the helpless child he has lost, but as a radiant and beautiful young maiden, the Bride of the Lamb, and talks with her about the joys of her heavenly abode. Recently it has been argued with great learning and ingenuity that the poet is a cleric and can have had no child, that he is a man who, being interested in the theological doctrine of grace, not works, as the basis of rewards in heaven, attempted to illustrate and enforce the doctrine by an imaginary case of a baptized child dying in infancy and receiving in heaven rewards equal to those given to the greater saints. There can be no doubt that, whether cleric or not, the poet was deeply versed in theology and believed ardently in the doctrine of grace, but no sufficient reason has been adduced for refusing to recognize the genuine personal tone of the poet's grief and love. That the child was not his own is reasonably clear from his remark that she was nearer to him than aunt or niece (line 233), and from the absence of the terms father and daughter in their conversation. But many a man has loved with great devotion a child not his own; Swinburne's charming poems (see p. 643 and the whole series entitled *A Dark Month*, written when the beloved child was away on a visit) may serve as a notable instance. That the bereaved heart of a lonely man here found consolation in the new and blessed doctrine of grace seems more likely than that a mere theologian devised this beautiful poem as the framework for promulgating a favorite dogma.

The technique of the poem is extremely elaborate. The stanza-form is intricate and difficult, requiring as it does two rhymes on one sound, four on another, and six on another, and demanding alliteration as an additional ornament. Moreover, the stanzas are linked together by the repetition in the first line of each stanza of some phrase or word from the last line of the preceding stanza; and, finally, the stanzas are bound together in groups of five by the possession of a refrain which is carried, with slight variations, throughout the group. (By some oversight or error the fifteenth group contains six stanzas instead of five.)

As the poem is too long to be presented in full, we have given a few stanzas outlining the story and illustrating the writer's power. Modern versions of the whole have been published by Dr. S. Weir Mitchell, Miss Sophie Jewett, and Dr. G. H. Gerould.

JOHN GOWER

Confessio Amantis

Pp. 51 ff. Gower is not a great poet, but through being contrasted with Chaucer he has had less than his due of recognition. Mr. Lowell, one of the most genial of critics, sought to enhance his praise of Chaucer by setting him off against a dark background and playfully celebrating his contemporary and friend Gower as superhumanly dull. But Chaucer needs no such setting; we now know his age to have been one of extraordinary mental activity and poetical production, and he shines with undiminished brightness above all its light. And Gower, though no artist and undeniably monotonous, is not altogether lacking in power of swift narrative and picturesque description, as the story of Medea and Eson clearly proves.

The simple fact in regard to Gower would seem to be that, though no poet in the high sense of the term, he was one of the best educated and most learned men of his time and one of the most thoughtful and intelligent. His Latin poems on social and political affairs are vigorous, intelligent and original. He also wrote in French a volume of social criticism called *Le Miroir de l'Homme* (or, as it was called in Latin, *Speculum Meditantis*). But education and general intelligence do not make a man a poet; and Gower remained only a well-trained man of letters.

In the fifteenth century, when literary taste was not exacting and men cared rather for material than for art, Gower was ranked as high as Chaucer. Nowadays, when we have learned that the subject matter of story-tellers is universal and impersonal, we value only those writers who have art, and consequently we care little for Gower.

The story here told is based principally on Ovid's *Metamorphoses*, VII, 164–293. Gower, however,

tells the story freely; and ll. 4039–4114, which are in the main original, or at least not derived from Ovid, are by no means the least picturesque. There are some errors, but they seem due in large part to the fact that Gower had an incorrect manuscript of Ovid. Thus in l. 3994, *Crete* is due to the reading *Cretis* or *Creteis* instead of *Threces* (l. 223) in Ovid; *Eridian*, l. 4005, for *Apidanus* (l. 228), is doubtless also based on a corrupt form; as is likewise *the Rede See*, l. 4011 (cf. Ovid, l. 267: Et quas Oceani *refluum* mare lavit harenas).

GEOFFREY CHAUCER

Pp. 56 ff. Many of the writers of English verse before Chaucer were educated and well-trained men. They had studied logic, rhetoric, and grammar in the schools, they were familiar with good examples of Latin literature, and they set a high value on accuracy of versification and of rhyming, as their verses prove. Such loose composition, such careless rhymes, such impossible or irregular metres as we now see daily in the verses of ignorant versifiers are practically unknown in English verse before 1400. It is a great mistake to suppose that Chaucer or his predecessors were untrained men who wrote without reflection and without standards of composition. But although logical structure and rhetorical skill are elements in works of art, art requires also taste, imagination, creative ability; and comparatively few of the predecessors of Chaucer had great poetic powers.

Chaucer was not only a well-trained and skilful man of letters, but also a great poet. Both his creative faculty and his artistic ability, however, seem to have developed comparatively late. *The Book of the Duchess*, written when he was nearly thirty, is a pleasant and skilful piece of work, but it is imitative, conventional, and lacking in individuality; and so far as we know, he produced nothing better than this until several years later. This slowness of development may have been due in part to his being too fully occupied with his official duties in these early years to devote much time to composition or to reflection on the aims and methods of art. We know too little of the details of his life to be able to say exactly when he obtained more leisure or came into contact with the literary world which gave him a new conception of poetry, but apparently both of these events occurred when he was between thirty and forty years of age.

In 1373 and 1378 he was sent on official business to Italy. Whether he had any knowledge of the language or literature of Italy before his first visit to that country is uncertain. Certain it is that in some way, at some time, he acquired a knowledge of some of the works of Dante, Petrarch, and Boccaccio, the three great Italian writers with whom the great age of Italian literature began. All three of these men had a richer, finer conception of the meaning and value of literature and were more powerful as thinkers and more skilful as artists than the French poets who up to this time had been Chaucer's models. After becoming acquainted with these new and stimulating masterpieces, Chaucer, for a time, translated and imitated them; but the new poetic material with which they provided him was very far from constituting their chief value to him. He obviously began to reflect upon the differences between the old and the new, to consider questions of literary art — of narration, of description, of characterization, of background, of tone, of structure — with the result that he developed a thoroughly original manner of thinking and of writing, indebted, to be sure, to all his models, English, French, Latin and Italian, but none the less original, individual, thoroughly his own. The poems of his mature years are those upon which his fame rests.

TROILUS AND CRISEYDE

Pp. 56 ff. The story of Troilus and Cressida is one of the most famous love stories of literature. It does not appear in Homer's account of the siege of Troy but was developed by Boccaccio, an Italian writer of the fourteenth century, from slight hints in the *Roman de Troye*, by Benoît de Sainte-More, a French writer of the twelfth century, and the *Historia Troiana* of Guido delle Colonne, an Italian of the twelfth century who turned Benoît's French verse into Latin prose. Chaucer got the story from Boccaccio and greatly improved it by changing the characters of some of the actors and making the motives of action more psychological. Shakespeare derived the plot of his play *Troilus and Cressida* largely from Chaucer, but he introduced many changes of character and motive, and produced a cynical, unpleasant story very different from the piteous and beautiful tragedy told by Chaucer.

Our first selection (p. 56) describes the first meeting of Troilus and Criseyde and his sudden love for her, in spite of all the sport he had previously made of love and lovers. The second (p. 57) describes Criseyde's first sight of Troilus, after Pandarus — her uncle and Troilus' friend

and confidant — had awakened her interest by telling her how desperately Prince Troilus, the best of all the Trojan knights except his brother Hector, had fallen in love with her. The third (p. 58) tells briefly and pathetically how she forsook Troilus for Diomede, the Greek, after she had been compelled by her father to leave Troy and join him in the camp of the besieging army.

THE PROLOGUE TO THE CANTERBURY TALES

Pp. 59 ff. *The Canterbury Tales* are a collection of tales which Chaucer represents as told by a group of men and women who, having met by chance in an inn in Southwark, made a pilgrimage together to the shrine of St. Thomas at Canterbury. *The Prologue* tells when and how they met, and how, finding that they were all going to the same place, they agreed to go together and to enliven their journey by telling tales as they rode along. At his own suggestion, the innkeeper, Harry Bailey by name, agreed to accompany them and to act as presiding officer and as judge of the merits of the tales. The teller of the best tale was to have a supper at the expense of the rest upon their return, and any one who refused to obey the orders of the presiding officer was to pay for all that the company spent on the journey.

Chaucer tells us that there were twenty-nine, including himself and not counting the Host (or innkeeper). They came from various parts of England and represented almost every occupation and station in life. The upper classes were represented by the Knight and his son the Squire, who were attended by a servant, the Yeoman. The church, in accordance with the large part it played in mediæval life, was predominant, with nine representatives: the Prioress, and her companions, the Nun and the Priest; the Monk, the Friar, the Pardoner, the Summoner, the Parson, and the Clerk (who had not yet obtained a benefice and was still studying at Oxford). Of the learned professions there were two representatives: the Doctor and the Sergeant-at-Law. From the country there were the Franklin (a large landowner), the Reeve (a sort of overseer of a large estate in Norfolk), the Miller, and a poor Plowman. From the city of London there were, besides Chaucer, who had recently been Comptroller of Customs for the post of London, a Merchant (or wholesale exporter), five tradesmen, a Cook, and a Manciple (steward of one of the organizations of lawyers). From the west of England there was a Shipman of Dartmouth (master of a sailing vessel and a rather disreputable character, though a good sailor) and a buxom, red-cheeked widow from Bath, skilful in weaving cloth and fond of gadding about.

The intention at first was that each of these persons should tell four tales, two on the way to Canterbury and two on the way back; but Chaucer seems to have decided later that one each way would be enough; and as a matter of fact he did not write enough tales to go once around. There are actually only twenty-four tales, and of these one is a second tale told by Chaucer himself after he had been stopped in the middle of his first tale by the Host's declaration that it was too dull, and another is an account of the tricks of an Alchemist who had overtaken them on the journey, given by his servant after the Alchemist had fled in shame at the revelations of his swindling methods.

Chaucer also intended to tell how each tale led to the next and to report the conversations and discussions which arose. These bits between the tales are among the liveliest and most interesting parts of Chaucer's work; but as he did not write all the tales necessary, so also he did not fill in all the bits that should have come between. No part of the work, however, is more artistic than these and the descriptions of the pilgrims which Chaucer gives in the Prologue. They have never been surpassed in humor or in brilliance of characterization.

P. 59. l. 8. In l. 1 Chaucer tells us that April had already begun. During April the sun is in the sign Aries until the 11th and in Taurus the rest of the month. Line 8 therefore means that it is now after April 11th. In fact, we learn from a later passage that the pilgrims met on the evening of April 16th.

l. 17. Thomas a Becket, at one time Chancellor of Henry II, upon being made Archbishop of Canterbury resisted the efforts of Henry to deprive the church courts of some of the powers they had possessed. In the quarrel that ensued, four of Henry's knights rode to Canterbury and murdered Thomas in the Cathedral (in 1170). Although Henry had not ordered the murder, he was held responsible for it, and Thomas was worshipped as a saint. His tomb at Canterbury became the most famous shrine in England and for three hundred and fifty years was visited by pilgrims from all parts of the country, who brought gifts of gold and jewels in return for the saint's services to them. When the shrine was destroyed by Henry VIII, cart-loads of treasures were taken away.

ll. 48 ff. When the Knight was not fighting for his lord, he sought service elsewhere. His campaigns were all against the heathen and fall into three groups: one in the orient (Alisaundre, Lyeys, Satalye, Tramissene, Turkeye), one against the Moors (Algesir in Granada, and Belmarye in northern Africa), and one on the borders of Russia and Prussia (Ruce, Pruce, Lettow). His battles ranged in time from 1344 to the date of the pilgrimage (see l. 77). The Grand Master of the Knights of the Teutonic Order in Prussia was famous for his wisdom, his skill in war, and his courtesy.

P. 60. ll. 85–6. The expedition here referred to was doubtless that under Bishop Henry of Norwich in 1383.

l. 115. Compare the images which Louis XI wore in his hat, in *Quentin Durward*.

ll. 118 ff. The nunnery over which the Prioress presided was probably in the main a finishing school for young ladies of the upper classes. Hence her manners are those prescribed in the books of etiquette of the day.

l. 120. Most ladies of rank swore pretty vigorously in ancient times; cf. what Hotspur says to his wife in I *Henry IV*, III, i, 252–261, and Clarke's note on the strong oaths of Queen Elizabeth. *By Seint Loy* was a very mild oath, quite in keeping with the delicate manners of the Prioress.

ll. 124–6. The French of Stratford-atte-Bowe (a nunnery near London) was boarding-school French.

l. 146. Nuns were so fond of little dogs that it was necessary to prohibit them from bringing them into the church.

P. 61. l. 162. *Amor vincit omnia* (Love conquers all things) is not a very appropriate motto for a nun, unless "Love" is taken in a spiritual sense.

l. 164. *Prestes three* is probably wrong. Only one is mentioned elsewhere; three would make the number of pilgrims 31, instead of 29 (see l. 24), and it is strange that Chaucer does not here describe the Nun and the Priest, as he does the other pilgrims. Perhaps he left the passage incomplete, intending later to compose descriptions of these characters.

ll. 165 ff. Many monasteries of Benedictine monks had become very wealthy through the increase in value of the lands given them at their foundation and later. Consequently the heads and other officials often needed to be, and became, much engrossed in business and scarcely distinguishable in manners and ideas from nobles and other great landholders. An interesting account of all this is given in Carlyle's *Past and Present*. The rule of St. Benedict, the founder of the order (*Seint Beneit*, l. 173), was revised often; once by St. Maurus (l. 173), who lived some fifty years later and introduced the Benedictine order into France. The *Austin* of ll. 187-8 was probably that St. Augustine who in 596 brought Christianity from Rome to England; he was a Benedictine monk. He should not be confused with St. Augustine, Bishop of Hippo (fourth century), or with the founder of the Augustinian order of friars (see footnote on l. 210). The worldliness of the monks was supposed to be shown by their fondness for sports. *Pricking* (l. 191) means tracking a hare by its footprints.

ll. 208 ff. The orders of *friars* were established in the thirteenth century to carry religion among the common people, as the Salvation Army of our own day was, and the methods of work of the two organizations have a few points of resemblance. To prevent such worldliness as had grown up among the monks, it was ordered that neither the individual friar nor the house to which he belonged could hold property. They were to be like the disciples who went out to convert the world after the death of Christ. They did a great work, and became influential. Then ambitious men entered the order and used it to advance their personal interests, with the result that in Chaucer's day need was felt within the Church for reforming the worldliness of the friars.

P. 62. ll. 285 ff. In the Middle Ages education was the best means for an able man who lacked wealth and social influence to attain eminence and power. The Church afforded great opportunities for many, and many entered the service of the government or of powerful nobles. All educated men were called clerks, whether they went into the service of the Church or not. The Clerk of this poem is a type of the devout scholar; he was devoted to the Church and to the philosophy of Aristotle.

P. 63. ll. 331 ff. A franklin is a landholder of free, but not of noble birth. This *Franklin* was rich and hospitable, but not a man of education or culture.

ll. 388 ff. The *Shipman*, though an able sailor, was, like most of his craft at that time, rather disreputable — dishonest and little better than a pirate.

P. 67. ll. 725 ff. Chaucer's excuse for some of the improper stories he tells is one of the earliest bits of social or moral criticism of literature in English. It serves here two purposes: it carries on the literary device that this was a real pilgrimage; and it thereby enables Chaucer to shift responsibility for the improper tales from himself to the characters — who are of course in reality his own creations.

A Roundel

P. 69. This roundel is sung by the birds of Chaucer's *Parlement of Foules* (Assembly of Birds) just before they fly away with the mates they have chosen for the ensuing year. The roundel is an elaborate form of light verse (*vers de société*) which originated in France and was much cultivated in the Middle Ages. It and the other forms similar to it died out in the fifteenth century but were revived in the nineteenth. Compare the structure of this roundel with that of the three by Swinburne, p. 643.

Balade de Bon Conseyl

The balade is also a conventional form of verse with much the same history as the roundel. There should always be three stanzas (or a multiple of three) with the same rhymes in the same order, and each stanza should close with the same line, called the "refrain." Usually there is an additional stanza, called "l'envoi" (or "the envoy"), which contains an address to the person for whom it was written. Chaucer's balades have a different structure from those of most later writers; cf. Rossetti's translation of Villon's *Balade of Dead Ladies*, p. 629.

The Compleint of Chaucer to his Empty Purse

This is also in form a balade with an envoy. It was addressed to Henry IV a few days after his accession to the throne and was immediately successful in procuring a pension for the aged poet. How serious was Chaucer's need it is hard to say, in view of the humorous tone of his Complaint.

Note the three claims which Henry has to the throne, as expressed in ll. 22, 23.

A Treatise on the Astrolabe

P. 70. An astrolabe (or astrolabie) is a simple instrument for taking rough observations of the positions of the heavenly bodies. Chaucer, who was much interested in astronomy and astrology, compiled a treatise on the use of this instrument for little Louis, who had shown ability and interest in mathematics. The Prologue to this treatise is the only bit of prose we have from Chaucer except certain translations.

JOHN DE TREVISA

HIGDEN'S POLYCHRONICON

P. 71. About the middle of the fourteenth century, Ralph Higden, a monk of the city of Chester, wrote in Latin a history of the world, with special regard to England, entitled *Polychronicon*. Thirty-five or forty years later John de Trevisa, of Cornwall, wishing to make this book accessible to those who could not read Latin, translated it into English. He included comments and additions of his own and to them he prefixed his name.

The section here given is a brief extract from the remarks of Higden and Trevisa on the languages spoken in England. These remarks show that although there was no scientific study of languages in the fourteenth century, educated men thought about the linguistic situation and had very sensible ideas concerning it. Trevisa's statements in regard to the change that occurred about the end of the first half of the century are very important for the history of literature in English (see above, p. 677). The two reformers of teaching whom Trevisa mentions seem from their names to have been Cornishmen.

THE END OF THE MIDDLE AGES

HOCCLEVE AND LYDGATE

Pp. 72 ff. Hoccleve (p. 72) and Lydgate (p. 73) are of historical interest only. Each professed himself a follower and devoted pupil of Chaucer's, and there can be no doubt of their affection and admiration, but both singularly failed to reproduce any of his characteristic qualities. Neither seems to have understood his versification or to have had the ability to adapt it to the language of their time. Chaucer's verse, as everybody now knows, is as smooth and musical as the best verse of any age, if the final vowels which were pronounced in his speech are sounded in his verse. Hoccleve and Lydgate knew that final *e* was sometimes sounded, but in their own speech apparently sounded it much less often than Chaucer, and consequently, when they read his verse with their own pro-

nunciation, it sounded to them as rough and uncertain as their own.

There must have been very great and sudden changes in the pronunciation of English during Chaucer's lifetime, especially in regard to sounding final *e*. He and Gower apparently spoke and wrote the more conservative speech of the upper classes. The younger generation, to which Hoccleve and Lydgate belonged, apparently spoke very differently. This may have been due to the sudden rise in social position of a vast multitude of people in consequence of the general political and social movements of the age. Such people would naturally try to acquire the pronunciation of the new class into which they had risen, but because of the multitude of them their own earlier habits of speech could not fail to exercise some influence upon standard English.

But it is clear also that neither Hoccleve nor Lydgate was possessed of much intellectual fineness or artistic sensibility. Neither of them understood the spirit and aims of Chaucer's work. To them, and, sad to relate, to most men for a century to come, Chaucer's merits were not those of a great artist, a true poet, but merely those of a voluminous writer of interesting stories and songs. Doubtless they enjoyed his work more than they did Gower's, but he and Gower seemed to them to belong essentially to the same class of writers. It is not strange, therefore, that Hawes and Skelton and other writers of the age of Henry VII and Henry VIII praised Chaucer and Gower and Lydgate in the same breath and with the same note of praise. The matter was all they could understand or appreciate; and Gower and Lydgate had as much material as Chaucer, if not more. In our own day the sudden addition to the reading public of a multitude of readers of uncultivated minds and undeveloped taste has resulted in a somewhat similar state of affairs. The success of a book — that is, of one of "the best sellers" — depends not upon its artistic qualities or its power and beauty of thought, but solely upon its presentation of the sort of material liked by the general public. Now, as in the fifteenth century, it is not even necessary that the material should be novel; the public swallows with avidity to-day absolutely the same story that it swallowed yesterday, provided the names of the hero and the heroine are changed. A century or two hence critics will find it as hard to account for the great vogue of some of our popular novels as we find it to account for the failure of the men of the fifteenth century to distinguish Chaucer from Gower and Lydgate.

DE REGIMINE PRINCIPUM

Pp. 72 f. Hoccleve's *De Regimine Principum* is a treatise on the duties of princes, addressed to Prince Henry, Shakespeare's Prince Hal. It has a Prologue of 2016 lines, telling how he came to write the poem, and an Address to the Prince of 147 lines (ll. 2017–2163). The Prologue contains much information about Hoccleve's misspent youth and his poverty, and incidentally throws much light on the life of the time. For nearly twenty-four years, he tells us, he had been a writer in one of the government offices, that of the Privy Seal. Now his back is bent and he has pains in "every vein and place of his body" from so much writing; he is married and his income is only four pounds a year, besides an annuity of twenty marks (£13 6s. 8d.), which is hardly ever paid. An old and wise beggar, who professes to be able to help him, advises him to write a book and present it to the Prince in the hope of getting a more lucrative position. The dialogue between Hoccleve and the beggar, which forms the greater part of the Prologue, is very interesting, as has just been said.

Hoccleve's devotion to Chaucer cannot be doubted; he neglects no opportunity to praise him. The first of the three passages given in our selection (ll. 1961–1974) is from the Prologue; the second (ll. 2077–2107), from the Address to the Prince. In both cases Hoccleve is lamenting his own lack of skill as a writer, and this naturally suggests to him the mention of his beloved master, the "flower of eloquence." The third passage (ll. 4978–4998) occurs in the treatise itself, when the author has just urged Prince Henry not to hold councils on holy days. Lines 4992–4998 refer to the portrait of Chaucer which Hoccleve caused to be inserted in the Manuscript at this point. We are not told who the artist was, but the likeness was probably a good one. It is reproduced in many modern books: see especially Garnett and Gosse, *Engl. Lit.* (ill. ed.), Vol. I, p. 140 (in color); Skeat's *Oxford Chaucer*, Vol. I, front.; Green's *Short Hist. of the Engl. People*, Vol. I, p. 419; Saunders, *Chaucer's Canterbury Tales*, etc.

THE STORY OF THEBES

Pp. 73 f. In the Prologue to the *Story of Thebes* Lydgate represents himself as having made a pilgrimage alone to Canterbury in gratitude for his recovery from illness. Upon reaching the inn, he finds there all Chaucer's Canterbury pilgrims and is invited by the Host to join them and ride home with them the next day. He accepts the invitation, and the next morning, before they have gone a bow-shot from the city, the Host calls upon him for a tale. The story of the Siege of Thebes is the story he tells. As Lydgate was only thirty years old when Chaucer died, and as he gives his age as "nigh fifty" when he meets the Canterbury pilgrims, it is obvious that we have here, not the account of a real meeting, but merely a literary device to introduce his story.

The story itself is more than twice as long as the *Knight's Tale*. It is concerned with the strife between Eteocles and Polynices (Polymyte is the form in Lydgate), the sons of Œdipus and Jocasta, for the kingdom of Thebes — the subject of Æschylus' great tragedy, *The Seven against Thebes*; but Lydgate's poem is not derived from the Greek play, which of course was unknown to him, but from an Old French prose romance.

The situation in our selection is as follows: Tydeus, the friend of Polynices, has come to Thebes with a message to Eteocles from Polynices demanding that he fulfil his promise of giving up the kingdom to Polynices after reigning for one year. Eteocles has refused, and Tydeus, after declaring that God will punish him for his unfaithfulness, has left Thebes alone on his journey back to Polynices at Argos. He has scarcely left the palace when Eteocles, in furious wrath, orders his Chief Constable with fifty chosen knights to pursue him and slay him. They steal out secretly and lie in ambush for him, as our selection tells.

In l. 1165, *squar* seems irreconcilable with *round;* I presume that it either is a mistake for *swar* (heavy) or has, by confusion, taken on the meaning of that word.

THE BALLADS

Pp. 74 ff. The *Ballads* here given are specimens of a kind of literature which has attracted a great deal of attention and aroused a great deal of controversy in modern times. Composed during the Middle Ages for the common people, they attracted scarcely any attention from cultivated men and played little part in literature until the second half of the eighteenth century. Sir Philip Sidney knew and loved "the old song of Percy and Douglas," Shakespeare and some of the other dramatists quoted brief snatches of them in certain of their plays, and Addison devoted a critique in the *Spectator* to one of the best of them; but they had no general literary standing until some men of the eighteenth century, sick of the conventionalities and prettinesses of the poetry of their day, turned for relief to the rude vigor and simplicity of these old poems. The book most influential in this introduction of them to modern readers was Bishop Percy's *Reliques of Ancient English Poetry*, published in 1765.

But, although obscure until the time of the Romantic Movement, the ballads, as has been said, were composed centuries before that time. Even approximate dates of composition can be set for very few of them, for they were not written down but only preserved in memory and transmitted orally through the centuries, and consequently in most cases no certain conclusions as to their dates can be drawn from the forms of the language in which they are expressed. But we know that some of those that have come down to us belong to the fifteenth, the fourteenth, and even the thirteenth century. Perhaps the earliest of those printed here is *St. Stephen and Herod* (p. 84), one of the most remarkable for a vivid simplicity which no art could improve. This and *Sir Patrick Spens*, by some curious chance, have precisely the artistic qualities which we look for in the best modern verse; the excellences of some of the others, such as the *Battle of Otterburn* and *Captain Car*, though perhaps as great in their way, belong to an ideal of art entirely different from that of the modern individualistic, conscious artist.

Robin Hood and Guy of Gisborne

Pp. 74 ff. Between l. 8 and l. 9 a number of verses have been lost. Apparently they told that Robin had a dream in which he was bound and beaten by two yeomen, who also took away his bow. From the later development of the story we learn that these are the Sheriff of Nottingham and Sir Guy of Gisborne. It does not appear from anything in the ballad that Robin recognized his foes, but he has at least been warned that there are two of them and he vows vengeance upon them. The story is told in the vivid, disconnected way characteristic of ballads and much is left to the imagination of the hearer. Thus we are not told how Robin knows that Little John has been captured by the Sheriff. He goes to Barnesdale to see how his men are faring (st. 45); perhaps he sees Little John bound and recognizes him at a distance.

Ballads were sung (usually to the accompaniment of a fiddle or other stringed instrument); see the quotation from Sir Philip Sidney in the notes on *The Battle of Otterburn*. The tunes of

AE

many of them are given in Chappell's *Popular Music of the Olden Time*.

The Battle of Otterburn

Pp. 77 ff. The words of Sir Philip Sidney, who knew both good fighting and good poetry, have been quoted a hundred times, but must be quoted again: "Certainly I must confess my own barbarousness. I never heard the old song of Percy and Douglas that I found not my heart moved more than with a trumpet; and yet it is sung by some blind crowder (fiddler), with no rougher voice than rude style: which being so evil apparreled in the dust and cobwebs of that uncivil age, what would it work trimmed in the gorgeous eloquence of Pindar!" Sidney's praise is justified, whether he had in mind *The Hunting of the Cheviot* or the older poem, *The Battle of Otterburn*.

Both of these famous ballads are founded on an actual historical event, the battle of Otterburn, which was fought between the English and the Scots on Wednesday, August 19, 1388. A detailed and admiring account of the real battle was given by the French chronicler Froissart and may be read either in Johnes's translation, Vol. III, Chaps. 126–128, or in the older translation of Lord Berners, Globe ed., pp. 370–380. Neither of the ballads is accurate historically, and curiously enough each entirely neglects the picturesque motive which was the real occasion of the battle, that is, Percy's vow to recover his pennon, which Douglas had captured a few days earlier in a combat before Newcastle. As we are studying the ballad not as history but as poetry, we need not discuss the history or the geography, further than to note that events are thoroughly distorted to the advantage of the English. Douglas really had only 300 lancers and 2000 other soldiers; Percy had 600 lancers and 8000 foot soldiers. Both Percy and Douglas were young men. "The chivalrous trait in st. 17 and that in the characteristic passage stt. 36–44," says Professor Child, "are peculiar to this transcendently heroic ballad." On stt. 43 and 49, he remarks that archers really had no part in this fight.

Sir Patrick Spens

Pp. 80 f. Whether this tragic ballad had any historical event as its basis is unknown and unimportant. It is one of the finest examples of Scottish balladry; and if its suppressions of details be due to accident, this is one case in which the half of the story is, as Professor Child says, better than the whole.

CAPTAIN CAR, OR EDOM O GORDON

Pp. 81 f. The reason for the double title of this ballad is that in some versions the villain is not Captain Car but Edom o Gordon (that is, Adam of Gordon). There was, in fact, in Scotland in the days of Mary Queen of Scots an able and gallant soldier Adam Gordon, whose fame is said to have been destroyed by the infamous deed of his man, Captain Ker. He sent his soldiers under the leadership of Captain Ker to the castle of Towie, demanding the surrender of the castle in the queen's name. In the absence of her lord, the lady of the castle refused, and "the soldiers being impatient, by command of their leader, Captain Ker, fire was put to the house, wherein she and the number of twenty-seven persons were cruelly burnt to the death." According to another account, nearly contemporary, Gordon himself was the inhuman leader. At all events, whether for his own deed or for failing to punish Ker, he was denounced and execrated by his contemporaries.

Lines 5–8 are a chorus or refrain. The tune of this ballad is given in Chappell's *Popular Music of the Olden Time*, old ed., p. 226, new ed., I, 74.

P. 82. Stanza 20 is not in this version of the ballad, but it is traditional. John Hamelton, of st. 22, is a servant, as l. 90 indicates.

LORD RANDAL

P. 83. This is not an historical ballad. Its origin lies in folk lore. Stories and ballads on this theme are very ancient and almost worldwide in their distribution, and versions of the ballad itself are still sung in parts of the United States. The eels of st. 3 are of course snakes.

HIND HORN

Pp. 83 f. This ballad is not derived from the romance of King Horn (p. 9), but is a variant of the same story. The refrain, which is sung between the lines, is very different in the other versions of this ballad, of which there are many. Most refrains are, like this, entirely meaningless; one of the most interesting is a Scottish version:

Near Edinburgh was a young son born,
　　Hey lilelu an a how low lan
An his name it was called young Hyn Horn.
　　An it's hey down down deedle airo.

ST. STEPHEN AND HEROD

P. 84. This is of course a traditional distortion of the story of St. Stephen, for which there is no warrant in sacred or secular history. But a somewhat similar story is told of Judas in the apocryphal Gospel of Nicodemus and the incident of the crowing of the cock is found in tales in many languages The picturesque ignorance of the Bible involved in placing the stoning of Stephen on the day after the birth of Christ is characteristic of the common folk of the Middle Ages. All that they knew was that in the Church calendar St. Stephen's day is the next after Christmas.

l. 2. *befalle,* befits; subjunctive for indicative.

l. 3. *boris hed,* the Christmas dish of old England, brought into the hall in procession with the singing of carols.

SIR THOMAS MALORY

MORTE DARTHUR

Pp. 84 ff. The *Morte Darthur* of Sir Thomas Malory has long been famous, not only as the source of most of the modern poems about King Arthur and his Knights, but also as one of the most interesting books in any language. It has recently been shown by Professor Kittredge that Sir Thomas was not, as some have supposed, a priest, but, as the colophon of his book tells us, a soldier, with just such a career as one would wish for the compiler of such a volume. He was attached to the train of the famous Richard Beauchamp, Earl of Warwick, and perhaps was brought up in his service. As Professor Kittredge says, "No better school for the future author of the *Morte Darthur* can be imagined than a personal acquaintance with that Englishman whom all Europe recognized as embodying the knightly ideal of the age." The Emperor Sigismund, we are informed on excellent authority, said to Henry V, "that no prince Cristen for wisdom, norture, and manhode, hadde such another knyght as he had of therle Warrewyk; addyng thereto that if al curtesye were lost, yet myght hit be founde ageyn in hym; and so ever after by the emperours auctorite he was called the 'Fadre of Curteisy.'"

Sir Thomas derived his materials from old romances, principally in French, which he attempted to condense and reduce to order. His style, though it may have been affected to some extent by his originals, is essentially his own. Its most striking excellence is its diction, which is invariably picturesque and fresh, and this undoubtedly must be ascribed to him. The syntax, though sometimes faulty, has almost always a certain naïve charm. On the whole, regarding both matter and manner, one can hardly refuse assent to Caxton when he says, "But thystorye (*i.e.*, the history) of the sayd Arthur is so gloryous and shynyng, that he is stalled in the fyrst place of the moost noble, beste, and worthyest of the Cristen men." With this version of the death of King Arthur the student should read Layamon's version (p. 5) and Tennyson's (p. 528).

WILLIAM CAXTON

Preface to the Booke of Eneydos

P. 86. William Caxton, the first English printer, was born in Kent about 1422. After serving his apprenticeship in London with the merchant Robert Lange, who became Lord Mayor, he went to Bruges and so prospered that in 1462 he was Governor of the guild of English Merchant Adventurers there. In 1469 he seems to have given up his business and entered the service of the Duchess Margaret of Burgundy, sister of Edward IV of England. For her he began in that year a translation into English of a French prose romance called *Le Recueil des Histoires de Troyes*. So many of those who heard of this translation wished to have a copy of it that he learned the new art of printing in order to provide enough copies. He says in the Epilogue to the Third Book: "And for as moche as in the wryting of the same my penne is worn, myn hand wery and not stedfast, min eyen dimmed with over moche lokyng on the whit paper, and my corage not so prone and redy to laboure as hit hath ben, and that age crepeth on me dayly and febleth all the bodye; and also because I have promysid to dyverce gentilmen and to my frendes to address to hem as hastely as I myght this sayd book; therfor I have practysed and lerned at my grete charge and dispense to ordeyne this sayd book in prynte after the manner and forme as ye may here see; and is not wreton with penne and ynke as other bokes ben, to thende that every man may have them attones (at once); for all the bookes of this storye named the *Recule of the Historyes of Troyes*, thus enpryntid as ye here see, were begonne in oon day and also fynyshid in oon day."

Whether he learned printing in Cologne, where he finished his translation in September, 1471, or in Bruges, he began to print in Bruges in partnership with Colard Mansion and produced, besides the *Troy Book*, a translation called *The Game and Play of the Chess Moralized*. In 1476 he removed to London and set up a press in Westminster Abbey. Such was his diligence that he translated, before his death in 1491, twenty large folio volumes (4900 pages) and printed nearly one hundred volumes (over 18000 pages).

With the exception of his continuation of Higden's *Polychronicon* (see p. 71), his original writings are confined to the prefaces, epilogues, etc., which he supplied to several of his publications. These are very interesting, both for their intrinsic value and for the charming garrulity of his style. The passage here chosen is from his preface to his translation of a French version of the story of Æneas. What he tells us of his difficulty in determining what sort of English to use is a classic in the history of the language (compare the passage given above from Trevisa, p. 71). I have tried to make it easier to read by breaking up into shorter lengths his rambling statements, — they can hardly be called sentences, — but I somewhat fear that, in so doing, a part, at least, of their quaint charm may have been sacrificed.

STEPHEN HAWES

The Pastime of Pleasure

Pp. 86 f. The main stream of English poetry in the fifteenth century was in name and claim Chaucerian, but in reality it showed rather the influence of Lydgate. With the exception of the Scottish Chaucerians, not represented in this volume, the later men were insensible to those qualities of the master which make him significant not for the Middle Ages only but for all time. The literary forms and the style which attracted them and which they most frequently try to reproduce are those which Chaucer himself in the course of his marvelous artistic development outgrew and abandoned. They imitate *The Boke of the Duchesse*, *The Prologue to the Legende of Goode Women*, *The Parlement of Foules*, and above all the *Roman de la Rose* or the translation of it. Allegory is the chosen form, abstractions are the favorite personages; the ancient conventional machinery of spring mornings and grassy arbors and dreams and troups of men and fair women is used again and again, though all its parts have become loose and worn with use and age and creak audibly at every movement. To all this they add a pretentious diction that smells of schools and musty Latinity. The flowers that deck their fields are withered blossoms that they have picked up and painted and tied to the bare and lifeless stalks. Gaudy they are, but odorless, lifeless, and obviously painted.

This outworn tradition was preserved in the beginning of the new age by one man of some note, Stephen Hawes, who regarded himself as the only faithful votary of true poetry in his age. His most important poem is an elaborate allegory in the form of a romance of chivalry. The full title of it is significant: *The Pastime of Pleasure; or the History of Graunde Amour and La Bell Pucell; conteining the knowledge of the seven Sciences and the course of mans life in this worlde.* All this is set forth in a series of incidents in which the hero, Graunde Amour (Love of Knowledge) falls in love with and wins La Bell Pucell (the beautiful maiden, Knowledge). Our extract gives a fair idea of the method and merits of the poem. After the marriage, Graunde Amour lives happily with his bride for many years; then, summoned by Old Age and Death, he dies and is buried, his epitaph being written by Remembrance.

The use of chivalric romance as the form of the allegory is both a link with the world that was passing away and Hawes's sole original contribution to the development of poetry. Even in Chaucer's day the spirit which had informed and vitalized chivalry as a social system was giving way before the new methods of warfare and the rising powers of commerce and industry; but the system remained much longer and the ideals were cherished with an almost fanatic zeal by many lovers of ancient forms of beauty. Malory's *Morte Darthur* — an unallegorical presentation of chivalry — was published shortly before Hawes wrote. And nearly a century later, Edmund Spenser found no form so suitable for the embodiment of his allegory of the moral virtues as the persons and incidents of chivalric romance.

JOHN SKELTON

Pp. 87 f. Skelton was the bitterest satirist of his time. His learning, which was of the old type, was very considerable, and his fondness for displaying it is thoroughly characteristic. He wrote verses on all sorts of subjects, but it is as a satirist of Cardinal Wolsey that he is best remembered. The language used in these satires is vituperative and often obscene, and the ideas are sometimes expressed with such obscurity that we who are ignorant of the petty details of court intrigue in those days are unable to discover their meaning. A brief specimen of his satirical verse

at its cleanest and clearest is given in the short extract from *Colyn Cloute* (p. 88).

The Boke of Phyllyp Sparowe (p. 87) was written for a young girl, Jane Scroupe, whose pet sparrow had been killed by a cat. The poem contains 1267 lines, not counting the additions (of 115 lines) in which he defends himself for having written as he did. The first 844 lines are supposed to be spoken by Jane; they are largely in the form of a dirge, with sentences and words interspersed from the Latin service for the dead. Some devout persons took offence at this, but Skelton explains that he meant no harm.

THE NUTBROWNE MAIDE

Pp. 88 ff. This is curiously modern in versification, in language and in tone. One would like to know who was the author—to what class of society he belonged, what education and experience of life were his, and whether he ever wrote anything else. The existence of such isolated originality as is shown in this poem, in *The Owl and the Nightingale*, in some of the Early Tudor lyrics, and a few other ancient poems, makes one slow to believe that our remote ancestors were less capable of excellence in literature than we are, and confirms the view that the variation in the number of good writers in different periods is due, not so much to differences in intellectual equipment, as to variation in the interests that attract the attention of different periods.

The poem was intended for recitation as a dialogue. The object is to set forth the manner in which a loving woman would overcome all obstacles separating her from her lover. It may be held that the attitude expressed in ll. 151-156 is, after the mediæval fashion, somewhat exaggerated. Professor Skeat thought the author was a woman; but the last stanza, especially l. 177, seems against this view, and the whole conception of woman's love seems rather that of a man (cf. Mrs. Browning's *Man's Requirements*).

EARLY TUDOR LYRICS

Pp. 92 ff. That *Lyrics* were written in great numbers before the influence of Italy seriously affected English poetry in the sixteenth century is well known, but most historians of English literature entirely neglect these lyrics and speak as if England owed all her wealth of song in the age of Elizabeth to Italian influence. That there was much imitation of sonnet and madrigal and other Italian forms of lyric poetry is beyond question, but in many of the most charming of the lyrics of the latter part of the century one hears, I think, the same notes and discovers the same poetic method that had marked English lyrics at the beginning of the century and for ages before. Only a few specimens of these "native wood-notes wild" are given here, but they will serve to enforce what has just been said. One of them, it will be remarked, is curiously unlike the rest and curiously modern. In both tone and poetic method the love song:

Lully, lulley, lulley, lulley!
The fawcon hath born my make away! (p. 94)

smacks, not of the Middle Ages, but of that interesting nineteenth century imitation of mediævalism associated with the Pre-Raphaelite Movement.

CHRISTMAS CAROLS

P. 93. I, l. 36. Some such word as *to* or *for* seems needed for the metre before *the* (= thee).

II. The refrain seems to represent a playful conversation between the Mother and the Babe. The Mother says, "What are you seeking, O little son?" The Babe replies, "O sweetest Mother, kiss-kiss!" The question is repeated; and the Babe replies, "Give me the kisses of approval." I take *ba-ba* and *da-da* to be the only remarks really made by the Babe, the rest of his speeches being the Mother's interpretation of this babble. *Ba-ba* and *da-da* are treated as Latin imperatives, the latter being taken from the actual imperative of *do*, and the former, as my friends Professors Hale and Beeson suggest, being based on the obsolete English verb *ba* (meaning "kiss").

CONVIVIAL SONGS

P. 94. II. The exclamations in this song are mere convivial outcries, having probably no very definite meaning. Sir James Murray says, however, that "Tyrll on the bery" means "Pass round the wine."

THE BEGINNING OF THE RENAISSANCE

SIR THOMAS MORE

A DIALOGUE

Pp. 95 f. Sir Thomas More is one of the most striking and charming figures in the brilliant court of Henry VIII, and is known to all students of literature as the author of *Utopia*. Unfortunately for our purposes, that interesting book was written in Latin and, though soon translated into English, cannot represent to us the author's English style. I have chosen a selection from his *Dialogues* rather than from the *History of Richard III*, partly because the style seems to me more touched with the author's emotion, and partly because the passage presents the attitude of the writer on a question which may interest many modern readers. It is characteristic in its mixture of dignity, good sense, prejudice, enlightenment, spiritual earnestness, and playfulness of temper. The question of making the Bible accessible to the laity was one of the burning questions of the day. Sir Thomas argued that the Church had done all it was safe to do in this matter and that more harm than good would arise from going further. Tyndale and his fellows, a specimen of whose translation follows, thought differently.

WILLIAM TYNDALE

THE GOSPELL OF S. MATHEW

Pp. 96 f. Tyndale's translation of the New Testament (1525) was the first of many translations into English that appeared during the sixteenth century. It passed through two editions of 3000 copies each almost immediately, although it had to be printed abroad and distributed surreptitiously. The opposition of the English bishops to its circulation was bitter and effective, and as Henry VIII had not yet broken with the Roman Church, he did not come to the aid of Tyndale as he did to that of Coverdale ten years later.

Tyndale's translation is one of the most important monuments of the English language. As will readily be seen, the Authorized Version of 1611 is greatly indebted to it in diction and phraseology; and it has directly or indirectly affected the language of all later writers and speakers of English.

WYATT AND SURREY

Pp. 97 ff. Most of the lyrics of Sir Thomas Wyatt and the Earl of Surrey were first printed in a little volume entitled *Songes and Sonettes written by the right honourable Lorde Henry Howard, late Earle of Surrey, and other*, but commonly known, from the publisher's name, as *Tottel's Miscellany*. With this volume modern English literature is usually regarded as beginning; its significance is duly emphasized in all histories of English literature.

The contribution of Wyatt, Surrey, and their fellows is twofold; partly in introducing new forms of verse, and partly in developing themes which were either new or freshly conceived and expressed. The principal new forms were the sonnet, which was destined to become the standard form for the brief expression of serious thought in poetic mood, and blank verse, which was destined to become the standard form for drama and serious narrative poetry.

THE LOVER COMPLAINETH

P. 98. This poem appears to be original, as also is the next. Lines 6–8 mean "My song may pierce her heart as soon as a tool of lead can engrave in marble or a sound be heard where there is no ear to hear."

A DESCRIPTION, ETC.

l. 4. The *l* in *should* is pronounced and the word rhymes with *gold* (l. 6).

l. 7. The printed editions have *tried*, but *tied* (the reading of the Mss.) is obviously correct. The poet says that he might be tied to one object of love if she possessed the charms he enumerates, and good sense (*wit*) in addition.

DESCRIPTION AND PRAISE OF HIS LOVE

P. 100. This sonnet was addressed to Elizabeth Fitzgerald, daughter of the great Irish Earl of Kildare, who was brought to England and imprisoned by Henry VIII. After her father's execution in 1534, Elizabeth was attached to the household of the Princess Mary. A very romantic story grew up about the love of Surrey for the fair Geraldine, as she was called; but his love poems were probably mere literary exercises, as Elizabeth was only nine years old when this poem is supposed to have been written. The Fitzgeralds claimed to have come from *Florence* in *Tuscany* (ll. 1, 2); *Camber* (l. 4) is Wales; *Hunsdon* (l. 9) and *Hampton* (l. 11) were royal residences. Surrey was imprisoned at Windsor in 1537 for having struck a courtier, and this poem (because of l. 12) is usually ascribed to that date; but he was also imprisoned there in 1542, and, after all, the passage may mean that Geraldine was at Windsor and he elsewhere.

THE MEANS TO ATTAIN A HAPPY LIFE

The epigram on this subject by the Latin poet Martial addressed to himself (*Ad Seipsum*), has been a favorite for translation. Surrey's version is very graceful as well as nearly literal.

VIRGIL'S ÆNEID

This is important as the earliest blank verse written in England. Although lacking the flexibility later developed by Shakespeare, Milton, and others, this earliest attempt is far less stiff and monotonous than much blank verse that followed it. The translation keeps pretty close to the original, though it lacks distinction and perfection of phrasing.

In this passage Æneas begins to tell Dido the story of the destruction of Troy and his wanderings.

ll. 10–11. The soldiers mentioned were enemies of Æneas.

l. 55. *Kindled* means excited. The punishment of Laocoön, related by Virgil in this same book, has become famous in literature and in art.

ROGER ASCHAM

THE SCHOLEMASTER

Pp. 101 ff. Ascham is of special interest for two reasons: his reforms in the methods of teaching Latin and his services to English criticism. His ideas on education, presented fully in his *Scholemaster*, were singularly enlightened. He believed in making the study of Latin as easy as possible; he held that the value of the classics lay, not in their difficulty, but in the world of great ideas and great men which they made accessible; and he counseled humane and gentle methods of instruction and discipline. His ideas prevailed for a time, but were long forgotten or disregarded and had to be rediscovered by schoolmasters of the last quarter of the nineteenth century. Much of his criticism of literature we now regard as mistaken, particularly his advocacy of classical metres for English and his mixture of ethics with æsthetics in his judgments; but his ideas of English style were in the main sound, and he aided not a little in preventing the language from being overrun with ornate words of Latin origin.

In some matters he was very conservative. He believed that the replacement of the bow by the gun would cause the decay of manhood and he therefore wrote a book, *Toxophilus* (Lover of the Bow), to revive and promote archery in England.

JOHN FOXE

ACTS AND MONUMENTS

Pp. 103 ff. This book, more commonly called Foxe's *Book of Martyrs*, is the work of a violent partisan. It purports to describe "the great persecutions and horrible troubles that have been wrought and practised by the Romish prelates, especially in this realm of England, and Scotland, from the year of our Lord a thousand unto the time now present" (1563). Probably no book ever written is more uncritical and unjust, or has done so much to create among Protestants a wrong conception of Queen Mary and the Catholics of the sixteenth century. Catholics like Sir Thomas More and Bishop Fisher and numerous others, who suffered the same sorts of deaths as the Protestant martyrs, Foxe regards as wicked men who were justly and not too severely punished by righteous and gracious Henry VIII. Foxe's book — a huge folio originally, eight octavo volumes in the modern editions — is an unrelieved orgy of blood and bitterness, but it was much relished by our Protestant ancestors.

THOMAS SACKVILLE, LORD BUCKHURST

A MIRROR FOR MAGISTRATES

Pp. 105 ff. This is a tremendous collection (over 1400 pages) of tragic stories of wicked and unfortunate kings and nobles of Great Britain, from 1085 B.C. to the end of the fifteenth century after Christ. In character and aim it is mediæval; its editor says in his address to the nobility (*i.e.*, those called magistrates in the title): "Here, as in a looking-glass, you shall see, if any vice be in you, how the like hath been punished in other[s] heretofore." The plan was derived from such mediæval works as Chaucer's *Monk's Tale* and Lydgate's *Falls of Princes*. Nine editions, not counting reprints, were published between 1554 and 1610, and it contributed greatly to the development of historical poems and plays on British history. The author of the *Induction* was Thomas Sackville, one of the authors of *Gorboduc*, the first English tragedy, who later, as Lord Buckhurst, was an eminent statesman. The subject of the *Induction* is a vision in which the goddess Sorrow shows the author the enemies of mankind and the sad plight of their victims.

l. 210. *Averne*, lake Avernus, near Cumæ, through which Æneas entered the underworld. This description is based on the *Æneid*, VI, 237 ff.

l. 219 etc. *Remorse of Conscience, Dread, Revenge, Misery*, etc., are personifications of the mediæval type.

P. 106. l. 294. Wealth and poverty are here contrasted in *Cræsus*, the fabulously rich king, and *Irus*, the beggar described in the *Odyssey*, Bk. XVIII.

l. 299. *The Sisters*, the Fates who spin and cut the thread of man's fate (cf. Lycidas, 75–6).

l. 330. This recalls the riddle of the Sphinx:

There lives upon earth a being, two-footed, yea,
and with four feet,
Yea and with three feet too, yet his voice continues unchanging:
And lo! of all things that move in earth, in heaven
or in ocean,
He only changes his nature, and yet when on
most feet he walketh,
Then is the speed of his limbs most weak and
utterly powerless.

The solution given by Œpidus was as follows:

Man is it thou hast described, who, when on
earth he appeareth,
First as a babe from the womb, four-footed creeps
on his way;
Then when old age cometh on and the burden of
years weighs full heavy,
Bending his shoulders and neck, as a third foot
useth his staff.

Tr. by Plumptre, *The Tragedies of Sophocles*, p. 1, notes 2, 3.

THE RENAISSANCE

EDMUND SPENSER

THE SHEPHEARDS CALENDER

Pp. 108 ff. About 300 B.C., when the social life of Greek cities had become highly artificial and sophisticated, there arose, just as there has arisen in our own time, a feeling of satiety and weariness, and a fad of celebrating the charm and the virtues of rural life — a movement "back to nature." The most important literary result of this fad was the *Eclogues* of Theocritus, a native probably of Sicily, and a dweller in the courts of Syracuse and Alexandria. In these *Eclogues* Theocritus represents goatherds as discussing the interests and incidents of their simple life, such as the care of their flocks, their contests in song, their loves, their joys and their sorrows. Three centuries later, when Roman society was similarly sophisticated, the Latin poet Vergil wrote, in imitation of Theocritus, poems of a similar character, his *Eclogues*. With the revival of classical learning in the period of the Renaissance came imitations of all types of classical literature, and among them of the eclogue. This type of poetry, the pastoral, as it is called, passed naturally from a celebration of the simplicity and innocent sweetness of country life to a contrasting of it with the complicated, wearisome, vicious life of men in cities, and the pastoral became very early a medium of social, religious, and political satire. Under these conditions, naturally enough, the pastoral was often allegorical or symbolical. Feeding one's flocks meant really something else — governing a kingdom, or ruling a diocese, or presiding over a college; contests in song meant really contests in politics, or religion, or some other affair of the great world; and the characters, though bearing the names of shepherds, were understood to be statesmen, or bishops, or scholars, or poets.

Spenser was not the first Englishman to write pastoral poetry, but his *Shepheards Calender* was the first English pastoral of real beauty or power. It is a series of twelve poems, one for each month, in which shepherds are represented as keeping their flocks and engaging in discussions of matters that interest them. Some of these poems, "ægloges" he calls them, are undoubtedly allegorical. That for February has been thought to be in reality a controversy as to the old and new religious establishments.

The vogue of the pastoral conception and its conventions explains the form and tone of many lyrics of the Elizabethan age, as well as Milton's choice of the pastoral eclogue as the form for *Lycidas*.

The language of the *Shepheards Calender* is archaic. Spenser wished to give it a rustic tone, and he did so, not by imitating the language of the rustics of his own day, but by imitating the spelling of older English and using some old words. He had particularly in mind the works of Chaucer, which had already been published in several editions. As he did not know how to pronounce fourteenth century English, it is highly probable that he thought that in some of the metres of the *Shepheards Calender* he was writing Chaucerian verse.

P. 108. Ægloga is so spelled because Spenser thought the word meant goat-song. The word is properly *eclogue* and means a choice or a chosen song. *Phyllis* (l. 63) and *Tityrus* (l. 92) are names

from Vergil (and Theocritus); *Thenot* (l. 25) is from the French poet Marot.

l. 40. Making music by blowing in pipes made of the straws or stems of oats was conventionally one of the chief occupations of the shepherds in pastoral poems. In England *corn* never means maize, Indian corn, but simply grain.

P. 109. ll. 65–66. A gilt girdle embossed with glass beads (buegle or bugle) was an appropriate gift to win the love of Phyllis, the country maid.

l. 92. By *Tityrus* Spenser usually indicates Chaucer, but this tale of the Oak and the Briar is not from Chaucer.

l. 116. *Thelement:* the element *par excellence,* *i.e.*, the air, the other three elements being earth, water, and fire.

THE FAERIE QUEENE

Pp. 111 ff. Spenser's design in writing the *Faerie Queene* is best told in his own words in a letter to Sir Walter Raleigh:

"The generall end therefore of all the booke is to fashion a gentleman or noble person in vertuous and gentle discipline: Which for that I conceived shoulde be most plausible and pleasing, being coloured with an historicall fiction, the which the most part of men delight to read, rather for variety of matter than for profite of the ensample, I chose the historye of King Arthure, as most fitte for the excellency of his person, being made famous by many mens former workes, and also furthest from the daunger of envy, and suspition of present time. . . . I labour to pourtraict in Arthure, before he was king, the image of a brave knight, perfected in the twelve private morall vertues, as Aristotle hath devised; the which is the purpose of these first twelve bookes: which if I finde to be well accepted, I may be perhaps encoraged to frame the other part of polliticke vertues in his person, after that hee came to be king. . . . In that Faëry Queene I meane glory in my generall intention, but in my particular I conceive the most excellent and glorious person of our soveraine the Queene, and her kingdome in Faery Land. And yet, in some places els, I doe otherwise shadow her. For considering she beareth two persons, the one of a most royall Queene or Empresse, the other of a most vertuous and beautifull Lady, this latter part in some places I doe expresse in Belphoebe, fashioning her name according to your owne excellent conceipt of Cynthia, (Phœbe and Cynthia being both names of Diana). So in the person of Prince Arthure I sette forth magnificence in particular; which vertue, for that (according to

Aristotle and the rest) it is the perfection of all the rest, and conteineth in it them all, therefore in the whole course I mention the deedes of Arthure applyable to that vertue which I write of in that booke. But of the xii. other vertues I make xii. other knights the patrones [*i.e.*, patterns, models], for the more variety of the history: of which these three bookes contayn three. The first of the Knight of the Redcrosse, in whome I expresse holynes: The seconde of Sir Guyon, in whome I sette forth temperaunce: The third of Britomartis, a lady knight, in whome I picture chastity. . . .

"The beginning therefore of my history, if it were to be told by an Historiographer, should be the twelfth booke, which is the last; where I devise that the Faery Queene kept her Annuall feaste xii. dayes, uppon which xii. severall dayes, the occasions of the xii. severall adventures hapned, which being undertaken by xii. severall knights, are in these xii. books severally handled and discoursed. The first was this. In the beginning of the feast, there presented him selfe a tall clownishe younge man, who, falling before the Queen of Faries, desired a boone (as the manner then was) which during that feast she might not refuse: which was that hee might have the atchievement of any adventure, which during that feaste should happen: that being graunted, he rested him on the floore, unfitte through his rusticity for a better place. Soone after entred a faire Ladye in mourning weedes, riding on a white Asse, with a dwarfe behind her leading a warlike steed, that bore the Armes of a knight, and his speare in the dwarfes hand. Shee, falling before the Queene of Faeries, complayned that her father and mother, an ancient King and Queene, had bene by an huge dragon many yeers shut up in a brasen Castle, who thence suffred them not to yssew; and therefore besought the Faery Queene to assygne her some one of her knights to take on him that exployt. Presently that clownish person, upstarting, desired that adventure: whereat the Queene much wondering, and the Lady much gainesaying, yet he earnestly importuned his desire. In the end the lady told him, that unless that armour which she brought would serve him (that is, the armour of a Christian man specified by Saint Paul, vi. Ephes.), that he could not succeed in that enterprise: which being forthwith put upon him with dewe furnitures thereunto, he seemed the goodliest man in al that company, and was well liked of the Lady. And eftesoones taking on him knighthood, and mounting on that straunge Courser, he went forth with her on that adventure: where beginneth the first booke, viz.

"A gentle knight was pricking on the playne, &c."

Of this plan he completed scarcely more in proportion than did Chaucer of his original scheme for the *Canterbury Tales;* of the twenty-four books planned, six are complete and there are portions of two others.

To get some idea of the length of the projected work, note that a single book contains more than 43,000 words — is about half as long as a modern novel. Consequently, Spenser was undertaking the equivalent of a dozen novels in addition to reducing all his material to an elaborate and artificial metrical form.

Aside from its length, *The Faerie Queene* as planned was impracticable. Mediæval poems, such as the *Roman de la Rose* and the romances of the Grail Cycle, had indeed personified abstract qualities and allegorized situations and actions; but Spenser's outline called, first, for a much more elaborate display of the virtues and vices and their conflicts with one another, and, secondly, for historical interpretations also of characters and scenes involved in the romance. In the First Book he succeeds fairly well with the efforts of the Red Cross Knight to free the church from Error, Hypocrisy, and the great dragon, Sin; but as the poem advanced, the plots inevitably became entangled, the characters and situations inconsistent, and the allegory obscured.

Moreover, the structural weakness of the poem, as shown in Spenser's outline, involves an intolerable degree of suspense if the work is to be regarded as a continuous whole. If, however, each book is read separately with the emphasis on the romance rather than on the allegory, the poem can scarcely fail to give great pleasure, both by its continual appeal to the imagination, and by its wonderful verse movement and perfect adaptation of sound to sense.

The nine-line stanza used was invented by Spenser and is named for him Spenserian. It consists of the ten-syllabled eight-line stanza which had been in common use earlier, plus an alexandrine, or twelve-syllabled line rhyming with the eighth line. The rhyme-scheme is, then, ababbcbcc. The movement is full of dignity, but necessarily slow (cf. Pope's clever gibe at the Alexandrine in the *Essay on Criticism*, II, 356–357).

The key to the allegory in the passages quoted is:

Canto I

The Red Cross Knight (l. 1), holiness, Church of England.

Gloriana (l. 20), glory, Elizabeth.

Dragon (l. 27), sin.

The Lady (l. 28), Una, truth.

The ass (l. 29), humility.

The milkwhite lamb (l. 36), innocence.

The dwarf (l. 46), prudence.

The aged sire, Archimago (the chief magician, l. 384), hypocrisy; also Jesuitism.

Canto III

The lion (l. 38), strength of mind.

Stanzas VIII to XXVIII tell how Error and her brood are overcome by the knight; but he and the lady then fall into the clutches of Hypocrisy.

P. 113. Canto I, l. 313. *file his tongue*, polish it so that it would utter smooth words.

l. 317. *sad humor*, heavy vapor.

l. 328. In late classic writers, Proserpine, the wife of Pluto (Hades), came to be associated and even confused with Hecate, the goddess of magic (l. 381). Cf. Gayley's *Classic Myths*, pp. 83, 84.

l. 332. *Gorgon, i.e.*, Demogorgon. This name was first given to Pluto, seemingly, by a writer of the fifth century A.D. It appears in Boccaccio's *Genealogia Deorum*, which is supposed to be the source of Ariosto. Spenser probably got it from Ariosto, and Milton (*Paradise Lost*, II, 965) from Spenser.

l. 333. *Styx* and *Cocytus* are two of the rivers in the kingdom of the dead. There were two or (according to some authors) three others.

ll. 343–387. The visit of a messenger to the house of Morpheus occurs in Ovid's *Metamorphoses* (XI, 592–632), and has been borrowed and worked up by many later poets, Chaucer among them. Chaucer in his *Death of Blanche the Duchess* (ll. 160–165) has just the hint of Spenser's wonderful description of the cave of sleep in the lines:

"Save ther were a fewe welles
Came rennyng fro the cliffes a-doun,
That made a deedly, slepyng soun,
And ronnen doun right by a cave
That was under a rokke y-grave
Amidde the valey, wonder depe."

l. 348. *Tethys*, a Titaness, *i.e.*, one of the older race of gods, overthrown by Jupiter (cf. Keats's *Hyperion*). She was the wife of Oceanus, the ocean, another of the same line. *his* refers to Morpheus, whose bed was beneath the sea.

Epithalamion

Pp. 115 ff. The custom of writing a poem to celebrate a wedding and to be sung at the bride's house by a procession of youths and maidens is classical. Such poems were called *Epithalamia*, or hymeneal songs.

l. 1. *learned sisters*, the Muses, who are regularly invoked by poets. Cf. Gayley's *Classic Myths*.

l. 7. Probably an allusion to Spenser's *Tears of the Muses*.

l. 16. *Orpheus*, cf. Gayley's *Classic Myths*; also Milton's *L'Allegro*, ll. 145–150, *Lycidas*, ll. 58–63, and notes on these lines.

l. 25. *Hymen*, god of marriage, represented in art as a winged youth bearing a lighted torch and the nuptial veil. He was supposed to lead the wedding procession or masque (l. 26).

l. 43. Flowers of early summer. Spenser was married June 11, St. Barnabas Day, which was then (cf. ll. 265–272) the date of the summer solstice.

l. 44. *truelove wise*, with truelove knots.

l. 75. *Tithon's bed.* Aurora, goddess of the dawn, is fabled to have loved Tithonus and to have procured for him from the gods the gift of immortality. Unfortunately she neglected to ask that he should never grow old. Tennyson's fine poem *Tithonus* depicts the distress which came from this neglect.

l. 83. *concent*, harmony, from Latin *concentus*, a singing together.

P. 116. l. 95. *Hesperus*, the evening star, is here mentioned only for its brightness; but Spenser can hardly have failed to remember the line in the *Wedding of Peleus and Thetis* in which Catullus speaks of Hesperus as bringer of what the husband desires (l. 328). Tennyson in *Locksley Hall Sixty Years After* calls Hesper the "bringer home of all good things" (cf. ll. 185–194).

l. 98. *Hours*, "the goddesses of order in nature, who cause the seasons to change in their regular course, and all things to come into being, blossom, and ripen at the appointed time."

l. 103. The three Graces, as well as the Hours, attended on Venus. *Cyprian*, because she was supposed to have first landed on Cyprus after her birth in the sea.

l. 190. *Medusa* was a maiden who dared to vie in beauty with the goddess Minerva. As a punishment her hair was changed into serpents and her appearance became such that all who saw her — "read her mazeful head" — were turned into stone. Read Shelley's lines *On the Medusa of Leonardo da Vinci*:

"Yet it is less the horror than the grace
Which turns the gazer's spirit into stone."

P. 117. l. 269. *the Crab*, the zodiacal sign Cancer, the first sign after the summer solstice, in which the sun seems to crawl slowly backward from the high point it had reached.

l. 433. The meaning seems to be: "May you (the song), instead of lasting only a short time, as would the ornaments you have taken the place of, be an eternal memorial of my love."

AMORETTI

Pp. 117 f. The *Amoretti* and the *Epithalamion* were published together in a small volume in 1595; and as the *Epithalamion* celebrates Spenser's own marriage, it has been assumed that the *Amoretti* celebrate his courtship of his wife. Recently this assumption has been attacked, and the theory maintained that the *Amoretti*, like so many of the sonnet-cycles of the time, were a mere literary exercise of courtly compliment. This may be true; at any rate, it is unsafe to regard these sonnets as strictly autobiographical and to use them as they have been used in writing Spenser's life. Other Elizabethan sonnet-cycles quoted from in this volume are Sidney's *Astrophel and Stella*, Daniel's *Delia*, Drayton's *Idea*, and Shakespeare's *Sonnets*. For later cycles, see Mrs. Browning and D. G. Rossetti.

VIII, l. 5. *the blinded guest*, the god of love.

P. 118. XXIV, l. 10. *Helice*, the constellation of the Great Bear, by which Greek sailors steered their course (cf. note on *L'Allegro*, l. 80).

PROTHALAMION

Pp. 118 ff. The subtitle reads: *A Spousall Verse made by Edm. Spenser in Honour of the Double Marriage of the Two Honorable & Vertuous Ladies, the Ladie Elizabeth and the Ladie Katherine Somerset, Daughters to the Right Honourable the Earle of Worcester and espoused to the Two Worthie Gentlemen Master Henry Gilford, and Master William Peter, Esquyers.* The occasion seems to have been a real water fête to celebrate the *spousall*, i.e., formal betrothal, of the two daughters of the Earl of Worcester. The bridegrooms were Sir Henry Guildford and William, Lord Petre. That a distinction between *spousall* and *marriage* was made at that time is clear (cf., for example, *Faerie Queene* (I, x, 4, 7)): "Though spoused, yet wanting wedlocks solemnize." That this poem celebrates such a contracting is indicated by ll.

175–179, which become perfectly clear if "at th' appointed tide" refers to the spousal ceremony while "their bridal day" in the refrain refers forward to the wedding, which did not take place until November 8. It seems certain that the poem was written between the two events.

The names *Somerset* and *Devereux* are punned upon in ll. 67 and 153–154 (happy: Fr. *heureux*).

Perhaps Spenser hoped for some reward for this occasional poem. He says that he has been disappointed after a long stay at court (ll. 5–10), and we know from the dedication of the *Four Hymns* that he was at Greenwich in September, 1596. His allusions to the favors that he had received from Leicester (ll. 137–142), to his love of London (ll. 127–131), and his laudation of the Earl of Essex's fame (ll. 145–158) and personal beauty (ll. 163–165) strongly suggest that he used the occasion to solicit Essex's influence with the Queen to secure for him a place that would enable him to live in London. Perhaps he aimed at this result both directly through Essex and indirectly through the Earl of Worcester. But the Queen was disappointed at the results of Essex's expedition (ll. 147–152), and he was for a time out of her favor. In any case, the poem seems to have brought no result, as Spenser soon after returned to Ireland.

If the poem is to be read literally as describing a real pageant, the party of the brides set out upon the Lea River (ll. 37–38, 114–118), which empties into the Thames opposite Greenwich, where the court then was; and on the Thames, near the place where the poet stood (near Greenwich?), they were met by the "nymphs" (from the Court, then at Greenwich) with flowers and songs, and so passed up the Thames to the Temple (ll. 132–136) or to Essex House which stood by it (ll. 137, 163), where they were met by Essex and the bridegrooms.

Compare the regular metre with the refrain at the end of each stanza, and the less regular verse of the *Epithalamion*.

ll. 42–44. For the story of Jove's changing himself into a swan to win the love of Leda, cf. Gayley's *Classic Myths*.

l. 63. *Venus' silver team*, doves.

P. 119. ll. 78–80. This district of Greece was famed for its beauty, and the name *Tempe* was generalized to mean any beautiful valley (cf. Keats's Ode on a Grecian Urn, l. 7).

l. 121. *Cynthia*, the moon; a compliment to Elizabeth, as the Virgin Queen, was also implied.

P. 120. ll. 147–149. The conquest of Cadiz by the English. Essex led the expedition. The pillars of Hercules are the two promontories separated by the strait of Gibraltar.

SPENSER'S HYMNS

Pp. 120 ff. In 1596 Spenser published a little volume entitled *Foure Hymnes*. The first two have as their subjects Love and Beauty, respectively; the second two, Heavenly Love and Heavenly Beauty. All four were written under the influence of the poetico-philosophical ideas known as neo-platonism — a mixture of parts of the philosophy of Plato with elements drawn from oriental mysticism and from Christian doctrine. "The two original *Hymnes in Honour of Love* and *of Beaulie*, taken together, suggest," as Professor Fletcher says, "the ascent from sensual to intellectual love. . . . The two later Hymns purge away all suggestion of romantic love, and develop at length the four higher grades of the soul's reascent to God. Thus the *Foure Hymnes* really constitute one complete doctrinal poem."

Our selections are from the second and fourth of the hymns. The first selection sets forth the view that every earthly thing is made after a divine pattern and is beautiful just in proportion as it partakes of the nature and qualities of its pattern. It is the infusion of this celestial power which kindles beauty and love in all things beautiful; "for of the soul the body form doth take." A beautiful body therefore must be the residence of a beautiful soul. Yet the poet is forced to admit that sometimes, by some perversion of nature, a beautiful soul is found in an ugly body and a wicked, ugly soul in a beautiful body; this however he reconciles poetically, though not logically, with his theory. The *Cyprian Queen* (l. 55) is Venus as goddess of love and fruitfulness.

The second selection shows how by contemplation of the beauty and goodness of created things we rise to a vision of the beauty and goodness and love of God.

SIR PHILIP SIDNEY

Pp. 122 ff. "The miracle of our age," Sidney was called by an enthusiastic contemporary, but the quality of his work does not account for his extraordinary influence upon the writers of his own day. This is rather to be explained by his strong enthusiasms, generous patronage of literature, social rank, physical prowess, personal charm, romantic love affair, and tragic early death, which, taken all together, touched the popular imagination. Fully two hundred memorials were pub-

lished at the time of his death, and for a generation after, Arcadian romance and sonneteering were literary fashions, while several plays drew their plots from episodes of the Arcadia.

ASTROPHEL AND STELLA

Pp. 122 f. Although Watson's sonnets were the first published as a series (1582), Sidney's were circulating in manuscript among his friends at that time; and it was their publication in 1591 that seems to have given the great impulse to sonnet writing. The series was called *Astrophel and Stella* (Star-lover and Star). Stella was Lady Penelope Devereux, the Earl of Essex's sister, who in 1581 married Lord Rich. A marriage between her and Sidney had been partly arranged by their parents, and the earlier sonnets seem to have been largely literary exercises. Only when it was too late did Sidney awaken to his love for her, and the later sonnets are believed to reflect real passion.

I. l. 6. *inventions*, methods of treating a theme; but in ll. 9, 10 *Invention* is creative imagination.

XV. ll. 5–6. *dictionary's method . . . rimes*. Sidney refers to alliteration, by which words beginning with the same letter are associated as, he says contemptuously, they are in the dictionary. For the use of alliteration, see *Piers the Plowman;* for its use combined with rhyme, see *Pearl*.

ll. 7–8. Sidney means that the English sonneteers lack originality. They are still sighing over the woes that Petrarch long ago expressed in his sonnets, and their ideas (*wit*) are not their own but his, naturalized (*denizen'd*).

P. 123. XXXIX. Compare Daniel's sonnet, No. LIV, Fletcher's *Invocation to Sleep*, Wordsworth's and Keats's sonnets entitled *To Sleep*, and *Macbeth*, II, ii, 37–40.

XLI. l. 1. The occasion referred to is probably a tournament which was held in the spring of 1581, in honor of a French embassy (l. 4).

ll. 6–7. A more fastidious judge declares too slight such praise as good form permits him to give; that is, he finds speech inadequate.

l. 10. The Sidneys were knights and soldiers as early as the time of Henry II. On his mother's side, Sir Philip was descended from the Dukes of Northumberland.

THE NIGHTINGALE

According to classical legend, Tereus, King of Thrace, married Procne, daughter of Pandion, King of Athens, and by her had a son Itys, or

Itylus. After five years, at the request of his wife, he went to Athens to persuade her younger sister Philomela to visit her; but falling in love with Philomela, he, on the way to Thrace, ravished her, and cut out her tongue in order that she might not be able to betray him. She, however, wove pictures of her wrongs in a web of cloth and sent it to Procne. The two sisters then, for revenge, killed Itys and served him up to his father to eat. When Tereus learned what they had done, he tried to kill them; but the gods changed him into a hawk, Procne into a swallow, and Philomela into a nightingale, and the pursuit and attempt to slay still continues. The story is frequently alluded to by Elizabethan poets. They had studied it in school in Ovid's *Metamorphoses* (VI, 412–674). Compare the love song on p. 94, Lyly's *Spring's Welcome* (p. 128), and *As It Fell Upon a Day* (p. 162). For modern versions, see Matthew Arnold's *Philomela* (p. 616), and Swinburne's *Itylus* (p. 642).

The *tereu* (*Spring's Welcome*, l. 3) and *teru* (*As It Fell Upon a Day*, l. 14) come from a fancied resemblance between the vocative *Tereu* and the nightingale's song.

HYMN TO APOLLO

Apollo is addressed in his double character as the sun and as the god of intellectual endeavor, as appears in ll. 1–2.

l. 5. *Python's skin*. The Python was a serpent-monster slain by Apollo near Delphi, as is related in Ovid's *Metamorphoses*, I, 416–451.

l. 8. *Doth teach to learn the good what travails do belong, i.e.*, what labor is involved in learning the good.

ARCADIA

Pp. 124 ff. Sidney's *Arcadia* was written to amuse his sister Mary, Countess of Pembroke. He seems to have considered it — what it is — mere elaborate trifling, and on his deathbed he asked to have the manuscript burned. His sister, however, took charge of its publication in 1590. Its influence on Elizabethan prose was pronounced although perhaps not so great as was that of the sonnets on verse. It is too leisurely in movement and too complicated in structure to be well illustrated by a continuous selection, except as to its style, but the passage here presented seems better suited than any other of similar length to convey an idea of the nature of the story and the sources of its charm for Sidney's contemporaries.

On the Countess of Pembroke herself (cf. Browne's *Epitaph*, p. 177).

JOHN LYLY

Pp. 127 f. The selection from John Lyly's *Euphues and his England* may seem to some teachers shorter than is warranted by Lyly's reputation and his indubitable services to English prose. But the characteristics of his style are such as can be exhibited in comparatively small compass, and its excessive ornamentation soon becomes monotonous and unendurable. Moreover, it is not by its ornamental but by its structural features that it rendered its services to English prose, and the most significant of these, as Professor Morsbach has shown, is exact balance of accents in correlative phrases and clauses.

P. 128. Lyly's classical comedies, which delighted Elizabeth's court, were written for the boy actors of St. Paul's and the Savoy, and were played by them. Some scholars have thought that the exquisitely fanciful lyrics scattered through the plays were not written by Lyly; but the weight of evidence seems to me entirely against this view, and I have therefore presented them here, under Lyly's name.

SPRING'S WELCOME

ll. 1–4. Cf. Sidney's *The Nightingale* (p. 123) and notes on it.

ll. 6–8. Cf. Shakespeare's sonnet XXIX, 11–12 (p. 139), and the first song from *Cymbeline* (p. 145).

THOMAS LODGE

Pp. 129 ff. The subtitle of *Rosalynde* shows that Lodge was one of the immediate heirs to Lyly's affectations. *Rosalynde* is quite as artificial as *Euphues* and much more sentimental. Shakespeare borrowed the plot of *As You Like It* from Lodge's novel; but he made many important changes in structure and characterization, and the difference in atmosphere between the two works is as great as between a perfumed, lighted room and a forest glade in the sunshine. Compare this passage with Act III, Sc. ii, and Act IV, Sc. i, of the play. Read the madrigal from this romance published in *England's Helicon*, p. 164 of this volume.

P. 129 a. *like the Syren*. Cf. the passage from Chapman's *Odysseys*, pp. 145 f.

P. 129 b. *Œnone . . . Paris*. See Peele's charming song, p. 161.

Sonnet. Cf. *Sonetto* on p. 131. Note that neither is in the conventional sonnet form.

P. 130 *b*. *with Ixion embrace Juno.* Ixion was a king of the Lapithæ, who, for boasting that he had won the love of Juno, was bound forever to a revolving wheel in Tartarus, the place of punishment for the wicked.

flew to the fist. When the falconer whistles, the bird flies back and settles on his fist. So Ganimede, *i.e.*, Rosalynde, recognized in Rosader her master and showed her preference for him, even though he did not know her and had not sent any "call."

Phyllis . . . Ariadne. Chaucer tells both stories, and also that of *Dido*, in his *Legend of Good Women* (ll. 2394–2561, 1886–2227, and 924–1367). Cf. Gayley's *Classic Myths*. Phyllis hanged herself in despair of the return of her lover Demophoön and was changed into an almond tree. Lodge calls the tree *philbert* (*filbert, i.e.*, hazel), evidently thinking that the name is derived from *Phyllis*. Ariadne helped Theseus to slay the Minotaur in the labyrinth, and was afterwards forsaken by him.

ROBERT GREENE

Pp. 131 ff. Robert Greene had the reputation of being one of the most dissolute and disreputable men of his time. Strangely enough his plays and his novels are singularly free from immorality and coarseness, and his songs are not only sweet and clean but have an astonishing accent of innocence and simplicity.

A GROAT'S WORTH OF WIT BOUGHT WITH A MILLION OF REPENTANCE

Pp. 133 ff. Although this purports to be a deathbed confession and admonition by Greene, it is probably, as some of his friends declared when it was published (after his death), the work of Henry Chettle. Professor Vetter's arguments against Greene's authorship (*Abhandl. d. 44ten Sammlung d. d. Schulmänner*, Teubner, 1897) seem to me conclusive, and it would not be difficult to add to them.

The extract given, however, is interesting as showing a contemporary Puritan view of Greene, and as touching upon the lives of several of his famous companions.

P. 133 *a*. *Delphrigus*, etc. Allusions to characters in plays and to plays of the time not now identified.

P. 133 *b*. *thou famous gracer of tragedians*,

Marlowe, who, for the unconventional utterances in his plays, especially *Tamburlane*, was regarded as nothing less than an atheist. In point of fact, he was a kind of Unitarian.

P. 134 *a*. *Machiavellian policy.* To the Elizabethans Niccolo Machiavelli was the devil incarnate, and from his name is said to come the term Old Nick. In reality he merely set forth in his treatise *The Prince* the methods which successful rulers used and still use. He recognized their immorality and brutality as clearly as any one.

perished as ill as Julian, the Emperor Julian the Apostate, nephew of Constantine the Great, who because of ill-treatment by Christians in his youth abjured their religion. He died of a spear-thrust in battle. He was one of the stock examples of the punishment of atheists.

young Juvenal, Thomas Nash, the bitterest satirist of the age, who was repeatedly referred to by that name.

thou no less deserving, perhaps George Peele; certainly the description fits him.

P. 134 *b*. *an upstart Crow . . . Johannes fac totum* (= Jack-of-all-trades) *. . . Shake-scene*, undoubtedly Shakespeare. The *Tiger's heart*, etc., is a parody of 3 *Henry VI*, I, iv, 137.

buckram gentlemen, imitation gentlemen. Buckram was a coarse linen cloth (often stiffened with glue or gum). It seems to have been worn only by the lower classes (see Falstaff's account of the "rogues in buckram" who robbed him, 1 *Henry IV*, II, iv), and was used as a general term of contempt: "Thou say (*i.e.* silk), thou serge, nay, thou buckram lord!" 2 *Henry VI*, IV, vii, 27.

CHRISTOPHER MARLOWE

HERO AND LEANDER

Pp. 135 ff. This unfinished poem was Marlowe's last work. He seems to have written only two books and a fragment of the third. Seemingly at his request, his friend Chapman, the translator of Homer, finished the poem and published it in 1598, five years after Marlowe's death.

The story of *Hero and Leander* is taken from a Greek poem, attributed to a pre-Homeric legendary poet named Musæus (l. 52). No genuine writings of Musæus, however, are known. Marlowe's original was written by an unknown author, probably in the fifth or sixth century after Christ. Of this work, however, Marlowe used little more than the bare outlines; the imaginative fire and strong power of visualization that enter into his wonderful pageantry of pictures are as much his own as is the rich and musical verse. To appreciate its splendor, read with it the selection from *Venus and Adonis* (p. 137), in which even Shakespeare, writing, as he undoubtedly did on that occasion, in a commercial spirit, lags far behind.

The First Sestiad. Sestiad is derived from *Sestos* as *Iliad* from *Ilium;* hence, *Sestiad* means a poem about Sestos as *Iliad* a poem about Troy (Ilium). But the Elizabethans used both words in the plural for the whole work and in the singular for each book.

Marlowe's familiarity with the classics appears from many allusions, which may be studied in Gayley's *Classic Myths* or in the special references given below with each.

ll. 12–14. Adonis was a huntsman and scorned the goddess of love. The outcome of the story as told by Shakespeare follows on pp. 137 ff.

ll. 45–50. Hero was so lovely that Nature wept because she took more than half of the beauty of the world; and as a sign of her loss, since Hero's time, half the people of the world have been black.

ll. 56–58. Jason's quest for the Golden Fleece of Colchis and his flight with Medea, the king's daughter, are told in Ovid's *Metamorphoses*, VII, 1–452, *Heroides*, VI, and in William Morris's *Life and Death of Jason*.

l. 59. *Sphere.* See the note on Milton's astronomy, p. 717 below.

P. 136. l. 65. *the white of Pelops' shoulder*, ivory. Pelops was killed and served as a banquet to the gods by his father Tantalus; but was afterwards restored to life. The only part missing, his shoulder, was replaced by one of ivory (*Metamorphoses*, VI, 403–411).

ll. 73–76. Narcissus, who fell in love with his own reflection in a pool and pined away because he could not embrace it (*Metamorphoses*, III, 339–510).

l. 77. *wild Hippolytus*, son of the Amazon Antiope, served Artemis (Diana); and was untamed by love (Ovid, *Heroides*, IV).

ll. 81–82. Thrace was a mountainous country. In classical times mountaineers were called barbarians, as over against the more civilized inhabitants of cities.

ll. 101–102. Phaeton, son of Apollo, tried to drive his father's chariot; the horses ran away with him and almost destroyed the world by fire (*Metamorphoses*, II, 1–400).

l. 105. Cf. Chapman's *Odysseys*, p. 146.

ll. 114–115. *Ixion's shaggy-footed race.* Ixion was the father of the Centaurs, a race of beings

half-man and half-horse (*Metamorphoses*, XII, 210–535).

l. 137. *Proteus* was a sea god, a shape-shifter, who could assume any form he wished (cf. *Odyssey*, IV, 384 ff., and Vergil, *Georgics*, IV, 387–452).

l. 158. *turtles' blood.* It should be noted that in Elizabethan English *turtle* always means "dove"; it was not until nearly a century later that it was applied to the water-tortoise.

l. 161. Love has two arrows: one, with a golden head, which causes successful love; the other, with a leaden head, causes unreciprocated love; cf. *Midsummer Night's Dream*, I, i, 170.

WILLIAM SHAKESPEARE

VENUS AND ADONIS

Pp. 137 ff. *Venus and Adonis* was Shakespeare's first work to be printed (in 1593) and, in his own words, "the first heir of" his "invention." It was dedicated to the Earl of Southampton in extremely formal and respectful language. That it met with his approval is shown by the affectionate tone of the dedication to him in 1594 of *The Rape of Lucrece*.

Venus and Adonis became immediately popular and continued so. It went through about a dozen editions within the next fifty years. The story was taken from Ovid's *Metamorphoses* (X, 519–739, with details from IV, 271–388, and VIII, 267–371) — a book familiar to every one who went to school in Shakespeare's time — with not a little added (perhaps through an intermediary) from the Greek pastoral writers. Cf. Andrew Lang's *Theocritus, Bion and Moschus* (in the Golden Treasury Series), especially *The Lament for Adonis* by Bion and the fifteenth idyl of *Theocritus*.

A familiar love story, with the fashionable idyllic background, and handled with the utmost license, was sure to succeed even though it showed little originality and only moderate imaginative fire.

The verse form and some details are borrowed from Lodge's *Scillaes Metamorphosis* (also derived from Ovid), published in 1589.

P. 138. ll. 1109–1116. Cf. Theocritus, *The Dead Adonis*, in *Idyl XXX*.

SONNETS

P. 139 ff. The only edition of Shakespeare's sonnets in his lifetime was seemingly unauthorized. We do not know for whom they were written or whether they are now placed in the order in which he meant them to be read. Although the critics agree that Nos. I–CXXVI are, for the most part, addressed to a young man who was at once patron and friend, and CXXVII–CLIV to a dark lady with whom the poet was in love, this conclusion is based entirely upon internal evidence, and does not explain some features of the texts as they stand. No attempt to identify the persons mentioned has been universally accepted as convincing.

The sonnets are very unequal in value, ranging from the extravagant commonplaces of conventional Elizabethan flattery to serious reflections of personal experience and opinion. It is best to judge each on its own merits without regard to the series as a whole.

In form they belong to the loosely-knit English type of three distinct quatrains, with a summarizing couplet that often has a tacked-on effect. The best sonnet writers of the nineteenth century — see the examples given below of Wordsworth, Keats, the Rossettis, and Mrs. Browning — returned to the Italian model.

XII, l. 10. *thou among the wastes of time must go*, thou must take thy place among things injured by time.

XV, l. 4. The stars comment upon the unsubstantial forms and events of life by making or marring them through their secret influence.

ll. 11–12. Time discusses with Decay how to change your youth to age.

ll. 13–14. Warring with Time because of my love for you, I, in my verses, give you life as fast as he takes it.

XVII, l. 11. Cf. what Theseus says of "the lunatic, the lover and the poet," *Midsummer Night's Dream*, V, i, 2–17.

l. 12. *stretched metre*, exaggerated verse.

XXIX, ll. 10–12. Cf. Lyly's *Spring's Welcome*, ll. 6–8, p. 128, Shakespeare's first song from *Cymbeline*, l. 1, p. 145, and *Par. Lost*, V, 198.

P. 140. LV, l. 1 ff. The traditional idea, which goes back to Horace, that a poem, as poetry, will live forever, does not necessarily involve any personal conceit on the part of the poet.

l. 4. Than uncared-for gravestone stained by Time.

l. 13. Till the Judgment Day that bids you rise from the dead.

LXIV and LXV are closely connected, and should be read together. The first is pessimistic, and the second returns to the traditional poetic hope.

LXIV, l. 2. Elaborate, expensive, and ancient monuments.

l. 4. Possibly suggested by Horace's *monu-*

mentum ære perennius, "a monument more enduring than brass"; but here *eternal* modifies *slave*. *Mortal rage* means, simply, violence that destroys. Cf. CVII, ll. 13–14.

l. 8. Shakespeare regards land as the positive element (*store* = abundance), water as the negative (*loss*).

LXV, l. 2. *sad mortality*, destruction, not limited to human beings, but applied to everything that exists.

l. 3. *hold a plea*, contend successfully.

l. 4. *action*, vigor.

l. 10. Time is supposed to take things from this world and deposit them in the oblivion of his jewel-chest.

P. 141. LXXI. Cf. Christina Rossetti's *Remember*, p. 652.

LXXIII, ll. 1–4. This is a double metaphor: first of his own condition as that of the leafless boughs among which no birds now sing; then of the condition of those boughs as that of the choir of a ruined abbey. At the disestablishment of the monasteries by Henry VIII many were stripped and ruined and left to decay. These, as Steevens points out, would have been familiar and impressive sights to Shakespeare.

l. 12. The fire is consumed by the burning of the fuel which maintains it.

XCVII, l. 5. *time removed*, time of absence.

ll. 4–10. The autumn is represented as ready to bring forth the fruit begotten by the spring (*the prime*, l. 7), but as the spring is dead, the autumn is a widow, and consequently the fruit hoped for will, when it is brought forth, be orphaned.

XCVIII, l. 4. Saturn, the planet whose metal is lead, is supposed to govern heaviness and melancholy, and therefore stands here for all dull and low-spirited creatures.

XCIX. The first line is introductory; the sonnet is complete without it. It is made to fit the rhyme scheme of the first quatrain thus: *babab*.

l. 7. *i.e.*, have stolen its fragrance, but some editors think that color (dark auburn) is meant.

l. 13. *canker*, canker-worm.

P. 142. CVII. Massey explained this as a song of triumph at the death of Elizabeth and the deliverance of Shakespeare's friend, the Earl of Southampton, from imprisonment in the Tower. Elizabeth would be the eclipsed *mortal moon* of l. 5. This seems impossible on any hypothesis. The reason why the augurs are sad and mock their own prediction (l. 6) is certainly that the moon has passed through her eclipse and now shines clear again; this could not apply to the death of Elizabeth. Rolfe thinks the moon represents Elizabeth; her survival of the eclipse represents, he thinks, the suppression of the Rebellion of Essex (1601); he also quotes with apparent approval Palgrave's suggestion that "the peace, completed in 1609 might answer to the tone of this sonnet," though it does not appear why, if Shakespeare wrote as late as 1609, he should speak of an event of eight years earlier which had lost all interest.

But all such interpretations are excluded by the fact that the sonnet is a love sonnet, celebrating an ideal love or friendship. Such a love would not be affected by the imprisonment of either lover or beloved (cf. sonnet CXVI). The subject of the sonnet is some threatened and predicted estrangement between the friends which has now been removed. The eclipse and the endless peace are figurative expressions of aspects of the love story; the *balmy time* of l. 9 is of the same nature and has nothing to do with "the weather at the time he writes," as Rolfe seems to think. Lines 3, 4, mean "none of these things can set limits to the duration of my love (which was falsely supposed to be nearing its end), because it is true and endless."

CIX, ll. 7-8. Prompt to the time, not changed by absence; so that, coming back as I do, I bring my own excuse.

CX, ll. 2-4. I have played the fool, done violence to my own thoughts, sold cheap what I prize most, committed grave offences by entertaining new affections. Line 2 contains a figure which may come from the stage (though household fools also wore motley), but ll. 7-8, 11-12 show that Shakespeare is not talking about his stage career but about this temporary interest in new friends, which had only made him love the old friend better.

ll. 10-12. I will never again whet my sword on newer armor (*i.e.*, on a new friend) in order to test an older friend to whom I am bound.

CXI. This strongly personal sonnet is a protest against the deterioration in manners and character caused by the profession of acting (l. 4).

CXVI, ll. 2-4. Love is not love if it alters when the loved one alters, or turns away (bends to remove) as the loved one withdraws.

ll. 5-7. Cf. Spenser's *Amoretti*, XXIV.

P. 143. CXLVI. In this splendidly impersonal and virile sonnet, Shakespeare gets away from convention and expresses, in grim and powerful phrasing, a fundamental creed. The soul is the citadel of the body (*sinful earth*) warred upon by its own rebellious faculties. Why, as the body necessarily has so short a lease of life, should it

AE

be cultivated at the expense of the soul? Are worms to devour all that which you spend upon the body and which would feed your soul? Then starve your body and feed your soul. Acquire ages in heaven (*terms divine*) by selling worthless hours. So shall you cheat death.

SONGS FROM THE PLAYS

LOVE'S LABOUR'S LOST

P. 143. This is merely a *genre* picture of winter in the country.

l. 13. *crabs*, crabapples, which, floating in spiced ale, made the dish called "lambs' wool."

A MIDSUMMER NIGHT'S DREAM

This song is sung by a fairy.

l. 9. *pensioners*. An allusion to the splendor of the dress of the gentlemen pensioners of the Queen, of whom Elizabeth, following the custom of her father, had fifty in attendance upon her. They were chosen for their fine physique and good looks.

AS YOU LIKE IT

P. 144. The first of these songs is sung by Amiens in praise of the free life which the Duke and his followers lead in the greenwood. The second (also sung by him) recalls the ingratitude of those whom the Duke had loved and befriended.

HAMLET

P. 145. l. 3. *cockle hat*. The cockle shell was worn on the hat by pilgrims who had visited the shrine of St. James of Compostella in Spain. Lovers in the old romances, when forbidden to see their sweethearts, often disguised themselves as pilgrims to escape recognition.

THE TEMPEST

The Sea Dirge is sung by Ariel — the dainty invisible spirit commanded by Prospero — in the hearing of Prince Ferdinand, who supposes his father has been drowned in the storm that has thrown them on the island. Its beauty is undeniable; its lightness of tone and lack of any hint of grief are perhaps due, not only to the inability of such a spirit as Ariel to understand death, but also to the fact that the father has not been drowned but has been conveyed by Ariel himself to a place of safety.

The second song is also sung by Ariel and gives a hint of his nature and character.

GEORGE CHAPMAN

THE TWELFTH BOOK OF HOMER'S ODYSSEYS

Pp. 145 f. At the time when Chapman made his translations of the *Iliad* and the *Odyssey*, the study of Greek in England was still uncommon. Chapman's work is full of errors, but by its vigor and picturesqueness it has held its own until this day. It was greatly admired by Dryden, himself a good translator, and Dr. Johnson said that Pope constantly referred to it in making his version; but the same criticism that Bentley, the eighteenth century classical scholar, made of Pope holds, in a different way, of Chapman — "a very pretty poem but not Homer." Pope (cf. p. 290) is too abstract, too sophisticated, too regular, for Homer's simple concreteness and the big wave-movement of his hexameters. Chapman, on the other hand, although he is concrete, is not simple. His style is full of Elizabethan "conceits," highly compressed and unnatural figures of speech, as, for example, in describing the sirens' song in ll. 284–285:

"This they gave accent in the sweetest strain
That ever open'd an enamour'd vein."

In the simple translation of Butcher and Lang, this reads: "So spake they, uttering a sweet voice."

Chapman in his *Iliad* uses a fourteen-syllabled rhyming couplet which comes nearer to the big swing of the Greek hexameters than the ten-syllabled couplet used in the *Odyssey;* but the longer measure also gave him more opportunity to get away from the plain directness of the original. Keats's sonnet *On First Looking into Chapman's Homer*, p. 478, shows, however, how profoundly the range and sweep of Chapman's translation impressed one who loved and knew fine poetry.

The Odyssey is an account of the adventures of Ulysses (Greek, Odysseus) and his companions, and later of himself alone, in his efforts to return to his home in Ithaca after the destruction of Troy, and of the means by which he punished the suitors of his wife and regained possession of his kingdom. Our selection tells how he managed to hear the fatal song of the Syrens and yet to escape in safety. He himself tells the story.

SAMUEL DANIEL

Pp. 146 ff. Daniel's connection with the Sidney family — he was tutor to the Countess of Pembroke's son, William Herbert, who became the third earl — probably explains his early venture into sonneteering. An unauthorized edition of some of his *Delia* sonnets appeared in the appendix to *Astrophel and Stella*, and the following year, 1592, the series of fifty-five was published, dedicated to Sidney's sister.

Daniel's sonnets are all on conventional themes, but his conceptions have individuality and his verse has dignity, sonority, and a fine rhythmical movement. No. XIX may be contrasted with Shakespeare's No. XCIX; No. LIV with Sidney's No. XXXIX and the others on the same topic; No. LV recalls to mind several of Shakespeare's.

EPISTLE TO THE LADY MARGARET, COUNTESS OF CUMBERLAND

Pp. 147 f. Daniel was tutor from 1595 to 1599 to Lady Margaret's daughter, Lady Anne Clifford (born 1590). He fretted at having to "bide with children" when he wished to be trying lofty flights of verse, as Spenser, who thought highly of his work, had urged him to do.

This description of the state of a man strong in character and confident in his strength shows him at his best.

MICHAEL DRAYTON

Pp. 148 ff. Drayton tried his hand at most of the forms of verse popular in his day, and achieved more reputation than he has been able to maintain.

Many students of Shakespeare's sonnets believe that Drayton was the rival poet, "the proud full sail of [whose] great verse" Shakespeare mentions in sonnet LXXXVI. This belief is to some extent confirmed by a comparison of Drayton's sonnet XX with Shakespeare's CXXVII–CXLIV. Others think the rival poet to have been Chapman.

IDEA

XXXVII. Compare this with the sonnets on Sleep — Daniel's and others.

LXI. This is one of the most famous sonnets ever written; but it is admired probably as much for its appeal to common experience as for its beauty of expression.

Ode XII

To the Cambro-Britans and Their Harp, His Ballad of Agincourt

Pp. 149 f. *Cambro-Britans*, the Welsh, whose national instrument was the harp. For the circumstances and leading figures of the battle of Agincourt, see Shakespeare's *Henry V*, especially III, v–vii, and IV.

l. 41. *Poitiers* (1356) and *Cressy* (1346), in which Henry's great-grandfather, Edward III, won amazing victories over the French, might well inspirit his men at Agincourt (1415).

l. 48. *the French lilies.* The French coat of arms was three fleurs-de-lys, often called lilies.

P. 150. l. 113. *St. Crispin's Day.* October 25, the day of the twin saints, Crispinus and Crispinianus. See *Henry V*, IV, iii, 40–67.

Nymphidia

The Court of Fairy

Compare Shakespeare's description of Queen Mab, *Romeo and Juliet*, I, iv, 53–69, and of Titania and her court, *A Midsummer Night's Dream*, II and III, i, 147–181. The influence of Shakespeare appears from ll. 150–152; but Drayton has borrowed no details, and his form is entirely different.

FRANCIS BACON

Pp. 150 ff. Bacon's essays are characterized by extraordinary compression of thought and richness of illustration. In reading them, it is necessary often to pause between sentences and to expand the thought in order to grasp the full meaning. Again, like all other writers to whom Latin was almost as familiar as English (notably Sir Thomas Browne and Milton, in this book), he uses words derived from the Latin with a significance not commonly given to them at the present day. For example, *imposeth* (p. 151 a) means "impresses itself as authoritative." For this reason, it is necessary to study his vocabulary with great care. His range of quotation and anecdote is very great, as will be seen from the following notes. His practice was, indeed, to jot down in a note-book whatever struck him as of special interest in his thinking or his reading, and these notes, classified by subjects and arranged in proper order, furnished nearly the whole frame-work of his essays.

On whatever subject Bacon is writing, his ideas show the same mixture of observation and shrewd common sense. His ideals are all governed by considerations of practicability, and he is never carried off his feet by imagination or by any sort of enthusiasm.

I. Of Truth

P. 151 a. *masks and mummeries and triumphs.* The masques, disguisings, and other elaborate entertainments at court were usually given in the evening by artificial light.

vinum dæmonum. Many of the early Christians were opposed to Greek and Roman literature and especially poetry, not so much because it was fiction as because it celebrated the gods.

The quotation from Lucretius is in his poem *De rerum natura*, Bk. II, ll. 1 ff.; that from Montaigne in his *Essais*, ii, 18; the prediction at the end of this essay is from *Luke*, xviii : 8.

VIII. Of Marriage and Single Life

P. 152 a. In the *Odyssey*, Bk. V, the nymph Calypso offers Ulysses immortality and eternal youth if he will remain with her. He refuses and returns to his old wife Penelope.

P. 152 b. *A young man not yet.* The saying is ascribed to Thales, one of the Seven Wise Men of Greece.

XI. Of Great Place

Pp. 152 ff. Of the Latin quotations, the first is from a letter of Cicero's to his friend Marius; the second from Seneca's tragedy, *Thyestes*, 401–403; the third is Bacon's Latinization of *Genesis*, i : 31; the fourth and fifth from Tacitus's *Historiæ*, I, 49 and 50.

XVI. Of Atheism

Pp. 154 f. Of the Latin quotations, the first is from Diogenes Laertius, the Greek biographer of philosophers (X, 123); the second from a sermon by St. Bernard of Clairvaux; the last from one of Cicero's *Orations*.

P. 154 a. *The Legend* is doubtless *The Golden Legend* (*Legenda Aurea*), a collection of Legends of the saints made by Jacobus de Voragine in the thirteenth century; the *Talmud* is a vast collection of stories, decisions, and sayings of Jewish Rabbis; the *Alcoran* (or *Koran*) is the sacred book of the Mohammedans.

Leucippus, *Democritus*, and *Epicurus* were Greek

philosophers who developed the atomic theory of matter. The *four mutable elements* are earth, air, fire, and water, of which, in Bacon's day, all things were supposed to be made. The *immutable fifth essence* (quintessence) was supposed to be an ethereal substance necessary to the existence of things and in a sense the soul of them. The theory which Bacon rejects is, in a modified form, that now dominant in science.

P. 154 *b*. *Diagoras* and *Bion* were Greek philosophers of the fifth and third centuries B.C.; *Lucian* was a Greek humorist and satirist (120?–200? A.D.).

XXIII. Of Wisdom for a Man's Self

P. 155 *b*. The setting of a house on fire to roast an egg may have suggested to Charles Lamb his amusing *Dissertation upon Roast Pig*.

P. 156 *a*. The deceitful weeping of the crocodile, reported by early travellers and naturalists, became proverbial in Shakespeare's day; cf. *2 Henry VI*, III, i, 226.

Sui amantes sine rivali is loosely quoted from a letter of Cicero to his brother Quintus (III, 8, 4).

XXVII. Of Friendship

The sentiment quoted in the first sentence is a modification of a statement by Aristotle: "He who is unable to live in society, or who has no need because he is sufficient for himself, must be either a beast or a god" (*The Politics of Aristotle*, translated by Jowett, I, i, 2).

falsely and feignedly. Bacon means that the stories told of them were not true. Epimenides was a Cretan Rip Van Winkle, who slept fifty years in a cave and came back with superhuman knowledge. Numa Pompilius, the second mythical king of Rome, retired into solitude to learn wisdom from the nymph Egeria. Empedocles threw himself into the crater of Ætna in order to seem to disappear like a god, instead of dying like a mortal. Apollonius of Tyana was an ascetic who was worshipped as a rival of Christ.

Pp. 157 *b*ff. The stories of *Pompey*, *Cæsar*, and *Themistocles* are told by Plutarch in his lives of those men, and *the parable of Pythagoras* (p. 157 *b*) is also reported by Plutarch (in a *Discourse on the Training of Children*); the anecdotes of the Roman emperors are recorded by Suetonius (in his *Lives of the Cæsars*) and Dion Cassius (in his *Roman History*). The famous maxim of *Heraclitus* (p. 158 *a*) is recorded by Diogenes Laertius.

XLII. Of Youth and Age

P. 159. The first quotation is from the life of Severus in the collection of biographies of the Roman emperors known as the *Augustan History;* the second (English) is from *Joel*, ii: 28; the third is from Cicero's *Brutus;* and the last is a paraphrase of a sentence of Livy's *History of Rome*.

Cosmus Duke of Florence (1519–1574), better known as Cosmo the Great, belonged to the family of the Medici, famous for their wealth, their political power, and their patronage of literature and art. Gaston de Fois (or Foix), Duc de Nemours (1489–1512), was a brilliant young general; after a great victory at Ravenna, in 1512, he was killed while pursuing the enemy.

MINOR POETRY

Song of Paris and Œnone

P. 161. Elizabethan lyrics are of two kinds. One is the formal, elaborate sonnet, not set to music, sometimes a mere tissue of conventional sentiments expressed in highly artificial terms, but often built around a striking thought. The other is the song, — madrigal, canzone, round, roundelay, etc., — which shows extreme variation in form, a minimum of thought, and a maximum of musical expression. In fact, the Elizabethan song is as near an approach to pure musical sound as has ever been made in words. Of this type no better example can be given than this roundelay (l. 11). It is sung by a man and a woman, first turn about and then together. With all the repetitions it contains more than forty lines and only sixty-two words.

Compare the lyrics taken from *England's Helicon*, pp. 162 ff., and the note on them.

Farewell to Arms

The occasion for this poem was the retirement of Sir Henry Lee from his office as queen's champion, November 17 (the anniversary of Elizabeth's coronation day), 1590. It was sung in a pageant presented before the Queen at Westminster. Sir Henry Lee, who had held his office ever since Elizabeth's accession, and who had come to be regarded as a model of knighthood, went through a ceremony of actually taking off his armor and putting on a civilian coat and cap, and then presented to the Queen his successor, the Earl of Cumberland.

l. 4. Youth (in years) wanes as youth (the young man) increases in age.

l. 10. *age his alms, i.e.,* age's alms. A pedantic affectation common among Elizabethan writers, based on the mistaken idea that the possessive arose from a contraction of the noun and the masculine possessive pronoun.

THE BURNING BABE

Pp. 161 f. No poet ever expressed his life and personality more completely in a few words than Southwell in this poem. The fiery religious zeal that it shows brought him to martyrdom for his faith as a Roman Catholic. Ben Jonson said that he would willingly have destroyed many of his poems to have written *The Burning Babe*.

ENGLAND'S HELICON

Pp. 162 ff. The success of Tottel's miscellany in 1557 (see note on Wyatt and Surrey, p. 697) set· the fashion for collections of lyric poetry. Tottel's book was in its eighth edition in 1587. *The Paradise of Dainty Devices*, published in 1576, was in its eighth edition when *England's Helicon* came out; and three other similar collections had also appeared before that time.

Undoubtedly the interest shown in lyric verse is to be associated with the great cultivation of music, which appears in the issue of song books by Byrd, Dowland, and other musicians, in the large use of songs in plays, and in the popularity of masques and pageants with musical accompaniments.

The Elizabethan songs were all practical, that is, they were written to fit the measures of tunes and to make immediate appeal to the senses. Consequently the ideas in them are few and simple while the verse forms show infinite variety. Cf. note on Peele's *Song of Paris and Œnone*, above. *England's Helicon* is the best of the poetical miscellanies. It contains lyrics by Sidney, Spenser, Drayton, Greene, Lodge, Breton, Peele, the Earl of Surrey, Watson, Marlowe, Shakespeare, William Browne, and other well-known poets. Some songs are signed with initials, some with the pen-name "Shepherd Tony," many are marked *Ignoto* (unknown). Of the one hundred and sixty poems in the collection, more than four-fifths deal with the conventional shepherds and shepherdesses.

PHYLLIDA AND CORYDON

Sung before Queen Elizabeth, to her great delight, in the entertainment given her, in 1591, by the Earl of Hertford.

AS IT FELL UPON A DAY

Attributed to Richard Barnfield. It had been published twice before, once with music. Barnfield published in 1594 the sonnet series entitled *Cynthia*, dedicated to Penelope, Lady Rich, Sidney's "Stella."

PHYLLIDA'S LOVE-CALL

P. 163. ll. 15–17. Only a short time before, Queen Elizabeth had been presented with her first pair of knit silk stockings, and was immensely delighted with them.

l. 50. *the golden ball,* the apple of Discord given by the shepherd Paris to Venus as the most beautiful of the three goddesses. Cf. Gayley's *Classic Myths*, p. 285.

THE SHEPHERD'S DESCRIPTION OF LOVE

Signed S. W. R. (Sir Walter Raleigh) in the edition of 1600; but in the extant copies a slip on which is printed *Ignoto* is pasted over the initials.

DAMELUS' SONG TO HIS DIAPHENIA

P. 164. H. C. was probably Henry Constable, author of the sonnet series called *Diana*.

ROSALIND'S MADRIGAL

From Lodge's romance of that name (cf. p. 129).

THE PASSIONATE SHEPHERD TO HIS LOVE

P. 165. Marlowe's only known song.

THE NYMPH'S REPLY

Attributed to Raleigh, but without grounds.

THE END OF THE RENAISSANCE

THOMAS DEKKER

THE SECOND THREE MEN'S SONG

P. 166. l. 12. *Ring, compass,* from an allusion of the year 1555 it seemingly means to form a circle. Perhaps there should be no comma after *ring*.

THE GULL'S HORNBOOK

Pp. 166 ff. Dekker's prose work is valuable chiefly for its vivid representation of contemporary life. His *Gull's Hornbook* is a sort of "Booby's Primer," ostensibly to teach a young man his way about town, incidentally but fundamentally to show up the follies and vices of the time. It is of course full of local hits and highly satirical.

P. 166 b. The Royal Exchange built by Sir Thomas Gresham in 1566–1567, and opened by Elizabeth in 1571, loomed so large in London life that the figure is very apt.

P. 167 a. *throne . . . lord's room* (place). These boxes were on each side of the balcony in which scenes in upper rooms were presented. Seats there were not as comfortable and did not give as good a view as a stool on the stage itself.

Cambises. In a popular play of that name written by Thomas Preston before 1569.

Persian lock, a fashion affected by the long-haired gallants of the time.

a signed patent to engross the whole commodity of censure, a monopoly to control the market of criticism. A hit at one of the abuses of the time.

P. 167 b. *a mere Fleet-street gentleman, i.e.*, one who lived between the merchants of the "city" and the nobility in the Strand, which was then the fashionable quarter.

P. 168 a. *counter amongst the poultry*, a pun. A counter was a debtor's prison. There were several of these in London. One stood in the street called Poultry (from the fact that it once contained a poultry market). Cf. the puns below on *sculler* and *scullery* (p. 168 b); on *frets*, troubles and marks on a musical instrument (p. 169); and on *hogshead* (p. 169).

P. 169 a. *Arcadian and Euphuised gentlewomen.* Dekker's hit shows how popular the works of Sidney and Lyly had become among women of rank.

BEN JONSON

Pp. 169 ff. Jonson is perhaps the earliest example in England of the all-round man of letters whose personal influence outweighed the critical judgment of his work by his contemporaries. Jonson did many things very well, nothing, perhaps, supremely well — though it would be hard to better some of his lyrics; but because of his versatility and his power as a critic, he became the outstanding literary figure of his time. See Dryden's tribute, pp. 233 f.

TO THE MEMORY OF MY BELOVED, MASTER WILLIAM SHAKESPEARE

These lines show that Jonson understood and appreciated Shakespeare as fully as any critic who has written about him. When a man who loved and imitated the classic drama could say that his contemporary equaled and surpassed ancient (ll. 31–54) as well as modern dramatists (ll. 27–30), the praise does honor to both. The tribute to Shakespeare's art (ll. 55–64), as well as to his natural gifts, is noteworthy as a corrective to the criticism that Jonson made of him on that ground in his *Conversations with Drummond of Hawthornden* (Shakespeare Society Publications).

Cf. Matthew Arnold's sonnet on *Shakespeare*, p. 602.

JOHN DONNE

Pp. 171 f. Dr. Donne's peculiar qualities as a poet were intellectual and temperamental. He played with thoughts as his immediate predecessors played with concrete images. So doing, he initiated a new method, and his method was imitated by many so-called "metaphysical" seventeenth century poets, among whom must be numbered Wither, Quarles, Carew, Suckling, Lovelace, Marvell and Cowley. They wrote a few poems that will be remembered; but the trouble with most of them was that they insisted upon the playing even when they did not have the thoughts. Donne, with his restless, intense, subtle mind, was sincere, but the others were more or less affecting a mode which was not natural to them.

JOHN FLETCHER

SWEETEST MELANCHOLY

P. 173. Compare with the opening lines of *Il Penseroso*, especially ll. 1, 2, 12, 31–36, 133–140, 67, and 74 of the latter. Note also the metrical resemblance: ll. 8–17 of Fletcher's poem are in the regular meter of *Il Penseroso;* the first lines of the two poems are identical in movement; while the opening and concluding lines of Fletcher's, taken together, may have suggested to Milton the form of his Introduction.

In Fletcher's day the cultivation of melancholy, as he describes it in these lines, was a fad of young men of fashion (cf. *King John*, IV, i, 15–17; and the melancholy Jaques in *As You Like It*). The melancholy invoked by Milton is of an entirely different cast.

FRANCIS BEAUMONT

P. 174. The difference between the poems of Beaumont and those of Fletcher shows two strongly opposed types of mind: Fletcher, musical, sensuous, almost effeminate; Beaumont, solid and reflective. In fact, Beaumont had no real lyric gift; he simply wrote tolerable verse.

The interest of the *Letter to Jonson* is entirely in its picture of the gatherings at the Mermaid Inn. For an illustration of the kind of wit that Beaumont had in mind, see the word contest between Mercutio and Romeo, *Romeo and Juliet*, II, iv, 38–106.

ll. 58–65. The meaning is: "My wit has gone to seed. I shall take to writing cheap ballads. I am getting to like country sports such as telling riddles and singing catches. Soon I shall even be proud of being able to use long words — so fast am I degenerating." For the kind of ballads that Beaumont means, see *Winter's Tale*, IV, iv, 262–296. In *sell bargains* (l. 62) he refers to a country sport known as the New Fair.

ll. 67–68. Our young men (in Leicestershire, where the poem was probably written) know little and talk much.

l. 69. They have vegetable souls, like the trees.

l. 79. Apparently refers to the finishing of a play, *The Coxcombe*, which Beaumont and Fletcher were working on in the summer of 1609.

WILLIAM DRUMMOND

P. 174. Drummond, whose picturesque country place at Hawthornden, near Edinburgh, is still visited by tourists, was a dilettante who played at poetry as he played at science. In his literary isolation in Scotland, he continued to imitate the Italians after their influence had ceased to be felt in England.

SONNET

l. 5. *Small*, capitalized because it refers to the *microcosm*, small universe, a term commonly applied to man, over against the *macrocosm*, the great universe.

l. 13. *this prince*, Prince Henry, son of King James I; his death was greatly lamented by the English people.

MADRIGAL I

Translated from the Italian of Guarini.

GEORGE WITHER

SONNET IV

P. 175. l. 14. *pelican*. According to ancient fable the pelican wounded her own breast and fed her young with the blood. Because of this, she was often used in religious poetry as a type of Christ.

In his own day, Wither was known as a bold and insuppressible satirist. But as his satire was of temporary and local interest and as his style, though vigorous, was simple and often diffuse, his satires are no longer read. His lyrics have grace and playfulness and this one, at least, has a permanent place in English anthologies.

WILLIAM BROWNE

BRITANNIA'S PASTORALS

Pp. 176 f. A copy of the first edition of this poem with notes written in Milton's handwriting points to the most significant fact about Browne, that he was a sort of bridge over which pastoral poetry passed from Spenser to Milton. It does not seem, however, that his influence on Milton was of much importance.

This passage is interesting as a seventeenth century attempt at a description of romantic nature.

ll. 141–144. Cf. Herrick's *Corinna's Going A-Maying* (p. 177).

l. 158. *frizzled coats*, apparently a conceit for foliage, *i.e.*, trees.

l. 163. *end the creek*. *of* is omitted for metrical reasons.

l. 173. *thronged*. The waters were crowded together as the creek grew narrow. The phrase is an instance of post-Elizabethan obscure subtlety.

ON THE COUNTESS DOWAGER OF PEMBROKE

P. 177. Nash wrote of her in 1591: "artes do adore [her] as a second Minerva, and our poets extol [her] as the patroness of their invention." See notes on Sidney's *Arcadia* and on Samuel Daniel.

ROBERT HERRICK

Pp. 177 f. Herrick has, in addition to the sweetness and melody of the Elizabethans, a sense of proportion and of the fitness of things to which they rarely attained. Where they are spontaneous and unrestrained, he has the repose that comes with a sense of art. One of the greatest charms of his work is the country freshness that he managed to get into it from long association with Devonshire. Another is an occasional flash of imaginative insight that fuses commonplace words into an immortal phrase, as when, in describing the movement of a woman's silk dress, he speaks of "the liquefaction of her clothes" (*Upon Julia's Clothes*, l. 3).

CHERRY–RIPE

P. 177. Cf. Campion's poem on the same subject, p. 162.

CORINNA'S GOING A-MAYING

The custom of maying in the sixteenth century is thus described by Stowe:

"In the moneth of May, namely on May day in the morning, every man, except impediment, would walke into the sweete meadowes and greene woods, there to rejoyce their spirites with the beauty and savour of sweete flowers, and with the harmony of birds, praysing God in their kind, and for example hereof *Edward Hall* hath noted, that *K. Henry* the eight, as in the 3. of his raigne, and divers other yeares, so namely in the seaventh of his raigne on May day in the morning with Queene *Katheren* his wife, accompanied with many Lords and Ladies, rode a Maying from Greenwitch to the high ground of Shooters hill, where as they passed by the way, they espied a companie of tall yeomen cloathed all in Greene, with greene whoodes [hoods], and with bowes and arrowes to the number of 200. One being their Chieftaine was called *Robin Hoode*, who required the king and his companie to stay and see his men shoote, whereunto the king graunting, *Robin Hoode* whistled, and all the 200. Archers shot off, loosing all at once, and when he whistled againe, they likewise shot againe, their arrowes whistled by craft of the head, so that the noyse was straunge and loude, which greatly delighted the King, Queene and their Companie. Moreover, this Robin Hoode desired the King & Queene with their retinue to enter the greene wood, where, in harbours made of boughes, and decked with flowers, they were set and served plentifully with venison and wine, by Robin Hoode and his meynie, to their great contentment, and had other Pageants and pastimes as ye may read in my saide Authour. I find also that in the moneth of May, the Citizens of London of all estates, lightly in every Parish, or

sometimes two or three parishes joyning togither had their severall mayings, and did fetch in Maypoles, with diverse warlike shewes, with good Archers, Morice dauncers, and other devices for pastime all the day long, and towards the Evening they had stage playes, and Bonefiers in the streetes."

l. 4. *fresh-quilted*. A homely country touch, with a world of associations of cottage life.

ll. 30–31. Each field is so full of people, and each street is so full of boughs.

GEORGE HERBERT

Pp. 178 f. Like Herrick, Herbert was a clergyman, but while Herrick was in feeling almost a pagan, Herbert was almost a saint. It seems extraordinary that he should have been the brother of the brilliant and worldly philosopher, Lord Herbert of Cherbury, and the friend of the subtle and thought-tormenting Dr. Donne, and still have developed his serene and unique genius. He is the poet who most nearly represents the early Christian ideal of ethics, the surrender of worldly things to the life of the spirit, yet without the mystic rapture of Vaughan and Crashaw.

IZAAK WALTON

Pp. 179 ff. The ironmonger who owned "half a shop" in Fleet Street, the nonagenarian whose life stretched across from Marlowe to Pope, the simple-minded gentleman who thought that he knew all about fishing and who somehow got himself the friendship of the most interesting literary men of his day, achieved fame seemingly without trying. There are critics who say that he made mistakes in his theory of fishing, but there are few readers who deny the spell of perfect naturalness and simplicity and the sense of being in the open air that comes when we begin to walk with him up Tottenham Hill. His *Compleat Angler* went through five editions between 1653 and 1676 — a fact which shows that England had other interests besides deposing and restoring kings and persecuting people for their religious beliefs.

THOMAS CAREW

P. 181. See the note on Waller, Carew and others, p. 717 below.

SIR THOMAS BROWNE

Pp. 181 ff. When the diarist Evelyn visited Sir Thomas Browne at Norwich, he found the house and garden of "that famous scholar and physitian," full of "rarities, and that of the best collections, especially medails, books, plants, and natural things." His mind likewise was stocked with "rarities" of thought. His curiosity in regard to out-of-the-way matters is illustrated by his *Hydriotaphia: Urn-Burial; or, a Discourse of the Sepulchral Urns Lately Found in Norfolk.*

The occasion of this discourse was the discovery in 1658 of between forty and fifty burial urns which Sir Thomas believed to be of Romans or Romanized Britons. His interest in the matter led him to write a discussion of the different methods of burial; and to conclude that the desire of the ancients to "subsist in lasting monuments, to live in their productions, to exist in their names . . . is nothing in the metaphysics of true belief."

Sir Thomas Browne is impressive because of a certain breadth of wisdom due to much reading and reflection, and perhaps even more because of the slow and rhythmical pacing of his rich and elaborate style.

EDMUND WALLER

Pp. 184 f. As Waller was the most notable of the love poets of the seventeenth century, and his long life almost covered the century, we may group with him others who distinguished themselves especially for this same kind of lyric verse, Carew and Suckling, and later, Lovelace, Sedley, and Rochester.

Waller's "sweetness," as Pope's criticism possibly implies (*Essay on Criticism*, II, 361, p. 275), at once made and marred his work. He lacks both ideas and virility, but such short lyrics as *On a Girdle* and *Go, Lovely Rose*, are pearls without a flaw.

Carew (p. 181) is somewhat violent in his imagery and the mental conceptions behind it. The idea of his *Song* is that his lady is the source of roses, the nightingale's song, the stars, and that she is the Phœnix's nest in which that unique and immortal bird is born again (cf. note on Crashaw's *Hymn*, l. 46, p. 724). This is a perfect case of a "metaphysical" conceit, that is, an extravagance of imagery based upon an elaborately ingenious idea.

Suckling (p. 214) is at the opposite pole from Carew, being simple, natural, and genial.

Lovelace (p. 218) is the noblest of the group, because the most sincere. Though not as simple as Waller and Sedley, he is not as sentimental. He lacks Suckling's humor and Rochester's wit, but he has an earnestness and a quaintness all his own.

Rochester (p. 244) has, like Suckling, a sense of humor, but he is sharp rather than sunny, to a degree not illustrated by the selections given.

Sedley (p. 243) is merely prettily sentimental, and falls far short of Waller.

THE STORY OF PHŒBUS AND DAPHNE APPLIED

P. 184. *Thyrsis* is Waller himself who professes adoration for a lady whom he calls *Sacharissa* (Dorothy, Countess of Sunderland); but the passion seems to have been purely literary. The classical myth here "applied" is told in Ovid's *Metamorphoses*, I, 452–567 (cf. also Gayley's *Classic Myths*, pp. 138–141).

THOMAS FULLER

Pp. 185 ff. Thomas Fuller was famous, both as preacher and as writer, for his quips and ingenious conceits. He had learning and native wit, and he came at a time when elaborate combinations of the two were allowed and praised.

The volume from which our selection is taken is a miscellaneous collection of sketches and moral essays.

JOHN MILTON

Pp. 189 ff. While all Milton's early work gives abundant evidence of his love of the classics and his study of classic methods, only *Lycidas*, among the poems here quoted, may be said to approach a classic model in form and in substance. The titles *L'Allegro* and *Il Penseroso* show Italian influence, while the use of nature in both poems is as English as Herrick's; *Il Penseroso* is decidedly romantic, after the first thirty lines even mediævally romantic, in treatment, while *On the Morning of Christ's Nativity* is a precursor of *Paradise Lost* in its blending of Greek and Hebraic elements.

ON THE MORNING OF CHRIST'S NATIVITY

This ode was begun, as Milton himself says in one of his Latin elegies (VI, ll. 81–90), on Christmas Day. The irregular metre, with its wonderful interlacing of short and long lines, gives an extraordinary effect as of leaping flames.

ll. 45–60. Milton emphasizes the idea that the Roman peace throughout the world at the time of Christ's birth was in preparation for the coming of the Prince of Peace.

l. 48. *the turning sphere*, perhaps specifically the Primum Mobile. Milton knew the Copernican system of astronomy, which regards the earth as one of a system of planets revolving round the sun; but in his poetry he preferred to make use of the older system known as the Ptolemaic. As this system is constantly referred to in our earlier literature, it may be explained here briefly: 1. The earth is the centre of the mundane universe. 2. Surrounding it at different distances, and revolving on it as a centre, are several hollow transparent spheres. 3. In the first seven of these are placed the seven planets, one planet in the surface of each sphere, in the following order: Moon, Mercury, Venus, Sun, Mars, Jupiter, Saturn. Each planet is carried about by the motion of its own sphere but has also its own motion in the surface of its sphere. 4. The eighth hollow sphere is that of the fixed stars, which are immovably set in its surface. 5. Outside of these eight spheres, according to the older view, was a ninth sphere, called the Primum Mobile or First Mover, which revolved round the earth daily from east to west and caused the succession of day and night. Its motion was so powerful and its adjustment to the other spheres of such a nature that it carried them all about with it in its diurnal revolution, though each of them had an independent motion from west to east and each of the planets was free to move within its sphere or orb, as has just been said. As the spheres were placed at harmonic intervals, they were supposed to make a divine music, inaudible by human ears. 6. By Milton's time this simple system had been found inadequate to account for all the motions of the heavenly bodies and a crystalline sphere had been added (between the Primum Mobile and the fixed stars), to account for certain irregularities (see *Par. Lost*, III, 481–483). 7. The Mundane Universe, consisting of this system of spheres, is surrounded on all sides by Chaos (unorganized matter). 8. The Mundane Universe is suspended from Heaven (or the Empyrean), which lies above it, by a golden chain (see Tennyson's *Morte D'Arthur*, 254–255). 9. Below the Mundane Universe, and distant from Heaven by three times the radius of that Universe, lies Hell (cf. *Par. Lost*, I, 72–4).

l. 68. *birds of calm*, halcyons, fabulous birds, identified with kingfishers, supposed to nest on the sea for seven days before and after the winter solstice. At this time the sea was always calm. For the story of Ceyx and Halcyone, see Ovid, *Metamorphoses*, XI, 410–748, or Gayley's *Classic Myths*, pp. 194–196. Cf. also Theocritus, *Idyls*, VII (the Song of Lycidas).

P. 190. l. 89. *Pan*, here Christ. The identi-

fication came about through the character of each as a shepherd (cf. *John*, x: 11).

ll. 125–132. The music of the spheres. It was a common idea that this could be heard by the pure of heart. In *Arcades* (ll. 61–73), Milton follows Plato in imagining the Muses (celestial sirens), as making the music of the spheres.

P. 191. ll. 173–180. The pagan religion has come to an end. Professor Shorey suggests that the form *Delphos* (l. 178) may be due to Milton's recollection of the striking passage in Æschylus' *Eumenides*, l. 16, in which the King of Delphi is called *Delphos*. He also points out that Sir Thomas Browne uses *Delphos* for *Delphi*. Marlowe has *Colchos* for *Colchis*.

ll. 181–188. The mourning is for the death of Pan, here symbolical of paganism, not of Christ, as in l. 89.

P. 192. ll. 229–231. Certainly a grotesque picture.

L'ALLEGRO AND IL PENSEROSO

Pp. 192 ff. Although these companion pieces are almost balanced in structure, Milton's preference for the thoughtful mood appears in two ways. He adds to *Il Penseroso* (ll. 167–174) a desire for a life of continued solitude which carries him outside his plan of giving a day for each mood; and furthermore, in *L'Allegro* he is throughout walking apart, merely the observer of the life of joy; not for a moment is he "admitted" to be of the "crew" of Mirth.

The plan of each poem is: (1) an introduction banishing the opposite mood; (2) the origin of the mood; (3) a day lived in each mood; (4) the poet's attitude.

In *L'Allegro*, the typical day begins with the lark and a sunshiny early morning in the country; continues with a rustic dinner and work in the fields, followed by country sports and tales; and ends with a description of evening life in cities, with social gatherings, marriages, comedies, and Lydian (secular) music.

In *Il Penseroso*, it begins with the nightingale, a moonlight walk, the study of astronomy and philosophy, the reading of tragedies and romances; continues with a stormy morning, a woodland walk; and ends with religious music in a cathedral.

It is interesting to work out minutely the balancing of detail; also to observe the difference in treatment due to Milton's personal preference. It is obvious that he is not interested in Nature except as a means of reflecting his moods; and equally clear that he is thoroughly interested in music for its own sake. Cf. *L'Allegro*, ll. 136–144, *Il Penseroso*, ll. 161–166, and *Paradise Lost*, I, 550–559 (in which he describes martial music). No one but a musician could have written so fully and so technically. Lines 139–144 of *L'Allegro* exactly describe the elaborations of the seventeenth century songs. Milton played both the bass viol and the organ. Observe also the prominence he ascribes to music in his scheme of education, p. 209.

Metrically, each poem begins with a ten-line introduction in alternate short and long lines, and then drops into the regular beat of the eight-syllabled iambic couplet. There is, however, a great difference in effect caused by the omission in more than a third of the lines of *L'Allegro* of the unaccented first syllable, which gives a tripping trochaic movement (cf., for example, ll. 25–34, and ll. 69–70, which are actually trochaic). In *Il Penseroso* this unaccented syllable is kept in more than seven-eighths of the lines and gives a slower, more regular movement (cf., for example, ll. 155–176).

L'Allegro

ll. 33–68. One long, loosely constructed sentence, the effect of which is to give a hurried, almost breathless movement. *to come* (l. 45) is parallel with *singing* (l. 42) and *begin* (l. 41), though it can scarcely be said to depend upon *hear* (l. 41); while *To hear* and *listening* (l. 53) are parallel and refer to the poet.

P. **193**. l. 83. *Corydon* and *Thyrsis*, neighbors, as in Vergil, *Eclogues*, VII (where they are called "Arcades ambo"). *Phillis* (l. 86), regularly associated with the former in pastoral verse and praised by both in the Eclogue just cited, is waiting on them. *Thestylis* here is apparently a woman's name, as in Theocritus, *Idyls*, II, and Vergil, *Eclogues*, II.

l. 102. *fairy Mab.* See Drayton's *Nymphidia*, p. 150, and the note on it.

l. 104. Apparently a confusion of will o' the wisp ("ignis fatuus") which appeared outdoors, and Friar Rush, a demonic apparition that haunted houses; *the drudging goblin* is Puck or Robin Goodfellow. See *A Midsummer Night's Dream*, II, i, 16–57.

l. 136. *soft Lydian airs*, voluptuous music.

ll. 145–150. Orpheus by his music persuaded Pluto, the god of Hades, to give him back his wife Eurydice, from the dead. But he broke Pluto's condition that he should not look back at her until they had left Hades, and so lost her again. Cf. Gayley's *Classic Myths*, pp. 185–188, Ovid, *Meta-*

morphoses, X, 1–77, and Vergil, *Georgics*, IV, 453–506.

Il Penseroso

The germ of this poem is in Fletcher's *Sweetest Melancholy*, p. 173 (cf. note on that poem).

P. **194**. ll. 83–84. *The bellman* was a night watchman who passed through the streets ringing a bell and calling out the hours and the weather. He also pronounced a blessing on the sleeping city.

l. 88. *thrice-great Hermes.* Hermes Trismegistus, the Greek god Hermes (Roman Mercury) who came to be identified with the Egyptian Thoth, and was the reputed author of magical, alchemical, and astrological works.

ll. 99–100. The three great subjects of the classical drama, of which Milton was a devoted admirer. That he cared less for the Elizabethan drama appears from ll. 101–102.

l. 104. See note on *Hero and Leander*, p. 706, above.

ll. 109–115. Chaucer. The persons named are in the unfinished *Squire's Tale*, to which Milton refers perhaps as a type of pure romance.

P. **195**. ll. 116–120. Probably *The Faerie Queene* which Milton admired and imitated.

ll. 156–160. The characteristic features of Gothic architecture: the cloister, which is always attached to a cathedral, the vaulted roof, pillars massive and strong, and stained-glass windows. But on this point Milton was not in accord with the taste of the times. About thirty years after he wrote these lines, Sir Christopher Wren rebuilt many of the churches destroyed by the Great Fire of London, in a very different style of architecture; and it was not until a century later that a liking for the Gothic was revived.

Lycidas

Contributed for the memorial volume of Latin poems published by the friends of Edward King, whose death is referred to in the note at the beginning of the poem. Milton had been five years away from Cambridge, with which King was still connected at the time of his death. There is no evidence, external or internal, of any special friendship between the men; and almost half the poem is given to Milton's own ideas and affairs (ll. 19–22 and 64–84), a lament over the corruption of the church (ll. 114–131), and elaborate embellishments in imitation both of classical elegiasts and of Spenser.

The framework of *Lycidas*, following the general conventions of the Greek pastoral, is as follows:

1. Invocation to laurels, ivy, and myrtles, of which the poet is to make a wreath for Lycidas (ll. 1–14). These plants may be, as some think, emblems of poetry, learning, and beauty, but they have no such significance when used by Theocritus and Vergil.

2. Invocation to the Muses (ll. 15–18), and a personal digression (ll. 19–22).

3. Story of the poet's association with Lycidas (ll. 23–36).

4. His mourning for Lycidas (ll. 37–49).

5. Appeal to the nymphs of the district in which Lycidas died, and allusion to the death of Orpheus (ll. 50–63), with a digression on the lack of reward for poetry (ll. 64–84).

6. Address to the Arethusa (a river in Sicily, where Theocritus lived) and the Mincio (in Italy, near Vergil's birthplace), as introductory to the story of Triton (l. 89), who has asked about the mishap and brought answer from Æolus (Hippotades, l. 96) that there was no wind, that the sea-nymphs (l. 99) were playing about, and that the fault lay in the ship (ll. 100–102).

7. The lament of Camus (god of the river Cam), representing Cambridge and St. Peter (ll. 109–110), representing the church (ll. 103–113). Digression on the corruption of the church (ll. 114–131).

8. Address to the pastoral streams of Arcadia and Sicily to bid the valleys bring all their flowers for Lycidas (ll. 132–151).

9. Lament for the body tossed about the seas (ll. 152–164).

10. Comfort that Lycidas is in heaven (ll. 165–185).

11. The shepherd's conclusion (ll. 186–193).

Milton's choice of the name Lycidas may have been determined by several considerations. Shepherds of that name are celebrated by the chief pastoral poets, Theocritus (Idyls, VII), Bion (Idyls, II and VI), and Vergil (Eclogues, IX). Moreover, Lycidas is spoken of in Theocritus' Idyl as "the best of men" and is addressed thus: "Dear Lycidas, they all say that thou among herdsmen, yea and among reapers, art far the chiefest flute-player;" and in Bion's sixth Idyl the poet says: "If I sing of any other, mortal or immortal, then falters my tongue, and sings no longer as of old, but if again to Love and Lycidas I sing, then gladly from my lips flows forth the voice of song."

P. 196. l. 36. *Damœtas* is a shepherd in Theocritus, *Idyls*, VI and in Vergil, *Eclogues*, II, III; in *Eclogues*, II, 36–38, Corydon says: "A flute is mine, with seven unequal hemlock stalks, which Damœtas

once gave me as a present, and dying said: 'That flute has now for its master you, second to me alone.'"

ll. 50–55. Imitated from Theocritus, Bion, Moschus, and Vergil.

ll. 58–63. The Mænads (Bacchantes) tore him to pieces for indifference to women after the death of Eurydice (Ovid, *Metamorphoses*, XI, 1–84) and Vergil, *Georgics*, IV, 507–527).

ll. 68–69. Conventional expressions for a life of ease and pleasure. Amaryllis is one of the nymphs most praised in Theocritus and Vergil (esp. *Idyls*, III, 1, and *Eclogues*, I, 4 f.); Neæra is mentioned by Vergil, *Eclogues*, III.

l. 75. *blind Fury*. The Fate, Atropos, is called a Fury, because she has slain Lycidas.

l. 77. In similar manner Phœbus touches the ear of the poet and reproves him in Vergil, *Eclogues*, VI, 3 f.

ll. 85, 132. The story of the river god Alpheus and the nymph Arethusa is charmingly told in the seventh Idyl of Moschus, and at greater length in Ovid, *Metamorphoses*, V, 572–661. Less simple is Shelley's *Arethusa*. The river Arethusa is invoked by Theocritus, Moschus, and Vergil as being to pastoral poetry and poets what the fountain Hippocrene was to epic poetry and poets, see especially Moschus, *Idyls*, III, where Homer and Bion are compared.

l. 106. The hyacinth, on the leaves of which are marks said to be AI, AI (alas); cf. Moschus, *Idyls*, III, "Now thou hyacinth, whisper the letters on thee graven, and add a deeper *ai ai* to thy petals; he is dead, the beautiful singer."

P. 197. ll. 130–131. Three interpretations have been given:

1. The axe of the Bible (*Matthew*, iii: 10, *Luke*, iii :9) which cuts down the unrighteous — identified with the executioner's axe.

2. St. Michael's two-handed sword, which finally overcame Satan when "with huge two-handed sway Brandisht aloft the horrid edge came down Wide wasting" (*Par. Lost*, VI, 251–253).

3. Parliament, with its two Houses, which Milton hoped would check the evils of episcopacy.

l. 132. *Alpheus* is invoked as the lover of Arethusa, see Moschus, *Idyls*, VII. Alpheus and the Sicilian Muse (Arethusa) are called on to return after the digression and resume the pastoral lament. The "dread voice" is the voice of denunciation that has just shrunk the pastoral stream of verse.

ll. 159–162. In his *History of England*, Milton had told a "fable" of the wrestling match between a British hero Corineus and a giant whom he overcame and hurled into the sea off the Cornish coast. The name *Bellerus*, used here instead of *Corineus*, seems to be coined from *Bellerium*, the Roman name of Land's End. St. Michael is supposed to have appeared in a vision, seated on a crag of the rocky island now called St. Michael's Mount. Milton conceives him as still sitting there and looking toward Spain (*Namancos* and *Bayona*, near Cape Finisterre). In l. 163, Milton bids him look back towards England and sympathize.

l. 189. *Doric, i.e.*, pastoral. Applied to the Sicilian poets, who were of Dorian extraction, and characterizing their affectation of simplicity.

l. 190. Perhaps an elaboration of what Vergil says of the shadows of the hills in *Eclogues*, I, 84, and II, 67, with a reminiscence of Hamlet's expression in *Hamlet* II, ii, 270.

l. 191. *western bay*, perhaps Chester Bay, from which King had sailed.

SONNETS

P. 198. Milton's sonnets return to the Italian form, but in matter they are, for the most part, absolutely original, and a direct expression of strong personal feeling. On Milton's relation to the earlier sonneteers, cf. Wordsworth's *Scorn Not the Sonnet*, p. 396.

WHEN THE ASSAULT WAS INTENDED TO THE CITY

Written in November, 1642, when an attack on London by the Royalist forces was expected. As Milton was an ardent Parliamentarian pamphleteer, his house, just outside one of the city gates, was in danger. The original title read: "On his dore when yᵉ city expected an assault," as if the sonnet had been really intended as a defence.

l. 13. A chorus from the *Electra* of Euripides, recited by a ministrel before the conquerors of Athens, caused them to spare the city.

TO THE LORD GENERAL CROMWELL, MAY, 1652

Cromwell had completed a series of victories over the Royalists on the river Darwen, and at Dunbar and Worcester, as a result of which Charles II was driven into exile. Meanwhile, the committee named in the subtitle was proposing religious reconstruction. Milton feared that the Presbyterians would establish a state system similar to the one just disestablished, and the sonnet is a plea to Cromwell to prevent this.

ll. 13–14. Compare *Lycidas*, ll. 119–131.

ON THE LATE MASSACRE IN PIEDMONT

Written in 1655 after the Duke of Savoy and Prince of Piedmont had cruelly massacred his Protestant subjects, the Waldenses or Vaudois, for refusing to turn Roman Catholic. Cromwell as Lord-Protector protested so strongly that the Vaudois were afterward allowed their own worship. Milton, as Cromwell's secretary, wrote the protests of the State; this sonnet expresses his personal views.

ON HIS BLINDNESS

P. 199. l. 2. He was forty-five years old when he lost his sight completely.

TO CYRIACK SKINNER

l. 11. His blindness had been hastened by his work, *Defensio Prima pro Populo Anglicano*, 1651, in reply to Salmasius, a Dutch professor who attacked the Commonwealth.

PARADISE LOST

The thorough fusion in Milton of the spirit of the Renaissance, the love of classical themes and treatment, and the spirit of Puritanism, the struggle towards a higher ethical plane by means of a revival of Hebraism, is unique in English literature. His avowed purpose to write "Things unattempted yet in prose or rime" (l. 16), in order to "justify the ways of God to men" (l. 26), is equalled in its daring only by the plan of Dante's *Divina Commedia*. His poetical achievement, however, is quite apart from his theological purpose, and lies in his marvellous power of reproducing in sound and rhythm the visions that came to his imagination, and in the tremendous swing and wonderful flexibility of his blank verse. Note how he gets variety by inverting his sentence order, as, for instance, in ll. 44–47, and by varying the number of stressed syllables in a line, as, for example, in ll. 209–215. Cf. Gray's appreciation of Milton in *The Progress of Poesy*, ll. 95–102, p. 318.

Milton's classical training and his many years of handling official correspondence in Latin made him so familiar with that language that he continually uses words derived from the Latin in a sense fully warranted by their origin but uncommon in English. For example, in l. 2, *mortal* has the meaning *deadly*, not the more usual sense *human;* in l. 187, *offend* means *injure*, not *anger*. For this reason Milton's vocabulary must be studied with the greatest care if his meaning is to be fully understood.

ll. 1–6. The subject of the poem is stated at once, as in the opening lines of the *Iliad* and the *Æneid*.

P. 201. ll. 197–209. The first example of the elaborately developed classical simile. For others, see ll. 230–238, 302–313, 338–346, 551–559, 768–775, 780–792.

P. 202. ll. 288–290. Galileo with the telescope discovered the uneven surface of the moon. *Fesole*, or Fiesole, is a village three miles from Florence, and *Valdarno* is the valley of the river Arno, which flows through Florence. This is a personal reminiscence. Milton visited Galileo who lived at Arcetri, just outside Florence, and later described him as "a prisoner of the Inquisition for thinking in astronomy otherwise than the Franciscan and Dominican licensers thought." Here speaks the author of the *Areopagitica*.

Pp. 204 f. ll. 392–521. Of these one hundred and thirty lines given up to descriptions of Satan's host, only seven name Egyptian gods (ll. 476–482), and fourteen Greek (ll. 508–521). More than a hundred lines are devoted to the various Semitic gods that appear in the Old Testament. Perhaps Milton's early love of the Greek deities kept him from over-emphasizing their transformation into devils; but, in any case, the Semitic gods are more in harmony with his theme, and after nearly twenty years of association with men who thought and talked in terms of the Old Testament, he would naturally have drawn most of his material from that source. Some passages contain scarcely a word not found in the Bible. For instance, ll. 396–422 are put together and fused out of *I Kings*, xi: 5, 7; *II Kings*, xxiii: 4–14; *II Samuel*, xii: 26–27; *Judges*, xi: 13, and 19–33; *Isaiah*, xv–xvi; *Jeremiah*, xlviii; *Numbers*, xxv: 1–5; *Deut.*, xxxii: 49. Lines 437–446 describe the idolatry of Solomon as told in *I Kings*, xi: 4–8; and in *Jeremiah*, vii: 18. Lines 446–457 tell about the worship of Thammuz (who is identified with the Greek Adonis, l. 450) as it was revealed to Ezekiel (*Ezekiel*, viii: 6–14). Lines 457–466 refer to the overthrow of Dagon by the ark of God as told in *I Samuel*, v. Lines 467–471 tell of the leper, Naaman the Syrian, *II Kings*, v: 1–18; and lines 471–476 of the idolatry of King Ahaz, *II Kings*, xvi: 7–18. Lines 482–489 refer to the worship of the golden calf (*Exod.*, xxxii: 1–6; cf. xi: 2), Jeroboam's Calves (*I Kings*, xii), and to the slaying of the first-born in Egypt (*Exod.*,

xii: 29, 51). Lines 490–505 refer to the sins of the sons of Eli (*I Samuel*, ii: 12, 22), to the purposed outrage in Sodom (*Gen.*, xix: 4–11), and that perpetrated at Gibeah (*Judges*, xix: 22–28). In l. 508 Milton connects the Ionian gods with the Old Testament (cf. *Gen.*, x: 2).

P. 206. ll. 575–576. Cf. ll. 780–781. The pygmies were supposed to have been 3½ inches tall. Their war with the cranes is mentioned by Homer, Aristotle, Ovid, and other writers.

ll. 576–577. *Phlegra*, in Thrace; according to Pindar the scene of the battle between the gods and the giants.

ll. 580–581. King Arthur and his Round Table.

ll. 582–587. Places celebrated in French and Italian epics and romances of Charlemagne and his knights: *Aspramont*, in Limburg; *Montauban*, in Languedoc; *Trebisond*, in Cappadocia; *Biserta*, in Tunis. The defeat alluded to was at Roncesvaux, a pass in the Pyrenees, in 778. Milton is wrong in saying that "Charlemain with all his peerage fell"; the fact seems to have been that his rearguard was attacked and routed by Basque mountaineers. The story was introduced into literature in the *Chanson de Roland*, an Anglo-Norman epic of the eleventh century, although ballads on the subject were sung earlier. William the Conqueror's minstrel, Taillefer, chanted a song of Roland as he went into the battle of Hastings (Senlac). This Roland, who in the *Chanson* is represented as Charlemagne's nephew and the hero of Roncesvaux, became one of the chief figures in the mediæval French epics. As Orlando he became in Italy the hero of the famous poems of Ariosto and Boiardo. His name was also introduced into English literature and tradition (cf. Browning's poem, p. 556, the title of which comes from an old song alluded to in *King Lear*, III, iv, 187). *Fontarabbia*, modern Fuenterrabia, is probably introduced for the beauty of the name itself. It is many miles from Roncesvaux, but far more musical than *Burguete*, which is geographically correct.

MILTON'S PROSE

Pp. 208 ff. Milton's prose has more movement and color than Bacon's, more vigor and less studied elaboration than Browne's. He writes as a practical man whose mind is burdened with what he has to say. His long years of secretarial work for Cromwell, although they may scarcely be said to have moulded his English prose style, had the effect of keeping him in good fighting trim.

Of Education

Milton's essay on Education is a small tract of eight pages. It was published in 1644 in response to a request for his views from his friend Samuel Hartlib, a man of a good Polish family who had come to England about 1628 and amid all the civil strife of the time had devoted himself to scientific studies for the improvement of education, agriculture, and manufactures. Milton's plan of study, as set forth in his tractate, is too ambitious for all but students of extraordinary abilities, but it is noteworthy that, like Hartlib's, his conception of education was distinctly modern. Although himself a great classical scholar and linguist, he treats of the languages as tools, instruments for helping the student to a knowledge of *things*, and suggests that most of them can be learned incidentally in odd moments of leisure. He emphasizes the study of the sciences and of the arts (particularly music); and he lays great stress upon training students as men who are to bear a responsible part in the life and government of the nation. The section on Exercise shows that, although he makes little provision for play, — aside from the recreation of music, — he believed in the cultivation of the body as well as of the mind. But in this he was in harmony with the general ideals of the Renaissance.

Areopagitica

Pp. 210 ff. June 14, 1643, Parliament appointed various committees to control the licensing of books. This restriction of the freedom of the press was due partly to the desire of the Presbyterians in power to prevent such publications as Milton's own pamphlet on divorce, for example, and partly to the effort of the Stationers' Company (the organization of printers and publishers) to protect their copyrights. Milton was called to account in 1644 for disregarding the new regulations, and November 24 of that year he published the *Areopagitica*, itself unlicensed. The title means: matters befitting the high court of the Areopagus, the famous Athenian tribunal, here, of course, referring to Parliament. It is easy to see that the theme was one after Milton's own heart.

P. 210 a. Cadmus sowed, at Athene's command, the teeth of a dragon that he had slain and so obtained a crop of armed men to help him with the building of Thebes. Cf. Ovid's *Metamorphoses*, III, 1–137. A similar story is told of Jason.

P. 210 b. *those confused seeds which were imposed on Psyche.* Psyche had fallen into the hands of Venus, who punished her, for having won the love of Cupid, by making her separate seeds of wheat, millet, poppy, vetches, lentils, and beans, mixed all together. She was to place each kind of seed in a separate heap and to finish the task by evening. As Psyche sat in despair, an ant took pity on her and summoning the whole tribe of ants, accomplished the work within the time set. The story of Cupid and Psyche is told in *The Golden Ass of Apuleius*, Bks. IV–VI.

P. 212 a. *the old philosophy of this island.* There was a theory that the Pythagorean and Zoroastrian doctrines were derived from the wisdom of the Druids, the priesthood of the early Britons.

as far as the mountainous borders of Russia and beyond the Hercynian wilderness. The mountains bordering Transylvania are a part of the Carpathians. The Hercynian wilderness was a mountainous tract of forest land in southern and central Germany (the name survives in *Harz* and *Erzgebirge*), many miles to the northeast of Transylvania. But Milton's geography is vague and rhetorical; he cared more for the sonority and associations of a geographical name than for its exact significance.

P. 212 b. *muing her mighty youth*, etc. Renewing her youth as an eagle renews its feathers by moulting. In mediæval bird-fable the eagle's keen sight was supposed to be actually kindled and her youth renewed by flying up near to the sun, as Milton says. See the Middle English "Bestiary" in Emerson's *Middle English Reader*, or in Morris and Skeat's *Specimens of Early English*. In Milton's figure the sun is truth; in the Middle English poem the sun is God and the eagle is the soul.

P. 213 a. *Ye cannot make us*, etc. You cannot make us again as we were before you gave us liberty. We, with our finer ideals, are the result of your own high ideals in the past, and to undo your good work now would be like a reversion to that barbarous ancient law which permitted parents to kill their own children. If you did, who would stand up for you and urge others to do so? Not such patriots as rose against illegal taxation.

Coat and conduct, the clothing and conveyance of troops. On this ground taxes were unjustly levied.

his four nobles of Danegelt, ship-money. *Danegelt* means literally Dane-money, and in Saxon times was a tax levied to protect England against the invasions of the Danes. It is not clear why Milton should have specified four nobles (26s. 8d.).

Lord Brook. Robert, second Lord Brooke, cousin and heir of Fulke Greville, Lord Brooke, the friend of Sidney and Spenser. Milton tells the chief facts about him. He was killed storming Lichfield, Jan. 7, 1643. The book mentioned is: *A discourse opening the nature of that Episcopacie which is exercised in England. Wherein, with all Humility, are represented some considerations tending to the much desired Peace and long expected Reformation of this our Mother Church.*

P. 214 a. *old Proteus.* Cf. note on *Hero and Leander,* l. 137, and especially Vergil, *Georgics,* IV, 387–414.

SIR JOHN SUCKLING

Cf. note on Waller, p. 717.

RICHARD CRASHAW

IN THE HOLY NATIVITY OF OUR LORD GOD

Crashaw at his best is full of intense religious fire combined with some degree of Milton's power of visualization; but he has a subtlety quite un-Miltonic and an extravagance of imagery that sometimes mars his work. See, for instance, l. 87, describing the Virgin's breast, l. 90, her double nature; also ll. 91–93, describing courtiers, especially the extraordinary figure in l. 93. It is interesting to compare Crashaw's Hymn not merely with Milton's, but with the simplicity of the early Christmas carols and Southwell's *Burning Babe,* pp. 92–94 and 161 above.

ll. 15–16. Observe that the shepherds have conventional classical names.

P. 215. l. 46. The phœnix is, because of its uniqueness, a frequent symbol of Christ in early Christian poetry. According to fable, the phœnix lives five hundred years, and, when it feels the time of its death approaching, gathers spices and fragrant woods, of which it builds a nest; it then sets fire to the nest and is consumed with it, but comes out from the ashes a young phœnix, new and yet the same. As the phœnix builds the nest for its own rebirth, so Christ himself chose where he would be born.

JEREMY TAYLOR

Pp. 216 f. Jeremy Taylor was a master of elaborate and involved prose rhythms and as such will always retain his place in the history of English

literature. Whether his fondness for themes of decay and death was due to a morbid liking for the subjects themselves, or to the value which religious teachers in general at that time attached to the contemplation of physical corruption, or whether such themes offered a specially favorable opportunity for lyrical movements in prose ending in minor cadences, may admit of discussion. Certainly one hears even in the most soaring strains of his eloquence the ground tone of the futility and vanity of life.

SIR JOHN DENHAM

P. 218. Denham was the first English poet after the Restoration who set out to be deliberately descriptive. To-day he seems colorless, but he was greatly admired in his own and the succeeding age, not so much for the descriptions themselves as for his moralization of his theme. See Pope's *Essay on Criticism,* II, 361.

RICHARD LOVELACE

Cf. note on Waller, p. 717.

THE GRASSHOPPER

Cf. Keats's sonnet *The Grasshopper and the Cricket,* p. 478.

ABRAHAM COWLEY

P. 219. Cowley's fame was greatest in his lifetime. His contemporaries buried him in Westminster Abbey by the side of Chaucer. But almost at once reaction set in, and he came to be recognized for what he was, a good verse-artisan but one of the most shallow and artificial thinkers among the followers of Donne. It is supposed that it was his precocity which Milton contrasted with his own late and slow development (as it seemed to him) in the sonnet *On his Having Arrived at the Age of Twenty-three* (see especially l. 8).

ANDREW MARVELL

Pp. 219 f. As Cowley is associated with the Stuart court, so is Marvell with Cromwell and the Protectorate. The vigor so striking in his work as a satirist and pamphleteer stiffens his lyrics and makes them to-day much fresher and more interesting than Cowley's work. His fancies are original and often quaint.

THE GARDEN

P. 220. l. 32. And out of the reed he made his flute. Cf. note on Waller's *The Story of Phœbus and Daphne Applied*, p. 717.

ll. 43-44. The idea that the mind contains an image of each external thing is a modification of Platonism.

TO HIS COY MISTRESS

Addison, in his *Hilpa and Shalum* (p. 269), developed the idea of this amusing extravaganza in great detail.

HENRY VAUGHAN

P. 221. A Welsh imitator of Herbert, and the most purely mystic of English poets. He was practically forgotten when Wordsworth rediscovered him. His influence on the *Ode on the Intimations of Immortality* (p. 391) is noticeable. It may be a question how far Wordsworth has improved upon his simple model, *The Retreat*.

THE TIMBER

This is a fanciful conceit which is redeemed from absurdity by the strength of the feeling that pervades it.

The tree is pictured first as alive in the forest (ll. 1-8), then as wood built into a house (ll. 9-12), which creaks in a storm (l. 13-16); and this "resentment after death" is supposed to be a survival of the old enmity between the tree and the winds (ll. 17-20).

THE RESTORATION

JOHN DRYDEN

Pp. 222 ff. Dryden was to the men of letters of the time of Charles II about what Ben Jonson was to those of Charles I — the dominant literary figure, yet without supreme talent in either prose or verse. He left a large body of work, of which the prose shows him to have been possessed of a kind of ample common sense, strikingly evinced, for example, in the *Essay of Dramatic Poesy*, while the verse has a large, easy movement without the fire and force of the best of the Elizabethans. The heroic couplet he developed and popularized to a degree that made it the chief vehicle of narrative poetry for the next half century (cf. Gray, *The Progress of Poesy*, ll. 103-111, p. 318).

AE

Dryden's satire is effective partly because of its lack of exaggeration and heat, its tone of well-bred superiority and amused self-possession, and partly because of its clearness, its rapidity, and its ease of movement. It was well fitted to be read and discussed and enjoyed by the miscellaneous assemblies in the coffee-houses (see p. 516), and it is still his chief credential to a high place in the history of English literature.

ABSALOM AND ACHITOPHEL

Pp. 222 f. July 2, 1681, the Earl of Shaftesbury was sent to the Tower. He was the leader of the movement to have the Roman Catholic Duke of York barred from the succession, and the illegitimate Duke of Monmouth recognized as heir to Charles II. Dryden's satire, which was not improbably written at the King's suggestion, was published only a few days before Shaftesbury's indictment and, although it did not prevent his acquittal, had an enormous popular success.

The use of the biblical story of David and Absalom must have appealed even to the Dissenting party, who thought in Hebraic terms, the more so as Shaftesbury had been dubbed Achitophel and Monmouth Absalom before the poem was written. This fact suggests that Dryden was shrewd enough to follow in the wake of popular imagination.

In the second selection, Zimri (l. 544) is the notorious Duke of Buckingham, against whom Dryden had a personal grudge for ridiculing him in the famous burlesque called *The Rehearsal*.

THE HIND AND THE PANTHER

Pp. 223 f. A religious satire in the form of a beast-fable, written after Dryden had become converted to Roman Catholicism. The key to the allegory is:

Hind — the Church of Rome.
Panther — the Church of England.
Bear — the Independents.
Quaking Hare — the Quakers.
Ape — the Free-thinkers.
Lion — the Court party, perhaps including the King.
Boar — the Anabaptists.
Reynard the Fox — the Unitarians, called Arians in the time of Athanasius, and Socinians after the early sixteenth century.

ll. 13-16. Caledonian. Not Scottish, but British. The reference is to the Roman Catholic martyrs.

ALEXANDER'S FEAST

Pp. 224 ff. Dryden's odes are cold and artificial, but remarkable for their sustained adaptation of sound and rhythm to produce musical quality.

For Pope's eulogy of this poem, see the *Essay on Criticism*, II, 374–383.

l. 9. According to tradition Alexander was induced by Thaïs to set fire to the capital Persepolis.

l. 20. Timotheus. A famous Athenian musician who, however, died just before Alexander was born.

P. 225. ll. 75–83. The particular force of this passage is that Alexander himself had conquered Darius in a series of hard-fought battles, and that his own memory would necessarily strengthen the impression which the musician wished to produce in his mind.

ll. 97–98. Cf. *L'Allegro*, ll. 135–150 (p. 193).

P. 226. ll. 161–165. St. Cecilia, a Roman martyr of the third century, is credited with the development of sacred music. Line 162 refers to her supposed invention of the organ.

ESSAY OF DRAMATIC POESY

Pp. 226 ff. This is at once an authoritative treatment of a big literary problem, a summary of dramatic criticism for an age, and a monument of common sense. The subject of debate is the respective merits of the classic (including the French), and the romantic (especially the English) ideals of the drama. Dryden presents each side with a fine balance and discrimination, but is obviously in sympathy with the English ideal.

The four talkers are Eugenius (? Lord Buckhurst, later Earl of Dorset, himself a keen critic, to whom the essay was dedicated), Crites (? Sir Robert Howard, author of some successful plays), Lisideius (Sir Charles Sedley, a well-known poet and wit,—the anagram of *Sidleius* makes this identification certain), and Neander (Dryden himself). To give informality to their discussion, the friends are represented as on a pleasure trip in a barge on the river. The supposed date of the excursion is June 3, 1665, when the Dutch and English fleets were engaged in battle; but the setting is, of course, a mere device for making the presentation of all sides of the question more convincing and more entertaining.

P. 233 a. *Mr. Hales of Eton*, John Hales, a famous scholar of his day. It is said that in an actual debate in Hales's chamber at Eton, to which many "persons of wit and quality" were invited, his opponents produced from a large number of authors the most striking expressions of many various subjects, and that he immediately produced from Shakespeare a better expression of each.

SAMUEL PEPYS

Pp. 234 ff. *The Diary* of Samuel Pepys is probably the most honest and unsophisticated self-revelation ever given to the world. This is due partly to the fact that Pepys did not suppose that it would ever be read by any one but himself, and partly to an intellectual clearness and candor which enabled him to describe his actions and feelings without self-deception. Other autobiographies — even the most famous — have, without exception, been written with half an eye on the public; either the author has, consciously or half-consciously, posed to excite admiration for his cleverness or to shock by his unconventionalities, or he has become secretive at the very moment when he was beginning to be most interesting. But Pepys shows himself exactly as he was — an extraordinarily human mixture of worldliness and religion, of loyalty and intrigue, of jealousy, immorality, good-heartedness, pettiness, generosity, weakness, and substantial personal worth. Yet the reader would judge unjustly who estimated Pepys's character solely on the basis of the Diary. He was in his own day regarded as a model of propriety and respectability and a man of unusual business capacity. He may be said, indeed, with little exaggeration, to have created the English navy: when he became Secretary to the Generals of the Fleet, the Admiralty Office was practically without organization; before the close of his career he had organized it and, as a recent Lord of the Admiralty says, provided it with "the principal rules and establishments in present use." That he was not altogether averse to what we now call "graft," is true; but in an age of universal bribery he was a notably honest and honorable official, and he never allowed his private interests to cause injury or loss to the service. No other document of any sort gives us so full and varied and vivid an account of the social life and pursuits of the Restoration period; Pepys is often ungrammatical, but he is never dull in manner or unprovided with interesting material.

The carelessness of his style is due in no small measure to the nature of his book. He wrote for his own eye alone, using a system of shorthand which was not deciphered until 1825. That he was a man of cultivation is proved by the society in which he moved, by his interest in music and the drama, by the valuable library of books and prints which he accumulated and bequeathed to Magdalene College, Cambridge, by his interest in the Royal Society, by the academic honors conferred upon him by the universities, and by his official writings.

SAMUEL BUTLER

Pp. 237 f. For an account of his career, see Oldham's *Satire*, p. 238, ll. 175–190. Butler himself wrote a quatrain saying that Charles II was never without his *Hudibras*.

JOHN OLDHAM

A Satire Dissuading from Poetry

P. 238. The passage quoted illustrates the distressing financial condition of writers in the time between the decay of the system of private patronage and the development of business relations with publishers which made it possible for authors to live upon the results of their labor. The term "Grub Street," given to writers who are struggling for a bare existence, arose during this time from the name of a street in which many of the hack writers actually lived.

JOHN LOCKE

The Conduct of the Understanding

Pp. 238 f. John Locke first extended the principles of the inductive method in philosophy into the field of mental phenomena. By his discussion of the nature and origin of ideas and the necessary limits of human knowledge, he introduced, not only into philosophy, but into the common thinking of educated men conceptions which have been fruitful ever since. Locke is also notable as a pioneer in the cause of civil and religious liberty and in more rational methods of education.

His style is not distinguished, but it has the great merits of clearness and of intelligibility to the general reader.

JOHN BUNYAN

Pp. 239 ff. Written in an age of subtleties and extravagances of style, Bunyan's prose is so simple and straightforward that children to-day can understand and enjoy it. A naturally vivid imagination strengthened by keen observation of life, intense religious feeling quickened by persecution, and much reading of the Bible are some of the factors that entered into the creation of his masterpiece, *The Pilgrim's Progress*.

P. 241 b. *Vanity Fair*. If instead of the allegorical *Vanity*, we substitute *Stourbridge*, or *Southwark*, or the name of some other town, we find in this passage a vivid and accurate description of the old-time fair, with only slight exaggeration for the purpose of the allegory. Fairs lasted usually only a day, or a few days, although at Stourbridge, on the outskirts of Cambridge, where a fair was held in September, after the harvest was in, it continued for three weeks. At such a fair every article used in England could be bought, and merchandise was imported from the Continent and the Far East. As Bunyan shows, there were also associated with the bartering all sorts of amusements, and much license and crime developed. Cf. Ben Jonson's amusing play, *Bartholomew Fair*.

MINOR LYRISTS

Pp. 243 f. See the discussion under Waller, p. 717.

THE CLASSICAL AGE

DANIEL DEFOE

Pp. 245 ff. Defoe had the type of mind, the training, and the experience that make a successful newspaper man. His invincible curiosity and love of experiment, his willingness to take risks, his argumentative ability, his instinct for what the people think and want, his memory for details, and his marvelous ability to add circumstantial evidence to make his fictions convincing, his talent as a "story-teller," and his keen eye to the main chance commercially — all these qualities would have helped him to success under any conditions; and, considering his time and his temperament, he made a considerable figure. He was not an originator, but by reason of his lucid and forceful English, he was a good disseminator of current ideas. His project for the education of women, for instance, was not original, but it reflects the most advanced thought of his time on the subject, and in a way that could not have failed to interest a wide public. The selection does not show Defoe's peculiar genius for making fiction read like fact, but it does show him as a man able to make English serve his ends.

JONATHAN SWIFT

Pp. 248 ff. Swift's satire is supreme by virtue of his style and his constructive imagination. The latter shows itself chiefly in his ability to assume a certain attitude toward a problem or a situation and carry out this attitude to its logical consequences in even the minutest details. Thus in *Gulliver's Travels* he shows human life as looked at successively by beings smaller than men, by beings larger than men, and by beings of other standards and ideals. In his *Modest Proposal* he emphasizes the low value set on human life — on the lives of children in Ireland — by assuming that they are worth only what they will fetch in the market, and consistently pushing that assumption to its logical but horrible consequences. The effectiveness of his method depends upon the fact that, whereas in most of our thinking inherited views and conventional opinions on particular points rise up to prevent us from developing any principle with relentless logic, this method presents a principle under such a form that our inherited views and conventional reactions are not aroused until after we have committed ourselves to what the simple logic of the principle implies.

His style is devoid of grace and charm because it is so set upon practical results and so direct and simple. He uses words with an exact sense of their intellectual values and force rarely equalled; but his clearness and simplicity are deceptive. A second meaning lurks always beneath the plain and simple surface.

A TALE OF A TUB

Pp. 248 ff. Swift himself explains his title thus:

"The wits of the present age being so very numerous and penetrating, it seems the grandees of Church and State begin to fall under horrible apprehensions lest these gentlemen, during the intervals of a long peace, should find leisure to pick holes in the weak sides of religion and government. To prevent which, there has been much thought employed of late upon certain projects for taking off the force and edges of those formidable inquirers from canvassing and reasoning upon such delicate points. . . . To this end, at a grand committee, some days ago, this important discovery was made by a certain curious and refined observer, that seamen have a custom when they meet a Whale to fling him out an empty Tub, by way of amusement, to divert him from laying violent hands upon the Ship. . . . The Ship in danger is easily understood to be its old antitype, the commonwealth." But this explanation is a part of Swift's jest; "a tale of a tub" had long

been a proverbial expression for an absurd or nonsensical story.

The treatise as a whole is a satire on the three great branches of the Christian Church: the Catholic (represented by Peter), the Church of the Reformation, including the English and the Lutheran branches (represented by Martin, *i.e.*, Luther), and the Presbyterians, Independents and other Dissenters (represented by Jack, *i.e.*, Calvin). The coats represent Primitive Christianity as delivered by Christ to his followers. The successive sections of the main satire describe allegorically the various changes which have been made in Christian doctrine and institutions from time to time. The section given in this volume is devoted entirely to the history of the Church before the split caused by the Reformation. A later section tells how Peter, claiming to be the oldest, assumed authority and kicked his brothers out of the house which he had taken possession of (see p. 252, last paragraph); and other sections narrate the adventures and deeds of the brothers after their separation.

That this satire should have given great offence to Protestants as well as to Catholics and effectually prevented Swift from ever attaining such a rank and position in the English Church as his intellectual ability clearly entitled him to, is not to be wondered at. It has been said that he was more favorable to Martin — the Church of England — than to the others; but no good Church of England man can have been pleased with the treatment Martin receives, especially in the brief section entitled *The History of Martin* which Swift added in some editions of the work. The fact is that every deviation from Primitive Christianity is represented as arbitrary, fraudulent, and ludicrous.

Some details of the allegory may assist the reader:

The seven years of obedience and the travels and exploits (p. 248 *a*) refer to the early centuries and the spreading of Christianity in foreign lands. The three ladies with whom the brothers fell in love (p. 248 *b*) are covetousness, ambition, and pride. the great vices which caused the first corruptions of the Church; and the social climbing (p. 248 *b*) represents the rise of Christianity to dominant power in the Roman Empire. The whole of p. 249 — in which readers of Carlyle will recognize the germ of his Clothes Philosophy in *Sartor Resartus* — is a general satire on mankind for its worship of externals, such as rank, wealth, etc., and at the same time a special satire on the Church for the development of an elaborate hierarchy and elaborate ceremonies. The idol sitting crosslegged (249 *a*) is in primary intention a tailor and secondarily, perhaps, the Pope, the origin of whose dignity and title some deduced from the Roman system of religion. Hell (*ibid.*) was a term applied in Swift's day to a box beneath the tailor's work-bench into which scraps were thrown, and also, say the satirists, such pieces of cloth as the tailor wished to steal from his customers. I do not understand the symbolism of the goose or of the yard-stick and the needle (*ibid.*). The shoulder-knots (p. 250 *b*) and the gold lace (p. 251 *a*) are symbolical of the additions made to the simple doctrines of early Christianity, and the discussions are a satire on the methods by which authority for these innovations was adduced. The nuncupatory will (*ibid.*) is tradition, to which the Catholics allow great authority. The flame-colored satin (p. 251 *b*) is the doctrine of Purgatory, which, according to views in vogue in Swift's day, had already appeared in Jewish rabbinical doctrine (my Lord C ——) and in Mohammedanism (Sir J. W.). The advice "to take care of fire and put out their candles before they went to sleep" (*ibid.*) means to shun hell and, in order to do so, to subdue and extinguish their lusts. The codicil (*ibid.*) figures the Apocryphal books of the Bible, and the dog-keeper is said to be an allusion to the Apocryphal book of Tobit. The interpretation of "fringe" as "broom-stick" (p. 252 *a*) alludes to mediæval methods of interpreting scripture. The embroidered figures (*ibid.*) are images of Christ and the saints. The strong box in which the will was locked up (p. 252 *b*) signifies the Greek and Latin languages, and the power of adding clauses (*ibid.*) to the will signifies the Pope's power to issue bulls and decretals. The lord whose house was usurped (*ibid.*) means the Emperor Constantine, from whom the Church was said to have received the donation of St. Peter's patrimony, the foundation of the temporal power of the Church.

A Modest Proposal

Pp. 253 f. Written in Swift's bitterest mood, to show the terrible condition of the poor in Ireland, and the utter heartlessness of the English in dealing with the situation. The terrific force of the satire is due largely to the matter-of-fact handling of details in a proposition subversive of all civilization. Some simple-minded persons have failed to understand Swift's irony and supposed him to be really in favor of the plan he advocates.

JOSEPH ADDISON AND RICHARD STEELE

Pp. 254 ff. Addison and Steele are as commonly thought of as inseparable as are Beaumont and Fletcher, and the two are as different as the earlier pair. Addison is always cool, level-headed, with a keen eye for the humorous side of life, and an occasional flight of fancy. Steele is usually hot-headed and warm-hearted, inclined to preach and to sentimentalize, at times rather in the manner of Thackeray. These differences are very evident in the passages chosen. Both writers owe much of their charm to their ease and unaffectedness, and to the sense of leisure — the play element — that pervades their work.

In No. 10 of the *Spectator*, Addison is at his best, chatting with his readers as if they were all personal friends; in No. 26, he is the man of taste (cf. Sir Thomas Browne on a similar theme, pp. 181–184, above); in No. 98, he is the satirist, amusing yet never sharp; in No. 159 and Nos. 584–585, he turns his imagination into Oriental fields and produces phantasies which show that even the most classical age has its romantic moods.

In No. 95 of the *Tatler* and No. 11 of the *Spectator*, Steele shows himself as a warm-hearted sentimentalist; in No. 167 of the *Tatler*, as a critic and philanthropist; and in No. 264, as a genial humorist.

The Campaign

P. 262. Addison was asked to celebrate in verse the Battle of Blenheim for the sake of helping the political party with which the Duke of Marlborough was connected. When he produced his *Campaign*, Godolphin, Marlborough's son-in-law, and the other leaders were so pleased that they gave him a political post made vacant by the death of John Locke, the philosopher (see p. 238). Later, as the poem was an immediate and pronounced success, they made him under-secretary of state. One of the most admired passages was the simile of the angel, ll. 287–292, which taken in connection with a terrible storm that passed over England in November, 1704, was obvious and commonplace enough to hit the popular fancy. I have quoted a short passage from the work as a good specimen of utilitarian verse. To-day it is of historical value only.

HILPA AND SHALUM

Pp. 269 ff. The idea of this extravaganza was perhaps suggested by Marvell's poem, *To His Coy Mistress*, p. 220.

MATTHEW PRIOR

P. 272. Although Prior lived well into the Classical Age, he, like Swift, began to write while Dryden was still at the height of his power. His first production, indeed, was a parody, — such as any clever school boy might write, — written in collaboration with Charles Montague (later Earl of Halifax), upon Dryden's *The Hind and the Panther*. It was entitled *The Hind and the Panther Transversed to the Story of the Country Mouse and the City Mouse* and began:

"A milk-white mouse, immortal and unchanged,
   Fed on soft cheese and o'er the dairy ranged:
   Without unspotted, innocent within,
   She feared no danger, for she knew no gin."

Later he wrote a successful travesty of Boileau's Pindaric ode in praise of Louis XIV. Most of his writing was called out by some special occasion and is distinguished by playfulness and wit, as are the brief selections here chosen to represent him. That he was capable of more serious efforts is shown by his *Carmen Sæculare*, an ode in praise of King William, but his life was devoted chiefly to politics and diplomacy.

ALEXANDER POPE

Pp. 273 ff. Pope was avowedly the pupil of Dryden, but within his more limited field, he far excelled his master. His immediate success was due not only to the fact that he voiced most perfectly the predominant spirit of the cultivated classes of the age in which he lived — the age of obedience to rule, and worship of form — but also to his remarkable faculty, however unconscious, of advertising himself by means of a host of friends and an even greater host of rivals and foes. His enduring success is based upon qualities very different from those so admired by his contemporaries. His ideas in criticism, which they regarded as infallible axioms, seem to us partly commonplace, and partly false; his theory of metaphysics, which they regarded with admiring awe, we smile at as superficial, and even so, as borrowed from Bolingbroke; his satires we are likely to read with half-impatient amusement, because they are so largely works of personal spite, and so often ascribe to his enemies qualities which they did not possess. But with all his glib ·superficiality and his petty malice, Pope has two qualities more highly developed perhaps than they are found in any other English poet: one is almost inexhaus-

tible wit, which spices his dullest subjects and his most objectionable satires; the other is an amazing instinct for the minor perfections of form.

AN ESSAY ON CRITICISM

I, ll. 68–91. The doctrine that creative artists should take Nature as their guide is one of the most astonishing doctrines of the critical theory of Pope and his fellows — the so-called classicists; for it seems to us that this is precisely the thing which they did not do, and the thing by doing which the leaders of romanticism, Thomson, Cowper, Wordsworth and others, introduced new subjects and new methods into English literature. The difficulty is cleared up, however, when we learn (from ll. 88–89, 126, 135, and especially 139–140), that the way to "follow Nature" is, not to observe things as they are, but to imitate and defer to the "ancients" — Homer (124), Vergil (129–130), and Aristotle (138).

That this official doctrine did not entirely satisfy Pope's native impulses may be seen from ll. 146–155, where he represents Pegasus, the winged horse of poesy, as boldly deviating "from the common track." See also the romantic sentiments expressed in *Eloïsa to Abelard*. In landscape gardening Pope's tastes were decidedly romantic. The classicism of his writings was therefore not so much the expression of anything fundamental in his nature as the result of deliberate conformity to a critical theory.

P. 274. l. 180. Horace, in his *Ars Poetica*, had admitted that even Homer sometimes nods; Pope suggests that when we suspect a good writer of writing poorly, the fault may be, not his, but our own.

P. 275. II, ll. 374–383. Compare *Alexander's Feast*, p. 224. Pope heightens the compliment by recalling the phrasing of the original.

THE RAPE OF THE LOCK

Pope's mocking spirit made him particularly successful in dealing with this petty quarrel as if it were a matter of national importance. The occasion of the poem was this: A young nobleman named Lord Petre had stolen a lock of hair from a well-known beauty, Miss Arabella Fermor, and a quarrel arose. Their common friend, John Caryll, suggested to Pope, whom he also knew well, that the poet write something to make peace. The first version of *The Rape of the Lock* was the result. At first, all parties to the quarrel were incensed by the satire, but eventually they were placated, and Miss Fermor allowed Pope to dedicate the second edition of the poem to her. In the first form the "machinery" of the sylphs was absent. In order that the reader may compare the two versions, Pope's later additions are shown within brackets; aside from these additions and a few minor verbal changes, the poems are identical.

The charm of the poem comes from its mock solemnity, its sudden bits of bathos, its delicious wit and sparkle, its light sketching of human vanities and follies, and the perfect art of its verse and phrasing.

I, l. 32. *silver token*, the silver penny which superstition said the elves would drop into the shoe of a maid who was tidy about her work. *Circled green*, the fairy ring (cf. the song from *A Midsummer Night's Dream* (p. 143), l. 8).

P. 278. II, ll. 112–115. Note that the fanciful name in each case tells the sylph's occupation: *Zephyretta*, little breeze; *Brillante*, shining one (for Belinda's earrings); *Momentilla*, little moment, *i.e.*, timekeeper; *Crispissa*, curly one (cf. IV, 99–102, from which it appears that Belinda's hair did not curl by nature).

II, ll. 134–135, and III, l. 106. The drinks served were chocolate and coffee. The chocolate was evidently brought in a hard ball or cake, as it is still prepared in the West Indies, and was ground in a hand mill, as were the roasted coffee berries.

Pp. 279 f. III, ll. 25–100. The popular Spanish game of ombre. Evidently Pope's description is accurate (cf. Lamb's *Mrs. Battle's Opinions on Whist*, p. 426). Most commonly it was played by three persons, one of whom made the trump and played against the other two. Nine cards were dealt (ll. 29–30). The *Matadores* (l. 33) were the principal trumps, in the order of importance (l. 34) as follows: (1) *Spadillio* (l. 49), the ace of spades; (2) *Manillio* (l. 51), with a black trump, the deuce (as here, cf. ll. 46–47), with a red trump, the seven; (3) *Basto* (l. 53), the ace of clubs; (4) *Pam* (ll. 61–62), the knave of clubs.

The game runs thus: Belinda leads successively the ace of spades (l. 49), the deuce of spades (l. 51), the ace of clubs (l. 53), the king of spades (l. 56), and takes four tricks: (1) two trumps (l. 50), (2) two trumps (l. 51), (3) a trump and another card (l. 54), (4) Pam and another card (ll. 61, 64).

Then she leads the king of clubs (l. 69) and loses the trick because the baron plays the queen of spades (ll. 66–68). The baron then has the lead and takes three more tricks with the king, queen, and knave of diamonds (the last trick including Belinda's queen of hearts, ll. 75–76, 87–88).

As Belinda and the baron have four tricks each,

the next trick will determine who wins the deal. The baron leads the ace of hearts (l. 95), but Belinda has the king (ll. 95–96), which, except when hearts are trumps, outranks the ace. Accordingly, she is saved from *codille* (l. 92), the failure of the person who makes the trump (Spanish: "yo suy *hombre*," "I am the man," which gives the name to the game) to take more tricks than her opponents.

P. 280. ll. 122–124. Scylla stole for her lover Minos the purple lock of hair of her father Nisus, on which depended the safety of his city. For this she was scorned by Minos and changed by the gods into a bird (Ovid, *Metamorphoses*, VIII, 6–151).

P. 281. IV, l. 20. In England, the raw wind that makes people blue and irritable. In Dickens's *Bleak House*, Mr. Jarndyce commented on all misfortunes with "The wind is in the East again."

P. 282. ll. 127–132. The irony of l. 132 is pointed by the proportion of oaths and expletives used, fully half of the four lines.

P. 284. V, ll. 125–126. Romulus, the founder of Rome, was believed by the Romans to have been carried up to heaven by his father Mars, while he was reviewing his troops during a thunderstorm. He was said to have appeared in a vision to Proculus, and to have bidden him tell the Romans that their city would become the greatest in the world.

ELOÏSA TO ABELARD

Pp. 285 f. This poem is a highly romantic effort in itself, and surprising as coming from the pen of the leading poet of the age of common sense. It is based upon an English translation made by Hughes in 1714 of a French version published in 1693 of the famous correspondence of Abelard and Heloïse. With the original Latin letters, the authenticity of which has been questioned, Pope's version has practically nothing to do.

The story, however, is as follows: Abelard, a famous scholar and teacher of the twelfth century, fell in love with his pupil Heloïse; but the lovers were separated by her uncle and both entered the religious life. The letters are supposed to have been written some years later, when Abelard was Abbot of St. Gildas in Brittany and Heloïse Abbess of the convent of the Paraclete.

ESSAY ON MAN

Pp. 286 ff. Whether or not Pope actually had in his hands a manuscript embodying the ideas of his friend Henry St. John, Lord Bolingbroke, his poem is little more than a skilful paraphrase of the deistic philosophy of the eighteenth century as expressed by him. It was at first published anonymously, and Pope took great delight in hearing the various comments upon it. Not until it had reached its fourth edition did he acknowledge authorship of it.

The poem had as great a success in Germany and France, in translations, as it had in England and America, where, notwithstanding its deism, it long remained a favorite with orthodox Christians of a mildly speculative turn. It was regarded as a model of cogent reasoning in verse.

EPISTLE TO DR. ARBUTHNOT

Pp. 288 ff. Dr. Arbuthnot, Queen Anne's physician, was one of Pope's most faithful friends. He also was a man of some literary skill, though he took no pains to preserve his writings — it was said that he let his children make kites of them. According to his contemporaries, he was one of the most brilliant, witty, and genial members of the famous Scriblerus Club. Cf. Dr. Johnson's opinion of him, p. 343.

The *Epistle* is interesting not merely as a satire on Pope's enemies but also as a defence of his own position and a study of his own character as he saw himself. It is impossible, however, to take him precisely at his own estimate. He had the double sensitiveness of the poet and the hunchback, which made him unable to bear the slightest unfavorable criticism, however good-natured, of his work or of himself. While it is true that many of his enemies deserved what he said of them, it is also certain that he was in most instances provoked by their failure to approve of him. For instance, the three singled out in l. 146 had all written against Pope. Thomas Burnet, son of the Bishop of Salisbury (satirized in *The Dunciad*, as G —— [Gilbert Burnet], IV, l. 608), had published *Homerides; or a letter to Mr. Pope occasioned by his intended translation of Homer, by Sir Iliad Doggrel,* and Pope suspected him (wrongly) of writing *Pope Alexander's Supremacy*. Pope retaliated upon him also in *The Dunciad*. Oldmixon was a Grub Street writer, one of the many who replied to *The Dunciad*, and had criticised Pope on other occasions. Cooke, who himself translated Hesiod, abused Pope in an article called the *Battle of the Poets*. Again, "gentle Fanny," l. 149 (Lord Hervey), had infuriated Pope by ridiculing his deformity and his birth. The passage in ll. 305–333 (not given here) is one of the bitterest denun-

ciations in all literature. It should be noted, however, that Pope, for reasons unknown, opened the war in his *Imitations of Horace* by scoffing at Lord Hervey for both his good looks and his pretensions to verse. In l. 151, he expressed his opinion that Gildon had been paid by Addison to defame him. In l. 153, what he says of Dennis might as justly have been applied to himself. Dennis had found fault with Pope's *Pastorals;* Pope ridiculed him in his *Essay on Criticism;* Dennis retorted in a violent pamphlet. The comments on Bentley and Tibbalds (Lewis Theobald), l. 164, were drawn by the "slashing" that the famous classical scholar gave to Pope's *Iliad* in calling it "a very pretty poem but not Homer"; while the "piddling" (trifling) of Theobald refers to his objections to Pope's Shakespearean emendations and guesses. Theobald later brought out a much better edition of Shakespeare than Pope's. Pope's contempt for Ambrose Phillips (ll. 179–180) seems to be a case of sheer jealousy of the praise bestowed upon Phillips's *Pastorals* and of Addison's friendship for him.

Over against these evidences of pettiness must be placed not only the list of men of letters and of social eminence by whom Pope's genius had been recognized and with whom he was on friendly terms (ll. 135–141), but also his own defence in ll. 125–134, with the tragic implications of l. 132. Granville, Baron Lansdowne (l. 135), was a statesman and himself a verse-writer and dramatist. He said of Pope when the poet was only seventeen or eighteen years of age that he promised "miracles." Pope dedicated to him his *Windsor Forest.* Walsh (l. 136) and Garth (l. 137) were themselves poets and men of taste. Congreve (l. 138) was one of the leading dramatists of the Restoration. Talbot (l. 139), Earl and Duke of Shrewsbury, rose to be lord chamberlain. He was, according to Swift, one of the most popular men of the time and also "the finest gentleman we have." Lord Somers (l. 139), lord chancellor, was a member of the Kit Kat Club and a patron of various members of it. He gave Addison his pension, and to him Swift dedicated his *Tale of a Tub.* Sheffield (l. 139), Earl of Mulgrave and afterward Duke of Buckingham and Normanby, was a munificent patron to Dryden. He wrote in both prose and verse, and his *Essay on Poetry* was praised by Dryden and Pope. Pope edited his collected works. Rochester (l. 140) was Francis Atterbury, Bishop of Rochester, one of Pope's special friends and himself a writer of polished prose. St. John (l. 141) was Lord Bolingbroke, by whom the *Essay on Man* was largely inspired.

l. 190. Pope uses Tate merely as a type. He has been described as the "author of the worst alterations of Shakespeare, the worst version of the Psalms of David, and the worst continuation of a great poem (*Absalom and Achitophel*) extant."

ll. 193-214. The three enemies of whom Pope drew elaborate pen pictures were Addison, Lord Halifax, and Lord Hervey. Against Lord Hervey he seems to have cherished some strong personal grudge (see note on l. 149, above); he railed against Halifax not only because the First Lord of the Treasury failed to bestow the pension he had promised, but also because Halifax had the bad taste to approve of the poet Tickell. While his attacks on these two men are marked by the most undignified vituperation, the lines on Addison show a certain restraint, as if Pope stood in some awe of the Atticus (Addison was already so called for his supposedly flawless style) of his age; a certain unwilling respect shows through his taunting phrases. We have omitted the portraits of Halifax and Hervey.

THE DUNCIAD

P. 290. The Dunce-epic had as its hero in the first edition (1728) Lewis Theobald, who had pointed out the faults in Pope's edition of Shakespeare. The poem was written in imitation of Dryden's *MacFlecknoe*, which deals with the appointment of Shadwell (who supplanted Dryden as poet laureate in 1688) to succeed Flecknoe, an obscure poet, as monarch of the kingdom of Dulness. Pope represented Dulness as a goddess who chooses Tibbald (Theobald) to succeed Settle (Elkanah Settle, a third-rate dramatist who had become a hack writer and died in 1724) as ruler of her land. In 1741 Pope added a fourth book; and in 1743, he published a revised edition with Colley Cibber, the actor-dramatist, as hero. The change was due to one of Pope's many quarrels. Cibber had introduced into a play some lines ridiculing a play that had failed, in which Pope had had a hand. For this reason Pope had satirized Cibber in the fourth book added to the original *Dunciad*. Cibber replied in a printed letter, but in a spirit of good-humored raillery. Pope was roused by this to the point of fury which is reflected in the revised *Dunciad*.

The passage quoted concludes the poem. It tells how the reign of Dulness becomes universal and absolute, even the poet's Muse yielding to her power. It is often cited as the most eloquent passage in all Pope's writings.

THE ILIAD

Cf. note on Chapman, p. 710, above.

JOHN GAY

Pp. 291 f. Gay, at the request of Pope, set out to burlesque the *Pastorals* of Ambrose Phillips, but having an eye for reality and a genuine though slight poetic talent, he produced in his *Shepherd's Week* a work of some interest and vitality. The same sense of reality and lightness of touch are displayed in his *Trivia, or Art of Walking the Streets* and in his *Fables*.

His *Black-eyed Susan* connects him with the romantic movement, in that it is an early eighteenth century song dealing sympathetically though artificially with the lives and emotions of the lowly.

His greatest success and his main claim to a place in the history of English literature came from his composition of the *Beggar's Opera*, a burlesque of fashionable Italian opera, in which the principal characters are thieves and vagabonds. It is in a sense the ancestor of modern comic opera.

EDWARD YOUNG

Pp. 292 f. Young's poetry has now entirely lost its appeal, but it is important historically. The tide of the Romantic Movement was rising when he began to write, and he was carried on with it so that his mediocre talent brought him a disproportionate success. His sententious moralizing, and his religious sentimentality appealed strongly to an age of rigid theoretical conventions and actual license.

His early satires were in the manner and form of the classical age; his later poems, from which our extracts are taken, are romantic, not merely in their background and emotion, but in their use of blank verse, the great vehicle of those writers who rebelled against the couplets of Dryden and Pope.

THE TRANSITION

LADY WINCHILSEA

P. 294. Lady Winchilsea finds a place here because of recent years the romantic qualities of her work, noted long ago by Wordsworth, have met with general recognition and have received special significance from their existence at a time when the Classical Movement seemed supreme.

Her sketch of the sights and sounds of night

(ll. 23–36) shows observation and simplicity worthy almost of Wordsworth himself.

ROBERT BLAIR

Pp. 294 f. Blair's one poem gave rise to a series of mortuary poems, and is important because it appealed to the same taste that took delight in Young's *Night Thoughts*, and so belongs to the same phase of the romantic movement.

JAMES THOMSON

Pp. 296 ff. Thomson is one of the earliest romantic poets to make the different aspects of Nature his main theme. The extracts from his *Seasons* show that he had really observed what he described, although he is not free from such indirectness of phrasing for mere effect as *the bleating kind* = sheep, *soft fearful people* = sheep, *plumy people* = birds, *watery gear* = fishing tackle, in which the classical school of poets delighted. He was preëminently the poet of the English middle classes until the nineteenth century, when Scott and then Tennyson took his place.

Pp. 298 ff. His *Castle of Indolence*, like Shenstone's *Schoolmistress* (pp. 312 f.) and other eighteenth century imitations of Spenser's *Faerie Queene*, was intended to be at least mildly humorous. Thomson uses comparatively few archaic words or constructions — just enough, perhaps, to secure the effect of quaintness and remoteness at which he aimed. It is hardly necessary to add that neither he nor any other eighteenth century writer was always accurate in his use of such words and constructions.

JOHN DYER

Pp. 300 f. Dyer wrote little but he had the eye of a careful observer and lover of Nature. For this he was perhaps indebted to his having been born and brought up in Wales among the mountains and dales of which he sings. It is just possible that the word "van" — rather curiously used in l. 3 — may have been suggested by the name of a mountain familiar to him — the Carmarthen Van, the second highest peak in southwest Wales.

DAVID MALLET

Pp. 301 f. David Mallet — his name was originally Malloch — lives in literary history by virtue of three rather curious circumstances: the title of one of his poems (*The Excursion*) had the

honor of being used later by Wordsworth; the famous song, *Rule Britannia!* (p. 300), was first sung in a musical comedy called *Alfred, a Masque*, composed by him and James Thomson ; and he was the reputed author of *William and Margaret* (p. 301), the most important ballad in the history of the Romantic Movement. Fate favored him in Wordsworth's choice of a title for his poem. She favored him in the second instance by letting the poet James Thomson die before *Alfred* was printed and before any public claim had been made to the great song which all scholars now ascribe to Thomson. She favored him the third time by allowing him to retain for over one hundred and fifty years credit in literary circles for the authorship of *William and Margaret*, a ballad which we now know to have been printed in slightly different form and sold about the streets of London while he was still a child. The importance of the ballad for the history of Romanticism lies partly in its real beauty, partly in the early date at which it attracted public attention and interest, and partly in the large amount of discussion to which it gave rise.

SAMUEL JOHNSON

Pp. 302 ff. Boswell's incomparable account of the life and conversation of Dr. Samuel Johnson not only proves that his personal supremacy in the literary society of his day was deserved, but also exhibits in almost bewildering detail the independence of character, the courage, the strong and clear common sense, the freedom from cant, the wit, and the personal vigor, by virtue of which he dominated all with whom he came in contact. All these qualities are exhibited also in Johnson's writings, though his wit is sometimes made clumsy by an affected ponderosity of diction, and his common sense sometimes sounds to our modern ears like oracular emptiness in the elaborate artificiality of his balanced clauses and phrases.

CONGREVE

In his *Lives of the English Poets*, which were written when he was nearly seventy years old, Johnson's style is seen at its best. His diction has become more simple and natural and the structure of his sentences more varied and flexible.

These essays are still valuable. Since they were written, research has cleared up many points which were then doubtful and has supplied much information which was then inaccessible; but in his judgments of men and affairs and his criticisms of the purely intellectual qualities of the writings he discussed Johnson has rarely been equalled. He was, however, not endowed with poetic imagination, and he had little sensitiveness to some of the finer aspects of beauty. Consequently, while he is nearly always right and convincing in his attacks on poor verse, his judgment as to what is best is not trustworthy. The passage in *The Mourning Bride* which he declares the most poetical paragraph in the whole mass of English poetry has impressed most good judges as mere rhetorical declamation — and not of the highest order at that.

P. 307 b. *our Pindaric madness.* Cowley was blamed by his successors for introducing into English a Pindaric ode that did not conform to the plan of Pindar, but in metre and rhythm was governed only by the writer's caprice. For the structural scheme of the classical Pindaric ode, cf. note on Gray's *Progress of Poesy*, pp. 736 f.

THE RAMBLER

Pp. 308 f. The *Rambler* was a periodical modeled on the *Tatler*, the *Spectator*, and their like. Johnson was unable to give his essays the grace, ease, playfulness, and infinite variety of tone and manner which made the success of Steele and Addison. His diction is here at its worst and his sentences, though clear and strong, rumble and creak; but even here the fine qualities of his mind are displayed. The subject and the ideas of the essay we have chosen as representative are from time to time re-discovered by social philosophers and exploited as a new contribution to human knowledge.

LONDON

Pp. 309 f. This is an imitation of the third satire of Juvenal. It was published in 1738 and in its bitterness bears evidence of the poverty, struggles, and lack of success which marked Johnson's life at that time. Satires were then much in vogue. An ambitious young author of that period wrote a satire as naturally and inevitably as he now writes a short story. This one is notable only for the author's sympathy with the poor and his expression of personal feeling in l. 173, which he caused to be printed in capital letters. In style, it shows many of the qualities and tricks which especially characterize his work, though they are not so fully developed as in the *Rambler* and *The Vanity of Human Wishes*.

ll. 158 f. Even the sedate tradesman, at the sight of a tattered cloak, wakes from his dream of wealth and labors to make its wearer the object of a scornful jest.

ll. 162–165. The thought was suggested by Juvenal.

P. 310. l. 169. Spain, under authority of a papal grant of the sixteenth century, claimed all lands more than 470 leagues west of the Azores.

THE VANITY OF HUMAN WISHES

This is an imitation of the tenth satire of Juvenal. It was published in 1749 and shows in style the further development of the qualities of sonorous diction and balanced sentence structure exhibited in *London*. The first couplet is often quoted as an example of tautology disguised by verbosity. The general theme of the satire is stated in the title. The method is to present successively examples of great ambitions unfulfilled or, when fulfilled, the source of disappointment.

ll. 191 ff. The meteoric career of Charles XII of Sweden was fresh in mind when Johnson wrote, and had been brilliantly described by Voltaire. Charles invaded Denmark, defeated the Russians, the Poles, and the Saxons, and conceived the design of overthrowing the Russian Empire. When the Czar wished to negotiate peace, he declared, "I will treat with the Czar at Moscow." From this time his career was a succession of misfortunes and failures. His army, weakened by famine and cold (ll. 207–208), was defeated and scattered at Pultowa, July 8, 1709, and he fled into Turkey, where he attempted by bribes and intrigues to enlist Turkey in his designs. But the Czar bribed and intrigued more effectively, and Charles was imprisoned. He escaped in disguise in 1714 and fled to Norway, where he was killed, at Frederickshall, Dec. 11, 1718, by some unknown person (l. 220).

P. 311. ll. 313 f. Solon is said to have told Crœsus to count no man happy till his death.

ll. 317–318. The duke of Marlborough, the greatest general of his time, was paralyzed in 1716, six years before his death, and spent his last days playing with his grandchildren, being quite out of public affairs. He was talked about for his petty economies; it was said that, old and infirm as he was, he would walk to save the expense of sixpence for a sedan chair.

Swift's mind began to fail in 1738, and he subsequently had paralysis and aphasia; in 1741 he was insane beyond hope and so continued till his death in 1745, four years before Johnson wrote these lines.

WILLIAM SHENSTONE

WRITTEN IN AN INN AT HENLEY

P. 311. These lines in praise of the comfort and freedom from care to be found in an old English inn have been much praised and the last stanza often quoted. Dr. Johnson was especially fond of them.

THE SCHOOL-MISTRESS

Pp. 312 f. Thomson's imitation of Spenser, in his *Castle of Indolence*, has, as he intended, the effect of remoteness and dreaminess. Shenstone mixes realism and pseudo-archaisms to secure a playful picturesqueness which perhaps justifies his method, though his ignorance of archaic English may cause distress to the student of language. Shenstone had seen such a school-mistress and such a school as he describes. He spent his life in the country and is mainly notable for his romantic taste in gardening and his sacrifice of his fortune to his hobby.

ll. 136–139. The Coronation Chair of Great Britain, which contains the ancient "stone of destiny" brought from Scone, in Scotland, where it formed part of the seat in which the kings of Scotland were crowned.

P. 313. ll. 156–158. A hornbook was a card on which were printed the letters of the alphabet, a few simple syllables and words, the nine digits, and the Lord's prayer; this was covered with a thin transparent sheet of horn and set in a frame with a handle. Later the term was used loosely for a primer of any sort.

ll. 165–167. In his *Faerie Queene* Spenser often expresses his sorrow and pity for the characters of his poem when they are in distress or danger; cf. I, iii, 1–18 (p. 114).

THOMAS GRAY

Pp. 313 ff. Gray is the best type of the eighteenth century scholar-poet, important for his influence in the Romantic Movement, though in his own poetry less interesting than some poets of less authority. His work is always artistic, often artificial, never spontaneous, and it abounds in abstractions and personifications of abstractions (cf. ll. 61–70 in the *Ode on . . . Eton College*, p. 314). It shows, however, a wide range of interests, of subjects, and of metres; and he was a pioneer in many fields. He was one of the first poets in his time to write sympathetically of the life of the poor villager; he experimented in the classical form of the ode, with the regular strophe, antistrophe, and epode; he translated from the Norse at a time when Norse literature was unknown in England; he enjoyed romantic scenery at a time when it was unfashionable to do so; he was interested to write of the misfortunes of the Welsh nation in *The Bard* and he gave practical aid to the Welsh poet, Llewellyn Jones.

ON A DISTANT PROSPECT OF ETON COLLEGE

As a child Gray was sent to school at Eton College, and he seems always to have retained his interest in that place and the beautiful country about it. This poem, written when he was twenty-six, reviews the sports and probable future destinies of the boys who play there as he played when a child. In the churchyard at Stoke Pogis, only a few miles from Eton, is shown an ancient yew-tree beneath which tradition says he wrote his famous *Elegy*, and his own grave there bears the epitaph with which the *Elegy* closes.

The *Ode* shows the fondness for personified abstractions, for apostrophes to inanimate objects, for "elegance" of diction, and for moralization, characteristic of the so-called Age of Classicism. *The Elegy* still retains the fondness for abstractions, but shows in other respects distinct tendencies toward saner ideals of style. Both poems exhibit that taste for melancholy which was a marked feature of the early productions of Romanticism.

ELEGY WRITTEN IN A COUNTRY CHURCHYARD

Pp. 314 ff. This poem has always been popular because of the combination of universality and democracy in its theme; but because by the neatness of its form it has lent itself to over-quotation, it has lost much of its freshness for us. None the less, it is sincere and touched with real feeling.

P. 315. l. 57. *Some village-Hampden.* Some one who will stand up for the rights of his neighbors against the injustice of a local landowner, as John Hampden stood up for the rights of his countrymen against the unjust taxation of King Charles I.

THE PROGRESS OF POETRY

A *Pindaric Ode*

Pp. 316 ff. Cf. note, p. 735 above, on Cowley's treatment of the Pindaric Ode. Gray had too exacting a sense of scholarship not to adopt the genuine classical form. The present poem consists of three strophes and antistrophes, each containing twelve lines, and of three epodes, each containing seventeen lines. The parts are balanced in rhythm and in the various rhyme schemes.

I. Strophe : invocation to music.

Antistrophe : the power of music (the lyre, which was invented by stretching strings across a tortoise shell) to soothe all cares and passions, and to subdue the god of war, and even the eagle of Jove, the ruler of storms.

P. 317. *Epode :* the voice and the dance are obedient to music, together with all the Loves and Graces who dance before Venus to its strains.

II. Strophe : the ills to which mankind is subject and the question whether music can lessen them.

Antistrophe : the power of music from the Pole (the Eskimos) to the Equator (Chili).

Epode : the passing of music from Greece to Rome and from Rome to England.

III. Strophe : Shakespeare as the poet of Nature who can play upon the human heart.

P. 318. *Antistrophe :* Milton as the poet of the supernatural, and Dryden as a lesser poet but still great in the management of the heroic couplet (ll. 103–106).

Epode : Dryden as a lyric poet (ll. 107–111); Gray's own ambitions. Though he cannot equal Pindar, he has cultivated verse since childhood, and he will mount higher than "the Great" (who are *not* poets), simply because of his calling as poet.

THE FATAL SISTERS

Pp. 318 f. In his simplicity and directness Gray has caught something of the Norse spirit; and the form he has chosen, with its short lines broken up by alternating rhyme, bears out the general effect.

The chief importance of this poem and of several of Gray's later compositions is that in them were introduced to English readers new and fruitful sources of poetic themes. *The Descent of Odin, The Triumphs of Owen,* and *The Bard* all testify to the range of Gray's studies and the catholicity and unconventionality of his taste.

This poem is supposed to be addressed to her sisters by one of the Valkyries or Battle Maidens of Norse mythology. They are, as their name indicates, "choosers of the slain" (see ll. 33–34) and they hasten with joy to the battle.

The battle was fought in the eleventh century between Sigurd, earl of the Orkneys, and Brian, King of Dublin.

WILLIAM COLLINS

Pp. 319 ff. Collins wrote little, but his verse is simple, natural, and of exquisite poetic quality. His work is in general free from the affectations and conventionalities of his time. His *Ode on the Popular Superstitions of the Highlands* especially shows his ability to break away from the conventional in the choice of poetical material.

ODE WRITTEN IN THE BEGINNING OF THE YEAR 1746

The occasion was the loss of a large number of English soldiers in the autumn of 1745 and January 1746, in the War of the Austrian Succession.

ODE TO EVENING

This is a notable example of an unrhymed stanzaic poem.

The influence of Milton's minor poems is apparent in such lines as 11, 12 and 31, yet the picture itself is freshly imagined and original.

THE PASSIONS

Pp. 320 f. Like Dryden's *Alexander's Feast* (pp. 224 ff.), this is an ambitious attempt to suit the verse and style to the sentiments, varying them according to each passion described. It concludes with a tribute to the power of music in inspiring emotions. The poem is not entirely free from the conventional diction and rhetorical figures of the time.

THOMAS WARTON

P. 322. Thomas Warton owes his position in the history of English poetry, not to the fact that he was poet laureate, but to his having contributed, both by his own verse and by his *History of English Poetry,* to the triumph of Romanticism. His *History of English Poetry,* which is still a standard treatise, brought to the attention of the reading public the rich but forgotten fields of English poetry from the twelfth to the close of the sixteenth century, the influence of which became dominant in the Romantic revival. His best poetry also expresses two of the principal characteristics of Romanticism — love of antiquity and love of nature. He is further notable as having helped to revive the sonnet as a form of English verse.

SONNET IV

In Salisbury Plain stand many gigantic stones set in two concentric circles surrounding two ellipses and a central altar, which have aroused much speculation as to their origin and purpose. Scholars now believe that they are in fact — as they were long ago reported to be — ruins of a temple of the Druids, remnants of that ancient system of religion held by the Celts in all parts of Europe in prehistoric times.

l. 5. *Hengist* and his brother Horsa were the traditional leaders of the first bands of Saxons that came from Germany to Britain and, with the aid of later reinforcements, conquered Vortigern, King of Britain.

l. 11. *Brutus* was, in the legendary history of Britain, a descendant of Æneas and the colonizer of the island Britain, which took its name from him.

OLIVER GOLDSMITH

Pp. 322 ff. Whatever may be the truth about Goldsmith's character, — and he seems to have been misrepresented by Boswell and misunderstood by most of his biographers, — his writings are usually full of sensible and independent thought as well as of grace and charm. His kindliness and his humor are all-pervasive, and the quality of his work, considering the amount he wrote and the conditions under which he worked, is amazing.

LETTERS FROM A CITIZEN OF THE WORLD

In 1721, Montesquieu made a sensation and started a literary fashion with his *Persian Letters* (*Lettres Persanes*), in which he criticised French society with much wit and effectiveness. Goldsmith in 1760 contributed to the *Public Ledger*, a daily paper, a series of letters purporting to be written by a Chinese to inform his friends of the manners and customs of the English. Two years later they were gathered into a book and published under the title given above. This device for criticism has been revived with success more than once in our own time.

THE DESERTED VILLAGE

Pp. 324 ff. Although Goldsmith was theoretically attached to the views held by the classicists, and although his first poem, *The Traveller*, is of the same general type as the philosophical disquisitions which so many of his predecessors published in verse, when he came to write about his own recollections and sensations his work is so simple and unaffected and his emotion so genuine that he achieves a permanent interest.

The Deserted Village is of course a highly ideal-ized picture, based probably upon memories of his childhood in Ireland and of the village Lissoy, where his brother lived; but it has a convincing naturalness, unforced humor and pathos, and it is as successful in the sketches of character as in the pictures of idyllic village scenes. Here and there we see the influence of his romantic contemporaries (cf. especially ll. 344 and 418), and here and there we have traces of traditional conventionality (cf. *swain*, l. 2, *unwieldy wealth*, l. 66, *mantling bliss*, l. 248, *shouting Folly*, l. 270, *fair tribes*, l. 338, and especially ll. 97–112).

ll. 137–192. Cf. Chaucer's sketch of the faithful parson, *Prologue*, ll. 477–528 (pp. 64–65).

ll. 275–280. Cf. Thomson's *Autumn*, ll. 350–359 (p. 298).

RETALIATION

Pp. 329 ff. In February, 1774, two months before Goldsmith's death, and some of his circle — Dr. Barnard, dean of Derry (l. 23), Edmund Burke (l. 29), Townshend, later Lord Sydney (l. 34), Cumberland, a dramatist (l. 61), Garrick, the great actor-manager (l. 93), Sir Joshua Reynolds (l. 137), and others — were having dinner at the St. James Coffee-house when some one proposed that they write mock epitaphs for one another. Although the accounts differ in detail, it appears that several members of the company continued the contest after the evening was over, and Goldsmith finally provided the epitaphs he had written with a humorous introduction. His poem was passed about in manuscript but was not published until after his death. It was the last thing he wrote.

P. 331. l. 137. *Reynolds.* Sir Joshua Reynolds was greatly beloved by the Johnson group, to which Goldsmith belonged. His pictures are gentle rather than "striking," persuasive rather than "resistless," and noble rather than "grand" (l. 139). He is not to be compared with Raphael or Correggio. But Goldsmith was no critic of art.

l. 146. *trumpet.* Reynolds was deaf.

EDMUND BURKE

SPEECH ON THE NABOB OF ARCOT'S DEBTS

Pp. 331 ff. The passage quoted is from a speech against government support of graft in the East India Company. The circumstances under which it was delivered were these: The company incorporated in 1600 for trading purposes in India had gradually acquired greater powers until in the eighteenth century it could make war and peace independently of the British government. In 1749 it began a series of conquests, but with these came a degree of mismanagement that led to the passing of several bills in Parliament and, in 1784, to the establishment of a parliamentary board of control. For some years it had been known that officers and members of the company had been making fortunes by helping the Nabob of Arcot to plunder his neighbors, receiving from him in return, not merely money to an extent impossible to estimate, but also the promise to pay several million pounds acknowledged as debt on his part to various individuals. Parliament demanded an investigation, and this was undertaken by the Directors of the East India Company and certain conclusions were reached. The Ministry, however, introduced another bill providing that the supposed debts of the Nabob to members of the Company should be raised out of the province governed by the Company and paid, practically without investigation. Fox challenged this bill, February 28, 1785, and there was a debate, in which Burke's was the last speech. The bill was lost by a large majority.

WILLIAM COWPER

Pp. 336 ff. Cowper's *Task* is a narrative poem in six books, of which the only interest lies in the digressions from the subject. Having been challenged by a friend, Lady Austen, to write a poem in blank verse on the subject of a sofa, Cowper set out upon his "task," and developed the work as a sort of poetical commonplace book into which he put his various experiences, impressions, emotions, and ideas. He touches the Romantic Movement in several ways: in his realistic descriptions of nature and of humble life (cf. the woodman and his dog, V, 41–57), in his democratic ideals (cf. his attitude toward slavery, II, 1–47), and in the unaffected simplicity of his style.

On the Loss of the Royal George

P. 338. August 29, 1788, while the flagship *Royal George* was being refitted at Spithead, through the shifting of the weight of the guns (of which she carried 108), she suddenly keeled over, and about eight hundred of the thousand sailors aboard were drowned. Admiral Kempenfelt himself was among the lost.

JAMES MACPHERSON

Pp. 340 f. Whatever may have been the real basis for Macpherson's so-called translation of the *Poems of Ossian*, the work exercised a great, and, indeed, almost immeasurable, influence upon English and other literatures. The question as to Macpherson's responsibility for the poems will probably never be entirely resolved. Celtic poems bearing some resemblance to his translations undoubtedly existed in considerable number, but it seems certain that his work was in no case merely that of a translator.

The *Battle of Loda* relates an adventure of Fingal, father of the poet Ossian, who, according to Macpherson, composed the Gaelic original. Fingal, king of Morven in Scotland, was shipwrecked on the coast of Norway and his men fought a skirmish with the people of that country in which his friend, Duth-maruno, was killed. During the night, while the two hosts were encamped face to face, and Fingal himself was still mourning at the grave of his friend, Starno, the king of Norway, told his son Swaran a story of his youth. He said that when the chief, Corman-trunar, came to the hall of his father Annir, his sister, Foina-bragal, fled with him. Annir and Starno pursued, but Corman-trunar prevailed in battle. Then Starno went in disguise to the lovers, and said that Annir was slain and that Starno had sent him to make a truce until Annir was buried. Being kindly received, he waited until the lovers were asleep and then killed them both, to the great rejoicing of his father. Starno then asks Swaran thus to steal upon Fingal and kill him. As Swaran indignantly refuses the treachery, Starno himself undertakes the task, is overcome and made captive, but is released when Fingal sees that his foe is Starno, the father of Agandecca, whom he had loved and lost in his youth.

JAMES BOSWELL

Pp. 341 ff. Boswell was a good observer and perhaps the best note-taker the world has ever known. Some persons have thought his accomplishment in the *Life of Dr. Johnson* one of so mechanical a nature as to deserve little credit; but none of his many imitators has approached him in effectiveness, and it is now admitted that although he was a faithful reporter and transcriber, he used no little artistic skill in the selection and organization of the events and conversations he reported, and in the management of the vast company of figures among which the Doctor moves. Boswell had strong prejudices and he was obviously unjust to Goldsmith, of whom he was jealous; but his faithfulness to his task of displaying Johnson exactly as he was, is such that he does not suppress even the occasional manifestations of narrowness, prejudice, bigotry, brutality, and coarseness. It is indeed just because we get Johnson as a whole that we are able to realize his greatness of heart and mind, his dauntless courage in facing life and its ills, and the robust individuality that challenged, aroused, and dominated his age.

P. 346 *a*. For three years Voltaire lived with Frederick the Great as his friend and literary adviser, but they quarrelled and parted.

Robert Levitt, a friend and dependent of Dr. Johnson's, was originally a waiter. He had picked up some knowledge of medicine and practised among the poor.

P. 348 *a*. *Great kings have always been social;* cf. what Bacon says on pp. 156 f.

JUNIUS

Pp. 351 ff. *The Letters of Junius* produced in their day a very great sensation, and their fame has been heightened by the mystery surrounding their authorship. Many of the prominent men of the time were accused of writing them, and not a few either shyly admitted or boldly claimed the credit and the infamy. The reason why the real author did not appear and establish his claims was, as De Quincey long ago pointed out, that he could not assert his right to the literary fame without at the same time convicting himself of having made improper use of his official position under the government to obtain the information which made his attacks so effective. Historians of English literature have long accustomed us to believe that these letters depended for their success solely upon their literary style, their bitterness of invective, and their sardonic irony; but, although they are remarkable as literature, the special feature which aroused the fears of the government was the fact that no state secret seemed safe from the author and that he might at any moment reveal matters which it was important to keep unknown. Recent researches have made it practically certain that Junius was Sir Philip Francis, who was a clerk in the war office during the period of the publication of the letters.

The Duke of Grafton was leader of the Whig party and prime minister in 1769. Junius sums up the political situation on p. 352. Lord Bute had been the favorite of George III and exerted enormous influence over him as Prince of Wales — an influence that persisted long after he was out of office.

THOMAS CHATTERTON

Pp. 353 ff. Thomas Chatterton wrote under his own name some poems of great promise for a boy (he was only eighteen when he died), but his most important and interesting poems he pretended not to have written but to have discovered. Most of them, he said, were composed by a monk named Rowley in the second half of the fifteenth century, and had been found by himself among old papers in the church of St. Mary Redcliffe at Bristol. In the present state of knowledge of the English language it is easy for any scholar to see that these poems could not possibly have been written in the fifteenth century. They are full of false archaisms and eighteenth century contractions, and other forms not in early use. Some persons suspected them when they were first produced; but to the majority even of the scholars of that day any imitation of old manuscripts, old writing, and old spelling was good evidence of age, and it seemed absolutely impossible that so young a boy — he was only twelve or thirteen when he began to produce these poems — could have composed the poems and fabricated the manuscripts. When the imposture was discovered, the critics, making no allowance for its having been the work of a mere child, were filled with high moral indignation, and the poor boy was allowed to starve, until, being able to endure his neglect no longer, he took poison and died. It has been thought strange that the poems written in this "fake" old English are better than those in the English of his own day; but the explanation seems easy psychologically. The imagination of the boy was specially excited both by the idea of the imposture he was carrying on and by the odd forms of words which he used. He felt himself transported to the times and scenes he was trying to reproduce and wrote with the picturesqueness and vigor which belong to such excited states of mind. Professor Skeat, in his edition of Chatterton, changed the old spelling of the poems to modern spelling, on the ground that the boy really thought in eighteenth century English and ought to be so represented. This sounds logical, but really is not. He may have thought thus, but we may be sure that he felt and imagined in these pseudo-archaic forms which made the antique world live again for him. Chatterton's method of old spelling is so simple also that it will give hardly any trouble. His first principle is to double letters as often as possible; his second is not to be too regular even in doing this; his third, to use any genuine old spellings that he happens to remember.

BRISTOWE TRAGEDIE

Sir Charles Bawdin. It has been supposed that the story was suggested to Chatterton by some account of the execution at Bristol in 1461 of Sir Charles Fulford, a zealous Lancastrian. *Kynge Edwarde* (l. 5) is Edward IV; *Canterlone* (l. 17) is Chatterton's mistake for Cantlow or Cantelowe; *Canynge* (l. 45) was mayor of Bristol under Henry VI and Edward IV.

THE ACCOUNTE OF W. CANYNGES FEAST

P. 358. Chatterton picked out archaic words from dictionaries and old glossaries, and as he did not know the connection in which they were used, he sometimes made rather ludicrous mistakes. In this poem he makes an unusual effort at archaism and consequently fails oftener than usual.

Sounde, l. 1, cannot be a past participle; *Byelecoyle*, l. 2, is a bad spelling of the French name of one of the allegorical characters in the translation of the *Roman de la Rose*, the name in English being Fair-Welcoming, *i.e.*, Favorable-Reception; *doe*, l. 2, cannot be singular; *cheorte*, l. 4, properly means "dearness, scarcity," but Chatterton thought it could be used as an adjective meaning "dear, delicious"; *lyche*, l. 5, is improperly used for "like" or "as"; *coyne*, l. 7, is used by Spenser to mean food for man; *heie*, l. 9, is an impossible form for "they"; *ha ne*, l. 9, is not good English for "have nothing"; *echone*, l. 11, is wrongly used for "each"; and *deene*, l. 11, is not proper for "dine." I have passed over some of the minor errors. What Chatterton intended this to mean may be given thus:

Through the hall the bell has sounded;
A fair welcome befits these serious men;
The aldermen sit around the table
And snuff up the delicious aroma
As wild asses in the desert waste
Do sweetly taste the morning air.

Such food they ate; the minstrels play —
A sound as of angels do they make;
Then they become silent; the guests, however,
    have nought to say
But nod their thanks and fall asleep.
Thus everyday it is my habit to dine
If one of my friends, Rowley, Iscamm or Tyb
    Gorges, is not seen (*i.e.*, does not come to dine
    with me).

AE

GEORGE CRABBE

TALES

The Lover's Journey

Pp. 358 f. Cf. Cowper's *Task*, I, 557–591, for a similar picture of gypsies. Cowper pities them and is not unaware of their picturesque qualities; Crabbe is unsympathetically realistic and throws a stone at each member of the group.

WILLIAM BLAKE

Pp. 359 f. Blake was an artist as well as a poet, and in both characters vision is the quality that distinguishes him — vision of invisible forms and relationships — what Pater calls "preponderating soul." Both his painting and his poetry are full of symbolism, but they represent very different phases of his personality. The pictures are extravagant to the point of madness; the poems, which are so misleadingly simple in phrasing that they have been abused by insertion into school readers, are extraordinarily subtle and elusive. The poet who most resembles Blake in this subtle simplicity is Emily Dickinson. To understand Blake's exquisiteness, compare his "To see the world in a grain of sand" (p. 360) with Tennyson's coarser, more obvious, hence popular, "Flower in the crannied wall," which phrases the same thought.

MINOR SCOTTISH POETS

Pp. 361 f. The Minor Scottish Poets here represented are mainly interesting as a background to Burns. In methods and ideals he was not an isolated phenomenon; freedom and individuality had not perished entirely. In London literary circles and throughout Great Britain wherever people tried to write or to criticise as they thought all "up-to-date" people were writing and criticising, the prevailing fashion of "classicism" was omnipotent. But wherever people wrote for the pleasure of saying a thing as they wished to say it, life, with its old joys and hopes and sorrows and fears and desires, ran fresh and strong, as an immediate fount of inspiration.

ROBERT BURNS

Pp. 362 ff. In reading Burns, it is easy to believe that poetry is indeed a matter of instinct and not of acquirement. On his own ground and in his own tongue, Burns rarely failed to find that perfect correspondence of sound to sense, that perfect suffusion of thought with emotion, which together create poetry; but as soon as he strayed from his "Scotsdom" in material, attitude, or language, he became commonplace and conventional. Compare, for instance, the last nine stanzas of the *Cotter's Saturday Night* with those that precede them. Compare the perfection of *To a Mouse* with the four-stanza lapse in *To a Daisy* (ll. 31–54).

Lines to John Lapraik

P. 364. Lapraik was himself a minor poet as well as a friend of Burns.

The Cotter's Saturday Night

Pp. 365 ff. The scene described is Burns's own home and his father is the Cotter. After his father's death, Burns himself led family prayers — impressively, it is said.

Robert Aiken was a lawyer in Ayr, the market town near which Burns was born.

Tam O'Shanter

Pp. 370 ff. The peculiar quality of this poem is its blending of the humorous and the horrible in a way that is characteristically Scottish.

Bonie Doon

P. 372. The Doon is a little river in Ayrshire near Burns's home. Burns made another version of this poem, more regular and literary and much less beautiful than this.

Ae Fond Kiss

P. 373. Sent to a Mrs. McLehose, of Edinburgh, with whom he had a love affair just before his marriage with Jean Armour.

Bonie Lesley

Bonie Lesley was Miss Lesley Baillie, daughter of Mr. Baillie of Ayrshire. He, on his way to England with his two daughters, called on Burns at Dumfries. When they left, Burns accompanied them fifteen miles on their way and composed the song as he rode home.

Highland Mary

Mary Campbell was a young nursemaid whom Burns met in the spring of 1786. In a time of reaction against Jean Armour, whom he afterwards married, Burns fell in love with her, and she promised to marry him, but she died in the autumn of that year. Burns never talked about her, but he seems to have felt her loss deeply, and some of his most beautiful poems are addressed to her.

Duncan Gray

P. 374. Cf., for spirit, with Suckling's *Why So Pale and Wan?* (p. 214, above).

Scots Wha Hae

This celebrates the Battle of Bannockburn, fought in 1314, between the Scots and the English. The Scots had been struggling for independence from England since 1296. Their leader, Sir William Wallace, had at first considerable success, but was reduced to fighting a sort of guerilla warfare, and was finally betrayed by one of his countrymen and executed in London in 1305. The struggle was, however, continued by Robert Bruce, who was crowned King; and at Bannockburn he won a victory that made Scotland free and independent until the kingdoms were united under James I (James VI of Scotland), son of Mary Stuart.

The poem is supposed to be spoken by Bruce himself just before the battle, as he stood on the hill where to-day the "bore-stone" is still pointed out as his standard holder. The English attacked from the lower land by the river, where the softness of the ground contributed to their defeat.

A Man's a Man for A' That

This sums up the democratic attitude which Burns consistently maintained. The ideas which came to practical political expression in the Declaration of Independence and in the French Revolution were making progress in Scotland and England also.

WILLIAM WORDSWORTH

The Preface to the "Lyrical Ballads"

Pp. 376 ff. This Preface was printed with the second edition of *Lyrical Ballads* (1800) and later expanded. By accident, one of the cuts made in our reprint is not indicated; there should be asterisks to indicate an omission on p. 378 *b*, after the words *Milton himself.*

In connection with this epoch-making essay, Jeffrey's criticism of Wordsworth's success in carrying out his theory (p. 416), and Coleridge's statement of a view opposed to the theory itself (p. 398) should be read.

The famous *Preface* is much more than a defence of the particular poems that it introduced; it is a protest against the entire method of the eighteenth century poets, and a statement of the principles which Wordsworth believed should govern poetry, and which his own theory and practice did actually introduce into the work of his contemporaries and successors.

The four points in which Wordsworth regarded his work as fulfilling the essential requirements of poetry are carefully stated in the opening sentence of our selection. The rest of the essay is devoted to explaining, illustrating, expanding, and defending these principles. Particular attention should be given to Wordsworth's note on p. 378, as it shows that he was not unaware or neglectful of the distinction between poetry and non-poetry (science, as he calls the latter) whether in verse or prose. It is in this sense that poetry is to be taken in some of those fine aphorisms which give to this essay so much of its value, as, for example: "All good poetry is the spontaneous overflow of powerful feelings;" "Poetry is the breath and finer spirit of all knowledge; it is the impassioned expression which is in the countenance of all Science;" and many others. What seems to be lacking in this exposition of Wordsworth's theory and what was sometimes lacking in his practice is that activity of the poet stated by Coleridge in the following terms (p. 399 *b*): "He diffuses a tone and spirit of unity, that blends, and (as it were) fuses, each into each by that synthetic and magical power, to which we have exclusively appropriated the name of imagination."

We are Seven

Pp. 382 f. In a passage omitted from our reprint of the *Preface to the Lyrical Ballads* Wordsworth explains that he intended in this poem "to illustrate the manner in which our feelings and ideas are associated in a state of excitement" by showing "the perplexity and obscurity which in childhood attend our notion of death, or rather our utter inability to admit that notion."

Although the theme is also stated explicitly in the first stanza of the poem itself, the poem contains no explicit moralizing, but the poet undoubtedly wished his readers to feel, as did the little girl, that loved ones are not separated from us, even when their bodies are laid in earth, and their spirits have passed to heaven. There is, of course, no logical transition to this conclusion from the utterances of an ignorant child, but the emotions may make the transition, if they have been sympathetically stirred. The main reason why the poem, for all its popularity, does not rank high as poetry is that it exhibits no "spontaneous overflow of powerful emotions," or, to use Coleridge's terms, that the images, thoughts and emotions are not fused by "that synthetic and magical power to which we have exclusively appropriated the name of imagination." In other words we have here perhaps raw materials for a poem, but the poem itself remains unwritten. The prosaic blemishes which Wordsworth sometimes allowed to creep into his poetry may be illustrated by the original form of l. 1: "A little child, dear brother Jim."

The verse, appropriately to the subject and material, is simple and familiar, — a four-line stanza, such as is used in many ballads, with four and three iambic feet in alternate lines, and with alternate rhymes. The only features worthy of special note are the first, tenth, and last stanzas. The incompleteness of l. 1 and the lack of rhyme between it and l. 3 — both due to the omission of words from the original line — cause this stanza to stand off from the rest of the poem, as the prologue should. The middle rhyme of ll. 37 and 39 is in imitation of many lines in the old ballads and contributes to the inartificiality characteristic of the poem. The extra line in the last stanza gives to it a slower and more dignified movement and causes the reader to reflect upon the story and its implications.

In reading this poem, one is inevitably reminded of the very different attitude toward the loss of a loved one by death expressed in the three poems on p. 386. It is, as has often been remarked, entirely uncertain whether the Lucy of these poems was a real person, or a creature of the poet's imagination. But certainly the tone of the concluding stanza of each poem suggests that she really existed and that the poems were written before the poet had recovered from the shock of personal loss and while his sensations of bereavement were still in entire control of his mind and heart. This is especially notable in the third poem, where the poet's thought dwells upon the purely physical aspect of death, and he thinks of the beloved body that seemed to defy the forces of change and death as now senseless clay,

"Rolled round in earth's diurnal course
With rocks and stones and trees."

Expostulation and Reply, and The Tables Turned

Pp. 383 f. In a note, Wordsworth tells us that these two poems "arose out of conversation with a friend who was somewhat unreasonably attached to modern books of moral philosophy." They are companion poems, though they do not present, as the titles might lead one to expect, different phases of the same subject. The tables are turned only in the sense that, whereas in the first poem the poet's friend had expostulated with him, in the second the poet takes his turn; but in both the poet makes his own ideas and attitude prevail.

The subject of both poems is Wordsworth's favorite doctrine of the powerful moral influence of nature — of birds and trees and flowers and beautiful streams, of sunrise and sunset and starlight — upon the character of any one who loves these things and lives in sympathetic communion with them. In another beautiful poem (*Three Years She Grew*, p. 386) he carries the doctrine still further and asserts that grace of form and beauty of face will pass from the graceful and beautiful objects of nature to the child who grows up among them (see especially ll. 19–24 and 29–30 of that poem).

If there is any difference at all between the doctrine set forth in *Expostulation and Reply* and that in *The Tables Turned*, it is merely that the influence of nature upon the passive mind is emphasized in the former, while in the latter a more active attitude is suggested by the words "That *watches* and receives," l. 32.

Lines Composed a Few Miles Above Tintern Abbey

Pp. 384 ff. Wordsworth had visited the valley of the Wye, one of the most picturesque spots in England, in 1793 — five years, as he tells us, before the visit in company with his sister recorded in this poem. A little below Monmouth the valley of the Wye contracts and is enclosed by steep, wooded hills. Lines 10–22 (especially 10–11 and 14–16) indicate that he is on the cliffs, with the valley spread out beneath him. The poem is notable not so much because it gives explicit expression to the three phases of the love of nature recognized by Wordsworth, as because it is, in intensity of spiritual emotion, in the novelty and truth of its poetical ideas, and in beauty and suggestiveness of phrasing, one of the most perfect poems ever written. In connection with it, the reader should by all means consult other passages in which Words-

worth has dealt with the same themes, notably *The Prelude*, Bk. I, ll. 401–463; Bk. VIII, ll. 340–356; and *The Recluse* (cf. especially the extract in this book, pp. 387 f.). It may aid the reader in following the course of the poet's thought to note that ll. 1–22 are devoted to his return to the scene after a long absence; ll. 22–57 express the influence of these beauteous forms in absence upon his feelings and his insight into the meaning of life; in ll. 57–65 he expresses the hope that this visit, by renewing the memories of these forms, may supply "life and food" in future years; ll. 65–85 paint his feeling for nature at the time of his former visit (age 23); ll. 85–111, his maturer feeling; ll. 111–119 tell how his former pleasures revive in the influence of nature upon his sister; in ll. 119–134 he prays that this influence may continue, and sets forth the elevating and soothing power of nature; in ll. 134–146 he exhorts his sister to experience all these sweet sensations and store them in memory as antidotes for future sorrows; and in ll. 145–159 bids her then remember him and his love for this landscape.

l. 29. Why "*purer* mind"?

ll. 25–30. Compare *The Reverie of Poor Susan* and *The Prelude*, Bk. VII, especially the last two paragraphs.

ll. 38–40. Compare *The Prelude*, Bks. XI and XIII.

ll. 43–46. Note the mysticism of this passage and compare it with the *Ode on Intimations of Immortality*, ll. 141–145, and the notes on Tennyson's *St. Agnes' Eve*.

P. 385. l. 54. *hung upon* is used rather curiously. It does not mean "depended upon," but "weighed upon."

ll. 93–102. These lines have sometimes been taken as pantheistic, but pantheism was not Wordsworth's creed; they express rather the presence of an immanent deity.

P. 386. l. 149. *past existence* refers here to past experiences of this life, not to preëxistence.

Lucy

This and the two following poems form a series devoted to the same person. Cf. what is said about them above in connection with *We Are Seven* and *Expostulation and Reply*.

Lucy Gray; or, Solitude

Pp. 386 f. Like *We Are Seven*, this presents a simple story almost without comment. This theme, however, is better suited to the ballad-like simplicity of treatment, and it contains a few memorable phrases. The secondary title has little to do with the theme.

THE RECLUSE

Pp. 387 f. *The Recluse* is a part of a great philosophical poem upon which Wordsworth worked at intervals for many years but which he never completed. The extract here given expresses in poetic forms his plans and aspirations as a poet.

By some oversight the lines of our selection were numbered without reference to their position in the poem; they come at the very end and the first line should be l. 754.

TO THE CUCKOO

Pp. 388 f. In beauty of conception and magic of phrasing few poems surpass or even equal this. It is very simple in subject and structure and needs only to be read thoughtfully and sympathetically to be fully understood. Its theme is the emotions of wonder and delight the author feels in hearing again the song of the bird and recalling the sensations with which it had been heard in boyhood. All poets are perhaps endowed with keener memories of past sensations than ordinary people. How large a part such memories played in Wordsworth's life may be noted not only in *The Prelude*, *The Recluse*, and *The Excursion*, but in many occasional poems such as this and the *Lines Composed above Tintern Abbey*. Even details, such as the peculiarity of the cuckoo's song referred to in ll. 3-4, 7-8, 15-16, and 29-32, are recalled more than once (cf. *The Recluse*, ll. 90-94).

> "Where'er my footsteps turned,
> Her voice was like a hidden bird that sang.
> The thought of her was like a flash of light,
> Or an unseen companionship, a breath
> Of fragrance independent of the wind."

THE SOLITARY REAPER

P. 389. This poem was suggested by the following words in Thomas Wilkinson's *Tour in Scotland* : "Passed a female who was reaping alone; she sung in Erse, as she bended over her sickle; the sweetest human voice I ever heard; her strains were tenderly melancholy, and felt delicious long after they were heard no more." Again, as in the poem *To the Cuckoo*, we have the witchery of music and mystery wonderfully rendered by the art of the poet. And here in addition we have a picture sketched without detail yet as

vivid to the imagination and as lasting in the memory as Millet's "Angelus." Perhaps the only obscurity in the poem — the reason why the poet does not know what she sings — is removed by Wilkinson's statement that she sang in Erse, the language of the Gaelic Highlanders.

ODE : INTIMATIONS OF IMMORTALITY FROM RECOLLECTIONS OF EARLY CHILDHOOD

Pp. 391 ff. Although this poem has long been a favorite of lovers of Wordsworth and though no one can deny the beauty of it, some of the Orthodox have objected to the doctrine that souls have a conscious existence in another world before being united with the body in this. Wordsworth himself is careful to disclaim this doctrine as a creed and to insist only upon his right to treat it poetically. It seems clear, however, that the doctrine made a powerful appeal to his imagination and affections. The beauty of the poem, both in parts and as a whole, will be felt by every reader, but as the exact relation of some of the parts to the general theme seems to have been missed by some, it may be well to give a closer analysis than usual of the course of thought.

I, II. Even though the poet sees and feels the beauty of the earth, he misses in it a glory it once possessed.

III, IV. While birds and beasts are full of joy, he alone feels sad, but utterance gives relief and he determines to share in the general joy and enumerates the sources of pleasure. But in vain, for the sight of a tree, a field, a flower, recalls thoughts of "the glory and the dream" that are gone and makes him ask what has become of them.

V, VI, VII, VIII. He expounds the theory that the new-born soul coming to earth from heaven brings a part of the glory of heaven with it and envelops in it all the sights and sounds of earth, but loses it as it journeys through the world. The whole theory is explicitly stated in V. The efforts of Earth to win her foster-child Man to love her alone are given in VI. The earthly attractions and interests that successively capture his heart and fill his life are set forth in VII. "Why, O Child, do you — endowed as you are with heavenly knowledge and glory — strive to become the slave of Earth?" is the substance of VIII.

IX. The poet utters thanks for the indestructible traces of our heavenly origin.

X. He reverts to the joy theme of III, IV, with recognition of the compensations afforded by "the philosophic mind" for the lost splendor and glory.

XI. He appeals to Nature whom he now loves even more deeply, because more seriously and maturely.

The argument in favor of immortality from hints of preëxistence forms the principal subject of Plato's *Phædo*, and is also finely set forth in *The Banquet* and *Phædrus*. The argument as given in the *Meno* is more sophistical and less interesting.

P. 392. l. 28. *the fields of sleep.* Professor Hales is probably wrong in explaining this as "the yet reposeful, slumbering, countryside," for not only the poet and the birds, but the shepherd boy of l. 35, the children of l. 45, and the whole countryside are awake. To the west of the poet, of course, the sun has not yet reached and awakened the people. The winds are therefore the western winds.

ll. 58–76. Compare Vaughan's beautiful poem *The Retreat*, p. 221.

l. 67. *prison-house*, life; cf. *Phædo*, 62.

l. 68. Note the stages of change indicated by *infancy* (66), *boy* (68), *youth* (71), *man* (75).

l. 81. Earth is conceived as the nurse of Man, not as his mother; his ancestry is divine.

P. 393. l. 103. *humorous stage.* The general conception comes from the speech of Jaques in *As You Like It*, II, vii, 139 ff. According to the ancient physiology a man's tastes and tendencies were determined by his predominant humor. "Humorous stage" therefore means here the part in life to which his nature impels him.

l. 124. *yoke*, of custom. Cf. l. 127.

ll. 141–165. Wordsworth himself explained that these lines refer to peculiar experiences much like those which we shall have occasion to note in connection with Tennyson's *St. Agnes' Eve*. He says, "There was a time in my life when I had to push against something that resisted, to be sure that there was anything outside of me. I was sure of my own mind; everything else fell away and vanished into thought." Such experiences suggested, of course, the unreality of the external world and the real existence of the soul.

l. 166. The poet has changed his imagery somewhat and speaks as if souls were brought to this world by the sea of immortality (*immortal sea*, l. 163). The children are, therefore, near the shore, while youths and men are further inland (cf. l. 162).

P. 394. l. 198. It is the poet's eye that hath kept watch o'er man's mortality, and he therefore sees with a soberer coloring the clouds which to the child were brilliant with the light of the setting sun and the "visionary gleam."

l. 199. This is rather obscure, but seems to mean that in one more contest man has been victorious, in the sense that he has attained to a deeper, more philosophic love of nature.

ll. 202–203. It cannot too often be insisted that the meaning of these lines is distorted if they are taken out of connection with ll. 200–201. It is not because of the love of nature, but because of the love of man that a flower can give the poet "thoughts that do often lie too deep for tears."

To A Sky-Lark

Cf. Shelley's *To a Skylark*, p. 465.

On the Extinction of the Venetian Republic

Venice, during the Middle Ages and early modern times one of the richest and most powerful cities of the world, began to lose its power soon after the discovery by the Portuguese of the route to India and China round the Cape of Good Hope. In the eighteenth century it had become a city of idle, unenterprising, pleasure-loving people. But its final humiliation came in 1797 when it was conquered by Napoleon and by him turned over to the rule of Austria. Very similar to the feelings of Wordsworth are those expressed by Byron some years later in the first canto of his *Ode* (p. 455).

In structure this sonnet varies from the regular Petrarchan model, as the octave falls into two quatrains, independent in rhyme and in syntax. Contrast with it in structure the sonnet *London, 1802*, which is perfect both as to the structure of the octave and the division of the theme between the octave and sestet, and that *Composed Upon Westminster Bridge*, which, though metrically perfect, continues the theme of the octave into the sestet.

Lines 7–8 refer to the well-known annual ceremony in which the Doge of Venice dropped a ring into the sea in token of the wedding of the city to it.

To Toussaint L'Ouverture

Dominique François Toussaint L'Ouverture, one of the most remarkable negroes known to history, was born in Haiti in 1743. Although a slave, he received an elementary education and attained prominence. He took part in the revolutions of 1791–94 and in the latter year became commander-in-chief; in 1801 he was made president for life with the power of nominating his successor. After a series of battles with the French forces sent by Bonaparte, he capitulated and was pardoned (May 1, 1802), but the next month he was arrested on a charge of conspiracy, sent to France, and imprisoned in the Castle of Joux, where he died in April, 1803. Wordsworth wrote this sonnet in August, 1802. Toussaint was notable for his protection of the whites and his attempts to give the negroes liberty and a stable organization of industry.

Thought of a Briton on the Subjugation of Switzerland

Cf. Byron's *Ode*, especially section IV (pp. 455 ff.).

The World is too Much with Us

P. 395. This is a passionate outcry against the absorption of men in worldly business and their lack of interest in Nature and its inspiring influences. The poet declares that, rather than be so absorbed, he would prefer even to be a pagan, that thus imagination might at times give him glimpses of the gods of nature, such as Proteus and Triton — gods of the sea.

To Sleep

Cf. the sonnets of Daniel (p. 147) and Keats (p. 478).

Scorn not the Sonnet

P. 396. Cf. Rossetti's sonnet on the sonnet (p. 630). Dante, Petrarch and Tasso were Italian writers who cultivated the sonnet; Camoëns was a Portuguese.

SAMUEL TAYLOR COLERIDGE

Biographia Literaria

Pp. 396 ff. In his *Biographia Literaria* Coleridge gives an interesting account of his literary career and opinions. Chapter XIV is especially valuable for its relation of the origin of the *Lyrical Ballads*, the joint volume in which he and Wordsworth gave to the world the first proofs of their great poetic powers, and also for its exposition of Coleridge's theory of poetry. It should be read in connection with Wordsworth's *Preface*. Characteristically, Coleridge is concerned, not with the external form, but with the nature of poetry.

Bathyllus and *Alexis* (p. 398 *b*) are revolting subjects. Petronius Arbiter (p. 399 *a*) was a Roman author of the time of Nero; he was renowned for his wit and his taste. Bishop Taylor (*ibid.*) is Jeremy Taylor, the celebrated pulpit orator; for an example of his poetic prose, see pp. 216 f. Thomas Burnet (1635?–1715), an English scholar, wrote a Sacred Theory of the Earth (*Telluris Theoria Sacra*) in Latin, in which he argued eloquently that the earth was originally constructed like an egg and that at the Flood the shell broke and let out the inner fluid and that the mountains are fragments of the shell.

Kubla Khan

Pp. 399 f. This poem, Coleridge tells us, he composed in a dream, when he had dropped asleep while reading a passage in *Purchas his Pilgrimage*. The passage is as follows: "In Xaindu did Cublai Can build a stately Pallace, encompassing sixteene miles of plaine ground with a wall, wherein are fertile Meddowes, pleasant Springs, delightful Streames, and all sorts of beasts of chase and game, and in the middest thereof a sumptuous house of pleasure." He goes on to say that he "continued for about three hours in a profound sleep, at least of the external senses, during which time he has the most vivid confidence that he could not have composed less than from two to three hundred lines; if that indeed can be called composition in which all the images rose up before him as things, with a parallel production of the correspondent expressions, without any sensation or consciousness of effort. On awaking he appeared to himself to have a distinct recollection of the whole, and taking his pen, ink, and paper, instantly and eagerly wrote down the lines that are here preserved. At this moment, he was unfortunately called out by a person on business from Porlock, and detained by him above an hour, and on his return to his room, found, to his no small surprise and mortification, that though he still retained some vague and dim recollection of the general purport of the vision, yet, with the exception of some eight or ten scattered lines and images, all the rest had passed away like the images on the surface of a stream into which a stone had been cast, but, alas! without the restoration of the latter."

The lines from *Purchas* seem indeed inadequate to the result, but great transformations are possible to dreamers and poets. Whether Coleridge, in writing down his dream poem, merely transcribed what he could remember, or recomposed it, may perhaps be doubted. He calls it a fragment, but it has unity and even a certain completeness. If he merely transcribed his memories, he apparently recalled the dream lines without a break or omission. Undoubtedly a continuation of the poem is conceivable, in which case the continuation would doubtless consist of a romantic narrative set against the background of these introductory lines.

The poem, as we have it, is a remarkable example of romantic description. The mysterious Kubla Khan, the sacred river, the measureless caverns, the sunless sea, the ancient forests, the sunny spots of greenery, the cedarn cover, the savage place, holy but enchanted, and many other details which will at once impress the reader, contribute to the establishment of an atmosphere of mystery and charm. The presence of caves of ice seems to have troubled some of the critics, who even go so far as to suggest that the poet may have thought of marble or alabaster. But there can be no doubt that he was really thinking of caves of ice, and that he did not regard them as poetically impossible in such a landscape (cf. ll. 35, 36).

Other critics have been disturbed by the introduction of an Abyssinian maid in connection with a scene in Tartary. But Coleridge does not connect the Abyssinian maid, who belongs to another vision, with the Tartar landscape, except as he might connect any other recollection with it. In this last stanza of the poem, he is concerned entirely with the possibility of the poet's rebuilding with his music the beauties of the stately pleasure dome. This he says he might accomplish if he could revive within him the symphony and song which he once heard in a dream. To produce such an effect the music must obviously be wild and exotic, and the poet has therefore chosen as the musical instrument the dulcimer, which, though he probably had only a vague idea of it, suggests by its very name infinite and mysterious possibilities. That the player was an Abyssinian maid and that she sang of Mount Abora may possibly be due to the poet's vague recollections of other passages in *Purchas*. But the matter of real importance to the poet and the reader is that Abyssinia and Mount Abora are poetic words of vague connotation which suit the general atmosphere of the poem. For both poet and reader the poem is merely an effort to reproduce in verse a vision of sensuous and mysterious beauty, and anything which interferes with the reader's emotional response to it is not only superfluous, but injurious.

THE RIME OF THE ANCIENT MARINER

Pp. 400 ff. This is also a poem which depends for its effect mainly upon the creation of an atmosphere of mystery. It deals with the supernatural, though it owes much of its power to its descriptions of the effects of the supernatural upon man and nature. It contains few difficulties. In the second edition of it, the poet added to it an outline of the narrative, printed in the margin. The purpose of this addition was probably not to aid the reader in understanding the story, but to increase the strangeness and weirdness of the poem. The archaic diction and syntax contribute to the same effect: cf. *may'st*, l. 8, *din*, l. 8, *eftsoons*, l. 12, *kirk*, l. 23, *bassoon*, l. 32, *sheen*, l. 56, *swound*, l. 62, *thorough*, l. 64, *I wist*, l. 152, *Gramercy*, l. 164, *gossameres*, l. 184, *quoth*, l. 198, etc. Notice also the effect of the repetition of words and lines.

But independently of its uncanny atmosphere, the poem possesses other merits of the highest order. The narrative holds the reader as the Mariner's eye held the restive wedding guest. The events and scenes are presented as vividly as pictures, and the phrasing is so perfect that much of it has passed into common currency. Notable lines are 15, 34, 103–104, 105–106, 109–110, 117–118, 121–122, 125–126, 127–128, 200, 226–227, 232–233, 236–239, 292–293, 369–372, 404–405, 414–417, 498–499, 568–569, 586–587, 599–600, 612–617, 624–625; but there are many others of less general application that are for the poem itself of equal effectiveness.

CHRISTABEL

Pp. 415 f. The subject and title were suggested to Coleridge by the old ballad *Sir Cauline*. He wrote the first part of it in 1797–98 — that brief period in which he produced all his greatest poems: *Genevieve*, *The Dark Ladie*, *Kubla Khan*, and *The Ancient Mariner*. He took it up again in 1800, but it was never finished and was published as a fragment in 1816. It is interesting, not only as one of Coleridge's most successful treatments of the mysterious and uncanny, but also because it introduced a new type of verse into modern poetry. Scott, who heard the poem recited, adopted the verse for his *Lay of the Last*

Minstrel. The theme of *Christabel* is the struggle of the heroine against the powers of evil embodied in a wicked enchantress, whom, in the form of a beautiful maiden, she rescues and brings into her father's castle. We give only the opening episode.

FRANCIS JEFFREY

Pp. 416 f. If Francis Jeffrey was unjust in his reviews of Wordsworth, lovers of Wordsworth — and who is not? — have been at least equally unjust in their treatment of Jeffrey. Sentences have been quoted, often in garbled form and always without the context, to illustrate the unfairness and stupidity and poetic insensibility of Jeffrey. Most sane critics of the present day differ from Jeffrey mainly in emphasis; they recognize that Wordsworth really had the defects which Jeffrey pointed out, and that they are grave. But in literature only the successes count, the failures fall away and should be forgotten. The selection here printed presents Jeffrey in his most truculent mood; another selection, the review of the Excursion, was planned for this volume, but the limitation of our space necessitated its omission.

SIR WALTER SCOTT

The Lay of Rosabelle

Pp. 417 f. In the *Lay of the Last Minstrel* this poem is supposed to be sung, after the espousal of Margaret of Buccleuch to Lord Cranstoun, by Harold, the minstrel of the house of St. Clair. It is composed in imitation of the ancient ballads and tells, dramatically but simply, the death of Rosabelle in the Firth of Forth as she was returning from Ravensheuch Castle to Roslin, and the supernatural prodigies which preluded it. The time is perhaps conceived as the fifteenth century.

The difficulties of the poem lie mainly, if not exclusively, in the diction; for the superstitions, if not well known, are at least easily understood. The words for which the dictionary may need to be consulted are: *firth*, l. 8, *inch*, l. 10, *panoply*, l. 36, *sacristy*, l. 38, *pale*, l. 38, *pinnet*, l. 41, and *sea-mews*, l. 10; *copse-wood*, l. 30, *battlement*, l. 41, *buttress*, l. 42, are known to most of us only from literature.

The first stanza gives, in the ancient manner, the minstrel's appeal for attention, and the nature and subject of his lay.

In the next five stanzas the minstrel presents dramatically the vain effort to persuade the lady not to tempt the storm, the real motive for her going being suggested by her protests (ll. 17, 22).

The next five describe the blazing portents above the castle and chapel of Roslin.

The last two tell the fate of the lady.

The poem has no other motive than that of causing our sympathies to dwell lightly for a moment upon an ancient tragic episode. An air of remoteness and unreality is produced by the archaic spellings *ladye*, *chapelle*, by the poetic syntax, and by the light versification.

l. 21. Riding the ring was a favorite sport of knights as late as the seventeenth century. The competitors, riding on horseback at full speed, tried to thrust a lance through a ring suspended at the proper height and carry it away. He who succeeded most often was the winner. The sport required fine horsemanship and an accurate aim. A form of it is practised nowadays at country fairs by the riders of the wooden horses of a merry-go-round — the same sport, but "Oh, how changed! how fallen!"

l. 32. *Hawthornden* — where Ben Jonson visited the poet Drummond in 1618 — is famous for its caves. There are two sets, the upper and the lower, both of them artificial, but of unknown date and purpose. The upper, and larger, consists of a gallery 75 feet long, a passage 24 feet long leading to a well, and two roughly shaped rooms 9 feet and 15 feet long respectively, — all of these 6½ to 7 feet wide and about 5 feet 8 inches high.

l. 39. Roslin chapel is still a place of exquisite beauty. Wordsworth and his sister Dorothy visited it September 17, 1803, and both were impressed with the abundance of carven foliage on walls and roofs and pillars. See her journal for an interesting account of this visit, and his sonnet, recording another visit in 1831. The chapel was repaired in 1842.

l. 50. The knell for the dead and the use of candles and the service book in the burial service are still well known in all Catholic churches.

Fitz-James and Roderick Dhu

Pp. 419 ff. This is an episode of Scott's interesting narrative poem *The Lady of the Lake.* King James V of Scotland, in disguise as the knight James Fitz-James, has penetrated to the island stronghold of the Highland clan Clan-Alpine in Loch Katrine and has there fallen in love with Ellen, the daughter of his enemy, the Earl Douglas. His disguise is discovered and on a second visit to the island he is led astray by his guide, one of the followers of Roderick Dhu, chief of Clan-Alpine. Discovering the treachery of the guide, he kills him and suddenly comes face to face with Roderick, who hates him, both because of jealousy of Ellen and because of the ancient enmity of the Highlanders for the Lowlanders. Fitz-James is speaking when our extract begins.

CHARLES LAMB

Pp. 422 ff. Either Charles Lamb captures his readers at once and keeps them as long as he cares to talk, or — if their minds are averse to his hobbies, void of curiosity as to the various manifestations of humanity in which he delights, and not attuned to his personality, especially his humor — they must forever do without him as a friend. He is the least formal, the most friendly, the most brotherly of writers. He meets his reader on the street, as it were, and takes him off, gossiping all the way, to explore odd corners and talk about odd people, and joke about everything that turns up, in the happy and not unfounded belief that people in general will be interested in him because he is interested in them. Cf. Swinburne's sonnet to Lamb on p. 644.

THE TWO RACES OF MEN

P. 422 b. *the primitive community.* Lamb refers, not to communism among primitive races, but to the system of the early Christians; cf. *Acts*, iv: 32.

Pp. 424 f. *Comberbatch, C.,* and *S. T. C.,* are different designations for Coleridge in different aspects. Mystifications of this sort are a feature of Lamb's whimsical methods.

P. 424 b. *a widower-volume,* not — as some say — because John Buncle married seven times, but because as there were two volumes originally, the one left was bereaved of his mate.

P. 425 a. *Was there not Zimmermann on Solitude.* The suggestion of a book on this subject as more suitable for the lady is a hint at her husband's leaving her alone when he went to France.

A CHAPTER ON EARS

P. 429 a. *the Temple.* Lamb was born there. His father was clerk and servant to one of the Benchers, who later procured Lamb's admission to Christ's Hospital.

even in his long coats. Lamb studied at Christ's Hospital, the famous Blue Coat School founded by King Edward VI. Until a few years ago,

when the school was removed to the country, the boys were one of the picturesque features of London. They still went hatless and wore a modification of the original uniform: a dark blue coat reaching to the heels and open in front to show a leather belt, knee breeches and saffron colored stockings, and buckled shoes. At Christ's Hospital was formed the lifelong friendship between Lamb and Coleridge. Cf. Lamb's essays: *On Christ's Hospital and the Character of Christ's Hospital Boys,* and *Christ's Hospital Five-and-Thirty Years Ago.*

THOMAS CAMPBELL

YE MARINERS OF ENGLAND

P. 431. l. 15. Robert Blake, a great English admiral under Cromwell, defeated both the Dutch and the Spaniards, who were then rivals of the English on the seas. He died at sea in 1657. Lord Nelson, perhaps the most famous of English admirals for his defeats of the navies of Bonaparte and his allies, was killed in the sea-fight at Trafalgar in 1805. But as this poem was written in 1800, the reference here must have been inserted later. The first edition of the poem (in the *Morning Chronicle*) is not accessible to me.

THOMAS MOORE

THE HARP THAT ONCE THROUGH TARA'S HALLS

Pp. 433 f. Since the Elizabethan age, when apparently every one could write songs that would sing, there have been few poets whose lyrics have so much of the singing quality as have those of Thomas Moore. Many of them have been favorites of the people ever since they were written. Some of his sweetest and most characteristic songs are those celebrating the past glories or lamenting the sorrows of Ireland (see the note on *Adonais*, l. 269). Tara, the seat of the high, or chief, kings of Ireland in her ancient days of mythical and historical splendor and power, is celebrated in epic and in history. Ireland was then famous for culture, for learning, for poetry, for religion, and for war.

LEIGH HUNT

RONDEAU

P. 434. This charming little poem is said to have been the result of Mrs. Carlyle's expression of delight when Hunt announced that the publishers had accepted Carlyle's *History of Frederick the Great*.

THOMAS DE QUINCEY

Pp. 434 ff. The *Confessions of an Opium Eater* is a literary elaboration of a class of experiences never before put into literary form. De Quincey began taking opium when he was a student at Oxford and continued all his life, although, after several severe crises, he succeeded in reducing the amount very greatly. His *Confessions* became immediately popular, doubtless rather through morbid interest in the theme than through appreciation of his art.

The fact is, however, that he gives singularly little definite information in regard to either the sensations or the dreams produced by opium. His method is to take a comparatively small body of experiential fact and play with it as a musician plays with a theme in a fugue or a symphony. His high place among writers of English prose is due chiefly to the elaborate and subtle rhythms he builds up in his long, involved sentences. For the suggestions of these he is indebted to the writers of the sixteenth and seventeenth centuries, especially Hooker, Sir Thomas Browne, Jeremy Taylor and Milton.

P. 435 b. *My knowledge of the Oriental tongues.* The reader might infer that De Quincey knew the Arabic and Turkish words he mentions at the time of the visit of the Malay, but this visit — if it ever occurred — is placed by him in 1816–1817 (see p. 438 a), at least two years before the publication of *Anastasius*. The fact is that De Quincey was a little vain in regard to his learning — even when, as here, it was very small — and rarely neglects an opportunity to insinuate it.

The quantity was enough to kill three dragoons and their horses. At the usual price of opium, this amount was an expensive gift for so poor a man as De Quincey to make. But the incident is picturesque.

P. 436 b. *as a witty author has it.* The reference is to Southey's *The Devil's Walk*, st. 8:

" He passed a cottage with a double coach-house,
    A cottage of gentility:
And he owned with a grin
That his favorite sin
    Is pride that apes humility."

P. 438 b. *as unlimited a command . . . as a Roman centurion*, an allusion to the reply of the centurion to Jesus: " I say unto this man ' Go,' and he goeth; and to another ' Come,' and he cometh." *Matt.* viii : 9.

P. 440 b. That Homer knew of opium and its effects is inferred from the account in the *Odyssey*, IV, 220–221, of the drug which Helen cast into the drink of the heroes who were lamenting those who had fallen in the Trojan war, to lull pain and cause forgetfulness; but there is no reason to believe that this implies that Homer had any personal experience of the drug.

P. 441 a. Observe how slight a use is made of the Malay after all the elaborate preparations of pp. 435–436. De Quincey seems often to secure his effects upon his readers rather by awakening enormous expectations and supplying eloquent generalizations than by given specific details of horror or obsession. The passage at the foot of p. 441 b has been greatly and justly admired, but except in it and the passages on pp. 442–443 he displays little faculty for visual imagery, despite what he says in p. 438 b. His method furnishes a remarkable example of the use and effectiveness of "atmosphere" — which he creates abundantly.

P. 442 a. *my children were standing, hand in hand, at my bedside.* At this date he had only one child — an infant in arms; he married Margaret Simpson — the "dear M." of p. 437 b — in 1816. The first child was born in 1817.

Easter Sunday. A dream-confusion; Easter cannot occur in May.

P. 443 b. *" I will sleep no more!"* But he did.

LORD BYRON

Byron is not a poet whose work requires to be studied in detail, though his powerful imagination often produces images and phrases that do not reveal their full significance without careful reflection. In general, it is the larger, broader phases of his work that demand attention, — his emotional power, his creative imagination. That much of his poetry is the product of hysterical sentimentality, partly natural and partly cultivated, is true, and this has been the cause of strange ups and downs in his reputation; but his genius is undeniable, and few English poets have exercised so powerful an influence upon foreign literature.

ENGLISH BARDS AND SCOTCH REVIEWERS

Pp. 443 ff. In 1807 Byron published his first volume of verse, *Hours of Idleness*. It was unfavorably reviewed in the *Edinburgh Review*, one of the two most influential magazines of the time.

This is his reply. That his judgments are the product, not of intelligence, but of emotion, may be inferred from the praise he lavishes upon forgotten versifiers such as Montgomery, Bloomfield, Gifford, Macneil, White and Shee. In his preface he says, referring, we may presume, to Scott, Wordsworth, and Coleridge: "But the unquestionable possession of considerable genius by several of the writers here censured, renders their mental prostitution the more to be regretted. Imbecility may be pitied or, at worst, laughed at and forgotten; perverted powers demand the more decided reprehension."

P. 445. ll. 235–238. "Mr. W., in his Preface, labors hard to prove that prose and verse are much the same, and certainly his precepts and practice are strictly conformable." *Byron's Note.*

CHILDE HAROLD'S PILGRIMAGE

The very title of this poem, no less than the occasional archaic diction, serves to create an atmosphere of artificiality appropriate to its *blasé* hero, steeped in the unconquerable melancholy of youth. There is, perhaps, no period in the life of an imaginative and sensitive man at which melancholy holds him so fast, — at which

> "the heavy and the weary weight
> Of all this unintelligible world"

bears so sadly upon him — as when he is just passing from youth to manhood. This was the period at which Byron began this poem, and he had, in addition to youth's natural causes of melancholy, some special ones, arising from his morbid pride and sensitiveness, accentuated by fits of nervous exhaustion and reaction from a life of excessive self-indulgence.

The poem is a series of more or less connected descriptions and meditations, suggested by the scenes through which his imaginary pilgrim took his proud and lonely way. The subjects are very varied, and it is interesting to note how the poet has made the Spenserian stanza respond to all the moods and movements of his themes.

The extracts give a few of the many famous passages.

The first (Canto I, ll. 1–197) describes the pilgrim and his departure on his pilgrimage. Note his pride in his profligacy and his unfaithfulness in love, his disbelief in friendship, his sullen aloofness, and — despite all this — his fundamental capacity for strong and genuine affection. His attitude is indicated in the very first stanza by his refusal to invoke the Muse.

l. 1. *Hellas*, ancient Greece.

l. 6. *Delphi*, the shrine of Apollo, god of music and poetry. He obtained the lyre from Hermes, who had stretched strings across a tortoise shell (see l. 8) and produced the first lyre.

l. 8. *Mote*, an ancient form meaning *may*. Other archaisms, for which the dictionary may be consulted, are *whilome* (l. 10), *in sooth* (l. 14), *Childe* (l. 19), *hight* (l. 19), *losel* (l. 23), *Eremite* (l. 36), *lemans* (l. 77), *feere* (l. 79), *Paynim* (l. 99).

l. 8. *the weary Nine*, the nine muses, who have been invoked by so many generations of poets.

P. 446. l. 61. *Paphian girls*. Paphos, in Cyprus, was the seat of one of the most famous temples of Aphrodite (Venus). Here the adjective is applied to devotees of sensual love.

l. 79. *Eros* (Cupid), the god of capricious sensual love. *feere*, an old word for companion, friend.

l. 81. *Mammon*, the Syrian god of wealth (see *Par. Lost*, I, ll. 678–688).

P. 447. The second extract (Canto III, ll. 181–252) begins with the ball in Brussels the night before the battle of Quatre Bras (two days before Waterloo) and passes almost immediately to the battle itself (ll. 200–207). The Duke of Brunswick was one of the first leaders to leave the ball and one of the first to fall in the battle. His father was mortally wounded nine years before in the battle of Auerstadt.

ll. 226–234. The memories of clan Cameron included the great deeds of Evan in the war of the Commonwealth and of his son Donald, called "the gentle Lochiel," in behalf of Prince Charles Stuart in 1745. A *pibroch* is a piece of warlike Scottish music played on the bagpipes; that of clan Cameron was "Cameron's Gathering."

P. 448. l. 235. The forest of Soignies, between Brussels and Waterloo, said by Byron to be a remnant of the ancient forest of Ardennes, is mentioned here on account of its associations with peace.

The third extract (Canto III, ll. 604–675) is devoted by the poet to setting forth his attitude toward Nature and Man and the effect of Nature upon himself.

P. 449. The three stanzas (Canto IV, ll. 694–720) demand some familiarity with the history of Rome. They need no other commentary.

And none seems needed by the two remaining extracts, devoted respectively to a cynical view of love (Canto IV, ll. 1081–1125) and to a contrast of the works of Man with the desert, the forest, and the ocean (Canto IV, ll. 1587–1656).

THE PRISONER OF CHILLON

Pp. 451 ff. Bonnivard, celebrated in the prefatory sonnet, was a Genevan patriot, imprisoned for six years in the castle of Chillon, four of which he spent in the dungeon. He was released by his own party and seems to have lived for some thirty-four years more. His story, though not very similar to that of "the prisoner," no doubt suggested the poem.

ODE

Pp. 455 ff. There can be no doubt of the genuineness of Byron's interest in political independence. It is attested not only by the sonnet on Chillon, this *Ode*, and many other passages in his writings, but by his devotion of his money and his life to the struggle for the independence of Greece. At the time this *Ode* was written, Venice, once a glorious and powerful republic, had been since 1797 a possession of Austria. Austrian governors sat in the ancient seat of the doges, and Austrian soldiers paraded with drums and guns in the streets and in the Piazza di San Marco; the ancient spirit of patriotism seemed dead or at least alive only in the hearts of a few conspirators, who held meetings in Byron's own apartments. Every reader will wish to read in connection with this *Ode*, Ruskin's *The Stones of Venice*, Vol. II, Chap. IV (cf. above, pp. 582 ff.), especially §§ xii–xv.

This *Ode* is very uneven in conception and execution. Cantos I and IV are well conceived and in general nobly expressed; Cantos II and III are awkward and uncertain in thought and awkward and involved in style.

After four lines of invocation to the city, Canto I is devoted to a merciless arraignment of the Venetians for cowardice and submission to the tyrant Austria. Even the carved Lion of St. Mark, the patron saint of the city, is made to appear subdued and spiritless (l. 19) and the city is compared to a dying man (ll. 37–55).

In Canto II (ll. 56–100) the same theme is continued in confused fashion, with almost unintelligible references to "the few spirits" who love freedom and are not appalled at thought of the crimes which the mob will commit in freedom's name when the prison wall is thundered down.

P. 456. Canto III recites some of the former glories of Venice and her services in preserving

freedom for Europe, and, finally, the poor requital she has received.

Canto IV predicts the disappearance of freedom from Europe with the subjugation of Switzerland and declares America to be its only remaining refuge.

PERCY BYSSHE SHELLEY

Pp. 458 ff. Shelley's poetry should be read in the light of his own views of the nature and value of poetry. These are given with clearness and eloquence in his *Defense of Poetry*, which, with the views of sixteen other poets, including Chaucer, Sidney, Spenser, Milton, Wordsworth, and Coleridge, is published in a small volume entitled *The Prelude to Poetry*, edited by Ernest Rhys (J. M. Dent and Co.). What the poets themselves thought about the nature and value of their own art is surely of greater interest to lovers of it than the disquisitions of critical system makers.

ALASTOR

Alastor is not the name of the hero or any other character in the poem — indeed there are no other characters. It is a Greek word meaning an evil spirit; Shelley's intention was to set forth solitude as evil and even fatal. "The Poet's self-centred seclusion was avenged by the furies of an irresistible passion pursuing him to speedy ruin." But Shelley's sympathy is so obviously engaged by his picture of the youth enamored of "his own imaginations" of "all of wonderful, or wise, or beautiful" and uniting them in " a single image," that the terror of the poet's fate is less impressive than the charm of his lonely and restless pursuit of loveliness and truth. The passage here given contains only the characterization of the youth and a general account of his early efforts in search of truth. The quotation from St. Augustine is from the *Confessions*, Bk. III, Chap. I.

HYMN TO INTELLECTUAL BEAUTY

Pp. 459 f. The basis of this poem is Plato's doctrine of beauty; cf. especially *The Banquet*. It gains new light and interest from a comparison with Spenser's *Hymn in Honor of Beauty* and *Hymn of Heavenly Beauty* (see pp. 120–122), which are based upon Neo-Platonism; that is, upon the ideas of Plato as modified by later Christian and non-Christian philosophers and poets.

The following quotation from Diotima's conversation, as given by Socrates in Plato's *Banquet*, gives the principal features of Plato's doctrine of beauty; the translation is Shelley's:

"He who aspires to love rightly, ought from his earliest youth to seek an intercourse with beautiful forms, and first to make a single form the object of his love, and therein to generate intellectual excellences. He ought, then, to consider that beauty in whatever form it resides is the brother of that beauty which subsists in another form; and if he ought to pursue that which is beautiful in form, it would be absurd to imagine that beauty is not one and the same thing in all forms, and would therefore remit much of his ardent preference towards one, through his perception of the multitude of claims upon his love. In addition, he would consider the beauty which is in souls more excellent than that which is in form. So that one endowed with an admirable soul, even though the flower of the form were withered, would suffice him as the object of his love and care, and the companion with whom he might seek and produce such conclusions as tend to the improvement of youth; so that it might be led to observe the beauty and the conformity which there is in the observation of its duties and the laws, and to esteem little the mere beauty of the outward form. He would then conduct his pupil to science, so that he might look upon the loveliness of wisdom; and that contemplating thus the universal beauty, no longer would he unworthily and meanly enslave himself to the attractions of one form in love, nor one subject of discipline or science, but would turn towards the wide ocean of intellectual beauty, and from the sight of the lovely and majestic forms which it contains, would abundantly bring forth his conceptions in philosophy; until, strengthened and confirmed, he should at length steadily contemplate one science, which is the science of this universal beauty.

"Attempt, I entreat you, to mark what I say with as keen an observation as you can. He who has been disciplined to this point in Love, by contemplating beautiful objects gradually, and in their order, now arriving at the end of all that concerns Love, on a sudden beholds a beauty wonderful in its nature. This is it, O Socrates, for the sake of which all the former labours were endured. It is eternal, unproduced, indestructible; neither subject to increase nor decay: not, like other things, partly beautiful and partly deformed; not beautiful in the estimation of one person and deformed in that of another; nor can this supreme beauty be figured to the imagination like a beautiful face, or beautiful hands, or any portion of the body, nor like any discourse nor any

science. Nor does it subsist in any other that lives or is, either in earth, or in heaven, or in any other place; but it is eternally uniform and consistent, and monoeidic with itself. All other things are beautiful through a participation of it, with this condition, that although they are subject to production and decay, it never becomes more or less, or endures any change. When any one, ascending from a correct system of Love, begins to contemplate this supreme beauty, he already touches the consummation of his labour. For such as disciplined themselves upon this system, or are conducted by another beginning to ascend through these transitory objects which are beautiful, towards that which is beauty itself, proceeding as on steps from the love of one form to that of two, and from that of two to that of all forms which are beautiful; and from beautiful forms to beautiful habits and institutions, and from institutions to beautiful doctrines; until, from the meditation of many doctrines, they arrive at that which is nothing else than the doctrine of the supreme beauty itself, in the knowledge and contemplation of which at length they repose."

Ozymandias

P. 460. This sonnet was written by Shelley in friendly competition with Leigh Hunt, who took the river Nile as his subject and, on this one occasion, proved himself Shelley's equal. The theme is taken from a passage in Diodorus Siculus, who describes the gigantic statue and records the inscription. Here, as elsewhere, Shelley is careless of rhyme and other details of form.

Lines Written among the Euganean Hills

The Euganean Hills are near Este in Italy, south of a line drawn from Padua to Verona. The view from Shelley's garden was a wide one east and south and west. The mood of the poem is due to Shelley's ill health and the recent death of his infant daughter.

P. 461. ll. 212 ff. Cf. Byron's *Ode* and Wordsworth's sonnet *On the Extinction of the Venetian Republic. The brutal Celt* (l. 223) is inaccurately applied to the Austrians.

l. 239. *Ezzelin.* Ezzelino da Romano (1194–1259), successively conqueror of Verona, Padua, Vicenza, Feltre, Trento and Brescia, aspired to the conquest of Milan and all Lombardy. His cruelty was such that his name became proverbial and the legend arose that his mother confessed that he was the son of Satan himself. He is placed by Dante, in the *Inferno*, among the tyrants expiating the sin of cruelty, and his career was the subject of the first modern tragedy, the *Eccerinus* of Albertino Mussato. The dice play by Sin and Death — two Miltonic figures — was, according to the poet, to decide whether he should continue his life of sin or die.

ll. 256 ff. Padua was the seat of one of the most famous universities of mediæval and early modern times.

P. 462. l. 292. *point of heaven's profound*, zenith of the fathomless depths of air.

l. 333. *Its*, the frail bark's (l. 331).

ODE TO THE WEST WIND

The poet, despondent and empty of energy, appeals for aid to the West Wind of Autumn. Stanzas I, II, and III are successive apostrophes to the Wind in various functions and aspects. In stanzas IV and V he makes his appeal for aid, and as his inspiration glows and his pulses quicken, he passes from appeals that he may be passively subject to the Wind's power — a leaf lifted and driven before it, or a lyre responding in mighty harmonies to its breath — to a prayer for active union in spirit and power to scatter his thoughts among men, and finally reaches a triumphant recognition that the coming of Winter is the promise of Spring.

The poem is very subtly and skilfully constructed. Not only do the last two stanzas recall all the activities of the first three, but ll. 64, 65 are beautifully associated with ll. 2–14, and the triumphant note of ll. 68–70 is prepared for by the words,

"Thou dirge
Of the dying year" (ll. 23, 24).

The stanzas are ingeniously formed from the *terza rima*, the verse of Dante's *Divina Commedia*. Strictly speaking, the *terza rima* [1] ends with the thirteenth line of each stanza; Shelley, in order to get a stanzaic effect, adds another line rhyming with the thirteenth. The *terza rima* gives him the continuity of movement within the stanza

[1] In *terza rima* the first rhyme and the last must appear twice and only twice, while each of the others must appear three times. The rhyme formula is ababcbcdc . . . xwxyxyzyz. *Terza rima* is rare in English. Other examples of it in this volume are Wyatt's *Of the Meane and Sure Estate* (p. 98) and Rossetti's fragment, *Francesca da Rimini* (p. 629), translated from Dante.

appropriate to his subject; the couplet rhyme gives the stanzaic structure necessary to his plan.

l. 9. *Thine azure sister of the spring* is not the South Wind, as has sometimes been supposed, for from ancient times the south wind has been dreaded in Italy (see Vergil's *Eclogues* and *Georgics, passim*). The wind meant is the West Wind of the Spring, sister to the West Wind of Autumn.

P. 463. l. 21. *Mænad.* The women who in ecstasy took part in the rites of Dionysus, with flying hair and flaming torches, were called Mænads (the frenzied ones). Everybody who has not already done so should read Professor Gilbert Murray's translation of the *Bacchæ* of Euripides.

l. 32. *A pumice isle* is one formed from the lava of a volcano. *Baiæ*, an ancient Roman pleasure resort, is the modern Baja, a few miles west of Naples, in a region where nearly extinct volcanoes still rumble and spurt feebly.

THE INDIAN SERENADE

There are several versions of this poem, all apparently originating with Shelley himself. This explains the variant readings, of which there are several, for example: *burning* for *shining* (l. 4); *As I must die on thine* (l. 15); *Beloved as thou art* (l. 16); *press me to thine own* and *press it close to thine again* (l. 23).

THE CLOUD

P. 464. ll. 17–30. Shelley conceives of the Lightning as the pilot of the Cloud and as itself following the movements of the genii that move in the sea. Wherever the Lightning dreams, the spirit he loves will be found below — under mountain or stream. But how does the Lightning dissolve in rain (l. 30)? One would expect the Cloud to do that.

TO A SKYLARK

Pp. 465 f. This flood of divine rapture is one of the many wonderful poems in English which have so impressed lovers of the beautiful, that even we Americans, to whom the cuckoo, the English skylark, and the nightingale are entirely unknown, think of these birds as sources of delight, and some of us who "meddle with making," as the old scribbler said, have even written about them without ever having heard a song from their throats. Nearly all the poem is devoted to the bird itself — the first six stanzas to pure lyric outcries, the second six to lyric comparisons with other forms of beauty, then six to a contrast of the bird's song of unalloyed happiness with human music with its constant undertone of incompleteness and longing; in the last three stanzas, reverting to the appeal of ll. 61-62, the poet longs for the skill of the bird.

ADONAIS

Pp. 466 ff. There has been much discussion as to the formation of this name, but no entirely satisfactory suggestion has yet been made. The suggestion that it is formed on the model of *Thebais*, a poem by Statius about Thebes, is obviously unacceptable, as Adonais is primarily the name, not of the poem, but of the subject of it. The name — pronounced, of course, as four syllables — is at any rate formed from Adonis (see note on l. 12), and is intended to suggest his beauty and lamentable fate.

Neither Shelley nor Byron approved of Keats's early poems. But Shelley, at least, said of the fragment *Hyperion* that it was "second to nothing that was ever produced by a writer of the same years," and he was sincerely concerned when he heard that Keats was ill. He wrote to Mrs. Leigh Hunt: "Where is Keats now? I am anxiously expecting him in Italy, where I shall take care to bestow every possible attention on him. . . . I intend to be the physician both of his body and his soul. . . . I am aware indeed, in part, that I am nourishing a rival who will far surpass me; and this is an additional motive, and will be an added pleasure." Keats, however, went to Rome, and Shelley, who was in Pisa, knew of his death only by report, which, as he says in his preface, accounts for the fact that he did not celebrate in the poem the friendship and care of the painter Severn, who "almost risked his own life and sacrificed every prospect to unwearied attendance upon his dying friend." The poem is no less the product of Shelley's indignation against reviewers in general and the writer of the savage criticism of *Endymion* in the *Quarterly Review* in particular, than of his sorrow for the death of Keats. And it perhaps suffers from what Shelley himself calls the "interposed stabs on the assassins of his peace and of his fame." Shelley was, of course, wrong in supposing that the unfavorable criticisms of the *Quarterly Review* (or the still more savage ones of *Blackwood's Magazine*) seriously affected the health of Keats. Keats himself said: "Praise or blame has but a momentary effect on the man whose love of beauty in the abstract makes him a severe critic of his own

works. My own domestic criticism has given me pain without comparison beyond what *Blackwood's* or the *Quarterly* could possibly inflict — and also when I feel I am right, no external praise can give me such a glow as my own solitary reperception and ratification of what is fine. J. S. is perfectly right in regard to the slipshod *Endymion*."

Adonais, though one of the most beautiful poems in the language, is one of the most difficult to read with thorough comprehension. This arises from two facts. In the first place, Shelley was at this time steeped in classical literature, and not only is his verse packed with classical allusions and reminiscences, but his diction also is subtle and often affected by classical usage. His confidence that the poem had not been "born to an immortality of oblivion" has, of course, been fulfilled. He was no less right in calling it a highly wrought *piece of art* than in declaring that "it is absurd in any review to criticise *Adonais* and, still more, to pretend that the verses are bad." In the second place, the mysticism of the poem, based in large part upon the ideas of Plato, though perhaps furnishing the sincerest and most effective stanzas, involves many difficulties of thought for readers who have not already become somewhat familiar with these ideas. The best, indeed the indispensable, method of understanding and appreciating the poem thoroughly is to read for the classical allusions and reminiscences Bion's *Lament for Adonis* (Idyl I), Moschus's *Lament for Bion* (Idyl III), Theocritus's *Song of Thyrsis* (Idyl I), Vergil's *Eclogues* V and X, and Milton's *Lycidas;* and for the mystical ideas, Plato's *Timæus, Phædrus*, and *Phædo*, Spenser's *Hymn in Honor of Beauty* (p. 120), and *Hymn of Heavenly Beauty* (p. 121), and Wordsworth's *Lines Composed Above Tintern Abbey*, ll. 93-102 (p. 385). For the doctrine of Plato's ideas, some readers may prefer to consult, instead of Plato himself, the summary and discussion by Walter Pater in *Plato and Platonism*, Chap. VII. It is not enough to consult the works enumerated above, when references are given in the notes. They should be read after the poem has been read carefully at least once, and then the poem should be read again; for the study of literary relationships becomes vital only when it is a study of related wholes, not of minor details.

The verse is the well-known Spenserian stanza. It is interesting to contrast the effect of it as used by Shelley with its effect as used by Spenser, on the one hand, and Byron, on the other. Although the same metrical scheme is used by each of these writers, the effects produced are as different as if the metrical schemes were entirely different.

The general outline of the poem may be briefly indicated. ll. 1–9, The subject stated. ll. 10–72, Appeal to Urania to come where Adonais lies. ll. 73–153, The lamentations of Dreams, Desires, Adorations, Morning, Ocean, Echo, Spring, and the Nightingale. ll. 154–189, Contrast between the renewal of nature and the fate of man. ll. 190–261, The visit of Urania to the bier of Adonais, and her lament. ll. 262–315, The visit of the "mountain shepherds." ll. 316–342, Attack upon the critic of the *Quarterly*. ll. 343–369, Denial that the passing away from earth is death. ll. 370–396, The incorporation of Adonais with "the loveliness which once he made more lovely" as his part in the work of the "One Spirit." ll. 397–414, The welcome accorded him by "the inheritors of unfulfilled renown." ll. 415–459, Rebuke of any one so foolish as not to recognize the fate of Adonais as a blessed one. ll. 460–495, The thirst of the soul for the Absolute, — the Eternal Beauty, Light, and Truth.

l. 1. Cf. Bion, ll. 1 ff.

l. 3. *so dear a head.* Horace's *Odes*, I, xxiv, 2.

l. 4. *Hour.* Not one of the classical *Horae*, but a personification of the hour made illustrious by the death of Keats (cf. *obscure* in the next line).

l. 10. *Where wert thou.* Cf. the *Song of Thyrsis* (Theocritus, *Idyl* I) and Vergil, *Eclogue* X.

l. 12. *Urania* is clearly the Uranian Aphrodite discussed in Plato's *Banquet*, 180, 187, etc., and there identified with the Muse, who is mentioned in the *Phædrus* in the following terms: "But to Calliope, the eldest, and Urania, the second of the nine, they bare tidings of those who pass their lives in philosophic study and the observance of their peculiar music, these we know being the muses who having heaven for their special sphere, and words both divine and human, pour forth the gladdest strains." It is the Uranian Aphrodite who is the mighty mother of all living things (l. 10). This phase of Aphrodite, or Venus, is not only celebrated by Plato and Greek poets, but is also the subject of the magnificent lines with which Lucretius begins his *De Rerum Natura*. This explains why Adonais is made the son of the Uranian Aphrodite in contrast to Adonis, the lover of the Pandemian Aphrodite.

l. 16. *melodies*, referring not merely to the *Ode to the Nightingale*, but to all the poems written by Keats after he became aware of his condition.

l. 20. *wake and weep.* Cf. Bion, ll. 3, 4.

l. 24. *where all things wise and fair descend.* Cf. Bion, l. 55.

l. 29. *He died.* Cf. Moschus, ll. 71 ff., who celebrates Homer as Shelley here does Milton.

AE

P. **467**. l. 36. *the third.* The other two are certainly Homer and Dante. See Shelley's *Defense of Poetry*, where he not only calls Homer, Dante, and Milton the three great epic poets, but speaks of Vergil as not among the highest.

l. 39. "Those who recognize their limitations"; perhaps a reminiscence of the words of Socrates in the *Phædrus:* "I possess something of prophetic skill, though no very great amount, but like indifferent writers just enough for my own purposes."

l. 46. Cf. Moschus, ll. 74, 75.

l. 47. Cf. Bion, l. 59.

ll. 48–49. A reference to Keats's poem *Isabella*.

l. 55. Cf. ll. 424–437.

l. 61. Cf. Bion, ll. 71 ff.

l. 63. *liquid* = serene. Cf. Vergil's *Georgics*, IV, 59; *Æneid*, X, 272.

l. 69. *The eternal Hunger*, the same as *invisible Corruption* (l. 67).

l. 73. *The quick Dreams*, the poetical conceptions of Keats, here take the place of the Graces, the Muses, etc., of Bion and Moschus.

l. 78. Cf. "Those thoughts that wander through eternity," *Paradise Lost*, II, 148.

l. 88. Cf. l. 14.

P. **468**. l. 127. *Lost Echo.* Cf. Bion, ll. 35 ff., and Moschus, ll. 30–31.

ll. 133, 140, 141. The well-known stories of Echo, Narcissus, and Hyacinthus may be found in Gayley's *Classic Myths* or any classical dictionary.

l. 145. Moschus (ll. 9 ff., cf. ll. 45 ff.) also calls upon the nightingale to lament for Bion, but Shelley has in mind Keats's *Ode to a Nightingale*, as is shown by *thy spirit's sister*.

ll. 154 ff. The contrast between the yearly renewal of the flowers and the finality of human death is also the subject of one of the finest passages in the *Lament for Bion*, ll. 101 ff.

P. **469**. l. 172. *The leprous corpse, i.e.,* earth.

l. 186. Mr. W. M. Rossetti's explanation that "in this our mortal state death is the solid and permanent fact . . . the phenomena of life are but like a transitory loan from the great emporium, death," seems out of harmony with the context. Throughout the stanza Shelley is talking about grief. Read the whole stanza carefully and note the *must* in l. 188 as well as in l. 186.

ll. 212–213. Cf. what Agathon says of the feet of Love in Plato's *Banquet*, 195.

l. 219. *Blushed to annihilation.* The figure is rather difficult until one remembers that the essential nature of death implies paleness. Blushing would imply the annihilation of death by changing it into life.

l. 224. The distress of Urania gives encouragement to Death, who becomes himself again.

l. 227. A literal translation from Bion, ll. 45, 46.

P. 470. l. 238. *The unpastured dragon* is the critic of the *Quarterly*, hungry for victims; but, as l. 240 shows, Shelley had in mind the story of Perseus and the dragon which was to devour Andromeda.

l. 240. *Wisdom, the mirrored shield*, is suggested by the polished shield of Athene (Goddess of Wisdom), which Perseus used as a mirror when he slew Medusa.

ll. 244 ff. The *wolves, ravens,* and *vultures* are the detractors of poets in general.

l. 250. *The Pythian of the age* is Byron; and the *one arrow*, his famous *English Bards and Scotch Reviewers*.

l. 261. Poets akin to the *god-like mind* of l. 258 as the *immortal stars* of l. 256 are to the *sun* of l. 253.

l. 262. The shepherds come to lament Daphnis in Theocritus, and Lycoris in Vergil, as Keats's fellow poets (poetically called shepherds) come to lament him.

l. 264. *The Pilgrim of Eternity* is Byron. The phrase was doubtless suggested by *Childe Harold's Pilgrimage*, Canto III, l. 629 (see p. 448).

l. 268. *Ierne* = Ireland.

l. 269. Thomas Moore wrote many songs about the ancient glories and modern sorrows of Ireland. *Her saddest wrong* refers not to any particular event, but to her calamitous history in general.

ll. 271–306. Shelley himself is the subject of these lines, which emphasize his love of beauty and his sense of ineffectiveness. Curiously enough, some of them, as well as the final lines of the poem, are strangely prophetic of the fate which actually overtook him.

l. 276. The fable of Actæon, who was changed into a stag and destroyed by his own hounds because he had gazed upon Artemis (Diana) bathing, may be found in Gayley's *Classic Myths*.

ll. 289–295. This picture seems strangely suggestive of the god Dionysus, whose mission as set forth in the *Bacchæ* of Euripides must have seemed to Shelley to resemble his own.

l. 298. What does *partial* mean here?

P. 471. l. 301. *The accents of an unknown land* most probably means "in imitation of Theocritus, Bion, and Moschus"; for the *gentle band* (l. 299) is composed of English poets, not of the classical personages earlier invoked.

ll. 307–315. Leigh Hunt. Shelley explains in his preface that he did not know of the services of Severn when the poem was written.

l. 316. Shelley returns to the attack on the critic of the *Quarterly*. Bion is also said by Moschus to have *drunk poison*, whether literally, or, like Keats, figuratively, is unknown.

l. 325. The critic, because he is anonymous, has not even the fame of infamy, as the burner of the Temple of Diana at Ephesus has (cf. p. 183).

ll. 338 ff. The remainder of the poem is largely indebted to Plato. The indebtedness is so general and pervasive that to appreciate it the reader must familiarize himself with the Platonic ideas of beauty, love, and the soul. Only a few special points will therefore be noted.

ll. 343–357. Cf. the words of Socrates in the *Phædo*, 106–110, 114–116.

ll. 345–348. The figure may have been suggested by the action of the raving Pentheus in the *Bacchæ* of Euripides. Dionysus says: —

"On that he rushed, and there,
As slaying me in vengeance, stood stabbing the thin air."

P. 472. l. 381. *plastic*, moulding, shaping. *The one Spirit* is the absolute existence, the "One" of Plato's philosophy as opposed to the "Many," *i.e.*, the phenomena of this world, all of which are manifestations of this "One." Cf. Spenser's *Hymn in Honor of Beauty*, ll. 29–49 (p. 120).

ll. 399 ff. Chatterton, Sidney, and Lucan are all appropriately mentioned as "inheritors of unfulfilled renown," because all of them were cut off by death in early manhood. Perhaps few will agree with Shelley in feeling that Lucan's suicide atoned for his willingness to betray his fellow conspirators, though Shelley may have felt that he was justified in the conspiracy. Shelley may have been influenced by Plato in ascribing conscious immortality to the souls of these and the *many whose names on earth are dark* (l. 406).

l. 412. *blind* = dark.

ll. 422–423. Apparently the meaning is "Keep thy heart light, lest thou be overwhelmed with a sense of the pettiness of earth and be tempted to follow Adonais."

ll. 438–449. This is a beautiful description of the place in which Keats lies buried, "the romantic and lonely cemetery of the Protestants in that city, under the pyramid which is the tomb of

Cestius, and the massy walls and towers, now mouldering and desolate, which formed the circuit of ancient Rome. The cemetery is an open space among the ruins, covered in winter with violets and daisies. It might make one in love with death to think that one should be buried in so sweet a place." — Shelley's Preface to *Adonais*.

P. **473**. l. 460. Cf. the note on l. 381.

l. 461. The same idea in different words. That earthly phenomena are shadows cast by the Heavenly Light is set forth in the seventh book of Plato's *Republic*.

l. 463. *The white radiance of eternity* was doubtless suggested by the description of heaven in Plato's *Phædrus*. "Real existence, colorless, formless, and intangible, visible only to the intelligence which sits at the helm of the soul . . . has its abode in this region." The comparison of life to a dome of many colored glass may conceivably have been suggested by the fable which Socrates tells Simmias in the *Phædo* to the effect that "this earth, if any one should survey it from above, is like one of those balls covered with twelve different pieces of leather, variegated and distinguished with colors," though that of course is really a different conception from this.

ll. 478–486. The ideas of this stanza are all Platonic.

FINAL CHORUS FROM HELLAS

Hellas is a lyrical drama inspired by the proclamation of Greek independence in 1821 and celebrating this event as preluding the return of the "Golden Age." Shelley tells us in a note that the Final Chorus was suggested by the prophetic visions of Isaiah and Vergil, that is, especially the sixty-fifth chapter of Isaiah and the fourth *Eclogue* of Vergil. The student may also compare Pope's *Messiah*, which was likewise suggested by Isaiah and Vergil.

ll. 1–18. A belief of the ancients was that at the end of many thousand years all the heavenly bodies would have returned to the positions they occupied at creation and the events of history would begin to repeat themselves. As the Golden Age of innocence and happiness was, in poetry and mythology, placed in the first age of the world, its return was also looked for. In this poem Shelley develops in detail this ideal of historic recapitulation. A new Greece (Hellas) shall arise with all the beauties and glories of ancient Greek history and poetry: the river Peneus, the vale of Tempe, the islands of the Cyclades shall again be scenes of pastoral sim-

plicity and delight; the great adventures of the search for the Golden Fleece, the descent of Orpheus to Hades to release his lost Eurydice, the return of Ulysses, shall all be relived.

P. **474**. ll. 19–24. Pursuing the same idea, the poet is shocked by the thought that the evil of the past will also be renewed — the Trojan War, the dark tragedy of Œdipus — and he prays that this may be averted.

ll. 31–34. "Saturn and Love were among the deities of a real or imaginary state of innocence and happiness. *All those who fell*, or the gods of Greece, Asia and Egypt; the *One who rose*, or Jesus Christ, at whose appearance the idols of the Pagan World were amerced of their worship; and *the many unsubdued*, or the monstrous objects of the idolatry of China, India, the Antarctic islands, and the native tribes of America, certainly have reigned over the understandings of men, in conjunction or in succession." — Shelley's Note.

JOHN KEATS

ODE TO A NIGHTINGALE

The poet, listening to the song of the nightingale, is affected to a passion of tearful delight in the happiness of the bird (ll. 1–10), and longs for a magical draught of summer that will cause him to follow the bird (ll. 11–20), leaving behind the fever and fret of the world (ll. 21–30). Imagination fulfils his desire, and he finds himself in the forest of his fancy (ll. 31–40), a place lighted only by moon-beams, and so dim that he discerns the flowers about him only by their odors (ll. 41–50).

Resuming the theme of the first stanza, he declares that, as he listens in the dark, death seems richer and sweeter at the thought that the bird's song is immortal (ll. 51–70).

His thoughts are brought back to himself and his sorrows by the word "forlorn," and as the song of the bird fades away in the distance, he questions whether it may not have been "a vision or a waking dream."

In music and suggestiveness of diction, in beauty of imagery, in sensuous richness of conception, this poem has never been surpassed even by Keats himself. It must be read, often and in many moods, for though its magical charm can be felt at a single reading, every rift, to borrow a phrase from Keats's advice to Shelley, is loaded with ore.

P. **475**. l. 9. The shadows are those cast by the full moon (see l. 36).

ll. 11–20. The draught that is to transport the poet away from the weariness and sorrow of life is no draught of earthly wine (cf. l. 32), for all its taste and color, but the wine of poetic inspiration (cf. ll. 16, 33).

l. 14. Provençal poetry, though he knew little about it, was always associated in Keats's imagination with romantic beauty (cf. *The Eve of St. Agnes*, l. 292, and *La Belle Dame Sans Merci*).

l. 16. *Hippocrene*, like *Lethe* (l. 4), *Dryad* (l. 7), *Flora* (l. 13), *Bacchus* (l. 32), is fully explained in Gayley's *Classic Myths*.

l. 32. *Bacchus* is here only the vulgar god of wine, not the mystical god Dionysus. There is no better way of appreciating these two different phases of the same Greek god than by reading in succession the *Cyclops* and the *Bacchæ* of Euripides (Shelley translated the former).

ll. 65-67. Cf. Wordsworth's *Solitary Reaper* for a picture much akin to this.

ll. 69-70. Why these lines suggest to the imagination the whole world of romance, it would be difficult to say.

ODE ON A GRECIAN URN

Pp. 475 f. This urn, like the deep bowl of ivy-wood which the Goatherd gave to Thyrsis for singing the *Affliction of Daphnis* (Theocritus, *Idyl* I), was carved with a succession of beautiful scenes and figures. No urn exactly answering to that in the poem is known; some editors think Keats had in mind a finely carved marble urn that stood in the garden of Holland House, but if so, he has not described it closely. "Description" is, indeed, hardly the term for his method of setting these sculptured scenes before our eyes. For him they live, and we learn what they are like only from the emotions and reflections they produce in him. The carvings of the Goatherd's bowl are perhaps no less beautiful, but the descriptions of them are simple and uncolored by emotion or reflection.

The urn seems to present two main scenes: (1) the rout of fleeing maidens and pursuing men of ll. 8-10; and (2) the sacrificial procession of ll. 31-37. The youth piping beneath the trees (l. 15) and the bold lover (l. 17) who has almost caught the maiden, are apparently details of the first scene; and the little town of silent streets (ll. 38-39) is obviously not in the picture, but only inferred by the poet from the crowd that follows the priest and the sacrificial victim to the forest altar, — which also is not visible except to the imagination of the poet.

The fundamental idea of the poem is, of course, the permanence of all these beautiful forms and the consequent permanence of their wild rapture

and quiet happiness, as contrasted with the transiency of human happiness and the cloying of human passion that wins to its goal.

l. 1. *unravished*, because preserving its purity and beauty.

l. 2. *foster-child*, because nursed by them.

l. 3. *Sylvan historian*, because telling tales of woods, as well as of men (cf. ll. 15, 21, 32, 43).

P. 476. l. 7. *Tempe* and *Arcady*, delightful regions in Greece, famous in mythology and poetry; for particulars, see Gayley.

ODE

P. 477. This charming ode, ascribing to the poets of the past, two lives, one in heaven, and the other, through their poems, here on earth, shows a sense of mirth and humor in dealing with a serious subject that seldom appears in Keats's verse, but is very frequent in his letters. In ll. 29-36 we have the same idea as in Wordsworth's *Personal Talk*, ll. 51-56 (p. 391).

LINES ON THE MERMAID TAVERN

This poem, a companion piece in the same metre and manner as the preceding, is even lighter in tone. Keats might have shrunk from being "disrespectful to the Equator," but he certainly treats the Zodiac with delightful levity.

The Mermaid Tavern was the resort of Beaumont and Fletcher, Ben Jonson, Shakespeare, and their fellows (see Beaumont's *Letter to Ben Jonson*, p. 174 of this volume).

l. 19. Why *new old-sign*?

l. 22. Which of the signs of the Zodiac is the Mermaid?

LA BELLE DAME SANS MERCI

The title of this poem (The Beautiful Lady without Mercy) is taken from one written in French by Alain Chartier about 1400. Keats seems to have thought it was written in Provençal (cf. *The Eve of St. Agnes*, l. 292). The English translation of it by Richard Ros was accessible to him among the poems ascribed to Chaucer in Chalmers' *English Poets*, but its mediocre quality did not prevent him from being fascinated by the title and writing a poem to suit it.

It is not a poem that the student should try to analyze or reason about. It is the expression of a romantic mood by means of a combination of romantic figures and imagery with wonderful verbal music. It should, however, be read with recognition of the art with which the withered sedge, the lonely lake, the fairy lady, the vision of the pale kings and princes who had been her victims, and, indeed, all the details, are combined to harmonize with the figure of the knight; and all to develop the suggestions of the title.

SONNETS

Pp. 478 f. Among the comparatively few masters of the sonnet, Keats ranks very high. The six chosen for this volume of selections illustrate various themes and moods. None of them requires any explanation. With that on *The Grasshopper and the Cricket* the student may compare Lovelace's *The Grasshopper*, p. 218. The pedant has long been shocked to note that in the one *On First Looking into Chapman's Homer* Keats has ascribed to Cortez a feat performed by Balboa, and has extended the bounds of Darien perhaps unwarrantably. But the poem as a poem is none the less admirable on those accounts.

Wordsworth has a fine sonnet *To Sleep* (p. 395), which it is interesting to compare with Keats's on the same subject. It is somewhat characteristic of the two poets that Wordsworth woos Sleep as the —

"Dear mother of fresh thoughts and joyous health,"

whereas Keats mingles with a sensuous pleasure in sleep itself a yearning for it as shutting out the cares and sorrows of life. Wordsworth's is a fine wholesome poem; Keats's is a subtle and rich work of sensuous art, almost every line of which is a masterpiece of thought and phrasing.

ENDYMION

Pp. 479 f. In this poem Keats follows that form of the Endymion myth which represents him as a shepherd lad. The scene is laid in ancient Greece, and the rivers, fountains, meadows, and forests are peopled by the beautiful creatures of Greek fancy — nymphs, dryads, oreads, fauns, etc. That the beauty of the poem is too elaborate, too rich, too overcharged with ornament and sentiment, Keats himself recognized; but it was a youthful production and he knew that he could free himself from the faults it contained and develop into greater solidity and strength the beauties it undeniably possessed. The fact is that Keats regarded all his work, as he says in his letters, as mere experiments, exercises in composition to prepare him for the great and serious work

which he planned to do when mind and character were riper and more richly furnished with the wisdom of life.

Lines 1–33 — a proem on the influence and value of beauty — give his reasons for choosing this subject. Lines 540–671 describe the first meeting of Endymion and the Moon Goddess, Diana.

HYPERION

Pp. 481 f. The subject of *Hyperion* is the overthrow of the older gods by the younger, especially of the old sun deity Hyperion by the new sun-god Apollo. The chief older gods, or Titans, were Oceanus and Tethys, Hyperion and Thea, Chronos (or Saturn) and Rhea, Japetus, Themis, and Mnemosyne. In the new order Oceanus was replaced by Neptune, Hyperion by Apollo, and Saturn by Jupiter. The theme is really the eternal conflict between the old order of established power and peace and the new order of aggressiveness and progress. Although the poem shows a great improvement in power and restrained beauty over *Endymion*, Keats did not finish it — perhaps because he felt that he was not yet mature enough for the great demands of such a theme.

l. 21. Gaea (or Earth) was the mother of the older gods; Uranus (or Heaven) their father.

l. 23. *there came one,* Thea.

l. 30. *Ixion* was bound to a revolving wheel in Tartarus (Hell) for boasting that Juno loved him.

l. 51. *To* = compared to.

ll. 83–4. A month had passed.

l. 129. What is implied by *metropolitan?*

THE EVE OF ST. AGNES

Pp. 482 ff. The poem is a simple story of two lovers separated, like Romeo and Juliet, by the enmity of their families, and of their elopement on St. Agnes' Eve. The scene is laid in feudal times, and the date chosen is the night on which, according to popular superstition, a girl may have a vision of her true lover if she performs certain ceremonies. The poem itself tells all that is necessary for its interpretation, but those who wish a prose account of the superstitions may consult Chambers' *Book of Days* or Brand's *Popular Antiquities.*

l. 1. *St. Agnes' Eve,* the night of January 20.

ll. 5 ff. *Beadsman,* a beadsman was one paid or maintained to pray for his benefactor or others. This one is represented as praying in the chapel of the castle before the picture of the Virgin. About him, on their tombs enclosed with iron railings or **in** oratories (alcoves along the walls), are the sculptured figures of the dead with their hands folded as if in prayer.

l. 71. On account of her name and her innocence the lamb (Latin *agnus*) is associated with St. Agnes. Eight days after her martyrdom, her parents, praying at her tomb, saw a vision of angels, among whom was their daughter, and beside her a lamb white as snow.

P. 484. l. 116. The nuns who weave the sacred wool of St. Agnes' lambs; of the ceremonies on her day in Rome, Naogeorgus, as translated by Barnaby Googe, says:

> "For in St. Agnes' church upon this day while masse they sing,
> Two lambes as white as snowe the nonnes do yearely use to bring,
> And when the Agnus chaunted is upon the aulter hie
> (For in this thing there hidden is a solemne mysterie),
> They offer them. The servants of the Pope, when this is done,
> Do put them into pasture good till shearing time be come.
> Then other wooll they mingle with these holy fleeces twaine,
> Whereof, being sponne and drest, are made the pals [palls] of passing gaine."

WALTER SAVAGE LANDOR

Pp. 487 ff. Landor's temperament was very erratic and volcanic. In singular contrast, his verse, as well as his prose, is distinguished by reserve and moderation of expression, sometimes, indeed, lapsing into the prosaic. He often has lines and short passages of an exquisite quiet beauty and suggestiveness, but never succeeds in maintaining a high poetic level throughout a long poem. It is not strange that only the finest of his poems, like *Rose Aylmer* and the others given here, have attained general currency. Each of these is written, as it were, in a single flash of inspiration, and each incorporates in a form of ultimate beauty thoughts and feelings that awaken an almost universal response.

Æsop and Rhodopè

The suggestion for this dialogue Landor took from Herodotus, who says that Æsop and Rhodopè were both slaves in the same household. Æsop was the famous writer of fables, of whom

little is known except that he was a Phrygian who lived about 600 B.C. Traditionally he was hunchbacked and ugly. Rhodopè or Rhodopis (the rose-faced) was a Thracian, whom her master Xanthus took to Egypt. Sappho's brother fell in love with her and purchased her freedom, as appears from one of Sappho's poems. Strabo tells of her a story which is the oldest form of one episode in the tale of Cinderella. It is that while she was bathing, an eagle flew away with one of her shoes and dropped it in the lap of the King of Egypt. He was so attracted by the beauty of the foot suggested by it and by the strangeness of the circumstance that he sent out messengers to find the owner of the shoe and married her.

The story of the way in which Rhodopè came to be a slave was invented by Landor.

Rose Aylmer

P. 492. This beautiful and suggestive elegy contains all the elements of the poetry of personal loss — the reflection that no virtue or power could save the beloved one, and the expression of the poet's own sorrows. Those prosaic souls who have objected that one night is little to consecrate to the memory of a friend so beloved are inaccessible to the effects of suggestion and incapable of understanding that the poet's sense of loss can be permanent unless he tells them explicitly that he will never get over it.

A Fiesolan Idyl

Fiesole (pr. Fee ay' sō le) is an ancient town situated at the summit of a small mountain of the same name that rises with a steep slope on the outskirts of Florence. The idyl is a sweet, small poem, presenting, as in a picture, a single, simple incident. The poet hears a rustling among the orange trees on the slope of the mountain, and, finding a graceful young girl gathering flowers, helps her pull down the branches that are too high for her to reach. Then comes the delicate embarrassment of both, when she wishes, but hardly dares, to offer him a large sweet blossom, and he dares not assume that she means to offer or that he ought to take it. Incidentally the poet's love and tender care of flowers is exquisitely expressed (ll. 16–33).

On His Seventy-Fifth Birthday

P. 493. The only thing that has ever been unfavorably criticised in this poetic summary of

Landor's life, and his contentment with what it has brought him, is the supposed egotism of the first line. But if a man loves nature and art and devotes himself to them (warming "both hands before the fire of life") and to the expression of his love for them, he may well feel that striving with other men is silly and unworthy of him.

THE VICTORIAN AGE

THOMAS CARLYLE

SARTOR RESARTUS

Pp. 497 ff. In reading *Sartor Resartus*, it is well to remember that Carlyle had a Scotch temperament and that he purposely adopted German modes of thought and phrasing. The first results in a picturesque half-suppressed violence in the utterance of the emotions with which his philosophy of life was surcharged, and the second gives his style the complexity and elaboration that characterize much German philosophical writing. He chose for the vehicle of the message embodied in *Sartor Resartus* an imaginary German professor whom he calls Teufelsdröckh of Weissnichtwo (Don't-know-where). Under the pretence that he has met this man and become impressed with his ideas, Carlyle represents himself as translating his biography into English. The materials of this biography, he says, reached him in the following form:

"Six considerable PAPER-BAGS, carefully-sealed, and marked successively, in gilt China ink, with the symbols of the Six southern Zodiacal Signs, beginning at Libra; in the inside of which sealed Bags lie miscellaneous masses of Sheets, and oftener Shreds and Snips, written in Professor Teufelsdröckh's scarce legible *cursiv-schrift;* and treating of all imaginable things under the Zodiac and above it. . . ."

By this device Carlyle obtains the greatest possible freedom in the expression of his ideas. He begins with the idea suggested by Swift in his *Tale of a Tub* (p. 248 above), choosing the title *Sartor Resartus* (the tailor re-tailored) to show that he meant to tear away the outward appearances of life in order to get at its real meaning. He sums up the purpose of the book thus:

"Have many British readers actually arrived with us at the new promised country; is the Philosophy of Clothes now at last opening around them? Long and adventurous has the journey been: from those outmost vulgar, palpable Woollen Hulls of Man; through his wondrous Flesh-Garments, and his wondrous Social Garnitures; inwards to the Garments of his very Soul's Soul, to Time and Space themselves! And now does the spiritual, eternal Essence of Man, and of Mankind, bared of such wrappages, begin in any measure to reveal itself? Can many readers discern, as through a glass darkly, in huge wavering outlines, some primeval rudiments of Man's Being, what is changeable from what is unchangeable?"

He criticises its character and value as follows:

"It was in this high moment, when the soul, rent, as it were, and shed asunder, is open to inspiring influence, that I first conceived this Work on Clothes: the greatest I can ever hope to do; which has already, after long retardations, occupied, and will yet occupy, so large a section of my life. . . ."

The three chapters given in this book form a thought-unit, showing Carlyle's growth from pessimism and despair to the foundation of his particular form of optimism, that the supreme need of the soul is to express itself in some sort of work.

There is much autobiography even in the details of the book, and as a spiritual history, it is entirely autobiographical.

THOMAS, LORD MACAULAY

Pp. 510 ff. The long selection from Macaulay's famous chapter on the state of England at the time of the Revolution of 1688 is out of proportion to his importance among writers of English prose; but teachers who are tired of reading over and over again his biographical sketches will doubtless welcome it as a change, and both teachers and pupils will surely find it valuable for the vivid picture it gives of the physical and social background against which so large a part of English literature must be seen if it is to be seen truly. Moreover, in style it presents Macaulay at his best, and Macaulay at his best is a triumph of clear and vivid common sense. He is, to be sure, one-sided; he was not a big enough man to have an all-round vision or a subtle enough man to observe distinctions and shades that make all the difference in the final accuracy of a picture, and he has no real philosophy of history. He is pompous, rhetorical, even blatant at times; but he is one of the first writers of history in English who gets beyond the point of stringing together and weighing events merely as events. He really constructs pictures that enable us to realize the times and the men about which he is writing.

JOHN HENRY NEWMAN

Pp. 518 ff. In 1851 the Catholics of Ireland founded a University in Dublin. Newman was called upon to speak on the occasion, and delivered nine lectures which were published under the title *The Idea of a University*. He himself was chosen as rector of the newly-founded university; but it was a failure from the first, partly through lack of government support, and partly because Newman himself lacked executive ability.

The lectures themselves may, perhaps, be summed up, in a phrase used by Newman himself in the passage chosen for this book, as inspired by "clear, calm, accurate vision." And it was largely this clearness, this poise, this precision, that made Newman such a power in his day.

ALFRED, LORD TENNYSON

THE LADY OF SHALOTT

Pp. 523 f. Like Keats's *La Belle Dame Sans Merci*, this poem seems to have been suggested by its title. In this case, as in the other, the piece from which the title was taken bears little relation to the poem suggested by it. The curious may read the story of *La Donna di Scalotta* in the old Italian *Cento Novelle Antiche*, where it is No. 81 (tr. Roscoe, *Italian Novelists*, Vol. I). This is Tennyson's first attempt to deal with a theme taken from the stories that clustered about King Arthur and his knights. Here the interest lies not in the story as such, but in the mood of the poet and the suggested but indefinite symbolism of the poem. The key to the symbolism of the poem is said by Tennyson's son to lie in ll. 69–72 and to consist in the entrance of human interests into the world of shadows in which the Lady had lived. It is hardly possible, and certainly unnecessary, to attempt to find a definite symbolic meaning for every detail of the situation and narrative.

The poem is divided into four parts, each devoted to a single phase of the theme. Part I sets before us the lonely situation of the Lady in the gray-walled island tower beside the thronged road to Camelot. Part II emphasizes her isolation from the world of realities and her contact with life only through the shadows in the magic mirror, which apparently she reproduces in her magic web as her fragment of the dream of human life. In Part III, half-sick of shadows as she has become, she sees the brilliant figure of Sir Lancelot in the mirror, and, in spite of the curse that will come upon her, she leaves her web and for the first time sees in direct vision the world of nature, represented by the water lily, and the world of mankind, represented by Lancelot, whom she has loved at first sight. In Part IV the curse has come upon her, and real life is broken for her, as was the mirror in which she saw the world of shadows. When the boat bearing her body floats down the stream to Camelot, Lancelot, though all unaware of her love for him, is touched by admiration and pity, and breathes a prayer for her.

A DREAM OF FAIR WOMEN

Pp. 524 ff. The style of this poem is rich and elaborate in three ways. In the first place Tennyson's imagination is largely pictorial; he visualizes the scenes and persons and objects of his story, and the reader who would perfectly recreate in his own mind the poet's conception must try to catch every hint given by the words of the poem and reconstruct the pictorial images. This is true not only of such striking figures as Cleopatra with her wild exotic beauty or Jephthah's daughter, the embodiment of maidenly sweetness and filial submission until, at the thought of the victory over Ammon, her face glows with a light that would be savage if it were not Biblical; it is true, also, of such incidentals as the dim red morn lying dead and pale across the threshold of the sun, and the bizarre emphasis given to the dark silent forest by the red anemone that *burned* among the lush green grasses. Everywhere, in almost every stanza, the reader must move slowly, must read carefully, must let every word play its due part in the elaborate and highly colored pictures that hovered in the poet's vision.

The second element of richness and elaborateness of effect is due to the fact that in the poet's mind many of the rich pictures of the poem itself exist in a very atmosphere of beauty and pathos created for him by poets and painters and sculptors who have treated these same things before him. As he sees in his vision Helen and Iphigenia, his memory is filled with the music of the *Iliad* and the choral measures of Æschylus and Sophocles, and he sees not only these women and the vivid picture of the death of one of them, but all the heroes who went out from Greece to battle on the windy plains of Troy, the fatal return of Agamemnon to his dishonored home, and the vengeance of Electra and Orestes. The disconnected pictures of ancient strife and wrong that pass before his eyes before he fully falls asleep — the lances in ambush, the attack on the walled city, the heated blasts bursting in the doors of defiled sanctuaries — all these come with a thousand recollections of wild tales in mediæval romances and chronicles. And the praise of Chaucer and of the great literature of the Elizabethan age are the echoes of hundreds of hours of delight spent in reading. There is no method, as has been said, of supplying the reader suddenly with all this experience of literature, with all these associations, with all this richness of emotional life. An editor may cite examples to explain every line, may pile up instance upon instance until the intellect is thoroughly convinced that such things were common, but not in this way can the reader gain those associations and memories which alone give significance and power to the great figures of history and romance and myth or the scenes and manners of past ages. The only method is to do as the poet himself has done, — read these poems and histories, and amass the associations and emotions of this experience with literature.

The third element is the rich and elaborate diction. Here, as with the first element, we are on easier ground; we are dealing with matters which the intellect and imagination can compass immediately by knowledge and native vigor. Such lines as, —

"The maiden splendours of the morning star,"
(l. 55),
"A daughter of the gods, divinely tall,
    And most divinely fair," (ll. 87–88),
"The star-like sorrows of immortal eyes," (l. 91),
"The stern black-bearded kings with wolfish eyes,"
(l. 111),
"A queen, with swarthy cheeks and bold black
    eyes,
    Brow-bound with burning gold," (ll. 127–128),

reveal their meanings at once to any one who has imagination. But sometimes Tennyson substitutes the ornate and elaborate for the simple and imaginative, and produces lines that require some ingenuity for interpretation. How many a reader has not beaten his brains to find out what is meant in l. 1 by "before my eyelids dropt their shade"! It is, indeed, a rather elaborate way of saying, "before I closed my eyes to sleep," and the feeling that it must mean more is so strong that some will still strive vainly for a more mystical interpretation, in spite of the fact that the poem obviously narrates the events of one night, when the poet, after reading Chaucer, passes through that stage of visions which precedes sleep, into a sleep of dreams and finally

wakes and tries to recall his dreams. "The crested bird that claps his wings at dawn" (ll. 179 f.) has also shed much ink. If Tennyson meant the cock and took this method of slipping that brilliant but rather prosaic fowl into his bediamonded poetry, we may be glad that it is possible to rescue him by arguing in favor of the crested lark of Theocritus and insisting that no modern student of poetry, as Tennyson was, could write

"That claps his wings at dawn,"

without remembering those exquisite lines of John Lyly's:

"Now at heaven's gates she claps her wings,
    The morn not waking till she sings."

Tennyson's poem, though obviously suggested by Chaucer's *Legend of Good Women*, bears only superficial and unessential resemblances to it. It is true that both poems deal with ill-fated fair women, that in both the poet dreams, and it is even possible that Tennyson has taken from other of Chaucer's poems the thoroughly conventional device of falling asleep after reading a book that determines the subject of his dream. But aside from the fact that Chaucer's style is simple and his mood relaxed and easy, while Tennyson's style is ornate and his mood one of the utmost intensity, the purely external features are very different. The scene of Chaucer's dream is a meadow filled with all the gladness of a May morning, — singing birds and blossoming flowers and "softe, swote, greene grass"; the scene of Tennyson's is an ancient wood, oppressive with huge elms, hanging vines, dark walks, a deadly silence, and a pale chill light from the dying dawn. Chaucer meets in his dream the brilliant God of Love and his queen, accompanied by a group of charming maidens, and for sufficiently valid reasons promises to write each succeeding year the story of some fair woman who had been faithful though unfortunate in love; Tennyson meets and converses for a few vivid moments with women, fair and unfortunate, but by no means chiefly "Love's martyrs." It seems not improbable that Tennyson may have been, consciously or unconsciously, influenced by the procession of noble ladies with whom Odysseus spoke in Hades (*Odyssey*, Bk. XI).

The structure of the poem is very simple and clear:

ll. 1–13. What the poet had been reading and the immediate effect of it.

ll. 13–52. He muses on what he has read, and

visions of ancient strife and wrong pass in vivid pictures before his eyes as he is falling asleep.

ll. 53–84. He then dreams he is in a great forest, made gloomy by its huge trees, its dank festoons of jasmine, its long, dark, dew-drenched walks, its uncanny silence, and the cold pale light that followed the fading of the first dim flush of morn. His melancholy is increased by the odor of hidden violets bringing memories of happier times, and a voice within him tells him he will always stay in this dark wood.

ll. 85–260. There come before him in his dream women like those of Chaucer's *Legend*, beautiful heroines of tragic story — Helen of Troy, Iphigenia, Cleopatra, Jephthah's daughter, and the ill-fated Rosamond.

ll. 261–272. Then as he slowly awakes, he catches glimpses of certain other ill-starred heroines, — Margaret Roper, Joan of Arc, and Eleanor, wife of Edward I.

ll. 273–288. With difficulty he recalled his dream and often vainly strove to strike again into the same dream.

Details that may deserve explanation or comment are the following : —

P. 525. ll. 17–52. The vividness of these hypnagogic figures approaches nearly to hallucination. Every one has, at times, in falling asleep slowly, had more or less vivid images pass before his eyes. Some persons have them constantly. Tennyson may have been more than usually sensitive to them. See the remarks on *St. Agnes' Eve* for what he says of his experiences of trance-like seizures, and compare also De Quincey, p. 438.

ll. 73–76. Apparently the poet makes the unblissful wood of his dream one which he had known in real life under happier circumstances. Dante's famous lines : —

> "Nessun maggior dolore
> Che ricordarsi del tempo felice
> Nella miseria,"

it will be remembered, had impressed him when he was a boy of twelve, long before he so tawdrily translated them as

"A sorrow's crown of sorrow is remembering happier things,"

and it may be that here and in ll. 77–80 he shaped his poem in accordance with them.

P. 526. l. 87. The beauty and self-sufficingness of this line sometimes make us forget, what the poet remembered, that Helen was, according to the myth, the daughter of Zeus, and therefore divinely tall.

ll. 100–116. In his picture of Iphigenia, Tennyson apparently follows the story as told in the first Chorus of the *Agamemnon* of Æschylus, with perhaps recollections of the *Electra* of Sophocles, but there are also expressions which indicate that the touching scenes of *Iphigenia in Aulis* were in his mind, though he necessarily rejected the vicarious sacrifice narrated by Euripides. There is no way to obtain the full effect of this passage but to read these plays.

ll. 118–120. These words of Helen's are almost a transcript of what she says in the *Iliad*, VI, 345 ff., to Hector when Paris seems slow to prepare for battle : —

"My brother, even mine, that am a dog mischievous and abominable, would that on the day when my mother bare me at the first, an evil storm-wind had caught me away to a mountain or a billow had swept me away before all these things came to pass."

ll. 127–128. Critics have chided Tennyson for forgetting that Cleopatra was a Greek, fair and blue-eyed ; but he saw the Cleopatra of romance, not her of history. And this one must be swarthy and bold-eyed, as Tennyson saw her ; a "gypsy" with a "tawny front" as she appeared to Shakespeare's Mark Antony.

P. 527. l. 174. Clearly Tennyson did not visualize this image, or he would have cancelled it. It is neither beautiful nor possible as a picture.

ll. 177–242. The story of Jephthah's daughter, in *Judges*, xi, should be read, even if it is already familiar.

P. 528. ll. 249–260. The romance of Rosamond and Henry II of England and her death at the hands of his queen, Eleanor, are told in almost every history of England.

l. 259. Some of the commentators seem to have missed the point of Cleopatra's mention of Fulvia. As she counsels Rosamond to use the dagger, her own rival, Fulvia, comes to her mind, as in Shakespeare's play, and, forgetting Rosamond and Eleanor, she herself becomes heroine and prime actor in the imagined event.

l. 266. The devotion of Margaret Roper to her father, Sir Thomas More, is one of the fine incidents of history. To feel it as Tennyson did, one must know, as perhaps one may from Green's *History of the English People*, the power and charm of Sir Thomas More and his tragic fate.

l. 268. This line, with its reticence and moderation, suggests to one familiar with the wonderful story of the Maid of Orleans all the glamour and beauty that attach to one of the most romantic and mysterious figures the world has ever seen.

ll. 285–288. This ending is weak, because it is very obscure. The difficulty is not so much with the rhetorical figures of the chosen words withering beneath the palate and the heart fainting in its own heat as with the doubt whether these four lines are to be taken with ll. 281–284, or whether they really connect in thought, though not in syntax, with the efforts of the poet to recall and record the glimpses of his dream.

MORTE D'ARTHUR

This is Tennyson's earliest attempt at the epic treatment of Arthurian romance, and the treatment is simply epic, not allegorical, as is the case with the *Idylls* written after 1859. The immediate source of the poem is Sir Thomas Malory's famous *Morte Darthur* (Bk. XXI, Chaps. 4 and 5). It will be observed that Tennyson follows Malory very closely, though there are some interesting changes.

Tennyson himself speaks of the poem as full of faint Homeric echoes, but there are few of any significance. The most interesting is ll. 105–106, which seem to echo the words of Hephaistos, *Iliad*, xviii, 400 ff.: "Nine years with them [the sea-nymphs Thetis and Eurynome] I wrought much cunning work of bronze, brooches and spiral arm-bands and cups and necklaces, in the hollow caves, while around me the stream of ocean with murmuring foam flowed infinite." There are also faint echoes of other classical writers, the most important being l. 60, a close rendering of *Æneid*, iv, 285, viii, 20, and l. 240, perhaps an echo of Lucretius, *De Rer. Nat.*, iii, 976 f.:

"Cedit enim, rerum nouitate extrusa, uetustas
Semper, et ex aliis aliud reparare necesse est";

for the idea, cf. also Plato's *Banquet*, 207–208.

l. 1. Chapter 4 of Malory's account tells how the battle raged all day long, till all were dead in both armies except King Arthur, Syr Bedwere, and his brother Syr Lucan.

l. 8. In Malory, Arthur is borne to the little chapel by the two brothers, but Syr Lucan dies soon after. Tennyson has omitted Lucan in order to concentrate attention on Arthur and Bedivere.

P. 529. ll. 38, 44. Note the epic repetition here. Collect other examples from the poem. This is, perhaps, due to the influence of Homer.

P. 530. l. 123. Note the archaic character of the syntax here and elsewhere. It is meant to give dignity to the language and to suggest antiquity.

ll. 169–170. The passage from the *Agamemnon*, 240, cited by Mustard does not seem to express the same idea as this: "She smote each of her sacrificers with a piteous glance from her eye, remarkable in her beauty as in a picture."

P. 531. l. 255. A Platonic idea, taken over directly or indirectly by many later writers, among them Boethius (cf. Chaucer's translation of Boethius, Bk. I, Metre v, and Bk. II, Metre viii, where the chain is Love).

ll. 260 ff. The relation of Avilion to other ideal lands is uncertain. These lines may have been suggested by the description of Olympus in the *Odyssey*, vi, 43 ff. But they are more like the description of the Earthly Paradise in Lactantius, *De Ave Phœnice*, 1–30, expanded into eighty-five lines in the Anglo-Saxon translation (Bright's *Anglo-Saxon Reader* contains both versions); for a modern English rendering see Cook and Tinker's *Old English Poetry*. The Celtic conception of the Otherworld is similar, and is given in several of the older poems.

l. 267. Tennyson cannot have failed to remember the beautiful passage in which Socrates argues that the dying swan does not sing for grief but as "foreseeing the blessings of the other world," *Phædo*, 85.

ULYSSES

P. 532. "*Ulysses*," says Tennyson, "was written soon after Arthur Hallam's death and gave my feeling about going forward and braving the struggle of life perhaps more simply than anything in *In Memoriam*" (*Alfred Lord Tennyson, a Memoir*, by his son, I, p. 196). It is based upon the following passage in Dante's *Divina Commedia*, Inferno, XXVI, 90–142: —

"When I departed from Circe, who had retained me more than a year there near to Gaeta, before Æneas had so named it, neither fondness for my son, nor piety for my old father, nor the due love that should have made Penelope glad, could overcome within me the ardor that I had to gain experience of the world and of the vices of men, and of their valor. But I put forth on the deep open sea, with one vessel only, and with that little company by which I had not been deserted. One shore and the other I saw as far as Spain, far as Morocco and the island of Sardinia, and the rest which that sea bathes round about. I and my companions were old and slow when we came to that narrow strait where Hercules set up his bounds, to the end that man may not put out beyond. On the right hand I left Seville, on the other already I had left Ceuta. 'O brothers,' said I, 'who through a hundred thousand perils have reached the West, to this so little vigil of your senses that remains be ye unwilling to deny the experience, following the sun, of the world that hath no people? Consider ye your origin; ye were not made to live as brutes, but for pursuit of virtue and of knowledge.' With this little speech I made my companions so eager for the road that hardly afterwards could I have held them back. And turning our stern to the morning, with our oars we made wings for the mad flight, always gaining on the left-hand side. The night saw now all the stars of the other pole, and ours so low that it rose not forth from the ocean floor. Five times rekindled and as many quenched was the light beneath the moon, since we had entered on the deep pass, when there appeared to us a mountain dim through the distance, and it appeared to me so high as I had not seen any. We rejoiced thereat, and soon it turned to lamentation, for from the strange land a whirlwind rose, and struck the fore part of the vessel. Three times it made her whirl with all the waters, the fourth it made her stern lift up, and the prow go down, as pleased Another, till the sea had closed over us.

It will be seen that Tennyson's conception of Ulysses is precisely the same as is Dante's in this passage. It is true Dante places Ulysses among the "evil counsellors" in the eighth pit of the eighth circle of Hell, but no hint of that appears in this passage. This is not the place to discuss the discrepancies between Homer's account and Dante's, but it may be noted that the death of Ulysses at sea is not one of them, as some commentators have said, for Tiresias explicitly tells Odysseus, *Odyssey*, xi, 136 ff.: —

"And from the sea shall thine own death come, the gentlest death that may be." Dante's notion that Ulysses sailed into the unknown west was apparently suggested by certain traditions connecting him with Scotland and Lisbon, according to Grion in *Il Propugnatore*, III, 1a, pp. 67–72. The main difference between Dante's account and Tennyson's is that in the former Ulysses sets out from Circe's island, while in the latter he sets out from Ithaca. In both, he and his companions are old. In both, the companions are apparently men who were with him at Troy and on the homeward journey, though, according to Homer, all these had perished.

Tennyson's poem is full of reminiscences of the classics, as is quite natural.

Every lover of poetry should note the fine application of ll. 51–53, and 62–70 in the last page of Huxley's eloquent "Romanes Lecture" on *Evolution and Ethics*, and read what he has to say about Tennyson and Browning in the appended note.

LOCKSLEY HALL

As poetry, this does not rank with Tennyson's best productions, but its mood of mingled melancholy and optimism hit the taste of the time when it was written (1842) and it has ever since been a favorite with youths who feel that the world is out of joint and at the same time cannot resist the strong tide of vital impulses.

The poem is not autobiographical but dramatic. It was suggested by an Arabian poem, translated by Sir William Jones, the great oriental scholar. Perhaps the most interesting lines of the poem to the present-day reader are the prophecies of social and scientific progress, ll. 117–138.

P. 535. Lines 135–136 shadow forth the slow attack of democracy upon ancient privilege and authority.

P. 536. ll. 181–182. Tennyson explained that when he first rode on a railway train he thought that the wheels ran in grooved rails.

ST. AGNES' EVE

P. 537. In a letter to Spedding in 1834 Tennyson says: "I daresay you are right about the stanza in *Sir Galahad*, who was intended as a male counterpart to St. Agnes." This seems to indicate that in the poem bearing her name St. Agnes is the speaker, and not, as the poem suggests, some unknown nun. St. Agnes' eve is January 20. It was threatened by her persecutors that she should be debauched in the public stews before her execution, but in answer to her prayers she was miraculously preserved from this fate by lightning. Eight days later at her tomb her parents saw her in a vision among a troop of angels.

This poem expresses her religious aspiration, which in stanza 3 becomes ecstatic mystical vision. This is the point Tennyson refers to when he speaks of Sir Galahad as the male counterpart of St. Agnes. The lines especially noteworthy in this respect in *Sir Galahad* are 25–48, 63–80. Such mystical ecstasy as finds expression in these two poems is common in the experience of mystics. Mystical vision is often preceded by other phenomena. Richard Rolle (see Horstman's

Works of R. Rolle, Vol. I), the greatest of mediæval English mystics, felt first a delightful warmth in his bosom, then tasted delicious food and heard heavenly music. Similar experiences are related of St. Catherine of Sienna and many others.

The tendency to fall into a mystic trance in which the external world seems unreal is characteristic of certain temperaments (see note on Wordsworth's *Ode on Intimations of Immortality*, ll. 141 ff.). Tennyson says of himself: "A kind of waking trance I have frequently had, quite up from boyhood, when I have been all alone. This has generally come upon me thro' repeating my own name two or three times to myself silently, till all at once, as it were out of the intensity of the consciousness of individuality, the individuality itself seemed to dissolve and fade away into boundless being, and this not a confused state, but the clearest of the clearest, the surest of the surest, the weirdest of the weirdest, utterly beyond words, where death was an almost laughable impossibility, the loss of personality (if so it were) seeming no extinction but the only true life." Note in this connection the weird seizures of the Prince, added to *The Princess* in 1851.

SIR GALAHAD

In mediæval romance the stories of the Holy Grail and the quest for it vary greatly. Tennyson follows Malory (Bks. XI, XIII, XVII), in making Sir Galahad the knight of the Grail and the Grail itself the sacred vessel containing some of the blood of Christ.

See note on *St. Agnes' Eve*.

IN MEMORIAM

Pp. 540 ff. *In Memoriam* is a series of elegiac poems, written between 1833 and 1850 and expressing various phases of Tennyson's grief at the loss of Arthur Hallam, his most intimate friend in boyhood and youth. No doubt the grief becomes monotonous to the reader if he undertakes to read the whole series at a sitting, but the themes — the aspects of grief — are many and varied, and it is to be borne in mind that they are a record of many years of permanent consciousness of loss. They contain some of Tennyson's sincerest and best work and have found responsive echoes in many bereaved hearts.

The Proem, written in 1849, is Tennyson's summary of his attitude toward the mystery of bereavement.

Cantos I and XXVII are closely connected in thought and feeling.

Cantos XXXI and XXXII form almost a single poem on a single theme.

Canto LIV is the last of a series in which the poet discusses the carelessness and waste of Nature as revealed especially in the geological records, which show that not only individuals but whole species have perished: in this canto he takes refuge in a vague hope and trust.

MERLIN AND THE GLEAM

Pp. 543 ff. Tennyson said: "In the story of Merlin and Nimue I have read that Nimue means the Gleam — which signifies the higher poetic imagination." His career as a poet is expressed in the symbols of the successive stanzas.

CROSSING THE BAR

P. 545. Written in Tennyson's eighty-first year. He instructed his son to put this at the end of all editions of his poems.

ELIZABETH BARRETT BROWNING

SONNETS FROM THE PORTUGUESE

Pp. 545 ff. These sonnets are not translations, as the title implies, but record the courtship of the Brownings. The title was adopted to disguise their intimate personal tone. Sonnets I and VII allude to the unhappy conditions of Mrs. Browning's life before her marriage. For years she had been an invalid, and her father's jealousy of her friends added to her distress. Her marriage with Browning transported her to a finer, freer life and was followed by many years of improved health. Browning's response to the Sonnets may be inferred from *One Word More* (pp. 564 ff.) and from his beautiful tribute in *The Ring and the Book* beginning:

"O lyric Love, half angel and half bird
And all a wonder and a wild desire, —
Boldest of hearts that ever braved the sun,
Took sanctuary within the holier blue,
And sang a kindred soul out to his face, —
Yet human at the ripe red of the heart."

The passage in Theocritus here alluded to (I, 1) is in the "Psalm of Adonis" in *Idyl XV*, ll. 104 f.: "Tardiest of the Immortals are the beloved Hours, but dear and desired they come, for always, to all mortals, they bring some gift with them." Another notable poem suggested by the Theocritan lines is Emerson's *Days:*

" Daughters of Time, the hypocritic Days,
  Muffled and dumb like barefoot dervishes,
  And marching single in an endless file,
  Bring diadems and fagots in their hands.
  To each they offer gifts after his will,
  Bread, kingdoms, stars, and sky that holds them
    all.
  I, in my pleachèd garden, watched the pomp,
  Forgot my morning wishes, hastily
  Took a few herbs and apples, and the Day
  Turned and departed silent. I, too late,
  Under her solemn fillet saw the scorn.

THE CRY OF THE CHILDREN

Pp. 547 ff. In the middle of the nineteenth century the conditions of industrial workers in England were as bad as they still are in many parts of the United States. There were no laws regulating the employment of women and children, and child-labor was extensively exploited by manufacturers in all lines of industry. This poem was suggested by a report on factory conditions written by Richard Hengist Horne, a friend who was himself a poet of real though intermittent genius.

ROBERT BROWNING

CAVALIER TUNES

Pp. 549 f. These songs are intended to express the feelings and opinions of the adherents of King Charles I in the Parliamentary War; they are supposed to be sung by them.

"HOW THEY BROUGHT THE GOOD NEWS FROM GHENT TO AIX"

Pp. 550 f. Browning said: "There is no sort of historical foundation about *Good News from Ghent*. I wrote it under the bulwark of a vessel off the African coast, after I had been at sea long enough to appreciate even the fancy of a gallop on the back of a certain good horse 'York,' then in my stable at home." But the imaginary object of this imaginary ride was apparently, in Browning's intention, the conveyance of the news of the "Pacification de Gant," a treaty of union of Holland, Zealand, and the southern Netherlands against Spain. As this was concluded in 1576, the date 16— at the head of the poem is perhaps

due to a failure of memory, just as some of the towns mentioned as lying on the route between Ghent and Aix are really not on the shortest and best route. The ride can easily be traced on the map; the distance is somewhat more than ninety miles.

SAUL

Pp. 552 ff. These two consecutive cantos from *Saul* give David's discussion of the power and love of God, ending in the prophetic vision of the God-Man, Christ. He has examined the works of God carefully and discovers in them evidences of law, wisdom, love, the will and the power to redeem mankind.

MY LAST DUCHESS

Pp. 554 f. This dramatic monologue is one of Browning's most successful efforts in this form of poetry.

The Duke of Ferrara is supposed to be talking with an ambassador who has been sent by an unnamed Count to discuss with him a proposition of marriage with the Count's daughter. When the poem opens, they are returning from the place of discussion to the company awaiting them (cf. ll. 47–48), and the Duke, as if by mere chance, calls attention to a picture, and explains, as coolly as if he had no personal concern in the matter, that this is the picture of his last Duchess, whose "smiles" he had ordered "stopped," because she had a heart "too soon made glad" and had wounded his pride by setting no higher value upon what he gave her than upon the trifling gifts of others. He puts her offence purely as one against taste and family pride. The object of the conversation is, of course, to let the ambassador understand what his next Duchess may expect if she fails to rate highly enough the honor of being his wife.

Fra Pandolf and Claus of Innsbruck are names invented by the poet.

A GRAMMARIAN'S FUNERAL

Pp. 555 f. At the revival of classical learning in Europe the revelation of the rich and highly developed life and literatures of ancient Greece and Rome affected many men like the discovery of a new world. Some, like Erasmus (see Green's *Short History of the English People*) and the Grammarian of Browning's poem (see J. A. Symonds, *The Revival of Learning*, or J. Burkhardt, *The Civilization of the Renaissance*, Pt. III), were ready to make all sorts of sacrifices, even to going without sufficient food, in order to devote their lives to these fascinating studies. The Grammarian is at heart an idealist and a poet, bewildered by this wonderful new world, and so entangled in the preliminaries to acquiring and applying the new ideals of life that he dies before he has completed his preparations for living. His enthusiasm and idealism he has communicated to his pupils, and a company of them bear his body on their shoulders to its last resting place. One of them is the speaker in the poem. He discusses the ideals and aims of his master and asserts that his life was not a failure, but a triumph. This is a favorite theme with Browning (cf. *Abt Vogler* (p. 567), *Apparent Failure*, and many other passages).

The poem is not difficult if the reader remembers that here, as in many other poems, Browning's speaker uses the rapid changes of tone and syntactical structure of conversation. This makes it necessary to watch the punctuation closely, as it is intended to hint at the tone and voice inflection. Note especially the parentheses and quotations.

l. 95. *Hydroptic* means "afflicted with such a thirst that the more one drinks the more he thirsts."

"Childe Roland to the Dark Tower Came"

Pp. 556 ff. Many have insisted upon regarding this poem as an allegory and have tried to find the allegorical meaning of each detail. Browning declared it was not so intended, but was a dramatic poem suggested by the words of the title. He admitted, however, that it might be regarded as having a symbolic significance suggesting faithfulness to any high moral quest in spite of the failure or desertion or treachery of companions, the interference of obstacles and dangers of all sorts, and the uncertainty of the final outcome. It seems also safe to recognize in ll. 175 ff. a suggestion of the sort of moral crisis that is not known as such until one is brought suddenly and unescapably into it, and when courage — even if only the courage with which a brave soul fronts the inevitable — is the only safe counselor. The right way to read the poem is to attend consciously only to its plain dramatic meaning; it will inevitably suggest to the emotions all the symbolic significance it has.

P. 557. l. 12. Notice that there is only a comma at the end of this line; the sentence goes on. Notice also ll. 30, 132. Notice further that the "No" of l. 61 is very closely connected with ll. 58-60.

P. 558. l. 80. *Colloped* usually means lying in folds of fat, but here it is used of the folds or ridges of the horse's gaunt, withered neck.

P. 559. l. 192. This line, though in quotation marks, is not spoken, but represents the supposed attitude of the hills, watching to see the adversary slay Childe Roland.

l. 203. Browning's fancy was sometimes captured by an old or odd word, and he used it without knowing exactly what it meant. *Slug-horn* is due to a misunderstanding of an old spelling of the word *slogan*. Browning seems to have got it from Chatterton, who uses it several times; cf. Skeat's ed., II, pp. 42, 64, 125, 129, 132, 199, and especially 162:

"Some caught a slug-horn, and an onset wound."
(*Battle of Hastings* II, xi.)

Fra Lippo Lippi

"Poor brother Lippo" (*i.e.*, Filippo) was in reality a great Florentine painter of the Quattrocento (fifteenth century), whose character and career are very accurately given in this poem. He was born in 1406, according to Berenson, and died in 1469. His teacher was Lorenzo Monaco, the *Brother Lorenzo* of l. 236, but he owes much more to Masaccio (= *Hulking Tom* (l. 277), the nickname of Tommaso Guidi, five years his senior, whom Browning mistakenly makes his pupil. He was also somewhat influenced by Fra Angelico (1387-1455), who is mentioned in l. 235. Lippo's comments on Giotto in the poem are, of course, unfair, and were intended by Browning to be so.

The cloister of the Carmine (l. 7) was then outside the city, a little south and west of the Ponte alla Carraia. When the poem opens, Fra Lippo is at work for Cosimo de' Medici in what is now the Palazzo Riccardi. As this palace was built in 1430 and Fra Lippo seems to be engaged in decorating the walls, the imaginary date of the poem is apparently before Fra Lippo left the cloister in 1432, as, indeed, l. 7 seems to indicate.

The other places mentioned are in or near Florence. The church of San Lorenzo (St. Laurence, l. 67) is less than a hundred yards from "the house that caps the corner" (l. 18). The convent of the *Preaching Friars* (l. 140), or Dominicans, better known as that of San Marco, is a few hundred yards north of San Lorenzo; Camaldoli, the seat of the *Camaldolese* monks (l. 139), lies about twenty miles east, while *Prato* (l. 324) is twelve miles northwest.

For the facts of Fra Lippo's career Browning relied upon the latest edition of Vasari's *Lives of the Painters* (G. Vasari, *Delle Vite de' più Eccellenti Pittori*, etc.), which misled him in regard to Masaccio. The snatches of song in the poem are said to be modeled on the type of folk song called stornello (pl. stornelli), though they do not conform to the examples I have seen. The picture conceived for Sant' Ambrogio's church (ll. 346 ff.) is the Coronation of the Virgin, now in the Accademia delle Belle Arti. The words *Iste perfecit opus* (l. 377, "This one painted the picture") are on a scroll pointing towards the figure of the monk.

The information just given may satisfy some natural curiosity about certain details. The poem itself, however, can be understood without this introduction; it, indeed, contains all the elements necessary to its interpretation as a poem. Browning has two objects in the poem: (1) to give a vivid dramatic presentation of the psychology of this type of artist and the conditions of his life in fifteenth century Italy; (2) to use him as a mouthpiece for some interesting and important views about realistic art.

One Word More

Pp. 564 ff. This poem was, as ll. 1–2 indicate, the final poem of the volumes entitled *Men and Women* (2 vols., 1855). It is a tribute to the poet's wife, as clear and simple as it is beautiful. Its general theme is stated in ll. 96–99 and 184–186.

Notes on a few details may be interesting : —

l. 5. Nothing is known of Rafael's (1483–1520) *century of sonnets;* according to Browning it disappeared while in the hands of Guido Reni (b. 1575, d. 1642).

l. 10. *Who that one?* Rafael's lady was Margareta (la Fornarina), whose likeness appears in many of his pictures.

P. 565. l. 32. Dante's account of his beginning to draw an angel on the completion of Beatrice's first year "in the life eternal" is given in *The New Life* (*La Vita Nuova*), section xxxv (see Professor Norton's translation, pp. 74 ff., and his note on p. 163).

l. 46. Browning called one of his own works *Parleyings with Certain People of Importance in Their Day* (pub. 1887).

l. 57. *Bice* (pronounced "Bee'chè") is a love-form of Beatrice.

P. 566. l. 148. *Fiesole,* cf. notes on Landor's *A Fiesolan Idyl.*

l. 150. *Samminiato,* a popular form of San Miniato, a small mountain southwest of Florence, famous for its scenery and its church.

P. 567. ll. 163–165. *Zoroaster* and *Galileo* are named as types of those who studied the moon as scientists; *Homer* and *Keats* as poets who wrote about it. Galileo's discovery of the mountains in the moon was one of the most famous results of the use of the telescope. Keats's *Endymion* is the most notable version of the well-known myth of the loves of Endymion and the moon goddess.

Abt Vogler

Georg Joseph Vogler (b. 1749 at Würzburg, d. 1814 at Darmstadt) was the son of a violin maker and was early devoted to the career of musician. He studied in Germany and Italy and taught and directed in Germany and Sweden. While in Rome he entered the priesthood and was appointed Apostolic Protonotary and Chamberlain. He was court chaplain and master of the chapel at Mannheim and Stockholm, and established schools of music at both places. He composed a great deal of music, but his principal interest for us is in his career as virtuoso. Having made a good many simplifications in the pipe organ, which resulted in a portable organ about nine feet in height, depth, and breadth, named by him an "orchestrion," he visited Denmark, Holland, and England with it and gave organ recitals with much success. This is the instrument upon which he has been improvising when Browning's poem opens (cf. l. 2).

The central ideas of the poem are expressed in ll. 69–82.

The musician has just built up with his playing a beautiful structure of music, as wonderful both in result and in mode of accomplishment as the legendary palace built by Solomon for the princess he loved. He reflects upon these resemblances (ll. 1–40), expressing first the wish (l. 9) that this palace of music might be permanent, not doomed to perish as the notes of the improvisation die away. Then (ll. 41–56) he contrasts the rational, intelligible processes of other arts — painting, poetry, etc. — with the mysterious and divine creative processes of music. Then he returns to the question whether music — even improvised music — does really perish when the tones cease here on earth, and he finds in his soul's demand for personal immortality (ll. 63–64) the assurance that music, and all that is good and beautiful, must exist eternally in and through the power and love of the Ineffable Name; and finds in the necessity for the completion of the incomplete and the final success of apparent earthly failure triumphant "evidence for the fulness of the days" (ll. 65–82), the reality of eternity. And conformably to what is said of the nearness of God to the musician in ll.

49–56, he declares in ll. 81–88 the divine revelation of these truths to musicians.

The rest of the poem is a real, and at the same time symbolic, return from these exalted thoughts and feelings through the emotional effects of music to the plane and the duties of common human life.

l. 3. Legends of Solomon's skill in magic arose very early out of what the Bible says of his wisdom. The Talmudists inferred from the simple Biblical statement that no sound of a hammer was heard in the building of the Temple, that he must have used supernatural means, and they devised a story of a wonderful animal that cut stone and glass and iron, discovered by Solomon by means of his knowledge of the language of birds (see S. Baring-Gould's *Myths of the Middle Ages* and *Legends of the Patriarchs and Prophets*). Later legends, hinted at in the *Koran*, put him in control of armies of angels and demons, able to execute every command.

l. 5. The demons had or assumed all shapes.

l. 7. The belief that the real name of God was unspeakable goes back to ancient Hebrew times — or at least to a time earlier than the Septuagint version of the Old Testament; see any good encyclopædia under *Jehovah* or *Jahveh*.

P. 568. l. 18. If *crest* here means anything more than "head" or "creature," it is used to imply the different natures or groups represented by different crests or cognizances.

l. 22. The lighting of the lamps around St. Peter's dome (l. 23) used, it is said, to be one of the great sights of Rome on festal occasions.

l. 34. *Protoplast* is usually taken here to mean "model" or "mold." It seems rather to mean "creator," "first maker," as in Browning's other use of it in *Fifine*, cxxiv.

l. 42. *visibly*, as if he had really seen the structure of music.

l. 51. *this* = the art of music.

P. 569. ll. 91–96. The symbolism of this passage is clear. The efforts of commentators to indicate the succession of chords are not entirely satisfactory. In l. 91 the *common chord* seems to mean the basal chord of the tonality in which he had been improvising, for he would hardly have begun his descent to the *C Major of this life* from any other tonality. That this was not itself C Major, as some suppose, is probable; for what reason would there then be for sliding into the minor and the ninth before finding the resting place in C Major? What seems clear is that, beginning on the heights of feeling induced by his improvisation, the musician resumes the tonality in which he was improvising and, modulating by semi-tones,

AE

slips into the minor, which characteristically arouses emotions of unrest, incompleteness, and longing; but he resolutely blunts this with the inharmonic ninth, and then resolves this into C Major — the tonality of common human life.

RABBI BEN EZRA

Rabbi Ben Ezra, or Ibn Ezra, was born in Spain about 1090. He travelled in Africa, the Holy Land, Persia, India, Italy, France, and England, and was a scholar and a poet. Some of the ideas which Browning here puts into his mouth were really expressed by him in his poems and his commentaries on the Bible.

THE EPILOGUE TO ASOLANDO

Pp. 572 f. The volume of which this little poem is the epilogue was published the day of Browning's death, December 12, 1889. It contemplates his own death and the feelings which his friends will have about it, and rejects their imagined pity, declaring that as on earth he was one who never feared or doubted, so after death he will continue his career, asking only that his friends cheer him though unseen and speed him onward. Note the contrast between midnight (l. 1) and noonday (l. 16).

WILLIAM MAKEPEACE THACKERAY

Pp. 573 ff. A typical John Bull among writers, Thackeray is nowhere more Bull-ish than in dealing with his fellow-humorist. The key to all that he has to say about Sterne is found in the last sentence of the selection; his mid-Victorian sense of what is due the conventions will not permit him to discuss Sterne without saying that he prefers Dickens for his children. This personal bias, on moral, not literary, grounds, pervades his presentation of the character. His study is not unsympathetic — far from it; it is appreciative, even kindly, but it never for a moment abandons the position of a paterfamilias in a frock-coat. He is scandalized — and, one may admit, not without reason; all the more scandalized because Sterne was a clergyman. Compare his study with Stevenson's treatment of Villon, pp. 662 ff.

The essay quoted is a good example of Thackeray's vigorous and genial English, his bluffness suffused with sentiment, his happy faculty of choosing the material that will give to his presentation vitality and charm.

ARTHUR HUGH CLOUGH

Pp. 578 ff. Clough perhaps gave fuller and sincerer expression than any other poet to the religious doubt and unrest characteristic of the middle of the nineteenth century. Others — even at their sincerest — give us only the conclusions they have reached and such steps in the progress of their thought as they think profitable for us; Clough allows us to be with him in all his falterings, his waverings, his inconsistencies. In *Easter Day*, we have, to be sure, first the doubts and then the faith, but in *The Questioning Spirit* and its sequel, *Bethesda*, the moods are reversed. In this sincerity lies his great value. He was a poetic thinker but only too seldom a poetic artist. This may have been due in part to his sincerity — his recording at the moment the thoughts of the moment. "All immortal verse," says William Sharp, " is a poetic resurrection," and he quotes Schiller as saying that "to live again in the serene beauty of art, it is needful that things should first die in reality."

QUA CURSUM VENTUS

The title is a phrase from Vergil's *Æneid*, III, 269, and means "whithersoever the wind directs the course." The situation in the *Æneid* bears no resemblance to that set forth in this poem. There Æneas, in relating his adventures, tells how he left the islands called the Strophades; "The winds," he says, "spread wide our sails; over the foaming waves we flee, whither the wind and the helmsman direct our course:" —

Tendunt vela Noti; fugimus spumantibus undis,
Qua cursum ventusque gubernatorque vocabat.

Our poem presents, under the figure of two ships that sail away into the night and are unintentionally separated, the common experience of friends who unintentionally and unwittingly drift apart in thought and feeling.

JOHN RUSKIN

THE STONES OF VENICE

Pp. 582 ff. Ruskin was a combination of types rarely combined — an artist and a reformer. Fundamentally, he was an artist; but as he was not content to observe and study and love the beautiful things that exist, but wished to see all the world beautiful, he inevitably joined the ranks of those who strive to hasten by human and artificial means the golden age when all hateful and hideous things shall be unknown.

Himself trained as a painter, Ruskin used words as he used pigments, to build up a composition that would convey an impression of objectivity colored by personality, very much as a painting of the same subject would do. For this reason his description of St. Mark's is one of the most wonderful pieces of word-painting ever produced. As he is writing for English readers to whom the word *cathedral* is rich in associations — and associations altogether foreign to the scene he is about to describe — he prepares the way by summing up the characteristic features of an English cathedral. Having set forth and banished these, he feels still that the reader's mind is not sufficiently ready to receive emotionally the impression of a church so unlike any other, and he prepares the way further by a long description of the incongruous scenes crowded into the paved alley leading to the piazza. And when expectation can bear no more, "we forget them all, for between those pillars there opens a great light. . . ."

Observe that the description of the cathedral itself fills only half a page, while almost as much space is devoted to contrasting it with the people who live round about it, and three times as much space is given to preparing for the description. But the word-picture, short as it is, is as vividly colored as any piece of English prose; it gives a clear impression of the general appearance of the church, and of its structure from the ground to the spires, and it bathes the whole scene in an atmosphere of suggestion by means of the words used, much as a painter gets atmospheric effects by combinations of color.

THE CROWN OF WILD OLIVE

Pp. 584 ff. The selection from *The Crown of Wild Olive*, though it contains less wonderful descriptive writing, is quite as beautiful in its way, and fully as characteristic of Ruskin. It shows the strength of his bitter hostility to the economic waste that produced nothing but ugliness for the expenditure of labor. It reveals the artist as an economist, a socialist, a lover of his fellow-men, and a wanderer in lonely paths of thought; and it contains a doctrine that he was eager to impress upon the hearts of his readers. The value of Ruskin's work grows with the growing recognition of political economy as the science, not of wealth, but of social well-being.

The meaning of the title is explained in the last paragraph of the selection.

FREDERICK LOCKER–LAMPSON

P. 590. Praed (p. 494) and Locker-Lampson are the advance guard of a host of writers of *vers de société* of exquisite delicacy and refinement. The ideal of such verse is elegant and ingenious trifling with only occasional touches of more serious sentiment — as a swallow circles bright and swift through the air, dips its wing for a moment in the water, and like a flash is off again in its careless flight. Some of the lighter verse of the sixteenth, seventeenth, and eighteenth centuries bears a close resemblance to the work of these later writers, but there is a difference in tone, in attitude, in personal concern with the sentiments expressed. Locker (or Locker-Lampson, to use the name he assumed upon his marriage to Miss Lampson) was far superior to Praed in tenderness, in reserve, in genuine poetic feeling, and in technique. His range of sentiments, of ideas, and of rhythms was greater; and he has had the greater influence upon later writers. With the lines *To My Grandmother* a curious analogy and contrast are afforded by Oliver Wendell Holmes's *The Last Leaf.*

SIDNEY DOBELL

P. 591. Sidney Dobell is a notable example of the rather large class of poets in the nineteenth century who gave evidence of true and even great poetic ability, but who failed in unity, in sustained power, in final and perfect utterance.

MATTHEW ARNOLD

Neither as poet nor as prose-writer did Arnold catch the ear of the great public, but in both characters he was eminent in his generation as one who taught and guided the teachers and guides of the educated world.

His prose is clear, vivacious, classical in its restraint and its definiteness of aim, and though often careless, its carelessness has always the effect of elegant negligence, not of slipshod ignorance. The importance of the ideas for which he contended and the unwavering and urbane persistence with which he supported a cause that could triumph only in the remote future are among the most admirable of his many admirable qualities.

His verse is more restrained than his prose and it lacks the lightheartedness, the spontaneity, the outward and obvious signs of power necessary for popularity. In his own day it found only a small band of lovers, but its permanent beauty and value

are steadily gaining wider recognition. It now seems probable that he and Browning will in the future be counted the most notable poets of the Victorian period.

The Scholar Gipsy

Pp. 617 ff. In a note, Arnold gave the following passage from Glanvil's *Vanity of Dogmatizing* (1661) as the foundation of this poem: —

"There was lately a lad in the University of Oxford, who was by his poverty forced to leave his studies there; and at last to join himself to a company of vagabond gipsies. Among these extravagant people, by the insinuating subtilty of his carriage, he quickly got so much of their love and esteem as that they discovered to him their mystery. After he had been a pretty while exercised in the trade, there chanced to ride by a couple of scholars, who had formerly been of his acquaintance. They quickly spied out their old friend among the gipsies; and he gave them an account of the necessity which drove him to that kind of life, and told them that the people he went with were not such impostors as they were taken for, but that they had a traditional kind of learning among them, and could do wonders by the power of imagination, their fancy binding that of others: that he himself had learned much of their art, and when he had compassed the whole secret, he intended, he said, to leave their company, and give the world an account of what he had learned."

EDWARD FITZGERALD

The Rubaiyat of Omar Khayyam

Pp. 621 ff. Fitzgerald's translation of *The Rubaiyat* of Omar Khayyam has long had a place in the hearts of lovers of high and serious poetry. Although a translation, it is in the truest sense an original poem and expresses as scarcely any other does the strange combination of doubt and defiance and sensuousness and religious yearning characteristic of much of the thought and feeling of the Victorian Age.

Rubáiyát is a Persian word, the plural of *rubái*, which means a quatrain. Omar, surnamed *Al Khayyám* (the tent-maker), was a distinguished Persian scholar and poet. He was regarded as a paragon of learning, especially in astronomy. In one of his quatrains he refers whimsically to his surname and in another to his reformation of the calendar. His quatrains circulated very widely in the Orient and produced many imitations —

some of which are indistinguishable from his own. He was born at Naishápúr in the second half of the eleventh century and died there in the first half of the twelfth. One of his school-fellows was the famous statesman Nizám-ul-Mulk, and another the infamous Hasan ben Sabbáh, the Old Man of the Mountains, from whose name the word *assassin* is said by some to be derived.

COVENTRY PATMORE

Pp. 623 f. Coventry Patmore has been the subject of the most widely divergent judgments. One contemporary critic says: "It may be affirmed that no poet of the present age is more certain of immortality than he." Another regards him as possessing no spark of the divine fire. The selections here presented seem to justify his claim to a unique and high position among the poets of his time, but his range was narrow — his vocal register had scarcely a tone that does not find utterance in these selections — and his voice obviously lacked resonance and power. Being incapable of self-criticism, he wrote much that is prosaic — some lines that even awaken inextinguishable laughter; but at its best his verse is simple, picturesque, passionate, of exquisite freshness and charm.

DANTE GABRIEL ROSSETTI

Pp. 624 ff. The vigor and intensity of Rossetti's thought is often lost sight of in consequence of the luxuriance and sensuous richness of his imagery and melody. But his poems are not involuntary cries of passion; they are planned and constructed with serious artistic care and wrought out with infinite attention to details. Of *The Blessed Damozel*, he said: "I saw that Poe had done the utmost it was possible to do with the grief of the lover on earth, and so I determined to reverse the conditions, and give utterance to the yearning of the loved one in heaven." It would be difficult to find two more impressive examples of logical structure and development than are afforded by this poem and *Sister Helen*.

The intellectual power of his verse may be seen also in the sonnets *On the Refusal of Aid between Nations, The Sonnet, The Landmark, The Choice, Vain Virtues* — indeed in practically every selection, for even the love-sonnets are as closely reasoned as if they were treatises instead of lyrics.

SISTER HELEN

Pp. 626 ff. The superstition that an enemy's life could be destroyed by making a figure of him

in wax and melting it before a slow fire — the whole process, of course, to be carried out with proper ceremonies of black magic — is a very ancient and almost world-wide belief. The most interesting variants of the belief, in classical literature, are perhaps those in the second Idyl of Theocritus. The whole Idyl is interesting to read in connection with this poem, though the heroine Simaetha is attempting, not to destroy her lover, but to bring back his love; cf. especially the following (ll. 23–31): —

"Delphis troubled me, and I against Delphis am burning this laurel; and even as it crackles loudly when it has caught the flame, and suddenly is burned up, and we see not even the dust thereof, lo, even thus may the flesh of Delphis waste in the burning!

"My magic wheel, draw home to me the man I love!

"Even as I melt this wax, with the god to aid, so speedily may he by love be molten, the Myndian Delphis! And as whirls this brazen wheel, so restless, under Aphrodite's spell, may he turn and turn about my doors!

"My magic wheel, draw home to me the man I love!"

Instances of the superstition in England and Ireland are discussed in Thomas Wright's introduction to *The Proceedings against Dame Alice Kyteler* (Camden Society Publications).

THE BALLAD OF DEAD LADIES

P. 629. l. 2. *Lady Flora.* The Roman goddess of flowers, or more probably the Roman lady mentioned by Juvenal, *Sat.* II, 49.

l. 3. *Hipparchia.* Villon has *Archipiada*, which is probably a distortion of *Alcibiades*. The beauty of Alcibiades was proverbial, and Villon may have thought he was a woman. Modern editors have substituted the name *Hipparchia*, but the name of this learned Greek lady of the fourth century B.C. was probably unknown to Villon. For *Thaïs* see *Alexander's Feast*, p. 224, l. 9.

l. 5. *Echo*, the mythical sweetheart of Narcissus, cf. Gayley's *Classic Myths*, p. 206.

l. 9. *Héloïse*, cf. Pope's *Eloïsa to Abelard* and the notes on it.

l. 13. *The Queen* who willed that Buridan should be thrown into the Seine was, according to legend, Marguerite of Bourgoyne, queen of Louis X.

l. 17. *Queen Blanche* is probably Blanche of Castile, mother of Louis IX of France (St. Louis): she died a nun in 1252.

l. 19. *Bertha Broadfoot*, according to tradition

the mother of Charlemagne, heroine of the old French romance *Berte aux Grans Pies*. *Beatrice*, apparently Beatrice of Provence, wife of Charles, son of Louis VIII. *Alice*, perhaps the wife of Louis VII; but many old French songs begin "Belle Aalis" (*i.e.*, Beautiful Alice).

l. 20. *Ermengarde* married the famous warrior Foulques d'Anjou in 1004.

l. 21. *Joan*, Jeanne d'Arc.

FRANCESCA DA RIMINI

As Dante, in the *Inferno*, passed among those whom guilty love had sent to hell, he entreated two to come and speak to him. They were the famous lovers Paolo and Francesca, and this passage is a part of Francesca's account of their love. She was given by her father in marriage to Giovanni Malatesta, a man of extraordinary courage and ability, but deformed. Unfortunately she fell in love with his younger brother, Paolo, and he with her. They were killed by Giovanni. Few love stories have attracted more sympathetic interest. Leigh Hunt wrote a narrative poem on the story, and it has been dramatized in English by G. H. Boker and by Stephen Phillips, and in Italian by Silvio Pellico and by Gabriele D'Annunzio. Pictures illustrating the story have been painted by Ingres, Cabanel, Ary Scheffer, G. F. Watts, and others.

WILLIAM MORRIS

Pp. 633 ff. To no poet of the Victorian period could the term "the idle singer of an empty day" be less appropriately applied than to William Morris. He not only was a chief factor in revolutionizing the general artistic taste of the English people and their house-decorations in particular, but also became a leader in the social reforms which are tending surely though slowly to the reorganization of society and the state. Such a career may seem strange for one whose whole interest as a young man lay apparently in mediæval romance and poetry; yet in reality the art-reformer and the social-reformer were logical and, one may almost say, inevitable developments of the lover of mediævalism, for his love of mediæval art taught him the hideousness of the work produced by modern artisans, and practical experience as a decorator soon brought the recognition that art is not possible under the conditions of modern industrialism, that beauty is the product of the free artist, working with a love of his art.

THE EARTHLY PARADISE

The Earthly Paradise was written under the influence of Chaucer (cf. Morris's *Prologue*, ll. 1–16) and, like the *Canterbury Tales*, is a collection of stories told by the members of a group of travelers. *The Lady of the Land* is a retelling of the story told briefly by Sir John Mandeville in his fourth chapter (see pp. 30 ff).

ALGERNON CHARLES SWINBURNE

Pp. 640 ff. From his youth, almost from his boyhood, Swinburne possessed a wealth of sensuously beautiful words and a facility in versification unsurpassed by any other English poet. Unfortunately both these gifts tempted him to verbosity. He always has a meaning but it is often obscured, if not entirely hidden, by the excess of words and the long and elaborate sentences in which it is expressed. His influence upon other English poets — both great and small — was for a time very notable: to the great he taught new lessons and presented new standards of melodious verse; to the small he worked injury, tempting them to produce sound without sense and to indulge in all sorts of hot-house *malaise* and eroticism. He himself grew steadily in power and seriousness of thought, but he never escaped from the involuted coils of his diction and his syntax. The republican poems written under the influence of Victor Hugo and Mazzini cannot be quoted here, but they should be read by any one who wishes a just idea of his significance in English poetry.

GEORGE MEREDITH

Pp. 644 ff. George Meredith was one of the most richly and variously endowed writers of the nineteenth century. He is best known as a novelist, but to many of his admirers he seems equally great as a poet. All of his work is notable for its combination of significance and beauty. In depth of insight, in subtle apprehension of life and of the problems which it presents to try the hearts of intelligent men and women, even such great writers as Scott, Dickens, Thackeray, and George Eliot are hardly his equals; and his sensitiveness to the beauties of nature and of the soul of man has a wider range and a finer delicacy. The same qualities are manifest in much of his poetry. But the gods gave him also the fatal gift of excessive intellectual ingenuity and a delight in the exercise of it; while the sole gift they denied him was self-restraint. Like his own Bellerophon, he had the winged horse and the golden bridle, and he, too,

> . . . could mount and sit
> Flying, and up Olympus midway speed;

but instead of riding straight and hard for the summit he too often, in mere exuberance of power and of delight in his steed, executes difficult feats of horsemanship on the lower slopes of the mountain.

Love in the Valley is not a logical, consecutive description of the beloved, but a series of glimpses of her in many moods and under many aspects. The poem may be said to resemble in structure a diamond with a hundred facets, each of which glows with its own transformation of the white light of beauty.

Pp. 648 f. *Juggling Jerry* affords a striking contrast with this poem in both subject-matter and style.

Pp. 649 f. *Bellerophon* is a remarkable imaginative reconstruction of a situation, the tragedy and pathos of which depend upon an appreciation of the career of the hero as set forth in classical mythology.

P. 650. The *Song of the Songless* and the *Dirge* give some hint of the beauty of the nature poetry which forms a notable part of his work. Taken together these selections illustrate the range as well as the beauty of Meredith's poetry.

CHRISTINA ROSSETTI

Pp. 650 ff. Christina Rossetti deserves a high, perhaps the highest, place among women poets of the nineteenth century, not by virtue of range of thought or volume of production, but because her verse is uniformly almost the perfection of simple passionate beauty.

JAMES THOMSON

Pp. 652 ff. James Thomson is one of the most curious and interesting figures of the Victorian period. No one has been more successful in catching the true poetic aspect of the pleasures of the lower middle classes of a great city. His "idyls of the London mob," as he calls them, are not echoes of Theocritus or Vergil, of the pastoral of the Italian Renaissance, or of the genuine bucolic poetry of Scotland and England; they are original and independent treatments of the material that he saw actually about him in the holiday excursions of the young people of cockneydom.

In striking contrast with these simple and charming pictures is the dark melancholy which finds expression in *The City of Dreadful Night* and other poems of his later years. These poems have often been admired, or condemned, as the ultimate expression of philosophical pessimism, and often the form and the ideas seem to justify such an interpretation; but there can be little doubt that they are in reality devoid of philosophical significance, though full of power and of far-reaching suggestion. The ideas and the imagery have the horrible fascination of a hideous dream. They are indeed the utterance of a poet of splendid original power and infinite aspiration for life and strength and beauty, whose vigor has been sapped by folly and misfortune, who with shattered nerves and strengthless hands strives vainly to clutch some good that has durability and three dimensions. *The City of Dreadful Night* is, as the poet explains, the city of darkness, peopled with sad forms by the insomnia which night after night tortures and weakens him and restores him to the day empty of strength and hope.

The selection *As I came through the desert* is one of the narratives of gloom and despair incorporated in Thomson's account of the dreadful City and the melancholy figures whom the poet meets in his wanderings. The poem is very difficult. It is clearly symbolic of the passage through life of some distressed soul, but the significance of the woman with the red lamp in her hand, of the two selves of the speaker, and of the woman's devotion to the corpse-like self will be differently interpreted by different students. Perhaps this poem no more admits of a definite interpretation of details than does *Childe Roland to the Dark Tower Came.*

WALTER PATER

STYLE

Pp. 654 ff. Pater's essay on *Style* is exemplified in *The Child in the House;* from *The Child in the House* it would be possible to deduce his principles of style, so completely in his case are critic and creator at one. He and Stevenson are the two supremely self-conscious artists of the nineteenth century; and yet in neither case does the expenditure of thought, love, and care upon the process itself detract from the beauty of the result.

Pater's mind worked in a perpetual probing, testing, balancing, for the purpose of finding shades of difference among resemblances, shades of resemblance where differences were obvious, ever approaching exactness in definition, ever defining relationships to the last degree of nicety. For that reason, his sentences often seem cumbersome; he was unwilling to relinquish his effort at expression until he had reached the end of the ramifications of his thought. Together with this went a love of words as words and a wonderful patience in seeking the exact word and the right combination of words to convey his meaning with such emotional suggestiveness as he himself felt in connection with it.

THE CHILD IN THE HOUSE

Pp. 657 ff. *The Child in the House* is to some extent autobiographical. It was written in 1878 when Pater was thirty-nine years old and had been away twenty-five years from the Enfield home (about ten miles from London). In the house itself the Watteau picture probably represents one by Jean-Baptiste Pater, Watteau's contemporary, to whose stock the English Paters were supposed to belong. For a study of Watteau and Pater, see Pater's essay, *A Prince of Court Painters*. Undoubtedly Florian Deleal represents Pater's own attitude as evolved by home influences, just as *Emerald Uthwart* reflects his own life at Canterbury School and its effect upon him.

ROBERT LOUIS STEVENSON

FRANÇOIS VILLON

Pp. 662 ff. Stevenson was exactly the man to write upon Villon; he was enough of a bohemian and enough of a poet to present with the utmost charity and clarity his sordid material. His interest in Villon appears further in his story, *A Lodging for the Night*, of which Villon is the hero.

The book upon which Stevenson bases most of his information is Longnon's *Étude biographique sur François Villon*, Paris, 1877; but he seems also to have consulted the *Bourgeois de Paris* (ed. Panthéon) and the *Chronique Scandaleuse* (ed. Panthéon), among other books. Further details and illustrative material about the life of Villon may be found in Champion's *François Villon*, Paris, 1913.

Stevenson's object is to reconstruct, out of the facts brought to light by research, the living image of a man. In this he succeeds admirably, partly by his sympathetic realization of what Villon must have meant to himself and to others, and partly by his clearness of presentation. An-

other source of charm is, as always, his racy and delightful English.

P. 664 *a*. *with specification of one work*, etc. Stevenson here misses the point. The book in question, *The Rommant du Pet au Deable*, was Villon's first work, now lost, a mock romance relating the pranks of students at the University of Paris while Villon was there. The *Pet au Deable* was a stone which lay before the house of a pious old woman. It was moved by the students to their quarter, and a great deal of merry-making and rioting grew out of the whole affair. Signs were also stolen from different parts of the city, and the doings finally led to a serious clash between the University and the city authorities. Without attempting to whitewash Villon or his lost poem, we may believe that his uncle might have received such a legacy without being insulted and still be a worthy ecclesiastic, but with a twinkle for the vagaries of students.

P. 668 *a*. *a whole improper romance*, etc. Stevenson omits the important point that this romance was Villon's lost composition referred to above. Tabary was a clerk, apparently a fellow-student with Villon, who describes him, in this very connection, as "a real man" (*homs veritable*); but his later career scarcely bore out the compliment.

P. 672 *a*. *Charles of Orleans . . . in the pages of the present volume*, that is *Familiar Studies of Men and Books*, in which is printed also Stevenson's essay on Charles of Orleans. He was nephew and cousin to kings of France, was captured at Agincourt in 1415, and kept prisoner in England for twenty-five years. He had a pretty skill in lyric verse and was a great patron of poets.

P. 675 *a*. *The date of the "Large Testament,"* etc. Since the essay was written, a few more facts have been discovered; but they are sordid details of two more arrests, the second ending in a sentence of death by hanging, which was afterward lightened to banishment from Paris for ten years. In this case, an unprovoked assault on a notary and his scribes, Villon seems to have been entirely innocent; but he was punished for being in bad company, and because his career was notorious. In 1463, then, he left Paris, and no more is known of him. He was broken in health, and without means of subsistence; and the sentence against him must have kept him continually exposed to danger. He was dead in 1489 when his works were first published.

TRANSLATIONS OF CLASSICAL AUTHORS

Every student of English poetry should have access to the chief Greek and Latin classics. As few can nowadays be expected to read the original texts, a brief list of cheap translations of the authors who have had the greatest influence upon English literature may be useful:

Iliad, translated by Pope (Astor ed., 50 cents); tr. Lang, Leaf, and Myers (prose), 80 cents.

Odyssey, tr. Palmer, 75 cents; tr. Butcher and Lang (prose), 80 cents.

Æschylus (Everyman's Library, 35 cents).

Sophocles (Everyman's Library, 35 cents).

Euripides (2 vols., Everyman's Library, 35 cents each).

Plato, *Five Dialogues on Poetic Inspiration* (Everyman's Library, 35 cents).

Theocritus, Bion, and Moschus, tr. Lang (prose), 80 cents.

Vergil, tr. Conington (Astor ed. 50 cents); tr. Lonsdale and Lee (prose), $1.25.

Horace (Everyman's Library, 35 cents).

Ovid, the only accessible translation at present is that in Bohn's Library 3 vols., $1.50 each (of which Vol. II is the most valuable); but Mr. Dent promises that a translation will soon be included in Everyman's Library.

Editions of all the classical texts with translations are planned for the Loeb Classical Library (the Macmillan Company); many of them have already been published.

INDEX OF AUTHORS

INDEX OF TITLES AND FIRST LINES

AE

DATE DUE